The History of the island of Antigua

one of the Leeward Caribbees in the West Indies, from the first settlement in 1635 to the present time (Volume III)

Vere Langford Oliver

Alpha Editions

This edition published in 2020

ISBN : 9789354049095 (Hardback)

ISBN : 9789354049590 (Paperback)

Design and Setting By
Alpha Editions
www.alphaedis.com
email - alphaedis@gmail.com

Preface.

MY original intention had been to limit this Work to two volumes, but owing to the great increase of material, and a desire not to omit anything which might be useful, I have been compelled to issue this Third and final Volume.

I wish to point out that owing to the shortness of my stay at Antigua in 1888-9, it was impossible for me to examine many of the later volumes of records—a matter for regret, as otherwise many pedigrees might have been more fully set out. In regard to marriage licences, which were formerly invariably granted by the Governor or his Deputy, present officials have no knowledge of their existence.

My thanks are due to the Publishers for the very able way in which they have carried out their difficult and troublesome work.

February, 1899.

List of Illustrations.

This Edition has been limited to 150 *copies,*
of which this is No. 70

Mitchell L Hughes.

The History of Antigua.

Pedigree of Pare.

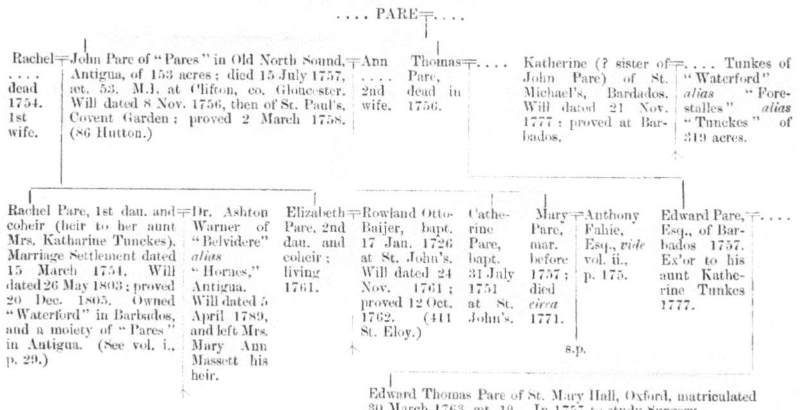

John Pare of Antigua, now living in St. Paul's, Covent Garden. Will dated 8 Nov. 1756; proved 2 March 1758 by Richard Oliver, Augustus Boyd, and John Bond, the Attorneys of Rachel Warner the wife of Ashton Warner, and of Elizabeth Otto-Baijer wife of Rowland Otto-Baijer, Esq., the daus. (86 Hutton.) To each of my grandsons John & Rowland Otto £50 at 18. To my granddau. Frances Otto £50 at 18. To my nephew Edw[d] Pare, son of my brother Tho. Pare, deceased, £50. To Cath. Wilson £200 at 16. To Ann Wilson £15 yearly for 7 years. All residue to my 2 daus. Rachel Warner & Eliz[th] Otto, & appoint them Ex'trices. Witnessed by Matthew Christian, James Bogle French, Joseph Sanders. Recorded also at St. John's 9 June 1758.

1st Codicil dated 15 March 1757. To my negro Pero £4 c. yearly, my friend M[r] Robinson Tudway of Bristol, hosier, to send him over to Antigua. Witnessed by Elizabeth Rudge, R. Tudway, Ro. Fullwood.

2nd Codicil dated 21 March 1757. To my son-in-law Anthony Fahie, Esq., £200. To Sam[l] Redhead of Antigua, Esq., £200. Witnessed by R. Tudway, John Powell, Ro. Fullwood.

3rd Codicil dated 25 March 1757. To Ann Wilson £20 c., not £15 a year. To my nephew Edw[d] Pare of Barbados, Esq., £20. To Sam[l] Redhead, Esq., £20. My nephew Edw[d] Pare to go to S[t] Thomas Hospital, London, for the better study of surgery, as my son-in-law D[r] Ashton Warner shall direct. Witnessed by Eliza Rudge, John Powell, R. Tudway.

1825, Nov. 19. In Park-street, Bath, the relict of Samuel Pare, esq. of Barbadoes. ('Gent. Mag.,' p. 190.)

PARISH REGISTER OF ST. JOHN.

Baptized.

1751 July 31 Catherine the D. of John Pare, Esq[r], and Ann his wife.

CLIFTON NEAR BRISTOL.

JOHN PARE, Esq. | of the Island of Antigua, | departed this Life 15 July 1757, aged 53.

(Bigland's 'Gloucestershire Collections,' p. 392.)

Pedigree of Parke.

ARMS.—*Azure, an eagle displayed argent, armed or, guttée de sang.*
CREST.—*An eagle's head or, spotted with ermine spots, murally collared sable.*

LIEUT.-COLONEL DANIEL PARKE of Virginia; "Col. Parkes" sent by Governor Sir W. Berkeley with a letter to the King 1669; Member of Council 1674. Will dated 11 Aug. 1677; proved 16 Sep. 1679. (120 King.) ═ (? dau. of .... Evelyn.)

Mrs. Katherine Chester, wife of Edward Chester, senior, of St. John's. — Daniel Parke, mortgagee of Colonel George Gamble's plantation of 316 acres for £6000 sterling, which descended to Lucy Chester-Parke; owned lands at Whitechurch, co. Hants, of £500 a year; was M.P. for that borough; expelled the House for bribery; Aide-de-camp to Duke of Marlborough 1704; Governor-General of Leeward Isles 1706—1710; shot during an insurrection and bur. at St. John's 9 Dec. 1710, æt. 41. Will dated 29 Jan. 1709-10; sworn 20 Dec. 1710; proved May 1711. (112 Young.) ═ ....

Evelyn Parke, mar. Gilbert Pepper, Esq.; both living 1712 and 1715-16.

Rebekah Parke, mar. ....

Jane Parke, mar. ....

Colonel James Parke, nephew of the Governor; Member of Assembly 1727. ═ Eleanor, dau. of Chief Justice Samuel Watkins; mar. 1707 at St. John's.

A dau., mar. 1st .... Wallace, s.p.; 2ndly Colonel Farley of Antigua.

Thomas Dunbar Parke, bur. 28 Nov. 1734 at St. John's. ═ Lucy Chester, mar. 10 Dec. 1720; obtained possession of "Gambles" 20 Nov. 1723; bur. 20 Nov. 1770 at St. John's.

Frances Parke, inherited the Virginia property. ═ (? John) Custis* of Virginia, Esq. Arms: *Three parrots.*

Lucy Parke, mar. .... Bird.

Daniel Dunbar Parke, bapt. 8 Feb. 1728 at St. John's; a lunatic 1767.

Alexander Simms, bur. at St. John's 26 Jan. 1770. ═ Elizabeth Dunbar Parke, born 1725; mar. at St. John's 3 Oct. 1746; bur. there 27 May 1759; died 26 May 1759, æt. 34.

Daniel Parke Custis. ═ Martha ═ George Washington, first President U.S.A., born 1732; mar. 1759; died 1799.

....

Fanny Parke Custis, living 1739. ═ William Winch of London, Virginia Merchant. Will dated 22 Jan. 1739; proved 4 Feb. 1739-40. (56 Browne.)

George Washington Parke Custis of Arlington House, Virginia; his dau. Mary mar. General Robert Lee, the Confederate ('Mis. Gen. et Her.,' Second Series, i., p. 107).

* Captain Edmund Curtis or Custis, a Commissioner nominated by Parliament to reduce Virginia 1651; a merchant 1654.

Daniell Parke of London, Esq. Will dated 11 Aug. 1677; proved 16 Sep. 1679 by Micajah Perry and Thomas Lane; power reserved to the others. (120 King.) To my son Daniell Parke my plantation and negros in Virginia & to his heirs male; heirs female to take my surname. To each of my daus. Eveling Parke (the eldest), Rebekah Parke, and Jane Parke £1500 at 18. Profits of sale of tobacco & shipping. All residue to my son Daniel at 21 & sole Ex'or. Loving friends Col. Edward Carter, Mr Michaiah Perry, & Mr Tho. Lane Ex'ors in trust for England, & Jas. Bray, Esq., & Mr Robt Cobb for Virginia, & £5 rings. Witnessed by Row. Place, jun., Samuel Pettit, John White, servant to Henry Faucon, scr.

Daniel Parke, Captain-General and Chief Governor of all the Leeward Islands. Will dated 29 Jan. 1709-10 at St. John's; proved May 1711. (112 Young.) All my estate in these islands to Tho. Long, Esq., & Mr Ceasar Rodney for Lucy Chester, dau. of Mistress Kath. Chester, but if she die under 21 to her mother, then to my godson Julius Cæsar Parke. Lucy Chester & her heirs to take my name & use my coat of arms which is yet of my family of the co. of Essex,* but if they refuse then to my godson Julius Ceasar Parke, then to the heirs of my dau. Frances Curtis, then to the heirs of my dau. Lucy Bird. To my dau. Frances Curtis all my estate in Virginia or England, then to the heirs of my dau. Lucy Bird, then to the yst dau. of Mistress Kath. Chester, then to the heirs of Julius Ceasar Parke, then to the poor of the parish of White Church in Hampshire. To my dau. Lucy Bird £1000. To Julius Ceasar Parke £50 a year. To my 3 sisters & their children £50 for rings. To each Ex'or £20. I appoint Tho. Long, Esq., of this island, & Mr Ceasar Rodney and Majr Saml

* A Pedigree of Parke of Gestingthorpe was entered in the Visitation of 1634. See also Morant and Wright's 'Essex.'

Byam Ex'ors for the Leeward Islands; Micajah Perry, Esq., Mr Tho. Laws, & Mr Richd Perry of London, mercht, Ex'ors for England & Virginia. Witnessed by Hubert Pember, John Birmingham, and William Martin.

Codicil dated 7 Dec. 1710. Mr Abraham Redwood to be Ex'or in the place of Col. Thos. Long, deceased. On 20 Dec. 1710 Hubert Pember, Esq., of Antigua, and William Martin of St. John's, vintner, were sworn before the Hon. Walter Hamilton, Esq., Lieut.-General and Commander-in-Chief of H.M. Leeward Charibbe Islands.

William Winch of London, Virginia Merchant. Will dated 22 Jan. 1739; proved P.C.C. 4 Feb. 1739 by Francis William Massey. (56 Browne.) By the deed of settlement at my marriage with my now wife Fanny Parke Winch, dau. of John Curtis of Virginia, Esq., I was to have received from him £1000, but he has not paid it. All my lands, negros, cattle, etc., to my cousin Mr Francis Wm Massey of Christ Church, London, apothecary, he & Messrs. Sam. Haswell, Tho. Brooks, & Wm Hunt to be Ex'ors. Witnessed by James Martin, Mary Martin, James Henry Kent.

James Parke. On 4 May adm'on of goods of James Parke, late of Antigua, but in St. Botolph's without Aldgate, deceased, granted to Henrietta Stevenson, wife of Thomas Stevenson, the widow and relict. Nov. 1741.

Hugh Parke, planter. Will dated .... My Ex'ors to send to Philadelphia, Pennsilvania, 4 heavy British guineas to Mr Archd Bingham to purchase 4 gold rings, one to be sent to Mr Jno Service in the said city or Virginia, another to my sister Hester, spouse of the said Archd, another to my sister Elizth, wife of the said John, & one to be kept by the said Archd in memory of me their affectionate brother. All residue to be divided. (Remainder of will has been lost.) Recorded at St. John's.

1674, Nov. 21. At a Court at James City, Virginia. Present: Sir William Berkeley, Knt., Governor, Lieut.-Colonel Daniel Parke, Sir Henry Chicheley, Knt., and others of the Council.

For a biography of Governor Parke see: "The History of Col. Parke's Administration Whilst he was Captain-General and Chief Governor of the Leeward Islands; With an Account of the Rebellion in Antegoa: Wherein he, with several others, were Murther'd on the 7th of December 1710. By Mr. George French. London, 1717, pp. 427, 8°." His portrait* is given, painted by Sir Godfrey Kneller and engraved by G. Vertue, with his arms: *Quarterly*—1 and 4, *Azure (? guttée), an eagle displayed; 2 and 3, Azure, a griffin passant, a canton argent.* Crest: *An eagle's head couped, gorged with a mural crown with three embattlements sable.* Died 7 Dec. 1710, æt. 41.

Letter from the Duke of Marlborough to Queen Anne.

August 13, 1704.

I have not time to say more, but to beg you will give my Duty to the Queen, and let her know her Army has had a glorious Victory. Mons Tallard and two other Generals are in my Coach and I am following the rest. The bearer, my Aide-Camp C. M. Parkes, will give her an account of what has pass'd. I shal doe it in a day or two by a nother more att large.

MARLBOROUGH.

(A copy of this is given in W. A. Paton's 'Down the Islands,' p. 77.)

1708, Feb. 4. Julius Cæsar Parke has been appointed youngest Ensign in Colonel Jones's Regiment.

* This has been reproduced in vol. i.

Memorial of Gilbert Pepper,* Esq., and Evelyn his wife, sister of the late Governor Parke, petitioning against the appointment of Edward Warner to the Council of Antigua. Received 21 March 1711-12. (B. T. Leeward Islands, vol. 12.)

1715-16, Feb. 11. Gilbert Pepper and Evelyn his wife complain to the Assembly against the Governor.

1723, Nov. 20. Cæsar Rodney, merchant, Ex'or of late Governor Parke, hands over to Thomas D. Parke and Lucy his wife Governor Parke's estate of 316 acres, formerly mortgaged by Colonel George Gamble.

1727, Dec. 11. James Parke, Esq., was returned as a Member of Assembly for Belfast Division.

1728, March 8. Petition of Thomas Dunbar Parke and Lucy Chester his wife for settlement of the late Governor Parke's affairs.

1729, March 9. Petition of Thomas Dunbar Parke that he married on 10 Dec. 1720 Lucy Chester, and hath now issue a son Daniel. Recites Governor Parke's will.

1734. Thomas Dunbar Parke and Lucy his wife claim £4364 as house rent voted to the late Governor Parke, and still owing by the Assembly. They refuse to pay it.

1736, Oct. A conspiracy discovered among the negros on the Widow Dunbar Parke's plantation.

1736, Dec. 22. Julius Cæsar Parke then Master of the ship "St. George."

1767, Aug. 15. Petition of Lucy D. Parke *re* her son Daniel Dunbar Parke, a lunatic, who is allowed £80 a year.

PARISH REGISTER OF ST. JOHN.

Baptized.

1728 Feb. 8 Daniell the s. of Thomas Dunbar Parke & Lucey his wife.
1732 Feb. 11 Patrick the s. of Thomas Parke & Margarett his wife.
1798 Oct. 10 Georgiana D. of William Park & Isabella his wife. B. the 13th March last.
1806 Feb. 25 Jennet D. of William Park and Isabella his wife. B. the 17th October last.

Married.

1707 (May or June) 9 James Parkes and Ellinor Wattkins. Lic.

Buried.

1710 Dec. 9 His Excellcy Daniel Parke, Esqr, Late Capt General, etc.
1732 Oct. 19 Thomas Parkes.
1734 Nov. 28 Mr Thomas Dunbar Parke.
1767 June 1 Andrew Park, Junr.
1770 Nov. 20 Lucy Dunbar Parke.
1775 Dec. 30 Daniel Parke.
1777 June 10 Robert Park.

PARISH REGISTER OF ST. PAUL.

Married.

1746 Oct. 3 Alexander Simms & Elizabeth Dunbar Parke; by Lic.

PARISH REGISTER OF ST. PHILIP.

Buried.

1795 Nov. 27 Mr Hugh Park.

* A Gilbert Peppar, son of Dennis Peppar of Aslackby, co. Lincoln, Gent., matriculated from Magdalen Hall, Oxford, 15 May 1632, æt. 16, of which family a pedigree is recorded in the Visitation of 1634.

Major-General John Pepper, M.P. for Staining, co. Sussex, died Oct. 1725. (Mawson's 'Obits.')

In St. Paul's, Covent Garden, is a M.I. to Mary wife of Gilbert Pepper, ob. 20 Nov. 1694. (Seymour's 'London,' p. 674.)

Family of Parker.

Frances Traverse. Will dated 27 Sep. 1757. To Jane Parker, dau. of my son-in-law Thos. Parker, 7 slaves, & in default of issue to my granddau. Henrietta Parker. I give the latter 5 negros. To my granddaus. Marg^{t} & Mary Parker each a negro, & to my granddau. Sarah Parker 7 negros. To my grandson Thos. Parker a negro & all demands I have against the estate of Henry Warner, sen^{r}, dec^{d}. To my godson Ashton Warner and my goddau. Sarah Warner each a negro. To my nephew Octavius Nibbs a ring of 3 gs. To my dau. Henrietta a negro, furniture, plate, & all residue. Tho. Warner, Esq., & my son-in-law Thos. Parker, Ex'ors. Witnessed by Richard Glover, Edward Monteigue, William Pigott. By his Excellency George Thomas was sworn Edward Monteigue 31 March 1759. Recorded 2 July 1759.

Richard Glover, carpenter, in his will dated 17 Oct. 1759 names his partner Thomas Parker.

Thomas Parker. Will dated 16 Jan. 1779. Whereas Henry Warner, late of Antigua, by his will dated 6 Feb. 1729 bequeathed Frances Haydon £3000 c., and there appears to be a large sum still due to the heir-at-law of Frances Headon, then Frances Traverse, as by her will dated 27 Sep. 1757 she gave to my son Tho. Parker, jun^{r}, her grandson, all such demands. My son Thos. Parker died an inf^{t}, & his legacy descended to me, & I bequeath all claims to my 4 daus. Jane Clapham, Sarah Nibbs, Henrietta Hawes, & Marg^{t} Parker. To my dau. Jane Clapham a negro. To my dau. Sarah Nibbs, wife of Jer. Nibbs, jun^{r}, a negro. To Sarah Nibbs the younger, their inf^{t} dau., a negro. To Henrietta Hawes, dau. of Martin & Henrietta Hawes, a negro. All residue to my dau. Marg^{t} Parker. Jer. Nibbs, John Martin Hawes, & John Hawes, Ex'ors. Witnessed by John Burton, E. Moore Mascall, Thomas Mackie. By his Excellency Thomas Shirley was sworn Edmund Moore Mascall 25 March 1786. Recorded 3 April 1786.

Thomas Parker of Antigua, planter. Will dated 26 April 1780. To my father and mother Isaac & Jane Parker of Gatesgill, co. Cumb., all estate. My friends and employers Mr Bertie Entwisle, Mr Jos^{h} Brown, Ex'ors. Witnessed by John F. Athill, Peter Corss. Before Thomas Jarvis, Esq., were sworn John F. Athill and Peter Corss. Recorded 10 Sep. 1781.

1786, Jan. 5. Will of John Parker, writing clerk.

1676, March 9. Ensign Robert Parker granted 100 acres by Colonel Philip Warner; surveyed 26 March 1677.

PARISH REGISTER OF ST. JOHN.

Married.

1735	....	1	Thomas Parker and Eliz^{a} Hill.
1743	July	23	Thomas Parker & Henrietta Warner; by Lyc.

Buried.

1743	July	5	Capt John Parker.
1785	Dec.	1	Edward Parker (Planter).

Pedigree of Parry.

John Symes of Montserrat from co. Gloucester. = ...

JOHN PARRY of Antigua, Esq.; in 1668 had a grant of 325 acres; Chief Secretary of Antigua 1671; styled Esq. in 1672 and 1678; living 1679. = Henrietta, widow of Mr. John Brand; living 1674.

Lieut. John Symes of Montserrat. Will dated 2 April 1709; proved 20 Jan. 1712. (249 Leeds.)

Catherine Symes. Will dated 11 Oct. 1721, sworn 1 Nov. following, then a widow. = Major Charles Lloyd of Antigua; in 1699 bought 300 acres called "Cinnamon Valley" of Colonel Henry Lyons; Member of Assembly 1710 and 1711 and a J.P.

Elizabeth Symes, living 1721. = Colonel Samuel Parry of Antigua. Will dated 6 Feb. 1724-5; sworn 9 April 1725. His five sons and six daughters all named therein.

Governor John Yeamans. Will dated 15 Dec. 1717. "Eliz. Symes dau. of my Wife's sister." "My cousin Sam. Parry & his s. John Parry." "Mr Paul Parry."

Sarah Lloyd. (See under Harman, vol. ii., p. 63.)

Dorothy Lloyd, bapt. 6 Jan. 1710 at St. John's; mar. Samuel Harman, Esq.; she died 29 May 1754, æt. 44; he died 27 Nov. 1759, æt. 63.

Amy Lloyd, mar. 2ndly Theodore Walrond; Marriage Settlement dated 11 Jan. 1731; bur. 27 March 1741 at St. Philip's. = John Parry, 1st son and heir, bur. 25 Nov. 1730 at St. Philip's.

Symes Parry-Symes, heir to his uncle Lieut. John Symes, whose name he took; under 17 in 1709; bur. 13 Aug. 1723 at St. John's. Adm'on granted May 1728 to his brother Samuel. = Elizabeth . . . .

Samuel Parry-Symes, æt. 20 in 1718; heir to his brother Symes 1728; dead in 1742. = ...

Amy Parry, only dau. Will dated 27 Nov. 1744 in London; proved 1 July 1745. (202 Seymer.)

Elizabeth Parry-Symes, mar. William Steele. Adm'on of estate of Symes Parry-Symes granted to her 1742.

Frances Parry-Symes.

Henrietta Parry-Symes, mar. Thomas Stevenson. Adm'on of estate of Symes Parry-Symes granted to her 1742.

Amy Parry-Symes, living 1721.

Catherine Loyd, widow. Will dated 11 Oct. 1721. To my nephew John Parry, 1st s. of my brother Col. Saml Parry, £200 st., now in the hands of Nathl Carpenter, mercht at London, also a riding horse & negros. To Henry, 1st s. of Mr Henry Symes of Willoughby Bay, £30 c. & a negro. To my niece Cath. Parry, dau. of Col. Saml Parry, negros. To Capt. John Roynon of Montserrat £50 c. To my sister Eliz. Parry £100 st. To Henrietta, Elizth, & Amy Parry, daus. of my nephew Saml Parry, £20 c. each. All residue to my 3 children Amy Loyd, Sarah Loyd, & Dorothy Loyd equally. My brother Col. Saml Parry & his son John Parry & Mr Henry Lyons, Ex'ors. Witnessed by Walter Sydserfe, Symes Symes. Before Walter Hamilton, Esq., were sworn Walter Sydserfe and Symes Symes 1 Nov. 1721.

Samuel Parry, sen. Will dated 6 Feb. 1724-5. To my daus. Kath. Parry, Mary Parry, Margt Parry, Henrietta Parry, Frances Parry, & Rebecca Parry £300 c. each at 21 or marriage. To my 3 sons Wm, Henry, & Geo. Parry £300 c. each & £60 c. for apprentice fee. To my wife Elizth a mulatto & all plate & furniture. To my loving son John all my estate. My wife, my son John, & Hon. Archibald Cochran, Wm Yeamans, Esq., Thos. Kerby, Esq., Mr Henry Lyons, Ex'ors & Guardians. Witnessed by N. Monk, jun., William Masters, Geff. Duncomb. By Edward Byam, Esq., was sworn [*blank*] 9 April 1725.

Amy Parry of London, spinster. Will dated 27 Nov. 1744; proved 1 July 1745 by Henry Lyons and Richard Boddicott, Esquires. (202 Seymer.) My sister-in-law Eliz. Walrond, now living with her mother-in-law at Exeter, £1000 at 21; if she die to the children of my aunt Dorothy Harman, at present wife of Samuel Harman of Antigua, planter. My uncle Henry Lyons of Antigua, Esq., £100, & to my aunt Amy his wife £100, & my cousins Joseph Lyons & John Lyons their sons £50 apiece. My friends Richd Boddicott of London, merchant, & Mary his wife & Eliz. Wilder £100 apiece. Richd Boddicott the younger their son £50. Mrs Mary Debeta of Spittlefields, schoolmistress, £50. Guinea rings also to Mary, Frances, Martha, & Ann Smith & Eliz. Cralb. All residue to the said Henry Lyons & Richd Boddicott the elder, & Ex'ors. Witnessed by Edward Coulter, Thomas Smith, Chain Street, Crutched Fryars, Jonathan Evendon, Copthall Court.

Close Roll, 18 Geo. II., Part 7, No. 11.

Indenture made the 7th Oct. 1744 between Amye Parry of London, spinster (only daughter of John Parry, late of Antigua, a planter, deceased), of the one part, and Henry Lyons of Antigua, Esq., of the other part, witnesseth that for docking, barring, and destroying all estate in tail, reversions, etc., made in or upon the negros hereinafter mentioned, and in consideration of 5*s*. Amye Parry has sold her 23 negro slaves, with their increase, in Antigua, late in the possession of Henry Lyons, and now in her possession, to Henry Lyons and his heirs for ever. Edward Coulter, Jonathan Evendon, witnesses.

1668. Mr. John Parry and Mrs. Anne Washington granted 335 acres by patent.

1671, Jan. 11. John Parry granted 150 acres by Governor Warner; surveyed 20 Jan. 1671-2.

1671, Feb. 1. John Parry then styled Chief Secretary of Antigua.

1672, Aug. 29. John Roane of Antigua, Chirgion. Letter of Attorney to John Parry, Esq., *re* 2100 lbs. Witnessed by Jane Knight, Ralph Gordges. Recorded in Secretary's Office 16 Nov. 1672.

1674, July 29. Warrant to divide the estate of Mr. John Brand, deceased—half to his widow Henrietta, now wife of Mr. John Parry, and half to his daughter Christian Brand. 16 Aug. 1674.

1679, Nov. 9. John Parry, Gent., exchanges 3 acres with Robert Starkey.

1680. John Parry, Esq., granted 10 acres by Colonel James Vaughan; surveyed 1680.

John Parry granted parcell of land 28 Feb. 1680 by Sir W. Stapleton; also 10 acres and one proportion on 22 May 1682.

1709-10, March 14. John Parry of Antigua, planter, sells to John King of Antigua, planter, 11 acres.

1718, Feb. 4. Deposition of Mr. Samuel Parry, Gent., aged 20.

PARISH REGISTER OF ST. JOHN.

Baptized.

1700	Feb. 16	John S. of John Parry.
1710	Jan. 6	Dorothy d. of Maj. C. Loyd & Catherine his wife.

Married.

1709	April 4	Thos Lewis & Ann Parry. L.

Buried.

1740	Jan. 20	Henry Simms Parrie.
1753	Dec. 5	Samuel Parry.
1771	Dec. 25	Sarah Parry.

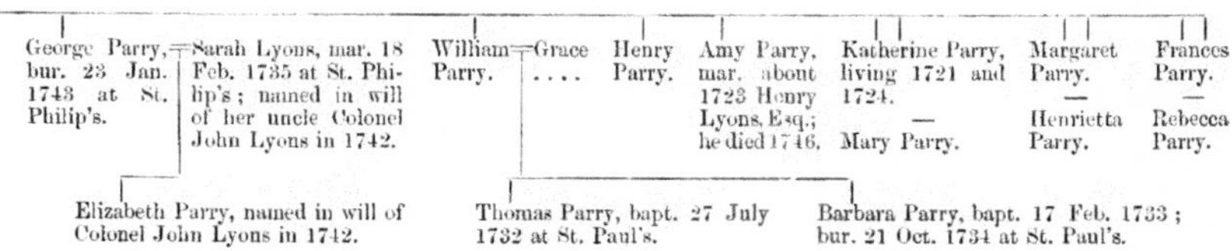

PARISH REGISTER OF ST. PHILIP.

Married.

1735 Feb. 18 George Parry to Sarah Lyons. L.
1741-2 Mar. 9 James Thibou to Rebeckah Parry.
1759 April 12 Jno Lydiatt & [*blank*] Parry.

Buried.

1697 Aug. 26 Alexander Parry.
1697 Oct. 14 Robert Parry.
1730 Nov. 25 John Parry.
1734 May 16 Rebecca D. of Saml Parry.
1743 Jan. 23 Mr George Parry.
1760 . . . . . . Robt Parry, jun^r.
1768 Jan. 3 Mrs Ann Parry.

PARISH REGISTER OF ST. PAUL.

Baptized.

1732 July 27 Thomas S. of William & Grace Parry.
1733 Feb. 17 Barbara D. of William Parry & Grace his wife.

Married.

1727 April 10 Mr Andrew Bodkin and Mrs Parry, Widdow; p^r L.
1731 Dec. 11 Samuel Parry & Eleanor Hunt; by L.
1740 June 19 Samuel Alford & Grace Parry; by Bans.

Buried.

1731 Nov. 23 Mrs Margaret Parry; at St Peter's, Parham.
1732 July 6 Thomas S. of William and Grace Parry.
1734 Oct. 21 Barbara D. of William Parry & Grace his wife.

BELFAST BURIAL-GROUND.

On a headstone:—

ROBERT JN^O PARRY
BORN THE 1 MAR. 1759
DIED APR. 12. 1760.

"Parrys," St. Peter's Parish, in 1852, contained 222 acres, and was owned by George W. Ottley.

Family of Patterson.

John Patterson. Will dated Jan. 1732. (Fragmentary.) My son Walter . . . . John . . . . & my dr. Sarah all my estate. Appoint D^r . . . . Sydserfe & Dr Stephen Mignan, Ex'ors, & my wife Sarah during her widowhood.

Codicil. I hereby bequeath to my son John a tankard, & to my dau. Sarah silver spoons. Witnessed by . . . . as Crawford . . . . Hawes . . . . Monteigne. Before Edward Byam, Esq., was sworn Thomas Crawford, merchant, 13 June 1733. Recorded 17 . . . .

Joseph Patterson, ivory-turner. Will dated 23 Aug. 1754. All my estate to my wife, & after her death to my 3 children. Witnessed by William Dickinson, Samuel Clayton. Recorded 27 Sep. 1759.

Elizabeth Becket, widow. Will dated 9 Nov. 1792. My former husb^d Roger Ashley left all his est. to me, which, after my marriage with Peter Becket, I sold for £500 c., having no children. To my late husband's bro. Ed. Ashley £500 c., & in default to his bro. Chr. Ashley. My goddau. Ann Becket Bray £100 st. My sist. Ann McPherson £30 c. a year. My neph. Peter Becket Patterson £1000 c. All res. to my niece Rebecca Patterson, wid. She & Isaac Eccleston, Ex'ors. Witnessed by Mary Martin, Langford L. Hodge, James Grant. By Edward Byam, Esq., was sworn James Grant, writing clerk, 28 March 1794. Recorded 29 March.

1773, Oct. 21. Joseph Pattison, jun., heir of Joseph Pattison, sen., deceased. (Minutes of Council.)

PARISH REGISTER OF ST. JOHN.

Baptized.

1708 Oct. 23 John S. of John Pattison & Hannah his wife.
1711 Jan. 27 Mary D. of John Patterson & Hannah his wife.
1715 April 3 Elizabeth D. of John Patterson & [*blank*] his wife.
1716 Oct. 29 Hannah d. of John Patterson & Hannah his wife.
1727 June 11 Alice the d. of John Patterson and Sarah his wife.
1728 Jan. 9 Sarah the d. of John Patterson and Sarah his wife.
1730 Jan. 15 Walter the s. of John Patterson & Sarah his wife.
1732 Jan. 7 John the s. of John Patterson & Sarah his wife.
1788 Feb. 1 John S. of Robert Patterson and Margaret his wife; b. the 4th May 1787.
1810 June . . George Infant S. of Captain William Patterson, R.N., and his wife.
1817 Mar. 29 Eliza Jane Josephine D. of John Patterson and Isabella his wife. B. 24th Nov. 1815.

Married.

1754 Nov. 19 Robert Patterson and Grace Abbott, Widow; by L.
1754 Dec. 26 John Patterson and Ann Murray, Spinster; by L.
1759 June 2 Walter Patterson and Ann Smith (Widow); by L.
1759 July 28 Galbraith Patterson and Frances Sawcolt; by L.
1759 Sep. 15 Peter Forster to Ann Patterson (Widow); by L.

Buried.

1711 Oct. 3 John s. of John Patterson.
1716 Nov. 1 Hannah Patterson.
1716 Dec. 22 Hannah Patterson.
1727 Sep. 28 Alice D. of John Patterson.
1733 June 10 Mr John Patterson.
1739 July 20 James Patterson, Chymist.
1748 Feb. 2 Henry Patterson.
1754 Feb. 1 Mary Patterson.
1763 Dec. 14 Walter Patterson, P.
1773 May 22 Robert Patterson.
1774 Dec. 20 Ann Patterson.
1775 Sep. 29 Frances Cressey Patterson.
1775 Nov. 23 Alexander Patterson.
1780 Feb. 25 John Patterson.
1780 June 8 Ann Patterson.
1788 Feb. 3 John Patterson, Infant.
1793 June 3 Captain Patterson.
1799 Dec. 29 Joseph Patterson.
1808 Nov. 4 William Patterson.

Family of Payne.

1700, July 7. Will of Peter Brozett of S[t] Giles in the Fields, who was married with M[rs] Anne de Clainenbrong, and issue was: Mary, Paulina, Peter, Cath., John, Jas., & Mary Brozett. Wife to be heiress, then children. Daniel Papon & Peter Soulegre* her sons-in-law, Overseers. Proved 26 July 1701. (91 Dyer.) Translated out of French.

1757, July. Abraham Payne of St. Christopher's, Esq., deceased. Adm'on to Mary Douglas, wife of James George Douglas, Esq., the dau., Anne Douglas the widow and relict renouncing.

1775, Aug. 7. Adm'on of George Thomas Payne, late of Antigua, Esq., bachelor, deceased, granted to Stephen Payne Galwey, Esq., the brother.

John Brozet. Will dated at Southampton 6 Jan. 1777; proved 20 April 1780 by Peter Guinard and Catherine Durban, spinster. (174 Collins.) All my estate to M[r] Peter Papon, M[r] Peter Guinard, & M[rs] Cath. Durban, & Ex'ors. Witnessed by Thomas Scott, Thomas Waight, James Gerard.

1st Codicil. 26 Dec. 1778. M[rs] Paine of S[t] Christopher's dying without a will I have administered as heir, & I divide the neat produce thereof into 15 shares. To Miss Brozet that lived with her 4 parts, & to M[r] Brozet her brother 2 parts. To M[r] John Brozet of S[t] Kitts 2 parts. To the late M[rs] Percival's (formerly Mary Brozet, spinster) children at S[t] Kitts 2 parts. M[r] Peter Brozet of Chelsea, Miss Cath. Durban, M[rs] Guinard, John Smith Budgen, Esq., & M[r] Papon my Ex'or, each 1 part. Witnessed by James Gerard, Joseph Norris, Thomas Scott.

2nd Codicil. 18 June 1779. Whereas Mary Pasquereau Payne, late of S[t] Christopher's, widow, died intestate, & all her real estate descended to me as her heir-at-law, & I took out letters of administration of her personal estate in the P.C.C., & have already received £1596. I give to my 2 friends M[r] Peter Guinard & M[rs] Cath. Durban all my real & personal estate in Trust to sell & divide into 15 shares (as in the will). Witnessed by Thomas Andrews, William Andrews, Thomas Adney Payne. Letter annexed refers to a dau. of Lewis Brozet, dated 25 Jan. 1779. Will translated from the French 10 April 1780.

* See his will later, under Woodley.

1778, July 13. Mary Payne, late of St. Christopher's, widow, deceased, adm'on to John Brozet, Esq., cousin german once removed and next of kin.

James Parson Ottley in his will dated 4 Feb. 1779 names his mother Lucretia Payne and John Willett Payne and William Payne.

1780, April 21. Further adm'on of goods left unadministered by John Brozet, Esq., deceased, now granted to Peter Guinard and Catharine Durban, his Ex'ors.

Close Roll, 3 Geo. III., Part 2, Nos. 4 and 5.

Indenture made the 4th June 1763 between Ralph Payne, late of St. Kitts, Esq., but now of St. George's Parish, Hanover Square (eldest son and heir, and likewise devisee named in the will of Ralph Payne of St. Kitts, Esq., his late father, deceased), of the one part, and Henry Wilmot of Gray's Inn, Esq., of the other part, witnesseth that for barring, docking, etc., all estates tail and all reversions and remainders in the messuages, etc., hereinafter mentioned, and in consideration of 5*s.* Ralph Payne grants, etc., to Henry Wilmot for one whole year all messuages, plantations, lands, etc., and negros and other slaves, etc., belonging to him in Nevis in America, late the estate of Ralph Payne, deceased, for the use of Ralph Payne and his heirs for ever, and Ralph Payne appoints, etc., Thomas Cottle of St. Kitts and Henry Sharpe of Nevis, Esquires, his Attornies in Nevis.

No. 5.

Indenture made the 3rd June 1763 between the same. (A mere counterpart.)

Pedigree of Payne.

ARMS.—*Gules, a fess between two lions passant argent.*
CREST.—*A lion's gamb erased, holding the lower part of a tilting-lance in bend.*

CAPTAIN PHILIP PAYNE of St. Christopher's in 1669 and 1673.

CAPTAIN SAMUEL PAYNE of St. Christopher's in 1673.

Colonel Stephen Payne of St. Christopher's; Member of Council in 1704; æt. 47 in 1707-8; died 10 Sep. 1711, æt. 50. M.I. in Middle Island Churchyard. =. . . .

Lieutenant Abraham Payne of St. Christopher's; Member of the Assembly 1683—1686.

Abraham Payne of St. Christopher's, Esq., æt. 28 in 1707-8; of Christ Church, Nicholas Town, 1711; appointed Member of Council on 21 April 1730; died 1740. A = Anne, dau. of Ralph Willet by Anne his wife; living 1711.

Sir Charles Payne, Bart. = ... See PEDIGREE A.

Nathaniel Payne of St. Anne, Sandy Point, St. Christopher's, 1735. = ...

Stephen Payne, died æt. 6. M.I. at Middle Island.

Samuel Payne, died æt. 9. M.I. at Middle Island.

Two daus.

A |

Alice, only dau. of Colonel Francis Carlisle of Antigua, and sole heir of her brother Francis Carlisle; mar. 8 July 1734 at St. John's. 1st wife. ╤ Ralph Payne of St. Christopher's, Esq., matriculated from Oriel College, Oxon, 17 Dec. 1722, æt. 16; Barrister-at-Law Middle Temple 1730; appointed 1759 Chief Justice of St. Christopher's; died 1762. ╤ Margaret, dau. of . . . . Gallwey of St. Christopher's; mar. before 1750; she died there 1760. 2nd wife.

Ralph Payne, Baron Lavington, P.C., K.B., 1st son and heir; inherited the paternal estate in Nevis; born 19 March 1739 at St. George's, Basseterre, St. Christopher's; M.P. Shaftesbury 1768; K.B. 1771; Governor of Leeward Islands 1771—1775; M.P. Camelford 1774, Plympton 1780, Woodstock 1795; created Baron Lavington 1 Oct. 1795; a second time Governor of Leeward Islands 1801 till his death Aug. 1807; bur. at Carlisles, in Antigua, 4 Aug. 1807. M.I. at St. John's. ╤ Françoise Lambertine de Kolbel, dau. of Frederick Maximilian, Baron de Kolbel, Maj.-Gen. in Imperial Service; mar. 1 Sep. 1767 at St. George's, Hanover Square; died 2 May 1830 at Hampton Court Palace.

s.p.

Elizabeth Payne, only dau., a minor 1753; mar. William Payne Georges of St. Christopher's. She mar. 2ndly Pickering, son of Dr. Lettsom, at Tortola, 22 Sep. 1808; he died 1 month after, æt. 27. (See vol. ii., p. 175.)

Stephen Payne-Gallwey of Tofts Hall, co. Norfolk; matriculated from Oriel College, Oxon 14 Feb. 1767, æt. 17; by Act of Parliament in 1762 assumed name and arms of Gallwey; died 31 March 1812, in Montague Street. ╤ Mary, dau. of Oliver de Lancey of New York; died 1795 at Salthill.

A son, a Captain in the Army, died 19 April 1795, æt. 18.

Charlotte Payne-Gallwey, only dau. and heir, æt. 14 in 1795; mar. 25 May 1797 John Moseley of Great Glenham, co. Suffolk.

PEDIGREE 3.

Sir Charles Payne, Bart., of St. Christopher's; æt. 24 in 1707-8; appointed Member of Council 1730; knighted before 1733; created a Baronet 31 Oct. 1737; died 21 Dec. 1744, æt. 62. M.I. in Middle Island Churchyard, St. Christopher's. ╤ . . . . dau. and coheir of William McArthur of St. Christopher's.

Abraham Payne, junior, matriculated from Oriel College, Oxon, 17 Dec. 1723; æt. 17 in 1729; Member of Council of St. Christopher's; living 1733; died v.p. ╤ . . . . dau. of Jeffrey Brown, Chief Justice of St. Christopher's.

Sir Gillies Payne, 2nd Bart., of Tempsford Hall, co. Bedford; died there 1801, æt. 80. ╤ . . . .

Frances Payne, posthumous and only surviving dau., mar. 30 March 1758, at St. George's, Hanover Square, William Woodley of St. Christopher's and later Governor of Leeward Islands; he died 1793 at St. Christopher's; she died 1813, æt. 75, at Bloxworth, co. Dorset.

Sir John Payne, 3rd Bart., died 1803. His legitimacy questioned. ╤ Mary, 1st surviving dau. and heir of Sir Philip Monnoux, Bart., of Wootton House and Sandy Place; mar. 2ndly, 20 Feb. 1811, J. F. Buckworth; she died 1850.

Mary Payne, died Dec. 1819 at Elstow near Bedford.

—

Christiana Payne, mar. 1st, Nov. 1788, George Sharpe of St. Vincent; 2ndly, 21 Sep. 1808, at St. Pancras, Thomas Swale; she died 25 Jan. 1816.

Charles Payne, died 1849. Claimed to be 4th Bart.

Rev. Coventry Payne, Vicar of Hatfield Pevered, co. Essex, 1823, and of Munden 1830; died 1849. Claimed to be 5th Bart. ╤ Henrietta, 3rd dau. of Peter Wright of Hatfield Priory, co. Essex.

Coventry Payne of Wootton House, co. Bedford, born 1821; died 1874. Claimed to be 6th Bart. ╤ Harriet, 1st dau. of John Wright of Wickham Place, co. Essex; first-cousin to her husband.

Philip Monnoux Payne of Wootton, co. Bedford, born 1858; of Magdalen College, Cambridge. Claims to be 7th Bart. ╤ Winifred, dau. of Richard Vigors Doyne; mar. 1880.

s.p.

Colonel Stephen Payne, living 1711; Member of Council, St. Christopher's, but resigned Dec. 1768.

Ann Payne, living 1711.

Eliza Payne, living 1711.

Willet Payne = ...

Clara Payne, mar. Stephen Adye of St. Christopher's; he died 1756.

John Willet Payne, Rear-Admiral R.N. = ...

Sir William Payne-Gallwey, Bart., Lieut.-General and Colonel of 3rd Dragoon Guards; created Baronet 8 Dec. 1812; in 1814 assumed name and arms of Gallwey; died 16 April 1831. = Harriet, dau. of Valentine, 1st Earl of Dunraven; mar. 19 Nov. 1804; died 13 Dec. 1845.

George Thomas Payne, bur. 7 June 1774 at St. John's; died bachelor. Adm'on granted 7 Aug. 1775 to his brother Stephen Payne-Gallwey.

Lucretia Payne.

Martha Payne.

Ralph Payne, matric. from Oriel College, Oxon, 14 Feb. 1767, æt. 17; B.A. 1770; M.A. 1773.

. . . . = A son, Rector of a parish in Barbados.

Sir William Payne-Gallwey, 2nd Bart., born 1807; Major in Army; M.P. Thirsk 1851—1881; died 19 Dec. 1881. = Emily Anne, 3rd dau. and coheir of Sir Robert Frankland Russell, Bart.; mar. 1847.

Henry John William Payne-Gallwey, Captain R.N.; died 25 May 1875.

Philip Payne-Gallwey, Captain 90th Light Infantry; died at Pilmoor Hall, Yorkshire, 23 Feb. 1894, æt. 82.

Rev. William Payne.

Charles Lane Payne, Barrister-at-Law Middle Temple, Acting Solicitor-General British Guiana. = ... dau. of . . . . Spence, and widow of . . . .

James F. Lavington Payne, Barrister-at-Law of Middle Temple; now of Grenada. = ... dau. of . . . . Gittens of Barbados.

Sir Ralph William Payne-Gallwey, 3rd Bart. = ...

Charles Payne of St. Christopher's; appointed Member of Council 1750; his death announced 27 Sep. 1765.

Sarah Payne, mar. 1st Thomas Butler, senior; 2ndly William Buckley of St. Christopher's, Barrister-at-Law, *circa* 1736, and died before 1761.

A dau., mar. . . . . Estridge, son of President Estridge; both living 1733.

Peter Payne, M.P., of Blunham House, Sandy, co. Bedford, died 1843. Claimed to be 3rd Bart. on the ground of the illegitimacy of his elder brother. = Elizabeth Sarah, only dau. of Samuel Steward of Stourton Castle, co. Stafford; mar. 1789 at Kinver, co. Stafford; died 23 April 1832 at Leamington, co. Warwick.

Elizabeth Payne, mar. 1790 Rev. Richard Palmer.

Janet Payne, mar. 1792 Richard Booth.

Susannah Payne, youngest dau., mar. 1797 Hugh Perry Keane of St. Vincent.

Charles Gillies Payne, matric. from Merton College, Oxon, 13 Dec. 1812, æt. 18; B.A. 1815; M.A. 1818; Barrister-at-Law Middle Temple 1823; died 21 May 1870. Claimed to be 4th Bart. = Mary Elizabeth, 1st dau. of Rev. Thelwall Salusbury, Rector of Graveley, co. Herts; died 8 Sep. 1855, æt. 54. M.I. at Offley, co. Herts.

Robert Henley Payne of Bordean, co. Hants, born 1795. = Louisa, dau. of Henry Chawner of Newton Manor, co. Hants.

Salusbury Gillies Payne, J.P., of Blunham House, Sandy, co. Bedford, only son and heir, born 1829; entered Rugby 25 April 1845, æt. 15; matriculated from Brasenose College, Oxford, 22 June 1848, æt. 19; B.A. 1852; Barrister-at-Law Middle Temple 1857. Claims to be 5th Bart. = Catherine Anne, 3rd dau. of Robert Chadwick of High Bank, Manchester; mar. 1858.

Henry Lavington Payne, born 1833; late of 2nd Dragoon Guards.

Other issue.

Charles Robert Salusbury Payne, 1st son, born 1859; Lieut. R.N. (retired). = Aline Cecilia, only child of James Henry Murray of 34 Ovington Square, London; mar. 22 Aug. 1893 at St. Paul's, Knightsbridge.

Alfred Lavington Payne.

Close Roll, 7 Geo. III., Part 14, Nos. 25 and 26.

Indenture made the 24th March 1767 between Sir Gillies Payne of St. Kitts, Bart., now residing at Roxton, Beds, of the one part, and John Willett of Broad Street, London, merchant, of the other part, witnesseth that in consideration of 5s. Sir Gillies Payne grants, etc., to John Willett those two messuages (late of Sir Charles Payne, Bart., his father, deceased), in the town of Sandy Point and in the parish of St. Ann, Sandy Point, St. Kitts, and the plantation in the tenure of Sir Gillies Payne called the French Ground Plantation containing 200 acres, and that other plantation in the tenure of Sir Gillies Payne in the said parish called Sandy Point Plantation containing 100 acres, and that other plantation in the tenure of Sir Gillies Payne in the parish of St. Thomas, Middle Island, called Half Way Tree Plantation containing 40 acres, and all the pasture and mountain lands, etc., and all messuages, etc., whatsoever for one whole year, yielding therefore one peppercorn if demanded, and Sir Gillies Payne appoints Hon. Colonel Stephen Payne, Walter Jodrel, and Archibald Esdaile, jun., Esquires, all of St. Kitts, his Attorneys.

No. 25.

Indenture made the 25th March 1767 between Sir Gillies Payne, of the one part, and John Willett, of the other part, witnesseth that for barring, etc., of all estates tail, remainders, and reversions expectant, etc., and in consideration of 5s. Sir Gillies Payne bargains, etc., to John Willett all those messuages, plantations, etc. (as in No. 26), to the use of John Willett and his assigns for ever, to the use of Sir Gillies Payne and his heirs and assigns for ever.

Close Roll, 7 Geo. III., Part 14, Nos. 23 and 24.

Indenture made the 24th March 1767 between Sir Gillies Payne of St. Kitts, Bart., now residing at Roxton, Beds, of the one part, and John Willett of Broad Street, London, merchant, of the other part, witnesseth that in consideration of 5s. Sir Gillies Payne bargains, etc., to John Willett all that plantation or ground land of Charles Payne, Esq., his brother, deceased, and heretofore of Sir Charles Payne his father, deceased, in the parish of St. Thomas, Nevis, containing 300 acres, part thereof cultivated cane land and the other part mountain land, and all messuages, etc., whatsoever of Sir Charles Payne and afterwards of Charles Payne, Esq., in Nevis, and all negros and other slaves, and all horses, mules, cows, sheep, and other cattle whatsoever for one whole year, and Sir Gillies Payne appoints the Hon. Colonel Stephen Payne, Walter Jodrel, Esq., and Archibald Esdaile, jun., Esq., all of St. Kitts, his Attorneys.

No. 23.

Indenture made the 25th March 1767 between Sir Gillies Payne, of the one part, and John Willett, of the other part, witnesseth that for settling and assigning to the uses mentioned and in consideration of 5s. Sir Gillies Payne grants, bargains, etc., to John Willett all that plantation, etc. (as in No. 24), to the use of Sir Gillies Payne and his heirs for ever, and to no other use, intent, or purpose whatsoever.

Close Roll, 8 Geo. III., Part 13, Nos. 1 and 2.

Indenture dated 3 March 1768. Ralph Payne, late of St. Christopher's, now of Queen Ann Street, Cavendish Square, Esq., 1st son and heir of Ralph Payne, Esq., deceased, for 5s. conveys to Valentine Henry Allott of Gray's Inn, Gent., all his plantations, slaves, and stock in Nevis, and nominates John Dasent, John Vanderpoole, and John Stanley, all of Nevis, his Attorneys.

No. 1.

Indenture tripartite dated 4 March 1768 between Ralph Payne, Esq., of 1st part, David Viscount Stormont and Henry Wilmot of Bloomsbury Square, Esq. of 2nd part, and Valentine Henry Allott of Gray's Inn, Gent., of the 3rd. Whereas by Indentures of 3 and 4 June 1763 Ralph Payne conveyed to Henry Wilmot all his lands in Nevis; and whereas by Indenture tripartite dated 31 Aug. 1767 between Ralph Payne, of the 1st part, Frances Kolbel, daughter of late Baron de Kolbell, Major-General in the Imperial Service, of the 2nd part, and David Viscount Stormont and Henry Wilmot, of the 3rd part, reciting the intended marriage (soon after solemnized) between Ralph Payne and Frances Kolbell, he agreed to secure to his wife £1000 a year if she survived him, and bound himself in £40,000 to Viscount Stormont and Henry Wilmot, and for 10s. granted to them a plantation called Walkers, or the Lower, or the Windmill in St. James Parish, and in Fig Tree Division of Nevis for 99 years in trust, now, to remove doubts and confirm the deed of 3 and 4 June 1763, and to secure the annuity, he conveys all his estates in Nevis to Valentine Henry Allott in trust, viz.: Walker's Plantation for Viscount Stormont and Henry Wilmot for remainder of term of 99 years. Walker's is bounded W. with John Ward, Esq., E. with the mountain, N. by the high road and lands of John Ward, S. by Ralph Willett, Esq., John Prater Pinney, Esq., Ralph Payne's other plantation called De Witts, all which lands had been heretofore purchased by his father Ralph Payne, deceased, of Thomas Walker, Esq.

Close Roll, 54 Geo. III., Part 49, Nos. 8 and 9.

Indenture made the 18th Nov. 1814 between Sir Charles Payne of Tempsford Hall, Beds, Bart. (eldest son of Sir John Payne, late of Tempsford Hall, Bart., deceased, who was eldest son of Sir Gillies Payne, formerly of Tempsford Hall, Bart., deceased), of the one part, and Thomas Farrer of Lincoln's Inn, Gent., of the other part, witnesseth that in consideration of 5s. Sir Charles Payne conveys to Thomas Farrer all that plantation, late in the tenure of Sir Gillies Payne, deceased, but now of . . . . in the parish of St. Ann, Sandy Point, in St. Kitts, called the French Ground Plantation, containing 200 acres, and all pasture and mountain land for one whole year. Thomas Atkinson, William Matthew Coulthurst, witnesses, both of 64 Lincoln's Inn, Gentlemen.

No. 8.

Indenture made the 19th Nov. 1814 between the above for barring and destroying all estate tail, etc., and Sir Charles Payne appoints the Hon. John Julius, Robert Cleghorn, Esq., and John George Goldfrap, Esq., all of St. Kitts, his Attorneys.

1668. Martyn Payne of Antigua granted a patent for 15 acres.

1669, March 22. Captain Philip Payne appointed one of the Commissioners to demand back the English portion of St. Kitts. In 1670 the inhabitants of that island petitioned that he and others, owners of estates in the Leeward Islands, might join the Commission. In 1673 it was reported that his estate and that of Captain Samuel Payne at St. Kitts had been devasted by the French since the peace. (Colonial Calendar, America and West Indies.)

1678, Nov. 12. Martin Paine, planter, sells a parcell of land at Popeshead to Jonas Langford.

1683-4. Abraham Payne then a member of the Assembly of St. Christopher's.

1686, Nov. 16. Lieut. Abraham Payne a member of the Assembly of St. Christopher's.

1704, Sep. 5. Stephen Payne, Esq., then a member of the Council of St. Christopher's. On 25 Nov. 1707 he was styled Colonel, and in 1712 his death was announced. (B. T. Leeward Islands, vol. 12.)

1707-8, Jan. List of inhabitants of St. Christopher's :—

	Age.		Men.	Women.	Boys.	Girls.
Stephen Payne, Esq.	47	White	3	2	2	1
		Negros	22	19	8	5
Charles Payne	24	White	1	1	2	
		Negros	4	5	1	1
Abraham Payne	28	White	1	2	1	1
		Negros	6	3	1	1

1711, Aug. 10. List of inhabitants of St. Christopher's:—

Christ Church, Nichola Town.

	White Woman.	White Children.	Servant.	Negros.
Abraham Payne	Ann Payne.	Ralph Payne. Stephen Payne. Ann Payne. Eliza Payne.	1	19

St. Anne's, Sandy Point.

	Man.	Woman.	Boys.	Girl.	Slaves.
Charles Payne. Esq.	1	1	3	1	19

St. Thomas, Middle Island.

	Men.	Women.
Col. Stephen Payne	2	2

1729-30. Governor Mathew appoints Abraham Payne, Esq., to a seat in the Council of St. Kitts.

1730. Mr. Ralph Payne produced his certificate of his having been called to the bar in London, and took the oaths previous to practising the Law here. (Minutes of Council, St. Kitts.)

1733, Dec. 20. Abraham Payne, jun., Esq., was recommended for a seat in the Council of St. Christopher's, but objection was made that several of his family were already Councillors, viz. his father Sir Charles Payne and his uncle Abraham Payne, Esq. A sister of his was also married to a son of President Estridge, and Mr. Joseph Phipps was distantly related to the Paynes.

1735. Sir Charles Payne petitions for a grant of land in St. John's, one of the Virgin Islands.

1740, May 20. Abraham Payne a member of the St. Kitts Council is dead. (B. T. Leeward Islands, vol. 55, p. 154.)

1748, June 30. At Whitehall. Ralph Payne, Esq., appointed a Councillor of St. Christopher's.

1750, March 29. Charles Payne, Esq., to be of the Council of Nevis. (America and West Indies, No. 103.)

1753, June 14. Petition of Ralph Payne, Esq., and Ralph Payne, jun., his son and Elizabeth Payne his daughter (these two being under 21) for leave to bring in a bill to confirm the agreement between John Gray, Esq., and Elizabeth his wife in regard to the settlement of certain plantations.

1755, Aug. 12. Stephen Payne, Esq., to be of the Council of St. Christopher's *vice* John White, Esq., resigned.

1759, Dec. 27. Ralph Payne appointed Chief Justice of St. Christopher's *vice* Richard Wilson, deceased.

1760. The wife of Ralph Payne, Esq., Mrs. Margaret Payne.

1763, Jan. 18. The death announced of Mr. Payne, Chief Justice of St. Christopher's.

1763, Aug. 4. Ralph Payne recommended for a seat at the Council Board of St. Kitts.

1765, Sep. 27. Governor Thomas announces the death of Charles Payne, Esq., of the Nevis Council.

1768, Dec. Stephen Payne, Esq., resigns his seat at the Council of St. Christopher's.

1771, May 15. Warrant ordered for Sir Ralph Payne to be Captain-General of the Leeward Islands.

1771, May 31. Stephen Payne-Gallway recommended to be of the Council of St. Kitts.

1778, Sep. 30. Governor W. M. Burt writes: "I am truly sorry to say Sir Gillies Payne, now in England, was always deemed a Strong North American Partizan. . . . . His Manager is an avowed supporter of that Party."

1789, Oct. 3. Sir Gillies Payne writes from Tempsford Hall that his father purchased Flat Island near Auguilla of a native of St. Christopher's sixty years ago.

1892, July 8. The gross value has been sworn at £401,525 and the net value at £399,866 of the personal estate of Mr. James Chadwick, late of 12 Queen's Gate Place, and Hints Hall, Tamworth, the principal partner in the Manchester firms of J. and N. Philips and Co., and James Chadwick and Brother, his share and interest in whose business he leaves to his nephews and partners Alfred Lavington Payne and Frank Morrison Genfield Grant. He bequeaths to each of them £1000, and to the former £6000 and the latter £12,000, advanced by the testator to them respectively as capital. The executors may leave in the business, whilst his said nephews remain partners therein, not exceeding £200,000 without security. Mr. Chadwick bequeaths £10,000 for distribution amongst charitable institutions in Manchester, Salford, and Birmingham. A sum of £200,000 is to be set apart to secure an annuity of £4000 for Mrs. Chadwick during her widowhood, or a life annuity of £2000 in the event of her re-marriage, and the remainder of the income of the trust fund is to be paid as to two-fifths thereof to the testator's brother Mr. Robert Chadwick, and as to one-fifth each to his sisters Mrs. Milne, Mrs. Grant, and Lady Payne. On the death of Mrs. Chadwick a legacy of £40,000 is to be paid to Mr. Robert Chadwick, and legacies of £20,000 each to the testator's three sisters. He bequeaths immediate legacies of £5000 to his wife; £2000 to his said brother; £2000 to his brother-in-law Sir Salisbury Gillies Payne, Bart.; £1000 to his partner Mr. William Morton Philips; £10,000 to his nephew James Melville Grant; £5000 each to his niece Eva Tatton and to Georgina Losack; £5000 in trust for Elizabeth Clapham and her son; £2000 to J. T. Barnett King; and life annuities of £200 each to Harriott and Elizabeth Barnett, the Rev. William Baring Hayter, and Colonel King. Mrs. Chadwick is to have the use and enjoyment for her life of Hints Hall and its furniture. The residue of the late Mr. Chadwick's property is left in trust for his nephews and nieces; but "I revoke this will," he states, "in case I shall have any child living at my decease, or born in due time afterwards."

1893, Aug. 23. Mr. Charles Robert Salusbury Payne, Lieut. R.N. (retired), eldest son of Sir Salusbury Gillies Payne of Blunham House, Sandy, Bedfordshire, was yesterday married at St. Paul's, Knightsbridge, to Miss Aline Cecilia Murray, only child of Mr. and Mrs. James Henry Murray of 34 Ovington Square. The bride's uncle, Mr. Frederick Sloane Stanley of Roche Court, Fareham, in the absence of her father through indisposition, gave her away. Mr. W. B. M. Bird was "best man." The service was conducted by the Rev. Walter Welby, uncle of the bride.

1894, Feb. 23. At Pilmoor Hall, Yorkshire, Philip Payne-Gallwey, late Captain 90th Light Infantry, aged 82.

EXTRACTS FROM THE 'GENTLEMAN'S MAGAZINE.'

1758, March 20. Wm Wordley of Hill Street, Esq — to Miss Payne of Hanover-square.

1763, Jan. Hon. Ralph Payne, Esq; of the island of St Kitts (p. 97).

1767, Sep. Ralph Payne, Esq; to Mademoiselle Köbel daughter of the late general. She came over with the Princess Poniatouski, Sister to the King of Poland (p. 478).

1769. Ralph Payne (elected) M.P. for Shaftesbury in expectation of the captain-generalship of the Leeward Islands (p. 632).

1771, Feb. 18. Ralph Payne, Esq., to be a K.B.

1771, Nov. Sir Giles Payne, Knt. at St Kitts (p. 522).

1774, Aug. At Antigua, George Thomas Payne. Esq; brother to his Excellency the Governour (p. 391).

1788, May. John Payne, esq. eldest son of Sir Gillies P. bart. of Temford-hall, co. Bedford, to Miss Campbell, of Blunham, in the same county (p. 561).

1788, Nov. At Tempsford, co. Bedford, Geo. Sharpe, esq. of St Vincent's, in the West Indies, to Miss C. Payne, 2d dau. of Sir Gillies P. bart. (p. 1026).

1789. At Kinver, co. Stafford, Peter Payne, esq. son of Sir Gillies P. bart. to Miss Steward, of Stourton-castle (p. 859).

1795, April 19. Capt. Payne-Galloway, only son of — Payne esq, who a few years ago, took the name of Galloway for an estate at Tofts, in Norfolk, and younger brother, by a second marriage, of Sir Ralph Payne, K.B., and married one of the three daughters of Oliver De Lancey, esq. of New York, who lost a large property by his attachment to Government in the American war. His lady died at Salt-hill, about 10 years ago, and left two children, the above young gentleman and a daughter, now in her 15th year etc. . . . . he was in his 19th year (p. 440).

1799. Capt. John Willett Payne to be rear admiral of the blue, & Lord Lavington appointed Govr of Leeward islands *vice* Majr Genl Chas. Leigh (p. 537).

1801. John Willett Payne to be Rear Admiral of the white (p. 178).

1801, lately. At Tempford, co. Bedford, after an illness of a few hours, aged 80, Sir Gillies Payne bart. so created 1737 (p. 189).

1803, Nov. 17. At his apartments in Greenwich hospital, after a few days illness of a paralytic stroke, in his 51st year, Jn. Willett Payne, esq. rear-admiral of the Red, vice-admiral of the coasts of Devonshire and Cornwall, treasurer of Greenwich hospital, comptroller of the household of his Royal Highness the Prince of Wales, and lord warden of the Stanneries, etc. (long notice of his life). On the 25th he was interred in the vault at N.W. corner of St Marg's Westmr (p. 1187).

1807, Aug. 1. Lord Lavington, governor of the West India Islands, and K.B.; of whom a more particular account in our next (p. 889).

Oct. Ralph Payne, Lord Lavington, K.B., Captain-general and Governor in Chief of his Majesty's Leeward Islands, and a Privy Counsellor, was born in 1738, and married Francoise Lambertine, Baroness de Kolbell, of a noble Saxon family, daughter of Frederick-Maximilian, Baron de Kolbel, a general in the Imperial Service, a lady eminently distinguished. Deceasing without issue, the barony of Lavington becomes extinct, making the sixth Irish peerage which has become extinct since the Union. Ralph Lord Lavington was a nobleman much endeared in private life; and in his public capacity esteemed and revered. He was descended from an antient family in Devonshire; and one of his ancestors eminently distinguished himself for his loyalty to Charles I.; but fled to the West Indies after the battle of Worcester. From a younger branch of this noble House descended the Baronet family of Payne of Tempsford-hall co. Bedford. At a very early age his Lordship discovered those shining talents which elevated him in life. After making the tour of Europe, on the General Election in 1768 he was chosen Representative for the borough of Shaftesbury; and served in the successive parliaments of 1774 and 1780 for Camelford and Plympton. In 1771, he was appointed Captain-general and Governor in Chief of the Leeward Islands; and continued in that station until 1775, when he returned to England, and was appointed Clerk of the Board of Green Cloth; in which department he continued during the existence of it. In 1772, his Lordship was invested with the military order of the Bath; and died the senior Knight of the Order. In 1795 he was returned to Parliament for Woodstock; and was advanced to the dignity of Baron Lavington in October in the same year: in 1801 he was again appointed Captain-general of the Leeward Islands, and sworn of his Majesty's most honourable Privy Council (p. 974).

1808, Sep. 21. At St Pancras, Thomas Swale, esq. of Little Barton-lodge Suffolk, to Mrs Sharpe, widow of George Sharpe esq. of the Views, Huntingdon, and one of the daughters of the late Sir Gillies Payne, bart. of Tempsford-hall, co. Bedford (p. 951).

1808, Sep. 22. At Tortola, Pickering Lettsom, esq. (son of Dr Lettsom) to Mrs Georges, widow of William Payne Georges esq. of Manchester-square, sister to Lord Lavington and Mother of Mrs Charles Combe (p. 1038).

1808, Sep. 29. At Tortola, Charles Combe, esq. youngest son of Dr Combe of Hart-street, Bloomsbury; a young gentleman whose untimely loss will long be regretted by many who well knew and justly estimated his merit (p. 1039).

1811, Feb. 20. J. F. Buckworth, esq. Lieut.-col. in the Royal Cheshire militia, to Lady Mary Payne, of Wooton, Bedford, widow of Sir John Payne, bt. of Timpsford-hall (p. 288).

1812, March 31. In Montague-street, Portman-square, Stephen Payne Galwey, esq. of Thetford, Norfolk (p. 397).

1816, Jan. 25. Christiana, relict of the late T. Swale, esq. of the Views, Hunts, and of Mildenhall, Suffolk, youngest daughter of the late Sir Gillies Payne, bart. of Tempsford-hall, co. Bedford (p. 187).

1817, June 10. At the estate of her late father, Joseph Rawlins, esq. at St Christopher's, where she went for the recovery of her health, Frances George, wife of Lieut. J. Rawlins Thomas, R.N. great niece of Gen. Sir William Payne bart. and of the late Lord Lavington. And Sep. 7, at Stonehouse, Devon, aged 8 months, Frances Anne, infant daughter of the above.

1819, Dec., Lately. At Elstow, near Bedford, Mary, eldest daughter of the late Sir Gillies Payne, bart. (p. 569).

1830, May 2. In Hampton Court Palace, the Right Hon. Frances Lady Lavington. She was a daughter of Frederick Maximilian Baron de Kolbel, a general in the Imperial service; and was left a widow by Ralph Lord Lavington, K.B. in 1807 (p. 477).

1831, May. Lately. Sir William Payne Gallwey, Bart. a General in the army, and Colonel of the 3d dragoon guards, half brother to the late Lord Lavington, and brother-in-law to the Earl of Dunraven. Long obituary notice follows (p. 466).

1832, April 23. Warwick. At Leamington, Eliz-Sarah, wife of Sir Peter Payne, Bart. M.P. of Knuston-hall, Northamptonshire. She was the only dau. of Samuel Steward, esq. was married in 1789, and has left a numerous family (p. 478).

1839, July 20. At Blunham, Beds, James Elsden Everard, of Congham, Norfolk, esq. to Isabella Emma, youngest dau. of Sir Peter Payne, Bart. (p. 308).

1841, Jan. At Feltham Hill, aged 47, "Sir" Charles Payne, formerly of Tempsford hall, Bedfordshire, and Captain of the 9th Lancers. This gentleman, as well as his uncle, "Sir" Peter Payne, claimed the title of Baronet, created in 1737; but their titles were equally defective. See Courthope's 'Extinct Baronetage' (p. 332).

1841, June 30. At Blunham House, Beds, the Rev. Peter Samuel Henry Payne, M.A. Fellow of Balliol college, Oxford. He was the youngest son of the soi-disant Sir Peter Payne, Bart. of Blunham House (pp. 215, 338).

1843, Jan. 23. At Blunham House Bedfordshire, in his 82nd year, Sir Peter Payne, Bart. formerly M.P. for that county. Sir Charles Payne, of St Christopher's, was created a Baronet in 1737; and his son Sir Gillies, the second Baronet, died 1801, when, says Courthope in his 'Extinct Baronetage, 1835,' the title became extinct. After a lapse of 27 years the title was assumed by Peter Payne, esq. claiming to be a legitimate son of the last Baronet. Burke in 'Peerage and Baronetage,' states that Sir Peter "succeeded to the title in 1828, in consequence of a decree of the Court of Chancery, confirming a report, finding him the eldest son born in wedlock of his late father Sir Gillies Payne, of Tempsford, in Bedfordshire." This was the cause Glascott *v.* Bridges. . . . . Sir Peter Payne married in 1789, Elizabeth-Sarah, only daughter of Samuel Steward, esq. by whom he had issue three sons: 1, Charles Gillies, who succeeds; he married Mary, eldest daughter of the late Rev. Thelwall Salusbury, Rector of Graveley, Herts, and niece of Sir Robert Salusbury, Bart. and became a widower in 1840; 2, Robert Henley; and 3, the Rev. Peter Samuel Henry Payne, M.A. Fellow of Balliol college, Oxford, who died June 30, 1841; and four daughters: 1, Maria-Mary, married to Joseph Webster, esq. of Penns, in Warwickshire; 2, Laura-Janet; 3, Elizabeth, married to Charles Barnett, esq. of Stratton Park, Bedfordshire; and 4, Isabella-Emma (p. 94).

1844, Feb. 9. At Bedford, aged 84, Frances, widow of John Macartha Sharpe, esq. Solicitor-Gen. of the Island of Grenada, and sister of the late Sir Peter Payne, Bart. (p. 440).

1845, Dec. 16. In Eaton-sq. aged 61, the Lady Harriet Payne Gallwey, sister to the Earl of Dunraven. She was the daughter of Valentine-Richard the 1st Earl by Lady Frances Muriel Fox-Strangways, 6th dau. of Stephen 1st Earl of Ilchester; was married in 1804 to the late Sir William Payne Gallwey, Bart. and left his widow in 1831 (p. 216, 1846).

PARISH REGISTER OF ST. GEORGE, HANOVER SQUARE, LONDON.

Married.

1758 Mar. 30 William Woodley, B., & Frances Payne, S. Licence.

1767 Sep. 1 Ralph Payne, Esq[r], of this parish, B., & Frances Kolbel of S[t] James's, Westm[r], S. Licence.

PARISH REGISTER OF ST. GEORGE, ANTIGUA.

Buried.

1807 Aug. 4 Lord Lavington in his Garden at Carliles.

PARISH REGISTER OF ST. JOHN.

Married.

1734 July 8 Ralph Paine, Esq[r], and Alice Carlile, married without Lycence by the Rev[d] M[r] Davis.

Buried.

1774 June 7 George Thomas Payne.

1807 Aug. 4 His Excellency the Right Honourable Ralph, Lord Lavington, Baron of Lavington, One of his Majesty's most Honourable Privy Council, Knight Companion of the most Honourable Order of the Bath, Captain-General and Governor in Chief, in each and over all His Majesty's Leeward Charibbee Islands in America, Chancellor, Vice Admiral and Ordinary of the same, etc.

ST. JOHN'S CATHEDRAL.

On a white marble slab lying loose on the floor in north transept. It was formerly part of the base of a very handsome mural monument which was thrown down by the earthquake in 1843, since which time it appears to have been neglected. I even saw fragments of it in the fernery of Dr. Freeland at Parham:—

[He] was born [in the ISLAN]D of Saint *Chriſtop[hers* of] an *Engliſh* Family, distinguished for its Loyalty and Public-Spirit. His Education |

[h]e [re]ceived in *England*, and it prepared him [for the] Diſtinctions which awaited his Return to his native Iſland, when he was elected a Member |

of the HOUSE of ASSEMBLY, and on its first Meeting, unanimously called to the CHAIR of the HOUSE, in which high Situation he gave an early |

Diſplay of those ſuperior Talents and eminent Qualifications, which afterwards ſecured to him the CONFIDENCE of his KING, and the |

ESTEEM of his COUNTRY. On his return to *England*, in 1762, he was elected a Member of the HOUSE of COMMONS for the Borough |

of *Plympton* in *Devonſhire*; and from his perfect knowledge of colonial Affairs, he was appointed, in the year 1771, a Period of great |

national Intereſt, to be CAPTAIN-GENERAL and COMMANDER-IN-CHIEF of the *Leeward* Islands, at which time he was also inveſted with |

the Moſt-honourable ORDER of the BATH. He remained in the Exercife of his Government until the year 1774, when he returned to *England* |

and was appointed a Member of the BOARD of GREEN-CLOTH. During the Period of his Residence in *England* he sat in five different Parliaments |

and in the Year 1795, HIS-MAJESTY was moſt graciously pleaſed to raise him to the Dignity of a PEER of *Ireland*, by the Style and Tit[le] |

of BARON LAVINGTON of *Lavington*. In 1799, he was ſworn of HIS-MAJESTY'S Most-Honourable PRIVY-COUNCIL, and *again* appointed |

to the CHIEF-COMMAND of the *Leeward* Iſlands; in the wiſe and able Adminiſtration of which important Truſt he paſſed his latter Years |

and cloſed his venerable Life.

This NOBLEMAN

was as revered for his public Qualities

as he was beloved for his private Virtues:

He blended the dignity of his high Office with the Affability of his Diſpoſition and the Gracefulneſs of his Manners, |

and at once commanded the Respect and conciliated the Affection of all Ranks of People |

within the Circle of his Government.

As a ſincere and laſting Teſtimony of their veneration and Regret, |

The LEGISLATURE of ANTIGUA have erected this Monument. |

He died at the Government-House of this Iſland, on the third Day of Auguſt, 1807, aged 68, and was interred at his Eſtate called *Carliſles*.

N.B. There is a good account of this monument in 'Antigua and the Antiguans,' vol. i., p. 226, from which I copied the following M.I.:—

Sacred
To the memory of
RALPH PAYNE LORD LAVINGTON,
Of the kingdom of Ireland,
One of His Majesty's most honourable Privy Council,
Knight of the most honourable Order of the Bath,
and Captain-general, and Commander-in-chief of
The Leeward Islands.

OFFLEY CHURCH, CO. HERTS.

In memory of Dame Mary Elizabeth Payne, the beloved wife of Sir Charles Gillies Payne, of Blunham, Co. Bedford, Bart., and eldest daughter of the Revd. Thelwall Salusbury, Rector of Graveley, in this County, who died the 8th September 1855, in the 55th year of her age, leaving a husband and five children, with many relatives, to lament her sudden and unexpected death. Arms above: *Gules, a fess between two lions passant argent, on an inescutcheon the Badge of Ulster*, for PAYNE: impaling, *Gules, a lion rampant argent, crowned or, between three crescents of the last*, for SALISBURY.

(Cussans's 'Herts,' vol. ii., p. 107.)

MIDDLE ISLAND CHURCH, ST. KITTS.

Sir Charles Payne, Knight and Baronet, Major General of His Majesty's Leeward Islands. Dyed the 21 Day of December 1744, aged 62 years.

In the churchyard:—

Here lyeth the bodies of Colonel Stephen Payne who departed this life, the 10th day of September 1711, in the 51st year of his age.

And also of his sons Stephen and Samuel Payne, who departed this life in the 7th and 10th years of their age.

(Communicated by Mr. N. Darnell Davis of George Town, Demerara.)

Family of Payne or Pain.

John Jardine. Will dated 10 Oct. 1715. All property in America, Antigua, and Scotland to my nephew James Paine, now resident in Antigua. Witnessed by Anthony Garrett, Bartholomew Bovine, Robert White, John Clerke. Before Walter Hamilton, Esq., were sworn Anthony Garrett, Robert White, and Bartholomew Bovine, Aug. 1719.

Richard Oliver, Esq., in his will dated 17 Sep. 1761, names his niece Margaret Payne and her son Arthur.

1708, May 31. In Chancery, Antigua. Richard Jarden of Cambridge, linendraper, son of Andrew Jarden, late of Cloughbray, co. Anoundell, Scotland, deceased, brother of William Jarden, late of Antigua, Gent., deceased, against Mr. John Wright, defendant. William Jarden of St. John's, merchant, by his will dated 29 June 1704, gave half of all his estate to his right heir. James Pain of Antigua claims to be son of a sister of testator. James Pain is son of William Pain of the parish of New Abby, co. Gallaway, Ireland, by Elizabeth his wife otherwise Elizabeth Jarden. She is half-sister to the deceased. John Jarden of St. John's, merchant, answers that the said Elizabeth Jarden or Pain is eleven years older than himself. Andrew and Richard Jarden are no relations of testator. James Dickson also says that he has known James Pain twenty-five years. It is claimed that Andrew Jarden was brother of testator William Jarden, deceased. Nine months given to the parties for proof.

1709. Mr. Richard Jardine, linendraper, of Cambridge, states that his near relation has died in Antigua, and that he has gone out there. (B. T. Leeward Islands, vol. 2.)

Parish Register of St. John.

Baptized.

1742 Dec. 12 Arthur the s. of Cap^tn James Pain & Margaret his wife.
1750 Feb. 21 Ann the D. of John Payne and Mary his wife.
1754 Jan. 9 Thomas the S. of John Payne and Mary his wife; b. Aug. 26th 1752.
1755 Nov. 15 Edward the S. of John Payne and Mary his wife.
1768 July 5 Ellinor Louise D. of John Payne by Rebecca his wife.
1769 May 4 John James S. of John Payne and Rebecca his wife.
1771 Feb. 3 Margaret Dam the D. of John Payne and Rebecca his wife.
1773 June 29 William the S. of John Payne & Rebeccah his wife.
1780 April 19 Elvira the d. of Thomas Payne & Mary his wife.
1781 Dec. 31 John Thomas s. of Edward Payne & Ann his wife.
1784 Mar. 7 Mary the D. of Edward and Anne Payne.

Married.

1714 (? Jan.) 20 James Payne and Jane Mackenny; by L. from Govr Yeamons.
1718 Feb. 10 George Paine and Mary Raine; by Banns Published.
1737 Feb. 16 James Paine & Margaret Turner. L.
1767 Feb. 14 John Payn to Rebecca Hanson. L.
1771 June 15 Thomas Halloran to Ann Payn. L.
1787 Jan. 26 John Burke (Lieut. in 28th Reg^t) to Margaret Payne, Spinster. L.
1789 June 27 George Halloran to Mary Payne, Widow. L.

Buried.

1701 Sep. 6 Mrs Eliz. Paine.
1738 Dec. 25 Mary ye D. of James Paine.
1744 Aug. 4 Henry Payne.
1773 June 30 Rebeccah Payne & William Payne.
1779 Oct. 13 Edward Payne.
1781 Nov. 25 Thomas Payne.
1784 Mar. 24 Mary Infant D. of Edward & Anne Payne.
1785 Jan. 29 John Thomas Payne, Infant.
1787 May 31 Achilles Gilles Payne, Infant.
1796 Oct. 7 Edward Payne.

Parish Register of St. Philip.

Married.

1738 July 8 Robert Symes to Elizabeth Payne; by Mr Rose.

Parish Register of St. George.

Buried.

1786 June 30 Ann Payne, from St John's.

Parish Register of St. Paul.

Married.

1781 Jan. 11 Edward Payne to Ann Saweolt; pr. L.

Pedigree of Paynter.

. . . . PAYNTER ═ . . . .

Lieut. Edmond Paynter of Old North Sound Division; had 5 children at the census of 1678; patent for 123 acres 1681; overseer to will of George Dewitt 1683; bur. 13 Jan. 1711 at St. Philip's. (See will of Col. Samuel Jones 1684.) ═ . . . .

Captain John Paynter, Member of Assembly 1698-9; of New North Sound 1707. Will dated 7 June 17 . . : sworn 5 Jan. 1712-13. ═ Ann . . . . living 1715.

John Paynter, Esq., 1st son and heir. ═ Elizabeth Pigott, mar. 8 Aug. 1734 at St. George's.

Colonel William Paynter, left "Painters" of 278 acres in New North Sound to William Gunthorpe, Esq. Will dated 11 June 1735; sworn 10 June 1736. ═ Sarah, dau. of Laurence Crabb by Sarah his wife; bur. 13 Oct. 1734 at St. George's.

Joseph and Benjamin Paynter, bapt. 27 July 1710 at St. John's.

Ann Paynter, mar. Colonel John Gunthorpe, who was buried 1 March 1740 at St. John's; she was bur. 17 Feb. 1761 at St. George's. Will dated 4 Dec. 1754; sworn 19 Feb. 1761.

A son, bapt. 1735 at St. John's.

John Paynter, bapt. 31 Oct. 1738 at St. John's.

Edward Paynter, ? bur. 22 March 1772 at St. Peter's. ═ Elizabeth Lony, mar. 11 Nov. 1753 at St. John's.

William Paynter, bapt. 28 Feb. 1758 at St. John's.

William Paynter, bapt. 12 Nov. 1759 at St. John's.

Nicholas Painter of Anne Arundell co., in the Province of Maryland, Gent., now residing in London. Will dated 8 Sep. 1684; proved 8 Oct. 1685 by Henry Bray. (123 Cann.) To my cozen Hen. Bray of London, glazier, 4000 acres in Dorchester co., Maryland. To my bro. Roger Painter of Andover, co. Hants, husbandman, 700 acres at Wye River in Talbott co. To my sist. Kath. Painter of Andover, spr, 700 acres in Anne Arundell co. To Mrs Barbara Trinder of Abchurch Lane, spr, 1050 acres in Cæcill co. To Kath. Keate, dau. to Jno Keate of Andover, 400 acres in Tuckahoe in Talbott co. To Wm Hawkins of London, scr, ½ of 1000 acres in Chester River in Talbott co., & of 1700 acres in Dorchr co., & of 900 a. in Cæcill co., all which were granted to me by patent. To Jno Hawkins of Lond., distiller, £5. My negros Tom & Sarah to be free. All res. to Hen. Bray, he sole Ex'or. Witnessed by William Evans, Joseph Huckebutt, John Jenkins.

John Paynter. Will dated 7 June 17—. To my wife Ann . . . . of estate in lieu of dower. To my son John all my estate subject to charges . . . . To my son Wm . . . . Benjamin Paynter £800 c. at respective ages of 21, & £60 yearly till then. To my dau. Ann . . . . To my dau. Hester the like sum of £800 c. . . . . Catherine £800 c. To . . . . the like sum. Mary . . . . my wife now enseint . . . . If my son John die without issue then to my son Wm, and in default to my son Joseph, then to my son Benjn. My brother Wm to have 6 years for payment of his debt. Col. Edwd Byam, Major John Tomlinson, Mr Francis Carlile, Capt John Duer, & my wife Ex'ors. Before Walter Douglas, Esq., was sworn Mr Richd Sherwood 5 Jan. 1712-13.

William Painter of Belfast Division, Antigua. Will dated 9 March 1721-2. To my wife Cath. my black horse & saddle of £20 & a negro. To my dau. Elizth £100 c. To my grandson John Barton £50 c. at 21 in lieu of a negro I promised my dau. his mother Elizth. To my dau. Cath. £400 c. at 21. To my dau. Mary the same at 21. To my son John the same at 21. To my son Saml the same at 21. To Peter Delany for the care his mother took of me £25 c. at 21. All my estate to my son Wm, & in default to my son John, then to my son Saml, then to my daus. equally. My wife, John Gunthorpe, Wm Painter, John Brunckhurst, & John Richards Ex'ors. Witnessed by Walter Sydserfe, Nathaniel Cramp, Henry Browne. Before Edward Byam, Lieut.-Governor, was sworn Nathaniel Cramp 27 Aug. 1724. Recorded 8 Dec. 1747.

William Paynter, Esq. Will dated 11 June 1735. Col. John Gunthorpe & Col. John Tomlinson to be Ex'ors, & to pay £500 out of the profits of my estate to each of my unmarried sisters Elizth & Mary Paynter above what is bequeathed them by my late brother's will. To my godson Saml, son of my brother Saml Martin, £100 c. All my plantation to my godson Wm, 2d son of my brother-in-law Col. John Gunthorpe, if he die without issue then to his brother George, the 3rd son. Witnessed by Rowland Ash, jun., Nicholas Collins. Before Edward Byam, Esq., was sworn Capt. Rowland Ash 10 June 1736. Recorded 7 Sep. 1736.

Mary Paynter of Antigua, spinster. Will dated 1 Sep. 1769. £50 c. for my funeral. To my sister Cath. White my negro. My negro woman to Billy Elliot, son of Saml Elliot, Esq., and in default of issue to his brother Saml Elliot, then to his sister Nancy Elliot. To my said sister my clothing & £100 c., & to her daus. £100 between the 3. To my cousin Ann Byam, widow of Wm Byam, £50 c., & £50 c. each to my cousin Mrs Harry Byam, Mrs Alice Eliot, wife of Saml Eliot, Esq., & to Mrs Anne, wife of Anthony Wyke, Esq., & £50 amongst Harry Byam's 3 daus. Polly, Nancy, & Hetty Byam. All residue to Billy Eliot. My cousin Ann Byam Ex'trix. Witnessed by Ashton Warner Byam. Before Hon. Thomas Jarvis, President of H.M.'s Council, was sworn Ann Warner of Antigua, widow, who stated that Ashton Warner Byam, Esq., late of Antigua, now of St. Vincent, had been absent for eight or nine years, 10 April 1781. Recorded 28 May 1781.

Margaret Paynter of Antigua, widow. Will dated 11 Sep. 1777. To Mary Monteigne 6 silver spoons & my sugar tongs. To my sister-in-law Mary Pigott my clothes. To Jas. Watson Roberts, son of Robt Roberts, 3 negros. To Robt Roberts, jun., son of Robt Roberts, a negro. To my niece Elizth Roberts, wife of Robt Roberts, my silver tankard & all furniture. Robt Roberts Ex'or. Witnessed by Benjamin Roberts, Mary Wilson. By Thomas Shirley, Esq., was sworn Mary Wilson 3 June 1783. Recorded 12 June 1783.

1671. Sir Tobias Bridge's Barbadoes Regiment. Captain-Lieut. John Painter went in that capacity, continued with the regiment, and stays in Barbadoes. (Colonial Calendar, 'America and West Indies,' p. 258.)

1676. Captain Samuel Painter, 75 acres. Surveyed 1676.

1678, July 20. Samuel Jones, Esq., leases 150 acres for 99 years to Edmond Painter and George Digby.

1679. Edmond Painter granted 4 acres on 7 Aug. 1677 by Colonel Philip Warner. Surveyed 12 March 1679.

1679, Dec. 26. Samuel Jones sells to Edmond Paynter 75 acres at New North Sound.

1681. Edmond Painter granted a patent for 123½ acres 23 July by Sir W. Stapleton.

16 Feb., 8 Queen Anne. John Paynter of Antigua, Gent., and Ann his wife for £1500 currency sell to John Richards of Antigua, Gent., 85 acres in Nonsuch.

Captain William Paynter of Belfast Division 1707; bur. 13 March 1721 at St. Philip's. Will dated 9 March 1721-2; sworn 27 Aug. 1724. = Catherine . . . . living 1721.

Elizabeth Paynter, 1735. — Hester Paynter.	Catherine Paynter, mar. 6 May 1729, at St. John's, William White; living 1769.	Mary Paynter, bur. 22 Sep. 1779, spinster, at St. George's. Will dated 1 Sep. 1769; sworn 10 April 1781.	William Paynter. — John Paynter, a minor 1721.	Samuel Paynter, living 1721. — Elizabeth Paynter, mar. . . . . Burton.	Catherine Paynter, mar. 3 Feb. 1732, at St. John's, John Hall.	Mary Paynter, mar. 18 June 1735, at St. George's, Thomas Pigott.

1715, April 6. William Lyell of Antigua, tailor, leases to Mrs. Anne Paynter, widow and relict of Captain John Paynter, 4 acres. (Her son Mr. John Paynter.)

1716, Aug. 1. William Painter petitions for 10 acres, lately belonging to John Hall, deceased, now descended to Samuel Hall who resides in Jamaica.

1726, Nov. 12. In Chancery. Heir of William Paynter, deceased, *v.* Ex'ors of John Paynter.

Paynters in St. George's Parish in 1852 contained 272 acres, and was owned by K. B. Osborn, M.D. In 1789 it consisted of 278 acres and 148 slaves. (See Gunthorpe Deed for its boundaries.)

About the year 1790 Mr. Samuel Painter, a free colored man of Antigua, and a member of the Methodist Society, came to reside in Grenada and to labour as a mechanic. (Dr. Coke's 'History of the West Indies,' vol. ii., pp. 68 and 86.)

PARISH REGISTER OF ST. JOHN.

Baptized.

1710	July 27	Joseph & Benjamin children of Capt John Painter & his wife.
1735	[*blank*]	S. of John Paynter & his wife.
1738	Oct. 31	John ye S. of John Paynter & his wife.
1758	Feb. 28	William the S. of Edward Paynter & Elizabeth his wife.
1759	Nov. 12	William the S. of Edward Paynter & Elizabeth his wife.

Married.

1729	May 6	William White and Catherine Paynter.
1732	Feb. 3	John Hall and Catherine Paynter. L.
1741	Jan. 6	John Painter and Mary Crawford.
1753	Nov. 11	Edward Paynter and Elizabeth Louy. L.

Buried.

1718	June 8	William Paynter.
1745	Mar. 31	Jarvis Painter.
1748	Nov. 22	Mary Paynter wife of John Painter.
1748	Feb. 27	John Painter.
1752	Nov. 22	.... Paynter.
1756	May 16	Rebeccah Paynter.
1764	April 4	Samuel Paynter, P.
1768	Dec. 30	Elizabeth Paynter.

PARISH REGISTER OF ST. GEORGE.

Baptized.

1735	......	S. of John Paynter & his wife.
1738	Oct. 31	John ye S. of John Paynter & his wife.

Married.

1734	Aug. 8	John Paynter, Esqr, & Elizabeth Piggott, Spinster.
1735	June 18	Thomas Pigott & Mary Paynter, Spinster.

Buried.

1734	Oct. 13	Sarah ye wife of Colle William Paynter.
1740	Jan. 6	Elizabeth Paynter.
1779	Sep. 22	Miss Mary Paynter.

PARISH REGISTER OF ST. PETER.

Buried.

1772	Mar. 22	Edward Painter.

PARISH REGISTER OF ST. PHILIP.

Buried.

1711	Jan. 13	Edmond Paynter.
1717	April 13	Ann Paynter.
1721	Mar. 13	Capt Willm Paynter.

ST. GEORGE'S CHURCHYARD.

On a head stone:—

Sacred to the Memory
of Samuel Paynter
Who departed this life
On 19th of April 1816
Aged 79 *years.*

In Ringwood Churchyard, co. Hants, there is a flat stone with an inscription to the memory of William Paynter who died 1711, and to a dau. of William and Joan Paynter who died 15 Jan. 1753, æt. 53, and on a shield these arms: .... *within a bordure* .... *three billets* .... (PAYNTER). Crest: *Three pheons handled* .... *two in saltire, one in pale.* These are approximately the bearings of the Cornish family whose pedigree was entered in the Visitation of that county.

Pedigree of Pearne.

.... PEARNE = ...

Henry Pearne of Antigua, Esq., Member of Council; Colonel of Militia; bur. 21 Jan. 1705 at St. John's. Will dated 17 Jan., and sworn 23 Jan. 1705-6. = Grace, dau. of Colonel Philip Warner, Deputy Governor of Antigua; mar. 21 March 1689 at St. Paul's; living 1714.

Captain William Pearne of Antigua; bur. 15 April 1726 at St. John's. Will dated 12 April 1726. = Mary, only child of John Slicer, and relict of Robert Freeman; mar. *circa* 1706.

Captain John Pearne. = (? Henrietta .... bur. 23 April 1730 at St. John's.)

Children of Henry Pearne:

- Robert Pearne, only son and heir, a minor in 1705; owned "Blubber Valley" of 1200 acres and "Musketo Cove" of 600. Will dated 12 July 1717; proved 11 Nov. 1718. (221 Tenison.) = Mary, youngest dau. of William Lisle, Esq., of Evenley, co. Northants; died 13 May 1756. M.I. at Evenley. Will dated 9 June 1750; proved 13 July 1756. (201 Glazier.)
- Jane Pearne, under 18 in 1705; living 1714.
- Elizabeth Pearne, under 18 in 1705; mar. Captain Toby Lisle, R.N., son of William Lisle of Evenley, Esq. Will dated 25 Jan. 1717; proved P.C.C. 21 July 1719.

Children of Captain William Pearne:

- John Henry Pearne, living 1726; dead 1749.
- Richard Hamilton Pearne, living 1726 and 1749.
- William Loolin Pearne, ? bur. 8 Jan. 1730 at St. John's; dead 1749.
- Mary Ann Pearne, mar. 1731, at St. Paul's, ... Barton; living 1749 a widow.
- Sarah Grace Pearne, living 1726; dead 1749.

Child of Captain John Pearne:

- Henrietta Pearne, living 1726.

Children of Robert Pearne and Mary Lisle:

- Robert Pearne, only son and heir, bur. 31 March 1757 at Evenley. Will dated 26 Jan. and proved 4 April 1757. (132 Herring.)
- Mary Pearne, only dau., under 17 in 1717; mar. Samuel Pateshall of St. George's, Hanover Square, Esq.; both living 1757.

Henry Pearne of Antigua, Esq. Will dated 17 Jan. 1705. To my wife Grace my plate, furniture, coach & horses, 3 negros, & ⅓ of all produce. To my 2 daus. Jane & Elizth Pearne £2000 st. each at 18, & £50 a year till then. To my brother Wm Pearne £300 c., my clothing & fusil. To my brother Capt John Pearne all the rents of my plantation in St Christopher's, now in the possession of Michael Lambert, Esq., till my son Robert be 21. To my sisters-in-law Mrs Ann Barnes & Mrs Mary Burgeois & my cozen Elizth Burgeois £20 c. each. To my friend Wm Nevine, Esq., my bay mare. To John Malson £10 c. All residue to my son Robt his heirs, & in default to any younger son, then to my daus. equally, then to my said 2 brothers John & W^m. My son Robt Ex'or, & during his Minority Col. Edwd Byam of Antigua, Esq., Archibald Hutchinson of the Inner Temple, Esq., Barry Tankard of Antigua, Esq., Capt. John Perry late of Antigua, Daniel Mackinen of Antigua, Chirurgeon, & my wife Ex'ors in Trust. Witnessed by Gousse Bonnin, Dorothy Crafford, Margaret Fowler. By John Yeamans, Esq., were sworn Gousse Bonnin, Chirurgeon, and Margaret Fowler, spinster, 23 Jan. 1705-6. Recorded 25 Jan. 1705-6.

Robert Pearne, Esq., of Antigua. Will dated 12 July 1717; proved 11 Nov. 1718 by Patrick Lisle, power reserved to the other Ex'ors. (221 Tenison.) To my wife Mary £3000 charged on my estate in Blubber Valley. To my dau. Mary Pearne £1000 at 17 (in case my wife is now enceint with a boy) & £10 yearly till then. If the child be a girl then the £1000 to be void, & to my 2 daus. all my estates & negros at 17. My wife to be Guardian. In case of failure of issue to my daus. my estate to go to such persons as are named in the will of my late father Henry Pearne, Esq. My worthy friends & relations Col. Edwd Warner, Capt. Patrick Lisle & Capt Toby Lisle, Ashton Warner, Esq., & Wm Pearne, Esq., Ex'ors, & £50 apiece. All residue of my personal estate to my dau. Mary & to the child to be born if a girl, but if a boy then all my estate to him. Witnessed by W. Hill, Muriel Mackenzie, Michael Arnald.

William Pearne, Gent. Will dated 12 April 1726. To my niece Henrietta, dau. of my late brother John Pearne, Esq., £100 c. to be paid out of the legacy left me by my brother Henry Pearne. All residue to my Ex'ors in trust to sell & invest proceeds & divide the same equally among my children John Henry Pearne, Richd Hamilton Pearne, Wm Loolin Pearne, Mary Ann Pearne, & Sarah Grace Pearne. Hon. Archibald Cochran, Esq., Chas. Dunbar, Henry Osborn, Ashton Warner, Esq., Ex'ors & Guardians. Witnessed by Roger Adams, W. Alexander, Edward Rickett. Before William Mathew, Esq., was sworn William Alexander.

Francis Pearn, shopkeeper. Will dated 9 Sep. 1729. All my estate to my wife Mary. To Mr Thos. Kerby, Mr Jacob Thibou, Mr Thos. Stevens Ex'ors with my wife, all my estate after my wife's death or marriage in trust for my children equally. Witnessed by Rachel Hughes, Robert Smith, George Jennings. Before Edward Byam, Esq., was sworn Robert Smith 26 Nov. 1729.

Mary Pearne. Will dated 9 June 1750. On 13 July 1756 adm'on to Robert Pearne the son. (201 Glazier.) £20 to my sister for mourning. My Mother orders £20 a year to be paid to my aunt Bridget Lisle, & after my aunt's death £4 a year to Anne South, wife of John South of Mixbury, & all residue between testatrix's son & dau. equally. Deed of gift new signed 26 Nov. 1753 & 26 March 1756. On 15 July 1756 were sworn Mary Pateshall, wife of Samuel Pateshall of St. George's, Hanover Square, only dau. of Mary Pearne late of Evenly, co. Northampton, and Bridget Vipont of Hampstead, widow, Robert Pearne and Mary Pateshall, the son and dau., being the only children of deceased.

Robert Pearne of Isleworth, Esq. Will dated 26 Jan. 1757; proved 4 April 1757 by the Right Hon. Sir John Willes, John Willes, and Charles Spooner, Esquires. (132 Herring.) The use of my plate, etc., as per schedule to my sister Mary Pateshall for life, then to her dau. Mary Pateshall to whom I give £1000 at 23. To John Willes, Esq., 1st son of the R^t Hon. Sir John Willes, K^t, 1st Lord Commissioner of the Great Seal & Lord Chief Justice of the Court of Common Pleas, my chariot & harness, my diamond shirt buckle, & my picture. To Edwd Willes, Esq., 2^d son of Sir John, my gold-headed cane & 20 gs. To Chas. Spooner, Esq., youngest son of John Spooner of Bloomsbury, Esq., my diamond ring with 2 large & 2 small brilliants. To the Hon. Mrs Marg^t Tufton & the Hon. Mrs Mary Tufton, aunts to the present Earl of Thanet, the pictures of my mother & my grandfather Wm Lisle, my silver tumbler & agate snuff box. To my servant Jas. Gulliver my clothing, the use of my silver watch for life, then to Jas. Byers, shopkeeper, of Brackley, co. Northants, also £10 a year. To my old coachman Thos. Tarman of Evenley £6 a year. To Jas. Gulliver my tenement in co. Northants with the use of the furniture & implements there for life, then to John Willes, Esq. £40 a year to Mrs Hannah Axford formerly Lightfoot, niece to the late Mr John Jefferyes, watchmaker in Holborn. The £4 a year given by my late mother Mary Pearne by will to Mrs Ann South of Mixbury, co. Bucks, to be continued. My Ex'ors to give to my cousin Eliz. Bowles, wife of the Rev. Dr Tho. Bowles, Rector of Brackley, the pedigree of my family. To Saml Pateshall, husband of my sister Mary, 5 gs. To each servant 10 gs. To the poor of Brackley & Evenley 10 gs. All residue of plate & household goods in my house at Isleworth to John Willes, Esq. All residue of personal estate to Sir John Willes & John Willes, Esq. (legacies to be charged on my plantation in Antigua), in Trust to pay £300 a year to my sister Mary Pateshall. ½ of my plantation in Antigua to Sir John Willes for life, then to his 1st son John Willes, then to Tho. Abney of Willesby, co. Derby, Esq., & to Nathl Worley in Trust for the 2^d son of John Willes, & in default to Chas. Willes, youngest son of Sir John. The other ½ to Chas. Spooner & his heirs, then to Chas. Willes. Sir John Willes, John Willes, Esq., & Cha. Spooner, Esq., Ex'ors. Schedule of plate follows. Mrs Collier's picture.

Close Roll, 14 Geo. II., Part 9, Nos. 4 and 5.

Indenture made 18 Dec. 1740 between Robert Pearne of the parish of Evenly, Northants, Esq. (son and heir of Robert Pearne, late of Antigua, Esq., deceased, grandson and heir male of Henry Pearne of Antigua, Esq., deceased), of the one part, and Drury Otley the younger and Charles Lavall Molineux of St. Kitts, Esquires, of the other part, witnesseth that Robert Pearne, in consideration of 5s., sells to Drury Otley and Charles Lavall Molineux all that plantation in the parish of St. Mary Cayon in St. Kitts, containing 120 acres, formerly the plantation of Robert Skerrit, deceased, and afterwards by letters patent under the Great Seal of H.M.'s Charibee Islands duly recorded, etc., and in a special verdict found by the jury on the tryal of an action of ejectment brought against William Otley and Elizabeth Otley his wife, and Margaret Willet the younger, on the demand of Robert Pearne in the Court of King's Bench and Common Pleas, held at the town of Basseterre, granted by King William III. unto Henry

Pearne therein mentioned, and to his heirs for evermore, and now in the tenure of Patrick Blake, Esq., and late in that of Martin Blake, Esq., and heretofore in that of Ralph Willet, Esq., and bounded at the foot with the common path, to the E. with the lands heretofore of Charles Nephew Francis Hicky and now of [*blank*], S. with the lands heretofore of Lewis and now of [*blank*], and W. with the lands of Clement Crook, Esq., and so to its extent to the mountains, and all other messuages and plantations, etc., whatsoever of Robert Pearne or of any person in trust for him in the said parish, and all messuages, pastures, feedings, mountain land, timber, trees, woods, underwoods, with the ground and soil of the same, waters, watercourses, etc., to have and to hold to Drury Otley and Charles Lavall Molineux for one whole year at the rent of a peppercorn, if demanded, to the intent and purpose only that they, by virtue of these presents and of the statute of transferring uses, may be in actual possession, and enabled to accept and take a grant and release of the reversion and inheritance to them and their heirs for ever. J. Spooner, John Sharpe, witnesses.

No. 4.

Indenture made 19th Dec. 1740 between Robert Pearne of the parish of Evenly, Northants, Esq. (son and heir, etc.), of the 1st part, William Otley and Elizabeth Otley his wife and Margaret Willet the younger of St. Kitts, singlewoman (which said Elizabeth and Margaret are the daughters and coheirs of John Willet, and cousins and coheirs of Ralph Willet, late of St. Kitts, Esq., deceased), of the 2nd part, and William Coleman of London, merchant, of the 3rd part, and Drury Otley the younger and Charles Lavall Molineux of St. Kitts, Esquires, of the 4th part. Whereas in the year 1736 an action of ejectment was brought against William and Elizabeth Otley and Margaret Willet on the demand of Robert Pearne in the Court of King's Bench and Common Pleas, etc., for the recovery from them of the possession of a messuage, 200 acres of land, 200 acres of cane land, and 100 acres of pasture, and 100 acres of wood in the parish of St. Mary Cayon, and the said William and Elizabeth Otley and Margaret Willet having appeared and pleaded the general issue of not guilty, the action came on to be tryed the second Thursday in June 1736 when the jury returned a special verdict, and afterwards upon the 15th June 1736 upon arguing the said verdict the Court gave judgment that Robert Pearne the lessee should recover against the others his term in the said 200 acres, etc., but Robert Pearne having released to them his action as to the messuage, and also remitted to them all damages, costs, etc., by him sustained, and also all judgments and executions thereon had, they were acquitted by the Court as to the messuage; and whereas William and Elizabeth Otley and Margaret Willet afterwards brought a writt of error from the judgment before the Governor and Council, and assigned the general error, and Robert Pearne having filed a joinder in error, the writt of error on the 31st Aug. 1737 came on to be argued before the Governor and Council as a Court of Errors, when the former judgment was affirmed with costs on the writt; and whereas William and Elizabeth Otley and Margaret Willet prayed and were allowed an appeal to the King's Most Excellent Majesty which is still depending; and whereas by articles of agreement of the 21st May last past between Robert Pearne, late of St. Kitts, but then residing in London, of the one part, and William Coleman (on behalf of the others), of the other part, reciting as above, it was further recited that in order to prevent any further litigation it was agreed that Robert Pearne should release and confirm all his right, etc., to William and Elizabeth Otley and Margaret Willet in consideration of £1000 sterling, £100 to be paid on the ensealing, and £900 on the 5th Sep. next ensuing in case St. Kitts continues till then in the possession of the Crown of Great Britain, and shall not be before taken by the Spaniards or any other enemy to the Crown of Great Britain, it was witnessed that William Coleman has paid Robert Pearne £100, and on payment of the residue Robert Pearne agrees to make proper conveyances. Now this Indenture witnesseth that Robert Pearne has granted, etc., to Drury Otley the younger and Charles Lavall Molineux the 120 acres, formerly the plantation of Peter Skerrit, deceased, etc., as to one moiety to the only use of Elizabeth Otley and her heirs, and the other moiety to the only use of Margaret Willet and her heirs for ever, and William Coleman transfers to Drury Otley and Charles Lavall Molineux and their Ex'ors the said judgments, etc., to the sole benefit of William Otley and Elizabeth his wife, and Margaret Willet.

Close Roll, 17 Geo. II., Part 20, Nos. 21 and 22.

Indenture made the 28th March 1743 between Robert Pearne of Evenly, Northants, Esq. (son and heir of Robert Pearne of Antigua, Esq., deceased, and grandson and heir of the body of Henry Pearne of Antigua, Esq., deceased), of the one part, and William Johnson of Sergeants' Inn, Chancery Lane, Gent., of the other part, witnesseth that in consideration of 5s. Robert Pearne grants, etc., to William Johnson Blubber Valley Plantation in the parish of St. Mary and division of Bermudian Valley, Antigua, containing 1200 acres, bounded E. with the lands of George Jennings, Esq., deceased, Thomas Stephens, Esq., deceased, William Allam, John Sedgwick, and Robert Christian, W. with the plantations of the Hon. Valentine Morris, Esq., lately deceased, and the lands of William Dunning and Sheers Stephens, N. with the plantation of the Hon. Samuel Watkins, Esq., and of George Jennings, Esq., deceased, and S. with the lands of Francis Franklyn, Robert Christian, and the late John Forster, deceased, and the dwelling house, etc., and all those negro and other slaves (names given), 45 men, 49 women, 15 boys, and 20 girls, and all those 50 horses and 100 head of cattle thereon, and all that other plantation called Musketo Cove in the said parish and division containing 600 acres, bounded E. with Perrie York's Plantation, W. with the sea, N. partly with the lands of George Leonard and partly with the sea, and S. with the plantation of Valentine Morris and the sea, and all that stock house, and also 20 horses and 100 head of cattle thereon, and also all that other parcel of land called James Red's Hill containing 30 acres in the said parish, bounded E. in part with the plantation of Valentine Morris and part with the sea, and W., N., and S. with the sea, to have and to hold for one whole year, yielding therefore one peppercorn, to the intent he may be in actual possession, and thereby enabled to take a grant and release of the reversion and inheritance.

No. 21.

Indenture made the 29th March 1743 between Robert Pearne, etc., of the one part, and William Johnson, of the other part, witnesseth that in consideration of 10s. Robert Pearne grants, etc., to William Johnson (as in No. 22), to the intent that all estates tail and remainders, etc., may be effectually barred and destroyed according to the laws of the Leeward Islands, to the only proper use of William Johnson and his heirs and assigns for ever. Hugh Hamersley, William Rowlandson, witnesses.

Close Roll, 19 Geo. II., Part 16, Nos. 1, 2, 3, and 4.

Indenture made the 14th March 1745 by which Robert Pearne conveys to William Johnson Blubber Valley Plantation, etc., and all the dwelling-house, etc., and also all and every those negro and other slaves (as in 17 Geo. II.), and also all Musketo Cove Plantation containing 600 acres, and 20 horses and 100 head of cattle, and also James Red's Hill containing 30 acres, and also all those 36 acres lately recovered by Robert Pearne from the said Valentine Morris, and now in the possession of Martin Blake, Esq., or his assigns for one whole year, and Robert Pearne appoints Stephen Blizard, Nathaniel Gilbert, and Martin Blake, all of Antigua, Esquires, his Attorneys. John Martin, Tobias Lisle, Harry Webb, witnesses.

No. 3.

Indenture made the 15th March 1745 between Robert Pearne, of the one part, and William Johnson, of the other part, witnesseth that in consideration of 10*s*. Robert Pearne conveys to William Johnson (as in No. 4), to the only proper use of William Johnson and his heirs.

No. 2.

Indenture made the 17th March 1745 between William Johnson, of the one part, and Robert Pearne, of the other part.

No. 1.

Indenture made the 20th March 1745 between the above (simply the reconveyance, with the same Attorneys and the same witnesses).

Close Roll, 29 Geo. II., Part 2, Nos. 1 and 2.

Indenture made the 3rd Dec. 1755 between Robert Pearne of Evenly, otherwise Imley, Northants, Esq. (only son and heir of Robert Pearne, heretofore of Antigua, Esq., deceased, who was only son and heir of Henry Pearne, heretofore likewise of Antigua, Esq., deceased), of the one part, and Robert Christian of Antigua, Esq., of the other part, witnesseth that in consideration of 5*s*. Robert Pearne conveys to Robert Christian all Shackerley's Plantation containing 300 acres, late in the tenure of Charles Dunbar or his tenants, and heretofore in the occupation of Francis Shackerley, ... Duncombe, or . . . . Martin, and formerly purchased by Henry Pearne the grandfather from John Barnes and Ann Barnes of Antigua, for one whole year. Thurston Blackman, William Marshall, witnesses.

No. 1.

Indenture made the 4th Dec. 1755 as above. Whereas Articles of Agreement were made and concluded on the 20th May 1752 between the said Robert Pearne (only son and heir-at-law of Robert Pearne, deceased), of the one part, Robert Christian, of the other part, by which after reciting that Robert Pearne claimed to be seised of certain lands in the parish of St. Mary in Antigua called Shackerley's Plantation, containing 300 acres, mostly wood and coppice, then in the occupation of Charles Dunbar, Esq., or his tenants, and heretofore (as in No. 2), and also after reciting that Robert Christian had contracted and agreed for the absolute purchase upon the conditions hereinafter mentioned, it was witnessed that in consideration of £500 Robert Pearne did agree to forthwith produce all deeds, etc., whereby it might appear he was seised of a good estate in fee simple, and also that he would (so that he was not compelled to travel above 20 miles from his usual place of abode), at the costs and charges of Robert Christian, convey to him the said plantation, free from incumbrances whatsoever, and Robert Christian did covenant and agree that on the execution of the said conveyance he would pay a further sum of £500 in full satisfaction of the purchase money, and it was agreed that if Robert Christian should not approve of the title Robert Pearne should nevertheless retain the first-mentioned £500, which should be forfeited, and also reciting that Robert Pearne was seised of divers other plantations, etc., in Antigua, but no other lands than those on the 7th March then last in the tenure of Charles Dunbar should be taken as any part of the lands contracted for by Robert Christian; and whereas Charles Dunbar hath by his Attornies William Dunbar and Thomas Warner, Esquires, by Indentures dated the 10th and 11th July last, conveyed to Robert Pearne the said lands and hereditaments called Shackerleys, to the only proper use of Robert Pearne and his heirs and assigns. Now therefore this Indenture witnesseth that for carrying the said Articles into execution, and in consideration of the £500 already paid, and also in consideration of £500 to be paid at or before the sealing of these presents, and to bar and destroy all estates tail and remainders, and vest in Robert Christian an absolute inheritance in fee simple, Robert Pearne grants and confirms to Robert Christian in his actual possession being all that plantation (as in No. 2), and Robert Pearne appoints, etc., Thomas Elmes, Francis Farley, Simon Farley, and John Jeffreson of Antigua, Esquires, or any three of them, his Attorneys.

1695. Henry Pearne conveys 300 acres (part of Jolly Hill Plantation) to General Codrington.

1696. Captain Henry Pearne, a member of the vestry of St. Mary's Parish, was rated on 750 acres and 74 slaves.

On 1701, Aug. 12, was read the Act to enable Hen. Pearne, Esq., to sell Blubber Valley Plantⁿ, reciting that Henrietta Warner, late yᵉ Wid. of Col. Philip Warner, decᵈ, owned the said plantⁿ of 380 acres, & by her deed of 1 Mar. 6 Wᵐ conveyed it to Esaū Burgois & to Wᵐ Barnes, late of Antigua, Gent., for 1 year, in trust for her own use for life, & then for Hen. Pearne, Gent., husbᵈ of Grace her dau., for his life, then to Grace Pearne for her life, then to their only s. & h. Robᵗ Pearne & his heirs, reserving power to charge the estate with 200,000 lbs. The Negros are all dead & Hen. Pearne has spent £3000 on the estate. (Minutes of Council.)

1706, June 7. Colonel Henry Pearne's estate in St. Mary's Parish was rated on 665 acres and 150 slaves.

1712. In the Court of King's Bench and Common Pleas Mary Lingham sued the Guardians of Robert Pearne, *re* the Blubber Valley and Musquito Cove Plantations of 1200 acres and 100 negro men, 20 women, 20 boys, and 20 girls.

1713. John Pearne, late Lieut.-Governor of Montserrat, has gone to England. (B. T. Leeward Islands, vol. 13.)

1714, March 1. Mrs. Jane Pearne of Antigua for £100 c. sells to her mother Mrs. Grace Pearne 4 negros.

1716. Mr. Pern was allotted pew No. 3 in St. Mary's Church.

1719, Aug. 12. William Pearne, Gent., has a plantation of 100 acres in Nonsuch Division, St. Philip's Parish, N. with Robert Freeman, Robert Hunt, deceased, and Thomas Skerrett, E. with Thomas Skerrett, Daniel Maningham, and Robert Freeman, S. with Robert Freeman and John Lucas, Esq., and Nicholas Lynch, W. with Nicholas Lynch and Robert Hunt, deceased. Patent granted.

Mary, widow of Robert Freeman who died 1705, married secondly Mr. Perne, possibly the above-mentioned William Pearne.

Robert Pearce (? Pearne), Esq., owner of large estates in Antigua and St. Kitts, married 28 Jan. 1744 the dau. of Mr. Pycraft, brewer, with 20,000*l*.

1749, Jan. 6. In Chancery. Charles Dunbar, Esq., Ashton Warner, Esq., the surviving Ex'ors of William Pearne, deceased; Richard Hamilton Pearne, Gent., and Mary Ann Barton, widow, the surviving children and legatees of William Pearne, Complainants, *v.* Elizabeth Freeman, Executrix of Arthur Freeman; John Tomlinson, Esq., Joseph Buckshorne, George Thomas, Esq., Alice Freeman, widow, Executors of Robert Freeman the younger, deceased.

No. 356. Private. An Act for vesting divers Slaves, late of Robert Pearne, of Isleworth in the County of Middlesex, in the Kingdom of Great Britain, Esq., now deceased, in Trustees, to be sold: and for laying out the Monies arising by such Sale, in the Purchase of other Slaves, to be settled upon the Trustees, and to the Uses of the Will of the said Robert Pearne. Dated 6th May 1771.

No. 135. Private. An Act to vest in Trustees for Sale certain Negro Slaves devised by the Will of Robert Pearne, Esquire, discharged from the Uses and Trusts declared, concerning the same in and by the said Will: and for investing the Money arising by such Sale in real or Government Securities in Great Britain, upon the like Uses and Trusts. Dated 28th March 1786.

For an account of the Pearne estate see the Lingham Papers.

PARISH REGISTER OF ST. PAUL.

Married.

1731 . . . . Barton & Mary Ann Pearne; by L.

PARISH REGISTER OF ST. JOHN.

Buried.

1705 Jan. 21 Coll° Henry Pearne.
1726 April 15 Capt William Pearne.
1730 April 23 Mrs Henrietta Pearne.
1730 Jan. 8 Mr Wm Pearne.
1731 June 12 Mrs Sarah Pearne.

EVENLEY CHURCH, CO. NORTHANTS.

Here lies Interred the Body of
Mrs MARY PEARNE
Wife of ROBERT PEARNE Esq
late of the Island of ANTEGOE
and youngest Daughter of
WILLM LISLE Esqr
late of Evenly
at whose feet she desired to be laid
on the left side of
Sister FRANCES LISLE
She Died May ye 13th 1756.

Pedigree of Perry.

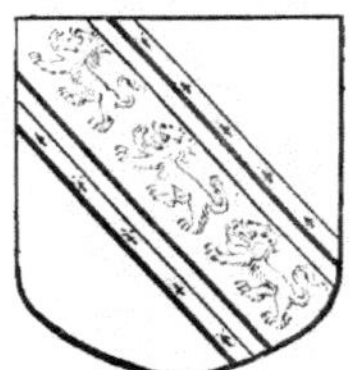

ARMS.—*On a bend . . . . between two cottises ermine three lions passant*, PERRY of London; granted 1700.

. . . . PERRY ╤ . . . .

Micajah Perry* of Leadenhall Street, Virginia merchant; aged 23 in 1663; Agent to Governor Hamilton in 1710; died 1 and bur. 10 Oct. 1721, aged, at St. Botolph, Bishopsgate. Will dated 22 Dec. 1720; proved 3 Oct. 1721. (185 Buckingham.) ╤ Ann, dau. of Dr. Richard Owen; marriage licence dated 20 Oct. 1663, then æt. 24; bur. 1 March 1701, æt. 66, in the chancel of St. Botolph, Bishopsgate.

Elizabeth Perry, uxor . . . . Evans 1720.

A dau. ╤ . . . . Lowe.

Richard Perry of Leadenhall Street, merchant. Will dated 15 April and proved 4 May 1720. (118 Shaller.) ╤ Sarah . . . . living 1725 and 1753.

Micajah Lowe of Charles Town, Virginia, and of Carshalton, co. Surrey, merchant. Will dated [illegible] Jan. 1702; proved 17 March 1702-3. ([illegible]3 Degg.) ╤ Sarah . . . . s.p.

Susanna Lowe, living 1720.

Johanna Lowe.

Mary Lowe, living 1720.

Micajah Perry, Esq., M.P. London 1727—1741; Alderman of Aldgate 1728—1746; Sheriff 1734, and Colonel of the Orange Regiment of Trained Bands; Lord Mayor 1738; died 22 Jan. 1753 at Epsom, co. Surrey. Adm'on 14 Aug. 1753. (See 'Notes and Queries' for July 1895.) ╤ . . . . dau. of . . . . Cock of London, linendraper; died 1738. s.p.

Philip Perry of London, merchant; under 24 in 1720; living 1753.

Sarah Perry, 1st dau., born 31 Aug. 1702; mar. 1 Oct. 1719 William Heysham of East Greenwich, Esq., M.P. for town of Lancaster. He was born 10 Dec. 1691, and died s.p. 14 April 1727, æt. 35. M.I. at St. Paul's Walden, co. Herts. Will dated 22 April 1725; proved 28 June 1727. (142 Farrant.) She was living 1753.

Elizabeth Perry, under 18 in 1720; mar. 1733 Salusbury Cade, Esq., son of Dr. Cade; his will proved 1775. (240 Stevens.)

* Richard Perry, of Newhaven 1640, had Mary, bapt. 4 Oct. of that year; Micajah, 31 Oct. 1641; Samuel, 8 June 1645; John, 11 July 1647; and Grace, 2 Sept. 1649. A Richard Perry, merchant, of London, was one of the Assistants named in the Royal Charter of 1629. (Savage's 'Gen. Dict. of New Eng.,' p. 400.)

William Perry was a Member of Council for Virginia in or before 1635. (Colonial Calendar.)

. . . . Perry ╤ . . . .

John Perry of Antigua, merchant; Provost Marshal-General of the Leeward Islands 8 William III.; born and died at Youghall, co. Cork. Will dated 24 Jan. 1708, then of St. James, Westminster; proved 4 April 1713. (89 Leeds.) ╤ Anne . . . .

Anne Perry, widow of . . . . Osborne 1708.

A dau. mar. James Nisbitt, Esq.

Samuel Perry, dead 1708. ╤ Mary . . . . living 1708.

Edward Perry of Antigua, Esq.; Registrar 1704; bur. 26 Feb. 1716-17 at St. John's. Will dated 24 Feb. 1714; proved 23 May 1717. (101 Whitfield.) ╤ . . . .

John Perry, bur. 16 Feb. 1700 at St. John's.

Anne Perry, 1st dau. and coheir; mar. when a minor; æt. 21 in 1722; died 1731. ╤ Richard Rigby of Misley Hall, co. Essex, Esq., son of Edward Rigby; formerly a woollen-draper in Paternoster Row, and factor to the South Sea Company; died 1730. Will dated 16 Aug. and proved 19 Nov. 1730. (315 Auber.)

Dorothy Perry, bapt. 28 Dec. 1703 at St. John's; a minor in 1722; mar. George Barker of St. Paul, Covent Garden, merchant; both living 1745.

Elizabeth Perry, died intestate under 17 before 1722.

Sarah Perry, bapt. 28 Dec. 1703 at St. John's.

Mary Perry, a minor in 1722; mar. John Cleland of St. Peter Poor, London, and of South Carolina; marriage settlement dated 14 Nov. 1728; both living 1745.

Edward Perry, bur. 12 Sep. 1691 at St. John's.

Samuel Perry, a minor in 1708.

Jonathan Perry, merchant, only son, brother-in-law of Hopefor Bendall 1727. (See vol. i., p. 40.)

Mary Perry, widow of . . . . Pullen 1714.

A dau., living 1708.

Right Hon. Richard Rigby, a Member of the English Privy Council; Master of the Rolls and Vice-Treasurer in Ireland; M.P. Tavistock; Paymaster in Ireland 1768—1782; died at Bath 8 April 1788, bachelor, aged 65 or 66. Will dated 31 Dec. 1781; proved 19 May 1788 (see 'Gent. Mag.' for 1788, pp. 370 and 462).

Anne Rigby.

Martha Rigby.

1673. Henry Perry of Antigua died intestate. Adm'on to Kath. Perry his relict 4 Aug. by Philip Warner, Esq.

1699. Henry Hartwell of Virginia, Esq., names Mrs Sarah Perry, wife of Mr Richd Perry, £5. Micajah Perry & Richd Perry of London, merchants & Ex'ors, £50. (134 Pett.)

Christopher Morgan of London. Will dated 22 March 1703-4. (45 Eedes.) Micajah Perry, Tho. Lane, & Richard Perry's bond dated 26 March 1700 for £2000, ditto & money £1000, debts in Virginia. My $\frac{1}{8}$ of the ship "Perry & Lane," $\frac{1}{16}$ of the ship "Hartwell," etc.

Micajah Lowe, late of Charles City, County and Colony of Virginia, now of Caschaulton, co Surrey, merchant. Will dated 20 Jan., proved 17 March 1702 by Micajah Perry. (53 Degg.) To my uncle Mr Micajah Perry, my mother-in-l. Mrs Eliz. Hamlin, my sisters Susanna Lowe & Johanna Jarrett & Mary Lowe, rings. All residue to my wife Sarah, she & my uncle Mic. Perry Ex'ors. Witnessed by Sarah Barnes, Jos. Cooper, Robert Dalley, Thomas Denbery.

John Perry, late of Antigua, now of St. James, Westminster, merchant. Will dated 24 June 1708; proved 4 April 1713 by Jonathan Perry the Guardian of Anne and Dorothy Perry, minors, daus. of testator, who was last of Youghall, deceased; proved 7 Oct. 1713 by Edward Perry; power reserved to Anne and Dorothy Perry; proved 23 May 1717 by Jonathan Perry, Edward Perry being dead; proved 25 Aug. 1722 by Anne Rigby *alias* Perry, now wife of Richard Rigby, and one of the surviving Ex'trices, she being now 21; power reserved to Dorothy Perry. (89 Leeds.) To the ministers & churchwardens of Youghall, co. Cork, where I was born, £300 c. to buy lands in the name of the bishop of the diocese, and the profits to be distributed to the poor every 29th of May at the church door. To the poor of Christ Church in the City of Cork £100 c. in the same way. To the parish of St John's, Antigua, £300 for the purchase of annuity of £30 c. to be distributed in the same way. To my sister-in-law Mary Perry, widow of my brother Saml Perry, £30 a year for life. To my sister Anne Osborne, widow, & to her daus. Mary Mills & Joyce Osbourne £200 c. apiece, & to each of her grandchildren £100 c. at 21, except John Freeman, son of Jas. Freeman, to whom I have already given that sum. To my nephew Saml Perry £1000 c. at 21. To my well beloved wife Anne Perry £100 a year for life in lieu of dower, & all plate & furniture. To my dau. Anne Perry £2000 which Major Long of Antigua owes me, & my house & land adjoining Major Long's plantation in the town & parish of St John's, & £500, equal to a portion of £3000. To my dau. Dorothy Perry all money due to me from Patrick Browne, late of Antigua, deceased, & if less than £2500 to be made up to that sum. To my dau. Eliz. Perry my moiety of a plantation in St Mary's parish with negros, etc., as lately rented by me to Patrick Browne, deceased, which cost me £2290, also £210. To my dau. Mary all my plantation in South Carolina & £500, equal to a portion of £2500. If my wife be with child then £2000 to it, & £500 less to each dau. All portions to my daus. at 18. To my nephew Jonathan Perry, son of my brother Edwd Perry, £1000 at 21 & £60 yearly till then, if he die then to his 2 sisters now living. My wife to be Guardian. To my brother Edwd Perry £50. To my worthy friend Archibald Hutcheson, Esq., £50. To Capt John Perne £10. All residue to my wife & children. Archibald Hutcheson, Mr Edward Perry, & my wife Guardians. My daus. Anne & Dorothy Perry & my brother Edwd Perry Ex'ors. Witnessed by Christopher Devonsheir, John Devonsheir, Christopher Devonsheir, all of Bristol. Recorded also at St. John's 3 Oct. 1714.

Edward Perrie of Antigua. Will dated 24 Feb. 1714; proved 23 May 1717 by Jonathan Perrie the son. (101 Whitfield.) My 1st dau. Mary Pullen of London, widow, £500. All estate to my only son Jonathan Perrie of London, merchant, & sole Ex'or. My friends Mr Hopefor Bendall, Mr Edward Chester, jun., & Mr Joseph Adams of Antigua, merchants, overseers, & a 3 gn. ring each. Witnessed by Samuel Payn, Samuel Galpine, Edward Morgon, Benjamin Rawleigh, John Helden, Thomas Holmes, George Forrest.

Codicil. 24 Jan. 1716. To each of my grandchildren £100 at 21. All plate with my coat of arms to my son Jonathan. Edward Chester, jr, my gold watch. Joseph Adams my bed furniture. My sister Nisbitt my common prayer book & my late brother John Perrie's seal. Mr Hopefor Bendall my sword, belt, & gun, & to his dau. my goddau. the silver tankard I expect out of England. Mr John Helden my gold-headed cane. Cath. Atkinson 40 pistoles & a silver tankard. I have in my chest £747 belonging to Mr Wm Moore of Barbados. Witnessed by Peter Hasell, James Chester, George Jenkins.

Richard Perry. Will dated 15 April at London, proved 4 May 1720 by Sarah Perry the relict. (118 Shaller.) To my wife Sarah my groundrent of Brewer's Key, now in the possession of the heirs of Mr Rob. Richardson, decd, at present £50 a year, & after her death to my s. Micajah Perry, the mortgage of Little Stanbridge, co. Essex, now let to Mr Joseph Tanner for £80 a year, with the manor & quitrents of 35*s.* a year, the money I have lent the Crown on it being much more than its worth, my rentcharge on lands in Sussex, now paid by Mr Tho. Medley, Esq., of Lewis, £50 a year, my groundrents in Hatton Garden 18 years to come, £50 a year, & I pay Lord Nottingham £6 a year, my groundrents in Moorfields £20 a year, also plate, jewels, & furniture. To my son Micajah Perry the ⅓ of Chester's Key, left him by Mr Tho. Lane after the death of Mrs Mary Lane his widow, also my ⅓. Whereas my father hath settled his estate in Leadenhall-str. on me, after his death I give it my son Philip, but my wife to have the house I live in rent free. I give her also the leases of my 2 houses in Leadenhall-str., let to Mr Motley & Mrs Walker, till my son Philip be 24, at £38 & £30 less groundrent of £13 6*s.* 8*d.* My dau. Sarah Perry I have sufficiently provided for. To my dau. Mary Perry £3000 bank stock. My dau. Eliz. Perry £1000 bank stock, payable to both at 18. My stock in trade with my father consists of a moiety, ⅓ of this to my son Micajah, ⅓ to my son Philip at 24, & ⅓ to my wife. The monthly draughts for it to be not less than £60 nor more than £90. I have sold my estate in Gravel Lane to John Blant, Esq., subject to 2 annuities of £40. My wife sole Ex'trix. Witnessed by John Ware, Charles Miller, James Johnston, John Walkeley.

Micajah Perry. Will dated 22 Dec. 1720 at London; proved 3 Oct. 1721 by Sarah Perry, widow, Micajah and Philip Perry. (185 Buckingham.) To Christ's Hospital £100. To the Work-house £100. Mary & Susanna Lowe £50 each. My sister Eliz. Evans £20 a year. To my 2 granddaus. Mary & Eliz. £1500 between them. Their father's will. I give them also my lease at Eaton, co Beds, which I hold of Trinity Coll., Cam. To my grandson Micajah Perry my ⅓ of Chester's Key. To my 2 grandsons Micajah & Philip all residue & my moiety in trade. To be buried in Bishop Church in the Middle Isle near the step into the chancell where my dear wife lies. My dau. Sarah Perry & her 2 sons Micajah & Philip Perry Ex'ors. Witnessed 27 Sep. 1721 by John Warr, James Johnston, John Walker.

William Heysham of East Greenwich, co. Kent, Esq. Will dated 22 April 1725; proved 28 June 1727 by Robert Thornton, and on 3 Feb. 1727 by John Marsh; power reserved to Robert Heysham. (142 Farrant.) My lands called Greaves, near Lancaster, to my heirs male, remainder to Mrs Mary Meller, then to the Corporation of Lancaster in Trust for 8 poor men. To be buried in the church of St Paul's Walden, co. Herts, near my deceased uncle Robt Heysham, Esq. £30 to the poor there. £300 to my wife & £20 to her mother Mrs Sarah Perry, & to my wife's brothers & sisters Micajah, Phillip, & Eliz. £10 each. My aunt Mrs Hester Barker, & her dau. Eliz., & her son-in-law Mr Pall, & my cousin Jane his wife £10 each. To my cousins Gyles & Robt Thornton £10 each. My friend Mr John Marsh of Haberdashers' Hall £10. Mr Robt Antrobus of Eaton £10. To my wife plate, coach, & horses. All freehold estate to the 1st son of my body, & to each younger child £2000. To my godson Wm Hall, son of Mr Hall by Jane my cousin his wife, £100. Mr John Green, surgeon in the Strand, £50. My cousin Robt Thornton £500. My friend John Marsh £1000. To Christ's Hospital £200. All residue to any children, but in case I leave no issue then to my cousin Robt Heysham, then to my cousin Robt Thornton. They & John Marsh Ex'ors. Witnessed by Robert Haynes, Thomas Roots, Charles Master.

Richard Rigby of Mistley, co. Essex, Esq. Will dated 18 Aug., proved 19 Nov. 1730 by Anne Rigby the relict; proved also 1 July 1742 by George Barker and Charles Gray, the probate granted to Anne Rigby having expired by her death. (315 Auber.) To my wife Anne my mansion house Mistley Hall, & confirm to her £150 a yr. by our marriage settlement, & I give her also £250 a yr. & the use of plate & furniture, coach & 4 horses, 2 saddle horses, & £200. All my lands to my brother-in-law Geo. Barker & Cha. Grey of Colchester, Esq., on Trust for my only s. Richd Rigby in tail male, remainder to the heirs male of my daus. Anne & Martha, my neph. Edw. Rigby, s. of my bro. Jas. Rigby. £1500 to ea. of my sd 2 daus. My niece Mary Venn £20. To my friends Sir Chas. Wager, Kt, & Sir John Eyles, Bart., & my brother Jas. Rigby, my brothers-in-law John Stewart & Geo. Barker, my kinsman Jonathan Perrie, & my good friends Edw. Pratter, Esq., of Jamaica, & the sd Chas. Grey, each a ring of 20 gas. My sd s. to be G. of my daus. My wife Ex'trix. Geo. Barker & Chas. Gray Ex'ors, & 50 gas each. Witnessed by William Bumpstead, Thomas Barron, Rose Rye.

Codicil 18 Aug. 1730. £1000 to my wife, payable out of the produce received from the West Indies for improving Mistley Hall. £300 for almshouses.

1753, Aug. 14. Micajah Perry, Esq., deceased. Limited adm'on to Philip Perry of East Greenwich, Esq. It has been alledged by Sarah Heysham, widow, & Gyles Thornton Heysham, Esq., that by Indenture tripartite dated 11 April 1739 between Robt Thornton of East Greenwich, Esq., the surviving Ex'or of Wm Heysham, of the 1st part, Micajah Perry, then Lord Mayor of London, but late of Epsom, Esq., deceased, & the said Philip Perry of London, mercht, but since of East Greenwich, Esq., of the 2d part, & Gyles Thornton Heysham, then of Stagnoe, co. Herts, Esq., of the 3d part, that in consideration of a marriage intended, & after solemnized, between Wm Heysham & Sarah Perry, one of the daus. of Richd Perry, Esq. (now the said Sarah Heysham, widow), £10,000 bank stock was assigned to Robt Heysham, Esq., Peter Godfrey, Esq., & Micajah Perry for her joynture, & if she died without issue for the use of her husband & his heirs, & this sum became eventually vested in Edwd Turnour of Bloomsbury Square, Esq., Micajah Perry, & Philip Perry. Wm Heysham died s.p. & appointed Robt Thornton, Robt Heysham, Esq., & John Marsh (both since dead) his Ex'ors. The £10,000 was ordered by the Court of Chancery to be sold, & the reversion of it was purchased by Gyles Thornton for £6100. Micajah Perry died intestate within 12 months since. Adm'on to Philip Perry concerning the £10,000 only. Limited adm'on of rest of goods passed Nov. 1757.

Another adm'on. Micajah Perry, formerly Lord Mayor of London, but of Epsom, Esq., deceased, widower, intestate, leaving Sarah Perry, widow, his mother, since deceased, Philip Perry, Esq., his brother, Sarah Heysham, & Eliz. Cade (wife of Salisbury Cade, Esq.) his sisters.

Close Roll, 20 Geo. II., Part 1, No. 25.

Indenture tripartite made the 1st Feb. 1745 between John Cleland, late of the parish of St. Peter Poor, London, but now of the province of South Carolina, Gent., and Mary his wife (one of the daughters and coheirs of John Perrie, late of St. James's, Westminster, Esq., deceased), of the 1st part, William Hamilton of Lincoln's Inn, Esq., George Barker of St. Paul's, Covent Garden, merchant, and Alexander Hamilton of Lincoln's Inn, Gent., of the 2nd part, and George Moncrieff of Antigua, Esq., of the 3rd part. Whereas by articles of agreement made previous to the marriage of the said Mary with John Cleland, dated the 14th Nov. 1728, between John Cleland, of the 1st part, Mary Perrie (one of the daughters of John Perrie, late of Antigua, merchant, deceased), of the 2nd part, and Richard Rigby, Esq., since deceased, and the said William Hamilton, George Barker, and Alexander Hamilton, of the 3rd part, Mary Perrie did covenant with Richard Rigby and the others that within six months after the solemnization of the marriage she would convey among other things the 3rd part of the messuages and lands, etc., hereinafter mentioned to them in trust, and it was further agreed that the said intended settlement should contain a provision that the said trustees might sell, etc., with the consent of John and Mary Cleland; and whereas the marriage was soon after solemnized and Richard Rigby is since dead, but no settlement has been made, and George Moncrieff has agreed with John and Mary Cleland for the purchase of her 3rd part. Now this Indenture witnesseth that in consideration of £1200 sterling paid to William Hamilton, George Barker, and Alexander Hamilton, and of 5*s.* each to John and Mary Cleland, they grant, etc., to George Moncrieff all that one-third of all that plantation in the parish of St. Mary, Antigua, containing 286 acres, according to an actual survey there taken by John Teatte, Sworn Surveyor General of Antigua, the 25th Feb. 1722, bounded N. with the creek, S. with the lands of John Roe, deceased, now belonging to the heirs of George Jennings, Esq., deceased, and the lands heretofore of John Gamble, deceased, now belonging to Samuel Watkins, Esq., W. with the lands formerly of Charles Callaham, deceased, now in the possession of William Smith, Esq., and E. with the lands of Samuel Martin, Esq., as fully and largely as now claimed and enjoyed by the said John Cleland and Mary his wife, and Richard Rigby, Esq. (son of Richard Rigby, late of Misley, co. Essex, Esq., deceased, by Ann his wife, also deceased, who was another of the daughters and coheirs of John Perrie), and the said George Barker and Dorothy his wife (the other of the daughters and coheirs of John Perrie), their managers, overseers, etc., and all messuages, etc., and all one-third part of the following slaves (names given), 25 negro men, 30 negro women, 11 negro boys, and 7 negro girls, and also one-third part of 2 bulls, 15 oxen, 15 cows, 8 bull calves, 3 cow calves, 5 mules, and 1 horse (all named), and of all hoes, etc., to George Moncrieff and his heirs and assigns for evermore; and whereas George Moncrieff hath not only agreed with them but with Richard Rigby and George and Dorothy Barker for the purchase of the remaining two thirds, but owing to the absence of John and Mary Cleland in South Carolina and the others in Great Britain it is not thought convenient to join them to this conveyance, etc., nevertheless for the better and more effectual conveyance, etc., it is hereby covenanted that John and Mary Cleland will at any time hereafter at the request of George Moncrieff join, etc. Peter Ham, J. Crosthwaite, William Stone, Archibald Liddell, Thomas Sumersett, Edward Hughes, Thurston Blackman, witnesses.

Close Roll, 19 Geo. II., Part 13, No. 20.

Indenture tripartite made the 10th Oct. 1745 between Richard Rigby of Misley Hall, Essex, Esq. (son and heir of Richard Rigby, Esq., deceased, by Anne his wife, also deceased, one of the daughters and coheirs of John Perrie, late of St. James's, Westminster, Esq., deceased), of the 1st part, George Barker of St. Paul, Covent Garden, merchant, and Dorothy his wife, another of the daughters and coheirs of John Perrie, of the 2nd part, and George Moncrieff of Antigua, Esq., of the 3rd part, witnesseth that in consideration of £2400 for the absolute purchase of the plantation, etc., hereinafter mentioned, Richard Rigby and George and Dorothy Barker grant, etc., to George Moncrieff, in his actual possession being, all those two-third parts of all that plantation in the parish of St. Mary, Antigua, containing 286 acres (as in Cleland and Moncrieff) as fully and largely as now claimed and enjoyed by the said Richard Rigby, George and Dorothy Barker, and John and Mary Cleland, to the use of George Moncrieff and his heirs and assigns for evermore. Thurston Blackman, Richard Capstack (?), witnesses.

1672. John Perry's land, granted 23 Dec., is surveyed 4 Feb. 1672.

1697. Edward Walrond, Esq., complains against Captain John Perrie who four years ago kept a tavern in St. John's Town, and was an incestuous person, having married his own brother's widow, and was prosecuted by the Assembly of Antigua for doing so. (B. T. Leeward Islands, vol. 5.)

In 1699 Mr. Weaver remarks of John Perrie, one of the Council of St. Christopher's, that he is "most infamous, yet made Provost Marshall, Com^{r} of Prizes, Dep^{ty} auditor of ye K^{s} accounts of all ye Is^{lds} whereby he has got great Riches. He drew Ale a few years ago." Archibald Hutcheson writes in 1698 that Captain John Perrie came as a merchant to the Leeward Islands and settled at Antigua, where he was concerned in a plantation which did not succeed well with him, and is Provost-Marshall and Deputy Auditor. (*Ibid.*)

1701, July 29. Edward Perrie of St. John's, merchant, grant of a proportion of land by Christopher Codrington.

1701, Oct. 10. John Perrie, Esq., Provost-Marshal General, granted a parcel of land in St. John's Town by Christopher Codrington.

Anne Reg. William III. appointed John Perry, Esq., Provost-Marshal General by patent. We do re-appoint him. At Westminster 4 Aug. 1 Anne. Recorded 17 Dec. 1703.

1704, May 18. John Perrie, Esq., granted 100 acres by Christopher Codrington.

1705, Aug. 13. Robert Amory, late of Antigua, now of Gallway, merchant, sells to John Perry half of 344 acres in St. Mary's Parish for 5*s.* Letter of Attorney to him.

In a letter of 1708 Edward Perrie is described as a rich merchant, one of the Commissioners of the Customs, whose brother is Provost-Marshal General.

1709-10. Mr. Micajah Perry is agent to Governor Walter Hamilton.

1710, March 3. Petition of Edward Perrie, Esq., and Thomas Trant, merchant, Attornies of John Perrie, Provost-Marshal General, that Governor Parke appointed Michael Ayon during John Perrie's absence, and he has consequently lost three years' fees. His leave of absence for two years dated 6 Aug. 1709 was read.

1714, July 23. Edward Perrie, Esq.'s commission read as Clerk of the Navy and Naval Officer of Antigua.

1716, Aug. 1. Edward Perrie in a letter says he has well known the island for thirty years, and the $4\frac{1}{2}$ per cent. duty was always collected at St. John's.

1717. Mr. Micajah Perry and Mr. Richard Perry of London offer to purchase a portion of the French lands at St. Christopher's.

1720, Jan. 14. Robert Heysham, Esq; elected Alderman of Billingsgate-Ward, in the Room of Sir William Ashurst, deceas'd. ('Historical Register,' p. 5.)

1721, Oct. 1. Dy'd Mr Micajah Perry, Virginia Merchant, at his House in Leaden-hall-street. ('Historical Register,' p. 39.)

1721, Nov. 14. Robert Heysham, Esq; Alderman of London for the Ward of Billingsgate, chosen President of Christ's Hospital, in the room of Sir Robert Child, deceas'd. (*Ibid.*, p. 43.)

Indenture. Richard Rigby of Misly Hall, co. Essex, Esq., now of Antigua, bound to Jamaica. John Perrie's will, dated 24 June 7 Anne, was proved P.C.C. Edward Perry, brother and Ex'or to said John Perry, is now dead, and Ann Perry his daughter is married to me and is 21. Dorothy the other daughter is not 21, and John Perry left two other daughters—Elizabeth died under 17 and intestate and Mary Perry is an infant. Letter of Attorney now granted to Thomas Kerby 21 Feb. 1722.

1723, Feb. 26. Dy'd Robert Heysham, Esq; Alderman of London, for the Ward of Billingsgate, and President of Christ's Hospital. ('Historical Register,' vol. 8, p. 14.)

1727, April. Christopher Tower, jun. Esq; elected Member of Parliament for the Borough of Lancaster, in the Room of William Heysham, Esq; deceas'd. (*Ibid.*, p. 17.)

1727. Micajah Perry was one of the four M.P.'s for the City of London.

1728, Feb. 24. Micajah Perry, Esq; unanimously elected Alderman of Aldgate Ward, in the Room of Sir Francis Porteen, Knt., deceas'd. ('Historical Register,' p. 14.)

Indenture dated 2 June 1724. Arthur Dabron, Esq., Deputy Provost-Marshall, and Slingsby Bethell, Esq., against Thomas Rome, by Richard Rigby, Esq., and his wife Anne and Dorothy Perrie, spinster, Ex'ors of will of John Perrie, deceased, merchant. 167 acres to said Slingsby Bethell were sold by outcry for £450 c. Slingsby Bethell now assigns to Sir William Codrington.

1733. Mr Cade, Son of the late Dr Cade, to Miss Perry, Sister to Mr Alderman Perry, a young Lady of 10,000*l.* Fortune. ('London Magazine,' p. 44.)

1734, July. At his Seat at Stagenhoe in Hertfordshire, Robert Heysham, Esq; only Son of Robert Heysham, Esq; formerly one of the Representatives in Parliament for this City: He being a Batchelor has left his whole Estate (except 5000*l.* to Mrs Robinson) to his first Cousins, Giles and Robert Thornton, Brothers. (*Ibid.*, p. 386.)

1734, Sep. Micajah Perry, Esq; Alderman of Aldgate Ward, chosen Sheriff of London and Middlesex for the year ensuing. (*Ibid.*, p. 24.)

1738, Sep. Micajah Perry, Esq; chosen Lord Mayor of the City of London, for the year ensuing. ('Historical Register,' p. 34.)

1738. At Epsom in Surrey, The Lady of Micajah Perry, Esq; Lord Mayor elect: She was the Daughter of Mr Cock, a very eminent Linnen Draper near Stocks-Market, and has left no Issue. (*Ibid.*, p. 41.)

1738, Oct. The Lady of Micajah Perry, Esq; Lord Mayor Elect. ('London Magazine,' p. 516.)

1740, Dec. 9. Petition of Captain Syer Allicock, Attorney to the heirs of Jonathan Perrie, deceased.

1753, Jan. 22. Micajah Perry, Esq; Lord Mayor of London in 1738. ('Gent. Mag.,' p. 53.)

1753, Jan. 25. The late Mr Alderman Perry, who had served the office of lord-mayor, and was formerly one of the representatives of the city of London, in parliament. ('London Magazine,' p. 93.)

For the Pedigree of the Heyshams see 'Miscellanea Genealogica et Heraldica,' vol. iv., New Series, p. 373.

LEYDEN UNIVERSITY.

Perrij, Carolus, Anglus, 5 Febr. 1723.
Perrij, Micajah, Hibernus, 8 Nov. 1712.
Perrij, Micajah, Hybernus, 25 Maii 1715.

PARISH REGISTER OF ST. JOHN.

Baptized.

1703	Dec. 28	Sarah Perry d. of John Perry & Anne his [*blank*].
1703	Dec. 28	Dorothy d. of John Perry & Anne.

Buried.

1690	Aug. 26	Doctr Samuel Perry.
1691	Sep. 12	Edward S. of Samuel & Mary Perrie.
1700	Feb. 16	John S. of John Perry.
1701	April 20	Thos. Perry, Carpenter of ye Lyon, Captn Burnside, Comdr.
1716	Feb. 26	Edward Perrie.
1741	Aug. 23	Mary Perrie.
1760	Nov. 28	John Perry.
1771	Nov. 10	John Perry.
1777	Jan. 2	Andrew Perry.

PARISH REGISTER OF ST. PHILIP.

Married.

1700	Aug. 4	John Elliott to Elizabeth Perry.

1663, Oct. 20. Micajah Perry, at St Mary le Bow, London, Haberdasher, Bachr, abt 23, & Ann Owen, of St Swithin's, London, Spr, about 24; consent of father Dr Richd Owen; at St Swithin's, or St Michael's, Crooked Lane. (Marriage Allegations: Vicar-General of Archbishop of Canterbury.)

ST. PAUL'S WALDEN, CO. HERTS.

On a flat stone in the Church:—

Here lieth interred the body of WILLIAM HEYSHAM, of Greenwich, in the county of Kent, esq., who was member of parliament ten years last past for the corporation of Lancaster. He married Sarah, daughter of Richard Perry, of London, esq., and died the 14th day of April, anno Domini, 1727, in the 36th year of his age.

Arms: *An anchor, and in chief three roundels;* impaling, *on a bend . . . . between two cottises ermine three lions passant . . . .*

('Gent. Mag.,' 1798, p. 758.)

"Rigbys" (? formerly "Perrys") in St. Mary's Parish in 1852 contained 263 acres, and was owned by Sir W. Martin.

Family of Pigott.

Thomas Pigott of Long Ashton, co. Somerset, Esq. Will dated 31 March 1670; proved P.C.C. 13 Feb. 1673-4 by Florence Pigott the relict. (23 Bunce.) To be buried according to the Liturgie of the Church of England. To my dau. Eliz. Pigott as a marriage portion £1500 out of my rents in Westmeath, Ireland. To my 2[d] son John Piggott chattel lease in Banwell, co. Som., & my copyhold in Queen's County, Ireland, after my mother's death, & £100. To my 1st son Poulett Pigott & his heirs all my lands & manor of Brockley, co. Som., my wife to have the same for life but paying £100 a year towards his maintenance & education. To my dau. Usher £20. To my son-in-law Sir Hugh Smyth, Sir Humphry Hooke, & their wives, my dau.-in-law Mrs. Eliz. Smyth, M[rs] Helena & M[rs] Ann Smyth, my son-in-law Tho. Smyth, Lord Poulett & my brother-in-law Francis Poulett, my brother M[r] Alex. Pigott & my sisters Mrs. Grove, Mrs. Phillips, & Mrs. FitzGerald, 40/ rings. All residue to my wife & Ex'trix. (Somersetshire Wills, vol. iv., p. 107.)

Florence Pigott of Ashton. Will dated 20 April 1676; proved P.C.C. 19 Feb. 1676-7 by Sir Hugh Smyth, Bart. (23 Hale.) To be buried in the vault where M[r] Pigott & Poulett Pigott were laid. My son Sir Hugh Smyth to be sole Ex'or. My dans. Florence Hooke, Eliz. Smyth, Helena Boorn, Anne Knitt, & Martha Usher, £50 each. Eliz. Halles £5. Poor of Ashton £20, Bedminster £15, Hinton S[t] George £10. My terme in Great Wembrow for my dau. Hook's children. Certain plate to my son John Pigott which were his father's, marken with armes, also the household stuff at Brockley.

Acquila Stoughton* of Antigua. Will dated 17 July 1690. To my brother John Stoughton 10,000 lbs. To Tho. & Sarah Turner, son & dau. of Tho. Turner of Popes Head, each 10,000 lbs. for mourning. To my wife Ffrances Stoughton all my goods, lands, tenements, negros, etc., & to be sole Ex'trix. Witnessed by Richard Traveis, Thomas Edgecombe, Ffrancis Jadine. By his Excellency the General was sworn Thomas Edgecombe. Recorded 21 June 1693. Thomas Gatewood, Deputy Secretary.

Francis Stoughton† of Antigua. Will dated 9 Sep. 1693. To my granddau. Ffrances Kerby 10,000 lbs. & an heifer. To my son John Pigott a negro, a mare, & colt. To my dau. Ffrances Pigott all my linen, bedding, & household stuff, plate only excepted, also a negro woman for life. To my 2 grandchildren John Gunthorpe & W[m] Gunthorpe all my estate real & personal equally, only my son John Pigott to keep my negros on my land at Falmouth for 5 years, then paying 15,000 lbs. to them. To my friend M[rs] Martha Edgeomb £5 for a piece of plate. To my son John Pigott £20 left me by Major John Gunthorp to buy mourning. To the 1st child my dau. Ffrances Pigott has £5 for a piece of plate. Major Edw[d] Byam, my son John Pigott, & my dau. Ffrances Pigott Ex'ors. Witnessed by W. Barter, Cutbord R. Parker, An Ashton. By his Excellency the General were sworn Anne Ashton and William Barter 8 Feb. 1693.

John Pigott of Kilcromin. Will dated 2 March 1708; proved in Ireland 1711. Bound on a voyage to the West Indyes. To my 3 youngest sons Rob[t], Benj[n], & John, £200 each. My dau. Eliz. £400. My 3 other daus. £300 each. My 1st s. to have ½ of my real & personal estate. My wife Frances shall live in y[e] house of Kilcromin during her widdow-hood. My brother Rob[t] Pigott, Lan[t] Sands, Esq., Cileavon & Major John Lyons & my wife Ex'ors. Witnessed by Thomas Pigott, Samuel Bowker, Ann Barrington. Recorded in P.R.O. of Ireland, Four Courts, Dublin.

Robert Pigott of Disart, Queen's County, Esq. Will dated 5 Jan. 1728. To be bur. in the vault in Disart Church near my father, mother, & wife. £1400 is due by bond from Richard Warburton of Garryhinch, Esq., & Capt. John Warburton his brother; £600 from Richard Warburton of Donecarney, Councelor; £100 from Capt. John Wheatley of Mountmelie; £50 from Sir Tho. Slade of Dublin; £50 from Dudley Cosby & Pole Cosby, Esq.; £900 due on my death by deed of sale of Disart, etc., which altogether amount to £3100. I give £1000 to Pigott Sands & Capt. Rich[d] Sands his brother in Trust for my nephew Thos. Pigott, 1st s. of my brother John Pigott, to pay the interest towards discharging the rent of the farm he holds of Warner Westenra, Esq. I give them also £350 to pay the rent of the farm of Coulereth held by my sister Martha Bowker, & at her death £100 to her 1st son John Bowker, £100 to her dau. Frances Bowker, & £150 equally to her youngest sons Sam[l] & Rob[t] Bowker. To my nephew Rob[t] Pigott, 2[d] s. of my brother John, £700. To my nephews Pigot Sands & Rich[d] Sands £300 in Trust for my brother Walter Pigott. To my niece Judith Pigott, youngest dau. of my brother John, £300. For my sister Phellipe £100, & at her death to go to her daus. Mary & Eliz. My niece Eliz. Pigott, dau. of my brother Alex[r], £100, & to his 2[d] son John Pigott £50, & to his youngest son Starkey Pigott £50, & to his 1st son Rob[t] Pigott £50. To my cousin Judith Pigott, wife of Emanuel Pigott,* Esq., my furniture. My brother Samuel Bowker. All residue to my nephew Thos. Pigott, s. of my bro. John. My said nephew Tho. Pigott, Pigott Sandes, Richard Sandes, & John Bowker my brother-in-law, Ex'ors. Witnessed by Warner Westenra, William Caulfield. Seal affixed bears:—*Ermine, three fusils argent.*

For the extracts from the Irish wills and records the author is indebted to Mr. William Jackson Pigott of Dundrum Manor House, co. Down.

Governor Codrington writes 3 July 1691 recommending Captain John Piggott, and says: "His father as I am inform'd is a Gentleman of a Considerable interest in Ireland, and hath been a very great sufferer by the present Rebellion of the Irish, who in the former were the Murtherers of his Grandfather." (B. T. Leeward Islands, vol. 43.)

1714, Aug. 5. Thomas Pigott, Esq., petitions for land formerly Mr. Edmond Brinsden's, who died 30 years ago, bounded N. with Newgate Street, S. with Thomas Lynch, W. with Jeffry Dooling.

1727, Dec. 23. Dy'd John Pigot, Esq.: aged 80 Years. He was son of Colonel Thomas Pigot, Master of the Court of Wards in Ireland. ('Historical Register,' 1728, p. 4.)

1759, May 2. Petition of William Piggott, Ex'or of Thomas Piggott.

* He was Deputy Secretary 1679 and a Member of the Assembly 1686. Frances his wife was probably widow of .... Proctor (? Lieutenant William Proctor) who was living 1678.

† Probably Frances widow of Acquila.

* Emanuel Pigot, son of Thomas of Chetwynd, Ireland, arm., matriculated from Pembroke College, Oxon. 9 July 1701, aged 17; student of Inner Temple 1702; migrated to the Middle Temple 1704; M.P. Cork City 1735-60; died 30 June 1762 (see Baronetage). He was grandson of Alexander, consequently second-cousin of testator.

Pedigree of Pigott.

ARMS.—*Ermine, three fusils conjoined in fess sable, on the centre one a crescent or for difference.*
CREST.—*A wolf's head erased argent, charged on the neck with a crescent gules for difference.*
(From the registry of Knighthood of Sir Robert Pigott, 1609.)

JOHN PIGOTT of Dysart in Queen's County, Ireland, Gent.; had a grant of a message with 766 acres by patent dated 28 Feb. 1562; died 27 April 1570. Inq. p.m. 9 April 1578.

Thomas Pigott, 1st son and heir, died a minor 7 April 1578.

Anne, dau. of William St. Leger, son of Sir Anthony St. Leger, Lord Deputy; died 9 Oct. 1599; bur. at Christ Church Cathedral, Dublin. (Funeral Entry, ii., 41.) 1st wife. = Sir Robert Pigott of Dysart, Knt., æt. 13 in 1578; had a grant by Privy Seal 25 May 1587 and patent 16 Oct. 1587 to hold as of the Castle of Maryborough *in capite* by the one-fourth of a knight's fee; knighted 30 Sep. 1609 at Loughrver; M.P. for Queen's County 8 April 1613; had a grant of Corbally, Capard, etc., by patent of 29 April 1622. Will dated 23 May 1641; proved 17 April 1644 in Ireland. = Thomasine, 3rd dau. and coheir of Sir Christopher Peyton, Auditor-General of Ireland, widow of Captain Baptist Castillion; of the Bedchamber to Queen Elizabeth. 2nd wife.

Anne Pigott (? mar. 1st . . . . Bridgewater); 2ndly Henry Packenham of Packenham Hall, co. Westmeath; he died 1691. See Earl of Longford.

John Pigott of Grangebeg, Queen's County, Major in the Army; M.P. for Queen's County 4 July 1634; murdered by the rebels under O'Farrel in his Castle of Dysart 1646; depositions in Trinity College. Will proved 14 April 1654. = Martha, dau. of Sir Thomas Colclough, Knt., of Tintern Abbey, co. Wexford; living 1670.

Alexander Pigott of Innishannon, co. Cork, Colonel in the Army.

Sibilla Pigott, mar. Barnaby Dunn of Brittas.

Dorothy Pigott, mar. Andrew Hoult of Aughenchely; died Dec. 1637.

Joan Pigott, mar. Edm. Savage, son of Sir Arthur Savage of Reban, Knt.

Robert Pigott of Dysart. = Anne, dau. of Sir William Gilbert of Kilminchy, King's Co., Knt.

Thomas Pigott of Long Ashton and Brockley Hall, co. Somerset; Privy Councillor; M.P. Queen's County 1661. Will dated 31 March 1670; proved 13 Feb. 1673-4. (23 Bunce.) = Florence, dau. of John, Lord Poulet, and widow of Thomas Smith of Long Ashton; mar. 1648. Will dated 20 April 1676; proved 19 Feb. 1676-7. (23 Hale.)

Thomas Pigott of Dysart, died 1687 at Dysart, and bur. there. = Elizabeth, dau. of William Weldon, Esq., of Rahenderry, co. Kildare, M.P. for Athy 1661; mar. lic. dated 28 April 1663; bur. at Dysart.

Paulet Pigott* of Long Ashton; matric. from St. Edmund Hall, Oxon, 10 March 1664-5, æt. 14; Student of Lincoln's Inn 1668; dead 1676.

John Pigott, died young.

John Pigott of Brockley. Will dated 1714; proved 1728. *A quo* Pigotts of Brockley Hall.

Martha Pigott, mar. Christopher Usher of Dublin; he died Jan. 1706.

Elizabeth Pigott, mar. . . . . Long of Bristol.

Robert Pigott of Dysart, and bur. there. Will dated 5 Jan. 1728; proved 30 April 1730. = ... bur. at Dysart. s.p.

John Pigott of Kilcromin, and of Antigua in the West Indies, Captain in Holt's Regiment 1694 at the Leeward Islands; killed in the Parke Riot at St. John's 7 and bur. 8 Dec. 1710. Will dated 2 March 1708; proved 1711 in Ireland. = Frances Proctor, spinster; mar. 1690; died 1712. See the will of her mother Mrs. Frances Stoughton, dated 9 Sep. 1693.

Thomas Pigott of Kilcromin and of Grange, 1st son and heir; living 1723; heir to his uncle Robert 1728. = Mary, dau. of Oliver Wheeler of Dublin; living 1723.

Robert Pigott of Dysart, M.P. for Maryborough. = ...

Benjamin Pigott, died a bachelor. By his will dated 1720 left his estate to his uncle Robert.

John Pigott. = ...

Elizabeth Pigott, mar. . . . . Knox.

Anne Pigott.

Martha Pigott.

Two sons, who died young.

Elizabeth Pigott.

Rev. Richard Pigott, B.A., D.D., of Dysart, Vicar of Holy Trinity; died Nov. 1782; bur. in Cork Cathedral. (Brady's 'History of Dioceses of Cork, Cloyne, and Ross.') = Dorothy Crosbie, dau. of Lord Brandon.

Anne Pigott, mar. Robert Shapland Carew of Castleborough, M.P. for City of Waterford and co. Wexford (died 29 March 1829), to whom she conveyed the Dysart estates, and was mother of Robert Shapland, first Baron Carew.

* A Paulet Pigot by the Irish Records died intestate in 1678.

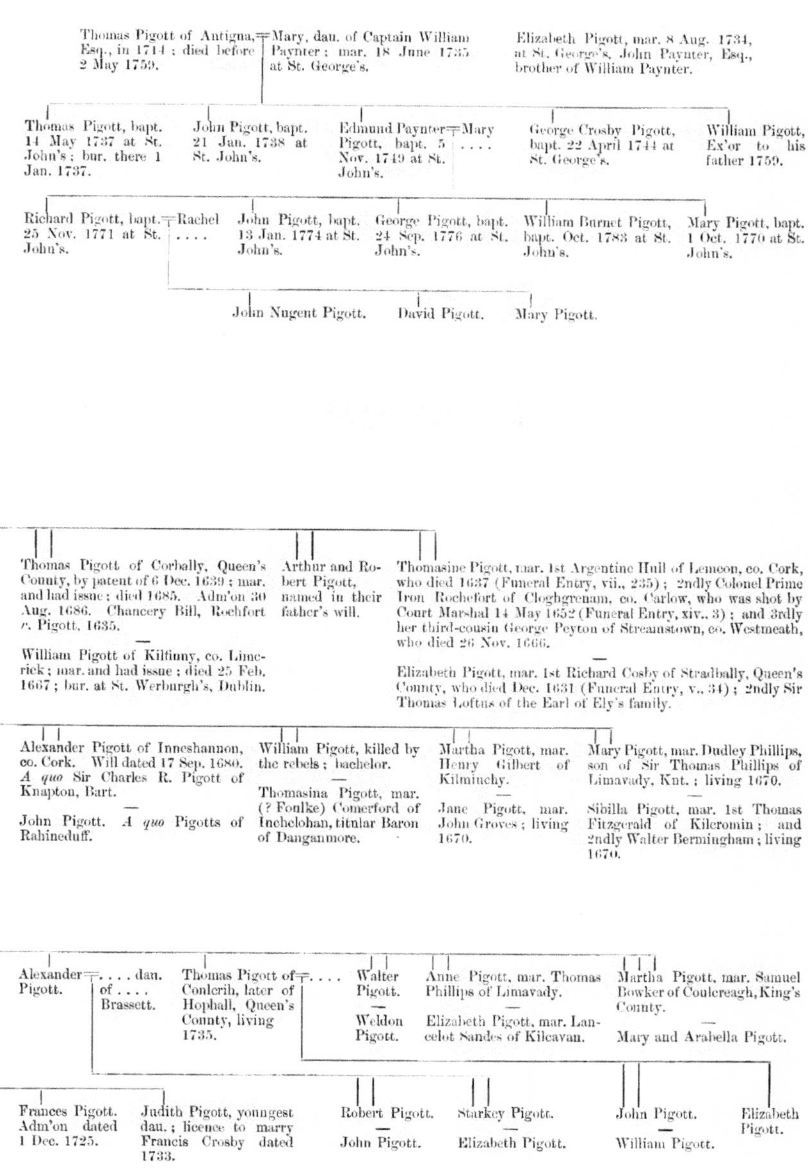

Thomas Pigott of Antigua, Esq., in 1714; died before 2 May 1759. ═ Mary, dau. of Captain William Paynter; mar. 18 June 1735 at St. George's.

Elizabeth Pigott, mar. 8 Aug. 1734, at St. George's, John Paynter, Esq., brother of William Paynter.

Thomas Pigott, bapt. 14 May 1737 at St. John's; bur. there 1 Jan. 1737.

John Pigott, bapt. 21 Jan. 1738 at St. John's.

Edmund Paynter Pigott, bapt. 5 Nov. 1749 at St. John's. ═ Mary ....

George Crosby Pigott, bapt. 22 April 1744 at St. George's.

William Pigott, Ex'or to his father 1759.

Richard Pigott, bapt. 25 Nov. 1771 at St. John's. ═ Rachel ....

John Pigott, bapt. 13 Jan. 1774 at St. John's.

George Pigott, bapt. 24 Sep. 1776 at St. John's.

William Burnet Pigott, bapt. Oct. 1783 at St. John's.

Mary Pigott, bapt. 1 Oct. 1770 at St. John's.

John Nugent Pigott. David Pigott. Mary Pigott.

Thomas Pigott of Corbally, Queen's County, by patent of 6 Dec. 1639; mar. and had issue; died 1685. Adm'on 30 Aug. 1686. Chancery Bill, Rochfort *v.* Pigott, 1635.

William Pigott of Kilfinny, co. Limerick; mar. and had issue; died 25 Feb. 1667; bur. at St. Werburgh's, Dublin.

Arthur and Robert Pigott, named in their father's will.

Thomasine Pigott, mar. 1st Argentine Hull of Lemcon, co. Cork, who died 1637 (Funeral Entry, vii., 235); 2ndly Colonel Prime Iron Rochefort of Cloghgrenam, co. Carlow, who was shot by Court Marshal 14 May 1652 (Funeral Entry, xiv., 3); and 3rdly her third-cousin George Peyton of Streamstown, co. Westmeath, who died 26 Nov. 1666.

Elizabeth Pigott, mar. 1st Richard Cosby of Stradbally, Queen's County, who died Dec. 1631 (Funeral Entry, v., 34); 2ndly Sir Thomas Loftus of the Earl of Ely's family.

Alexander Pigott of Inneshannon, co. Cork. Will dated 17 Sep. 1680. *A quo* Sir Charles R. Pigott of Knapton, Bart.

John Pigott. *A quo* Pigotts of Rahineduff.

William Pigott, killed by the rebels; bachelor.

Thomasina Pigott, mar. (? Foulke) Comerford of Inchelohan, titular Baron of Dangannore.

Martha Pigott, mar. Henry Gilbert of Kilminchy.

Jane Pigott, mar. John Groves; living 1670.

Mary Pigott, mar. Dudley Phillips, son of Sir Thomas Phillips of Limavady, Knt.; living 1670.

Sibilla Pigott, mar. 1st Thomas Fitzgerald of Kilcromin; and 2ndly Walter Bermingham; living 1670.

Alexander Pigott. ═ .... dau. of .... Brassett.

Thomas Pigott of Conlcrih, later of Hophall, Queen's County, living 1735. ═ ....

Walter Pigott.

Weldon Pigott.

Anne Pigott, mar. Thomas Phillips of Limavady.

Elizabeth Pigott, mar. Lancelot Sandes of Kilcavan.

Martha Pigott, mar. Samuel Bowker of Coulcreagh, King's County.

Mary and Arabella Pigott.

Frances Pigott. Adm'on dated 1 Dec. 1725.

Judith Pigott, youngest dau.; licence to marry Francis Crosby dated 1733.

Robert Pigott.

John Pigott.

Starkey Pigott.

Elizabeth Pigott.

John Pigott.

William Pigott.

Elizabeth Pigott.

Copy of Inquisition (Exchequer), No. 1 Queen's County, P.R.O., Ireland.

Inquisitio capta apud Mariborowe in Com' le Quenes Countie ixº die Aples Anno d'ni 1578 et regni d'ne Elizabethe dei gracia Anglie ffrauncie hibericque Regine vicesimo Coram Joh'e Whitney generoso deputato Joh'is Crofton Armigeri generalis Scactoris et ffeodar deo d'ne Regine Regni sui hibernie virtute Comissionis einsd'm Escaetoris sibi direct ad inquirendu infra Comitat' le Quenes Countie predictum p' Sacrum legaliu' hominu' einsd'm comitat' quorum nomina subsequunt'.

Robertus Bowen de balliaddam, Mulmurry McEdmund de Rahen, Petrus Ovinden de Tankerdeston, Robertus Dyer de Kilvinchen, Alexander Cosby de ffarmpriori, Edmundus Ketinge de . . . . David Hetherington de ballirone, Richardus Chapman de Mariborough, Joh'es Ovinden de balliffoill, Georgeus hetherington de Tullie, Will'mus Beard de Coult, Richardus ffox de Mariborough.

Qui jurati dicunt super sacrum' sun' quod Joh'es Pigott nuper de dizart in Com' le Quenes Com' generosus fuit seisitus dominico suo ut de feodo . . . . uno castro sive ffortilogio lapideo voct' le dizart in Com' le Quenes Com' ac eitiam de villis villatis sive hambletis de dizart Dirry al's Rathina . . . . Cloyder Colchri. Mollenekawer Rathinuskie Cargeneparke Keltelough Ballicarrould et Collarne cu' omnibz et singulis Castris messagiis cottagiis terr' . . . . advocacionibz, doncio'bz presentacionibz Juribz patronatis ecclesiarum rectoriarum et vicariaru' pratis pascius com' unibz viis rampuiis custumis col . . . . peiis Clausuris aquis piscariis stagnis gurgitibz molindinis aquaru' curibz moris moriscis turbariis terris montanis silvis bocis subbocis et aliis . . . . temporalibz quibuscumqz cu' suis p'tinenciis prefatis Castro et villis de Dizart Dirry el's Rathinusk Ballicloyder Colchri Molenekawer Rathinuskie Carg . . . . parke kell . . . . lough ballicarrould et Collarne aut eoru' alicui spectantibz sive ptinentibz et ea tenuit de d'na Regina ut de castro suo de Mariborough in Capit' p' servitui' militare viz. p' xxm partem anius feod militis quondo scutagi'm currit et p' annuallem reditu' de ix Dxis monete hiberie ac unu' custumarii diem vocat' a plowe day de quolibet arratro q'd erit arrando dictas terras arrare aut talem laborem et opera facere ad tale tempus et locu' infra Com' p' dick quale p' constabularin' castri de Mariborowe tempori existent' limitabitu' sive appunctuabit' vell tres solidos quolibet custumario dei ad Libitu dict Joh'is vell heredu' sur et q'o ipse tenebit et maun tenebit de tempore in tempus quatuor habiles equites defencione Cum' p'dict' Quiquidem Joh'es Pigott sic existens suisitus de castro terris ten'ts ac de o'ibz aliis hereditamentis predict' et superius specificat' diem obiit extremu ex indeseisitu xxviiº die Aprils' aº 1570 post cuius mortem Thomas Pigott primus felius et heres predicti Joh'is captus fuit in custodia d'ne Reginæ ut warda dict d'ne Regine quiquidem Thomas Pigott sic extremu' viz septimo die Ap'les p'terit Ao dni 1578 et Regni nunc Regine xxº It'm dicunt quod Robertus Pigott secundus ffellius predicti Joh'is Pigott et ffrater dicti Thome Piggot est legitimus et p'pinquis' heres antedictoru' Joh'is Pigott patris sui et Thome Pigott ffratri sui et est etatis circiter xiii annoru et non maritatus. In cuius rei testimonii tam predic'us Joh'es Whitney Deputat' Escaet' quam prenominati Juratores p'sentibz sigilla alternatim apposuerunt. Dat Aº die et loco Sup dictis Quenes County Th. Pygot. Quenes County. Thomas Pigot & Thomas Piggot.

Deliba't' fuit ista inquis' vii die Novemb
Anno Regni regine Elizabeth } xxmo.

I certify that the foregoing is a true and authentic Copy made pursuant to the Statute 30 & 31 Vic., ch. 70.

Samuel Ferguson, D.K.,
8th Sep. 1873.

Ross Corporation Books, co. Wexford.

1700, Aug. John Pigott signed as one of the Grand Jury of the Queen's Co. relative to wool exportation (p. 121).

1725, Nov. 6. Rev. Harfinch Pigott admitted freeman & free burgess; last appearance 12 Aug. 1738. 7 Sep. 1727 app. overseer of Trinity Hospital.

1734. Wm Pigott is named as one of the Brethren of the Poor (p. 143).

1741. Aug. 12. Wm Pigott s. of the Revd Harfinch Pigott was admitted and made a free burgess same day (p. 45).

1746, Oct. 11. Certain lands canted to Mr Wm Pigott for lives renewable for ever, at 4s. *2d.* per acre, next adjoining the "Maudlin" (p. 144).

1781, Oct. 6. Renewal of lease of part of the commons to Wm Pigott, Esq., in place of Johanna Pigott (p. 151).

1802, June 29. Renewal of lease of the commons to Wm Pemberton Pigott. Esqr, new lives in place of Wm Pigott & Cæsar Sutton, Jun., decd (p. 155).

1818, June 29. Wm Pemberton Pigott, Esq., of Slevoy, admitted & made free burgess (p. 53); his last appearance 29 June 1831.

1818, Sep. 29. Renewal of lease for life of Cha. Cæsar Pigott, aged 7 (p. 159); renewal of ditto 29 June 1824 & 28 Aug. 1841.

1824, June 18. John Pigott of Charlotte St., Esqr, and Elizth Maguire, 1st dau. of Mr Wm Maguire of Peter's Place, married. (William Maguire was father of the Rev. Dr. Edward Maguire, present Dean of Down; J. Pigott was uncle of William Jackson Pigott.)

1825. Alexr Pigott, esq., of Sunbury Lodge, Queen's Co., 2d s. of late Genl Tho. Pigott of Knapton, Queen's Co., mar. but s.p.

The following Piggotts have been High Sheriffs of Queen's County:—

1663	Thomas.	1754	John, of Brockley Park, Queen's County.
1670	Thomas.		
1690	Thomas.	1778	George.
1705	John.	1803	William.
1712	Robert.	1808	Thomas.
1727	Southwell.		

Consistorial Marriage Licences, Dublin.

1663	April 28	Thos. Pigott of Dysart, Queen's Co., Esqre, & Elizabeth Weldon of Dublin Castle, Spr.
1667	Dec. 19	John Pigott . . . . Nicholas citra & Dorothea Gifford, Spr. St Werburghs.
1730	April 3	Francis Cosby . . . . Anne Pigott, Spr. St Michan's.
1733	[*blank*]	Francis Cosby, Gent., & Judith Pigott, Spr. St Catherine's.
1740	Aug. 2	John Pigott, Dublin, Esqr, & Catherine Babington, Widow. St Bridget's.
1794	Dec. 19	Wm Pemberton Pigott, co. Wexford, Esq., & Eleanor Haughton, Spr. St Anne's.
1806	July 26	Welman Harvey, Esq., Lieut. 9 foot, & Abigail Pigott, Spr. St Andrew's.

1755, March 14. Alexr Pigott bur. St Anne's, Dublin.
1756, March 19. Southwell Pigott bur. ditto.

Parish Register of St. John.

Baptized.

1737	May 14	Thomas the s. of Thomas Pigott and Mary his wife.
1738	Jan. 21	John ye s. of Thomas Pigott & Elizabeth his wife.

1749 Nov. 5 Edmund Paynter the s. of Thos. Piggott and Mary his wife.
1770 Oct. 1 Mary the D. of Edmund Pigott & Mary his wife.
1771 Nov. 25 Richard the S. of Edmund Pigott and Mary his wife.
1774 Jan. 13 John the S. of Edmund Pigott & Mary his wife.
1776 Sep. 24 George the S. of Edmund Pigott and Mary his wife.
1783 Oct. . . William Burnet the S. of Edmund Pigott and Mary his wife.
1805 June 26 John Nugent S. of Richard Pigott and Rachel his wife. B. the 26th December 1804.
1808 Mar. 23 David S. of Richard Pigott and Rachell his wife. B. the 18th November last.
1813 June 21 Mary D. of Richard Pigott and Rachel his wife. B. the 18th November 1808 and was Baptized on the day following but omitted to be recorded.
1820 July 6 Ann D. of Richard Piggot and Catherine his wife. B. the 11th April 1820.
1822 Nov. 14 William Horatio Nelson S. of Richard Pigott and Catherine Bowman his wife. B. September 29, 1822.

Married.

1754 Aug. 1 William Pigott and Susanna Sedgwick. L.
1763 Feb. 16 Charles Libert to Elizth Pigott.
1816 Nov. 30 Richard Pigott to Catherine Bowman Rose, Spinster. L.

Buried.

1710 Dec. 8 Captn John Piggott.
1772 Oct. 2 Richard Pigott.
1785 July 11 John Pigot, Infant.
1814 July 14 Rachel Piggot.

PARISH REGISTER OF ST. GEORGE.

Baptized.

1744 April 22 George Crosby the S. of Thomas Pigott and Mary his wife.

Married.

1734 Aug. 8 John Paynter, Esqr, & Elizabeth Piggott, Spinster.
1735 June 18 Thomas Pigott & Mary Paynter, Spinster.
1800 Feb. 25 Henry Greenway Gore, Planter, & Mary Pigott, S.; by L.

Buried.

1737 Jan. 1 Thomas Pigott, infant.
1745 Jan. 12 George Crosby Pigott.
1748-9 Ann Pigot died 15th Feb., buried ye 16th Feb. 1748-9.

PARISH REGISTER OF ST. PETER.

Baptized.

1814 June 19 William Bladen S. of Henry Tucker Pigot & Sarah his late wife, b. Decr 26, 1812, & Henry S. of Henry Tucker Pigot & Sarah his late wife, b. March 3d, 1814; at Mr Bladen's Cotton N. Work.
1818 Nov. 1 Eliza Ann Billinghurst D. of Henry Pigott and his Wife; privately at Vernon's Estate.
1821 Oct. 8 Henry Alexander Moore s. of Henry T. Pigot and his Wife; at Vernon's Estate.

Buried.

1813 Dec. 29 Henry Bladen Pigot, Infant; from Cotton New Work.
1814 April 13 Sarah Ann Pigot; from Garden Estate.
1814 June 24 Henry Pigot, Infant; from Cotton New Work.
1818 Nov. 11 Eliza Ann Billinghurst, Infant D. of Henry Tucker Pigot & his Wife; in Parham Church Yard, from Vernon's Estate.

PARISH REGISTER OF ST. PHILIP.

Baptized.

1782 Jan. 1 Elizabeth dau. of Richard & Mary Pigot.

Married.

1777 Aug. 14 Richard Pigot & Mary Hicks, spinster.

Buried.

1781 Nov. 16 Mary Pigot.
1783 May 28 William Pigot s. of [*blank*] Pigot.
1843 Jan. 28 Prudence Pigot. Villa. 34.

PARISH REGISTER OF ST. GEORGE, BERMUDA.

Married.

1812 Sep. 12 Edward Moore, Town Major of this garrison and Eliza Tudor Pigot, spinster; by Lic.

ST. JOHN'S CHURCHYARD.

THIS STONE ERECTED
BY
THOMAS PIGOTT
In Memory of
HIS TWO BELOVED WIFES
AND TWO INFANT (TWIN) CHILDREN
ELIZA MARY, THE FIRST
DEPARTED THIS LIFE 8TH AUGUST 1834,
AGED 18 YEARS AND 5 MONTHS.
ELIZA MARY, THE SECOND
DEPARTED THIS LIFE 10TH JANY 1852
AGED 37 YEARS
GEORGE WILLIAM HENRY
DEPARTED THIS LIFE 30TH SEPTR 1849
AGED 7 WEEKS
ELIZA JANE ANN,
DEPARTED THIS LIFE 17TH FEB. 1850
AGED 7 MONTHS.

PARHAM OLD BURIAL-GROUND.

On a ledger:—

SACRED TO THE MEMORY
of
HENRY BLADEN PIGOT
WHO DEPARTED THIS LIFE
DECEMBER 28. 1813
AGED 6 YRS
AND
ELIZA ANN PIGOT
WHO DEPARTED
THIS LIFE
NOVEMBER 11 1818
AGED 11 MONTHS.

Pedigree of Pollington.

. . . . POLLINGTON, owned a message and 120 acres in Slaugham, co. Sussex=. . . .

Alexander Pollington of the "Three Bells" in Lombard Street, Citizen and Haberdasher; owned "Nowells" in Nuthurst, co. Surrey, and "Fig Tree," the "Body," and "Pollingtons" in Antigua. Will dated 4 Jan. 1669; proved 25 Nov. 1672. (141 Eure.)=Dorothy . . . . living 1669.

John Pollington, died before 1658 at Antigua.

Richard Pollington, died 1658 at Antigua.

William Pollington, born 15 and bapt. 28 April 1633 at St. Mary Wolnoth; entered Merchant Taylors' School Oct. 1644; died 1658 at Antigua.

Thomas Pollington, born 1 April and bapt. 11 May 1634 at St. Mary Wolnoth; entered Merchant Taylors' School Oct. 1644 (? 2nd surviving son 1669; of Queen's College, Cambridge, B.A. 1658, M.A. 1664).

Samuel Pollington, born 18 Dec. 1636 (*sic*); bapt. 10 Nov. 1636; entered Merchant Taylors' School Oct. 1644; living 28 Oct. 1662; died 1666 at Antigua.=Mary . . . .

Maurice Pollington, bapt. 21 Sep. 1638.

Alexander Pollington, bapt. 29 and bur. 30 Aug. 1662.

Edward Pollington, only surviving child 1669.

John Pollington, born 10, bapt. 17, and bur. 19 Dec. 1678.

Alexander Pollington, only son and heir, of "Nowells" in Nutthurst, bapt. 7 Dec. 1679; living *circa* 1711 (? bur. 5 Sep. 1714).=. . . .

John Pollington, inherited "Nowells" in Nuthurst in 1711, then under 8.

Mary Pollington, only surviving dau. and heir; heir to her aunt Mrs. Elizabeth Brooke; living 1732.=Daniel Betts of St. Giles in the Fields, shagreen-case maker; living 1732.

George Thompson of Antigua. Will dated 13 March 1649; proved 6 April 1649 by Alexander Pollington and Richard James. (40 Fairfax.) To my sister Eliz. Small, wife of John Small, 4000 lbs. of tobacco, & to her dau. Hester Small 2000 lbs. To my sister Frances, wife of John Waite of [*blank*], n^r Leeds, 500 lbs. To my godchild Geo., son of Robt Nanton, 1000 lbs. To my godchild Edwd, son of Wm June, 500 lbs. To Rich^d, son of Thos. Stevenson, 500 lbs. To my landlord Humfrey Knowles 500 lbs., all payable out of my plantation in Antigua. All residue equally to Mr Alex^r Pollington of London, haberdasher, & Mr Richd James of London, merch^t, whom I appoint Ex'ors. To Geo. Blanchard of Antigua 1000 lbs. Witnessed by Ralph Webster, Humfrey Knowles, George Blanchard.

Alexander Pollington, Citizen and Haberdasher of London. Will dated 4 Jan. 1669; proved 25 Nov. 1672 by Dorothie Pollington the relict. On 21 May 1706 commission to Alexander Pollington the son *re* goods left unadministered by Dorothie Pollington *alias* Grumbridge. (141 Eure.) Am possessed of a part of a plantation bought of Marke Mortemer in Monsurrat, & of 2 others in Antigua called Figgtree & the Body, all which are to be sold & the proceeds laid out in negros for my other plantation in the Leeward Division of Antigua, now or late in the possession of Master John Frye my overseer, which I bequeath after the death of my Ex'trix to my 2 sons now living, Tho. & Alex^r, & to my grandson Edwd Pollington, only child of my late son Saml, the latter to give up the poll deeds I made to his father on 28 Oct. 1662. My son Alex^r to manage all affairs, & I give him my new built house in Lombard Str. called the 3 Bells for the term of my lease, with all goods & wares therein & presses in the shopp, also my house in Threddneedle Str. & the lease, also my house & land called Nowles in Nutthurst, co. Surrey, according to the desire of my son Rich^d, dec^d, also my house & 120 acres in Slaugham, co. Sussex, which my father mortgaged to Anthony Gouldsmith for £200. All debts to be got in from Virginia, New England, Monsurrat, Barbados, Nevis, Antigua, & Ireland. All residue & my lands called Oxlepitts in Kent to my wife Dorothie & sole Ex'trix, & after her death to my 2 sons Tho. & Alex^r. Witnessed by John Clarke, Richard Colebourne, John Cox.

Richard Pollington of Eltham, co. Kent, smith. Will dated 19 Jan. 1671; proved 18 April 1672 by Anne the relict. (51 Eure.) Children Geo., Rich^d, Sarah, & Anne £30 each. Bro. Jno Pollington & his son Jno 50s. each. My adventure out at sea. Wife Anne, Ex'trix.

1691, Feb. 26. Adm'on of the estate of Sarah Pollington, late of St. Mary Wolnoth, deceased, granted to her husband Alexander Pollington.

Alexander Pollington, Citizen and Haberdasher of London. Will dated . . . . Queen Anne; proved 4 Feb. 1711 by Elizabeth Pollington the dau.; and on 10 May 1721 adm'on to John Foster, Gent., the administrator of Elizabeth Brooke *alias* Pollington, deceased, the said dau. (35 Barnes.) ½ of my personalty among my children "by the custome of the city of London," the other ½ is at my own disposal, & I give it to my dau. Eliz. Pollington, also all my lands called Nowells *al's* Knowls in Nutthurst, co. Sussex, according to deed, & then to my dau. Martha Pollington. My house in Threadneedle Str. n^r the Royal Exchange, now in the tenure of John Barton of London, cordwayner, to my dau. Eliz. To my loving friends Mr Wm Proutine & his wife Rebecca, in trust for my dau. Eliz. for life, all my plantations in the Leeward Division of Antigua, now under the management of Col. John Frye of Antigua, Esq., she paying my debts, & also to my younger dau. Martha on her day of marriage (except she marry my journeyman Mr Tho. Ruffe) £500. All my lands at Apsley Guise, co. Bedford, to my dau. Eliz. ½ of my personal estate I leave to my 3 children Eliz., Martha, & Alex^r, the other ½ to my dau. Eliz. I give Nowells *al's* Knowls in Nutthurst, now occupied by Saml Mathews, to my loving cousins Mr Wm Prouting & Rebecca his wife for my dau. Eliz., to receive the rents & make leases during the minority of John

Elizabeth . . . . bur. Feb. 1684. 1st wife. = Alexander Pollington of London, Citizen and Haberdasher, bapt. 17 March 1640; 1st surviving son and heir 1669; bur. 3 Jan. 1711. Will dated temp. Anne; proved 4 Feb. 1711. (35 Barnes.) = Sarah . . . . died 24 and bur. 27 Feb. 1689. Adm'on 26 Feb. 1691 to her husband. 2nd wife.

Aron Pollington, bapt. 26 May and bur. 29 July 1648.

Moses Pollington, died 1666 at Antigua.

Samuel Brooke the elder, inherited his son's plantation at Antigua in 1720 (? bur. 22 Sep. 1729 at St. John's). = ...

Samuel Pollington, bapt. 7 and bur. 10 Nov. 1682.

Thomas Pollington, bapt. 21 and bur. 28 April 1684.

Mary Pollington, born 15 May and bapt. 6 June 1675.

Margaret Pollington, born and bapt. 25 Feb. 1677.

Martha Pollington, living a spinster 1711; mar. before 1720 . . . . Wakeman.

Elizabeth Pollington, born and bapt. 19 Feb. 1676; only surviving sister and heir of her brother Alexander Pollington; inherited the estates in Antigua; dead 1721. = Samuel Brooke the younger of St. Mary, Newington Butts, Gent., died v.p. Will dated 11 May, proved 26 Oct. 1720. (209 Shaller.)

Pollington, infant son of my son Alex^{r} Pollington, & to pay for his education till he is 8 or 12, then he is to be taught navigation on some vessel trading to the Leeward Islands, & all other sons in like manner, & after their age of 21 the said lands to my son Alex^{r} & his 1st son & his heirs, then to my daus. Eliz. & Martha. The house in Threadneedle Str. to descend in like manner. All my plantations in Antigua to Mr Wm Prouting & Rebecca his wife for my dau. Eliz. absolutely, she paying my debts. All my lands at Apsley Guise also to her (she being my 1st child now living), & appoint her sole Ex'trix. Mr Wm Prouting, citizen & apothecary of London, & Rebecca his wife to be joint trustees, & I give them £5 each. On 4 Feb. 1711 appeared Mr. Samuel Brooke of St. Mary, Newington Butts, Gent., and Mrs. Elizabeth Haycock of ditto, and swore they knew testator who was of St. Mary, Newington. Recorded also at St. John's.

Samuel Brooke the younger of Newington Butts, Gent. Will dated 11 May 1720; proved 26 Oct. 1720 by John Forster; power reserved to Samuel Brooke the father. (209 Shaller.) To Mrs Martha Wakeman my late wife's sister £20. To my good friend Mr John Forster £50. To my honoured father Samuel Brooke the elder my plantation in Antegoa & the lands I have there in Rendezvous Bay, with the negros, Christian slaves, etc., & all other my estate. My father, Samuel Brooke, & John Forster Ex'ors. Witnessed by Thomas Skeffington, W. Hutchinson, George Worrall.

Close Roll, 6 Geo. II., Part 16, No. 16.

Indenture made the 24th Aug. 1732 between Daniel Betts of the parish of St. Giles in the Fields, shagreen-case maker, and Mary his wife (late Mary Pollington, only surviving daughter and heir of Alexander Pollington, deceased, who was only son and heir of Alexander Pollington the elder, late of the City of London, haberdasher, also deceased, and the said Mary being also niece and heir of Elizabeth Brooks, late the wife of Samuel Brooks the younger of Newington Butts, Surrey, Gent., deceased, the said Elizabeth being only sister of the said Alexander Pollington, father of the said Mary, party hereto), of the one part, and Daniel Gohard of the parish aforesaid, shagreen-case maker, of the other part, witnesseth that in consideration of £500 sterling Daniel Betts and Mary his wife grant and confirm to Daniel Gohard all that plantation in the Leeward Division of Antigua *alias* Antegoa situated in Rendezvous Bay in the said island in the parts beyond the seas, late under the management of Colonell John Frye of the said island, Esq., and all lands, etc., belonging to the said plantation, to the only use and behoof of Daniel Gohard and his heirs and assigns for ever. Elizabeth Rawlinson, Elizabeth Rawlinson, jun., Burrell Blyttie (?), William Shield, witnesses.

Lieut. John Frye purchased a large tract of land at Bermudian Valley of Mr. Alexander Pollington of London, by virtue of a deed of sale under his hand dated in London 19 Oct. 1664.

1667. Road. Mr. Alexander Pollington, 32 mens land bought of Gowin Hill; also 22½ mens land formerly John Collinson's, and by bill of sale granted by latter.

On 5 May 1685 was read: "The Humble Petition of Alexander Pollington for making out his title to lands in Antigoa.

"Sheweth,

"That your Pet^{rs} ffather being one of the most antient Planters of the Island of Antigoa in America, who did expend there at least 3000^{lbs} and lost 5 Sons—which all dyed in the said Island and being seized or possessed of a considerable Plantation with a good stock of Negroes and Cattle therein, and having a just Right to two other Plantations Known by the Name of The Body and Fig-Tree Plantation, dyed before he had settled the same: By means whereof the wrongful Possessors still unjustly detain the said Lands; and your Pet^{r} very lately understanding that there is some Act of that Country sent over to be confirmed, which will defeat your Pet^{r} of a very considerable Estate" prays his Title may be first made out. It further recites that:

"Henry Hunckes Govr of Antigua by a Com^{n} from the Earl of Carlile did by his patent da. 10 Sep. 1638 in the 4th year of that Colony grant to Rowl^{d} Tompson Esq. a parcell of land at ye Body 240 paces wide & 1½ miles long & on the following day granted a warr^{t} for its survey. 400 acres were measured out & the s^{d} Row. Tompson settled the lands & by his will da. 20 Dec. 1641 devised them to his only s. & h. Edwd Tompson & made Alex^r Pollington & John Collyton his Ex'ors & dyes there. Edwd Tompson before going out there made his Will dated 20 March 1647 & gave his estate to Alex^r Pollington his sole Ex'or. Alex^r Pollington intending to go into partnership with Edwd Tompson sent over with him his 1st son Jno Pollington who lived some years & died there. Edwd Tompson dying on his voyage to Antigoa a Kinswoman of his then residing there married Wm Warrington cousin to the then Govr & got letters of adm'on & possession of the estate & kept Alex^r Pollington out of his rights many years. Alex^r Pollington having interest in 3 plant^ns there sent out 2 sons viz.: Rich^d & W^m & about 1657 Rich^d as att^y to his father recovered the Body plant^n by Law & for damages & costs had the Fig Tree plant^n from the said Warrington. In 1658 Rich^d & W^m both dyed. In 1661 he sent over two other sons Sam^ll & Moses who both dyed there in 1666. Pet^r is s. & h. of s^d Alex^r Pollington & now petitions against the Act of 1668."

1703, Nov. 19. Alexander Pollington of London, Citizen and Haberdasher. Letter of Attorney to Colonel Rowland Williams of Antigua, Esq., but for the great age of said Williams appoints Captain John Frye, Esq., in his place.

PARISH REGISTER OF ST. MARY WOOLNOTH, CITY OF LONDON.*

Baptized.

1633 April 28 William son of Alexander Pollington, Haberdasher.

1634 May 11 Thomas son of Alexander Pollington, Haberdasher.

1636 Nov. 10 Samuell son of Alexander Pollington, Haberdasher.

1638 Sep. 21 Maurice son of Alexander Pollington, Haberdasher.

1640 Mar. 17 Alexander son of Alexander Pollington, Haberdasher.

1648 May 26 Aron son of Alexander and Dorothy Pollington, Haberdasher.

1662 Aug. 29 Alexander son of Samuell and Mary Pollington.

1675 June 6 Mary daughter of Alexander and Elizabeth Pollington; born May 15.

1676 Feb. 19 Elizabeth daughter of Alexander and Elizabeth Pollington, Haberdasher of Hatts; born Feb. 19.

1677 Feb. 25 Margaret daughter of Alexander and Elizabeth Pollington; born Feb. 25.

1678 Dec. 17 John son of Alexander Pollington, Haberdasher; born Dec. 10.

1679 Dec. 7 Alexand son of Alexander and Elizabeth Pollington.

1682 Nov. 7 Samuel son of Mr Alexander and Elizabeth Pollington, Haberdasher of Hats.

1684 April 21 Thomas son of Mr Alexander and Elizabeth Pollington.

Buried.

1648 July 29 Aron son of Alexander Pollington.

1662 Aug. 30 Allexander son of Samuell Pollington.

1678 Dec. 19 Dyed, John son of Allexander Pollington, Haberdasher of Hatts; bur. Dec. 20.

1682 Nov. 10 Dyed, Samuell son of Mr Allexander Pollington, Haberdasher of Hatts; bur. Nov. 12.

1684 April 28 Dyed, Thomas son of Mr Allexander Pollington, Haberdasher of Hatts; bur. April 30.

1684 Feb. — Ellizebeth wife of Mr Alexander Pollington.

1689 Feb. 24 Dyed, Sarah wife of Mr Alexander Pollington, Haberdasher; bur. Feb. 27.

1711 Jan. 3 Buried, Alexander Pollington, brought from Newington.

1714 Sep. 5 Buried, Alexander Pollington.

PARISH REGISTER OF ST. JOHN.

Married.

1725 April 20 Thomas Brookes and Mary Buckley. L.

1757 July 25 Baptist Looby and Sarah Brooke. L.

Buried.

1717 June 23 Willm Brooke.

1729 Sep. 22 Mr Samuel Brooke the elder.

1739 June 6 Richard Brookes.

1741 May 26 Mary Brooks, Widow.

1747 Sep. 25 Robert Brooks.

1747 Feb. 9 Robert Brooks.

* See the transcript of these Registers, by Rev. J. M. S. Brooke, Rector, and Mr. Cornelius Hallen, M.A., etc., 1886.

Family of Powell.

1663, July 23. Nicholas Roe in the West Indies, deceased. Adm'on to Marco Cottle, Gent., pending the cause between Merial Roe the relict and George Roe the brother and Maria Roe the sister.

1693, Nov. 24. By His Excellency the General. Edward Powell of Antigua died intestate. Saml Martin, Ex'or of John Ravenscourt, the greatest creditor, appeared before me to have adm'on of goods. Capt Richd Powell & his brethren were summoned before the Council, but refused. Adm'on is therefore granted to Saml Martin, he having given security in the Sec. Office to pay all just debts due. Inventory to be exhibited 20 days after date & a just account required by myself or successors.

C. CODRINGTON.

Recorded 24 Nov. T. Gatewood, Sec.

1696, Oct. 10. By Christopher Codrington. Elizabeth Powell, late of Antigua and wife of Captain Garret Powell, died intestate. Adm'on to him. Recorded 17 Dec. 1696.

1697, Aug. 31. Order to appraise goods of Garrett Powell of Antigua, deceased, George and Richard Powell his administrators, to Captain Henry Pearne, Captain John Roe, and Captain Peter Lee. Inventory recorded 24 Sep. 1697.

Christian wife of George Powell. Will dated 11 Oct. 1785. Whereas by Indenture da. 7 Jan. 1756 between me Christian (then) Knight & Geo. Powell & Saml Nibbs, late of Antigua, Esq., in order to marry with the said Geo. Powell it was agreed that Saml Nibbs should receive £800 c. to which I was entitled by the will of my father Henry Knight, dec^d, & the further sum of £200 c. given to my sister Alice Knight, dec^d, to pay the interest to Geo. Powell for life, then to me, & if I died first it w^d be lawful for me to dispose of the same after his death. I give to my dau. Frances Nibbs, wife of Nich^s Rowe, planter, the £800 & £200, & free my negro woman Rachel & her dau. Betty. Hon. Jas. Nibbs & my son-in-law Nich^s Rowe, Ex'ors. Witnessed by Mary Humphreys, William Bowie. Before Thomas Jarvis was sworn Dr. William Bowie 22 Oct. 1785.

Pedigree of Powell.

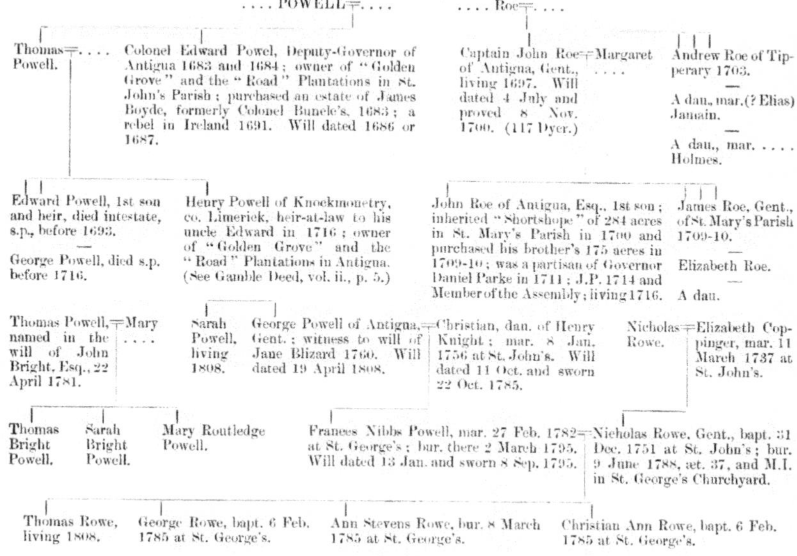
. . . . POWELL ═ . . . .
. . . . Roe ═ . . . .
Thomas ═ . . . . Powell.
Colonel Edward Powel, Deputy-Governor of Antigua 1683 and 1684; owner of "Golden Grove" and the "Road" Plantations in St. John's Parish; purchased an estate of James Boyde, formerly Colonel Bunele's, 1683; a rebel in Ireland 1691. Will dated 1686 or 1687.
Captain John Roe ═ Margaret . . . . of Antigua, Gent., living 1697. Will dated 4 July and proved 8 Nov. 1700. (117 Dyer.)
Andrew Roe of Tipperary 1703.
A dau., mar. (? Elias) Jamain.
A dau., mar. . . . . Holmes.
Edward Powell, 1st son and heir, died intestate, s.p., before 1693.
George Powell, died s.p. before 1716.
Henry Powell of Knockmonetry, co. Limerick, heir-at-law to his uncle Edward in 1716; owner of "Golden Grove" and the "Road" Plantations in Antigua. (See Gamble Deed, vol. ii., p. 5.)
John Roe of Antigua, Esq., 1st son; inherited "Shortshope" of 284 acres in St. Mary's Parish in 1700 and purchased his brother's 175 acres in 1709-10; was a partisan of Governor Daniel Parke in 1711; J.P. 1714 and Member of the Assembly; living 1716.
James Roe, Gent., of St. Mary's Parish 1709-10.
Elizabeth Roe.
A dau.
Thomas Powell, ═ Mary . . . . named in the will of John Bright, Esq., 22 April 1781.
Sarah Powell, living 1808.
George Powell of Antigua, ═ Christian, dan. of Henry Gent.; witness to will of Jane Blizard 1760. Will dated 19 April 1808.
Christian, dan. of Henry Knight; mar. 8 Jan. 1756 at St. John's. Will dated 11 Oct. and sworn 22 Oct. 1785.
Nicholas ═ Elizabeth Cop- Rowe.
Elizabeth Coppinger, mar. 11 March 1737 at St. John's.
Thomas Bright Powell.
Sarah Bright Powell.
Mary Routledge Powell.
Frances Nibbs Powell, mar. 27 Feb. 1782 ═ at St. George's; bur. there 2 March 1795. Will dated 13 Jan. and sworn 8 Sep. 1795.
Nicholas Rowe, Gent., bapt. 31 Dec. 1751 at St. John's; bur. 9 June 1788, æt. 37, and M.I. in St. George's Churchyard.
Thomas Rowe, living 1808.
George Rowe, bapt. 6 Feb. 1785 at St. George's.
Ann Stevens Rowe, bur. 8 March 1785 at St. George's.
Christian Ann Rowe, bapt. 6 Feb. 1785 at St. George's.

John Roe of Antigua, Gent. Will dated 4 July 1700. To my wife Margarett the furniture of her chamber, plate, a horse, & a negro boy and girl. To my 1st son John Roe my plantation called Shortshope of 284 acres in St. Mary's parish with the mill, stills, coppers, &c., & ½ of all my negros & cattle at 21. To my younger son James Roe my plantation in New Division of 175 acres near Five Islands Harbour with the mill, stills, & coppers, & ½ of all my my negros & cattle at 21. To each of my daus. £1000 to be paid in England at marriage, if either die the survivor to have £1500. My 2 sons Ex'ors. My friends Henry Pearne, Esq., Robt Amory, & John ffry, gent., & my loving brother Andrew Roe guardians. Witnessed by Samuel Martin, Elias Jamain, Thomas Gateward. On 8 Nov. 1700 commission to John Darby the uncle and guardian of John, James, and Elizabeth Roe, minors, the children of John Roe at Antegoa, deceased, Margaret Roe his relict being there resident. Proved 20 Aug. 1701 by Andrew Roe the brother, the adm'on being revoked. Proved 3 Sep. 1708 by John Roe the son, power reserved to James Roe the son. (117 Dyer.)

Frances Nibbs Rowe, widow of Nicholas Rowe. Will dated 13 Jan. 1795. Whereas I am entitled on the death of my father Geo. Powell to £800 & £200 settled on my late mother Christian Powell by Indenture of 7 Jan. 1756, the interest to my son Thos. Rowe till 21, then the whole sum to him, & in default to Dr John Muir of Antigua, to whom all residue, he & Hon. Tho. Norberry Kerby Ex'ors. Witnessed by Anthony Brown. Before Edward Byam was sworn Anthony Brown 8 Sep. 1795. Recorded 10 Sep. 1795.

George Powell of Antigua, Gent. Will dated 19 April 1808. To my grandson Tho. Rowe, planter, £5. To my sister Sarah Powell all residue, she & Chas. Chesser, Esq., Ex'ors. Witnessed by Samuel Pettierew, Thomas Lynch. On 25 May 1816 appeared Adam Gordon, James Hill, and John Proudfoot of Antigua.

1668. Robert Powell had a patent for 20 acres.

1672, Nov. 2. Indenture of sale. Elkina Rowe of Antigua, planter, sells 20 acres to John Atkinson and John Lurenm of Antigua, planters.

1681, Feb. 17. James Jolly sells land to William Roe.

1683, Sep. 17. Colonel Edward Powell granted a patent for 380 acres.

1684, Dec. 27. Colonel Edward Powell, Governor, granted a patent this day for 380 acres in St. John's Division, formerly called "Paul's" and now "Golden Grove."

1685, March 30. Mr. Garret Powell granted a patent for 6 acres in St. John's Town.

1689, June 17. Richard Powell, joyner, granted a patent for 70 acres.

Letter from Andrew Roe, dated at Tippery 20 [*blank*] 1703, to Messrs. Jamaine and Holmes. Dear Brothers. Mr Abrose Minchin goes to Manage the Estate of my Brother deceased & his children. A cask of tongues for my sisters. Recorded 15 June 1704.

Indenture 28 Feb. 1709-10. James Roe of St. Mary's Parish, Gent., sells to John Roe his brother 128 acres and 47½ acres, lately in the possession of Captain John Roe, Gent., deceased.

1713, May 12. Captain John Roe petitions for land, W. with Mr. James Low, N. with Baldwin Johnson, E. waste, W. with James Street.

1713, July 27. Richard Powell petitions for land in Parham Town, E. and W. 60 feet, N. and S. 80 feet, E. with Corbett Lane, N. with High Street, W. and S. waste.

1714, July 16. John Roe, Esq., petitions for £90 due.

1714, Sep. 2. John Rowe of St. John's Town, Esq., petitions for land bounded N. with Baldwin Johnson, W. with Mr. Laferty, S. with Nevis Street, E. waste.

1716, March 31. Isaac Royall of Antigua, Esq., and Elizabeth his wife sell to John Roe, Gent., a parcell of land in St. John's Town for £1000 c.

PARISH REGISTER OF ST. JOHN.

Baptized.

1727 Dec. 20 Marg^t the D. of Peter Roe and Mary his wife.
1751 Dec. 31 Nicholas the S. of Nicholas Row and Elizabeth his wife.
1808 Jan. 2 Thomas S. of Benjamin Powell and Elenor his wife. B. the 27th September last.

Married.

1732 Feb. 25 John Burn and Sarah Roe; by Banns.
1737 Mar. 11 Nicholas Roe & Elizabeth Coppinger; by L.
1738 April 22 Thomas Teague & Rachel Powell. Banns.
1756 Jan. 8 George Powell and Christian Knight.

Buried.

1700 Oct. 2 [*blank*] Powell, Widdow.
1717 Sep. 30 [*blank*] Roe, a child.
1717 Oct. 22 Rolie Roe.
1724 Oct. 7 Mrs Ann Row.
1730 Oct. 1 Mr Peter Roe.
1732 May 23 Isaac Rowe.
1747 Jan. 13 Ann Roe; in the Country.
1748 Mar. 3 Benjn Rowe.
1772 Dec. 2 John Powell.
1785 Nov. 7 Thomas Powel (Planter).

PARISH REGISTER OF ST. PHILIP.

Married.

1712 Jan. 4 Thomas Powel & Elizabeth Hamilton.

PARISH REGISTER OF ST. GEORGE.

Baptized.

1738 Feb. 24 Robert the S. of Thomas Powel.
1742 Aug. 28 Robert Powel the s. of Thos Powel and his wife.
1785 Feb. 6 Christian Ann & George D. and S. of Nicholas Rowe.

Married.

1742 Dec. 11 Isaack Hughes and Elizabeth Powel, Spr.
1767 Aug. 31 Arthur McCormick, Gentleman, & Ann Powell, Spr.
1782 Feb. 27 Nicholas Rowe, Planter, & Frances Powell, Spr.

Buried.

1750 Mar. 17 Sarah Powell, Widow.
1755 Jan. 29 Mary Roe.
1780 Jan. 18 Thomas Powel, Junr.
1782 Jan. 29 George Powel.
1785 Mar. 8 Ann Stevens D. of Nicholas Rowe.
1788 June 9 Nicholas Rowe.
1795 Mar. 2 Frances Rowe, from St John's.
1816 [*blank*] George Powell, from Town; in Fitches Church Yard.
1819 Nov. 10 Sarah Powell; in Fitch's Church Yard, aged 85 years; from St John's.

ST. GEORGE'S CHURCHYARD.

On a ledger at the west door of nave:—

NICHOLAS ROWE
e vita decessit
A.D. 1789
Æ.S. 37.
In memoria et menti et beneficii
R.K.
hic hoc posuit.

Family of Poyntz.

From 'The Vindication of Collonel Generall Points, 1648,' it appears that while in command of the seven Northern Counties, as Major-General, he was by the orders of Cromwell and Fairfax forcibly seized on 25 July 1647 at York, where he was residing with his wife and family, and removed from his post.

1651-2, Jan. 12. Surrender of Barbados by the Royalists. Article XIII. That such particular persons as are in this island, together with Sir Sydenham Pointz, who have estates in Antegoa, may peaceably return thither . . . .

"About 5 Dec. 1658, I, Henry Nicoles Survey^r then bounded out for Capt Wm Poyntz 100 acres at Soldiers Gut at the sea side on west next to Edwd Newman & John Cash, drawn from my old field book, 1 Mar. 1677—80."

1679, April 30. Cassava Garden of 1000 acres bounded West with Sir Sydenham Poines.

1680, July 7. Samuel Hilder and Mary his wife and Henry Steenman and Abigail his wife *re* a plantation of 300 acres formerly belonging to Captain Robert Poyntz, deceased, who left the same to his said two daughters Mary and Abigail his coheirs. Estate to be equally divided. By the Hon. Valentine Russell, Governor, Lieut. Samuel Hilder and Mr. Henry Steenman, in right of their wives Mary and Abigail, have obtained judgment against Jonas Langford for a plantation called Soldiers Gutt of 100 acres. Warrant for possession. Witnessed by Robert Hamilton.

In 1681 James 4th Duke of Courland entered into a contract with Captain Poyntz, granting 12,000 acres of the Island of Tobago to him and company, upon very advantageous terms. ('Gent. Mag.,' 1781, p. 416.)

Capt. John Poyntz (of the Iron-Acton family) wrote and published: "The present Prospect of the famous and fertile Island of Tobago, etc., with Proposals for the Encouragement of all those that are minded to settle there." Lond., 1683, in 7 sh. in qu. (Wood's 'Athenæ Oxonienses,' vol. iii., p. 715.)

1730, Jan. 13. Samuel Malcher Esq; an eminent Portugal Merchant of London, marry'd to Mrs. Jane Poyntz, only Daughter of William Poyntz, Esq; Brother of Stephen Poyntz, Esq; his Majesty's third Plenipotentiary at the Congress of Soissons. ('Historical Register,' p. 8.)

1731, May 21. Stephen Poyntz, Esq; made Governor to his R. Highness the Duke. ('Gent. Mag.,' p. 222.)

1733, Feb. Stephen Poyntz, Esq; to Mrs. Anna-Maria Mordaunt, and receiv'd £3000 as of Royal Bounty, she having been Maid of Honour to her Majesty. (*Ibid.*, p. 100.)

1735, Jan. William Poyntz, Esq; Brother to Stephen Poyntz, Esq; to the Relict of Sir Thomas Frederick, Bart. ('Historical Register,' p. 8.)

1735, June. The Lady of Stephen Poyntz, Esq; Preceptor to the Duke of Cumberland, deliver'd of a Son and Heir. (*Ibid.*, p. 27.)

To Mr Rich, the second English Governor of St Christopher's, succeeded Mr Everard, who continued in the Government, several Years; and by what we can understand, was in that Office when the Rump usurped the supreme Power in England. The Leeward-Islands refusing to acknowledge their Sovereignty, King Charles the IId. appointed Major General Poyntz to be Governor, and he was in Possession of St Christopher's when Sir George Ayscue arrived at Barbados and reduced that Island. After which he sailed to Nevis and St Christopher's; but Major General Poyntz not being strong enough to defend himself against the Power Sir George brought with him, withdrew before his Arrival, and ship'd himself for Virginia, the only Retreat for Cavaliers. (Oldmixon's 'British Empire in America, 1741.')

1748, Oct. 15. William Poyntz, Esq; treasurer to the excise and brother to the Hon. Stephen Poyntz, Esq; ('London Mag.')

1748, Nov. 1. Jacob Ricketts of Jamaica, Esq; marry'd to Miss Hannah Poyntz, niece to Stephen Poyntz, Esq; ('Gent. Mag.,' p. 524.)

1749, June 27. Capt. Robert Poyntz, nephew to Stephen Poyntz, Esq; (*Ibid.*, p. 284.)

1750, Jan. 9. Dean Poyntz, Esq; Capt. of a company in Guise's reg. of foot and nephew to the Hon. Stephen Poyntz, Esq. ('London Mag.')

1750, Dec. 17. Rt. Hon. Stephen Poyntz, Esq; one of his Majesty's most Hon. privy-council, formerly preceptor to his royal highness the duke of Cumberland, and at the time of his death steward of his household etc. (*Ibid.*)

1756, Dec. 26. Hon. John Spencer, Esq; to Miss Poyntz. ('Gent. Mag.,' p. 42.)

PARISH REGISTER OF ST. JOHN.

Married.

1716 June 7 James Gamble and Rachell Hilder. L. (See their marriage settlement under "Gamble.")

Buried.

1701 Feb. 6 Mrs Mary Hilder.

ST. MICHAEL'S, CORNHILL, LONDON.

Baptized.

1661 Sep. 19 Francis s. of Francis Poynes & Katherine his wife; born 4 Sep.

1663 April 26 Katherine d. of Francis Pointz & Katherine his wife.

1664 May 1 Sarah Pointz d. of Francis Pointz & Katherine his wife.

1674 April 5 Mary d. of William Poynes & Mary his wife.

1676 April 9 Martha d. of William Poyntzs & Mary his wife.

1678 Mar. 31 John s. of William Poynes & Mary his wife.

1684 Mar. 26 Jane Poyntz d. of William Poyntz & Jane his wife.

1685 Nov. — Stephen Poyntz s. of William Poyntz & Jane his wife.

1687 April 17 Deane Poyntz s. of Wm Poyntz & Jane his wife.

1689 Nov. 3 John Poyntz s. of Wm Poyntz & Jane his wife.

1691 June 7 Joseph Poyntz s. of Wm Poyntz & Jane his wife.

Buried.

1674 Oct. 25 Henry s. of Henry Poynes & Mary his wife; in the upper new vault in S. isle.

1679 Jan. 3 Mary Poyntz wife of William Poyntz; in the upper vault of S. isle.

1679 Jan. 19 John Poyntz s. of William Poyntz and Mary his late wife; in the upper vault of S. isle.

KINGSTON, JAMAICA.

On a white marble slab in the churchyard:—

Arms: *Barry of eight, on the third bar a crescent.*
Crest: *Over an esquire's helmet a dexter hand closed.*

.... LYES THE BODY OF | JOSEPH POYNTZ | OF KINGSTON IN YE ISLAND | OF JAMAICA | MERCHANT | WHO DEPARTED THIS LIFE ON | .... 24 OF SEPTEMBER 1728 | AGED 37 YEARS.

(Lawrence Archer's 'M.I. of the West Indies,' p. 128.)

Pedigree of Poyntz.

ARMS.—*Barry of eight or and gules.*
CREST.—*A dexter hand closed.*

SIR ROBERT POYNTZ, twelfth in descent from Hugh Poyntz; died 1519; bur. in the Gaunts' Chapel, Bristol. Will dated 19 Oct. 1520. (28 Ayloffe.) ═ Margaret, natural dau. of Anthony Woodville, Earl Rivers; dead 1520.

Sir Anthony Poyntz, 1st son and heir, died 1534.

John Poyntz, 2nd son, died 1544. ═ Margaret, dau. of Nicholas Saunder of Charlewood, co. Surrey, Esq. 2nd wife.

William Poyntz of Reigate, co. Surrey. ═ Elizabeth, dau. and coheir of Thomas Newdigate of Newdigate, co. Surrey. Will dated 15 May 1600; proved 16 Aug. 1602. (58 Montague.)

A

A

John Poyntz of Reigate, co. Surrey; Ex'or to his mother 1600. = Anne, dau. of .... Sydenham of Nympsfield, co. Gloucester.

Sarah, dau. of N. Foxley of Harringworth, co. Hants. 1st wife. = Newdigate Poyntz of Reigate, co. Surrey, Gent.; died 1643. Will dated 26 March 1639, then of Benefield, co. Northants; proved 27 Feb. 1644-5. (34 Rivers.) = Mary, dau. of Aden Parkyns of co. Notts, Esq. 2nd wife.

Mary .... bur. 3 Jan. 1679. 1st wife. = William Poyntz of the Goat in St. Michael's, Cornhill, Citizen and Upholder; traded with the Leeward Islands; living 1684. = Jane, dau. of Stephen Monteage of London, merchant; his will proved 1687. (140 Foot.) 2nd wife.

Newdigate Poyntz.

John Poyntz.

Charles Poyntz.

Francis Poyntz of St. Michael's, Cornhill, Citizen and Upholder. Will dated 8 Sep. 1684 and proved 18 Feb. 1684-5. (26 Cann.) = Catherine ....

Mary Poyntz, bapt. 5 April 1674.

Martha Poyntz, bapt. 9 April 1676.

John Poyntz, bapt. 31 March 1678; bur. 19 Jan. 1679.

William Poyntz of St. James, Westminster, Esq., a minor 1685; Receiver-General of the Excise 1736; died, s.p.m., Oct. 1748. Will dated 7 April 1747; proved 19 Oct. 1748. (307 Strahan.) = Mary Moncreif, dau. of John Aston and relict of Sir Thomas Frederick, Bart. Her father's will proved 1715. (63 Fagg.)

Right Hon. Stephen Poyntz of Midgham, co. Berks, Governor to the Duke of Cumberland; Ambassador to Sweden; Privy Councillor 1735; died 17 Dec. 1750. Will dated 16 Dec. 1738; proved 4 Jan. 1750. (18 Busby.) = Anna Maria, dau. to Henry Lewis Mordaunt, grandson to John Earl of Peterborough; mar. Feb. 1733.

William Poyntz of Midgham, bapt. at St. Margaret's, Westminster; matriculated from Christ Church, Oxon, 17 Jan. 1752, æt. 17; B.A. 1756; bur. 20 May 1809. = ...

Charles Poyntz, born June 1735; matriculated from Christ Church, Oxon, 13 Dec. 1752, æt. 17; B.A. 1756; M.A. 1759; D.D. 1769; Rector of North Creak, co. Norfolk, 1760.

Margaret Georgina Poyntz, mar., 27 Dec. 1755, John, Earl Spencer; he was born 18 Sep. 1734, and died 1783.

William Stephen Poyntz of Midgham and Cowdray, M.P.; matriculated from Christ Church, Oxon, 29 June 1787, æt. 17; died 8 April 1840.

Pedigree of Prynn.

James Hurd of Plymouth, co. Devon, merchant, and formerly of St. John's, Antigua. Will dated 15 Jan. 1696; proved P.C.C. = Mary .... living 1696.

Jane Hurd, died v.p. 1st wife. = JOHN PRYNN of Antigua, merchant. Will dated 13 Oct. 1714; sworn 25 April 1715. = Mary .... living 1714. 2nd wife.

John Prynn, appears to have removed to Stratford, Fairfield County, Connecticut; living 1745. = Mary .... living 1743.

Francis Prynn of Antigua. = Elinor ....

William Prynn, apparently 1st son and heir 1714.

Malham Prynn, a minor 1714.

Mary Prynn, in 1714 wife of .... Bezoon.

Sarah Prynn, in 1714 wife of .... Richard.

Ann Prynn, in 1714 wife of .... Brewster.

Henrietta Prynn, a minor 1714; mar. 20 Dec. 1729, at St. Paul's, John Francis.

John Malham Prynn. Francis Prynn. William Prynn, a minor 1745. Mary Prynn.

James Hurd of Plymouth, co. Devon, merchant. Will dated 15 Jan. 1696. Aged. To my wife Mary Hurd all my houses in St. John's, & after her death to my son-in-law Caleb Tyley & his heirs. To the 3 children of my late dau. Jane Prynn, viz. Mary Prynn, Sarah Prynn, & Ann Prynn, a guinea each, & to their father Jn° Prynn 1s. All residue to my wife Mary, she to be Ex'trix; after her death all res. to my son-in-law Caleb Tyley & wife Mary. Witnessed by Jonah Lavington, Thomas Edgcumbe, Joseph (? Hosper), William Pattey. Copy sent from P.C.C.

Sir Sydenham Poyntz,* Knt., Major-General for the Parliament; Deputy-Governor of St. Christopher's; retired to Virginia 1663; died before 1667, leaving Colonel Charles Ghest of Antigua his Ex'or. ⊤ Elizabeth .... living 1647.

Captain Robert Poyntz of Antigua; owned 300 acres; dead 1667. ⊤ Abigail .... mar. 2ndly .... Belcher.

Captain William Poyntz of Antigua; owned 100 acres in 1658.

Lieut. Samuel Hilder, living 1680. 1st husband. ⊤ Mary Poyntz, dau. and coheir; living 1716 and 1719. ⊤ .... Thornton, bur. 19 May 1705 at St. John's. 2nd husband. ⊤ Edward Mann, Gent., mar. 18 Nov. 1710 at St. John's; living 1716 and 1719. 3rd husband.

Abigail Poyntz, dau. and coheir; in 1680 wife of Henry Steenman.

Deane Poyntz of Jamaica, bapt. 17 April 1687. ⊤ ....

John Poyntz, bapt. 3 Nov. 1689.

Joseph Poyntz of Jamaica, merchant, bapt. 7 June 1691; died 24 Sep. 1728, æt. 37. M.I. at Kingston, Jamaica. ⊤ Hannah .... living 1747.

Rachel Hilder, mar. 7 June 1716, at St. John's, James Gamble of Antigua, Gent.

Deane Poyntz, Captain in Guise's Regiment of Foot. Will dated 21 Feb. 1746; proved 16 Feb. 1749. (55 Greenley.) ⊤ .... dau. of Mrs. Florence Blechynden.

Robert Poyntz of Padworth, co. Berks; heir to his brother Deane. (? Captain in Army, and died 27 June 1749.)

Molly Poyntz, mar. Dec. 1747, George Hinde.

Hannah Poyntz, dau. and coheir; mar. 1748. ⊤ Jacob Ricketts of Midgham, Jamaica. (See Burke's 'Landed Gentry.')

William Deane Poyntz, matriculated from University College, Oxon, 4 June 1767, æt. 18; created M.A. 9 July 1773.

George Poyntz Ricketts, born 1750; mar. 13 Dec. 1772; Governor of Barbados 1794; died 8 April 1800 at Liverpool.

* For an account and portrait of him see 'A Survey of England's Champions,' 1647. He defeated Sir Marmaduke Langdale at Rowton Heath, near Chester.

John Prynn of Antigua, merchant. Will dated 13 Oct. 1714. To my dau. Mary Bezoon 1s. for her rebellious & undutiful conduct. To my dau. Sarah Richard £5 c., & 20s. to each of her children. To my dau. Ann Bruster £5 c., & 20s. to her son. All these 3 daus. married contrary to my consent & knowledge. To my dau. Garthrud Prynn, my s. Jn° Prynn, my dau. Henrietta Prynn, & my sons Francis Prynn & Malham Prynn £150 c. each at 21. To my wife Mary my house at Willoughby Bay Town, a horse, a negro, a cow, £100 c., & my furniture. All residue to my son Wm Prynn. M^r Jn° Richards & Mr Hen. Symes & my Wife Ex'ors. Witnessed by Sygismond Cooper, Ambrose Marchant, John Colborn. By John Yeamans, Esq., was sworn Sigismond Cooper 25 April 1715.

John Bezune, Gent., planter. Will dated 20 April 1720. To my wife Eleanor the use of all my estate for her & my children equally, & after her death or marriage to my 5 sons equally, viz. Tho., W^m, Edwd, Anthony, & Joseph. To my dau. Eliz. £400 c. To my sons Edwd, Joseph, & my grandchildren Nich^s, John, & Elsina Bezune certain negros. All residue to my wife, Saml Martin, Esq., John Greenway, & John Bradston, planters, as Ex'ors in Trust. Witnessed by Thomas Hanson, Robert Delameer, Robert Hughes. Before Walter Hamilton, Esq., was sworn Thomas Hanson 5 April 1721.

Roger Beffin. Will dated 3 Aug. 1743. .... Mrs Mary Pryn, wife of Mr John .... all residue to Marg^t Marchant .... Benj. Marchant .... Saml .... Stratford, co. Fairfield, Connecticut, New England, Ex'or. Wm Furnell of Antigua, merch^t, Ex'or. Signed, ROGER BEFFIN.

Recorded in Probate Court, Fairfield, Connecticut. Copy signed by John Burr, Judge of the Court of Probate, Stern district of Fairfield county, at Fairfield 17 April 1744. Per Ephraim Curtiss, J.P. for the said county. Mr. John Prynn and Mary his wife, of lawful age, swore that Mr. Roger Beffin of Antigua, a resident at their house at Stratford in Fairfield county, departed this life 28 Oct. 1743.

Francis Prynn, planter. Will dated 8 Jan. 1745. To my son Francis £400. To my son W^m & my dau. Mary £400 each at 21. To the child my wife now goes with £400. To my bro. John Prynn £100. To my godson Francis Malun Francis £25. To my wife Elinor £100. All residue to my son John Malum, & in default to my son Francis, then to my dau. Wm Skerrit, Jas. Michelson, & Saml Lyons Ex'ors. Witnessed by Henrietta Francis, George Heuitt, Thomas Morris.

1699, Dec. 2. John Bezune, an alien, took the oaths. He was born at sea, his father was Welch and his mother Dutch. Recorded at St. John's.

1706. Mr. John Bezune, sen., taxed on 22 negros and 70 acres. Mr. John Bezune, jun., taxed on 12 negros and 33 acres. (St. Mary's Vestry Book.)

PARISH REGISTER OF ST. PAUL.

Married.

1727 Dec. 20 John Francis, Gent., & Henrietta Pryn, Spr.

Family of Pyle.

William Pyle, sen., merchant. Will dated 2 Aug. 1791. Within 2 years of my decease £21,500 c. shall be placed in the Bank of Philadelphia, & the interest of £5000 is to be p[d] annually to Ralph Pyle of Baltimore for life, & after his death to be drawn out & given to his children. Interest of £5000 annually to Joseph Pyle of Chester in Pennsilvania, & after his death to be given to his children. The Interest of £5000 to Mary, wife of Peter Hendrick, sen[r], of Newcastle in Delaware, & after his death to his children. The Interest of £5000 to Sarah, wife of . . . . Geniston of Newcastle in Delaware. The interest of £1000 to Eliz[th], wife of John Porter. £500 to Susannah, dr. of Mary, wife of . . . . Frame of Chester in Pennsilvania, but if she die under 21 then to W[m], s. of Rob. Robertson of Newcastle, & to Ralph Pyle, son of John Pyle of same place. To Ralph Pyle & W[m] Robertson £1500 c. each. Certain slaves to be free. All residue to W[m] Pyle the younger. Jos. Pyle, W[m] Pyle, jun[r], Jn[o] Morton, merch[ts] in Philadelphia, & Jn[o] Taylor Ex'ors. Witnessed by Ste. Rose, James Bird, John Brooke. Before his Excellency William Woodley, Esq., was sworn James Bird, writing clerk, 29 Feb. 1792. Recorded 1 March 1792.

William Pyle, jun. Will dated 16 March 1792. To my wife Eliz[th] £2000 st. To my mulatto Will. £200 & his freedom. ½ of residue to my wife & ½ to my son W[m] Pyle at 21. To any future child £2000 at 21, & in default of any surviving issue to my wife £5000 st., & all residue to my bro. Ralph Pyle, now of Newcastle, Delaware. Jn[o] Taylor, Jn[o] Smith, Ph. Hicks, & my wife Ex'ors. Witnessed by Edward Gamble, H. Greenway, James Bird. Before Edward Byam, President of H.M. Council, was sworn James Bird, clerk, 27 April 1792.

1807, Nov. 12. At Antigua, Alexander Coates, esq; a gentleman who did as much good to that Island as any one had done for a century. Many individuals might have had their estates out of the possession of their families, had he not stept forward and paid the mortgages, and allowed them the privilege of sending the produce of their Sugar Plantations where they pleased. The illiberal mind cannot say a word against such a character, as M[r] Coates might have placed his money in the British Funds, which would have been of much greater advantage, particularly in the time of War. Money lent as his was worth twelve per cent.; but he had the lawful interest of the Country; and their consigning their crop to whom they chose was an incalculable advantage, and what is unusual on such loans. But the time when M[r] Coates shewed himself was in the year 1805, when the Legislature, sanctioned by the late Lord Lavington, Captain-general of the Leeward Islands, etc. allowed the Treasurer a vote of credit for £5000. M[r] Coates was applied to; but he did not at that moment think proper to lend it, that it might not be insinuated that he lent it, not by the way of doing good for the Government, but through fear of the Combined Fleets and Armies of France and Spain, who at that time threatened the Island with destruction, and which were making the greatest preparation at Martinique to attack Antigua. Those Combined Fleets and Armies sailed close to Antigua, June 7, 1805; but his Majesty's Troops, the Officers and Seamen of the Royal Navy, who were at that time on the Island, united by the unanimous wish of the Inhabitants, which was much to their honour, turned out, at 2 in the morning, to oppose the Enemy's landing, but they proceeded on Northward. On the 12th of the same month, the late Admiral Lord Viscount Nelson appeared off Antigua, with his gallant ten sail of the line, in pursuit of the 22 sail of the line of French and Spanish ships, besides frigates, etc. However, during the stay in the West Indies of so great a Naval Force of the Enemy, and of Troops to the number of 13,000, the Government of Antigua was under the necessity of incurring considerable expences, by a military encampment of all ranks of the Inhabitants, which lasted 40 days, when the Enemy made their appearance; which, when they did, their timidity was such that they passed by without an attempt to invade. The encampment broke up; M[r] Coates then came forward; nor was it the first time that he had assisted the Government. He, now, under the sanction of the late Lord Lavington and the Legislature, lent £10,000, which was double the sum at first requested, and at a time when all danger had blown over. This may be much better seen and known by inspecting the Public Records of Antigua. His Majesty never had a more loyal subject than M[r] Coates; and in this particular he set a most laudable example to his family. Until he was infirm with the gout, he was a tall, portly, and elegant person; his face was most manly, and very commanding. He was born April 16 (o.s.) 1734; and the Almighty, whom alone he feared, was pleased to take him from this life, after having sustained an untarnished reputation for 73 years. The great wealth of which he died possessed, except a few legacies, which were immediately paid, he nobly and equally bequeathed to his family. His funeral was numerously and respectably attended. ('Gent. Mag.,' p. 1188.)

1810, June. Lately. At Towcester, R. Coates, esq. of the island of Antigua; a son of the gentleman whose death is noticed in our vol. 68, p. 1188. (*Ibid.*, p. 677.)

Parish Register of St. John.

Baptized.

1792 June 11 William Egan S. of William Pyle, Jun[r], dec'ed, and Elizabeth his wife. B. 9th March 1791.

Married.

1792 Dec. 1 John Coates to Elizabeth Pyle, Widow; by Lic.

Buried.

1789 April 12 Robert Pyle, Inf.
1792 July 12 William Egan Pyle (Infant).

St. John's Churchyard.

On a headstone:—

In Memory
of Robert Egan Pyle
Born 16th *November* 1788
Died *April* 12th 1790
Also of William Egan Pyle
Born 9 *of March* 1791
Died 14th *of July* 1792
Son of William & Eliz[th] Pyle
of this Island.

Family of Redhead.

Samuel Redhead of Antigua, now residing in London, Esq. Will dated 21 June 1784; proved 6 April 1785 by Marmaduke Trattle, Esq., and Charles Comyns; power reserved to Thomas Jarvis, jun., John Lindsay, John Blair, and Thomas Fraser. (307 Ducarel.) All my household furniture to Sarah Bullock who resides with me. All my tenement in Long Street, St. John's, Antigua, now in the occupation of Mr John Lindsay, to Joseph Redhead and Henry Redhead my natural or reputed sons by Sarah Bullock at 21. To Sarah Sheffield, dau. of a mulatta lately dead, Fanny Sheffield, the use of a room in the same house on my plantation for life. My mulatta Mary Crawford to Sarah Sheffield for life, then to Jane Comyns, dau. of Sarah Bullock. All residue of my personal estate to Tho. Jarvis, jun^r, of Antigua, Esq., John Lindsay of Long Street, St. John's, John Blair of Antigua, Gent., Marmaduke Trattle & Tho. Fraser, both of London, merch^ts, & Chas. Comyns of London, hatter, on Trust to pay debts and legacies. To Eliz. Anderson, dau. of Mr Wm Anderson of Antigua by Ann his late wife, £200 c. at 15, but if she die to her sister Mary. To Grace Redhead & Mary Payne, 2 daus. of my late son Nathl Redhead, £400 c. apiece. To Sarah Bullock £1000 & £50 at once. To Sarah Ann Redhead, another dau. of Sarah Bullock, £1000 at 21. To Joseph & Henry Redhead £1000 apiece. To Jane Comyns £12. To John Lindsay £100 c. To Marmaduke Trattle & Chas. Comyns 10 gs. each. To Tho. Jarvis 10 gs. To John Blair £20 c. All my plantations & negros to my trustees to pay the following annuities, viz.:—£20 c. yearly to my grandson Wm Redhead, son of my late son Nathl Redhead, till 21. £20 c. a year to Sarah Sheffield. £15 c. a year to Jane Comyns, dau. of Sarah Bullock, & after her death to her son Saml till 16. £400 c. a year to my son George Redhead & all my estates for life, then to his son Saml & his heirs male, then to his 2^d son George, then to my grandson Wm Redhead. My son Geo. may charge the estate with £500 for his younger children & £120 c. a year for his wife Marg^t. All produce to be consigned to Marmaduke Trattle. Trustees to be Guardians & Ex'ors. Witnessed by Alexander Williams of Antigua, John Moore Plunkett of Broad Street, London, Thomas Dunn of Bloomsbury Square.

Codicil dated 28 Dec. 1784. To Mrs Sarah Bullock my negro Hester, now in the possession of Mary, dau. of Eliz. Davy of St John's, also my mulatto W^m, then to Sarah Ann Redhead my natural dau., also £50. To each of my said 3 natural children £500. £1000 c. to my dau. Ann Athill, widow of Dr James Athill, late of Antigua, deceased. £100 to my grandson Saml Comyns, son of Mrs Jane Comyns, at 21. Witnessed by William Norris, Old Jewry, John Moore Plunkett, Broad Street, London Wall, William Biddle, Henrietta Street, Covent Garden. Recorded also at St. John's 6 June 1785.

Margaret Redhead, wife of George Redhead. Will dated 1 April 1786. To my son Saml Redhead, my dau. Anne Redhead, my son Geo. Redhead, my dau. Mary, to Eliz^th Redhead, my son Byam Crump Redhead, my son Cusack Munton Redhead, & my dau. Alicia Elliot Redhead certain negros. All my estate real & personal to my children Ann, Geo., Mary, Eliz., Byam Crump, Cusack Munton, & Alicia Elliot Redhead equally. Witnessed by William Baxter, John Gloster. Recorded 3 April 1794.

Close Roll, 28 Geo. III., Part 8.

Indenture made the 17th Nov. 1788 between George Redhead, late of Antigua, but now of Newman Street, Oxford Street, Esq., and Margaret his wife, of the one part, and James Trecothick, Francis Thwaites, and Charles Apthorpe Wheelwright of Bucklersbury, merchants, of the other part. Whereas George Redhead now stands justly indebted unto James Trecothick, Francis Thwaites, and Charles Apthorpe Wheelwright in the sum of £5500 sterling for money lent and paid for his use, and they have considerable transactions with him in the West India trade, and a current account is kept open between them; and whereas in the course of future transactions it may happen that George Redhead may have occasion for further sums, and on the balance of accounts may become further indebted, for securing the said £5500, and such further sums, with interest, George Redhead has agreed that he and his wife shall convey to the others by way of mortgage the several hereditaments hereafter described, *i.e.* a certain estate called Cusacks, and now known by the name of George Redhead's, in the parish of St. Philip in the division of Nonsuch or Willoughby Bay, of which George Redhead is seised in fee, together with the dwelling-house and all the slaves, cattle, sheep, and other stock thereon, and also all slaves belonging to a plantation called Fryes in the parish of St. Philip and division of Willoughby Bay which George Redhead or Margaret his wife now are or at any time hereafter may be seised of, and also the crops of sugar and other produce (rum only excepted), both from Cusacks and Fryes, and has agreed also to assign to them all his personal estate in Antigua and Great Britain, as hereinafter mentioned. Now this Indenture witnesseth that in pursuance of the agreement, and in consideration of the £5500 now justly due, and for securing the repayment, and for conveying and assigning the plantation, etc., and for barring and conveying the estate, right, interest, dower and thirds of Margaret Redhead, and in consideration of 10s., George Redhead and Margaret his wife convey to James Trecothick, Francis Thwaites, and Charles Apthorpe Wheelwright all that plantation called Cusacks, but now George Redhead's, containing 320 acres, together with the dwelling-house and all the live and dead stock, and 87 slaves, now on the plantation called Fryes, and all crops of sugar and produce (rum only excepted), and also all personal estate in Antigua and Great Britain, to the only use of James Trecothick, Francis Thwaites, and Charles Apthorpe Wheelwright for ever, subject nevertheless to the proviso that if George Redhead do pay the said £5500, and all further sums, and all interest at 5 per cent., on the 17th May 1789, this Indenture shall be absolutely null and void; and lastly George Redhead and Margaret his wife nominate William Dickinson and Edward Rigge, Esquires, both of Antigua, their Attorneys. Philip Wyatt Crowther, Edward Peale, Guildhall, witnesses.

Pedigree of Redhead.

JOSEPH REDHEAD of Antigua, carpenter; living 1722; dead 1725. (See the will of William Glanville, dated 1724.) = (? Mary, dau. of Thomas Gilliat, living 1714.)

Samuel Redhead of Antigua; in 1763 purchased "Fryes" of 420 acres for £20,000; died 15 March 1785, æt. 81, in Bennet Street, Blackfriars. Will dated 21 June 1784; proved 6 April 1785. (307 Ducarel.) = Anne, dau. of George Crump, senior, Esq.; bur. 16 Jan. 1742 at St. John's.

William Redhead, Surgeon; is stated to have removed to America. = Frances Watson, mar. 16 Feb. 1735 and bur. 25 Dec. 1772 at St. Philip's.

Nathaniel Redhead, 1st son; died v.p., bur. 26 Jan. 1778 at St. John's. = Elizabeth . . . .

George Redhead of "Fryes" and "Cusacks" in Antigua, 2nd son, bapt. 11 Nov. 1737 at St. Paul's; died 5 Dec. 1801, æt. 64, in Upper Berkeley Street. = Margaret, dau. and coheir of Dr. Patrick Cusack of Antigua; died 5 and bur. 6 Oct. 1793 at St. John's. Will dated 1 April 1786 and recorded 3 April 1794.

Samuel Redhead, bapt. 8 Sep. 1770 and bur. 26 Aug. 1776 at St. John's.

William Redhead, bapt. 20 Dec. 1772 at St. John's; a minor 1784.

Elizabeth Redhead, bapt. 8 Oct. 1758 at St. John's.

Grace Redhead, bapt. 11 July 1759, and mar. 26 April 1784, at St. John's, Richard T. Shervington.

Anne Redhead, bapt. 11 July 1759, and mar. 5 April 1777, at St. John's, William Anderson.

Mary Redhead, bapt. 23 July 1760, and mar. 21 Jan. 1779, at St. John's, Thomas Payne.

Elizabeth Redhead, bapt. 24 and bur. 25 Feb. 1763 at St. John's.

Samuel Redhead, 1st son, bapt. 7 March 1768 at St. Philip's; lost at sea *circa* 1795–97.

Close Roll, 35 Geo. III., Part 5, No. 7.

Indenture made the 30th July 1795 between Samuel Redhead of Antigua, and of Vere Street, Middlesex, Esq. (eldest son and heir-apparent of George Redhead of Antigua, Esq.), of the 1st part, George Redhead aforesaid of Antigua, but now of Bath, Esq., of the 2nd part, Anthony Munton of London, Esq., Samuel Athill, Esq., and the Hon. Rowland Burton, both of Antigua, and Francis Thwaites and Charles Apthorpe Wheelwright, both of Bucklersbury, merchants, as trustees, of the 3rd part, and the said Francis Thwaites and Charles Apthorpe Wheelwright (as creditors of George and Samuel Redhead), of the 4th part. Whereas the plantation called Fryes in the parish of St. Philip and division of Willoughby Bay in Antigua stands settled and limited to George Redhead for life, and after his decease to his son Samuel Redhead for life, and to his son, successively in tail male, with several remainders over; and whereas by Indentures made the 16th and 17th Nov. 1788 between the said George Redhead and Margaret his wife, since deceased, of the one part, and James Trecothick, Esq., and the said Francis Thwaites and Charles Apthorpe Wheelwright, of the other part, in consideration of £5500 then due from George Redhead to Francis Thwaites and Charles Apthorpe Wheelwright, George Redhead and Margaret his wife granted to James Trecothick and to them a plantation called Cusacks, of which George Redhead was then seised in fee simple, with the live and dead stock thereon, and also 87 Negro and Mulatto slaves belonging to George Redhead and Margaret, or one of them, which were then on the plantation called Fryes, and did grant to them also the crops of sugars, etc., except as therein excepted, with provision of redemption on payment of the £5500 and all other sums; and whereas soon after the execution of the Indentures the plantation, etc., became vested in Francis Thwaites and Charles Apthorpe Wheelwright alone, absolutely discharged from the estate of James Trecothick; and whereas George Redhead did some time since request and direct Francis Thwaites and Charles Apthorpe Wheelwright to allow to Samuel Redhead £300 a year from the consignments of sugar, etc., to discharge certain debts contracted by Samuel Redhead in England, and they did so, although under the Indentures they were entitled to retain the whole amount of the produce towards the diminution of the debt due to themselves; and whereas in January 1791 they lent to Samuel Redhead upon his own account £1198 18*s*. 8*d*., and some time after George Redhead, at the request of his son, directed them to charge the same to his account; and whereas they have paid other debts on account of Samuel Redhead, and at his like request to his father they are charged to his account, and the sum amounted on the 30th April last to £4369 as Samuel Redhead acknowledges; and whereas on an account between them and George Redhead on the said date George Redhead is indebted to them in the sum of £8731 11*s*. 1*d*., including the £4369, and they have agreed to pay for him several other sums amounting (inclusive of £2000 and upwards, for which they ? have provisionally given bills of exchange) to £4000 and upwards; and whereas they did a short time since resolve to proceed against George Redhead and the mortgaged premises; and whereas Samuel Redhead has contracted divers other debts in England amounting to £2000 and upwards, and his creditors have consented to discharge him on receiving bills of exchange, to be drawn by Samuel Redhead and accepted by George Redhead, payable at three years after date, with interest at 5 per cent., and meantime the payment to be guaranteed by Francis Thwaites and Charles Apthorpe Wheelwright if Antigua continue under the Government of Great Britain; and whereas George Redhead at the request of Samuel Redhead, and in consideration of the counter security and indemnity hereinafter given by him in respect of the money, George Redhead has engaged to pay, did agree to accept the bills, and to allow Samuel Redhead £120 a year for his support and maintenance during their joint lives, and also to concur with him in the arrangement for settling his affairs hereinafter mentioned to have been proposed to Francis Thwaites and Charles Apthorpe Wheelwright; and whereas to induce Francis Thwaites and Charles Apthorpe Wheelwright to desist from putting into force their remedies for recovering the moneys due to them and to guarantee the bills of exchange, and to secure a provision both for Samuel Redhead during the joint lives of himself and his father, and for George Redhead during his life, Samuel Redhead and George Redhead did lately propose to Francis Thwaites and Charles Apthorpe Wheelwright that if they would provisionally guarantee the bills of exchange, and from the consignments of sugar, subject to the interest of the money due to them,

Elizabeth Redhead, mar. 28 May 1726, at St. John's, William Garrett.

Sarah Redhead, mar. 17 March 1725, at St. John's, Robert Jacobs.

Grace Redhead, mar. 17 Sep. 1726, at St. John's, Edward Monteague; both living 1764.

Samuel Redhead, bapt. 23 Dec. 1739 at St. Paul's.

Anne Redhead, only surviving dau., born 22 March 1737; mar. 1 Aug. 1757 Dr. James Athill.

Mary Redhead, bapt. 31 Jan. 1741 at St. Paul's; died young.

George Redhead, bapt. 1771 at St. Peter's, 1st surviving son and heir; Lieut. 3rd Foot Guards; Capt. 18th Foot in 1797; retired 1803; resided at Ramsgate. = Susannah, dau. of Joseph Hayter, Esq., of Christchurch, co. Hants, and relict of John Cooper.*

Byam Crump Redhead, bapt. 10 Sep. 1778 at St. Peter's; Commissary-General in the Army; settled later at Trinidad. = ... mar. at Trinidad.

Cusack Munton Redhead, died s.p. 1820.

Anne Redhead, 1st dau., bapt. 14 May 1770 at St. Philip's; living 1786.

Mary Redhead, bapt. 11 Jan. 1773 at St. Peter's; mar. 6 Aug. 1789, at St. Philip's, John Athill, Esq.

Elizabeth Redhead, bapt. 24 April 1773 at St. Peter's; living at Boulogne, spinster, 1852.

Alicia Elliot Redhead, living at Boulogne, spinster, 1852.

Letitia Redhead, born 4 March and bapt. 1 Oct. 1769 at St. Philip's.

George Redhead.

Edward Redhead.

Ellen Redhead, only dau., mar. James Athill, son of John Athill of Antigua, Esq.; first-cousin to her husband.

Samuel Redhead.

* By her first husband she had a dau. Susannah Elizabeth Cooper, who died single in 1829 at Caen, the residence of her uncle Benjamin Hayter, R.N. He died 1860 at Coburg in Canada.

---

and to the necessary expenses of the plantations, pay unto Samuel Redhead £120 a year during the life of his father, and unto George Redhead £600 a year for life; in such case Samuel Redhead would assign to Anthony Munton, Samuel Athill, Rowland Burton, Francis Thwaites, and Charles Apthorpe Wheelwright the said plantation and estate called Fryes and the slaves, etc., and Francis Thwaites and Charles Apthorpe Wheelwright have acceded, and George Redhead has agreed to pay £6369; and it was agreed between Samuel Redhead and his father that if the said sum was paid by the latter out of his own proper monies, or if he should die before it was paid, or if with interest it should amount in his lifetime to £12,000, in either case the plantation should be charged with the said sum for George Redhead and his Ex'ors, and in the meantime should be charged with the yearly sum of £600 for the younger children of George Redhead living at his death; and whereas in pursuance of the agreement Samuel Redhead has lately drawn several bills of exchange to the amount of £2000 and upwards upon George Redhead, payable at the end of three years from their dates, and George Redhead has accepted them, and Samuel Redhead by his bond dated the 25th May last is become bound to his father in £12,738 with a condition for making it void. Now this Indenture witnesseth that in further pursuance of the agreement Francis Thwaites and Charles Apthorpe Wheelwright agree from the residue of the consignments to pay to Samuel Redhead £120 a year and to George Redhead £600 a year, but if there is any deficiency in the amount of residue the annuities to be proportionably abated, and if any surplus it is to be retained by them towards the diminution of the money due to them; and further witnesseth that in further pursuance Samuel Redhead in consideration of the premises and of 10s. conveys to Anthony Munton, Samuel Athill, Rowland Burton, Francis Thwaites, and Charles Apthorpe Wheelwright all that plantation called Fryes for 99 years from the decease of George Redhead in trust, immediately after his decease to enter in and take possession and to pay to Francis Thwaites and Charles Apthorpe Wheelwright 5 per cent. on all sums of money not exceeding £12,000, and to Samuel Redhead during the continuance of the trusts £500 a year, and amongst all younger children of George Redhead now born or hereafter to be born £600 a year, as George Redhead shall by deed appoint, and if no other child living than Samuel Redhead, to pay the £600 a year to the Ex'ors of George Redhead during the continuance of the trusts, and lastly they constitute and appoint John Athill and Robert Clogstones, both of Antigua, Esquires, their Attorneys. John Peale, John Inskip, Thomas Hewson, John Coleman, witnesses.

Close Roll, 37 Geo. III., Part 5, No. 2.

Indenture made the 20th July 1797 between George Redhead of Antigua, and of Burton House in the parish of Ringwood, Hants, Esq., of the one part, and Francis Thwaites and Charles Apthorpe Wheelwright of Bucklesbury, London, merchants and copartners, of the other part. Whereas the plantation called Fryes in the parish of St. Philip and division of Willoughby Bay stands limited to George Redhead party hereto for life, and after his decease to George Redhead, Esq., his eldest son, a Captain in H.M.'s 18th Regiment of Foot, for life, and to his sons successively in tail male with several remainders over; and whereas by Indentures made the 16th and 17th Nov. 1789, between George Redhead and Margaret his wife, since deceased, of the one part, and James Trecothick, Francis Thwaites, and Charles Apthorpe Wheelwright, of the other part, for the considerations therein mentioned a certain plantation called Cusacks was conveyed to the latter in trust; and whereas by Articles of Agreement dated the 1st of May last past between George Redhead, party hereto, and George Redhead the younger, of the one part, and Francis Thwaites and Charles Apthorpe Wheelwright, of the other part, reciting as before recited, and that Francis Thwaites and Charles Apthorpe Wheelwright had from time to time lent to George Redhead divers considerable sums of money, and on making up their account to the 30th April it appeared that the sum due to them was £7216 5s. 7*d.*, independently of divers other sums they had made themselves liable to pay, and reciting that George Redhead, party hereto, had requested them from the consignments of the produce of the said plantation to pay to him £60 per month, and also from time to time to allow for the use of his children so long as he should think proper the following sums, that is to say, for Miss Redhead £30 a year, for Miss Eliza Redhead £30 a year, for the said George Redhead the younger £120 a year, for Lieut. Byam Crump Redhead £40 a year, and for Cusack Redhead £60 a year, and in case it should happen that on the 30th April 1798 the balance due to them should be less than £5000, then George Redhead, party hereto, might be at liberty to draw on them for what sum the said balance should be short of the £5000, provided the accounts of the then ensuing crop should appear to them adequate to the outgoings of the year, and when the debt should be reduced to £4000 George Redhead might be permitted to draw for £80 per month, to be reduced again to £60 when the debt should exceed £4000; and George Redhead had also requested them to discharge a debt due from him in respect of the said estate to the Ex'ors of Charles Kerr, Esq., deceased, as follows, £1000 in Oct. 1797, £1000 in Oct. 1798, and the balance in Oct. 1799 if not more than £1000 sterling; and also reciting that, instead of making further advances, Francis Thwaites and Charles Apthorpe Wheelwright had a right to retain all consignments in satisfaction of their debt, and that having some little time previous resolved to proceed against George Redhead and the mortgaged premises which would have materially injured him, George Redhead, party hereto, and George Redhead the younger, to induce them to desist had proposed that four-fifths of the crops should be consigned to them till the whole debt was paid, and that in the event of the death of George Redhead the younger they should insure the life of George Redhead, party hereto, for the whole amount; and George Redhead the younger had consented to the consignment of the crop in the event of his coming into possession, but with such allowance made to him as is therein expressed, and he had proposed that when the whole debt should not exceed £3000 he should be allowed £20 per month instead of £10 if his father agreed and authorized them to pay it; and it is by the said Articles witnessed that George Redhead and his son, to effectuate the said purposes and in consideration of the premises, covenant to convey, etc.; and whereas in pursuance of the covenant George Redhead the younger, by Indenture bearing even date with these presents, has granted to Francis Thwaites and Charles Apthorpe Wheelwright all that plantation called Fryes, etc., in trust for 99 years from the decease of his father. Now this Indenture witnesseth that for confirming the said Articles of Agreement, with respect to the debt due to the Ex'ors of Charles Kerr and the other considerations Francis Thwaites and Charles Apthorpe Wheelwright agree to pay £1000 in October yearly till the said debt is paid, and to pay to George Redhead the younger £10 per month, to Ann Redhead the eldest daughter £30 a year, to Eliza Redhead £30 a year, to Byam Crump Redhead the second son £40 a year, and to Cusack Redhead the third son £60 a year; and George Redhead, party hereto, in consideration of the premises grants and confirms to Francis Thwaites and Charles Apthorpe Wheelwright all those plantations called Fryes and Cusacks; and lastly George Redhead constitutes the Hon. Rowland Burton, Samuel Athill, and John Athill, all of Antigua, Esquires, his Attorneys. Archer Brumell. Joshua Morris.

1707, Aug. 9. Joseph Redhead, carpenter, and Thomas Hall, carpenter, petition that they don't own a foot of land, and ask for 10 acres of waste at the Body. Joseph Redhead, carpenter, signs his deposition in 1710.

1711, April 9. Joseph Redhead, carpenter, working on Monk's Hill, petitions for food.

1712, May 13. Joseph Redhead is paid £646 for work done.

1 Geo., June 3. Hon. William Byam of Antigua, Esq., Nathaniel Crump of Antigua, Esq., Francis Carlile of Antigua, Esq., and Archibald Cochran of Antigua, Esq., Ex'ors of Samuel Phillips and guardians of his children, lease to Joseph Redhead, carpenter, two proportions of land in Parham.

Thomas Gillyat by his will dated 8 Jan. 1714 bequeathed 1*s.* to his dau. Mary Redhead.

1722, March 8. In Chancery. William Glanville, complainant, against Joseph Redhead, defendant.

1725, Feb. 26. The Ex'ors of Joseph Redhead are paid £63 c. by order of the Assembly.

1726. Samuel Redhead then a clerk in the Registrar's Office.

1745, Aug. 4. William Redhead petitions for land at Parham; granted.

1748, Sep. 19. Samuel Redhead returned for Willoughby Bay.

1785, March 15. In Bennet-str. Blackfriars-road, aged 81, Samuel Redhead, esq. of Antigua. ('Gent. Mag.,' p. 237.)

1815, April. At Pennington, Hants, the wife of George Redhead, esq. (*Ibid.*, p. 376.)

PARISH REGISTER OF ST. JOHN.

Baptized.

1758	Oct.	8	Elizabeth the D. of Nath[l] Redhead and Eliz. his wife.
1759	July	11	Ann and Grace the D's of Nath[l] Redhead and Elizabeth his wife.
1760	July	23	Mary the D. of Nathaniel Redhead and Elizabeth his wife.
1763	Feb.	24	Eliz[th] and [*blank*] twins of Nathaniel Redhead & his wife.
1770	Sep.	8	Samuel the S. of Nathaniel Redhead and Elizabeth his wife.
1772	Dec.	20	W[m] the S. of Nath[l] Redhead and Eliz[a] his wife.

Married.

1725	Mar.	17	Robert Jacobs and Sarah Redhead; by L. from Lieut. Gen[l] Mathew.
1726	May	28	W[m] Garrett and Elizabeth Redhead; by L. from Lieut. Gen[l] Mathew.
1726	Sep.	17	Edward Monteague and Grace Redhead; by L. from Gov[r] Byam.
1777	April	5	William Anderson to Ann Redhead. L.
1779	Jan.	21	Thomas Payne to Mary Redhead. L.
1784	April	26	Richard T. Shervington to Grace Redhead, Spinster.

Buried.

1742	Jan.	16	Ann Redhead w. of Sam[l] Redhead.
1763	Feb.	25	Eliz[th] Redhead (Child).
1763	Mar.	9	[*blank*] Redhead (Child).
1776	Aug.	26	Samuel Redhead.

1778 Jan. 26 Nathaniel Redhead.
1781 Jan. 17 Elizabeth Redhead.
1793 Oct. 6 Margaret Redhead.

PARISH REGISTER OF ST. PAUL.

Baptized.

1737 Nov. 11 George S. of Mr Samuel Redhead and Anne his wife.
1739 Dec. 23 Samuel S. of Mr Samuel Redhead and Anne his wife.
1741 Jan. 31 Mary D. of Mr Samuel Redhead & Anne his wife.

PARISH REGISTER OF ST. PETER.

Baptized.

1771 [*blank*] George the s. of George Redhead & Margaret his Wife.
1773 Jan. 11 Mary the D. of George Redhead and Margaret his Wife.
1773 April 24 Elizabeth the D. of George Redhead and Margaret his Wife.
1778 Sep. 10 Byam Crump S. of George Redhead and Margaret his Wife.

Buried.

1775 July 30 William Redhead.

PARISH REGISTER OF ST. PHILIP.

Baptized.

1768 Mar. 7 Samuel s. of George & Margaret Redhead.
1769 Oct. 1 Letitia d. of George & Margaret Redhead; b. March 4.
1770 May 14 Anne d. of George & Margaret Redhead.

Married.

1735 Feb. 16 William Redhead, Surgeon, to Frances Watson; by L.
1789 Aug. 6 Jno Athill to Mary Redhead; by L.

Buried.

1742 Jan. 16 Anne Wife of Mr Samuel Redhead. Buried in St John's.
1772 Dec. 25 Frances Redhead.

Family of Redwood.

William Redwood of Bristol, feltmaker. Will dated 17 Nov. 1668; proved 2 March 1668 by Anne Redwood the relict. (36 Coke.) To be buried in St Thomas' Churchyard. 20*s.* to the poor. To my wife my house for her life, then to my son Wm & his heirs male; remainder to my sons Isaac, Jacob, Abraham. To my son Wm Redwood £200. To my dau. Ann Redwood £200 at 21 & the house where John Dorny & Walter Thorne dwelleth in St Thomas' street for the remainder of the term. My s. Isaac Redwood £200 & the house where John Abbotts, tobacco-pipe-maker, liveth at 21. My dau. Sarah Redwood £200 & the house where John Jones liveth in the long Row in Temple parish adjoining John Abbotts at 21. My dau. Hester £200 at 21. My s. Jacob £200 at 21 & the house in the greene in Temple street where John Milles, Tho. Curnock, & the widow Synderlin liveth. My son Abraham £200 at 21. My brother John Redwood his bond. My cousin Israel Lane, Michael Lane, & Mary Kelson, & her dau. Mary Kelson 20*s.* each. Arthur, Judith, & Jeane Redwood, children of Arthur Redwood, 20*s.* each. Eliz., dau. of John Redwood, 20*s.* My wife may give to my cousin Mary, dau. of Richard Redwood, my little house in Redcliffe Hill in the holding of . . . . Cornish. All residue to my wife Anne & Ex'trix. Mr Mathew Rogers & my kinsman Israel Lane overseers, & 20*s.* each. Witnessed by Isaac Haywood, Robert Langford, Israel Lane, Notary Public, Michael Lane.

Codicil. To my son Wm & my dau. Ann each £100 more.

1672, Sep. 11. Robert Redwood of Bristol, deceased. Adm'on to Sarah Redwood the relict. (P.C.C.)

Amy Borlase of Newton St. Loe, co. Somerset, spinster, by her will made 31 Oct. 1673 bequeathed to Anne Redwood, dau. of Mr. William Redwood of Bristol, £50 at 21 or marriage. ('Genealogist,' New Series, vol. i., p. 292.)

Ann Bourne of Bristol, widow. Will dated 4 Aug. 1692; proved 10 Nov. 1692 by Thomas Bourne the son. (196 Fane.) Mother Ann Redwood. Sister Sarah Redwood. Son Tho. Bourne a messuage. Sister Heaster Sandford, now wife of Richd Sandford of Bristol, barber chirurgeon. Sister-in-law Eliz. Bourne. Brother Abraham Redwood £10. Ann, dau. of late brother Wm Redwood. Isaac, son of late brother Isaac Redwood, £8. Quaker poor. To be buried near husband. Poor of Temple parish 20*s.* All residue to my son Tho. Bourne & Ex'or. Mathew Rogers & John Hawkins overseers. Witnessed by Thomas Bisse, James Cooke, Jon Gregory.

Anne Redwood of Bristol, widow. Will dated 1 May 1711. To my grds. Wm Hopper £50, my diamond ring, & silver plate marked S. P. To my grds. Jno Hopper £5. To my grds. Tho. Hopper 2 gs., & to my grddrs. Anne & Eliz. Hopper 2 gs. ea. All res. to Onesipherus Tyndall of B'tol, drysalter, on T. to pay over to my dr. Anne Hopper, wife of Tho. Hopper, hosier. Witnessed by Henry ffane, Anne Peate. Sworn 17 Dec. 1717 by O. Tyndall. Recorded at Bristol.

John Avery of Bristol, plumber. Sarah Redwood £250, dau. of my sister Kath. Plomer, wife of Tho. Plomer. Proved 1713. (18 Aston.)

Thomas Redwood of St. James, tobacconist. Will dated 17 May 1718. To my s. Jno Redwood my leasehold mess. at Stokes Croft, St Jas. P'sh. My dr. Margt Harbin. My grddr. Mary Harbin. My ten. the Three Cupps in Mount Str. Grds. Tho. Richards. My dr. Sarah. My grddr. Rachael Peake, dr. of Jno Peake, baker, decd. My grddr. Mary Paradise, wife of Geo. Paradise, farrier. My grddr. Margt Redwood, dr. of my s. Tho. Redwood. My bro. Wm Redwood. All res. to my s. Jno Redwood & my dr. Margt. Witnessed by John Hickes, John Saunders. John Redwood sworn 25 May 1719. Recorded at Bristol.

John Redwood of Bristol, tobacco rowler. Will dated 2 Jan. 1729; proved 17 Feb. 1729 by Christopher Harbin. Wife Sarah. Neph. Tho. Richards £15 at 21, & to his bro. Jno Richards, Marr, £15. Kinsman Geo. Evans my apprentice. My kinswoman Margt, wife of [*blank*]. My tent in Broadmeed to kinsman Chr. Harbin. Witnessed by John Hobbs, Joseph Murrow, Thomas Blagden. Recorded at Bristol.

Pedigree of Redwood.

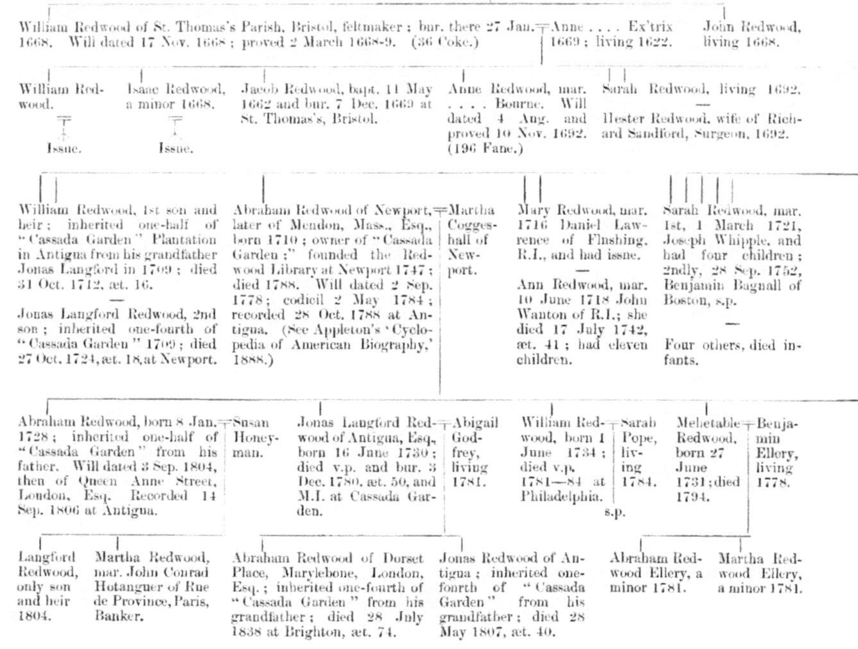

.... REDWOOD of Bristol=....

William Redwood of St. Thomas's Parish, Bristol, feltmaker; bur. there 27 Jan. 1668. Will dated 17 Nov. 1668; proved 2 March 1668-9. (36 Coke.) = Anne .... Ex'trix 1669; living 1622.

John Redwood, living 1668.

William Redwood. = Issue.

Isaac Redwood, a minor 1668. = Issue.

Jacob Redwood, bapt. 11 May 1662 and bur. 7 Dec. 1669 at St. Thomas's, Bristol.

Anne Redwood, mar. .... Bourne. Will dated 4 Aug. and proved 10 Nov. 1692. (196 Fane.)

Sarah Redwood, living 1692.

Hester Redwood, wife of Richard Sandford, Surgeon, 1692.

William Redwood, 1st son and heir; inherited one-half of "Cassada Garden" Plantation in Antigua from his grandfather Jonas Langford in 1709; died 31 Oct. 1712, æt. 16.

Jonas Langford Redwood, 2nd son; inherited one-fourth of "Cassada Garden" 1709; died 27 Oct. 1724, æt. 18, at Newport.

Abraham Redwood of Newport, later of Mendon, Mass., Esq., born 1710; owner of "Cassada Garden;" founded the Redwood Library at Newport 1747; died 1788. Will dated 2 Sep. 1778; codicil 2 May 1784; recorded 28 Oct. 1788 at Antigua. (See Appleton's 'Cyclopedia of American Biography,' 1888.) = Martha Coggeshall of Newport.

Mary Redwood, mar. 1716 Daniel Lawrence of Flushing, R.I., and had issue.

Ann Redwood, mar. 10 June 1718 John Wanton of R.I.; she died 17 July 1742, æt. 41; had eleven children.

Sarah Redwood, mar. 1st, 1 March 1721, Joseph Whipple, and had four children; 2ndly, 28 Sep. 1752, Benjamin Bagnall of Boston, s.p.

Four others, died infants.

Abraham Redwood, born 8 Jan. 1728; inherited one-half of "Cassada Garden" from his father. Will dated 3 Sep. 1804, then of Queen Anne Street, London, Esq. Recorded 14 Sep. 1806 at Antigua. = Susan Honeyman.

Jonas Langford Redwood of Antigua, Esq., born 16 June 1730; died v.p. and bur. 3 Dec. 1780, æt. 50, and M.I. at Cassada Garden. = Abigail Godfrey, living 1781.

William Redwood, born 1 June 1734; died v.p. 1781—84 at Philadelphia. = Sarah Pope, living 1784. s.p.

Mehetable Redwood, born 27 June 1731; died 1794. = Benjamin Ellery, living 1778.

Langford Redwood, only son and heir 1804.

Martha Redwood, mar. John Conrad Hotanguer of Rue de Province, Paris, Banker.

Abraham Redwood of Dorset Place, Marylebone, London, Esq.; inherited one-fourth of "Cassada Garden" from his grandfather; died 28 July 1838 at Brighton, æt. 74.

Jonas Redwood of Antigua; inherited one-fourth of "Cassada Garden" from his grandfather; died 28 May 1807, æt. 40.

Abraham Redwood Ellery, a minor 1781.

Martha Redwood Ellery, a minor 1781.

Richard Redwood of Bristol, mariner. Will dated 6 June 1726; proved 30 Dec. 1731 by Elizabeth Davie the mother. (314 Isham.) To Eliz. Davie, wife of James Davie of Bristol, dyer, all my goods, & Ex'trix. Witnessed by Henry Churchman, Thomas Dando.

Richard Redwood of Bristol, shipwright. Will dated 16 Nov. 1736; proved 30 Nov. 1736. To my brother Abraham Redwood 1*s*. All my estate to my wife Elizth Redwood for her life, then to my son-in-law Jas. Linford. My wife Ex'trix. Recorded at Bristol.

Abraham Redwood, late of Newport, State of Rhode Island, and Providence, now of Mendon, Worcester, and State of Massachusetts Bay, Esq. Will dated 2 Sep. 1778. To my dau. Mehetable Ellery, wife of Benjn Ellery, £3000 st., negros, coach, chariot, chaise, horses, plate, furniture, house, and land in Newport bought of my brother Wm Redwood, & the dwelling house on the farm at Mendon. To my granddau. Martha Redwood Ellery, dau. of the said Mehetable Ellery, the house & land purchased of Nathl Green of Boston in Massachusetts Bay. To my son Wm Redwood my dwelling house in Newport where I lately lived, & in which my son Abraham now lives, & a lot of land in Newport of 9 acres, also my farm in Portsmouth, Rhode Island, with the sheep & cattle, also my farm at Mendon, excepting what I have given to my dau. Mehetable, also my library of books & clothing, & £8000 st. to be paid out of my plantation in Antigua called Cassava Garden, *i.e.* £4000 to be p^{d} him by my son Jonas Langford Redwood out of his share, & £4000 by my son Abraham out of his share. I give him also all money in the funds or bank, & sugar & money in the hands of Messrs. Trecothick & Apthorp, merchants, of London, & Messrs. Rich^{d} & Tho. Oliver, merchants, of London. To my sons Jonas Langford Redwood & Abraham Redwood all my plantation called Cassava Garden in Antigua, negros, & cattle equally between them. To my grandson Abraham Redwood, son of Benjn & Mehetable Ellery, my gold watch, chain, & seal. To the poor of Newport 100 Spanish silver milled dollars. All residue to my son Wm Redwood. Joseph Clark of Rhode Island & my son Abraham Ex'ors. Witnessed by William Ellery, David Earl, Robert Lawton.

1st Codicil. 14 March 1781. To my brother Wm Redwood that portion of my estate bequeathed to my son Jonas Langford Redwood, now deceased, to hold until my grandson Jonas Redwood, son of the said Jonas Langf^{d} Redwood, be 21, then the said share of Cassava Garden to be equally divided between my 2 grandsons Abraham and Jonas Redwood, sons of the said Jonas L. Redwood, dec^{d}, & my brother to pay out of the rents £100 st. yearly to my dau. Abigail Redwood, widow of my said son. To my granddau. Martha Redwood, dau. of Benjn & Mehetable Ellery,

Mehetable, dau. of Jonas Langford of Popeshead, Antigua, a Quaker planter; died 1715. 1st wife. = Abraham Redwood, bapt. 2 July 1665 at St. Thomas's, Bristol; master of a London ship in the Jamaica trade; went to Antigua 1687; merchant there 1690; removed to Salem, Mass., 1712, and seventeen years later to Newport, Rhode Island, where he died 17 Jan. 1729, æt. 64. = Patience, relict of . . . . Phillips, and dau. of Joseph Howland of Duxbury, Mass.; mar. 14 Aug. 1716; died 11 Dec. 1745 at Newport. 2nd wife.

Patience Redwood, born in Salem, Mass., 24 Aug. 1719; mar. 17 April 1735 John Easton of Rhode Island, great-grandson of Governor John Easton; she died 1772 in Philadelphia; had seven children.

Rebecca Redwood, born in Salem 24 Aug. 1719; mar. 1st, 5 April 1739, Dr. Walter Rodman; 2ndly, 31 Oct. 1754, Joseph Clarke, and had three children.

Mehetable Redwood, born in Salem 16 Sep. 1722; mar. 13 Sep. 1739 Benjamin Hazzard, and had three children.

Lydia Redwood, born in Salem 14 Dec. 1724; died infant.

Hannah Holmes of Newport. 1st wife. = William Redwood, born in Salem 21 Dec. 1726; died 16 Jan. 1815. = Sarah Saunders, mar. 18 Jan. 1776. 2nd wife.

Martha Redwood, born 1733; died 1734.

Elizabeth Redwood, born and died 1735.

Samuel Holmes Redwood, born 13 Dec. 1765; died 20 May 1790 at Philadelphia.

Sarah Redwood, born 18 Dec. 1755; died 14 Aug. 1847.

Hannah Redwood, born 25 Sep. 1759; died 11 April 1796 at Philadelphia.

Elizabeth Redwood, born 18 July and died 9 Oct. 1767.

William Redwood, junior, born 23 April 1778; died 22 Nov. 1838.

Mary Redwood, born 18 Nov. 1776; died 14 Aug. 1777.

£700 st. at 21. To my grandson, their son Abraham Redwood Ellery, £1000 st. at 21. To my brother Wm Redwood £100 st. Of the residue, ¼ to the sons of my late son Jonas L. Redwood, ¼ to Mehetable Ellery, ¼ to my son Wm Redwood, & ¼ to my son Abraham Redwood. Witnessed by David Earl, Robert Lawton, Levi Albee.

2nd Codicil. 24 March 1781. My brother Wm to pay £200 yearly to the widow of Jonas L. Redwood for the maintenance of children till 21, & to Abraham Redwood £200 a year after 21 till his brother Jonas attain that age.

3rd Codicil. 2 May 1784. My son Wm Redwood being now dead the sum of £8000 is to be merged in Cassava Garden. My dwelling house in Newport to my dau. Mehetable Ellery. To my son Abraham my library & clothing. Of the money in the hands of merchts in London ⅓ to my brother Wm in trust for my grandsons, ⅓ to my son Abraham, ⅓ to my dau. Mehetable. To Sarah, widow of my late son Wm Redwood, £100 st. yearly. Witnessed by Andrew Peters, Levi Albee, Benjamin Lincoln, jun. Recorded 28 Oct. 1788.

Abraham Redwood of Queen Ann Street, co. Middlesex, Esq. Will dated 3 Sep. 1804. All my personal estate to my son Langford Redwood. All my plantation called Cassada Garden in Antigua to Thos. Norbury Kerby of Antigua, Esq., & Ambrose Weston of Fenchurch Street, Esq., on Trust for my son Langford Redwood & his heirs, charged with legacys & with £5000 for my dau. Martha, wife of John Conrad Hotanguer, Banker, Rue de Province, Paris. My 2 trustees & my said son Ex'ors. If my son die all my estate to my dau. Witnessed by James Bogue, William Todd, Fenchurch Street, London, Charles Hope, Featherstone Buildings, London. Sworn under £6000.

Abraham Redwood, formerly of Queen Ann Street, Esq., late of Duchess Street, Portman Place, St. Marylebone, deceased. Adm'on to Thomas N. Kerby, Esq., power reserved to Langford Redwood, Esq., the son. (P.C.C.) Recorded 14 Sep. 1806 at Antigua.

Close Roll, 36 Geo. III., Part 1, No. 11.

Indenture made the 18th Jan. 1796 between Abraham Redwood, late of Antigua, but now of London, Esq., of the one part, and Francis Thwaites and Charles Apthorp Wheelwright, both of London, merchants, of the other part. Whereas Abraham Redwood, formerly of Newport in the County of Newport in the State of Rhode Island, and Providence Plantation, but late of Mendon in the County of Worcester and State of Massachusetts Bay, Esq., deceased (paternal grandfather of Abraham Redwood, party hereto), made his last will dated 22 Sep. 1778 (will recited), and afterwards died; and whereas Abraham Redwood and Jonas Redwood have respectively attained to 21; and whereas several of the legacies have been paid; and whereas Francis Thwaites and Charles Apthorp Wheelwright have, at the request of Abraham Redwood, accepted three bills of exchange to secure the payment thereof. This Indenture witnesseth that Abraham Redwood grants, etc., his share, etc., to Francis Thwaites and Charles Apthorp Wheelwright in trust, etc., and he constitutes the Hon. Thomas Norbery Kirby and the Hon. Rowland Burton, both of Antigua, his Attorneys.

In the year 1613, Robert Redwood, a good old Puritan, gave his garden house on the city wall for a library; the alterations were finished in 1614, and Richard Williams, the Vicar of St. Leonard's, was appointed as the first librarian; the books were free to all citizens. This was, we believe, the first free library ever established in England. ('Old and New Bristol,' p. 277.)

1623, Aug. 13. 'Visitation of Gloucester.' Disclaymed at Bristoll "Robert Redwood of Bristoll no gent."

1654, July 12. Mountserrat. Dutch accounts. Sar^t Robert Redwood owes 53 lbs. of sugar. Sarj^t Redwood owes 310 lbs. (Egerton MS. 2395, British Museum.)

"This 4° Novemb^r 1668 William Redwood Haberdatir' was Admitted into the Liberties of this Citty for that hee was ye sonn & Apprentice of William Redwoode. And hath taken ye Oath of Allegiance & pd. 04 06." (Burgess Roll, Bristol City.)

1690. Abraham Redwood signs a petition at Antigua. (America and West Indies, No. 550, p. 387.)

1699, May 22. George Gamble of Antigua, Esq., sells to Abraham Redwood of Antigua, merchant, 10 acres.

1807, May 28. In his 41st year J. L. Redwood, esq. late of the island of Antigua. ('Gent. Mag.,' p. 593.)

1838, July 28. At Brighton, aged 74, Abraham Redwood, esq. of Dorset-place, St Marylebone, and of Antigua. (*Ibid.*, p. 341.)

Mr. Ledeatt of Antigua inherited Cassada Garden from his godfather Redwood.

A Rev. Mr. Redwood was living at Antigua *circa* 1863.

Redwood Family. A detailed genealogical account of the Redwood family, formerly of Bristol, who settled in America in the last century, may be found in the first number of the 'Newport Historical Magazine' (July, 1880), issued by the Historical Publishing Company, Newport, Rhode Island, U.S.A. [For a copy of a portion of this the Author is indebted to Mr. Richard Bliss, Librarian of the Newport Library.]

PARISH REGISTER OF ST. JOHN.

Married.

1729	Mar. 24	Richard Redwood and Eliz^a White.	L.
1738	Aug. 31	John Hawes & Elizabeth Redwood.	L.

Buried.

1694	May 13	Georg Redwood, carpenter of the Falcon ship of Bristol. Richard Redwood, Commander.
1731	April 14	John s. of Alex^r Ellery.
1731	Sep. 14	Capt Rich. Redwood from Bristoll.
1733	Oct. 31	John Ellery.
1740	Nov. 19	William Ellary, a child.
1780	Dec. 3	Jonas Langford Redwood.
1840	June 6	Norman Langford Redwood. St John's. 19.

ST. THOMAS, BRISTOL.

Baptized.

1659	April 17	Arthur s. of Arthur Redwood baptised.
1662	May 11	Jacob the s. of William Redwood.
1663	May 31	Joane d. of Arthur Redwood.
1665	July 2	Abraham s. of Wm Redwood.

Married.

1653	May 1	Arthur Redwood and Judeth Marten.

Buried.

1665	Mar. 14	John s. of John Redwood.
1668	Jan. 27	William Redwood.
1669	June 9	Jane d. of Judith Redwood.
1669	Dec. 7	Jacob s. of ye widd. Redwood.
1669	Jan. 28	Judeth d. of widd. Redwood.

CASSADA GARDEN.

At the private burial-ground, close to the present shooting butts.

On a white marble ledger:—

Sacred to the Memory
of
JONAS LANGFORD REDWOOD ESQ^R
Who departed this life the 3^d day of
December 1780
Aged 50 Years.

There is a smaller vault near the above, but without any ledger or M.I.

In 1852 "Cassada Garden" in St. John's Parish contained 599 acres, and was owned by the heirs of J. L. L. Redwood.

Pedigree of Richardson.

JOHN RICHARDSON of Parham, Antigua; granted 100 acres in 1679. = ... Will dated 20 Oct. 1705.

John Richardson of "Barnes" in North Sound, only son and heir. Will dated 7 Sep. 1731; sworn 15 Feb. 1734-5. = Margaret . . . . Ex'trix 1731.

- Elijah Richardson, ob. v.p. = ...
- Zephaniah Richardson, living 1731.
- John Richardson of St. Martin's 1731.
- Anna Richardson. = Arthur Williams, junior, planter. Will dated 3 March 1756.
- . . . . Blizard, dead 1724. 1st husband. = Margaret Richardson. = John Ellyatt. Will dated 14 July 1733. 2nd husband.

Issue of Elijah Richardson:

- John Richardson, heir to his grandfather in 1731; a physician 1744; Ex'or 1756 to Arthur Williams. = Amelia, dau. of Jacob Thibou, bapt. 28 Dec. 1728; mar. April 1744 and bur. 30 June 1759 at St. John's.
- Elizabeth Richardson, living 1731.

Issue of Anna Richardson and Arthur Williams:

- Catherine Williams, bapt. 23 Jan. 1714 at St. John's; named in the will of her grandfather John Richardson 1731.
- Rebeckah Williams, named in the will of her grandfather John Richardson; dead 1731.

Issue of Margaret Richardson and . . . . Blizard:

- Frances Blizard, mar. 5 March 1734 John Ellyatt; named in the will of her grandfather John Richardson 1731.

Issue of John Richardson and Amelia Thibou:

- Elizabeth Richardson, named in the will of W. H. Doig 1765.
- Dorothy Halsal Richardson, bapt. 24 Feb. 1744 at St. George's; named in the will of W. H. Doig 1765; bur. 26 Sep. 1816.
- Amelia Richardson, bur. 3 Nov. 1753.

John Richardson of Parham Town. Will dated 20 Oct. 1705. To my son Jno Richardson all my estate. Appoint Col. Wm Codrington, Mr Sam. Philips, & Wm Glanvile Ex'ors. Witnessed by Thomas Blake, John King, William Balfour. (See Goble Pedigree.)

The following portion of a will has no name of testator attached to it:—

John [*blank*] Will dated 7 Sep. 1731. My wife Marg^t^ Richardson. My late son Elijah Richardson. My grandson John. To my said wife a horse. I formerly gave to my granddau. Rebeccah Williams, deceased, a heifer, now in the possession of my granddau. Cath. Williams. To my son Zephaniah Richardson 19 acres he now holds of my plantation called "Barnes" in North Sound Div^n^ to hold for life, he paying to my grandson Jno Richardson .... To my dau. Marg^t^ Elliott £100 c. To my granddau. Frances Blizard, dau. of my dau. .... Elliott a £30 negro. To my granddau. Cath. Williams maintenance. To my granddau. Eliz^th^ Richardson, dau. of my son Elijah Richardson, 3 negros. To my son John Richardson in the island of St Martin's my gold-headed cane. £15 to be laid out to wall in a burial-place on my plantation 50 feet square. All residue to my grandson John, son of Elijah Richardson, dec^d^. My wife Marg^t^, Hon. Edwd Byam, & my son Zephaniah Ex'ors. Witnessed by Arthur Williams, Joseph Gillyatt, George Jennings. Before Hon. Edward Byam was sworn Joseph Gillyatt 15 Feb. 1734-5. Recorded 25 Feb. 1734-5.

Close Roll, 4 Geo. IV., Part 18, No. 17.

Indenture made the 11th August 1823 between John Young of Brock Street, Bath, Esq., and Jane his wife, of the 1st part, Eliza Gumbes Bradshaw, formerly of Antigua, but now residing in the Colony of Trinidad, widow (only child and heiress-at-law of Frances Bishop Richardson, late of Antigua, widow, deceased), of the 2nd part, and John Cornelius Gibbs of Antigua, Esq., and John Halloran of Antigua, Gentleman, of the 3rd part. Whereas John Young and Jane his wife did in 1802 contract with Frances Bishop Richardson for the sale to her and her heirs of the fee simple of the messuage hereinafter mentioned for the price of £400 currency or £200 sterling; and whereas the said sum was shortly after paid to Thomas Norbury Kerby, late of Antigua, but now deceased, Esq., Attorney of John and Jane Young; and whereas John Young and Jane his wife did in a certain deed duly executed, dated in Oct. 1805, grant and confirm to the said late Frances Bishop Richardson the said piece of land; and whereas the said deed having been omitted to be duly stampt has been rendered of no effect in Antigua; and whereas Frances Bishop Richardson died in 1809, leaving Eliza Gumbes Bradshaw her only child and heiress-at-law, who is now entitled to the fee simple and inheritance; and whereas she hath applied to John Young and Jane his wife to execute a valid conveyance. Now therefore this Indenture witnesseth that in consideration of the £400 currency paid John Young and Jane his wife grant and confirm to Eliza Gumbes Bradshaw all that piece of land in High Street, in the town of St. John in Antigua, containing in length from E. to W. 38 feet, in breadth from N. to S. 76 feet 8 inches, bounded E. by lands formerly of Langford Lovell and Ann his wife, but late of George Green, deceased, and now in the possession of Rachel Rose, spinster, to whom the same was bequeathed by the will of George Green, W. with lands formerly of John and Jane Young, but now of the Hon. Samuel Warner, N. with High Street, and S. with Long Street, together with the dwelling house standing thereon to Eliza Gumbes Bradshaw and her heirs and assigns for ever; and John Young and Jane his wife appoint, etc., John Cornelius Gibbes and John Halloran to be their Attorneys. John Maule, witness.

1672. For an account of William Richardson, merchant, see under Rodney.

1679, March 18. John Richardson granted 100 acres by Jeremiah Watkins; surveyed 7 Dec. 1679.

1724. John Richardson then President of Nevis.

1748-9, Feb. 3. John Richardson to be of the Council of Nevis.

1808, Nov. 9. At Bath, Major-general Richardson, to Mrs. Scott, widow of the late David Scott esq. of the island of Antigua. ('Gent. Mag.,' p. 1039.)

1828, May 29. Col. J. F. Browne, Bristol, 28th Reg., to Grace, relict of the late Hon. John Richardson, of the Island of Nevis. (*Ibid.*, p. 640.)

PARISH REGISTER OF ST. JOHN.

Married.

1723	April 13	Zacchariah Richardson and Eliz^a^ Hodge; by L.
1736	Aug. 7	George Traut and Jane Richardson; by Banns published.
1736	Sep. 2	Alexander Richardson and Sarah Patterson; by L.
1739	Nov. 24	Cæsar Roach & Elizabeth Richardson; by L.
1739	Nov. 24	Samuel Jones & Sarah Richardson; by L.
1739	Dec. 6	Stephen Richardson & Margaret Welch; by B. p.
1741	Oct. 24	Thomas Richardson and Sarah Reynolds.
1744	April —	Doctor John Richardson & Amelia Thibou.

PARISH REGISTER OF ST. PAUL.

Married.

1776	[*blank*]	John Richardson (planter) to Elizabeth Knewstub, Spinster; by L.

Buried.

1830	Dec. 3	William Richardson, Major 86 Reg. Ridge. 42.

PARISH REGISTER OF ST. GEORGE.

Baptized.

1744	Feb. (24?)	Dorothy Halsal the D. of John Richardson and Amilia his wife.

Buried.

1743	Jan. 25	Mary the D. of Thos Richardson and Mary his wife.
1753	Nov. 3	Amelia Richardson D. of Doc^t^ Richardson & Amelia his wife buried in the Plantation by Licence from the Hon. Andrew Lesly, Ordinary. W. Topham, Cler.
1759	June 30	Amelia the Wife of Dr Jno Richardson.
1816	Sep. 26	Dorothy Hazael Richardson; in the Family Burying Ground at High Point.
1818	Oct. 30	Amelia Richardson, from Town; in the Family Burying place at High Point.

PARISH REGISTER OF ST. PHILIP.

Married.

1771	Nov. 26	William Richardson, Esq., & Margaret Lavicount, Spr.

Pedigree of Roach.

JAMES ROACH of Antigua had 20 acres in 1678.

Major John Roach of St. John's Parish, Antigua, bur. 24 May 1729. Will dated 20 Feb. 1728-9; sworn 31 March 1729. ═ Mary, dau. of William Halliday, mar. 6 May 1708; living 1729; named in the will of her sister Mrs. Elizabeth Yeamans 1750.

Jane Cooper, mar. 27 May 1730 at St. Paul's; bur. there 27 Dec. 1734. 1st wife. ═ John Roach, bapt. 24 Sep. 1713. ═ Sarah .... 2nd wife.

Cæsar Roach, bapt. 14 Jan. 1719; heir to his aunt Mrs. Elizabeth Yeamans 1750; Ex'or 1762 to Mrs. Rachel Denbow. ═ Elizabeth Richardson, mar. 24 Nov. 1739.

George Roach, bap. 3 April 1723; bur. 4 Feb. 1724.

Katherine Roach, bapt. 18 Dec. 1715.

John Roach, bapt. 3 Aug. 1735. ═ Mary ....

George Roach, bapt. 24 Feb. 1736 and bur. 31 May 1737.

Cæsar Roach, bapt. 21 June and bur. 10 July 1738.

John Roach ═ Margaret .... died 3 Dec. 1840, æt. 70. M.I.

Sarah Gylliat Roach, bapt. 11 March 1764 at St. George's.

Franzes Eliza Roach, born 8 Oct. 1788; bapt. 2 Dec. 1789.

Sarah Roach, born 3 Oct. 1792; bapt. 20 Oct. 1793.

Catherine Roach, born 7 May 1801, bapt. 9 March 1803; bur. 2 June 1827, æt. 26.

John Roach, Gent. Will dated 20 Feb. 1728-9. To my sister Mary £10 c. yearly. To my son John my pair of silver trumpets, my diamond ring, large gold snuff box, gold seal with coat of arms, pair of gold shoe buckles. All residue to my sons John & Cæsar equally. Wm Yeamans, Esq., Ashton Warner, Tho. Kerby, Richd Sherwood Ex'ors. Witnessed by Joan Lodge.

Codicil. To my wife her gold snuff box & pocket case. Before Edward Byam, Esq., was sworn Joan Lodge 31 March 1729.

Elizabeth Yeamans, by her will which was sworn 31 Aug. 1750, bequeathed all residue of her estate to her nephew Cæsar Roach, son of her sister Mary Roach.

1678. James Roach, 20 acres by Colonel James Vaughan; surveyed 15 Nov.

1711, May 22. John Roach of Antigua, Gent., and Mary his wife sell two negros to William Yeamans.

1711, May 22. George Roch of Pensilvania, now of Antigua, merchant, releases all claim to William Glanvill of Antigua, merchant, to three proportions of land in St. John's Town, and with Cæsar Rodney of Antigua, merchant, gives bond for £1500.

Parish Register of St. John.

Baptized.

1702-3	Mar. 25	Rachel d. of George Roache & Penelope his wife.
1704	[*blank*]	George s. of & Lydia d. of Thomas Roache & Lydia his wife.
1713	Sep. 24	John s. of John Roach & Mary his wife.
1715	Dec. 18	Katherine d. of John Roach & Mary his wife.
1717	Dec. 22	Ann D. of .... Roach & Ann his wife.
1719	Jan. 14	Casar s. of John Roach & Mary his wife.
1723	April 3	George s. of John Roach & Mary his wife.
1735	Aug. 3	John s. of John Roach & Sarah his wife.
1736	Feb. 24	George the s. of John Roach and Sarah his wife.
1738	June 21	Cæsar ye s. of John Roach & Sarah his wife.
1741	Nov. 3	William the s. of William Roach and Catherine his wife.
1789	Dec. 2	Frances Eliza D. of John Roach and Margaret his wife. B. 8th October 1788.
1793	Oct. 20	Sarah D. of John Roach and Margaret his wife. B. the 3rd October 1792.
1803	Mar. 9	Catherine D. of John Roach and Margaret his wife: b. 7th May 1801.

Married.

1702	[*blank*]	Anthony Montero & Eliz. Roche.
1708	May 6	John Roach & Mary Holliday.
1732	Jan. 4	John Barnes and Ann Roach. L.
1739	Nov. 24	Cæsar Roach & Elizabeth Richardson. L.

Buried.

1700	Mar. 18	Rachel Rooch, Widdow.
1715	Dec. 22	Katherine Roach.
1717-18	Mar. 20	Robert Roach of the Eliz. Com^r Geo. Long.
1719	Oct. 11	Lewis Roach.
1724	Feb. 4	George s. of John Roach.
1729	May 24	Maj^r John Roach of this Parish.
1734	Jan. 1	Thomas Roach.
1737	May 31	George s. of John Roach.
1738	April 11	Jane ye wife of John Roach.
1738	July 10	Cæsar ye s. of John Roach.
1742	May 23	John Roach.
1744	Nov. 17	George Roch.
1827	June 2	Catherine Roach. St John's. 26.

Parish Register of St. Paul.

Married.

1730 May 27 John Roche & Jane Cooper; by Banns.

Buried.

1734 Dec. 27 Jane W. of John Roach.

Parish Register of St. George.

Baptized.

1764 Mar. 11 Sarah Gylliat the D. of John Roach & Mary his wife.

St. John's Churchyard.

On a brass plate on a tomb within lofty railings:—

Sacred to the Memory | OF MARGARET ROACH | WHO DEPARTED THIS LIFE ON THE | 3RD DEC. 1840 AGED 70 YEARS | ALSO OF | ANN HESTER | *His beloved wife* (three lines follow) DEPARTED THIS LIFE ON THE | 16 Augst 1841 Aged 46 Years. (Six lines follow.)

Pedigree of Rodney.

ARMS.—*Or, three eagles displayed purpure.*

SIR JOHN RODNEY, Knt., died 18 Hen. VIII. Sixteenth in descent from Walter Rodeney who lived *temp.* Stephen. ═ . . . .

George Rodney, 2nd son; owned the manors of "Over-Badgeworth" and "Congresbury," co. Somerset; died 1580, æt. 80. ═ . . . .

Sir John Rodney, Knt., son and heir, born 1549 at Stoke; matriculated from Christ Church, Oxford, 1568, æt. 18; High Sheriff; M.P.; knighted 1 Jac.; died 1612. ═ Jane, dau. of Sir Henry Seymour, brother of Edward, Duke of Somerset; living 1595.

William Rodney, 3rd son; named in the Visitation of Somerset 1623. ═ . . . . dau. of Sir Thomas Cæsar,* Knt.

Cæsar Rodney of Bristol, merchant ═ Sarah . . . .

- Alice Rodney, bapt. 8 April 1666 at Christ Church, Bristol.
- Cæsar Rodney of "Rodney Stoak," Antigua, Gent., Captain of Militia; Agent at Nevis for his brother 1672; Provost-Marshal 1679—82; granted 213 acres in 1680; Speaker of Antigua 1684. ═ Lydia More, mar. 10 July 1701 at St. John's; bur. there 15 June 1723.
- Frances, dau. and heir of Stephen Mall of Nevis, and relict of William Richardson of Nevis, merchant; latter living 1666. 1st wife. ═ Captain John Rodney of Nevis 1668; Officer in the Guards 1659—66; Lieut. in Bridge's Regiment 1666; Captain 1668—71; Member of Council of St. Christopher's 1689; later of Antigua. ═ Ann . . . . 2nd wife.
- Two younger brothers of John and Cæsar at Nevis *circa* 1672.

- Lydia Rodney, bapt. 1706 at St. John's; mar. there, 26 Jan. 1722, Edward Trant.
- Dorothy Rodney, bur. 27 Feb. 1708 at St. John's.
- Alice Rodney, bapt. 21 Oct. 1708 at St. John's; mar. there, 12 Feb. 1722, John Panton (? brother of Christina, wife of George Dewar, Esq., of St. Kitts).
- Grace Rodney, bapt. 21 Feb. 1710 at St. John's; bur. 13 June 1712.
- Cæsar Rodney of St. John's Town, Gent., 1731; quitted the Island Aug. 1737 in debt.
- John Rodney, bur. 4 Feb. 1690 at St. John's.

* He was born 1561, became a Baron of the Exchequer and was knighted 1610; mar. 3rdly in 1592, at Stepney, Susan, dau. of Sir William Ryther, Knt., and Alderman of London, by whom he had three sons and five daughters. His burial is thus entered in the Parish Register of St. Helen's, Bishopsgate:—"1610, July 18. Sir Thomas Cæsar, Kt., one of the Barons of the King's Ma'ties Exchequer: died the same day in his house in Chancery Lane." ('The Annals of St. Helen's, Bishopsgate,' by Rev. J. E. Cox, D.D.)

List of stock and goods left by John Rodney upon his plantation in Nevis in 1668, made by him by direction of the Secretary of the Council for Plantations, viz., 33 negros and Indians, great and small; 4 white servants; 9 cattle; 2 sugar mills; 7 coppers, with stills, coolers, and other necessaries, besides house and near 100 acres of canes, all fit to make sugar within one year after Cole had possession.

1671. Lieutenant John Rodney, now a captain in Sir Tobias Bridge's Regiment, went over lieutenant, was made captain in 1668, left those parts 11th June same year, and desires a lieutenant's place. In 1666 His Majesty sent forces to Barbadoes under Sir Tobias Bridge, when Captain Rodney quitted the Guards, where he had served seven years under Sir P. Howard, to go lieutenant to Major Andros, but fifteen months after had a commission for a company of foot, which he kept till the regiment was disbanded in July 1671.

1672, Nov. Petition of John Rodney and Frances his wife to the King. That Stephen Mall, deceased, was seised of an estate in Nevis worth £500 per annum; petitioner Frances, his daughter & heir, married Wm. Richardson, merchant, deceased, who had some small dealings with Tho. Cole; that after said Richardson's death petitioners intermarried, & some time after returned for England. In their absence said Cole, pretending Richardson to be indebted in 60,000 weight of sugar (about £300), James Russell, then Governor, & his intimate friend, caused some proceedings to be had against said Richardson (according to some pretended law in that island), & said plantation to be sold by outcry, at which Cole was admitted to buy the same for 60,000 weight of sugar, etc., etc.

1672, Nov. 30. Sir James Russell writes from Bristol that Captain Rodney had no injury done him, unless by his profuse and idle brother and agent Cæsar Rodney.

1673, April 21. Sir James Russell says that Rodney sent his brother as agent, who, with two younger brothers, ruined his estate. This business was still under discussion in Feb. 1674. Richardson was in possession in 1666. (Colonial Calendar, America and West Indies.)

1678. Nevis. Cæsar Rodney. 6 white men and 1 woman; 3 negros.

1678. Antigua. Thomas Poole, mason, sells to Mr. Cæsar Roedney of Nevis, Gent., 40 acres in the Road Division.

1679, Sep. 1. Cæsar Rodeney signs papers as Provost Marshal. (Colonial Leeward Islands, 48.)

1680, Oct. 17. Cæsar Rodney granted a patent for 213 acres by Sir W. Stapleton.

1680 and 1689. John Rodeney signs as a member of the Council of St. Christopher's. (*Ibid.*, Colonial Entry Book, 46, and America and West Indies, No. 550, p. 68.)

1682. Nevis. Cæsar Rodeney then Marshal.

1684, March 27. Captain Cæsar Rodney and Mr. John Sampson granted a patent for 200 acres called Rodney Stoak. The former was one of the gentlemen of St. Mary's Vestry.

1684, Sep. 30. Cæsar Rodeney returned to the Assembly for the Road Division; was at the same time chosen Speaker *vice* Captain John Yeamans.

1711, June 14. Cæsar Rodney and others owners of the Virgin Queen.

1731. Cæsar Rodeney, Gent., two proportions of land in St. John's Town; surveyed.

PARISH REGISTER OF ST. JOHN.

Baptized.

1706	 6	Lydia D. of Cæsar Rodney & Lydia his wife.
1708	Oct. 21	Alice D. of Cæsar Rodney & Lydia his wife.
1710	Feb. 21	Grace ye d. of Cæsar Rodney & Lydia his wife.

Married.

1701	July 10	Cæzar Radney & Leadiatt More, Spinster.
1722	Jan. 26	Edward Trant and Lydia Rodeney. L.
1722	Feb. 12	John Panton and Alice Rodeney. L.

Buried.

1690	Feb. 4	John the s. of Captn Jno Radney & Ann his wife.
1708	Feb. 27	Dorothy D. of Cæsar Rodeney & Lydia his wife.
1712	June 13	Grace Rodeney.
1723	June 15	Mrs Lydia Rodeney.

CHRIST CHURCH, BRISTOL.

Baptized.

1666	April 8	Alce the daughter of Cesar Rodney by his wife Sarah was baptised. [Several children of Mr. Wm. Rodney were baptised about the same time at another city church, viz., St. John's.]

Pedigree of Ronan.

PHILIP RONAN, Trustee for the Crabb Family 1727; of St. John's Division 1753; dead 1759. = ...

John Ronan, senior, of St. John's Division 1753. Will dated 26 Nov. 1765; sworn 5 March 1766. = Tryphany, dau. of Henry Nibbs; a minor 1741. Will dated 5 Sep., then of Parham, sworn 17 Oct. 1789.	Philip Ronan, junior, of St. John's Division 1753; named in his brother John's will 1765.	Ann Ronan, 1765.	Margaret Ronan, 1759.

John Ronan, junior, Ex'or to his parents 1766 and 1789; Member of Assembly for Belfast 1774, 1781, 1788, 1801, 1807, 1810. = Hester, dau. of Mrs. Mary Collins; mar. 4 March 1771 at St. Philip's; living 1789.

John Collins Ronan, bapt. 7 Oct. 1773 at St. Philip's. (? joined in the purchase in 1806 of Robert Burnthorn's estate for £33,000 c.) Living 1810.	Nicholas Ronan, named in the will of his grandmother Mrs. Collins 1782; living 1789.	Christopher Ronan, living 1789.	Tryphena Ronan, living 1789; goddaughter of Patience Freeman 1798.

John Ronan, carpenter. Will dated 20 Nov. 1765. To my sister Ann Ronan a negro. All residue to my wife Tryphany Ronan & my s. John Ronan. My wife during her widowhood & Hon. Steph. Blizard, Esq., Guardians of my son. My brother Philip Ronan, Geo. Hurst, & Jas. Bridges, planters, Ex'ors. Witnessed by John Burton, Nathaniel Gilbert. Before Governor George Thomas was sworn John Burton 5 March 1766. Recorded 10 March 1766.

Tryphena Ronan of Parham. Will dated 5 Sep. 1789. All my houses in St John's Town & lime kiln, furniture, plate, & stock to Hon. Tho. Norbury Kerby, Jos. Lyons Walrond, Isaac Eccleston, & John Burke, Esqrs, in Trust to sell. Wooden legged Jack & Rose to be free & £10 c. yearly apiece. All my slaves to my trustees for my grdchildren John, Nich., Chr., & Tryphena Ronan at 21. My house in Parham & certain slaves & all residue for my son John Ronan, but if liable for his debts to his wife & children, & after his death for my grds. John Ronan. Trustees to be Ex'ors. Witnessed by Grace Haslom, George Crump, Nathaniel Crump. Before Hon. John Nugent, Commander-in-Chief, was sworn George Crump of Antigua, Esq., 17 Oct. 1789. Recorded 20 Oct. 1789.

Close Roll, 45 Geo. III., Part 27, No. 12.

Indenture made the 29th March 1805 between Robert Burnthorn of Antigua, Esq., and Abigail, now residing in Middlesex, his wife, of the 1st part, Abigail of Antigua, a negro girl slave, of the 2nd part, and Anne Goolsby of Antigua, widow, a trustee on behalf of the said negro girl slave, of the 3rd part. Whereas Robert Burnthorn and Abigail his wife are now seised of the said Abigail in their demesne as of fee in right of Abigail Burnthorn, and it has been agreed between Robert Burnthorn, with the consent of his wife, and Anne Goolsby that in consideration of £66 currency to be paid by Anne Goolsby to Robert Burnthorn, they shall manumit the said Abigail and also all her present and future issue. Now this Indenture witnesseth that in consideration of £66 Robert Burnthorn and Abigail his wife manumit, etc., and they appoint William Burnthorn, Esq., and John Harris, Esq., now resident in Antigua, their Attorneys. Margaret Eales, Eleanor Montague, witnesses.

Close Roll, 50 Geo. III., Part 26, Nos. 8 and 9.

Indenture made the 15th Feb. 1810 between Robert Burnthorn,* late of Antigua, but now or late of the colony of Demerara, Esq. (by Emanuel Lousada of London, merchant, his Attorney appointed by Deed Poll dated the 24th July last past, and duly recorded in Antigua), and Abigail Burnthorn his wife, now residing in New North Street, Red Lion Square, Middlesex, of the one part, and Robert Hyndman of Antigua, merchant, of the other part; witnesseth that in consideration of 10*s*. Robert Burnthorn and Abigail his wife convey to Robert Hyndman all that plantation containing 207 acres, 3 r., and 7 p., in the parish of St. Philip and the divisions Nonsuch and Willoughby Bay in Antigua, bounded E. by the lands of or in the possession of Samuel Byam Athill and the lands heretofore of Thomas Elmes, deceased, but now in the possession of Thomas Rogers and others, N. by the lands of Thomas Duberry Harman and the lands now or late of Samuel Harman, W. by the lands of John Lyons, and S. by the lands of the said Samuel Byam Athill and the sea of Willoughby Bay, and the following slaves (names given), 49 males and 58 females, being the slaves which were on the plantation on the 1st Aug. 1806, or such as are now in existence, and 4 bulls, 4 oxen, 6 cows, 2 calves, 2 horses, 1 mule, and 7 asses, being the stock on the plantation at the said date, for one whole year, and Robert Burnthorn and Abigail his wife constitute Thomas Hyndman and Thomas Saunderson of Antigua, merchants, their Attorneys. Thomas Street, Philpot Lane, London, George Frederick Street, same place, witnesses.

No. 8.

Indenture made the 16th Feb. 1810 as above. Whereas Robert Burnthorn is seised in his demesne as of fee in certain lands, etc., in Antigua, and on the 1st Aug. 1806 did agree to sell them to John Ronan the younger and Richard Garland of Antigua, Esq., for the price of £33,000 currency, and John Ronan and Richard Garland in pursuance of the agreement were then let into the possession and still continue in the possession thereof; and whereas the said lands, etc., are encumbered by mortgages in several considerable sums, amounting to or nearly to their value, and no part of the principal of the purchase hath been paid, nor hath any part of the moneys due on the mortgages been paid by John Ronan and Richard Garland or either of them. Now therefore this Indenture witnesseth that for the purpose of conveying and assuring the said lands to John Ronan and Richard Garland, in case the £33,000 currency with interest at 6 per cent. from the 1st Aug. 1806 shall be fully paid or duly accounted for, and if not for the intent and purpose of providing a fund for the payment of the mortgages by the sale of the lands, and in consideration of 10*s*., and also in consideration of £250 sterling, Robert Burnthorn and Abigail his wife convey to Robert Hyndman all that plantation (as in No. 9) to the use of John Ronan and Richard Garland if they pay, and to pay the moneys arising from the same to the discharge of a mortgage made by Robert Burnthorn on the 18th Dec. 1802 to James Donovan, for the payment of £10,000 currency, and a mortgage of the said premises made by Robert Burnthorn to Daniel Sharry on the 29th April 1809 for £5000 currency, and a mortgage made by Robert Burnthorn the 30th April 1805 for £6320 sterling to Warwick Pearson and Robert Hyndman, and a mortgage made the 11th April 1799 by John Elliott the elder and Catharine his wife unto John Duberry, deceased, affecting and being an encumbrance on part of the plantation for securing the payment of £6000 currency, upon which mortgage is only now due £2000 or thereabouts with interest, and upon trust to pay any surplus to Robert Burnthorn and his Ex'ors, but if the said purchase money shall not be paid or accounted for in trust to sell the said lands, etc., and to apply the moneys as before.

* He married at St. John's, 6 May 1795, Abigail Goolsby, widow. William Burnthorn married Margaret Burton (baptized 1782), dau. of John Burton, Esq.

PARISH REGISTER OF ST. JOHN.

Baptized.

1827 Sep. 27 James Thompson the s. of John Joseph & Elizabeth Ann Ronan. St John's. Merchant.

Married.

1700 Feb. 12 William Boone & Mary Ronan; by Lyc.
1754 Feb. 14 Joseph Ronan and Jane Weeks, Widow.
1802 April 22 James Farley to Sarah Ronan, Spr.

Buried.

1775 Feb. 27 Jane Ronan.
1828 Jan. 4 James Thompson Ronan, infant.
1829 May 31 Clement Ronan. 17.

PARISH REGISTER OF ST. GEORGE.

Buried.

1781 Jan. 30 Mary Ronan, an Infant.

PARISH REGISTER OF ST. PHILIP.

Baptized.

1773 Oct. 7 John Collins Ronan.
1775 [*blank*] [*blank*] Ronan [*blank*] Ronan.

Married.

1736 April 8 Peter Lavicount to Sarah Ronan.
1771 Mar. 4 John Ronan & Hesther Collins.

Buried.

1844 Aug. 8 John N. Ronan. Parham. Infant.

PARISH REGISTER OF ST. PETER.

Baptized.

1771 Jan. 1 Sarah the D. of Joseph Ronan & Elizabeth his wife.

Married.

1834 Feb. 3 George Richard White of St Peter's, planter, & Tryphena Ronan of St John's, Spr.

Buried.

1824 Feb. 3 John Ronan, Junior, from Parham, in Church Yard.

ST. JOHN'S CHURCHYARD.

On a white marble flat-stone:—

SACRED | TO THE MEMORY OF | J. J. RONAN | LATE HARBOUR MASTER | *of* | *St JOHN'S ANTIGUA.* | WHO DIED APRIL 2ND *1850* | AGED 62 YEARS.

To the memory of | William Ronan [remainder illegible].

Pedigree of Rose.

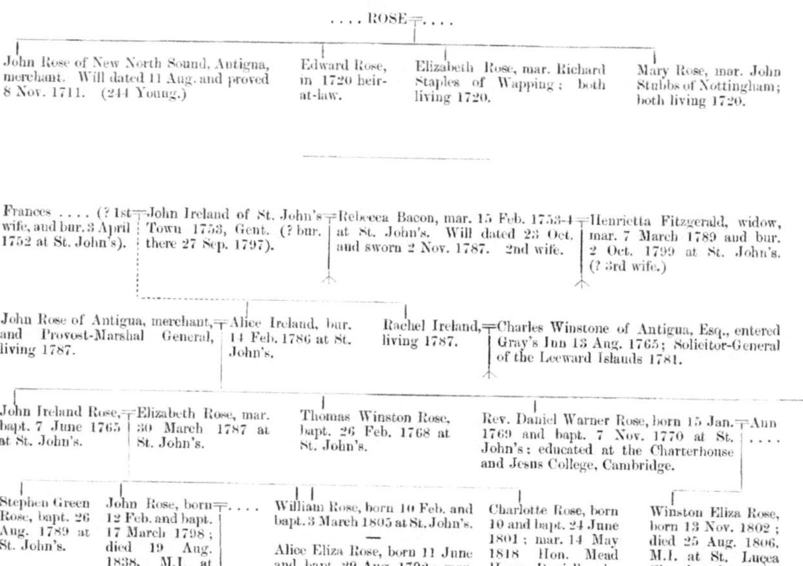

.... ROSE = ...
John Rose of New North Sound, Antigua, merchant. Will dated 11 Aug. and proved 8 Nov. 1711. (244 Young.)
Edward Rose, in 1720 heir-at-law.
Elizabeth Rose, mar. Richard Staples of Wapping; both living 1720.
Mary Rose, mar. John Stubbs of Nottingham; both living 1720.
Frances .... (? 1st wife, and bur. 3 April 1752 at St. John's).
John Ireland of St. John's Town 1753, Gent. (? bur. there 27 Sep. 1797).
Rebecca Bacon, mar. 15 Feb. 1753-4 at St. John's. Will dated 23 Oct. and sworn 2 Nov. 1787. 2nd wife.
Henrietta Fitzgerald, widow, mar. 7 March 1789 and bur. 2 Oct. 1799 at St. John's. (? 3rd wife.)
John Rose of Antigua, merchant, and Provost-Marshal General, living 1787.
Alice Ireland, bur. 14 Feb. 1786 at St. John's.
Rachel Ireland, living 1787.
Charles Winstone of Antigua, Esq., entered Gray's Inn 13 Aug. 1765; Solicitor-General of the Leeward Islands 1781.
John Ireland Rose, bapt. 7 June 1765 at St. John's.
Elizabeth Rose, mar. 30 March 1787 at St. John's.
Thomas Winston Rose, bapt. 26 Feb. 1768 at St. John's.
Rev. Daniel Warner Rose, born 15 Jan. 1769 and bapt. 7 Nov. 1770 at St. John's; educated at the Charterhouse and Jesus College, Cambridge.
Ann ....
Stephen Green Rose, bapt. 26 Aug. 1789 at St. John's.
John Rose, born 12 Feb. and bapt. 17 March 1798; died 19 Aug. 1838. M.I. at St. John's.
....
Seven children.
William Rose, born 10 Feb. and bapt. 3 March 1805 at St. John's.
Alice Eliza Rose, born 11 June and bapt. 29 Aug. 1792; mar. 6 Sep. 1810, at St. John's, John Brook Donaldson.
Charlotte Rose, born 10 and bapt. 24 June 1801; mar. 14 May 1818 Hon. Mead Home Daniell; she died 28 Jan. 1839, æt. 38; he died 6 Sep. 1852, æt. 73.
Winston Eliza Rose, born 13 Nov. 1802; died 25 Aug. 1806. M.I. at St. Luçea Churchyard, Hanover Parish, Jamaica.

John Rose of Antegoa, merchant. Will dated 11 Aug., proved 8 Nov. 1711 by Richard Staples; power reserved to the others. (244 Young.) To my loving brother Edward Rose, & my sister Mary Rose of Nottingham, & to my brother-in-law Rich[d] Staples of Wapping, & to their familys all my estate real & personal. Edw[d] Perrie, Esq., Tho. Kerby, & my brother Rich[d] Staples, & M[r] Edw[d] Chester, jun., all of Antigua, except Staples, Ex'ors, & they are to discharge my debt to M[r] John Hill, late of London, deceased. My dear friend M[r] Hopefor Bendall to aid my Ex'ors, & a suit of mourning. Witnessed by Daniel Mackinen, George Forrest, Eleazr. Allen.

Rebecca Ireland, wife of John Ireland of Antigua, Gent. Will dated 23 Oct. 1787. By Indenture of 16 Oct. 1769 between myself & husband & John Rose of Antigua, merchant, I can dispose of certain lands & slaves, & I give 3 slaves to my g[t] g[d]dau. Rebecca Greene (dau. of David Greene, now of N. America, merchant, & my gr[d]dau. Rebecca Greene), a negro to my gr[d]son Tho. Winstone Merrick, & all residue to John Rose on Trust to pay the profits to my husband for life, then to sell & pay all residue to my dau. Rachel Winstone, wife of Chas. Winstone, Esq., my grandson Tho. W. Merrick, & my gr[d]children, the sons & daus. of my late dau. Alice Rose by John Rose, equally. John Rose Ex'or. Witnessed by William Roberts, John Johnston. Before Sir Thomas Shirley was sworn William Roberts 2 Nov. 1787. Recorded 1 Feb. 1788.

Benjamin Ireland, planter. Will undated. To my wife Ann ½ my real estate, all furniture, plate, my horse, & whiskey, etc. To Susannah & Eliz. Jones of Mile End Green, sprs., £100 st. each. My brother W[m] Ireland £100 st. To Hannah Wood & Eliz. Warner, servants, who attended my dec[d] mother, £50 each. Tho. Brown, master of the ship "Margaret and Eliza," 10 gs. All residue to my father Benj. Ireland, late of Essex str., Strand, baker, & after his death to the children of my brother W[m] Ireland & Eliz. Hodgson. Recorded 22 Oct. 1793.

Richard Bowman. Will dated 22 Nov. 1797. To my wife Marg[t] negros. My dau. Ann Rose all residue. Witnessed by Archibald Douglas, James Cummings, Andrew McClure. Sworn and recorded 13 May 1800.

Eleanor Rose, wife of John Rose and widow of Muir. See her affidavit 2 Sep. 1799 to will of Henrietta Cook in the Smith Pedigree.

The will of Henrietta Ireland, widow, was recorded 5 Dec. 1799.

Indenture dated 30 Dec. 1710 between Robert Weir of Antigua, planter, and Mary his wife, of the 1 part, and John Rose of Antigua, merchant, of the other, the latter agrees to let his plantation in New North Sound to the former, late in the occupation of William Glanville of Antigua, merchant, for lease of twelve years at £300 a year.

Stephen Rose of Antigua, bur. 15 Nov. 1776 at St. John's. = Catherine, dau. of James Delap, merchant; mar. 30 May 1767 at St. John's.

William Warner Rose, bapt. 23 Oct. 1769 and bur. 9 Aug. 1796 at St. John's. = Elizabeth McPherson, mar. 5 March 1787 at St. John's.

Stephen Rose, bapt. 14 Oct. 1772 at St. John's. = Ann, only child and heir of Richard Bowman, whose will was dated 22 Nov. 1797 and sworn 13 May 1800; mar. 1794 at St. John's.

James Rose, bapt. 14 Nov. 1772 at St. John's.

Isaac Eccleston Rose, bapt. 12 and bur. 16 June 1776 at St. John's.

John Rose, bapt. 12 March 1779 at St. John's.

Margaret Carding Rose, bapt. 12 June 1776 and mar. 9 March 1793, at St. John's, John Roberts.

Isaac Eccleston Rose, born 16 April and bapt. 30 May 1789 at St. John's.

Alexander McPherson Rose, born 12 Aug. and bapt. 27 Dec. 1790 at St. John's.

Stephen Rose, born 18 Sep. and bapt. 20 Oct. 1795 at St. John's.

Richard Jacobs Rose, born 18 Oct. 1797; bapt. 13 March 1798 at St. John's.

George Bowman Rose, born 18 Jan. 1799; bapt. 15 Dec. 1800 at St. John's.

Stephen Thornhill Rose, born 19 Oct. and bapt. 19 Dec. 1804 at St. John's.

Horatio Nelson Rose, born 6 Jan. and bapt. 23 April 1806 at St. John's.

Edward Fitzroy Rose, born 18 March and bapt. 1 Aug. 1808 at St. John's.

Catherine Bowman Rose, born 4 Aug. and bapt. 22 Sep. 1796; mar. 30 Nov. 1816, at St. John's, Richard Piggott.

Mary Ann Rose, born 5 Dec. 1798; bapt. 6 Aug. 1799 and mar. 3 Dec. 1818, at St. John's, R. H. Mason.

Rebecca Clement Rose, born 4 Oct. 1802 and bapt. 21 Jan. 1803 at St. John's.

Joseph Warner Rose, bapt. 12 June 1773 at St. John's. = Harriet ....

Stephen Blizard Rose, bapt. 3 June 1776.

Alice Rose, bapt. 7 Nov. 1770 and bur. 15 April 1777 at St. John's.

Elizabeth Akers Rose, bapt. 12 March 1779 at St. John's.

Catherine Rose, bapt. 14 March 1760 at St. John's.

Anne Rose, bapt. 29 Nov. 1762 at St. John's.

Rebecca Rose, mar. 13 Nov. 1777, at St. John's, David Greene, who was in 1787 of North America, merchant.

Joseph Rose, born 15 Dec. 1802; bapt. 13 Jan. 1803 at St. John's.

John William Rose, born 31 May and bapt. 11 July 1810 and bur. 1 June 1811 at St. John's.

William Payne Rose, bapt. 12 and bur. 13 Oct. 1811 at St. John's.

Harriet Payne Rose, born 5 and bapt. 16 Feb. 1804 at St. John's.

Elizabeth Burling Rose, born 14 May and bapt. 4 Dec. 1807; bur. 3 July 1810 at St. John's.

Rebecca Green Rose, born 3 April 1809 and bapt. 11 July 1810 at St. John's.

Josephine Rose, born and bapt. 13 Feb. 1815 at St. John's.

Indenture dated 27 June 1720 between Edward Rose of Great Britain, brother and heir-at-law of John Rose of Antigua, merchant, and Richard Staples and Elizabeth his wife, sister of said John Rose, and John Stubbs and Mary Stubbs, also sister of John Rose, and Edward Chester, sen. Sale.

In Chancery. 31 Dec. 1723. Colonel Robert Weir *v.* Thomas Kerby, Ex'or of Rose.

1774. Mr. Stephen Rose, then printer of the 'Antigua Mercury.'

Parish Register of St. John.

Baptized.

1760	Mar. 14	Cathrine the D. of John Rose and Alice.
1762	Nov. 29	Ann the D. of John Rose and Alice his wife.
1765	June 7	John Ireland the S. of John Rose and Alice his wife.
1768	Feb. 26	Thomas Winston S. of John Rose and Alice his wife.
1769	Oct. 23	William Warner S. of Stephen Rose and Catharine his wife.
1770	Nov. 7	Daniel Warner the S. of John Rose and Alice his wife; b. the 15th day of January 1769.
1770	Nov. 7	Alice the D. of John Rose and Alice his wife; b. the 18th day of January 1770.
1772	Oct. 14	Stephen the S. of Stephen Rose and Catherine his wife.
1772	Nov. 14	James the S. of Stephen Rose and Catharine his wife.
1773	June 12	Joseph Warner the S. of John Rose & Alice his wife.
1776	June 3	Stephen Blizard the S. of John Rose & Alice his wife.
1776	June 12	Margaret Carding the D. of Stephen Rose & Catharine his wife.
1776	June 12	Isaac Eccleston the S. of Stephen Rose & Catharine his wife.
1779	Mar. 12	John the S. of Stephen Rose, dece'd, & Catharine his widow.
1779	Mar. 12	Elizabeth Akers the d. of John Rose & Alice his wife.
1789	May 30	Isaac Eccleston S. of William Warner Rose and Elizabeth his wife. B. the 16th April 1789.
1789	Aug. 26	Stephen Green S. of John Rose, Jun., and Elizabeth his wife. B. the 21st June 1789.
1790	Dec. 27	Alexander McPherson S. of William Warner Rose and Elizabeth his wife. B. the 12th August 1790.
1792	Aug. 29	Alice Eliza D. of John Rose, Junior, and Elizabeth his wife. B. the 11th June 1792.
1795	Oct. 20	Stephen S. of Stephen Rose and Ann his wife. B. the 18th September 1795.
1796	Sep. 22	Catherine Bowman D. of Stephen Rose and Ann his wife. B. the 4th August 1796.

1798 Mar. 13 Richard Jacobs S. of Stephen Rose and Ann his wife. B. the 18th October 1797.
1798 Mar. 17 John S. of John Rose, Jun., and Eliza his wife. B. the 12th February 1798.
1799 Aug. 6 Mary Ann D. of Stephen Rose and Ann his wife. B. the 5th December 1798.
1800 Dec. 15 George Bowman S. of Stephen Rose and Ann his wife. B. the 18th January last.
1801 June 24 Charlotte D. of John Rose, Jun., and Eliz. his wife. B. the 10th June 1801.
1802 Mar. 16 Elizabeth Jacobs D. of Stephen Rose and Ann his wife. B. the 21st August 1801.
1803 Jan. 13 Joseph S. of Joseph Warner Rose and Harriet his wife. B. the 15th December 1802.
1803 Jan. 21 Rebecca Clement D. of Stephen Rose and Ann his wife. B. the 4th October 1802.
1804 Feb. 16 Harriet Paine D. of Joseph Rose and Harriet his wife; b. 5 Instant.
1804 Dec. 19 Stephen Thornhill S. of Stephen Rose and Ann his wife; b. 19 Octr. last.
1805 Mar. 3 William S. of John Rose and Elizabeth his wife. B. the 10th of February 1805.
1806 April 23 Horatio Nelson S. of Stephen Rose and Ann his wife. B. the 6th January last.
1807 Dec. 4 Elizabeth Burling D. of Joseph Rose and Harriet his wife. B. the 14th May last.
1808 Aug. 1 Edward Fitzroy S. of Stephen Rose and Ann his wife. B. the 18th March last.
1810 July 11 Rebecca Green. B. the 3rd April 1809. John William. B. the 31st May last. } D. and S. of Joseph Warner Rose and Harriet his wife.
1811 Oct. 12 William Payne S. of Joseph Warner Rose and Harriet his wife. B. this day.
1815 Feb. 13 Josephine D. of Joseph Warner Rose and Henrietta his wife. B. this day.

Married.

1754 Feb. 14 John Ireland and Rebecca Bacon.
1767 May 30 Stephen Rose to Cathrine Delap. L.
1777 Nov. 13 David Greene to Rebeccah Rose. L.
1780 May 11 Samuel Jeaffreson to Ann Rose. L.
1785 Dec. 24 Benjamin Ireland to Ann Jones, Spr. L.
1787 Mar. 5 William Warner Rose to Elizabeth Macpherson, Spinster.
1787 Mar. 30 John Rose, Junior, to Elizabeth Rose.
1789 Mar. 7 John Ireland to Henrietta Fitzgerald, Widow. L.
1793 Mar. 9 John Roberts to Margaret Carden Rose, Spinster. L.
1794 [*blank*] Stephen Rose to Ann Bowman, Spinster. L.
1808 [*blank*] Nathaniel Donaldson to Elizabeth Rose, Widow. L.
1810 Sep. 6 John Brook Donaldson to Alice Eliza Rose, Spinster. L.
1816 Nov. 30 Richard Piggott to Catherine Bowman Rose, Spinster. L.
1818 May 14 The Honorable Meade Home Daniell to Charlotte Rose, Spinster. L.
1818 Dec. 3 Richard Holmes Mason to Mary Ann Rose, Spinster. L.

Buried.

1745-6 Feb. 21 John Ireland, a child.
1752 April 3 Frances Ireland, wife of John Ireland.
1766 June 9 Alexander Rose.
1773 Feb. 2 Charles Winstone Merrick.
1773 Feb. 10 James Rose.
1776 June 16 Isaac Eccleston Rose.
1776 Nov. 15 Stephen Rose.
1777 April 15 Alice Rose.
1785 Nov. 21 Anna Maria Ireland.
1786 Feb. 14 Alice Rose, Wife of John Rose, Esq.
1795 Mar. 1 John Rose, Junior.
1796 Aug. 9 William W. Rose.
1797 Sep. 27 John Ireland.
1799 Oct. 26 Henrietta Ireland.
1803 Jan. 23 Joseph Rose, Infant.
1803 Jan. 25 Rebecca Clement Rose, Infant.
1803 Dec. 9 Eleanor Rose.
1804 Feb. 2 John Rose.
1804 Dec. 6 Elizabeth Rose.
1808 Aug. 4 Edward Fitzroy Rose, Infant.
1808 Oct. 25 Horatio Nelson Rose, Infant.
1810 July 3 Elizabeth Burling Rose, Inf.
1811 June 1 John Wm Rose, Infant.
(? 1811 or 1812) Oct. 13 William Payne Rose, Infant.
„ . . . . 3 Ann Rose.
„ [*blank*] Stephen Rose.
1814 Oct. 9 Rebecca Rose, Infant.
1823 Aug. 16 John Rose.
1823 Dec. 11 Richard Rose.
1824 Dec. 6 Catherine Rose.

PARISH REGISTER OF ST. MARY.

On a scrap later than 1823:—

Buried the body of Mr Stephen Rose, a white man, aged about 37 years, at Valley ch. yard, March.

PARISH REGISTER OF ST. PAUL.

Buried.

1754 Aug. 27 Mr Henry Rose. First Lieutenant of his Majesties Ship the Advice.

PARISH REGISTER OF ST. PHILIP.

Baptized.

1834 April 27 Leonora Arabella d. of John & Mary Martin Rose. Sandersons. Planter.

ST. JOHN'S CHURCHYARD.

On a ledger over brick vault:—

AS A TOKEN OF LOVE
NO LENGTH OF TIME CAN ALTER
THIS STONE
IS PLACED OVER AN AFFECTIONATE HUSBAND
WHO HAS LEFT
A WIDOW AND SEVEN YOUNG CHILDREN
WHO LAMENT A LOSS NEVER TO BE REPLACED
JOHN ROSE BORN 12 FEBRUARY 1798
DEPARTED THIS LIFE 19 AUGUST 1838

(Three lines follow.)

On a marble ledger over brick vault:—

HERE LIES THE BODY OF
ELIZABETH ROSE
WHO DEPARTED THIS LIFE ON THE
FIRST DAY OF JULY ANNO DOMINI 1832
AGED 50.

ST. LUCEA CHURCHYARD, HANOVER PARISH, JAMAICA.

HERE LIES THE BODY OF WINSTON ELIZA ROSE THE DAUGHTER OF THE REVD. D. W. ROSE BY ANN HIS WIFE, BORN 13 NOV., 1802; AND DIED 25TH AUGUST, 1806.

(Eight lines follow.)

(Archer's 'M.I. in the West Indies.')

THE REVD. DANIEL WARNER ROSE, SON OF JNO. ROSE, PROVOST MARSHAL GENL. OF ANTIGUA, WAS EDUCATED AT CHARTER HO., LONDON, & JESUS COLL., CAMB. (*Ibid.*)

Pedigree of Rossington.

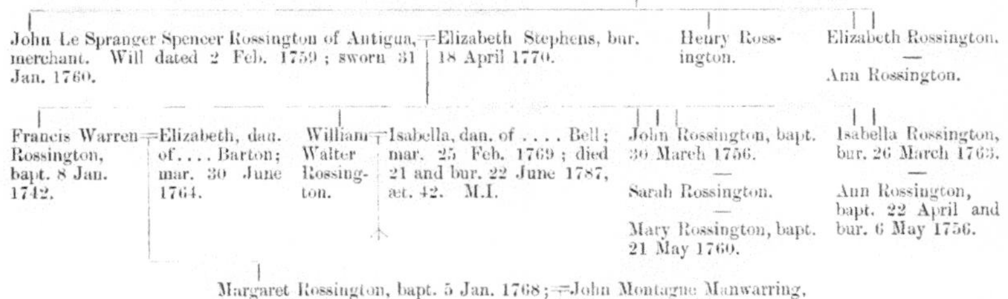

FRANCIS ROSSINGTON of Mallow, Ireland=Elizabeth . . . .

John Le Spranger Spencer Rossington of Antigua, merchant. Will dated 2 Feb. 1759; sworn 31 Jan. 1760.=Elizabeth Stephens, bur. 18 April 1770. | Henry Rossington. | Elizabeth Rossington. — Ann Rossington.

Francis Warren Rossington, bapt. 8 Jan. 1742.=Elizabeth, dau. of . . . . Barton; mar. 30 June 1764. | William Walter Rossington.=Isabella, dau. of . . . . Bell; mar. 25 Feb. 1769; died 21 and bur. 22 June 1787, æt. 42. M.I. | John Rossington, bapt. 30 March 1756. — Sarah Rossington. — Mary Rossington, bapt. 21 May 1760. | Isabella Rossington, bur. 26 March 1763. — Ann Rossington, bapt. 22 April and bur. 6 May 1756.

Margaret Rossington, bapt. 5 Jan. 1768;=John Montague Manwarring, mar. 24 March 1787. Ensign 67th Regiment.

John L. Spranger Spencer Rossington of Antigna, merchant. Will dated 2 Feb. 1759. To my wife Eliz. Stephens Rossington all my furniture, linen, plate, jewels. To my dear father Francis Rossington of Mallow in Ireland £100 st., but if dead to my mother Elizth Rossington, & if dead to my 2 sisters Elizth & Ann Rossington. To my wife Elizth S. Rossington & my 6 chⁿ, viz., Francis Warren Rossington, Wm Walter Rossington, Jno Rossington, Sarah Rossington, Mary Rossington, & Isabella Rossington, all residue equally, the two youngest not yet baptised. My brother Henry Rossington. I appoint my good friends Nathl Gilbert, Esq., Wm Mackinen, Fra. Farley, & Wm Warner, Esq^{res}, Ex'ors & Guardians. Witnessed by John Webb, John Lindsey, jun., Abraham Marshall. Before Governor Thomas appeared John Webb and John Lindsey, jun., and were sworn 31 Jan. 1760. Recorded 14 April 1760.

Parish Register of St. John.

Baptized.

1742	Jan. 8	Francis Warren s. of John La Spranger Spencer Rossington and Elizabeth his wife.
1750	Sep. 14	Sarah D. of John Le Sprainger Spencer Rossington and Elizabeth his wife.
1756	April 22	Ann the d. of Jno Le Spraing^r Spenc^r Rossington & Eliz. his wife.
1756	Mar. 30	John the S. of John Le Spraing^r Spenc^r Rossington & Eliz. his wife.
1760	May 21	Mary the D. of John Le Spranger Spencer Rossington and his wife.
1768	Jan. 5	Margrett D. of Francis Warren Rossington & Elizabeth his wife.

Married.

1764	June 30	Francis Warring Rossington to Eliz. Barton.
1769	Feb. 25	William Walter Rossington to Isabella Bell.
1787	Mar. 24	John Montague Manwarring (Ensign of 67th Reg^t) to Margaret Rossington, Spinster; by Lic.

Buried.

1745	Nov. 17	John Rossington.
1756	May 6	Ann Rossington, a Child.
1763	Mar. 26	Isabella Rossington (child).
1770	April 18	Elizabeth Rossington, Widow.
1772	Aug. 15	Thomas Rossington.
1787	June 22	Isabella Rossington.

Parish Register of St. George.

Buried.

1769	[*blank*]	Henry Rosington.

St. John's Churchyard.

On a ledger:—

Here lieth the Body
of
ISABELLA ROSSINGTON
who departed this life
on the 21st day of June
1787
Aged 42 Years
And
Near this . . . . lieth the Body
of
THOMAS BELL
. . . .
Brother to the above named
ISABELLA ROSSINGTON who died
the 21st day of April
1779
Aged 29 Years.

Pedigree of Royall.

ARMS.—*Azure, three garbs, two and one, or.*

WILLIAM RYALL, cooper, settled at Salem in 1629; was at Casco Bay 1635; removed 1675 to Dorchester, Mass., where he died 15 June 1676. ═ Phœbe, dau. of Mrs. Margaret Greene, widow; died 16 July 1678.

William Royall of North Yarmouth and Dorchester, carpenter, died 7 Nov. 1724, æt. 84. M.I. ═ Mary ....

Elizabeth, dau. of Asaph Eliot and widow of .... Oliver; born 1 Feb. 1679-80; mar. 1 July 1697 at Boston. 1st wife. ═ Isaac Royall, born 1672; settled as a merchant at Boston, later at Antigua; in 1732 purchased Governor Usher's estate of 500 acres at Medford for £10,350; died there 7 June and bur. 16 June 1739 at Dorchester. Will dated 27 Dec. 1738; sworn 9 July 1739. Recorded at Antigua. ═ Elizabeth, dau. of .... mar. Isaac Royall 1707 at St. John's; died 21 April 1747 at Medford; bur. at Dorchester from the house of Dr. Oliver. Will dated 4 April 1747. 2nd wife. ═ James Brown of Antigua. 1st husband.

Asaph Royall, born in Boston 1 May and died 24 July 1699; bur. at Dorchester.

John Royall, bapt. 15 Jan. 1712 at St. John's.

Elizabeth Royall, bapt. 30 June 1709 at St. John's.

Isaac Royall, bapt. 23 Sep. 1719 at St. John's; J.P. 1753; Member of Council for Mass. 1751—74; in 1761 Brigadier-General of the Artillery Company at Boston; his estates were confiscated by the rebels; died in London Oct. 1781. Will dated 26 May 1778. ═ Elizabeth McIntosh, mar. 27 March 1738; died 14 July 1770 at Medford; bur. at Dorchester.

Penelope Royall, bapt. 10 Sep. 1724 at St. John's; mar. 28 Jan. 1742 Colonel Henry Vassall of Cambridge, Mass.; he died there 17 March 1769; she died at Boston 19 Nov. 1800, æt. 76.

Elizabeth Royall, born 7 June 1740; died 9 July 1747.

Mary McIntosh Royall, born 10 Jan. 1744-5; mar. 4 Jan. 1775 George Erving of Boston, merchant. She died 11 Nov. 1786, æt. 42. M.I. at Froyle, co. Hants. He died in London 1806, æt. 70.

Elizabeth Royall, born 30 Oct. 1747; mar. 12 Nov. 1767; died at sea 8 Oct. 1775. ═ Sir William Pepperell Sparhawk of Kittery, Maine; owner of Royalls, Antigua; created Baronet 29 Oct. 1774; died in London 18 Dec. 1816, æt. 70.

William Royall Pepperell, only son, born 5 July 1775; matric. from Christ Church, Oxford, 18 Feb. 1794, æt. 18; died a bachelor 27 Sep. 1798 at Cowes, Isle of Wight.

Elizabeth Royall Pepperell, born 17 April 1769; mar. Rev. Henry Hutton; living 1814.

Mary Hirst McIntosh Pepperell, born 2 Nov. 1771; mar. 11 July 1799 Sir William Congreve of Aldermaston, co. Berks; she died 3 Feb. 1839.

Harriet Pepperell, born 17 Dec. 1773; mar. 14 July 1802, at St. Marylebone, Sir Charles Thomas Hudson, Bart., of Wanlip Hall, co. Leicester.

Isaack Royal of Charlestown, New England. Will dated 27 Dec. 1738. To my dau.-in-law Ann, wife of Robt Oliver of Antigua, now in New Engld, 2 negros & their 10 children. To my wife Elizth Royal the use of all plate, furniture, 2 negros, my chariot & horses, & after her death to my son Isaac & my dau. Penelope equally. To my dau. Penelope 2 negros & their 6 children & £200 c. yearly till 21, also ½ my estate in Antigua. To my son Isaac the other ½ of my estate, also all my lands in Prov. of Maine, N.E., & in Massachusetts Bay between Springfield & Hadley. To my sister Mary Bird £20 c. To my sister Martha, widow of Benjn China (*sic*, ? Cheney) of Dorchester, £20 c. To my sister Sarah Dunton £20 a yr for life. To my brother Saml Royal release debts. All residue, including my land & houses in Charlestown, with the negros & cattle, also 40 acres in Medford purchased of Mr John Foye of Charlestown, & a wood purchased of Capt Isaac Dupee in Woburne, & a farm in township of Stoughton, & a farm in Freetown Co., Bristol, where my bro. Saml Royal now lives, to my brother Jacob Royal of Boston, mercht, in trust for my son Isaac Royal for life & his heirs, & in default to my dau. Penelope, her heirs in such case to take my sirname, then to Wm, his sons, Saml Winthorp, Jacob, Elia, sons of my bro. Saml Royall, successively. My wife Elizth Royal, now in Charlestown, Ex'trix in New England & Antigua, & in Antigua Tho. Watkins & Jacob Thibou, & in New England my bro. Jacob Royal, Wm Taylor, and Edmund Quincey, mercht, of Boston, Ex'ors & Guardians. Witnessed by Simon Tuffs, Benjamin Wills, Randall Stuart, Mass. Bay. Copy sworn to 9 July 1739. Recorded at Antigua 5 Nov. 1739.

Isaac Royall, late of Medford, co. Middlesex, in the province of Massachusetts Bay, New England, now of Kensington, co. Middlesex, in England. Will dated 26 May 1778; proved 15 Nov. 1781 by Sir W. Pepperell, Bart. (553 Webster.) I left Medford 16 April 1775. My estates in Mass., also one in Antigua, I disposed of by a will dated 12 Jan. 1775 & another 11 May 1776 at Halifax. To my uncle Sam[l] Royall 5 guineas a year. M[rs] Abigail Royall, wife of my late uncle Jacob Royall, Esq., dec[d], 5 guineas a year. My kinswoman Sarah Clark, wife of Jonas Clark, merchant, 3 guineas a year. Rebecca, wife of Jos. Thomson, kinswoman to my late wife, £3. My Ex'ors D[r] Simon Tofts, Oliver Wendall, & Francis Dana, Esq[res], £10 each. Rev[d] Sam[l] Cook of Cambridge, N. Eng., & the church of Medford £10. Rev. M[r] Turill & Rev[d] M[r] Osgood, Hon. D[r] Winthorpe, professor of Mathematics in Cambridge & President of Harvard Coll., & my friends the Hon. John Owing & James Bowden, & Jeremiah Powell, Esq., of Boston, & M[r] Willis Hall, M[r] Seth Sweetzer of Charles Town, & Chas. Pelham, Esq., of Newtown, gold mourning rings; likewise to Lady Dowager Pepperell, & my sister M[rs] Eliz. Sparrowhawk at Kittery, & my kinswoman Hannah Potter, wife of Col[o] Potter of Bristol, N.E. My attorney D[r] Simon Tufts & his 1st dau. Lucy Tufts, my kinsmen Jacob Royall & W[m] Royall, sons of my uncle Samuel, Jacob Cheney, son of my late aunt Cheney, heirs of Allen Cary, late of Bristol, N.E., & Jonathan Sawton of Freetown, N.E., forgive debts. To my dau. Mary M[c]Intosh Erving, wife of the Hon. Geo. Erving, Esq., a gold box with my father's picture, ½ my library, my chariot & chaise. The other ½ of my library to my granddau. Eliz. Royall Pepperell. To my grandson W[m] Pepperell, son of Sir W[m] Pepperell, my own & my late wife's pictures, & those of M[r] Thos. Palmer & his own parents. All my estate in the Island of Antigua to be sold,

[*Continued below.*

Isaac Royall of Dorchester, carpenter, bur. 17 Jan. 1729, aged=. . . . Waitestill, died 29 Nov. 1732. 2nd wife.

Waitestill Royall, 3rd dau., bapt. 26 July 1685 at Dorchester; mar. 9 Sep. 1708, at St. John's, Antigua, Captain John Haddon.

Robert Royall, 4th son, carpenter, born 12 Jan. 1687-8 at Dorchester; died 1757. = Mercy, dau. of Ebenezer Billings; born 22 June 1687; died 29 Jan. 1773 at Dorchester.

Ann Brown, mar. 3 Feb. 1721-2 at St. John's; living 1738. = Robert Oliver, Esq., 3rd son of Hon. Colonel Richard Oliver of Antigua; in 1738 purchased lands at Dorchester, Mass., for £2515; in 1747 leased his 148 acres at Popeshead, Antigua, to Isaac Royall and Henry Vassall for seven years; died *circa* 1762 at Dorchester. Will dated 3 Aug. 1761. Recorded at Boston.

Joseph Royall, born 13 May 1721 at Dorchester; in 1778 of Portman Street, and late of Jamaica; died in Great Cumberland Street 3 June 1814, æt. 93. = Catherine, sister of John Morse.

Miriam Royall, mar. 23 Dec. 1773 Thomas Savel, and had issue.

Thomas Oliver of Cambridge, Mass., Esq., born 5 Jan. 1733-4 at Antigua; B.A. Harvard 1753; Lieut.-Governor of Mass. 1774; his estates were confiscated by the rebels; died at Bristol, England, 1815, æt. 83.

Isaac Oliver.

Richard Oliver.

& out of the proceeds £200 to my son-in-law Sir Wm Pepperell, 20 guineas to Tho. Palmer, Esq., & to my sons-in-law Sir Wm Pepperell & Geo. Erving, Esq., my sister Penelope Vassall & my nieces Eliz. her dau., wife of Dr Chas. Russell, & to Eliz. Vassall, wife of John Vassall, Esq., to my nephews his Honour Tho. Oliver, Richard Oliver, & Tho. Palmer, Esq[res], my kinsman Joseph Royall, Esq., late of Jamaica, now of Portman Street, £10 each. My late dau. Lady Pepperell. My friends the Hon. Tho. Pownall, Joseph Paice, Daniel Leonard, Tho. Danforth, & Tho. Brattle, Esq[res], now in Eng., mourning rings. Of the residue of the proceeds of the sale ½ to my dau. Mary M[c]Intosh Erving, £500 to my granddau. Eliz. Royall Pepperell, & then the remainder to the 4 children of my late dau. Pepperell, viz., Eliz. Royall Pepperell, Mary Hirst M[c]Intosh Pepperell, Harriot Pepperell, & W[m] Pepperell. My estate in Bristol, colony of Rhode Island, called Mount Hope Farm, of 375 acres, to my granddau. Eliz. Royall Pepperell. To the Town of Medford 100 acres in the township of Grandby, formerly known as South Hadley, towards the erection of a free school, & the remainder of the tract, about 8 or 900 acres, & 978 acres in co. Worc., which I bought of the Mass. Bay colony on 28 Dec. 1752 in company with the Hon. James [*blank*], Esq., John Chandler, Esq., & Capt. Caleb Daney, to Harvard Coll. for the endowment of a professorship of laws. My kinsman Jacob Royall 100 acres, lot 105, in Royallsborough, co. Cumb., Mass., & to his son Isaac Royall. My kinsman W[m] Royall 100 acres in ditto, lot 104. To Isaac Royall, son of my kinsman Samuel Winthorpe Royall, 100 acres in ditto. The residue of the said lands in Royallsborough, & in cos. Cumb. & Linc., & in Royallston, co. Worc., to my 3 grandchildren Mary Hirst M[c]Intosh Pepperell, Harriot Pepperell, & W[m] Pepperell. To my granddau. Harriot Pepperell 4 lotts in Medford. All other my real estate, my mansion-house in Medford, co. Midx., & my lands in Stoughton, co. Suffolk, to D[r] Simon Tofts of Medford, my kinsmen Joseph Royall, Esq., late of Jamaica, & Tho. Palmer, Esq., late of Boston, now supposed to be in Surinam, in trust for my dau. Mary M[c]Intosh Royall, wife of Geo. Erving, Esq.; remainder to my grandchildren W[m] Pepperell, Eliz. Royall Pepperell, Mary Hirst M[c]Intosh Pepperell, & Harriot Pepperell, then to Eliz. Russell, W[m] Royall & his brothers Jacob Royall & Sam[l] Winthorpe Royall, Elia Royall, Joseph Royall, late of Jamaica, & in default of issue ½ for a hospital in co. Midx. & ½ to Harvard College. My tomb in Dorchester. Of the residue of my est., both real & pers., ¼ to my dau. Mary & ¾ to my 3 granddaus. Eliz. Royall Pepperell, Mary Hirst

McIntosh Pepperell, & Harriot Pepperell. My son-in-law Sir Wm Pepperell, my neph. Tho. Palmer, Esq., & Joseph Royall, Esq., Ex'ors for Antigua & Great Britain; Dr Simon Tufts, Oliver Wendall, & Francis Dana, Esq^{res}, for New England. Witnessed by Richard Taylor, James Belher Ball, John Rawling, jun., Thomas Butts.

Codicil. 31 Dec. 1779. The Hon. James Borodoine, Esq., & Mr Willis Hall, merchant in Medford, to be Ex'ors for New Eng. To my kinswoman Hannah Potter, wife of Simeon Potter, Esq., in Bristoll, Rhode Island. 200 acres, lot 18, in Royallston to Medford for a free school; lot 104 of 200 acres to Harvard Coll.; lot 1 of 200 acres in ditto to Isaac Royall, son of Saml Winthorpe Royall in N. Yarmouth. Witnessed by John Fosbrook, James Bechel Hall, William Dalley, Thomas Butts.

John Morse in his will proved 1781 (204 Webster) names Joseph Royall of Portman Street, Esq., his Ex'or, and "my sister Cath. Royall."

Joseph Royall of Great Cumberland Street, London, Esq. Will dated 25 May and proved 25 June 1814. (373 Bridport.) To Mrs Mary Hirst Congreve, wife of Wm Congreve, Esq., £4000. To Mrs Eliz. Royall Hutton, wife of Rev. Mr Hutton, £4000. All my estates in trust for Kath., wife of Fra. Geo. Smyth of Temple Druid, co. Pemb., now of Upper Brook Str., & to her dau. Cath. Smyth. Adm'on 1854 to said Dame Harriet Cath. Capel, formerly Cath. Smyth, the dau.

1710, Jan. 3. Justice Royall was accused by the Assembly of fomenting disturbances. After the death of Governor Parke he was very active in obtaining depositions, etc., in his favour. He wrote a long letter from Antigua 23 April 1711 to his friend Michael Ayon. (America and West Indies, No. 52, fo. 149.)

1712, Jan. 5. Isaack Royall, Esq., granted 6 acres at Popeshead by Governor Walter Hamilton. For further details of this family see 'The New England Royalls, by Edward Doubleday Harris, a reprint (1885) from the New England Hist. and Gen. Reg., with additions'; also the 'Herald and Genealogist,' vol. iii., p. 430, for an engraving of the shield from the tomb at Dorchester, Mass.

1712, Aug. 9. Major Royal was confined to the Fort for reporting "that he heard Your Excellency say certain words reflecting on your honour."

1754. Sir Wm. Pepperell Bart. Col. of a 2^d Reg^t of foot to be raised in America. ('Gent. Mag.,' p. 484.)

1789, Nov. 25. At Kittery, in New England, Lady Pepperell, widow of the late Sir Wm. P. bart. (who commanded his Majesty's troops at the conquest of Louisbourg, in 1745,) and grandmother to the present Sir Wm. P. (*Ibid.*, p. 179.)

1798, Sep. 27. At West Cowes, in the Isle of Wight, William Royall Pepperell, esq. the only son of Sir Wm. P. bart. of Upper Seymour-str. (*Ibid.*, p. 909.)

1802, July 14. At St Mary-la-Bonne, Charles Thomas Hudson, esq. eldest son of Sir Charles Grave H. bart. of Wanlip-hall co. Leicester, to Miss Pepperell, youngest dau. of Sir Thos. P. bart. of Dorset-street, Portman-squ. (*Ibid.*, p. 685.)

1814, June 3. In Great Cumberland-street, aged 93, Joseph Royall, esq. (*Ibid.*, p. 699.)

1816, Dec. 18. In Dorset-street, Portman-square, universally regretted, aged 70, Sir Wm Pepperell, bart. He was created a baronet Oct. 29, 1774. He married in 1767, Elizabeth daughter of the Hon. Isaac Royall, of his Majesty's Council in Massachusetts Bay, Esq. and by her had three daughters and a son who died in 1798. The title is extinct. (*Ibid.*, p. 573.)

1839, Feb. 3. At Tunbridge Wells, Mary, wife of William Congreve, esq. of Aldermaston-House, Berks, dau. of the late Sir W. Pepperell, Bart. ('Gent. Mag.,' p. 331.)

The following description of the Royall mansion (Hobgoblin Hall) at Medford, Mass., has been taken from 'Our Colonial Homes,' by Samuel Adams Drake. This house stands at the left side of the old Boston road not half a mile out of the village. "The grounds, once laid out in most correct taste, were separated from the highway by a low brick wall. From the gateway, flanked by tall wooden columns, a broad avenue, bordered with aromatic box, led straight up to the house, situated at some seventy paces back from the road. The space between was embellished with shrubbery, fruit, and shade trees. To the right as you looked toward the mansion was the driveway, with a massive stone gatepost of imposing size standing at either side .... Imagine a very large, three-story brick house, sheathed entirely in wood, except at one end, and having, as is customary when the upper story is lower studded, the upper tier of windows smaller than those underneath them. All the spaces below the windows of the east front, toward which I was looking, were filled in with panels, so that from ground to cornice the windows rose in the form of columns .... Sufficient unto himself, no doubt, with his gardens, his slaves, and his rich wines, was the old Antigua merchant, Isaac Royall, who came in 1737 from his tropical home, bringing his tropical habits with him, to rear what passed for a palace in his day, in the country village, for such he found it. Isaac Royall the first, the author of this charming country-seat, soon died, and was succeeded by Isaac the second, who inherited the five hundred paternal acres, "turf and twig," with the mansion, human chattels, and other worldly possessions of his deceased sire.

"The carriage-drive terminated at the back of the mansion in a court-yard paved with small, smooth beach stones, through the interstices of which the grass grew thickly. To the right of the drive were the stables, while just beyond the house were the slave-quarters, fronting on the court-yard, which was thus enclosed upon three of its sides. The two-story brick building occupied by the negroes was still remaining, the last visible relic of slavery in New England. The deep fire-place in which the blacks had prepared their food was still there .... On the fourth side of the court-yard there rose a high brick wall, similar to that already mentioned, which opened by an arched gate-way into another beautiful garden, in which some of the old box-trees and clumps of lilacs were still growing here and there. A gravelled walk led to the farther end of the garden, where an artificial mound with two terraces had been raised to make a base for a summer-house on which a dilapidated figure of Mercury, *minus* wings and arms, was poised, unable to fly, unwilling to fall. The garden front of the house overlooked this enclosure, evidently the favorite resort of the family in the cool of the evening. The summer house, a veritable curiosity, displayed much beauty of design, with its panels, its fluted pilasters, and its bell-shaped roof. An artist made the plan for this little structure, now so delightfully ruinous and picturesque. There was a trap-door in the floor, which, when raised, disclosed a cellar, formerly used for the storage of ice, so that beauty and utility were here combined.

"The Royall mansion was modelled after that of a nobleman at Antigua ...."

After the battle of Lexington Isaac Royall retired to Boston, and later he "seems to have fully made up his mind to go back to Antigua, but had too long delayed. He now took passage for Halifax; and finally, when Howe, with his long train of refugees, arrived from Boston, he also departed for England, and there died, sighing for his beautiful home in America, and striving to the last, though always unsuccessfully, to avert the forfeiture of his estate

. . . . Lingering in the entrance hall only long enough to admire the elaborately carved balusters and the panelled wainscot, I first passed into the suite of apartments at the right, the reception-rooms proper of the house. These rooms were separated by an arch, in which sliding doors were conceiled; and from floor to ceiling the walls were panelled in wood, the panells being of single pieces, some of which were a full yard in breadth. In the rear of these apartments, and opening to the north, were two alcoves, each flanked by fluted pilasters, on which rested an arch set off with mouldings and carved ornaments . . . .

"The second floor was furnished with four chambers, all opening on one spacious and airy hall. Of these, the north-west room only demands special description, because it was the best. It had alcoves similar to those already mentioned in the apartments below; only, instead of panelling, the walls were covered over above the wainscot with hangings of leather, stamped in gorgeous colors of red, green, and bright gold, with flowers, birds and beasts of Chinese creation. On this side only were seen the original windows, with their heavy frames and small panes, the kitchen, with its enormous brick oven, still in perfect repair, and its iron chimney-back, handsomely embossed with the Royall arms."

In the same book is an illustration of the Pepperell mansion at Kittery on the sea coast of Maine, where Sir William Pepperell, 1st Bart., the conqueror of Louisburg, lived and died. Until the death of the elder Pepperell in 1734 this house was occupied by his own and his son's families. The lawn in front reached quite down to the water, and an avenue of ¾ mile in length skirted by trees led all the way to the house of Colonel Sparhawk, a little east of the village church. It used to be said that Sir William could ride to the Saco, 30 miles distant, without going off his own possessions. By his will he made the son of his daughter Elizabeth and Colonel Sparhawk his residuary legatee. The latter took the name of Pepperell, and was created a Baronet; as a loyalist he went to England in 1775, and had his estates confiscated. In Longfellow's Cambridge mansion there is, or was, a portrait of two children, William and Elizabeth Royall Pepperell, by Copley. A picture of the victor of Louisburg, painted by Smibert in 1751, is in the Essex Institute at Salem. His tomb is at Kittery.

Parish Register of St. John.

Baptized.

1709 June 30 Eliz. D. of Isaac Royall & Eliz[a] his wife.
1712 Jan. 15 John s. of Isaac Royall & Eliz[a] his wife.
1719 Sep. 23 Isaac s. of Isaac Royall & his wife.
1724 Sep. 10 Penelope the d. of Isaac Royall & Eliz[th] his wife.

Married.

1707 (? June) 3 Isaac Royall & Elizabeth Browne. Lyc. from Generall Parke.
1708 Sep. 9 John Haddon & M[rs] Waitestill Royall.
1766 Aug. 2 W[m] Royall to Eliz. Lee. L.
1792 April 12 John Foster to Barbara Royal, Spinster. L.

Buried.

1724 Sep. 10 Eliz. D. of Isaac Royall.
1724 Nov. 8 George Royall.
1786 Sep. 5 William Royal.
1800 Nov. 28 Elizabeth Royal.

Parish Register of St. Paul.

Baptized.

c. 1773—1775 Barbara D. of Will[m] and Elizabeth Royall.

Dorchester, Mass.

On a slab over the Royall tomb in the burial-ground:—

Here lyeth y[e] Body of WILL[M] ROYALL
of North Yarmouth in the PROVINCE
of MAIN, who departed this Life
Nov[bre] y[e] 7th 1724, in y[e] 85th year of his Age.
this Stone is Erected in ye Pious memory
of his Father by his Eldest Son ISAAC
as the last Act of a dutifull remembrance.

On another tomb:—

Arms: . . . . *three garbs* . . . .

Here lyes the Body
of the Honble ISAAC ROYALL Esq.
who departed this Life at his Seat in Charlestown
June ye 7th Anno Dom[ni] 1739 Ætatis 67.
He was a Gent[n] of Superiour natural powers & great
acquired knowledge
Civil affable, courteous & Just to all Men
Dutiful to his Parents,
Kind to his Relations & Charitable to ye poor
He was a faithfull Husband, a tender Father, a kind Master,
and a True Friend
Delighted in doing good.
He was highly esteemed & respected during his residence at
Antigua |
which was near 40 years.
And advanced to y[e] most Honorable and important Public
employments Civil & military
which he discharged with y[e] highest reputation & fidelity.
He returned with his Family to New England His Native
Country |
July 27th 1737
Where his death which soon followed was greatly lamented
by all who knew Him
But as He Lived a Virtuous Life
So He was removed by a peaceful Death.
Leaving a SON & DAUGHTER
To inherit a plentifull Fortune which He was Bles'd with
At His desire His Remains were here
Interred with his Parents For whom He Erected This
MONUMENT.

Froyle, co. Hants.

On an achievement in the chancel:—

Arms: *Argent, a chevron gules between three pineapples vert, on a canton gules a fleur-de-lis argent* (Pepperell). *On an escocheon of pretence: Azure, three garbs, two and one, or* (Royall).

Crest: *Out of a mural crown argent, with three laurel-leaves proper in the embrasures, an arm embowed, holding a banner argent.*

Motto: *Peperi.*

The achievement of Sir William Pepperell, Bart. He was Governor of New England, and married one of the daughters and coheirs of Isaac Royall, Esq., of New England, but of a Scotch family. Lady Pepperell's mother was a coheiress of the Highland family of McIntosh. The wife of W. Congreve, Esq., of Aldermaston, co. Berks, was a daughter of Sir William Pepperell.

In the churchyard is a railed monument to:—

Isaac Royall, Esq., late of Medford, in New England, who died Oct. 16, 1781, aged 62, as also of his daughter Mary McIntosh, wife of George Erving, late of Boston, in New England, Esq., died Nov. 11, 1786, aged 42.

('Collectanea Top. et Gen.,' vol. viii., p. 216.)

Pedigree of Russell.

ARMS.—*On a bend . . . . three swans . . . .*

. . . . RUSSELL ═ . . . .

Frances, 2nd dau. of Edmund Kaynell of Haslebury, co. Dorset (*sic* Le Neve); he was living 1677. 1st wife. ═ Lieut.-Colonel Randal Russell, settled in 1637 at St. Kitts under Sir Thomas Warner; Deputy-Governor of Nevis 1668; his death announced 29 June 1678. Will dated 17 March 1677; proved 30 June 1683. (76 Drax.) ═ Margaret . . . . 2nd wife.

Sir James Russell, Knt., Governor of Nevis 1632—71; knighted 10 May 1672; died 15 Nov. 1674, æt. 74; bur. and M.I. at St. James's, Bristol. Will dated 6 Nov. and proved 10 Dec. 1674. (147 Bunce.) ═ Margaret Hunt, sister of Robert Hunt; bur. Sep. 1677 at St. James's, Bristol, intestate.

Colonel Sir James Russell, Knt., 1st son and heir; heir to his uncle Sir James Russell; Member of Council, Nevis, 1672. Will dated 16 July 1687; proved 4 July 1688. (99 Exton.) ═ Penelope, dau. of Sir Timothy Tyrrell of Shotover, Knt.; mar. 13 Jan. 1675 at Camberwell, co. Surrey; died in London 3 Dec. 1707.

Valentine Russell, matriculated from Trinity College, Oxford, 4 Nov. 1673, aged 15; Secretary of Nevis 1678; Member of Council of Antigua 1680; dead 1713. ═ Mary, dau. of Colonel Philip Warner, Deputy-Governor of Antigua; (?) mar. 1677.

Elizabeth Russell, 1st dau. and coheir; living 1687.

Frances Russell, 2nd dau. and coheir, mar. 1st, her first-cousin, Sir William Stapleton, 2nd Bart., of Nevis. His will was dated 6 Dec. 1699 and proved 14 March 1700. (43 Dyer.) She mar. 2ndly, Walter Hamilton, Captain-General of the Leeward Islands. His will was dated 16 April 1722 and proved 22 Feb. 1723. (29 Richmond.) Her will was dated at Cheltenham 17 Oct. 1743 and proved 26 March 1746. (100 Edmunds.)

Colonel Martin Madan of Hertingfordbury, co. Herts; a minor 1703; M.P. for Wooton Bassett 1747—54; died 1756. Will dated 23 Oct. 1750; proved 22 March 1756. (75 Glazier.) ═ Judith, dau. of Mr. Justice Spencer Cowper, uncle of Earl Cowper; mar. Dec. 1723; living 1756.

James Russell Madan.

Rev. Martin Madan, 1st son and heir; matriculated from Christ Church, Oxford, 9 Feb. 1742-3, æt. 17; B.A. 1746; Barrister-at-Law Inner Temple 1748; died at Epsom 2 May, æt. 63, and bur. 8 May 1790 at Kensington. Will dated 4 April 1778; proved 12 May 1790. (252 Bishop.) ═ Jane, 2nd dau. of Sir Bernard Hale of King's Walden, co. Herts.

Right Rev. Spencer Madan, D.D., entered Westminster School 1742; B.A. Cambridge 1749; Bishop of Bistol 1791, then of Peterborough 1794; died 8 Nov. 1813, æt. 85, at the Palace, Peterborough. (See 'Gent. Mag.,' vol. 83.) ═ Lady Charlotte, 2nd dau. of the 1st Earl of Cornwallis; mar. 1756; died 11 March 1794 at Bath, æt. 68. M.I. in Worcester Cathedral. (See 'Gent. Mag.,' vol. 75.) 1st wife.

Rev. Spencer Madan, D.D.; M.A. Cambridge 1779; Rector of Thorpe, co. Stafford, 1809, and of Ibstock, co. Leicester, 1832; Chancellor and Prebendary of Peterborough.

William Charles Madan, Colonel in the Army.

Charlotte Madan, only dau.; mar. 1781 General George Ward of Woodland Castle, co. Glamorgan; she died 29 Aug. 1832, æt. 75.

Captain John Russell of Antigua, bur. 28 Oct. 1732 ═ Gertrude . . . .

. . . . Fletcher. 1st husband. ═ Mary Russell. Will dated 29 Oct. and sworn 27 Nov. 1747. ═ William Spencer, shoemaker, bur. 15 Nov. 1727. 2nd husband.

Gertrude Russell, bur. 3 May 1720.

Charles Russell. ═ Eliza Ervin, mar. 4 Aug. 1715.

Anthony Fletcher, living 1747.

William Spencer, bur. 5 April 1725.

Russell Spencer, bapt. 13 June 1726.

Dorothy Spencer, living 1747.

Gertrude Spencer, mar. . . . . Hamilton; bur. 12 Dec. 1760.

Erwin Russell, bur. 6 June 1745 at St. John's. ═ Susannah, dau. of Mrs. Elizabeth Gibson; bur. 8 June 1745.

Elizabeth Russell, bapt. 1 Jan. 1719.

John Russell, bapt. 27 July 1744. Named in the will of his grandmother Mrs. Elizabeth Gibson dated 1 July 1745.

Charles Russell, bapt 8 June 1745; bur. 17 April 1751.

. . . . Russell = ...

James Emra of Nevis, later of Antigua, Esq., mar. 13 July 1749 at St. Paul's; died 28 Dec. 1759, æt. 37. M.I. at Parham. 1st husband. = Rachell, dau. of William Yeamans of Millhill, Antigua, Esq.: bapt. 22 Aug. 1731 at St. Paul's. Will dated 9 Sep. and sworn 12 Oct. 1809. = William Woodley Parson of St. Kitts, Esq. Will dated 4 Nov. 1766; proved 7 Aug. 1770. (307 Jenner.) 2nd husband. = Major Lockhart Russell of Antigua, mar. *circa* 1773; died 8 Jan. 1798 at Southampton. Will dated 2 Dec. 1797; sworn 9 Feb. 1798. 3rd husband.

. . . . Russell. = ...

Elizabeth Russell, only surviving sister 1797.

Francis Russell of Blackhall, co. Kincardine, N.B., Advocate; owner of "Millhill" of 333 acres and "Gardeners" in Old Road, Antigua, which he inherited from his uncle Lockhart Russell. Will dated 13 Jan. 1803; proved 8 Jan. 1807. = Mary Bannerman.

Lockhart Russell. James Russell. Jane Russell. Frances Russell.

Sir Thomas Warner, Knt., Governor of St. Kitts and Lieut.-General of ye Caribbee Isles; died 10 March 1648. M.I. at the Old Road, St. Kitts. 1st husband. = Anne Russell. Will dated 16 July 1692; proved 27 Feb. 1693. (35 Box.) = Sir George Marsh, Knt., of Nevis, later of Limehouse. Will dated 27 March 1672; proved 9 Nov. 1676. (117 Bence.) 2nd husband.

Randall Russell, under 18 in 1677. = Margaret . . . . (?) remar. before 1682 Colonel Thomas Hill, Deputy-Governor of St. Kitts. His will dated 5 April and proved 20 Oct. 1697. (201 Pyne.)

Edmond Russell, under 14 in 1677.

Anne Russell, mar. 1671, at Nevis, Sir William Stapleton, 1st Bart., Captain-General of the Leeward Islands. His will dated at London 1 April and proved 28 Oct. 1686. (141 Lloyd.) Her will dated 14 May 1719; proved 26 July 1722. (147 Marlborough.)

Frances Russell, æt. 15 and spinster in 1681; mar. Joseph Jory of Nevis, who was a Lieut. 1680, Captain 1683, Colonel 1719; Agent at London 1702. He died at Bethnal Green (? 1725). His son Randolph matriculated from St. John's College, Oxford, 3 Nov. 1699, æt. 16. Adm'on at Oxford 26 Nov. 1702.

Penelope Russell, 3rd dau. and co-heir. = Martin Madan, Esq., of Nevis in 1687. Will dated at London 17 and proved 20 March 1703. (69 Ash.)

Edmund Russell, living 1697.

Elizabeth Russell, mar. 1st, Robert Jeaffreson of St. Kitts; 2ndly, before 1681, Captain John Vernon of Antigua. His will dated 17 June 1704; proved 2 Nov. 1705. (231 Gee.) She died 1737.

Richard Madan. Will dated 31 Aug. 1759; proved 17 Nov. 1762. (470 St. Eloy.) = Bridget Maria, only dau. and heir of Hugh Stafford, Esq., of Pynes, and relict of Sir Henry Northcote, Bart., who died 1743.
s.p.

Penelope Madan.

John Madan.

Charles Madan, Ensign Foot Guards, died 1 April 1761 in Germany.

Frederick Madan, Lieut.-Colonel 1st Foot Guards, died in North America. Adm'on 9 Feb. 1785.

Penelope Madan, mar. 6 July 1754, at St. George's, Hanover Square, General the Hon. Sir Alexander Maitland, son of Charles, 6th Earl of Lauderdale.

Maria Frances Cecilia Madan, mar. before 1750 William Cowper, Esq., her first-cousin.

Hon. James Russell of Charlestown, Mass., son of Hon. Daniel Russell, and descended from Richard Russell who settled there 1640; born there 1715; Member of Council 1774; died 1798, æt. 82. = Catherine . . . .

Colonel Henry Vassall, born 25 Dec. 1721 in West Indies; in 1748 leased Robert Oliver's 140 acres at Popeshead, Antigua, in partnership with Isaac Royall; died intestate 17 March 1769 at Cambridge, Mass.; bur. at Christ Church. = Penelope, dau. of Isaac Royall of Antigua and Mass.; mar. 28 Jan. 1742; died 19 Nov. 1800, æt. 76, in Boston.

Charles Russell, born 27 Dec. 1738 at Charlestown; B.A. Harvard 1757; M.D. Aberdeen 1765; banished 1778; died 27 May 1780 at Antigua. = Elizabeth Vassall, only surviving child and heir, bapt. 17 Dec. 1742 at Cambridge; mar. 15 Feb. 1768; died 23 Feb. 1802 at Plymouth, Mass. Of her ten children six died infants.

Penelope Russell, born 17 March 1769 in Lincoln; bapt. 9 April 1769; mar. 7 Nov. 1808 Hon. Theodore Sedgwick of Stockbridge, Mass.; he died 24 Jan. 1813, æt. 67; she died s.p. 18 May 1827 in Boston, and was bur. in William Vassall's Vault under King's Chapel.

Elizabeth Russell, born and died 27 Jan. 1770.

Elizabeth Vassall Russell, born 10 Jan. 1771; mar. 12 June 1797 Charles Furlong Degen, an English Merchant of Leghorn; he died 28 Aug. 1824 in Marion, co. Miss., and left issue.

Catherine Graves Russell, born 9 Jan. 1772; died a spinster 5 Sep. 1847 at Roxbury, and bur. in Colonel Henry Vassall's Vault beneath Christ Church, Cambridge.

Rebecca Russell, born 20 Feb. 1773 in Lincoln, Mass.; mar. 1st, 6 or 7 Nov. 1793, David Pearce of Gloucester, Mass., by whom she left issue; 2ndly, in 1813, Joseph Ruggles of Roxbury; she died 15 Dec. 1825 at Philadelphia and was bur. there.

Charles Thomas Jarvis Russell, bapt. 23 and bur. 24 Oct. 1779 at St. John's, Antigua.

(D'nus.) George Marche of Limehouse in Stepney, Esq. Will dated 27 March 1672; proved 9 Nov. 1676 by Dame Ann March the relict. (117 Bence.) I own a parcel of land called the Dusthill in Limehouse with a mansion house thereon with gardens, orchards, etc., all which I give to my loving wife Dame Anne Warner for 80 years, & after her death to Edward Younger, citizen & cutler, of London, Chas. Porter of the Middle Temple, Esq., & Francis Pemberton, Esq., for 99 years on trust to pay debts & legacies, & when paid I give the estate to Rich[d] Fowke, 2[d] s. of my sister Joice Fowke, & his heirs male, with remainder to her other sons John, Thos., & Geo. Fowke. My interest in the light house in the parish of Leede, co. Kent, called Dungenness, & all my lands in that county I give to my wife on trust to pay the following annuities, viz., To the poor of Limehouse £20, Edw[d] Younger of S[t] Clement Danes £20, Chas. Porter of the Middle Temple, Esq., £20, Geo. Fowke, youngest s. of my sist. Joice Fowke, John Minterne of Limehouse, public notary, £20, Francis Pemberton of the Inner Temple, Esq., £20. I give to my wife all my plantations, Indians, negros, & stock in the Island of Nevis or elsewhere in the West Indies, & all residue & Ex'trix. Witnessed by John Whiteing, John Carter, Jo. Fyrchild.

James Russell, late of Neivis, now living in Bristoll. Will dated 6 Nov., proved 10 Dec. 1674 by Margaret Russell the relict. On 26 Jan. 1676 new Probate to Dame Margaret Russell because Sir James Russell did not state his title in his will. On 9 Oct. 1677 commission to Robert Hunt the brother and adm'or of Dame Margaret Russell, deceased. (147 Bunce.) To M[r] Tho. Horne, Minister of S[t] Jas., £5, & £10 to the poor. To my lov. bro. Col. Randall Russell my saddle horse, pistols, rapier, & coat of armes to be sent to him at Nevis. To my sist. M[rs] Kath. Fenton if living in Irel[d] £50. To the Lady March a 20s. ring. All est. in Eng[d] to my wife Marg[t] Russell, she to be sole Ex'or, & I give her all the right of the S[t] X'pher's plant[n] that was formerly hers. As to my own proper plant[n] in Nevis, leased out to my bro. Col. Randall Russell for 5 years at £400 a year, 1½ years yet to run, I give my wife the residue of the rent, & then all the plant[n] & slaves to my neph. Cap[t] Jas. Russell, he to pay £200 a year in sugar or indigo to my wife as long as she remains my widow, & she may live in the house there. Jas. Russell Ex'or for Nevis. Witnessed by Thomas Cole, George Morris.

Randall Russell of Nevis. Will dated 17 March 1677; proved 30 June 1683 by Sir James Russell, Knt.; power reserved to Margaret Russell the widow and relict. (76 Drax.) To my wife Margaret ⅓ my real & personal estate or else £1500 st., all my jewels, & those negros formerly belonging to Sir Samuel Windall, deceased. To my son Sir James Russell my white gelding left me by my brother & sent from Bristoll. My dau. Ann Stapleton £100. My grandson James Stapleton £100. My dau. Frances Russell £1500 st. at 16, ½ to be paid here & ½ out of the monies in the hands of Capt. Gabriell Deane & M[r] Geo. Morris, merchants of Bristoll, if she die £800 to her brother Randall & the other to my Ex'ors. My said dau. to have ⅓ of my plate. My son Randall to be sent to England for his education, & £50 a year till 18, then £800. To my son Edmond Russell £500, & £12 a year till 14, £25 a year till 18. My dear sister Lady Ann March £5 for a ring. My former wife left negros to my dau. Frances which I confirm to her. My son Valentine Russell £100 at the birth of his 1st child. My father-in-law M[r] Edmond Kaynall £12 a year. To the parish of S[t] James 1000 lbs. To Capt. W[m] Burt my red plush saddle given me by the general. To Charles Pym my red scarfe, & to Ensign Samuel Gardiner my gold belt & sword. M[r] John Ley 1000 lbs. My wife to take her ⅓ of my estate then at her death equally to my sons Randall & Edmond Russell. All other my estate, money, plantations, slaves, cattle, mills, coppers, stills, etc., to my son Sir James Russell, he & my wife Ex'ors. My friends Cap[t] W[m] Burt, Chas. Pym, & Ensign Samuel Gardiner feoffees in Trust & overseers. Witnessed by Christopher Julian, Ja. Rolt, Ali. Duvall, ffra. Matham, George Thornehull.

1677, Oct. 9. Dame Margaret Russell of St. James, Bristol, widow, deceased. Adm'on to Robert Hunt the brother.

Sir James Russell, Knt., of Nevis. Will dated at Nevis 16 July 1687; proved 4 July 1688 by Dame Penelope Russell the widow. (99 Exton.) To my daus. Eliz[th] Russell, Penelope Russell, & Frances Russell ½ my estate in Nevis, the other ½ to my wife Penelope Russell. To my bro. Randolph Russell £5. To my 3 daus. all my personal estate & ½ my estate in Antigua, the other ½ to my wife, she to be Ex'trix. Witnessed by Thomas Hill, ... Tyrrell, John Smargin, Martin Madan.

Dame Anne Marsh, widow and relict of Sir George Marsh, late of Limehouse, co. Middlesex, Knt. Will dated 16 July 1692; proved 27 Feb. 1693. (35 Box.) My loving friends Anthony Bowyer of Camberwell, Esq., & Edmond Portington, Gent., Ex'ors, & to dispose of my estate & all arrears of my annuity in the West Indies. Witnessed by Charles Carrington, Richard Lee, Mary Cotton, Jane Trappes.

Codicil. To my neece M[rs] Louice Stapleton, dau. of my niece the Lady Stapleton, widow of Sir Wm. Stapleton, £500 out of my arrears in the West Indies. To Edmund Russell, s. of Col. Russell, £200. M[rs] Judith Portington £200. M[r] Steyner & his wife & children £200. M[rs] Anne Stapleton, dau. of the said Lady Stapleton, £100, & to the other dau. of M[rs] Frances Stapleton £100. To my Ex'ors £300. M[rs] Mott my servant £200.

Martin Madan, late of Nevis, now of London, Esq. Will dated 17 and proved 20 March 1703 by Joseph Martyn, William Fellowes, and Thomas Andrews. (69 Ash.) To my 1st son Martin, over & above the plantation called Russells with the negros which myself & wife have settled on him by deed lately made in England, £2000 at 21. To my dau. Penelope Madan £3000. To my son James Russell Madan £2000 at 21 over & above the two plantations in Nevis I settled on him. To my youngest son Richard Madan £2500 at 21. To my wife Penelope, on whom the plantations in Nevis are settled for life, all goods, plate, jewels, coach, horses, & £500. To my mother-in-law Dame Penelope Russell £20 & £20 a year. To my sister Geraldine in Dublin £50. To my brother Robert Madan £50. To my sister Margaret (whose surname I don't know) £30. To my sister Dame Frances Stapleton £25. To my loving friend Col. Wm. Ling of Nevis 20 French pistoles & to aid my Ex'ors. £10 to my servant Margaret Wroth, & £5 to the others. To my friends M[r] Joseph Martyn of London, merchant, & his two sons-in-law M[r] Wm. Fellowes & M[r] Tho. Andrews £20 each & to be Ex'ors. All residue in trust for my 4 children. Witnessed by W. Cockburne, P. Allix, William Bolton.

? 1726, Jan. 11. Commission to Nathaniel Hedges of Bethnall Green, Esq., to administer the goods of Joseph Jory of ditto, Esq.

Mary Spencer, widow. Will dated 29 Oct. 1747. My dau. Gertrude Hamilton, wid., negros, dau. Dorothy Spencer negros. My son Anth^o Fletcher my silver watch. All interest I have in the estate bequeathed by my father Jno Russell, dec^d, to my said s. Anthony & my daus. Gertrude & Dorothy. Richd Hosier Ex. Witnessed by Jos. Monteigne, Thomas Sawcolt. Before Josiah Martin, Esq., was sworn Thomas Sawcolt 27 Nov. 1747. Recorded 4 Dec. 1747.

Martin Madan of St. George's, Hanover Square, Esq. Will dated 23 Oct. 1750; proved 22 March 1756 by Judith Madan, widow, the relict, Ashley Cowper, and William Cowper. (75 Glazier.) I have purchased 6 £50 exchequer annuities in the names of my 6 younger children, & having preferred my 1st dau. Maria in marriage with Wm Cowper, Esq., I give my younger dau. Penelope Madan Maria's said annuity. By the settlement on my marriage with my wife Judith £400 a year is to be paid her after my death. £50 a year more to my dau. Penelope. All my plantations at Nevis & St Christopher's to my 1st son Martin Madan, remainder to my 2^d s. Spencer, 3^d John, 4th Chas., & 5th Frederick. John, Duke of Rutland, & my brother James Russell Madan, Esq., Trustees. All residue of my personal estate to my wife Judith. My said trustees with my wife Ex'ors. Witnessed by Elizabeth Jefferson, W. Bromfeild, William Inguire.

Codicil. 25 Nov. 1752. I revoke the appointment of John, Duke of Rutland, & my brother James Russell Madan, & make my brother Ashley Cowper & my son Wm Cowper Ex'ors in their place. Witnessed by Charles Torriano, John Laurence, John Marshall.

Richard Madan of Clarges Street, co. Middlesex, Esq. Will dated 31 Aug. 1759; proved 17 Nov. 1762 by Spencer Schutz, Esq.; power reserved to the Rev. Martin Madan. (470 St. Eloy.) To my wife Bridget Maria Madan, styled Lady Northcote, all arrears of rents. My 2 nephews Rev. Martin Madan & Spencer Schutz all my S. Sea stock in Trust for my wife to educate Richd Madan, s. of Mrs Eliz. Turnley, now at the free school at Bath. My 2 nephews Chas. Madan & Fred. Madan. My sister Schutz £100. Nephew Spencer Schutz ½ the mortgage of Sir John Osborne's estate in Ireland. All residue to my nephews Rev. Martin Madan & Spencer Schutz on trust for my wife for life, then to the said Richd Madan at Bath, if he die then all real estate to my nephew Rev. Spencer Madan, & my personal estate to my nephews Chas. Madan & Fred. Madan. Martin Madan & Spencer Schutz Ex'ors. Witnessed by W. Jones, Doro. Scott, Lewis Clutterbuck.

1st Codicil. 27 Oct. 1760. £1709 has become due from the estate of the late Sir Henry Northcote, Bart., Kelland estate in the Southams, co. Devon, & £876 which I lent to my son-in-law Ensign Henry Northcote. I give £1000 more to my wife.

2nd Codicil. 28 March 1761. My nephew Chas. Madan has died so my nephew Chas. Schutz to stand in his place.

On 16 Nov. 1762 appeared Bridget Maria Northcote of Upton Pine, co. Devon, spinster, and John Henry Merttins, jeweller, of St. Bennet Fink, London, and swore to handwriting of testator who was late of Upton Pine.

William Woodley Parson of Great Marlboro' Street, Esq. Will dated 4 Nov. 1766; proved 7 Aug. 1770 by Rachael Parson the relict; power reserved to the others. (307 Jenner.) All my estate to my wife Rachael, but if she die before me then to Wm Maxwell of Carredon in Scotland, Esq., £500, & £100 each to Mrs Mary Udny, widow of Mr Ernest Udny, Mrs Charity Benonville, Mr Tho. Yeomans Elliott, & Mr Chas. Yeomans Martin, all these nephews & nieces of my wife. £100 also to Mrs Grace Patterson her particular friend, & then all residue to my sisters Lucretia, Bridget, & Frances at 21. My wife Rachael, my father Edward Parson, & Wm Maxwell Ex'ors. Witnessed by Henry Wilmot, John Lancaster, Valentine Henry Allott.

Martin Madan of Epsom, co. Surrey, clerk. Will dated 4 April 1778; proved 12 May 1790 by Jane Madan the widow and relict. (252 Bishop.) All my lease of the plantation in St Christopher's, made to me by Mrs Stapleton of Harrow on the Hill & her 2 daus. Anna & Frances, & all my negros purchased since the death of my father, to my wife Jane, & sole Ex'trix.

1785, Feb. 9. Frederick Madan, Lieut.-Colonel of the 1st Regiment of Foot Guards, Esq., in North America, deceased. Adm'on to Walter Lewis a creditor; Judith Madan, widow, the mother dying, and Rev. Martin Madan, Rev. Spencer Madan, Clerk, D.D., Penelope Maitland, wife of Alexander Maitland, Esq., and Maria Frances Cecilia Compton, widow, the brothers and sisters, renouncing.

Major Lockhart Russell. Will dated 2 Dec. 1797. My wife Rachel & Francis Russell of Blackhall, N.B., Ex'ors. All my estate in trust. To my wife all produce for life, & after her death to my nephew Francis Russell, & then to my godson Lockhart Russell, son of the said Francis. To my wife absolutely plate, linen, & furniture. 1st I confirm my obligation under the marriage articles of my nephew Francis Russell & Mary his wife, over & above that sum £100 per ann. to my said niece Mary for life. To my only surviving sister Eliz^th Russell £40 a year. To my niece Stewart Russell £40 a year. To my niece Isabella Russell £50 a year. To my cousins Eliz^th & Isabella Philips £10 a year each. To my niece Euphemia, wife of John Innes, Esq., £50 a year. To my niece Mary, wife of Lucas . . . . Smyth, Esq., £10 a year. To my servant Jno Bell £25 a year. My wife & my nephew Francis Ex'ors. Witnessed by John Mackie, M.D., Thomas Mears. John Mackie of Southampton sworn there 9 Feb. 1798. Copy sent out from P.C.C. and recorded 5 April 1798.

Francis Russell, Advocate at Blackhall, co. Kincardine. Will dated 13 Jan. 1803; proved 8 Jan. 1807 by Mary Russell the widow, under £5000 in P.C.C. To my wife Mary Bannerman *al's* Russell all my estate of Milhill & Gardiners in Old Road Div^n, Antigua, charged with the life interest of Mrs Rachel Russell, widow of my uncle Lockhart Russell, also £10,000 in the 3 per cents., with furniture & stock, & £600 a year during the life of Rachel Russell by John Innes, Esq., of (Darries?). My wife to take all estate in trust to pay herself & £1000 extra, & secure £3000 each to our children Jane, Frances, & Jas. Russell at 25, & pay £6667 due to John Innes, Esq., on the death of Mrs Rachel Russell. All residue to our children. My wife sole Ex'trix & Guardian to Lockhart Russell my 1st s., to Jas. Russell my y^st s., to Jane Russell my 1st d., to Frances Russell my y^st d. My 1st son to be heir to my landed estate in Scotland. Witnessed by James Bryce, William Henderson, John Moir. Recorded at St. John's, copy sent from the Court of Sessions, Scotland.

Rachel Russell of Antigua, widow. *Codicil* dated 9 Sep. 1809. I left my will with my friend Daniel Mackinnen, Esq., in Great Britain. My Ex'ors Edwd Jones & Danl Hill of Antigua are to pay to my niece Eliz^th Eliot £100. Witnessed by Isaac Taylor, Daniel Hill. Before Edward Byam, Esq., was sworn Isaac Taylor 12 Oct. 1809.

Close Roll, 13 Geo. III., Part 5, Nos. 8 and 9.

Indenture made 1st Nov. 1773 between Lockhart Russell of Berners Street, St. Marylebone, Major, and Rachel Russell his wife (late Rachel Parson, widow), of the one part, and John Russell of Castle Street, London, Esq., of the other part. In consideration of 5*s.* paid by John Russell, Lockhart and Rachel Russell grant to him all that plantation called Young's Lane of 40 acres in the parish of St. Mary, Antigua, and 175 slaves upon it, and their other plantation in the division of Old Road in Antigua to hold for one year, yielding therefore one peppercorn if demanded, that John Russell may be in possession and enabled, etc., to the uses of an Indenture to bear date the day after these presents, and Lockhart and Rachel Russell appoint, etc., Samuel Eliot and David Potter, both of Antigua, Esquires, their Attornies.

No. 8.

Indenture made 2nd Nov. 1773 between Lockhart Russell of Berners Street, etc., Major, and Rachel his wife (late Rachel Parson, widow), of the one part, and John Russell of Castle Street, St. Marylebone, Esq., of the other part. Whereas Rachel Russell is seised of an estate of inheritance in the plantation, etc., hereinafter mentioned, now for destroying all estates tail, and extinguishing all dower in the said premises, and for assuring the same, and in consideration of 10*s.*, Lockhart and Rachel Russell grant to John Russell Young's Lane Plantation, containing 40 acres in the parish of St. Mary, Antigua, butted and bounded E. with the lands of James Emra, Esq., deceased, N. with the lands of Ashton Warner, Esq., deceased, and W. and S. with the lands of Edward Williams, now in the possession or occupation of Lockhart Russell, together with the 175 negros, etc., to have and to hold to John Russell and his heirs, etc., to his own use, but nevertheless in trust for Lockhart Russell and his heirs for ever.

1660, Sep. 12. Colonel James Russell commissioned as Governor of Nevis. (Nevis Acts.)

1670, Aug. Lieut.-Colonel Randolph Russell of Nevis to be a Commissioner for the rendition of St. Kitts.

1671. Colonel James Russell then Deputy-Governor of Nevis.

1671, June 15. Governor Stapleton was gone to Nevis to marry Lieut.-Colonel Russell's daughter.

1671, July 14. Colonel Russell referred to as late Governor of Nevis.

1671, Dec. 9. Nevis has a regiment of trained bands (under Colonel Russell, a great support of the Government), and a militia troop under Captain James Russell, eldest son to the Colonel.

1672, March 6. Nevis. Colonel Russell the principal man of the island.

1672, May 25. Governor Stapleton commissioned Lieut.-Colonel Randolph Russell as Deputy-Governor of Nevis.

1672, June 11. Captain James Russell of the Council of Nevis.

1672, Nov. Sir James Russell then in England.

1673, April 25. Sir James Russell, then at Bristol, writes to his "cousin Warner." (Colonial Calendar, America and West Indies, 1669—74.)

1673, March 18. Mr. John Jory, brother of Mr. Joseph Jory of Nevis, merchant, enters his protest. (Records at St. John's.)

1675, Dec. 20. Deposition of Colonel Randolph Russell, Deputy-Governor of Nevis. Deponent, in July 1637, arrived out of Europe into St. Christopher's, and was received into the house of Sir Thomas Warner, and there lived in his employ several years. (Colonial Entry Book, 46.)

1676-7, Jan. 16. Hon. Lieut.-Colonel Randolph Russell granted 511 acres in Antigua by Colonel Philip Warner. Surveyed 1676.

1678, Aug. 1. Valentine Russell, Gent., Secretary of Nevis, granted a patent for 511 acres in Falmouth by Sir W. Stapleton, at the annual rent of an ear of Indian corn.

Sir James Russell, Governor and Commander-in-Chief of Nevis and the Caribee Leeward Islands, wrote "In the event of the decease of ye Capt Genl and ye Govr of Nevis is to take up the gov^t^ . . . . Wm Stapleton made me Dep. Govr of Nevis." (No date.)

Nevis. Colonel Randoll Russell, Mrs. Margaret Russell, 2 boys, 1 girl (white children); 103 negros, 23 boys, 23 girls, 2 mulattos.

Sir James Russell, 11 white men, 1 woman, 9 children; 70 negro men, 70 women, 18 children.

1678, June 29. Colonel Randall Russell, Deputy-Governor of Nevis, is dead.

1680, June 15. Valentine Russell signs as a Member of Council of Antigua.

1680, June 19. James Russell signs as a Member of Council of Nevis.

1680, Feb. 9. John Parington sells 50 acres to the Hon. Valentine Russell of Antigua.

1680, March 3. Sir James Russell and Nicholas Raynsford, Esq., granted a patent for 1050 acres in Antigua, formerly Colonel Thomas Middleton's ground, by Sir W. Stapleton. Surveyed 8 March 1680. Confirmed 28 Nov. 1681, and a further grant of 100 acres of flashes made on 15 March 1684.

1681. Hon. Valentine Russell styled Governor of Antigua in various deeds.

1682. Nevis. Sir James Russell, Deputy-Governor. He is entered in a later list as "Sr Jas. Russell K^t^ Judge of St Jas. P'sh. who also commands one Reg^t^ of Militia, and as eldest Collonel both ye Reg^ts^."

1687, Aug. Sir Nathaniel Johnson wrote that since his return from St. Kitts to Antigua he has heard of the death of Sir James Russell, Lieut.-Governor of Nevis. (Colonial Entry Book, 47.)

1700, Sep. 13. Letter from Joseph Jory, agent for Nevis, dated at Bethnall Green. The seal has: . . . . *a double-headed eagle displayed* . . . . ; impaling . . . . *on a bend* . . . . *three swans*. Two étoiles are visible in chief, but part of the base of the seal is missing. (B. T. Leeward Islands, vol. 7.)

1707-8. Census of Nevis. Colonel Joseph Jory, 33 slaves.

1711-12, March 19. John Russell, late Governor of James Fort, was appointed without pay, etc. On 16 July 1714 he was described as a Captain of Artillery.

1719. Joseph Jory still agent.

No. 170. Private. An Act for the Encouragement of Rudhall Russell, Back-maker, in his Projection of Stills compounded of Wood and Copper, within this Island. Dated 26th June 1721. (Laws of Antigua.)

1723, Dec. Martin Madan, Esq; marry'd to Mrs Judith Cowper, only Daughter of Spencer Cowper, Esq; Uncle of William Earl Cowper. ('Historical Register,' p. 56.)

1725, Aug. 24. Dy'd . . . . Jory of Abury-Hatch in the County of Essex, Esq; formerly a West-India Merchant. (*Ibid.*, p. 39.)

1732, April 20. Dy'd at her House near Grosvenor-Square, the Lady Penelope Russel, a Widow Lady. (*Ibid.*, p. 20.)

1732, April. The Lady Penelope Russel, at her House near Grosvenor-Square. ('London Mag.,' p. 42.)

1748, Sep. 1. Dr. James Russell licensed to practise medicine and surgery.

1761, April 1. At Paderborn, in Germany, Ensign

From Johnson's Account, 1830 (*reduced*).

Charles Madan of the foot-guards. ('Historical Register,' p. 188.)

1767. James Russell rated on 300 acres and 153 slaves. (St. Mary's Vestry Book.)

1780. Lockhart Russell rated on 199 acres. (*Ibid.*)

1786. On p. 609 of the 'Gent. Mag.' is an account of the plot among the slaves on the plantation of the Hon. Major Lockhart Russell.

1798, Jan. 8. At his house at Southampton, Major Lockhart Russell. ('Gent. Mag.,' p. 87.)

Elizabeth Vassall, only surviving child of Colonel Henry Vassall, by Penelope his wife, daughter of Isaac Royall, born about 1742, baptized at Cambridge, Mass., 17 Dec. 1742, married Charles Russell, M.D., 15 Feb. 1768. He was the son of James and Catherine Russell, born in Charlestown, Mass., 27 Dec. 1738, studied medicine with Dr. Ezekiel Hersey of Hingham, and afterwards in England with Drs. Colin Mackinzee and William Hunter at St. Thomas's Hospital, took a degree of M.D. at Aberdeen 1765, returned to New England and settled at Lincoln, Mass., where he had inherited an estate from his uncle, Judge Chambers Russell. He sailed for Martinico April 1775, and his wife, if she did not accompany him, soon followed with her mother, then a widow. Dr. Russell was exiled by the Act of 1778, and his property confiscated. He died at Antigua 27 May 1780. His widow died at Plymouth, Mass., 23 Feb. 1802. Of their ten children the births of but four are recorded in Mass. Some of the others were perhaps born in the West Indies. ('The Vassalls of New England,' by E. D. Harris, 1862.)

1832. Leicestershire, Aug. 29. At the house of her brother the Rev. Dr. Madan, Ibstock Rectory, aged 75, Charlotte, relict of Gen. George Ward, late of Woodland Castle, Glamorganshire, the only dau. of the Right Rev. Spencer Madan, D.D. late Lord Bishop of Peterborough, by Lady Charlotte, sister of the first Marquis Cornwallis. ('Gent. Mag.,' p. 286.)

PARISH REGISTER OF ST. JOHN.

Baptized.

1719 Jan.	1	Elizabeth D. of Charles Russell and Elizth his wife.
1721 Aug.	26	John s. of John Russell junr & Henrietta his wife.
1741 July	27	John the s. of Edwin Russell and Susannah his wife.
1745 June	8	Charles the s. of Evin Russell and Susannah his wife.
1779 Oct.	23	Charles Thomas Jarvis the s. of Docr Charles Russell and his wife.

Married.

1710 Oct.	3	Thomas Fletcher and Eliza Ervin.
1715 Aug.	4	Charles Russell and Eliza Ervin.

Buried.

(? 1702 or 3)		James s. of Peter Russell & Mary his wife.
1720 May	3	Gertrude Russell.
1722 Sep.	13	Gertrude wife of John Russell.
1724 July	16	Mrs. Hannah Spencer.
1725 April	5	William s. of William Spencer.
1726 June	13	Russell s. of Wm. Spencer.
1727 Nov.	15	Mr. William Spencer, shoemaker.
1732 Oct.	28	Capt John Russell.
1745 June	6	Ervin Russell.
1745 June	8	Susannah Russell, widow.
(? 1751) April	17	Charles Russell, a Child.
1755 Mar.	19	Mary Russell.
1756 Sep.	13	Bristoll Roussell.
1769 Sep.	28	Doctr James Russell. P.
1779 Oct.	24	Charles Thomas Jarvis Russell.
1780 April	27	Docr Charles Russell.

ST. GEORGE, HANOVER SQUARE, LONDON.

Married.

1754 July 6 The Hon. Alexander Maitland, Esq., B., & Penelope Madan, S. L.A.C.

CAMBERWELL, CO. SURREY.

Married.

1675 Jan. 13 Sr Ja. Russell, knt and Mrs Penelope Tyrrell, daughter to Sr Tim. Tyrrell.

('Collect. Top. et Gen.,' vol. iii., p. 163.)

ST. JAMES'S CHURCH, BRISTOL.

On the north side of the altar, beneath a fractured entablature, supported on two Corinthian columns, is this inscription:—

Here lyeth the body of James Russell, Knt., late of Nevis, one of the first setlers in that Island, who was ye first mayor and coilonel there, and after, by commission of King Charles 2nd (bearing date ye 12th day of Septr. in ye 13th yeere of his reign), appointed governor of ye said Island, and so continned till 1671; by whose wisdom and valor (uncer God) it was preserved, when that and ye rest of those islands were endangered by the French and Dutch, in 1666; who, after obtaininge leave of His Majesty to come for England, here departed this life ye 15th day of November, 1674, aged 74 years.

No mention is here made of Lady Russell, but an entry in the church accounts shews that she was interred in the same tomb with her husband:—1677, September 13th. "Received for breaking ground in the chancel for ye Lady Russell, £1."

('Bristol Past and Present,' vol. ii., p. 44.)

N.B. The author visited St. James's Church in Aug. 1891, and found that this monumental tablet was placed so high up on the north side of the nave wall, first bay, near the altar, that without the help of a long ladder the inscription was invisible.

KENSINGTON.

Rev. Martin Madan, buried May 8, 1790. Son of Martin Madan, Esq., of Hertingfordbury, near Hertford, member of parliament for Woottonbasset, and Groom of the bedchamber to Frederick, Prince of Wales. His mother was daughter of Spencer Cowper, Esq., and niece of the Lord Chancellor, an accomplished lady, and author of several poems of considerable merit.* Mr. Madan was originally bred to the law, and had been called to the bar; but afterwards quitted that profession, entered into holy orders, became chaplain at the Lock hospital, and a popular preacher. In the year 1780 he published a book called Thelypthora, which from the singularity of its doctrines, being a defence of polygamy, was much read and talked of when it first came out. It is somewhat remarkable that Mrs. Manley in the Atlantis speaks of Lord Chancellor Cowper as maintaining the same tenets. Mr. Madan published also a literal translation of Juvenal and Persius; Thoughts on executive Justice with respect to the Criminal Law; and some single Sermons. He died at Epsom in the 64th year of his age.

(Lysons's 'Environs of London,' iii., 224.)

* 'Abelaird to Eloisa'; the 'Progress of Poetry'; 'Verses on the Death of Hughes,' etc.

Pedigree of Salmond.

ARMS.—*Sable, three salmons or.*
CREST.—*An armed arm sable, holding a falchion or.*

.... SALMOND ╤ ....

Captain James Salmond of Antigua, planter, born 1694; died 1 and bur. 2 Oct. 1746 at St. John's. Will dated 9 Sep. 1741; sworn 4 Oct. 1746. ╤ Lydia, dau. of William Kennedy of Antigua; died 24 April 1748. Will dated 31 March and sworn 28 April 1748.

Katherine Salmon, mar. 1st .... Simes, and 2ndly Andrew Rickards of London, tailor.

Elizabeth, dau. of J. Chalmers of Edinburgh; mar. 22 Aug. 1759; died 18 July 1760. 1st wife. ╤ William Salmond of Seaforth, Antigua, Esq., born 4 Aug. 1737; Agent for Antigua 1776; died 4 Aug. 1779. ╤ Jane, 1st dau. of Edward Hasell of Dalemain, co. Cumberland; born 22 April 1745; mar. 3 Oct. 1765; died 11 Aug. 1820. 2nd wife.

Euphemia Salmond, only child, born 7 June 1760; mar. C. Thorne, and had issue.

Louisa, 1st dau. of David Scott, Esq., of Dunninald, M.P.; mar. 2 July 1798; died 20 June 1805. 1st wife. ╤ James Hanson Salmond of Waterfoot, near Penrith, co. Cumberland, Esq., born 17 Nov. 1766; Major-General E.I.C.S.; died 1 Nov. 1837. ╤ Rachel Mary Ann, 2nd dau. of Venerable Thomas Constable of Beverley, Archdeacon of Yorkshire; born 1770; mar. 17 Aug. 1808; died Feb. 1847. 2nd wife.

James Salmond of Waterfoot, Esq., born 15 June 1805; entered Rugby, Midsummer 1815, æt. 10; matriculated from Oriel College, Oxford, 16 Nov. 1822, æt. 17; B.A. 1826; Student of the Inner Temple 1826; Captain 2nd Dragoon Guards, J.P., etc.; died 24 Nov. 1880. ╤ Emma Isabella, dau. of D'Ewes Coke of Brookhill Hall, Derbyshire, Esq.; mar. 16 Aug. 1832; died 8 March 1886.

Edward Salmond, born 3 April 1809; died 14 May 1821.

Charles James Salmond, Captain E.I.C.S., born 11 Nov. 1833; entered Rugby Feb. 1847, æt. 13; killed near Cawnpore 6 Dec. 1857.

Francis Salmond, born 20 Sep. 1837; died 4 Feb. 1838.

Henry Salmond of Waterfoot, Esq., J.P., Captain R.N., born 31 Dec. 1838.

William Salmond, Lieut.-Colonel R.E., born 25 Aug. 1840. ╤ Emma Mary, youngest dau. of William F. Hoyle, Esq., of Hooton Levett Hall, Yorkshire.

David Salmond, born 16 Oct. 1843; died 11 April 1856.

William Geoffry Hanson Salmond, born 19 Aug. 1878. John Maitland Salmond, born 17 July 1882. Three daus.

A portion of this Pedigree is from Burke's 'Landed Gentry.'

James Salmond. Will dated 9 Sep. 1741. To my wife Lydia a riding horse, plate, & furniture for life. To my 1st dau. Jane negros & £500 c. at 21 or marriage. To my dau. Mary £500 c. & negros. To my yst dau. Elizth £500 c. & negros. All residue to my Ex'ors in trust to pay the purchase money of my estate called .... Hill according to the agreement between Wm Codrington & Ann his wife & myself, & work the same till my son Wm be 21, if he die without issue then to my dau. Jane, then to my dau. Mary, then to my dau. Elizth, then to my wife ½ absolutely, the other ½ to my nephew .... James & Mary Sims, children of my sister Kath. Rickards, now residing in England. My wife, Robt Christian, Jas. .... Mackinnen, Esqres, & Col. John Tomlinson, Gent., Mr Robt .... & Francis Hanson, planters, Ex'ors. Witnessed by William Simms, Absolam Zeagers.

Codicil. 3 April, 8 Geo. II. To my dau. Jane certain negros. To my 2d .... negros. To my yst dau. Elizth negros. To my nephew Alexr Simms, now resident on this island, my riding horse, demi poke saddle, blew cloth housen & honlster caps, old silver handled sword, boots, iron spurs, & pair of pistols. To Ex'ors a guinea ring, as also to Mrs Mary widow of Saml Hanson, decd, Mrs Anne widow of Capt John Martin, & her daus. Elizth Gray & Mary Martin, Rebecca Martin & Nancy Martin, & to be delivered in London to Andrew Rickards, taylor in London, & his wife Kath. my sister, & her sons Jas., Wm, & John Simms, & daus. Mary & Jane Rickards. Sworn 4 Oct. 1746.

N.B. Large portions of this will have been destroyed.

Lydia Salmond, widow. Will dated 31 March 1748. To my 1st dau. Jane negros & £500 c. at 21. To my dau. Mary £500 c. To my yst dau. Elizth £500 c. & £30 for a negro. All my real estate to my son Wm & his heirs, then to my daus., then to Robt Gray, planter, & to the children of my sister Ann Martin ½ each. John Tomlinson, Wm Mackinnen, Robt Christian, & Jas. Doig Ex'ors. Witnessed by Martha Horsford, Merriel Turnbull, Hill Dasent. Before Josiah Martin, Esq., was sworn Merriel Turnbull 28 April 1748.

Mary Salmond. Will dated 27 Nov. 1791. All my negros to be sold & the proceeds to my nephews & nieces Wm, Jas., Lydia, Mary, Elizth, Cath., & Jenne Gilchrist, sons & daus. of my sister Jane Gilchrist, & to Euphemia Thorne, Jas. Salmond, Wm Salmond, Francis Salmond, Julia Salmond, & Maria Salmond, sons & daus. of my late brother Wm Salmond, & to Wm Salmond Loving, son of my sister Elizth Loving, equally. Witnessed by John McConnell, Nathaniel Marchant. Before Edward Byam, Esq., was sworn Nathaniel Marchant, Doctor in Physic, 8 Dec. 1791. Recorded 14 Dec. 1791.

Mrs. Jane Gilchrist in her will dated 1794 names her nephew William Salmond.

1743. James Salmond, Esq., then a member of the vestry of St. Mary's Parish.

1767. William Salmond rated on 306 acres and 177 slaves, and in 1780 on 456 acres and 242 slaves. (St. Mary's Vestry Book.)

1772, May 12. William Salmond, Esq., recommended to be of the Council of Antigua *vice* William Warner, deceased.

Jane Salmond, a minor 1748; mar. Dr. John Gilchrist of Antigua. Her will dated 25 March 1794, and his will in 1782.

Mary Salmond, died a spinster. Will dated 27 Nov. and sworn 8 Dec. 1791.

Elizabeth Salmond, mar. 1st . . . . Campbell, 2ndly . . . . Wilson, 3rdly . . . . Loving.

Edward Salmond, born 8 April and died 13 June 1768.

William Salmond, Collector at Curaçoa 1801; Inspector-General of Taxes for cos. Berks, Oxford, etc.; Captain Cumberland Militia; born 20 Oct. 1769; died 15 Dec. 1838, bachelor.

Francis Salmond, Master Attendant, Fort Marlborough, Sumatra; born 28 Nov. 1770. = Anne, dau. of Charles Salmon; born 13 April 1791; mar. 21 Dec. 1805; died 22 Aug. 1812.

Four daus., died single.

George Edward Salmond, Captain 5th Derbyshire Regiment, born 24 Jan. 1845; educated at Rugby; of Queen's College, Oxford; matriculated 30 Oct. 1863; B.A. 1867; M.A. 1872.

Richard Arthur Salmond, Lieut. R.A., born 16 June 1847.

Walter Salmond, Captain 5th Derbyshire Regiment; J.P. for Notts; born 7 Feb. 1851. = Mary Augusta, 2nd dau. of William C. Smith of Ivy Lodge, Wandsworth; mar. 25 Jan. 1877.

Albert Louis Salmond, Captain 5th Derbyshire Regiment, born 9 Sep. 1852. = Henrietta Margaret, dau. of William S. Coke of Brookhill Hall, co. Derby; mar. 3 Sep. 1881.

Three daus.

Hugh Austen Bentinck Salmond, born May 1881.

Three daus.

James Sacheverell Constable Salmond, born 1 June 1882.

A dau.

Parish Register of St. John.

Married.

1732 June 27 Thomas Salmon and Dorothy Carley. B.
1738 Oct. 29 Thomas Salmond & Margaret Lister. B.
1744 Dec. 19 George Bingham and Alice Salmon, Widow.

Buried.

1737 June 4 Robert Salmond, Merchant from Maryland.
1737 June 15 Robert Simes Nephew to Mr James Salmond.
1742 Jan. 6 Thomas Salmon.
1746 Oct. 2 James Salmond.
1748 April 3 Francis Salmon.

Parish Register of St. George.

Married.

1747 Jan. 24 Benjamin Salmon & Luisa Asty, Spinster.

Buried.

1748 June 10 James Salmon S. of Benjamin Salmon and Lucia his wife.
1759 July 11 Benja Salmon.

Parish Register of St. Paul.

Baptized.

1819 Feb. 7 Sarah Elizabeth D. of James Farley Salmon & Louisa his wife was baptised at the Estate of Robert French Esq. called Cochran's; b. on the 23 Dec. 1818.

1837 Dec. 23 Louisa Jane D. of James Farley & Eliza Rawson Salmon of Cochrans, planter.

1839 May 4 Mary Eliza Burgess D. of James Farley & Eliza Rawson Salmon of Cochrans, planter; b. March 25.

1842 Aug. 20 Jas. Francis Nelson s. of James Farley & Eliza Rawson Salmon of Cochrans, planter; b. 18 April.

Buried.

1826 June 12 Louisa Salmon wife of James Farley Salmon of Cochrans, aged 34.

1838 July 27 Louisa Jane D. of James Farley Salmon of Cochrans, aged 8 months.

ST. PAUL'S CHURCHYARD.

On a marble ledger over stone tomb:—

Sacred
To the Memory of
LOUISA CAMILLA SALMON
Wife of *JAMES FARLEY SALMON, Esqre*
who departed this Life
the 11 June 1826
Aged 36 years.
(Five lines follow.)

"Seaforths" in St. Mary's Parish of 622 acres was formerly owned by the Salmonds.

Pedigree of Sampson.

.... SAMPSON ═ ....

Mr. Nathaniel Humfryes of St. Michael, Crooked Lane, London, Citizen and Ironmonger. Will dated 17 March 1681; proved 1 June 1682. (72 Cottle.) ═ Mary ....

Colonel John Sampson of St. James's Parish, Barbados, 1679; living 1685. (? died s.p.) His nephew John was his heir.

Francis Sampson of London, merchant; Secretary to the Assembly of Antigua 1668. Will dated 26 Oct. 1663; proved 10 Feb. 1668. (23 Coke.) ═ Mary, sister of Isaac Legay;* sold her 500 acres in 1670 to Jonas Langford, and her ¼ of "Barbuda" in 1673 to Governor Stapleton. Will dated 12 Nov. 1677, then of Kennington, co. Surrey, widow; proved 23 Jan. 1677. (8 Reeve.)

Sir William Humfryes, Knt. and Bart., Citizen and Ironmonger of London; Alderman of Bridge Without; knighted 26 Oct. 1704 when Sheriff; created Bart. 30 Nov. 1714 when Lord Mayor; Colonel of the Green Regiment of Militia; Commissioner of Greenwich Hospital; M.P. for Marlborough; mar. twice; he had a grant of arms in 1717; died 4 Oct. 1735. Will dated 27 Nov. 1731; proved 13 Nov. 1735. (228 Ducie.)

Elizabeth Humfryes, mar. licence dated 4 March 1681-2, then æt. 20; mar. 2ndly John Berringer, Esq., of Barbados, who was dead 1695. Will dated 5 July 1690; proved 6 April 1695. (59 Irby.) Recorded 17 June 1692. ═ John Sampson of London, merchant, son and heir, æt. 27 in 1681-2; died 1689 at Barbados. Will dated 26 Nov. 1688; proved 6 April 1695. (59 Irby.)

Peter Sampson, living 1688.

Martha Sampson, in 1688 wife of .... Withers.

Nathaniel Sampson, Gent., of Antigua, youngest child; Agent to the Royal African Company 1698 — 1701; owned "Cassada Garden"; bur. 11 May 1701 at St. John's. ═ Mary, dau. of Lieut.-Governor John Yeamans; mar. 2ndly, 30 Oct. 1701, at St. John's, Colonel William Byam.

John Sampson, æt. 18, 1702; inherited the Barbados estate of his great-uncle Colonel John Sampson. Will dated 12 May 1724, then of St. Thomas's Parish, Barbados; sworn 27 Oct. 1724. ═ Susanna ....

Francis Sampson, bur. 23 July 1705 at St. John's, a minor.

William Sampson, a minor 1688.

Mary Sampson, a minor 1705.

Codrington Sampson, a dau., died 1701—1704, infant.

Ann Sampson, a minor 1724.

* Jacob Butler, a Barbados merchant, who died 1669-70, married Katherine Legaye, sister of Jacob Legaye, and an Isaac Legay, his cozen, was overseer to his will. The will of Peter Legay of London, merchant, brother of Isaac and son of Peter Legay, Esq., was proved P.C.C. 1660. (269 Nabbs.)

Francis Sampson of London, merchant. Will dated 26 Oct. 1663; proved 10 Feb. 1668 by Mary Sampson the relict. (23 Coke.) Shortly about to undertake a voyage beyond the seas for the settling of my affairs with my brother John Sampson, in whose hands lieth a great part of my estate. My loving brothers Edward Palmer of London, wine cooper, & Isaac Legay of London, merchant, stand bound with me to Josiah Child of London, merchant, in two obligations for the payment of £500, which said £1000 is my own proper debt. Edward Palmer is bound with me to Tho. Harrison, Gent., for £200, & I owe the former £515 & my friend Mr Robt Thorner £150. I give all my estate beyond the seas or in England to my said brothers Edward Palmer & Isaac Legay & my friend Robt Thorner in Trust. Sums owing my sister Thorowgood to be paid. £50 to my dear brother Tho. Chaplyn & 2 per cent. commission for selling the produce of my estate. £5 to Mr Nathaniel Robinson for the poor, & £5 to Mr Anthony Palmer. To my father & mother, my wife, her father & mother, mine & her brothers & sisters, each a gold ring, & to Robert Thorner & his wife. ⅓ of all residue to my wife Mary & ⅔ among all my children. Witnessed by John Heavedyn, Mary Knapton, Thomas Jones.

Mary Sampson of Kennington, co. Surrey, widow. Will dated 12 Nov. 1677; proved 23 Jan. 1677 by John Sampson; power reserved to Isaac Legay. (8 Reeve.) Ex'ors to use my estate for bringing up & apprenticing my youngest child Nathaniel, but not to exceed £50 for this purpose. All residue for my 4 children John, Peter, Nathaniel, & Martha. My loving brother Isaac Legay & my son John Sampson Ex'ors. Witnessed by Jo. Jerrom, Harry Langford.

Nathaniel Humfreys, Citizen and Ironmonger of London. Will dated 17 March 1681; proved 1 June 1682. (72 Cottle.) Have already paid the portions of my children Thos. Humfreys, Wm Humfreys, Samuel Humfreys, Mary late wife of Richd Read, deceased, & Eliz. now wife of John Sampson; do now therefore give to my s. Samuel Humfreys & my dau. Eliz. Sampson 20s. apiece, my dau. Mary Read £50, my s. Wm Humfreys £100. To my grandchildren Martha, Orlando, & Sarah Humfreys £10 apiece. My sister Kath. Richards 40s. a year. My cozen Humphrey Richards 40s. To the poor of St Michael, Crooked Lane, 40s. All residue to my wife Mary & Ex'trix. Witnessed by F. Gillolk, sen., John Wheatley, Ed. Jolland.

John Sampson of Antigua, planter. Will dated 26 Nov. 1688; proved 6 April 1695 by William Humfreys, the uncle and guardian of John, Francis, and Mary Sampson the children of testator, he having died at Barbados and Elizabeth the relict having also died; proved by him again 20 Jan. 1702, the said John Sampson, jun., being 18. Entered 5 Aug. 1689. (59 Irby.) Bound for Barbados. My 1st son John to be heir to all my estate there bequeathed to me by my late uncle Col. John Sampson, except £1000 to be paid to my wife Eliz. over & above her thirds. I give her also all my jewels, plate, & household stuff. To my dau. Mary Sampson £2000 at 21 charged on my Barbados estate. To my sister Martha Withers £100. To my brother Nathl Sampson £100 & £20 a year for life. To my son Francis all my estate in Antigua, he to pay my youngest son Wm £2000 at 21. My wife sole Ex'trix. If my son John die under 21 without issue, Francis to have the estate in Barbados & Wm the one in Antigua, & in that case £300 to my sister Martha Withers' children, & £100 apiece to my brothers Peter & Nathl Sampson, & £100 to Martha Withers, & £400 to the poor. If my dau. Mary die under age then £2000 to my wife, & if Wm should be my sole heir then £1000 to his sister Mary, & if the latter shall come into my estate she shall pay £3000 to my wife. Col. Rowland Williams, Cap. John Fry, Capt Wm Wainwright trustees for Antigua, & . . . . Eastchurch & Mr John Thomas for Barbados. Witnessed by Peter Sampson, William Snurfy. Recorded also at St. John's Oct. 1694.

Elizabeth Berringer* of Barbados, formerly the wife of John Sampson of Antigua, deceased. Will dated 5 July 1690; proved 6 April 1695 by William Humfreys, John Beringer having died. Entered 17 June 1692. (59 Irby.) My now husband John Beringer to have all the benefits I receive under the will of my former husband John Sampson & to manage the estates. Witnessed by Randolph Vawrdrey, Francis Vawdray, Joseph Morton.

Codicil. To my sons John Sampson, Francis Sampson, & my dau. Mary Sampson, & the child I now goe with £100 apiece at 21. To my said dau. Mary my necklace of pearls with 2 strings, my gold lockett with diamonds, 1 large silver tankard, & 1 silver plate. If my husband die before they are 21 then my loving brother Mr Wm Humphries of London to be their Guardian.

John Sampson of Antigua, planter. My 1st son John to be heir of all my lands & negros in Barbados. Recorded 1701.

* The will of Benjamin Berenger of Iver, co. Bucks, and Barbados was dated 7 April 1656 and recorded in the Court of Delegates. (See 'Genealogist,' Jan. 1895.)

John Sampson of the parish of St. Thomas in the island of [*blank*]. Will dated 12 May 1724. To my dau. Ann [*blank*] at 21. All residue to my wife Susana, she to be Ex'trix. Witnessed by Burch Hothersall. By Henry Worsley at Barbados was sworn Burch Hothersall 27 Oct. 1724.

In 1630 Robert Sampson, son of John Sampson of Kersey, co. Suffolk, accompanied John Winthrop, Esq., to New England. His pedigree was entered in the visitation of that county.

Indenture of sale dated 6 Dec. 1671. Mary Sampson, widow and executrix of Francis Sampson of Antigua, deceased, and John Sampson his son and heir, by deed dated 2 Feb. 1670 made over title to all estate in Nevis or elsewhere in the West Indies to Lieut.-Colonel Randolph Russell, Captain George Holman, Joseph Palmer, and Samuel Jones of Nevis, as recorded in the Registrar's Office of this island; and whereas Samuel Jones, jun., is empowered by Captain George Holman and Joseph Palmer of Nevis to dispose of estate of Francis Sampson in Antigua, he in consideration of 70,000 lbs. of Muscovado sugar hath sold to Jonas Langford a moiety of a plantation of about 1000 acres in St. John's division called Cassavia Garden, bounded E. by land of Timothy Snapes, N. by Captain Giles Blizard, W. by Sir Sidenham Poynts, S. by Colonel Bastian Bayer; also a moiety of 60 feet square of land in St. John's Town, being a storehouse erected by Justinian Holliman, deceased, and a moiety of all houses, woods, timbers, provisions, negros, canes, stock, etc., as nominated in a schedule hereunto attached. (Liber A.)

Whereas on 26 Dec. 1671 Samuel Jones, on behalf of Captain George Hollman, Joseph Palmer, and himself, by letter of attorney from Mary, widow of Francis Sampson, and John Sampson his son and heir, sold 500 acres in North Sound Division to Jonas Langford. Confirmed the same to Samuel Jones 1 June 1673.

1673, April 1. Mary Sampson of Kennington in Newington Parish, co. Surrey, widow and relict of Francis Sampson, Esq., by her surviving Attorney Samuel Jones, grants to Captain-General William Stapleton her ½ share of the lease of Barbooda.

1679, April 3. John Sampson of London, Gent., son and heir of Francis Sampson, late of Nevis, Esq., deceased, for 10,000 lbs. sells to Captain Samuel Jones a plantation granted by William, Lord Willoughby, to my father, of 500 acres in New North Sound.

1679. Captain John Sampson owned 25 acres in St. James's Parish, Barbados.

1685. Colonel John Sampson then at Barbados.

1686, April 19. Mr. John Sampson one of the gentlemen of St. Mary's Vestry.

Nathaniel Sampson, Gent., was a Member of Assembly at a meeting held on 27 Jan. 1698-9, he was returned in the next election on 1 Feb. 1699-1700 for Belfast Division, and again on 16 Jan. 1700-1 for St. John's Division. On 30 May following he was dead, and his seat declared vacant.

1701, Jan. 27. Letter of attorney from George Turney of London, merchant, to James Read of Antigua, merchant, to recover sum due from Mary Sampson of Antigua, widow and relict of Nathaniel Sampson of Antigua, merchant, deceased.

Warrant from P.C.C. Adm'on to William Humphreys of London, guardian, the uncle, dated 18 Jan. 1702. Nathaniel Sampson now (? not) 21, his brother John dead. The relict now wife of Thomas Byam. I, William Humphreys, Citizen and Ironmonger of London, uncle and guardian of John Sampson, a minor, he being nephew and heir of Nathaniel Sampson of Antigua, merchant, deceased, grant letter of attorney to Samuel Proctor of Antigua, merchant, 22 Jan. 1702.

1703. Samuel Procter of London, merchant, now resident in Antigua, owes £2000 c. to William Byam, Gent. He was partner with Nathaniel Sampson, and William Byam, after Nathaniel Sampson's death, married Mary Sampson his relict. Letter of attorney to William Byam dated 12 Aug. 1703. Witnessed by Gilbert Hamilton, Surgeon.

1704, April 1. Affidavit of John Willson, planter, aged 60, before the Hon. Colonel George Gamble, Chief Justice of Antigua, that on 25 July 1701 he began working as overseer on the plantation of Nathaniel Sampson, merchant, deceased, called Cassada Garden, and was there two years and four months, and planted five pieces of cane between the death of Nathaniel Sampson and that of his infant daughter Codrington Sampson. Recorded 30 Nov. 1704.

1704, May 23. William Humphreys, Citizen of London, guardian of John and Francis Sampson, minors, sons of John Sampson, deceased. Letter of attorney to Thomas Cox of London, merchant.

1705, April 24. Sir William Humphreys, Knt., and Sheriff of London, guardian of John, Francis, and Mary Sampson, minors, children of John Sampson, deceased. Letter of attorney to Colonel George Gamble, Esq., and Thomas Cox of Antigua, merchant.

1705, Aug. 15. Warrant *re* Francis Sampson, deceased. Chattels £135 18s. 6*d*. George Gamble administrator. His plantation at the Road. Recorded 12 Oct. 1705.

1708, Aug. 5. Colonel William Byam, who lately married the widow and Ex'trix of Nathaniel Sampson, deceased, who was Agent to the Royal African Company from 1698 till his death a few months back, before Ed. Chester was appointed, is to give account of all negros sold by the Company.

Parish Register of St. John.

Buried.

1701 May 11 Nathaniel Samson of ye Island.
1705 July 23 Franciss Samson.
1754 June 9 Abraham Samson.

1681-2, March 4. John Sampson, of St Mary Magdalen, Milk Street, London, Mercht, Bachr, abt 27, & Elizabeth Humfreyes, of St Michaell, Crooked Lane, Spr, abt 20, with consent of her father Mr Nath. Humfryes; at St Mildred's, Poultry, or Allhallows in the Wall, Lond., or [*blank*]. (Marriage Licences.)

Pedigree of Saunders.

JOHN SAUNDERS of Wotton-under-Edge, co. Gloucester, mercer. Will dated 17 Aug. and proved 21 Nov. 1660. (296 Nabbs.) = ...

Rev. Samuel Saunders of Antigua; of Redcliff, Bristol, in 1732; died at Wotton-under-Edge, co. Gloucester. Will dated 20 Aug. 1733; proved 16 June 1739. (140 Henchman.) = Margaret . . . . died 1733—39.

John Saunders. = ...

Rev. William Saunders of Balliol College, Oxon; matriculated 10 Oct. 1732, æt. 17; living 1739.

John Saunders of Wootton-under-Edge, co. Gloucester, mercer. Will dated 17 Aug. and proved 21 Nov. 1660. (296 Nabbs.) My sons John, Saml, & Tho. £5 each, & sons Nathl, Joseph, Achilles, & Benjn £20 each at 21. My daus. Anne, Mary, Damaris, Deborah £30 each at 21. Wife Margery. Brother-in-law Jonah Cakes.

Christopher Woodward of Chewstoke, co. Somerset, merchant, dated his will 21 April 1677 (105 Reeve) and named his wife Elizabeth, daus. Ann, Elizabeth, and Abigail, son Christopher, son-in-law Ed. Hippisley, and grandson Ed. Hippisley, to whom he gave 15,000 lbs. of Nevis sugar.

Thomas Sanders of Wotton-under-Edge, clothier. Proved 1678. (117 Reeve.) My brother Nathaniel.

Francis Woodward* of Grimsbury in Britton, co. Gloucester, Gent. Will dated 2 Dec. 1730; adm'on 10 March 1730 to Elizabeth Woodward and the three trustees as guardians for Francis Woodward the son; proved P.C.C. 4 Sep. 1751 by Francis Woodward the son now 21. Whereas at a Court of Chancery held at St John's Town, Antigua, in 1724 a considerable sum was decreed to me & my wife in a cause wherein we & others were Complainants & Samuel Saunders, clerk, & others Defendants, I give this to James Hopkins of Stanton Drew, co. Som., Gent., Joseph Lewis, Esq., of Bristol, & Robert Blanch of Whitechurch, co. Som., Gent., on Trust for my wife Eliz. & my 2 younger children Francis & Richard, & to pay the principal to them at 21. To my wife the furniture, etc., in the room over the kitchen & the green room. My son Newton £1000. To my trustees £1000 for my wife for her life, then £600 to my s. Francis & £400 to my s. Richard. £1000 in trust for my son Richard. The children of my sons John & Newton. To my trustees 10 gns. each. The interest of £10 for 10 poor widows in the hamlet of Oldland on Michaelmas day for ever. All residue to my son Francis & sole Ex'or. My wife & trustees guardians. Witnessed by Lazarus Underhill, Walter Cookey, William Owen.

* For copies of the M.I. of several of his descendants see 'Gloucester Notes and Queries,' vol. ii., p. 79, also the 'Herald and Genealogist,' vol. iv., p. 297.

Penelope Sellick names in her will her nephews John and Newton Woodward, sons of Francis Woodward of co. Gloucester.

Antigua. Samuel Saunders, clerk. Will dated 20 Aug. 1733; proved 16 June 1739; adm'on to William Saunders, clerk, the son of testator, who was late of Antigua, but at Wotton-under-Edge, co. Gloucester, widower, deceased,

Margaret Saunders the wife being dead and John Gunthorpe, Esq., William Yeamans, Esq., not appearing, and Samuel Saunders and Thomas Vines renouncing. (140 Henchman.) To my wife Margaret all my estate with maintenance to my son Wm Saunders, & after her death all to him, remainder to the children of my sister Mary Vines of Wotton-under-edge, co. Glouc. John Gunthorpe, Esq., & Wm Yeamans, Esq., both of this island, Mr Samuel Saunders of Tedbury & Mr Tho. Vines of Wotton-under-edge Ex'ors & Guardians. Witnessed by Fran. Carlisle, Jonas Langford, Stephen Blizard.

Thomas Woodward, son of Christopher Woodward, was of Nevis in 1668, and married Anne, widow of Captain Laurence Broadbelt of that Island.

The three families of Saunders, Vines, and Adey of Wotton-under-Edge all had representatives settled in the Leeward Islands.

1678, April 30. Simon Vines and Mary Vines *alias* Mary Delanoy, dau. of John Delanoy, deceased, for 8000 lbs. sell to Olliver Enderby 10 acres in New North Sound, also land to Thomas Gilliatt on 3rd May.

1678, June. Deed of gift. Mary Saunders, widow and Ex'trix of Peter Saunders, deceased, recites his will dated 19 Oct. last, and gives her estate to "our 4 children surviving," viz., Elizabeth, Mirriam, Petter, and John Saunders.

1678, Nov. 14. John Saunders, planter, sells a parcel of land at Popeshead to Philip Chapman.

1678-9, Feb. 15. John Sanders and Henry Walden for 8500 lbs. sell 12½ acres to Ambross Yorke and William Mares.

1680, April 19. Symon Vaines, planter, sells 10 acres to Roger Compline.

1680, Aug. 14. Simon Vines, planter, and Mary his wife, late dau. of John Delanoy, deceased, sell 10 acres in New North Sound to Roger Complin, Gent.

PARISH REGISTER OF ST. JOHN.

Baptized.

1720	May 14	Richard s. of Samuel Saunders & his wife.
1774	Nov. 8	Henry the S. of Docr Wm Sanders & Eliza his wife.

Married.

1700	Aug. 17	Francis Saunders of St Tully, Southwark, and Sarah Read of St John's, Widdow.
1705	May 16	Francis Sanders & Sarah White. L.
1758	May 27	Richard Jones and Rachel Saunders. L.
1773	Feb. 20	William Saunders (Surgeon) to Elizabeth Horne. L.

Buried.

1691	Oct. 6	Doctr William Sanders.
1700	Feb. 3	Elizabeth D. of Francis Saunders & Sarah his wife.
1701	Sep. 29	John S. of Francis Sanders and Sarah his wife.
(1702-3)	[*blank*]	Joseph S. of Franciss Sanders & Sarah his wife.
1706	July 22	Sarah Sanders.
1719	Sep. 1	John Saunders, a child.
1742	Jan. 3	Francis Woodward, Doctor of Capt Edward Coulter.

PARISH REGISTER OF ST. GEORGE.

Buried.

1734	Nov. 11	John Saunders.

Pedigree of Sawcolt.

Colonel JOHN SAWCOLT of "Sawcolt's Road" Plantation in St. Mary's Parish and "Sawcolt's Body" Plantation in St. John's Division; Captain of Militia 1706; J.P. 1711; Member of Assembly 1713; bur. 2 Jan. 1748 at St. John's. Will dated 30 Nov. 1746. His six daus. inherited his estates. = Elizabeth, dau. of Colonel John Yeamans, Deputy-Governor of Antigua; bur. 18 Sep. 1711 at St. John's.

William Sawcolt, bapt. 26 Sep. 1708 at St. John's.

A child, bapt. 8 April 1710 at St. John's.

Henry Sawcolt, bapt. 15 April 1714 at St. John's.

John Sawcolt, bapt. 6 July 1725 and bur. 22 Sep. 1755 at St. John's. Will dated 20 Sep. 1755.

Henrietta Sawcolt, mar. 23 May 1740, at St. John's, George Horsford.

Elizabeth Sawcolt, mar. 17 Oct. 1747, at St. John's, Thomas Burton, Esq.; both dead 1776.

Mary Ann Sawcolt, bapt. 27 Nov. 1712 and bur. 2 Nov. 1759 at St. John's, spinster. Will dated 13 Sep. and sworn 1 Dec. 1759.

Rachel Sawcolt, bapt. 23 Aug. 1715 and mar. 8 April 1749, at St. John's, Samuel Horne; he died 1766; she was bur. 15 May 1776 at St. John's.

Frances Sawcolt, bapt. 17 Sep. 1718 and mar. 28 July 1759, at St. John's, Galbraith Patterson.

Barbara Sawcolt, bapt. 8 May 1722 and mar. 5 March 1760, at St. John's, George Frye; she died his widow before 1776.

Mr. Thomas Sawcolt of Antigua, bur. 16 March 1733 at St. John's. = Mary, dau. of Mr. Richard Denbow of St. John's, vintner; mar. 21 May 1724 at St. John's; named (1767) in her mother's will.

Thomas Sawcolt, bapt. 28 March 1726 at St. John's; named (1755) in the will of his uncle William Denbow.

John Sawcolt, bapt. 27 Jan. 1728. = Mary ....

Denbow Sawcolt (? bapt. 1731 at St. John's). = Mary Ellyat, mar. 15 June 1754 and bur. 16 Dec. 1767 at St. John's.

John Sawcolt, bapt. 19 April 1752 at St. John's.

Thomas Henry Sawcolt, bapt. 1 Jan. and bur. 3 March 1757 at St. John's.

John Sawcolt, bapt. 21 May 1762 at St. George's; bur. 18 July 1792 at St. John's. Will dated 7 Nov. 1789; sworn 19 July 1792. = Sarah .... dead 1789.

Denbow Sawcolt, bapt. 29 Jan. 1765 at St. John's.

Ann Sawcolt, bapt. 19 Nov. 1755 at St. John's; mar. 11 Jan. 1781, at St. Paul's, Edward Payne.

Elenor Denbow Sawcolt, bapt. 2 Sep. 1760 at St. John's; mar. there, 17 Dec. 1777, Richard Battyson.

Mary Sawcolt, bapt. 12 June and bur. 16 Dec. 1767 at St. John's.

John Sawcolt. Will dated 20 Sep. 1755. My sister Ma . . . . My nephew Yeamans Horsford. All residue amongst my sisters . . . . Negro to my sister Mar . . . . Sawcolt. My brothers-in-law Mr Thos. Burton, Saml Horne, & my friend . . . . Ex'ors. James Athill swore that he saw . . . . (? John) Sawcolt . . . .

Mary Ann Sawcolt, spinster. Will dated 13 Sep. 1759. To my nephew John Burton a mulatto of £50 c. To my nephew John Horsford £10 c. for a ring. To my nephews Isaac Horsford, Wm Edwd Yeamans Horsford, Saml Horsford, & Geo. Horsford £50 c. each. To Wm E. Y. Horsford a negro & a cow & calf. To my nephew Edwd Horne & my niece Lydia Horne £50 c. To Mrs Elizth Burton of St John's, widow, £12 c., to her dau. Cath. £12 c. To Elizth wife of Rowld Ash, Esq., £12 c. To my sister Mrs Frances Patterson 12 silver table spoons. To my sister Barbara Sawcolt my chaise & horse & all residue. Rowld Oliver, Tho. Warner, & my brother-in-law Thos. Burton Ex'ors. Witnessed by Robert Fellows, John Vulliamoz (?). Before his Excellency George Thomas was sworn Robert Fellows 1 Dec. 1759. Recorded 29 Dec. 1759.

John Sawcolt, Gent., first brother and heir-at-law to Thomas Sawcolt, late of Antigua, who died intestate, from whom I inherit certain slaves. Will dated 7 Nov. 1789. To my niece Ann dau. of Mr Edwd Payne £100 c. My Ex'ors are to free the slaves I possess thro' a deed of settlement between my late wife Sarah & my brother Tho. Sawcolt. All residue to Mr Wm McDowal, merchᵗ, & Mr Jno Cuthbert, planter, my Ex'ors in trust, to give the rents to Capt John Robinson & Elinor his wife, my niece, for her & her children. Witnessed by Alexander Proctor, John Harris, Joseph Hoskins. Before Edward Byam, Esq., was sworn Alexander Proctor, Gent., 19 July 1792. Recorded 19 July 1792.

Close Roll, 16 Geo. III., Part 17, Nos. 14 and 15.

Indenture made the 3rd April 1776 between John Burton, late of Antigua, but now of Lincoln's Inn, Esq. (son and heir-at-law of Elizabeth Burton late wife of Thomas Burton, late of Antigua, Esq., both deceased, and also one of the nephews and devisees of Barbarah Frye, late of Antigua, widow, deceased, which said Elizabeth Burton and Barbarah Frye were two of the daughters and devisees of John Sawcolt, late of Antigua, Esq., deceased), of the one part, and Samuel Turner the younger of London, merchant, of the other part, witnesseth that in consideration of 5*s*. John Burton grants, etc., to Samuel Turner all that his undivided 6th part in Sawcolt's Road Plantation in the parish of St. Mary and division of Old Road, bounded E. by the lands of Messrs. Dean and Adney and with the lands of Messrs. Byam and Johnson, S. by the land of Lockhart Russell and John Gilchrist, and W. and N. by the lands of George Byam, and also in Sawcolt's Body Land Plantation in the parish and division of St. John's, bounded E. by the lands of Thomas Warner and Daniel Mathew, N. by the lands of Thomas Warner, W. by the lands of the heirs of Rowland Oliver, deceased, and S. by the lands of Daniel Mathew, formerly the estate of John Sawcolt, deceased, and all negros, for one whole year. Tobias Pickering, Thomas Sermon, witnesses.

No. 14.

Indenture made the 4th April 1776 between the above. Whereas John Burton is, under the will of John Sawcolt dated the 30th Nov. 1746, and as heir of Elizabeth Burton his mother, deceased, seised of one undivided 6th part in all those two plantations (as in No. 15) as tenant in tail with remainders over. Now this Indenture witnesseth that for barring and docking all estates tail, etc., and in consideration of 10*s*., John Burton grants, etc., to Samuel Turner, in his possession being, all that his 6th part, to the use of John Burton and his heirs for ever; and John Burton constitutes John Burke and Bertie Entwisle, Esquires, both now residing in Antigua, his Attorneys.

1713, April 4. Thomas Sawcolt petitions for 10 acres granted to Mr. John Dncoster, bounded S. with land formerly Mr. Richard Cheshire's, E. with widow Byam, formerly Waldron's, N. with Mr. Elliott, W. with Mr. Preston.

PARISH REGISTER OF ST. JOHN.

Baptized.

1708	Sep. 26	William S. of John Sawcolt & Elliz. his wife.
1710	April 8	[*blank*] Sawcolt [*blank*] of Sawcolt & his wife.
1712	Nov. 27	Marian D. of John Sawcolt & Elizth his wife.
1714	April 15	Henry S. of John Sawcolt & Elizabeth his wife.
1715	Aug. 23	Rachell d. of John Sawcolt & Elizth his wife.
1718	Sep. 17	Frances D. of John Sawcolt & [*blank*] his wife.
1722	May 8	Barbara D. of John Sawcolt & Elizth his wife.
1725	July 6	John the s. of John Sawcolt and Elizabeth his wife.
1726	Mar. 28	Thomas s. of Thomas Sawcolt and Mary his wife.
1728	Jan. 27	John the s. of Thomas Sawcolt & Mary his wife.
1731	[*blank*]	Denham the s. of Thos. Sawcolt & Mary his wife.
1752	April 19	John the S. of John Sawcolt & Mary his wife.
1755	Nov. 19	Ann the D. of Denbow Sawcolt & Mary his wife.
1757	Jan. 1	Thos Henry the S. of Denbow Sawcolt & Mary his wife.
1760	Sep. 2	Elinor Denbow the D. of Denbow Sawcolt and Mary his wife.
1765	Jan. 29	Denbow the S. of Denbow Sawcolt and Mary his wife.
1767	June 12	Mary the D. of Denbow Sawcolt and Mary his wife.
1767	Dec. 15	Mary Sawcolt (an Infant who dy'd Immediately after being Christened) D. of Denbow Sawcolt by Mary his wife.

Married.

1724	May 21	Thomas Sawcolt and Mary Denbow.
1740	May 23	George Horsford & Henrietta Sawcolt.
1747	Oct. 17	Thomas Burton and Elizabeth Sawcolt.
1749	April 8	Samuel Horne and Rachel Sawcolt.
1754	June 15	Denbow Sawcolt and Mary Ellyat. L.
1759	July 28	Galbraith Patterson to Frances Sawcolt. L.
1760	Mar. 5	George Frye to Barbara Sawcolt. L.
1777	Dec. 17	Richard Battyson to Eleanor Denbow Sawcolt. L.

Buried.

1733	Mar. 16	Mr Thomas Sawcolt.
1734	Oct. 12	Mr Samuel Sawcolt.
1741	Sep. 18	Elizabeth Sawcolt w. of Collo John Sawcolt.
1746	Nov. 16	William Sawcolt.

1748 Jan. 2 Coll° John Sawcolt.
1755 Sep. 22 John Sawcolt.
1755 Nov. 10 Mary Sawcolt, a Child.
1756 Jan. 30 John Sawcolt, a Child.
1757 Mar. 3 Thomas Henry Sawcolt, a Child.
1757 April 14 Andrew Sawcolt, a Child.
1759 Nov. 2 Mary Ann Sawcolt [*blank*].
1767 Dec. 16 Mary Sawcolt Wife of Denbow Sawcolt.
1767 Dec. 16 Mary Sawcolt, an Infant.
1768 Jan. 26 Sarah Sawcolt Wife of Jn° Sawcolt. C.P.
1774 May 19 Mary Sawcolt.
1782 Feb. 3 Thomas Sawcolt.
1787 Nov. 23 John Sawcolt, junior.
1788 Aug. 10 Denbow Sawcolt, jun.
1792 July 18 John Sawcolt.
1795 July 2 Mary Sawcolt.
1800 May 30 Edward Sawcolt.

PARISH REGISTER OF ST. PAUL.

Married.

1781 Jan. 11 Edward Payne to Ann Sawcolt ; p^r L.

PARISH REGISTER OF ST. GEORGE.

Baptized.

(*c.* 1738) John the S. of John Sawcolt & his wife.
1762 May 21 John the S. of Denbow Sawcolt and Mary his wife.

Buried.

1747 June 6 Mr Sweal (*sic*).

PARISH REGISTER OF ST. PHILIP.

Married.

1758 July 13 John Sawcolt & Sarah Minchan, Widow.

"Sawcolts" is in St. Mary's Parish. In 1852 it contained 234 acres, and was owned by Sir R. Horsford.

Family of Scholes.

William Entwisle. Will dated 7 March 1798. To John Scholes my signet ring, & to W^m his son my silver tankard.

John Scholes of St. John's Town. Will dated 19 Nov. 1804. To my wife Rachel £300 c. yearly & my house, 4 negros, horse, & whisky, & all furniture. All residue to my son Wm. My friends Hen. Benskin Lightfoot, Ed. Byam Wyke, Geo. Wm White, & Rich. Lovely Nanton, Esq^res, & my wife Ex'ors. Before President Byam was sworn William Collins of Antigua, Esq., 30 Jan. 1808. Recorded 10 Feb. 1808.

Mrs. Eliza Oliver, widow, of Antigua, in her will of 20 Aug. 1823 bequeathed jewellery to her cousin Eliza Scholes.

1806, Oct. 1. At Polefield, near Manchester, the wife of John Entwistle Scholes, esq. ('Gent. Mag.,' p. 1077.)

1846, Feb. 7. At Cawsand, near Plymouth, Mary, wife of J. Entwisle Scholes, esq. (*Ibid.*, p. 331.)

PARISH REGISTER OF ST. JOHN.

Baptized.

(? 1785) [*blank*] William Entwisle Infant S. of John Scholes and Elizabeth his wife.
1789 Mar. 11 Eliza Jane D. of John Scholes and Elizabeth his wife. B. the 10th Feb. 1789.
1806 Aug. 18 Elizabeth Ash D. of William Scholes and Anna his wife. B. the 23rd July last.

Married.

1794 Oct. 23 John Scholes to Rachel Thibou, Sp^r ; by L.
1825 June 25 James Douglass, M.D., and Elizabeth Ash Scholes of this Parish, Sp^r ; by L.

Buried.

1790 Aug. 9 Elizabeth I. Scholes, Infant.
1807 Sep. 29 John Scholes.
1808 Nov. 7 Rachael Scholes, Infant.

Family of Scotland.

John Scotland. Will dated 27 March 1788. To my wife Mary £100 c. a year & my house in Newgate Street, my chaise, whiskey, certain slaves, etc., & after her death to my s. Thos. To my s. Thos. £1000 above what I have p^d for his commission on condition my Ex'ors obtain a full discharge of £1000 st. from John Deffell, merch^t of London, which I stand guaranteed for my said son, otherwise I give him but 1*s*. All residue equally to my sons Benjn, Jas., & Geo., & my daus. Marion-Mary & Jane-Eliz^th. Thos. Oliver, Esq., of London, merch^t, Langford Lovell, & Wm Dickenson, Ex'ors. Witnessed by Charles Ross, Joseph Dowdy, John Burke. Before Edward Byam, Esq., was sworn Charles Ross 2 Jan. 1793.

Codicil (same date as will). To my said sons & daus. my brick tenement in Livingston's Row at the corner of the Parade I recently purchased. Recorded 9 Jan. 1793.

John Scotland. Will not dated. To my wife £100 c. yearly & the use of my house in Newgate Str., certain negros, etc. To my s. Thos. £400 st., also £600 st. p^d for an Ensigney or Lieutenantcy in the army, & £1000 to John Deffel, Esq., of London, for security. To my dau. Marion wife of John Hall £1000 st., having already p^d her husb^d for her use £1000 st. To my s^s Benjn, Jas., Geo., & daus. Mary & Jean-Eliz^th £2000 st. apiece. All residue to my s. Benjn, Jas., & Geo., & daus. Marion-Mary & Jean-Eliz. equally. To my bro. Wm Scotland of Edinburgh £10 a yr. Whereas my sister Jean wife of John Ballandine left certain monies to be equally divided among her bros. & sisters, my share to be placed at interest for my brother Wm Scotland. The expense of my son James, now going to Cambridge University, to be p^d by my Ex'ors & not to exceed £200 st. a year. My son Jas. to be sent to the Charter House at the age of 12, & then to the university or other public school. Testator died 12 Dec. 1792 leaving the will unsigned. Adm'on granted to John Scotland, Langford Lovell, and Mary Scotland on 27 Jan. 1794. Recorded 18 Feb. 1795.

Pedigree of Scotland.

. . . . SCOTLAND ═ . . . .

John Scotland of Antigua, merchant, died 25 Dec. 1792, æt. 63 years and 9 months. M.I. at St. John's. Will dated 27 March 1788; sworn 2 Jan. 1793. ═ Mary . . . . (? bur. 30 March 1818). M.I. now obliterated.

Jean Scotland, mar. John Ballandine.

William Scotland of Edinburgh.

Abigail . . . . died 23 Aug. 1815 at Hextable House, co. Kent. 1st wife. ═ Thomas Scotland, Ensign in the Army 1788; Deputy-Paymaster at Jamaica; Registrar of Antigua 1826. ═ Sarah, dau. of James Haverkam of Antigua, Gent., by Mary Kirwan his wife; mar. 2 Aug. 1817. 2nd wife.

Deffell Scotland, born 9 April 1789; bapt. 22 July 1790.

Thomas Colley Scotland, Lieut. R.N., born 6 Dec. 1790; bapt. 17 May 1792; bur. 20 Dec. 1812.

George Otto Scotland, born 6 Jan. and bapt. 22 April 1794.

Sir Colley Harman Scotland, Knt., born 16 June and bapt. 14 Nov. 1818; Barrister-at-Law Middle Temple 1843; Chief Justice of Madras 1861, then knighted; Vice-Chancellor of Madras University 1862—71; of 44 Queen's Gate Gardens 1894. ═ Sarah Anne, only surviving dau. of John Joseph Bygrave; mar. 21 Dec. 1853; died 1859.

. . . . ═ . . . .

Haverkam Forrest Horne Scotland, born 26 March 1825 and bapt. 31 Dec. 1826.

Mary Ann Scotland, born 15 Sep. 1822 and bapt. 14 May 1823.

Harriet Jesse Scotland, only child, mar. 8 April 1875 ═ Robert Harry Lingen Burton.

Rev. Horace Scotland of Kingston, Jamaica, 1889.

1812, Dec. In the Island of Antigua, Lieut. Thos. C. Scotland, R.N., son of Thomas S. esq. of that Island. ('Gent. Mag.,' 1813, p. 284.)

1815, Aug. 23. At Hextable-house, Kent, the wife of T. Scotland, esq. of Antigua. (*Ibid.*, p. 281.)

1865, Jan. 31. At Kensington, aged 82, Geo. Scotland, esq., C.B. late Chief Justice of the Island of Trinidad, West Indies. (*Ibid.*, 394.)

Parish Register of St. John.

Baptized.

1790	July 22	Deffell S. of Thomas Scotland and Abigail his wife; b. the 9th April 1789.
1792	May 17	Thomas Colley S. of Thomas Scotland and Abigail his wife. B. the 6th December 1790.
1794	Jan. 2	William S. of John Scotland and Mary his wife. B. the 7th March 1793.
1794	April 22	George Otto S. of Thomas Scotland and Abigail his wife. B. the 6th January 1794.
1794	Dec. 7	Ann Margaret D. of John Scotland and Mary his wife. B. the 3rd May 1794.
1798	Feb. 19	Mary Catherine D. of John Scotland and Mary his wife.
1803	Mar. 9	Anna D. of John Scotland and Mary his wife. B. the 25th November 1802.
1807	Mar. 8	Benjamin S. of Benjamin Scotland and Elizabeth his wife. B. the 5th Instant.
1807	Oct. 30	Mary Anna D. of Benjamin Scotland and Elizabeth his wife. B. the 18th July 1807.
1808	Sep. 9	Esther D. of James Scotland and Esther his wife, deceased. B. the 7th May 1803.
1813	April 2	Jane Elizabeth D. of Benjamin Scotland and Elizabeth his deceased Wife. B. the 18th Nover. 1809.
1816	June 26	George S. of George Scotland and Sarah his wife. B. the 11th April 1815.
1818	Nov. 14	Colley Harman S. of Thomas Scotland and Sarah his wife. B. 16th June.
1823	May 14	Mary Ann D. of Thomas Scotland and Sarah his wife. B. September 15, 1822.
1825	Aug. 13	B. the 5th Nov. 1823 Sarah Maria D. of Thomas & Sarah Scotland. Registrar of Deeds.
1826	June 7	Esther Scotland D. of Thomas & Sarah Scotland. Registrar of Deeds. B. April last.
1826	Dec. 31	B. 26 Mar. 1825 Haverkam Forrest Horne S. of Thomas & Sarah Scotland. St John's. Registrar of Deeds.

Married.

1800	Feb. 24	Benjamin Scotland to Elizabeth Hamilton, Spr. L.
1817	Aug. 2	Thomas Scotland to Sarah Haverkam, Spr. L.
1818	May 6	Richmond Cumming to Mary Scotland, Spr. L.
1822	July 12	James Scotland, Junior, Esquire, to Barbara Foster, Spr. L.
1822	Aug. 1	Robert Scotland to Maria Colley Scotland, Spr. L.
1822	Oct. 25	Thomas Ferguson, M.D., to Esther Scotland, Spr. L.

Buried.

1812	Dec. 20	Thomas C. Scotland, Lieut. R.N.
1818	Mar. 30	Mary Scotland.
1819	Dec. 1	Mary Ann Scotland.
1820	April 6	Samuel Watts Scotland, Infant.
1821	Nov. 17	Benjamin Scotland.

James Scotland, Master in Chancery of Antigua. = Esther ....

Benjamin Scotland. = Elizabeth, dau. of .... Hamilton; mar. 24 Feb. 1800.

George Scotland, C.B., Chief Justice of Trinidad; died 31 Jan. 1865, æt. 82, at Kensington. = Sarah ....

Maria Scotland.

Jean Scotland.

Elizabeth Scotland.

Sarah Maria Scotland, born 5 Nov. 1823 and bapt. 13 Aug. 1825.

Esther Scotland, born April and bapt. 7 June 1826.

Esther Scotland, born 7 May 1803; bapt. 9 Sep. 1808; mar. 25 Oct. 1822 Thomas Ferguson, M.D.

Benjamin Scotland, born 5 and bapt. 8 March 1807.

Mary Anna Scotland, born 18 July and bapt. 30 Oct. 1807.

Jane Elizabeth Scotland, born 18 Nov. 1809; bapt. 2 April 1813.

George Scotland, born 11 April 1815; bapt. 26 June 1816.

Rev. John Scotland, 2nd son, matric. from St. John's College, Oxford, 11 May 1836, æt. 19; B.A. 1840; Student Inner Temple 1841; died 26 May 1865.

Henry Scotland, 4th son, matric. from St. John's College, Oxford, 6 June 1840, æt. 18; Barrister-at-Law Middle Temple 1849; Member Legislative Council, New Zealand.

St. John's Churchyard.

On a white marble tomb:—

Sacred
To the memory of
JOHN SCOTLAND
late of this Ifland Merchant,
He died 25th Day of December
1792
Aged 63 Years and 9 Months.

On a loose broken stone:—

In Memory of
MARY CATHA-
RINE and ROBERT
Third Daughter and
Second Son of John
Scotland the Younger
The former Died the 2 .
November 181 .
. ged 22 . . ars
. he latter . . . .
. . Mar . . . .

On a broken head-stone:—

In Memor . . . .
MARY Wife of . . . .
SCOTLAND . . . .
Wh . . . .

In 1852 the heir of James Scotland owned "Nantons" of 76 acres.

Family of Sedgwick.

1685. Henry Sedgwick of Nevis, chyrurgeon. Wife Mary. (50 Cann.)

Ann Sedgwick of Antigua, widow. Will dated 11 Feb. 1731. To my son Tho. Sedgwick all my estate, he paying legacies. To my son John Sedgwick £100. To my dau. Mary Sedgwick £100. To my granddau. Cath. Hagan £50 c. at 21. Messrs. Thos. & Saml Hanson Ex'ors. Witnessed by Edward Bezune, Edmund Hagan. Before his Excellency William Mathew was sworn Edward Bezune, planter, 13 July 1739. Recorded 6 March 1740.

John Sedgwick, planter. Will dated . . . . To my dau. Susannah Sedgwick £300 c., to . . . . £300 c. To my son Tho. Sedgwick £300 c. To my son Saml all residue, he to pay my said daus. Susannah & Ann £100 c. each. Robt Christian, Jno Brookes, & Saml Martin Ex'ors.

Codicil. My Ex'ors to be kind to my sister Mary Monk & my son Jeremiah, & to latter certain negros. Recorded 19 March 1750.

Samuel Sedgwick, Gent. Will dated 7 Dec. 1792. To my wife Sarah 113 acres in Falmouth Divn, St Paul's parish, with all the buildings, also my land in Ratcliff Str., St John's. To my son Saml, my son John, my dau. Barbara Sedgwick negros. To my son Saml 35 acres in St Mary's parish, subject to the maintenance of my 2 youngest children John & Barbara. To my son John & my dau. Barbara each £400 at 21. My wife Sarah Ex'trix. Witnessed by William Burnett. Recorded 13 Dec. 1793.

Samuel Sedgwick of Antigua, writing clerk. Will dated 23 May 1800. My son Samuel. My wife Elizth. All residue to her, she to be Ex'trix. Witnessed by Mary Bird, Robert Hyndman.

Sarah Sedgwick of Antigua, widow. Will dated 22 March 1812. To my grandson Saml Sedgwick a cocoa nut porter cup & a negro. To my granddau. Eliza Sedgwick 1 guinea. All sums due for dower for land rented to Wm Shervington. Mrs Elizth Sedgwick & Mr Richd Garland Ex'ors. Witnessed by Valentine Weston, John Crawford. Before his Excellency was sworn John Crawford April 1812.

In 1780 Samuel Sedgwick was rated on 35 acres and 24 slaves. (St. Mary's Vestry Book.)

Pedigree of Sedgwick.

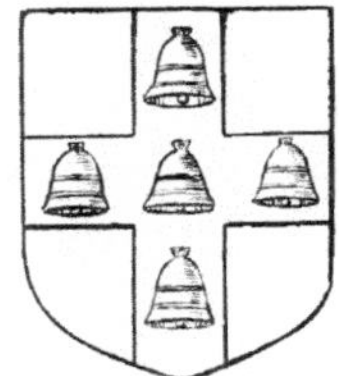

ARMS.—*Or, on a cross gules five bells of the first.*
CREST.—*A hand erect holding a white rose.*
MOTTO.—*Ne tentes aut perfice.*

(? JOHN) SEDGWICK (? from Dent or Kerby Moorside, Yorkshire). = Ann . . . . Will dated 11 Feb. 1731, then a widow; sworn 13 July 1739. Recorded at St. John's.

Charity . . . . 1st wife. = John Sedgwick, planter, bapt. 18 March 1706 at St. John's. Will recorded 19 March 1750. = Sarah Bawn, mar. 22 Dec. 1733 at St. Paul's. 2nd wife.

Thomas Sedgwick.

Mary Sedgwick (? mar. . . . . Monk).

Jeremiah Sedgwick, bapt. 13 May 1733 at St. Paul's.

Samuel Sedgwick, merchant, owned 113 acres in St. Paul's and 35 in St. Mary's; bur. 4 Sep. 1794 at St. John's. Will dated 7 Dec. 1792. = Sarah, dau. of Dr. Francis Jarvis; bapt. 5 Feb. 1758; mar. 15 Feb. 1776 at St. Paul's. Will dated 22 March and sworn April 1812.

Thomas Sedgwick.

—

Susannah Sedgwick, mar. 1 Aug. 1754, at St. John's, William Pigott.

Ann Sedgwick, mar. 16 April 1757, at St. John's, David Barnet.

Samuel Sedgwick, died 15 May 1800. M.I. at St. John's. Will dated May 1800. = Elizabeth Thompson, mar. 15 March 1797; died 2 June 1842, æt. 74. M.I. at St. John's.

John Sedgwick, a minor 1792.

Barbara Jarvis Sedgwick, mar. 27 June 1797, at St. Paul's, Chester Fitch, Master Attendant of English Harbour.

Eliza Sedgwick.

Samuel Sedgwick, M.D., of St. Peter's, Parham, born 7 Jan. and bapt. 19 March 1798 at St. John's; died 27 Oct. 1861; bur. at Brompton Cemetery, London. = Elvira, dau. of Dr. Walter Murray of St. Paul's by Eliza Nanton his wife; mar. 6 April 1826 at St. Paul's; died 14 March 1878, æt. 71. M.I. at St. George's.

Sarah Jarvis Sedgwick, born 12 Jan. 1799 and bapt. 31 Jan. 1800 at St. John's.

Eliza Sedgwick, born 8 Dec. 1800 and bapt. 1 Jan. 1801 at St. John's; mar. 5 May 1818 William E. Ledeatt, Esq.

Samuel Sedgwick, born 21 April and bapt. 8 July 1827 at St. Paul's; died 30 Nov. 1827. M.I. at St. John's.

—

Walter Murray Sedgwick, M.R.C.S. Eng., born 17 Sep. and bapt. 24 Oct. 1828 at St. Peter's; mar. 1855, at St. John's, Letitia M. B. Moore; he died 3 April 1857, bur. and M.I. there.

Elvira Crichton Sedgwick, born 15 Aug. 1830; mar. 29 Feb. 1848, at St. Peter's, Richard Nugent, M.R.C.S. Eng.; she died 10 Feb. 1879 in Dublin. Had issue three sons and two daus.

—

Elizabeth Sarah Sedgwick, born 10 Jan. and bapt. 19 March 1833 at St. Philip's; mar. 1 Dec. 1857, at St. Peter's, Rev. A. F. M. Berkeley.

Samuel Jarvis Sedgwick, born 8 Feb. 1835; died 4 Jan. 1881. M.I. at St. George's. = Selina H. Rossi, mar. 2 Aug. 1860 at St. Marylebone, London.

Henry Nanton Murray Sedgwick, M.R.C.S. Eng., L.S.A. London. (retired) Deputy Inspector-General of Hospitals, born 2 and bapt. 22 Dec. 1840 at St. Peter's; mar. 21 June 1880, at St. Jude's, Southsea, Mary Constance Aldous.

—

Louisa Vinale Sedgwick, born 9 Dec. 1841.

Eleanor Anne Sedgwick, born 1 April and bapt. 5 Aug. 1847 at St. Peter's; died 6 Dec. 1864. M.I. at St. John's.

—

Annette Grant Sedgwick, born 14 and bapt. 19 Nov. 1850 at St. Peter's; died 26 Nov. 1850 and M.I. at St. John's.

Samuel Louis Sedgwick, planter, born 5 March 1862.

—

Louisa Elizabeth Sedgwick, born 20 July 1863.

Ellen Sedgwick, born 9 Feb. 1865.

—

Minnie Ernestine Sedgwick, born 2 Aug. 1867.

Walter Henry Sedgwick, born 5 July 1868.

—

Charles Murray Sedgwick, born 4 Jan. 1870.

Stephen Leonard Sedgwick, born 29 Aug. 1871.

—

Edith May Sedgwick, born 26 Feb. 1874.

Bernard Sedgwick, born 10 May 1875.

—

Lena Sedgwick, born 12 Nov. 1876.

For additions and corrections to this Pedigree I am indebted to Deputy Inspector-General H. N. M. Sedgwick.

PARISH REGISTER OF ST. JOHN.

Baptized.

1706 Mar. 18 John S. of John Sedgwick & Anne his wife.
1798 Mar. 19 Samuel S. of Samuel Sedgwick & Eliza his wife. B. the 7th Janry. 1798.
1800 Jan. 31 Sarah Jarvis D. of Samuel Sedgwick & Eliza his wife. B. the 12th January 1799.
1801 Jan. 1 Eliza D. of Samuel Sedgwick, deceased, & Eliza his wife. B. the 8th December 1800.

Married.

1754 April 18 Peter Becket and Sarah Sedgwick. L.
1754 Aug. 1 William Pigott and Susanna Sedgwick. L.
1757 April 16 David Burnet (Planter) and Ann Sedgewick (Spinster). L.

Buried.

1794 Sep. 4 Capt. Samuel Sedgwick.
1800 Feb. 28 Sarah Sedgwick.
1800 May 24 Sarah Sedgwick.

PARISH REGISTER OF ST. PAUL.

Baptized.

1733 May 13 Jeremiah S. of John Sedgwick & Charity his wife.
1827 July 8 Samuel s. of Samuel & Elvira Sedgwick of Parham. Practitioner of Physic. B. 21 April.

Married.

1733 Dec. 22 John Sedgwick & Sarah Bawn; by L.
1776 Feb. 15 Mr Samuel Sedgwick, Merchant, to Miss Sarah Jarvis; pr L.
1797 June 27 Chester Fitch, Mastr Attendt of Eng. harbour, to Barbara Jarvis Sedgwick, spr.; by L.
1826 April 6 Saml Sedgwick, B. of St Peter's, & Elvira Murray, Spr. L.

PARISH REGISTER OF ST. PETER.

Baptized.

1828 Oct. 24 Walter Murray S. of Samuel & Elvira Sedgwick of Parham, Physician.
1830 Sep. 8 Elvira Crichton D. of Samuel & Elvira Sedgwick of Parham, Physician.
1840 Dec. 22 Henry Nanton Murray S. of Samuel & Elvira Sedgwick, Doctor of Medicine.
1847 Aug. 5 Eleanor Anne D. of Samuel & Elvira Sedgwick, etc., M.D.
1850 Nov. 19 Annette Grant D. of Samuel & Elvira Sedgwick, etc., M.D.

Married.

1818 May 5 William Eales Ledeatt, Esqr, & Eliza Sedgwick, spr; by L.

PARISH REGISTER OF ST. PHILIP.

Baptized.

1833 Mar. 19 Elizabeth Sarah d. of Samuel & Elvira Sedgwick of Parham, Physician.

ST. JOHN'S CHURCHYARD.

On a ledger within an iron grill:—

In
Memory of
MR SAMUEL SEDGWICK
who died May 15th 1800
Aged 28 Years.
ELIZABETH SEDGWICK
died June 2nd 1842 Aged 74.
SAMUEL SEDGWICK
died November 30th 1827 Aged 7 months and . . . .
ANNETTE GRANT SEDGWICK
died November 26th 1850 Aged 12 days.
WALTER MURRAY SEDGWICK
died April 3rd 1857 Aged 28.
ELEANOR ANN SEDGWICK
died December 6th 1864 Aged 17.

ST. PETER'S, PARHAM.

Inside the church, on a white marble monument on black:—

Arms: *Or, on a cross gules five bells of the first.*
Crest: *A hand erect holding a white rose.*
Motto: NE TENTES AUT PERFICE.

SACRED TO THE MEMORY OF
WALTER MURRAY SEDGWICK,
MEMBER OF THE ROYAL COLLEGE OF SURGEONS
OF ENGLAND
ELDEST SON OF SAMUEL SEDGWICK M.D.
AND HIS WIFE ELVIRA
BORN ON THE 17TH DAY OF SEPTR 1828
DIED ON THE 3RD DAY OF APRIL 1857
HIS REMAINS LIE INTERRED
IN THE FAMILY ENCLOSURE IN THE CEMETERY
OF THE CATHEDRAL OF THIS ISLAND.

ST. GEORGE'S, FITCHE'S CREEK.

On a broken pillar in the churchyard, in an enclosure of six graves:—

TO THE MEMORY
OF
SAMUEL JARVIS SEDGWICK
DIED JANRY 4TH 1881
AGED 46 YEARS.

On a white marble cross:—

SACRED TO THE MEMORY OF
ELVIRA,
WIDOW OF THE LATE,
SAMUEL SEDGWICK M.D.
DIED MARCH 14TH 1878 AGED 71.

On a wooden cross:—

LOUISA ELIZABETH SEDGWICK
DIED JUNE 7TH
1867
AGED 8 YEARS 11 MONTHS.

Pedigree of Shand.

ARMS.—*Azure, a boar's head couped argent, on a chief of the second three mullets gules.*
CREST.—*A dove with wings displayed, holding in its beak an olive-branch.*
MOTTO.—*Virtute duce comite fortuna.*

Maurice Berkeley, junior, from co. Gloucester, went out to St. Christopher's in 1731 in Captain Tobin's ship the "Apollo." = ... dau. of . . . . Tobin of Nevis; living 1731.

William Hart (? of St. Kitts). = Sarah, dau. of John Johnson by a dau. of . . . . Milliken; mar. 31 Jan. 1748.

Abraham Hardtman. = ...

Benjamin Amory, senior, born 13 Aug. 1739; died 21 Sep. 1806. = Mary, dau. of Anthony Somersall; born 22 Nov. 1744; died 11 Aug. 1808.

Henry Berkeley. = Mary Earle. Had 7 sons and 2 daus.; 2 sons and 1 dau. died infants.

Maurice Berkeley, died a bachelor.

James Lapsly of North Woodside, Glasgow. = Elizabeth Hart, born 26 May 1750.

Jacob Hardtman. = Isabella Amory.

Maurice Berkeley. = Elizabeth Sarah Manning. Her mother was Ann, dau. of Robert Howard by . . . . Pelham.

John Rawlins (son of Stedman Rawlins, President of St. Kitts 1817). = Sarah Johnston Hart, sister of Sir Anthony Hart, Vice-Chancellor of England, K.B., 30 April 1827.

William Wilson of Glasgow. = Elizabeth Susannah Lapsly, born 30 Oct. 1776; bapt. at St. George and St. Peter, St. Kitts; mar. there 24 April 1797.

Thomas Allman Hardtman, born 15 April 1799; died 23 Dec. 1852. = Ann Howard Berkeley, coheir, born 10 Aug. 1800 in Martinique; mar. 7 Feb. 1822; died Jan. 1854.

Anthony Rawlins, Barrister-at-Law.

John Hart Rawlins, Lieut. 13th Regiment. = Martha Wilson.

FRANCIS SHAND of Woolton Wood near Liverpool, West India merchant; Mayor 1856-7. Owned large estates in Antigua. = Lydia, dau. of Sir William Byam of Cedar Hill, Antigua; mar. 16 March 1837 at St. George's.

Thomas Berkeley Hardtman of Shadwell, St. Kitts, and Cedar Hill, Antigua, born 14 Jan. 1824; President of the Federal Council of the Leeward Islands; died 6 Nov. 1881. = Alice Hart Rawlins, born 3 Jan. 1828; now living.

William Alfred Byam Shand, youngest son, matriculated from Balliol College, Oxford, 17 Oct. 1877, æt. 19; B.A. 1882; M.A. 1886; Barrister-at-Law Inner Temple 1884.

Charles Arthur Shand of Fitche's Creek, Antigua, 1st son and heir, educated at Harrow; Member of Council 1895. = Alice Howard Hardtman-Berkeley, mar. 30 Oct. 1877 at St. George's.

Annie Hardtman, mar. 23 Oct. 1873 Hon. Arthur Wyndham A'Court of Antigua, 6th son of the 2nd Lord Heytesbury, and has issue.

Sir Henry S. Berkeley Hardtman, Solicitor-General of the Leeward Islands; Chief Justice of Fiji 1895; knighted 1896. He sold Cedar Hill.

Francis Byam Berkeley Shand, 1st son and heir, born 11 Aug. 1879; in 1895 at Derby School.

William Kenrick Willoughby Shand, born 11 July 1891; living 1895.

A dau., dead.

The above Pedigree has been compiled from papers in the possession of Charles A. Shand, Esq.

A Miss Braithwaite mar. 1st Mr. Ledeatt of Cassava Garden, Antigua, by whom she had an only dau. Lena Redwood Ledeatt, wife of Frank H. Moore of Barbados; and 2ndly Walter Shand, cousin of the present proprietor of Fitche's Creek Estate.

1695, Sep. 4. Captain Heartman's sloop referred to. (Colonial Entry Book, No. 48.)

1707-8. Census of St. Christopher's.

	Age.	White Men.	White Women.	White Boys.	Slaves.
John Hardtman	33	1	1	3	1
Joan Hardtman	40		1	4	2
Eliz. Hardtman	22		1	2	3

1711. St. Thomas, Middle Island.

	White Men.	White Women.	White Boys.	Slaves.
John Hartman	1	1	2	1
Joan Hartman		1	4	3

1726, Feb. 17. Deposition of Peter Hardtman, jun., of St. Kitts.

1814, Sep. 25. Aged 58, Isaac Hartman, esq. of St Croix. ('Gent. Mag.,' p. 499.)

1825, April 22. Mrs. Sarah Amory, Relict of the late Jos. Amory, Esq.; aged 85. (Almanack of St. Christopher.)

1825, May 7. Miss Susannah Berkeley, aged 52. (*Ibid.*)

1839, Jan. 7. In the island of Grenada, aged 55, John Berkeley, esq. ('Gent. Mag.,' p. 558.)

1842, July 12. In London, Major W. H. Hartman, 9th Regt. to Mary, widow of Thos. Berkeley, esq. of Grenada, West Indies. (*Ibid.*, p. 312.)

1865, Feb. 24. Thomas Berkeley Hardtman, esq., to be a Member of the Legislative Council of the Island of St. Christopher. (*Ibid.*, p. 496.)

Amory Family.

Copy of a letter written to Captain Jack Hardtman Berkeley of St. Kitts :—

Dear Sir,—I hope you will pardon a stranger for making some inquiries about my progenitors ; I have from circumstances in a measure had imposed upon me the collection of material for the history of my name and family. Captain Train tells my nephew Arthur Amory that you possibly can give me some information about Robert, brother of my grt. grt. gr'dfather Mr Jonathan Amory, who died in Carolina about 1698. They were sons of Robert Amory of Somersetshire, England, & of the sister of Eliot ; & their father Robert, we have reason to believe, was the son of the Rev. Anthony Amory or d'Amorie, who died rector of Ashott in Somerset 1620, where he had been rector of the manor of white Chapelle in Bishops . . . . in Devon, which estate & other manors went to his gr'ddau. Frances Amory, who mar. Edward Giblon 1675. Giblon—who after her death mar. the dau. of Sir Courtenay Pole, at which time he is called "of white Chapell, the paternal inheritance of Frances"—died *c.* 1709 & was bur. at Tiverton where his monument stands . . . . see vol. 7 Collins' 'Peerage,' "Damer," & see Dr Rob. Amory in 'Gent. Mag.,' 1788. My grt. grt. gr'dfather who d. in Carolina 1698 mar. thrice, 1sty Rebecca Cunningham of Craigends who d. in Barbados, & was Mother of my grt. gr'df. whose portrait is over my mantel, & whose half-brother thro' her was Alexr Hamilton of Grange in Renfrew in Scotland, & whose half-sister, by my grt. grt. grdfather's 2d wife Martha, was Sarah who mar. Gov. Arthur Middleton of South Carolina in 1706, from whom all the best people in S. Carolina seem to have descended. The 1st brother of Jonathan & Robert of Antigua—Thomas,* mar. Eliz. Fitzmaurice, dau. of the 19th Lord Kerry, 1667, ancestor of the Govr Genl of Canada.† He died 1667, leaving an only son Thos. Amory of Bunratty Castle in Clare who died in 1728. Their brother John died in 1733 at the age of 94 in that county. In one of the family letters from Julia O'Connor she says that Robert of Antigua left her brother Tho. Amory of Bunratty Castle £800 a year rental. From this I had inferred that Robert left no Son, but he may have had daus., or the £800 rental may have reverted on Robert's death about 1710 to the main stem, & not passed by inheritance to his children . . . . In the family is an old silver pitcher with arms like the Ludwells, left in 1698 by Mrs Martha, Mother of this Gov. Arthur Middleton, to my grt. gr'df. Thos. Amory . . . . Govr Clarke was Govr‡ of Antigua & had mar. a dau. of Govr Ludwell whose 2d Wife was the Widow of Govr Sir Wm Berkeley of Virginia. ? was she Martha Ellis . . . .

* Described in Burke as one of the victuallers of the Navy.
† The Marquess of Lansdowne.
‡ I do not think that he could have been Governor.

Arms : *Quarterly,* 1 *and* 4, *Azure, a boar's head couped argent, on a chief of the second three mullets gules* (Shand) ; 2 *and* 3, Byam : impaling, 1 *and* 4, *Gules, a chevron argent between six Maltese crosses above and four below, a crescent for difference ;* 2, *Sable, a demi-man in armour couped at the hip, holding in his dexter hand a battle-axe* (Hardtman) ; 3, *Gules, a bend sinister wavy or, with three mullets of the first between two crescents of the second.*

Crest : *A dove with wings displayed, holding in its beak an olive-branch* (Shand).

Motto : *Virtute duce comite fortuna.*

Crests of Berkeley and Hardtman : *A bishop's mitre.* "*Dieu avec nous.*" *Out of a ducal coronet a demi-man grasping a raised battle-axe with both hands, between two wings.* "*Touch not.*"

Parish Register of St. George.

Married.

1837 Mar. 16 Francis Shand, Esqr, Bach., & Lydia Byam, Spr, of St Peter's. Lic. ; by Robt Holberton, rector of St John's.

1877 Oct. 30 Charles Arthur Shand, Bach., & Alice Howard Hardtman-Berkeley. Banns. By Edwin Elliott, rector of St John. Witnesses, T. Berkeley, Kate Cassin, H. S. Berkeley.

St. Peter's Church, Antigua.

North wall. On a white marble shield :—

IN LOVING REMEMBRANCE OF | THE HONOURABLE | THOMAS BERKELEY HARDTMAN BERKELEY | OF "SHADWELL" | IN THE ISLAND OF ST KITTS, | AND "CEDAR HILL" IN THIS ISLAND, | PRESIDENT OF THE FEDERAL COUNCIL OF THE | LEEWARD ISLANDS | WHO DIED AT CEDAR HILL, ON THE 6TH NOV. 1881 | AGED 57 YEARS | THIS TABLET | IS ERECTED BY HIS SON HENRY, | THE SOLICITOR GENERAL, | TO THE MEMORY OF A BELOVED AND | DEEPLY MOURNED FATHER.

Bath Abbey.

South wall of south transept :—

Sacred to the Memory of
ANN STEPHENS AMORY
(daughter of BENJAMIN
and
POLLY EARLE AMORY,
late of the Island
of Saint Christopher)
who departed this Life
8th June 1817
In the 11th year of her age.
Also the above named
BENJAMIN AMORY
who departed this Life
the 20th January 1819
Aged 51 Years.

Pedigree of Shephard.

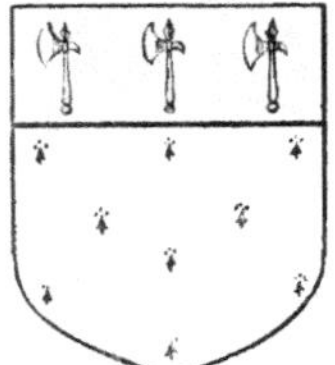

ARMS.—*Ermine, on a chief . . . . three battle-axes . . . .*
CREST.—*A stag courant-regardant.*

. . . . SHEPHARD of Cerne, co. Dorset ═ . . . .

Elizabeth, dau. of . . . . Byam ; mar. 8 Aug. 1730 at St. Philip's ; died 26 and bur. 27 Sep. 1732, æt. 21, at St. John's. 1st wife. ═ Thomas Shephard of Antigua, merchant, bur. 14 May 1749 at Cerne. Will dated at London 5 April and proved 9 May 1749. (160 Lisle.) ═ Rachel, dau. and coheir of Colonel Jacob Morgan ; bapt. 14 Feb. 1711 at St. John's ; mar. 29 Nov. 1733 at St. Philip's. (? bur. 29 Aug. 1780 at St. George's.) 2nd wife.

Thomas Shephard, Esq., 1st son and heir, died s.p. 23 Dec. 1769 at Bath. Will dated 4 July 1767 ; proved 9 Jan. 1770. (30 Jenner.)

Richard Shephard, died s.p. before his brother Thomas. (? bur. 1768 at St. George's.)

Jacob Shephard, a lunatic 1790.

Elizabeth Shephard, mar. 30 June 1764, at St. George's, Samuel Byam, Esq. ; he died 1786 ; she died after 1790 in London.

Mary Shephard, bapt. 20 Oct. 1744 at St. John's. (? bur. 20 Jan. 1793 at St. George's.)

Susannah Shephard, mar. . . . . Braham ; living 1790. (See Hanson Pedigree.)

Thomas Bridges, bapt. 4 Aug. 1757 ; living 1779 ═ Rebeccah . . . . living 1779.

Elizabeth Bridges, bapt. 24 May 1755.

Thomas Lovely Bridges, bapt. 25 Oct. 1780.

Henry Bridges, bapt. 2 Nov. 1787.

Lydia Bridges, bapt. 9 July 1783.

Elizabeth Ross Bridges, born 27 July 1783.

Anne Sanderson Bridges, born 6 June 1784.

1658, Feb. 14. Peter Stoodleigh of Bridport, co. Dorset, deceased. Adm'on to Joane the relict.

John Stoodley, Clerk, Rector of Winterborne Abbas, co. Dorset. Nuncupative will dated Dec. 1658 ; proved 8 June 1659 ; commission to Joane Stoodley the sister. (312 Pell.) £5 to the poor. Mourning cloaks to my 4 brothers. All residue to my sister Joane. Witnessed by Giles Studdley, Joseph Stoodley.

Edward Stoodley of Malswood, co. Dorset, yeoman. Will dated 15 Jan. 1670 ; proved 6 June 1671 by Margery Stoodley the relict. (82 Duke.) To John Wills & Grace his wife £40. Daniel Stoodley £20. Ann Ding £20. Mary Conner £30. Kath. Hext £10. Mr Solway £5. Robert Bartlett £5. Hugh Cooke 40*s*. Mag^d Cooke 1*s*. Nich. Cooke 40*s*. James Bagg 5*s*. My brother Joseph Stoodley £5 14*s*., being a debt from Wm Pinney of Broad Winsor. All residue to my wife Margery & sole Ex'trix. Witnessed by Robert Kedger, Henry Byshopp.

John Bridges of Antigua, merchant. Will dated 15 May 1672. To my friend Cap. Wm Thomas of Antigua, Gent., my mare. To my friend Geo. Hawkins of Antigua, planter, 5000 lbs. of sugar charged on my plantation called "Taylor's Ridge" in St John's Div^n, & to his wife Amy my ring. To Elias Buckly, planter, 1000 lbs. of tobacco, & to his son Richd Buckly 500 lbs. To my brother Richd Bridges in England 3 negros & all residue, & I appoint him Ex'or, & Cap. Wm Thomas & Geo. Hawkins feoffees to whom I give 20*s*. rings. Witnessed by Richard Buckley, John George, Jacob Hill. On 11 Nov. 1672 appeared Richard Buckly of Popeshead, planter, and William Thomas, and on 13 Nov. John George, cooper, before Governor P. Warner. Recorded 27 Nov. 1672.

John Eyre of Bristol, ironmonger. Will dated 12 April, proved 10 July 1680. (95 Bath.) To be buried in the parish of St Thomas near my brothers. My sister Mary Lewis, widow of John Lewis of Bristol, cooper, 20*s*. My sister Sarah Stoodly, wife of Chr. Stoodly of Dorchester, grocer, 20*s*. All residue to my wife Mary & Ex. My brothers-in-law Mr Samuel Clarke, Mr Robert Allen, & Mr John Ewens of Bristol, overseers.

John Eyre of Poole, Dorset. Will dated 10 July, proved 8 Nov. 1682. (129 Cottle.) My father bequeathed me his farm in Purbeck, the rent of which I give to my wife Sarah. My dau. Mary Lewis, widow, £50. Grandsons John & Chr. Stoodley £10 each, son Stoodley my signet ring, & my dau. his wife that ring from her brother Eyre. Worth Maltravers where I was born.

Robert Shephard of Cerne Abbas, co. Dorset, innholder. Will dated 10 March 1689 ; proved 18 Feb. 1692. (35 Coker.) To be buried near my wife Leatice. Joan White, Geo. White, Eliz. White, Anne White, & Joane White, children of Geo. White, tallow-chandler, deceased. My kinsman Newton Shephard of Lewes, co. Sussex, cordwinder, £10. All residue to Richd Shephard, s. of my brother Tho. Shephard, dec^d, & sole Ex'or.

Charles Stoodley of Dorchester, co. Dorset, yeoman, dead 1693. ═ Sarah .... Adm'on 25 Oct. 1693 to her son Christopher.

Christopher Stoodley of Antigua, merchant, bur. 23 Dec. 1731 at Richmond, co. Surrey. Will dated 23 July and proved 31 Dec. 1731. (316 Isham.) ═ Mary .... bur. 13 Oct. 1745 at Richmond. Will dated 26 Jan. 1744; proved 14 Oct. 1745. (282 Seymer.)

Rev. Timothy Stoodley, matriculated from Wadham College, Oxford, 3 April 1693, æt. 18; B.A. 1 March 1697; Vicar of Sydling St. Nicholas, co. Dorset, 1702; died 27 and bur. 29 Dec. 1724, æt. 49. M.I. at Sydling. ═ Elizabeth .... bur. 13 Feb. 1730-1 at Sydling.

Mary Stoodley, bur. 29 June 1738 at Sydling.

Jonathan Sheppard of Southwark, co. Surrey, brother-in-law of Christopher Stoodley 1731 ═ ....

Robert Shephard of Cerne 1749.

Susannah Shephard, mar. .... White.

Catherine Shephard, mar. .... Balcocke.

William Sheppard, living 1731.

Sarah Sheppard.

Elizabeth Sheppard, mar. 22 April 1721 at St. John's; living 1731 at Southwark. ═ Bartholomew Saunderson of Antigua, merchant, 1711; Member of Assembly for St. John's Town 1721-2; bur. 1 Nov. 1724 at St. John's.

Samuel Wickham Sanderson of Antigua, later of London, merchant. Will dated 5 Oct. and proved 26 Nov. 1762. (484 St. Eloy.)

Sarah Sanderson, living 1779. ═ Thomas Bridges, builder. Will dated 8 Feb. 1760.

Rachel Sanderson,* mar. Rev. Samuel Lovely, Rector of St. Peter's; she bur. 16 Nov. 1785 at St. John's. Her will dated Nov. 1779.

Anne Sanderson, spinster 1779.

Christopher Saunderson, living 1731 and 1744.

John Bridges, 2nd son, bapt. 29 Sep. 1759 ═ Mary Penony.

Henry Bridges, born 1762; bapt. 6 Feb. 1763.

John Richard Bridges, bapt. 13 Aug. 1785. ═ Amy ....

Samuel Lovely Bridges, bapt. 10 Jan. 1786. = Jane Edwards, mar. 10 Aug. 1808.

Sarah Bridges, bur. 15 March 1782.

John Richard Bridges, bapt. 12 May 1810.

* In the Coull Pedigree, vol. i., p. 177, she has been erroneously styled sister of Patrick Coull.

Joh. Sheppard of St. Leonard's, Shoreditch. Gr'dsons Math. & Tho. sons of my s. John. (9 Hene.)

1693, Oct. 25. Sara Stoodley of Dorchester, co. Dorset, widow, deceased. Adm'on to Christopher Stoodley the son.

Richard Sheppard of Lothbury, London, merchant. Will dated 17 April, proved 13 Jan. 1730. (18 Isham.) Sister M[rs] Frances Sheppard of Dorchester, Dorset. All est. to only son M[r] Thos. Sheppard.

Christopher Stoodly, late of St. John's Town, Antigua, now of London, merchant. Will dated 23 July, proved 31 Dec. 1731 by Thomas Tryon; power reserved to William Tryon and William Chase. (316 Isham.) To my wife Mary £1000, furniture, plate, linen, chariot, horse, & chaise, also my lease of 21 acres with buildings in S[t] John's parish, which were demised to me by Bayer Otto-Bayer, Esq., & have since been by me demised to Geo. Byam, Esq., in trust to pay all profits to my nieces Sarah Shepard, Eliz. Sanderson, widow, Mary Sheppard, Mary Stoodly, Sarah Stoodly, & Eliz. Stoodly. By a certain agreement duly enrolled the Hon. Valentine Morrice of Antigua, Esq., now holds a plantation & has to pay myself & wife £400 a year for our lives, & at the death of the survivor of us £2500. In case of the conquest of the island, however, this agreement becomes void, & in such case I give the plantation to Ashton Warner & Edw[d] Chester of Antigua, Esq[rs], & Tho. Sheppard of Antigua, merch[t], in trust to be sold & the proceeds to my wife. To my nephew W[m] Sheppard, son of Jonathan Sheppard of Southwark, co. Surry, my house in S[t] John's town, lately occupied by W[m] Dunbar, Gent., he to pay £10 a year to my niece Sarah Stoodly & 2s. weekly to my negro Sarah Sibill. I manumit Sarah Sibil & Tho. Tomson. To my niece Mary Stoodly, dau. of my beloved brother Timothy Stoodly, late vicar of Sydling, co. Dorset, £500. To my brother-in-law Jonathan Sheppard £100. To Christopher Sanderson, son of Eliz. Sanderson of Southwark, widow, £100. To Eliz. Northall £10. To my godson John Watkins, son of Giles Watkins, Esq., of Antigua, £10. To each Ex'or £10. To Ashton Warner, Edw[d] Chester, & Tho. Sheppard all residue of my real estate in trust to sell, as also all my ships & personalty for my said nieces Sarah Sheppard, Eliz. Sanderson, Mary Sheppard, Mary Stoodly, Sarah Stoodly, & Eliz. Stoodly. Ashton Warner, Edw[d] Chester, & Tho. Sheppard Ex'ors for America, & W[m] Tryon & Tho. Tryon, merch[ts] in London, & W[m]

Chase of London, linendraper, Ex'ors for G[t] Britain. Witnessed by John Long, John Wise, Jonathan Evendore, all in Abchurch Lane.

Codicil dated 28 Aug. 1731. The lease of 21 acres to go to my wife absolutely, not to my nieces. Witnessed by John Wise, William Frye, Jonathan Evendore.

Joseph Stoodley was Ex'or 1737 to Edward Sanderson of London, merchant. (See vol. i., p. 119, for the latter's will.)

Joseph Studley, Gent. Will proved 1743. (136 Boycott.) To my wife Eliz. my presentation to the rectory of West Knighton, co. Dorset. My late sister Jane Beer. My sister Eliz. Butter, etc.

Mary Stoodly of Richmond, co. Surry, widow. Will dated 26 Jan. 1744; proved 14 Oct. 1745 by Elizabeth Northall. (282 Seymer.) To be buried at Richmond near my late husband. To my goddau. Henrietta Horn, wife of Edward Horn, Esq., now in Antigua, £120. To M[rs] Frances Morrice, dau. of Col. Valentine Morrice, deceased, my gold snuffbox. To Christopher Sanderson, son of Eliz. Sanderson, widow, £400. To each servant £5. To Sarah Maynard £5 more. To my negro Sarah Sibbell £5. To Eliz. Northall, sp[r], dau. of the late Capt. Geo. Northall, my lease of 31 acres in S[t] John's Parish, which were demised to my late husband Christopher Stoodly by Bayer Otto-Bayer, Esq., & afterwards let to Geo. Byam, Esq. No claim for improvements to be made against Henry Meyler in whose house I dwell. All residue to Eliz. Northall & appoint her Ex'trix. Witnessed by William Chase, A. Chase, Henry Collins.

Thomas Shephard, late of Antigua, now of London, merchant. Will dated 5 April, proved 9 May 1749 by George White, Richard Bingham, Esq., and Robert Shephard; proved 22 March 1756 by Stephen Mingnan *alias* Mignian; power reserved to the others. On 7 Sep. 1767 adm'on to Thomas Shephard, Esq., the son, Ashton Warner, Daniel Warner, and Richard Boddicot dying without taking on them the execution, and Thomas Warner, Esq., renouncing. (160 Lisle.) To my dear wife Rachael all my household goods, jewels, linen, & use of plate, but the latter after her death to my dau. Eliz. Shepherd. I give my wife also £300, she to assent to all leases of my plantations & of all houses here or at Philadelphia, & if so ⅓ of rents. To each child of my sister Cath. Bulcocke £50. To all my sons except my heir-at-law all my houses in S[t] John's, Antigua, & in Philadelphia as joint tenants & £1200 each at 21. The like sum to each dau. at 21. The legacies to my wife & children are in full bar of all claims they have under the will of the late Col. Jacob Morgan, my wife's father. To my brother Robert Shephard & to my sister Susannah White each £15 yearly & £30. My negro London to be free & 3 shillings c. a week. All residue to my son Thos. Shephard. Ashton Warner, Tho. Warner, Dan[l] Warner, all of Antigua, Esq[rs], Geo. White of Antigua, merch[t], Rich[d] Bingham of Melcomb, Dorset, Esq., Rob[t] Shepherd of Cern, Dorset, Gent., & Rich[d] Boddicot of London, merch[t], Ex'ors & Guardians & 2 gs. each. Witnessed by Peter Mauleverer, Clement's Lane, Lombard Street, Alexander Malcolm, clerk to Mr. Shephard, Thurston Blackman, Clifford's Inn.

Memo. Instructions to Mr. Richard Boddicot, dated 7 April 1749. My body to be buried at Cerne with the rest of my family. My brother Rob[t] to have £5 a year for maintenance of each of my children during the break up for the holidays, & £10 for charity. Witnessed by Thomas Hunsdon.

1st Codicil dated 8 April 1749. My wife to have her own plate which she had before her marriage with me absolutely. Stephen Mignian of London, surgeon, but going to Antigua, to be an Ex'or. Witnessed by Peter Mauleverer, Thurstan Blackman.

2nd Codicil dated 29 April 1749. To each child except my heir £300 more. Witnessed by Robert Moncrieff, Thurston Blackman. On 9 May 1749 was sworn Thurston Blackman of Clifford's Inn, Gent. Testator was of St. Edmund the King. Recorded also at St. John's 9 March 1749-50 (fo. 131).

John Wickham, Esq., by his will dated 1750 bequeathed property to his godson John Wickham Sanderson, son of Captain John Sanderson, provided he took the name of Wickham. A William Wickham Sanderson was also named in a Wickham will of *c.* 1743.

Thomas Bridges of Antigua, carpenter. Will dated 8 Feb. 1760. To my wife Sarah my house in S[t] John Street, now in the occupation of Archibald Gloster, surgeon, also the use of my furniture, plate, china, & £60 c. yearly, & 2 negros, after her death to my son John Bridges. To my son Thos. Bridges 6 proportions of land in Broad Str., S[t] John's Town, & the house now in the occupation of Geo. White, merchant, also 7 negros. To my son John Bridges 8 negros. To my dau. Eliz. Bridges 3 proportions of land in Popeshead Str., S[t] John's Town, & the house & 5 negros. All residue to my wife. Hon. Francis Farley, Esq., Rev[d] Samuel Lovely, clerk, Samuel Martin, & Samuel Wickham Sanderson, merchants of Antigua, Ex'ors. Witnessed by Edmond Griffith, George Jordan.

1st Codicil dated 26 Feb. 1762. My wife Sarah is now with child. £500 to my Ex'ors for the said child.

2nd Codicil dated 9 April 1763. I revoke the appointment of Samuel Martin as Ex'or & nominate my kinsman James Bridges of the city of Bristol. M[r] Samuel Wickham Sanderson being since dead I appoint M[r] Samuel Gunthorpe of Antigua, merchant, Ex'or. Witnessed by R. Lovely, Samuel Gunthorpe, John Haslewood. Antigua: before Governor Thomas appeared Samuel Gunthorpe, merchant, and John Haslewood, Gent., 27 April 1763. Recorded 27 April 1763.

Samuel Wickham Sanderson, late of Antigua, now of London, merchant. Will dated 5 Oct., proved 26 Nov. 1762 by James Bridges; power reserved to the others. (484 St. Eloy.) Funeral not to exceed 50 guineas. Most of my estate is in the hands of my partner Mr. James Taylor of London, merchant, which I estimate at about £3500. To Tho. Bridges, son of Tho. & Sarah Bridges of Antigua, John Bridges their 2nd son, Eliz. Bridges their dau., & to their last child £200 apiece at 21. James Taylor £50. My brother-in-law Rev. Samuel Lovely, rector of S[t] Peter's at Falmouth in Antigua, £50 for a better horse to ride to church. To Mary, Eliz., & Eleanor Morris, daus. of Chas. & Eleanor Morris of Antigua, £20 apiece. My sister Sarah Bridges, wife of Tho. Bridges, 2 negro boys. My sister Rachel Lovely, wife of Rev. Samuel Lovely, 2 negros. My sister Anne Sanderson 2 negros & all my plate. My father by will left her a legacy which shall be paid. My father's sword to my nephew John Bridges. My negro Jack his freedom. All residue to my friends James Bridges of Bristol, architect, Langford Lovell, & Samuel Gunthorp of Antigua, merchants, & Tho. Bridges of Antigua, builder, in Trust for my said 3 sisters. Trustees to be Ex'ors. Witnessed by Thomas Symonds of Bristol, attorney, G. N. Viner, his clerk.

Codicil. 8 Oct. 1762. Revoke appointment of Langford Lovell.

Thomas Shephard, late of London, now of Antigua, Esq. Will dated 4 July 1767; proved 9 Jan. 1770 by William Gunthorpe, Samuel Byam; power reserved to the others. (30 Jenner.) To my mother £300 st. To each of my 3 sisters Eliz. Byam, wife of Samuel Byam, Esq., Susannah Shephard, & Mary Shephard £150 st. To my Ex'ors 10 guineas each. £40 st. to the poor of Cerne Abbas, co. Dorset. To Kitt a free negro, formerly slave of my father, now a servant in my mother's family, £10 a yr. Hon. Byam Freeman, Esq., Wm Gunthorpe, Esq., Oliver Nugent, Esq., Edwd Byam, jun., Esq., & the said Samuel Byam Ex'ors in Trust. All my plantations, slaves to my brother Richard Shephard for life, then to the said Ex'ors in Trust for his children in tail, then to my sister Eliz. Byam, my sisters Susannah Shephard & Mary Shephard. All residue to my said brother. Witnessed by John Hoskins, John Newman, William Higgins.

Codicil. 4 July 1767. My brother Jacob Shephard is a lunatick, but should he not be so at my death then all my estate to him, otherwise to my brother Richard Shephard.

Charity Shepherd of Dickinson's Bay. Will dated 17 April 1782. To my mother Sarah all my slaves on condition she take care of my son John, & after her death 1 negro to the child I am now with, & all residue to my son John. Robt Christian, Wm Mackinnen, Jas. Nibbs, Esqres, Ex'ors. Witnessed by Samuel McKinnen. Before Thomas Jarvis, Esq., was sworn Samuel McKinnen 23 Aug. 1785. Recorded 2 Sep. 1785.

John Sheppard. Will recorded 10 Aug. 1799. All the remainder destroyed.

Close Roll, 10 Geo. III., Part 2, Nos. 18 and 19.

Indenture made the 5th Feb. 1770 between Samuel Byam, late of Antigua, but now of Featherstone Buildings, Holborn, Esq., and Elizabeth his wife (which said Elizabeth is the eldest sister of Thomas Shephard, formerly of Antigua, but late of the city of Bath, Esq., deceased), of the one part, and William Gunthorp, late of Antigua, but now of Cecil Street, Strand, Esq., of the other part, witnesses that in consideration of 5s. Samuel and Elizabeth Byam have sold to William Gunthorp all that plantation, etc., in the division of New North Sound in the parish of St. George, Antigua, formerly the estate of the said Thomas Shephard, deceased, with all slaves, etc., for one year at the rent of one peppercorn that he may be in actual possession, to the uses of an Indenture to be made. Joseph Pickering, Tobias Pickering, witnesses.

No. 18.

Indenture made the 6th Feb. 1770 between Samuel Byam and Elizabeth his wife, of the one part, and William Gunthorp, of the other. Whereas Thomas Shephard duly executed his last will dated 4th July 1767 (will recited), and died the 23rd Dec. 1769, at which time Jacob Shephard his brother, by an Inquisition taken the 31st Jan. last past, was found to be a lunatic from August 1763, so that the devise in the said codicil to Jacob and his sons and daughters did not take effect; and whereas Richard Shephard the other brother died in the lifetime of Thomas intestate s.p., Elizabeth Byam became seised as tenant in tail general of the said plantations, now this Indenture witnesses that in consideration of 10s. Samuel and Elizabeth Byam bargain to William Gunthorp all that plantation (as in No. 19) to hold to him and his heirs to the intent that they may be seised thereof, and qualified to convey them to Samuel Byam and Elizabeth, and lastly Samuel and Elizabeth Byam appoint Edward Byam, Esq., and Samuel Henry Warner, Esq., both residing in Antigua, their Attorneys.

Close Roll, 10 Geo. III., Part 15, No. 6.

Indenture made the 5th Oct. 1770 between Stephen Shepherd of Deptford, shipwright, and Mary Susanna his wife, of the one part, and Peter Alsop of Antigua, Esq., of the other part, witnesseth that in consideration of 10s. Stephen Shepherd and Mary Susanna his wife convey to Peter Alsop and his heirs, etc., all that piece of land in the town of Falmouth in Antigua, containing four proportions, bounded E. with land belonging to the heirs of Edward Tyley, deceased, W. with a street leading north and south, N. with the lands of Charles Hozier, and S. with an east and west street, and also the dwelling house, etc., thereon, and also two negro men Gosport and Valentine, and two negro women Jenny and Sally, which said lands, etc., were late the property of William Hart of Antigua, shipwright, deceased, in trust to sell and to remit the money to Stephen Shepherd and Mary Susanna his wife, and they appoint, etc., John Burke of St. John's, Antigua, Gent., their Attorney. Martin French, David Young, witnesses.

In the Visitation of Kent 1619 is a pedigree of Studley from Wimborne Minster, co. Dorset. Arms: *Argent, on a fess vert three stags' heads caboshed or.* Crest: *A stag's head or, transfixed obliquely by an arrow barbed sable.*

1623. Giles Studley of Broad Windsor and John Studley of Marchwood were disclaimed by the Heralds at Bridport.

1636. Mr. Charles Studly was rated for the higher farm. (Churchwarden's Book, Langton Long Blandford. 'Somerset and Dorset Notes and Queries,' vol. iii., p. 58.)

There are several entries of Stoodley of co. Dorset in Foster's 'Alumni Oxonienses.'

Circa 1670. A Mr. Giles Studley was living in a house called Kaites near Pensbury in Gillingham, co. Dorset. ('Motcombe Past and Present.')

1693. Timothy Stoodley. M. 3 April 1693 (fil. Caroli Stoodley de Dorchester, Dorcestr pauperis æt. 18). C.M. received as Servitor 7 Mar. 1693 & restored 4 Ap. 1698. Goodbridge Exhibitioner 1693 & 1694. B.A. 1 Mar. 1697. (Registers of Wadham College, Oxford.)

1705, Aug. 20. Christopher Stoodly, two proportions of land in St. John's Town by grant from John Yeamans, Esq. Surveyed 3 Sep.

1730, July 20. Christopher Stoodly having gone to England his seat in the Assembly for St. John's Town was declared vacant.

1744-5, Feb. 28. Mr. Shephard hath purchased Henry Osborn's Estate and gives £10,500 for it, ye Crop on the ground and 30 negroes, a great purchase in these times.

1790, Dec. 2. Petition of Elizabeth Byam, Susanna Braham, and Mary Shepherd, sisters of the whole blood and presumptive heirs of Jacob Shepherd a lunatic, for leave to bring in Act to sell his real estate.

Act *re* estate of Jacob Shepherd of St. John's, a lunatic, read 24 June 1791.

Parish Register of St. John.

Baptized.

1744	Oct.	20	Susannah the D. of Thos Sheppard and Rachel his wife.
1744	Oct.	20	Mary the D. of Thos Sheppard and Rachel his wife.
1755	May	24	Eliz. the D. of Thos Bridges & Mary his wife.
1757	Aug.	4	Thos. the S. of Thos Bridges & Sarah his wife.
1759	Sep.	29	John the S. of Thomas Bridges & Sarah his wife.
1760	Nov.	15	Abigail the D. of John Shephard and Ann his wife.
1763	Feb.	6	Henry the S. of Thomas Bridges and Sarah his wife.

1777 Mar. 3 Edward the S. of the Revd John Shephard and his wife.

1780 Oct. 25 Thomas Lovely the s. of Thomas Bridges & Rebeccah his wife.

1781 July 31 Sarah the d. of James Bridges & Mary his wife.

1783 July 9 Lydia the D. of Thomas Bridges and Rebecca his wife.

.... 13 John Richard the S. of John Bridges and Mary his wife.

.... 21 Elizabeth Ross. B. 27 July 1783. Anne Sanderson. B. 6 June 1784. } Daus. of Thomas Bridges and Rebecca his wife.

1786 Jan. 10 Samuel Lovely Infant S. of John Bridges and Mary Penony his wife.

1787 Nov. 2 Henry s. of Thomas Bridges and Rebecca his wife. B. 7 Feb. 1787.

1810 May 12 John Richard S. of John Richard Bridges and Amy his wife. B. 10th Instant.

Married.

1721 April 22 Bartholomew Sanderson and Eliza Sheppard; by L. from the Generall.

1783 April 5 Alexander Neilson to Abigail Shepherd. L.

1808 Aug. 10 Samuel Lovely Bridges to Jane Edwards, Spinster. Lic.

Buried.

1724 Nov. 1 Bartholomew Saunderson, Mercht.

1732 May 16 Mr William Sheppard.

1732 Sep. 27 Mrs Elizabeth Shephard.

1733 June 9 Richard Shephard, a child.

1738 June 14 Mary ye D. of Thomas Shephard.

1761 Sep. 4 Capt John Shepherd.

1779 Sep. 28 Mary Bridges.

1782 Mar. 15 Sarah Bridges the D. of John Bridges and Mary his wife.

PARISH REGISTER OF ST. PHILIP.

Married.

1730 Aug. 8 Thomas Sheppard and Eliza Byam; by L. from Genl Mathew.

1733 Nov. 29 Thomas Sheppard and Rachell Morgan; by L. from Genl Mathew.

PARISH REGISTER OF ST. GEORGE.

Married.

1764 June 30 Samuel Byam, Esqr, and Elizabeth Shephard, Spinster.

1769 July 24 John Shephard, Merct, & Mary Sephard (*sic*), Spinster.

Buried.

1768 ...... Richard Shephard.

1770 July 9 Thomas S. of John Shephard and Mary his wife.

1780 Aug. 29 Rachael Shephard.

1793 Jan. 20 Mary Shephard.

PARISH REGISTER OF ST. PETER.

Married.

1817 Oct. 1 John Sheppard, Planter, and Mary Powell Bladen, Spinster, at Cotton New Work. L.

PARISH REGISTER OF ST. MARY WOOLNOTH, LONDON.

Married.

1714 Aug. 6 Jonathan Shipperd of St Saviour, Southwark, Bachelor, and Mary Hawkins of the same Parish, Spinster; by licence, London.

SYDLING ST. NICHOLAS, CO. DORSET.

Buried.

1724 Dec. 29 Timothy Stoodly, vicar of Sydling St Nicholas.

1730-31 Feb. 13 Mrs Elizabeth Stoodly, widow.

1738 June 29 Mrs Mary Stoodly.

CERNE ABBAS, CO. DORSET.

The Vicar (Rev. H. D. Gundry) wrote me in 1895, "I find the following children of Richard Shephard were baptized at Cerne .... I find no record of Robert."

Matilda 18 Dec. 1694.
Katherina 11 May 1699.
Thomas 19 Mar. 1701.
Susannah 7 Feb. 1703.
Richard 17 Jan. 1707.
John 23 Oct. 1710.

Buried.

1749 May 14 Thomas Sheppard, Merchant.

ST. JOHN'S CHURCHYARD.

On an altar-tomb:—

Arms: *Ermine, on a chief .... three battle-axes ....* (SHEPHARD); impaling .... *three wolves' heads erased ....* (BYAM).

Crest: *A stag courant regardant over helmet and wreath.*

Here lyeth the Body of
ELIZABETH SHEPHARD
wife of THOMAS SHEPHARD
of this Iſland who departed
this life ye 26th of September
1732 in ye 22d Year of her Age.

SYDLING ST. NICHOLAS, CO. DORSET.

On a monument in the south aisle:—

TIMOTHEUS STOODLEY,
hujus ecclesiæ
per annos viginti et amplius
Vicarius diligentissimus.
(Thirteen lines follow.)
Obiit Dec. 27, Anno Dom. 1724,
Æt. 49.
Posuit hoc frater ejus amantissimus,
Christopherus Stoodley,
ad insulam de Antego
mercator non incelibris.

(Hutchins.)

CERNE ABBAS, CO. DORSET.

On an altar-tomb in the churchyard:—

Here lies the body of ROBERT WHITE, who died Jan. 6, 1753, | aged 46; after having been upwards of 20 years in Antigua in | South America, and returning home with a good character, which | is well known by the best sort of people in that island. (Hutchins's 'Dorset.')

Pedigree of Sheriff.

ARMS.—*Azure, on a fess or between three griffins' heads erased . . . . a fleur-de-lis between two roses.*
CREST.—*A lion's paw erased, holding a sprig.*
MOTTO.—*Esse quam videri.*

These arms were granted in 1559 to Sheriffe of Warwick (Edmondson).

WILLIAM SHERIFF of Nonsuch 1753. = Rachel Wallis, mar. 28 Feb. 1760 at St. Philip's. (? bur. there 4 July 1792.)

John Sherriff, joins the Troop 1754. Witnessed John Wise's will 1755.

Children of William Sheriff and Rachel Wallis:

- William Elmes Sheriff, born 3 April and bapt. 7 Oct. 1767 at St. Philip's.
- John Sheriff, bapt. 11 Sep. 1768 at St. Philip's.
- Samuel Harman Sheriff, bapt. 17 Nov. 1771 at St. Philip's.
- Samuel Harman Sheriff, bapt. 4 Feb. 1774 at St. Philip's. = Joyce Claudia Dickman, mar. 7 Dec. 1797 at St. John's.

Children of Samuel Harman Sheriff and Joyce Claudia Dickman:

- Samuel Marchant Sheriff, born 14 Jan. and bapt. 19 Feb. 1799 at St. John's. = ...
- James Watson Sheriff, born 5 Oct. and bapt. 15 Nov. 1803 at St. John's; Barrister-at-Law of the Inner Temple 1838; Speaker 1845; Solicitor-General 1846; Attorney-General of the Leeward Islands 1848—1852; President of Nevis; died there 9 March 1866. M.I. at St. John's.
- John Dickman Sheriff, born 12 July and bapt. 11 Sep. 1806, and bur. 17 March 1825 at St. John's.
- Elmina Ledeatt Sheriff, born 3 and bapt. 6 July, and bur. 6 Nov. 1810 at St. John's.
- Mary Harris Sheriff, born 24 June and bapt. 15 July 1801; mar. 18 May 1820 Anthony Musgrave, M.D., Treasurer; he died 24 Feb. 1852, æt. 58.

Children of Samuel Marchant Sheriff:

- William Anthony Musgrave Sheriff* of the Middle Temple 1864; Barrister-at-Law 1867; Attorney-General of Grenada 1872, and of Bahamas 1879; Chief Justice of British Honduras 1882; Puisne Judge of British Guiana 1893.
- Robert Ffrench Sheriff, Q.C., Barrister of Inner Temple Nov. 1862; Attorney-General of Leeward Islands 1874, and of Gibraltar 1877—1892.

* This gentleman wrote to me from Barbados 20 March 1895: "I beg to state that I take no interest whatever in my ancestors, and consequently your work is one with which I have no sympathy."

1749-50. From a letter: "As for Billie Sheriffe . . . . he lived some time with Mr. Watkins to settle Coll° Martin's accounts . . . . Mr. Watkins thought him honest and sober, but inclined to be idle, he proposes doing business as a town agent."

1866, March 9. At Nevis, West Indies, from the effects of a severe carriage accident, James Watson Sheriff, esq. President administering the Government of that island. The deceased was the representative of an old English colonial family in Antigua, W.I., in which island he had inherited considerable property. He was called to the bar by the society of the Inner Temple in 1838, and soon after his call commenced practice in Antigua, where he speedily became the recognised leader of the bar, and acquired a reputation as a lawyer that was by no means confined to his native island. Mr. Sheriff was elected Speaker of the House of Assembly in 1845, and upon his retirement from that post was voted an address and a donation of 200 guineas; Mr. Sheriff had been previously distinguished for his eloquence as a member of the Assembly. In 1846 Mr. Sheriff was appointed Solicitor-General and in 1848 Attorney-General, in which office he shewed great ability in framing and passing several most important measures of financial and legal reform, for which he several times received the thanks of the Home Government. Upon the retirement in 1856 of Sir Robert Horsford, Chief Justice of Antigua, the greatest dissatisfaction was felt, both by the bar and the public, that Mr. Sheriff was not appointed his successor; and in consequence of this slight, Mr. Sheriff then resigned the Attorney-Generalship and retired from the bar. In 1860 Mr. Sheriff became a member of the Executive Council of Antigua, and in 1864 he accepted the presidentship of Nevis, in the administration of which island he made himself universally beloved. Mr. Sheriff's acquirements as a lawyer were of the first class; as a speaker, he had a commanding presence, a pleasing voice, and considerable eloquence; and he brought the most indefatigable zeal and energy to bear upon whatever he undertook, whether as a lawyer, politician, or administrator of public affairs. (Law Times, 'Gent. Mag.,' p. 755.)

PARISH REGISTER OF ST. JOHN.

Baptized.

1799 Feb. 19 Samuel Marchant S. of Samuel Sheriff and Joyce Claudia Sheriff. B. the 14 January 1799.

1801 July 15 Mary Harris D. of Samuel Sheriff and Joyce Claudia his wife. B. the 24th June 1801.

1803 Nov. 15 James Watson S. of Samuel Sheriff & Joyce Claudia his wife; b. 5 Octr last.

1806 Sep. 11 John Dickman S. of Samuel Sheriff and Joyce Claudia his wife. B. 12th July last.

1810 July 6 Elmina Ledeatt D. of Samuel Sheriff and Joyce Dickman his wife. B. 3d Instant.

Married.

1797 Dec. 7 Samuel Sheriff to Joyce Dickman, Spinster. L.

1806 Mar. 3 Thomas Sheriff to Eliza Shirley, Widow. L.

1820 May 18 Anthony Musgrave, Esquire, M.D., to Mary Harris Sheriff, Spr. L.

Buried.

1766 Mar. 19 John Sheriffe.

1810 Nov. 6 Elmina Ledeatt Sheriff, Infant.

1811 April 20 Joyce Sheriff.

1825 Mar. 17 John D. Sheriff.

PARISH REGISTER OF ST. PHILIP.

Baptized.

1767 Oct. 7 William Elmes s. of William & Rachel Sheriffe; b. Apl. 3.

1768 Sep. 11 John s. of William & Rachel Sheriffe.

1771 Nov. 17 Samuel Harman s. of William & Rachel Sheriffe.

1774 Feb. 4 Samuel Harman s. of William Sheriffe.

Married.

1760 Feb. 28 William Sheriff & [*blank*] Wallis.

1777 Dec. 14 John Coleburn & Rachael Sheriffe, spinster.

1778 Dec. 31 Benjamin Reynolds & Grace Sheriffe, spinster.

Buried.

1770 Feb. 8 William Sheriffe.

1776 April 14 William Sheriffe.

1792 July 4 Rachel Sheriffe. Fam. b.g.

CHRIST CHURCH, NICHOLA TOWN, ST. CHRISTOPHER'S.

Baptized.

1726 Nov. 2 Wm McDowel S. of John & Eliz. Sherriff.

1729 May 3 Alexander S. of John & Eliz. Sherriff.

ST. JOHN'S CATHEDRAL.

On the east wall of the south transept :—

Arms : *Azure, three griffins' heads erased* [*or*], *on a fess or a fleur-de-lis . . . . between two roses . . . .*

Crest : *A hand* erased, holding a sprig of . . . . over wreath and helmet.*

Motto : *Esse quam videri.*

SACRED
TO THE MEMORY OF
THE HONOURABLE JAMES WATSON SHERIFF,
OF THE INNER TEMPLE,
BARRISTER AT LAW,
LATE PRESIDENT OF NEVIS.
A NATIVE OF THIS ISLAND.
MR SHERIFF FOR MANY YEARS FILLED SOME OF
THE HIGHEST PUBLIC OFFICES OF ANTIGUA,
INCLUDING THAT OF HER MAJESTY'S ATTORNEY-GENERAL.
BORN 15TH OCTOBER 1804,
DIED AT NEVIS, FROM A CARRIAGE ACCIDENT,
9TH MARCH 1866,
UNIVERSALLY ESTEEMED AND LAMENTED.

ST. GEORGE'S CHURCHYARD, FITCHES CREEK.

On a small white marble cross :—

EDITH MARY
INFANT DAUGHTER OF
W. M. SHERIFF DIED NOVR 6TH 1868.

* The crest used by Mr. W. A. M. Sheriff is: *A lion's jamb erased* [*or*] *holding a laurel branch* [*vert*], and in Fox-Davies's revised edition of 'Fairbairn's Crests' this is given as S. of Scotland, so that it is possible that "a hand erased" is either an error on my part or on that of the sculptor.

Pedigree of Shervington.

Rev. WILLIAM SHERVINGTON of St. John's Town 1753; bur. 30 Dec. 1763 at St. John's. ╤ Catherine Toole, mar. 14 Feb. 1750-1 at St. John's.

Tyrrill Shervington, a dau., bapt. 19 Dec. 1756 at St. John's.

Richard Tyrrell Shervington. ╤ Grace, dau. of Nathaniel Redhead, Esq.; bapt. 11 July 1759 and mar. 26 April 1784 at St. John's.

. . . . Appleton ╤ . . . .

Hon. Tyrrell Shervington, Puisne Baron of Antigua 1852. ╤ Lucy Jane Appleton, mar. 27 Aug. 1831 at St. George's; died 25 April 1833, æt. 24. M.I. at St. John's.

Louisa Appleton, died 13 April 1833, æt. 28. M.I. at St. John's. ╤ Joseph Shervington, Esq., Deputy-Treasurer of Antigua 1852; Master of St. John's Lodge of Freemasons.

Hon. Tyrrell Mildmay Shervington, Attorney-General of Grenada, dead 1889. His mother died 1886 at Antigua. ╤ Eliza Amelia (2nd dau. of George Athill of Antigua, merchant, and of Bridge Place, Canterbury, by Eliza his 1st wife; she died in 1845, and he Jan. 1857, æt. 50), cousin to her husband; bapt. 11 March 1836 at St. John's; dead 1889.

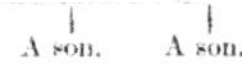

A son. A son.

1801. William Shervington then member of the Assembly.

PARISH REGISTER OF ST. JOHN.

Baptized.

1756 Dec. 19 Tyrrill the D. of the Rev[d] W[m] Shervington & Cath. his wife.

Married.

1750-51 Feb. 14 William Shervington and Catherine Toole. L.

1784 April 26 Richard T. Shervington to Grace Redhead, Sp[r]. L.

Buried.

.... Sep. 27 William Shervington.
1763 Dec. 30 Rev[d] W[m] Shervington, C.P.
1794 Sep. 25 Catherine Shervington.
1798 Dec. 4 William Shervington, Inf.
1804 Jan. 20 William Shervington.

PARISH REGISTER OF ST. GEORGE.

Married.

1831 Aug. 27 Tyrrell Shervington of S[t] John & Lucy Jane Appleton of S[t] John. Lic.

ST. JOHN'S CHURCHYARD.

On a marble ledger:—

97—SACRED | TO THE MEMORY OF TWO SISTERS! | LOUISA, WIFE OF JOSEPH SHERVINGTON, | AND | LUCY JANE, WIFE OF TYRRELL SHERVINGTON. | THEY WERE BOTH CALLED FROM THIS LIFE | WITHIN THE SHORT PERIOD OF TEN DAYS. | THE FORMER ON THE 13TH APRIL 1833, | AGED 28 YEARS, | THE LATTER ON THE 25TH OF THE SAME MONTH | AGED 24 YEARS.

(Three lines follow.)

Family of Shirley.

Memorial of Major-General Thomas Shirley, Governor-in-Chief of the Leeward Islands, that your petitioner is lineally descended from, and is heir male of, Thomas Shirley of Preston, co. Sussex, Esq. (as appears by annexed pedigree* from the College of Arms), whose 1st son Anthony was created a baronet 6 March 1665. In 1705 Sir Richard Shirley, grandson of the said Anthony Shirley, ob. s.p., and though William Shirley, petitioner's father, became heir male of the said Sir Anthony Shirley as grandson of his brother William, he could not succeed to the title as it was limited to the heirs male of Sir Anthony. Lieut.-General William Shirley, petitioner's father, was appointed Governor† of Massachusetts in 1741, and in 1745 planned the expedition against Cape Breton under the command of Mr. Pepperell, a provincial General, and Admiral Sir Peter Warren. They were both made Colonels in the Army and General Pepperell a baronet, but William Shirley declined that title. William Shirley was appointed Commander-in-Chief in North America in 1755 and there lost two sons; one was secretary to, and fell with, Major-General Braddock at Ohio in 1765; the other, a Captain in the Army, died near Oswego; and William Shirley died in 1771 after 40 years' service, leaving petitioner his only surviving son. Petitioner has served in the Army since 1745 at Louisbourg, Minorca, Belle Isle, and as Lieut.-Colonel in Portugal. Petitioner married Anne the granddaughter of Mary sister and coheiress of Sir Richard Shirley, in whom the title became extinct in 1705. Asks for the revival of the title in himself.

In a letter of 19 Nov. 1783 he says William Hutchinson, Esq., was his A.D.C. and served as Lieut.-Colonel at Brimstone Hill, St. Kitts.

1786, Oct. 3. Governor Shirley writes that he has heard from his nephew Hutchinson that his name has been put on Lord Sidney's List, and that he has been created a baronet.

* Pedigree missing from the Memorial.

† Governor Shirley was superseded in 1756 (Hutchinson's 'History of Mass.,' p. 48), but some time after obtained the small government of the Bahamas.

For further information see 'Stemmata Shirleiana,' Horsfield's 'Sussex,' vol. i., p. 171, Berry, and the Visitation of 1634.

Family of Skerrett.

Robert Skerrett of St. Christopher's, merchant. Will dated in London 27 Aug., proved 3 Sep. 1731 by John Blake; power reserved to Nicholas Gallwey. (240 Isham.) Now in the small pock. Reversion of my estate to my dear father Nich[s] Skerrett & Mary Skerret in Monserrat. My brother-in-law John Blake & my kinsman M[r] Nich[s] Gallwey of S[t] Christopher's Ex'ors in Trust.

William Skerrett. Will dated 13 Jan. 1750. .... by the said Indenture of release da. 16 Aug. 1735 to prevent the said Thibou Skerrit his heirs enjoying .... the said Thibou Skerrit is a professed Roman Catholic, the said mortgaged premises have been sold for £20,704 7*s.* c. to Stephen Lynch, Esq., which is more than will pay off the mortgage, whereby I hope to have decree to have all surplus monies paid me, & if Thibou Skerrit succeed to any of my estate, & by that or any means it prove deficient to pay the legacies, notwithstanding Eliz[th] Warner, Thos. Elmes, & Thos. Warner shall not abate any of their legacies. Thos. Elmes & Thos. Warner Ex'ors. Witnessed by William Warner, Charles Bromhall, William Glun (?).

Codicil dated 22 April 1752. .... the injury I did my relations by giving the residue of my estate from them .... I give to the parish of S[t] Peter's £50 c. To the children of my kinsman Peter Skerritt of Gallway, Ireland, & those of Owen Heyne & Christian his wife, dau. of my uncle Rob[t] Skerritt (? of) Gallway, dec[d], all residue real & personal after payment of the legacies left in my will, except that to the Incorporated Society at Dublin which I make void. Witnessed by Edward Coulter, William Colburn, Ambrose Marchant. Before John Tomlinson, Esq., was sworn William Warner 19 May 1752. Recorded 24 June 1752. (Much of the above will destroyed.)

Pedigree of Skerrett.

ARMS.—*Vert, a chevron or, between two squirrels counter-sejant in chief and one in base proper.*
CREST.—*A squirrel sejant proper.*

THOMAS SKERRETT of Antigua ;═. . . . purchased 50 acres in 1705 ; granted 214 acres in 1707.

Robert Skerrett of Galway,═. . . . uncle of William Skerrett of Antigua ; dead 1752.

William Skerrett of Antigua, Esq. ; was in possession of the above mentioned 50 acres 1731 ; Ex'or to Nicholas Brown 1740 ; bur. 8 May 1752 at St. Philip's. Will dated 13 Jan. 1750 ; codicil 22 April 1752.

. . . . Skerrett,═Mary . . . . bur. 22 Sep.═Major Anthony Brown 2nd husband. | 1760 at St. Philip's, very aged. Will dated 20 Nov. 1759 ; sworn 15 Nov. 1760. | of St. Philip's Parish, Antigua ; bur. there 23 Jan. 1723. 1st husband.

Robert Skerrett of "Nugents" *alias*═Antonetta, dau. of Walter Nugent, Esq. ; mar. "Skerretts" of 500 acres, planter. (? bur. 1771 at St. Pancras, co. Middx.) Will dated 26 Dec. 1769 ; proved 12 Aug. 1771. (357 Trevor.) | 14 Nov. 1753 at St. John's ; died insolvent *circa* 1785. "Skerretts" *alias* "Nugents" *alias* "Clare Hall" passed to the Codringtons. s.p.

Mary Skerrett, living 1769.

Eleanor Skerrett, mar. . . . . Power ; living 1769.

Nicholas Skerrett of Montserrat, living 1731═Mary . . . . living 1731.

Robert Skerrett of St. Christopher's, merchant. Will dated at London 27 Aug. and proved 3 Sep. 1731. (240 Isham.)

Mr. Skerrett of Antigua═Henrietta, dau. of Edward Frye of Montserrat, Esq. ; (? from Montserrat). | named 1776 in her mother's will.

Walter Frye Skerrett, Esq., of Whitehall, co. Middx.,═Albinia Mathias, and Heckfield Park, co. Hants ; named 1776 in the will of his grandmother Mrs. Mary Frye ; died 27 Jan. 1828. | mar. 29 March 1791.

Marianne Skerrett, many years in Her Majesty's service ; died 29 July 1887, æt. 93, at 41 Beaumont Street, Marylebone. (See vol. i., p. 285.)

Elizabeth Skerrett of Cork, spinster. Will dated 15 May, proved 22 Dec. 1758 by the Ex'trices. (382 Hutton.) To Hellena Cottor, Teresa Moran, & Eleanor Tuite of Cork, spinsters, £1200 for which I have the bond of my uncle Mr Nicholas Tuite of London, & sole Ex'trices. (See the latter's will in the Carter Pedigree.)

For the will of Mrs. Mary Skerrett dated 1759 see the Brown Pedigree, vol. i., p. 75.

Robert Skerrett, late of London, now of Antigua, planter. Will dated 26 Dec. 1769 ; proved 12 Aug. 1771 by Antonetta Skerrett the relict. (357 Trevor.) To my clerk Mr Jas. Tinkler £100. To Master Joseph Lynch, son of my kinsman Steven Lynch of Antigua, now in England, £500 at 18. To my sister Eleanor Power £2000 in 10 years & 4 %. till then. To my sister Mary Skerrett £2000 in like manner. To each Ex'or 50 gs. All my lands & all residue to my wife Antonetta Skerrett, & appoint her & Mr John Bradshaw of London, broker, & Mr Chas. O'Hara of Montserrat, mercht, Ex'ors. Witnessed by John Bowsen, Thomas Morton, Thomas Osborn.

Close Roll, 40 Geo. III., Part 3, No. 5.

Indenture made the 16th Nov. 1799 between John Daly of Cobbins, co. Essex, Esq., of the one part, and Walter Frye Skerret of Whitehall, Middlesex, Esq., of the other part, witnesses that in consideration of £1347 7*s.* sterling paid to John Daly he grants to Walter Frye Skerret all that piece of land called Concessie ? in the colony of Demerary on the W. side of the river Demerara, and adjoining to a plantation called Belle Vue, and abutted on the N. by canal No. 2, and on the S. by a plantation called the Goede Intentie, which said piece of land containing 97 acres, valuing at 100 florins per acre, and is planted with 11,249 coffee trees, valuing each tree at 11½ stivers per tree, and at the exchange of 12 florins to £1 sterling making the above sum, and also all belonging to the said piece of land to have and to hold to the only proper use of Walter Frye Skerret and his heirs absolutely for ever, and John Daly and Walter Frye Skerret appoint Joseph Hamee, Henry Ryan, Francis Martin, and David Lynch, all of the colony of Demerara, their Attorneys. James Pinniger, Richard Pr. Broome of Gray's Inn, witnesses.

1707, Feb. 17. Thomas Skerret, planter, granted a patent for 214 acres at Nonsuch in St. Philip's Parish by Governor Daniel Parke.

1712. Montserrat, Leeward Division. Losses from the French capture:—

George Skerrett, jun.	£496
Robert Skerrett	2325
Edward Skerrett	110
Nicholas Skerrett	943
George Skerrett, sen.	979

1731, Dec. 11. Fifty acres, now in the possession of William Skerritt, were purchased by Thomas Skerritt in 1705.

1731, Jan. 15. George Skerrit paid for a negro.

1745, Sep. 1. "Robertus Skerret, Americanus," graduated at Leyden University.

1746, Sep. 16. William Skerrett, Esq., returned for Nonsuch Division.

1791, March 29. Walter F. Skerrett, esq. of New-street, Spring-gardens, to Miss Albinia Mathias of Scotland-yard, Whitehall. ('Gent. Mag.,' p. 380.)

1828, Jan. 27. Walter Fry Skerrett, esq. formerly of Berners-street, and Heckfield Park. (*Ibid.*, p. 188.)

The Skerretts were one of the old clans settled in the City of Galway.

There was a tomb in St. Pancras Churchyard to Robert Skerret, Esq., 1771 (Lysons, vol. iii.), probably of Antigua.

PARISH REGISTER OF ST. JOHN.

Baptized.

1753 Mar. 16 Margaret the D. of . . . . Skerret and Mary his wife.

1755 Feb. 4 Mary the D. of Jeremy Skerret & Mary his wife.

Married.

1749 Jan. 16 Jeremy Skerret and Mary French. L.

1753 Nov. 14 Robert Skerret, Esqr, and Antonetta Nugent.

Buried.

1746 Dec. 14 Mrs Skerrett.

PARISH REGISTER OF ST. PHILIP.

Buried.

1715 Feb. 8 Ann Skerrett.

1723 Oct. 8 Dominick Skerrett.

1724 Jan. 29 Thomas Skerrett.

1729 Sep. 7 Robert Skerrett.

1734 Oct. 3 George Skerrett.

1752 May 8 Willm Skerrett.

1760 or 1761 Sep. 22 Mrs Skerrett.

"Skerretts" is in St. Philip's Parish. In 1852 it contained 314 acres, and was owned by Oliver Nugent. For an account of the estate see NUGENT.

Pedigree of Smith.

ARMS.*—*Gules, on a chevron or, between three bezants, as many crosses formée fitchée sable.*

. . . . SMITH ╤ . . . .

Obadiah Smith, ╤ . . . . dead 1670.

Michael Smith of Nevis, Serjeant-Major. ╤ Elizabeth . . . . Will dated 1 Nov. 1670; proved 7 Oct. 1675. (104 Dycer.)

Daniel Smith of Nevis, merchant. Will dated 20 July 1647 at Bristol. (181 Fynes.) ═ Barbary . . . .

Francis Smith, a minor 1670.

Michael Smith of Nevis, appointed Member of Council 1685, then a Captain; Lieut.-Colonel 1692; died 1700. ╤ . . . .

Elizabeth Smith, a minor 1670. — Margaret Smith.

Penelope Smith, æt. 45 in 1707. Will dated 31 Aug. 1733; proved 23 March 1735. (106 Ducie.) ╤ William Mead of Nevis, Member of Council of St. Kitts 1689; Captain 1693; Commissioner of Customs 1695; President of St. Kitts 1698—1701. Will dated 23 July 1702; proved 26 July 1704. (36 Ash.)

Francis Smith. — John Smith. — Barbary Smith.

Michael Smith of Nevis, appointed Member of Council 1708; nephew of Penelope Mead 1733; President 1731—39. ╤ Anne . . . . A

Daniel Smith of Nevis, Member of Assembly 1688; of the Council and Captain 1692, later President; æt. 40 in 1707; died 23 April 1722 at Battersea. Will dated 17 April and proved 4 June 1722. (126 Marlborough.) ╤ Elizabeth Mead. B

. . . . ═ Henry Carpenter of Nevis 1685, appointed Secretary-General of the Leeward Islands 27 Nov. 13 William III. Will dated 19 Nov. 1703; proved 27 Nov. 1704. (227 Ash.) See vol. i., p. 117.

* These are the arms of Smith *alias* Harris, whose pedigree was recorded in the 'Visitation of Leicestershire in 1619."

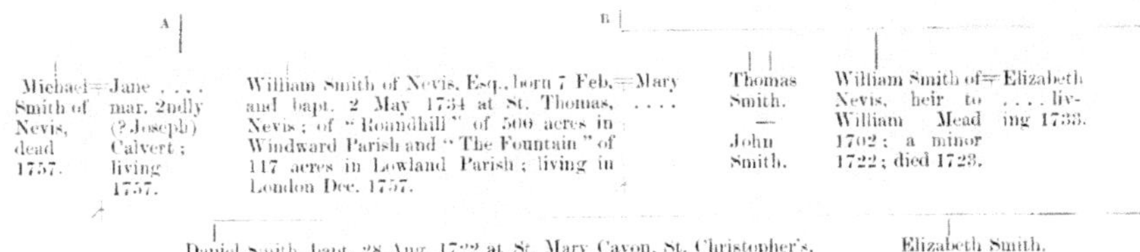
A
B
Michael Smith of Nevis, dead 1757. = Jane . . . . mar. 2ndly (? Joseph) Calvert; living 1757.
William Smith of Nevis, Esq., born 7 Feb. and bapt. 2 May 1734 at St. Thomas, Nevis; of "Roundhill" of 500 acres in Windward Parish and "The Fountain" of 117 acres in Lowland Parish; living in London Dec. 1757. = Mary . . . .
Thomas Smith.
John Smith.
William Smith of Nevis, heir to William Mead 1702; a minor 1722; died 1723. = Elizabeth . . . . living 1733.
Daniel Smith, bapt. 28 Aug. 1722 at St. Mary Cayon, St. Christopher's.
Elizabeth Smith.

Daniell Smyth of Nevis, marchant. Will dated 20 July 1647 at Bristol. (181 Fynes.) My eldest brother Michaell Smith of Nevis my black tabby suite. My brother Obadiah Smith a cloth suite & cloke. My wife Barbary Smith & my children Francis, John, & Barbary all my estate. My wife & said brother Michaell Ex'ors. Friends Mr Edward Knight & Mr John Knight of Bristol, merchants, Master Francis Heath, Capt. John Jennings, & Mr Humphry Richardson of London, merchants, overseers, & 40s. each. Witnessed by Ja. Brent, Simon Bowyer, John Hartwell. On 16 Aug. 1647 commission to Humphry Richardson, a supervisor, Barbary Smith and Michaell Smith being absent.

English Smith of Bristol, merchant. Will dated 12 Sep., proved 14 Sep. 1661. (104 Bruce.) My old plantation called the Bath in the Island of Nevis & the stock to my 1st son Thos. Smith, now residing at Nevis. My new plantation called the Saddle Hills to my 2^d son John Smith & his youngest brother English Smith. My wife Dorothy £200. My dau. Eliz. £300 at 21. My dau. Mary wife of Tho. Curtis £200. My 2^d son John, now a minor, sole Ex'or. My friends Mr Tho. Ellis, Mr Philip Roots, & Mr Gabriell Deane overseers. Witnessed by John Gwynn, Edmond Sweper, Samuel Lloyd, Christian Upcott.

Michael Smith, Esq., Sergeant-Major of Nevis. Will dated 1 Nov. 1670; proved 7 Oct. 1675 by Michael Smith the son; power reserved to Elizabeth Smith the relict. (101 Dycer.) Sick and weake. Elizabeth Smith, eldest daughter, £800 ster. (from money in the hands of Mr Richard Chandler, merchant, of London, & Mr George Morris, merchant, of Bristol) at 21 or marriage, & sufficient maintenance & education from his plantation. If she marries in Nevis $\frac{1}{3}$ of all his plate, which on her marriage is to be equally divided between her & his Executor & Executrix. In case of her mortality before 21 or marriage the £800 between Michael Smith, sonne, & Penelope Smith & Margaret Smith, 2 youngest daughters. He confirms to daughter Elizabeth a negro girl Black Besse (given her by Maddam Russell), & also the mare given her by Doctor Nicholson, & gives her besides a negro boy Jack son of Toney to be kept on the plantation till she is 21 or married. Penelope Smith & Margaret Smith, daughters, each £500 at 21 or marriage, & sufficient maintenance, etc. Francis Smith £100 ster. at 21 (son of Mr Obediah Smith, brother, dec.). Anne Nelson, widow, 1000 lbs. Muscovado sugar a year as long as she remains in Nevis towards the maintenance of herself & her children. Daniel Slow & Barbara Slow each 1000 lbs. good merchantable Muscovado sugar at 16 (children of William Slow, chirurgeon). Elizabeth Smith, beloved wife, & Michael Smith, loving sonne, Ex'ors, & to divide equally all estate real & personal. Immediately after his death wife & son are to enter into a joynt partnership & to manage & enjoy the whole estate joyntly during their lives, if wife continues his widow, but they are also to advise with & adhere to the counsell of the overseers of his will. Elizabeth Smith, wife, $\frac{1}{2}$ of his estate, if a widow, & power to give the same to all or any one of the children she may think most fit. If she marries son is to pay her £800, & she is then to relinquish the estate to him; provided nevertheless that she shall have choice of what furnished roome she pleases on the plantation, of any one negro boy & girle to waite on her, & any one horse. If son dies before 21 his part to daughters equally. Lt Coll. Ran^ll Russell, Cap^tn Daniel Lankaster, Cap^tn Francis Morton, & Lieut. John Cade, loving friends, supervisors & overseers, each 500 lbs. of sugar to buy a beaver hatt. Witnessed by George Spigurnell, Barbara Gardner her marke, William Slowe, Michael Yorke, cl.

William Mead, late of Nevis, now of London, Esq. Will dated 23 July 1702; proved 26 July 1704 by Joseph Martyn and Penelope Mead the relict. (36 Ash.) Funeral not to exceed £150. Revoke deeds by which I formerly conveyed most of my property on trust to Hen. Carpenter, Danl Smith, Phil Broome, & Wm Smith, son of said Danl Smith. To my mother Bridgett Mead of Haitesbury, co. Wilts, wid., £30 a year. To my bro. Tho. Mead £500, & to his son Wm Mead £1000 at 21, & to each of his daus. £500. £500 among all the children of my sister Joan Townsend, wife of . . . . Townsend, grasier, at 21. £200 among the children of my bro. Richd Mead at 21. To Mr Jos. Martyn, Mr Tho. Andrews, & Mr Richd Savage £10 ea. for mourning. To Madam Martha Andrews, wife of Mr Thos. Andrews, my charriott & horses. To my godson Wm Smith, s. of my son-in-law Danl Smith, £300, & to my granddau.-in-law Anne Smith, dau. of Danl Smith, £300. All residue of my estate to my d^r wife Penelope for life, then to Wm Smith, s. of Danl Smith. Mr Jos. Martyn to be Ex'or for all my personal est. in Engl^d, & residue of such for my wife, whom I appoint full Ex'trix. My friends Mr Danl Smith & Mr Hen. Carpenter to be overseers in America. Witnessed by John Fellowes, Charles Kesar, John Blake.

Daniel Smith, Esq., Lieut.-Governor of Nevis, now residing in Leicester Street, St. Anne, Westminster. Will dated 17 April, proved 4 June 1722. (126 Marlborough.) To my wife Eliz. Smith all my jewells, plate, £500, & the moiety of the rents of my plantations. To my grandson Daniel Mathew, son of Wm Mathew, Esq., Lieut.-Govr of St Christopher's, by my dau. Anne, £1000 at 21. To my daus. Penelope Smith & Frances Smith & my sons W^m & Daniel £2000 apiece at 21 & £60 a year till then. To the Minister & Churchwardens of St John's, Nevis, £50. All residue to my 2 sons. My wife Eliz., Lawrence Brodbelt, & Jas. Symonds of Nevis, Esq^res, William Coleman of London, merch^t, & Col. Tho. Butler guardians, & all except the last named overseers.

Penelope Mead, widow of William Mead of St. Christopher's, Esq. Will dated 31 Aug. 1733; proved 23 March 1735 by William Coleman; power reserved to General William Mathew and John Williams. (106 Ducie.) To my grandson-in-law Genl Wm Mathew 100 gs. for a ring & £100 for mourning, but if he be dead then to his son

Anne Smith, died 5 April 1730, æt. 31. M.I. at Sandy Point, St. Christopher's. 2nd wife. = General William Mathew, Captain-General of the Leeward Islands seventeen years; died 14 Aug. 1752.

Daniel Smith, a minor 1722; appointed Member of Council 1731; at London 1739.

Frances Smith.

Penelope Smith, 2nd dau., a minor 1722; mar. Thomas Budgen,* M.P. for co. Surrey; he died 3 March 1772 and was bur. at Dorking; left a son and heir Thomas Smith Budgen, who was born 28 June 1741 and died 25 May 1805.

William Buckley, Esq., of St. Christopher's, Barrister-at-Law; Treasurer 1736; mar. 1745; died 1754 intestate. (See vol. i., p. 82.) = Penelope Smith, only surviving child and heir; divorced from her 1st husband in 1745; died 6 Feb. 1756. = Daniel Mathew of Felix Hall, co. Essex, Esq.; mar. 4 Feb. 1736; bur. at Kelvedon 3 June 1777. 1st husband. = Mary, dau. of George Byam of Antigua; mar. 8 May 1750 at St. Philip's, æt. 21 on 13 July 1751; bur. at Kelvedon 25 Oct. 1814, æt. 84. = Joseph Lyons of "Lyons" of 400 acres; matriculated from Exeter College, Oxford, 23 March 1742-3, æt. 17; mar. 21 June and bur. 9 Oct. 1748 at St. Philip's.

* See Berry's 'Surrey' for pedigree of Budgen.

Daniel Mathew. To my nephews Michael & John Williams, Esq^res, £100 each; if Michael be dead then to his dau. Sarah Williams. To my nephew Michael Smith of Nevis, Esq., £100. To John & James Williams, sons of my nephew John Williams, sen^r, & to my nieces Ann Stanley, Eliz. Peterson, & Ann Abbott £50 each. To Rev. Francis Smith £50, but if dead to his granddau. Mary Smith. To my nephews Wm Leader, Nathl & Jeffery Gateward £20 each. To Penelope Gateward, dau. of my nephew Nathl Gateward, £100; if dead to her 2 sisters equally. To my granddau.-in-law Eliz. Smith, relict of my grandson Wm Smith, deceased, £50. To W^m son of Genl Wm Mathew £20. To my great-grandson Daniel son of Genl Wm Mathew the interest of all my exchequer annuities for his life, & then to his brothers Abednego & Edwd. To Sarah Williams, dau. of my nephew Michael Williams, £200, & to each of his other children, except his dau. Peterson, £40. To Frances wife of my nephew John Williams £20. To Anne wife of my nephew Michael Williams £20. To the children of my cousin Eliz. Peterson £20. To my nephew Henry Simes of Antigua £100. To Lucinia Garrique, wife of John Francis Garrique, £10, & to her brother John Bezune £10. To the poor of St Mary Cayon 6 barrels of Irish beef yearly for 4 years. To Billingsley Smith & Eliz. his wife each £40 c. To Wm Flower £20. To my great-granddau. Penelope Smith all my lands, £50, & my large silver Monteith. To my great-grandson Daniel Mathew my large silver cistern, & to his sister Penelope Mathew my gold striking watch. To my grandson-in-law Genl Wm Mathew, Wm Coleman of London, merch^t, my nephew John Williams, & Wm Fenton, both of St Christopher's, Esq^res, all residue, to sell & divide the proceeds between my grandchildren Daniel Smith & Penelope Budgen, wife of Tho. Budgen, & my great-grandchildren Daniel, Abednego, Penelope, & Edward Mathew. My g^t granddau. Penelope Smith to have all my slaves & stock at a valuation. My trustees Ex'ors. Witnessed by Russel Fenton, William Russel, John Collet.

Codicil dated 9 Oct. 1734. Billingsley Smith & his wife Eliz. are both dead; of the £80 c. formerly given to them £60 c. to the 1st child of Mrs Marg^t Mathew, wife of Genl Wm Mathew, depending on her affectionate care of my dear g^t grandchild Penelope Mathew. To Mrs Eliz. Holleran of St Christopher's the other £20 c. To my g^t granddau. Penelope Mathew all china & plate. My worthy friend Wm Fenton has desired to be excused as Ex'or. Witnessed by Louise Burt, William Pym Burt, Pat. Blake.

Close Roll, 13 Geo. II., Part 18, No. 21.

Indenture made the 7th June 1739 between Thomas Walker of Kirby Street, Hatton Garden, Esq., of the one part, and Daniel Smith of Nevis, now residing in London, Esq., of the other part, witnesseth that in consideration of 5s. Thomas Walker grants, etc., to Daniel Smith all those his Leeward Plantations in the south-western division of Nevis, containing the parcels of land hereinafter mentioned, that is to say, all those 29 mens lands broad from Hurleston Path till it comes a great gutt, bounded with the lands of one David Phillips, thence running along to the common path in the mountain with an uneven breadth, bounded at the foot or W. end with Hurleston's Path, at the head or E. end with the common path in the mountain, on the N. side with the lands sometime of John Coker and David Phillips, with the land sometime of one Mr. Stoakes *alias* Scot, and one Joseph Sweeper, and also all the angle of land containing 16 mens lands at the head being 12,000 plants ground, lying on the N. side of the 29 mens lands and running from a certain wall and a little gutt, running from a slobb (?) to a stone wall, sometime of the said David Phillips and John Coker, and also all that other parcel of land lying in the mountain being 14 mens lands, beginning at the common path and running to the figtree extent, bounded on the N. side with the lands sometime of Nicholas Raynsford and John Lapworth to Springgutt, and the lands sometime of Philip Lee, on the S. side with the lands sometime of Ensign John Smith and Christopher Spencer, and also all that other parcel of land containing 40 mens lands, bounded on the W. end with the lands sometime of the said David Phillips and part of the common path, and at the E. end with part of a great gutt and the plantation sometime of the said Philip Lee, on the N. side with the plantations of the said Ensign John Smith and Christopher Spencer, on the S. side therein first adjoining to it 3½ mens lands according to the old marks, bounded at the foot with the common path, and at the head with a great gutt as the 40 mens lands is, and on the S. side with the lands sometime of one Mr. Townsend and one Mr. Coleby, sometime in the possession of John Smith of Saddlehill, and also all that the plantation whereon the said David Phillips heretofore lived (and by him devised to James Walker, father of Thomas Walker, party hereto), bounded N. with the lands sometime of Lieutenant John Smith and Richard Wade, W. with the lands sometime of John Coker, E. with the mountain common path, and S. with the lands of the said James Walker and John Coker, and also all that plantation containing 100 acres purchased by James Walker of John Spencer and Mary Spencer his wife, situated in Nevis, abutting E. on the lands now or late of Philip Dewit, N. and S. on the lands of the said James Walker, and W. on the lands now or late of Richard Wade, and all negros, etc., to have and to hold to Daniel Smith for one whole year, yielding therefore one peppercorn that he may be in actual possession and thereby enabled to accept and take and grant a release of the reversion and inheritance.

No. 20.

Indenture made the 8th June 1739 between Thomas Walker, of the one part, and Daniel Smith, of the other. In conformity with an Act of the Commander-in-Chief, etc., made 4 Queen Anne to supply the want of fines, and for settling an estate in fee simple in Daniel Smith, and in consideration of 5s., Thomas Walker grants to Daniel Smith all those lands (as in No. 21) to the use of Thomas Walker and his heirs for ever.

Close Roll, 31 Geo. II., Part 12, Nos. 7 and 8.

Indenture made the 13th Dec. 1757 between William Smith of Nevis, Esq., now residing in London, of the one part, and Martin Kynck van Mierop, Richard Maitland, and Thomas Lucas, all of London, merchants, of the other part, witnesseth that in consideration of 10s. William Smith sells to them all that plantation in the Windward Parish in Nevis called Roundhill, containing 500 acres, bounded towards the S. by the lands of John Canty, W. and N. by the sea, and E. by the lands of David Gardiner, and all that other plantation in the Lowland Parish in Nevis called the Fountain, containing 117 acres, bounded towards the S. by the lands of Charles Payne, W. by the lands of Dr. William Jones, N. by the lands of the said William Jones and of William Burt Weeks, and E. by the lands of . . . . Madding (?), widow, and all that mansion house standing on the last mentioned plantation, and all that other plantation in the Lowland Parish called the Lower Grounds, containing 37 acres, bounded S. and E. by the lands of Matthew Mills, W. by the sea, and N. by the lands of Dr. William Jones, and also all those 150 slaves, to have and to hold for one whole year. Thomas Bennett, Jonathan Price, witnesses.

No. 7.

Indenture made the 14th Dec. 1757 between the above. Whereas William Smith is justly indebted to Martin Kynck van Mierop in the principal sum of £1230 15s. sterling besides interest, by virtue of a bond dated the 1st Dec. instant in the penal sum of £2461 10s. to be void on payment of the principal and interest on the 10th Dec. instant, and also to Richard Maitland and Benjamin Boddington, merchant of London, in partnership, in the principal sum of £607 15s. 11d. besides interest, by virtue of another bond dated the 2nd Dec. instant in the penal sum of £1215 11s. 10d. to be void on payment of the principal and interest on the 10th Dec. instant, and also to Thomas Lucas and William Coleman, sen. and jun., of London, merchants, in partnership, in the principal sum of £913 6s. 8d. besides interest, by virtue of a bond dated the 1st Dec. instant, in the penal sum of £1826 13s. 4d. to be void on payment of the principal and interest on the 10th Dec. instant, and also stands justly indebted by simple contract to several persons whose names are set down in a schedule annexed. Now this Indenture witnesseth that for making a provision for the payment of the said debts herein and in the schedule mentioned, and in consideration of 10s., William Smith grants and sells to Martin Kynck van Mierop, Richard Maitland, and Thomas Lucas, in their actual possession being by a lease for a year, all those plantations, etc. (as in No. 8) in trust to sell either entire or in parcels, and after the deductions of their costs, etc., and of such sums not exceeding £300 sterling as they may advance to answer the present occasions of William Smith, and of all incidental expenses relating to the management of the plantations, etc., till sold, and to the execution of the trusts, to pay to William Smith £200 a year for life, and to distribute all residue among themselves and all other creditors, and after all are paid to convey the residue to the use of William Smith. The trustees are to work the plantations and to lay out the money necessary and from time to time to sell the sugars, molasses, rum, and other produce, and they may employ such Attorneys and managers, etc., and allow them out of the trust money such sums for their trouble as they the said trustees shall think fit, and the said plantations are hereafter to be held in trust as aforesaid without any lett, suit, or hindrance from William Smith or any persons lawfully claiming under him or under Michael Smith his late brother, deceased, or under Michael Smith his late father, deceased, or under any of the ancestors of William Smith, and free from all incumbrances except one annuity of £225 sterling, payable from the said plantations, etc., to Jane Calvert (formerly wife and widow of Michael Smith the brother, deceased), for life and in lieu of dower, etc., and except the right and title of dower of Mary Smith, wife of William Smith, if she should survive him, and except the portions and maintenance which Thomas Smith and John Smith, brothers of William, are entitled to receive from the said plantations, etc., not exceeding £1000 currency and the interest thereon, and lastly for rendering these presents more valid William Smith impowers James Tobin, Esq., and the Rev. Edwin Thomas, Clerk, both of Nevis, to act in all things as his true and lawful Attorneys.

Schedule.—William Smith. Debtor to sundrys.

	£	s.	d.
To Van Mierop, Esq. . .	1230	15	0
To Coleman and Lucas . .	913	6	8
To Maitland and Boddington .	607	15	11
	£2751	17	7

Bills Protested.

	£	s.	d.
Edward Kendrick . . .	180	7	6
Ann Ripley	133	0	0
Wells, Wharton, and Doran .	242	0	0
Joseph Calvert	40	0	0
William Wells	100	0	0
Joseph Calver	185	0	0
John McDougall . . .	100	0	0
William Ravenstan . . .	50	0	0
William Burke, sen. . . .	180	0	0
Lachlan Fraser	40	0	0
Thomas Wharton . . .	47	3	9
Alexander Douglas . . .	100	0	0
Remseach (?) and Fraser . .	270	0	0
John Calvert	160	0	0
	£1907	11	3

	£	s.	d.
Keefe (?) and Burke . . .	17	0	0
Benjamin Lees (this John Richard Herbert)	57	18	10
R. Herbert (this is Lees' debt) .	50	0	0
Smith and Baillie . . .	310	0	0
Allen Popham	46	17	3
David Gibson	121	0	0
Stephen Cottam . . .	28	0	0
John Richardson Herbert . .	30	1	3
Peter Merchant . . .	27	3	9
John and Thomas Mills . .	51	3	7
	£796	13	8
	1907	11	3
	£2704	4	11
	2751	17	7
	£5456	2	6
Benjamin Braithwaite . .	£56	18	6

£	s.	d.
£5456	2	6
56	18	6
£5513	1	0

1670. Major Smith of Nevis named as a proper person to serve as a Commissioner.

1671, July. Lieut.-Colonel Michael Smith a Commissioner for Sir Charles Wheeler.

1672, July. John Smith then a Member of the Nevis Assembly.

1673, June 11. Petition of John Smith, junr., son of English Smith, deceased, to the King and Council. Petitioner's father possessed two plantations called the Sadhill and Bath Plantations, stocked with sugar canes, cattle, and servants, and a parcel of pasture in Nevis, and died leaving by Will the Bath Plantation to his eldest son Thomas, and 700*l.* to his wife and children, and petitioner sole executor. That said Thomas having set up a Deed of Gift which his father made to him in the usurper's time to keep his estate from being sequestered. His Majesty on petitioner's petition ordered the Governor to enquire into the state of the case, and relieve the parties injured, upon which the Deed of Gift was laid aside and the will proved in 1664. But said Governor being removed Thomas pretended the pasture belonged to the Bath Plantation, and petitioner for the sake of concord permitted him to enjoy it; but not content therewith, on a suggestion that there were several cattle on that ground, he sued for 11 cattle, 2 colts, and a negro boy, and obtained judgment against petitioner in his absence for 25,000 lbs. sugar, though neither ground nor cattle belonged to the Bath Plantation. Prays his Majesty to order the Governor of Nevis to stay execution or award restitution, and that the said Thomas may be sent for over, that both parties may be heard before his Majesty in Council, petitioner being willing to pay cost if judgment be given against him. *In margin:* "Recd June 11, read 12, 1673. Recd & read 23 June, '73." *Annexed:* Order of the King in Council referring above petition to the Council for Trade and Plantations to examine and report to his Majesty what is fit to be done for Petitioner's relief. Whitehall, 1673, June 20.

1673, Aug. 29. Petition of John Smith, son and executor of English Smith, late planter in Nevis, to the King. Recites his former petition. Prays an order to the Governor of Nevis to award restitution to petitioner for the present, and that said Thomas, being now in England and about to transplant himself to New England, may be summoned to appear before his Majesty to make good his title to said cattle if he can, petitioner being ready to put in security as his Majesty shall think fit, to abide judgment and answer all costs. *In margin:* "Recd and read in Council, Aug. 29, '73."

A second petition was presented on 24 Sep. and a third one on 24 Oct., which was followed by—

Order of the King in Council on above petition. That Thomas Smith be required to attend the Board on 21st Nov. to answer petitioner's complaint, whereof he is not to fail at his peril, and that petitioner give 500*l.* security to answer said Thomas Smith's damage by the delay of his voyage, if it be found petitioner had no just cause of complaint. Oct. 31, 1673.

Costs and charges sustained by Thomas Smith, planter, of Nevis, by reason of a petition preferred against him by John Smith to the King, and an order obtained whereby said Thomas was required to attend the Council Board, total 35*l.* 1*s.* 7*d.* besides 100*l.* damage sustained by being stopped of his voyage. *In margin:* "Recd. Dec. 10, '73."

(Colonial Calendar, America and West Indies.)

1678. Nevis. Lieut.-Colonel John Smith of the Council.

	White.			Black.		
	Men.	Wom.	Childn.	Men.	Wom.	Childn.
Captain John Smith's family . . .	14	1	2	27	28	21
Ensign John Smith .	8	2		6		

1680. John Smith, member of the Council and Lieut.-Colonel of one of the two militia regiments.

1680. Captain Nicholas Meade then of the Council of Montserrat, also in 1684 and 1688.

1685, March 30. Captain Michael Smith is sworn a member of the Council of Nevis.

1688, Nov. Captain Michael Smith is sworn a member of the Council of Nevis, and Daniel Smith then of the Assembly.

1689. William Mead of the Council of St. Christopher's.

1692-3, March 17. Lieut.-Colonel Michael Smith and Captain Daniel Smith both of the Council of Nevis.

1693, June 2. Captain William Meade an assessor of Charles Town, Nevis.

1695, July 22. Nevis. William Mead, Esq., a Commissioner of H.M. Customs.

1697. Nevis. Colonels Michael and Daniel Smith of the Council.

Mr. Weaver remarks of Michael Smith of Nevis that he is "of ordinary capacity for Governmt and of small Estate," and of Daniel Smith that he is "Of good Estate, but one of ye Genls Supernumeraries." (B. T. Leeward Islands, vol. 6.)

1700, Oct. 18. A letter dated this day at Nevis announced the death of Colonel Michael Smith.

Petition of William Mead, for three years President of St. Christopher's, is told that in the new list he is last but one of the members of Council; received 6 June 1701.

On 23 June 1701 he is stated to be off to England to lay complaints against Governor Codrington. (B. T. Leeward Islands, vol. 7.)

Petition of William Mead, Esq., of Nevis. Your petitioner and his wife have owned the lease of a plantation here called Harveys for upwards of 25 years. A low fellow one Thomas Herbert claimed it. Colonel Codrington openly favoured him, and petitioner was turned out losing his crop worth £3000. Petitioner held under Thomas Harvey a minor. Received 23 Dec. 1701. (*Ibid.*)

27 Nov., 13 Wm. III. Patent for Henry Carpenter to be Secretary of Leeward Islands *vice* Ed. Parsons, deceased. (*Ibid.*)

In 1702 Mr. Freeman and William Mead exhibited articles to the House of Commons against Christopher Codrington chiefly about the Harvey Plantation. A paper in favour of Codrington was signed in 1701 by "Daniel Smith, Son-in-Law to Mr Mead," one of the Nevis Council.

Colonel Codrington writes 1 May 1702, "With you Collo Pearne I wou'd be more Particular, you have a more than ordinery freindship and familiarity with all Mr Mead's family, you Lodg'd with Mr Carpenter, one of Mr Mead's Sons in Law, and saw Collo Smith the other, as well as Mrs Mead every day." (B. T. Leeward Islands, vol. 7.)

1703, Dec. 27. Death of Hon. Michael Smith of Nevis announced, and on 15 May 1704 that of Mr. William Mead, collector of the 4½ per cent. duty.

1707. St. Christopher's.

		White.		Black.			
	Age.	Men.	Wom.	Men.	Wom.	Boys.	Girls.
Daniel Smith, Esq.	40	1		20	20	6	1
Penelope Mead	45		3	56	60	16	21
Nevis.							
William Smith		3	1	5	5		
Colonel Daniel Smith		2		12	10		
Michael Smith		1	1	8	17		

1707. Colonel Daniel Smith to have the next vacancy as Lieut.-Governor of Nevis. (B. T. Leeward Islands, vol. 10.)

1708, July 11. Order for Michael Smith to be of the Council of Nevis.

1711, Aug. 10. St. Christopher's.

	White.			
	Men.	Wom.	Child.	
Madam Penelope Mead	2	4	1	157 negros.
Mr. William Smith / Mr. Henry Willet	2	3		17 men, 14 women, 9 children.

1717, Nov. 22. Anguilla Census. Spanish Town. William Smith of Nevis, Mary Smith, 4 children; 8 negros. (B. T. Leeward Islands, vol. 15.)

1721. Colonel Michael Smith, Lieut.-Governor of Nevis, died in London.

1722, April 23. Dyed Danl Smith, Esqr, Governr of Nevis, at Battersea. (Mawson's 'Obits.')

1723. Petition of Daniel Smith, Esq., and Elizabeth widow of William Smith, Esq., deceased, sons of Colonel Daniel Smith, late Lieut.-Governor of Nevis, that the latter did great services lately towards the extirpation of the French, and in consideration thereof the Governor after the peace granted to him 109 acres of uncultivated woody land in the French part of the Island, which he at very great expense cultivated and improved and put Daniel and William your petitioners into possession thereof, who continued to improve the land, but Colonel Daniel Smith dying in England last year, William Mathews, Esq., who had formerly obtained grants of two plantations on Nevis and sold them, prevailed with the present Governor to grant petitioner's plantation to him on pretence their interest determined on the death of their father, and William Mathews having privately obtained the grant entered on the crop and possessed himself of the land. Your petitioners came to England, but William Smith dyed on the journey before he could reach London, leaving Elizabeth and three young children destitute.

1731. Michael Smith then President of Nevis.

1731, May 12. Daniel Smith takes his seat at the Council of Nevis.

1749, Nov. 2. Deposition of William Smith, Gent., aged 28.

1763, May 26. In an Antiguan deed of this date Thomas Meade, Esq., was described as residuary devisee and legatee of Thomas Meade of Montserrat, deceased.

1772, Nov. 30. John Browne recommended to be of the Council of Nevis *vice* James Smith, deceased.

PARISH REGISTER OF ST. MARY CAYON, ST. CHRISTOPHER'S.

Baptized.

1722 Aug. 28 Daniel s. of Wm & Eliz. Smith.

PARISH REGISTER OF ST. THOMAS, NEVIS.

Baptized.

1734 May 2 William s. of ye Honble Michael Smith, Esqr, & Anne his Wife. B. Febry 7 last. Baptized this day.

Pedigree of Smith.

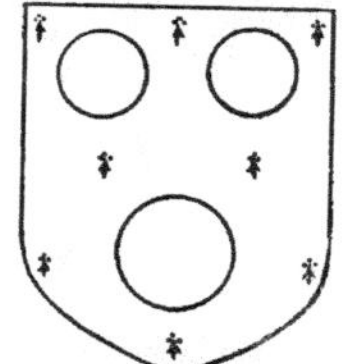

ARMS.—*Ermine, three roundles* . . . .
CREST.—*Out of a ducal coronet a plume of feathers.*
MOTTO.—*Ne differ in an* . . . .

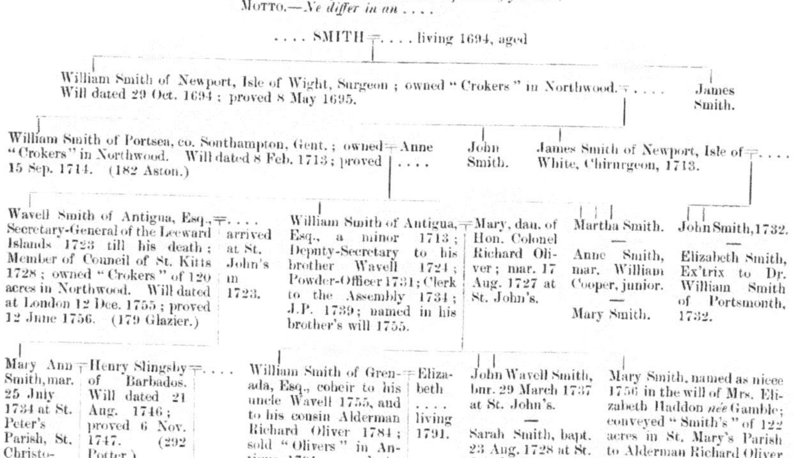

. . . . SMITH = ... living 1694, aged

William Smith of Newport, Isle of Wight, Surgeon; owned "Crokers" in Northwood. Will dated 29 Oct. 1694; proved 8 May 1695. = ...

James Smith.

William Smith of Portsea, co. Southampton, Gent.; owned "Crokers" in Northwood. Will dated 8 Feb. 1713; proved 15 Sep. 1714. (182 Aston.) = Anne . . . .

John Smith.

James Smith of Newport, Isle of White, Chirurgeon, 1713. = ...

Wavell Smith of Antigua, Esq., Secretary-General of the Leeward Islands 1723 till his death; Member of Council of St. Kitts 1728; owned "Crokers" of 120 acres in Northwood. Will dated at London 12 Dec. 1755; proved 12 June 1756. (179 Glazier.) = ... arrived at St. John's in 1723.

William Smith of Antigua, Esq., a minor 1713; Deputy-Secretary to his brother Wavell 1724; Powder-Officer 1731; Clerk to the Assembly 1734; J.P. 1739; named in his brother's will 1755. = Mary, dau. of Hon. Colonel Richard Oliver; mar. 17 Aug. 1727 at St. John's.

Martha Smith.

Anne Smith, mar. William Cooper, junior.

Mary Smith.

John Smith, 1732.

Elizabeth Smith, Ex'trix to Dr. William Smith of Portsmouth, 1732.

Mary Ann Smith, mar. 25 July 1734 at St. Peter's Parish, St. Christopher's. 1st wife. = Henry Slingsby of Barbados. Will dated 21 Aug. 1746; proved 6 Nov. 1747. (292 Potter.) = ...

s.p.

William Smith of Grenada, Esq., coheir to his uncle Wavell 1755, and to his cousin Alderman Richard Oliver 1784; sold "Olivers" in Antigua 1791; owned the "Diamond" and "Resolution Hall" estates in Grenada. = Elizabeth . . . . living 1791.

John Wavell Smith, bur. 29 March 1737 at St. John's.

Sarah Smith, bapt. 23 Aug. 1728 at St. John's; coheir to her uncle Wavell 1755; living 1804.

Mary Smith, named as niece 1756 in the will of Mrs. Elizabeth Haddon *née* Gamble; conveyed "Smith's" of 122 acres in St. Mary's Parish to Alderman Richard Oliver 1772. Will dated 15 May 1804, then of Bulstrode Street, Marylebone, spinster; proved 14 Feb. 1806.

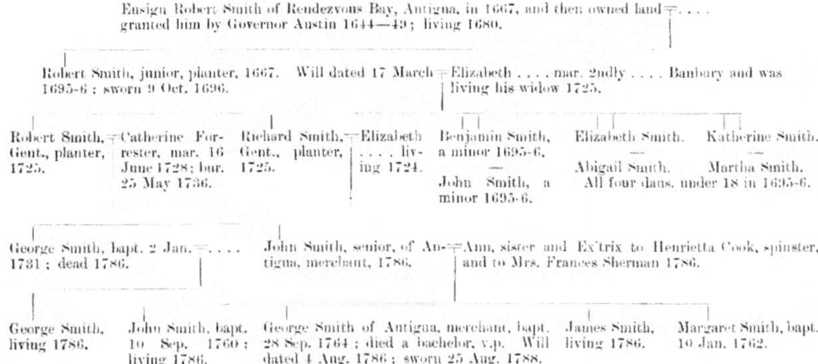

Ensign Robert Smith of Rendezvous Bay, Antigua, in 1667, and then owned land ╤ . . . . granted him by Governor Austin 1644—49; living 1680.
Robert Smith, junior, planter, 1667. Will dated 17 March 1695-6; sworn 9 Oct. 1696. ╤ Elizabeth . . . . mar. 2ndly . . . . Banbury and was living his widow 1725.
Robert Smith, Gent., planter, 1725. ╤ Catherine Forrester, mar. 16 June 1728; bur. 25 May 1736.
Richard Smith, Gent., planter, 1725. ╤ Elizabeth . . . . living 1724.
Benjamin Smith, a minor 1695-6.
John Smith, a minor 1695-6.
Elizabeth Smith.
Katherine Smith.
Abigail Smith.
Martha Smith.
All four daus. under 18 in 1695-6.
George Smith, bapt. 2 Jan. 1731; dead 1786. ╤ . . . .
John Smith, senior, of Antigua, merchant, 1786. ╤ Ann, sister and Ex'trix to Henrietta Cook, spinster, and to Mrs. Frances Sherman 1786.
George Smith, living 1786.
John Smith, bapt. 10 Sep. 1760; living 1786.
George Smith of Antigua, merchant, bapt. 28 Sep. 1764; died a bachelor, v.p. Will dated 4 Aug. 1786; sworn 25 Aug. 1788.
James Smith, living 1786.
Margaret Smith, bapt. 10 Jan. 1762.

Thomas Smith of Newport, Isle of Wight. Will dated 26 Oct. 1575; proved 4 May 1576. My bodie to Caresbrook. Children Wm, Tho., Richd, & James. Wife Ex'trix. Wm Thomas & Tho. Andrews overseers. Witnessed by William Thomas, John Crowther, John Andrews, Jeffrey Tarrant.

John Smith of Caresbrook. Will dated 20 Aug. 1661; proved 31 May 1662. Wife Anne. Brother Wm Smith of Castlehold. Kinsman James Smith.

Joseph Chun of Antigua, carpenter. Will dated 27 March 1693. To John Smith, jun., ye son of John Smith of Antigua, planter, all my est. & sole Ex'or. Witnessed by Joseph Mathews, Daniel Rayne, and John Knight. Sworn 12 March 1693-4.

William Smith of Newport, chirurgeon. Will dated 29 Oct. 1694; proved 8 May 1695. Daus. Anne & Eliz. tenement called Crokers *alias* Crockers in the parish of Northwood. Sons Wm & John. Aged mother. Son James all residue & Ex'or. Brothers James & Wm overseers.

Christmas Smith of Antigua, died intestate. Adm'on to John Tankerd, Esq., and Robert Amory 19 Nov. 1695. Recorded 28 Nov. 1695.

Jeremiah Smith, Commander of the ship "Barbary" of Culraine in Ireland. Codicil dated 25 Oct. 1695. To my wife what I left in the hands of my cousin Saml Smith my Ex'or. To my 2 children Robt & Jeane Smith all residue. Jas. Neale, Thos. Speare, & Jas. Robertson Ex'ors. Witnessed by James Rowan, Lawrence Murphy, Andrew Adam, Robert Mitchells. By Christopher Codrington was sworn James Rowan, merchant, 7 Dec. 1695. Recorded 12 Dec. 1695.

John Smith of St. John's. Will dated . . . . To Henry Smith my Ex'or 1 proportion of land 80 feet by 60 feet. To Frances Birde of St John's 1 proportion of land 80 feet by 60 feet when she is of age. To Henry Smith my clothing & share in the sloop Capt. Redman commands, & in the briganteen Capt. Wm Henry O'Brian Comr. Henry Smith to be Ex'or. Witnessed by John Oudes, Robert Jeaffreson, John Rain, John Mackarty. By the Deputy-Governor was sworn Robert Jeaffreson, John Rain, and John Mackarty. Recorded 27 Nov. 1696.

Robert Smith of Antigua. Will dated 17 March 1695-6. To my son Benjn Smith 10,000 lbs. at 21. To my son John Smith 10,000 lbs. at 21. To my daus. Elizth Smith, Abigail Smith, Kath. Smith, & Martha Smith 10,000 lbs. each at 18 or marriage. To my wife Elizth Smith a horse. All residue to my sons Richd & Robt Smith, they to be Ex'ors. My good friends Edward Byam, Esq., Edwd Walrond, Esq., Cap. John Otto, & Isaack Horsford trustees. Witnessed by Thomas Franklyn, Richard Boraston, Katherine Chapman. By Christopher Codrington were sworn Thomas Franklyn and Richard Borraston 9 Oct. 1696. Recorded 12 Oct. 1696.

William Smith of Portsea, co. Southampton, Gent. Will dated 8 Feb. 1713; proved 15 Sep. 1714 by Daniel Wavell, James Smith, and William Cooper. (182 Aston.) Sick & weak in body. Anne Smith, my loving wife, all my farm called Crockers in Northwood in the Isle of Wight, now in the possession of Peter Cook, & at her death to Martha Smith, Wavell Smith, Anne Cooper, wife of William Cooper, jun., Gent., William Smith, & Mary Smith my children, & to their heirs & assigns for ever, as tenants in common, & not joint tenants. Martha Smith, my daughter, £200 within 3 years. Daniel Wavell of Hayling in the county aforesaid, Clerk, James Smith of Newport, Isle of Wight, chirurgeon, my brother, & William Cooper, my son-in-law, & to their heirs for ever, in trust to sell all that new erected tavern the "Ship & Castle" in West Dockfield in Portsea, near the Dock gate, now in the occupation of Simon Urwin, & also all that my dwelling house with garden in or near the said Dock field, in a street called Chappell Row, which I purchased of Sir William Gifford, Kt., now in the occupation of Philip Varloe, & likewise all my moiety of ½ an acre in Seavill (? Furlong) in West Dockfield, which for many years past has been used for a rope walk, & was late in the occupation of David Aldridge, & lastly all that quitt-rent or yearly sum of £2 10s. issuing out of 4 new erected messuages now or late John Cleverleys, situate in Chappell Row in West Dockfield, near her Majestie's Dock, & all other my messuages, lands, etc., in the parish of Portsea, & my said trustees also to sell my personal estate, & from the money raised by the sale of the lands they are to allow as much as is requisite towards putting out son William as an apprentice or clerk to some trade or profession, and pay daughter Martha's £200, & all residue to be divided among Wavell Smith, Anne Cooper, William Smith, & Mary Smith my children equally, the shares of Wavell & Anne to be paid within a month after the death of Anne my now wife, of William at 21, & of Mary at 21 or marriage. All household goods, pay, wages, ready money, debts, rents, & other goods & chattells before mentioned to be sold, to be divided in the same way as the said residue. If either William or Mary dies before 21 the share between the survivor & daughters Martha & Anne, if both die all to said daughters. Until the lands are sold the rents, etc. (except the quitt-rent) are to be paid to Anne my wife towards the maintenance & education of Martha, William, & Mary. When sold the money is to be invested as trustees think proper, & the interest & profits of the shares of Wavell & Anne to be paid to wife for her own use for life, & of the shares of William & Mary for their maintenance & education. My trustees to be also my Ex'ors & Guardians of William & Mary during their minority. Witnessed by Elizabeth Maynard, Thomas Yerbury, John White.

William Smith* of Portsmouth, co. Southampton, Doctor in Physic. Will dated 9 Feb. 1732; proved 23 Feb. 1732 by Elizabeth Smith, sole Ex'trix. (67 Brice.) To the Dean & Canons of Christ Church, Oxford, the free chapel & farm of East Standen in Arreton, Isle of Wight, in trust for a Grammar School in Portsmouth to pay £50 a year to a Master & £30 a year to an Usher. Mrs. Eliz. Smith living with me, dau. of Mr. James Smith of Newport, I. of Wight, £2000. Rev. Samuel Du Gard, son of Rev. W^m Du Gard of Fareham £500. Wm Smith, son of Tho. Gleed of Carisbrooke, my manor of Wymering, co. Southampton, which I purchased of John Walton, Clerk, Rector or Vicar of Bottley, remainder to John, son of the said James Smith of Newport. Wm Smith to become M.B. Oxford. Eliz. Smith sole Ex'trix.

Harry Slingsby of Barbados. Will dated 21 Aug. 1746; proved 6 Nov. 1747 by Wavell Smith, Esq., William Smith, Esq., and William Post, three of the surviving Ex'ors; power reserved to Ann Slingsby the relict and Jonathan Blenman, Esq. (292 Potter.) I intend shortly a voyage to Europe. If I leave no child all my estate to my wife & her heirs. If I leave a child my estate to go as if I had made no will. To my cosen Ann Beale, sister of Mr Post of London Bridge, my mahogany chest & its contents now in the hands of Mr John Post of Maidstone, co. Kent. To Wm Smith of Antigua, Esq. (uncle of my 1st wife) the debt due to me from Henry McCallough & Henry Howson, & all debts due in Antigua & St Kitts for the use of his son Wm Smith & his dau. Sarah Smith. I discharge my wife's father Wavell Smith of all sums due on 2 bonds for £1700, & give him for life my 2 farms Hale Place & Bedwells, co. Kent, subject to £100 a year I pay to my cosen Alex^r Beale, & after his death the 2 farms to Wm Post of London Bridge & my cosen Mary his wife for their lives, then to her heirs, they paying to her sister Anne Beale £50 a year. To each of my wife's brothers £100 c. Hon. Jonathan Blenman & Burch Hothersall, both of Barbados, Esq^res, Wm Smith of Antigua, Esq., Wavell Smith, Esq., & Wm Post of England, & my wife Ann Ex'ors, & to each £100 c. All residue to my wife. Witnessed by Thomas Lake, Samuel Hill, Thomas Thomas.

* William Smith, s. of William of Newport, Isle of Wight, doctoris, matric. from Christ Church 30 June 1702, aged 16, B.A. 29 Jan. 1705-6, bar.-at-law Middle Temple 1712 (his father of Portsmouth). 1733 Feb. 4 William Smith, Esq.; and Alderman of Portsmouth, also Doctor of Physick, and reputed worth upwards of 20,000*l*. He left his Dwelling House to be a Charity School for Grammatical Learning, and 100*l*. per Ann. to endow it. ('Gent. Mag.,' 101.)

He is stated to have been an M.D. of Leyden, and to have been incorporated at Oxford University 20 June 1696.

James Smith. Will dated 8 Dec. 1754. All to my children Mary & Sarah & . . . . Wm Allen, Gent., my son-in-law Will . . . . & my wife Jane Ex'ors . . . .

London. Wavell Smith, Secretary of H.M. Leeward Charibbee Islands in America. Will dated 12 Dec. 1755; proved 12 June 1756 by William Smith, Esq., the brother; power reserved to George Thomas, Esq., William Sharpe, Esq., Gregory Sharpe, LL.D., Rowland Oliver, Esq., and William Smith, Esq., the nephew. (179 Glazier.) To Geo. Thomas, Esq., Govr of the Leeward Islands, I give 2 pictures, the one "the Old Man," & the other "the Queen of King Chas. I." To my neph. Wm Smith all my other pictures. To my friends Wm Sharpe, Esq., a clerk of the Privy Council, & his bro. Dr Gregory Sharpe £50 each. My farm called "Crokers" of 120 acres in the parish of North Word, Isle of Wight, to the said Geo. Thomas, Wm Sharpe, Dr Gregory Sharpe, & Rowl^d Oliver of Antigua, Esq^res, for ever. By letters patent granted to me & Savile Cust, Esq., by Geo. I. I am entitled to the office of Sec^ry & Clerk to the Crown in the Leewards Islands for our joint lives, & I give all my interest therein to them, they to take my said farm & the office of Sec^ry & all residue of my est. on Trust, ½ for my neph. Wm Smith, & ½ for his sister my niece Sarah Smith. My said 4 Trustees with my brother Wm Smith & my neph. Wm Smith, now my deputy at St Christopher's, to be Ex'ors. Witnessed by William Bush, William Mackay.

Samuel Smith, Gent. Will dated 1 Nov. 1758. To my brothers Robt, W^m, & John, to my sisters Eliz^th Patterson & Martha Watson, all of Ireland, 1s., all residue to Leah Levington. Mr Robt Gray, Saml Martin, merch^t, Ex'ors. Witnessed by Cornell Kennedy, William Alexander. Before George Thomas, Esq., was sworn William Alexander 16 Nov. 1758. Recorded 16 Nov. 1758.

John Smith of Princess Street, London, merchant. Will dated 31 Oct. 1775; proved P.C.C. 2 March 1776 by Ingham Foster, Daniel Hobson, and Samuel Smith, Esquires; proved 12 March 1777 by John Halliday, Esq.; power reserved to Richard Oliver, Esq., Alderman of London, John Burke, and John Delap Halliday; proved 25 Aug. 1810 by John Burke, Esq., only surviving Ex'or. All my est. to my friends Richd Oliver, Esq., Alderman of Lond., John Halliday of Queen Ann Str., Cavendish Sq., now of Antigua, Esq., John Burke of Antigua, Esq., John Delap Halliday of Queen Ann Str., Ingham Foster of Clement's Lane, ironmonger, Danl Hobson of Copthall Court, merch^t & insurance broker, & Saml Smith of St Mary Axe, Gent., on Trust to invest £10,000 in the funds & the residue in lands, & to pay £100 a yr. to my dau. Marg^t Smith till 16, then £200 a yr. till 21, then £10,000 at 25 or marriage, & all residue in trust for her & her heirs. My Trustees to be Guardians & Ex'ors & £50 ea. My partner Robt Christian, Esq. My neph. the s^d John Burke not to be pressed for payments for 7 years. Witnessed by John Readshaw, Thomas Smart, Charles Gurney.

Codicil. Dated at Kentish Town 23 Dec. 1774. To my aunt Joanna Guard, now of Youghall, £20 a yr. To my aunt Alias (*sic*) Hake of Cork £20 a yr. Mr Daniel Hobson £500. To my serv^t Martha Watson £100 & £20 a yr. Mr Richd Beahan & Mr Geo. Thompson £100 ea. My dau. to remain with M^r & Mrs Stevenson till 18. £100 to Mrs Stevenson. Witnessed by Jos. Barber, Christian Barber. On 28 Feb. 1776 appeared George Thompson of St. Christopher's Le Stocks who knew testator, who was also of that parish.

George Smith, merchant. Will dated 4 Aug. 1786. Negros to my brother John Smith & my mother Ann Smith. Mourning rings to my aunts Miss Henrietta Cook, Mary Cooke, M[rs] Frances Sherman. My negro woman to be free & to have £12 c. a year. All residue to M[r] Joseph Lyons Walrond & Sam[l] Atthill in trust for my mother Ann Smith, & if my father survive her then to him, & after to my brothers John & Jas. equally, & in default to George son of my uncle Geo. Smith, dec[d]. Joseph Lyons Walrond, Samuel Atthill, John Smith, sen[r], & Ann Smith Ex'ors. Witnessed by Henry de Ponthien, Cornelius Sherman, Elias Ferris. By John Nugent, Esq., Lieut.-Governor, was sworn Elias Ferris 25 Aug. 1788. Recorded 23 March 1789.

Henrietta Cook, spinster. Will dated 25 July 1787. To my sister Ann, wife of John Smith, sen[r], Merch[t], a negro. To my sister Frances Sherman & her 2 dans. Ann & Frances £50 c. each if there be sufficient from the debt owing me by Boyce Ledwell the surviving partner of Alex[r] Scott, dec[d]. All residue to my sister Ann Smith, & after her death to her son Jas., she to be Ex'trix. Witnessed by Elias Ferris, W. Richards, Elinor Muir. Before Edward Byam was sworn Eleanor Rose, wife of John Rose and widow of . . . . Muir, 2 Sep. 1799. Recorded 18 Oct. 1799.

Jane Smith, widow. Will dated 9 Jan. 1793. My house & slaves to Benj[n] D'Harriett Smith of Grenada, Merch[t]. To Walter, son of M[rs] Eliz[th] Oliver, £20 c. Alex[r] Brodie & Eliz. Oliver Ex'ors. Witnessed by Henry M[c]David. Before Edward Byam, Esq., was sworn Henry M[c]David, writing clerk, 2 May 1793. Recorded 14 June 1793.

Mary Smith of Bulstrode Street, St. Marylebone, spinster. Will dated 15 May 1804; proved 14 Feb. 1806 by James Nibbs, Esq. To Jas. Nibbs & Thos. Kerby of Antigua, Esq[res], my plantation called "New Division" in trust for my sister Sarah Smith, to receive the rents then to sell. My clothes to my old servant Sarah Corps. My late brother W[m] Smith, Esq., by his will da. 15 July 1793, gave me an annuity of £50 charged on his Grenada estate, viz., ⅔ on the Diamond estate (⅓ of which estate he gave to my late cousin Geo. Griffin of Monmouth, Esq., deceased) & ⅓ on his Resolution Hall estate, which latter estate he gave to Rich[d] Oliver Smith, son of Sarah Dean. There is due to me £450 for arrears, the interest of which I give to my sister, & after her death to go towards payment of a debt on the estate of Geo. Griffin due to Thos. Oliver, deceased, for monies advanced by Thos. Oliver towards the settlement of the Diamond estate. The repayment of the said £2000 was secured by Geo. Griffin with the late W[m] Cooke by agreement da. 19 June 1797. M[rs] Cath. Griffin, widow of Geo. Griffin. The interest of all arrears due from the Resolution Hall estate to my sister for life & then to Rich[d] Oliver Smith. All residue of my personal estate to my sister Sarah, & after her death the following legacies to be paid, viz., £20 a year to Sarah Corps. £15 a year to my servant Sarah Light. To Jas. Nibbs £200. To Thos. Kerby £100. To Ann Frost £200. To Arabella French of Marybone Str., widow, £30, & then all residue to the 7 godchildren of my sister & myself, viz., Lucy Ann Blois, sp[r], dau. of Sir John Blois, Bart., Ann Mildmay & Letitia Mildmay, sp[rs], daus. of Sir Henry S[t] John Mildmay, Bart., & Eliz[th] Ann Griffin & Mary Griffin, sp[rs], daus. of Geo. Griffin, Jn[o] Clerk, son of John Clark of Worting, n[r] Basingstoke, Esq., & Mary Ann Ricketts, sp[r], dau. of Geo. W[m] Ricketts of Lainston, n[r] Winchester, Esq. Jas. Nibbs & my sister Sarah Smith Ex'ors. Witnessed by Anne Lessly, Welbeck Street, Catherine Mills, Queen Anne Street, Westminster, Robert L. Appleyard, Lincoln's Inn.

Codicil. 2 March 1805. 5 guineas to Sarah Corps. On 2 Jan. 1806 appeared Robert Langley Appleyard of Lincoln's Inn, Gent., and Humphrey Gilbe of Great Winchester Street, London, Merchant. Sworn under £1000. Recorded 25 Oct. 1806.

Close Roll, 12 Geo. III., Part 2, No. 13.

Indenture made the 7th April 1772 between Mary Smith of Golden Square, spinster, of the one part, and Richard Oliver, Esq. and Alderman of London, of the other part, witnesseth that for docking and barring all estates tail or remainders in the plantation, lands, etc., and negros or slaves hereinafter mentioned, and for conveying the same to and for such uses, and in consideration of 5s. Mary Smith grants to Richard Oliver and his heirs for ever all that plantation in the parish of St. Mary, Antigua, containing 122 acres, called Smith's, abutting N. on the lands now or late of Isaac Thibou, S. on the lands now or late in the possession of Samuel Watkins, E. on the lands now or late in the possession of George Moncrieff, and W. on the lands now or late in the possession of Nesbit Darby and Samuel Watkins, together with all negros or slaves late in the occupation of W. Smith, Esq., and she appoints Stephen Blizard, Esq., and Jeremiah Blizard, Esq., both of Antigua, her Attorneys. William Smith, George Daniel, witnesses.

Circa 1667. Rendevous Bay. Ensigne Robert Smith, 20 mens land by grant from Governor Austin. Robert Smith, jun. (by gift of his father Ensign Robert Smith), half of 83 acres by will of John Stanworth. (Book of Claims.)

1668. Henry Smith patent for 100 acres.

1671, Jan. 11. George Smith, 10 acres by Governor Warner; surveyed 20 March.

1678. Mr. George Smith. Exchange Island by warrant from the Hon. Paul Lee, Esq.; surveyed 2 Dec.

1678, July 1. Lieut. Henry Smith, planter, sells to John Smith, jun., planter, 25 acres.

1679, May 21. Alexander Rollo, planter, sells to Ensign Robert Smith 21 acres at Rendesvouz Bay Division.

1680, May 19. John Marchant, planter, leases to George Smith, planter, 50 acres at Belfast at the rent of 5s. a year for two years. Witnessed by Jacob Laroux.

1680, July 12. Robert Barker and Margery his wife sell to Ensign Robert Smith 23 acres at Rendezvous Bay.

1680, Sep. 1. Henry Smith sells 60 acres to Francis Bagwell.

1686-7, March 24. Deposition of Thomas Smith, aged 36. (Colonial Entry Book, 48.)

1688. Mr. Thomas Smith rated on 14 slaves and 450 acres.

1692. Mr. Thomas Smith of Nevis rated on 450 acres and no slaves.

Simon Smith, A.M., about to be a Chaplain in Jamaica by licence dated 12 Dec. 1694 from Henry, Bishop of London. Recorded 10 Nov. 1703. He states that he has taken the oath of Supremacy and allegiance. Affidavit of Richard Lawrence *re* the accusation against Simon Smith, Rector of Falmouth, that he was imprisoned in New York for clipping and coyning. The accusation is utterly false. 29 Nov. 1703. Recorded 1 Dec.

1708, Sep. 23. Rev. Simon Smith, Rector of Falmouth, is accused of bigamy and of having forged the Bishop's Seal. The Bishop of Bath and Wells did not ordain him on Trinity Sunday 1692. Mrs. Smith lives in Town (his primitive wife). He was married to Mrs. Elliot, the wife he now lives with, in the Governor's house, and Mrs. Yeamans gave Mrs. Elliot away. He married Mrs. ffower (who is now living in St. John's Town) at New York, and had previously cohabited with her for some years. Certificate also from Mr. John Lambert, Rector of Nunny, co. Somerset, who married them.

William Smith of Portsea (will 1714) was an official in the dockyard; both he and William Smith, M.D. (will 1732), were Aldermen of Portsmouth, and the latter was Mayor one year. The seal he then used bore for arms a lion sejant, and a crest a horse's head. (? the coat of Heatherington.)

In Chancery, 1721, Sep. 2. Simon Smith, Dr. of Physic, plaintiff, *v.* John Galway, merchant, defendant.

1722, Oct. 15. Wavell Smith, Esq; appointed Secretary and Clerk of the Crown for Life, to the Leeward Caribbee Islands, in the Room of John Knight of Gosfield in the County of Essex, Esq; who resign'd. ('Historical Register,' p. 46.)

1723, Aug. 7. Governor's Commission to the Council to swear in Wavell Smith as Secretary of the Leeward Islands, his patent dated 29 July last under the Great Seal. Mr. James Smith is to be his clerk. (Minutes of Council.)

1723, Sep. 9. Petition of Wavell Smith for two proportions of land in St. John's Town; granted.

1723, Oct. 4. Wavell Smith writes that his wife was on board one of the ships in the harbour during the hurricane, but got safely ashore during a lull, and complains that he has probably lost all his effects. (America and West Indies, No. 451, p. 37.)

1723, Jan. 23. Mr. William Smith to be Deputy-Secretary.

1724, April 10. Wavell Smith on 23 Jan. last appointed his brother his deputy, is about to go to England, and has complaints against the Governor in regard to his fees. Six Members of Council sign a letter in his favour.

1724, April 29. Richard Smith of Antigua, Gent., and his wife Elizabeth and Robert Smith sell 10 acres to John Sawcolt, Esq.

Indenture dated 7 May 1725 between Richard and Robert Smith of Antigua, planters, sons of Robert Smith of Antigua, deceased, and Elizabeth Banbury, widow and relict of said Robert Smith, deceased, of the one part, and Jacob Thibou, merchant, of the other.

1727, July 23. Wavell Smith seals his letter. Arms: *Ermine, three roundles.* Crest: *A plume of feathers out of a ducal crown.* Motto: *Ne differ in ann* . . . . (America and West Indies, No. 53, p. 2.)

1728, Nov. 30. Wavell Smith appointed by Lord Loudonderry to a seat at the Council Board of St. Christopher's.

1730, Oct. 12. Petition of Richard Oliver as guardian of Richard Smith, a minor, for payment of negro.

1731, Oct. 9. William Smith is appointed powder-officer.

1734, June 5. Petition of William Smith, Esq., Clerk to the Assembly, for £102 as one year's salary.

1736, March 17. Fred. Cope, Esq., to act as clerk during the absence of William Smith, Esq.

1738, Nov. 29. Mr. William Smith one of the Attorneys to Wavell Smith the Secretary.

1739, Aug. 21. William Smith, jun., struck out of Troop.

1739, Aug. 29. Mr. William Smith, Clerk to the Assembly, is so disordered that he must go abroad.

1739, Sep. 13. William Smith is sworn a J.P. Mr. William Smith being sick Mr. William Smith, jun., is sworn in as clerk.

1742, July 9. William Smith, Esquire's, accounts as late Collector of Powder Duty.

William Smith, Deputy-Secretary of St. Christopher's, writes on 13 Nov. 1754 that he was so appointed by his uncle. Seal: *A royal crown over a double-headed eagle displayed.*

1767. Ann Smith rated on 4 acres and 14 slaves. (St. Mary's Vestry Book.)

1780. Mary Smith rated on 160 acres and 59 slaves. (*Ibid.*)

1792, Nov. 5. Wm. Smith, esq. of Grenada, to Miss Johnstone of Liverpool. ('Gent. Mag.,' p. 1054.)

Robert Snow and William Collis of Cork were appointed to be Attorneys for William and John Smith of Cork to administer the estate of their brother Willson Smith. (No date.)

William Smith of Barbuda graduated 23 June 1823 at Leyden University, and another William of ditto on 14 June 1830.

PARISH REGISTER OF ST. JOHN.

Baptized.

1728	Aug. 23	Sarah the d. of Mr William Smith & Mary his wife.
1750	April 27	William the s. of William Smith and Ann his wife.
1760	Sep. 10	John the S. of John Smith, Jun., and Ann his wife.
1762	Jan. 10	Margaret the D. of John Smith and Ann his wife.
1764	Sep. 28	George the S. of John Smith, Junr, and Ann his wife.
1782	June 12	Samuel and George William the Ss. of William Smith and Mary his wife.
1783	Sep. 10	William the S. of The Reverend William Smith by Jane Bertie.
1789	Sep. 23	Mary Hurst D. of William Smith and Mary his wife. B. the 8th February 1784.
1789	Sep. 23	Sarah Farley D. of William Smith and Mary his wife. B. the 23rd December 1787.
1795	Sep. 4	Thomas S. of Thomas Smith, deceased, and Clementina his wife. B. the 16th August 1795.

Married.

1708	June 8	Peter Horne & Ann Smith. B.
1715	Nov. 15	Richard Mercer and Mary Smith. L.
1727	Aug. 17	William Smith and Mary Oliver.
1727	Mar. 1	The. Stil. Smith and Ann Bullock.
1728	June 16	Robert Smith and Catherine Forrester.
1731	July 26	William Smith and Mary West. L.
1739	Jan. 27	William Smith & Ann Bryant. L.
1747	Dec. 18	James Smith and Jane Hamilton.
1759	June 2	Walter Patterson and Ann Smith (Widow). L.

Buried.

1691	Sep. 5	Henry Smith.
1695	Oct. 26	Jeremia Smith, Comandr of the ship Babora of Coleraine.
1696	April 12	John Smith.
1712	Sep. 7	John Smith.
1713	Aug. . .	Jane Smith.
1713	Oct. 5	Benj. Smith.
1714	May 9	Mary Smith.
1714	Sep. 26	Benjamin Smith.
1715	Oct. 1	John Smith.
1720	June 4	James Smith.
1721	Feb. 13	Mary w. of Simon Smith.
1725	Mar. 11	Ensigne Henry Smith.
1728	Mar. 31	Henry Smith.
1728	May 19	Docr Simon Smith.
1728	Feb. 16	Elinor Smith, widow.
1728	Feb. 27	Mr James Smith of this Island.

1729 Aug. 19 Capt John Smith, Comr of H.M.S. the Sapphire from Guinea.
1730 June 14 George Smith.
1730 Feb. 2 Mrs Mary Smith.
1732 Oct. 16 Henry Smith.
1736 May 25 Catherine wife of Robert Smith.
1737 Mar. 29 John Wevell s. of Mr William Smith.
1737 Aug. 10 Sarah Smith.
1737 Mar. 16 Samuel Smith, infant.
1740 Nov. 23 Mary Smith w. of William Smith.
1741 May 26 John Smith.
1743 June 15 James Smith.
1743 June 21 Capt Edward Smith of His Majesty's ship the Burford.
1743 Dec. 13 Doctor Saint George Smith.
1745 Oct. 12 Robert Smith, a child.
1747 Nov. 29 Margt Smith in the country.
1750 Oct. 29 John Smith.
1754 Sep. 13 Capt Isaac Smith.
1778 Jan. 2 William Smith.
1778 Nov. 30 John Smith, Senr.
1779 Sep. 3 William Smith.
1780 Jan. 17 John Smith.
1784 Oct. 29 John Smith (Planter).
1809 Sep. 13 Francis Smith, Captain R.N.

Parish Register of St. Peter.

Married.

1779 .... 8 William Smith & Mary French.

Parish Register of St. Paul.

Baptized.

1731 Jan. 2 George S. of Robert Smith & his wife.

Married.

1786 Oct. 6 Thomas Smith, planter, to Clementina Anderson, Spinster; by L.

Buried.

1727 Feb. 27 Captn Richard Smith.
1827 Nov. 23 James Smith, Cap. late R. W. I. Rangers. English Harbour. 51.
1828 Feb. 22 John Hankey Smith, Lieu. 93d Highlanders. Ridge. 22.

St. Peter's, St. Christopher's.

Married.

1734 July 25 Henry Slingsby and Mary Ann Smith.

St. John's Churchyard.

On a headstone:—

Here Lyeth
the Body of
SAMUEL SMITH
who departed this life
the XXIII of November
Ann. Dom. 1758
aged XXXIII years.

Family of Sones.

Richard Sones. Will dated 27 March 1719. To my son Richard the house & land joining Mr John Russell, he paying £20 c. to his sister Jane Sones at his age of 21. To my said dau. Jane Sones the little shop next the said house, with bed, furniture, etc. To Eliz. Skelton a ring of a pistole. To Eliz. Ford ditto. Mr John Vincens, Chirurgeon, & Mr Joseph Lee, planter, Ex'ors. Witnessed by William Cooper, Thomas Delamar, John Ford. Sworn 18 Dec. 1719.

Elizabeth Chelton of Antigua. Will dated 3 May 1730. To my granddau. Eliz. Chelton, dau. of Roger Chelton, £50 c., & in default of issue to the children of my dau. Rachel Sones. Nathl & Eliz. Whitle, s. & dau. of my son Nath. Whitle. All residue to my dau. Rachel Sones & Ex'trix. Witnessed by Jasper King, Roger Beffin. Sworn 29 Aug. 1735. Recorded 16 Feb. 1740.

1712, May 6. Patent for one proportion of land to Richard Soanes, vintner.

Parish Register of St. John.

Baptized.

1800 Jan. 4 Amelia Gamble D. of Richard Sones and Mary his wife.
1804 Nov. 15 Hester Hunt D. of Richard Sones and Mary his wife; b. 15 June 1804.

Married.

1691 Jan. 31 Daniel Sones and Katheren Thomas.
1733 Mar. 11 Joseph Boone and Rachell Soanes.

Buried.

1701 Jan. 9 Franciss S. of Richard Soanes & Jane his wife.
1729 Nov. 24 Daniel Soanes, a child.
1736 Mar. 7 Marianne the D. of John Soanes.
1741 April 10 John Soanes.

Parish Register of St. Philip.

Baptized.

1788 Nov. 15 Richard Murrough s. of Richard & Mary Soans.
1802 Aug. 14 Joseph B. s. of Richard & Mary Sones; b. 5 Nov. 1801.

Married.

1783 Dec. 20 Richard Soanes to Mary Hunt.

Parish Register of St. George.

Buried.

1737 Oct. 12 Mark Soan.

Parish Register of St. Paul.

Baptized.

1726 Feb. 26 Richard the S. of Richard Soanes & Rachel his wife.
1732 Aug. 25 Thomas S. of Richard Soanes & Rachel his wife.
1785 May 10 Elizabeth D. of Richard Sones & Mary his wife; b. Nov. 1. £3 6 0.

Married.

1732 Oct. 28 Daniel Fox and Elizabeth Soanes; by B.
1734 Feb. 26 Jasper Oakes & Rachel Soanes; by L.
1734 Mar. 22 John Martin & Jane Soanes; by L.
1751 Mar. 30 Richard Soanes and Anne Barnes; by L.
1786 Oct. 10 Thomas Sones, planter, to Diana Knewstub; by L.

Buried.

1733 June 10 Richard Sone.
1753 Jan. 3 John S. of Richard Soanes and Anne his wife.

Family of Stapleton.

Sir William Stapleton of London, Knt. and Bart. Will dated 1 April 1686; proved 28 Oct. 1686 by Dame Anne Stapleton the relict and Sir Edward Scott, Knt.; power reserved to Richard Grace, Esq., and Sir James Cotter, Knt. (141 Lloyd.) £100 for charity. To my loving wife Dame Anne Stapleton my plate, jewells, household stuff, & ½ of my lands in Nevis & my storehouse in Charles Town, or in lieu £500 a year. To my Ex'ors my interest in the plantation of Phillip Noyell in St Christopher's, which is to be sold after his death. To my son Wm all my lands in Montserrat, & his heirs, then to my other 2 sons, viz. ½ to my son James & ½ to my son Miles. To my 1st dau. Ann Stapleton £1500. To my dau. Louise Stapleton £1000 & to my dau. Frances £1000 at 18. To my dau. Louise all my interest in the potwork in Nevis with the 20 acres & negros. All my monies to be invested in land in Ireland for my son James, then to my sons Wm & Miles. My trustees to be guardians of my 3 sons. ½ of all my lands in Nevis after my wife's death to my son Jas. To my brother Andrew of Cork £30 a year for 12 years for his care of my sister's children. To my brother Redmond Stapleton all debts due from him or from my brother Edmond, deceased. All residue to my son Jas. at 21. Sir Edmond Andros, Kt, Sr Edwd Scott, Kt, Col. Richd Grace, Sr Jas. Cotter of Ballinspeny, co. Corke, & Patrick Trant of St Gyles in the Fields, Esq., Ex'ors, & give them each £11. Witnessed by Thomas Newcomen, Ja. Nibell, Thomas Butler.

Codicil dated 5 July 1686. Now in Paris. Revoke appointment of Sr Edmond Andros & Patrick Trant as Ex'ors & appoint my wife in their stead. I give her also ½ of the lands to be purchased in England or Ireland & ½ stock in Nevis. Witnessed by William Trumbull, Walter White, Frances Lambe, George Denham.

Sir William Stapleton of Nevis, Bart. Will dated 6 Dec. 1699; proved 14 March 1700 by Dame Frances Stapleton. (43 Dyer.) All debts to be first paid, particularly for mine & my brother's education in Paris. My father Sir Wm Stapleton by his will gave a legacy to a relative in Ireland, which is to be paid. To my dearly beloved bro. Miles a suit & £200 charged on my Montserrat estate & my library. To my mother Dame Anne Stapleton & my sisters Anne Louise & Frances Stapleton mourning & £30 each. Guinea ring to Col. Jos. Jory, Mr Randall Jory, Mr Jos. Martin, Col. Wm Burt, Col. Jas. Morton, Col. Thos. de la Wall, Majr Spencer Broughton, Cap. Rupert Billingsley, Cap. Fra. Collingwood, & Mr David Digony. To my mother-in-law Dame Penelope Russell, my brother-in-law Martin Madan, & my sister his wife £20 each. £10 c. to the poor. To my dear son not yet christened to be called Jas. £1000 at 21. To my cousin Mrs Briget Rogers a guinea ring. To my dear wife Dame Frances Stapleton ½ of all my estate & jewells. My servt Blanch Lemon £3 & to Jno Gray 30s. All residue to my 1st s. & h. Wm Stapleton. My wife, mother, bro. Miles, and brother-in-law Martin Madan Ex'ors in Trust. Witnessed by Spencer Broughton, Joseph Chapman, William Semple.

Mem. 8 Dec. 1699 appeared Major Spencer Broughton and Mr. Joseph Chapman and on 13 Jan. William Semple before William Burt, Esq.

Dame Anne Stapleton of St. James's, co. Middlesex, widow of Sir William Stapleton, Knt. and Bart. Will dated 14 May 1719; proved 26 July 1722 by Anne and Frances Stapleton the two daughters. (147 Marlborough.) All my estate to my daus. Anne & Frances Stapleton, & appoint them Ex'trices. Witnessed by Thomas Elliott, Elizabeth Bowery, Nicholas Fitz-Gerald, scrivener.

Miles Stapleton of Harrow-on-the-Hill, co. Middlesex, Esq. Will dated 16 June, proved 25 Aug. 1730 by Elizabeth Stapleton the widow. (246 Auber.) All my lands in Gt Britain & St Christopher's to my wife Eliz., she to pay £100 a year to my sister Mrs Anne Stapleton, spr. After my wife's death all my lands to my son Miles Stapleton. To each of my 2 daus. Anna & Frances £100 at 21. All residue to my wife, she to be sole Ex'trix. Witnessed by Harry Gibbes, Ri. Collibee, Thomas Croome.

Penelope the wife of James Russell Stapleton, Esq. Will dated 24 March 1737; proved 18 June 1739 by James Russell Stapleton, Esq. (140 Henchman.) By virtue of a common recovery in the great sessions for the co. of Flint, & by a certain deed, I have power to dispose of the moiety of the estate of Sir John Conway my late father, deceased. I give all my estate to my husband Jas. Russell Stapleton, whom I appoint sole Ex'or. Witnessed by Gibson Lucas, Peter Guerin, John Crofts.

James Russell Stapleton, Esq. Will dated 1 Jan. 1739; proved 3 Oct. 1743 by Dame Frances Stapleton, widow, the surviving Ex'or. (322 Boycott.) To my 5 daus. all my estate equally at 21, & in default of issue to my brother Sir Wm Stapleton, Bart., but in that case to be charged with £1500 for his younger children. My said brother & my honoured mother Lady Stapleton to be Ex'ors. Cancel all debts due from my mother-in-law Lady Conway. Witnessed by John Stevens, William Ives, Fs. Blandy.

Sir William Stapleton of co. Oxon, Bart. Adm'on granted on 5 July 1741 to Lady Catherine Stapleton the widow.

Dame Frances Stapleton of Cheltenham, co. Gloucester, widow. Will dated 17 Oct. 1743; proved 26 March 1746 by Dame Penelope Conway, widow; power reserved to Martin Madan, Esq., Elizabeth Conway, spinster, and Augustus Schutez; proved also 10 June 1746 by Eleanor Conway, spinster, the only daughter of Dame Penelope Conway, deceased, by mistake called Elizabeth in the will; power reserved to Martin Madan and Augustus Schutez. (100 Edmunds.) To my trustees all my lands at Stoke Pogis & Wexham, co. Bucks, & my plantation in St Christopher's, on trust to pay the rents for discharge of £11,000 I agreed to secure on the marriage of my son Sir Wm Stapleton, Bart., deceased, & then all my said lands in co. Bucks to my grandson Sir Tho. Stapleton, Bart., together with the furniture at Stoke Podges. £8000 to be raised from my plantation in St Christopher's, £3000 of which I give to my grandchildren, the younger children of my son Sir Wm, & £5000 to all my grandchildren, the children of my late son Jas. Russell Stapleton, Esq.; after the payment of the £8000 the said plantation to my said grandchildren as tenants in common. I confirm the settlement of my plantation in Nevis on my son Jas. Russell Stapleton. The above legacy of £3000 includes £2000 charged on the Nevis plantation. To my granddau. Cath. Stapleton, dau. of my son Jas. Russell Stapleton, my house building in Cheltenham & all my lands there, also the lease of my house in Grosvenor Str., St Geo., Hanover Sq., & my jewells. All residue to Ex'ors in Trust. Lady Conway & my nephew Martin Madan, Esq., & Mrs Eliz. Conway, dau. of Lady Conway, & my nephew Augustus Schutez trustees & Ex'ors. Witnessed by Mary Greene, Elizabeth Woods, W. De La Bere.

Close Roll, 11 Geo. II., Part 5, No. 14.

Indenture made the 7th Nov. 1737 between Sir William Stapleton of Braywick, Berks, Bart., of the one part, and William Fenton of Montserrat, but now residing in London, Esq., of the other part. In conformity with an Act made 4 Queen Anne for supplying the want of fines, and in consideration of £2500 sterling, Sir William Stapleton grants to William Fenton and his heirs and assigns all that Water Work Plantation in the parish of St. Peter, Montserrat, containing 600 acres, bounded E. with the top of the mountain and certain lands of Richard Cooke, Esq., and thence running W. to the Old Road River, S. with the river and other lands of Richard Cooke, and N. with certain lands of Colonel John Bramble, which plantation now is or lately was in the tenure of Colonel George Wyke his undertenants, etc., to the only proper use of William Fenton and his heirs for ever. Thomas Hook, George North, witnesses.

1669, April 30. Sir Tobias Bridge reports that Lieut.-Colonel Stapleton writes from Montserrat that he will be very diligent in collecting the 4½ per cent. duty. William, Lord Willoughby, reported that Colonel Stapleton being appointed Deputy-Governor of Montserrat, after the capture of that island by the French Jan. 1666, and the country not being in a condition to support a Governor, he settled upon him and his heirs the Waterwork Plantation. (Colonial Calendar, America and West Indies.)

1671, Feb. 24. Sir Charles Wheeler was required by his commission to continue Lieut.-Colonel William Stapleton, Lieut.-Governor of Montserrat, for the good opinion his Majesty has of his abilities. He was also commissioned a Captain of one of H.M. companies of Foot. (*Ibid.*)

1671, June 15. Nevis. Sir Thomas Lynch, Lieut.-Governor of Jamaica, wrote that Governor Stapleton was gone to Nevis to marry Lieut.-Colonel Russell's daughter. (*Ibid.*)

1671, July 5—15. Major-General William Stapleton one of the Commissioners for settling the differences about the rendition of St. Kitts. (Colonial Calendar, America and West Indies.)

1671, July 6. Sir Charles Wheler writes of Colonel Stapleton, Deputy-Governor of Montserrat, whom he has made Major-General of Militia of the islands. He was at the first raising, and in 1671 Lieut.-Colonel of Bridge's Barbadoes Regiment. On Dec. 20 he was commissioned Captain-General and Governor-in-Chief of the Leeward Islands *vice* Wheler recalled. (*Ibid.*)

1671. James Cotter then a Captain in Bridge's Barbadoes Regiment. The following year his name appears as Senior Captain of the Barbadoes Regiment of Dragoons.

(? 1672.) Petition of James Cotter, Esquire, to the King. Shewing that William Stapleton, Captain-General of the Leeward Islands, has, notwithstanding his power to dispose of all places under him in those islands, given him leave to beg of his Majesty the places of Secretary and Marshal of said islands. Prays therefore, in consideration of his long service and late losses in his Majesty's service, a patent for 21 years of the places of Secretary and Marshal of Nevis, St. Christopher's, Montserrat, and Antigua. (Colonial Calendar, America and West Indies, p. 457.)

1674, May 6. Garrett Cotter a witness to an agreement between the Lords Proprietors of Carolina. (*Ibid.*, p. 577.)

1676, Nov. 22. Colonel William Stapleton writing home stated that the then Governor of Montserrat was his brother Edmond Stapleton.

1678. Antigua. James Stapleton and William Stapleton, jun., Esquires, had a grant of 1025 acres from Colonel James Vaughan, which lands were surveyed on March 7.

1679, Jan. 1. Redmond Stapleton, Esq., received a patent for 1025 acres, which tract was to be a manor with all royalties and other rights, at the annual rent of an ear of Indian corn. By deed dated at Montserrat 6 July 1682, witnessed by Nicholas Meade, he conveyed this to Sir William Stapleton for 100,000 lbs.

1680. Ran. Stapleton signed papers as a member of Council of Montserrat. (Colonial Leeward Islands, 48.)

Pedigree of Stapleton.

ARMS.—*Argent, a lion rampant sable.*
CREST.—*Out of a crown or a Saracen's head proper.*

Sir JOHN STAPLETON, Knt., settled in Ireland *temp.* Henry VI.=. . . .

Richard Stapleton, living 1566=Eleanor Butler.

John Stapleton=Margaret Bourke.

. . . . Stapleton=. . . .

John Stapleton of Thorlesbegg, co. Tipperary=Sarah McEgan.

Redmond Stapleton of Thorlesbegg, Esq.=. . . . dau. of Cornelius Fogarty, Esq., of Devey.

A

A |

. . . . Stapleton, 1st son (? Andrew Stapleton of Cork, living 1686); died s.p.

Edmond Stapleton, 2nd son, Deputy-Governor of Nevis; died s.p. before 1686.

Sir William Stapleton of Nevis in the West Indies, Knt. and Bart., 3rd son; Colonel of Militia; Deputy-Governor of Montserrat 1669—72; Captain-General of the Leeward Islands 1672—86; created Bart. 20 Dec. 1679; died at Paris 3 Aug. 1686. Will dated 1 April and proved 28 Oct. 1686. (141 Lloyd.) = Anne, dau. of Colonel Randolph Russell, Deputy-Governor of Nevis; mar. *circa* June 1671. Will dated 14 May 1719; proved 26 July 1722. (147 Marlborough.)

Sir James Stapleton, 2nd Bart., 1st son and heir, born 24 Sep. 1672; died s.p.

Sir William Stapleton, 3rd Bart., of Nevis, 2nd son, born 14 Nov. 1674. Will dated 6 Dec. 1699; proved 14 March 1700. (43 Dyer.) = Frances, 2nd dau. and coheir of Sir James Russell, Knt., of Nevis, first-cousin to her husband, æt. 15 and unmar. in 1681; mar. 2ndly, before 1716, Walter Hamilton, Captain-General of the Leeward Islands, who died 18 April 1722. Her will dated 17 Oct. 1743; proved 26 March 1746. (100 Edmunds.)

Sir William Stapleton, 4th Bart., M.P. for co. Oxford 1727; created D.C.L., Oxford, 11 July 1733; died 12 Jan. 1739-40 at Bath. Adm'on granted Jan. 1741 to his relict. = Catherine, only dau. and heir of William Paul of Braywick Grove in Bray, co. Berks, by Lady Catherine Fane; died 28 June 1753.

James Russell Stapleton, Captain 3rd Regiment of Guards; died Aug. 1743. Will dated 1 Jan. 1739; proved 3 Oct. 1743. (322 Boycott.) = Penelope, dau. and heir of Sir John Conway, Bart., of Botrythan, co. Flint; died May 1739 at Harding, near Henley-on-Thames. Will dated 24 March 1737; proved 18 June 1739. (140 Henchman.)

William Stapleton, 1st son, Lieut. R.N.; killed 8 May 1754, æt. 27. M.I. at Port Royal, Jamaica.

Sir Thomas Stapleton, 5th Bart., of Rotherfield Greys, co. Oxford, born 24 Feb. 1727; matriculated from St. Mary Hall, Oxford, 27 Feb. 1743-4, æt. 17; created D.C.L. 3 July 1754; M.P. for Oxford, 1759—68; died 1 Jan. 1781. = Mary, dau. of Henry Fane of Wormsley, co. Oxford; mar. 27 Nov. 1765; died 26 Feb. 1835, æt. 90, at Greys Court.

James Stapleton, died a bachelor.

Catherine Stapleton, mar. Sir James Wright, H.M. Resident at Venice.

Frances Stapleton.

Sir Thomas Stapleton, 6th Bart., 22nd Baron Le Despencer, born 10 Nov. 1766; died 1 Oct. 1831, æt. 64. = Elizabeth, 2nd dau. of Samuel Eliot of Antigua, Esq.; mar. 1 July 1791; died 3 Jan. 1848.

Thomas Stapleton, 1st son and heir, born April 1792; died v.p. 1 June 1829 in Devonshire Street. = Maria Wynne, 2nd dau. of Henry Bankes of Kingston House, co. Dorset; mar. 2 Feb. 1816; died 15 Oct. 1823.

William Stapleton, an Officer in the Army; died 26 Sep. 1826 at Barrackpore.

Mary Frances Elizabeth Stapleton, 23rd Baroness Le Despencer, of Mereworth Castle, Kent, only surviving child, born 24 March 1822; succeeded her grandfather 1831; mar. 29 July 1845; died 20 Nov. 1889. Will dated 17 Jan. 1890. = Evelyn Boscawen, 6th Viscount Falmouth, born 18 March 1819.

Evelyn Edward Thomas Boscawen, 7th Viscount Falmouth, of Tregothan Castle, Cornwall, C.B.; Lieut.-Colonel Coldstream Guards; born 24 July 1847.

Hugh Le Despencer Boscawen, Lieut. 1st Life Guards; born 28 Feb. 1849. = Lady Mary Wentworth, 3rd dau. of the 6th Earl Fitzwilliam, K.G.; mar. 23 May 1872.

John Richard De Clare Boscawen, Lieut. Oxford Militia; born 19 Dec. 1860.

Three daus.

1687, Aug. 10. Sir Nathaniel Johnson reported the death of Colonel Redmond Stapleton, Lieut.-Governor of Montserrat. (Colonial Entry Book, vol. 47, p. 272.)

1688. Montserrat. John Stapleton a member of the Assembly, and Redmond Stapleton of the Council.

Charles II. in 1679 granted a patent to Garrett Cotter as Secretary and Marshal of the Leeward Islands during the lives of Captain James Cotter and Mary his wife and James Cotter his nephew. Mary Cotter, James Cotter the nephew, and Garrett Cotter are dead. Captain James Cotter is a Papist and rebel. Opinion of H.M. Attorney-General. Read before their Lordships 11 Nov. 1689. (America and West Indies, No. 550.)

A plantation of 240 acres in St. Christopher's, granted by letters patent dated 1 May 1696 to Dame Anna Stapleton and Sir William Stapleton and their heirs and assigns for ever (formerly the plantation of the Father Hermit), descended to Miles Stapleton, third son of Dame Anna, and was in 1767 the property of his two daus. and coheirs Anna Stapleton, spinster, and Frances wife of William Lake of Hanwell, and let at £600 a year to the Rev. Martin Madan for two terms which would expire in 1803. (Mrs. V. T. C. Smith.)

1702, May 20. The estate of Sir William Stapleton, 125 acres. 6100 lbs. owing for taxes.

1706, Dec. 9. Petition of traders to and inhabitants of Nevis signed by Miles Stapleton. (B. T. Leeward Islands, vol. 9.)

1707-8. Nevis. Lady Stapleton, 51 male and 54 female negros.

1712. Montserrat. Lady Stapleton's loss by the French invasion was £1100.

1716-17, Jan. 9. Lieut.-General William Mathew wrote from St. Kitts: "I am sorry to hear Lady Stapleton has been indisposed."

Colonel Redmond Stapleton, 4th son, Deputy-Governor of Montserrat 1676—87; died *circa* 1687. = ...

A dau., mar. . . . . Andrew of Cork.

Miles Stapleton, 3rd son, died June 1730 at Bath. Will dated 16 June and proved 25 Aug. 1730. (246 Auber.) = Elizabeth, only dau. and heir of Sir Charles Gerrard, Bart., of Flamberds in Harrow, and relict of Warwick Lake of Cannons, who died 1712.

Mary Stapleton, mar. (1st wife) Sir James Cotter, Knt., M.P. for co. Cork; Provost-Marshal and Secretary of the Leeward Islands 1676; she died s.p. before 1688; he died 1705.

Anne Stapleton, living 1686 and 1730.

Louise Stapleton, living 1686.

Frances Stapleton, living 1686 and 1722.

Honora Stapleton.

Miles Stapleton, died a bachelor s.p.

Anna Stapleton, 1st dau. and coheir, a minor in 1730; living 1767.

Frances Stapleton, 2nd dau. and coheir, mar. William Lake of Hanwell.

Penelope Stapleton, 1st dau. and coheir, mar. 10 May 1753, at Camberwell, co. Surrey, Ellis Yong of Acton Park, co. Denbigh; she died 1788.

Catherine Stapleton, of Cheltenham in 1743, 2nd dau.

Elizabeth Stapleton, mar. Watkins Williams of Perevyd.

Frances Stapleton, mar. Robert Cotton, son of Sir Lynch Cotton of Llenay.

William Stapleton, Lieut.-General in the Army, born 6 June 1770; died 1826 at Douglas. = Anna Maria, 1st dau. of Hon. Frederick Keppel, Bishop of Exeter; mar. 1790; died 1836.

James Henry Stapleton, born 29 June 1777; died 1842.

Maria Stapleton, died 20 March 1858.

Catherine Stapleton, died April 1863.

Rev. Miles John Stapleton, Rector of Mereworth and Vicar of Tudeley, co. Kent, born 1801; matriculated from Worcester College, Oxford, 18 May 1819, æt. 18; B.A. from Magdalene College, Cambridge, 1827; died 11 June 1830. = Anne Byam, only child and heir of Thomas Norbury Kerby, Esq., of Antigua; mar. 29 Dec. 1820; died 1842.

s.p.m.

Rev. Sir Francis John Stapleton, 7th Bart., Rector of Mereworth, co. Kent; born 6 Aug. 1807. = Margaret, 1st dau. of Lieut.-General Sir George Airey; mar. 17 May 1830 at Florence.

A quo the present Baronet.

John Horace Thomas Stapleton, Colonel in the Army; mar. 1st, in 1814, Georgiana Maria, 1st dau. of George, 2nd Lord Southampton; and 2ndly, 1834, Charlotte Georgiana, dau. of Hon. Sir William Ponsonby; he died 7 Nov. 1836.

6 Geo., Sep. 2. In Chancery. Sir William Stapleton, Bart., a minor, by Ashton Warner, Esq., his guardian, and Dame Anne Stapleton, widow, plaintiffs, against Rowland Ash, Gent., defendant.

1724, Dec. 11. It was stated in the Assembly that on 11 May 1682 an Act gave Sir William Stapleton 200,000 lbs. yearly, that he had been Captain-General 10 years and 3 months, but did not receive anything because he never made Antigua his residence as was required by the Act.

1736, March. The Lady of Sir William Stapylton, Bart., Member of Parliament for the County of Oxford, of a Son. ('Historical Register,' p. 24.)

1736, March. The new-born Son of Sir William Stapleton, Bart., Knight of the Shire for the County of Oxford. (*Ibid.*, p. 27.)

1743, Aug. Col. Stapleton, Brother of the late Sir William Stapleton, Bart., and Colonel of a Comp. in the Third Reg. of Foot Guards. ('London Mag.,' p. 413.)

1746, Jan. 14. Frances Lady Dowager Stapleton, of the small pox, near Windsor, Bucks; she was mother to late Sir Wm Stapleton. ('Gent. Mag.,' p. 45.)

1753, June 28. Lady Stapleton, relict of the late Sir William Stapleton, Bart. (*Ibid.*, p. 340.)

1754, Dec. 9. James Wright, of Warwickshire, Esq; to Miss Stapleton, only daughter of the late Sir William Stapleton, a 30,000*l.* fortune. ('London Mag.,' p. 571.)

1817, Dec. At Paris, Hon. Col. Packenham, brother of the Earl of Longford, to Hon. Emily Stapleton, dau. of Lord le Despenser. ('Gent. Mag.,' p. 628.)

1826, March 5. At Douglas, aged 55, Lieut.-gen. William Stapleton, brother of the present Lord Le Despencer . . . . etc. (*Ibid.*, p. 368.)

1827, Sep. 26. At Barrackpore, the Hon. Wm. Stapleton, 2d son of Lord Le Despenser, and aid-de-camp to the Commander-in-chief, Lord Combermere. (*Ibid.*, p. 478.)

1829, June 1. In Devonshire-street, aged 37, the Hon. Thomas Stapleton, eldest son of Thomas Lord Le Despencer. He married Jan. 29, 1816, Maria-Wynne, second daughter of Henry Bankes, esq. M.P., and by that lady, who died 25 Oct. 1823, has left an only daughter surviving, born in 1822, to whom, on her grandfather's death, the Barony of Le Despencer, being one by writ, will descend. (*Ibid.*, p. 572.)

1830, May 17. At Florence, the Hon. F. J. Stapleton, youngest son of the Right Hon. Lord Le Despencer, to Margaret, eldest dau. of Lieut.-Gen. Sir Geo. Airey, K.G.H. (*Ibid.*, p. 641.)

1831, Oct. 1. In London, aged 64, the Right Hon. Thomas Stapleton, Lord le Despencer (by writ 1264), and a Baronet (1787). A long obituary notice follows. ('Gent. Mag.,' p. 465.)

1834, July 8. At Kensington, Lieut.-Col. Stapleton, nephew of the late Lord Despencer, to Charlotte Georgiana, 2nd dau. of the late Hon. Sir W. Ponsonby. (*Ibid.*, p. 208.)

1835, Feb. 26. Oxon. At Grey's-court, aged 90, Mary widow of Sir Thomas Stapleton, Bart. and great-grandmother of the Baroness le Despencer. She was the daughter of Henry Fane, esq. of Wormesley, brother to Thomas, 8th Earl of Westmoreland, by his second wife, Anne, daughter of Dr John Wynne, Lord Bishop of Bath and Wells; was married Nov. 27, 1765, and was left a widow, Jan. 1, 1781, with three sons and two daughters, of whom the eldest was the late Lord le Despencer. (*Ibid.*, p. 445.)

1835, Aug. 25. At Ash Cottage, Old Brompton, aged 32, the Hon. Frances Stapleton, daughter of the late Right Hon. Lord le Despencer. (*Ibid.*, p. 441.)

EXTRACTS FROM THE JEAFFRESON PAPERS.

1679, Sep. 9. By the death of Colonel Stapleton (His Excellency's brother) Mountserrat, as well as Antigua, is without a governor. (Vol. i., p. 243.)

1683, Sep. 25. Sir William Stapleton is expected here (London) the next Spring, having obtained leave to come home for a tyme. (Vol. ii., p. 83.)

1683-4, Feb. 12. Sir Nathaniell Johnson is the person that will succeed Sir William Stapleton. (*Ibid.*, p. 99.)

1683-4, March 10. Sir William Stapleton is returning to Europe, of his own free will. (*Ibid.*, p. 111.)

1684, July 1. Mr Blackburne shewed me a letter of your Excellency's wherein I was mentioned, as one of the persons he was to advise with about removeing the young gentlemen, your sons, from Camberwell to Westminster Schoole; but I understand the Lady Marsh is too tender of them to part with them to such harsh masters, as the masters of that schoole are reputed to be. (*Ibid.*, p. 118.)

1684, Dec. 6. Sir Nathaniell Johnson makes preparations, as if he designed still for the Generalship; but I am persuaded he will not go till our Generall comes over, and not then, if Sir William Stapleton desires to retourne. (*Ibid.*, p. 157.)

1685, June 6. Sir William Stapleton and all our friends, that were the compagnions of his voyage, are in good health at present. Our General is very well received by the King, and will probably make his enemies ashamed of the injustice they have done him in his absence. (Vol. ii., p. 202.)

1685-6, Jan. 28. Sir William Stapleton designes to try if the French air will recover his health, and Ensign William Matthews accompanies him into France, and Lady Stapleton goes also, which voyage is intended in the month of March. (*Ibid.*, p. 265.)

1686, Aug. 3. I just now received a letter which brings me the sad intelligence of the death of our Generall, Sir William Stapleton. He dyed and was buried at Paris, to the great loss and grief of all under his government.

1686, Sep. 8. By my last I gave you the sad news of Sir William Stapleton's death, whose lady is now at Camberwell with Lady Marsh. The French priests were very unkind to her, and still detain her sons out of some religious pretence, with no small addition to the grief of her ladyship, who is deprived at once of a husband and her sons. The General was so sensible before he died of the designs of some, that he had entrusted with the execution of his will, that it much discomposed him in his extremity, and he endeavoured to make some alterations, and would have done more, if death had not prevented him. (*Ibid.*, p. 315.)

1686, Sep. 11. The Lady Stapleton is retourned; but to add to her sorrow, the French detain her three sons; and unless our King will be pleased to demand them, they will not be permitted to come from the colledge where they are in the custody of men barbarously devout; who were so bloody zealous, as to send the lady word they had rather stick a dagger to her sons' hearts, and see the blood of them, than that they should go with her to be bred hereticks (as they term it), but the young baronet has the courage, that he tells them to their faces, if they keep him for eleven years there, he will never depart from his faith, which is great resolution for one of his age. (*Ibid.*, p. 321.)

CAMBERWELL, CO. SURREY.

Married.

1753 May 10 Ellis Young, Esqr, of St George, Hanover Sq., Wr, & Penelope Stapleton of the same, Spr. By the Bp. of St Asaph.

('Collect. Top. et Gen.,' vol. iii., p. 383.)

Family of Swete.

Nicholas Tripe of Exeter, goldsmith. Sons Thomas & Anthony. Proved 1685. (126 Cann.)

Adrian Swete of Train, co. Devon, Esq. Will dated 1 May 1716; proved 4 Dec. 1733 by Main Swete, Esq., the brother. (319 Price.) To my wife Honour Swete & my sister Philippa Swete £40 for the purchase of a flagon for holy communion for the church at Modbury. To my wife £700 & all that is due in the name of my late mother-in-law Mrs Petronella Fownes, & all chattels that were hers (my wife was her Ex'trix), & all her plate & household goods, & the use of the plate bearing the coats of arms of myself & wife except my large Montiffe. To my sisters Philippa & Loveday Swete £300 apiece. To my cousin Mr Richd Norris £100, he to discharge 2 bonds for £650 I signed with him as his surety. To my cousin Geo. Norris a bond of £95 & my books if he takes orders. To my brother Main Swete & Mr Wm Ley of Holbeton my tenement called Fursdon als South Fursdon in Holbeton, co. Devon, for 80 years, to pay the rents to my cousins Arthur . . . . Eliz. & Honour Penhay. To my cousins Edwd, Dennis, John, & Eliz. Philippa Russell (the 4 children of my cousin Ann Russell the wife of Mr Dennis Russell of Penryn) a debt of £50 their uncle Joseph Archer owed me at his decease. To John Voysey £40. To my cousin Mr Peter Courtney & his wife of London £40. A guinea ring to each godchild, also to my cousin Tho. Luscombe, Esq., Mr Richard Luscombe, Mrs Sarah Archer, Mrs Anne Russell, & Mrs Eleanor Norris. To my wife & 2 sisters £15 each. A gown to the Minister & a suit to each servant & 20s. ring. To my brother Main Swete my tenement called Scadownes in Modbury, & all other lands, & all residue of my personal estate, & appoint him Ex'or. My sister to take charge till he come to Modbury; if he be dead then to my 2 sisters. Witnessed by H. Legassicke, Pas. Legassicke, James Legassicke.

Main Swete of Train, co. Devon, Esq. Will dated 27 June 1735; proved 10 July 1736 by Esther Swete the widow, Philippa Swete, and Hugh Coplestone. (163 Derby.) My beloved wife Esther is entitled to £2000 under our marriage settlement, & I give her also £100 a year. To my sister Philippa Swete £200. To my cousin Anne Russell of Penryn in Cornwall, widow, £100. To my cousin Rebecca White, now wife of Adam White of Newton Abbott, Devon, surgeon, £20. To my cousin Esther Norton, wife of Nich^{s} Norton of Dartmouth, mariner, the £20 lent her by my late brother Adrian Swete. To Hugh Coplestone of Modbury, Gent., £50 in trust for his son John Coplestone. To my kinsman Benjn Swete of London, Esq., 3 guineas. To my sister-in-law Mrs Honor Swete a single Johannes, a piece of Portugal coin of 36s., & the like to my kinswoman Mrs Eleanor Norris of Modbury & to my cousin Dorothea Coplestone. To my wife Esther, my sister Philippa, & to Hugh Coplestone all my real estate that is not entailed in England & all my plantations & slaves in Antegoa in Trust to sell to pay legacies & to terminate any suits at law. All residue to my only child Adrian John Swete at 21, & if he dies without issue then my wife to have £1000 more, the children of my cousin Anne Russell £100 each, & the like sum to each of the children of my kinsman John Archer of Trelewick, co. Cornwall, Esq., deceased, & then all residue of trust money to my sister Philippa Swete. My wife Esther, my sister Philippa Swete, & Hugh Coplestone Ex'ors & Guardians. If the latter die Jas. Legassicke of Modbury, Gent., to act. To my wife Esther all her father's plate & her jewels. Witnessed by Christopher Savery, Gilbert Isaack, Ralph Wakeham. Sealed afresh 30 June 1735.

Benjamin Swete, Esq., widower, of Norfolk Street, St. Clement Danes, Strand. Will dated 26 Oct. 1743; proved 3 Dec. 1744 by Robert Weston, Edward Baughem, James Hudson, and Rev. J. Peters. (294 Anstis.) To be buried at Beggars Brook, co. Oxford, in the churchyard, a brick vault to be built, & my name & arms to be engraved on a stone. 10 gs. to the minister who shall preach my funeral sermon. £300 to the Mayor, Bayliffs, & Commonalty of Oxford for aiding the completion of their town hall. £100 towards completing the library at Christ Church, Oxford. £200 to the charity school for boys & girls in St Clement Danes & £400 to be distributed among poor housekeepers of that parish. To my worthy friend the Hon. Col. Guise, Major of the 1st Reg^{t} of Foot Guards, now Major-Genl, a diamond ring. To the Directors of the E.I. Co. £150 pursuant to what I subscribed March 1726 for their disabled seamen. To my housekeeper Bridget Sell £200. To Eliz. Pitmore £200. To my cook Sarah Calfe £200. To my servant Joseph Waracker £200. £10 to the poor of Beggars Brooke & of Yarnton, co. Oxford, & of St Thomas, Oxford. To the S.P.G. Society £100. To St Bartholomew's Hospital £100. £300 for 53 poor families of seamen of E. Greenwich for binding apprentices. To Mrs Mary Murray, widow of Mr Geo. Murray (she lodges at Mr Moodey's in Knightsbridge), £50. To Madame Weston, widow, & her dau. Mrs Mary Weston, my next door neighbours in Norfolk Str., 2 diamond rings. To Madame Hawkins of Norfolk Str. a like ring. To Madame Weston my bible fo, 2 vols. in Turkey blue leather with my arms thereon, & another to her dau. printed at Cambridge fields, also a gold watch by Quare. £200 to the 2 daus. of Edwd Baughem, Esq. To my servant Martha Wheaton £50. To my friend Mr Edwd Baughem a gold repeater made at Amsterdam by Mr Clarke. To Mr Wm Beamish, a midshipman on H.M.S. "Shrewsbury," Capt. Townshend Commander, £200. To St Bartholomew's Hospital £100. To Capt. John Swete in Col. Poulett's Reg^{t} of foot marines £500; he married Mrs Cockle of Greenwich. To Benjn Swete, Esq., £10,000; he lives at Kinsale in co. Cork, they being brothers & sons of the late Richd Swete, Esq., of a Devonshire family. To Miss Cath. dau. of Francis Fulford of Fulford near Exeter, Esq., £500. All my linen & plate to Mrs Weston & Mrs Hawkins to sell, & the proceeds for decayed gentlewomen of ancient family. To my godson Mr Furlay, son of Mr Furlay, merch^{t}, of Essex near Sir Joseph Eyles', £50. To my godson the son of Mr Tribe, apothecary, of Oxenden Str., Westminster, £50. —— Weston, Esq., Councillor-at-law, my next door neighbour, Edwd Baughem, Esq., of Hatton Garden, deputy-auditor to Esquire Benson, the Rev. Dr Peters, preacher at St. Clement Danes, & Capt. Hudson of the 1st Reg^{t} of Guards of Petty France, Trustees & Ex'ors, & to sell all my personal estate, then to hand in their accounts to the Govr, dep^{ty} Govr, & Directors of the Bank of England, viz.: to —— Carbonnell, Esq., Govr, —— Brookshanks, Esq., Govr: 1, Sir Edwd Bellamy, K^{t} & Alderman; 2, Bryan Benson, Esq.; 3, John Bance, Esq.; 4, Mr John Eaton Dodsworth; 5, Saml Holden, Esq.; 6, Sir Wm Jolliff; 7, Sir John Lequesne, K^{t}, Alderman & Sheriff; 8, Mr Robt Thornton; 9, Mr Benjn Lomquet; 10, Mr Benjn Mee; 11, Chas. Palmer, Esq.; 12, Moses Raper, Esq.; 13, Mr John South; 14, Sir John Thompson, K^{t} & Alderman; 15, Mr Saml Trench; 16, Mr Mark Weyland; 17, Tho. Cooke, Esq.; 18, Wm Fawkener, Esq.; 19, Jas. (? Jno) Gualtier, Esq.; 20, Mr Wm Hunt; 21, Henry Neale, Esq.; 22, Chas. Savage, Esq.; 23, Jas. (or Jno) Spelman, Esq.; 24, Alex^{r} Sheaf, Esq. $\frac{1}{4}$ of the residue of my personal estate to be divided among 50 persons, the widows or daus. of Naval officers, $\frac{1}{4}$ to 100 of those of seamen, $\frac{1}{4}$ to 50 of those of officers in the army, & $\frac{1}{4}$ to those of soldiers. The receipt of the Commissioners of the Navy to be sufficient, viz., of: 1, Richd Haddock, Esq.; 2, Sir Jacob Ackworth; 3, Tho. Pearse; 4, Geo. Purvis; 5, Geo. Crowle, Esq.; 6, John Phillipson; 7, John Fowler; & of the general officers, viz.: Genl Sir Chas. Wills & Lieut.-Genl Geo. Wade, Hatton Compton, Philip Honywood, Lord Mark Kerr, Robt Naper, Tho. Panton. To my Ex'ors £100 apiece. The above are the same officers as in my will of 1741. Guinea rings to the Governors & 24 Directors of the Bank of England. £120 for the girls & £80 for the boys at the schools at Greenwich. £159 to St Clement Danes for the Charity boys & girls. As to my real estate, my house & land in Yarnton, co. Oxford, called "The Freise," of 153 acres, in the tenure of Tho. Field, I give to my cousin Adrian John Swete, Esq., of Train by Modbury, co. Devon, charged with £30 a year to my cousin Mrs Mary Murray, widow, & £10 a year to my servants Bridget Sell & Eliz. Pitmore, & £50 a year to Mrs Hester Swete his mother. All my lands in Yarnton in the tenure of Richd Roberts, consisting of one farm of 42 acres & another of 62, I give to my cousin Francis Fulford, Esq., of Fulford, subject to £10 a year for my servant Sarah Calfe & Jos. Wareker. All my lands in the tenure of John Rooper at Beggars Brooke of 64 acres & Barley Wood in my own occupation, my dwelling house & furniture, & its 26 acres for the daus. of Francis Fulford, Esq. My 83 acres at Medley, co. Oxford, I give to the Rev. Dr Shipping, Principal of Brazen Nose Coll., Oxf^{d}, & Rev. Dr Leigh, head of Balliol, to keep in repair the cottages, house, & the chapel now building, & to pay 15s. to some minister for prayers & sermon there on Sunday morning & prayers in the afternoon, & the house for their own entertainment. My house at Crum Hill, E. Greenwich, I give to Capt John Swete. My house in Norfolk Str. which is leasehold I leave to Mrs Weston & Mrs Hawkins to allow 4 poor gentlewomen to reside there, & the sparrows & other birds to be fed as hithertoe. To my servant Charlotte £50. To Benjn Swete, Esq., of Kinsale, £5000. 6 or 7 pieces of tapestry representing the Siege of Troy to Dr Leigh to be hung in the house at Medley. Witnessed by John Burgess, Charles Judd, Lad. Mabert.

1st Codicil dated 9 March 1743-4. To Capt John Swete £1000, & to his brother Benjn Swete of Kinsale £1000. The lands in tenure of Richd Roberts to go to Francis Fulford's youngest son, & those in tenure of John Roper & Burley Wood to his daus. Francis Fulford, his wife, & her nephew Sir John Chichester, Bart., to be their Trustees. Rev. Mr Blackwell also to be Ex'or. To Mrs Wood £50. To Capt. Jas. Thompson of the "Star" brewhouse in Southwark £50. If Adrian John Swete die without heirs then the lands to Capt. John Swete. Witnessed by Rowland Simon, James Browne, Richard Bath.

Memorandum. 9 March 1743. I have burnt all my account books relating to the payment of the English & other forces in the Low Countries. My bay gelding worth 100 gs. to be sold & the proceeds given to Joseph Warcker.

2nd Codicil. 2 March 1743-4. I have paid Mr Thor, surgeon, £50.

Susannah Tripe of Exon, deceased 24 July. Commission to Nicholas Tripe the brother Jan. 1738.

John Archer of Trelewack names in his will his six younger sons Swete Nicholas Archer, Edward Archer, Samuel Archer, Addie Archer, and Nicholas Archer; sister Anne Russell; aunt Philippa Swete and uncle Adriane Swete. ('Memorials of the Archer Family.')

John Swete of Richmond, co. Surrey, Esq. Will dated 27 Jan. 1746; proved 19 March 1755 by Alicia Swete the widow. On 7 June 1762 adm'on of goods of testator, heretofore of Richmond, but at Plaistow, co. Essex, Esq., deceased, unadministered by Alicia Swete the relict, now deceased, granted to John Cottle, Esq., her brother. (93 Searle.) My house on Crump's Hill, E. Greenwich, to my wife Alicia for life, then to my brother Benjn Swete of Ireland, Esq., for his life, then to my sister Mrs Dorothy Beamish, then to my niece Miss Young, dau. of my sister Mrs Mary Young. My moiety of the Ridgwick estate, co. Sussex, under lease to the Bishop of Chichester, lately my dear wife's sister's Susannah, I give to my wife Alicia. £700 to my brother Benjn Swete, & to my brother-in-law Mr Tho. Beamish, attorney-at-law of Ireland, for my 4 sisters Catn, Ann, Mary, & Dorothy, viz., the interest of £200 between my sisters Mrs Cath. White, widow, & Mrs Anne Sullavan, then after their death £100 to my sister Mrs Dorothy Beamish & £100 to my niece Young. The interest of £200 to my sister Mrs Mary Young. The interest of £300 to my sister Mrs Dorothy Beamish. To each sister £10 for mourning, also to brother Benjn & his wife, my brother-in-law Mr Tho. Beamish, & Jas. Young. My gold repeating watch & seals to my sister Mrs Dorothy Beamish. To Cross Outing, Esq., £20. To my servant Mrs Ann Britton £100 & £10 for mourning. £5 to each other servant. All residue to my dear wife Alicia Swete & appoint her sole Ex'trix. Witnessed by Elizabeth Willey, Mary Fish, John Willey.

Adrian John Swete of Train, co. Devon, Esq. Will dated 10 Dec. 1755; proved 22 Jan. 1756 by Esther Swete, widow, the mother. (21 Glazier.) To be buried at Armington. To Mr Edmond Andrews of Ugborough £100 for his faithful services. To the St Luke's Hospital for lunaticks £100 & to the S.P.G. £100. To Mr Robt Vansittart my esteemed friend the £50 he owes me. To my honoured mother Esther Swete of Train, widow, & to her heirs all my barton of Train & all other lands, plantations, etc., & all residue, & appoint her Ex'trix. Witnessed by Robert Cawley, W. Usticke, Mary Abbott. Recorded at Registrar's Office, St. John's, 12 Feb. 1757.

Esther Swete of Bath, widow. Will dated 30 Nov. 1778; proved 3 Feb. 1784 by Rev. John Tripe and Henry Beeke (miscalled Harry Beke in the will) and Hugh Hammersley, Esq. (97 Webster.) To be buried at Armington, co. Devon. To my relations Mrs Esther Yard, Mr Nicholas Yard & Mrs Jane Yard, all living at Chudleigh, co. Devon, £20 a year for life. To my friend Mrs Rebecca Lee £100 a year for life. All these annuities charged on my plantation in Antigua, leased to Daniel Mathew, Esq., deceased. To my servant Leonard Fryer £50 a year. All my estate in Antigua & all my manors in Devon to Robert Child & Robert Dent, bankers in London, in trust for Rev. John Tripe, son of —— Tripe, surgeon at Ashburton, co. Devon, for life, then to his heirs, & failing such to Harry Beke, son of Mr Beke of King Staunton, co. Devon, & his heirs, then to my kinsmen Edward Archer, Esq., and Samuel Archer, Esq. The heir to take the surname & arms of Swete only & within a year to obtain an Act of Parliament for that purpose. To the children of my cousin Rebecca Yard, except the said Nicholas, Esther, & Jane, £100 apiece, & the like sums to each of the children of my kinswoman Rebecca Jones, widow of —— Jones, clerk, deceased. To my dear friend Miss Eliz. Theobalds my best pair of diamond earrings. To John Tripe all my other jewels. Mr & Mrs Hammersley £200 each. Mrs Margt Ayleworth £100. My steward Edmund Andrews £200 & to his son John my godson £100. The hospital at Bath £100 & the pauper scheme £100. My woman Hannah Abdy £100 & clothing. Poor of Armington & Modbury £20 each. My friends Mrs Theobald, Lady Stapylton, Sir Edward & Lady Dering, Mr & Mrs Winchester, Mrs Mary Weston, Mrs Hay of Bath each a 10 gn ring. To John Tripe £1000 & to Harry Beke & Hugh Hammersley of Spring Gardens, Esq., £500 each, they to be Ex'ors. They are to recover & sell my lands in Jamaica which were given to me by my friend Miss Mary Hynes, deceased. To Alice Longstaff, spinster, £20 a year. My godson Robert Charles Dering, son of Sir Edward Dering, £200 at 21. My kinsmen Edward & Samuel Archer £500. My physician Dr Harrington £100. Mr Cawley my late apothecary £100. All residue to my trustees to invest in lands. Witnessed by Peregrine Courtney, Edward Cary, Thomas Bowdler.

Codicil. 1 June 1779. Legacies to be paid in stock. Mathias Harris my coachman £20. Witnessed by John Andrews. On 1 Feb. 1784 appeared John Edgar of St. George's, Bloomsbury, Gent. Recorded 3 Oct. 1789 at Antigua.

Richard Sweet was Bailiff of Exeter in 1540 and 1572, and at his death in 1590 Receiver-General; Robert Sweet was Bailiff 1541; Gilbert Sweet Bailiff 1613, Receiver 1627, and Mayor 1633; and Richard Sweet Mayor 1650.

John Sweete of Devon subscribed £25 to the Armada Fund.

1701. The plantation of Captain Main Swete at Falmouth of 337 acres was surveyed on July 15, and a plan of this is recorded in the Surveyor's Book, fo. 54.

1704, Aug. 3. Captain Main Sweete then a member of the Assembly.

1744, April 15. Benjamin Sweete of Norfolk-street, Esq; aged 93. He was Paymaster to the Army under the D. of Marlborough. ('Gent. Mag.,' p. 228.)

1817, Dec. 31. J. Beaumont Swete, esq. of Oxton-house, Exeter, to Mary eldest dau. of Henry Line Templer, esq. of Teignmouth. (*Ibid.*, p. 628.)

1820, April 6. Rev. Richard Ellicombe, Prebendary of Exeter, to Elizabeth, dau. of the Rev. John Swete, of Oxton House. (*Ibid.*, p. 369.)

1831, Dec. 10. At Springfield-lodge, Camberwell (the residence of her son-in-law, M. F. Gordon, esq.) aged 67, Charlotte, relict of the late Rev. John Sweete, of Oxton, Devon. (*Ibid.*, p. 570.)

1840, July 7. At South Bovey, Devon, Henry John Beaumont Swete, esq. of Oxton to Camilla Shafto, dau. of the Rev. R. P. Carrington. ('Gent. Mag.,' p. 311.)

1846, July 16. At Belle Vue Mupoorie Hills, Bengal, aged 19, Lieut. George Henry Walter Sweete, 56th Regt. B.N.I. fourth son of John Beaumont Sweete, esq. of Oxton, Nottinghamshire (*sic*). (*Ibid.*, p. 558.)

1844, Oct. 3. At Meerut, Bengal, aged 19, Ensign Adrian John Sweete, third son of John Beaumont Swete, esq. of Oxton. (1845, *Ibid.*, p. 222.)

1863, April 16. At Shanghae, after a short illness, aged 27, John Montagu Swete, esq. of the Imperial Customs, Ching Kiang. He was eighth son of John Beaumont Swete, esq., late of Oxton-house, Exeter. (*Ibid.*, p. 244.)

Mr. Charles Worthy of Exeter wrote me on 18 Sep. 1888: The Swetes succeeded to Trayne or Traine in succession to the "Scoos" family, now spelt "Skews," *circa* 1550. John, who died in 1690, gave a house and land to poor of Modbury by deed dated Dec. 10th, 1684. The Tripes were an old Dawlish family who ultimately settled at Ashburton and built the large Inn there known as the "Golden Inn" for a residence. They represented the Martins, Barons of Barnstaple, as you will see from the enclosed extract of Pedigree which I compiled from Martin de Turon 1066, some time since for my late friend the Rev. H. Ellicombe of Clist St. George. The Swetes also owned an estate called Preston in Ermington Parish.

In 1696 Adrian Swete (Ex'or of Rev. John Swete) was patron of St. Keverne, Cornwall. John Swete was Vicar of this parish 1664 to 1696. In the Registers is recorded the marriage "1621, June 4, Samuel Sweete, Vicar of Rennar (?), to Alice the daughter of Richard Downynge, Vicar of St Keverne." ('Western Antiquary,' 1888, pp. 52 and 88.)

PARISH REGISTER OF ST. JOHN.

Buried.

Circa 1702 . . . . Mr Anthony Sweet.

1687, Jan. 27. Benj. Sweet of St Marg[t], West., B., æt. 30, & Dame Anne Markham *al's* Crabb of Stepney, Wid. (Marriage Licences: Archbishop of Canterbury.)

WANSTEAD, CO. ESSEX.

On a ledger in churchyard:—

Arms: (*Gules*) *two chevrons between as many mullets in chief and a rose in base* (*argent*), *seeded* (*or*), *barbed* (*vert*); impaling . . . . *a bend* . . . .

Crest: *An helmet and mantling, a mullet* (*or*) *pierced* (*azure*) *between two gillyflowers* (*proper*).

JOHN SWETE ESQ[R]
of Plaistow in this Covnty
Died the 15 of Avgvst 1752.

Pedigree of Swete.

ARMS.—*Gules, two chevrons between two mullets in chief and a rose in base argent, seeded or.*
CREST.—*A mullet or pierced azure between two gillyflowers proper.*

. . . . SWETE* of Trayne in Modbury, co. Devon ╤ . . . . dan. and heir of . . . . Scoos of Trayne, mar. *circa* 1550.

Thomas Tripe ╤ . . . . of Dawlish, Gent.

John Swete ╤ . . . . of Trayne.

Rev. Lewis Swete, D.D., Fellow of All Souls, Oxford, 1563, Rector of Uplowman 1579; Canon of Exeter and Archdeacon of Totnes 1583; died 1613. Will recorded 1615 at Exeter. ╤ . . . .

Andrew Swete ╤ . . . . of Modbury, Gent.

Rev. Nicholas Tripe, matriculated from Exeter College, Oxford, 22 Feb. 1702-3, æt. 17; B.A. 1706; Vicar of Chudleigh, co. Devon, 1710—18; bur. there 26 April 1718. ╤ Susanna, 2nd dau. of Nicholas Martyn, Esq.; mar. 7 Dec. 1710 at Dawlish.
A

Rev. John Swete of Trayne, Esq., Vicar of St. Keverne, co. Cornwall, 1664—95; died 2 and bur. 6 Aug. 1695, æt. 60. M.I. at Modbury. ╤ . . . . Loveday, bur. 8 Jan. 1697 at Modbury.
B

Rev. Richard Swete, matriculated from Broadgates Hall, Oxford, 3 April 1596, æt. 19; B.A. 1599; M.A. 1602; Rector of Uplowman 1615.

John Swete, matriculated from Exeter College, Oxford, 24 May 1639, æt. 15; B.A. 1642; Fellow 1647; died 1713, æt. 89.

* The first three generations are very doubtful.

A | B |

Hester Sowter of Ashburton, mar. licence dated 2 Aug. 1738. 1st wife. = Nicholas Tripe, Surgeon, bapt. 12 Nov. 1711 at Dawlish; inherited "Oxton" of 320 acres from his cousin William Clifford Martyn, Esq., 1770; died 12 June 1790 at Ashburton. = Rebecca Yarde of Kingsteignton: mar. licence dated 18 Jan. 1748. 2nd wife.

Susannah Tripe of Exeter, bapt. 1714 at Chudleigh. Adm'on Jan. 1738 to her brother Nicholas.

Esther Tripe, bur. 6 Dec. 1745 at Ashburton.

John Tripe, bapt. and bur. 1750 at Ashburton.

Charlotte ....; died 10 Dec. 1831, æt. 67. = Rev. John Tripe of Oxton, Prebendary of Exeter, bapt. 1752 at Ashburton; matriculated from University College, Oxford, 19 Oct. 1770, æt. 18; B.A. 1774; M.A. 1777; inherited Trayne from Mrs. Esther Swete, and took the name and arms of Swete by Royal Licence 1781; died 1821. = Grace Palk of Ashburton; she remar. James Mogridge.

Nicholas Tripe, bapt. 1753 at Ashburton.

John Beaumont Swete of Oxton, matriculated from Oriel College, Oxford, 16 Oct. 1806, æt. 19; B.A. 1810; High Sheriff of Devon; died 4 March 1867; sold Oxton. = Mary, 1st dau. of Henry Line Templer of Teignmouth; mar. 31 Dec. 1817.

Rev. William Swete of Wrington Lodge, co. Somerset; matriculated from Oriel College, Oxford, 16 April 1817, æt. 19; B.A. 1822; M.A. 1824; died 27 Aug. 1878.

John Beaumont Swete, Lieut.-Colonel R.A.; died 20 Jan. 1895, æt. 63.

Adrian John Swete, 3rd son, Ensign in the Army; died 3 Oct. 1844, æt. 19, in Bengal.

George Henry Walter Swete, 4th son, Lieut. 56th Regiment; died 16 July 1846, æt. 19, in Bengal.

John Montagu Swete, 8th son, of the Imperial Customs, Ching Kiang; died 16 April 1863, æt. 27, at Shanghai.

Ermington, co. Devon.

A marble tablet of the period in the south aisle commemorates Adrian Swete, Esquire, Main Swete, Esquire, Mrs. Philippa Swete of Train in this county.

Arms: *Gules, two chevronels between in chief two mullets argent, pierced of the field, and in base a rose of the second.*

DIED
A. S. 27 Sept., 1733.
M. S. 5 July, 1735.
P. S. 15 Feb., 1747.

Near the last, another monument records Mrs. Esther Swete of Train, in the parish of Modbury, who died in January 1781, aged 68, to whose memory this tablet was erected by her only son Adrian Swete, Esq., who died aged 24 years. "Joⁿ Swete de Oxton." Arms, as on the last. Crest, A mullet argent pierced, between two lilies (or iris) of the last, stalked and leaved vert.

Close to the above tablets is a hatchment, the field all sable: Arms, Swete as before, the crest being the same, except that the mullet is gules, pierced or. Motto, In cœlo quies. By the side of this is an iron spike, on which a helmet was hung, part of a gauntlet, and the staff to which was fixed the bannerole, which at the time these notes were taken was lying rolled up on the Strachleigh tomb. The bannerole was of canvas, painted black, with on one side the arms of Swete as already given, with the motto "Festinat Lethum," while on the other side is displayed this crest, A mullet or, pierced gules, between two lilies (or iris) argent, stalked and leaved vert. Also the motto "Memento Mori." The helmet was a funeral one, which had found a resting-place, together with a spur, and an actual helmet which may have seen service in the Wars of the Roses, on the tomb with the bannerole.

In the north aisle of Modbury Church are two memorials to this family—one a mural monument for John son of John Swete of Train and Loveday his wife. He was of Exeter College, Oxford, and died 22 August 1690, aged 25 years. Arms, Swete as above. The other is a floorslab commemorating the Rev. Mr. John Swete, late of Train, who died 2nd August 1695. On this stone is cut a shield with these arms: two chevronells between in chief two mullets, and in base a rose; impaling, Per fess, in chief, three towers (Argent, three towers azure, Haviland; Argent, three towers gules, Castell), in base, on a cross five pheons (Or, on a cross azure five pheons of the first, Harrison).

The accompanying Register Extracts give additional data for this family:—

Ermington Parish Register.

Married.

1608	Jan.	8	Richard Pearse and Agnes Sweete.
1613	Aug.	15	Adrian Sweete and Judith dau. of John Mayne.
1660	Feb.	12	Mayne Sweet of Modbury, gent., and Mrs. Susan Trevillian.
1660	Feb.	12	Sampson Hurrell of Lodyswell, gent., and Mrs. Judith Sweet of Modbury.
1669	Mar.	6	Philip Champernoun and Elizabeth Sweet.
1675	July	7	Richard Sweet and Susanna Bowden.
1695	Nov.	9	Adryan Sweet, Esqr., and Honour Founes.

Buried.

1617	Mar.	22	Tamsin Sweet.
1622	June	4	John Mayne, gent.
1678	Feb.	6	Joseph s. of Richard Sweet.
1701	Feb.	18	Elizabeth dau. of Richard Sweet of Modbury.
1733	Sep.	30	Adrian Swete, Esq.
1735	July	8	Main Swete, Esq.
1747	Feb.	18	Madam Philippa Swete of Modbury.
1756	Jan.	10	Adrian Swete, Esq.
1781	Jan.	28	Madam Esther Swete.

Esther Tripe, mar. 25 April 1728 at Kingsteignton: died Jan. 1781, æt. 68, at Bath: bur. 28 Jan. 1781 at Ermington, co. Devon. M.I. Will (97 Webster). = Main Swete, 3rd son, of Antigua, Esq., 1701; Member of Assembly 1715; succeeded to Trayne 1733; died 5 July 1735. Will dated 27 June 1735; proved 10 July 1736. (163 Derby.) = Grace .... living 1721.

John Swete, 1st son and heir; matriculated from Exeter College, Oxford, 26 March 1680, æt. 13; Student of Inner Temple 1683; died 22 Aug. 1690, æt. 25. M.I. at Modbury.

Adrian Swete, 2nd son, of Trayne, Esq.; died 27 and bur. 30 Sep. 1733 at Ermington. Will dated 1 May 1716; proved 4 Dec. 1733. (319 Price.) = Honour, dau. of Mrs. Petronella Fownes; mar. 9 Nov. 1695 at Ermington; living 1735.

Philippa Swete of Modbury, died 15 and bur. 18 Feb. 1747 at Ermington.

Loveday Swete, living 1716.

Judith Swete, mar. 1683 Edward Archer, son of Rev. John Archer, Rector of Carhayes, co. Cornwall.

Adrian John Swete of Trayne, Esq., only child and heir, bapt. 17 Sep. 1731 at Modbury; matriculated from Balliol College, Oxford, 12 Oct. 1747, æt. 16; created M.A. 19 Oct. 1751; died a bachelor, æt. 24, and bur. 10 Jan. 1756 at Ermington. Will dated 10 Dec. 1755; proved 22 Jan. 1756. (21 Glazier.)

Elizabeth Swete, mar. 6 April 1820 Rev. Richard Ellicomb, Prebendary of Exeter, father of Rev. H. Ellicomb of Clyst St. George.

Caroline Swete, 5th dau., mar. 31 Aug. 1820 F. M. Gordon of Abergeldie.

Susan Swete, 6th dau., mar. Adam Gordon, brother of F. M. Gordon.

Modbury Parish Register.

Baptized.

1618 Sep. 1 Marjorie dau. of Adrian and Judith Sweet.
1620 Jan. 14 Adrian and Mary children of Adrian and Judith Sweet.
1626 Mar. 27 Judith dau. of Adrian and Judith Sweet.
1631 June 26 Adrian s. of Adrian and Judith Sweet.
1650 April 10 Elizabeth dau. of Mr Maine Sweet and Honour his wife.
1731 Sep. 17 Adrian John s. of Mr Maine and Mrs. Esther Swete.
1731 Feb. 4 Mary dau. of Mr William and Mrs. Amy Swete.
1744 Aug. 30 Elizabeth Jane dau. of Mr. William and Mrs. Amy Swete.

Married.

1613 June 28 Edward Ellot and Peternell Sweete.
1620 Mar. 15 Nicholas Pullibank and Abigail Sweete.

Buried.

1606 Aug. 8 Henry Sweet.
1623 April 17 Alice Sweete.
1627 Dec. 12 Adrian Sweet.
1633 Aug. 21 Joane Sweet.
1635 Sep. 22 Edward Sweet.
1647 Aug. 23 Mr Adrian Sweet.
1657 Jan. 26 Mrs. Judith Sweete, widow.
1661 Dec. 24 Mrs. Susanna Sweet, wife of Mr. Maine Sweete, Esq.
1670 April 29 Mr. Adrian Sweet.
1682 Jan. 12 Mayne Swete, Esq., died 30 Dec.
1689 Dec. 31 Mrs. Elizabeth Swete.
1695 Aug. 6 John Sweet, Esq., clerk.
1697 Jan. 8 Mrs. Loveday Swete.

Kingsteignton Parish Register.

Married.

1728 April 25 Mr. Maine Swete and Mrs. Esther Prickman. By Licence.

Bishop's Registry, Exeter.

Marriage Licences.

1725 Dec. 16 John Sweet of Great Torrington and Ulalia Blackmore of the same place, spinster.

1728 April 24 Maine Sweet of Modbury, Esq., and Esther Prickman of Torrington Regis, spinster.

Bishop's Transcripts, Exeter.—Gittisham.

1730 May 4 Mr. John Sweet and Mrs. Mary Bayley, both of Ottery St Mary.

Probate Registry, Exeter.

Index Principal Court.

1608 Philip Sweet of Georgeham.
1615 Lewis Sweet, Rector of Uplowman.

Totnes Archdeaconry.

1710-11 Mar. . . Sampson Sweet of Plymouth.

These are only fragmentary notes, no regular search for the name having been made. (Article on Ermington, co. Devon, by Arthur J. Jewers, F.S.A., in 'Western Antiquary,' vol. xi.)

Exeter Marriage Licences (by Vivian, part i.).

1597 July 30 Richard Sweete of Exeter, Merchant, and Elizabeth Payne.
1615 Aug. 22 Richard Sweete of Uplowman and Joanna Crosse of Tiverton.
1626-7 Jan. 11 Mathew Sweete of Barnstaple and Martha Puggesly, widow, of the same.

Modbury, co. Devon.

There is a tablet in the north aisle of the church to John son of John Swete of Train and Loveday his wife, who died 22 Aug. 1690, æt. 25. On a ledger in the same church: "Here lyeth the body of the Revd Mr John Swete, late of Train, who (after [? forty or fifty] years' service of Jesus Christ in the work of the ministry) departed this life the 2nd day of August 1695." On a conduit in Modbury:—

"DONO . ADRIANI
SWETE . EQUITIS .
DE . TRAIN : AN :
DOM : 1708
IN . HUNC SITUM .
E . MEDIA . VIA."

Pedigree of Symes.

ARMS.—*Azure, three escallops in pale or.*
CREST.—*A demi-hind salient erased or.*

JOHN SYMES of Barwick. Adm'on granted 4 Sep. 1563 to Jane the relict. ═ Jane .... living 1563.

Robert Hill of Yard, near Taunton, co. Somerset. Will dated 21 April and proved 15 June 1581. (26 Darcy.) ═ Alice Clerk. 1st wife.

William Symes of Chard, then of Poundsford in Pitminster, co. Somerset, merchant; held manors of Barwick, Boure, and Stoford, co. Somerset, and Frankham, co. Dorset. Will dated 4 June and proved 27 July 1597. (66 Cobham.) ═ Elizabeth Hill, living 1597.

John Symes of Poundsford, D.L., J.P., born 4 March 1572; matriculated from Exeter College, Oxford, 23 Feb. 1587-8, æt. 14; B.A. 9 July 1591; Student of Lincoln's Inn 1589; M.P. for Somerset 21 James I.; High Sheriff; died 21 Oct. 1661, æt. 88; bur. and M.I. at Frampton Cotterell, co. Gloucester. Will dated 5 Oct. 1658; proved 19 Dec. 1661. (206 May.) ═ Amy, dau. of Thomas Horner of Mells, Esq.

Henry Symes of Poundsford, matriculated from Exeter College, Oxford, 23 Feb. 1587-8, æt. 13; B.A. 9 July 1591; Student of Lincoln's Inn 1591. Will dated 19 March 41 Eliz.; proved 15 June 1599. (54 Kidd.)

John Symes of Poundsford. ═ Abigail, dau. of Arthur Arscott of Tetcott co. Devon.

Harry Symes of Frampton Cotterell, co. Gloucester, Esq.; B.A. from New Inn Hall, Oxford, 25 Jan. 1630-31; M.A. 11 Dec. 1634; Student of Middle Temple 1628; died 1 Nov. 1682, æt 73. M.I. at Frampton Cotterell (see the 'Visitation of Gloucester 1682-3'). Will dated 28 Jan. 1678; proved 12 Feb. 1682. (26 Drax.) ═ Amy, dau. of Sir John Seymour, Knt., of Bitton: she died 25 May 1686. s.p.m.

William Symes, æt. 6 months, 1623, at the Visitation of Somerset. (? Will dated 30 Nov. and proved 16 Feb. 1687 at Taunton.)

Grace Symes, 1623.

Thomas Symes, junior, of Barwick, Esq.; matriculated from Christ Church Coll. Oxford, 21 April 1657; Barrister-at-Law of Lincoln's Inn 1666; bur. at Barwick 22 Nov. 1681, æt. 46. M.I. Will dated 18 Nov. 1681 and proved 14 Jan. 1681-2. (10 Cottle.) ═ Merriel, youngest dau. of Sir John Horner of Mells, Knt.; mar. settlement dated 6 Oct. 1666; bur. at Barwick. Will dated 4 July 1710; proved 26 July 1717. (145 Whitfield.) See 'Misc. Gen. et Her.,' vol. iv., p. 163.

John Symes, of Montserrat, Esq., "Capt." and Member of Council 1678; dead 1687. ═ ....

Edward Symes, bapt. 1645 at Doynton, co. Gloucester; living 1675 and 1712.

Rev. Charles Symes, matriculated from Magdalen Hall, Oxford, 2 March 1665-6, æt. 17; B.A. 1669; M.A. 1672; Rector of Compton Martin, co. Somerset, 1674; Canon of Wells 1679; bur. at Compton Martin 1709. ═ Anne, dau. of .... Creed of Salisbury: mar. licence dated 21 June 1686, then æt. 28; bur. 21 Oct. 1726 at Compton Martin.

John Symes, only son and heir, born 26 Aug. 1667; of Exeter College, Oxford; matriculated 20 March 1683-4; Student of Lincoln's Inn 1686; died 6 July 1687, æt. 20. M.I. in Exeter College Chapel.

John Symes of Montserrat, only son and heir, Captain in the Army; killed at Port Mahon 9 Oct. 1710. Will dated 2 April 1709; proved 20 Jan. 1712-13. (249 Leeds.) ═ .... s.p.

Elizabeth Symes. ═ Colonel Samuel Parry of Antigua.

Katherine Symes, mar. Major Charles Loyd of Antigua; her will dated 11 Oct. 1721.

Amy Symes, mar. Thomas Thompson of Montserrat.

Captain Thomas Symes, bapt. 1689 at Compton Martin; Churchwarden 1710—18; died 21 Nov. 1724, æt. 65. M.I. at Compton Martin. Fought under Marlborough. ═ Christian .... bur. 9 March 1732 at Compton Martin. M.I. there.

Symes Parry-Symes, æt. 5, 1712; inherited the manors of Barwick and Stoford, co. Somerset; bur. 13 Aug. 1723 at St. John's. ═ Elizabeth ....

Samuel Parry-Symes of Antigua. ═ Rachel .... bapt. 27 Feb. 1729 at St. John's.

Thomas Symes, Churchwarden 1742, 1743, 1758, and 1769.

Richard Symes, died an infant.

Elizabeth Symes, mar. William Steele; he living 1742; she joined her sister in the sale of the manor of Barwick to John Newman in 1750.

Henrietta Symes, mar. Thomas Stevenson; both living 1742.

Frances Parry-Symes, bur. 18 Dec. 1734 at St. John's.

John Symes of Weston, Somerset, deceased. Adm'on 25 May 1563 to Nicholas Norden of Milverton, Somerset, during the minority of Joan Symes, sister of defunct.

John Symes of Barwick, Somerset, deceased. Adm'on 1 Sep. 1563 to Jane Symes the relict.

William Symes of Poundsford (in Pitminster), co. Somerset, merchant. Will dated 4 June and proved 27 July 1597 by Elizabeth Symes the relict. (66 Cobham.) Poor of Chard & Pitminster. Rt Hon. Sir Ed. Seymour, Knt. Lord Seymour of Pomeroy, Devon, by deed of 29 Nov. 31 Eliz. hath granted me an annuity of 100 marks out of the demesne of Bury Pomeroy for 99 years, if Eliz. my wife & Hen. & James my sons shall so long live. To my s. John Symes £2000 according to the covenants betw. me & Sir John Popham, Knt., Chief Justice, & Tho. Horner, Esq. To my s. Hen. 1000 marks. My s. Robt £500. My s. Wm. £500 at 21. My d. Eliz. 1000 marks. My dau. Margt 1000 marks at 21 or marriage. My dau. Margery Pyne 100 marks. Jasper Pyne my s.-in-l. living in Charde. My Manors of Barwick, Bowre, & Stoford, co. Som., & Frankham, co. Dorset. Mill in West Coker & lands in Taunton. My manor-house in Charde to Eliz. my wife for her life, & she to be Ex'trix. John Pyne, Esq., Roger Hill, Gent., & my bro.-in-l. Hugh Hill, Gent., to be Supervisors.

Henry Symes of Poundsford, co. Somerset, Gent. Will dated 19 March 41 Eliz.; proved 15 June 1599 by John Symes the brother. (54 Kidd.) To be bur. at Pitminster. To my sisters Jane Howe, Alice Hodges, & Margery Pyne 4 angels. My brother John Symes. Witnessed by Roger Hill.

Robert Symes.

William Symes, a minor 1597. — James Symes.

Jane Symes, mar. Roger Howe of London. — Alice Symes, mar. William Hodges.

Elizabeth Symes, mar. William Mallett. — Mary Symes, mar. Robert Hendy.

Margaret Symes, a minor 1597. — Margery Symes, mar. Jasper Pyne of Charde, co. Somerset.

Thomas Symes, senior, of Winterbourne, co. Gloucester, later of Poundsford, Esq., 1667. = Amy, dau. of Edward Bridges of Keynsham; his will dated 7 Nov. 1638; proved 22 Aug. 1639 (143 Harvey); mar. 1640.

Jane Symes, mar. Sir John Seymour, Knt. — Susan Symes.

Elizabeth Symes, mar. Nicholas Martyn of co. Devon. — Katherine Symes.

Amy Symes. — Elinor Symes.

Dorothy Symes. — Edith Symes.

Lieut. George Symes of Antigua, merchant; Member of Council 1678; granted 260 acres in 1681; Speaker 1688. = Dorothy, dau. of Thomas Everard; mar. 2ndly, before 1717, Arthur Freeman of Antigua, Esq.; her will dated 5 July 1721; proved 26 March 1737.

Captain Henry Symes of Antigua, bapt. 16 Nov. 1653 at Doynton; granted 100 acres 1682; Registrar of Antigua; bur. 9 July 1714 at St. John's. Will dated 19 June and sworn 13 July 1714. = Henrietta, widow of . . . . sister of Elizabeth, wife of Governor John Yeamans, 1717.

William Symes, living 1675. — Richard Symes of Blackheath; mar. thrice; died 27 May 1728, æt. 72. M.I. at Lewisham. Will dated 17 July 1723; proved 20 Aug. 1728. (250 Brooke.)

Amy Symes. — Catherine Symes. — Mary Symes. All living 1675.

Elizabeth Symes. Will dated 22 Nov. 1675, then of Doynton, spinster; proved 12 July 1676 at Gloucester.

Rev. William Compton Symes, matriculated from Balliol College, Oxford, 16 Dec. 1710, æt. 19; B.A. 1714; M.A. 1717; Master of St. Saviour's School, Southwark; Rector of Compton Martyn 1717. = Jane . . . .

Henry Symes, living 1720. — Elizabeth Symes (? mar. . . . . Athy).

Captain Henry Symes, junior, Deputy-Registrar to his father 1707; of Willoughby Bay 1721; nephew of Mrs. Penelope Mead 1733; bur. 2 Aug. 1742 at St. Philip's. = Sarah Lynch, sister of Fra. Lynch; mar. 9 Feb. 1715 at St. Philip's.

Richard Symes. — James Symes. — Elizabeth Symes.

Jane Symes, bapt. 22 July 1731 at Compton Martin.

Henry Symes, bur. Dec. 1792, æt. 75, at St. Philip's. Will dated 29 May 1787; sworn 3 May 1794. = Elizabeth, dau. of William Hunt; mar. 28 May 1748 at St. Philip's; her father's will was dated 1757.

John Symes. = Catherine, dau. of Colonel Samuel Harman; mar. 20 Dec. 1753 at St. Philip's.

William Symes. Will dated 8 June 17—; recorded at St. John's. = Elizabeth, dau. of Theodore Walrond, Esq.; mar. 29 Dec. 1753 at St. Philip's.

Henry Symes = Mary Marshall, mar. 17 March 1770 at St. John's.

Nicholas Symes.

John Symes.

Francis Symes, bur. 20 Dec. 1765 at St. Philip's.

Henry Lynch Symes = Sarah Powell Nanton, mar. at St. Paul's 1 May 1800.

Sarah Nanton Symes, bur. 11 July 1809 at St. Philip's. — Rowland Nanton Symes, bur. 19 March 1810 at St. Philip's.

Catherine Symes, bur. 16 March 1818 at St. Philip's. — Mary Symes, bur. 1 April 1718 at St. Philip's.

Kitty Garland Symes, born 28 Feb. 1805; bapt. 27 July 1806 at St. Philip's. — Catherine Marshall Symes, born 16 March 1818; bapt. 14 March 1819 at St. Peter's.

John Symes of Poundsford, co. Somerset. Will dated 5 Oct. 1658; proved 19 Dec. 1661. (206 May.) To be bur. at Frampton Cotterell, co. Glouc. To my neph. Arthur Symes £100 at the end of his apprenticeship. I am possessed of many years to come & undetermined of the Mansion of Poundsford, my Ex'ors shall convey it to Wm Symes, 1st s. of Jno Symes, decd, he not to vex or prosecute any suit against Hen. & Tho. Symes. To my 2 nieces Eliz. & Grace Symes £800 to be pd out of Poundsford. John & Ed. Symes, sons of my s. Tho. Symes. All residue to my sons Hen. & Tho. Symes, Ex'ors.

Sir John Seymour of Bitton, Gloucester, Knt. Will dated 14 June 1663; proved 17 Feb. 1663-4 by Thomas Seymour the son. (21 Bruce.) My dau. Ann (*sic*) Symes all household goods at Frampton Cotterell; her 5 children. Hen. Symes, Esq., Trustee, etc.

Elizabeth Symes of Doynton, co. Gloucester, spinster. Will dated 22 Nov. 1675; proved 12 July 1676. (Gloucester Will.) To be bur. at the disposing of my aunts Mrs. Eliz. Langton & Mrs. Kath. Bridges. To my brothers Hen., Geo., & Richd Symes £5 each. Rings to my brothers Edw. & John, my sisters Amy, Kath., & Mary Symes, my cousin Eliz. Guise, my cousin Still, my aunts Langton & Bridges, & my brother Wm Symes. Poor of Doynton. To my uncle Geo. Bridges 20*s.* & a ring. To Mr Robt Wilkes for a sermon 20*s.* To Mary Seymer 7*s.* To my brother Tho. Symes a ring. To my uncle Mr Guise a ring. To my bro. Chas. a silver cup. £5 to my brothers Ed. & Jno Symes. Residue to my sisters Amy & Kath., Ex'trices.

Henry Symes of Frampton Cotterell, Gloucester, Esq. Will dated 28 Jan. 1678; proved 12 Feb. 1682 by Amie Symes the relict. (26 Drax.) To my wife Amie messuages, etc., of the late dissolved free chapel called Stirthall *al's* St Luke's, Dorset, & after her death to my s. John Jacob & my friends Tho. Edwards, Gent., & Nath. Friend the Yr in Trust to permit my dau. Jane wife of Ed. Bisse, Gent., to take the profits thereof. Ed. Gorges of Wraxall owes me £3000 on mortgage of lands in Wraxall. John Jacob & Susan his wife shall have £1500 thereof, & the other portion to my wife Amie & my trustees as Jane Bysse shall appoint. My est. in the Manor of Matherne, co. Monm., granted to my dau. Jane, now wife of Ed. Bysse, by Geo. Milborne, Gent. To my gr'dchild Amy Berkley & heirs my inheritance in tenements in Frampton. My niece Eliz. Coleman £5. Adm'on (de bonis non) granted to Ann Berkeley (nepti) 11 Oct. 1686, Amye Symes the relict being deceased. Further adm'on 12 March 1690 to Susanna Jacob, dau. of testator and wife of John Jacob. Another grant 23 Dec. 1708 to Ann Hale, niece from the dau. of Henry Symes, and wife of Gabriel Hale.

Thomas Symes of Barwick, Somerset, Esq. Will dated 18 Nov. 1681; proved 14 Jan. 1681-2 by Meryell the relict. (10 Cottle.) Bonds, bills, etc., & residue granted to Sir Jas. Hayes & Mr Tho. Fountayne. My wife Meriel Ex'trix.

George Berkeley of Stoke Gifford, Gloucester. Will dated 24 June 1684; proved 7 May 1685. (54 Cann.) My grandmother Ann Symes. My grandfather Harry Symes, Esq. My father-in-l. Maurice, Lord Visc. Fitzhardinge.

William Symes of Poundisford in Pitmister, Somerset, Esq. Will dated 30 Nov. 1687; proved 16 Feb. 1687-8. (Archdeaconry of Taunton.) All my goods to my wife, Ex'trix. If not money enough to pay my debts to sell my est. & to return the overplus to my brother Hen. Symes of Bristol, Gent., my brother-in-l. John Bluett of Holcombe Regus, Devon, Esq., & my brother Fra. Bluett to be my friends in Trust. Estate of Hanereech & West Monckton. Geo., John, & Ellinor children of my brother Hen. Symes £100 each. To my cousin Rachel Davison, dau. of Jos. Davison of Freshford, Gent., £500 out of Poundsford at 21. Poor of Pitmister £10. To my brother John Bluett my young strawberry mare. To my brother Mr Fra. Bluett my silver hilt sword & all my arms. Heraldic Seal. Inventory, £116 6*s.* 8*d.*

Rachel Symes of Poundsford in Pitmister, Somerset, widow, relict and Ex'trix of William Symes, Esq. Will dated 19 May 1689; proved 21 Feb. 1692 by John Bluett. (Archdeaconry of Taunton.) My sister Johanna wife of Jos. Davison of Freshford, Som., Gent., & their children John, Eliz., Anna, Frances, & Rachel. My brother John Bluet of Holcomb Rogus, Eliz. wife of John Bluet. Residue to my sister Johanna Davison. My brothers John & Francis Bluet Ex'ors. Heraldic Seal.

Henry Symes, late of Bristol, now of London, Gent. Will dated 15 May and proved 8 June 1693. (100 Coker.) To be bur. at Ryson (Ruishton), Som. Est. given me by my late brother Wm Symes' Will. My wife Eleanor. My yst. s. Geo. Symes £200. My dau. Elianor. My s. John shall have my est. Ed. & Robt Westcombe, sons of my late sister Abigail.

Edward Bisse of Frampton Cotterell, Gloucester, Gent. Nuncupative will dated 18 April and proved 10 Sep. 1696 by Jane Bisse the relict. (179 Bond.) Residue to my wife Jane Bisse. Witnessed by Amy Hale, Abigail Symes.

Elizabeth Langton of Doynton, co. Gloucester, widow. Will dated 12 Feb. 1696; proved 24 April 1703. (71 Degg.) To be buried in the chancel of Keynsham if my nephew permit, otherwise at Winterborne near my sister Symes. Brother Sir Tho. Bridges 50 gs. Cozen Edwd Symes £100, cozen Harry Symes £100, cozen Geo. Symes his children £5 each, cozen Chas. Symes his children £5 each, cozen Edward Symes his children £5 each. Nephew John Symes his widow £5, & to his son John £20, & each of his 2 daus. £5. To Wm, Tho., & Richard sons of my nephew Wm Symes £10 each, & their sister Amy Symes £10. Mary wife o[f] my nephew Richd Symes £5. Ann wife of my nephew Chas. Symes £5.

John Symes of Poundsford, Somerset, deceased. Adm'on 20 May 1698 to his sister Elianor wife of Fra. Duncombe.

Thomas Symes of Stoke near Guildford, Surrey, Gent., deceased. Adm'on 14 Sep. 1698 to Elizabeth Symes his mother.

John Symes of Mountserrat in parts beyond the seas, Esq. (in the Regiment of Lieut.-General Witham at Port Mahon). Will dated 2 April 1709; proved 20 Jan. 1712-13 by Samuel Parry. (249 Leeds.) My plantations, negros, etc., in Mountserrat, & my estate in the manors of Berwick & Stoford, co. Som., held by Merriel Symes, widow of Tho. Symes of Berwick, decd, & other messuages to my nephew & godson Symes Parry, son of Samuel Parry of Antigua, gent., by Elizabeth my sister; remainder to the 2d son of the said Sam. Parry in tail male. The heir to assume my name. £500 to the children of my sister Amy Thompson, decd, late wife of Tho. Thompson, late of Mountserrat. £100 each to the children of my sister Kath. Loyd, wife of Chas. Loyd of Antigua, gent. To each of the other children of my sister Eliz. Parry £50. £100 to my kinsman John Roynon, who shall continue manager of my plantations till my nephew Symes Parry is 17. To my uncle Chas. Symes of Compton Martin, Som., clerk, £100 for mourning for him & his family, & his son Wm Symes to be presented to the vicarage of Berwick when vacant. To my uncle Henry Symes of Antigua £50. To Eliz. Symes, dau. of Richd Symes, late of Bristol, mariner, £50 at 17. My uncle Chas. Symes & my brother-in-law Sam. Parry to be trustees of my will during the minority of Symes Parry my Ex'or, to whom all residue.

Further adm'on 31 Jan. 1718.

Another grant 27 May 1727 to Samuel Symes, brother of Symes Parry Symes, deceased, the Ex'or and residuary legatee of John Symes, deceased.

Another grant 12 May 1742 to Henrietta Stevenson, wife of Thomas Stevenson, and Elizabeth Steele, wife of William Steele, daughters and surviving heirs of Samuel Parry Symes, deceased, brother of Symes Parry Symes the sole Ex'or and residuary legatee of the will of John Symes, the said Samuel Parry Symes surviving the testator but dying without having taken upon him the execution of the said will, and Elizabeth Parry, widow, mother of the said Symes Parry Symes, deceased, not appearing.

Meriell Symes of Barwicke, Somerset, widow. Will dated 4 July 1710; proved 26 July 1717 by William Guidott. (145 Whitfield.) To be bur. privately with my dec^d husb^d in Barwick Church or near my son in Exeter Coll., Oxf., & £100 for my funeral. To my Ex'or £50. To my kinsman Tho. Horner, Esq., £500, he to give bond not to alienate from his family the real estate left him by his father my neph. Horner. To John Horner, brother of Tho. Horner, my wrought bed in my house at Barwicke. To Ann Chaplin, dau. of Rob. Chaplin by my niece Ann Harrington, dec^d, £600 & my pearl necklace. My share in Norwood Park, Som., to the Rector & Fellows of Exeter Coll. for a Scholarship, they to appoint a son of Mr Jas. Lacey of Sherborne to a scholarship. To Mrs. Edith Phillips, yst. dau. of Sir Ed. Phillips, my set of gilt knives, forks, & spoons. To Mrs. Ann Jennens £10 for a Tankard. To Anth^o Guidott of Linc. Inn, Gent., my gold watch. To my kinswoman Ann Gibbs £100 & my wearing apparel. To Mrs. Fra. Wyndham my sable tippet. To Mrs. Jane Phelips, wife of Wm Phelips of Preston n^r Yeovil, 5 guineas. To Lady Nevill, wife of the late Judge Nevill, 5 guineas. To my niece Mrs. Eliz. Deer in London £10. To my goddau. Mrs. Mary Meredith, dau. of John Meredith, my divinity books & £10. To the Charity School at Yeovil £20. To Wyndham Harbin & Wm Phelips, Esq^res, £20 for binding apprentices at Barwick. I am entitled to £100 on my conveying to my cousin Wm Mallett, Esq., 1st s. of Baldwin Mallett, Esq., of St Andries, Som., the Rectory & tenements of Yarcombe. Residue to Wm Guidott of Linc. Inn, my Ex'or.

Codicil. 19 July 1714. To my cousin John Horner my linen, brass, pewter, chariott, horses, corn, etc., at Barwick so as he inhabit my house.

Codicil. 8 July 1716. The above bequest to John Horner ratified whether he lives in my house or not. To my brother Richd Symes 20 guineas. To Mrs. Edith Philipps £10.

Henry Symes of Antigua, Esq. Will dated 19 June 1714. To my wife Henrietta all my plate & household goods, she to be sole manager of my estate. All cattle reputed theirs to be given to my son Rich^d & my dau. Eliz^th. To my said dau. my green velvet side saddle & £100 c. My said children Jas., Rich^d, & Eliz^th to have maintenance. My Ex'ors Capt Thos. Oesterman & Mr Thos. Traut to sell my estate after my wife's death, & the residue equally to my children & to my wife's children equally with my own. My wife & 2 trustees to be Ex'ors. Witnessed by Edward Trant, Richard Rice, Elizabeth Parry. By John Yeamans, Esq., were sworn Edward Trant and Richard Rice 13 July 1714. Recorded 11 Jan. 1725.

Richard Symes of Lewisham, co. Kent, Esq. Will dated 17 July 1723; proved 20 Aug. 1728 by Richard Symes. (250 Brook.) To be bur. at Lewisham. A monument of £50. My late wife Charlotte Bridgman. Est. settled on Richd Symes, s. of my neph. Tho. Symes, remainder to the 1st s. of s^d Thos., remainder to his brother Wm Symes, cl'k, & to his sons. My neph. Tho. Harris £1000. His sister my niece Cath. Harris. My neph. Capt. Tho. Symes £300, & to his brother Wm Symes £100. My neph. John Meredith £100. My neph. Richd Symes Ex'or.

Richard Symes of Bristol, merchant. Will dated 10 Dec. 1723; proved 15 March 1726 by Henry Comb, Esq., Thomas Shute, and John Roberts. (75 Farrant.) Confirm the agreement made on my marriage with Eliz. my now wife by which I purchased of Griffith Curthoys of Olveston, Gent., lands in Oldbury upon Severne in the manor of Thornbury, co. Glouc., for our lives. To Tho. Shute of Stoakehine, co. Som., Gent., & John Roberts of Bristol, mariner, all my estate in trust to sell, & of the proceeds ⅓ to my brother Hen. Symes, ⅓ to my niece Edith Rogers, & ⅓ to her son Richd Rogers at 21. ½ of my plate & household goods to my wife Eliz., to lose it if she marry or leave the Church of England. Hen. Coombe of Bristol to be Ex'or & Trustee. Witnessed by John White, John Greene, William Dickinson.

Symes Parry Symes, late of Antigoa, bachelor, deceased. Adm'on 12 Nov. 1728 to Slingsby Bethell the Attorney of Samuel Symes the brother. Elizabeth Parry the mother having been first cited.

William Hunt of Antigua, planter. Will dated 20 Aug. 1757. To my wife Sarah my best horse & a negro boy. To my dau. Eliz. Simes, wife of Henry Symes, £500 c. To my son John & to my daus. Sarah & Marg^t £500 each at 21. To my s. W^m all residue. Robt Christian, Esq., & my son-in-law Henry Symes Ex'ors & Guardians. Witnessed by John Harman, Esq., James Tweedy, Archibald Ramsay. Sworn 1 Feb. 1758. Recorded 6 Aug. 1764.

William Simms. Will dated 8 June 17 . . My wife Eliz^th & the child she now goes with. My wife, my brother . . . . & Main Swete Walrond & Saml Harman, jun^r, Ex'ors. (From a much mutilated will.)

Elizabeth Simms, widow, of St. John's Parish. Will dated 23 June 1786. To my cousin Anna wife of Wm Anderton £5 c. To Ann Boudinott £40 c. To Dr Richd Martin £30 c. To my cousin Sarah Scandrett all furniture, except a bed & easy chair to my niece Cath. Hardcastle. My negros to be sold & the money given to John Hardcastle for Eliz^th Hardcastle & my godchild Cath. Hardcastle. To Sarah Scandrett 9 slaves, & after her death to Hester Scandrett her dau. All residue in trust to Elias Ferris, John Hardcastle, Wm Anderton, Esq., for my cousin Sarah Scandrett till her d. Hester be 21, then ½ to each. Trustees Ex'ors. Witnessed by Lucy Carlile, Thomas T. Wise, Christian Showercraft. Before Governor Shirley was sworn Thomas T. Wise 14 July 1786. Recorded 18 July 1786 at St. John's.

Henry Symes, sen. Will dated 29 May 1787. My house in the town of Willoughby Bay to my son John. My negros & whatever else I possess equally between my wife Eliz^th & my sons Nich^s & John Symes & my grandson

Henry Lynch Symes. To my son Henry 20s., he having already had large sums of money. Witnessed by Samuel Athill, James Watson, jun., Richard Hunt. Before Edward Byam, Esq., was sworn Richard Hunt, Gent., 3 May 1794. Recorded 9 May 1794.

James Simms. Will dated 4 Aug. 1789. All my estate, including that belonging to my late wife, to the Rev. Jas. Coull, Chas. Kerr, & Robert Farquhar, Esq., in trust to pay the profits to my nephew Stewart Simms, & in default of issue to my nephew John Simms his brother. To my Ex'ors 5 guineas each for a ring. To my sister-in-law Eliz. Urlin £150. My sister Eliz. Simms, wife of Wm Johnston, £150. All residue to my brother John Simms. Witnessed by Frederick William Fisher, Thomas Roberts, Joseph Seyton. Recorded at St. John's.

Many of the preceding wills have been taken from Brown's 'Somersetshire Wills.'

Chancery Proceedings before 1714, Collins 466.
Parry *alias* Syms *v.* Foy.
Emendat p. Ordin. Cur. Gerend. dat. 18 Feb. 1712.

23 June 1712. Humbly complaining Symes Parry *al's* Parry Symes of Antegoa, an Infant of about 5 years of age, by Samuel Parry of Antegoa his Father, Nathaniel Carpender the elder, and Nathaniel Carpender the younger, both of London, Merchants, his Prochein Amys, that Thomas Symes, late of Winterbourne, co. Gloucester, Esq., your Orator's great-grandfather, deceased, being seised in his demesne as of fee of and in the Manor (obliterated) Defford (?) and Hundred of Berwick, co. Somerset, and also of the right of presentation to the Rectory, together with other lands, etc., in Berwick, and also of several other Messuages in the Parishes of Yarcombe and Membery, co. Gloucester, by Indenture dated the 6th Oct. 1666 between the said Thomas Symes of Winterbourne, Esq., of the one part, and Thomas Symes the younger, his Sonne and Heire apparent, and Meriell Horner, Spinster, of the other part, in consideration of the marriage then shortly to be had, did convey the said Manors to the use of Thomas Symes the elder for life, and after his death to Thomas Symes the younger and Meriell, and to their heirs, in Trust for 1000 years to pay £1000 to the younger Brothers of Thomas Symes the younger, and by Indenture tripartite dated 23rd Aug. 1667 between Thomas Symes the younger, of the 1st part, Sir Thomas Bridges of Ravisham, co. Somerset, K[t], of the 2nd part, and Thomas Symes the elder, of the 3rd, reciting as before recited, and by Indentures dated the 19th and 20th June 1669 between Thomas Symes the younger and Meriell his wife, of the 1st part, John Symes their Son and Heir apparent, of the 2nd part, and James Hayes, Esq., afterwards Sir James Hayes, K[t], Thomas Fountaine, Esq., and Walter Foy, Gentleman, of the 3rd part, Thomas Symes and Meriell his Wife in consideration of their natural love and affection for John Symes their Son, and for settling the said Manors, etc., to come and remain in the blood and family of Thomas Symes the Son, and for divers other considerations, did grant and convey the said Manors, etc., to the said Trustees to the use of John Symes and his Heirs male lawful, and for default to the Heirs of Thomas Symes for ever (will of Thomas Symes recited), and Thomas Symes had issue at his death 14th Jan[y] 1681 the said John Symes, an Infant, to whom all the said Manors, etc., descended, but Meriell entered on all and received the Rents in her own right and that of the Infant, who happened to die in 1687 before he attained to 21, upon whose death all descended to John Symes, your Orator's Uncle, as only Son of John Symes of Montserrat, 2nd Son of Thomas Symes the elder, as Heir-at-Law to Thomas Symes the younger, and John Symes the Infant who died without Heirs, and therefore John Symes, your Orator's Uncle, ought to have received the Rents from the death of the Infant, save what was settled on Meriell for jointure, but the said John Symes living beyond the Seas and being a stranger to the said Settlement and Conveyances and the other Transactions aforesaid, which were kept secret from him, nor was he informed thereof till many years after the Infant's death, being himself an Infant at the time, but soon after he had information he came into England and acquainted Meriell that he was Heir-at-Law to the said Thomas Symes the elder, Thomas Symes her late Husband, and John Symes her Son, then all deceased, who did acknowledge him to be the Heir-at-Law, but pretended she had a right to the said Manors for life, but would not discover her title; and your Orator further sheweth that John Symes his Uncle being a Captain in the Army was soon after such discourse obliged to go with his Regiment to Port Mahon, where he died without leaving any issue living, having before he went from Great Britain made his Will (Will recited), soon after making which Will, viz., on the 9th Oct. 1710, he died, and your Orator hoped that the said Will being made when John Symes was of sound mind he should be let in at once to the Manors, but so it is Meriell Symes having got possession of the Deeds, etc., pretendeth sometimes that she is entitled to the whole estate for life and no longer, and sometimes that she hath a conveyance of some part in fee, but refuseth to discover, and insisteth she is at liberty to dispose of the same, humbly prayeth.

Answer of Edward Symes, 3rd Son of Thomas Symes the Father.

Answer of Meriell Symes, Widow, one of the Daughters of Sir John Horner of Mells, K[t]. Indenture as in the Bill of Complaint between Thomas Symes and herself, of the 1st part, Sir James Hayes of Beckington, co. Somerset, of the 2nd part, and Thomas Fountaine of Lincoln's Inn, Esq., and Walter Foy of Yeovill, of the 3rd part, and she is seised for life in the said Manors, and saith further she was in her own right till very lately seised of an Estate and inheritance in a part of Norwood Park, co. Somerset, which she no ways settled on her Husband in marriage or otherwise, and which she hath lately conveyed to the Rector and Scholars of Exeter College, Oxon, for a Charity, and hath no other Lands from her late Husband, deceased. Sir Thomas Bridges is dead, and his Ex'ors Harry Bridges and George Radney Bridges have assigned the Trust to Anthony Guidott, and Sir James Hayes and Thomas Fountaine are dead, and she believeth Walter Foy is living, and she doth deny all combination with Edward Symes, or that the Settlement, etc., were kept secret from John Symes, and believeth John Symes may be the Heir-at-Law.

Answer of Anthony Guidott.

Answer of Walter Foy. He was Steward to Thomas Symes the elder and Thomas Symes the younger.

Close Roll, 3 Geo. III., Part 2.

Indenture made the 28th Feb. 1763 between Amy Thomson, Henrietta Thomson, and Ann Thomson, all of Middlesex, spinsters (only surviving daughters and heirs-at-law of James Thomson, late of Montserrat, Gentleman, deceased, eldest son and heir of Thomas Thomson, late of Montserrat, deceased, and also only sisters and heirs-at-law of Lieut. John Thomson, lately deceased), of the one part, and Earle Daniel of Montserrat, Esq., of the other part, witnesseth that in consideration of £600 sterling Amy, Henrietta, and Ann Thomson grant to Earle Daniel (in his actual possession by virtue of a bargain for one whole year made the day before these presents) all that plantation in the parish of St. Anthony, Montserrat, late the land of

Thomas Thomson their said grandfather, deceased, containing 16 acres, bounded N. with the lands late of Captain Thomas Nugent, E. with the plantation of Colonel Roger Bentley, S. with the lands of Major Nicholas Meade, and W. with the lands of Timothy Popplewell, together with the dwelling house, by virtue of the entail created by their grandfather's will for the proper use and behoof of Earle Daniel and his heirs. Lastly they appoint Thomas Dorset and Thomas Dubery, Esquires, both of Montserrat, their Attorneys.

1588. Armada list of subscribers. "Maye William Symes of Chard, tercio Maii, £50."

Rectory of Barwick, co. Somerset—Patrons: John Syms, arm., 1643; Merilla Sims, vid., 1703 and 1708.

Rectory of West Coker, co. Somerset—Patrons: Joh. Syms de Chard, arm., 1619; Hen. Syms, arm., 1663.

St. John's, Yeovil—Patrons: Rob. Spendley and Tho. Symmes 1547; Joh. Symmes, S.T.B., instituted Rector 24 May 1547, deprived 1560.

Rectory of Compton Martin. "Car. Symes, A.M." Incumbent 15 June 1674 till his death in 1710. "Will. Symes, gen., fil. C.S., a.c. per Tho. Bridges, mil.," patron 1710. "Will. Symes, A.B.," instituted Rector on 18 Jan. 1716. ('Somerset Incumbents,' by Rev. F. W. Weaver.)

1649. John Syms of Poundford. Sequestration of an annuity of £80 taken off, he having assigned it for his sons Henry and Thomas, and the farm. He is accused of having omitted £3000 from his composition at Goldsmiths' Hall. (Calendar of Committee for Compounding Royalist Estates, p. 993.)

1670, Nov. 7. Thomas Simes of Antigua, planter, sells 7½ acres to John Knight and John Short, planters of Antigua.

1671, 11 Jan. Thomas Syms, 20 acres by Governor Warner; surveyed 16 Jan. 1671-2.

1678. Montserrat. Captain John Symms of the Council, also 1684.

1679, April 2. John Vernon of Old North Sound, Gent., of the one part, and George Symms, merchant, and Dorothy his wife, dau. of Thomas Everett, Gent., deceased, of the other part, in consideration of a marriage lately had between George Symms and Dorothy his wife, John Vernon gives to them and their heirs a plantation called Wakering Hall in Old North Sound.

1679, April 19. William Stephens, planter, sells to Thomas Symes, planter, 10 acres in Popeshead.

1681, May 23. Lieutenant George Symes, 260 acres by Sir W. Stapleton.

1682, May 8. Mr. Henry Symes, 100 acres by Sir W. Stapleton.

1684, Feb. 6. Henry Symes, Gent., 65 acres by Sir W. Stapleton.

1684, Feb. 20. Henry Symes, parcell of land in St. John's Town by Sir W. Stapleton.

1688. George Syms then Speaker of Antigua.

No. 96. Private. An Act enabling Henry Simes of the aforesaid Island, Gentleman, to convey and sell a certain Plantation, or Parcel of Land in this Island, late belonging unto Nicholas Rainsford, late of the same Island, Esquire, deceased, for the payment of his Debts and Legacies. Dated 1 Sep. 1697.

Deed dated 17 July 1707. Henry Symes. I appoint my son Henry Symes my Deputy-Registrar.

1710, Nov. 17. Henry Symes, jun., 10 acres granted; surveyed 12 Jan. 1710-11.

1711. "Collon[l] Samuell Parry of this Island applyed himself to the Lieu[t] Generall for Letters of Administration on the Estate of Capt[n] John Syms of Mountserrat, Brother in Law to the said Parry, who was kill'd in Spaine, w[ch] Letters was denyed him, the said Parry alleg'd to the Lieu[t] Generall Letters would be granted in Mountserrat to another Brother in Law there."

1712. Losses at Montserrat from the French Invasion: John Roynon for "Symes" Plantation in the Leeward Division, £244.

1714. At the request of Captain Henry Symes and with the consent of Mrs. Henrietta Symes, widow and relict of Captain Henry Symes, deceased, 20 acres surveyed for Captain Henry Symes 23 Sep.

Act. No. 159. Confirmed 19 May 1720 by Order of the King in Council. Private. An Act to enable Arthur Freeman and Dorothy his Wife to sell and convey a certain Plantation within the said Island, to raise Portions and make Provisions for Henry Symes and Elizabeth Athy, Children of the said Dorothy by her former Husband George Symes, deceased. Dated 1 March 1717. (Laws of the Leeward Islands.)

1720, April 13. Captain Henry Symes, one proportion of land at Willoughby Bay granted; surveyed 30 April.

1759, March 3. John Symes to be of the Council of Montserrat. He was the Rector of St. Anthony's, and his death was announced on 6 May 1777.

PARISH REGISTER OF ST. JOHN.

Baptized.

1729	Feb. 27	Rachel Parry the wife of M[r] Samuel Symes.
1783	July 9	Isabella the D. of [John Sims & his wife] (*sic*).

Married.

1723	Aug. 20	William Newgent and Elizabeth Symes.
1746	Oct. 3	Alexander Simms & Elizabeth Dunbar Parke; by L.
1770	Mar. 17	Henry Symes, Jun[r], to Mary Marshall. L.

Buried.

1691	Dec. 7	Thomas Simes.
1714	July 9	Cap[tn] Henry Symes.
1716	Feb. 29	Andrew Symes.
1724	Oct. 21	Richard Symes.
1759	May 27	Eliz[th] Simms Wife of Alex[r] Simms.
1759	Aug. 27	John Simms.
1770	Jan. 26	Alexander Symes.
1789	Mar. 14	Elizabeth Symes.

PARISH REGISTER OF ST. PHILIP.

Baptized.

1776	Mar. 24	William Higgins Symes.
1806	July 27	Kitty Garland infant d. of M[r] Henry Lynch Symes & Sarah Powell Symes; b. 21 Feb. 1805.

Married.

1715-16	Feb. 9	Henry Symes & Sarah Lynch.
1738	July 8	Robert Symes to Elizabeth Payne.
1748	May 28	Henry Symes to Elizabeth Hunt.
1748	Dec. 29	John Williams to Elizabeth Symes.
1753	Dec. 20	John Symes & Catharine Harman.
1753	Dec. 29	William Symes & Eliz[th] Walrond.

Buried.

1723	Aug. 13	Symes Symes.
1728	Oct. 26	James Symes.
1734	Dec. 18	Frances Parry D. of Samuel Parry Syms.
1742	Aug. 2	M[r] Henry Symes.
1765	Dec. 20	Francis S. of M[r] Henry Symes.
1775	Dec. 18	William Symes.
1781	May 8	William Higgins Symes.

1790 Dec. . . Henry Symes.
1792 Dec. . . Henry Symes, aged 75.
1809 July 11 Sarah Nanton Symes the Infant D. of Mr Henry Lynch Symes and Sarah his Wife in Willoughby Bay Church Yard.
1810 Mar. 19 Rowland Nanton Symes S. of Mr Henry Lynch Symes and Sarah Powell Symes his Wife at Willoughby Bay.
1811 June 14 Mrs Mary Symes at Willoughby Bay in the Church Yard.
1811 Nov. 19 Mrs Elizabeth Symes at Willoughby Bay in the Church Yard.
1818 Mar. 16 Catherine Symes inft d. of Mr Henry Lynch Symes & Sarah his wife (not *verbatim*).
1818 April 1 Mary Symes inft d. of Mr Henry Lynch Symes & Sarah his wife (not *verbatim*).
1833 Mar. 8 Henry Lynch Symes. 62.

PARISH REGISTER OF ST. PAUL.

Married.

1778 April 20 Cornelius Halloran (Planter) to Elizbth Sims, Widow; pr L.
1800 May 1 Henry Lynch Symes to Sarah Powell Nanton, spinstr; by L.
1835 Sep. 3 David Mortimer Malone, B., & Sarah Eliza Symes, Spr. Lic.

PARISH REGISTER OF ST. PETER.

Baptized.

1819 Mar. 14 Catherine Marshall D. of Henry Lynch Symes & Sarah his wife was baptised on Mathews Estate; b. the 16th March 1818.

Married.

1774 Jan. 6 William Symes & Elizabeth Burton.
1818 May 26 Mr Darius Davey & Eliza Symes, spinster, L.

COMPTON MARTIN, CO. SOMERSET.

1689 Thomas son of Charles Symes & Anna his wife was baptised.
1709 Rev. Mr Charles Symes, Rector of the Parish, was buried.
1726 Mrs Anne Symes (wife of the Rev. Charles Symes) was buried Oct. 21, 1726.
1731 Jane the daughter of Wm. Symes & Jane his wife was baptised July 22, 1731.
1732 Christian Symes wife of Captn Thos Symes was buried in the Chancel March 9, 1732.

DOYNTON REGISTERS, CO. GLOUCESTER.

('Gloucester Notes and Queries,' vol. ii., p. 435.)

Baptized.

1645 Ash Wednesday Edward s. of Mr Thomas Symes and Amy his wife.
1653 Nov. 16 Henry s. of Mr Thomas Symes.
1687 Feb. 26 Richard s. of William Symes, Gent., and Mary (posthumous).
1692 Feb. 5 Mary d. of John Symes and Rebecca of Bath.

Married.

1676 Jan. 15 Mr Samuel Truman, Rector of Dyrham, and Mrs Ann Symes.
1679 Oct. 28 Thomas Harris of Bristol and Katherine Syms.
1692 April 28 John Symes of Bath and Rebecca Nichols of Deinton.

1686, June 21. Charles Symes, Rector of Compton Martyn, co. Somerset, Bachr, 36, & Ann Creed, of the Close of Salisbury, Spr, 28, at her own disposal: at St Martin in the Fields, Middx., or St Dunstan in the East, London. (Marriage Licences: Faculty Office, Archbishop of Canterbury.)

FRAMPTON COTTERELL CHURCH, CO. GLOUCESTER.

Here lyeth the Body of | Anne Symes, Widow, | and Relict of Harry Symes, Esq. | who departed this Life | on the 25th Day of May A.D. 1686. | She was the Daughter of | Sir John Seymour, Knight, | formerly of this Parish, | by Dame Anne his first Wife, | the Daughter of William Poulett, | of Cottles, in the County of Wilts, Esq. | son of my Lord Giles Poulett, | Marquis of Winchester, and | Lord High Treasurer of England. (Three lines follow.)

Their dau. Amy ob. 9 Jan. and was bur. 13 Jan. 1678.

(Bigland's 'Gloucestershire Collections.')

Arms: *Azure, three escallops in pale or.*

Here lyeth the Body of | Harry Symes, Esq. | son of John Symes, Esq. | under the adjacent Marble, | who marryed the Daughter of | Sir John Seymour, Knight, | formerly of this Parish. | He departed this Life | the 1st Day of November, | Anno Domini 1682, ætatis suæ 73 | He was a loving Husband, a good | Father, and ever a cordial Friend, | where he professed Friendship. (*Ibid.*)

EXTRACT FROM 'BARWICK AND ITS CHURCH,' BY JOHN BATTEN, F.S.A.

The family of Roger, or Rogers, whose chief seat was at Bryanston, Dorset (see Hutchins's 'Dorset,' i., 250), held Barwick for six generations, extending to the latter part of the reign of Queen Elizabeth, when Sir Richard Rogers, knight, sold the manor and advowson to William Symes, of Chard, merchant.

This gentleman married Elizabeth, daughter of Robert Hill of Poundisford, near Taunton, a very old Somersetshire family, and he was succeeded at his death by his son and heir, John Symes, who at the close of his life left Poundisford for the residence of his son, at Winterborne, in the parish of Frampton Cotterell, Gloucestershire, where he died, and was buried. The remarkable career of this "Somersetshire worthy" is minutely detailed in the monumental inscription to his memory in Frampton Church. It is engraved on a brass plate surmounted with the arms of Symes: *Azure, three escallops in pale or*; impaling those of Horner: *Sable, three talbots passant argent, two and one.*

"Here lyeth the body of *John Symes of Poundisford*, in the Parish of Pitminster in the county of Somerset, Esquire, he was born on the 4th day of March, 1572 (in the 12th year of Queen Elizabeth). He lived soberly, righteously, and godly, and died on the 21st day of October, 1661.

"Reader, thou treadest on the sacred ashes of John Symes, Esq., who in the late unhappy times of rebellion, was forced (for his signal loyalty to his Prince) to leave his former habitation at Poundisford, in the parish of Pitminster, in the county of Somerset, and to seek a repose for his old age in this parish. He was a man greatly renowned for wisdom, justice, integrity, and sobriety, which talents he did not hide in a napkin, but religiously exercised in the whole conduct of his life, especially in the government of that county, wherein he bore all the honourable offices incident to a country gentleman (as Knight of the shire, elected *nem. con.*), for the Parliaments held at Westminster in the 21st year of King James, High Sheriff, Deputy Lieutenant for many years, and Justice of the Peace for 40 years and upwards, and as he was careful and solicitous to discharge his duties to God, his soveraigne, and his country, so God was pleased to bestow on him several badges (also) of his special favour, as length of days, accompanied with a most healthy constitution of body for above 80 years, and of his mind to the last, as also a numerous posterity even of children and children's children, to the number of 100 and upwards, descended from his loynes (by his only wife Amy, the daughter of Thomas Horner, of Cloford, in the county of Somerset, Esquire).

"And when he was full of days and honour, having lived 88 years 7 months and 17 days, and seen the safe return of his Prince to his crown and kingdom, after a long and horrible exile, and thereby the flourishing condition both of Church and State. Having finished his work on earth, he cheerfully resigned his soul to God that gave it, the 21st day of October, anno domini 1661, in full assurance of a joyful resurrection."

The grandson of this extraordinary old gentleman was Thomas Symes, who resided at Barwick, and obtained, 23 Charles II., a Charter for a second fair, to be held on the 17th of September. He renewed the alliance with the Horner family by his marriage with Merilla, younger daughter of Sir John Horner, of Mells, and died at Barwick A.D. 1681, leaving his wife and only son, John Symes, surviving. There stood against the west end of the north aisle of the church a mural monument to his memory, surmounted with the arms of Symes and Horner as above. On it is the following inscription (Coll., Som., ii., 338):—

"Heic subter sepultus jacet Thomas Symes armiger annos natus 46 a febri ereptus 22 die Novembris anno Verbi Incarnati 1681; mœstissimam reliquit viduam Merillam, filiam natu minorem Johannis Horner de Mells in Agro Somrsetensi equitis aurati per quam filium unicum Joharonem et unicam filiam habuit quorum hœc infans 6 die Septembris 1671, occubuit, heic etiam sepulta ille, una cum matre supertite monumentum hoc posuit; pientissima conjux, memoriam mariti sui pie colens hunc etiam sui locum sepulchri statuens cum Deo. opt. Max. visum fuerit."

The remains of the mourning widow were, in accordance with her wish so pathetically expressed, deposited by the side of her husband in the vault immediately beneath this monument, but we regret to say that, during the recent restoration, the monument itself has been unceremoniously taken down and shifted to the opposite side of the church, where—the opening words of the inscription being no longer applicable—like another more celebrated one, it "lifts it's head and lies." The only extenuation for the offenders probably is that they did not understand Latin.

We cannot refrain from observing that this removal was a clear violation of the law. Whatever may be done by the Bishop, in the exercise of a wise discretion with regard to a monument recently erected without his licence, the law will presume an ancient one to have been lawfully set up, and (subject to rare exceptions) no authority, civil or ecclesiastical, can justify its removal or disturbance, without the consent of the family of the deceased (in this case by no means extinct), to whom it absolutely belongs.

John Symes, only son of the above Thomas, survived his father but a few years. He was intended for the Bar, but was carried off by small-pox, A.D. 1687, when only 20 years of age, and his fond mother recorded his many virtues and talents on a monument erected by her to his memory in Exeter College Chapel. A copy of the Latin inscription will be found in Le Neve's 'Mon. Angl.' vol. iii., p. 91. As this young man died unmarried, Barwick, under a family settlement, devolved, first, on his cousin, John Symes, of Mount Serrat, in the West Indies, and then on his nephew, Samuel Parry, who assumed the name of Symes. His coheiresses sold it in 1750 to John Newman, father of the worthy gentleman of that name, who enjoyed it for his long life, respected by all who had the good fortune to know him.

As to the registers, the earliest commences in 1560, thirteen years after Edward VI. ordered parish registers to be kept. The following entries occur in one of them:—"Memorandum a pulpit cloak, a cushion, and carpet, given by Merral Symes, lady of the manor, in the year 1708, and a Communion table, bought in the year 1708, likewise. Item: A large silver flagon, given to ye Church of Barwick by Mrs. Merril Symes, lady of the manor, ye 25th of December, in ye year 1709, having her cress engraved thereon. Memorandum: A gallery set up in the year 1709, at the charge of the singers, with consent of Merral Symes, lady of the manor of Barwick, and Mr. Sydenham Burch, Mr. William Pearse, *rector*, and George William, churchwarden, and on consideration of its being an ornament to the Church they do agree and own it to be their own as land for them for ever, and their heirs after them without obstruction."

Several entries relate to the family of Horners, whose chief seat was at Mells, in this county, and who, as we have seen, became connected with Barwick by the marriage of Merilla, daughter of Sir John Horner, Knight, with Thomas Symes, of Barwick, Esquire, who died 1681. John Horner, a nephew of Merilla, married Ann, one of the two daughters and coheiresses of Edward Phelips, of Preston Plucknett, Esquire, and took up his residence at Barwick.

Exeter College Chapel.

Against the south wall of south aisle:—

Arms: *Azure, three escallops in pale or* (Symes); impaling, *Sable, three talbots passant argent* (Horner).

Crest: *A demi-hind salient erased or*

H. S. E.
Joannes Symes,
Thomæ Symes de Berwick in agro Somesfetenfi Arm.
Et Merillæ Conjugis lectiffimæ,
Filiæ Johannis Horner de Melis in eodem agro Eq. Aur.
Filius unicus.
Quem fub ipfa pœne infantia patre orbatum
Mater pientiffime artibus et difciplinis honeftis
Mature imbui curavit;
Primum hic Oxonii Philofophiæ,
Dein Londini in hofpitio Lincolnienfi Juris Anglicani
Studio operam dedit Juvenis egregius:
In quibus tantopere profecit,
ut magnam defe fpem excitaverit.
Morum infuper candore, et vitæ innocentia admodum fpectabilis; |
Tandem Variolarum morbo correptus,
Intra paucos dies puriffimam animam Deo reddidit.
Bonis omnibus trifte relinquens fui defiderium,
Cum vixiffet annos plus minus viginti.
Obiit fexto die Julii An. Dom. MDCLXXXVII.
Mater filio chariffimo mœrens P.

On a gravestone:—

JOANNES SYMES ARM.
NATUS XXVI AUGUSTI
ANNO DOM. MDCLXVII.
OBIIT VI JULII MDCLXXXVII
QUI COLLEGII EXON.
SOCIO COMMENSALIS
PRÆCEPS VITA FLUIT, BREVIS AC INCERTA JUVENTUS:
VIVERE FESTINA, JAM CITO DISCE MORI.

(Gutch's 'Antiquities of Oxford,' p. 119.)

Lewisham Old Church, co. Kent.

On south side of chancel:—

Mary, wife of Mr Richard Symes of Blackheath, ob. 4 Nov. 1701. She was dau. and heiress of Edm. Hawks of Mounckton, co. Dorset.

Richard Symes of Blackheath, ob. 27 May 1728, æt. 72, son of Tho. Symes of Winterbourne, co. Glouc., Esq., who mar. Mary sister of Sir Tho. Bridges of Keynsham, co. Somers., Knt., by whom he had 12 sons and 4 daus. The above Ric. was the 10th son, and directed by will that a monument should be erected in memory of him and his 2nd wife, Charlotte, dau. of Sir Orlando Bridgeman of Ridley, co. Chester. She died 3 March 1718, æt. 37. His 3rd wife was Elizab., eldest dau. of the Rt. Hon. Mathew Ducie Morton, Baron Morton of Morton, co. Staff., who survived him. Arms (beneath): *Azure, three escallops in pale or;* impaling, *Argent, ten plates sable, on a chief argent a lion passant sable.* The Hon. Elizab. Morton, the relict, afterwards married Francis Reynolds of Strangways, Esq. Her elder brother dying without issue, the honours of the house devolved on her descendants, of whom the present Earl Ducie is chief.

(Drake's 'History of the Hundred of Blackheath,' p. 267.)

Bristol Cathedral.

On a ledger in north aisle:—

HERE LYETH
THE BODY OF CAP[T]
RICHARD SYMES WHO
DEPARTED THIS LIFE THE
21ST OF JAN. 172$\frac{9}{0}$ IN THE
58 YEAR OF HIS AGE.
[Intervening space here on the stone.]
HERE ALSO LYETH ELIZ[H]
SYMES HER MOTHER WHO
DEPARTED THIS LIFE Y[E] 13TH
OF OCT[R] 1719 AGED 49.
HERE LYETH THE BODY OF
ELIZ[H] DAUGHT[R] OF RICHARD
AND ELIZ[H] SYMES WHO
DEPARTED THIS LIFE Y[E] 12
OF SEPT[R] 1711 AGED 19 YEARS.

St. John's Churchyard.

On a ledger:—

Here lieth the Body of
ELIZABETH SIMMS the wife of
ALEXANDER SIMMS who
Departed this life the 26th day
of May 1759 Aged 34 Years.

Pedigree of Tankard.

RICHARD TANCKRED of Antigua, on 18 Oct. 1639 sold 20 mens land, and later 33 more.

Captain John Tankard of Antigua, Esq., Member of the Assembly 11 July 1692; proposed for the Council 1699. Had relatives in Ireland. Will dated 13 . . . . 1699, on record at St. John's, but now illegible. He purchased a plantation of Marcus Kirwan. ═ Mary, dau. of Nathaniel Monk, senior; living 1696. Will recorded 1699.

Joseph Tankard of Antigua, named 1699 in his brother's will.

John Tankard, heir to his father; under 14 in 1697; died 1711—14. ═ Mary, dau. of . . . . mar. 2ndly . . . . Howard. Her will dated 10 Nov. and sworn 23 Nov. 1762.

Barry Tankard of "Tankards" (now "Tyrrells") in St. Paul's Parish; Member of Assembly 1699—1700; J.P. 1704; Member of Council 1704—16; died 10 July 1726, æt. 58. M.I. on his estate. ═ Anne (? dau. of Col. Valentine Russell), living 1709; bur. Dec. 1738 at St. Paul's.

Joseph Tankard. — Nathaniel Tankard.

Elizabeth Tankard. — Ann Tankard. — Martha Tankard.

. . . . Tyrrell of Ireland. ═ . . . . died 26 Feb. 1771, æt. 99, in Little Ormond Street.

John Tankard, named in the will of William Pike 1714; died s.p.; bur. 28 March 1757 at St. Paul's. Will dated 9 May 1756; sworn 4 April 1757.

Edward Chester, junior, of "Briggins," Antigua, mar. 24 Oct. 1726 at St. Paul's. Will dated 1743; proved 11 April 1745. 1st husband. ═ Russell Tankard, only child and heir, living 1709. Will dated 25 May 1751; sworn 11 Feb. 1765. ═ Richard Tyrrell, Esq., R.N., Admiral of the White 1762 and Commander-in-Chief of the Leeward Islands station; mar. 18 Nov. 1747 at St. Paul's; died 27 June 1766, and was bur. at sea. M.I. in Westminster Abbey. Will dated 20 Feb. 1765; proved 5 Aug. 1766. (323 Tyndall.) 2nd husband.

s.p. s.p.

Anne Tyrrell. ═ . . . . Barnes.

Catherine Tyrrell, mar. . . . . Reily and had issue.

Richard Tyrrell Barnes, Esq., of Crown Court, Prince's Street, Soho Square, in 1802; inherited "Tyrrells" or "Orleans" from his uncle Richard Tyrrell; died intestate.

Catherine Barnes. Adm'on to her 1821 of Admiral Richard Tyrrell's estate, as sister and ad'trix of Richard Tyrrell Barnes; then a widow. ═ . . . . Ford.

CAPTAIN RICHARD TYRRELL, R.N.

FROM A PROOF ETCHING BY WORLIDGE.

John Tankard of Antigua, Esq. Will dated 13 . . . . 1699. To . . . . Tankard of Ireland. My brother Joseph. My dau. Elizth Tankard. My dau. Martha Tankard. My son Joseph Tankard. My sons Nathl & John Tankard. To my son John the plantation I bought of Marcus Kirwan . . . . Recorded fo. 42. (This will is almost completely illegible from discolouration due to damp.)

Mary Tankard. Will recorded fo. 44. *Circa* 1699. (Illegible.)

Barry Tankard of Antigua. Will dated . . . . 17 . . Witnessed by Jacob Morgan, Walter Sydserfe, John Hodges. Before John Hart, Commander-in-Chief, was sworn Walter Sydserfe. Recorded 12 April 1750. (The will is missing.)

Russell Tankerd Tyrrell, wife of Richard Tyrrell, Esq. Will dated 25 May 1751. To be buried in the garden between my father & mother. To my husband Richd Tyrrell £1000 c. & request him to permit my cousin Margt Looby to possess the land now under lease from my former husband, Edwd Chester, Esq., & myself to Messrs Bodkin & Tully for life clear of charges, & after her death to permit Anthony Chester, a free negro, formerly Edwd Chester's & a faithful servant to me, to enjoy 8 acres for his life. To Miss Peggy Mascol, dau. of Margt Mascoll, widow, £100 c. Mrs Cath. Carty my former servant £100 c. To Miss Lætitia Cusack, dau. of Patrick Cusack the Elder, £100 c. To Miss Russell Cusack my goddau. £100 c. To Margt Looby £50 c. for charities. To Anthony Chester, free negro, £500 c. My mulattos Giles, Lucinda, & Sukey, & my negro Betty. To Margt Looby £1000 c. & clothing & ornaments, also 10 negros & all residue. Patrick Cusack, Senr, planter, Edwd Davy, book keeper, & Margt Looby Ex'ors. Witnessed by James Athill, Dudly Sweeny. Before his Excellency George Thomas were sworn Dudly Sweeny, planter, and Dr. James Athill 11 Feb. 1765. Recorded 12 Feb. 1765.

Sir Peter Warren,* K.B. Will dated 26 July, proved 30 Oct. 1752 by Dame Susannah Warren; power reserved to the others. (266 Bettesworth.) To my wife £3000, £300 for rings, & $\frac{1}{3}$ of the interest of my personal estate, & all residue to my 4 daus. If they all die then $\frac{1}{3}$ of my personal & $\frac{2}{3}$ of my real estate to my nephew Capt. Richd Tyrrel, & $\frac{1}{3}$ of my personal estate to my nephews & nieces. His 2 sisters. My nephews & nieces, children of Chr. Johnson. My nephew Wm Johnson. My nephew Capt. Warren Johnson I advanced £1100 & my nephew John Johnson £500 which I cancel, & the latter may hold the lands of Warrenstown of 448 acres at £160 rent. My wife, her brother James Delancey, chief justice of New York, & my nephew Capt. Richard Tyrrel Ex'ors.

On 14 Feb. 1772 adm'on of the estate of testator, late of St. Marylebone, but in Ireland, deceased, left unadministered by Dame Susan, was granted to the Hon. Ann FitzRoy, wife of the Hon. Charles FitzRoy, Susannah Skinner, wife of William Skinner, Esq., and Charlotte, Countess of Abingdon, wife of Willoughby, Earl of Abingdon, the daus., the other Ex'ors being dead.

John Tankard of Antigua. Will dated 9 May 1756. To my mother Mrs Mary Howard the use of my . . . . & slaves, but not to be let to any but Mr Patrick Cusack for the use of his 4 daus., & all to them after her death & all residue. Mr Patrick Cusack, Senr, Ex'or. Before Governor Thomas was sworn Hon. Andrew Lesly, Esq., 4 April 1757, and John Hart, Esq., and M. S. Walrond of Antigua, Esq., was present 27 March last at the house of the late John Tankard with William Lyons, Esq., and found the will. On 4 April 1757 Edward Davy, Gent., and Laurence Nihell, merchant, were sworn. Recorded 13 April 1757.

Mary Howard of Antigua, Gentlewoman. Will dated 10 Nov. 1762. By Indenture dated 30 June 1753 between myself, of the 1st part, Patrick Cusack the Elder of Antigua, Esq., of the 2d, & John Tankard of Antigua, planter, my son, of the 3rd part, I granted a certain plantation & slaves to Patrick Cusack to the use of John Tankard for life with remainder to his 1st son, but my son is dead without issue & all powers are therefore vested in me. To Elizth, dau. of my niece Sarah Walrond by her husbd Main Swete Walrond, Esq., £1000 c. at 21, & in default to her brothers Main Swete Walrond & Lyons Walrond. To Chas. Wills Walrond, son of my niece Sarah, £500 at 21, 7 negros to Elizth Walrond at 21, & in default to her sisters Sarah Lyons Walrond. To Elizth Walrond £100 a yr. for 4 years. To Margt, dau. of Robt Christian, Esq., £100 c. To Main Swete Walrond, son of my niece Sarah, a negro. To Chas. Wills Walrond a negro. $\frac{1}{2}$ of the rent due to me from Mr Patrick Cusack to Main S. Walrond the husband of my niece Sarah. To the latter £150 c. yearly for life. I give my plantation & all residue to my nephew Wm Lyons & his heirs, then to my niece Sarah Walrond. Wm Lyons & M. S. Walrond Ex'ors. Witnessed by Henry Symes, James Athill, Samuel Harman. Before Hon. Thomas Jarvis, President of Antigua, in absence of the Governor, was sworn Dr. James Athill 23 Nov. 1762 and Henry Symes 24 Feb. 1762. Recorded 24 Feb. 1763

Hon. Richard Tyrrell, Rear-Admiral and Commander-in-Chief at the Leeward Islands. Will dated 20 Feb. 1765; proved 5 Aug. 1766 by Alexander French, Robert Fulton, and Sarah Aylon; power reserved to William Maxwell, Esq., Hon. Robert Christian, Esq., Hon. Francis Carlisle, Esq., and Alexander Willock, Esq. On 16 Jan. 1802 adm'on to Richard Tyrrell Barnes, the nephew, of the goods left unadministered by Alexander French, Robert Fulton, and Sarah Aylon, spinster, now also deceased, Alexander Willock the surviving Ex'or being dead. On 1 June 1821 adm'on of effects of Richard Tyrrell, late of H.M.S. "Princess Louisa," widower, left unadministered by Alexander French, Robert Fulton, Sarah Aylon, as also by Richard Tyrrell Barnes, Esq., deceased, granted to Catherine Ford, widow, sister and administratrix of Richard Tyrrell Barnes, all the other Ex'ors having died without taking on the execution. (323 Tyndall.) By an Indenture da. 23 Aug. 1748 between myself & Russell my wife, of the 1st part, His Excellency Wm Mathew, since deceased, Walter Nugent, since deceased, & Patrick Cusack, planter, of the 2d part, being a settlement of certain lands in Antigua & Jamaica, & by another Indenture da. 8 Feb. 1752 between myself & Russell my wife, of the 1st part, & Wm Maxwell of Antigua, surgeon, & John Tankard of Antigua, planter, since deceased, of the 2d, we were minded in case there were no children to charge the estate with £5000 c., & granted the estate to them for 99 years as duly recorded in the Register's Office, & my wife Russell being now dead I am become sole possessor of the estates. To Sarah Aylon of Fulham, spr, my intended wife, $\frac{1}{2}$ of all my rents for life & the use of coaches, cattle, plate, jewels, & ship furniture. The sum of £5000 is due to me by mortgage on the estate that belonged to Henry Sharpe, Esq., in St Kitts, which he has since sold. The other $\frac{1}{2}$ of my rents for the mainten-

* Sir Peter Warren, Vice-Admiral of the Red, was made K.B. in 1749, sat as M.P. for Westminster, and died 29 July 1752. M.I. in Westminster Abbey. He married Anna 1st dau. of Stephen De Lancey by Ann 2nd dau. of the Right Hon. Stephen Van Cortlandt of New York. Lady Warren died in Grosvenor Square 19 Nov. 1771.

ance of the children of my sisters Cath. Reily & Ann Barnes. All my estates after payment of legacies & after the death of Sarah Aylon to Rich[d] Tyrrell Barnes, son of my sister Anne Barnes, & his heirs, charged with £10,000 c. for the children of my 2 sisters. I give him also all plate, etc. If he die without heirs then all to John Ambrose, younger son of Admiral John Ambrose, then to my secretary Rob[t] Fulton. Cancel debts of M[r] Luke Bourke, Lieut. of Marines. My negros W[m] Thomas, Tommy, & Delia his mother, Lucy & Sucky & their 2 children to be free. To s[d] negro W[m] Thomas £100 c. To Eliz. Susannah Ambrose £1000 c. due from her father Admiral John Ambrose. To Eliz. French, dau. of Alex[r] French of Rotherhithe, merch[t], £1000 c. To Mary Norris, dau. of Geo. Norris of Chelsea, gardiner, £1000 c. To Col. W[m] Dowling of Barbados £200 c. To Chas. Hart my overseer £500 c. W[m] Maxwell of Antigua, Esq., Rich[d] Reddy of Antigua, planter, Alex[r] French of Rotherhithe, merch[t], Rob[t] Fulton my secretary, now of Antigua, & Sarah Aylon of Fulham, sp[r], Ex'ors. Witnessed by Fras. Grant, David Williams, Galbraith Patterson.

Codicil dated 26 Oct. 1765. Sarah Aylon, now of Little Chelsey, to have her choice of £1000 a year or half my rental. My books & instruments to be sold & the proceeds sent to her. My box of papers to be sent to her locked & sealed with my armes. Chas. Hart is since dead. Mary Norris to have £1000 s. not currency. Hon. Rob[t] Christian, Hon. Francis Farley, & Alex[r] Willock, all of Antigua, Esq[res], additional Ex'ors, & Rich[d] Reddy to be struck out as too old & infirm. Witnessed by Robert Fulton, William Trant, Henry Harvey.

Codicil dated 20 June 1766. Eliz. Susanna Ambrose & Eliz. French £1000 s. each, not currency. Witnessed by Archibald Cobham, Robert Fulton.

Robert Fulton of Little Chelsea, co. Middlesex, Esq. Will dated 10 Nov. 1770; proved 6 Sep. 1771 by Sarah Tyrrell, widow. My sister Mary Ann Fulton £1000. My brother-in-law Alderman James Chatterton £300, & his dau. Hannah Chatterton £600. My natural son W[m] Sinnot £600, & his mother Mary Ann Sinnot £200. Miss Mary Norris 20 g[ns]. My chamber N[o] 8 New Inn. "I give and bequeath unto my dearly and well beloved ffriend Sarah Tyrrell of Little Chelsea aforesaid (who is my intended wife)," all residue of my estate & Ex'trix, & in case the plantation & slaves of Orleans in the Island of Antigua, left to me by the will of the late Rear Admiral Richard Tyrrell for want of issue of his nephew Richard Tyrrell Barnes & John Ambrose, jun., should come to me, then I give it to her.

Close Roll, 42 Geo. III., Part 1, Nos. 14 and 15.

Indenture made the 19th Jan. 1802 between Richard Tyrrell Barnes of Crown Court, Princes Street, Soho Square, Esq., of the one part, and David Sands of Winch (?) Street, Pall Mall, Esq., and Richard England of Leicester Square, Esq., of the other part, witnesses that in consideration of 5*s*. Richard Tyrrell Barnes sells to David Sands and Richard England all that plantation called Tyrrells or Orleans in Antigua, and all slaves, cattle, and stock which were devised to Richard Tyrrell Barnes by the will of Richard Tyrrell, Admiral of the White, for one whole year. Harry Thomas King and Jonathan Lodge, clerks to Messrs. Shawe, New Bridge Street, witnesses.

No. 14.

Indenture made the 20th Jan. 1802 between Richard Tyrrell Barnes, of the one part, and David Sands and Richard England, assignees of his estate and effects by virtue of an Act of Parliament passed in the 38th year of his present Majesty for the relief of certain insolvent debtors, of the other part. Whereas by virtue of the last will of Richard Tyrrell, late of Antigua, Rear-Admiral of the White, dated the 20th Feb. 1765, Richard Tyrrell Barnes is entitled to an estate tail in the plantation called Tyrrells or Orleans; and whereas Richard Tyrrell Barnes in October 1797 obtained his discharge under the said Act, and David Sands and Richard England were appointed assignees of his estate for the purposes of the Act; and whereas Richard Tyrrell Barnes is indebted to David Sands £200 for money advanced since the passing of the Act, with some arrears of interest thereon; and whereas Richard Tyrrell Barnes has agreed to convey the said plantation late of Richard Tyrrell, deceased, to David Sands and Richard England for the purposes hereinafter mentioned, the same not having effectually passed to them under the Act. Now this Indenture witnesses that for docking and destroying the estate tail of Richard Tyrrell Barnes and all remainders, and for vesting the same in fee simple in David Sands and Richard England, and in consideration of 10*s*. Richard Tyrrell Barnes sells to David Sands and Richard England in their actual possession being all the said plantation, slaves, cattle, horses, mares, and mules, and to their heirs for ever, subject only to such claims as may be made against the plantation under the will of Richard Tyrrell, deceased, in trust nevertheless to cultivate and manage the plantation and slaves as they shall think most advantageous, and to employ Attorneys in Antigua, and to consign and dispose of the crops, and from the moneys received in the first place to pay all expenses connected with the plantation, and subject thereto to divide the residue amongst the persons entitled to receive a dividend and distribution of the effects of Richard Tyrrell Barnes already vested in David Sands and Richard England, and especially to deduct the money owing to David Sands, and after full payment of all in trust to convey the plantation to the use of Richard Tyrrell Barnes, his heirs, Ex'ors, etc., for ever; and lastly Richard Tyrrell Barnes, David Sands, and Richard England constitute Rowland Burton, Samuel Athill, John Athill, and Richard Oliver Athill of Antigua, Esquires, their Attorneys.

Close Roll, 55 Geo. III., Part 7, No. 11.

Indenture made the 11th May 1815 between Sir John Tyrell of Boreham House near Chelmsford, Essex, Bart., and Dame Sarah his wife, of the one part, and Charles Cheshire of Antigua, Esq., Master Attendant of H.M.'s Naval Yard in Antigua, of the other part. Whereas by Articles of Agreement made at Antigua the 6th Oct. 1814 between Sir John Tyrell and Dame Sarah his wife (by the Hon. Samuel Athill of Antigua, Esq., their Attorney), of the 1st part, the said Hon. Samuel Athill, of the 2nd part, and Charles Cheshire, of the 3rd part, Sir John Tyrell and Dame Sarah did agree to sell to Charles Cheshire absolutely in fee simple a piece of land in the parish of St. Paul and division of Falmouth called Buckshornes, and formerly cultivated as a sugar plantation, containing 200 acres, bounded N. with land heretofore of Admiral Richard Tyrell, deceased, E. by land late of Captain Grant Gordon but now of Margaret Harcum, S. by the lands of the said Samuel Athill and the devisees of Mary Willis, deceased, and W. by the lands then or late of William Maxwell, and all buildings, etc., thereon, and also three negros, for the sum of £1500, to be paid by one bill of exchange of £600 drawn by Charles Cheshire on Messrs. Cook and Halford of Norfolk Street, London, merchants, and payable at thirty days sight to Alexander Bolt of Antigua, Esq., or his order, to be indorsed by him, and another bill of exchange of £900 drawn as above and payable at eight months to Alexander Bolt, Charles Cheshire having on the 6th Oct. delivered to Samuel Athill the two bills. This Indenture witnesseth that for the above considerations Sir John Tyrell and Dame Sarah his wife grant to Charles Cheshire the piece of land aforesaid, and to his heirs for ever, and they appoint Alexander Bolt, Esq., and the Hon. Samuel Athill, Esq., their Attorneys. John Jessopp of Clifford's Inn, William Lyddon, Carey Street, Lincoln's Inn, witnesses.

Circa 1667. Thomas Clerack of Road Division has 21 mens land by sale from Richard Tanckred 18 Oct. 1639 purchased from John Lapthorne. (Book of Claims.)

1688, Aug. 8. Thomas Haynes and his wife convey to John Tankard 10 acres in Willoughby Bay Division.

Captain John Tankerd, planter, grant of the land formerly in the possession of George Gray and his wife and Mary Weale, George Gray's mother, and late in that of Lieut. William Burden, deceased, a former husband of Mary Weale; also 235 acres formerly Roger Jones', a former husband of Mary Weale; also 165 acres bought of Marcus Kirwan and Mary Weale by patent granted 6 Aug. 1697 from Christopher Codrington.

1701. Petition of Barry Tankard for a patent for his 590½ acres formerly Colonel Valentine Russel's, deceased.

1701, Sep. 10. Barry Tankerd, Gent., granted a patent by Christopher Codrington for 590½ acres at St. Paul's, bounded north with Kean Osborne, Gent.

1708, Feb. 16. Governor Parke stated that Barry Tankard had insulted him and challenged him to fight. He and his brother John Tankard had armed their negros and guarded the paths leading to their plantation. On 15 March following he was bound over in £1000 c. to appear at the next Court of Sessions.

1709, Feb. 23. Dennis Macklemore, planter, having been killed in a duel with Barry Tankard, Esq., a warrant was issued for the latter's arrest. (Minutes of Assembly.) On 3 April following allusion was made to Barry Tankerd's wife and daughter.

1709, June 8. Barry Tankard, who had been often asked to take his seat as a Councillor and refused, was this day removed from that Board by Royal Instructions. He was a Member of Council before 14 July 1704.

1711, Nov. 1. John Tankard conveys to Victorious Looby 60 acres in Willoughby Bay including the 10 acres conveyed in 1688.

John Tankard, jun., of Antigua, Gent., sells to Victorious Looby of Antigua, Gent., 60 acres in Willoughby Bay for £400 c.

1715-16, March 13. Barry Tankard states that his affairs do not permit him to attend as Member of Council and resigns.

1717, Jan. 13. In Chancery. Ellinor Tankerd, widow, plaintiff, *v.* Hon. Archibald Cochran and Baptist Looby, defendants; publication to pass.

1759, March 6. The Right Hon. the Ld. Anson introduced Capt. Tyrrel, of the Buckingham, to the King at St. James's, to inform him of the progress of his majesty's forces in the West Indies. ('Gent. Mag.,' p. 143.) In June following he was promoted to the Foudroyant, 84 guns. (*Ibid.*, p. 294.)

1766, June 27. Rear-Admiral Tyrrel, on board the Princess Louisa, at sea, in his way home. His body was, by his own desire, thrown overboard, with the usual ceremonies. (*Ibid.*, p. 342.)

1767, May. Robert Fulton, Esq; to relict of late admiral Tyrrel. (*Ibid.*, p. 279.)

1771, Feb. 26. Mrs. Tyrrell, mother to the late Admiral, aged 99, in Little Ormond-street. (*Ibid.*, p. 142.)

1771, Sep. 4. Robert Fulton, Esq; at Little Chelsea. (*Ibid.*, p. 426.)

Mr. W. P. W. Phillimore of 124 Chancery Lane informs me that he possesses a fine portrait of Admiral Richard Tyrrell and his wife, which with other relics descended to him through his great-grandmother Sarah Stiff (*née* Norris) of Chelsea. The miniatures are on panels 5¾ inches by 4½ inches.

Captain H. S. Knight, late of the 67th and 19th Regiments, of The Observatory, Harestock, near Winchester, writes me: "My grandmother Mrs. Sparkes was a niece or grandniece of Admiral Richard Tyrrell, and in conjunction with her two brothers Captain George Pattoun and Lieut.-Colonel Robert Pattoun, who was killed at the siege of Moultan in India, inherited the Tyrrell estate in Antigua, where I was quartered when serving with the 67th Regiment under Lieut.-Colonel Basil Brooke; during part of the year 1853 we were quartered at Brimstone Ridge and Shirley Heights within a few miles of the Tyrrell property. Mrs. Sparks was an infant at the time of the Irish Rebellion."

PARISH REGISTER OF ST. JOHN.

Buried.

1694 May 15 Bartholemy Tankerd.

PARISH REGISTER OF ST. PAUL.

Married.

1726 Oct. 24 Edward Chester, Junr, Esqr, and Miss Russel Tankard; p^r^ L.

1747 Nov. 18 Richard Tyrrell, Esqr, Commander of his Majesty's Ship the Centaur, and Mrs Russel Tankard Chester, Widow; by L.

Buried.

1726 July 12 Barry Tankard.

1738 Dec. — Mrs Anne Russel Tankard.

1757 Mar. 28 Mr John Tankard.

AT TYRRELLS.

On a large ledger over a broken vault:—

Here lies Interr'd
the Body of the
Honble Barry
Tankard Esq. who
departed this life
the 10 Day of July
Anno Domini
1726 Aged 58 years.

WESTMINSTER ABBEY.

Arms (sculptured and painted): *Ermine, on three bars gules seven crosses patée, three, three, and one, in chief a demi-lion issuant out of the second.* (Neale's 'History of Westminster Abbey,' vol. ii., p. 236.)

Sacred to the Memory of RICHARD TYRRELL, Esq. who | was descended from an Ancient Family in Ireland, and died Rear | Admiral of the White, on the 26th day of June, 1766, in the | 50th year of his Age. Devoted from his Youth to the Naval | Service of his Country, and being formed under the Discipline, | and animated by the Example of his renown'd Uncle Sr Peter | Warren, He distinguished himself as an able and Experienced | Officer, in many Gallant Actions; particularly on the 3^d^ of | Novr 1758, when commanding the Buckingham of 66 Guns | and 472 Men, he attacked and defeated three French Ships of | War, one of which was the Florissant of 74 Guns and 700 | Men: but the Buckingham being too much disabled to take | possession of her, after she had Struck, the Enemy, under | cover of the Night, escaped. In this Action he received several | Wounds, and lost three Fingers of his Right Hand. Dying | on his return to England from the Leeward Islands, where he | had for three Years commanded a Squadron of his Majesty's | Ships, his Body according to his own desire was committed to | the Sea, with the proper Honours and Ceremonies.

One of the most curious monuments, perhaps, in the Abbey is that near the cloister door, in the south aisle of the nave. It commemorates Vice-Admiral Richard Tyrrell, commander of the Buckingham, who died in 1766, whilst on his return to England from the Leeward Islands, after an engagement with the French. His body, the inscription informs us, "according to his own desire, was committed to the sea, with proper honours and ceremonies." "To comprehend this monument," says Mr. Malcolm, "the spectator must suppose himself in a diving-bell at the bottom of the sea. When he has shaken off the terrors of his situation he will find on his right hand the Buckingham, of sixty-six guns, jammed in a bed of coral. Directly before him he will perceive a figure pointing to a spot on a globe, either intending to shew where the deceased body was committed to the deep, or the latitude where an action mentioned in the inscription was fought." The figures introduced into this piece of monumental composition are History, Navigatian, and Hibernia; they are represented among the rocks, with the sea above their heads; above all is the Admiral himself, ascending amidst heavy clouds—the latter being highly suggestive of ill-made pancakes. ('Old and New London,' by E. Walford, vol. iii., p. 417.)

Pedigree of Tempest.

JOHN TEMPEST of Antigua, dead 1725. = Frances, dau. of Governor Philip Warner; mar. 21 March 1689 at St. Paul's, Falmouth; bur. 1 June 1733 at St. John's.

Warner Tempest of Moulsey, co. Surrey, and Antigua, Esq., J.P. 1738; bur. 15 Dec. 1753 at St. John's. = Mary, 1st dau. of Colonel William Byam of Cedar Hill; mar. 12 March 1738 at St. George's.

- Warner William Tempest, bapt. 6 Sep. 1743 at St. John's.
- Lydia Tempest, bapt. 5 Oct. 1741 and bur. 18 April 1743 at St. John's.
- Henrietta Tempest, bapt. 13 Aug. 1747 at St. John's; mar. 8 Nov. 1766, at St. George, Hanover Square, Marmaduke Dayrell of Shudy Camp, co. Cambridge. He died 15 April 1790, æt. 67. (*Vide* Burke's 'Landed Gentry.')
- Frances Tempest, bapt. 5 Feb. 1749 at St. John's.

1718, Sep. 18. John Tempest, mariner, petitions.

1722. John Otto-Baijer refers in his will to his house in the tenure of Mrs. Frances Tempest.

1725. Thomas Tempest witnessed the will of Mrs. Ann Otto-Baijer, and Warner Tempest that of Mrs. Margaret Terrey.

Indenture dated 17 Nov. 1725 between Frances Tempest of St. John's Town, widow, and Warner Tempest of ditto, Gent., of the one part, and Ashton Warner, of the other. Sale of a negro.

1727, Oct. 26. Warner Tempest signs as powder officer. (B. T. Leeward Islands, 19.)

1738, Oct. 3. Warner Tempest takes the oaths as a J.P. He was an inhabitant of St. John's Town in 1753.

PARISH REGISTER OF ST. JOHN.

Baptized.

1741 Oct. 5 Lydia the D. of Warner Tempest and Mary his wife.

1743 Sep. 6 Warner William the s. of Warner Tempest and his wife.

1747 Aug. 13 Henriatta the D. of Warner Tempest and Mary his wife.

1749 Feb. 5 Frances the D. of Warner Tempest and Mary his wife.

Buried.

1730 Oct. 26 Mr Thomas Tempest.

1733 June 1 Madc Frances Tempest.

1743 April 18 Ledia Tempest D. of Mr Warner Tempest.

1753 Dec. 15 Warner Tempest.

PARISH REGISTER OF ST. GEORGE.

Married.

1738 Mar. 12 Warner Tempest and Mary Warner Byam.

ST. GEORGE, HANOVER SQUARE.

Married.

1766 Nov. 8 Marmaduke Dayrell, Esqr, B., & Henrietta Tempest, a minor, with consent of the Guardian. L.A.C.

Family of Thaxter.

William Thaxter, planter. Will dated 8 Dec. 1716. To my son W[m] all my estate at 21, remainder to my son Joseph. My son Joseph £500 c. at 21. My wife certain negros & the management of my estate during my sons' minority. My wife during her widowhood, James Grigg, & Jeremiah Nibbs Ex'ors. Witnessed by George Forrest, Edward Montague, Mary Westin. Sworn 21 May 1717.

.... Will dated 20 Dec. 1740. To my wife Eliz. all my estate, but if she have no issue then at her death all to my cousin Jane Thaxter, wife of Richard Thaxter. My uncle James Griggs* a ring of 2 pistoles. Appoint James Griggs & Jeremiah Nibbs Ex'ors. .... W[m] Thaxter. Witnessed by John Leacock, William Mercer, John Watkins. By Edward Byam, Lieut.-Governor, was sworn John Leacock 13 Jan. 1740. Recorded 15 Jan. 1740.

William Thaxter of Antigua, planter. Will recorded *circa* 1740. To my brother Joseph Thaxter 2 negros & £15 a year. (This fragment may belong to the above.)

John Thaxter of Antigua, windmill carpenter. Will dated 30 May 1762. All my negros to my son Joseph Farley Thaxter. A horse & all furniture to my wife Mary. I appoint the Hon. Stephen Blizard, Esq., M[r] Joseph Farley, sen[r], Ex'ors & Guardians. Witnessed by Joseph Nibbs, Joseph Farley, jun. Before Governor George Thomas was sworn Joseph Farley, jun., 8 June 1762; recorded same day.

* See his will in vol. i., p. 237.

PARISH REGISTER OF ST. GEORGE.

Married.

1734	Oct. 3	William Thaxter & Elizabeth Welch, widow.
1737	.....	Abrahamus Nibbs et Jana Thaxter juncti fuerunt Matrimonio vicesimo nono die Martis Anno Prædicto.
1741	April 16	John Greenway and Elizabeth Thaxter, widow.

Buried.

1737	Jan. 21	Benjam. Thaxter.
1740	Dec. 22	Willm Thaxter.
1740-1	Mar. 4	Joseph Thaxter.
1743	Oct. —	Sarah the D. of Benjamin Thaxter and his wife.
1751	June 15	Benjamin Thaxter, junior.
1757	July 16	Mr James Griggs, buried in his own Estate by a Licence from his Excellency George Thomas, Esq[r].
1762	June 2	John Thaxter.

Family of Thibou.

Lewis Thibou. Will dated .... To my wife Kath. plate & furniture .... All my estate .... for my 6 children, viz., J .... Fraise & Daniel .... my son John Thibou .... my dau. Eliz[th], my son Fraise .... Before Edward Byam, Esq., was sworn John Williams a witness, Daniel Barbotain and Robert Baker were the other witnesses, 24 Feb. 1732-3. Recorded 1 March 1732-3.

Gabriel Thibou, Gent. Will dated *c.* 1746. To my wife Mary my land & tenements in S[t] John's, furniture & plate for life, then to my son John Thibou. To Eliz[th], dau. of my son Gabriel, a negro after my wife's death. To Mary wife of my son Gabriel a negro. To my son Gabriel £5. To my dau. Jane Cooe my brick house & wooden store adjoining, & if she marry, then to her children. Witnessed by Richard Sheepshanks, Samuel Martin, Richard Lee ....

Jacob Thibou, late of Antigua, now of Petersham, co. Surrey, Esq. Will dated 11 May 1747; proved 16 March 1747 by Esther Thibou, widow. (102 Strahan.) All residue after payment of debts to my dear wife Esther, & appoint her sole Ex'trix. Witnessed by Richard Gem, Mary Seal. Recorded also at St. John's.

See vol. i., p. 195, for the will of Dorothy Delap, formerly wife of Jacob Thibou of Antigua, merchant, dated 1 Nov. 1757.

Judith Thibou of Antigua, widow of Peter Thibou, Gent. Will dated 22 April 1760. To my son Peregrine Thibou a negro woman given me by John Dunn. To my son Isaac Thibou 2 negros left me by my late husband's will. To my dau. Judith Dunn Thibou a negro. To my dau. Marg[t] a negro & £60 c. All residue to my said 2 daus. at 21. My beloved friend John Dunn & my dau. Judith D. Thibou at 21 Ex'ors. Witnessed by Neill Campbell, James Butler. Before Governor Thomas was sworn Neill Campbell 22 May 1760. Recorded 22 May 1760.

(? Will of Judith Thibou.) To my dau. Judith Dunn Thibou. my dau. Marg[t], my house & land adjoining the negro burial ground, also negros, & my other children to give her at 21 as follows, my son Peregrine £200 c., my son Isaac .... my daus. Eliz[th] & Judith £66 c. each. (Fragment.)

Mary Thibou. Will dated 13 Nov. 1786. To my mulatto called Kath. 6 silver teaspoons. All residue to my son Isack now in Tobago. M[r] John Rose, Jun[r], M[r] W[m] Shervington Ex'ors. Witnessed by Richard Hunter, Nathaniel Berwick. Before his Excellency Thomas Shirley was sworn Richard Hunter 20 Nov. 1786. Recorded 20 Nov. 1786.

Close Roll, 29 Geo. II., Part 13, No. 10.

Indenture made the 28th Jan. 1755 between George Blount of Henley-upon-Thames, co. Oxford, Esq., and Hester his wife (late widow and relict of Jacob Thibou the younger, formerly of Antigua, but late of London, Esq., deceased, son and heir and residuary legatee of Jacob Thibou the elder, late of Antigua, merchant), of the one part, and Thomas Jarvis of Antigua, Esq., of the other part. Whereas Jacob Thibou the elder made his last will the 28th Nov. 1741 and did give to Jacob Thibou his son all residue of his real and personal estate, but if Jacob died before 21 or having attained to 21 without issue, testator gave all to his daughter Rachel, now wife of Thomas Jarvis, and to her heirs for ever; and whereas Jacob Thibou intermarried with Esther, and after the marriage attained to 21 and became seised in tail general of the real estate devised subject to the dower of his mother, widow and relict of Jacob Thibou his father, now wife of Francis Delap of Antigua, Esq.; and whereas Esther Thibou on the death of her husband became dowable in ⅓ of the said real estate; and whereas Stephen Blizard of Antigua, Esq., hath in pursuance of authority given him by George Blount come to an agreement with Thomas Jarvis to lease the dower of Esther to him for her life at the rate of £580 currency a year. Now George Blount and Esther his wife grant, etc., to Thomas Jarvis all her dower from the lands and negros of Jacob Thibou the younger in Antigua or in Long Island adjoining, which is by law deemed part of Antigua, all which estates are now in the possession of Thomas Jarvis in right of Rachel his wife, or by virtue of deeds executed by them since their intermarriage, to have and to hold for 99 years if Esther Blount so long lives and to determine upon her death, yielding therefore on the 1st August yearly £580 currency at the south door of the Court House in the town of St. John's free from all taxes, and Thomas Jarvis is not to send off any slaves charged with the dower of Esther, save from Antigua to Long Island or from Long Island to Antigua under a penalty of £50 currency for each slave, and lastly George Blount and Esther his wife constitute Stephen Blizard and Thomas Warner of Antigua, Esquires, and William Warner of Antigua, merchant, their Attorneys.

Pedigree of Thibou.

Arms.—. . . . *a chevron between a badger in base and a fleur-de-lis between two mullets in chief.*
Crest.—*Three plumes.*

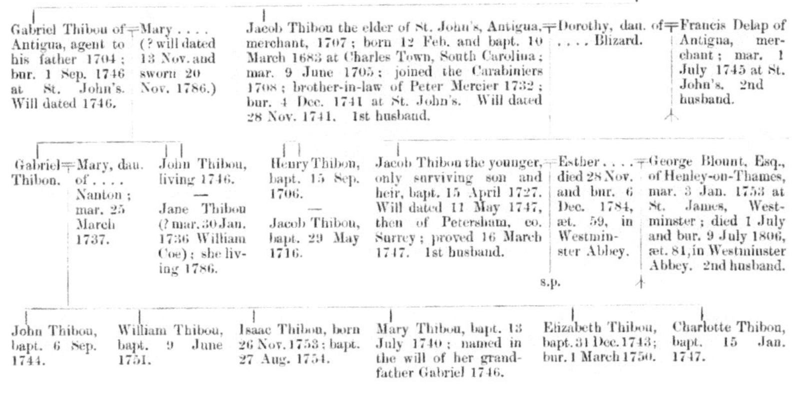

LEWIS THIBOU, born in the Province of Orleans, France; of Charles Town, South Carolina, merchant, 1683; settled at Antigua 1699; of Philadelphia 1704; bur. 5 April 1726 at St. John's. = Susan . . . .

Gabriel Thibou of Antigua, agent to his father 1704; bur. 1 Sep. 1746 at St. John's. Will dated 1746. = Mary . . . . (? will dated 13 Nov. and sworn 20 Nov. 1786.)

Jacob Thibou the elder of St. John's, Antigua, merchant, 1707; born 12 Feb. and bapt. 10 March 1683 at Charles Town, South Carolina; mar. 9 June 1705; joined the Carabiniers 1708; brother-in-law of Peter Mercier 1732; bur. 4 Dec. 1741 at St. John's. Will dated 28 Nov. 1741. 1st husband. = Dorothy, dau. of . . . . Blizard. = Francis Delap of Antigua, merchant; mar. 1 July 1745 at St. John's. 2nd husband.

Gabriel Thibou. = Mary, dau. of . . . . Nanton; mar. 25 March 1737.

John Thibou, living 1746.

Jane Thibou (? mar. 30 Jan. 1736 William Coe); she living 1786.

Henry Thibou, bapt. 15 Sep. 1706.

Jacob Thibou, bapt. 29 May 1716.

Jacob Thibou the younger, only surviving son and heir, bapt. 15 April 1727. Will dated 11 May 1747, then of Petersham, co. Surrey; proved 16 March 1747. 1st husband. = Esther . . . . died 28 Nov. and bur. 6 Dec. 1784, æt. 59, in Westminster Abbey. s.p. = George Blount, Esq., of Henley-on-Thames, mar. 3 Jan. 1753 at St. James, Westminster; died 1 July and bur. 9 July 1806, æt. 81, in Westminster Abbey. 2nd husband.

John Thibou, bapt. 6 Sep. 1744.

William Thibou, bapt. 9 June 1751.

Isaac Thibou, born 26 Nov. 1753; bapt. 27 Aug. 1754.

Mary Thibou, bapt. 13 July 1740; named in the will of her grandfather Gabriel 1746.

Elizabeth Thibou, bapt. 31 Dec. 1743; bur. 1 March 1750.

Charlotte Thibou, bapt. 15 Jan. 1747.

1699, Nov. 30. Lewis Tibiau, a Frenchman born in the province of Orleance, took the oaths as an alien before two J.P.'s.

Carolinia. I, Jacob, the Son of Mr Lewis Thibbou and Suisan his Wife, was borne the twelfth of February 1683 at Charles Towne in South Carolina, and was baptized the tenth of March following by Joseph Harrison, Minister of the Gospell in Charles Towne, Captn Gardaratt and Mrs Susanna Vairin, God father and God Mother.

A true Copy from the Registry. Examined this 2nd day of March 1702, p^r Thomas Booth (Reg^r). Affidavit of Jas. Moore, Esq., Govr of S. Carolina, 24 Mar. 170½.

Indenture dated 30 Aug. 1704. Louis Thibou, formerly of Antigua, now of Philadelphia in Pennsilvania, merchant, letter of attorney to my son Gabriell Thibou, now bound to Antigua. Recorded 12 Oct. 1704.

1708. Deposition of Jacob Thibou, merchant, and constable of St. John's, aged 25.

Isaac Thibou (? son of Lewis Thibou of Charles Town and Susan his wife), died 14 Sep. 1768, æt. 78. M.I. at St. John's. ╤ Catherine, dau. of Rev. James Field, Rector of St. John's; bapt. 3 Nov. 1710, and mar. 1 May 1739 at St. John's.

James Field Thibou, bur. 31 Jan. 1740.	Walter Thibou, ╤ Jane . . . . bapt. 16 Feb. 1741 at St. John's; living 1774.	Peter Thibou, bapt. 13 Aug. 1748; bur. 24 May 1750. — James Thibou, bapt. 27 April 1746.	William Thibou, bapt. 8 June 1751. [Catherine widow of William Thibou, Esq., living 1774.]	Dr. Isaac Field Thibou, witnessed the will of James Hutchinson 1788.	Rachel Thibou, bapt. 24 Oct. 1754; died 14 April 1769, æt. 14½.

Ann Thibou, bapt. 26 June 1773 at St. John's.

James Doig, mar. 22 Oct. 1787 at St. John's. 1st husband. ╤ Margaret, dau. of Dr. John Hurst by Margaret his wife; bapt. 12 Jan. 1763; bur. 13 Sep. 1837, æt. 75, at St. John's. ╤ Walter Thibou, Esq., Ex'or 1800 to Mrs. Ruth Atkinson his first-cousin; mar. 28 Jan. 1808 at St. Mary's. 2nd husband.

Lewis Thibou (? son of Lewis Thibou of Charles Town and Susan his wife). ╤ Mary Catherine Fraise, mar. 6 Aug. 1702.

Lewis Thibou, bapt. 8 Oct. 1707.	Elizabeth . . . . bur. 5 Nov. 1739. 1st wife. ╤ Peter Thibou, Gent., bapt. 1709; died 5 Oct. 1753, æt. 44. M.I. at St. John's. ╤ Judith Henzell, born at Glass Houses, Newcastle; mar. 3 Feb. 1739; died 10 May 1760, æt. 40, and M.I. at St. John's. Will dated 22 April and sworn 22 May 1760. 2nd wife.		James Thibou, bapt. 9 Sep. 1716. — Isaac Thibou, bapt. 4 Feb. 1718.	Lewis Isaac Thibou, bapt. 26 Aug. 1719. — Catherine Thibou, bapt. 30 March 1711.	Margaret Thibou, bur. 2 Oct. 1707. — Sarah Thibou, bapt. 29 Aug. 1714.

James Guilliem Thibou, bapt. 25 Sep. 1736; bur. 19 June 1737. — Mary Thibou, bapt. 5 May 1734.	Elizabeth Thibou, bapt. 19 April 1738. — Catherine Sarah Thibou, bapt. 26 Aug. 1739; bur. 4 May 1740.	Peter Henzill Thibou, bapt. 18 Jan. 1742; bur. 20 May 1746. — Peregrine Thibou, bapt. 28 Nov. 1744; living 1760.	Isaac Thibou, bapt. 22 Aug. 1746; living 1760. — Judith Dunn Thibou, bapt. 18 June 1741; living 1760.	Elizabeth Thibou, living 1760. — Margaret Thibou, bapt. 30 May 1749; living 1760.

Rachel Thibou, mar. 31 May 1749, at St. Paul's, Thomas Jarvis, who inherited through her "Thibous" and "Long Island."	Dorothy Thibou, bapt. 13 Oct. 1709; mar. 1 July 1727 James Doig. He was bur. 15 July 1759 at St. John's.	Sarah Thibou, bapt. 30 March 1711; mar. 2 April 1728 Joseph Mathews. — Ann Thibou, bapt. 30 Jan. 1714; mar. Richard Gem.	Alice Thibou, bapt. 6 Sep. 1719; mar. 11 April 1737 Charles Read. — Elizabeth Thibou, bapt. 21 May 1721; mar. 2 Dec. 1740 Nisbitt Darby.	Grace Thibou, bapt. 17 Dec. 1723; mar. 1 Feb. 1738 Rev. Thomas Wilson. — Lydia Thibou, bapt. 2 Dec. 1724; mar. 15 Jan. 1740 Francis Hanson.	Amelia Thibou, bapt. 28 Dec. 1728; mar. April 1744 Dr. John Richardson. — Charlotte Thibou, bapt. 1 Sep. 1731.

1711, Aug. 9. St. Christopher's Census. St. Anne's, Sandy Point. Mr. Gabriell Thibou. 1 white male, 1 female, 1 boy, 3 girls, and 2 slaves.

1717, Nov. 22. Anguilla Census. Isaac Thiboue. 1 white man, 1 ditto woman, 1 ditto child; 3 negros.

1753, Jan. 2. George Blount, of Henley upon Thames, Esq; to Mrs. Thibou, relict of Jacob Thibou, of Antigua, Esq. ('London Mag.,' p. 43.)

In 1767 Isaac Thibou was rated on 120 acres; in 1780 Walter Thibou on 120 acres.

From a Chancery case at St. John's to be heard 20 May 1774. Catherine Thibou, widow, and William Thibou, Esq., Complainants, *v.* Benjamin Graham, merchant, defendant. On a demurrer. It recites that Catherine Thibou being possessed of a plantation in St. John's Parish with buildings, slaves, and cattle, by Indenture of demise dated 10 Dec. 1768, made between her of the 1 part, and Walter Thibou, Esq., of the other, assigned her estate to him for 99 years, at the yearly rent of £700 for the first year and £800 a year after. The defendant and one John Morrison, late of the island, merchant, deceased, executed a bond of £10,000 on 10 Dec. 1768 for the due payment of the rents by the defendant. In 1773 Catherine Thibou drew bills for £600 in favour of William Thibou for arrears. The bills were not accepted and the defendant paid them.

PARISH REGISTER OF ST. JOHN.

Baptized.

1706 Sep. 15 Henry S. of Jacob Thibou & Dorothy his wife.

1707 Oct. 8 Lewis S. of Lewis Thibou & Mary Catherine his wife.

1708 Aug. 1 Jane D. of Gabrielle Thibou & Mary his wife.

1709 . . . . . . Peter ye s. of Lewis Thibou & Catherine his wife.

1709 Oct. 13 Dorothy child of Mr Jacob Thibou & Dorothy his wife.

1711 Mar. 30 Sarah D. of Jacob Thibou & Dorothy his wife.

1711 Mar. 30 Catherine D. of Lewis Thibou & Catherine his wife.

1714 Aug. 29 Sarah D. of Lewis Thibou, Junr, & his wife.

1714 Jan. 30 Ann D. of Jacob Thibou & Dorothy his wife.

1716 May 29 Jacob the s. of Jacob Thibou & Dorothy his wife.

1716 Sep. 9 James s. of Lewis Thibou and Mary his wife.

1718 Feb. 4 Isaac s. of Lewis Thibou, Junr, & his wife.

1719 Aug. 26 Lewis Isaac s. of Lewis Thibou & Sarah his wife.

1719 Sep. 6 Alice D. of Jacob Thibou & Dorothy his wife.

1720 Feb. 26 John s. of Lewis Thibou & Elizabeth his wife.

1721 May 21 Eliz. the D. of Jacob Thibou & Dorothy his wife.

1722 Aug. 23 Dorothy D. of Isaac Thibou & Elizth his wife.

1723 Dec. 17 Grace D. of Jacob Thibou & Dorothy his wife.

1723 Jan. 5 Jacob the s. of Isaac Thibou & his wife.

1724 Dec. 2 Lydia the D. of Jacob Thibou and Dorothy his wife.

1727 April 15 Jacob the s. of Jacob Thibou and Dorothy his wife.

1728 June 9 Fraise the s. of Lewis Thibou and Catharine his wife.

1728 Dec. 28 Amelia the D. of Mr Jacob Thibou and Dorothy his wife.

1730 April 12 Daniell the s. of Lewis Thibou and Catharine his wife.

1731 Sep. 1 Charlotte the D. of Jacob Thibou & Dorothy his wife.

1733 May 21 . . . . of Jacob Thibou & Dorothy his wife.

1734 May 5 Mary the D. of Peter Thibou & Elizabeth his wife.

1736 Sep. 25 James Guilliem the s. of Peter Thibou and Elizabeth his wife.

1738 April 19 Elizabeth ye D. of Peter Thibou & Elizabeth his wife.

1739 Aug. 26 Catherine Sarah ye D. of Peter Thibou & Elizabeth his wife.

1740 July 13 Mary ye D. of Gabriel & Mary Thibou his wife.

1741 Feb. 16 Walter the s. of Isaac Thibou and Catherine his wife.

1741 June 18 Judith Dunn the D. of Peter Thibou and Judith his wife.

1742 Jan. 18 Peter Hensill the s. of Peter Thibou and Judith his wife.

1743 Nov. 1 Field the s. of Isaac Thibou and Mary his wife.

1743 Dec. 31 Elizabeth the D. of Gabriel Thibou and Mary his wife.

1744 Sep. 6 John the s. of Gabriel Thibou and Mary his wife.

1744 Nov. 28 Peregrine the s. of Peter Thibou and Judith his wife.

1744 Feb. 2 . . . . Thibou the D. of John Thibou and Mary his wife.

1746 April 27 Isaac the s. of Isaac Thibou and Catherine his wife.

1746 April 27 James the s. of Isaac Thibou and Catherine his wife.

1746 Aug. 22 Isaac the s. of Peter Thibou and Judith his wife.

1747 Jan. 15 Charlot the D. of Gabriel Thibou and Mary his wife.

1747 Jan. 25 Catherine the D. of John Thibou, Snr, and Mary his wife.

1748 Aug. 13 Peter the s. of Isaac Thibou and Catherine his wife.

1749 May 21 Lewis the s. of John Thibou, Snr, and Mary his wife.

1749 May 30 Margaret the D. of Peter Thibou and Judith his wife.

1749 June 18 Elizabeth the D. of John Thibou, Snr, and Mary his wife.

1751 June 8 William the S. of Isaac Thibou and Catharine his wife.

1751 June 9 William the S. of Gabril Thibou and Mary his wife.

1751 Oct. 11 Mary the D. of John Thibou, Senr, & Mary his wife.

1752 July 19 John Gallaway the S. of John Thibou & Eliza his wife.

1754 Aug. 27 Isaac the S. of Gabriel Thibou & Mary his wife; b. November 26th, 1753.

1754 Oct. 5 Jacob the S. of John Thibou, Senr, and Mary his wife; b. October 5th, 1754.

1754 Oct. 24 Rachel the D. of Isaac Thibou & Catharine his wife.

1755 Mar. 15 Peter Thibou the S. of John Thibou & Eliz. his wife.

1755 Dec. 3 John the S. of John Thibou, Senr, & Mary his wife.

1758 April 16 Gabriel the S. of John Thibou & Eliz. his wife; b. in Novemr 1757.

1761 Feb. 15 . . . . the D. of John Thibou and Elizabeth his wife.

1766 Jan. 10 Eliz. the d. of John Thibou and Mary his wife.

1773 June 26 Ann the D. of Walter Thibou & Jane his wife.

1773 Oct. 24 James the S. of James Thibou, Senr, by a Neg.

1837 Jan. 11 John Watkins s. of John George Watkins & Mary Octavia Thibou. St John's. Merchant.

Married.

1702 Aug. 6 Lewis Thibou & Mary Catharine Fraise.

1705 June 9 Jacob Thibou & Dorothy Blissard; by L.

1727 July 1 James Doig and Dorothy Thibou. L.

1728 April 2 Joseph Mathews and Sarah Thibou. L.

1730 July 26 Stephen Baker and Ann Thibou. L.

1736 Sep. 25 James Thibou and Mary Guillenne; by L. from Genl Mathew.

1736 Jan. 30 William Coe and Jane Thibou; by L. from Genl Mathew.

1737 April 11 Charles Read and Alice Thibou; by L. from Genl Mathew.

1737 Mar. 25 Gabriel Thibou & Mary Nanton; by L. from Genl Mathew.

1738 Feb. 1 The Revd Mr Thomas Wilson & Grace Thibou; by L. from Genl Mathew.
1739 May 1 Isaac Thibou & Catherine Field Thibou; by L. from Genl Mathew.
1739 June 2 George Morgan & Elizabeth Thibou; by L. from Genl Mathew.
1739 Feb. 3 Peter Thibou & Judith Henzell; by L. from Genl Mathew.
1740 Dec. 2 Nisbit Darby & Elizabeth Thibou.
1740 Jan. 15 Francis Hanson & Lydia Thibou. L.
1743 Oct. 27 John Thibou and Mary Wheland.
1744 April — Doctor John Richardson & Amelia Thibou.
1745 July 1 Francis Delap, Esqr, and Dorothy Thibou.
1746 Jan. 22 John Thibou and Mary Dixon.
1750 Aug. 22 John Thibou and Elizabeth Gallway.
1767 Nov. 14 James Thibou to Thomazin Start. L.
1778 July 18 Joseph Berry to Thomazin Thibou, Widow. L.
1779 Sep. 9 John Crooke to Elizabeth Thibou. L.
1780 Dec. 23 Thomas Scholar to Mary Thibou. L.
1789 Oct. 17 James Morgan to Catherine Thibou, Spinster. L.
1792 Nov. 22 Joseph James Farley to Anna Thibou, Spinster. L.
1794 Oct. 23 John Scholes to Rachel Thibou. L.
1809 Dec. 14 John Thibou to Jane Watkins.
1837 Dec. 5 James Byam Thibou, Bach., of this Parish, to Louisa Susannah Hill, Spinster, of this Parish. L.
1840 May 5 Henry Jarvis Thibou, Bach., of this Parish, & Mary Maria Hatley of this Parish. L.

Buried.

1707 Oct. 2 Margarett D. of Lewis Thibou & Mary Catherine his wife.
1713 Oct. 22 Jane Thibou.
1715 July 22 Ann D. of Lewis Thibou.
1716 Sep. 22 Jacob Thibou.
1720 May 27 Isaac Thibou, a child.
1722 Aug. 23 Dorothy D. of Isaac Thibou.
1723 July 7 Dorothy the D. of Isaac Thibou.
1724 Nov. 24 Mrs Charlotte Thibou.
1726 April 5 Mr Lewis Thibou.
1731 July 25 Henry Thibou.
1732 April 15 Mr Lewis Thibou.
1734 Aug. 16 Mary D. of Peter Thibou.
1735 Oct. 9 Mrs Mary Thibou.
1737 June 19 James Guillem ye S. of Peter Thibou.
1737 Jan. 3 Elizabeth ye wife of Isaac Thibou.
1739 May 20 Isaac Thibou of this Island.
1739 Nov. 5 Elizabeth ye wife of Peter Thibou.
1740 Jan. 31 James Field Thibou s. of Isaac Thibou.
1740 Dec. 20 Mary Thibou wife of James Thibou.
1741 Dec. 4 Jacob Thibou, Merchant.
1744 April 7 Field Thibou, a child.
1744 Mar. 6 Mary Thibou, a child.
1745 Dec. 13 John Thibou, a child of Gabl Thibous.
1746 April 10 Jacob Thibou s. of Isaac Thibou.
1746 May 4 Catherine Sarah Thibou.
1746 May 20 Peter Thibou s. of Peter Thibou.
1746 Sep. 1 Gabriel Thibou.
1746 Mar. 19 Mary Thibou widow of Gabl Thibou, decc'd.
1747 Aug. 14 .... Thibou, a child of Isaac Thibou.
1749 Jan. 31 .... Thibou wife of John Thibou.
1750 May 24 Peter Thibou s. of Isaac Thibou, from the country.
1750 Mar. 1 Elizabeth Thibou, a Child of Gabriel Thibous.
1753 Oct. 6 Peter Thibou.
1755 Mar. 2 John Gallwey Thibou, a Child.
1755 April 19 Peter Tyson Thibou, a Child.
1758 April 20 Gabriel Thibou (a Child).
1760 May 11 Judith Thibou.
1760 Oct. 1 John Thibou.
1761 July 21 Gabriel Thibou.
1762 June 28 Cathrine Thibou. C.
1764 Aug. 8 Rebecca Thibou. C.P.
1766 Feb. 23 Eliz. Thibou. Child.
1768 Sep. 15 Isaac Thibou, aged 80 years. Cr C.P.
1769 April 15 Rachel Thibou. C.P.
1769 Sep. 14 John Thibou. P.
1774 Mar. 28 Mary Thibou.
1774 June 15 James Thibou, Sen.
1775 Feb. 14 Rachel Thibou.
1775 Aug. 6 Peregrine Thibou.
1778 Dec. 6 William Thibou.
1780 Sep. 2 Catherine Thibou.
1780 Sep. 25 Elizabeth Thibou.
1783 May 25 William Thibou.
1786 Nov. 17 Mary Thibou.
1803 Jan. 5 James Thibou.
1837 Sep. 13 Margaret Thibou. St John's. 75.
1843 July 5 Mary Ann Thibou. St John's. 54.

PARISH REGISTER OF ST. PHILIP.

Married.

1741 Mar. 9 James Thibou to Rebeckah Parry; by L.

PARISH REGISTER OF ST. PAUL.

Married.

1749 May 31 Thomas Jarvis, Esqr, and Mrs Rachael Thibou; by L.
1835 Feb. 16 Charles Thwaites of St Philip's, widower, & Rebecca Thibou, Spr.; by L.

PARISH REGISTER OF ST. MARY.

Married.

1808 Jan. 28 Walter Thibou, Esqr, to Margaret Doig, Widow.

REGISTER OF WESTMINSTER ABBEY.

Buried.

1784 Dec. 6 Mrs Esther Blount;* died Nov. 28th, aged 59: in the West Cloister.
1806 July 9 George Blount, Esq.:† died the 1st, aged 81: in the West Cloister.
1847 Mar. 26 George-Lane Blount;‡ 84 Baker Street, Portman Square; died the 19th, aged 91: in the West Cloister.

* Wife of George Blount, Esq. (see his burial 9 July 1806), to whom married, at St James, Westminster, 3 Jan. 1753, as Esther Thibou, of that parish, widow. See her son's burial 26 Mch. 1847.

† See his wife's burial 6 Dec. 1784. In their marriage allegation at the Faculty Office, dated 1 Jan. 1753, he was described as of Henley-on-Thames, co. Oxford, a bachelor, aged twenty-eight. His will, as of Pall-Mall, St James, Westminster, Esq., dated 7 Mch. 1795, was proved 23 Dec. 1806 by his eldest son, George-Lane Blount, residuary legatee. To his youngest son, John-Burrell Blount, he gave all his investments in the five per cent. annuities. His only other bequests were fifty guineas to Mr Hugh Rowland, of St James's Palace, Gent., and to two servants. See his son's burial 26 Mch. 1847.

‡ Eldest son of George Blount, Esq. (see his burial 9 July 1806), by Esther his wife (see her burial 6 Dec. 1784). He was born 22 Sep., and baptized at St Margaret's, Westminster, 20 Oct. 1756. His will, dated 22 Aug. 1844, was proved 19 Apl. 1847 by his cousin John-Henry Belli, Esq., and James-Gascoigne Lynde, Esq., the former being his principal legatee. The Funeral Book says that he died in his ninety-first year, and adds: "This was the First Cloister Funeral that the corpse was taken into the Abbey, and the whole of the Funeral Service read over, previous to its interment.

(Colonel Chester's 'Registers of Westminster Abbey.')

ST. JOHN'S CHURCHYARD.

Here lyeth the Body
of PETER . . IBOU who Departed this
life the 5th of October 1753 Aged 44
years and 10 Months
Here lyeth also the Body of
JUDITH his Wife who was born
at the Glafs-houfes near Newcastle
upon Tyne and Departed this Life
the 10th of May 1760 Aged 40 Years
This stone was Erected to her memory
By JOHN DUNN.

On a ledger over altar-tomb:—

Arms: . . . . *a chevron, in base a badger, in chief a fleur-de-lis between two mullets* . . . .

Crest: *Three plumes over wreath and helmet.*

Here lies the Body of
MR ISAAC THIBOU
who departed this life
the 14 of September 1768
in the 79th Year of his Age.
His Daughter RACHELL is Alfo
Interred in the fame Vault who at the
tender Age of 14 Years and 6 Months
Finifhed Her courfe of Life
the 14 of April 1769.

(Six lines follow, by which it appears that her mother survived her.)

In 1872 Dr. Jessee W. Thibou, M.R.C.S.E., was Medical Officer of St. John's Parish, member of Assembly for St. John's Division, and owner of "Briggins" of 440 acres. The Hon. James B. Thibou was also member of Assembly for St. John's City, and owner of "St. Clare" in St. John's Parish of 384 acres.

Family of Thomas.

Edward Thomas of Antigua. Will dated 5 Oct. 1694. To my wife Patience Thomas a negro & a horse. All est. to my goddau. Ann White, dau. of my present wife. Mr Jas. Parke & Nath. Crump Ex'ors in Trust. Witnessed by John Kerr, Henry Walden, Thomas Morton. Sworn 22 and recorded 23 Sep. 1698. By the Deputy Governor Sep. ye 22, 1698, Captain John Ker and Mr. Thomas Morton, persons of good fame and respect, swore to the will before John Yeamans, Esq. Recorded 23 Sep. 1698. Recorded from attested copy Jan. 1756.

William Thomas, late of Antigua, now in London. Will dated 20 Aug. 1718, 4 Geo.; proved 28 Nov. 1718 (testator was late of Bushey Hall, co. Herts, but died in the parish of St. Christopher, London) by Hon. Colonel Edward Byam and Daniel McKenin, and by George Thomas the nephew by a brother residuary legatee. (227 Tenison.) To my wife Anne Thomas £500 & £400 a year so long as she remains my widow, only £100 a year if she marry, also all plate, household goods, chariot & horses. If she reside in Antigua I give her the use of 100 acres called "Barnes" adjoining Mr Francis Carlil's, & the use of 20 negros & 5 slaves called Benaba, Sipio, Beck, Deda, & little Dick. To my loving nephew Wm McKenin £1000. To my niece Jane McKenin £500 at 18 or in lieu 100,000 lbs. of Muscovado. To my grandniece Alice Carlile £500 at 18 or 100,000 lbs. To my grandnephew & godson Francis Carlile a silver punch bowl to cost £120 to be filled with punch & given to him at his house in Antigua on his attaining 21. To my niece Lydia Byam £1000 at 16. To my nephew Wm Thomas Martin £500 at 26 & £50 a year till then if he reside so long in Gt Britain. To my nephew Francis Byame £200 for an apprentice fee & £500 when he becomes free of his apprenticeship. To my nephew Saml Thomas £200 when free of his apprenticeship. To my nephew Edwd Thomas £200 to be paid him in Bristol when free of his apprenticeship. To my nephew Wm Thomas 50,000 lbs. To Anne Stuteville for her honest & faithful service £600 & £100 a year. My loving brother the Hon. Col. Edwd Byame & Dr Daniel McKenin Ex'ors, giving them £50 c. apiece. All residue of my personal & all my real estate to my nephew Geo. Thomas, his heirs male, with remainder to Wm Thomas, my nephew Wm McKenin, Mr Francis Byame, my sister Eliz. McKenin, the heirs male & female of Lidia Biam. Witnessed by Joseph Matcham, Samuel Clarke, Sarah Clarke, Thomas Tryon. Recorded at St. John's in Libro "Q."

William Thomas, jun. Will dated 1 May 1728. To my wife £100 c. & negros. All residue to my son Wm & his heirs, then to my brother Geo. Thomas. To my dau. Elizth Thomas £500 c. & if her brother die £500 c. more. My brother George, Wm Yeamans, Esq., Capt Wm Mackinnen, & Capt Wm Lavington Ex'ors. £500 to any child my wife may go with at my decease. Witnessed by Mary Lavington, Elizabeth MacKinen, Joshua Archibould. Before Edward Byam, Esq., were sworn Joshua Archibould, Elizabeth MacKinen, 16 Jan. 1728-9.

Edward Thomas, late of Antigua, now of Barbuda. Will dated 27 May 1749. If I die here to be buried by my nephew Geo. Thomas. All my estate to my wife Ann, my son Wm, & my dau. Elizth equally. Mr Robt Bannister of Parham, Mr John Addis of Barbuda, & Mr Edwd . . . . (Evanson) of Guana Ex'ors. Witnessed by William Horne, George Lucas, ... Belt. By William Mathew, Esq., was sworn George Lucas, Esq., 27 June 1749. Recorded 9 Feb. 1750.

Walter Sydserfe,* late of Antigua, now of Dean Street, St. Ann's, Westminster. Will dated 16 May 1759; proved 1 April 1760 by William Thomas, Esq.: power reserved to Richard Oliver the elder, Esq., William Garratt, and Walter Tulledeph, Esq. (170 Lynch.) £8000 among the younger children of my dau. Margt Thomas at 15. All residue to my dau. Margt, wife of Wm Thomas of Yapton, co. Sussex, Esq. Richd Oliver, senr, of Low Layton, Esq., my son-in-law Wm Thomas, Esq., & my brother-in-law Wm Garrat of Antigua, Gent., Ex'ors. Witnessed by John Hogarth, T. Rhodes, H. Leighthesier. Recorded also in the Registrar's Office, St. John's, 19 Nov. 1760.

Codicil dated 20 Jan. 1760. Walter Tulledeph of Dundee, Esq., also Ex'or. Witnessed by John Hogarth, Thomas Durham.

* He was born 1692, son of John Sydserf of Dunbar, merchant, who was third son of Alexander Sydserf of Ruchlaw, co. Haddington. He registered his arms 1740.

Philip Thomas of Antigua. Will dated 9 Dec. 1761. To my nephew Philip Thomas, s. of Geo. Thomas, dec^d, my gold headed cane & 5s., nothing further. To my neph. John Lindsay, jun^r, my case of pistols & my long gun. All residue to my wife Jehodan Thomas. She & her bro. Mr John Davis Ex'ors. Witnessed by Dugald Campbell, Kean Osborne. Before Governor George Thomas was sworn Kean Osborne 20 Jan. 1763. Recorded 10 Jan. 1764.

William Thomas of Antigua. Will dated 17 Aug. 1762. To my sister Eliz^th Thomas all my estate. My friends W^m McKinen, Wm Maxwell, Robt Christian, Saml Elliot, Esq^rs, & my sister, Ex'ors. Witnessed by Elizabeth Fraser, Lydia Charity Mackinen, Edward Horne. By Governor Thomas was sworn Edward Horne 23 Sep. 1762. Recorded 12 Nov. 1762.

Sir George Thomas, late Captain-General and Governor-in-Chief of H.M. Leeward Charibbee Islands, now of Yapton Place, and Ratton, co. Sussex, Bart. Will dated 29 April 1773; proved 20 Feb. 1775 by Sir William Thomas, Bart., Richard Oliver, Richard Neave, and Gibbs Crawfurd; power reserved to Arthur Freeman, Thomas Warner, Francis Farley, and George White, Esquires. (74 Alexander.) To my Ex'ors £4000 for my dau. Lydia White for life, then to her son Geo. White & his heirs. To my Ex'ors £4000 for my dau. Marg^t Freeman & her children. To my Ex'ors £6000 for my dau. Eliz. Thomas for life, then to my dau. Marg^t Freeman & her children. To each of my 3 daus. £100 for mourning. To my dear sister Eliz. Dunbar £50. To my grandson Geo. White £50 for a ring. I am empowered by the articles made on the marriage of my son Wm Thomas, Esq., with the dau. of Dr Walter Sydserfe to charge £1000 on the New North Sound estate, which I conveyed to him, & I give this sum to the daus. of my said son equally, but not to be raised till 1 year after my grandson Geo. come into the estate. My cook Roque Ferdinando to be free & to have £20 a year. All residue of my personal estate to my son Wm Thomas. All my manors & lands in England & all my plantations, slaves, etc., in Antigua to my son W^m for life, then to my son-in-law Arthur Freeman of Antigua, Esq., Tho. Warner, Esq., Attorney-Genl of the Leeward Islands, Francis Farley, now living in Antigua, Esq., Richd Oliver, Alderman of the City of London, Esq., Richd Neave of London, merch^t, & Gibbs Crawfurd of Saint Hill, co. Sussex, Esq., in trust for the following purposes:—My Ratton estate near Bourne which I lately purchased of Saml Durrant of Lewes to my grandson Inigo Freeman, son of my dau. Marg^t Freeman, & his heirs in tail male, & in default to her 2^d son Geo. Thomas Freeman, etc., then to my grandson Geo. White, son of my dau. Lydia White, & his heirs male. My lands in Yapton, Warburton, Climping, Slindon, Little Hampton, etc., for my grandson Geo. White & his heirs male, then to my grandson Inigo Freeman, then to Geo. Tho. Freeman. My Antiguan estates to Geo. Tho. Freeman & his heirs male, then to Inigo Freeman, then to Geo. White. In default of issue in any of the above cases all my estates to my 3 daus. equally. My reason for not making any provision in this my will for my grandson Geo. Thomas is on account of his marriage with a foreign woman. My grandsons who may be heirs to my estates to take my name & use my coat of arms. Power to grant leases for 21 years. To my cook Roque Ferdinando 15 gs., & a year's wages to my other servants. My son-in-law Arthur Freeman, Tho. Warner, Wm Thomas, Geo. White, Richd Oliver, Richd Neave, & Gibbs Crawfurd, Esq^res, Ex'ors, & give them 10 gs. each. Witnessed by George Tilsley, Charles Sawyer, Francis Ellis.

Codicil. Proved 13 Sep. 1777 by Sir William Thomas, Bart., the son, Richard Oliver, Richard Neave, and Gibbs Crawfurd, Esquires; power reserved to the others. (401 Collier.) Sir George Thomas, Bart. Heads of a codicil to my will which is in the hands of Gibbs Crawfurd, Esq. The land purchased of the heirs of Pellett to go to the heirs of my Ratton estate. In case of the death of my son Wm Thomas before me my grandsons Geo. White & Inigo Freeman to be my residuary legatees, & in case of nonage of the latter my Ex'ors to act in trust for him. To my granddau. Lydia Frances Freeman who has been brought up in my house & maintained by me £1000 at 20. On 12 April 1776 were sworn William Hunter of Yapton, co. Sussex, Gent., & George Dunbar of St. George, Bloomsbury, Esq.; testator was of St. George, Hanover Square, and died Dec. 1774.

Sir William Thomas of New Norfolk Street, St. George, Hanover Square, Bart. Will dated 26 June 1777; proved 2 Jan. 1778 by William Roe, and Michael Lovell, Esquires; power reserved to Thomas Oliver, Arthur Freeman, Francis Farley, and Langford Lovell, Esquires. (11 Hay.) £4000 each to my 2 daus. Mary & Lydia Thomas. To my grandson Geo. Lyons £1000. To my grandson Wm Roe £1000. To Mrs Frances Giles of 52 Marg^t Str., Cavendish Sq., £500 & confirm the settlement made to her by a clause in the marriage settlements with my late wife Marg^t. I charge my North Sound estate in Antigua with £4000 for my 3 daus. Susannah Roe, Mary Thomas, & Lydia Thomas. To Mr Wm Hunter 100 gs. £12 each to my servant Allan Mason & his wife Mary. £10 each to 5 servants & 5 gs. apiece to 2 others. To Mrs Frances Williams, late Thomas, now wife of John Mongroe Williams, 1s. for her undutiful behaviour. All my plate, china, & furniture (except that at Ratton which I give to my nephew Inigo Freeman), books, carriages, & horses to be sold. All residue to my only son Geo. Thomas & his heirs male. My son-in-law Wm Roe, Tho. Oliver, & Michael Lovell, merch^ts in London, & Arthur Freeman, Esq., Francis Farley & Langford Lovell, Esq^rs, of Antigua, Ex'ors. To be buried at Yapton near my late wife. On 29 Dec. 1777 was sworn William Roe of St. Mary le bonne, Esq. Testator died at Bath. On 30 Dec. 1777 was sworn Thomas Dawson of Walnut Tree Walk, St. Mary, Lambeth, Gent., and Hugh Wilson of Hart Street in St. Olave, Hart Street, Gent.

Close Roll, 34 Geo. II., Part 11, Nos. 10 and 11.

Indenture made the 17th June 1760 between William Thomas of Yapton, co. Sussex, Esq., and Margaret his wife (only daughter, heir-at-law, and devisee named in the will of Walter Sydeserfe, formerly of Antigua, but late of Dean Street in the parish of St. Ann, Westminster, Esq., deceased), of the one part, and Richard Oliver the younger of London, merchant (son-in-law of Richard Oliver of Low Layton, Essex, Esq.), of the other part, witnesseth that in consideration of 5s. William Thomas and Margaret his wife grant to Richard Oliver the younger all that plantation late the estate of Walter Sydeserfe containing 450 acres in the parish of St. John's and division of Five Islands, bounded E. with the Flushes and the ponds called the Salt Ponds, late of Walter Sydeserfe, and part of Five Island Harbour, W. with the plantation belonging to the Hon. George Thomas, Esq., Captain-General and Commander-in-Chief, and the plantation now or late belonging to Duncan Grant, Esq., N. with the plantation late of James Gamble, deceased, and now of Edward Otto-Bayer, Esq., and S. with the sea, and also all that other plantation of Walter Sydeserfe containing 120 acres in the parish of St. Philip and division of Belfast, bounded E. with the plantation now or late belonging to William Garratt, Esq., W. with the plantations late of John Jefferson, and also another plantation late belonging to Joseph and Benjamin Wickham, N. with the plantation late belonging to John Myers [Mayer] and another plantation late of Benjamin Hull, and S. with the plantations late of Philip Lyddit [Ledeat] and now of Robert Gray, and also all negros and slaves and horses, asses, mules, and cattle for one whole year, and William Thomas and Margaret his wife appoint Patrick Grant, William Garratt, and William Thomas, all of Antigua, Esquires, their Attorneys. Henry Wilmot, John Lancaster, witnesses.

No. 10.

Indenture tripartite made the 18th June 1760 between William Thomas and Margaret his wife, of the 1st part, Richard Oliver the younger, of the 2nd part, and Patrick Grant of Antigua, M.D., of the 3rd part, witnesseth that for docking and barring all estates tail and remainders, etc., and in consideration of 5s. paid to William and Margaret Thomas by Richard Oliver, they grant to him in his actual possession being all those plantations, etc. (as in No. 11), in trust to the use of Patrick Grant for 99 years, and subject thereto to the use of William Thomas and his assigns for life, and after his death to Margaret Thomas for life, and at her death, and charged as she shall appoint, to George Thomas, son of William and Margaret, and to preserve the contingent remainders to his sons, and for default to all daughters of William and Margaret Thomas equally as tenants in common and to their heirs, and if but one to her and her heirs, and failing all to the right heirs of Margaret Thomas for ever ; and as to the 99 years to Patrick Grant in trust yearly during the life of William Thomas and Margaret to raise £600 a year from the rents and pay it as Margaret Thomas shall appoint, and failing her appointment into her own proper hands.

Close Roll, 42 Geo. III., Part 3, Nos. 17 and 18.

Indenture made the 1st Feb. 1802 between Sir George Thomas of Dale Park, co. Sussex, Bart., and Dame Sophia his wife and William Lewis George Thomas his son and heir apparent, of the one part, and Andrew Edwards of Antigua, Esq., of the other part, witnesseth that in consideration of 5s. Sir George Thomas, Dame Sophia, and William Lewis George Thomas convey to Andrew Edwards all that plantation of 286 acres 3 roods and 28 perches in the parish of St. Philip and division of Belfast in Antigua, bounded as to 266 acres 2 roods and 37 perches, part thereof, E. by the lands of John Mayor, but now of Walter Colquhoun, N. by the lands of the said John Mayor and now of Walter Colquhoun and the lands heretofore of Anthony Garratt, deceased, but now of John Taylor, and the lands late of Robert Jeaffreson, but now of John Taylor, and S. with the lands heretofore of Joseph Wickham, deceased, but now of John Yeates, and the lands late of John Gray, deceased ; and as to 28 acres and 31 perches, other part thereof, E., W., and S. by the lands of John Mayor, but now of Walter Colquhoun, and N. with land late of Christopher Bethell, deceased, but now of . . . . Codrington, and the land late of James Grant, but now of the said John Taylor, together with the dwelling house and all those 142 negros, mulattos, and other slaves (names given), and also 1 bull, 14 oxen, 4 steers, 1 heifer, 4 bull and 3 cow calves, 7 cows, 12 mules, and 4 horned cattle, and also all that parcel of land containing 60 acres in the said parish and division, bounded E. by country lands, W. by country lands and the lands late of John Ledeatt, deceased, N. by country lands and lands late of Thomas Montgomery, deceased, and S. by country lands and the sea, for one whole year, and they constitute the Hon. Thomas Norbury Kerby and John Burke of Antigua, Esq., their Attorneys. Robert Blake, Robert Sandham, Richard Wilkins of Dale Park, Gent., George Mant, Attorney-at-Law, Arundel, Sussex, Charles Beere, 5 Fetter Lane, John Call Manfield, Dorchester, Dorset, Gent., witnesses.

No. 17.

Indenture made the 2nd Feb. 1802 between Sir George Thomas and Dame Sophia his wife, of the 1st part, William Lewis George Thomas, only son and heir apparent, of the 2nd part, Thomas Edwards of Antigua, Esq., of the 3rd part, and Andrew Edwards of Antigua, Esq., of the 4th part. Whereas by articles of agreement made at the town of St. John in Antigua, dated the 19th Jan. 1801, between Sir George Thomas and William Lewis George Thomas, by the Hon. Thomas Norbury Kerby their Attorney, of the one part, and Thomas Edwards, of the other part, Sir George Thomas and his son agree to sell to Thomas Edwards and his heirs in fee simple a plantation therein described for the price of £22,000, to be paid as follows : £2000 on the 20th Jan., on which day possession should be given, and £6000 on the 1st August then next ensuing, and the residue as therein mentioned, in trust for 5000 years to Thomas Norbury Kerby (?) to secure the payment ; and whereas Thomas Edwards did pay the £2000 and entered upon the plantation and has since paid the £6000. Now this Indenture witnesseth that in consideration of the £2000, and the £6000, and the term of 5000 years, and of 20s. each, Sir George Thomas and William Lewis George Thomas grant to Andrew Edwards in his actual possession being all that plantation (as in No. 18) in trust for Thomas Edwards and his heirs for ever.

Close Roll, 43 Geo. III., Part 8, No. 3.

Indenture made the 29th July 1803 between William Lewis George Thomas (only son and heir apparent of Sir George Thomas of Dale Park, co. Sussex, Bart.), and Elizabeth Lucretia Thomas his wife, of the 1st part, Thomas Edwards of Antigua, Esq., of the 2nd part, and Andrew Edwards of Antigua, Esq., of the 3rd part. Whereas at the time of making the aforesaid Indentures of 1 and 2 Feb. 1802 (recited), William Lewis George Thomas was married, for more surely conveying the said plantation and slaves, etc., Elizabeth Lucretia Thomas his wife might claim therein, Thomas Edwards has requested them to convey. Now this Indenture witnesseth that in pursuance of the agreement and in consideration of 20s. William Lewis George Thomas and Elizabeth Lucretia Thomas his wife grant to Andrew Edwards all their interest in the said plantation and slaves, and lastly they appoint the Hon. Thomas Norbury Kerby, Esq., and John Burke, Esq., both of Antigua, their Attorneys.

Close Roll, 55 Geo. III., Part 9, Nos. 13 and 14.

Indenture made the 8th June 1815 between Sir William Lewis George Thomas of Dale Park, Sussex, Bart., of the one part, and Robert Blake of Essex Street, Strand, Gent., of the other part, witnesseth that in consideration of 5s. Sir William Lewis George Thomas grants and confirms to Robert Blake all that plantation in the division of Old North Sound, sometime called Thomas's Hill, and now known by the name of Colonel Thomas's North Sound Plantation, and also the mansion house thereon, as comprised and conveyed in and by Indentures made the 2nd and 3rd April 1766, the release being of six parts between George Thomas, Esq., of the 1st part, William Thomas his eldest son and heir apparent, of the 2nd part, Walter Tullideph, Esq., of the 3rd part, Stephen Blizard, Esq., of the 4th part, Patrick Grant, Esq., of the 5th part, and Samuel Martin, Thomas Warner, and William Warner, Esquires, of the 6th part, save and except such parts as in 1801 were sold by Sir George Thomas, Bart., deceased, and Sir William Lewis George Thomas to Thomas Edwards, then of Antigua, Esq., and all negros and other slaves, horses, mules, cows, oxen, sheep, cattle, and stock whatsoever for one whole year. Richard White, Essex Street, John Goble Blake, Essex Street, witnesses.

No. 13.

Indenture made the 9th June 1815 between Sir William Lewis George Thomas, Dame Elizabeth Lucretia his wife, of the one part, and Robert Blake, of the other part. Whereas by Indentures made the 2nd and 3rd April 1766 (as in No. 14) all that plantation together with the mansion house and slaves (as in No. 14) were settled to the use of George Thomas the elder and his assigns for life, and to the use of Samuel Martin and Thomas and William Warner during his life in trust to support the contingent remainders, to the use of Stephen Blizard for 99 years, to the use of William Thomas for life and to preserve the contingent remainders, to the use of Patrick Grant for 100 years, to the use of George Thomas, afterwards Sir George Thomas (son of William Thomas by Margaret Thomas his late wife), for life, to the use of Samuel Martin and Thomas and William Warner to support the contingent remainders to the first and other sons of Sir George Thomas, the trusts of 99 and 100 years are either satisfied or become incapable of taking effect; and whereas Sir William Lewis George Thomas is the only son of Sir George Thomas, and he and Dame Elizabeth Lucretia his wife are desirous of barring the estate tail and of settling the plantation, etc., freed from it and from the dower of Dame Elizabeth Lucretia, to the uses to be expressed. Now this Indenture witnesseth that in consideration of 10s. Sir William Lewis George Thomas and Dame Elizabeth Lucretia his wife grant to Robert Blake in his actual possession being all that plantation (as in No. 14) in trust for such persons as Sir William Lewis George Thomas shall appoint, and so far as his appointment shall not extend to the use of him and his assigns for life, and after his death to his heirs, and lastly Sir William Lewis George Thomas and Dame Elizabeth Lucretia constitute [*blank*] of Antigua their Attorneys.

Close Roll, 6 Geo. IV., Part 9, Nos. 17 and 18.

Indenture made the 1st March 1825 between Sir William Lewis George Thomas of Cowes, Isle of Wight, Bart. (only son of Sir George Thomas, late of Dale Park, Sussex, Bart., deceased, who was the only son of Sir William Thomas, formerly of Yapton, Sussex, Bart., deceased), and Dame Elizabeth Lucretia his wife, of the 1st part, Dame Sophia Thomas of Madehurst Lodge, Sussex (widow of Sir George Thomas, deceased), of the 2nd part, and Richard White of Essex Street, Strand, Gent., of the 3rd part. Whereas by virtue of Indentures made the 17th and 18th June 1760 (see *ante*): and whereas Sir William Thomas and Margaret his wife both died before 1780, and Margaret did not in any way exercise her power; and whereas by an Indenture made the 18th June 1781 between Sir George Thomas, of the one part, and John Montagu and the said Dame Sophia Thomas, then Sophia Montagu, spinster, of the other part, being the settlement previous to and in consideration of a marriage between Sir George Thomas and Sophia Montagu, which was shortly after solemnized, it was witnessed that in consideration of the marriage Sir George Thomas by virtue of the power contained in the said recited Indenture of the 18th June 1760 did appoint the said plantation to the use of Dame Sophia for life, and in bar of dower, but Dame Sophia might accept the yearly sum of £200 in commutation of the rents; and whereas Sir George Thomas departed this life in May 1815 leaving Sir William Lewis George Thomas only son and heir-at-law and Dame Sophia him surviving; and whereas Sir William Lewis George Thomas and Dame Elizabeth Lucretia his wife are desirous of barring the estate tail created in part by the said recited Indenture of Settlement, and of conveying the plantation, etc., freed from all right and title of dower of Dame Elizabeth Lucretia, to Richard White in trust, and to enable Sir William Lewis George Thomas to make the said conveyance Dame Sophia Thomas hath agreed to join. Now this Indenture witnesseth that for barring and destroying the estate tail of Sir William Lewis George Thomas and all other estates tail, and the right or title of dower of Dame Elizabeth Lucretia, and in consideration of 10s., Sir William Lewis George Thomas and Elizabeth Lucretia his wife and Dame Sophia Thomas grant to Richard White all that plantation containing 450 acres in the parish of St. John and division of Five Islands, bounded E. with the flushes and lands called the Salt Ponds and part of Five Island Harbour, W. with lands formerly belonging to Sir George Thomas, great-grandfather of Sir William Lewis George Thomas, and certain other land belonging to Duncan Grant, Esq., N. with the plantations formerly of James Gambell, deceased, and afterwards of Edward Otto-Baijer, Esq., and S. with the sea, and all other lands, etc., comprised in the said settlement and all negros in trust to reconvey, and they appoint, etc., John Billinghurst of Antigua and [*blank*] their Attorneys. W. P. Shuckburgh, 14 Essex Street, clerk to Messrs. Blake, White, Ainge, and Blake, John Goater, waiter, George Inn, Winchester, witnesses.

No. 17.

Indenture made the 2nd March 1825 between Richard White, of the 1st part, Dame Sophia Thomas, of the 2nd part, Sir William Lewis George Thomas, of the 3rd part, and John Goble Blake of Essex Street, Strand, Gent., of the 4th part, witnesseth that in performance of the trust reposed in him Richard White grants and conveys to John Goble Blake all that plantation, etc. (as in No. 18), in trust for Sir William Lewis George Thomas and his heirs and assigns for ever.

Circa 1667. Roger Thomas, 13 acres at Willoughby Bay bought of Mary Townsend ye daughter of James Townsend, deceased, and 13 acres as administrator to his partner George Williams, deceased, who bought it of said Mary Townsend 8 July 1665. (Book of Claims.)

1667, March 24. Lieut. William Thomas, 100 acres at Old North Sound by warrant; surveyed 4 Aug. 1668.

1668. Lieut. William Thomas, patent for 122½ acres at Old North Sound.

1670, March 7. Deposition of William Thomas, aged about 30.

William Thomas was appointed by Commission of H.M. Customs, dated 10 Jan. 1673, Collector of all rates as per Act of Parliament, 25 Charles II., an Act for the Encouragment of the Eastland and Greenland trades and for the better securing the Plantation, trade, etc., and promises to remit all the said rates to Richard Mounting, Esq., H.M. Cashier-General of the Customs and Stores, to Guy Molesworth, Esq., H.M. Storehouse-Keeper in the port of London. 31 July 1674.

1674. Roger Thomas, 10 acres bought of Colonel Nathaniel Clarke; surveyed 10 July.

1675, April 11. Captain William Thomas, 25 acres granted by Governor Warner, also "Bird," now called George Island; surveyed 12 June. Delivered to him according to ye ancient custom of England with turff and twig.

1677, March 27. Edward Thomas, 50 acres by Governor Warner; surveyed Aug.

1678, Nov. 4. Edward Thomas, 180 acres by Colonel James Vaughan; surveyed April 1680.

1679, Nov. 15. Edward Thomas and Elizabeth his wife, widow of Thomas Reynolds, sell 25 acres to William Coomes, planter, and the latter sells 20 acres to Mr. John Brimingham.

1680. By Indenture dated 6 Oct. Anna Thomas, wife of Captain William Thomas, gives to her husband her plantation and negros in North Sound Division.

Pedigree of Thomas.

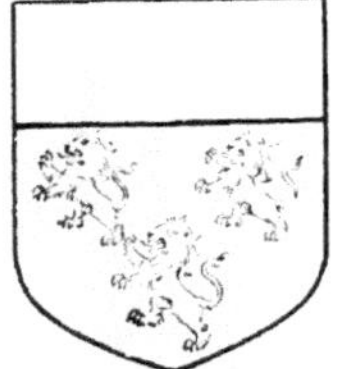

Arms.—*Argent, three lions rampant gules, a chief azure.*
Crest.—*A demi-lion rampant gules.*
Motto.—*Honesty is the best policy.*

WILLIAM THOMAS of Antigua, Esq., granted 100 acres in 1667; æt. 30 in 1670; Lieut. and Member of Council 1671; Captain 1672; Collector of Customs 1673; Major 1682; living 1690. = Lydia, dau. of . . . . Tomlinson; mar. at St. Augustine's, Bristol.

William Thomas of Antigua, Esq., Member of Assembly 1708, later Member of Council. Will dated 20 Aug. and proved 28 Nov. 1718 (227 Tenison), of Bushey Hall, co. Herts, but at St. Christopher's, London, deceased. = Ann . . . . conveyed her estate to her husband in 1680; living 1718. s.p.

Colonel George Thomas, Member of Assembly for Five Islands 1700, and for Bermudian Valley 1706; died 13 and bur. 14 May 1707 at St. John's. = Sarah, only dau. and heir of Joseph Winthrop (2nd son of Governor Samuel Winthrop of Antigua); he died 1679.

Sir George Thomas, 1st Bart., of Antigua, later of Yapton and Ratton, co. Sussex, heir to his uncle William 1718; Governor of Pennsylvania 1738; Governor of Leeward Islands 1752; created a Baronet 1766; died 31 Dec. 1773, æt. 79, at Upper Brook Street; bur. and M.I. at Willingdon, co. Sussex. Will dated 29 April 1773; proved 28 Feb. 1775. (74 Alexander.) = Elizabeth, dau. of Captain John King; mar. 18 April 1717 at St. Philip's; died 24 and bur. 25 Sep. 1763, æt. 61, and M.I. on the family estate at Old North Sound.

Sir William Thomas, 2nd Bart., of Yapton Place, near Bognor, M.P.; High Sheriff of Sussex 1767; owned the "New North Sound" estate; died 19 Dec. at Bath, bur. 30 Dec. 1777, æt. 56, and M.I. at Yapton. Will dated 26 June 1777; proved 2 Jan. 1778. (41 Hay.) = Margaret, only child and heir of Dr. Walter Sydserfe; bapt. 19 Jan. 1724 at St. John's; mar. 1742-3 in the Chapel of Somerset House; died 4 and bur. 12 Dec. 1763, æt. 39, and M.I. at Yapton.

George Thomas, died a bachelor.

Elizabeth Thomas, bapt. 17 Jan. 1721 at St. John's; died a spinster.

Jane Louisa, dau. of Alexander Sales, a foreigner; mar. at Geneva. 1st wife. = Sir George Thomas, 3rd Bart., disinherited by his grandfather; M.P. for Arundel; inherited the estate at North Sound; some time of Dale Park; sold his plantation of 286 acres in 1802 for £22,000 to Thomas Edwards; died 6 May 1815; bur. at Madehurst. = Sophia, dau. of Admiral Montagu; mar. settlement dated 18 June 1781; living 1825. 2nd wife. s.p.

Sir William Lewis George Thomas, 4th Bart., of Dale Park in Madehurst, born *c.* 1768; died 24 Aug. 1850. = Elizabeth Lucretia, dau. of Richard Welsh, Esq.; died 21 Jan. 1848.

George Thomas, Midshipman R.N., died v.p. 11 July 1821, æt. 17, at Trincomalee.

Thomasine, dau. of Captain Henry Haynes, R.N.; mar. 1843; died 6 March 1863. 1st wife. = Sir William Sidney Thomas, 5th Bart., born 1807 at Whippingham, Isle of Wight; entered the Navy 1820; Lieut. 1828; Commander 1842; Captain retired list 1860; died 27 April 1867, æt. 59, at Great Malvern. = Fanny Louisa, youngest dau. of John Coulson of Clifton Wood, co. Gloucester, Esq.; mar. 14 Aug. 1856; died 9 Nov. 1870. 2nd wife. s.p.

Sir George Sidney Meade Thomas, 6th Bart., born 12 Feb. 1847; some time of Caius College, Cambridge; of the Nimrod and New Travellers' Clubs 1895. = Edith Margaret, elder dau. of Morgan Hugh Foster, Esq., C.B., of Brickhill, co. Beds; mar. 9 May 1874 at Constantinople; living at Southsea 1895.

Montagu Sidney Thomas, born 23 Feb. and died 22 April 1880.

George Alan Thomas, born 14 June 1881 at Pera.

Isabel Edith Thomasine Thomas, living 1895.

Ruby Grace Thomas, living 1895.

1680, Dec. 8. Mathew Hunter and Mary his wife sell 30 acres to Major William Thomas for 6000 lbs. of sugar.

1681, May 9. Arundell Thomas conveys land to Dennis Kieph.

1681, Oct. 24. Major William Thomas, Gent., patent for 25 acres and 12½ mens land and four proportions and Bird Island granted by Sir W. Stapleton.

1684, Feb. 18. Edward Thomas, patent for 180 acres.

1684, Feb. 18. Edward Thomas, planter, patent for 50 acres granted by Sir W. Stapleton.

1703, June 11. William Thomas, Esq., of Antigua. Letter of attorney to my brother George Thomas of Antigua, Gent., and my beloved friends Daniel Mackinen of Antigua, Gent., Edward Byam of Antigua, Esq., and Robert Oliver of Antigua, Gent.

No. 164. Private. An Act for the better securing and confirming the Title of George Thomas, Nephew and Heir to William Thomas, late of the said Island, Esquire, deceased, to certain Lands and Negroes purchased of John Barnes, Gentleman, by the said William Thomas. Dated 13 July 1719.

1731, June 25. Dr. Walter Sydserfe's 32 acres at Belfast surveyed.

1738. Letter from Colonel George Thomas of Antigua, dated 12 May, petitioning against his removal from the Council board by Governor Mathew, on account of his having been appointed Governor of Pennsylvania. He arrived at Antigua last Feb. Memorandum annexed about Major George Thomas who had been presented to the King by Lord Carteret, and had applied to be made a Member of Council at the next vacancy. (America and West Indies, No. 451.)

Elizabeth Thomas, mar. Daniel Mackinen, Surgeon; he died 26 and was bur. 27 March 1719-20, æt. 62, and M.I. at St. John's; she was living his widow in 1728.

Lydia Thomas, mar. 1st, 28 Jan. 1691, at St. John's, Samuel Martin, Esq., and 2ndly in 1703, at ditto, Governor Edward Byam. Her will dated 6 Oct. 1744, then of Harding, co. Herts; proved 28 March 1747. (64 Potter.)

Samuel Thomas, living 1718.

Edward Thomas, an apprentice at Bristol 1718.

Elizabeth Thomas, mar. 7 May 1716, at St. John's, William Dunbar; he died 1749; she was living his widow 1773.

William Thomas. Will dated 1 May 1728; sworn 16 Jan. 1728-9. ═ . . . . dau. of John Yeamans; living 1728.

Lydia Thomas, mar. 25 Oct. 1744, at St. George's, John White of Montserrat, Esq.; he was later of Chichester, and died 6 and was bur. 12 Feb. 1776, æt. 75, and M.I. at Yapton; she died 14 and bur. 22 Aug. 1794, æt. 76, and M.I. at Yapton. (For their issue see the PEDIGREE OF WHITE.)

Margaret Thomas, mar. c. 1765, at Antigua, Arthur Freeman, Esq.; he died 30 Jan. 1780, æt. 56; bur. and M.I. at Willington; she died 1 Sep. 1797, æt. 51; bur. and M.I. at ditto. (For their issue see PEDIGREE OF FREEMAN.)

William Thomas, died 30 Aug. 1762, æt. 35. M.I. in Willoughby Bay Churchyard. Will dated 17 Aug. and sworn 23 Sep. 1762. Recorded at St. John's.

Elizabeth Thomas (? mar. 25 June 1774, at St. Paul's, Francis Farley, Esq.); sole heir to her brother 1762.

Elizabeth Thomas, mar. Col. Andrew Lyon of Edinburgh.

Susannah Thomas, mar. 1775 William Roe of London, Esq., Chairman of Board of Customs; she died 1822.

Mary Thomas, mar. General Popham.

Lydia Thomas, mar. 17 Dec. 1783 Alexander Adair of Flexton Hall, co. Suffolk.

Ann Thomas, mar. 17 Nov. 1771 Stephen Popham of Lincoln's Inn Fields.

Frances Thomas, mar. July 1777 John M. Williams of Chichester, Esq.; she died 1829.

Montagu Thomas, Captain R.N., died 1895 at Weymouth. ═ Isabella, youngest dau. of Rev. John Bowie of Salisbury; mar. 22 July 1845.

Helen Thomas, mar. 8 May 1830 Captain James Brymer.

Sophia Thomas, died 25 Feb. 1846.

Louisa Leonora Thomas, mar. 1841, at Weymouth, ... Browne of 41st Regiment, later a Colonel.

Elizabeth Thomas, living 1886.

Frederick Louis Charles Thomas of 1st Battalion Royal Dublin Fusiliers, born 27 Feb. 1853; matriculated from Brasenose College, Oxford, 27 Jan. 1872, æt. 18. ═ Eveline M., dau. of Charles Shand of Colombo, Esq.; mar. 22 Sep. 1881.

Lucy Elizabeth Thomas, mar. 14 Sep. 1869 Lieut.-Colonel Arthur James Shuldham, late 108th Regiment.

Isabella Montagu Jane Thomas.

1743, Sep. 29. Dr. Walter Sydserfe pays £32 an acre for Witts lands at Belfast and £25 an acre for Nicholas Hall's lands, all escheated.

1746. Dr. Mathew Sydserfe named in Thomas Kerby's will.

1753, Feb. 7. The draught commission for George Thomas, Esq., as Governor of the Leeward Islands, was read at St. James's. (B. T., vol. 103.)

1774, Nov. 17. Stephen Popham, Esq; of Lincoln's-inn-fields, to Miss Anna Thomas, grand-daughter of Sir Geo. Thomas, Bart. ('Gent. Mag.,' p. 541.)

1775. An account of the character of Sir Geo. Thomas, Bart. (*Ibid.*, p. 421.)

1777, July. John Williams, Esq. of Bagshot-place near Farnham, in Surry, to Miss Thomas, daughter of Sir William Thomas, Bart., of Yapton-place, Sussex. (*Ibid.*, p. 351.)

1777, Dec. 26. Sir Wm. Thomas, Bart. of Yapton-place, Sussex. (*Ibid.*, 1778, p. 45.)

1783, Dec. 17. Alex. Adair, esq: to Miss Lydia Thomas, dau. of the late Sir Wm. Thomas, bart. (*Ibid.*, p. 1064.)

1793, Feb. 11. George Thomas writes to the Lordships expressing a hope that he may be appointed Governor.

1804. James Thomas, Esq., has been appointed to the Council of St. Kitts, and is of a very old family there; his elder brother,* President of St. Kitts, acted as Commander-in-Chief *pro tem.* (Colonial Correspondence, vol. 41.)

1815, May 6. Sir George Thomas, bart. of Dale Park, Sussex. He succeeded his father Sir William, Dec. 28, 1775; married, first, at Geneva, Mad. Scales, of Pregny le Tour; secondly, Miss Montague, by whom he has one son, William-Lewis-George, who married Miss Welch, by whom he had one daughter, Sophia. ('Gent. Mag.,' p. 567.)

1821, May 6. At Brighton, Susanna, wife of William Roe, and daughter of the late Sir William Thomas, bart. (*Ibid.*, p. 570.)

1821, July 11. At Trincomalee, in his 18th year, Mr. Thomas, Midshipman of the Leander, eldest son of Sir Geo. Thomas, bt. (*Ibid.*, p. 185.)

1841, May 21. At Weymouth, Melville-Gore-Beckwith Browne, esq. 41st regt. son of Col. Melville Browne, to Louisa-Leonora, youngest dau. of Sir George Thomas, Bart. (*Ibid.*, p. 199.)

1843, June 29. At Clifton, W. S. Thomas, Comm. R.N. eldest son of Sir George Thomas, Bart. to Thomasine-Oliver, only dau. of the late Capt. Henry Haynes, R.N. (*Ibid.*, p. 200.)

1867, April 27. At Great Malvern, aged 59, Sir William Sidney Thomas, Bart. The deceased was the eldest son of the late Sir William Lewis George Thomas, Bart., of Yapton, Sussex, by Elizabeth, daughter of R. Welsh, Esq., and was born at Whippingham, Isle of Wight, in 1807. He entered the Navy in 1820, passed his examination in 1826, and in 1828 he was made lieutenant on board the Asia, flag-ship of Sir Pulteney Malcolm in the Mediterranean, where in the same year he was transferred to the Revenge. He returned to England about the close of 1830; but subsequently proceeded to the East Indies, where, after serving for a time on board the Melville and Alligator, he was appointed to the command of the Algerine. In 1840 he was transferred to the command of the Ferret, on the coast of Africa, and in the following year, to that of the Royal George yacht. He was advanced to the rank of commander in 1842, and became a captain on the Retired List in 1860. He succeeded to the title, as 5th baronet, on the death of his father in 1850. The late baronet was twice married: first, in 1843, to Thomasine, daughter of the late Capt. Henry Haynes, R.N. (she died in 1853); and secondly, in 1856, to Fanny Louisa, youngest daughter of the late John Coulson, Esq., of Clifton Wood, co. Gloucester. He has left issue by his first wife two sons and two daughters. His eldest son, George Sidney Meade, who succeeds to the title, was born in 1847. (*Ibid.*, p. 814.)

* President Thomas died 15 April 1797.

HADDINGTON HEIR SERVICES.

('Genealogist,' Jan. 1895.)

Name of heir.	Name of ancestor and lands.
1560, March 10, John Sydserf	father Patrick Sydserf of that Ilk—lands of Nether Sydserf.
1561, Jan. 26, Patrick Sydserf	brother Archebald Sydserf of Ruchelaw—lands of Ruchelaw.
1569, Dec. 5, John Sydserf of that Ilk	father's sister Agnes Sydserf.

PARISH REGISTER OF ST. JOHN.

Baptized.

17 (? 1701)		George the s. of George Thomas & Elizabeth his wife.
170 .	Dec. 18	Samuel the s. of George Thomas & Elizabeth his wife.
17 . .	. . . . .	Elizabeth d. of George Thomas & Elizabeth his wife.
1707	July 29	Lydia D. of George Thomas & Elizabeth his wife.
1721	Jan. 17	Elizabeth D. of . . . . Thomas & Eliz^th his wife.
1724	Jan. 19	Margaret the d. of Walter Sydserfe and Margaret his wife.
1727	Dec. 12	John the s. of Walter Sydserfe and Margaret his wife.
1736	Aug. 3	David Sweegle and Daniel the sons of Mathew Thomas & Cornelia his wife.
1738	April 23	David Sweegle ye s. of Mathew Thomas & Cornelia his wife.
1738	Feb. 18	John ye s. of William Thomas & Mary his wife.
1741	Nov. 15	James Griggs the s. of William Thomas & Mary his wife.
1742	Aug. 22	Elizabeth the D. of William Thomas & Mary his wife.
1742	Aug. 22	Mary the D. of William Thomas & Mary his wife.
1743	Jan. 1	William the s. of Philip Thomas and Jehojadan his wife.
1744	April 1	William the s. of William Thomas and Mary his wife.
1766	July 21	Edward the S. of Wm Thomas, Ann his wife.
1770	May 14	Archibald the S. of Bridgwater Thomas and Ann his wife.
1770	May 14	Elizabeth Dupee the D. of Bridgwater Thomas and Ann his wife.
1772	Sep. 23	Alice Bayley Kirwan the D. of Wm Bridgewater Thomas and Elizabeth his wife.

Married.

1691	Jan. 28	Samuel Martin, Esqr, and Lydia D. of William Thomas, Esqr, & Lidia his wife.
1691	Jan. 31	Daniel Sones and Katheren Thomas.
1708	9ber 17	John Luxford & Margarett Thomas.
1710	June 28	William Thoruton & Elizabeth Thomass.
1716	May 7	William Dunbar and Eliz^a Thomas. L.
1734	Aug. 10	William Thomas and Mary Griggs. L.

1771 Feb. 9 Edward Tyley to Lucy Thomas. L.
1792 Nov. 5 Henry Pickering (Ens[n] 60th Reg[t]) to Elizabeth Dupee Thomas, Spinster. L.
1815 Feb. 26 Captain Thomas Reed of the 4th W. I. Reg[t] to Anne Thomas, Widow. L.

Buried.

1707 May 14 Coll. George Thomas.
1707 Aug. 5 Lydia D. of Geo. & Elliz. Thomas.
1721 Mar. 22 Elizabeth Thomas, a child.
1722 April 20 M[r] Richard Meynell, Killed by William Thomas.
1724 Oct. 12 Eliz[th] D. of Walter Sydserfe.
1730 May 15 Richard Thomas.
1730 Nov. 22 John s. of Walt[r] Sydserfe.
1733 June 6 John Thomas.
1736 Oct. 9 David s. of Mathew Thomas.
1736 Nov. 7 Daniel the s. of Mathew Thomas.
1744 April 4 William Thomas, a child.
1745 (? Aug. or Sep.) William Thomas.
1746 June 19 W[m] Thomas, a child.
1755 Nov. 14 Susanna Thomas, a child.
1808 Oct. 26 George Thomas, Infant, } in one
Maria Ann Thomas, Infant, } grave.
1831 Dec. 27 Henry B. Thomas. S[t] John's. 44.

PARISH REGISTER OF ST. PAUL.

Baptized.

1725 Mar. 13 William the S. of M[r] William Thomas and his Wife.
1727 Jan. 26 Elizabeth the D. of M[r] William Thomas & his Wife.
1738 Mar. 26 William S. of William Thomas and Jane his Wife.

Married.

1725 Mar. 20 Robert Thomas and Mary Greatrix; p. L.
1733 ..emb[r] 9 William Thomas & Jane Greatrix; by Banns.
1774 June 25 The honourable Francis Farley, Esq[r], to Miss Elizabeth Thomas; p[r] L.

Buried.

1740 July 10 Tabitha D. of William Thomas and Jane his Wife.

PARISH REGISTER OF ST. GEORGE.

Married.

1744 Oct. 25 John White and Lydia Thomas, Spinster.

Buried.

1763 Sep. 25 Elizabeth the Wife of his Excellency George Thomas, Esq[r].
1767 Sep. 10 George Thomas.

PARISH REGISTER OF ST. PHILIP.

Married.

1717 April 18 George Thomas & Elizabeth King.

YAPTON, CO. SUSSEX.

Buried.

1758 Jan. 12 Mary Wife of Walter Sydserfe, Esq[r].
1760 Mar. 21 Walter Sydserfe, Esq., buried.
1763 Dec. 12 Margaret the Wife of Will[m] Thomas, Esq.
1777 Dec. 30 Sir William Thomas.

SOMERSET HOUSE CHAPEL, LONDON.

Married.

1742-3 ...... William Thomas, esq., to Margaret Sydserfe of Stoke Newington, co. Middlesex.

NORTH SOUND PLANTATION.

On a ledger over a marble tomb in a cane piece:—

Here lies the Body of
ELIZABETH THOMAS
Who Died the Twenty fourth Day
of September One Thoufand
Seven Hundred and Sixty three
In the Sixty fecond Year of her Age
She was forty fix Years the prudent
faithful and Affectionate Wife of
GEORGE THOMAS Efq Captain General and
Governour in Chief of the Leeward Iflands
Who from a just Sense of her Virtues
hath caused this Monument to be erected
to her Memory.

WILLOUGHBY BAY OLD BURIAL-GROUND.

On a large ledger:—

To the Memory of
WILLIAM THOMAS Efq[r]
who departed this life Auguft 30th 1762
Aged 35 Years.

YAPTON CHURCH, CO. SUSSEX.

On the north wall of the chancel is a tablet surmounted by the marble medallion of a woman:—

UNDERNEATH LYE THE REMAINS OF M[RS] MARGARET THOMAS
WHO DEPARTED THIS LIFE DECEMB. 4TH 1763
AGED THIRTY NINE.
WHEN LIVING EMINENT FOR HER MATERNAL CARE
AND CONJUGAL AFFECTION, FOR PIETY, CHARITY
UNIVERSAL GOODNESS, NOW DEAD AS EXTENSIVELY LAMENTED.
IN THE SAME SEPULCHRE ARE ALSO DEPOSITED
THE REMAINS OF HER PARENTS WALTER SYDSERFE
ESQ[R] AND MARY HIS WIFE, FROM WHOSE VIRTUOUS
EXAMPLES THEIR DAUGHTER BECAME THAT EXCELLENT
WOMAN |
TO THESE THIS MONUMENT IS ERECTED
BY AN AFFECTIONATE MUCH AFFLICTED HUSBAND
AND GRATEFUL SON IN LAW WILLIAM THOMAS.

Below the above is the following on an oval white marble tablet:—

In
The Vault beneath
Are deposited
The remains
of
SIR WILLIAM THOMAS BART
Who died
Dec[r] 19th 1777
Aged 56.

1852. Sir George Thomas, Bart., owned "Upper and Lower Five Islands Estates" of 703 acres in St. John's Parish and "North Sound Estate" in St. George's Parish of 602 acres. This latter was sold to the late George Estridge, Esq., about 30 or 40 years ago, and is now vested in his daughter. Mary Thomas owned "Friar's Hill" of 230 acres in St. John's Parish. "Thomas's" in St. Paul's Parish of 520 acres was owned by James W. Sheriff.

Pedigree of Tobin.

ARMS.—*Or, three (? holly) leaves.*

WALTER TOBIN of Nevis 1707 = ...

. . . . Tobin of Nevis, living at the date of his son's marriage. [Mr. John Tobin of Nevis living 1724 and 1727.] = ...

Captain Tobin of the ship "Apollo" bound to Nevis 1731. = Henrietta . . . . living 1731.

A dau., mar. Maurice Berkeley, junior; both living 1731.

James Tobin of Nevis, Esq., recommended to be of the Council 1776; settled as a merchant at Bristol 1783. His bookplate above. = ... dau. of George Webbe, Esq. (of Nevis, merchant, at one time of Stratford Manor House, Old Sarum, later of Bristol *c.* 1783, and died 22 June 1804 at Bourne House, co. Cambridge); mar. 7 July 1766.

John Tobin of St. James Parade, Bath, died 12 Dec. 1794, æt. 61. M.I. in Bath Abbey.

James Webbe Tobin, 1st son and heir, matriculated from Wadham Coll., Oxford, 9 Nov. 1787, æt. 20; B.A. 1791; died 30 Oct. 1814 at Nevis. = ...

George Tobin, C.B., Admiral R.N., born 13 Dec. 1768 at Salisbury; died 10 April 1838, æt. 69, at Teignmouth, co. Devon. = Dorothy, widow of Major William Duff of the 26th Foot and dau. of Captain Gordon Skelly, R.N.; mar. 13 June 1804.

Elizabeth Tobin, mar. 4 Jan. 1808; died 20 May 1824, æt. 52. = John Cobham of Barbados, Esq., died 26 Oct. 1811, æt. 48. M.I. at St. Paul's, Bristol.

John Tobin, born 26 Jan. 1770 at Salisbury; of Lincoln's Inn 1784; dramatic writer; died off Ireland Dec. 1804, æt. 35.

Charles Meadows Tobin, matric. from Wadham College, Oxford, 9 Nov. 1792, æt. 17; B.A. 1797.

Henry Hope Tobin, Esq., dead 1812. = Lucy, dau. of Thomas Oliver of Bristol, Esq., formerly Lieut.-Governor of Mass.; died 16 Jan. 1857, æt. 86. M.I. in Clifton Churchyard.

Henry Hope Tobin, drowned at Heidelburg 5 June 1831, æt. 17.

Eliza Lucy Hope Tobin, died 11 March 1834, æt. 23, at Bath.

George Webbe Tobin, only surviving son, of the 2nd Dragoon Guards, died 21 Sep. 1840, æt. 33. M.I. at St. Paul's, Bristol. = Susannah Christian Cobham, only dau., died 2 Jan. 1840. M.I. at St. Paul's, Bristol.

James Cobham, died 4 Dec. 1818, æt. 9. M.I. at St. Paul's, Bristol.

Lucy Tobin, mar. Butler Claxton of Bristol, Esq.; living 1812.

Thomas Ayson of Bristoll, merchant, now residing at Nevis and bound to Bristoll. Will dated 21 April 1664; proved 11 Nov. 1665 by Elizabeth Ayson the relict. (135 Hyde.) Poor of Madly, co. Hereford, £5 4*s.* 0*d.* per annum for bread, payable by the churchwardens & overseers out of my tenement there in the occupation of my father-in-law Joseph Symonds, & after the death of my wife Eliz. Ayson, his dau., £4 16*s.* 0*d.* per annum for apprenticing. My dau.-in-law Mary Hurlock 30,000 lbs. of shugar out of my plantation. My kinsman John Brewett 20,000 lbs. To the poor in these two divisions, viz. Capt. John Smith's Company & Capt. Freeman's, 20,000 lbs. My wife Eliz. all residue & Ex'trix. My friends Capt. Walter Symonds, Esq., Capt. John Smith, & Tho. Nicholson overseers & 5000 lbs. each. Witnessed by Walter Symonds, John Haddow, Joseph Symonds, Edward Scott.

Codicil. 23 Sep. 17 Car. II. Revoke 30,000 lbs. to dau.-in-law, & in lieu bond to her husband Wm Beach. Witnessed by Thomas Wickham, Thomas Cole, Richard Gutch.

Elizabeth Combes, wife of John Combes of Bristol, merchant, and relict of Thomas Ayson. Will dated 29 Nov. 1685. (148 Cann.) My plantation in Nevis & slaves after the death of my said husband to my kinsman Walter Symonds. My kinswoman Eliz. Symonds, dau. of my brother John Symonds, 100,000 lbs.

John Combes of Bristol, merchant. Will dated 11 April, proved 13 May 1689 by Susanna Combes the mother. (61 Ent.) To be buried in S[t] James churchyard near my former wife. Mother Susanna Combes sole Ex'or. Wife Mary £500, coach, & horses. Brother Adam Combes ⅓ of the ship "William & Anne" of which he is Master. Sister Eliz. Herrin £20. Brother James Combes of Antego 10,000 lbs. out of his debt. Sister Mary Combes £150. Wife ½ of negros & stock on my plantation in the West Indies, sister Eliz. Herrin's 2 daus. Susan & Eliz. ⅙, sister Mary Veale ⅙, sister Mary Combes ⅙, sister Rebecca March ⅙, brother W[m] Combes ⅙, Ex'ors ⅔. Sister Martha Dorrill £50. W[m] Minor & John Streton, late of Bristol, now of the West Indies, merchants, to sell the plantation I purchased of the widow Jones & "Crooks" & the land bought of Rob[t] Harrison in the low ground at Nevis adjoining the plantation of my late wife. Brother-in-law Henry March. Brother Rich[d] Veale. Witnessed by J. Owen, William Cox, Notary Public, John Yeamans, jun., Francis Buckstun.

Adam Combes of Bristoll, marriner. Will dated 19 Sep. 1691; proved 6 April 1692 by Joanna Combes the relict. (64 Fane.) Wife Joanna, dau. Eliz. by my 1st wife Eliz., 100,000 lbs. of sugar payable by M[r] Walter Symonds of Nevis. My 2 children Eliz. & Susanna & wife all residue & Ex'ors. Witnessed by Phil. Skrine, Nathaniel Coates, Ra. Barrow, Thomas Sampson, Jonah Jackson, Ed. Dorville.

(Sir) James Tobin of Bedford Rowe, St. Andrew's, Holborn. Will dated 26 March 1732; proved 9 July 1735 by the four Ex'ors. (162 Ducie.) All my estate to my friends M[r] Thos. Beckford of Mark Lane, merchant, M[r] Alex[r] Hume of Thames Str., on Trust to pay my nephew Edmond Tobin, son of my late brother Robert Tobin, £1000, to my sister Mary Tobin *al's* Binke £1000. M[r] Tho. Beckford, M[r] Alex[r] Hume, M[r] Philip Cantillion, M[r] Gregory Byrne, £200 each & Ex'ors. To James Arlond, son of the late Capt. Edward Arlond, £500. To the poor of Kilkenny where I was born £200, & the like sum to the Roman Catholic clergy, to be distributed by my brother Tho. Tobin. M[r] Henry Byrne of Oporto £200, various legacies to friends & merchants. To my loving brother Thos. Tobin £50 a year. £4000 to trustees for special purpose. All residue to my nephews James Tobin & Edmond Tobin, sons of my brother Edmond Tobin, dec[d]. James to be educated a merchant & to go to Cadiz.—Burke, dau. of my sister Mary Tobin *al's* Burke.

Codicil. 3 March 1732-3. The £4000 is for the boy called Michaell.

Jos. Symonds, s. Walter, of the island of Nevis, gent. Christ Church, matric. 10 Dec., 1697, aged 18; brother of John 1705.

John Symonds, s. Walter, of the island of Nevis, gent. Christ Church, matric. 30 Oct., 1705, aged 19; B.A. from Magdalen Hall 1708 (as Symons); perhaps a student of Lincoln's Inn 1705; brother of Jos. 1697.

1699, July 7. Walter Symonds of the Nevis Council dead. He was Speaker in 1668.

1707-8. Census of Nevis. Walter Tobin. 4 white males, 4 white females; 20 black males, 22 black females.

1723. James Symonds a member of the Council of Nevis.

1724. Deposition of Mr. John Tobin of Nevis that his sister Symonds had not had an illegitimate child.

1727. Census of Nevis. Thomas Tobin. John Tobin.

1731, Nov. About the middle of Oct. last some persons arm'd broke into the House of M[r] Spike at Cove in Ireland, where lodg'd M[r] Maurice Berkley, jun. his Wife, Wife's Sister, and a Servant Maid, Passengers in the Apollo, Capt. Tobin for Nevis. They went up into the Chamber, where Mrs. Henrietta Tobin lay, took her out of Bed, and carry'd her off with only her Shift on. The Principal in this Fact was one William Power, who had lately been several Times in her company. M[r] Berkley took his Sword, engaged and wounded a Person who stood Centinel at the Door; then pursu'd them to the Strand, where he was again oppos'd by three Men armed with Swords and Pistols. Upon which he cry'd out Murder, etc. two or three coming to his assistance, they follow'd them to the Water side, took Boat, and coming up with them, rescued her amidst all their Fire. The account she gave of their Usage was, that they forced her on Horseback before William Power, which with struggling, she had quitted several Times, and was as often remounted by his assistants. ('Gent. Mag.,' p. 498.)

There is a tomb to Sir James Tobin, Bart. (*sic*, ? Knt.), 1735, in St. Pancras Churchyard. (Lysons, vol. iii.)

Sir Richard Everard, fourth Bart., of Fethard, co. Tipperary, married Catherine dau. of James Tobin, Esq., of Cumpshinagh in said county.

1735, May. At the Bath, Sir James Tobin an Irishman; he pretended that he was ill used by the East-India Company here, and therefore went over to Ostend, where he offered his Service and was accepted: He was the first that sail'd from that Port to the East-Indies to China, and made such vast Returns, there being then no Directors to swallow up the Profits of the Voyage; that the Emperor Knighted him. ('Historical Register,' p. 24.)

1743, June 10. M[r] Walter Symonds, possess'd of several Plantations in the W. Indies. ('Gent. Mag.,' p. 333.)

1743, July. John Buttler Symmonds, Esq.; of the Island of Nevis at his lodgings in Fenchurch Street. (*Ibid.*)

1743, Aug. 1. John Buttler Symmonds, of the Island of Nevis, Heir to 1500*l.* per Ann. By the Death of his Brother. (*Ibid.*, p. 443.)

1757. Death of President Symonds of St. Christopher's announced. (B. T. Leeward Islands, vol. 33.)

1761, Nov. 19. James Symonds,* Esq; of Margaret-street, Cavendish-square. ('Gent. Mag.,' p. 539.)

1766, July 7. Ja: Tobin of Salisbury, Esq; — to Miss Webbe of Stradford, with 10,000*l.* (*Ibid.*, p. 342.)

1776, Dec. 3. James Tobin recommended as a Councillor of Nevis.

1794, Dec. 12. At his house on S[t] James's parade, Bath, John Tobin, esq. ('Gent. Mag.,' p. 1157.)

1804, June 13. Capt. Tobin, R.N. to Mrs. Duff, of Richmond, co. York, widow of the late Major D. of the 26th foot. (*Ibid.*, p. 595.)

1808, Jan. 4. At Bristol, John Cobham, esq. of that city, to Miss Tobin, dau. of James T. esq. (*Ibid.*, p. 85.)

1811. The Hon. James Weekes of Nevis wrote that Mr. J. W. Tobin was first met by John Peterson 25 years ago, and that the former's mother's family was connected with the latter.

1811. See an extract of Mr. James Tobin's letter in Southey's 'West Indies,' p. 498.

1814, Oct. 30. Died at his father's estate in Nevis, of a fever, James Webbe Tobin esq. (A long eulogy follows.) He was brother to the late Author of 'The Honey Moon' and other dramatic pieces. ('Gent. Mag.,' 1815, p. 178.)

* For his will see under Dunbar.

1815, Dec. 8. Whitehall. Capt. George Tobin R.N. to be a Companion of the most Honourable Military Order of the Bath. ('Gent. Mag.,' p. 629.)

1817, Oct. 6. At Bristol, at an advanced age, James Tobin, esq. (*Ibid.*, p. 562.)

1831, June 5. While bathing at Heidelberg, in his 18th year, Henry-Hope, youngest son of the late James Webbe Tobin, esq. of the Island of Nevis and of Bristol. (*Ibid.*, p. 561.)

1834, March 11. At Bath, aged 23, Eliza Lucy Hope, only dau. of Capt. Tobin, R.N. C.B. (*Ibid.*, p. 566.)

1838, April 10. "At Teignmouth, Devonshire, aged 69, Rear-Admiral George Tobin, C.B. This excellent officer was the second son of James Tobin, esq. of Nevis, a gentleman of high literary attainments. He was born at Salisbury on the 13th Dec. 1768." Entered the Navy 1780; Lieut. 1791; Commander 1798; Post Captain 1802; C.B. 1814. "He married in 1804, Dorothy, daughter of Capt. Gordon Skelly, R.N. (who was drowned at sea about 1774-5) and wife of Major William Duff, of the 26th regiment. She survives him, with one son, George Webbe Tobin, esq. late of the 2nd dragoon guards." Capt. Horatio Nelson married a relation of his mother, Mrs. Nesbitt of Nevis. (*Ibid.*, p. 101.)

1840, Jan. 2. At Clifton, Susanna-Christian, wife of George Webbe Tobin, esq. only dau. of the late John Cobham, esq. of Barbadoes. (*Ibid.*, p. 218.)

1840, April 2. At Nantes, aged 78, James Tobin, esq. (*Ibid.*, p. 670.)

1851. Sir John Tobin, Mayor of Liverpool, knighted 10 May 1820; died 27 Feb. 1851, aged 88.

John Tobin.

Born in the house now occupied by Mr. Foot, solicitor, in Endless Street, January 26, 1770. His father had been destined for one of the liberal professions, and his mother was the daughter of Mr. Webb, an opulent West Indian, who then resided in the Manor House at Stratford. At the commencement of the American war Mr. Tobin repaired to Nevis, to take charge of an estate in that island, which had been resigned to him on his marriage by his father. He left the subject of this article, and two brothers, under the care of their maternal grandfather, Mr. Webb, by whom they were placed in the school of Dr. Mant, at Southampton. Even at this early period young Tobin evinced a decided taste for dramatic representations.

On the conclusion of peace in 1783, Mr. Tobin returned to England, and settled in a mercantile business at Bristol; and his father-in-law in consequence removed to Redland in the neighbourhood. In the ensuing year John Tobin was articled to Mr. Wildman, an eminent solicitor in Lincoln's Inn. He passed through his clerkship, without acquiring a partiality for his profession, and devoted his leisure to the cultivation of literature, especially poetry.

On the expiration of his term he was admitted into partnership with his late master. His inclination for the drama became, however, still more decided. He composed several pieces, and was subjected to all the mortifications, difficulties, and disappointments, which generally await the early efforts of a writer for the stage. At length, in 1803, he obtained for a farce entitled "All's fair in Love," the honour of a representation; but it was coldly received. He however persevered, and, by the influence of Mr. Wroughton, procured the acceptance of "The Honey Moon," to which he owes his reputation. At this period his constitution suffered from the effects of his studious and sedentary habits. He spent the winter in Cornwall, for a change of air and scene; but the appearances of consumption becoming more marked and alarming, he was induced to undertake a voyage to the West Indies. He embarked at Bristol, with aggravated symptoms, in the latter end of 1804, and sailed to Cork. From thence he took his departure on the 7th of December: and the first night proving boisterous, exhausted the sinking powers of his enfeebled frame. On the ensuing morning he was found dead in his bed, and his remains were carried back for interment at Cork.

"The Honey Moon" was represented at Drury Lane on the 31st of January following, and received with that applause, which it has never since failed to call forth. Subsequently his other productions were offered to public notice. "The Curfew," was acted in 1806; "The School for Authors," in 1808; and "The Faro Table," in 1816; but all without attaining that rank which was at once assigned to his principal composition.

(Miss Benger's Memoirs of Tobin in Hoare's 'History of Wilts,' vol. vi., p. 653.)

Parish Register of St. John, Antigua.

Married.

1725 Jan. 23 Gustavus Christian and Frances Tobin.

Buried.

1757 Oct. 19 Thomas Tobin.

Cove, Ireland.

In the parish church is a plain marble tablet with the following inscription:—

Sacred to the memory
of
John Tobin, Esq. of Lincoln's Inn,
whose remains are deposited under
the adjacent turf.
He died at sea,
near the entrance of this Harbour,
in the month of December
1804,
on his passage to a milder climate,
in search of better health,
aged 35.

('Gent. Mag.,' 1815, p. 178.)

Clifton Churchyard.

On a stone tomb in Gothic characters:—

Lucy widow of the late Henry H. Tobin Esqr and last surviving daughter of Thomas Oliver Esqr | formerly Governor of the | Massachusetts North America died at Clifton XVI of January MDCCCLVII aged LXXXVI years.

Bath Abbey.

M.I. to John Tobin, who died 12 Dec. 1794, aged 61.

St. Paul's Church, Bristol.

On a tablet under the tower:—

Susannah Christian Tobin wife of George Webb | Tobin Esq. daughter of late John Cobham | Esq. of Applethwaite Spring Barbadoes. | George W. Tobin Esq. of Queens Bay | died at Anglesea Villa 21 Sept. 1840 | aged 33 years.

On another tablet (not copied *verbatim*):—

John Cobham of Barbadoes | died 26 Oct. 1811 æt. 48 | Eliz. his wife daughter of James Tobin died at Clifton 20 May 1824 aged 52. James Cobham (?) their son died at Bristol 4 Dec. 1818 aged 9.

Pedigree of Tomlinson.

Walter Philips of Antigua, Gent., granted a patent for 170 acres on 18 Feb. 1684; owned 264 acres and 16 negros in St. Philip's Parish. 1st husband. = Elizabeth . . . . = JOHN TOMLINSON of Antigua, Major 1706; had a grant of Walter Philips's 264 acres and 16 slaves in 1709; J.P. 1712; bur. 9 Oct. 1739 at St. John's. 2nd husband.

John Tomlinson, junior, Esq., joins the Troop 1717-18; Chief Baron of Exchequer 1744; Member of Council 1745; æt. 51 in 1749; President and Colonel of Militia 1752; bur. 11 June 1753 at St. John's. Will dated 29 May 1753. = Jane, dau. of Daniel Mackinen, Surgeon; bur. 9 Oct. 1736 at St. John's.

Mary Tomlinson, only surviving dau., bapt. 4 Aug. 1703; mar. 26 Feb. 1726, at St. John's, Michael White of Montserrat, Esq.

Elizabeth Tomlinson, bapt. 4 Aug. 1703 at St. John's; dead 1726.

John Tomlinson, Esq., died a bachelor. Will dated 17 Dec. 1760, then of Bath; proved 21 Jan. 1761. (38 Cheslyn.)

William Tomlinson, bapt. 19 Nov. 1721 at St. John's.

Elizabeth Tomlinson, bur. 7 Aug. 1723.

Mary Tomlinson, bur. 23 Sep. 1727.

Mary Tomlinson, bapt. 1731; bur. 31 Jan. 1731.

Alice Tomlinson, bapt. 29 Dec. 1733; living 1760.

Elizabeth Tomlinson, living 1760.

Penelope Tomlinson, bapt. 19 May 1735; bur. 19 Sep. 1806. Will dated 18 July 1802; sworn 12 Sep. 1806.

Mahitabell Tomlinson, bapt. 29 Sep. and bur. 7 Oct. 1736 at St. John's.

Jane Tomlinson, living 1760.

Lydia Tomlinson, mar. Delacourt Walsh, Captain 38th Regiment, Secretary of Antigua; she was bur. 4 Dec. 1800 at St. John's; he was bur. 2 July 1784 and M.I. at Richmond, co. Surrey. His will dated 21 Sep. 1783; proved 11 Aug. 1784. (480 Rockingham.) He mar. 1st, 1 Jan. 1748, Mary, dau. of John Gamble. (See his will, vol. ii., p. 5.)

John Thomlinson, Esq. Will dated 29 May 1753. To my dau. Lydia 2 negros & £1000 st. To my dau. Jane 3 negros & £1000 st. To my dau. Elizth 2 negros & £1000 st. To my dau. Alice 2 negros & £1000 st. To my dau. Penelope 2 negros & £1000. Free certain negros. To my said 5 daus. my title to the house now in possession of John Hoskins. All residue to my son John. He & Wm Mackinnen & Harry Webb, Esqres, Ex'ors & £20 c. each. Witnessed by Thomas Fraser, Ashton Warner, Dr. William Millar.

Codicil. My Ex'ors to repair my said dwelling house in St John's. To my 5 daus. equally my furniture, linen, plate, china, wine, sheep, & 30 pistoles. Witnessed by James Scott, Thomas Fraser. Before Hon. Gilbert Fleming, Lieut.-Governor, was sworn Thomas Fraser 13 . . . . 1753. Recorded 4 July 1753.

John Tomlinson of Antigua, Esq., now residing at Bath, co. Somerset. Will dated 17 Dec. 1760; proved 21 Jan. 1761 by James Scott, Esq.; power reserved to William Mackinen, Steven Blizard, Francis Farleigh, Robert Christian, and Oliver Nugent. (38 Cheslyn.) To Mary dau. of Henry & Eliz. Stokes of Ravenshall, near Betley, co. Stafford, £50 a year, & to her son John which she had by me £50 a year for life & £1000 at 21. Ex'ors to use £300 of it for his advancement after the age of 12. To Mary Stokes £50. To Frederick Nicholas of London, sugar baker, £100. To Jas. Scott & to Jas. Langford, both late of Antigua, Esqres, £200 apiece. Jas. Scott, Wm Mackinen, Steven Blizard, Francis Farleigh, Robt Christian, & Oliver Nugent, all of Antigua, Esqres, Ex'ors, & give them each a 20s. ring. All residue to my 5 sisters Lydia, Jane, Eliz., Alice, & Penelope Tomlinson. Witnessed by Lacon Lambe of Bath, Michael Fletcher, servant to Mr. Tomlinson, Charles Bolton of Bath. Exemplification recorded in Registrar's Office, St. John's, 7 May 1761.

Penelope Tomlinson of Antigua, spinster. Will dated 18 July 1802. To Hon. Thos. Norberry Kerby & Thos. Oliver of London, merchts, my Ex'ors £50 each. £800 to be equally divided amongst Saml McKinnen, Chas. Mackinnen, Thos. Mackinnen, & Lydia Hanen, children of Charles Mackinnen. To my Ex'ors £200 in trust to pay to Elizth wife of Geo. Molineaux Montgomery, dau. of Michl White, decd. To John White, son of Michael White & Mary his wife (late Mary Hussey) & grandson of the said Michl White, decd, £200 st. at 15, & if he die then to his sister Lydia White £100, & to his sister Elizth Hamilton White £100. To Wm White, son of the said Michl White & Mary (heretofore Lee), £200 st. To Ann Byam Kerby, dau. of Thos. N. Kerby, £105 st. All residue to my Ex'ors in trust to pay rents to Wm White for life, & then to his 1st son, & in default to his brother Michael White, then to his brother Robt White. Trustees to be Ex'ors. Witnessed by Richard S. Byam, Mark Atkinson. Before Ralph, Lord Lavington, was sworn Richard Scott Byam, Doctor, 12 Sep. 1806.

1st Codicil dated 5 Jan. 1805. Power to trustees to let my plantation called Tomlinsons & houses in High Street, St John's.

2nd Codicil dated 28 Nov. 1805. All my real estate to my kinsman Wm White of Antigua, Esq., in fee simple & not in trust. Witnessed by Rowland Burton, George McKerran. Before Lord Lavington was sworn George Ross McConell of Antigua, writing clerk.

1669, Aug. 31. Richard Glanfeild of Antigua, planter, leases 10 acres to Richard Mathews and Jonathan Tomlinson of Antigua, planters.

1708, June 3. John Tomlinson petitions that Walter Philips, late of this island, Gent., deceased, died seised in fee simple of 264 acres and 16 negros in Nonsuch Division and St. Phillip's Parish, which he by will gave to his two sons Walter and William Philips and his dau. Rachel Philips, all of which are since dead without heirs, and the said property escheated. Petitioner is married to the widow of Walter Philips, and has been an inhabitant for several years past, and has a large family of children. He is granted a patent.

1709, June 3. John Tomlinson, Esq., 264 acres (Joseph French, Esq., escheator) granted by Daniel Parke.

1744, May 8. John Tomlinson, Esq., appointed Chief Baron of the Exchequer.

1745, Feb. 20. John Tomlinson, Esq., now Member of Council; his seat in the Assembly vacant.

1746, July 23. John Tomlinson, Esq., appointed Member of Council *vice* Daniel Mathew resigned. (B. T. Leeward Islands, No. 55, p. 279.)

1749, Nov. 2. In a deposition of this date Hon. John Tomlinson was aged 51.

1753, Sep. 2. Hon. John Tomlinson, Esq: deputy-governor of Antigua. ('London Mag.,' p. 439.)

There was a family of Tomlinson in Bristol during the seventeenth century.

PARISH REGISTER OF ST. JOHN.

Baptized.

1703	Aug. 4	Mary d. of John Tomlinson & Elizabeth his wife.
1703	Aug. 4	Elizabeth d. of John Tomlinson & Elizabeth his wife.
1721	Nov. 19	Wm S. of John Tomlinson, Junr, & Jane his wife.
1731	......	Mary d. of John Tomlinson & Jane his wife.
1733	Dec. 29	Alice D. of John Tomlinson, Jnr, & Elizth his wife.
1735	May 19	Penelope D. of John Tomlinson, Jnr, & Jane his wife.
1736	Sep. 29	Mahitabell the D. of John Tomlinson, Junr, and Jane his wife.
1753	April 4	Rachel the D. of the Hon'ble John Tomlinson, Esqr, by a Mulattoe.

Married.

1726	Feb. 26	Michael White and Mary Tomlinson. L.
1775	Oct. 7	William Lytton to Jane Tomlinson. L.

Buried.

1723	Aug. 7	Elizabeth the D. of John Tomlinson, Junr, & Jane his wife.
1723	Nov. 9	Mrs Riddle, mother in law to Major John Tomlinson.
1727	Sep. 23	Mary the D. of John Tomlinson, Junr.
1731	Jan. 31	Mary D. of Jno Tomlinson.
1736	Oct. 7	Mehitabell the D. of Colle John Tomlinson.
1736	Oct. 9	Jane wife of Colle John Tomlinson.
1739	Oct. 9	John Tomlinson, senr, of this Island.
1740	July 16	Robert Tomlinson, Merchant, from Boston.
1753	June 11	Hon'ble Govr John Tomlinson.
1772	Dec. 16	Jonathn Thomlinson.
1774	June 24	Mary Thomlinson.
1797	Dec. 20	Jane Thomlinson.
1799	July 18	Elizabeth Tomlinson.
1800	Dec. 4	Lydia Walsh.
1806	Sep. 19	Penelope Thomlinson.

Pedigree of Trant.

ARMS.—*Per pale azure and gules, two swords in saltier argent, hilts and pommels or, between three roses of the third.*
CREST.—*A demi-eagle displayed.*

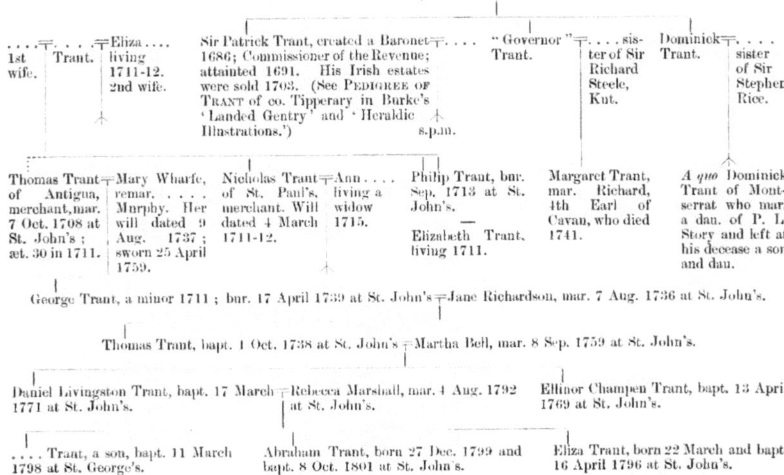

Edward Trant, senior, of Antigua, Esq., joined the Troop 1716; bur. 15 Nov. 1760 at St. John's. Will dated 12 Oct. and sworn 1 Dec. 1760. = Lydia Rodney of Old Road 1753; mar. 26 Jan 1722 and bur. 13 July 1782 at St. John's. Will dated 24 Feb. 1779; sworn 25 Jan. 1783.

William Trant, bur. 10 May 1785 at St. John's. = Mary Taylor, mar. 9 April 1760 at St. John's; living 1779.

Edward Trant, junior, bapt. 10 April 1726 and bur. 30 Sep. 1759 at St. John's. = Mary .... Will dated 19 July 1791.

Drury Trant, bur. 12 Feb. 1731 at St. John's.

Drury Trant, bapt. 26 Oct. 1740 and bur. 29 Nov. 1745 at St. John's.

A son, bur. 9 March 1754 at St. John's.

Lydia Rodney Trant, bapt. 19 Jan. 1723 at St. John's; mar. Lawrence Nihell, merchant.

Ann Trant, bapt. 24 Aug. 1729 at St. John's; dead 1791.

Penelope Trant, bapt. 25 April 1742 at St. John's; dead 1791.

Henrietta Trant, bapt. 21 June 1743 at St. John's; living 1779.

Sarah Trant, living 1779.

Alice Trant, 2nd wife of Stephen Lynch, Esq.; dead 1758.

Edward Trant, bapt. 30 Jan. 1766 at St. John's.

James Taylor Trant, bapt. 30 Jan. and bur. 1 Feb. 1766 at St. John's.

Alice Trant, bapt. 12 March 1761, and mar. 7 May 1781, at St. John's, James Boutein.

Paulina Trant, bapt. 9 July 1762 and bur. 8 Jan. 1766 at St. John's.

Elizabeth Sarah Trant, bapt. 28 June 1764 at St. John's.

Elizabeth Trant, bapt. 21 Feb. 1768 at St. John's; died in a convent at West Dean, co. Wilts; bur. 14 Dec. 1797, æt. 30.

Richard Trant, late of Barbados. Will dated 7 July, proved 8 Aug. 1684 by Patrick Trant. On 26 Jan. 1699 commission to Thomas Trant, principal creditor of Richard Trant, deceased, of all goods left unadministered by Patrick Trant, deceased, John Trant the son having renounced. On 20 Oct. 1701 commission to Ann Trant the relict and administratrix of Thomas Trant, deceased. (106 Hare.) Near & dear kinsman Patrick Trant of London, Esq., sole Ex'or & Guardian of my son John Trant. John Reid & Lawrence Trent of Barbados, Esq[res], & Tho. Trant of Barbados, Gent., overseers. Witnessed by James Nihell, Richard Nagle, Richard Comerford.

Nicholas Trant. Will dated 4 March 1711-12. To my wife Ann my furniture, jewels, plate, horse called Blackbird. To my brother Philip Trant my Indian boy Bermudos, a 2 masted boat, & my part of the sloop Ann & Mary, my horse Bell, trooping furniture, & best sword, gun, & pistols, also £100 c. To Geo. Trant, son of M .... Murphew, £100 c. at 21 & schooling. To my sister Eliz[th] Trant £60 c. To my stepmother Eliza .... *alias* Trant £10 c. To my aunt Gallway .... c. To the poor of Falmouth parish £10 c. For a church in Falmouth £10 c. To my wife Ann all rents for her life, then to .... mas Trant, then to Philip Trant. My brother .... my friend Bartholomew Sanderson, & .... Trant Ex'ors. Sworn 19 July 1712.

Mary Murphy. Will dated 9 Aug. 1737. To Mary wife of Thos. Sawcolt the free use of my chamber & kitchen, etc., in my house as she now uses for life. To Thos. Hanson, jun[r], & John Watkins all my estate, slaves, etc., in trust for my son Geo. Trant for life, provided his present wife Jane be in no way dowable therein, & after his death to the child his wife now goes with. To my slave Molly her freedom & use of dwelling room. The use of the shedd rooms to Jane wife of Geo. Trant during widowhood. To George's godsons, viz. W[m] Holborn, son of John Holborn, & .... each a negro girl. All residue to Mary Sawcolt. Thos. Hanson & John Watkins Ex'ors. Witnessed by James Fogo, Sarah Richardson, Hesiah Richardson. Before George Thomas, Esq., was sworn Sarah Jones for Richardson 25 April 1759.

Edward Trant of Antigua, Esq. Will dated 12 Oct. 1760. I gave to my 1st dau. Lydia when she was married to M[r] Lawrence Nihell 5 negros valued at £350 c., & have since given him £200 c., & do confirm the same. My son W[m] with each of my daus. to have the like sum of £550 c. To my dear wife Lydia my house I bought of Cap. W[m] King, & my daus. Anne, Sarah, & Penelope, & Henrietta to dwell there. To my wife all my furniture. On the marriage of my dau. Alice with M[r] Stephen Lynch I gave her 4 negros worth £222 c., she is since dead, & I give the said 4 negros to Stephen Lynch with £328 c. To my dau. Ann a negro woman & 3 children worth £180 c. & £370 c. To my son W[m] a negro worth £51 4*s.* c. & £498 16*s.* c. To my dau. Sarah £550 c. To my dau. Penelope a negro & 2 children worth £93 c. & £457 c. at 21. To my dau. Henrietta £550 at 21. All residue to my daus. Ann, Sarah, Penelope, & Henrietta, my son W[m], & my sons-in-law Lawrence Nihell & Stephen Lynch. My wife & my friends Rich[d] Kirwan & Rich[d] Ottley, Esq[res], my son W[m], & my son-in-law Stephen Lynch Ex'ors & Guardians. Witnessed by Richard Tuite, Mary Trant, Ebenezer Lovell. By Governor Thomas was sworn Ebenezer Lovell 1 Dec. 1760. Recorded 16 Jan. 1761. On 20 May 1761 before Governor Thomas appeared Richard Ottley, Esq., and renounced execution. Recorded 5 Oct. 1761.

Lydia Trant of Antigua, widow, relict of Edward Trant, sen. Will dated 24 Feb. 1779. To my son W[m] Trant £5 c. yearly. To my dau. Lydia Nihell £20 s. To my dau. Sarah Trant £5 a year. To my dau.-in-law M[rs] Mary Trant & to each of my grandchildren £19. All residue to my daus. Ann, Penelope, & Henrietta. Langford Lovell, Esq., & my grandson John Nihill, my dau.-in-law Mary Trant, & my daus. Lydia Nihill & Ann Trant Ex'ors. Witnessed by Elizabeth White, Elias Ferris. By Thomas Jarvis, Esq., was sworn Elias Ferris, planter, 25 Jan. 1783. Recorded 11 March 1783.

Stephen Lynch, Esq., by his will dated 16 May 1786 gave all his estate to his aunts Ann Trant and Penelope Trant and his kinsman Edward Nihell, clerk.

Mary Trant, widow, of East Street, Red Lion Square, London. Will dated 19 July 1791. To Miss Ann & Miss Penelope Trant the use of the negros they now have in Trinidad. To D[r] Lawrence Nihill of Bedford Str. 2 negros. To Sam[l] Boutein of S[t] Vincent's, controller, 5 gs. All residue to Sam[l] Turner of London, merch[t], & Langford Lovell of Antigua, planter, in trust to permit my niece M[rs] Alice Boutein to have my watch, plate, furniture for life, then to her dau. Alice, the income of my property to accumulate during the lives of Sam[l] & Alice Boutein & then to be equally divided amongst their children, & after the education of Edw[d] Trant Boutein her son my trustees are to advance £200 for his benefit & £500 at 21. Sam[l] Turner & Langford Lovell Ex'ors. Witnessed by Mary Freeman, Elizabeth Horne, Margaret Ramsay. Recorded 9 Aug. 1792.

From the Mackinen Petition it appears that William Bridges, Esq., holding Golden Grove in trust for Mr. Thomas Trant, a Roman Catholic, deceased, by his letter of attorney dated Nov. 1698 appointed Mr. Garret Trant of Montserrat, Mr. David Rice, and Mr. Thomas Trant, jun., of London, etc., to sell or let that estate, and two of them accordingly in 1702 granted a lease of it for 99 years to Dr. Daniel Mackinen at £100 a year.

1709, Oct. 3. Nicholas Trant of Falmouth, merchant, is refused any grant of land because in the late war he had been in the French service.

1710, Jan. 3. Nicholas Trant petitions for four parcels of land in Falmouth Town, bounded E. and W. with the main street, N. with the cross street, S. with the sea. Granted.

1712. Losses at Montserrat. Garrot Trant £151, in the Windward Division. (America and West Indies, No. 52.)

1713, June. Deposition of Thomas Trant of Antigua, merchant, aged 30. (George French's 'History.')

1714, Sep. 2. Thomas Trant petitions for land N. with Wine Street, S. with the sea, E. with Richard Buckeridge, Esq., W. with land and sea.

1715, Dec. 24. Ann Trant, widow of Nicholas Trant of Antigua, merchant, grants lease to Rowland Ash, Gent.

Martin French of Montserrat referred in his will of 1724 to his friend Dominick Trant, then about to settle as a merchant in London.

1729-30. Montserrat Census. Dominick Trant, Esq., Counsellor. 2 cattle mills, 3 men, 1 girl under 8, 80 negro men, 70 women, 75 children, 5 in family, 250 acres of cane, 25 cattle, and 27 mules.

Martin Blake, Esq., of St. Kitts, mar. 1742 Sarah daughter of Dominick Trant, Esq., of Montserrat; he died the following year, æt. 29, but she was living in 1760 in Paris.

1767. Mary Trant rated on 177 acres and 123 slaves.

1798, Dec. At St Luke's, Chelsea, James Trant, esq of Montserrat, to Miss Barrett, only daughter of the late Wisdom B. esq of Jamaica. ('Gent. Mag.,' p. 1147.)

1803, Dec. 10. At Montserrat, in the West Indies, aged 29, Dominick James Trant, esq. (*Ibid.*, 1804, p. 182.)

Mr. Fitzgibbon Trant of Dovea, co. Tipperary, informs me that: "Sir Patrick Trant having left Ireland with James II. his estates were confiscated and all records lost. We believe he was one of a very large family located in the County Kerry. My great-grandfather Dominick Trant mentions in one of his letters the amount of income he received from his 'cozen' in the West Indies—some £700 a year, and he also mentions meeting his relation Mr. Trant of Montserrat during a tour on the Continent about 1759.

"There is still an estate in St. Kitts called Trant's Estate, now held by the Rev. William R. C. Adamson, but by a deed dated 6 Oct. 1775 Dominique Henry Trant and Sarah Blake conveyed this estate in trust to Sir Richard Neave, Bart., and John Willet. In the 'Last Colonel of the Irish Brigade,' by Mr. M. J. O'Connell, are to be found some notes and a pedigree of the Trants prior to Sir Patrick Trant, and in King James II. army list (infantry) are to be found some more particulars."

PARISH REGISTER OF ST. JOHN.

Baptized.

1723 Jan. 19 Lydia Rodeney D. of Edward Trant & Lydia his wife.

1726 April 10 Edward the s. of Edward Trant & Lydia his wife.

1729 Aug. 24 Ann the d. of . . . . Trant and Lydia his wife.

1738 Oct. 1 Thomas ye S. of George Trant & Jane his wife.

1740 Oct. 26 Drury the s. of Edward Trant & Lydia his wife.

1742 April 25 Penelope the D. of Edward Trant & Ledya his wife.

1743 June 21 Henrietta the D. of Edward Trant & Lydia his wife.

1761 Mar. 12 Allis the D. of William Trant and Mary his wife.

1762 July 9 Paulina D. of Tho[s] Trant and Martha his wife.

1764 June 28 Eliz[th] Sarah the D. of W[m] Trant and Mary his wife.

1766 Jan. 30 Edw[d] & James Taylor the S. of W[m] Trant and Mary his wife.

1768 Feb. 21 Elizabeth D. of William Trant and Mary his wife.

1769 April 13 Ellinor Champen D. of Thomas Trant and Martha his wife.

1771 Mar. 17 Daniel Livingston the S. of Thomas Trant and Martha his wife.

1796 April 16 Eliza D. of Daniel L. Trant and Rebecca his wife. B. 22[d] March 1796.

1801 Oct. 8 Abraham S. of Daniel L. Trant and Rebecca his wife. B. the 27th December 1799.

1803 Jan. 11 Maria Hall D. of Daniel L. Trant & Rebecca his wife. B. the 18th January 1802.

Married.

1708 Oct. 7 Thomas Trant & Mary Wharfe.
1715 Jan. 12 Henry Douglas and Mary Trant. L.
1722 Jan. 26 Edward Trant and Lydia Rodeney. L.
1736 Aug. 7 George Trant & Jane Richardson.
1759 Sep. 8 Thomas Trant to Martha Ball. L.
1760 April 9 William Trant and Mary Taylor. L.
1781 May 7 James Boutein to Alice Trant. L.
1792 Aug. 4 Daniel Livingston Trant to Rebecca Marshall, Spinster. L.

Buried.

1713 Sep. . . Philip Trant.
1731 Feb. 12 Drury s. of Edward Trant.
1739 April 17 George Trant of this Island.
1742 Dec. 27 Henry Trant.
1745 Nov. 29 Drewry Trant s. of Edward Trant.
1754 Mar. 9 Cæsar Trant.
1758 July 22 Peter Trant.
1759 Sep. 30 Edward Trant, Junr.
1760 Nov. 15 Edward Trant, Senr.
1766 Jan. 8 Paulina Trant, Child.
1766 Feb. 1 James Trant, Child.
1771 April 10 Mary Trant.
1782 July 13 Mrs Lydia Trant.
1785 May 10 William Trant.
1793 April 2 Jane Trant.
1797 Aug. 13 Eliza Trant, Infant.
1802 Jan. 21 Martha Trant.

PARISH REGISTER OF ST. GEORGE.

Baptized.

1798 Mar. 11 . . . . S. of Daniel Trant & his wife.

PARISH REGISTER OF WEST DEAN, CO. WILTS.

Buried.

1797 Dec. 14 Elizabeth Trant, one of the ladies in the convent, daughter of William Trant & Mary *olim* Taylor of Antigua; aged 30.

Family of Traveis.

Robert Travis of St. Giles without Cripplegate, Citizen and Salter. Will dated 18 Sep., proved 24 Sep. 1667. (120 Carr.) Wife Grace.

John Travis, Citizen and Salter of London. 13 Oct. 1680. (157 Bath.) Brother Gilbert Travis, sister Mary Katherine, cozen Joseph Travis.

John Travis of St. Olive, Southwark, Gent. (174 Bath.) Children Bryan & Mary £40 each.

Anne Traveis of Fleete Street, London, widow. Will dated 19 Feb. 1693; proved 1 May 1694 by Henry Traveis. (110 Box.) To be buried in the Poultry Church near my late husband. My mother Mrs Mary Spire £600. My son-in-law Henry Traveis £400. Sarah Allen £20, & to her son Henry Whiteing £10. To my cousin Mrs Sarah Clarke £10, & to her son Henry Newberry £20. My cousin Brockett & his wife £20, & to them & their dau. Sara 40s. rings. Dennis Skinner £4. My maid Mary Connors £5. Nurse Smith 40s. Mr Wm Chapman & Mr John Chapman £5 each. Mrs Ruth Averett 40s. Capt. Smith & his wife & sister 40s. rings. My cousin Greene. My brother-in-law Mr Henry Traveis my silver mugg, & Ex'or. Witnessed by Mary Connors, Benjamin Bragg, Daniel Keylway.

Richard Traveis, now living in or near London, but late of Antigua, Gent. Will dated 5 March 1694; proved 24 April 1695 by Sarah the widow. (60 Irby.) To the 3 sons of Nathl Gale, senr, by his 2d wife Anne Gale, viz., John, Joseph, & Nathl Gale, 10,000 lbs. of Muscovado sugar apiece. To Nathl Gale, senr, after the decease of my wife Sarah, all the profits of my real estate in Antigua, then to my wife's heirs. I give him £10 & a guinea ring, as also to his wife. To Mrs Eliz. Freeman £5 & a guinea ring. To Mr Robt Amory £10 & a guinea ring. To Mr Tho. Botely & his wife Eliz. guinea rings. To my brother James & to such of my relations as may claim it 1s. All my estate, both real & personal, to my wife Sarah, & appoint her Ex'trix. Nathl Gale, senr, & Tho. Botely overseers. Witnessed by John Monck, Thomas Heath, Nathaniel Wickham. Recorded at St. John's 12 March 1696-7.

By an inventory recorded at St. John's it also appears that testator was owner of one-eighth of the ship "ye Happy Return."

Mary Traveis. Will dated 5 May, proved 10 May 1703. Commission to Daniel Puckle, guardian of William and Mary Helmes and of Henry Traveis till 21. On 4 Nov. 1707 commission to Richard Merryweather, guardian of Mary Helmes, Daniel Puckle being dead. (138 Degg.) To my son Wm Helmes & my dau. Mary Helmes all my property, they to pay to my dau. Mary Smith & my dau. Anne Cary & my son Henry Traveis £300 apiece. To Mr Azariah Penny, mercht, £5, & he to be trustee for Wm & Mary Helmes. To Mr Daniel Puckle £100, & to be trustee for Henry Traveis. To Mrs Mary Cope £100. To my uncle Henry Traveis £10. To my coachman Jos. Wilkinson £5. That part of my estate I hold in right of my husband I freely give to my son Henry Traveis. Witnessed by Anne Pery, Sarah Cocburn, Anne Walford, John Jarman. On 10 May 1703 was sworn Anne Pery, wife of John Pery of St. Andrew, Holborn, Esq., and John Jarman of ditto, Gent. Testator died in her house at Hatton Garden of small-pox, within two or three doors. Dr. Coles attended her. She could not sign as she was then blind.

Henry Traveis. 4 March. Adm'on to Fisher Tench, Esq., Guardian of Henry Traveis, a minor, son of said Henry Traveis, late of St. Bridget *alias* St. Bride's, but at Nevis, deceased. Mary Traveis was his widow and relict. Sep. 1708. Former grant 10 May 1703.

By Governor Sir William Mathew. Whereas Mrs. Mary Traveis, widow, deceased, of Antigua, by her will dated 3 May 1703, appointed Aezariah Penny of Antigua, merchant, trustee to her son William Helmes and her daughter Mary Helmes, which said children are in Europe and under age. Letters of Guardianship now granted to him 16 Feb. 1703-4. Recorded 17 Nov. 1704.

1704, July 14. Azariah Penny, guardian of William Helme, son and heir of Major William Helme, formerly of Antigua, deceased. Letter of Attorney to Edward Perrie of Antigua, Esq. Recorded at St. John's.

Henry Traveis the elder of St. Michael Bassishaw, Gent. Will dated 29 May, proved 7 Nov. 1706 by Fisher Tench, Esq., and Samuel Thayer, Gent. (248 Eedes.) My loving kinsmen Fisher Tench of Low Layton, co. Essex, Esq., & Saml Thayer of Bridgwater Square, London, Gt, Ex'ors in T., & on the death of either my coz. Fra. Asty, mt, to be co-Ex'or, & if survivor die my lov. frd Jno Young of Lond., mt, a co-Ex'or. I give them all my personal estate on Trust, & they shall be each paid £15 a year for 15 years if my neph. Hen. Traveis so long live. £300 to be laid out for setting up Hen. Whiteing, s. of my late niece Sarah Allen, decd, & 2 years after his setting up he shall be pd £200 more. All my personal est. to be laid out in the purchase of lands, houses, or ground rents, that when my neph. Hen. Traveis the younger, an infant son of my late nephew Hen. Traveis, decd, shall attain 21 my trustees shall settle the same on him & his heirs, & in default $\frac{1}{3}$ to Hen. Whiteing & $\frac{2}{3}$ to be held for such persons as I shall appoint, & for want of such $\frac{1}{2}$ to each of my said trustees. My messuage in London which I lately purchased to sd trustees, to go with my other lands. To St Bartholomew's Hospl £20. All my lands in cos. York & Lincoln to be settled on 9 trustees for support of certain poor children of the 3 parishes of Thorne & Hatfeild, co. York, & Wroot, co. Linc., according to the draft scheme I have drawn up. To my bro. Chester's dau., now wife of Thos. Fountaine, Esq. (if my brother do pay £51 to my Ex'ors due from my late coz. Edwd Chester, decd), the pearl necklace of 2 rows & a gold watch & fosset diamond ring my late wife's. My other pearl necklace of 1 row & my emerald ring to my neph. Hen. Traveis as heirlooms. To my coz. Eliz. Hardy my wrought bed with its hangings. To my Ex'ors & their wives £10 ea. Poor of Bexley, co. Kent, £10. To my coz. Martha Traveis & to Mrs Daniel where I now live £10 ea. To Jno Squibbs of Linc. Inn, Esq., £10. To be bur. at Bexley, co. Kent, nr my late dear wife. £50 for funeral. My said coz. Tench's bond to me of £750. Witnessed by Gratian Bale, John Allbright, Benjamin Powney, John Squibb.

Pedigree of Traveis.

ARMS.—*Argent, a saltier between four butterflies sable, in centre point a crescent.*
CREST.—*A right forearm couped erect, vested argent and sable, the hand proper holding a club or.*

RICHARD TRAVEIS of London, merchant ╤ . . . .

- John Traveis of London, merchant ╤ . . . .
- Margaret Traveis, mar. Sir Thomas Blanck, Knt., Lord Mayor of London. He was knighted at Greenwich 5 May 1583.

James Traveis of London, merchant ╤ Margaret, dau. of Robert Cocke.

- Richard Traveis of London, merchant, 1st son and heir, bapt. 21 April 1594 at St. Mary Woolnoth: mar. licence dated 23 Feb. 1624-5, then of St. Martin in the Vintry, mercer; died 27 Sep. 1661 at Mitcham, co. Surrey. Signed his Pedigree in the 'Visitation of London, 1633-5.' ╤ Mary, dau. of Thomas Roe of London, draper, and widow of Thomas Dorrell of All Hallows, Lombard Street, silkman.
- Jane Traveis, bapt. 3 June 1599 at St. Mary Woolnoth.

Children of Richard Traveis and Mary:

- James Traveis, living 1694.
- Richard Traveis of St. Botolph, Aldgate, and Antigua, bapt. 19 Aug. 1629 at Mitcham; settled as a planter at Antigua later than 1666. Will dated 5 March 1694-5; proved 24 April 1695. (60 Irby.) ╤ Sarah . . . . proved her husband's will. s.p.
- Margaret Traveis.
- Mary Traveis.
- Martha Traveis, living 1706.
- Henry Traveis the elder of St. Michael Bassishaw; bur. at Bexley, co. Kent. Will dated 29 May and proved 7 Nov. 1706. (248 Eedes.) ╤ . . . . bur. at Bexley, co. Kent. s.p.

Pedigree of Tremills.

Lieut. WILLIAM TREMILLS of Antigua, carpenter, granted 300 acres in St. Mary's Parish 1678. Will dated 17 March 1686; sworn 5 Jan. 1692. ╤ . . . . living 1686.

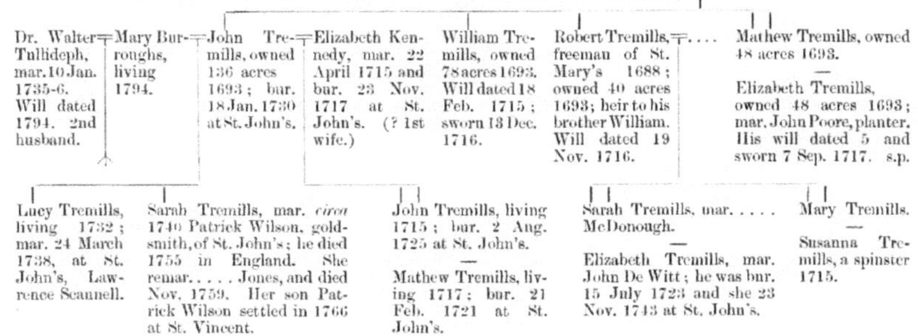

- Dr. Walter Tullideph, mar. 10 Jan. 1735-6. Will dated 1794. 2nd husband. ╤ Mary Burroughs, living 1794. ╤ John Tremills, owned 136 acres 1693; bur. 18 Jan. 1730 at St. John's. ╤ Elizabeth Kennedy, mar. 22 April 1715 and bur. 23 Nov. 1717 at St. John's. (? 1st wife.)
- William Tremills, owned 78 acres 1693. Will dated 18 Feb. 1715; sworn 13 Dec. 1716.
- Robert Tremills, freeman of St. Mary's 1688; owned 40 acres 1693; heir to his brother William. Will dated 19 Nov. 1716. ╤ . . . .
- Mathew Tremills, owned 48 acres 1693.
- Elizabeth Tremills, owned 48 acres 1693; mar. John Poore, planter. His will dated 5 and sworn 7 Sep. 1717. s.p.

- Lucy Tremills, living 1732; mar. 24 March 1738, at St. John's, Lawrence Scannell.
- Sarah Tremills, mar. *circa* 1740 Patrick Wilson, goldsmith, of St. John's; he died 1755 in England. She remar. . . . . Jones, and died Nov. 1759. Her son Patrick Wilson settled in 1766 at St. Vincent.
- John Tremills, living 1715; bur. 2 Aug. 1725 at St. John's.
- Mathew Tremills, living 1717; bur. 21 Feb. 1721 at St. John's.
- Sarah Tremills, mar. . . . . McDonough.
- Elizabeth Tremills, mar. John De Witt; he was bur. 15 July 1723 and she 23 Nov. 1743 at St. John's.
- Mary Tremills.
- Susanna Tremills, a spinster 1715.

From Johnson's Account, 1830 (*reduced*).

1646, April 13. Richard Traves of London fined £60 on his houses in Cornhill. (Calendar of Committee for Compounding, P.R.O.)

1678, Feb. 21. Richard Travis in the ship "Fellowship" from Barbados for Antigua, Thomas Pim Commander: time out. (Hotten's 'List of Emigrants,' p. 410.)

PARISH REGISTER OF ST. JOHN.

Buried.

1723 June 9 Peter Travers, Mercht, of a snow; from Londonderry.
1758 April 3 Frances Travers.

PARISH REGISTER OF ST. MARY WOOLNOTH, CITY OF LONDON.

Baptized.

1594 April 21 Richard s. of James Traves, Merchaunt.
1595 May 25 James s. of James Traves, Merchaunt.
1599 June 3 Jane d. of James Travers, Merchante.

Buried.

1689 Feb. 9 Thomas Travvis, Bookeseller. Dyed Feb. 7.

1624-5, Feb. 23. Richard Travis of St Martin in the Vintry, London, Mercer, & Mary Dorrell, of All Hallows, Lombard Street, London, widow of Thomas Dorrell, Silkman; at St Mary Somerset, Lond. (Marriage Licences: Bishop of London.)

Samuel Baker of London=. . . .

James Traveis of London, merchant, bapt. 25 May 1595 at St. Mary Woolnoth. Signed his Pedigree in the 'Visitation of London, 1633-5.'=Jane Baker. | Margaret Baker, mar. Humphrey Thayer of St. Dionys Backchurch. His Pedigree in the 'Visitation of London, 1633-5.' | Mabell Baker.=Nicholas Tenche of London, merchant; had a grant of arms 1 July 1628, 4 Charles. His Pedigree in the 'Visitation of London, 1633-5.'

James Traveis (? mar. 2ndly Anne, dau. of Mrs. Mary Spire. Her will dated 19 Feb. 1693; proved 1 May 1694. (110 Box.))=. . . . | Elizabeth . . . . bur. 7 Aug. 1663 at St. Dionys Backchurch, London. 1st wife.=Nathaniel Tench of St. Dionys Backchurch 1662-3, later of Low Layton, co. Essex, merchant; Alderman of London; died 2 April 1710, æt. 78. M.I. at Layton.=Anne, dau. and heir of William Fisher, Alderman of London; mar. *circa* 1667; died 25 April 1696, æt. 50. Had issue eight sons and three daus. 2nd wife.

Major William Helmes of Antigua, brother of Robert Helmes of Nevis. 1st husband.=Mary . . . . died in Hatton Garden, London. Will dated 3 and proved 10 May 1703. (138 Degg.)=Henry Traveis the younger of St. Bride's, London, but died at Nevis *circa* 1703. Adm'on granted 10 May 1703. 2nd husband. | Sir Fisher Tench of Low Layton, co. Essex, 1st Bart., only surviving son; High Sheriff 1712; created a Baronet 8 Aug. 1715; died 31 Oct. 1736, æt. 63. He built the "Great House" designed by Inigo Jones and decorated by Sir James Thornhill.=. . . .

William Helmes, son and heir, an infant 1703. | Mary Helmes, an infant 1703 and 1707. | Henry Traveis, a minor 1703; heir to his great-uncle Henry Traveis 1706; matriculated from Trinity College, Oxford, 14 Oct. 1717, æt. 17. | Sir Nathaniel Tench of the Great House, Low Layton, 2nd and last Bart., died a bachelor 2 June 1737, æt. 40. His estate was sold to Richard Oliver of Antigua in 1750.

Family of Tremills.

William Tremills, carpenter, of New Division. Will dated 17 March 1686. To my wife ⅓ of my real estate. All my goods & plate among my children, viz., my sons Wm, Robt, & John, & my dau. Elizth. My wife's ⅓ after her death to be also equally divided among them. My sons to be Ex'ors. Witnessed by Ambrose York, William Grace, John Butler. By Christopher Codrington was sworn John Butler 5 Jan. 1692.

William Tremills. Will dated 18 Feb. 1715. To my sister Eliz. Poore £40 c. To my neph. Jno Tremills £20 c. To my niece Sarah McDonough £20 c. To my godson Wm McDonough £5 c. To my nieces Eliz. Dewitt & Mary Parre & Susannah Tremills 40s. c. each. To Eliz. McDonough, Geo. Dewitt, Thos. Dewitt, children of said nieces Sarah & Elizth, 40s. c. each. All residue to my bro. Robt Tremills. He & Capt. Ambrose Yorke Ex'ors. Witnessed by William Kenedy, Peter Mathews, Thomas Pearce. Before Walter Hamilton, Esq., was sworn William Kenedy 13 Dec. 1716.

Robert Tremills of St. John's. Will dated 19 Nov. 1716. To my dans. Sarah McDonough, Elizth Dewitt, Mary Peared, Susannah, certain negros, & to the latter maintenance till 17. All residue equally among my 4 dans. Jno Tremills, Jno McDonough, Jno Poore Ex'ors. Witnessed by William Kenedy, James Pain. Before Walter Hamilton, Esq., was sworn William Kenedy 13 Dec. 1716.

John Poore, planter. Will dated 5 Sep. 1717. To Leonard Allen £60 c. to buy 2 negros for his children. To my godson Lawrence Seannel £60 c. to purchase negros as his uncle David Seannel & my widow think fit. To my godson Mathew Tremills £10 c. & "ye whole duty of man." To my godson Math. Barton £10 c. To Edw[d] Trant £20 c. To Thos. Trant Creagh, 2[d] son of my cousin Pierse Creagh, £20 c. To my sister Julian Torrington of co. Kerry, Irel[d], £500 c. due to me from Jn[o] Nibbs, Jas. Nibbs, & Thos. Hawes. 6000 lbs. to the children of my father after my own mother's decease to be shipped home. To Leonard Allen, Edw[d] Trant, & Pierse Creagh each a ring of 30*s*. All residue to my wife Eliz., she & Leonard Allen Ex'ors, & Edw[d] Trant & Pierse Creagh overseers in T. Witnessed by William Hillhouse, jun., John Tremills, Thomas Hanson. Before Edward Byam, Esq., was sworn William Hillhouse 30 Sep. 1717.

Peter Mercier, merchant. Will dated 2 Oct. 1732. To my mother Susannah Mercier of London, wid., £20 a year. To my wife Lucy all residue, she to be Ex'trix, & Geo. Jennings & Jacob Thibou Ex'ors in Trust, & to each a ring of a pistole. Witnessed by Robert Delamere, Josiah Wakelin, Gabriel Thibou.

Codicil. 4 Sep. 1733. Having obtained judgment against the estate of John Tremills, dec[d], for £918 c. I bequeath it to his widow Mary Tremills, my d[r]-in-law, & to her 2 daus. Lucy & Sarah, but if she re-marry to my bro.-in-law Jacob Thibou for their benefit. On 27 Oct. 1733 Gabriel Thibou was sworn by Edward Byam, Esq.

1678, Aug. 20. Lieutenant William Tramill granted 300 acres by Colonel James Vaughan. Surveyed 6 Sep.

1679, Nov. 7. William Tremills in the sloop "Hopewell" from Barbadoes for Antegua, William Murphy Comander; time out. (Hotten's 'List of Emigrants,' p. 412.)

33 Chas. II., 1681, Aug. 22. William Tremill, 300 acres. (Patent Book.)

1686, Nov. 11. Levy on land. On the back occur the names of Lieutenant William Tremills, B. Tremills, William Tremills, John Tremills, and Robert Tremills. (St. Mary's Vestry Book.)

1688. Levy at Bermudian Valley. Lieutenant William Tremills. 7 negros; 300 acres. Same date Robert Tremills is taxed 100 lbs. as a freeman.

1688, March 25. Peter Mercier, Suzanna his wife, Peter, James, Suzanna, and Ann their children, aliens born to receive letters of denization. (Camden Soc. Pub., p. 52.)

1693, Jan. 15. Levy. St. Mary's Parish.

	Acres.	Negros.
W[m] Tremills . . .	78	2
Rob. Tremills . . .	40	2
Jn[o] Tremills . . .	136	5
Eliz[th] Tremills . . .	48	1
Mathew Tremills . . .	48	0

1706, June 7. Levy.

	Acres.	Negros.
M[r] W[m] Tremills . . .	30	2
M[r] Rob[t] Tremills . . .	—	—
M[r] John Poor . . .	96	13

1709, March 1. John Poore of Antigua, planter, and Elizabeth his wife lease 50 acres to Robert Hanson, jun., of Antigua, planter, for 15 years for 12,000 lbs. rent. Bond of Robert Hanson, sen. and jun.

1712-13. Robert Tremills was uncle and guardian of the wife of Samuel Lightfoot. (Vol. ii., p. 183.)

1716, April 26. Pew No. 12 was allotted to John Tremills, and No. 13 to Mr. Denbow and the land of William Tremills.

Parish Register of St. John.

Married.

1715	(? April) 22	John Tremills and Eliz[a] Kennedy; by L.
1715	Oct. 30	Peter Mercier and Lucy Burroughs; by Lic.
1738	Mar. 24	Lawrence Seannell & Lucy Tremills; by L.
1743	July 11	William Mercer and Lucy Burroughs.

Buried.

1717	Nov. 23	Eliz[th] Tremill.
1721	Feb. 21	Mathew the s. of John Tremills.
1725	Aug. 2	John s. of John Tremills.
1730	Jan. 18	M[r] John Tremills.
1733	Sep. 13	M[r] Peter Mercier.
1744	Feb. 6	Lucy Mercier.

Family of Tudway.

Clement Tudway of London, merchant. Will dated 12 Dec., proved 8 Feb. 1688 by Rachel Tudway, Bastiaen Baijer, William Barnes, and John Pratt. (26 Ent.) To my dear wife Rachel ⅓ of the profits of my plantation called Parham Hill in Antigua & of Long Island, & of my ½ share of the Swan taverne in Old Fish-street, London, also all jewels & moneys given her by myself or by her mother Eliz. Clarke, & ⅓ of all my personal estate. All residue to be secured by my Ex'ors Bastiaen Baijer & W[m] Barnes, jun[r], for the education & maintenance of my children Eliz., Rachell, Sara, & Clement Tudway till 21, & all residue of profits to be divided among them at 21. Each of their shares to be made up to £1000. If any dau. die ⅓ of her share to my wife & ⅔ to her surviving sisters. If my son Clement die under age without issue then all the rents & profits to my daus. If I have but one son then all my plantations in Antigua to him at 21, if 2 sons the younger to have £500 in addition. If I have several sons then my estates to go to my 1st son, then to my next son, then to my daus., & after the death of my wife & children to the heirs male of my 1st son, then failing issue ⅓ to my brother Thos. Tudway, ⅓ to my brother Rich[d] Tudway, & ⅓ to my brother Chas. Tudway, & the ½ share of my estate in Old Fish Str. to my sisters Eliz. Clousley & Sara Floyer. My wife to relinquish all claim to dower, if not to have but ¼ & not ⅓ of the profits. My brother Chas. Tudway to manage my plantations in Antigua & to have 12 % of the profits. My Ex'ors to grant leases up to 11 years. To my mother Anne Tudway £90, & £6 a year, & £10 for mourning, & a 20*s*. ring. To my brothers & sisters Thos., Rich[d], & Chas., Ann Turner, & Eliz. Whitfield £5 apiece & 20*s*. rings. To my sister Susanna Tudway £15 & a 20*s*. ring. To my mother Eliz. Clarke £10, to her & my sister Eliz. Clousley & my brother & sister Peter Floyer & Sara his wife 20*s*. rings. My wife Rachel Tudway & W[m] Barnes the Younger Ex'ors, & Bastiaen Baijer, W[m] Barnes the Elder, Francis Carlisle, W[m] Barnes the Younger, & John Pratt Guardians. Witnessed by Jos. Blackburne, John Carthitch, Henry Paulson, servants to Mr. Floyer, Elizabeth Bort, servant to Mr. Tudway.

Memorandum dated 27 Dec. 1688. John Pratt to be Ex'or. I intend making a mortgage of ½ of my estate in Antigua & Long Island which I purchased of Geo. Turney, deceased, as a security to Sarah Turney, Geo. Turney, & Anthony Turney, his widow & children, for £2300 due to them, viz., for £1050 with 6 % interest due 1 Nov. 1690 & £1250 on 1 Nov. 1691. My Ex'ors are to draw up this mortgage. Witnessed by Andrew Binks in Watling Street, Charles Tincker, Jane Crocker, servants to Mr. Floyer, Mary Prince, servant to Mrs. Clarke.

1692, April 16. Thomas Tudway of Reading, co. Berks. Adm'on to Thomas Tudway the son.

Charles Tudway of Antigua, Gent. Will dated 16 July 1692. Bound to England. After my funeral expenses are paid, to my father-in-law Mr John Robinson & to my mother-in-law Mrs Mary Robinson & to my brothers Tho. & Richd & my sisters Ann, Elizth, & Susanna Tudway 40s. each. To my mother Mrs Anne Tudway of London £20. To my sister-in-law Mrs Rachell Tudway, relict of my brother Clement Tudway, Esq., decd, £20. To Francis Carlile, Esq., £20. To Nathl Barnes £20. ½ of all residue to my wife Mary Tudway of Wells, co. Som., & ½ to my son Chas. Tudway at 21. My wife & my father-in-law Mr John Robinson Guardians. My wife, Mr John Robinson of Wells, & my friends Francis Carlile & Nathl Barnes of Antigua Ex'ors. Witnessed by Robert Strode, John Murray, Nicholas Godman, William Bayley. By Hon. Thomas Duncomb, Esq., Member of H.M. Council, was sworn Robert Strode, Gent., 7 April 1693. Recorded 20 May 1693. Order to appraise the estate of the late Captain Charles Tudway dated 27 May 1693 by John Yeamans to Benjamin Wickham and James Porter. Inventory appended, four men, six women, etc., total value 46,290 lbs., one house at Parham, 10 June 1693.

1692, Nov. Charles Tudway, at one time of St. Martin's in the Fields, London, later of Antego, but in the city of Canterbury, deceased. Mary Tudway the widow and relict states that five years ago her said husband went to Antego and left behind him herself and his only child Charles Tudway, then aged about three, and returned in Oct. 1692 and died at Canterbury. Commission 26 Nov. 1692 to Richard Tudway the brother.

Thomas Tudway of Reading, co. Berks, mercer. Will dated 1 April, proved 28 May 1695. (82 Irby.) 3 daus., Hester, Eliz., & Mary.

Richard Tudway of London, merchant. Will dated 11 Jan., proved 3 Feb. 1707 by Joseph Whitfield; power reserved to Thomas Hawes Clarke. (46 Barrett.) To my honoured mother Anne Tudway, widow, £50 & £10 a year. To my dau. Eliz. Tudway £800 at 21, if she die before then without issue then £200 to my brother Dr Tho. Tudway of Cambridge University, £200 to my loving friends Guinnett Freeman, citizen & haberdasher, & Benjn Henshaw of London, mercht, on trust to pay to those persons my sister Eliz. the wife of Joseph Whitfeild may appoint, £100 to my nephew John Whitfeild, £100 to my sister Ann Cooper, widow, £50 to Mary widow of my brother Chas. Tudway, deceased, & to Chas. Tudway her son £50, they to release all claims against me on account of the estate of my brother Chas., £50 to Joseph Whitfeild my brother-in-law, £50 to my brother-in-law Tho. Hawes & my sister Anne his wife, to my brother Dr Tho. Tudway & my sister Eliz. Whitfeild £50 each, to my brother-in-law Joseph Whitfeild & Eliz. his wife, to my brother-in-law Tho. Hawes & Anne his wife, & to my sister Anne Cooper £10 each. To Mary, my brother Chas.' widow, & to her son Chas. Tudway £20 & £5, each, & I give them my tenement in Parham Town, Antigua. All residue to my dau. Eliz. Joseph Whitfeild & Tho. Hawes Ex'ors. Witnessed by Frederick Hare, Richard Elford, Robert Waple.

Codicil. If my dau. Eliz. die under 21 then ¾ of residue to my sister Eliz. Whitfeild & ¼ to my brother-in-law Tho. Hawes & his wife Anne. To my 2 Ex'ors 1 guinea each. My servant Eliz. Warwick £10. To be buried at St Cath., Coleman Str., near my late wife.

Anne Tudway of Brentwood, co. Essex, widow. Will dated 24 Feb. 1707; proved 4 March 1715 by Elizabeth Whitfield, widow of Joseph Whitfield, deceased. (60 Fox.) Aged. My late son Clement Tudway bequeathed to me £100 which is still unpaid & my son Richd Tudway bequeathed to me £50 also unpaid. To my dau.-in-law Mrs Rachael Tudway £5. To my grandson Clement Tudway £5. To my granddaus. Rachael & Sarah Tudway 50s. apiece. To my son Dr Tho. Tudway of Cambridge £30. To my granddau. Eliz. Tudway £20, but if she die £10 to my son Dr Tho. Tudway & £10 to my daus. Anne Cooper & Eliz. Whitfield. To my dau. Cooper £25 & to her son Tho. Turner £5. To my dau. Eliz. Whitfield £30. To my grandson John Whitfield £5. To my grandson Chas. Tudway £5. To my grandson Chas. Shugburgh £5. To my granddau. Letitia Shugburgh & my grandson John Shugburgh 50s. apiece. My wedding ring to my son Dr Thos. Tudway, & to him & to my 2 daus. Cooper & Whitfield each a broad piece of gold of 23s. 6d. To my granddau. Eliz. Cooper 40s. To the widow Poole of Brentwood what she owes me by bond. All residue to my son-in-law Mr Joseph Whitfield & appoint him Ex'or. Witnessed by Mary Lawes, Thomas Warren, Charles White.

Rachaell Tudway of London, widow. Will dated 25 July 1730; proved 3 Feb. 1732 by Clement Tudway the son. (67 Brice.) My dau. Rachaell Tudway £20, sister Eliz. Clowdesley £10, sister Dame Sarah ffloyer £20, niece Letitia ffloyer £10, cousin Sush Clowdesley 5 gns, s.-in-l. John Cresswell £10, cousins Wm Cartlitch & Eliz. Smith a ring. My 3 attorneys in Antigua, Col. Edwd Byam, Col. Nathl Crump, & Geo. Byam, Esq., £5 apiece. Daniel Dodson of Lincoln's Inn, Esq., a ring. Tho. ffenton, if living on Parham plantn in Antigua as manager, £10. To my s. Clement Tudway my leasehold messuage called the Indian Queen in Blow Bladder Str., London, now in the tenure of Richd Llewellyn, which I lately purchased of Mrs Mary Arnold, charged with £20 a yr. for my dau. Rachaell Tudway & £20 a yr. for my unfortunate sister Eliz. Clowdesley. All residue to my son Clement & Ex'or. Funeral not to exceed £40. Witnessed by Jacob Shelton, Basinghall Street, Pope Gregory, clerk to Mr. Hamond in Dove Court, Lombard Street, Jonathan Fullagar, clerk to Mr. Hamond.

Pedigree of Tudway.

ARMS.—*Ermine, a lion rampant gules between three roses azure.*
CREST.—*A demi-lion rampant gules, holding a rose azure slipped proper.*

THOMAS TUDWAY, Gentleman Clerk of St. George's Chapel, Windsor; bur. there 25 Nov. 1671. ═ Anne, 5th dau. of Richard Plat, 1st son of Sir Hugh Plat of Bedwell Green, co. Middlesex, Knt. Will dated 24 Feb. 1707, then of Brentwood, co. Essex; proved 4 March 1715. (60 Fox.)

Clement Tudway of Parham Hill, Antigua, and of London, merchant, 1st son, born 1649. Will dated 12 Dec. 1688; proved 8 Feb. 1688-9. (26 Ent.) ═ Rachel, dau. of Major Clowdesley of London; bur. at St. Alban's, Wood Street. Will dated 25 July 1730; proved 3 Feb. 1732. (67 Brice.)

Thomas Tudway, Mus. Doc., Professor of Music at University of Cambridge, died 23 Nov. 1726. ═ Margaret, dau. of Samuel Rix of Canterbury.

Richard Tudway, born 1656 at Bradfield, co. Essex; of St. Margaret Moses, London, æt. 34, 1691-2; master mariner in the Antiguan trade; bur. at St. Catherine, Coleman Street. Will dated 1 Jan. and proved 3 Feb. 1707, then of London, merchant. (16 Barrett.) ═ Elizabeth Steele of Winchester; mar. allegation dated 26 Jan. 1691-2.

Clement Tudway of Parham Hill, Antigua, Esq., only son and heir, died s.p.; bur. at St. Alban's, Wood Street, London. Will dated 18 Nov. 1748, then of London; proved 20 March 1748-9. (91 Lisle.)

Elizabeth Tudway.

Rachel Tudway.

Sarah Tudway.

Elizabeth Tudway, only dau., a minor 1707.

Thomas Tudway, born 8 and bapt. 20 Jan. 1707.

Charles Tudway of St. Andrew, Wells, born 2 Nov. and bapt. 19 Nov. 1713; sole heir in 1748 to his cousin Clement. Will dated 9 Sep. 1765; proved 2 Oct. 1770. (380 Jenner.) ═ Hannah . . . . living 1765.

Richard Clement Tudway, born 10 and bapt. 16 Dec. 1716; living 1765.

John Tudway, born 4 and bapt. 26 April 1719; living 1748.

Clement Tudway of Wells, born 8 Oct. 1734; J.P. and M.P. 1760—1815; died s.p. 7 July 1815. M.I. at St. Cuthbert's, Wells. Will dated 22 Dec. 1814; proved 30 Aug. 1815. ═ Elizabeth, younger dau. of Sir Rowland Hill, 1st Bart., of Hawkestone, co. Salop; mar. 7 June 1762; died 13 Feb. 1828, æt. 88. s.p.

Charles Tudway, Alderman of Wells, died a bachelor May 1810.

Robert Tudway of Wells, died there 1 Dec. 1800. ═ Mary, dau. of Rev. John Paine, Sub-Dean of Wells; born 1745; died 27 March 1823.

John Paine Tudway, born 21 April 1775; J.P. and M.P. for Wells 1815—30; sole heir to his uncle Clement, from whom he inherited the Parham Plantation, Antigua; died July 1835, æt. 60. ═ Fanny Goold, dau. of Lucas Pulsford of Wells; mar. 1806.

Rev. Clement Tudway, born 20 May 1782; Lieut. 16th Dragoons; Vicar of Chiseldon, Wilts, 23 Aug. 1814; died 26 Feb. 1830. ═ Elizabeth Pappod, dau. of Thomas B. Calley of Burderop Park, Wilts; mar. 7 April 1807; died 18 May 1836.

Robert Tudway, died a bachelor.

Christopher Tudway, died a bachelor.

Robert Charles Tudway of The Cedars, Wells, J.P., and of Parham, Antigua, born 6 July and bapt. 30 Sep. 1808; High Sheriff of Somerset 1842-3; died 20 Oct. 1855. ═ Maria Catherine, 1st dau. of Sir William Miles, 1st Bart., of Leigh Court, co. Somerset, M.P.; mar. 3 March 1846.

Henry Goold Tudway, matriculated from Trinity College, Oxford, 11 July 1846, æt. 19; B.A. 1851; M.A. 1853; Rector of Walton, co. Somerset, 1855, till his death there 13 Feb. 1866. ═ Mary, dau. of John Phipps of Leighton House, Wilts; mar. 1856.

Lady Edith Nelson, dau. of Horatio, 3rd Lord Nelson; mar. 5 July 1870; died 24 Aug. 1877. 1st wife. ═ Charles Clement Tudway of The Cedars, Wells, Stoberry Park, co. Somerset, and 17 Lower Berkeley Street, London, only surviving son, born 23 Nov. 1846; educated at Harrow. Owner of Parham Hill and Parham Lodge, Antigua. ═ Alice Constance, youngest dau. of Sir Frederick H. Hervey Bathurst, Bart.; mar. 15 Jan. 1884. 2nd wife.

Madeleine Constance Tudway, only child, born 18 April 1873.

A son, born 23 Sep. 1888 at 17 Lower Berkeley Street.

Charles Tudway of Parham, Antigua, Gent., born 1660 at Windsor; Captain of Militia; died at Canterbury. Will dated 16 July 1692; sworn 7 April 1693. Recorded at Antigua. ╤ Mary, dau. of John Robinson of Wells, co. Somerset, by Mary his wife.

John Tudway, bur. 1 Oct. 1662 at St. George's Chapel, Windsor.

William Tudway, bapt. 15 Oct. 1665 at St. George's Chapel, Windsor; died young.

Elizabeth Tudway, mar. Joseph Whitfield; living 1707.

Ann Tudway, mar. .... Cooper; living 1707.

Charles Tudway of New Street in Wells, yeoman, only child, bapt. 24 Aug. 1684 and bur. 24 April 1723 at St. Cuthbert's. ╤ Mary Cook, mar. 26 Dec. 1706 at St. Cuthbert's; living 1765.

Robinson Tudway of Bristol, hosier, born 9 and bapt. 19 Nov. 1721. Will dated 5 April and proved 10 Dec. 1763 at Bristol. ╤ Anne ....

Elizabeth Tudway, born 2 and bapt. 24 Feb. 1708; mar. 25 Nov. 1735 Robert Holloway.

Rachel Tudway, born 29 Nov. and bapt. 14 Dec. 1710; mar. 1 Nov. 1738 William Davis.

Mary Tudway, born 3 and bapt. 21 Sep. 1712. (? bur. 28 Dec. 1715.)

Mary Tudway, born 9 and bapt. 15 Nov. 1715.

John Tudway.

Elizabeth Tudway, mar. Rev. Francis Drake of Seaton, Devon.

Mary Tudway, a minor 1765; mar. June 1773 Rev. Rowland Hill, 3rd son of Sir Rowland Hill, Bart; she died 1830; he died 1833, æt. 88.

Richard Tudway.

Ann Tudway.

Jane Tudway.

Sarah Tudway.

Martha Tudway.

Elizabeth Tudway.

Fanny Tudway, mar. William Melliar of Wells, Esq.; he was born 14 Feb. 1757 and died 7 Aug. 1840; she died 11 March 1795. M.I. at St. Cuthbert's, Wells.

Mary Tudway, mar. Rev. Edward Foster, Prebendary of Wells.

Sarah Tudway.

Elizabeth Tudway, mar. Rev. Richard Thomas Whalley, Rector of Yeovelton, Somerset; she died 1830.

Harriet Tudway, mar. July 1815 Richard Burford, Lieut. 23rd Regiment; she died s.p. 1821.

Caroline Tudway, mar. 11 Aug. 1819 Andrew Carrick, M.D., of Clifton; she died s.p. June 1837.

Jane Tudway, mar. 23 Nov. 1825 Rev. Thomas Boucher Coney, Vicar of Pucklechurch; she died 1874.

Frances Henrietta Tudway, mar. 23 May 1837 Arthur Constantine Phipps of Shepton Mallet.

Emma H. S. Tudway, died 2 Jan. 1895 at Caledonia Place, Clifton.

Letitia Sarah Tudway, mar. George Fillingham.

Augusta Tudway, mar. Rev. Francis Fleming Beadon, Vicar of Shepton, Somerset.

Mary Tudway.

Harriet Henrietta Tudway.

Clement Tudway of London, only son, born 7 April 1809; died 26 April 1867 in London.

Elizabeth Pappod Tudway.

Caroline Tudway.

Clement Tudway of London, Esq. Will dated 18 Nov., proved 20 March 1748 by Charles Tudway. (91 Lisle.) To be buried near my mother's grave at St Alban's, Wood Str. To my cousin John Tudway £700 & forgive debts. To my cousin Robinson Tudway £1000. To my cousin Holloway, wife of Mr Robt Holloway, £500. To my cousin John Shuckburgh £300. To the dau. of my cousin Chas. Shuckburgh, deceased, £300 & forgive debts. £20 to each of my attorneys in Antigua. To my cousin Mrs Mary Tudway, widow, £10. To my cousin Mrs Letitia Woolley £21. To my cousin Mrs Susannah Clowdesley £10. To Mrs Mary Stockeld £10. To Mrs Jane & Mrs Alice Wickham £10 each & forgive debts due from them or their grandfather Mr John Fawkes & their father & mother John & Jane Wickham. To my cousin Letitia Wotton £21. To Mr John Wilson, now of Grantham, £50, & to his sister Mrs Mary Fotherby £10. To my goddau. Lenten, dau. of Mr Rossiter Lenten, £100. 2 gs. to each servant. To the poor of St Paul in the Bayle of Lincoln £10. To Mrs Anne Ealand, wife of Robt Ealand, £20 if in my service at my death. My good friends Mr Jas. Douglas of Fan Court, London, mercht, Mr Wm Wooley of Cheapside, hosier, & Mr Anthony Pollet of the Tower of London trustees & to have each £200 & a guinea ring. All my plantation called "Parham Hill" & a plot of ground with warehouse in Parham Town, Antigua, & negros, etc., to my cousin Chas. Tudway & his heirs male for life in trust, then to my cousin Richd Clement Tudway, then to my cousin John Tudway, then to my cousin Robinson Tudway, then to their daus. similarly, but they to take my name. To my said trustees £3000 South Sea stock & £3000 bank stock to pay these annuities, viz., £10 a year to my cousin Mrs Mary Tudway, mother of my Ex'or, £20 a year to my cousin Mrs Susannah Clowdesley, then to her niece Mrs Eliz. Child, then to the latter's sister Judith (her husband's name I forget), £30 a year to my cousin Mrs Eliz. Arnold, £10 a year to Mrs Mary Fotherby, sister of John Willson of Grantham, her present husband Tho. Fotherby, £5 a year to my footman Joseph Rowley, 25 gs. a year to my servant Ann Ealand, wife of Robt Ealand, £10 to my cousin Tho. Tudway the Elder brother of my Ex'or. The dividends of £1000 S. S. stock to my cousin Richd Clement Tudway, then ½ for his widow & ½ for his children at 21, but in case they die the £1000 between the children of my cousins Holloway, wife of Robt Holloway, & Rachael Davis, also in trust to pay to my cousin Rachel Davis the dividends of £500 S. S. stock, then to her children at 21. All residue to my cousin Chas. Tudway. Witnessed by William Hopkins, William Burford, Charles R. Porter.

Codicil dated 26 Feb. 1748. To my trustees £1000 stock to pay the interest to my good friend Edwd Hales, Esq., brother of Sir Christopher Hales, Bart., & son to the late Sir Edwd Hales, Bart. To my cousin Letitia Wooley a rose diamond ring given me by my mother & a gold locket & certain furniture in my house at Lincoln. The ring of Chas. 1st head to Mrs Jane Wickham, then to her sister Alice Wickham. To my godson Clement Harrison £50. To Anthony Pollett 20 gs. To Eliz. Barber 10 gs., & to each servant 2 gs. 1 g. each to Mr Saml Hughson of Dunholme, nr Lincoln, Rev. Mr Park, & Rev. Moses Terry, Mr Watkinson Wildman, & Mr Richd Wheeler, Mrs Thouroughton, wife of Robt Thouroughton, & my cousins Eliz. Arnold, Sarah Hopegood, Mary Whitick, Anne Wyvill, Rebecca Theldwall, 5 of the daus. of my late aunt Floyer. To Mr Wm Houghton of Lincoln, apothecary, 5 gs. To my housekeeper Anne Ealand 10 gs. Witnessed by William Hopkins, John Ellington, Charles R. Porter.

Robinson Tudway of Bristol, hosier. Will dated 5 April, proved at Bristol 10 Dec. 1763 by Anne Tudway the relict. To my s. Richd £500 at 21. To each of my daus. Ann, Jane, Sarah, Martha, & Eliz. £300 at 21. To Jas. Ireland, sugar baker, 5 gs. All residue to my wife Anne Tudway, she to be Ex'trix, & with Jas. Ireland Guardians. Witnessed by William Wood, Richard Room.

Charles Tudway of the Liberty of St. Andrew in Wells, co. Somerset. Will dated 9 Sep. 1765; proved 2 Oct. 1770 by Clement Tudway, Esq. (380 Jenner.) To be buried in the parish church of St Cuthbert in Wells. To my wife Hannah £100 & to reside in my new built house for 1 year, then the house & furniture to my son Clement Tudway except £100 worth of furniture my wife shall choose. I give her the 5 closes I purchased of Dr Saml Cresswicke, Dean of Wells, of 30 acres in the tything of Dulcott in St Cuthbert's parish which I hold by lease of the Bishop of Bath & Wells, & after her death to my son Clement. I give her also in like manner all the messuage I purchased of John Holden, Gent., at Easton & Dursdown in St Cuthbert's, all in lieu of dower. By the powers contained in my son Clement's marriage settlement, da. 16 Ap. 1762, I give £12,000 to my son Chas. Tudway & £5000 to my son Robt Tudway. To my son Clement £3000 in trust for my dau. Mary Tudway at 21, also £1200 for my dau. Eliz. Drake, wife of Rev. Francis Drake, & then to her younger children. To my honoured mother £10 & a guinea ring. To my brother Clement Tudway £30. To my sister Eliz. Raynes, widow, £20. To my sister-in-law Margt Tudway, widow, £10. To each of my brothers & sisters-in-law a guinea ring. To my dau. Eliz. Drake £50. To my servant Jas. Green £30, & my servant David Taylor £20. To my uncle Tho. Moore & Mr Richd Slade a guinea ring, & the like rings to the Mayor, Masters, Common Council, & Town Clerk of the City or Borough of Wells. All residue of my estate both real & personal as well at Antigua as in England to my son Clement Tudway, he to be Ex'or. Witnessed by Jos. Bacon, Charles Bacon, George Tuson.

Codicil dated 23 June 1766. Having lately given a bond of £1200 to my son Chas. I give him 10,800 instead of £12,000.

Sir Rowland Hill, Bart. Will dated 11 Jan. 1769. (26 Rockingham.) Names his 1st dau. Elizabeth wife of Clement Tudway, Esq., to whom he gave a considerable portion, and by his codicil dated 19 Nov. 1779 he bequeaths her £1000.

Close Roll, 6 Geo. II., Part 5, Nos. . . . .

Indenture made the 20th Dec. 1732 between Rachel Tudway of London, widow (and relict of Clement Tudway, late of London, merchant, deceased), and Clement Tudway their only son and heir, of the one part, and James Douglas of London, merchant, of the other part, witnesseth that in consideration of 5s. Rachel and Clement Tudway grant to James Douglas all that plantation in the division of Old North Sound in the parish of St. Peter, Parham, Antigua, called Parham Hill, bounded N. with the town of Parham and the lands now or late of Sarah Waynell (?), E. with the lands of Sir William Codrington, S. with John Pare, Esq., and Archibald Cochran, Esq., and W. with John Vernon, Esq., and all slaves and cattle and all that storehouse 60 feet by 80 in Parham Town, bounded to the N. with the sea, E. with the house and lands of Captain John Goble, now or late in the possession of Richard Hillhouse, S. with Broad Street, and W. with Crosse Street, for one whole year, paying therefore one peppercorn that he may be in actual possession, to the uses of an Indenture to be made the day after these presents. George North, Humphrey Hackshaw, witnesses.

No. . .

Indenture made 21st Dec. 1732 as above, witnesseth that Rachel and Clement Tudway grant to James Douglas the said plantation, one third to the use of Rachel Tudway for life, and at her death to Clement Tudway and his heirs for ever.

Close Roll, 2 Geo. III., Part 12, Nos. 21 and 22.

Indenture made the 25th Feb. 1762 between Charles Tudway of Wells, co. Somerset, Esq., and Clement Tudway of the Middle Temple, Esq., his eldest son, of the one part, and Henry Wilmot of Gray's Inn, Esq., of the other part, witnesseth that in consideration of 5*s.* Charles and Clement Tudway grant and sell to Henry Wilmot all that plantation in the division of Old North Sound and parish of St. Peter, Parham, in Antigua, called Parham Hill, in the tenure or occupation of Charles Tudway or his assigns, bounded (as before), and also all the negros, cattle, and quick stock whatsoever thereon, and all that storehouse 60 feet by 80 in Parham Town, bounded N. with the sea, E. with the house and lands of Captain John Goble, now or late in the possession of Robert (*sic*) Hillhouse, etc., for one whole year, and they constitute the Hon. Stephen Blizard, Esq., Chief Justice of Antigua, and Francis Farley and Robert Bannister, both of Antigua, Esquires, their Attorneys. John Lancaster, Valentine Henry Allott, witnesses.

No. 21.

Indenture made the 26th Feb. 1762 between Charles Tudway, Hannah his wife, and Clement Tudway, of the 1st part, Henry Wilmot, of the 2nd part, and Samuel Wildman of the parish of St. Mary le Bow, goldsmith, of the 3rd part, witnesseth that for barring and destroying all estates tail and remainders, and for releasing the dower, etc., of Hannah Tudway, and in consideration of 5*s.*, Charles Tudway and Hannah his wife and Clement Tudway grant and confirm to Henry Wilmot in his actual possession being all that plantation (as in No. 22) in trust for Charles Tudway and Samuel Wildman and their heirs and assigns for ever, and as to the estate and interest of Samuel Wildman in trust for Charles Tudway and his heirs and assigns for ever.

Close Roll, 46 Geo. III., Part 6, No. 1.

Deed Poll. Manumission of a slave. Know all men by these presents that I, Clement Tudway of Wells, co. Somerset, in that part of the Kingdom of Great Britain and Ireland called England, Esq., in consideration of £100 sterling paid by Edward Byam Wyke of Antigua, Esq., have manumised, enfranchised, and set free, etc., from all slavery and servitude whatsoever, for ever absolutely discharged, a mulatto man slave named Alick Dow, so that neither myself nor my heirs, Ex'ors, etc., or any other person can, shall, or may at any time hereafter have claim, challenge, or demand either in law or equity, any estate, right, title, etc., into or out of the said mulatto, or to his labour or service in any manner whatsoever, but of and from all such estate, right, title, etc., shall and will from henceforth be utterly debarred and for ever excluded, and I do hereby nominate the Hon. Rowland Burton and Thomas Norbury Kerby, Esq., both of Antigua, to appear before the Register of Deeds, etc., 19th June 1806. George Brookes, Leicester Square, H. R. Rogers, clerk to Mr. Brookes, witnesses.

Close Roll, 10 Geo. IV., Part 12, No. 1.

Indenture made the 6th July 1829 between John Paine Tudway of Wells, co. Somerset, Esq., of the 1st part, Robert Charles Tudway of the same place, Esq., his eldest son and heir apparent, of the 2nd part, the Rev. Richard Thomas Whalley, late of Henstridge, but now of Yeovilton, co. Somerset, clerk, of the 3rd part, William Wilkins Dyne of 61 Lincoln's Inn Fields, Gentleman, of the 4th part, Edwin Lovell of 6 Coventry Street, Gentleman, of the 5th part, the Rev. Charles Henry Pulsford of the Liberty of St. Andrew in Wells, Clerk, of the 6th part, William Melliar of Wells, Gentleman, of the 7th part, and the Hon. Samuel Athill, the Hon. Nicholas Nugent, M.D., George Weatherill Ottley, Esq., and John Freeland, Esq., all of Antigua, of the 8th part. Whereas Clement Tudway, late of Wells, Esq., did publish his last will dated the 22nd Dec. 1814, and after making certain devises in favour of John Paine Tudway aforesaid and Francis Drake, Esq., his nephews, devised all his manors and freehold estate in Great Britain and Antigua to the Rev. Edward Foster, Clerk, the Rev. Richard Thomas Whalley aforesaid, and John Holloway, Esq., in trust as to certain specific parts to the use of Elizabeth Tudway his wife (since deceased) and her assigns for 50 years if she should so long live, for her own use and benefit, and subject thereto to the use of Rowland, now Lord Hill by the name of Sir Rowland Hill, for 1000 years on trust to raise and pay certain annual sums to certain persons who, with the exception of Mary Hill and Mary Davis, have all departed this life, and subject thereto to John Paine Tudway and his assigns for life, with remainder to the trustees to preserve the contingent remainders to the sons of John Paine Tudway with divers remainders over, and declared it should be lawful for John Paine Tudway, after he should come into actual possession, to exchange the said freehold, copyhold, and leasehold property with any person, or corporation, or body politic or corporate, capable of making such exchange so that it should be fair and just, and such exchange made by John Paine Tudway as tenant for life should be as good, valid, and effectual as if he were absolutely seised, but on condition the lands exchanged should be subject to the same provisoes as by his will limited, and also devised all his messuages to the said trustees as to certain specific parts at Walcombe upon certain trusts for the benefit of Elizabeth Tudway his wife for life, and after her death those parts and all other messuages to the person who should have the freehold estates, and gave to the said trustees all residue and all personal estate (except the slaves and stock belonging to his plantation in Antigua) to sell and to invest in the purchase of freehold messuages and lands, etc., in fee simple with liberty to purchase copyhold or leasehold if convenient, free from all charges except fee, farm, or quit, or other rents, in England, to be conveyed to the same uses as before; and whereas Clement Tudway departed this life in July 1815 and his will was proved on the 30th Aug. 1815; and whereas Elizabeth Tudway his widow has since departed this life; and whereas by virtue of the power contained in the said part recited will certain specific parts have been exchanged, and such lands exchanged have been duly conveyed and settled according to the trusts; and whereas all just debts and legacies, etc., have been paid from testator's personal estate, and all residue has been invested in the purchase of lands; and whereas Robert Charles Tudway is the eldest son of John Paine Tudway and attained his age of 21 on the 4th July instant; and whereas for making an immediate provision for him and for other purposes it has been proposed and arranged between John Payne Tudway and Robert Charles Tudway that all estate tail, etc., in the aforesaid manors, etc., devised by the will of Clement Tudway, shall be barred and destroyed and settled to the uses to be mentioned. Now this Indenture witnesseth that in consideration of the premises and for barring and destroying the estate tail in remainder of Robert Charles Tudway in the aforesaid manors in England, hereinafter more particularly described, and also in consideration of 10*s.*, John Payne Tudway, Robert Charles Tudway, and Richard Thomas Whalley grant and convey to William Wilkins Dyne all the manors of Dulcot, otherwise Dulcote Wensley, otherwise Wellesly, Walcombe, Pen, and Wookey, all in co. Somerset, and the various messuages delineated in the first five schedules and described as freehold, which said messuages, farms, etc., are in the in and out parishes of St. Cuthbert in Wells, the liberty of St. Andrew in Wells, and the parishes of Dinder, Croscombe, Wookey, Westbury, West Harptry, Priddy Meare, Wedmore, East Brent, and Berrow, co. Somerset, and all other manors of which John Payne Tudway is tenant-at-law or in equity for life, and Robert Charles Tudway in remainder in tail, to have and to hold for the joint lives of John Payne Tudway and Robert Charles Tudway, and it shall be lawful for Edwin Lovell before the end of the present Trinity Term to sue forth out of His Majesty's Court of Chancery one or more writs of entry sur disseisin en le post against William Wilkins Dyne, in trust as they shall appoint, and in default that Robert Charles Tudway may receive £400 a year from the said manors during the life of John Payne Tudway, and subject thereto to Charles Henry Pulsford for 50 years in trust, and after the determination of that term to the use of John Payne Tudway for life, and after his decease to William Melliar in trust during the life of Robert Charles Tudway to support the contingent remainders to the first and other sons of Robert Charles Tudway in succession, and for default to Henry Tudway, second son of John Paine Tudway, for life and to support the contingent remainders to his first and other sons, and for default to John Paine Tudway and his heirs for ever, and as to all residue to John Paine Tudway and his heirs and assigns for ever; and whereas the terms limited to the above use are particularly mentioned in Schedules 4 and 5, and further witnesseth that for settling the leasehold estates of Clement Tudway for lives, and in consideration of 10s., and for settling the leasehold estates of Clement Tudway for terms of years, and in consideration of 10s., and for settling the copyhold estates of Clement Tudway, and in consideration of 10s., John Paine Tudway, Robert Charles Tudway, and Richard Thomas Whalley grant and convey them to William Melliar in trust (as for the freehold estates), and also witnesseth that in conformity with an Act of the General Assembly of H.M.'s Leeward Charibbee Islands, 4 Anne, and for docking and destroying all estates tail in possession or remainder vested in John Paine Tudway and Robert Charles Tudway, and all remainders whatsoever, and in consideration of 5s. each, John Paine Tudway, Robert Charles Tudway, and Richard Thomas Whalley convey to William Wilkins Dyne all that plantation in the division of Old North Sound and the parish of St. Peter, Parham, Antigua, called Parham Hill Plantation, formerly in the tenure or occupation of Charles Tudway, Esq., and afterwards of the said Clement Tudway, his agents and tenants or assigns, and now of John Paine Tudway, bounded N. with the town of Parham and the lands heretofore of Sarah Maynell, E. with the lands now or late of Sir Bethel Codrington, S. with the lands now or heretofore of John Pare, Esq., and Archibald Cockran, Esq., and W. with the lands now or heretofore of John Vernon, Esq., and which plantation is now divided into three plantations called Parham Old Work, Parham New Work, and Parham Lodge, and also a parcel of land reputed to belong to the plantation in or near Parham Town, whereon is a building used for a storehouse, bounded N. with the sea or the seashore, E. with the house and lands formerly of Captain John Goble, S. with Broad Street, and W. with Cross Street leading to the sea, and all negros and other slaves mentioned in the several lists 1, 2, and 3:—1, Parham Old Work (all names given), 197 men, women, and children; 2, Parham New Work, 95 men and boys, 103 women and girls; 3, Parham Lodge, 106 men and boys, 88 women and girls—as by registration founded on returns made by George Weatherill Ottley and John Freeland as Attorneys to John Paine Tudway, and all cattle as delineated in the sixth and last schedule in trust (as for the manors, etc.), the tenant in possession to have power to charge for any one child any sum not exceeding £2000, and the term of 50 years is so limited for the better securing the £400 a year to Robert Charles Tudway and John Paine Tudway, Robert Charles Tudway and Richard Thomas Whalley constitute, etc., Samuel Athill, Nicholas Nugent, George Weatherill Ottley, and John Freeland their Attorneys. Joseph Lovell Lovell, Edward Lovell, Wells, witnesses.

Close Roll, 11 Geo. IV., Part 10, No. 11.

Indenture made the 21st April 1830 between John Paine Tudway of Wells, co. Somerset, Esq., of the 1st part, Robert Charles Tudway, Esq., of the same place, his son and heir apparent, of the 2nd part, the Rev. Richard Thomas Whalley, late of Henstridge, but now of Yeovilton in the said county, Clerk, of the 3rd part, William Wilkins Dyne of 61 Lincoln's Inn Fields, Gentleman, of the 4th part, and the Hon. Samuel Athill, the Hon. Nicholas Nugent, M.D., George Weatherill Ottley, Esq., and John Freeland, Esq., all of Antigua, of the 5th part. Whereas Clement Tudway, late of Wells, Esq., duly made his will, dated the 22nd Dec. 1814, will recited, and the will was duly proved by Edward Foster and Richard Thomas Whalley; and whereas Edward Foster and John Holloway have departed this life; and whereas Robert Charles Tudway is the eldest son of John Paine Tudway and was born at his house in Wells on the 4th July 1808 and was baptized in the parish church of St. Cuthbert in Wells on the 20th Sep. 1808; and whereas by virtue of an Indenture dated the 6th July 1829 and of a common recovery suffered in performance thereof in Trinity Term now last past, wherein William Wilkins Dyne was tenant, Edwin Lovell demandant, John Paine Tudway first vouchee, and Robert Charles Tudway second vouchee, it was witnessed that by force thereof certain farms, etc., were assigned to the use of the persons mentioned and to such uses as John Paine Tudway and Robert Charles Tudway should appoint, with power of revocation and new appointment by them during their joint lives, and by the said Indenture it was witnessed that for barring and destroying all estates tail and remainders and for the nominal considerations mentioned Richard Thomas Whalley and John Paine Tudway and his son did grant and convey to William Wilkins Dyne all those plantations to the like uses and trusts; and whereas it is apprehended that some difficulty may hereafter arise in proving the time of birth of Robert Charles Tudway and that he was of age at the time of the hereinbefore recited Indenture, the persons who can testify to such facts being few in number and of advanced ages, it has therefore been agreed that a new bargain and sale of the said plantations shall be executed. Now this Indenture witnesseth that in conformity with an Act of the Leeward Caribbee Islands, and in consideration of 5s. each, John Paine Tudway, Robert Charles Tudway, and Richard Thomas Whalley convey to William Wilkins Dyne all that plantation in the division of Old North Sound and parish of St. Peter, Parham, called Parham Hill Plantation, and all those slaves as by three schedules annexed, and lastly they constitute Samuel Athill, Nicholas Nugent, George Weatherill Ottley, and John Freeland their Attorneys. Edward Lovell, solicitor, Wells, Ann Lovell, servant to John Paine Tudway, John Westmore and James Shaw, clerks to Mr. Dyne, 61 Lincoln's Inn Fields, witnesses.

1696-7. Richard Tudway signed the petition of 22 London merchants trading to Nevis. (B. T. Leeward Islands, vol. 5.)

Of the musical composers living in Anne's reign . . . . there was Tudway, who composed an anthem ("Thou, O God, hast heard my Vows") on the occasion of Queen Anne visiting the University of Cambridge in 1705, which gained him his doctor's degree, and he was afterwards made public Professor of Music to that university, where he was longer remembered for his punning proclivities than for his musical talents. (Ashton's 'Social Life in the Reign of Queen Anne,' vol. ii., p. 35.)

From the Royal African Accounts it appears that Richard Tudway was in 1700 Master of the ship "Codrington."

Indenture dated 30 Aug. 1711 between Hon. Colonel Edward Byam of Antigua and John Otto Bayer of Antigua, Esq., Attorneys to Madam Rachell Tudway of London, widow and ex'trix of Clement Tudway, late of London, merchant, deceased, and John Lightfoot of Antigua, Gent. and merchant. Lease to John Lightfoot of 20 acres in Old North Sound for seven years at £13 st. yearly rent: bond for £250 c. given.

1726, Nov. 23. Dy'd Dr Thomas Tudway, Professor of Musick in the University of Cambridge. ('Historical Register,' p. 43.)

1749, March 14. Clement Tudway of Lincoln, esq. ('Gent. Mag.,' p. 141.)

1749, March 15. Clement Tedway, Esq; a gentleman of a large estate in Lincolnshire. ('London Mag.,' p. 145.)

1770, Sep. 4. Charles Tudway, Esq; late Memb. for Wells, Somersetshire. ('Gent. Mag.,' p. 441.)

1773, June. Rowland Hill, Esq; (now the rev. Mr Rowland Hill) to Miss Mary Tudway, youngest daughter of the late Charles Tudway, Esq; and sister to the present member for Wells. ('Town and Country Mag.')

The arms of Clement Tudway, M.P., impaling Hill are engraved in William Tunnicliff's Survey 1789.

Clement Tudway was rated for St. Peter's, Parham, 1796—1825, and John P. Tudway 1821—1828.

1800, Dec. 1. At Wells, co. Somerset, after a long and painful illness, Robert Tudway, esq. a truly valuable man. ('Gent. Mag.,' p. 1294.)

1807, Jan. 1. At Wells, co. Somerset, the wife of John Paine Tudway, esq. of a daughter. (*Ibid.*, p. 88.)

1809, Oct. 26. Rev. Edw. Foster, prebendary of Wells Cathedral, to Mary eldest surviving daughter of the late Robert Tudway, esq. and niece to Clement Tudway, esq. M.P. (*Ibid.*, p. 1073.)

1815, July 9. At Wells, Clement Tudway, esq. M.P. for that city such a series of years, that he has long been considered the father of the House of Commons. He was first elected in 1761. (*Ibid.*, p. 184.)

Map* of the Parham Plantations in Antigua, the property of John Paine Tudway, Esq., surveyed by T. Baker in 1819.

Arms: *Quarterly, 1 and 4, Ermine, a lion rampant between three roses; 2 and 3, A chevron gules between three stags;* impaling . . . . *a cross flory argent.*

Crest: *A demi-lion couped, holding in its dexter paw a rose slipped.*

	Acres.	Roods.	Poles.
The Old Work . .	645	3	17
The New Work . .	451	0	13
	1096	3	30

1819, Aug. 11. A. Carrick, M.D. of Clifton, to Caroline, youngest dau. of Rob. Tudway, esq. of Wells, and sister of J. P. Tudway, esq. M.P. for that city. ('Gent. Mag.,' p. 178.)

1823, March 27. At an advanced age, the relict of Robert Tudway, esq. and mother of Payne Tudway, esq. M.P. for Wells. (*Ibid.*, p. 477.)

1825, Nov. 23. At Wells, the Rev. T. B. Coney, Rector of Chedzoy, to Jane, dau. of J. P. Tudway, esq. M.P. (*Ibid.*, p. 560.)

* In the possession of the Hon. T. D. Foote, Mr. Tudway's Attorney at Parham Hill.

1828, Feb. 13. At Wells, aged 88, Elizabeth, relict of Clement Tudway, for more than 50 years Member for that city, and aunt to Gen. Lord Hill. She was the only surviving dau. of Sir Rowland Hill, the fourth Bart. by Jane, eldest dau. of Sir Brian Broughton, third Bart. of Broughton, Staffordshire, and was married June 7, 1762. ('Gent. Mag.,' p. 189.)

1833, April 11. At his house in the Blackfriars Road, aged 88, the Rev. Rowland Hill, M.A. the celebrated Minister of the chapel in that place. (*Ibid.*, p. 565.)

1835, June 28. At Wells, aged 60, John Paine Tudway, esq. (*Ibid.*, p. 221.)

1836, May 13. At Cirencester, aged 53, Mrs. E. P. Tudway, widow of the late Rev. C. Tudway, formerly of Wells, sister to T. Calley, esq. of Burderop-park, Wilts. (*Ibid.*, p. 674.)

1837, May 23. At Wells, A. Constantine to Fanny Henrietta, dau. of the late J. Paine Tudway esq. M.P. (*Ibid.*, p. 82.)

1846, March 3. At Henbury, Robert Charles Tudway, esq. of Wells, to Maria Catherine, eldest dau. of William Miles, esq. M.P. of Leigh-court, Somerset. (*Ibid.*, p. 535.)

1846, July 1. At Harrow, Emily B. youngest dau. of Clement Tudway, esq. of Edsleigh-st. Tavistock-sq. (*Ibid.*, p. 220.)

1866, Feb. 13. At Walton Rectory, Somerset, aged 36, the Rev. Henry Tudway. He was educated at Trinity College, Oxford, where he graduated B.A. in 1851, and proceeded M.A. in 1852. He was appointed rector of Walton in 1855, having previously held the curacy of Priddy, near Wells. (*Ibid.*, p. 599.)

1867, April 26. In London, aged 58, Clement Tudway, esq., only son of the late Rev. Clement Tudway, vicar of Chiseldon, Wilts. (*Ibid.*, p. 825.)

1873. C. C. Tudway, Wells, 2827 acres, gross rental £4511. Henry Tudway, Wells, 18 acres, gross rental £46. Mrs. Tudway, Wells, 54 acres, gross rental £180. (Parliamentary Return of Owners of Land.)

PARISH REGISTER OF ST. PHILIP.

*Buried.**

1832	July 13	Gretta Tudway. Parham Lodge.	75.
1832	Aug. 22	Brunsmell Tudway. P. Lodge.	51.
1832	Dec. 13	Thercia Tudway. Parham Hill.	65.
1833	Mar. 24	Hammond Tudway. P. L.	61.
1833	July 14	London Tudway. P. L.	28.

REGISTER OF ST. GEORGE'S CHAPEL, WINDSOR.

Baptized.

William Tudway, son of Mr Thomas Tudway, was borne the 14 of September and baptized the 21, 1662.

Susanna Tudway, daughter of Mr Thomas Tudway, baptized the 15 of Octo^r 1665.

Buried.

John Tudway, son of Mr Tho. Tudway, one of the Clarks of this Church, was buried the first daye of October 1662.

Mr Thomas Tudway, one of the Gent. Clarks of this Church, was buried the 25th of November 1671.

[The entries for the years 1652—60 are missing.]

REGISTER OF WELLS CATHEDRAL.†

Baptized.

1670 . . . . . . Robert s. of Robert and Mary Tudway; born 9 May, and received at Church Sep. 7.

* These entries probably relate to coloured persons.

† From 'Wells Cathedral,' by A. J. Jewers, F.S.A.

1671 . . . . . . Charles s. of Robert and Mary Tudway; born 23 March, and received at Church July 26.

Married.

1735 Nov. 25 Robert Holloway & Elizabeth Tudway: by l.

PARISH REGISTER OF ST. CUTHBERT, WELLS.*

Baptized.

1684 Aug. 24 Charles s. of Charles and Mary Tudway.
1707 Jan. 20 Thomas s. of Charles and Mary Tudway of East Wells; born 8 Jan.
1708 Feb. 24 Elizabeth dau. of Charles and Mary Tudway of East Wells; born 2 Feb., priv. bap., brought to Church 15 March.
1710 Dec. 14 Rachel dau. of Charles Tudway of East Wells; born 29 Nov.
1712 Sep. 21 Mary dau. of Charles Tudway of East Wells; born 3 Sep.
1713 Nov. 19 Charles s. of Charles Tudway of East Wells; born 2 Nov.
1715 Nov. 15 Mary dau. of Charles Tudway; born 9, priv. bap., and brought to Church Nov. 24.
1716 Dec. 16 Richard Clement s. of Mr Charles Tudway; born 10 Dec., priv. bap., brought to Church Jan. 5.
1719 April 26 John s. of Charles Tudway; born 4 April, priv. bap., brought to Church April 30.
1721 Nov. 19 Robinson s. of Mr Charles Tudway; born 9 Nov., priv. bap., brought to Church 7 Dec.; of New Street.
1731 Jan. 6 Mary dau. of Thomas Tudway of Sadler Street; born 4 Jan., priv. bap., brought to Church 17 Jan.
1734 Aug. 25 Thomas s. of Thomas Tudway of Southover; born 1 Aug.

Married.

1706 Dec. 26 Charles Tudway, yeoman, and Mary Cook, both of St Cuthbert par. Licence.
1738 Nov. 1 William Davis and Rachael Tudway.

Buried.

1708 May 10 Mr John Robinson.
1708 July 20 Mrs Robinson, widow, of East Wells.
1715 Dec. 28 Mary dau. of Charles Tudway of East Wells.
1723 April 24 Mr Charles Tudway of New Street.

1625, Dec. 3. Thomas Tudway, of New Windsor, co. Berks, Gent., & Amy Gibson, of St Giles, Cripplegate, London, Spinster, dau. of William Gibson, of Arnham, co. Notts, Yeoman; at St Alphage, London. (Marriage Licences: Bishop of London.)

* From 'Wells Cathedral,' by A. J. Jewers, F.S.A.

1691-2, Jan. 26. Richard Tudway, of St Margaret Moses, Lond., Mercht, Bachr, abt 34, & Mrs Elizabeth Steele, of Winchester, Spr, above 21, with consent of her guardian Mr Fifield, her parents dead; at St Clemts Danes, Midd. (Marriage Licences: Vicar-General of the Archbishop of Canterbury.)

ST. CUTHBERT'S CHURCH, WELLS.

On a white marble tablet on the south side of the choir:—

TO THE MEMORY OF
CLEMENT TUDWAY ESQR,
ELDEST SON OF CHARLES TUDWAY ESQR OF THIS PLACE |
AND HANNAH HIS WIFE.
WHO WAS BORN OCTOBER 8TH 1734
AND DIED JULY 7TH 1815.
HE MARRIED ELIZABETH YOUNGER DAUGHTER OF
SIR ROWLAND HILL
OF HAWKESTONE SHROPSHIRE BART
BY WHOM HE HAD NO ISSUE.
HE SERVED THE OFFICE OF MAYOR
OF THIS CITY TEN TIMES,
AND HAD THE HONOUR TO BE ONE OF ITS
REPRESENTATIVES IN PARLIAMENT
FROM THE YEAR 1760
TO THE TIME OF HIS DEATH.

Adjoining the above:—

Arms: . . . . *three birds* . . . . *on a chief engrailed gules three annulets, a canton ermine*; impaling, 1, *Ermine, a lion rampant between three cinquefoils*; 2, *Vert, a chevron ermine between three stags.*

IN MEMORY OF
WILLIAM MELLIAR, ESQUIRE.
OF THIS PARISH,
WHOSE MORTAL REMAINS ARE DEPOSITED
IN A VAULT BENEATH.
HE WAS BORN 14TH FEBRUARY 1757.
AND DIED 7TH AUGUST 1840.
ALSO
IN MEMORY OF FRANCES HIS WIFE
DAUGHTER OF ROBERT TUDWAY ESQUIRE
WHO DIED 11TH MARCH 1795
AND OF FRANCES MARY,
THEIR ONLY CHILD
WHO DIED 4TH DECEMBER 1806,
AGED 11 YEARS.

Above is a large stained-glass window:—

IN MEMORY OF JOHN PAINE TUDWAY. ALSO OF FRANCES GOULD | HIS WIFE AND THEIR THREE DAUGHTERS LETITIA AUGUSTA AND | HENRIETTA.

WELLS CATHEDRAL.

On a white marble cross in the cloisters:—

HARRIET HENRIETTA TUDWAY
BORN SEPTEMBER 17TH 1824,
DIED SEPTEMBER 3RD 1854.

Pedigree of Tullideph.

CREST.—*A stag's head.*

. . . . TULLIDEPH, had five children=. . . .

Rev. Thomas Tullideph, 1st son, of Edrom near Berwick-on-Tweed; Professor of Divinity at St. Andrews 1734; living 1794.=. . . . died 15 June 1758.

Dr. Walter Tullideph, educated at the High School, Edinburgh; went out to Antigua *circa* 1726 at the invitation of his cousin Dr. Walter Sydserfe; Lieut.-Colonel in Militia Dec. 1752; Member of Council 1755; owned the "New Division" and "Musketo Cove" Plantations; purchased an estate at Dundee 1760. Will dated 28 May 1794.=Mary, dau. of Leonard Burroughs and widow of John Tremills; mar. 10 Jan. 1735-6; living 1794.

W. Tullideph

1734.

David Tullideph of Wisbeach, merchant, formerly of Antigua, which island he left 17 Aug. 1734; æt. 47 in April 1752; living 1794.=Ann . . . . died 1749.

A dau.=Rev. Alexander Trotter, living 1754.

Robert Tullideph, Lieut. in the Army 1759.

. . . . Tullideph, 1st dau. 1737.

Peggy Tullideph, mar. 1746.

Mary Tullideph, 1745.

Walter Tullideph, only son, born 29 March 1745; died 10 June 1752 at Antigua.

Mary Margaret Tullideph, born 6 Oct. 1739; mar. Hon. Lieut.-Col. Alexander Leslie; she died v.p.

Charlotte Tullideph, born 30 Oct. 1737; educated at Chelsea; mar. 1754.=Sir John Ogilvy, 5th Bart., of Invercarity, co. Forfar; Member of Council of Antigua 1782; died 1802.

Katherine Tullideph, 3rd dau., born 16 Nov. 1740; died 7 Oct. 1743.

A child, born and died March 1741.

A child, died 1739.

Ann Tullideph, 1740.

John Trotter, merchant at London 1744, at Antigua 1745, at Glasgow 1752, at Jamaica 1754, at Philadelphia 1757.

Thomas Trotter, taken prisoner by the Spaniards 1743-4; died at Jamaica 1745.

Two daus., one of whom was mar. in 1752.

Sir Walter Ogilvy, 6th Bart., born May 1755; going to Eton 1766; died a bachelor 1808.

Sir John Ogilvy, 7th Bart., born *circa* Oct. 1756; died a bachelor 1819.

David Ogilvy, born 10 April 1758; Lieut.-Colonel; killed 1801 in Egypt.

Sir William Ogilvy, 8th Bart., born 5 April 1759; Rear-Admiral R.N.; died 1823. *A quo* the present Bart.

James Ogilvy, died in the East Indies.

Alexander Ogilvy, mar. and left issue.

Thomas Ogilvy, died in the the East Indies.

Ramsay Ogilvy, Lieut. 44th Regiment, killed at the capture of St. Lucia.

Adam Ogilvy, murdered on his father's plantation in Antigua 29 July 1799.

Mary Ogilvy, born 31 March 1760.

Charlotte Ogilvy, born 1766.

. . . . Thibou=Charlotte . . . . bur. 24 Nov. 1724 at St. John's.

Leonard Burroughs of Antigua, an Englishman. 1st husband.=Lucy Thibou, born in London of French parentage; under 50 in 1736; purchased "Tremills," which she conveyed to Dr. W. Tullideph on his marriage; bur. 6 Feb. 1744 at St. John's.=Peter Mercier, merchant, mar. 30 Oct. 1715 and bur. 13 Sep. 1733 at St. John's. Will dated 2 Oct. 1732. 2nd husband.

Isaac Thibou, Esq., living 1753.

Benjamin Burroughs of Bermuda 1737—1748; "a poor relation 1756."=. . . .

John Tremills of Antigua, bur. 18 Jan. 1730 at St. John's. 1st husband.=Mary Burroughs, living 1794.=Dr. Walter Tullideph, mar. 10 Jan. 1735-6. Will dated 1794. 2nd husband.

Leonard Burroughs, 1st son, of St. Croix, where he died *circa* July 1764.=Mary . . . . mar. at St. Croix and there resident 1764.

Benjamin Burroughs, 2nd son 1751.

A 3rd son.

Lucy Burroughs, mar. 11 July 1743 Dr. William Mercer, partner of Dr. Walter Tullideph.

Martha Burroughs, living 1748.

Alexander Wilson, living 1734; mar. 6 Jan. 1738, at St. John's, Elizabeth Coppin. [Mar. 13 April 1734 William Coppin and Elizabeth Hues.]

Patrick Wilson, goldsmith, of Antigua 1734; mar. April 1740; died in England 1755.=(? Sarah) Tremills, died Nov. 1758. (See *ante*, p. 144.)=. . . . Jones (? Charles Jones, a sugar refiner of Antigua).

Three children 1764.

Patrick Wilson, only son and heir, at school in England 1754; æt. 16 in 1760; a merchant at Antigua 1764; settled an estate at St. Vincent 1766.

A dau., born 18 and died 19 April 1755.

Alexander Sydserfe of Ruchlaw, co. Haddington ═ . . . .

John Sydserfe of Dunbar, merchant, 3rd son ═ . . . .

Dr. Walter Sydserfe of Antigua, "cousin" of Dr. Walter Tullideph, born 1692; bur. 21 March 1760 at Yapton, co. Sussex. Will dated 16 May 1759; proved 1 April 1760. (170 Lynch.) See *ante*, p. 128. ═ Mary or Margaret . . . . living at Bath 1740; bur. 12 Jan. 1758 at Yapton, co. Sussex.

- John Sydserfe, bapt. 12 Dec. 1727 at St. John's; died of consumption in 1752 at Lisbon.
- Thomas Sydserfe, living 1752. (? died young.)
- Margaret Sydserfe, bapt. 19 Jan. 1724 at St. John's; at school in Chelsea 1736; mar. 1742-3; died 4 and bur. 12 Dec. 1763, æt. 39, at Yapton. ═ Sir William Thomas of Yapton, 2nd Bart.

Walter Tullydeph of Tullydeph Hall, co. Forfar, and formerly of Antigua. Will dated at Edinburgh 28 May 1794. To the Rt Hon. Geo., Earl of Dalhousie, Geo. Dempster, Esq., of Dunnichin, advocate, Sir John Ogilvy of Invercarity, Bart., Dame Charlotte Tullydeph *al's* Ogilvy his wife, my 1st dau., Rev. Tho. Tullideph, principal of the United College of St Andrews, Mr David Tullideph, merch^t at Westbeach, & Rev. Chas. Roberts, minister at Dundee, in trust, all my New Division estate, containing the lands formerly Tremills & Devereux's & the lands I bought of Mr Wm York & Capt Saml Martin. I have bargained to sell to Mr Morris of Antigua my Musketto Cove estate for £18,000 st. All other my lands in Antigua & Montserrat & all personalty to my trustees, they to be Ex'ors. To my wife Mrs Mary Burroughs *al's* Tullideph £400 a year, the life rent of Tullideph Hall is also settled on her, which will make up £600 a year, & £100 for mourning, 6 cows & 4 horses, use of furniture, then to my dau. Lady Charlotte Ogilvy. To my granddau. Mary Ann Leslie, d. of the Hon. Lt Col. Alexr Leslie & of Mrs Margt Tullideph, decd, my youngest dau., £100 a year till 21, then £3000 st. To Hellen Ogilvy, 1st d. of Sir John Ogilvy, £1000 at 21. To his other children, except the eldest, £4000 amongst them. All my estate to Dame Charlotte Ogilvy for life, then to Walter Ogilvy, 1st son of Sir John Ogilvy. If she die before Sir John then I give him £200 a year, & £300 a year to Walter. Trustees may sell estates . . . . Recorded at St. John's. (The remainder of the will is missing.)

1731, Dec. 2. Dr. Tullideph to attend the Governor's Regiment.

1748, Feb. 23. Walter Tullideph elected a Member of Assembly *vice* William Furnell resigned.

1750. James Doig a near relation of Dr. Tullideph's.

1754, Dec. 10. Walter Tullideph called up to the Council vacates his seat in the Assembly.

1767. Walter Tullideph rated on 144 slaves and 236 acres, and in 1780 his estate on 325 slaves and 536 acres. (St. Mary's Vestry Book.)

1782, March 7. Mandamus for Sir John Ogilvie, Bart., to be a Councillor of Antigua. His youngest son Adam was living at Antigua in 1794, and was murdered by a slave on his father's plantation 29 July 1799.

Dr. Walter Tullideph's Letter-books.*

1734.

June 25. Antigua. To Hon. Sir Hans Sloane, Bart., P.R.S. and C.P.: refers to his last letter of 28 April 1729 by his brother; offers to promote natural history of these parts.

June 20. Mr. Thomas Tullideph his Brother, who has been made Professor of Divinity in the new College of St. Andrews. "Your wife and bairns."

June 27. Mr. William Dunbar, his merchant in London, a frequent correspondent.

July 10. Patrick Wilson and his brother Alexander. Wrote same time to John Chrystie per Captain Oliver.

Aug. 20. To his brother Thomas: Brother David sailed the 17th; your estates in Fyffeshire. Mr. Dunbar arrived.

Aug. 20. Mrs. Elizabeth Cleghorn: a will made by your brother James Cleghorn wherein he leaves all to Walter Scott, apothecary in Canon Street. Mr. Hodge his administrator.

Aug. 27. Mrs. Martha Murray at Dorchester, South Carolina: your suit is determined thus, that the negroes shall continue on the estate till the old man's debt of £300 is paid; your share will be four negroes.

Sep. 3. Dr. Mathew Cargill's death at Spanish Town; his widow.

Aug. 29. John Chrystie administrator of his brother Alexander, deceased: bill of Edward Otto-Baijer drawn on Mr. Thomas Redhead at Mr. Gines, goldsmith in lumbard street.

1734-5, March 24. "Hon. Colonel George Lucas, Esq. . . . . owed above £30,000 c., his Estates subject to severall mortgages, finding himself thus incumbred he calls all his Creditors together, offers his Estates to be delivered up and sequestred till each of their debts should be discharged, reserving to himself his Company in Brigadier Jones's Regiment and his Estate in South Carolina, to which they all agreed . . . . he has lately sold one of his Estates for £13,000 and has two very good ones besides." James Gamble, Esq., a Gentleman of estate and Lieutenant in Jones's Regiment. William Crab's legacy upon his brother's estate.

1735.

May 19. Dr. Scott's death last November . . . . his effects are fallen into the hands of one Samuel Redhead who administered.

June 19. Captain Partis dyed a few days agone.

June 21. Messrs. Rowland and Samuel Frye, merchants in London, *re* his sugars.

Oct. 22. To Mrs. Ann Cargill at Mr. Edward Lothieu, jeweller, in the Parliament Cross, Edinburgh: your father and mother out here; your sister.

Oct. 22. Brother Thomas Tullideph: our aunt Sandilands; *re* my degrees—when I was in France. Dr. Sydserfe's letter for me to come out to these parts.

Nov. 8. Mrs. Martha Murray at Colonel Blake's, South Carolina: ? your little girl; *re* the negroes; when Dr. Murray was here. "Your Sister Bettey is married to a Scotch Taylor who has good business here in Town named George Swan."

Jan. 20. "Silver embroidered stagg's head as my Coat of Arms."

1736.

April 28. Brother Thomas: "I was married January 10th last to an agreeable Young Widow, by whom I have

* In the possession of Sir Reginald Ogilvy, Bart., who very kindly allowed me to make these extracts.

got Possession of a very fine Estate." "I have laboured very hard these ten years past . . . . there is only the breadth of a Bay about two Miles betwixt Cousin Sydserfe's Estate and mine." His daughter Peggy went to London last summer to a school at Chelsea; our cousin Hepburn at Chelsea; your wife and all friends at Edrom. "The Old Lady her Mother (not being 50) conveyed the Estate to me in fee simple for ever: per Captain Samuel Oliver."

May 23. "I received yours of ye 31st January per ye Fanny, Thomas Oliver."

July 16. To his brother David Tullideph, that he has let his (David's) store for £42 a year: per the Resolution, Thomas Oliver.

Oct. 12. John Burke's death. Died lately Mr. Jennings, Colonel Williams, Jacob Williams, and Captain Green.

1737.

May 25. "Samuel Oliver arrived here from Calis about 10 days agone and in 6 days sailed directly for London." Johnny Martin sails in Thomas Oliver with Thomas Martin's wife and children . . . . "sent a bill of Exchange for £30 sterling drawn by Captain Oliver on Messrs. Rowland and Samuel Frye, Merchants in London."

June 11. David Tullideph and his wife's 5 negros: were I to sell my Estate now it would produce no more than £5000 sterling. "My mother in Law's first husband's name was Leonard Burroughs, an Englishman, she of French Parentage, but born in London, named Lucey Thibout, my wife's maiden name. Mary Burroughs was married first to one John Tremills, a Creole of this Island, an honest, good natured man, but his hospitality bordered on profuseness, by which his Estate was mortgaged, and by virtue thereof sold to my mother in Law, now named Mrs. Lucey Mercier, by Order of high Court of Chancery, and by her conveyed to me and my heirs for ever."

Aug. 15. Dr. Sydserfe has purchased John Martin's and John Manwareing's estates at Five Islands. Cesar Rodenay is walked off, but Sydserfe has got all his negroes but 3 or 4 he carried with him. Royall is gone to New England.

Oct. 3. Refers to Copy of Colonel Williams's will, to whom Mr. Oliver and self are Executors . . . . about Jack Yeaman's Marriage.

Oct. 24. My brother David settled in England; his 6 negros to be sold.

Dec. 21. To Brother Benjamin Bourroughs: your sloops. "We had a girl born the 30th of October, and is named Charlotte after your grandmother," after Mercier's mother, "after my mother Mercier's mother." Lucy Tremills has been very ill.

1737-8, Feb. 28. "When Alexander Middleton went to Boston some years ago."

1738.

April 10. To William Dunbar: If Alexander Middleton is not in London he is at Glasgow; he is nephew to Colonel Middleton, and came out here with your brother some years agone. "The purchase of 50 Acres of Land I made of William Yorke two years agone for which I gave him £750 our money. I hear from Tortola that he is lately dead, now he has a wife that lives with her poor parents near Chatham or Rochester . . . . she is in extream want."

April 17. "If you are in London in June you will have the pleasure of seeing Dr. Sydserfe's Lady, Son, and Daughter."

May 29. Dr. Young's purchase of Dabron's estate.

Aug. 8. Received yours of June 26 per Samuel Oliver; mentions Michael Lovell.

Aug. 14. "John Yeaman's Creditors have allowed him five years' liberty, and his father has offered to plead for him at the Barr for some years till John can do it himself, and give all the profitts to John in the meantime." "Colonel Lucas is gone home about the Majority of this Regiment."

Nov. 3. I have resigned all business in favour of my partner Dr. William Mercer, it was too great fatigne, and he allowed me in consideration £300, and I still hold all business that side of the creek next myself, which may be £200 per annum. Have practised much inoculation for the small-pox.

1738-9, March 16. To Mr. Stephen Bayard, merchant in New York: I knew your brother Samuel when here.

1739.

April 14. To Mr. Thomas Martin at Cork: "Samuel Frye's Widow . . . . informed you have interest with her sister Gamble . . . . she has been paying large debts every year." Am Guardian to her (fatherless) children.

May 23. To William Dunbar: your cousin James Mackie's debts here; his goods worth £600.

June 5. To Brother Davie: Have built large works and lent my neighbour Leonard £600; am concerned for the loss of your child.

July 1. Since Dr. Sydserfe left.

July 1. Major Murray was married 11 days agone to Mrs. Otto, and go to New England to-day with John Frye and his family, but Murray will return again before Christmas.

Aug. 3. To Hon. George Thomas, Governor of Pennsylvania, at Philadelphia.

Sep. 1. To Walter Sydserfe, Esq., and Mrs. Thibou in London.

Oct. 15. Sum due to Burke's estate for money advanced to Onozephorus Gamble. "My wife was delivered of another girl the 6th instant, to be called Mary." Also to Mrs. Elizabeth Gamble at Cork: your sister Frye's debt.

Oct. 16. "Colonel Gilbert's Courtship, but believe he is now married to the widow Gaynor." Dr. W. Sydserfe's estates at Five Islands and Belfast. "Mr. Cope dyed some weeks agone, Old Tomlinson about 8 dayes agone; he dyed suddenly of fitts. Thomas Crawford dyed lately and left Walter Paterson a negroe boy and his sister a girl. James Gamble is made Gunner of James's Fort and has 14*s.* a day."

Oct. 16. To brother David: glad brother Thomas is advanced to the chair of St. Leonard's.

Nov. 18. Captain King's death.

1740.

April 22. £400 given to Mr. Pattrick Wilson, goldsmith, who was married to one of my wife's daughters.

April 26. To Brother Davie: congratulate you on the increase to your family.

June 23. I have shipt 8 hogsheads sugar to Colonel Samuel Martin in Bristoll . . . . for about 15 years agone I came to this Island in his employ . . . . also to Mrs. Mary Sydserfe at Bath.

July 5. "To Mrs. Elizabeth Gamble at Corke: Madam. I received yours of December 30th, 1739, since which have seen a letter from Mr. Samuel Lyons to his friend here wherein he mentions his haveing purchased Golden Grove of you for £1200 Irish money, which has prevented me from proposeing anything relateing thereto to Mr. Mackinnen . . . . I paid Miss Maly Frye's passage; she behaves well, and is well respected by Mrs. Frye and her friends." Also my 2 daughters Miss Charlotte and Mary Margaret.

Aug. 28. To Slingsby Bethel, Esq.: "Mr. Ephraim Jordin is a very industrious man who by the interest of Colonel King and self as his securitys has rented a pretty large Estate at £350 Sterling per annum."

1741.

Sep. 25. Thomas Hanson's and Dr. Young's death. Miss Turner's marriage.

Nov. 12. Cesar Rodenay's death.

Dec. 3. Halladay going to be married. Governor Byam and Jacob Thibou a-dying.

1741-2, Jan. 9. Dr. Ranken selling his house and going to Jamaica. Governor Byam's and Jacob Thibou's death.

Feb. 5. Mr. Gunthorpe's marriage. Dr. Dunbar's death.

March 13. My wife delivered of a dead child.

1742.

June. Per Captain Arthur Payne. Per Captain James Payne.

June 28. Mr. Andrew Murray, merchant in Dublin. Samuel Martin, Esq., merchant in London.

July 3. Dr. William Mercer ? at New York.

July 27. To Walter Sydserfe, Esq.; also to "Thomas Tullideph: wrote him with one inclosed to Mr. Hamilton from his sister Oliver."

Aug. 30. Cousin Lucy Burroughs.

Oct. 15. Mr. George Dunbar, merchant in Edinburgh: his brother might owe £1000; I advise his sisters to send a power to his Executors.

Oct. 18. John Watkins hath rented the Judges for £450 sterling.

Nov. 15. Samuel Lyons, merchant in Dublin.

1742-3, Feb. 2. Proposes offering £400 sterling a year for Mr. Smith's and £200 or £250 for Rigby's.

March 2. Nichols's and Mrs. Blizard's death.

1743.

Oct. 12. Ye Antigua Packett, Samuel Oliver.

1743-4, Jan. 28. To William Yeamans, merchant in Carolina.

Various accounts with—

1731—4. Mr. Robert Martin; Mr. Francis Francklyn £620; Mr. Thomas Powell; Mr. Samuel Hanson £492. 1732, Mr. William Bowers. 1733, Messrs. William, Edward, Anthony, and Joseph Bezunes; Mr. John Bezune. 1734, Philip Darby. 1733, Mr. Robert Dunning. 1733, Mr. Perrie Yorke. 1733-4-6, Mr. William Hillhouse. 1733, Mr. Robert Martin mortgaged £620. 1734. Mr. Thomas Hanson. 1734, Mr. Ephraim Jerdin. 1735, William Gerrish, Esq. 1735, Captain Charles Goore; Mr. Ed. Gregory. 1734-5, Mr. Robert Allen; Robert Dunning's estate, ye widow. 1735, Mr. Jacob Thibout; Mrs. Mary Tremills; Mr. Thomas Dunning. 1734, Mr. James and Mr. Charles Murray. 1735, Mr. James Mackie. 1735, Mr. Samuel Martin in New Division; Mr. W. Yorke £750; Mr. Robert Delamere. 1736, Dr. William Boyle. 1735, Mr. Joseph Mathews; Mrs. Judith Leott; Estate of John Tremills, deceased; Peter Mercier an Executor 1736. 1738-9, Mr. George Leonard; Mr. John Fyffe. 1739, Thomas Hanson, senior, Esq.

[*End of Volume I.*]

1743-4, March 3. Thomas Trotter, a nephew of mine, taken by a Spaniard, with other passengers.

1744.

April 24. Rev. Thomas Tullideph, his son Robin, his daughter Mary.

July 21. To William Smith, Esq.

Aug. 13. Have prevented the forced sale of Mrs. Frye's estate.

Sep. 15. Young Carlisle would have attained 21 in 1738. Several letters to Philadelphia merchants.

Oct. 28. Mr. Samuel Lyons, merchant in Dublin; per Captain Samuel Oliver. Thomas Oesterman Williams, Mr. Rowland Oliver and self.

1744-5, Feb. 28. Colonel Martin hath laid aside business (in London). "Mr. Shephard hath purchased Henry Osborn's Estate, and gives £10,500 for it and 30 negroes." Dr. Richardson, Grandson to ye Old man, inclines to rent his, but expects £500 sterling rent. To cousin John Trotter in London, brother of Thomas Trotter: your father; signed, your affectionate uncle W. Tullideph.

March 14. Mr. James Fyffe: your sister; your brother's death and will. Mr. Earl Daniel.

1745.

March 30. "Yesterday my wife was safely delivered of a fine boy."

French war this year.

July 12. To Mrs. Elizabeth Gamble: to settle your affair with Mrs. Moncrieff.

Aug. 8. Robert Martin, manager of Governor Thomas's estate is a creole; he was forced to sell his estate to his brother; is a single man.

Aug. 13. I hear John Trotter's brother died at Jamaica. Martin Goble's estate here is a very good one. Mr. James Stevenson is gone into partnership with Dr. Samuel Young.

Oct. 5. To Governor Thomas: Harry Hodge arrived yesterday from London; I hear he is confirmed a Lieutenant; congratulate you on the birth of your daughter: Dr. Sydserfe has gone to St. Kitts to see Mr. Willet, who hath been long in a bad way.

Oct. 17. Mr. Willet died the day before Dr. Sydserfe arrived.

Nov. 16. To his brother Thomas Tullideph: your daughter's marriage; Mr. Spooner hath rented Blubber Valley from young Pearne.

Nov. 18. *Re* death of Thomas Trotter.

1746.

March 26. To Ferdinando John Paris in Surrey Street.

Aug. 27. Nephew John Trotter has arrived.

Aug. 27. To his nephew Robert Tullideph (Robin), son of Rev. Thomas Tullideph; also to Mr. David Tullideph at Wisbeach: I made 110 hogsheads.

Aug. 28. Steeven's estate owes to Captain Partis's estate £4000 currency.

Oct. 29. To brother Thomas Tullideph: your daughter Peggy so well married.

1747.

April 4. Ambrose York, the heir to Yorke's estate: his father's Executors: believe that estate owes £5000 sterling to Mr. Young.

Aug. 15. To brother Thomas Tullideph: Mr. Dewar has arrived; I have purchased the equity of redemption of Yorke's, an adjacent estate, for £8000 from Yorke's heir; cousin Cecil; your family at Kilmux.

Aug. 22. John Fyffe died in very bad circumstances .... his brother James died at Montserrat 18 months agone .... the youngest of John's daughters and the eldest hath old Jefferies's estate close by General Mathews. Mr. Robert Baker, Surveyor of this Island, proposes a draught of this.

Oct. 11. Brother Benjamin Burroughs at Bermuda.

1747-8, Feb. 7. *Re* Mr. James Fyffe, deceased; his niece Frances Fyffe, my goddaughter.

1747-8, March 16. Old Colonel Frye died a few days agone.

1748.

June 25. "A few months agone a Cousin of ours, Dr. James Russell, son to Cousin Betty Tullideph's at Pearth, arrived here."

June 27. Michael Lovell's account. Dr. Walter Sydserfe back in London.

Oct. 22. Brother Benjamin Burroughs: your daughter Martha's letter; your uncle Mr. Stephen Outerbridge at Bermuda.

Nov. 7. Mr. Francis Sanders in Nevis: "I understand by Mr. Rowland Oliver that you were lately married to Miss Martha Williams." Her father's affairs in my hands: about £800 due to her and 16 negros.

Dec. Old Ambrose York died in 1716, and left Thomas Hanson his Executor, who ruined the estate.

Feb. 14. May add the Bear Garden to Yorke's, which will cost £9000 currency; it owes Mr. Bannister, our Collector, £5000 sterling, to whom I have now lent £2100 sterling.

1748-9, March 2. To Peter van Brugh Livingston, merchant in New York: at the recommendation of Mr. Livingston I consign you 10 hogsheads rum.

1749.

April 3. The Marshall .... is married to a sister of Francis Farley's. "As for James Gamble, Mr. Kerby is like to fall in his debt £5000 this money, which is to be divided amongst his Creditors; his son Ned hath gone to pott, owes £5000, they say nothing to be gott there till Man's Estate comes to him on the death of his Mother. Colonel Martin's son George dyed about 14 days agone suddenly of a fitt, the fruits, I fear, of intemperance." Have not struck with Mr. Steevens for Bear Garden.

June 4. I have purchased Bear Garden for £9000 currency; hope to make 250 hogsheads at ye 3 estates at 20*s.* to 22*s.* per cwt. Ned Thomas's death; death of brother David's wife.

June 4. To George Thomas, Esq.: "Your Brother Ned Thomas and Son went Over to Barbuda about 3 weeks agone for ye recovery of your Brother's health, where he dyed Saturday ye 27th past. Your son (George) tells me that he made a will there a few hours before his death, and had left Messrs. Bannister, Evanson, and Addis his Executors." Recommend George to your favour again.

June 4. Duncan Grant part-owner in a cargo. "John King hath sold his estate to Robin Gray, and hath 60 or 80 negroes reserved for his wife's Dower." "Our Great Fortune Miss Thibou was married about 3 weeks agone to Dr. Thomas Jarvis of Popeshead by the Consent of the family, and Mrs. Berry was married about ten days agone to young Dr. Frazer, who hath not been here 12 months as yet; he lived with his cousin the other Dr. Frazer, and is a likely young man."

Nov. 11. Mr. Doeg sells £4000 bank stock and gives him a bill of £2800 on Slingsby Bethell.

Nov. 22. To George Thomas, Esq.: your agreeable purchase in England. Colonel Lessly lost his Second Son David of a fever, William Yeamons lost his wife a few weeks agone, and the Old man is now fond of his Son John, but whether he will pay his debts I know not. "Jack Yeamans's mother dyed a few weeks agone."

Dec. 18. To Brother Benjamin Burroughs: Cousin Patty to tell me when of age to receive £60 from her grandmother's estate.

Jan. 20. Mr. William Dunbar's death.

1749-50, March 20. As for Billie Sheriffe .... he lived some time with Mr. Watkins to Settle Colonel Martin's Accounts .... Mr. Watkins thought him honest and sober but inclined to be idle, he proposes doing business as a Town Agent. "I was Inclined to Ship 20 or 30 hogsheads to Major Oliver as a grateful Sense of his former favours to me."

1749-50, March 20. To Richard Oliver, Esq., *re* consignments; also to Mr. George Dunbar in Edinburgh: your brother's affairs; Dr. William Mercer who upon remitting your Brother to be his Partner: your sisters.

1750.

April 20. Mr. Frazer, the Collector at Parham, was this morning given over by the Doctors .... ill of a fever .... of which he died the next day.

May 14. Our great Man .... his son Daniel was married last Tuesday to Mrs. Lyons, the daughter of George Byam and Widow of Henry Lyons's Son.

June 3. Levy on Kerr's estate in right of Jack Yeamon's wife .... Parson Grant some time past Dyed at Tortola .... Duncan Grant .... Stapleton Dunbar hath been down at Nevis. I spoke to his brother William.

June 27. Death of our worthy friend Mr. Thomas Martin. 10 hogsheads to Major Oliver, also to Richard Oliver, Esq., merchant in London.

July 11. James Doeg, Esq., a near Relation of mine.

1751.

[Walter Tullideph was in London in January.]

April 3. Brother Benjamin Burroughs: your 2nd son Benjamin. I arrived at Antigua 10th ultimo.

April 8. To George Thomas, Esq., Yapton Place, near Chichester.

April 13. To Walter Sydserfe: your brother Garrett. Dr. Dewar was married 14 days agone to a daughter of Dr. Bennets of St. Christopher's, an agreeable Lady. Mr. White lost his son William a little before my arrival. Old Senegatt and his wife, George White and his, Charles Alley and his, Alexander Dow and his wife, and Robert Baker's wife have all dyed in my absence, as did Charles Mathews a few days before my arrival.

April 14. Arrived here 10th of last month after a passage of 5 weeks. He left his daughter Charlotte at school in England. Richard Oliver, Esq., is now his Merchant and Correspondent *vice* William Dunbar, deceased.

May 12. I have a Refining house. Rum 2*s.* 6*d.*; Sugar 30*s.* to 35*s.*; Double refined Sugar 21*d.* per pound; Single refined ditto 15*d.*; Bastards 9*d.* (a large coarser loaf). Mr. John Trotter went home last year. Mr. Ephraim Jordin acting for him. The North Sound sugars of George Thomas, Esq., were usually consigned to S. Bethell and James Douglass of London.

June 28. Mrs. Rebecca Oaterbridge and Mr. Stephen Oaterbridge at Bermuda. B. B. rent paid.

July 8. To Walter Sydserfe: Charles Dunbar and his son Billy have sold Witts of 16½ acres for £600 sterling, which I bought for you; your brother Billie.

July 12. Stapleton Dunbar's brother the Doctor. James Delap is dead since my arrival.

Dec. 14. Mr. George Lucas Osborne, merchant in Philadelphia; he was at Antigua in October.

1752 (? New Style).

Feb. 3. Mr. George Leonard at Tortola: expect your return to your family; your boy George's education; your wife indisposed; Miss Ruth and Miss Durham; your Mother ailing; your works suffered much. "Dr. Turnbull makes a Demand of your Sister Turnbull's fortune in favour of his Two Sons."

March 4. List of losses to my works. Billie Garrett and his wife. Miss Fanny Wier.

March 4. Jack Sydserfe in danger of a consumption. *Re* £265 paid to Mr. Davison. Mr. Halliday in settling his accounts with his uncle William Dunbar.

March 25. To George Thomas, Esq.: Mr. McKinnen's sister Mrs. Carlisle *re* her renting George Thomas's Winthorpes. Your Brother Ned's Son Billie died here some time past; I made Enquiry of Colonel Gilbert who were his heirs; he told me as your Brother had left his Estate equally to be divided between his wife and Children, and the Wife had survived the Children, that she was Intitled to the whole.

March 25. Mr. Doeg hath purchased Mr. Moncrief's Estate and given £10,000 sterling.

April 11. Richard Oliver as Executor to late Thomas Martin. Charlotte Tullideph under Richard Oliver's care during Dr. Sydserfe's absence at Lisbon; also to Mrs. Mary Hanson; have paid Mr. William Dening your £40, and Mrs. Weatherill £11 13s. 4d. for 10 months' board of William French Dening to the 10 March 1750-1, when he dyed.

May 6. To Rev. Thomas Tullideph: Mr. Gregory was Surgeon to Captain Tyrrel, a worthy brave Officer, who married a Lady of great fortune here; Young Doeg goes home next month with his 2 eldest sisters, and will see you on his way to Montrose.

May 9. To Brother David Tullideph: last April you were 47.

May 11. Mrs. Jordin hath gott a Cancer of her breast; our friend Ephraim. No rain since Christmas.

May 25. Mr. Joseph Merry of Kingston in Jamaica: Your uncle Anthony Garratt and family here; you will not be of age till April 1754, will be then entitled to £600; the way you left us; your debts; Anthony Garratt and self your guardians; your relations at Barbadoes; return here in 1753.

May 30. To Richard Oliver: There is a young Gentleman, a kinsman of mine, Mr. William Dewar, who proposes comeing out here in a Mercantile way; his brother Dr. Dewar here.

June 14. My dear Son (Waltie), who was Carried off with a malignant fever and Ulcerated Sore throat on the 10th Instant. Also to Richard Oliver, Esq.: "I was not sure but you might be confined with the gout."

July 7. "John Lyndsey (who was married last week to Mr. Doeg's eldest daughter)."

July 8. "Mr. McKinnon's Daughter was married last week to Young Dr. Frazer, he who was formerlie married to Mrs. Barry, and Mr. Pare's eldest daughter is to be married next week to Dr. Ashton Warner."

July 15. To Walter Sydserfe: death of Jack; Dr. Grant hath purchased Jack Yeaman's part of Kerr's Estate, which is where the workes Stand; Mr. Jeffreson hath bought Simon Farley's part of said Estate, 39 acres I think, and given about £80 per acre; Pattrick Byrne lost his wife a few days agone; she has left 2 daughters.

Wrote Mr. George Leonard August 3 *re* sale of his uncle Hanson's estate 29 August.

Aug. 19. General Mathew departed this life the 14th instant at 10 o'clock.

Sep. 22. To George Thomas, Esq.: Mr. Martin (your Manager) moved from North Sound the 18th Instant, and is Succeeded by Mr. Edward Hamilton, a son of Rowland Hamilton, who hath the Character of an Honest, Active, Humane Man and a good Planter; is married, but not likely to have any children.

Sep. 22. To Walter Sydserfe: "When Mr. Watkins surrendered up the lease last month to Mr. Jennings the reappraisement was £1500 in Watkins's favour. I askt him how he expected to be paid, to which he replyed he had two very good Men his Securitys, meaning you and Major Oliver."

Nov. 9. To Mr. John Trotter, Glasgow: your father, aunt, and sisters.

Nov. 9. Richard Oliver, Esq.: I am glad the gout hath been so favourable these two years past. Mr. Delap's widow who hath a great many Sickly Children.

Nov. 12. To Walter Sydserfe: your son Thomas.

Dec. 3. Mathew Mills's death.

Dec. 25. Cousin John Trotter at Edrom near Berwick on Tweed: your sister's marriage; your other sister.

Dec. 26. Mr. Fleming hath sent me a Commission for Lieut.-Colonel.

1753.

Jan. 24. Mr. Joseph Merry at Philadelphia.

April 16. Mr. Robert Dewar's store.

April 29. Richard Oliver, Esq.: "I would choose that you should get lodgeings for us in Upper Greenidge."

[The last letter from Antigua was dated 19 June 1753. James Doig acts as his Attorney.]

Aug. 16. Arrived at Dover 7th instant after a passage of 7 weeks.

Sep. 29. London. Are moving into our house in Poland Street.

Oct. 13. The Brigantine Sally, Captain William Hindman, from Glasgow. Blast still troublesome. Our Island sugars rarely fetch 35s., but some of Mr. R. Ash's Mr. Oliver hopes to get 45s. 6d. for.

Oct. 18. Mr. Peter Desmonts, Junior, "cousin," who is in Holland and going to St. Kitts. Mrs. Wise's youngest daughter went to St. Martin's with Mrs. Desmonts; also to Mrs. Ann Desmonts *re* her said son Peter . . . . Mr. Desmonts . . . . at St. Kitts. To Mr. Peter Tyson at St. Kitts: have seen your brother and your son.

Oct. 23. To Ephraim Jordin: Remember me to uncle Isaac Monroe; my worthy uncle Isaac Thibou, Esq.

Dec. 22. Charles Alexander, Esq., and to Mr. William Garrett Hillhouse.

1754.

Feb. 14. Brother David Tullideph: your sister Buxton.

April 4. To Pattrick Wilson, who was off to Antigua the 10th ult.: his son Pattrick at school in England. Mrs. Wilson at Antigua. Mr. Francis Delap's Daughter being married.

April 8. To cousin John Trotter, merchant at Kingston, Jamaica: I wrote to Mr. Dewar of Vogrie.

May 30. Who hath Joseph Merry married? To Pattrick Wilson: a letter from Patie to his grandmother about Charlotte's marriage.

June 15. Brother Rev. Alexander Trotter at Edrom sent me a bill from his son's factor at Antigua.

July 11. *Re* marriage articles and Sir John Ogilvy; going to spend 4 weeks in Scotland.

[The last letter was dated at London 20 July, no others for this year.]

1755.

Antigua. Jan. 10. Arrived here.

Jan. 20. To Walter Sydserfe, Esq.: much sickness. Upon the death of Colonel Gunthorpe the General was pleased to press me again to take my seat in Council which I accordingly did last month, and Thomas Jarvis hath been since appointed another. My debt to Mr. Oliver.

Feb. 10. I arrived here the 22nd November after a passage of 32 days besides 14 lying at Falmouth.

Feb. 24. Mr. Robert Tullideph: dear cousin Robin *re* his love affair, he the 1st son. "My father had 5 Children, his Estate was such that he could not give more to your father, although his eldest son, than he gave us."

Feb. 24. The large fortune I have acquired; our cousin Thompson. Mr. Otto was swore into the Councill last meeting and stands next to Colonel Lesley our President, at same time was Colonel Byam who is the next above me, Mr. Oliver and Mr. Jarvis below me. A turtle for Sir John and my wife.

Feb. 24. To Sir John Ogilvy, Bart.: your £3000 settled. The Musketo Cove, Charlotte's estate, will make 150 hogsheads. By the 19th of June the day you were married.

April 5. To Mr. George Leonard, separated from his wife; his son George a promising youth, and daughter now grown up. £4000 debt paid off his estate of his own contracting since he went away. I gave my daughter £5000 fortune.

April 21. To Richard Oliver, Esq.: Mrs. Wilson was delivered of a Girl the 18th Instant who dyed next day.

May 18. Mr. William Delap, merchant in Dublin: Your brother, my worthy friend, recommended me to you.

July 14. Captain Alexander's lady has died.

July 25. To Sir John Ogilvy: yours of 21 May acquainted me with Charlotte's delivery of a boy to be called Walter. About 14 days agone Mr. William Simms dyed of a fever, he hath dyed in good Circumstances.

Aug. 30. To Walter Sydserfe: Captain Blair's addresses to Polly. I owe Mr. Oliver £3000, he may lend £5000 more for Polly's fortune. My New Division estate, containing that formerly Tremills, William Yorke's, and Samuel Martin's, is for Polly. My Muskito Cove, containing York's and Bear Gardens, is for Lady Ogilvy; latter worth £3000 more than former. 110 negros to be mortgaged with Polly's estate. Captain Blair's Mother; his intailed estate.

Sep. 29. Colonel William Byam dyed at Barbada ye 25th or 26th instant and was there buried; he was a good man and is a great loss to the Island.

Oct. 22. Mr. Patrick Wilson, silversmith here, went home and is dead.

Nov. 12. Miss Watkins's marriage to Byam Freeman. Mr. Thomas Elmes dyed suddenly one day last week.

Dec. 20. To Sir John Ogilvy, Bart., of Invercarity, near Dundee: your house at Kinnordy.

Dec. 28. I could have sold Pollies for £12,000 sterling. Mr. John Wise dyed lately. Mr. Dring the Taylor, John Blane, and Robert Cullen's wife; he continued a widower only 3 months and is married to the young Widow Glanville.

1756.

Jan. 10. Richard Oliver, Esq.: I wish to rent Pearne's Point of Mr. Pearne, West of Yorke's Mill, 200 acres, but great part of it rocky and hilly, and 50 acres of a salt pond; offer £60 sterling a year for it.

March 13. Colonel Horne's marriage. Mrs. Wilson's uncle Mr. Benjamin Bourroughs, a poor relation.

June 22. Young Mr. George Leonard at Cambridge.

Oct. 12. Charlotte bravely recovered, and the little boy thrives.

Oct. 20. Mr. Weir is a worthy, deserving young Gentleman. I owe Mr. Oliver £3137.

Nov. 8. Helen Thompson's marriage, and Maly Thompson's death.

1757.

Jan. 2. To Richard Oliver, Esq.: Please to send me out by Convoy two Tombstones of White Marble for my two Children; write on them thus, in black letters: Katherine Tullideph the third Daughter of Walter Tullideph, Esq., and Mary his Wife, born Sunday November 16th, 1740, and dyed Fryday October 7th, 1743. Walter Sydserfe Tullideph, only Son of Walter Tullideph and Mary his wife, born March 29th, 1745, and dyed June 10th, 1752.

March 16. To Sir John Ogilvy: Mr. Auchenleck is not yet arrived . . . . I shall do him what service I can.

March 24. Mr. John Desmont's son John's brigantine. Mr. Peter Desmont had gone to St. Martin's to escape from his creditors. Dr. James Russell is to manage estates of Dr. Walter Tullideph.

May 16. To Andrew Aiton, Esq., merchant in Glasgow: You and I were school-fellows att the high School of Edenburgh some 30 odd years agone.

May 31. To William Thomas, Esq.: cozen Thomas was likely soon to bless you with another child.

[Last letter from Antigua 3 June 1757, next one from London 1 August 1757.]

Oct. 29. At Kinnordy. To Mr. Duncan Grant: Mr. Jordin's death and will.

Dec. 20. To John Trotter at Philadelphia: When you came out in 1746 you had a cargo of £1200, etc.; your difficulties.

1758.

Jan. 31. Mr. Hart hath purchased Hamilton's Estate.

Feb. 10. Provost Doig of Montrose, brother of James Doig, Esq., of Antigua. Mrs. Sydserfe's death.

Feb. 21. To Dr. James Dewar: I spoke to Vogrie about your proposals to your father. Mr. Doig went up to London with his father (James Doig, Esq., had arrived in England 2 February); his wife was yesterday delivered of a fine boy.

March 4. To Mr. Charles Jones, sugar refiner at Antigua, and his wife.

March 16. Young Mr. Dewar of Vogrie declared his inclination for Miss Polley, but it is now all over as she did not like him.

April 11. Lady Ogilvy was yesterday morning safely delivered of another fine Boy.

April 22. To Right Rev. Mr. Thomas Tullideph.

May 30. To Mr. Pattie Wilson, who is to become a Hamburgh merchant: Your grandmama and I. To Walter Sydserfe, Esq.: I saw your brother and family here lately. Am furnishing a house at Dundee.

June 30. Have been over to St. Andrews to the Funeral of my brother's wife who dyed the 15th.

Oct. 16. This is the 1st letter to Richard and Richard Oliver, merchants in London; also to David Doig, Esq., Provost at Montrose.

Nov. Dundee. I have purchased a small estate (no house upon it) within a mile of this town, which will cost me near £6000.

1759.

Jan. 19. My nephew Robert Tullideph, a Lieut. in the army. The Balgay writings.

Jan. 31. Mrs. Wilson's, now Jones's, death announced in letter of November 20.

Feb. 21. Mr. Pattie Wilson: the loss of your mother lately.

[The last letter in this book is 28 March 1759.]

[*Volume III. begins 2 April* 1759.]

April 9. Mr. Charles Ogilvy, a brother of Sir John's, who will be 21 next Aug., hath lived with a wine merchant as prentice. Lady Ogilvy was safely delivered the 5th instant of another fine boy (4th); owe Olivers £1115. Wilson estate, the appraisement £7294, houses above £1600; total £8894.

June 6. Dr. Boag dead.

Nov. 12. Mr. Doig's death. I saw Billie Doig's son 23rd ultimo, but hear he is dead. Saw Mrs. Darby at Richmond about 7 weeks agone, she was delivered of another fine girl. Miss Dolly, her 1st daughter, is a fine woman. About 2 months agone I bought another estate within 2 miles of Dundee, which cost me £8000, so that I am greatly in debt. James Corss to go out to learn plantation business, a relation of Lord Gray; also George Ramsay, indentured.

1760.

Jan. 16. Propose to leave the "Bank" to Lady Ogilvy and "Balgay" to Polley; thought to rent Yorke's and Bear Garden for £1500 sterling. The number of renters surprises me much . . . . is it £1400 sterling Uncle Thibou gets for his estate?

Jan. 23. To Mr. James Crawford, merchant in Rotterdam: Your worthy brother. The bearer Mr. Pattrick Wilson nearly related to me is 16 years old.

Feb. 15. The Highland name of Tullideph signifies Hindhill, so call Balgay that and the other Tullideph Hall.

Feb. 25. To Mr. Henry Hancock, merchant in London: asking him to lend 6 or £7000. "Messrs. Oliver have advanced so largely for the Gentlemen of our Island, and cannot soon call it in." I owe them about £1000.

In a letter of the 22nd he wrote: "I have some reason not to be so well pleased with the Olivers, they are shy in advancing money equal to my wants on account of a late purchase." Duncan Grant in England.

March 28. Dr. Sydserfe's death; am sending barley and peas meal for the negros.

April 7. To William Thomas, Esq.: your father Sydserfe's will dated 16 —— 1759; his sister Weir's small annuity; he died 13 March. Lady Ogilvy was safely delivered of a fine girl the 31st ultimo.

[Letters now are dated from Tullideph Hall, Dundee.]

July 31. Borrows £2000 at 4½ per cent. from Lord Panmure.

Aug. 2. Sugar sold at 42*s.* 6*d.* netts, £20 sterling a hogshead.

[Loose letter dated 5 October 1758, London, from Richard and Richard Oliver: "Death of Colonel King, who has left his Estate to the Son of Peter Lavicount."]

1761.

[There is here a gap between 3 November 1760 and 5 August 1761, but *no* leaf torn out.]

1762.

April 6. I hope Mr. Oliver, Senior, is got well again.

1763.

Aug. 2. This letter is addressed to Thomas Oliver, Esq.

Aug. 22. Mr. Oliver's death; consign as before.

Aug. 29. To Thomas Oliver, Esq.: "My very worthy friend, your deceased father, for whose Death I am heartily concerned." If R. Oliver comes home this year.

Aug. 31. To Colonel Lesley (in Ireland): your dear child with us.

Sep. 10. Have started a Company at Dundee with Patty Wilson. Captain Peter Ogilvy commander of the snow.

1764.

Arrived at Antigua 6 January; hope to make a £4000 sterling crop.

June 7. To Andrew Dewar, Esq., Collector at Dominica: Mr. Symes of Montserrat, to whom I have lent £5000 sterling on mortgage at 8 per cent.: I propose settling in London as a merchant with brother David; Lieut. Ballingall of the 38th Regiment, a Fyffeman born, who married one of Mrs. James Delap's daughters, may rent Tullideph Hall; they sailed from here yesterday.

July 3. Mr. Thomas's Daughters have had a severe loss by the Death of their Mother. To Hon. Colonel Alexander Leslie: your business in the sale of the houses; Lady Mary Walker the Daughter and coheir.

July 3. To Mr. Francis Pearce, merchant at St. Croix: You knew my Wife's Brother Benjamin Bourroughs had three Sons; the eldest, named Leonard, was married at your Island; he is Dead; his Widow, who subscribes herself Mary Bourroughs, writes me she hath three Children. I saw your Sister three days agone.

Aug. 3. Offers to sell Yorke's and Bear Garden for £20,000 sterling, 400 acres good land, 115 negroes, stone mill, works, etc.

Aug. 11. The ship Charlotte and Mary hath cost me near £1200 sterling. There is one Dr. Walker in London who is married to Lady Mary Walker, a Sister of my Colonel Leslie.

Aug. 11. Messrs. Richard and Thomas Oliver alone.

Oct. 27. I have rented out my Musketo Cove Estate to Dr. Russell for £1100 sterling for 15 years. The Marshall's sale of Mr. Dunbar's estates.

1765.

Aug. 26. Have taken possession of Symes's estate at Montserrat. Mr. Samuel Auchinleck still with me.

1766.

Jan. 16. Yours of 7 October last informing me Lady Ogilvy was safely delivered of a fine Girl. Wattie going to Eton. Pattie Wilson has settled a Freehold estate at St. Vincent.

Jan. 19. Mr. William Daniel at Montserrat.

March 22. To Earl Daniel, Esq.

April 17. Mr. Daniel is my Attorney at Montserratt, a most worthy man; he comes home this year to borrow £7000 sterling to pay off all his debts; not many years agone his father dyed and left him burthened with £26,000 sterling, which he hath now discharged excepting the above sum; his Estates make above 300 hogsheads. Mr. William Daniel. Edie and Laird are Dr. Tullideph's merchants this year, not Olivers.

July 2. I sail hence the 6th instant.

[The next letter is from London, 12 September 1766.]

Sep. 12. Mr. Earl Daniel at London; he owes me £1380; his brother William who is on Symes's estate.

Sep. 12. Mr. Benjamin Ailhaud my manager.

1767.

[The last letter is dated from Tullideph Hall 18 April.]

PARISH REGISTER OF ST. JOHN.

Baptized.

1745 May 30 Walter Sydserfe the S. of Dr Walter Tullideph and Mary his wife.

Buried.

1752 June 11 Walter Tullideph, a Child of Docr Walter Tullideph's.

1770 Aug. 31 John Ogilvie.

1793 July 25 Alexander Ogilvy.

1804 Nov. 7 Thomas Ogilvy, M.D.

PARISH REGISTER OF ST. PAUL.

Buried.

1777 April 9 William Ogilvie, Mid.

Family of Turner.

Thomas Turner. Will dated the two and twe . . . 1695. To my dau. Sarah Rutherford £200 c. & a silver cup formerly Erastus Riaston's, decd. To my sister-in-law Cammell a negro girl, & to her daus. Elinor & Susanna 1000 lbs. each, & to the yst dau. Mary 1000 lbs. To Mary dau. of Saml Boon my goddau. 1000 lbs. at 11. To my godson Wm Walters 1000 lbs. at 10. To my brother Joshua Turner 2 negros & 15 acres adjoining Harry Blizard, & after his death to . . . . Thomas & his heirs. To my only son Thos. Turner all my estate & my plantation in Five Island & his heirs, & in default to my brother Joshua. Thos. Turner Ex'or. Witnessed by John Perrie, Joshua Turner, Elizabeth Turner. By Christopher Codrington was sworn Joshua Turner 26 Aug., and Captain John Perrie in Oct. 1695.

Sarah Turner of Antigua. Will dated 10 Nov. 1696. To my goddau. Susanna Evens my clothes & £10 c. To my prentice girl Margt Worlan my worse clothes. To my son-in-law David Rutherford & to Sarah his now wife all my estate in England & Antigua & 2 negros, 5000 lbs. in the hands of Tho. Turner, & 7 negros. David & Sarah

Rutherford to be Ex'ors. Witnessed by Peter Rogers, Elizabeth Rogers, John Moore. By Christopher Codrington, Esq., were sworn Peter Rogers and John Moore 22 Dec. 1696. Recorded 28 Dec. 1696.

Elizabeth wife of Thomas Turner of Antigua and North America, Gent. Will dated 13 June 1775. By Indenture da. 9 March 1744 between Ann Reynolds of Antigua, widow, Stephen Blizard, & myself by the name of Eliz[th] wife of Thos. Turner, the said Ann Reynolds conveyed to Stephen Blizard 43 negros in trust for her life, then to me for my life, then to my sons in tail, then to my daus., then to such uses as I will. I now free Sammy, Giles, & George, carpenters, Sophia & Ailey, Daniel, Billy, Mary, & Barry. To Sammy £12 c., & to the others £6 c. yearly each. All my other slaves to Barry Conyers Hart my friend & clerk. By Indenture da. 29 Dec. 1749 between my husband, myself, & Sam[l] Young we conveyed to the latter a parcel of land in Popes Head Div[n], S[t] John's parish, of 86 acres with house & negros for use of my husband for life, then to myself & heirs, & by another Indenture made 12 Aug. 1751 between Tho. Turner of Antigua, planter, & Rowl[d] Oliver, John Watkins, John Wise, merch[t], which, after reciting that Tho. Turner was much in debt, he demised to them the 85 acres for 99 years on trust, & my trustee Stephen Blizard commenced an action against Tho. Turner for sums due, & on 2 July 1765 obtained judgment for £494 8s. 8½*d*. c. with costs. By another Indenture da. 28 Sep. 1767 between Sam[l] Henry Warner, dep. Prov. Marsh., & Stephen Blizard, the former for £400 c. granted to the latter all rights to the said plantation, which was done on my behalf. I now bequeath the said estate to Barry Conyers Hart & any other my estate. Mimba to be free & to have £6 c. yearly. £50 c. a year to be paid to my husband Tho. Turner at present of New London, N. America. £12 c. yearly to Frances a mustee dau. of Madlene a mulatto, as also to her sons & dau. John, W[m], Eliz[th], Lydia, & Grace. Hon. Steph. Blizard, Esq., Hon. Tho. Jarvis, Geo. Savage, Esq., & Barry Conyers Hart Ex'ors. Witnessed by Thomas Hughes, Charles Mathews, Joseph Bowyer. By Thomas Jarvis, Esq., was sworn Thomas Hughes 14 Sep. 1785.

1st Codicil dated 8 May 1777. Barry Conyers Hart has been my faithful steward & steady friend. I have no children or near relations. I give Giles to Steph. Blizard, Esq., as he is void of discretion & will be less happy free. Witnessed by John Jackson, jun., James Tenant, Joseph Bowyer. Before Thomas Jarvis, Esq., was sworn James Tenant 14 Sep. 1785.

2nd Codicil dated 19 May 1784. Stephen Blizard being dead I free my mulatto Giles. To Eliz[th] Clearkly, dau. of Francis Turner, all plate & furniture, & to Ann Hart, d. of Barry C. Hart, 2 negros. To Tho. Jarvis & Geo. Savage £50 each. Witnessed by James Tenant, James Warden. Before Thomas Jarvis, Esq., were sworn James Tenant and James Warden 14 Sep. 1785. Recorded 24 Sep. 1785.

Samuel Turner of Mincing Lane, London, merchant, and late an Alderman. Will dated 24 July 1776; proved 5 March 1777 by Elizabeth Turner the relict and Samuel Turner, Esq., the son. (136 Collier.) To be bur. in the vault I built in S[t] Dunstan's in the East in 1765. To my wife Eliz[th] £10,000. To my s. Sam. & my dau. Eliz. £5000 in Trust to pay the interest to my wife for life, then to my s. Sam. I give my wife also my freehold house at Farnham, her late father's, for life, then to my s. Sam[l], also the interest of £1000 mortgage on my late estate at Wapping M[r] Tho. Kibbell purchased of me, then to my dau. Eliz., also £40 a year & £100 for mourning, & all furniture, plate, jewels, linen, books, china, & pictures for life, then to my children, & all wine, coach horses, & live stock at Southend, & the lease of my house in Mincing Lane & that at Southend. To my dau. Eliz. Turner £3000 Orphan Stock & £2000. To my dau. Jane Turner 200 shares of the London Assurance Corporation & £2000. To my s. Sam. & my dau. Eliz. £2000 in Trust to pay the interest to my sister Sarah Farr. To my dau.-in-law M[rs] Anne Turner £100 for mourning. To my grds. Tho. Turner £100 at 21, my gold watch & seals, the sword which was my dear s. Thomas's, books, etc. To my grddau. Eliz. Turner £50 at 21, & like sum to all my gr'dchildren at 21. To my aunt Mrs. Diana Hodges 20 guineas & to her children. To my cousin Sam. Hayward, Esq., of Gloucester 20 guineas, & to his lady & s. & dau. 5 guineas each. To the Rev[d] Sam. Markham & to my niece his wife 20 guineas each. To M[r] W[m] Longman of Aldershott 20 guineas, & to his wife & dau. 10 guineas each. To M[r] John Longman of Farnham & his wife 10 guineas. To my friends Sir Geo. & Lady Colebrook 20 g[as] apiece. To the Minister & church-wardens of S[t] Dunstan's 20 guineas for the poor. To the treasurer of the charity school Tower Ward 30 g[ns]. To my wife ½ ready money & the other ½ to my 2 daus. Eliz. & Jane. All residue to my s. Sam. £32 a yr. to Tho. Woodward of Farnham. To my son my ring in memory of my late dear Mother & the picture of his brother. My wife & s. Ex'trix & Ex'or. Witnessed by John Barker, Alexander Aubert, Arnold Mello.

Colonel Turner of Tobago, Esq. Will dated 3 June 1810. To my friends Rob[t] Paul of S[t] Vincent, Esq., John Balfour of Tobago, Esq., Alex[r] Innis of London, merch[t], & Colin M[c]Lachlan of Glasgow, merch[t], £200 c. To my friend D[r] Rob[t] Smith of Tobago £100 c., & to my goddau. Charlotte his dau. £200 c. To Duncan Turner, overseer on Riseland estate in Tobago, £200 c. To Henrietta Gordon, a free coloured woman, all my furniture & £200 c. All my real estate in Tobago to trustees, viz., my plantations called King's Bay, Friendsfield, & Belvidere to sell & pay legacies & £50 yearly to each of my 2 sisters Janet & Marg[t]., all residue to their children & to those of my sister Ann who died many years ago. Rob[t] Paul, John Balfour, Alex[r] Innis, & Colin M[c]Lachlan Trustees & Ex'ors. Witnessed by Robert Newton, Alexander Paul, Thomas Gerard. Before Sir William Young, Bart., Governor of Tobago, was sworn Alexander Paul, planter, 9 Sep. 1812.

Codicil dated 4 Sep., sworn 14 Oct. 1812. Witnessed by John Glanville, C. Hamilton, George Cumine.

This will was proved 9 Sep. 1812 by John Balfour and Robert Paul. Copy of will sent to Antigua 1 Aug. 1815 by John Balfour, President Commander-in-Chief of Tobago.

1667, March 2. Thomas Turner and John Bridges, 266⅔ acres by Governor Winthrop; surveyed 8 July 1668. This grant is recorded in the Book of Patents for 1668. The land was in St. John's.

1669, Jan. 1. Jane Turner, deed of gift of all her plantation to her husband Thomas Turner.

1671, Oct. 31. Thomas Turner and Alice his wife, late widow of William Milman, deceased, for 21,000 lbs. sell to John Polton of Antigua, carpenter, and William Morgan of Antigua, planter, 35 acres at Popeshead.

1672, Feb. 13. Alliee wife of Thomas Turner, planter, deed of gift to him of all her right to the plantation of her father Lawrence Jones, deceased, by will after the decease of her mother-in-law Mrs. Ann Jones. Her dau. Sarah Turner.

1673, Aug. 14. John Polton of Antigua, carpenter, and William Morgan of Antigua, planter, sell to Thomas Turner, Gent., 35 acres at Popeshead.

1678, Dec. 16. Thomas Turner, Gent., sells to George Smith, Gent., 30 acres in Nonsuch Division.

Pedigree of Turner.

ARMS.—*Per pale gules and azure, three hounds in full cry argent.*
CREST.—*An antelope sejant ermine, attired or, reposing, the dexter foot on an escutcheon of the last.*
(? Granted 1769. *Vide* Edmundson's 'Heraldry.')

SAMUEL TURNER of London, a West India Merchant, Lord Mayor 1768; died 23 Feb. 1777. Will dated 24 July 1776; proved 5 March 1777. (136 Collier.) ═ Elizabeth, dau. of . . . . Wright of Farnham, co. Surrey; mar. 1739.

Samuel Turner, born 21 July and bapt. 9 Aug. 1745 at Stoke Newington; died 24 Feb. 1815 and bur. at St. Dunstan's in the City of London. ═ Anne, dau. of Dr. John Athill of Antigua: born 9 Oct. 1753, bapt. 30 May 1757, and mar. 24 July 1770 at St. John's; died 16 Aug. 1833; bur. at St. Dunstan's in the East.

Elizabeth Turner.

Jane Turner.

Thomas Turner, M.D., of Curzon Street, Mayfair, Physician Extraordinary to William IV., M.D. Camb., F.R.C.P., etc. (see Munk's Roll); mar. 2ndly, many years after 1826, his cousin Dorothy, widow of Dr. Hackett, by whom s.p.; died 10 March 1865, æt. 93. ═ Lucretia Grace, 1st dau. of Sir John Blois, 5th Bart.; mar. 14 Jan. 1805; died 23 Dec. 1826.

Samuel Turner of London, Esq. ═ Elizabeth Rachel, dau. of Gilbert Slater. s.p.

Charles Turner of Liverpool, merchant. ═ Maria, dau. of Samuel B. Athill of Antigua; cousin to her husband.

Rev. Samuel Blois Turner, B.A., in 1876 Rector of South Elmham, Suffolk. ═ Mary, dau. of . . . . Day.

Henry Blois Turner, E.I.C.S., of Bombay. ═ . . . .

Samuel Athill Turner of Antigua, educated at Eton; Baron of Exchequer and Lieut.-Colonel of Militia; died 1849 at Bath. ═ Emily, 1st dau. of Dr. Nicholas Nugent of Antigua; mar. there. s.p.

A son.

Richard S. Turner, 4th son.

Charles Agnew Turner, 5th son, matriculated from Trinity College, Oxford.

1680, April 15. John Bushoone and his wife Elizabeth widow of John Thurland, deceased, sell 10 acres at Dickenson's Bay to Thomas Turner.

1680, May 7. Jonas Langford and Edmund Hull in right of Aron Atkins (John Atkins being deceased), lease $11\frac{1}{2}$ acres at Popeshead to Thomas Turner. Schedule: 2 negros, 1 mare, etc.

1689, July 8. Mr. Thomas Turner, planter, 90 acres late Lieutenant Roger Complin's, deceased, and 4 proportions at 1*s*. e. yearly rent; patent granted by Sir Nathaniel Johnson.

1724, Dec. 7. Richard Oliver, Esq., of Antigua, Ex'or of Thomas Turner and guardian of Thomas Turner, jun., infant, leases 162 acres to Philip Reynolds. Inventory appended.

1731, April 12. Petition of Richard Oliver, Esq., as guardian of Thomas Turner, a minor.

1755, Aug. 26. Petition of Rowland Oliver, John Watkins, and John Wise, merchant, trustees for Thomas Turner.

1777, Feb. 23. Samuel Turner, Esq; late Alderman of Tower Ward, London. He had served the first offices of the city, with honour and applause, and had retired from public business, on account of his ill state of health. ('Gent. Mag.,' p. 96.)

1822, June 7. At Liverpool, John Hayward Turner, esq. youngest son of the late Samuel Turner, esq. of Upper Wimpole-street, to Elizabeth, third daughter, of the late Nicholas Crooke, esq. of Liverpool. ('Annual Register,' p. 248.)

1826, Dec. 23. Lucretia-Grace wife of Thos. Turner, of Curzon-st. M.D. and half sister of Sir Charles Blois, bart. She was the eldest dau. of Sir John the fifth and late bart. by his second wife Lucretia, dau. of — Ottley, of the island of St Christopher, esq; and was married to Dr Turner, Jan. 14, 1805. ('Gent. Mag.,' p. 645.)

1865, March 10. In Curzon-st., Mayfair, aged 92, Thos. Turner, M.D. formerly Physician to St. Thomas' Hospital. He gradnated at Trinity College, Cambridge, (M.B. 1799, M.D. 1804,) and was a Fellow of the College of Physicians, being censor 1807, 1817, 1827, 1829; consiliarius 1836, 1844—1846; and treasurer 1823 to 1845. He delivered the Harveian Lecture 1822, and has a paper in the Medical Transactions. (*Ibid.*, p. 533.)

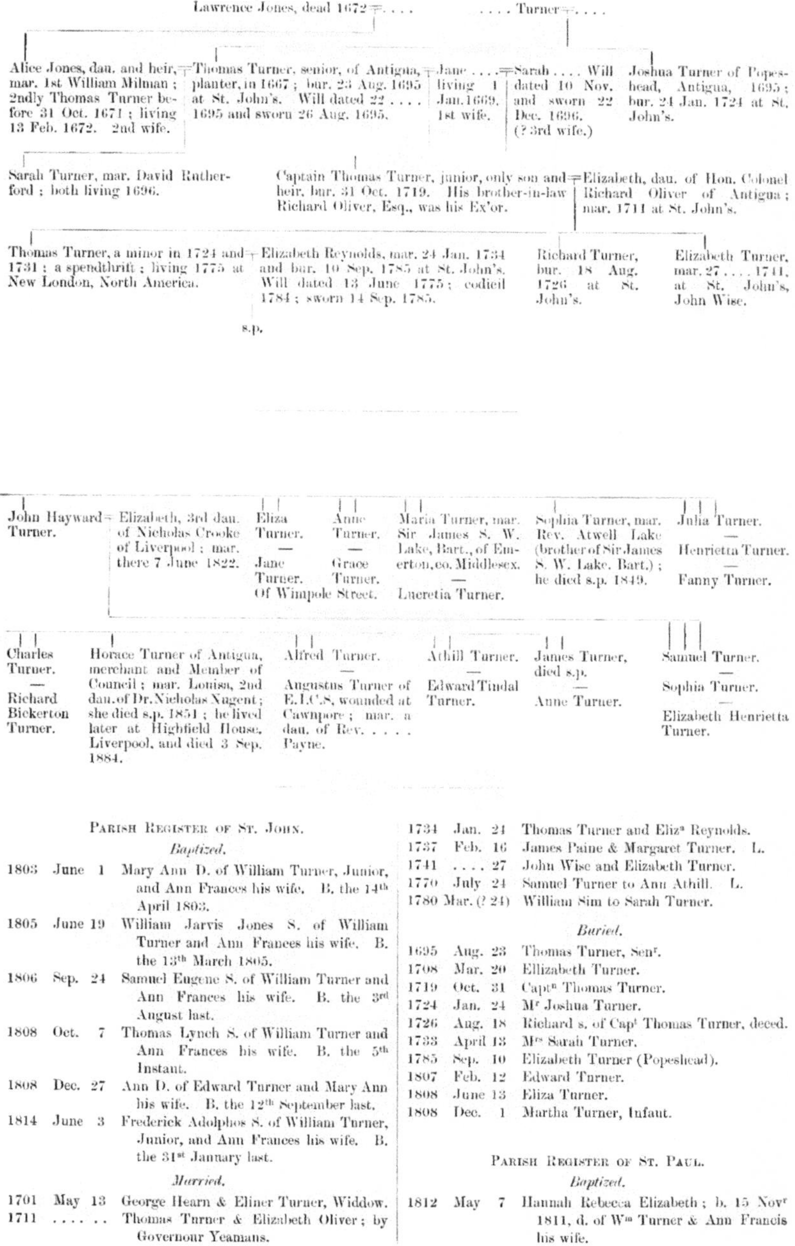

Lawrence Jones, dead 1672 = ...

. . . . Turner = ...

Alice Jones, dau. and heir, mar. 1st William Milman; 2ndly Thomas Turner before 31 Oct. 1671; living 13 Feb. 1672. 2nd wife. = Thomas Turner, senior, of Antigua, planter, in 1667; bur. 23 Aug. 1695 at St. John's. Will dated 22 . . . . 1695 and sworn 26 Aug. 1695. = Jane . . . . living 1 Jan. 1669. 1st wife. = Sarah . . . . Will dated 10 Nov. and sworn 22 Dec. 1696. (? 3rd wife.)

Joshua Turner of Popeshead, Antigua, 1695; bur. 24 Jan. 1724 at St. John's.

Sarah Turner, mar. David Rutherford; both living 1696.

Captain Thomas Turner, junior, only son and heir, bur. 31 Oct. 1719. His brother-in-law Richard Oliver, Esq., was his Ex'or. = Elizabeth, dau. of Hon. Colonel Richard Oliver of Antigua; mar. 1711 at St. John's.

Thomas Turner, a minor in 1724 and 1731; a spendthrift; living 1775 at New London, North America. = Elizabeth Reynolds, mar. 24 Jan. 1734 and bur. 10 Sep. 1785 at St. John's. Will dated 13 June 1775; codicil 1784; sworn 14 Sep. 1785. s.p.

Richard Turner, bur. 18 Aug. 1726 at St. John's.

Elizabeth Turner, mar. 27 . . . . 1741, at St. John's, John Wise.

John Hayward Turner. = Elizabeth, 3rd dau. of Nicholas Crooke of Liverpool; mar. there 7 June 1822.

Eliza Turner. — Jane Turner. Of Wimpole Street.

Anne Turner. — Grace Turner.

Maria Turner, mar. Sir James S. W. Lake, Bart., of Emerton, co. Middlesex. — Lucretia Turner.

Sophia Turner, mar. Rev. Atwell Lake (brother of Sir James S. W. Lake, Bart.); he died s.p. 1849.

Julia Turner. — Henrietta Turner. — Fanny Turner.

Charles Turner. — Richard Bickerton Turner.

Horace Turner of Antigua, merchant and Member of Council; mar. Louisa, 2nd dau. of Dr. Nicholas Nugent; she died s.p. 1851; he lived later at Highfield House, Liverpool, and died 3 Sep. 1884.

Alfred Turner. — Augustus Turner of E.I.C.S, wounded at Cawnpore; mar. a dau. of Rev. . . . . Payne.

Athill Turner. — Edward Tindal Turner.

James Turner, died s.p. — Anne Turner.

Samuel Turner. — Sophia Turner. — Elizabeth Henrietta Turner.

Parish Register of St. John.

Baptized.

1803	June 1	Mary Ann D. of William Turner, Junior, and Ann Frances his wife. B. the 14th April 1803.
1805	June 19	William Jarvis Jones S. of William Turner and Ann Frances his wife. B. the 13th March 1805.
1806	Sep. 24	Samuel Eugene S. of William Turner and Ann Frances his wife. B. the 3rd August last.
1808	Oct. 7	Thomas Lynch S. of William Turner and Ann Frances his wife. B. the 5th Instant.
1808	Dec. 27	Ann D. of Edward Turner and Mary Ann his wife. B. the 12th September last.
1814	June 3	Frederick Adolphos S. of William Turner, Junior, and Ann Frances his wife. B. the 31st January last.

Married.

1701	May 13	George Hearn & Eliner Turner, Widdow.
1711	. . . . .	Thomas Turner & Elizabeth Oliver; by Governour Yeamans.
1734	Jan. 24	Thomas Turner and Eliza Reynolds.
1737	Feb. 16	James Paine & Margaret Turner. L.
1741	 27	John Wise and Elizabeth Turner.
1770	July 24	Samuel Turner to Ann Athill. L.
1780	Mar. (? 24)	William Sim to Sarah Turner.

Buried.

1695	Aug. 23	Thomas Turner, Senr.
1708	Mar. 20	Ellizabeth Turner.
1719	Oct. 31	Captn Thomas Turner.
1724	Jan. 24	Mr Joshua Turner.
1726	Aug. 18	Richard s. of Capt Thomas Turner, deced.
1733	April 13	Mrs Sarah Turner.
1785	Sep. 10	Elizabeth Turner (Popeshead).
1807	Feb. 12	Edward Turner.
1808	June 13	Eliza Turner.
1808	Dec. 1	Martha Turner, Infant.

Parish Register of St. Paul.

Baptized.

1812	May 7	Hannah Rebecca Elizabeth; b. 15 Novr 1811, d. of Wm Turner & Ann Francis his wife.

Pedigree of Turney.

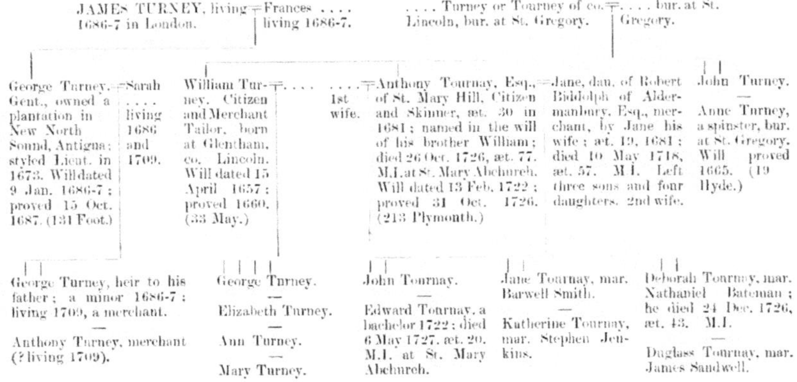
JAMES TURNEY, living 1686-7 in London. = Frances .... living 1686-7.
.... Turney or Tourney of co. Lincoln, bur. at St. Gregory. = ... bur. at St. Gregory.
George Turney, Gent., owned a plantation in New North Sound, Antigua; styled Lieut. in 1673. Will dated 9 Jan. 1686-7; proved 15 Oct. 1687. (131 Foot.) = Sarah .... living 1686 and 1709.
William Turney, Citizen and Merchant Tailor, born at Glentham, co. Lincoln. Will dated 15 April 1657; proved 1660. (33 May.) = ...
.... 1st wife. = Anthony Tournay, Esq., of St. Mary Hill, Citizen and Skinner, æt. 30 in 1681; named in the will of his brother William; died 26 Oct. 1726, æt. 77. M.I. at St. Mary Abchurch. Will dated 13 Feb. 1722; proved 31 Oct. 1726. (213 Plymouth.) = Jane, dau. of Robert Biddolph of Aldermanbury, Esq., merchant, by Jane his wife; æt. 19, 1681; died 10 May 1718, æt. 57. M.I. Left three sons and four daughters. 2nd wife.
John Turney.
Anne Turney, a spinster, bur. at St. Gregory. Will proved 1665. (19 Hyde.)
George Turney, heir to his father; a minor 1686-7; living 1709, a merchant.
Anthony Turney, merchant (? living 1709).
George Turney.
Elizabeth Turney.
Ann Turney.
Mary Turney.
John Tournay.
Edward Tournay, a bachelor 1722; died 6 May 1727, æt. 20. M.I. at St. Mary Abchurch.
Jane Tournay, mar. Barwell Smith.
Katherine Tournay, mar. Stephen Jenkins.
Deborah Tournay, mar. Nathaniel Bateman; he died 24 Dec. 1726, æt. 43. M.I.
Duglass Tournay, mar. James Sandwell.

William Turney, Citizen and Marchant Taylor of London. Will dated 15 April 1657; proved 12 Feb. 1660 by the two Ex'ors. (33 May.) S. Geo. lands in Asleckby* & Kingbyrby† & Glentenn,‡ to pay £60 a year to his 3 sisters Eliz., Anne, & Mary. Brother Anthony Turney £10. Wm s. of Edward Turney 20s. e. Poor of St Gregory by Paul's. Poor of Candey & Glentenn where I was born. Friends Roger Rines, grosser, & Robt Sewell, cit. & marchant taylor, Ex'ors, & £25 each. Witnessed by James Etheridge, Edmund Sawyer.

Anne Tourney, spinster. Will proved 1665. (19 and 22 Hyde.) Bro. Geo. Tourney. Brother-in-law Ralph Copinger & my sister Mary Copinger. To be buried at St Gregory near my father & mother.

William Turney of Lambeth, Gent. Will dated 1670. (104 Penn.) Sister Eliz. Heyward. Cozen Barnard Turney of Northall, brother of Wm Turney, sen. Cozen Tho. brother of Wm & Barnard. Bro. Jas. Turney. To be bur. at Mitcham, etc.

Bernard Turney of co. Bucks, Esq. 1682. (123 Cottle.)

Antigua. George Turney. Will dated 9 Jan. 1686-7; proved 15 Oct. 1687 by John Vernon, John Frye, and John Yeamans. (131 Foot.) My wife Sarah obtained a deed of jointure before her marriage, by which she is entitled after my death to the half of my plantation & negros in New North Sound Division. I give her $\frac{1}{3}$ of all my personal estate if she release to my son Geo. Turney her right to the said moiety of my lands. I give him also all my plantation & negros & $\frac{1}{3}$ of my personal estate. To my son Anthony $\frac{1}{3}$ of my personal estate. If my wife refuse to give up all claim to my plantation then all my personal estate to be paid over to Jacob Lucie of London, Esq., for my said 2 sons at 21, he to be their Guardian. My Ex'ors may lease out to Jeremiah Blizard for 10 years all that part of my plantation not already leased to Tho. Everett, the rent for the 1st year to be 15,000 lbs. & for each subsequent year 20,000 lbs. of Muscovado sugar. To John Vernon, Esq., £100 out of the money due to me from Mr Clement Tudway of this island in Oct. 1687, & to John Yeamans, Esq., £100 & my bay horse, also all my negros (except those rented to Tho. Everett) being those I had from Blubber Valley. To Eliz. Carlisle, dau. of Francis Carlisle of Antigua, Esq., 30,000 lbs. of sugar due from her father. To Tho. Everett 10,000 lbs. To John Nibbs 10,000 lbs. To the 2 daus. of John Fry of Antigua, Esq., each 5000 lbs., being the balance due from their father. To Mr Roger Royston, Clerke, 2000 lbs. after preaching my funeral sermon. All residue to my son Geo. Turney. My beloved friends John Vernon, John Frye, & John Yeamans, Esqrs, Ex'ors. Witnessed by Francis Carlisle, Esaii Burgeois, Jeremiah Blizard.

Memorandum. To my loving father & mother Jas. & Frances Turney £200 out of my estate in London.

Before Hon. Colonel Edward Powell, Deputy-Governor of Antigua, were sworn Captain Francis Carlisle and Jeremiah Blizard, carpenter, 14 Jan. 1686-7. Recorded in Secretary's Office 18 Jan. 1686-7. Walter Quarme, Deputy-Secretary of Antigua.

Edward Powell, Esq., Deputy-Governor and Ordinary. On 18 Jan. appeared before me Francis Carlisle, Esq., aged about 38 or thereabouts, & Jeremiah Blizard, Gent., aged 26, persons well known, & of good fame, credit, & estimation, & made affidavit as to having seen Geo. Turney sign his will, etc., & that he died within 3 days. Dated 8 Feb. 1686, 3 James II. We did see Edwd Powell, Esq., sign this certificate. James Ingle, Jno Osborn.

2 Anne. Sarah Turney of London, widow and relict of George Turney of Antigua, Gent., deceased, and guardian and mother of Anthony Turney, one of his sons. George Turney's will was dated 9 Jan. 1686-7, and he gave all residue to his sons George and Anthony, and John Vernon, one of his Ex'ors is since dead. Letter of Attorney to Edward Perry of Antigua, Gent., to get sums from John Fry and John Yeamans the other Ex'ors. Recorded 2 March 1703-4.

Anthony Tournay, Citizen and Skinner of London. Will dated 13 Feb. 1722; proved 31 Oct. 1726 by John Tournay the son. (213 Plymouth.) My son John £2000, & his wife my chariot & horses, my father's picture, my own, & my brother John's, those of my aunt Awdrey, & Sir Fra. Drake. My son Edward £1000. My son-in-law

* Aslackby, a parish in the wapentake of Aveland, co. Lincoln.
† Kingerby, a parish in the wapentake of Walshcroft, co. Lincoln.
‡ Glentham, a parish in the wapentake of Aslacoe, co. Lincoln.

Barwell Smith & his wife Jane my dau. £30, & to their children £100 each. My son-in-law Stephen Jenkins & Kath. his wife my dau. £30, & to their children £100 each. My son-in-law Nath[l] Bateman & his wife Deborah my dau. £30, & to her & their children £200 each. My son-in-law James Sandwell & his wife Duglass my dau. £30, & to their children £100 each. My cousin Hester Kitchin & to her children £20 each. To Christ Church & Bethlem £100 each. All residue to my said 6 children. My son John Ex'or. Witnessed by Benjamin Betts, William Myors, Seth Harrison.

Aliee, daughter of Peirce Morgan of Blackfryars, Gent., was wife of John Tourney at the date of the Visitation of London, 1634.

1673, Sep. 24. Lieut. George Turney, 93 acres New North Sound, surveyed.

1686, April 26. Thomas Horsnell mortgages his moiety of Jolly Hill to George Turney and his heirs.

1686, Nov. 3. George Turney, 132 acres granted by Sir James Russell, Knt. (Captain-General *pro tem.*).

1709. By Indenture George Turney, merchant, Sarah Turney, widow, and Anthony Turney, merchant, all of London, release to William Codrington and Valentine Morris their title to half of Jolly Hill, containing 200 acres.

1715. Barbados Census. St. Philip's Parish. Mr. Robert Turney, 36; Mrs. Aviss Turney, 35; Mrs. Jane Grant, widow, 70; Henry Turney, 13; Mary Ross, 12½; Elizabeth Turney, 10; Ann Ross, 10; Frances Turney, 7; Frances Ross, 7; Dorothy Turney, 5; Thomas Turney, 2; Mary Turney, widow, 50; Mary Turney, spinster, 25; Ann Turney, 18; Hannah Turney, 15; Sarah Turney, spinster, 15; Thomas Turney, 38; Elizabeth Turney, 25; Rebecca Turney, 4; Henry Turney, 2; Thomas Turney, 2 months.

A Pedigree of Turney of Cavenby was entered in the Visitation of co. Lincoln. (Harl. MS. 1550, fo. 113 b.)

St. Michael's, Cornhill.

Baptized.

1692 Jan. 20 Barnard Turney son of John & Elizabeth his wife.

1694 Mar. 28 Margarett Turney dau. of John Turney & Elizabeth his wife.

1695 June 30 Ann Turney dau. of John Turney & Elizabeth his wife.

1696 Aug. 22 Anthony Turney son of John Turney & Elizabeth his wife.

1701 July 13 John son of John Turney & Elizabeth his wife.

1702 Nov. 15 Thomas son of John Turney & Elizabeth his wife.

1705 April 15 Harry son of John Turney & Elizabeth his wife.

1706 Nov. 10 Anne dau. (posthumous) of John Turney & Elizabeth his wife.

Married.

1692 Jan. 26 Nathaniell Peacock, of S[t] Leonard, Shorditch, and Mary Turney, of S[t] Giles, Cripplegate; by D[r] Meriton; by lic.

Buried.

1706 May 4 M[r] John Turney, of this par.; in the lower vault.

1726 Mar. 19 Elizabeth Turney, widow; in the chy[d].

1626, June 21. W[m] Turney of Corbye, clk., æt. 30, & Eliz. Turney, of same, sp[r], æt. 22. (Lincoln Marriage Licences.)

1681, Nov. 1. Anthony Tourney, of S[t] Mary Hill, Lond., Citizen & Skinner, Wid[r], ab[t] 30, & Mrs Jane Biddolph, of S[t] Mary Aldermanbury, Lond., Sp[r], ab[t] 19, with consent of her mother Mrs Tymme *alias* Biddolph & the Ld Mayor & Aldermen of Lond.; at S[t] Mary Aldermanbury, S[t] Andrew, Holborn, or Gray's Inn Chapel. (Marriage Licences: Vicar-General of the Archbishop of Canterbury, p. 77.)

St. Mary Abchurch.

Jane Tournay, dau. of Robert Biddulph of Aldermanbury, Esq., merchant, late wife of Anthony Tournay, Esq.; she died 10 May 1718, æt. 57, and left three sons and four daus. Also Anthony Tournay, Esq., from co. Lincoln, died 26 Oct. 1726, æt. 77. Also Nathaniel Bateman, their son-in-law, died 24 Dec. 1726, æt. 43. Also Edward Tournay, youngest son, died 6 May 1727, æt. 20. (Seymour's 'London.')

Family of Tyley.

Edward Tyley of Antigua, merchant. Will dated 29 May 1761; proved 23 Sep. 1762 by John Freeman the elder and John Freeman the younger; power reserved to Robert Scott, Esq., Samuel Redhead, Esq., and William Dickinson. (403 St. Eloy.) My dwelling house & lands at Ampthill, co. Beds, lately purchased of Maj[r] W[m] Gordon, to my dau. Eliz. Tyley & her heirs, then to my niece Eliz. Murr, dau. of John Murr of Bristol, staymaker, & to my sister his wife £20 a year. To Eliz. Murr £100. To each Ex'or 10 gs. All my lands & stock in Antigua to my son Edw[d] Tyley. Rob[t] Scott of Peackham, co. Surrey, Esq., & my cousins John Freeman, sen[r], & John Freeman, jun[r], of Bristol, merch[ts], Sam[l] Redhead, Esq., & M[r] W[m] Dickinson, both of Antigua, Ex'ors. Witnessed by Robert Bannister, Mark Ward. Before his Excellency George Thomas, Esq., were sworn Robert Bannister, Esq., and Mark Ward of Antigua, Gent., 8 Oct. 1761. Recorded also at St. John's in Libro "C."

Parish Register of St. John.

Baptized.

1745 June 25 Elizabeth the D. of Edward Tyley by Mary.

1749 Mar. 5 Edward the s. of Edw[d] Tyley and Mary his wife.

1752 July 16 George the s. of Edw[d] Tyley and Elizabeth his wife.

1772 Mar. 4 Margaret Scent the D. of Edward Tyley and Lucy his wife.

1810 Sep. 14 Eliza Frances D. of John Tyley and Jane his wife. B. the 2nd Feb. last.

1813 April 7 Sarah Usher D. of John Tyley and Jane his wife. B. the 2nd Nov. 1811.

Married.

1771 Feb. 9 Edward Tyley to Lucy Thomas; by Lic.

Buried.

1746 June 16 George Tyley.
1752 July 17 George Tyley, a Child of Edw[d] Tyley.
1752 Aug. 13 Elizabeth Tyley.
1757 Oct. 30 Catherine Tyley.
1781 Dec. 13 Mark Tyley.
1784 June 4 Elenor Tyley.
1798 June 5 Luke Tyley.
1801 Mar. 29 Francis Tyley, Infant.
1802 Mar. 17 Mathew Tyley.
? 1811 Aug. 21 Mark Tyley.

Pedigree of Vaughan.

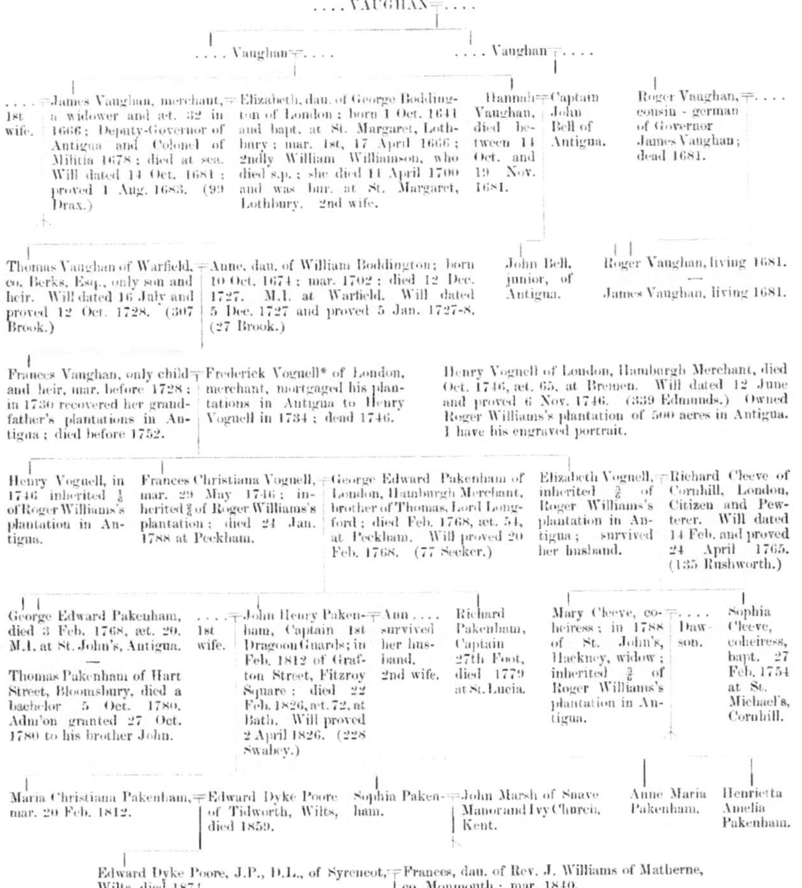

. . . . VAUGHAN ⊤ . . . .
. . . . Vaughan ⊤ . . . .
. . . . Vaughan ⊤ . . . .
. . . . 1st wife.
James Vaughan, merchant, a widower and æt. 32 in 1666; Deputy-Governor of Antigua and Colonel of Militia 1678; died at sea. Will dated 14 Oct. 1681; proved 1 Aug. 1683. (99 Drax.)
Elizabeth, dau. of George Boddington of London; born 1 Oct. 1641 and bapt. at St. Margaret, Lothbury; mar. 1st, 17 April 1666; 2ndly William Williamson, who died s.p.; she died 11 April 1700 and was bur. at St. Margaret, Lothbury. 2nd wife.
Hannah Vaughan, died between 14 Oct. and 19 Nov. 1681.
Captain John Bell of Antigua.
Roger Vaughan, cousin-german of Governor James Vaughan; dead 1681.
. . . .
Thomas Vaughan of Warfield, co. Berks, Esq., only son and heir. Will dated 16 July and proved 12 Oct. 1728. (307 Brook.)
Anne, dau. of William Boddington; born 10 Oct. 1674; mar. 1702; died 12 Dec. 1727. M.I. at Warfield. Will dated 5 Dec. 1727 and proved 5 Jan. 1727-8. (27 Brook.)
John Bell, junior, of Antigua.
Roger Vaughan, living 1681.
James Vaughan, living 1681.
Frances Vaughan, only child and heir, mar. before 1728; in 1730 recovered her grandfather's plantations in Antigua; died before 1752.
Frederick Vognell* of London, merchant, mortgaged his plantations in Antigua to Henry Vognell in 1734; dead 1746.
Henry Vognell of London, Hamburgh Merchant, died Oct. 1746, æt. 65, at Bremen. Will dated 12 June and proved 6 Nov. 1746. (339 Edmunds.) Owned Roger Williams's plantation of 500 acres in Antigua. I have his engraved portrait.
Henry Vognell, in 1746 inherited ⅓ of Roger Williams's plantation in Antigua.
Frances Christiana Vognell, mar. 29 May 1746; inherited ⅓ of Roger Williams's plantation; died 24 Jan. 1788 at Peckham.
George Edward Pakenham of London, Hamburgh Merchant, brother of Thomas, Lord Longford; died Feb. 1768, æt. 54, at Peckham. Will proved 20 Feb. 1768. (77 Secker.)
Elizabeth Vognell, inherited ⅓ of Roger Williams's plantation in Antigua; survived her husband.
Richard Cleeve of Cornhill, London, Citizen and Pewterer. Will dated 14 Feb. and proved 24 April 1765. (135 Rushworth.)
George Edward Pakenham, died 3 Feb. 1768, æt. 20. M.I. at St. John's, Antigua.
Thomas Pakenham of Hart Street, Bloomsbury, died a bachelor 5 Oct. 1780. Adm'on granted 27 Oct. 1780 to his brother John.
. . . . 1st wife.
John Henry Pakenham, Captain 1st Dragoon Guards; in Feb. 1812 of Grafton Street, Fitzroy Square; died 22 Feb. 1826, æt. 72, at Bath. Will proved 2 April 1826. (228 Swabey.)
Ann . . . . survived her husband. 2nd wife.
Richard Pakenham, Captain 27th Foot, died 1779 at St. Lucia.
Mary Cleeve, coheiress; in 1788 of St. John's, Hackney, widow; inherited ⅙ of Roger Williams's plantation in Antigua.
. . . . Dawson.
Sophia Cleeve, coheiress, bapt. 27 Feb. 1754 at St. Michael's, Cornhill.
Maria Christiana Pakenham, mar. 20 Feb. 1812.
Edward Dyke Poore of Tidworth, Wilts, died 1859.
Sophia Pakenham.
John Marsh of Snave Manor and Ivy Church, Kent.
Anne Maria Pakenham.
Henrietta Amelia Pakenham.
Edward Dyke Poore, J.P., D.L., of Syrencot, Wilts, died 1874.
Frances, dau. of Rev. J. Williams of Matherne, co. Monmouth; mar. 1840.

For much of the above Pedigree the Author is indebted to Mr. Reginald S. Boddington, many of whose notes have been published in 'Miscellanea Genealogica et Heraldica,' Second Series, vols. iv. and v.

* The grandfather of Sir Julius Vognell, K.C.M.G., Premier of New Zealand, was a London Merchant in the West Indian and South American Trade. ('Illustrated London News,' 1875, July 3.)

James Vaughan of Antigua, Esq. Will dated 14 Oct. 1681; proved 1 Aug. 1683 by Elizabeth Vaughan the relict; power reserved to the son and other Ex'ors. (99 Drax.) Rings of a mark each for my bearers who shall be 6 of the superior officers of my regiment. To my sister Mrs Frances Jones £50 st. To my sister Mrs Hannah Bell 4 negros & a pickoninge to be delivered to her husband, Cap. Jno Bell, he to settle them with the land I granted to him when I was Govr on himself, his wife, & his son Jno Bell, junr, & their heirs. To my honble mother Mrs Hannah Boddington a 20s. ring. To my sister Elizth Wight, my bro. Geo. Boddington & his wife, my bro. Jas. Boddington & his wife, & my sister Sarah Boddington rings of a mark. To my dearest wife Elizth Vaughan & my son Thos. Vaughan (whom I appoint my Ex'ors) all my personal estate equally, & I give her ½ the profits of my real estate for her life, the other ½ to him, & after his mother's death the whole to him & his heirs, & in default to Jas. Vaughan, son of my cozen german Roger Vaughan, decd, & his heirs male, then to Roger Vaughan, bro. of said Jas. Vaughan, then to my heirs genl, then to the Bayliffs of the town & corporation of Tewkesbury (?), co. Glouc., for repairs of the great Abby Church, the Ministers, free school, & the poor of that town. My honoured friends Col. Rowld Williams, Mr Tho. Duncomb, & Mr Tho. Erskin of this island Ex'ors & Trustees, & I give to each a £5 ring. Inventory of debts due as appears by my books, 450 acres in the Body, 20 negros & 3 pickoninges as per list, 27 acres with a house, stable, cook-room, & pidgeon house by St John's Town, 27 acres at the Point with a crabb to heave down ships. Witnessed by Thomas Duncombe, John Willford, Thomas Ærskin, Roger Randall his +, Mark Toker his +.

Codicil. 19 Nov. 1681. Whereas my sister Mrs Hannah Bell is since dec^{d}. I revoke the legacy of 5 negros. Witnessed by Thomas Duncombe, Thomas Ærskin. On 9 Aug. 1682 appeared Thomas Duncombe, Esq., John Willford, and Marke Toker and swore they saw testator Colonel James Vaughan sign.

John Bell of St. Mary's, Bermudian Valley. Will dated 25 May 1698. All estate to my children John & Wm Bell & ye child my wife now goes with. Cap. Robt Martin of Five Islands & Mr Wm Duning of Bermudian Valley Ex'ors. Witnessed by William Dining, Robert Tremill. Sworn 19 July 1698 and recorded 1 Aug. 1698 at Antigua.

Anne Vaughan, wife of Thomas Vaughan of Warfield, co. Berks, Gent. Will dated 5 Dec. and proved 5 Jan. 1727 by Thomas Vaughan the husband. (27 Brook.) My will for so much as my late mother Mrs Frances Boddington bequeathed to me, the most valuable part of which she left with Lovelace Hercy, Esq., & Mr Richd West her Ex'ors in T. by her will da. 12 Dec. 1726. I give all my Bank of England & South Sea stock to my husb^{d} for life, & all linen, plate, jewels, etc., that were my mother's, & all bonds & bills, & after his death to my son-in-law Mr Fred. Voguell, but he to add the same to my dau. Frances his wife's joynture & to give bond, otherwise everything to my husband absolutely. Witnessed by Elizabeth Russell, Thomas Lacy, Sarah Day.

Thomas Vaughan of Warfield, co. Berks, Esq. Will dated 16 July and proved 12 Oct. 1728. (307 Brook.) To my uncle Jas. Boddington, Esq., & my aunt Mrs Sarah Ford, my cousin Mrs Hannah Jones, Mr Hen. & Miss Sophia Voguell, Mr Richd West, Lovelace Hercy, Esq., Mrs Rebecca McWilliam, Mrs Anne Hercy & her sister Mrs Mary Parmenter, £10 st. each. To Rev. Bernard Mould, Mrs Fra. Foster, & Mrs Sarah West £50 each. Mrs Sarah Milward £20. Each servant £5. £100 for funeral. To the poor of Warfield who don't receive parish alms the interest of £200 for ever, providing the Minister & churchwardens within 3 years agree for the purchase of land. To my grandchild Fra. X'ian Voguell all jewels, silver plate, & £1000 at 20. My son-in-law Mr Fred. Voguell & his wife Ex'ors to whom all residue. Rev. Bernard Mould & Mr Edwd Clive, jun., to take an inventory of all my securities. To Mr Edwd Clive £50. Witnessed by David Lawes, Elenor Breghton, Samuel King.

Henry Vognell of London, merchant. Will dated 12 June and proved 6 Dec. 1746 by Robert Nettleton, Esq., and James Heywood; power reserved to Gerard Van Neck, Esq. (339 Edmunds.) If I die in Eng. to be bur. in Camberwell ch. y^{d}, co. Surrey, Mr Geo. Edwd Pakenham of L., merch^{t}, to build a vault there. Funeral £150. By 2 Ind. da. 7 & 8 June 1734 my kinsman Fred. Vognell, late of L., merch^{t}, dec^{d}, conveyed to me sev. freehold est., also a leasehold one, on T. for paying $\frac{2}{3}$ of £15,700 owing by him & his partner Anth^{o} Furstenau to Fra. Strengfellow, w., & I, having advanced the money to pay the same & other debts amounting to more than the value of the est., give all said estates to Hen. Voguell, Fra. Pakenham, wife of said Geo. Edwd Pakenham, & Eliz. Voguell, the 3 ch^{n} of Fred. Vognell, viz., $\frac{1}{6}$ to Hen. Voguell at 21, $\frac{3}{6}$ to Fra. Pakenham, & $\frac{2}{6}$ to Eliz. Voguell at 21. Their aunt Mrs Fra. Strengfellow has promised to provide for them. A partnership was lately carried on between me & Anth^{o} Furstenau & John Adolph Schroder. All my freehold messuages to Hen. Uhthoff, jun^{r}, s. of Hen. Uhthoff of Bremen, merch^{t}, then to Gottfried Molling, now living with Mr Gotthelff Bagge of Hamburgen, merch^{t}. Messuages at Billington, co. Lanc., & in Mumford's Court *al's* Page's Alley in St Mary Magdalen, Milk Str., L., to Hen. Uhthoff, jun^{r}, then to Gottfried Molling. If they as aliens cannot inherit then to Eliz. Voguell. To Fred. Ludowick Metzner of L., m^{t}, £100. To Hen. Klausing, 1st s. of X'an Klausing of Harford in Westphalia, organ maker, £500, & to Ann Francisca Klausing, dau. of the same X'ian Klausing, £500 at 21. To Gerhard Arnold Walther, s. of Wm Walther of Goest in Westphalia, apothecary, £100 at 21. John Thorbeck of L., m^{t}, & Ann his wife are separated, she liv. with his parents at Hamburgh, & if she shall again cohabit with him I give her £1000. To . . . . Thalitzer, wid. of Zachary Thalitzer, late of Berlin, m^{t}, £500. To Christoph. Mathias Molling, Minister of Drubeck, n^{r} Halberstad in Germany, £20. To my gods. John Hen. Haddon, living with me, £100. To my neph. Peter Shuter, Minister of Dornberg in Westphalia, £500. To Fra. Henrietta late wid. of Johan Fred. Von Laer of Harford, m^{t}, dec^{d}, but since married again, £20. To the wife of Becker of Beilfeld in W-phalia, D^{r} of phys., & dr. of Jobst. Hen. Stembolmer of Usthow, W-phalia, m^{t}, £20. To Hen. Uhthoff, sen^{r}, of Bremen, m^{t}, £200. To Chr. Mathias Molling, rector of Harford, 1st s. of Herman Chr. Molling, late Min^{r} of Iselhorst in W-phalia, dec^{d}, £20. Bequests to divers friends. To my cousin Hen. Otto Voguell, Burgemaster of Harford, £100 To Hen. Julius Speckboetell of Harford, m^{t}, £50. To Johana Voguell, only d^{r} of John Hen. Voguell, late of Hamburgh, m^{t}, dec^{d}, £100. To the Lutheran Ch. in Trinity-lane, L., £200, & to the Min^{r} there 10 g^{s}. To the Lutheran Ch. at Harford £150. To Anth^{o} Furstenau £50, & to Sophia Ernestina his wife £100. To the ch^{n} of my neph. Conrade Smith of Bristol, my 2^{d} cousin Sophia Ernestina Furstenau, my g^{t}niece Cath. Toderhorst, wife of Diedrich Wm Fred. Pritzler of Well Close Sq., Goodman's Fields, Mid^{x}, sugar refiner, & my 3^{d} cousin Fra. Pakenham, to every male child of aforesaid £1000 each. To my partner Theophilus Pritzler £5000 out of the £15,000 lent him. To my other partner Mr Geo. Amyand £1000. To my 2^{d} cousin John Fred. Molling at Bristol & to his bro. Gottfried Molling £1000 each. To John Rule, apprentice to Arch^{d} Maclane in Cheapside, £1000. To Eliz. Vognell all my furniture, plate, & goods (except pictures) in my house at Peckham. My landlord Mr Jas. Strengfellow of Manchester. To my niece Christina wife of X'ian Klausing of Harford, organ maker, £40 yearly. To Marg^{t} Eliz. wife of John Siegfried Dorrien of Minden in Germany £40 yearly. To Amelia Francisca wife of Geo. X'ian Luders of Hamburgh, m^{t}, £40 yearly. To Sophia Molling, wid. of Herman Christoph. Molling, Min^{r} of Iselhorst, £10 yearly. To Cath. Eliz. Andre, wid. of . . . . Andre, late Min^{r} of Soest, £10 yearly, & to Margt. Eliz. Andre, wid. of . . . . Andre, also late Min^{r} of Soest, £4 yearly. To Eliz. Eleanora Rule, wid. of X'ian Rule, £10. To John Hen. Voguell, only s. of John Hen. Vognell, late of Hamburgh, m^{t}, dec^{d}, £20 yearly. To Clara Eliz. Vognell of Harford, sp^{r}, d^{r} of Conrade Hen. Vognell, late Min^{r} of Deeshold in Hanover, dec^{d}, £20 yearly. To Anth^{o} Ernest Klausing, 2^{d} s. of X'ian Klausing, £30 yearly for 5 years. Gerrard Van Neck, Esq., m^{t} of L., Robt Nettleton of L., m^{t}, & Jas. Heywood of L., linen draper, Ex'ors & £500 each, & if either die Mr Fred. Ludowick Metzner an Ex'or. Witnessed by Edward Grubb, John Humpage, jun., Stephen Totton, jun.

Richard Cleeve, Citizen and Pewterer of London. Will dated 14 Feb., proved 24 April 1765 by Charles Hatt, Esq., Samuel White, Esq. (by mistake in the will called Thomas White), and Charles Green. (135 Rushworth.) £3000 in trust to Edward Furstenean & Geo. Ed. Pakenham to the uses of my marriage settlement. To my wife Eliz. household goods & plate with our joint coat of arms. The will of my bro. Benj. Cleeve, dec^d. All estate in trust to my brother-in-law Cha. Hatt, Esq., & friends Tho. White of Enfield, Esq., & Chas. Green of Christ's Hospital, Gent., my Ex'ors, for my daus. Sophia & Mary Cleeve at 21.

Thomas Pakenham, late of St. George, Bloomsbury, Middlesex, Esq., bachelor, deceased. Adm'on 27 Oct. 1780 to his brother John Henry Pakenham, Esq., his mother Frances Christiana Pakenham, widow, renouncing.

Close Roll, 5 Geo. II., Part 7, No. 21.

Indenture made the 16th Nov. 1730 between Frederick Vognell of London, merchant, and Frances Vognell his wife, of the one part, and Richard Oliver of Antigua, Esq., of the other part. Whereas by Indentures of Lease of 4th Nov. 1730 tripartite between Frederick Vognell and Frances Vognell his wife (daughter and only child of Thomas Vaughan, late of Mills, Berks, Esq., deceased, who was son and heir of James Vaughan, Esq., deceased, formerly Lieut.-Governor of Antigua), of the 1st part, Richard Oliver, Esq., of the 2nd part, Gilbert Fleming of St. Kitts, formerly of Antigua, Esq., of the 3rd part, Frederick Vognell and Frances his wife demised to Richard Oliver, among other lands, all that Roger Williams's plantation, containing 470 or 500 acres, in St. John's and New Divisions in Antigua, bounded N. with the lands formerly sold by James Vaughan to Thomas Duncombe, S. with the lands formerly belonging to Luke Child and John Coker, now or late in the possession of William Horne, W. with the lands formerly of one Fletcher, now or late possessed by Samuel Martin, Esq., E. with the lands formerly of John Lucas and John Traverse, but now or late in the possession of Edward Byam, jun., Esq., and the heirs of one Penny, deceased, to hold from the 17th Aug. then last past for 21 years, with a covenant to leave on the premises all works, buildings, etc., mentioned in a schedule annexed to the Indenture, valued at £111 currency; and whereas the title of the said demised plantation has been but lately recovered at law in Antigua by Frederick Vognell and Frances his wife from William Gregson of London, Gentleman, under an intail thereof created by the last will of James Vaughan aforesaid, deceased, dated 14th Oct. 1681, and on which recovery William Gregson has brought a writt of error before the Commander-in-Chief of the Leeward Islands and the Council of Antigua, upon which writt of error and the judgment to be given an appeal is intended to be brought to the King in Council by either party against whom the Commander-in-Chief and Council shall give judgment; and whereas it is agreed by the Indenture of Lease that if it is finally determined on the appeal that the title is not in Frederick Vognell and Frances his wife (in right of Frances) but in William Gregson and his heirs, who claim the same under Roger Williams, formerly of Antigua, planter, that the intail created by James Vaughan's will is sufficiently docked and barred, then the said lease shall be void from the beginning; and whereas Richard Oliver is minded to build a windmill and also, if he shall then proceed, to erect a convenient and necessary small dwelling-house, which will be to the advantage of Frederick and Frances Vognell, but it is not provided for by the lease. Now this Indenture witnesseth that in consideration of the said Indenture of Demise and of 5*s.* Frederick Vognell and Frances his wife agree to pay to Richard Oliver the half part of the full value of such erections, the value to be settled by four indifferent men which shall be then inhabitants of Antigua, and if the appeal confirms the right of Frederick and Frances Vognell, then the lease to Richard Oliver to remain in force.

[A copy of above deed was recorded at Antigua in Libro Y, and it is therein stated that the estate was leased for £200 sterling a year.]

Close Roll, 5 Geo. II., Part 4, Nos. 1 and 2.

Indenture made the 11th Feb. 1731 between Frederick Vognell of London, merchant, and Frances Vognell his wife, of the one part, and Anthony Furstenau of London, merchant, of the other part, witnesseth that in consideration of 5*s.* Frederick and Frances Vognell grant, etc., to Anthony Furstenau and his Ex'ors, etc., all that Roger Williams's plantation, containing 470 or 500 acres, and another plantation, containing 53 acres, also in St. John's Division, bounded E. with part of St. John's Cove and St. John's Harbour, S.W. on St. John's Harbour, N.E. with the land formerly of Anthony Racson [Royerson], the other part bounded with the sea, and also another plantation, containing 27¼ acres, in the parish of St. John's, situated at the N.E. angle of the town land of St. John's, and bounded N. with the land late of Roger Complin, E. with the land formerly of Carolina Guess [Guest] and late in the possession of Thomas Dunbar Parke, and to all the other parts with the town land of St. John's, and all those 15 negro slaves (names given), 3 men, 4 boys, 4 women, and 4 girls, all which premises are now in the possession and occupation of Richard Oliver of Antigua, Esq., or his under-tenants, by lease thereof to him, and all other lands and late the estate of James Vaughan, deceased, and which were devised by his last will in tail, in fee, or otherwise, to the said Thomas Vaughan, or which descended or came to the said Frances Vognell as daughter and heir to Thomas Vaughan, and all reversions to Anthony Furstenau for one whole year, paying therefor one peppercorn only at the Feast of St. Michael now ensuing, that he may be in actual possession, etc., and enabled to accept and grant and release, etc.

No. 1.

Indenture made 12th Feb. 1731 between Frederick Vognell of London, merchant, and Frances Vognell his wife (daughter and only child of Thomas Vaughan, late of Mills, Berks, Esq., deceased, who was son and heir of James Vaughan, Esq., deceased, formerly Lieut.-Governor of Antigua), of the one part, and Anthony Furstenau of London, merchant, of the other part, witnesseth that for docking and destroying all estates tail, reversions, and remainders created either by the last will of James Vaughan, deceased, dated 14th Oct. 1681, or by any other will deed, and to the intent to vest the fee and inheritance in Frederick Vognell and Frances Vognell his wife and their heirs, and in consideration of 5*s.* they grant to Anthony Furstenau, in his actual possession now being, and to his heirs and assigns for ever, all the above plantations, to the intent and purpose that he shall stand seised thereof only to the use and behoof of Frederick and Frances Vognell and their heirs, etc., for ever.

Close Roll, 29 Geo. II., Part 14, Nos. 4 and 5.

Indenture made the 3rd July 1755 between Richard Cleeve of Cornhill, London, merchant, Citizen and Freeman, and Elizabeth his wife, of the one part, and Anthony Furstenau and George Edward Pakenham, both of London, merchants, of the other part, witnesseth that in consideration of 5*s.* Richard and Elizabeth Cleeve grant, etc., to Anthony Furstenau and George Edward Pakenham all those three undivided sixth parts, making one full moiety, of Roger Williams's plantation, containing 470 or 500 acres, for one whole year. Richard Wyatt, John Potter, witnesses.

No. 4.

Indenture made the 4th July 1755 between the above. Whereas by articles tripartite made the 2nd June 1752 between Richard Cleve, of the 1st part, Elizabeth Vognell of London, spinster (one of the children of Frederick Vognell, late of London, merchant, by Frances his wife, both then deceased), of the 2nd part, and Anthony Furstenau and George Edward Pakenham, of the 3rd part, reciting that a marriage was then intended to be had and solemnized between Richard Cleve and Elizabeth Voguell, and that Frederick Voguell in his life-time had by Indentures of Lease and Release made the 7th and 8th June 1734 granted and conveyed to Henry Voguell, deceased, among other things, the several freehold plantations, etc., therein mentioned, in Antigua to him and his heirs, upon the several trusts therein mentioned, and particularly upon the trust, either by sale or from the rents and profits, to raise and pay two third parts of a debt of £15,700 then due from him and his then late partner Frances Strongfellow,* widow, since deceased, to whom, as therein mentioned, he demised the said premises for 1000 years for securing repayment with interest at 4 per cent., and Henry Voguell had become bound to Frances Strongfellow for the payment, and also reciting that Henry Voguell did make his last will dated the 12th June 1746 (recited), and also reciting that the money advanced by Henry Voguell in his life-time and by his Ex'ors since his death amounted to £21,000, and that Elizabeth Voguell had then attained to 21 and was thereupon become seised of three-sixths of the said several freehold plantations, etc. (subject to such right and equity of redemption as Henry Voguell (son and heir of Frederick) might possess), and in consideration of the marriage she agreed to convey to Anthony Furstenau and George Edward Pakenham all those her three-sixth parts in trust; and whereas the marriage soon after took effect, and the said recited articles were sent to Antigua to be recorded, but being delayed in the passage did not arrive within the time prescribed by the Acts for Registering Deeds after the execution thereof; and whereas it is necessary that the articles should be carried into execution by a proper conveyance. Now this Indenture witnesseth that in performance of the several trusts and agreements contained in the articles of the 2nd June 1752, and in consideration of 10s., Richard Cleeve and Elizabeth his wife grant, etc., to Anthony Furstenau and George Edward Pakenham in their actual possession now being all those three undivided sixth parts in trust for 99 years in case Richard Cleeve and Elizabeth shall live so long, to permit Elizabeth Cleeve and her assigns during her life to receive the rents to her sole use, and after her death to the use of Richard Cleeve for life, and after the death of the survivor to all children as they may appoint, and failing their appointment to the first son and his heirs male lawful, etc., and if Henry Voguell, son and heir of Frederick, should pay to Anthony Furstenau and George Edward Pakenham the two-thirds of the £21,000 and discharge the mortgage of the 7th and 8th June 1734, they are to receive the money and lay it out in lands in fee simple in England, and they are to receive all rents till a son of Richard and Elizabeth Cleeve is 21, and to apply a sum not exceeding £100 a year meantime towards the education and maintenance of such eldest son, and not exceeding £50 a year for each younger child till 21, and all residue to increase the portions of younger children, the said lands are free from all claims, etc., save one Indenture made the 13th July 1750, purporting to be a lease of the said plantations, etc., in Antigua, and granted by Henry Voguell, George Edward Pakenham and Frances Christiana his wife, and Elizabeth Voguell (now Elizabeth Cleeve) to Richard Oliver, Esq., for 9 years from the 18th Aug. 1751, and lastly they constitute Thomas Warner and Stephen Blizard of Antigua, Esquires, their Attorneys.

Close Roll, 28 Geo. III., Part 3, Nos. 6 and 7.

Indenture made the 9th May 1788 between Mary Dawson of the parish of St. John's, Hackney, widow (one of the two daughters and coheiresses-at-law of Richard Cleeve, late of London, merchant, and Elizabeth his wife, both deceased, which said Elizabeth was one of the children of Frederick Voguell, late of London, merchant, by Frances his wife, both also deceased), of the one part, and Joseph Eyre of Christ's Hospital, Gentleman, of the other part, witnesses that for extinguishing all estates tail and remainders, etc., in those three-sixths of the plantation in Antigua hereinafter mentioned, and that the fee simple and inheritance may be vested in Mary Dawson, and in consideration of 10s., Mary Dawson grants, etc., one moiety of those three-sixths in all that plantation called Roger Williams's, containing 470 or 500 acres (as in Voguell and Furstenau), to have and to hold to Joseph Eyre that he may be in actual possession, etc., and Mary Dawson constitutes John Burke, Esq., H.M.'s Solicitor-General, and Thomas Fairbairne of Antigua, M.D., her Attorneys. Hester Chowner, Hart Street, Bloomsbury, John Eyre, Christ's Hospital, witnesses.

No. 6.

Indenture made the 10th May 1788 between Joseph Eyre, of the one part, and Mary Dawson, of the other part. Whereas by Indenture of the previous day Mary Dawson granted to Joseph Eyre in trust to reconvey. Now this Indenture witnesses that in pursuance of the trust and in consideration of 10s. Joseph Eyre grants, etc., all that moiety of three-sixths (as above) to Mary Dawson and her heirs for ever in fee simple.

Close Roll, 38 Geo. III., Part 3, No. 15.

Indenture made the 30th June 1798 between John Henry Pakenham of Catesfield, co. Southampton, Esq., of the one part, and Robert Pitches of Swithin's Lane, London, Gentleman, of the other part, witnesseth that for barring and destroying all estates tail and remainders in two-sixths, intended to be hereby granted, of the plantation hereinafter mentioned, and in consideration of 10s. John Henry Pakenham conveys to Robert Pitches all those two-sixths of him John Henry Pakenham in Roger Williams's Plantation, containing 470 or 500 acres, in trust to the only use of John Henry Pakenham and his heirs and assigns for ever. Samuel Sampson, clerk to Robert Pitches, witness.

1675, Jan. 29. James Vaughan, Barnard Schenckingh, and Arthur Middleton, merchants, letter of attorney to Vincent Goddard of Antigua, merchant.

1678. Colonel James Vaughan then Deputy-Governor of Antigua.

Mr. Thomas Vaughan 600 acres, Governor Colonel James Vaughan 328 acres. Warrant dated 26 March 1679 from Colonel James Vaughan; hath patent. Surveyed 22 April 1679.

1679, May 2. Captain John Bell received a patent for 62½ acres.

1679. Colonel James Vaughan, 600 acres for ever paying an ear of Indian corn. Patent from Sir William Stapleton dated 26 April.

1679, July 8. Colonel James Vaughan grants to Major Jeremiah Watkins 100 acres in St. John's Division in exchange for 70 other acres.

1679-80, March 15. Colonel James Vaughan to Mr. Thomas Duncombe and Hannah his wife, sale of 500 acres at St. John's.

1680, May 6. Nevis. Walter Symonds of Nevis, Esq., sells to Colonel James Vaughan of Antigua 600 acres in Antigua.

Mr. Cornelius Vaughan is named in a will of 1703.

1728, Sep. 17. Dy'd Thomas Vaughan, Esq.; of — near Windsor in the County of Berks, formerly a Turky Merchant. ('Historical Register,' p. 51.)

Francis Fane, Esq., reports on 16 Oct. 1730 *re* an Act concerning Vaughan's estate of which he strongly disapproves,

* St. Mary Aldermary. Mar. 1707. Oct. 28. William Strengfellow, Rector of St Dunstan's in the East, single man, & Frances Bodington of the same parish, single woman, by Licence.

because the plantation was sold without the sanction of the mortgagor. He recites the will of James Vaughan, Esq., and goes on to say that his widow married William Williamson and by deed quadrupartite of 10 and 11 Feb. 1696 between Thomas Vaughan, son and heir of James Vaughan, Esq., William Williamson and Elizabeth his wife, of the 2nd part, Roger Williams, of the 3rd part, and Joseph French, of the 4th part, Thomas Vaughan and William Williamson and Elizabeth his wife for £500 conveyed to Roger Williams the said plantation. (This was a mortgage.) Roger Williams in 1713 owed £1200 to William Gregson, and mortgaged the estate to him. Roger Williams by will left it to Allen Smith and William Gregson. (B. T. Leeward Islands, vol. 21.)

[The Act for the sale of these lands was evidently negatived by the King, as Mrs. Frances Voguell in 1730 stated that she had just succeeded in recovering possession of them. Francis Fane was the legal adviser to the Privy Council and all Acts, etc., passed through his hands, the King and Council acting on his written report.—V. L. O.]

1746, May 29. Geo. Edw. Paeckenham, Esq; Hamburgh merchant in Lime-street, — to Miss Voguel of Nicholas-lane. ('Gent. Mag.,' p. 272.)

1746, Oct. Henry Voguel,* Esq; an eminent Hamburgh Merchant in Nicholas-Lane, Lombard-street, noted for his many Acts of Generosity and Kindness in his Life-time. He died at Bremen. ('London Mag.,' p. 534.)

1780, Oct. 5. Tho. Pakenham, esq; of Hart-str. Blooms. ('Gent. Mag.,' p. 495.)

1826, Feb. 22. At Bath, aged 72, John Henry Pakenham, esq. formerly of the 1st Dragoon Guards. (*Ibid.*, p. 285.)

PARISH REGISTER OF ST. JOHN.

Married.

1705 Sep. 10 James Vaughan & Sarah Tuch.
1725 Mar. 5 Edward Vaughan and Frances Monke.

* The Author has an engraving of him, the margin of which has unfortunately been cut off: it is noted in pencil "Henry Voguel, London, Merchant, æt. 65. Schmidt 1746."

Buried.

1708 Nov. 6 Sarah Vaughan.
1732 Aug. 27 Robert Vaughan.
1733 Dec. 28 Rachell Vaughan, a child.

1666, April 12. James Vaughan, of Hackney, Midx., Merchant, Widr, abt 32, & Mrs Elizabeth Bodington, of St Lawrence Jewry, London, Spr, abt 20; consent of father George Bodington, Gent.; at Hackney, Newington, or Islington, co. Midx., or St Botolph, Bishopgate, London. (Marriage Licences: Vicar-General of the Archbishop of Canterbury.)

ST. JOHN'S CHURCHYARD, ANTIGUA.

On a headstone:—

To the Memory of
GEORGE EDWARD PAKENHAM Jun Efq
who departed this Life the 3 Day of
February 1768 in the
21st Year of his Age.
(One Greek line above and two Latin ones below.)

WARFIELD CHURCH, CO. BERKS.

Herevnder lyeth the Body of
ANN lately ye Wife of Tho. VAUGHAN Efqr.
She was born the 10th Octr 1674 and
Departed this life ye 12th Decr 1727.
(Six lines follow.)

CAMBERWELL, CO. SURREY.

At the south-east end of this churchyard is a very neat monument:—

To the memory of
MARY VOGUELL,
Wife of HENRY VOGUELL, Esq.
Who died 28th of *February*, 1775, aged 28 years.
('A Collection of Epitaphs,' 1802, p. 265.)

Family of Vernon.

Thomas Everard, Gent. Will dated last of Jan. 1662. To my sister Mrs Dorothie Everard £10 st. for a diamond ring. To John Jarssie, s. of Wm Jarssie of Antigua, 300 lbs. To my loving kinsman Edward Sewster, mercht, my silver-handled rapier & belt. To my friend Mr Nichs Hartnoll of St Christopher's 1000 lbs. All residue to my wife Elizth Everard, my 1st dau. Dorothie Everard, & my youngest dau. Elizth Everard equally, to the latter at 18. If both die without issue then to my sister Mrs Dorothie Everard. My wife Ex'trix. If she marry before my daus. are 18 then Capt Saml Winthrope, Mr Hen. Meyer, & Mr Hen. Clarke feofees in trust & 20s. apiece. Witnessed by Thomas Allen, George Carter. Recorded 1678, Lib. B, fo. 30.

Thomas Hill, Esq., Lieut.-Governor of St. Kitts, by his will dated 5 April 1697, bequeathed £500 c. to Elizabeth Vernon, dau. of his wife Margaret, provided Captain John Vernon her then husband made her joynture of £2000 in England according to promise before marriage. (See Vol. II., p. 72.)

John Vernon, late of Antigua, now of St. James in the Liberty of Westminster, Gent. Will dated 17 June 1704; proved 2 Nov. 1705 by Elizabeth Vernon the widow; also 23 Dec. 1710 by Nathaniel Carpenter, Elizabeth Vernon having married again; power reserved to Sir William Mathew, Colonel Rowland Williams, Colonel Edward Byam, Archibald Hutcheson, Esq., and Major Edward Nott. (231 Gee.) To my wife Eliz. £500 & all my jewels, plate, furniture, & ½ of monies in England & ½ the produce of my plantation in Antigua in lieu of dower, but ⅓ only if she marry, subject nevertheless to the payment of ½ of the legacies given by my father John Vernon, deceased. My wife to have the care of my plantation, but if she marry, then His Excellency Sir Wm Mathew, Col. Rowld Williams, Col. Edwd Byam of Antigua, & Archibald Hutcheson, Esq., Major Edwd Nott, & Mr Nathl Carpenter of London to have charge of it. To my daus. Mary Vernon £1500 & Eliz. Vernon £1000 at 21. To my sons Tho. & Jas. Vernon £1000 apiece at 23, they to be brought up for the University, to have £40 for books & £80 a year till 23. To Robt Jefferson, son of Saml Jefferson of Antigua, £200 c. All residue to my 1st son John; if he die under 23 without issue then to my son Thos., he paying to my daus. Mary, Eliz., & my son Jas. £500 each, then to my son Jas., he paying to my daus. £500 apiece & £500 more to Robt Jefferson, then to my wife, then to Robt Jefferson, then to the 1st son of Geo. Sims, formerly of Antigua. My wife sole Ex'trix, but if she marry then my trustees to be Ex'ors. To Mary & Sarah Carpenter, daus. of Nath[l] Carpenter, £50 each. Witnessed by Ann Fisher, Charles Humfrey, Lucy Ladd. Recorded also at St. John's, fo. 99 in Libro N, 1714.

Anne Vernon *alias* Lysons of Wivenhoe, co. Essex. Commission to John Vernon, Esq., the husband, May 1733.

William Rawdon Vernon of Frodsham, co. Chester, Gent. Will dated 29 July, proved 22 Aug. 1755 by James Vernon the brother. (229 Paul.) My brother Jas. Vernon of London, merch[t], to pay all my debts, etc., & I give him all my lands in Over, co. Cambridge. To M[r] Joseph Keeling & his wife Hester of Fingringhoe Hall, co. Essex, & to M[r] John Miller & M[r] John Codrington of London, merch[ts], each a ring. My best silver-laced hat to Master Edw[d] Custard, son of M[r] Corbett Custard of Frodsham. All residue to my brother Jas. Vernon, he to be Ex'or. Witnessed by William Lowndes, George Whitley, D. Astley.

John Vernon of Barking, co. Essex, Esq. Will dated 30 Aug., proved 1 Oct. 1765 by James Vernon, Esq., the son; power reserved to Sir Edmund Thomas, Bart., Martin Madan, Charles Spooner, and William Brown; proved also 28 May 1773 by William Brown, Esq.; power reserved to Sir Edmund Thomas, Martin Madan, and Charles Spooner. (393 Rushworth.) All my real estate in Antigua to Sir Edmund Thomas of Winvoe Castle, co. Glamorgan, Bart., Rev. Martin Madan, Cl'k, & Cha. Spooner, Esq., both of St. Christopher's, & W[m] Brown of Cursitor Str., co. Midd., Gent., in Trust for my son Jas. Vernon & his heirs male, then to raise £3000 for each of my son's daus. at 21, then to my son John Joseph James Vernon (whom I had by my late wife Eliz. Weston) & his heirs male, then in default his daus. to have £3000 apiece, & then ½ for my dau. Hester & her children & ½ to my dau. Teresa Susanna. To my son Rob[t] (by my late wife Eliz. Weston) £100. To my son John Joseph James £1000 at 21 & £100. To my dau. Hester £120 a year & £100. To my dau. Teresa Susanna £3000 at 21 & £100. To Chas. Spooner of S[t] Christopher's, Esq., £20. To Martin Madan £20. To W[m] Brown £20. To M[rs] Eliz. Murphy of Bolton Row, Piccadilly, £40 a year for her fidelity & £50. I charge all my real estate in Antigua & at Egham, co. Surrey, called Little Foster House, with the payment of annuities, & my personal with debts & legacies. To Joseph Keeling of Clerkenwell, Esq., & my son Jas. Vernon £200 in trust for Jas. Asser, the natural son of my son Jas., at 21, as likewise £200 for Joseph son of Eliz. Murphy at 21 & £10 a year. All residue of my personalty to my sons & daus., Rob[t], John Joseph James, Hester, & Teresa Susanna at 21. Trustees to be Ex'ors. Witnessed by Christopher Musgrave, W. Rayment, William Jackson, Attorney in Winchester Street, London. Recorded also at St. John's 24 April 1766.

James Vernon of Egham, co. Surrey, deceased. Adm'on 30 Aug. 1769 to Margaret Vernon the widow.

Thomas Vernon of Bristol, Esq. Will dated 8 Feb. 1765; proved 5 April 1777 by Elizabeth Vernon the widow. (188 Collier.) I confirm the deed made by myself & my wife Eliz. with my son-in-law M[r] W[m] Browne & my dau. Jane Eliz. Browne his wife since their marriage, & he is to be paid £1000 as agreed. To my wife £1000 in trust to pay the interest to my other dau. Eliz. Isabella Vernon, & the principal if she marries with her consent. Under the settlement & will of Sir Harry Tyrrell, Bart., father of my 1st wife Frances Vernon, deceased, I became entitled to, & by a decree of the Court of Chancery recovered, £750, part of £3000 belonging to the 4 younger children of Sir Harry Tyrrell, of whom my late wife was one, & my wife left an only child by me called Frances Penelope Vernon, who after her mother's death married M[r] W[m] Watkins & died leaving 2 children, to whom I give the £750 at 21. To my son-in-law M[r] W[m] Browne, attorney-at-law, all my law books. To my wife Eliz. my house called the Long Room at Clifton, now leased to M[r] Rob[t] Morgan, & my 2 other houses leased to M[r] John Daport, & all stocks, plate, & all residue, appointing her sole Ex'trix. Witnessed by Paul Methuen, Joseph Blisset of the Six Clerks' Office, John Davis.

1st Codicil dated 19 Feb. 1767. My dau. Eliz. Isabella has married without my consent; the interest of her legacy to her for life, then the principal to her children. Witnessed by H. Burnes, Laz. Venables, William Roberts.

2nd Codicil dated 7 July 1772. Late of Bristol, now of St. George the Martyr, Esq. By the death of my nephew Jas. Vernon, Esq., I as his paternal uncle & heir-at-law am entitled to a messuage called Little Foster House at Egham, which I give to my wife Eliz. Witnessed by John Wynde, Richard Hatch, Thomas Perry.

Elizabeth Vernon of St. George the Martyr, widow. Will dated 21 July 1783; proved 17 May 1788 by William Browne; power reserved to Paul Methuen and Jeremy Bentham, Esquires. (275 Calvert.) All my messuages, farms, & lands at Highwood Hill & at Sanders Lane in the parish of Hendon to my son-in-law W[m] Brown of Lamb's Conduit Str., Esq., for his life & for that of my dau. Jane Eliz. Brown his wife, & after their death to such of their children as my dau. shall appoint, & in default of such appointment to her daus. Eliz. & Arethusa Martha Brown. All my messuages, farms, & lands at Totteridge, co. Herts, to my dau. Eliz. Isabella Barclay, widow, of G[t] Ormond Str., S[t] Geo. the Martyr, on condition she do not reside in Scotland or the East Indies; if she does the estate to go to her dau. Ann Eliz. Barclay, then to her son Jas. Barclay my grandson. All my lands in Dole Str., Hendon, to my grandson Jas. Barclay on the same conditions, otherwise to go to his sister. All my lands at Clifton, co. Glo'ster, & my estate called Little Foster House, Egham, to my daus. Jane Eliz. Browne & Eliz. Isabella Barclay, subject as regards Clifton to the payment of £500 to M[r] Hancocks & £500 to M[r] Moss, given to them by the will of M[r] Sandford. To my dau. Jane Eliz. Browne my brilliant diamond hoop ring & my single brilliant diamond ring. To my granddau. Arethusa Martha Browne my silver inkstand & all other rings. To my granddau. Eliz. Brown a 5-moidore piece of gold & the garnett bracelets with the pictures of her father & her aunt Barclay thereon. To Arethusa Martha Browne my gold watch & chain with the picture of my late husband set in gold. All residue of plate & linen to Jane Eliz. Browne & Eliz. Isabella Barclay. All household goods & pictures to my son-in-law W[m] Browne. To Paul Methuen of Holt, co. Somerset, & Jeremy Bentham of Lincoln's Inn, Esq., 10 gs. each. All residue of personal estate to my 4 grandchildren Eliz. Browne, Arethusa Martha Browne, Jas. Barclay, & Anne Eliz. Barclay. Paul Methuen & Jeremy Bentham, Esq[res], & my son-in-law W[m] Browne to be Ex'ors. Witnessed by Jo. Allen, David Colvard, Jo. Allen, jun.

Codicil. 15 Aug 1787. My granddau. Arethusa Martha Browne is dead. To my granddau. Eliz. Browne my Brussels lace & Turkey hoop ring. To my granddaus. Miss Browne & Miss Barely all my china. To my granddau. Eliz. Anne Barely, in case her aunt Browne do not change the watch left to Arethusa, a gold watch & rose diamond cluster ring, & diamond & emerald ring. To my grandson Jas. Barclay a ring with his grandfather's hair set round with brilliant diamonds. To my cousin M[rs] Sarah Cookson £100. To my cook Mary Childs £20. To my maid Fanny Wad all clothes. To my 3 servants 5 gs. each. To be buried near Arethusa. On 7 May 1788 were sworn John Alexander, jun., of Bedford Row, Gent., and Ann Pierson, wife of James Pierson of Brownlow Street, taylor.

Pedigree of Vernon.

Arms.—I., *Or, on a fess (azure) three garbs (of the first)*, Vernon; II., *Gules, a saltire argent*, Andrews: impaling, I., *Quarterly, 1 and 4, Sable, a lion rampant argent*, Casamajor; *2 and 3, Argent, a crescent . . . .*; II., *Gules, three antique crowns or*, Grant.

Crest.—*A demi-figure of Ceres, habited azure, crined or, holding a garb or in sinister arm and a reaping hook in dexter hand.*

Motto.—*Semper te digna sequare.*

Colonel Clement Everard of St. Christopher's 1647; appointed Deputy-Governor 1654 by Cromwell; displaced 1660; residing at Barbados 1665; Member of Council 1672. = ...

. . . . 1st wife. = Capt. JOHN VERNON, born 1610; clerk in the Secretary's Office, Antigua, 1670; one of the two persons chosen to take care for the relief of poor for North Sound 1671; Member of Assembly 1675-6; inhabitant of Old North Sound 1678; Captain of Militia 1680; one of the two representatives for Antigua at the General Council and Assembly of the Leeward Islands 1681; Speaker 1682; Member of Council 25 May 1683; died 1689. = Elizabeth, dau. of Randall Russel of Nevis, Esq., and relict of Robert Jeaffreson of St. Christopher's; remar. 1663—72. = Thomas Everard of Antigua, Gent., died *circa* 1663. Will dated 31 Jan. 1662. Owned the "Wakering Hall" Plantation in Antigua.

Dorothy Everard, 1662.

Clement Everard, junior, of Antigua, Gent., 1668; had 160 acres at Popeshead.

John Vernon of "Vernons" in St. Peter's Parish, Antigua, born 1650; recommended as a Member of Council 1699; died at his house in Golden Square; bur. 23 June 1704 at St. Edmund, Lombard Street. Will dated 17 June 1704, then of St. James, Westminster; proved 2 Nov. 1705. (231 Gee.) His estate was disintailed by Act of 1724 on the petition of William Moore and Elizabeth his wife. = Elizabeth . . . . mar. before 1681; Ex'trix 1704; remar. 29 June 1710, at St. Edmund, Lombard Street, William Moore; both living 1724; she died 1737.

Dorothy Everard, 1st dau., under 18 in 1662; owned half of 380 acres in 1672 in her own right, which she conveyed by Act of 1678 to her stepfather John Vernon; mar. George Symes in or before 1679, when "Wakering Hall" was settled on them.

Elizabeth Everard, 2nd dau., dead 1678.

Anna, only dau. and heir of George Lysons of Lincoln's Inn and co. Gloucester, by Magdalene, dau. of Sir Marmaduke Rawdon of Barbados and co. Herts; stated to have died 1732 at Wivenhoe, co. Essex. Adm'on May 1733 to her husband. 1st wife. = John Vernon of "Vernons" in Antigua, and of "Little Fosters," Egham, co. Surrey, 1st son and heir, born 1696; Major 1736; Member of Council (resigned 1742-3); bur. 26 Sep. 1765 at St. Edmund, Lombard Street. Will dated 30 Aug., then of Barking, co. Essex, and proved 1 Oct. 1765. (393 Rushworth.) = Elizabeth Weston, died 1760 at Barking; bur. with her parents at Paddington Church. 2nd wife.

John Vernon, died s.p.

James Vernon of "Vernons" in Antigua and of "Little Fosters," Egham, and of London, merchant, died 16 and bur. 22 Aug. 1769 at St. Edmund, Lombard Street. Adm'on 30 Aug. to his widow. = Margaret, dau. of Sir Crisp Gascoigne, Knt., Lord Mayor of London; he died 28 Dec. 1761. s.p.

George Vernon, died s.p. — William Rawdon Vernon of Frodsham, Cheshire. Will dated 29 July and proved 22 Aug. 1755. (229 Paul.)

Magdalen Vernon. — Elizabeth Vernon.

Katherine Vernon. — Hester Vernon. — Teresa Susanna Vernon.

John Vernon, born 1773; of St. Peter's College, Cambridge, 1795, M.A., Sen. Opt.; Colonel of 18th Hussars and Quartermaster-General; died 1859 at Boulogne. = Elizabeth Grace, 2nd dau. of Justinian Casamajor* of Potterells, co. Herts, by Mary, dau. of Duncan Grant of Antigua; mar. 17 Oct. 1808 at North Mimms.

Joseph Vernon, Captain in the Army. = Sarah, dau. of . . . . Fowler.

Seven others, who all died s.p.

John Vernon, died s.p. 1831.

Justinian Vernon, Captain 15th Hussars; assumed the name and arms of Casamajor by the will of his grandfather Justinian Casamajor dated 2 Sep. 1816; died s.p. 1842.

George James Vernon, Captain 47th Regiment, died s.p. 21 Dec. 1844 at Potterells, co. Herts.

Henrietta Vernon.

Cecilia Vernon, mar. Christopher Musgrave, son of Dr. Anthony Musgrave of Antigua.

Emma Vernon.

* See Vol. II., p. 29; also 'Miscellanea Genealogica et Heraldica,' New Series, vol. i., pp. 87—90.

Close Roll, 7 Will. IV., Part 11, No. 9.

Indenture made the 4th March 1836 between Justinian Vernon of Boulogne-sur-Mer, at present in London, Lieut. in H.M.'s 4th Light Dragoons, of the 1st part, William Jenkins of London, merchant, of the 2nd part, and Robert Grant and James Farley Salmon of Antigua, Esquires, of the 3rd part, witnesseth that in order to bar the estate tail of Justinian Vernon in the property hereinafter mentioned, and all estate which may take effect after the determination of the said estates tail, and also in confirmation of Indentures of Lease and Release dated the 24th and 25th April 1835, the release being between John Vernon (father of Justinian Vernon), of the 1st part, Justinian Vernon, of the 2nd part, and William Jenkins and George Allfree, his then co-partner in trade, of the 3rd part, and of an Indenture dated the 28th Dec. 1835 between the said John Vernon, of the 1st part, Justinian Vernon, of the 2nd part, and William Jenkins, of the 3rd part, Justinian Vernon, with the consent of William Jenkins in whom the first estate of freehold is vested, grants to William Jenkins all that plantation in the parish of St. Peter and division of New North Sound, containing 400 acres, and also all the compensation sums of money payable to the owners of the plantation in respect of the late slaves belonging to the same, and all other real and personal property whatsoever comprised in the aforesaid Indentures to have and to hold in confirmation of the said Indentures, subject to the right of redemption reserved by the said mortgage securities, but with all such powers and rights as were thereby vested in the said mortgagee. Lastly Justinian Vernon appoints, etc., Robert Grant and James Farley Salmon to be his Attorneys to appear before the Secretary in Antigua to acknowledge the present Indenture, and also the Indenture of release before mentioned dated the 25th April 1835, and also the Indenture dated the 28th Dec. 1835. Justinian Vernon, Thomas Smith, Raymond Buildings, Gray's Inn, Thomas Hanson Peile, Old Broad Street, witnesses. William Jenkins, Thomas Hanson Peile, Old Broad Street, W. I. McKellar, 2 Judd Place East, New Road, witnesses.

1647, Jan. 10. Samuel Winthrop writes to his father of "Cap'an Clement Everet (of St Christopher's), a justice of peace, who being o^r country man & hearing o^r name, vsed me verry courtiously, and assisted me much in my law suites, which were there verry many. Justice Froth,* who was of yor acquaintance in England (as he informs me), was his grandfather. I have left in his handes my businss in S^t X'per's." ('Winthrop Papers,' part iv., p. 239.)

It is probable that this Clement Everard was a member of the Essex family whose pedigree may be seen in the Visitation of that county.

1659. Twelve articles of complaint were drawn up against Colonel Clement Everard the Deputy-Governor of St. Christopher's, but the petition and sentence have been lost. (Calendar of Colonial Papers, 1574—1660.)

1665, July 5. Clement Everard of St. Christopher's, Esq., now resident at Barbados and bound for England. Letter of attorney to Peter Hancock of Barbados, merchant, for goods worth 18,528 lbs. Valued by Richard Jelly, Richard Morris.

1668. Clement Everard, Gent., jun., 160 acres at Popeshead. (Book of Claims.)

1670. Colonel Clement Everard, an owner of estates in the Leeward Isles, named in a petition of St. Kitts' inhabitants. In June 1672 he was a member of Council of St. Christopher's. It was stated in 1673 that his estate had been devastated by the French since the notice of the Peace.

* Governor Winthrop married 16 April 1605 Mary daughter of John Forth, Esq., of Great Stambridge, co. Essex. The latter died 15 May 1613.

James Vernon, youngest son, under 23, 1704.

Mary Vernon, a minor 1704; mar. William Oxenden of co. Kent, Esq.

Elizabeth Vernon, a minor 1704; mar. Thomas Hurst of Stamford, Esq.

Frances, dau. of Sir Harry Tyrrell, 5th Bart. 1st wife. = Thomas Vernon of Bristol, Barrister-at-Law, 2nd son, bur. 11 April 1777 at St. Edmund, Lombard Street. Will dated 8 Feb. 1765; proved 5 April 1777. (188 Collier.) = Elizabeth Nicoll of Hendon, co. Middlesex, mar. 1736 at Somerset House Chapel. Will dated 1 July 1783; proved 7 May 1788. (275 Calvert.)

Robert Vernon, elder son, died s.p.

Mary, dau. and heir of Rev. Randal Andrews,* Vicar of Preston, co. Lancaster. 1st wife. = John Joseph James Vernon of "Vernons," Antigua, Esq., succeeded 1769; born 1744 at Montauban, France; Capt. 4th Dragoon Guards; died 1823 at Chester. = Hannah, dau. of Miles Mason of Westhouse, Dent, Yorkshire. 2nd wife.

Frances Penelope Vernon, only child, mar. William Watkins; she died v.p.

Jane Elizabeth Vernon, mar. William Browne, Attorney-at-Law; both living 1783.

Elizabeth Isabella Vernon, mar. 1765—67 . . . . Barclay; living his widow 1783.

Susan, dau. of Dr. Kemball of Maldon. 1st wife. = Rev. William Vernon, born 1792; M.A. Cant.; Perpetual Curate of Grindleton, Yorkshire, 1822; Vicar of Patcham and Littlehampton; died 1871. = Elizabeth . . . . 2nd wife.

Henry Vernon, had an only child Henrietta. = H. Parker of Bury, co. Lancaster. s.p.m.

Eleven others, who all died s.p.

John James Vernon, scholar of St. Catherine Hall, Canterbury, died s.p. 1850.

William James Vernon, B.A. and Sen. Opt. St. John's College, Cambridge, 1855. Sent account of family to 'Gent. Mag.' 1867.

Susan Mason Vernon, died young.

Henry Hannotte Vernon, M.D. Edinburgh 1853; M.R.C.S. England 1854; of Southport, co. Lancaster, 1896. = ...

Elizabeth S. Vernon.

Frances M. J. Vernon.

Caroline H. Vernon.

Helen Victoria Vernon.

Henriette Vernon.

John Justinian Vernon, M.B. Edinburgh 1889; of Southport 1896.

* Randal Andrews, only son of Randall Andrews of Wellington, co. Salop, pleb., matriculated from Magdalen College 10 Oct. 1728, aged 18, B.A. 1732, became next year Curate of St. George's Chapel, Preston, and was instituted Vicar 30 April 1743, and died Aug. 1782 and was buried 7 Aug., having had by Elizabeth his wife two sons, of whom the younger Randal survived and became Vicar of Ormskirk, and three daughters. ('History of Lancashire,' by Baines and Croston, vol. v., p. 325.)

1672, Feb. John Vernon and Elizabeth his wife on behalf of Dorothy Everard, of the one part, and George Towes of Antigua, of the other, lease of 20 acres, part of 380 acres.

1673, April 30. Mr. John Vernone, 60 acres at Old North Sound by the Governor; surveyed 22 Feb. 1674-5.

1676, March 30. Captain John Vernon, 50 feet by 80 feet, St. John's Town, by Governor Williams; surveyed 6 April 1676.

Captain John Vernon, 260 acres. The first warrant, dated 1674, by Governor Warner was for 60 acres, and the second by Governor Williams, dated 5 Sep. 1675, for 100 acres, and the third, dated 11 Oct. 1677, for 100 acres by Governor Warner in Old North Sound; surveyed 4 Oct. 1677.

1678. Petition of Dorothy Everard, infant, by Major William Barnes and John Parry, Esq., her guardians. She recites her father's will . . . . my sister dead, my mother married Captain John Vernon. My father died about fifteen years ago. His plantation ruined by the French, my father-in-law resettled, and my share of it 190 acres I wish to convey to him for 10 negros; petition for Act which follows. Recorded in Secretary's Office at Falmouth. (Lib. B, fo. 32.)

Indenture dated 3 Sep. 1678 between Dorothy Everard, daughter of Thomas Everard, Gent., deceased, and Captain John Vernon, Gent., sale of her claim to 380 acres.

Act. No. 49. Antigua. An Act for the enabling Mrs Dorothy Everard, by Major William Barnes and John Parry, Esq; her Guardians, to make a firm conveyance of her part of a certain Plantation in the Old North Sound, late the Estate of Mr Thomas Everard her father, deceased, unto Captain John Vernon her now Father in law. Dated 4 Sep. 1678.

1678, Feb. Captain John Vernon and Captain Archibald Cochran, 200 acres by William Stapleton at North Sound; surveyed 7 June 1679.

John Vernon, Gent., on 2 April 1679 conveyed to George Symes and Dorothy his wife (recently married) and daughter of Thomas Everett, Gent., deceased, a plantation in Old North Sound called "Wakering Hall."*

1680, March 8. Captain John Vernon, 84 acres granted by Sir W. Stapleton.

Christopher Jeaffreson writes on 5 May 1681: "Mr Thomson haith taken up his aboad wth Capt. Vernam of Antegoa (who married o^r Cousen Robert Jeaffreson's Widdow). I saw him at Nevis and proffered my service to him."

1681, Jan. 1. Thomas Everet granted 45 acres by patent.

1684. Thomas Everard was one of the freeholders of St. Mary's Parish.

1724, April 8. Petition of William Moor and Elizabeth his wife to dock the intail of the estate of John Vernon, Esq., deceased. Colonel Nathaniel Crump dissented because John Vernon died possessed of a large clear estate (except legacies to his children), and of 5 or £6000 in England. Archibald Cochran dissented, saying it would be prejudicial to the immediate heir in reversion. The bill was, however, approved of by the majority of the Council, and an Act to sell was passed. (Minutes of Council.)

Act. No. 178. Private. An Act for cutting off the Intail of certain Lands, and Tenements, and Hereditaments, in Antigua, belonging to John Vernon, of the Parish of Saint James's, Westminster, Esquire. Dated 1 May 1724.

1743, May 4. John Vernon, Member of Council, in France. Daniel Mathew is appointed in his place. (B. T. Leeward Islands, No. 55, p. 236.)

* Great and Little Wakering are adjoining parishes in the Hundred of Rochford, co. Essex, and the manors passed from the Copes to the Highams and the Tyrrells. (Wright's 'Essex,' vol. ii., p. 615.)

1769, Aug. 16. Ja. Vernon, Esq; of Egham in Surry. ('Gent. Mag.,' p. 415.)

Justinian Casamajor was rated for St. Peter's, Parham, 1796—1824, and J. J. Vernon 1822—32.

1808, Nov. 17. At North Mimms, Middlesex, John Vernon, esq. of the 22d Light Dragoons, to Elizabeth, second daughter of Justinian Casamajor, esq. of Potterells, Herts. ('Gent. Mag.,' p. 1039.)

1809. At Potterells, Herts, the seat of her father (Justinian Casamajor esq.) the wife of Capt Vernon, of the 12th Light Dragoons, a son. (*Ibid.*, p. 981.)

1840, Jan. 11. At Farley Hill Castle, near Reading, Emma, fourth dau. of the late Justinian Casamajor, of Potterells, Herts, esq. (*Ibid.*)

1844, Dec. 21. At Potterells, Herts, George James Vernon, esq. late Capt. in the 47th Inf. (*Ibid.*, 1845, p. 217.)

1847, Feb. 16. At Potterells, aged 67, William Charles Casamajor, esq. (*Ibid.*, p. 452.)

A Map* of the Estate of Captain John Vernon in Old North Sound Division and St. Peter's Parish, surveyed in 1822 by F. Baker, Surveyor-General.

	Acres.	Roods.	Poles.
Cane pieces . .	285	3	9
In Pasture . .	105	3	14
The Island . .	24	2	14
	416	0	38

The shield of Vernon, given on page 174, is emblazoned on this Map, but the colours have faded.

The Vernon Family.

Mr. Urban,—I should be much obliged to any of your correspondents who may be able to give me some particulars respecting the family of Vernon of Antigua, formerly of Egham, Surrey, St. James's, Westminster, and Lombard Street. My father (whose eldest son I am) is the present representative of this family. The Antigua estate was a grant, made in 1664-5, by Lord Willoughby of Parham, and Sir W. Stapleton, Captain-General of the Leeward Islands, to my ancestor Colonel John Vernon, an officer in the Royalist Army. The chief matters concerning which I desire information are:—1. The Christian name of this Colonel Vernon's father. 2. The name of Colonel Vernon's first wife. 3. The name of his eldest son's wife. From what I gather from family records I think these two latter names are two of the following: Boyle, Carew, Clifford, Moore, Phipps, Duncombe, Robartes, Hedges, Berkeley. Manning and Bray in their 'History of Surrey,' mention the old mansion of this family, Little Foster Hall, now called Egham Lodge, as "belonging to the Vernons formerly." Little Foster Hall or Egham Lodge was in the possession of my great uncle, James Vernon, at the time of his death, and soon after my grandfather came into the property in the West Indies, Little Foster Hall seems to have ceased to belong to the Vernons; it subsequently became the property of a Mr. Blaythwayte. The arms of this family are, Or; on a fesse azure, three garbs or; crest, on a wreath or, a demi-figure of Ceres, habited azure, crined or, holding a garb or in the sinister arm, and a reaping-hook in the dexter hand. Motto "Ver non semper viret." The above-named Colonel John Vernon was born about 1610, and died in 1689 (I think in the West Indies, for I cannot find his will at Doctors' Commons). His second wife was Elizabeth Everard, widow of Thomas Everard, Governor† of the Leeward Islands. His eldest son by his first wife (whose name

* If I recollect rightly this Map was shewn to me by the Hon. Thomas D. Foote at Parham Hill.—V. L. O.

† This is incorrect. A Colonel Clement Everard, perhaps father of Thomas, was Lieut.-Governor of St. Kitts in 1659.

I wish to discover) was John Vernon, born 1650, died 1704, concerning whom I find the following among family records:—John Vernon, Esq. of Golden Square and Antigua, died at his house in Golden Square, 1704. Will in Doctors' Commons, proved in November 1705. The Antigua estate is therein devised to his eldest son John, a third of the nett profits being left annually to his wife Elizabeth (who died in 1737). The said John Vernon was a cousin of Mr. James Vernon, Secretary of State to King William III., and father to Admiral Vernon,—and his funeral was attended by Lord Radnor, Mr. Secretary Vernon, Mr. Vernon of the Exchequer, Sir Charles Hedges, and Mr. Constantine Phipps of the Temple. A list of the same, in the handwriting of the said John Vernon, is in the hands of a Mr. Martin of the Heralds' Office. The Executors of this John Vernon were Sir William Mathew, K.B., Colonel Rowland Williams, Colonel Edward Byam, Major Edmund Nott, Archibald Hutchinson.* and Nathaniel Carpenter. This John Vernon had by his wife Elizabeth (whose surname I wish to ascertain) three sons and two daughters. The eldest son, John Vernon, born in 1696, died 1765, was I believe a colonel in the army, and was a privy councillor for Antigua. He married (1) Anne Lysons, only daughter and heiress of George Lysons, of Lincoln's Inn, and of Gloucestershire, by Magdalene, daughter of Sir Marmaduke Rawdon of Hoddesdon, Herts. Their four sons and three daughters all died s.p. One of the sons, James Vernon, succeeded to the estate in 1765, but died s.p. in 1769, having married Margaret Gascoyne, daughter of Sir Crisp Gascoyne of London, and sister of Bamber Gascoyne, M.P. for Truro, and high steward of Southwark, etc. John Vernon (1696—1765) married (2) Elizabeth Weston, who died in 1760, and was buried at Paddington Church. They had two sons and two daughters. The eldest son, Robert, died s.p. The second John Joseph James Vernon, born 1744, died 1823, succeeded in 1769 to the estates. He was a captain in the 4th Dragoons. He married (1) Mary only dau. and heiress of the Rev. Randal Andrews, vicar of Preston, Lancashire, and by her had nine children, who all died s.p. except the eldest son. John Vernon, born 1773, died 1859, a lieut.-colonel in the army (23rd Fusiliers, and subsequently 18th Hussars). He married (2) Hannah, daughter of Miles Mason, Esq., of Westhouse, Dent, Yorkshire, and by her had thirteen children, of whom the eldest son, William Vernon, M.A. in holy orders, and formerly Vicar of Littlehampton, and of Patcham, Sussex, is now the head of the family. Lieut.-Colonel John Vernon, married Elizabeth Grace Casamajor, daughter of Justinian Casamajor, Esq., of Potterells, Herts; but their three sons, John, Justinian (a captain in the 15th Hussars), and George James (a captain in the 8th Hussars), all died s.p. The executors of John Vernon (1696—1765) were Sir Edmund Thomas, Bart., of Wenvoe Castle, Glamorganshire, Charles Spooner, and the Rev. Martin Madan of St. Christopher's, West Indies, and W. Brown, of Cursitor Street, Middlesex. The two sisters of this John Vernon married respectively, Thos. Hurst, Esq., of Stamford, and William Oxenden, Esq., of Kent. I have found among the family papers various deeds and other MSS. relating to the families of Boyle, Carew, Clifford, etc., but none of these enable me positively to determine the points I have above indicated as the objects of my inquiry. The peerage of the late Francis Vernon, Baron Orwell of Newry, co. Down, Ireland, Viscount Orwell, and Earl of Shipbrooke, who died in 1783, was considered on his death to be only dormant; and my grandfather (the late Captain Vernon, of Antigua, Egham, and White Hall, near Clitheroe, Lancashire) was considered as having a claim to it, but he did not take his claim to the House of Lords; and my uncle, the late Lieut.-Colonel Vernon, has frequently asserted that he had in his possession all the documents necessary to substantiate his claim, but where all these are I cannot discover, for he left most of his papers I believe to a stranger. Lord Shipbrooke was the nephew and heir of the celebrated Admiral Vernon, and I believe he claimed the barony of Orwell in right of his mother Lady Arethusa Boyle, daughter of Charles Boyle, Baron Clifford, of Lanesborough, eldest son of Richard Boyle, 2nd Earl of Cork and 1st Earl of Burlington.—

I am, etc.

Leek, Aug., 1867. W. J. Vernon.

('Gent. Mag.,' Sep. 1867, pp. 358—360.)

* Hutcheson.

Parish Register of St. John.

Married.

1710 . . . . 29 Charles Everard & Elizabeth Woodman.

Buried.

1725 Sep. 6 Charles Everard.
1734 Feb. 13 Capt. James Everard.

Parish Register of St. Philip.

Buried.

1722 Oct. 17 Mary Everard.

Parish Register of St. Peter, Parham.

Baptized.

1772 Nov. 3 Justinian the S. of Justinian Casamajor & Mary his Wife; born the 16th June 1772.

Parish Register of St. Edmund, Lombard Street, London.

Married.

1710 June 29 William Moore of St Bride's, widdower, & Elizabeth Vernon of St James in the feilds, co. Midd., widdow. T. L.

Buried.

1699 Aug. 2 William Vernon, son, W.
1704 June 23 Mr John Vernon, W.
1730 Sep. 4 Mrs Ann Vernon.
1765 Sep. 26 John Vernon, 'from Barking in Essex.'
1769 Aug. 22 James Vernon, Esq., from Chigwell.
1771 April 2 Esther Vernon.
1777 April 11 Thomas Vernon, Esqr.

Register of the Chapel of Somerset House.

Married.

1736 . . . . . . Thomas Vernon, esq., widower, to Elizabeth Nicoll, of Hendon, Midlx.

Family of Walrond.

Roger Walrond* of Wells, co. Somerset, Gent. Will dated 13 May 1562; proved 27 Oct. 1563. (Wells Registry.) My dans. Kath. & Mary. My wife Agnes. My s. Nich^{s}.

Humfrey Walronde of See in Somerset, Esq., Master in the Court of Chancery. Will dated 12 Feb. 1577; proved 14 Oct. 1580 by Henry Walronde. Adm'on (de bonis non) 25 Oct. 1617 to William Walrond "nepoti ex filio" of deceased, Harry Walrond being dead. (36 Arundell.) Money for maintenance of a schoolmaster at Ilminster. Debts of my bro. Roger Walronde forgiven, also those of my bro. Wm Walronde. To my wife Kath. the cup of silver I bought of Humphrey Walronde of Charde. My tenement at Buckland Mary. My s. Harry Walronde, his wife Elizth, & his s. Hum. Walronde. Jas. Walronde, s. of my bro. Roger. My cousin Ham. Walronde of Charde. Wm Poole of Shute, co. Devon, & my bro. Wm Walronde Overseers.

Katherine Walrond of Buckland Mary, Somerset. Will dated 9 May 28 Eliz.; proved 26 May 1593 by John Popham. Adm'on 6 May 1622, Humphrey Walrond of Sea, Somerset, to Humphrey Walrond his son. (46 Neville.) 10*s.* to the Church of N. Petherton where I was born. To John Popham, Esq., H.M. Attorney-General, my best goblet gilted. His wife Mrs Anne Popham my best bracelets of gold. To Miss Mary Popham my chaine. To Mrs Ellinor Warre a bedde. To Mrs Frances Popham my beere cup. Mr Alex. Warre £5. My goddau. Mrs Kath. Rogers my wedding ring. My neph. Ph. Warre, esq., £3, & to his sister £40. My neph. Hannam my great rone mare, & to his wife Mrs Penelope Hannam my ring graven with E. & S. My gods. Mr Wm Poule. My s.-in-l. Hen. Waldron the mare which I bought of my sister Clarke. To my gods. Geo. Walron one Conce. All residue to Mr John Popham Ex'or.

Henry Walrond of Sea, co. Somerset, Esq. Will dated 9 Oct. 1616; proved 26 May 1617 by William Walrond the son. (31 Weldon.) To be bur. at Ilminster. £20 to the poor of that parish. Poor of Chard, Isle Brewers, & Doniett. My wife Elizth. Messuages in Isle Brewers conveyed to Nich^{s} Denton (now dec^{d}) & John Hanke, G^{t}, to the use of me, my wife, my s. W^{m}, then to Humphry Walrond, younger s. of Humphry Walrond my 1st s., then in succession to Maurice Walrond, Edwd Walrond, & John Walrond, other sons of Hum. Walrond the Elder. Manor of Earnshill, co. Som., settled on my s. W^{m}. My s. Hen. Walrond £900. Kath. d. of Hum. Walrond. My s. W^{m} Ex'or. Inventory follows.

Elizabeth Seaman, widow of Dr. John Seaman, Chancellor of Gloucester. Will dated 20 Aug. 1 Chas.; proved 14 Feb. 1626. (8 Skinner.) To be buried at Painswick with my husband. My d. Grace Wallrond. My s.-in-law Humphrey Wallrond, Esq. My daus. Eliz. & Mary & sons Sam., Edw., & W^{m}.

Dr. John Seaman died 1623, æt. 59, and was buried at Painswick.

Maurice Walrond of All Saints, Honey Lane, London, deceased. Adm'on 2 Oct. 1639 to Elizabeth Walrond his relict.

Elizabeth Walrond of St. Mary Aldermanbury, London. Adm'on 6 May 1661 to her daughter Elizabeth Donner *alias* Walrond of goods not administered to by Maurice Watrond the son (Oct. 23, 1657), now also deceased.

1673, Nov. 15. Christabell Walrond of Isle Brewers, co. Somerset. Adm'on to Henry Walrond the husband.

* See Brown's 'Somersetshire Wills.'

Sir Alexander Walrond, Knt. Will dated 11 April, proved 7 May 1677 by Thomas Henchman. (57 Hale.) To be embalmed & sent over to Barbadoes & be buried with my mother in St Philip's Ch'yard, my wife to ask leave of the Vestry. My s. Alex^{r} Walrond. My dau. Cornelia Walrond. My 2 bros. Henry & Edwd Walrond. To my s. & dau. my 3 negroes Cuffee, Oliver, & Cromwell. My sister Elizth Walrond. My diamond ring to my sister Jane Walrond. My father Henry Waldon Ex'or. My mother.

Codicil. 13 April 1677. If I cannot conveniently be buried at Barbadoes then to be carried to Temple Ch. Mr Tho. Henchman Ex'or for this purpose.

(111 Cann.) Millicent Jennings of Barbados, widow, names Mrs. Mary Walrond, widow of Mr. John Walrond, and her son Edward Walrond, and the latter's uncle Job Brookes.

John Standfast of Bristol, now of Barbados. Will proved 1687. (54 Foot.) My 100 acres in St James parish called Mount Standfast, also 270 acres called Fontabell.

Thomas Spiar of Barbados, Esq. (54 Foot.) My brother-in-law Tobias Frere & his wife. Fontabell in which Madam Eliz. Walrond, now wife of Col. Thos. Walrond, hath an interest, for her life.

Bridget Crofts *alias* Walrond of Barbadoes, widow, but deceased in St. James, Westminster. Adm'on 26 June 1688 to Henry Walrond, Esq., her brother.

1698, March 2. Commission to Charles Walrond, brother of Edward Walrond, late of Barbados, but at Gambia in parts beyond the seas, bachelor, deceased.

Henry Walrond, only son of the Right Hon. Lieut.-General Henry Walrond. Will undated; proved 28 Sep. 1720 by Elizabeth Savile *alias* Walrond *alias* Burdyn, late wife of Charles Savill, and only heir and Ex'trix of deceased. (206 Shaller.) All my est. to Eliz. Burdyn my lawful wife.

Edward Walrond of East Greenwich, co. Kent, Gent. Will dated 28 Nov., proved 21 Jan. 1720 by Mary Walrond the widow. (18 Buckingham.) To my aunt Mrs Sarah Duncombe £100. To Mr Robt Meese, attorney of New Inn, £100. To the poor of E. Greenwich £100. To Mr Edwd Warner of Antigua my nephew £500 South Sea stock. To Mr Ashton Warner of Antigua my nephew £500 like stock. To Mr Wm Stevenson, son of Mrs Jane Stevenson, widow, £500 like stock notwithstanding his minority. To the poor of Queen Eliz. College in E. Greenwich £1000. To my 2 servants £5 apiece. To Saunder Ewers, waterman, £20. All residue to my dear wife Mrs Mary Walrond, & appoint her sole Ex'trix. Witnessed by John Brown, Charles Smith.

Mary Walrond, widow of Edward Walrond, late of East Greenwich, Esq. Will dated 17 Aug., proved 6 Nov. 1727 by Colonel Edward Warner and Robert Peirson. (279 Farrant.) To be buried in the vault in East Greenwich church near my husband, but my Ex'ors are to have a vault built in the churchyard & our bodies are to be moved to it, & I give £50 to the poor if this is done. £100 for funeral. To my Ex'ors £500 for my friend Mrs Jane Hammond, wife of Anthony Hammond, Esq., dau. of Sir Walter Clarges, deceased. To their son Jas. £1000 at 21. To Col. Edwd Warner, late of Antigua, now of Eltham, co. Kent, £500 & all my books, & to his brothers Mr Ashton Warner & Mr Henry Warner £500 apiece. To Mrs Phyllis Warner, wife of Mr Henry Warner, £200. To Jane Johnson, dau. of Eliz. Johnson & niece of my late husband Walrond, £200 at 21, also her mother's picture. To Cecill Tufton, Esq., son of Sir Chas. Tufton of Twickenham, & to his lady Mrs Eliz. Tufton £100 apiece, also a ring with King Chas. 1st head, a fine needlework picture, & their own pictures. To Mr Richd Knightly £100. To Mrs Deborah Knightly, sister of Mr Tufton, £100. To my couzin Edwd Turner of Tharefeild, nr Royston, co. Herts, my nearest relative by my father's side, £500. To my couzin Mr Richd Warner, son of Mr John Warner, late of Lambeth, deceased, who was my mother's brother, £500. To my couzin Mr John Bayspoole, son of Tho. Bayspoole, Esq., living with the Rev. Chas. Reeve, minister of Blofield, nr Norwich, £200. To my goddau. Mrs Martha Brockhurst, dau. of Mrs Martha Avis of E. Greenwich, £100. To my goddau. Mary Paulett, dau. of Mrs Susan Paulett & granddau. of Mr Robt Watson of Greenwich, £100, & £20 to the latter. To Mrs Phillis Stubbs, dau. of Mr Archdeacon Stubbs, £100. To Mr Peter Heyton, nephew of Mr Robt Heyton my 1st husband, £100. To my couzin Mr Luke Singleton of Norton, nr Gloucester, £100, to his younger son my godson £500, & to the former's 3 sisters Mary, Eliz., & Sarah £50 apiece. To Mr Robt Meese of London, Gent., £100. To Mr Tho. Elder of Greenwich, writing master, £50. To Mr Lawrence Singleton, druggist in Cheapside, £50. To Mrs Eliz. Warner, wife of Mr Ashton Warner, all my dressing plate. To Mrs Eliz. Harding, who keeps a coffee house, £10. To Mrs Eliz. Andrews, wife of my son-in-law Tho. Andrews, Esq., my diamond cross & string of diamonds, all my plate, also a diamond hoop ring which was my dau.'s, & to each of her nieces now living with her 1 of my best snuff boxes. To Mr Tho. Andrews & Eliz. his wife £50 apiece. On the marriage of my late dau. with Tho. Andrews, Esq., a clause was put in the settlement which caused afterwards some difference, & the matter having been referred to Mr Archdeacon Stubbs I executed a deed promising to pay 500 gs. to Tho. Andrews so that the estate reverted to me, of which I am in peacable possession. My estate in Greenwich consists of the house I now live in, most of its rooms hung with tapestry, a yard, garden, & appurtenances valued at £35 a year, a house in the occupation of Capt Strutt at £15 a year, 2 houses let on lease to Mr John Barber, bricklayer, at £15 a year, 6 others let to him at £25 a year, a house occupied by Mrs Eliz. Harding as a coffee house at £16 a year, a house occupied by Jas. Nichols, a cooper, at £13, called the "Boar," & a house occupied by Mr Avis at £21 a year. All these houses are to be sold & Mr Archdeacon Stubbs, chaplain to the Royal Hospital at Greenwich, is to offer them to the Govr & Directors at 20 years' purchase. Otherwise to be sold to the highest bidder, then £500 to be paid to the said hospital for completing the quire of the chapel, & £200 for repairing the great church of St Alban's. I bequeath the houses to Col. Edwd Warner, Robt Pearse of Doctors' Commons, Gent., Dr Richd Morton, & Rev. Mr Philip Stubbs Archdeacon to sell the same. To Dr Richd Morton & Rev. Archdeacon Stubbs £50 each. To Richd Pearse my gold watch, chain, & 2 seals, & 2 cases of silver spoons. To Mr Peter Heyton my silver tankard, 2 salvers, & 3 castors, all having his uncle's coat of arms on them. To Mr Edwd Turner's lady of Tharefield my silver teapott & lamp. To my 2 servants £5 each. All residue to Col. Edwd Warner in Trust for his 2 daus. Grace & Eliz. Anne. I appoint him & Robt Peirson Ex'ors, & give the latter £100. Witnessed by John Strutt, Thomas Peete, John Everatt.

Pedigree of Walrond.

ARMS.—*Argent, three bulls' heads cabossed sable, armed or.*
CRESTS.—1, *An heraldic tiger sable pelleté*; 2, *On a mural crown an heraldic tiger sable pelleté.*
MOTTO.—*Bienfaictz payeray malfaictz rangeray.*

OSMUND WALROND, younger son of John Walrond of Bradfield, co. Devon.═Emlyn, dau. of . . . . Buckthought of co. Devon.
(See Vivian's 'Visitations of Devon' for the earlier generations.)

Their children:

- Elizabeth, dau. and coheir of John Brokehampton of Sea, 1st wife.═Humphrey Walrond of Sea in Ilminster, co. Somerset, Esq., a Master in Chancery. Will dated 12 Feb. 1577; proved 14 Oct. 1580. (36 Arundell.)═Katherine, dau. of Sir John Popham, Knt.; born at North Petherton. Will proved 26 May 1593. (46 Nevill.) 2nd wife. s.p.
- Roger Walrond of Wells. Will dated 13 May 1562; proved 27 Oct. 1563 at Wells.═Agnes, dau. of John Mansell.
- William Walrond of Fysett, 1577.═Margaret Dolman.

Children of Humphrey Walrond and Elizabeth:

- John Walrond, died s.p.
- Henry Walrond of Sea, admitted to Inner Temple 15 June 1562; died 18 Feb. 1616. Will dated 9 Oct. 1616; proved 26 May 1617. (31 Weldon.)═Elizabeth, dau. and coheir of William Devenish of Hellingleigh, co. Sussex, Esq., coheir to the Barony of Welles.
- Humphrey Walrond, s.p.
- Mary Walrond, s.p.

Children of Henry Walrond and Elizabeth:

- Humphrey Walrond of Sea, Esq., died 17 Feb. 1621. Inq. p.m. at Yeovil June, 20 Jac. I. A═Elizabeth, dau. of Humphrey Colles of Barton, co. Somerset, by Elizabeth his wife, dau. of Roger Darcy and sister of Thomas, Lord Darcy, of Chiche; died before 1616.
- William Walrond of Islebrewers, co. Somerset, under 21, 1580; compounded for his estate 1646; died 24 Aug. 1662, æt. 80; bur. and M.I. in Wells Cathedral.* Will dated 29 May 14 Charles II.; proved 9 Dec. 1662. (160 Land.)═. . . .
- Henry Walrond, 1616.

* *Vide* 'Wells Cathedral,' by Arthur J. Jewers, for his M.I.

A |

Humphrey Walrond of Sea, Esq., æt. 19½ in 1621; compounded for his estate 1645, then had ten children; created 1653 Marquis de Vallado by the King of Spain; settled in Barbados; President of Council there 1660; living at London 1664. = Grace, dau. of Dr. John Seaman, Chancellor of Gloucester; mar. 1624; living 1668.

Maurice Walrond, Citizen and Goldsmith of London, bur. 30 Sep. 1639 at All Saints, Honey Lane. Adm'on 20 Oct. 1639. (*Vide* 'Visitation of London, 1633.') = Elizabeth, dau. of Gilbert Harrison, Sheriff of London. Adm'on 23 Oct. 1657 to Maurice her son.

Frances, 5th dau. of William Coryton of West Newton, Cornwall, Esq.; bapt. 16 April 1616 at St. Mellians; bur. there 13 Sep. 1665. 1st wife. = George Walrond of St. Philip's, Barbados, Esq., a minor 1645. Will dated 14 Aug. 1688; proved 18 Dec. following at Barbados. = ... 2nd wife.

Humphrey Walrond, a minor 1645. = Joan, 2nd dau. of Thomas Pennoyer of the Moor in Clifford, co. Hereford.

A dau., bapt. 21 Feb. 1653 at St. Mellians.

Theodore Walrond of St. Philip's, Barbados, 2nd son. Will dated 13 Sep. 1704; proved at Barbados 7 June 1706. = Elizabeth, dau. of Margaret Smith and sister of Captain William Smith, Esq.

George Walrond, 1st son, not 21, 1688.

Grace Walrond, mar. Le Conte of New York 1688.

Elizabeth Walrond, ux. William Wills of Wivelscombe in St. Stephen's, near Saltash, Esq., 1688; he born 8 and bapt. 19 Jan. 1658 at St. Stephen's, and bur. there 28 Feb. 1717; she bur. with him 5 Jan. 1723. Her will dated 3 April 1722; proved at Bodmin 7 May 1723.

Frances Walrond, bapt. 6 Aug. 1668 at St. Philip's; mar. there 16 Feb. 1687; ux. Richard Michell, junior, Surgeon, 1688.

Elizabeth, dau. of Thomas Wills of Wivelscombe; mar. licence dated at Exeter 1 Oct. 1724. (? bur. 23 Nov. 1726 at St. Philip's.) Adm'on 18 Dec. 1733 to her husband. (P.C.C.) 1st wife. = Theodore Walrond of Antigua, Esq., purchased lands of Main Swete 30 April 1726; bur. on his estate in St. Philip's, Antigua, 12 June 1750. He had other issue, but probably not surviving. = Amy, relict of John Parry; mar. settlement dated 11 Jan. 1731; bur. 27 March 1741 at St. Philip's, Antigua. 2nd wife. = Mary Keynell of Barbados, died 1 July 1766, æt. 70; bur. at St. Marylebone. Adm'on 2 Aug. 1768. 3rd wife.

George Walrond of of St. Philip's, Barbados, planter: not 21, 1704; died and bur. 23 Aug. 1743 at St. Philip's. Will dated 22 Aug. 1743. = Dorothy Pickering, mar. 9 July 1724 at St. Philip's.

Mary Walrond, not 21, 1704.

Main Swete Walrond of Antigua, Esq., only child, born 1725; bur. 1790 at St. Philip's. Will dated 16 May 1786; sworn 5 July 1790. Recorded at Antigua. = Sarah, dau. of Joseph Lyons of Antigua, Esq., and sister of William Lyons of Antigua, Esq.; born 4 Sep. 1731; mar. settlement dated 21 March 1748; died 2 Jan. 1764. M.I. at "Upper Walronds," St. Philip's, Antigua.

Charles Loyd Walrond, bur. 14 Jan. 1738 at St. Philip's, Antigua.

Catherine Walrond, bur. 21 Jan. 1738 at St. Philip's, Antigua.

Rowland Walrond, bur. 23 Feb. 1738 at St. Philip's, Antigua.

Catherine Walrond, bur. 16 Jan. 1743 at St. Philip's, Antigua.

Theodore Walrond, born 7 May and bapt. 1 June 1750 at St. Paul's; entered Merchant Taylors' School 1762; entered Gray's Inn 15 Jan. 1767; died a bachelor at Bristol 1771.

Joseph Lyons Walrond of Antigua, and of Montrath House in Broadhembury, co. Devon, Esq.; entered Merchant Taylors' School 1762; of St. John's College, Oxon, matric. 6 July 1770, æt. 18; Fellow 1770—72; died 13 Jan. 1815, æt. 63; bur. at Kentisbeare. M.I. = Caroline, dau. of Edward Codrington of Dodington, Esq.; mar. 28 Dec. 1797 at St. George's, Hanover Square; died 6 Nov. 1833 at Lasborough Park, co. Gloucester.

Charles Wills Walrond, born 21 Oct. 1754 at Antigua; entered Merchant Taylors' School 1764; medical student at Edinburgh; died 1795 at Tortola. = Elizabeth, dau. of John Day of Antigua, Esq., and sister of Capt. William Day, R.N., Governor of Sierra Leone; mar. 18 May 1777 at Edinburgh.

Lyons Walrond, born 21 April 1800; of Christ Church College, Oxford, matric. 11 Dec. 1818, æt. 18; died a bachelor 21 May 1819, æt. 19; bur. at Kentisbeare.

Bethell Walrond of Montrath House, J.P., D.L., M.P. for Sudbury and Saltash, born 10 Aug. 1801. Recorded his pedigree at College of Arms in 1829. Claims Barony of Welles. = Lady Janet St. Clare Erskine, only dau. of James, Earl of Rosslyn; mar. 10 Nov. 1829.

Main Swete Walrond, bapt. 25 Aug. 1779 at St. John's and bur. there 2 Sep. following.

Henry Walrond, born 30 July 1830; died 19 Aug. 1831.

Harriot Walrond, born 10 March 1832.

A dau.

Henry Walrond of Dulford House, J.P., born 9 Nov. 1841; of Christ Church College, Oxon, matric. 19 Oct. 1859, æt. 17. = Caroline Maud, dau. of W. J. Clark, J.P. and D.L., of Buckland Toussaints, Devon; mar. 1861.

Henry Humphrey Walrond of Dulford House, Devon, born 1862; of Exeter College, Oxon, matric. 20 Oct. 1881, æt. 19; B.A. 1886.

Ernest Adolphus Walrond, born 1863.

Francis Arthur Walrond, born 1866.

Herbert Walrond, born 1868.

Conrad Montagu Walrond, born 1869.

Stewart Basil Walrond, born 1876.

Four daus.

Most of this Pedigree has been copied from one recorded at the Heralds' College.

Edward Walrond of the Middle Temple, 10 Sep. 1624.

John Walrond, 1616; Secretary of Barbados *circa* 1660.

George Walrond, living 1632.
—
Katherine Walrond, 1616.

Elizabeth Walrond, mar. Henry Sydenham of Cholworthy and Claringdon, co. Wilts, Esq., 1623.

Henry Walrond, a minor 1645; Lieut.-General in the Army and Governor of Barbados; of St. John's Parish, Barbados, 1679; Chief Justice of the Court of Common Pleas. Will dated 22 Oct. 1690; proved 3 March 1693. ╤ Deborah .... bur. before 1677 in St. Philip's Church-yard.

John Walrond of Barbados, mar. and had issue.

Thomas Walrond, Col. in the Army, Member of Council of Barbados; of Christ Church Parish 1679.

Edward Walrond.
—
Three daus.

Sir Alexander Walrond of Barbados, matric. from Brasenose College, Oxford, 12 Dec. 1671, æt. 17; student of Inner Temple 27 April 1672; knighted 20 June 1672; bur. 14 May 1677 in the Temple Church. Will dated 11 April and proved 7 May 1677. (57 Hale.) ╤ Mary, dau. of James Cornelius of Barbados, merchant; mar. allegation dated 22 Sep. 1669.

Henry Walrond of St. John's Parish, Barbados, 1679. (? Lieut.-General 1720.) ╤ . . . .

Edward Walrond of Antigua, Esq., Ex'or 1695 to Thomas Warner, Esq. Will dated at Greenwich 28 Nov. and proved 21 Jan. 1720. (18 Buckingham.) ╤ Mary, widow of Robert Heyton, Esq. Will dated at Greenwich 17 Aug. and proved 6 Nov. 1727. (279 Farrant.)
s.p.

Jane Walrond, a spinster 1677; mar. Thomas Warner, son of Colonel Philip Warner, Governor of Antigua; he died Nov. 1695.
—
Elizabeth Walrond, a spinster 1677; mar. .... Johnson.

Alexander Walrond of St. Joseph's, Barbados, 1680. ╤ Mary, dau. of Tobias Frere (by Abigail, dau. and coheir of John Turner of Turner's Hall) and sister of John Frere, Governor of Barbados (latter's will 1721); born 9 Oct. 1678.

Cornelia Walrond.

Henry Walrond, only son (? of Antigua 1697, and then æt. 22). Will proved 28 Sep. 1720. ╤ Elizabeth Burdyn, Ex'trix to her husband.

Abigail Walrond.

Elizabeth, dau. of Charles A. Chabart, Governor of St. Eustachia; mar. 1778. 1st wife. ╤ Main Swete Walrond* of Manadan, Lieut.-Col., died 16 May 1817. ╤ Elizabeth, dau. and coheir of Humphrey Hall of Manadan, Esq.; mar. Feb. 1803 at Plymouth; living 1828; remar. Sir William Elford, Bart. 2nd wife.

Lyons Walrond, died s.p.
—
Elizabeth Walrond, mar. Admiral John Holloway; he died June 1826, æt. 84, at Wells; she living a widow 1828.

Sarah Lyons Walrond, mar. 1st, 17 July 1782, at St. Philip's, Captain Thomas Flucker; and 2ndly General Vaughan Lloyd, Commandant at Woolwich; he died there June 1817, æt. 80.

Catherine Walrond, mar. 1784 John Lyons of Antigua, and St. Austin's, co. Hants; she was born 21 Dec. 1763 and died 12 Dec. 1803; he was born 20 Oct. 1760 and died 6 Feb. 1816.

Theodore Walrond, bapt. 20 March 1782 at St. John's.

Five daus.

Theodore Walrond of Calder Park, co. Lanark, J.P., D.L., born 8 Jan. 1788; died 31 Dec. 1864. ╤ Jane, dau. of Sir Charles Holland Hastings, K.C.H.; mar. 11 Sep. 1820.

Main Sweete Walrond, of Hereford, M.D., born 22 Nov. 1779; mar. and had issue.

Jane St. John Hall Walrond, only child, died 18 April 1809, æt. 3½.

Henry Wood Walrond, born 30 June 1821; entered at Rugby 30 June 1834, æt. 13; died 1841 at Trinity Coll., Cambridge.

Theodore Walrond, C.B., born 17 Feb. 1824; entered at Rugby 12 Feb. 1834, æt. 10; matric. from Balliol College, Oxford, 10 March 1842, æt. 18; Scholar 1842—50; B.A. 1846; Fellow 1850—57; M.A. 1851; C.B. 1871; Assistant Master Rugby 1848; Examiner Civil Service 1856—63; Secretary 1863—75; Commissioner 1875—77; died 16 June 1887. ╤ . . . .

Rev. Main Swete Walrond, M.A., Vicar of St. Lawrence Jewry, born 30 May 1834. ╤ Fanny Mina, dau. of John Marston; mar. 10 Dec. 1867.

Francis Charles Walrond, born 17 Sep. 1836. ╤ Eliza, dau. of Hunter Morrison; mar. 24 Nov. 1868.

Charles Wills Walrond, late Capt. R.A., born 30 Dec. 1837.
—
Three daus.

* I have a letter of his, dated 17 Feb. 1801 from 12 Bond Street, Bath, referring to his little property in Dominica. (Matson Letters.)

1733, Dec. 18. Commission to Charles Dunbar, Esq., the attorney of Theodore Walrond, husband of Elizabeth Walrond *alias* Wills of Antigua, deceased. Theodore Walrond now residing in Antigua.

Gilbert Kennedy of Lincoln's Inn Fields, Doctor in Physic. Will dated 1778. All estate in Cornwall in trust. To my nephew David Kennedy of Barbados ½ for life. To Mary Waldron of Barbados another ½.

Maine Swete Walrond. Will dated 16 May 1786. To my dau. Cath. Lyons, wife of John Lyons, a negro, & to her husband a 5 guinea ring. To my dau. Eliz^th Holloway £1000 c. To my dau. Sarah Lyons Flucker £1000 c. To my son Main Swete a negro & £500 c. To my son Chas. Willes Walrond £500 c. To Hon. John Gray a 3 guinea ring. To John Burke, Esq., a 2 guinea ring. Certain slaves to be free. All residue to my son Joseph Lyons Walrond, he & John Gray to be Ex'ors. Witnessed by William Burnett, Moses Glover, John Smyth.

1st Codicil dated 14 Feb. 1788. £500 more to each of my sons Main Swete Walrond & Chas. Willes Walrond. To my dau. Eliz^th Holloway £35 st. for a negro, & to John Holloway her son a 5 guinea ring. To my dau. Sarah Lyons Flucker £100 st. & a negro. Witnessed by John Smyth. By Thomas Shirley, Esq., was sworn John Smyth 5 July 1790.

2nd Codicil dated 17 Feb. 1789. To my 2 daus. Eliz^th Holloway & Sarah Lyons Flucker all monies due to me from Clement Tudway of Wells, Somerset. Sarah L. Flucker to have the use of my horses, carriages, etc., for a year. Witnessed by John Burke, John Smith. Before Sir Thomas Shirley was sworn John Smith, merchant, 5 July 1790. Recorded at Antigua.

1645. Humphry Walrond of Sea, co. Somerset, now a prisoner in the Gate House of Westminster. Grace his wife and George his first son. (Calendar of Committee for Compounding Royalists' Estates, p. 937.)

1647, Jan. 29. Humphrey Walrond of Sea fined £300. On 14 Feb. 1651 this was reduced to £40 on account of his debts of £2143. (*Ibid.*, p. 764.)

In 1664 Humphrey Walrond appeared before the Privy Council and complained that Lord Willoughby had unjustly deprived him and his son of their estates in Barbados. The petitioner was however committed to the Fleet Prison, as he had quitted Barbados without the Governor's permission.

Circa 1666. In a pamphlet of this date, in which the writer described the transactions of Francis, Lord Willoughby of Parham at Barbados, it is stated that his lordship had seized the plantation of Colonel Waldron, who consequently fled.

1679. Census of Barbados. St. John's Parish. Henry Walrond, sen., Esq., 423½ acres, 1 bought servant, 8 hired servants, 198 negros. Henry Walrond, jun., Esq., 137½ acres, 6 bought servants, 1 hired servant, 70 negros.

Christ Church Parish. Thomas Walrond, 340 acres, 18 white servants, 170 negros.

St. Joseph's Parish. Alexander Walrond, 80 acres.

St. Philip's Parish. Captain George Walrond, 150 acres, 2 white servants, 28 negros.

1693. Order to Mr. Ed. Walrond for 1750 lbs. for rent of his storehouse in Parham, taken up by Charles Tudway. (Colonial Entry Book, No. 48.)

In B. T. Leeward Islands, vol. 5, are several original letters written to the Lords of the Plantations by Mr. Edward Walrond, making various charges against General Codrington the Governor; some are sealed with his arms . . . . three bulls' heads . . . .

In 1696 there had been some complaints made against Captain Robert Arthur, R.N., and the deposition is recorded of Henry Walrond, æt. 22, who was at his cozen Walrond's house at Antigua, sworn 19 Feb. 1696.

On 2 Aug. 1697 Edward Walrond, Esq., writes to their Lordships and says Colonel Charles Pym of Nevis, a great friend of the General's, is a Jacobite. Henry Walrond is later ordered into custody. On 4 Sep. 1697 was signed by John Perrie the Provost-Marshal the warrant for arresting Edward Walrond, Esq. In another deposition Henry Walrond, æt. 22, states that in 1697 he was a volunteer on H.M.S. Jersey. Edward Walrond escaped to England after having given £500 bail, and on 6 July 1698 writes from Islington to their Lordships on behalf of his friend Mr. John Lucas, who was being cruelly illused by the Governor, and he renews all his charges against the latter. The death of the General on 20 July 1698 seems to have put an end to the matter. John Lucas writes from prison in Antigoa to his friend Edward Walrond and says, "There is an Execution against your estate for £500 st.: they w^d have taken 20 of your negros, but your attornies objected & raised the money. Your brother Pern," dated 28 May 1698, and later mentions the illness of "your brother Burgis."

1697-8. The Lieut.-Governor, Council, and Assembly of Montserrat declare Edward Walrond's charges against General Codrington to be false and scandalous. (B. T. Leeward Islands, vol. 5.)

1715. Census of Barbados. Christ Church Parish. James Eliot, æt. 23. Elizabeth his wife, æt. 26. Bridget Walrond, æt. 40.

St. John's Parish. Deborah Walrond, æt. 70, and Jane Walrond, æt. 66.

1771, *circa* Oct. Theodore Waldron, Esq; at Bristol. ('Gent. Mag.,' p. 474.)

1780. Main Swete Walrond has resigned his commission as J.P. because, as Governor Burt says, a licence had been granted for his daughter to marry Captain Halway. On 28 Sep. Main Swete Walrond petitioned that he was appointed a Justice of the Court of Common Pleas on 2 July 1774 by patent, also Governor of Monk's Hill in 1779, has been J.P. twenty years, and in the Militia thirty years. (B. T. Leeward Islands, vol. 37.)

1785, Sep. 22. Nathaniel Walrond an insolvent debtor.

1786, Feb. 18. Mr. Walrond, to whom it is said the office of Chief Justice has been promised, has lately had a paralytic stroke.

On 7 June it was stated that Rowland Burton had been appointed Chief Justice, and that there was no foundation for the report about Walrond.

1803. Mary Walrond then living in Barbados.

1815, Feb. Lyons Walrond, esq. of Mortrath, near Collumpton. ('Gent. Mag.,' p. 187.)

1829, Nov. 10. At the Earl of Rosslyn's, St James's-sq. Bethell Walrond, esq. M.P. of Montrath, Devonshire, to the Right Hon. Lady Janet St Clair, only daugh. of the Earl of Rosslyn. (*Ibid.*, pp. 462, 558.)

1831, Aug. 31. Aged 12 months, Henry, only child of Bethell Walrond, esq. M.P. (*Ibid.*, p. 283.)

1833, Nov. 6. Gloucester. At Lasborough Park, the widow of Joseph Lyons Walrond, esq. She was sitting by herself after dinner and dozing, when her cap caught fire at the candle, and in attempting to extinguish it, her sleeves, and ultimately her whole dress, were in a blaze; and before it could be extinguished, the unfortunate lady was so dreadfully burnt as to cause her death on the following afternoon. Mrs. Walrond was sister to Sir C. Bethel Codrington, Bart., and mother to Bethel Walrond, esq. late M.P. for Saltash. (*Ibid.*, p. 476.)

1840, Sep. Lately. At Bath, Anne, relict of Alex. Walrond, esq. of Barbados. (*Ibid.*, p. 330.)

1841, May 31. Aged 84, Barwick Bruce M.D. of Barbadoes also on 29 July Amabel his widow dau. of late Nath. Walrond descended from Col. Humphry W. Govr of Barbadoes 1660 . . . . both died at Hartford in Connecticut. ('Gent. Mag.,' p. 331.)

1844, July 16. At Barbados, aged 57, Benjamin Walrond, esq. Provost Marshal General of the island, a Commissioner of the Peace, Serjeant at Arms to the Court of Chancery, and Common Pleas. He was lineally descended from Col. Humphry Walrond, "the gallant old Royalist," Governor of Barbados in 1660. (*Ibid.*, p. 334.)

1846, Oct. 27. At Bradfield Villa, St John's Wood, Nicholas Humphrey Walrond, esq. of the island of Barbados. (*Ibid.*, p. 664.)

1864, Dec. 31. At Calder-pk., Lanarkshire, aged 76, Theodore Walrond, esq. Mr. Walrond was nearly related to the family of Walrond, in Devonshire. He married a dau. of Sir Chas. Hastings, K.C.H. (a distinguished officer who was severely wounded and lost his arm at the battle of Copenhagen,) by whom he leaves four sons and three daughters. (*Ibid.*, p. 258.)

1867, March 31. At 37 St. George's-road, Eccleston-square, Anna Maria Louisa, wife of the Rev. Theodore A. Walrond. (*Ibid.*, p. 688.)

1867, Dec. 10. At Ealing, the Rev. Main Swete Alexander Walrond, second son of the late T. Walrond, esq., of Calder Park, Lanarkshire, to Fanny Mina, third dau. of J. Marston, esq., of Ealing. (*Ibid.*, 1868, p. 104.)

PARISH REGISTER OF ST. JOHN.

Baptized.

1779 Aug. 25 Main Swete the S. of Charles Walrond & Eliz. his wife.

1782 Mar. 20 Theodore the S. of Charles Wills Walrond and Elizabeth his wife.

Married.

1722 May 27 John Weir and Jane Waldrum. L.

Buried.

1774 Oct. 7 John Walrond.

1779 Sep. 2 Main Swete Walrond.

PARISH REGISTER OF ST. PHILIP.

Married.

1753 Dec. 29 William Symes & Elizth Walrond.

1782 July 17 Capt Thomas Flusher to Sarah L. Walrond, spinster.

Buried.

1726 Nov. 23 Mrs Elizabeth Waldron.

1738 Jan. 14 Charles Loyd s. of Theodore Walrond.

1738 Jan. 24 Catherine D. of Theodore Walrond.

1738 Feb. 23 Rowland S. of Theodore Walrond.

1741 Mar. 27 Mrs Amy Walrond.

1743 Jan. 16 Catherine D. of Theodore Walrond.

1750 June 12 Mr Theodore Walrond of St Philip's Parish. Buried in his own Plantation.

1753 Oct. 21 William Walrond.

1759 Oct. 27 Cath. Walrond, an Infant.

1762 Sep. 19 Baptized Mary Walrond & buried her the 31st.

1764 Jan. 3 Sarah Walrond.

1766 Oct. 14 Lyons Walrond.

1790 . . . . . . Mainswete Walrond, Fam. B.G.

PARISH REGISTER OF ST. PAUL.

Baptized.

1750 June 1 Theodore S. of Mr Main Sweet Waldron and Sarah his wife of St Philip's Parish, Willoughby Bay.

PARISH REGISTER OF ST. GEORGE, HANOVER SQUARE.

Married.

1797 Dec. 28 Joseph Lyons Walrond, Esqr, B., & Caroline Codrington, S. Licence. Ch. H. Codrington & Christn Codrington, witnesses.

1669, Sep. 22. Alexander Walrand, aged about 18, son of Henry Walrand, of the Barbadoes, Esq., & Mary Cornelius, Spr, about 12, dau. of James Cornelius, of ye Barbadoes, Merchant, both fathers consenting; alleged by Michael Hall, of Seething Lane, London, Grocer; at [*blank*]. [Not signed nor noted in the margin.] (Marriage Allegations: Vicar-General of the Archbishop of Canterbury.)

1698-9, Jan. 27. Edward Walrond, of St Dunstan in the West, London, Gent., Widr, & Mary Reeves, of Greenwich, Kent, Widow; at Greenwich afsd or [*blank*]. (*Ibid.*)

UPPER WALRONDS.

In a small walled enclosure surrounded by dense scrub, on a ledger over a stone tomb, the ledger being cracked across and a plant growing up through it:—

In Hopes of a Blefsed Refurrection
Here are deposited
The Remains of
MRS SARAH WALROND
The Beloved Wife
of
MAIN SWETE WALROND Efqr
Of this Ifland of ANTIGUA
Born Sepr 4th 1731
She departed this Life
Alas too Soon
In her 33d Year January 2d 1764.

(Six lines follow.)

CHRIST CHURCH, BARBADOS.

Arms: *Within a bordure compony . . . . three barrulets wavy; on an escutcheon of pretence . . . . three bulls' heads cabossed.*

Crest: *An elephant's head.*

HERE LIES THE BODY OF
THE HONBLE JAMES ELLIOT, ESQRE.
HE MARRIED ELIZABETH, DAU. OF THE HONBLE THOMAS WALROND,* ESQ. |
HE WAS SNATCHED AWAY FROM US
THE 14TH DAY OF MAY, ANNO DOM. 1724.
IN THE 24TH YEAR OF HIS AGE.

(Major Archer's 'M.I. in the West Indies.')

"Upper Walronds" of 222 acres and "Lower Walrond" of 154 acres are both in St. Philip's Parish. In 1852 they were owned by Bethel Walrond, Esq.

* Probably by Elizabeth who was his wife as stated by Thomas Spiar in 1687. In Burke's 'Landed Gentry' it is stated that this Colonel Thomas Walrond married Frances daughter of Sir Jonathan Atkins (Governor of Barbados, 1674—80), and had an only child Frances wife of William Adams.

Pedigree of Warner.

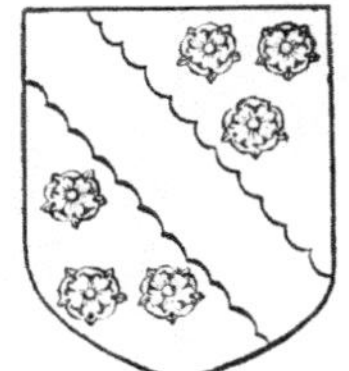

ARMS.—*Or, a bend engrailed between six roses, three and three, gules.*

This Pedigree has been drawn up from various ones in Davy's Suffolk Collections (Add. MS. 19,154), more especially from a seventeenth century one still in the possession of the Warners of Antigua and Trinidad. The earlier generations require further elucidation and proof.

JOHN WARNER of Great Waltham,* co. Essex. M.I. there: "Orate pro anima Johannis Warner Ar."=. . . .

John Warner of Warner's Hall in Great Waltham. M.I. there: "Hic jacet Johannes Warner quondam filius Johannis Warner Armigeri, qui obiit 9° Februarii 1439."=Jane, dau. of William Maldon and sister and sole heir of John Maldon.

. . . . 1st wife. s.p.s.=John Warner of "Warners," Esq., son and heir; æt. 18 at his father's death; died 13 Edward IV., 1473.=Elizabeth, dau. and heir of John Helyon. 2nd wife. (See the 'Visitations of Essex.')

John Warner, died s.p.

Edmund Warner, died s.p.

Henry Warner of "Warners," had the inheritance 20 Henry VII.; died 21 March 1504.=. . . .

Robert Warner, younger son, went into Suffolk.=Christian, dau. of George Seckford of Seckford, co. Suffolk, Esq.

John Warner of "Warners," 1st son and heir, æt. 19 in 1504; died 2 Sep. 1552.

Henry Warner of "Warners," heir to his brother John; æt. 10 in 1504; sold or gave away his lands; died s.p. 4 March 1556.

Two daus.

. . . . 1st wife.=Robert Warner of Wingfield, co. Suffolk, and Winfarthing, co. Norfolk, died 32 Henry VIII.; Inq. p.m.=Joan . . . . 2nd wife.

William Warner of Wingfield, 1st son and heir, æt. 30 in 33 Henry VIII., 1542.=. . . .

Robert Warner of Winfarthing; married.

Margaret Warner, ux. John Buxton of Tibenham, co. Norfolk; died 1572.

Anthony Warner of Stradbrook, Gent., younger son. Will dated 14 April and proved 25 May 1601 at Norwich. Inq. p.m. 43 Elizabeth.=Elizabeth . . . . s.p.m.

Alice, dau. of . . . . Spalding. 1st wife.=Robert Warner of Wingfield.=Christian, dau. of . . . . Powle. 2nd wife. (s.p. by 1st wife)

Robert Warner, died young, s.p.

William Warner of Framlingham.=Margaret, dau. of George Jernegan of Bilstede, son and heir of Sir John Jernegan of Somerleyton, Knt.

Francis Warner, son and heir.=Mary, dau. of . . . . Godfrey of Wingfield.

Robert Warner of Cratfield, died 1654, æt. 80. M.I. there.=Elizabeth, dau. of Alexander Courthope of Cranbrook, co. Kent. M.I. at Cratfield.

Sarah, dau. of Walter Snelling of Dorchester. 1st wife.=Sir Thomas Warner of St. Kitts, Coloniser of the Leeward Islands; knighted 4 Oct. 1629; patent as Governor 13 Sep. 1 Charles I.; died 10 March 1648. M.I. at St. Christopher's.=Rebecca, dau. of Thomas Payne of Surrey; living 1629. 2nd wife.=Ann . . . . 3rd wife. She mar. 2ndly Sir George Marsh or Marche of Limehouse, Knt. His will dated 27 March 1672; proved 9 Nov. 1676. (117 Bence.) Her will dated 16 July 1692; proved 27 Feb. 1693. (35 Box.)

Francis Warner, æt. 8 in 1612.

John Warner, æt. 2 in 1612.

Three daus.

Robert Warner, 1st son and heir, born 1611; died 1641; M.I. at Cratfield.

Francis Warner, Sheriff of London 1660.

Mary Warner, bur. 29 Dec. 1635 at Putney.

Edward Warner, Capt. in the Army; in 1628 Deputy-Governor of St. Christopher's; first Governor of Antigua; æt. 18 in 1629; died s.p. His wife and child were carried off by Caribs in 1640.

Sir Thomas Warner, admitted to Inner Temple 29 Jan. 1660; called to Bar 1666; knighted by Chas. II.; bur. 23 July 1679 at St. Michael, Barbados. Had two daus. Ann and Grace.=Grace, only dau. and heir of Gerard Fowke, Major-General in service of Charles I. and II.; remar. William Bean, son and heir of the Bishop of Landaff. Her will dated 18 Nov. 1700; proved 12 Nov. 1705. (232 Gee.) s.p.m.

* There was formerly an estate called "Warners" in Great Waltham which was held by Edmund Warner in 1360; it was sold by the family in 1536. A shield of Or, a bend engrailed between six roses, three and three, gules, for Warner, is carved on the roof of the south aisle of the Church. The Warners also held the Manor of Halstead before 1576.

Edward Warner, Citizen and Merchant Taylor of London. Will dated 13 June, proved 31 Oct. 1628 by Francis Warner the nephew. (87 Barrington.) To the poor children of Christ's Hospital £10. To the hospitals of Bridewell & Bethlehem each £50. For a dinner at my funeral £10. To the merch^t taylors £30 for a dinner, & to the clerk & beedle each £3. £30 for a supper to my friends. £6 10*s.* each to the widows in the almshouses of the merch^t taylors. To the same Company my 3 guilt silver wine boles, to be new gilded & my arms to be thereon engraven. £10 to the 5 following prisons, viz., the Counters in the Poultry, Woodstreete, Ludgate, Newgate, & the King's bench in Southwarke. To my cousin Francis Ashley of Graye's Inn, Gent., 40*s.* for a ring, & the like sum to Frances Ashley his mother. To Wm Wansey of London, bricklayer, 40*s.* To my good friend Isias Waller of London, grocer, living at the sign of the Green Dragon in Friday Str., £10. To my sister Ann Warner, late wife of my brother Edmund Warner, deceased, £10, & to my nephews his sons, viz., Henry, John, & Robt Warner, £100 each at 21. To another of his sons Edwd my godson £200 at 21. To my said brother's daus., viz., Ursula, Ann, Dorothie, & Mary Warner, £100 each at 21. To my brother Henry Warner £100, & to his wife 40*s.*, & to his son Francis £50 at 21, & to his dau. £50 at 21. To my brother-in-law Tho. Covell £10 & release him of debt of £6 13*s.* 1*d.* To Mary Savage, one of my late wife's sisters, £5, & to Sarah Hall, another one, £10. To John Okins my late apprentice £20. 40*s.* to each servant. To my cousin Robt Warner of Cratfield, co. Suffolk, £20, & to his wife 40*s.* To his brother Tho. Warner £20, & to Edwd Warner my godson, son of said Thos. Warner, £20 at 21, & to the dau. of the said Thos. Warner, who lives with my sister Covell in Suffolk, £10 at 21. To Mary Gurling, widow, late wife of my cosin Wm Gurling,* late of Graie's Inn, deceased, 40*s.* To Mrs Roberts, late widow of Edwd Roberts, deceased, 40*s.*, if she be dead then to her daus. To my loving friend Robt Graye £5 for a supper to my friends Mr Elnor, Mr Underhill, Mr Mildmay, etc. To my son-in-law Wm Lewis & Abigail his wife, the dau. of my late wife Marg^t Warner, deceased, £10 each if they give up all claim to benefit by her will. All residue to my nephew Francis Warner of the Inner Temple, Gent., son & heir of my late brother Edmund Warner, deceased, & appoint him sole Ex'or. A monument to be erected to my memory with my armes engraven thereon. To my sister Eliz. Covell, wife of Thos. Covell, £20 a year charged on my lands in Parham, Hacheston, Eson, & Framlingham, co. Suffolk, & £10 6*s.* a year for ever to buy bread to be distributed to 40 poor people, viz., 12 in Parham, 12 in Hacheston, & 16 in Framlingham.

By the codicil of 17 Oct. 1628 some additions were made to the various legacies.

* George Girling, son and heir of William Girling of Stradbrook Esq., deceased, entered Gray's Inn 21 Nov. 1627, and William Girling of Stradbroke, co. Suffolk, son of William Girling of Gray's Inn, deceased, on 11 Feb. 1632-3.

Elizabeth, dau. and heir of Robert Apleyard, Esq., of Framlingham. His will dated 10 Oct. 1558. 1st wife. = Francis Warner of Parham and Framlingham, Gent., born at Winfarthing; bur. 14 Jan. 1605 at Parham. Will dated 5 Jan. 3 James; proved 14 May 1606. (28 Stafford.) = Mary, dau. and coheir of Sir Edmund Rouse, Knt. 2nd wife.

Anne, ux. . . . . Norton. Her will dated 24 Oct. 4 James; proved 4 May 1607. (46 Hudleston.)

Edmund Warner, heir to his uncle Anthony 1601; died 20 Sep. 1617; bur. at Parham. = Anne, dau. of Robert Gosnold of Otley, Esq.; died 26 Sep. 1652; buried at Parham.

Edward Warner, 2nd son, Merchant Taylor of London; mar. twice, but died s.p.m. 28 Oct. 1628; bur. and M.I. at St. Andrew Undershaft. Will dated 13 June and proved 31 Oct. 1628. (87 Barrington.)

Henry Warner of Cransford, mar. and had issue.

Thomas Warner.

John Warner, bapt. 24 Aug. 1576 at Cratfield; died s.p.

Raynold Warner.

Ann Warner.

Margaret Warner.

Katherine Warner.

Elizabeth, dau. of Sir John Rous of Henham, Knt.; died 3 Nov. 1649; bur. at Parham. 1st wife. = Francis Warner, 1st son and heir, bapt. 12 May 1603; of the Inner Temple 1627; heir to his uncle Edward 1628; died 5 Sep. 1658; bur. at Parham. = Anne, dau. of Anthony Everard of Stow Park, Esq., and relict of Sir Thomas Pettus, Bart. 2nd wife.

s.p.

Edmund Warner, born 2 July 1610; entered Merchant Taylors' School 1618-19.

Henry Warner, bapt. 31 Aug. 1607; apprenticed 1627; bur. 10 April 1630 at Parham.

John Warner, bapt. 22 June 1609 at Parham; of St. Kitts 1629. Will dated 20 Jan. 1629; proved 10 Aug. 1630. (72 Scroope.)

Robert Warner.

Edward Warner, bapt. 19 Aug. 1612 at Parham; Physician to Car. II.

Ursula Warner, bapt. 19 Nov. 1601 at Parham.

Ann Warner, bapt. 4 Dec. 1610; bur. 25 May 1642 at Parham. Will dated 24 May and proved 28 June 1642 at Ipswich.

Dorothy Warner, bapt. 5 Feb. 1614.

Mary Warner, bapt. 22 July 1617.

Col. Philip Warner, Governor of Antigua 1672—75; died 23 Oct. and bur. 24 Oct. 1689 at St. Paul's. Left two sons and four daus. = Henrietta, sole dau. of Colonel Henry Ashton, Governor of Antigua, and sole heir 1667 to her brother Henry Ashton; bur. 31 Aug. 1697 at St. Paul's. Will dated 5 . . . . 1697; sworn 4 Oct. 1697.

Sir John Warner, Bart., born 14 and bapt. 24 May 1638 at Parham; created a Baronet 1660; a Jesuit 1665. = Trevor, dau. of Sir Thomas Hanmer of Hanmer, co. Flint; took the veil 1665; died 26 Jan. 1670.

s.p.m.

Francis Warner, bapt. 23 April 1643 at Parham.

Edmund Warner, bapt. 2 Oct. 1644; mar. and left issue; died 26 June 1696; bur. at Parham.

Gertrude Warner.

Henrietta Warner, mar. Colonel John Frye; she died 1703—13; he died 6 March 1747, æt. 78.

Thomas Warner. = Jane Walrond.

See PEDIGREE A, page 186.

Ann Warner, mar. William Barnes; he born Dec. 1656 and died 16 Nov. 1695, æt. 39; she bur. 13 Feb. 1745 at St. George's.

Frances Warner, mar. 21 March 1689, at St. Paul's, John Tempest: he was dead 1725; she was bur. 1 June 1733 at St. John's.

Grace Warner, mar. 21 March 1689, at St. Paul's, Colonel Henry Pearne; he died 1705 at Antigua; she living 1714.

Mary Warner, under age 1673; mar. Valentine Russell, Member of Council of Antigua, 1680. (? remar. Dr. Isaiah Burgeois, who died 1707.)

PEDIGREE A. (See page 185.)

Thomas Warner of the "Folly" and "Savannah" Plantations, bur. 11 Nov. 1695 at St. Paul's. Will dated 27 Sep. and sworn 19 Nov. 1695. 1st husband. = Jane, dau. of Henry Walrond, Chief Judge of Court of Common Pleas at Barbados, by Deborah his wife, and sister of Edward Walrond of Antigua, Esq. = Richard Lightfoot, Esq. 2nd husband.

Edward Warner, Colonel in the Army, Member of Council for Antigua, bur. 19 Feb. 1732 at Eltham, co. Kent. Will dated 27 Dec. and proved 21 Feb. 1732. = Elizabeth, dau. and heir of Richard Scott of Barbados, Esq.; died 13 Aug. 1723, æt. 37: bur. at Antigua. Arms: *Argent, three Catherine wheels sable* (SCOTT).

Ashton Warner, Attorney-General of Leeward Islands; entered at Gray's Inn 28 June 1716; died 11 Feb. 1752, æt. 61; bur. 12 Feb. 1752 at St. John's. Will dated 6 July 1750; sworn 13 Feb. 1752. = Elizabeth Ann, dau. of George Clarke of Clarke's Hill and widow of Major Samuel Byam; mar. 8 April 1714; died 2 June 1748, æt. 58; bur. 4 June 1748 and M.I. at St. John's.

Richard Scot Warner, died v.p.; bur. 2 Sep. 1729 at Eltham, co. Kent.

Grace Warner, born 13 Oct. 1717; mar. 1st Samuel Byam (he bur. 14 Jan. 1738 at St. George's); 2ndly, 24 May 1742, at Lee, co. Kent, William Fauquier; she died 31 May 1754.

Elizabeth Ann Warner, born 1718; mar. 1 Jan. 1739-40, at Lee, co. Kent, John Johnson, Esq., of Bloomsbury Square.

Jane Warner, born 11 Sep. 1720 at Christ Church, Barbados; mar. 2 Jan. 1738, at St. John's, Rev. Francis Byam; he died 1757; she died 1758.

Thomas Warner the elder, born Oct. 1716; entered Gray's Inn 17 April 1735; Attorney-General of the Leeward Islands 1758—79; Speaker 1769—77; died 2 and bur. 3 June 1779 at St. John's. = Elizabeth, dau. of Thomas Kerby; mar. 18 Feb. 1741 at St. George's, Hanover Square; died 15 Aug. 1763, æt. 40. M.I. at St. John's.

s.p.

William Warner of Dominica, 1st son and heir, dead 1833. = Mildred Johns, died 1 Nov. 1833, æt. 81, at Ralf House, Eltham.

Elizabeth, dau. of Richard Ottley of St. Vincent, Esq.; she was first-cousin to her husband; bapt. 20 May 1757 at St. John's, Antigua; died 29 April 1801 at Sea, co. Hants. 1st wife. = Joseph Warner, 2nd son, died 2 Sep. 1833, æt. 77; bur. at Wrington, co. Somerset. = Laura Elizabeth, dau. of Rev. Robert Hoadly Ashe, D.D.; mar. 11 May 1802 at St. Marylebone; died 28 May 1836 at Bath. 2nd wife.

See PEDIGREE B, page 188. See PEDIGREE C, below.

Joseph Thomas Warner, 1st son.

William Warner, 3rd son.

Ashton Warner, 4th son.

Edward Warner, 2nd son, Colonel in the Army; purchased estates in Trinidad; died 28 Aug. 1849. (See obituary in 'U.S. Mag.,' p. 477.) = Catherine Jane Mathew, 1st dau. and coheir of Major-Gen. Sir Charles Shipley, Knt., R.E., who carried out the fortifications at Antigua; died in London 4 Aug. 1863; mar. 1804.

Mary Pelham Warner, died an infant.

Eliza Hungerford Warner, died young.

Jane H. Warner.

Isabella Ann Carmichael, born 6 Feb. 1802; mar. 10 March 1829 at Worcester; died 29 March 1841 in London. M.I. at Gray's Inn Lane. 1st wife. = Charles William Warner, C.B., only son and heir, Barrister of Lincoln's Inn; Solicitor-General of Trinidad 1842; Attorney-General 1844—70; died there 1887, æt. 72. = Ellen Rose Garcia de Cadiz, mar. 26 Feb. 1848; now of 4 Neville Street, Onslow Gardens. 2nd wife.

Mary Warner.

Shipley Ashton Warner, born 11 Dec. 1830 at Trinidad.

Charles Edward Warner, born at Trinidad 8 Dec. and died 13 Dec. 1832.

Edward John Rudyerd Warner, born 3 Nov. 1838 at Trinidad; matriculated from St. John's College, Oxford, 3 Dec. 1856, æt. 18; of Middle Temple 23 Nov. 1859; Barrister 26 Jan. 1864; Advocate-General North-West Provinces India 1874—77; died in India. = ...

Charles William Pole Warner, born 13 March 1841 in London.

Isabella Jane Warner, born 20 April 1834 at Trinidad; mar. 10 Feb. 1859 Robert Farquhar Shaw-Stewart, 3rd son of Sir Michael Shaw-Stewart, Bart.

Margaret Frances Warner, born 3 April 1836 at Trinidad.

Robert Stewart Aucher Warner, born 9 May 1859.

Raymond John Richard Warner, born 19 July 1861.

Pelham Francis Warner, born 26 Oct. 1873.

Four daus.

Shipley Charles Warner, the present heir-general to Sir Thomas Warner, the founder and first Governor of the Leeward Isles.

Harold Warner.

Augusta Warner.

Mildred Buller Warner.

PEDIGREE C. (See above.)

Joseph Warner = Laura Elizabeth Ashe. 2nd wife.

Joseph Warner, born 12 July 1804.

John Warner, born 13 Sep. 1816.

Robert Edward Warner, born 11 Sep. 1806 at St. Vincent; died 29 Dec. 1858 at Dublin. = Margaret, dau. of Captain Bowie; died 1863.

William Kerby Warner, born 15 Oct. 1811. = Frederika Elizabeth, dau. of George Battye; mar. 3 Aug. 1841.

Laura Warner, born 10 June 1808; mar. 15 Sep. 1836 Fred. Angelo Bradburn of Chichester, and has issue.

Robert Edward Warner, born 7 Oct. 1852; died 1863.

Margaret Laura Sophia Warner, born 25 Dec. 1845.

Mary Warner, born 21 and died 31 Jan. 1847.

Agnes Emma Warner, born 21 Dec. 1850.

William Bannatyne Warner, born 8 Aug. 1842.

Ellen Morris Warner, born 29 July 1845.

Henry Warner, born 1693; Clerk of Assembly in 1724; died 17 and bur. 18 Sep. 1731, æt. 39, and M.I. at "Savannah" Estate. Will dated 26 Feb. 1729. = Phyllis Maria . . . . mar. before 1715; she mar. 2ndly Captain Francis Kirke before 1732; she living 1736. Thomas Smith, Esq., her Ex'or, 1763.

Philip Warner, bapt. at St. Paul's; living 1700.

Jane Johnson *alias* Ker, living 1732.

A

Joseph Warner, F.R.S. and M.R.C.S. from Guy's, of 35 Hatton Street, born 16 and bapt. 22 Dec. 1717: in 1786 settled "Clarke's Hill" on his first son William; owned the "Hatton Garden" Estate in Dominica; died 24 July 1801, æt. 83; bur. at St. Andrew's Ground, Gray's Inn Lane. M.I. = Elizabeth Sanders, born 1710; mar. 1735; died 16 March 1804, æt. 88. M.I. in Gray's Inn Lane.

Dr. Ashton Warner, President of Council, Antigua; born 10 Dec. 1721; owner of "Hornes" or "Belvidere;" practised in London: bur. 7 April 1789 at St. John's. Will dated 5 April 1789. = Rachel, dau. and coheir of John Pare, Esq.; heir to her aunt Mrs. Katherine Tanckes of Barbados. Will dated 26 May 1803; proved 20 Dec. 1805. s.p.

Philip Warner, born 23 June and died 24 Sep. 1723; bur. at St. John's.

B

Mary Warner, eldest child, died a spinster.

Thomas Warner.

Ashton Warner.

Anne Warner, mar. . . . . Hadley; died s.p. before 1786.

Elizabeth Warner, youngest dau., mar. at St. Andrew, Holborn, Robert Thornton of Muggerhanger, co. Beds; he was born 9 Jan. and bapt. 4 Feb. 1734 at Allhallows Stayning, and died 29 Nov. 1803, and bur. in Warner Vault in Gray's Inn Lane; she died s.p. sup. 9 Jan. 1817, æt. 63.

Ashton Warner, born 29 July and bapt. 20 Aug. 1750 at St. John's; died young in London.

Thomas Warner, born 12 Feb. and bapt. 17 Dec. 1753 at St. John's; of Bristol in 1800 and 1814; died 25 Dec. 1825 at Sevenoaks, co. Kent; bur. there. = Dorothy, dau. of Francis Frye, Esq.; bapt. 30 May 1770 at St. John's; mar. 12 Feb. 1790 at St. Mary's; died 30 April 1837, and bur. at St. Margaret's, Rochester.

C

Rebecca Dorothy Warner, born 31 Oct. 1790; bapt. 12 Feb. 1791 at St. George's; mar. 5 March 1816, at Clifton, Archibald Armstrong of Grenada; living 1837.

Elizabeth Grace Jane Warner, born 9 Sep. 1792; bapt. 21 Aug. 1793 at St. George's; bur. 3 March 1795 at St. John's.

Daniel Francis Warner,* born 9 June 1795; of Magdalen College, Oxon, matriculated 1 Nov. 1813, æt. 18; B.A. 1817; M.A. 1820; B.D. 1828; Master of Grammar School, Rochester; Vicar of Hoo St. Werbargh, Rochester, 1836, till his death 17 Nov. 1870. = Sylviana Maria, dau. of Robert Walter Vaughan of St. Stephen's, Bristol; born there 28 Aug. 1791; mar. 15 July 1818 at St. Pancras; died 4 Sep. 1864, æt. 73.

Thomas Warner, born 16 June 1819; died at sea 11 Oct. 1833.

Daniel Warner, born 4 Dec. 1828; bapt. at Rochester Cathedral.

Edward Warner, born 21 May 1831; bapt. at Rochester Cathedral; died 1832; bur. at St. Margaret's, Rochester.

Ashton Warner, born 21 July 1833; bapt. at St. Margaret's, Rochester; a Surgeon of Children's Hospital, London.

John Warner, born 11 Aug. 1836; bapt. at St. Margaret's, Rochester; died 7 Sep. 1836; bur. there.

Catherine Warner, born 27 Nov. and bapt. 7 Dec. 1820.

Maria Warner, born and bapt. 8 Aug. 1822.

Elizabeth Warner, born 24 Dec. 1824; bapt. at Meopham, co. Kent.

Jane Warner, born 15 Oct. 1826; died 1829; bur. at St. Margaret's, Rochester.

PEDIGREE D. (See page 188.)

Hannah Dove, dau. of Rev. Robert Hoadly Ashe, D.D.; mar. 19 May 1808; died 30 Oct. 1832. 1st wife. s.p. = Richard Warner, Captain 5th Foot, born 19 April 1782 at Hatton Garden, London; died 24 April 1863 at Snitterby. = Emma Bridget, dau. of Thomas Artemidious Russell of Cheshunt Park, co. Herts; born 3 March 1816; mar. 2 June 1834; died 16 March 1889. 2nd wife.

Anne Geraldine, only dau. of Marmaduke Jefferies of Hemel Hempstead, co. Herts; mar. 21 Jan. 1868; died 5 July 1871. 1st wife. = Ashton Cromwell Warner, born 11 Aug. and bapt. 18 Sep. 1835; died 29 Nov. 1879. = Florence Louise Piers, mar. 20 Nov. 1872. 2nd wife.

Rev. Richard Edward Warner, born 28 Nov. 1836; bapt. 6 Jan. 1837; Rector of Snitterby, Canon of Lincoln, Vicar of Gainsborough and Rural Dean. = Mary Jametta Hale, dau. of Major Constantine Yeoman; born 6 Sep. 1844; mar. 23 June 1864 at Sibson.

Wynyard Huddleston Warner, born 15 Sep. and bapt. 18 Oct. 1838; died 18 March 1883. = Jane Davidson, dau. of W. Bell. s.p.

Ashton Darell Cromwell Warner, born 30 Nov. 1868; died 2 Sep. 1871.

Lionel Ashton Piers Warner, born 30 April 1875.

Bridget Nora Cromwell Warner, born 1874.

Marjorie Ellin Warner, born 1877.

Esther Hastings Warner, born 11 July 1878.

Leonard Ottley Warner, born 7 March and bapt. 9 May 1867.

Basil Hale Warner, born 21 Jan. and bapt. 19 Feb. 1871.

Richard Cromwell Warner, born 16 and bapt. 30 March 1872.

Laurence Dundas Warner, born 3 and bapt. 17 Aug. 1873.

Wynyard Alexander Warner, born 2 and bapt. 18 May 1875.

Marmaduke Warner, born 9 and bapt. 19 Feb. 1878.

Constance Emma Cromwell Warner, born 27 Aug. and bapt. 24 Sep. 1865; mar. 5 April 1888 George Edward Weigall, Captain R.A.

Mary Chaloner Warner, born 25 Oct. and bapt. 30 Nov. 1868.

* He recorded the Family Pedigree at the College of Arms 8 Jan. 1838.

A

Daniel Warner, Treasurer, born 10 and bapt. 22 June 1724; killed on H.M.S. "Virgin" 25 March 1760. Will dated 21 Jan. 1759; proved 12 Aug. 1760. (412 Cæsar.) = Rebecca, dau. of Thomas Freeman, Esq.; born 30 Aug. 1726; mar. 2 Feb. 1746; died 13 June 1790.

Edward Warner of London, merchant, born 11 and bapt. 29 July 1725; Will dated 28 Feb. 1771, then of Austin Fryars, Esq.; proved 28 Feb. 1771. (152 Taverner.) = Catherine Johnson of Eltham, co. Kent; mar. 22 Sep. 1746 at Lee; living 1767. s.p.

William Warner, Member of Council and Treasurer, born 8 Nov. and bapt. 5 Dec. 1728; died 11 and bur. 12 Oct. 1771, æt. 43, at St. John's. Will dated 7 Dec. 1770. = Elizabeth, dau. of Stephen Blizard, Esq.; mar. 14 Feb. 1754 at St. George's; she mar. 2ndly, 2 Nov. 1775, at St. John's, Martin Byam, Esq. s.p.

B

Daniel Warner, born 20 Oct. 1754; bapt. 18 March 1755 at St. John's; bur. there 20 Nov. 1784, a bachelor.

Joseph Warner, born 15 Feb. 1756; bapt. 23 Nov. 1758 at St. John's; living 1788; died a bachelor.

Rebeccah Warner, born 1 and bapt. 22 July 1747 at St. John's; mar. there 5 Dec. 1775 John Gray; she died in Antigua. His will dated 1792.

Elizabeth Warner, born 8 Oct. 1748; mar. 18 March 1773, at St. John's, Dr. Jonas L. Blizard; he died 1794; she died May 1798.

Grace Warner, born 12 Nov. and bapt. 2 Dec. 1751 at St. John's; died 9 Nov. 1772.

C

Thomas Shirley Warner, born 24 May 1797 in Antigua; Clerk of the Council there 1831; Editor of the 'Antigua Herald' 1835; Stipendiary Magistrate of Montserrat; died in Trinidad. = Rebecca, dau. of Henry Hamilton of Montserrat, Esq.; mar. 9 May 1825.

Rev. Samuel Ashton Warner, born 30 May 1799 in Park Street, Bristol; bapt. there; Rector of St. George's in 1826. = Mary, only surviving dau. of Stephen Rose Willock of Antigua, Esq.; mar. 10 June 1824 at St. Mary's.

Hamilton Shirley Warner, born 27 May 1826 at Montserrat.

Samuel Gray Warner, born 1 June 1828 at Antigua.

Fergus Ashton Savage Warner, born 6 Nov. 1831; died 8 Sep. 1833.

William Ashton Warner, born 15 June 1838 at Antigua.

Gertrude Agnes Warner, born 29 Nov. 1833 at Antigua.

Henrietta Ann Warner, born 13 Dec. 1835.

Rebecca Grace Warner, born 10 Nov. 1840 at Montserrat.

PEDIGREE B. (See page 186.)

Joseph Warner* = Elizabeth Ottley. 1st wife.

Ashton Warner, Chief Justice of Trinidad, born 12 Aug. 1780; educated at Harrow; died 4 Sep. 1830. = Elizabeth Jane, 1st dau. of Dr. Ross of St. Vincent; mar. 1809.

Richard Warner. See Pedigree D, page 187.

Jane, dau. of J. Johnson, Chief Justice of Trinidad; mar. 1836; died at sea 14 June 1839, æt. 20; 1st wife. = Thornton Warner of the Colonial Civil Service, born 10 March 1812 at Trinidad; educated at Harrow. = Harriet Anne, dau. of Captain Span, late of the Indian Army; mar. 24 May 1845.

Henry Warner, born 23 Oct. 1813 at Trinidad; Barrister-at-Law; died 25 July 1843 at Jamaica. = Louisa Gumbs.

Frances Warner, born 1842.

Eliza Jane Warner, born 1843; mar. Col. Hawley and has issue.

Ashton Henry Warner, Colonel in the Army, born 10 Nov. 1838; now of Launceston, Tasmania. = ... dau. of Surgeon-Major Hastings; mar. 186–.

Lucie, dau. of E. Mathieu, Esq.; mar. 1871; died Sep. 1873. 1st wife. = Oliver William Warner, born 1 April 1846; now of Darjeeling, India. s.p. = Leila, dau. of Col. Justice; mar. 15 Dec. 1885. 2nd wife.

Thornton Harry Warner, born 13 Feb. 1853. = ... dau. of Colin M. Dick; mar. 1880.

Oliver Clive Warner, born 18 Sep. 1887.

Charles Thornton Warner, born 29 Aug. 1889.

Leila May Warner, born 14 Feb. 1891.

* Louisa, dau. of a Joseph Warner, married General Edward Buckley Wynyard, C.B. He was born 6 Sep. 1788 and died 24 Nov. 1864; she died 6 July 1870, æt. 77. ('Mis. Gen. et Her.,' vol. ii., New Series.)

John Warner. Will dated 20 Jan. 1629; proved 10 Aug. 1630 by Henry Warner the brother. (72 Scroope.) To be buried wher the R[t] Wor[ll] & my truly affectionate & loving cosin Sr Thomas Warner may think best. To my mother Mrs Anne Warner £10 for a ring. To my sister M[rs] Ursula Warner £15. To my loving brothers M[r] Edward Warner, M[r] Robert Warner, & my sisters M[rs] Anne Warner, M[rs] Dorothie Warner, & M[rs] Marie Warner £10 each. To my cosin My Lady Rebecca Warner a diamond ring. To my loving cosin Cap. Edward Warner £5. To my cosin M[rs] Mary Warner £5 & a picture case. To my cosin Sir Tho. Warner a diamond ring. My brother M[r] Henry Warner sole Ex'or & to receive all monies from S[t] Christopher's & England, & Sir Tho. Warner director & overseer of my servants in S[t] Christopher's. To my careful surgeon M[r] Luke Atkins 40 lbs. of tobacco. To M[r] Bolton, minister & preacher, the £5 he owes me, & to M[r] John Featly, minister, 30 lbs. of tobacco. Witnessed by Sir Thomas Warner, John Featley, minister, & Luke Atkins, chirurgeon.

Margaret Marchant, mar. 2 Feb. 1748 at St. Paul's. 1st wife. = Samuel Henry Warner, Deputy Provost-Marshal, born 11 and bapt. 27 Dec. 1733 at St. John's; died 13 and bur. there 11 Feb. 1779. = Ann Ash, mar. 20 Dec. 1755 at St. George's. 2nd wife.

Jane Warner, born 3 Jan. 1715; mar. Jonas Langford, Esq.; she died 26 July 1741; bur. at St. John's; he died 1758, æt. 50. M.I. at St. George the Martyr.

Barbara Warner, born 9 May 1720; mar. 30 Nov. 1738, at St. John's, William Dunbar of Machermore, Scotland, and of Antigua.

Ann Warner, born 3 and bapt. 29 Aug. 1726 at St. Paul's; mar. 13 May 1746, at St. John's, Hamilton Kerby, Esq.; he bur. 1767 at Eltham; she died 26 April 1804 at Castle Street, Southwark.

Elizabeth Warner, born 17 and bapt. 23 June 1735 at St. John's; mar. there 25 Oct. 1753 Richard Ottley of St. Vincent, Esq.; she died 28 Aug. 1766. M.I. at St. John's. He died 1775, æt. 45.

Ashton Warner, planter, bapt. 21 Feb. 1750 at St. Paul's. = Sarah, dau. of Anthony Brown, Esq.; mar. 5 Sep. 1776 at St. Philip's.

Sarah Warner, mar. 28 July 1773, at St. John's, Dr. John Dunbar. Her will dated 5 Aug. 1780; sworn 2 March 1787; her brother Ashton Warner Ex'or.

Samuel Warner, bapt. 26 April 1770 at St. John's; President of H.M. Council 1831—35; bur. 9 April 1838, æt. 70, at St. John's. = Ann Hurst, mar. 15 Nov. 1791 at St. John's.

John Warner, bapt. 16 July 1778 at St. John's.

Ashton Warner, bur. 30 Sep. 1779 at St. Philip's.

Charles James Warner, born 25 May and bapt. 13 July 1792 at St. John's.

Margaret Warner, bapt. 30 July (? 1785) at St. John's.

Agnes Warner, bapt. 5 April and bur. 21 April 1787 at St. John's.

Elizabeth Anna Warner, born 9 Nov. 1789; bapt. 23 Feb. 1790 at St. John's.

Joseph Wesston Warner, born 26 May 1825 and bapt. at St. George's, Antigua; died 28 Jan. 1833.

Thomas Warner, born and bapt. 11 Dec. (? Nov.) 1826 at St. John's.

Samuel Bott Warner, born 2 Feb. 1829 at Antigua; bur. 8 Dec. 1845 at St. John's.

Robert Holberton Warner, born 11 Dec. 1831 at Antigua.

Joseph Weston Warner, born 1 Nov. and bapt. 6 Dec. 1833 at St. John's; died 11 Jan. 1834.

Frances Mary Warner, born 12 Nov. 1836 at Paterson, New Jersey.

Georgiana Woodford Warner, born 10 Sep. 1819 in London; mar. 10 Sep. 1840 Anthony Clogstown of Trinidad.

Frederick Warner, of the Middle Temple 10 Oct. 1835; Barrister-at-Law 29 Jan. 1841; Member of Council and Solicitor-General of Trinidad; died 1890. = Jeanetta Maria, dau. of Rev. W. Ganthorpe of Antigua; mar. 20 June 1843 at St. Marylebone.

Richard Albert Warner, born 23 March 1817 at Trinidad; Rector of St. Patrick and St. David, Tobago; died 15 Dec. 1845, æt. 28, at Plymouth.

Reginald Richard Warner, born 15 Oct. 1850; a bachelor.

Henry Charles Warner, born 16 March 1854; a bachelor.

Catherine Eliza Warner, born 16 Nov. 1855; mar. 1885 H. Anson and has issue.

Emily Maud Warner, born 7 Jan. 1858; mar. 1878 Edmond Wilder and has issue.

Frederick Warner. = ... dan. of . . . . Grove.

Broderick Shipley Warner, born 9 Nov. 1847; Barrister-at-Law 186–; died 1881.

Alice Louisa Warner, born 7 Feb. 1846; mar. Rev. E. Murray and has issue.

Georgiana Frances Warner, born 9 March 1850; mar. N. Cox of Colonial Civil Service; s.p.

Jeanetta Warner, born 27 April 1857; dead.

Benjamin Warner, Citizen and Haberdasher of London. Will dated 2 Feb. and proved 8 March 1658. (148 Pell.) To be buried at St Michael, Cornhill. My wife Katherine & sons Thos. & John Warner. My brother Tho. Birkhead. Thos. Warner & Robt Warner & Eliz. Greene, sons and dau. of my 1st brother Thos. Warner, deceased. John Warner, 1st son of my y^st^ brother John Warner.

Francis Warner of Parham, co. Suffolk, Gent. Will dated 5 Nov. 1664; proved 4 Sep. 1667 by Edmund Warner. (121 Carr.) There is due to Mr Robt Carter of St Giles in the Fields, Gent., £800 on assigument of 2 mortgages of lands in Stradbrooke upon my purchase of them of my brother Sir John Warner. There is also due by me to Mathew Bedingfield of Bruxell, Esq., £1500 & £500. I give all my lands in Stradbrooke to Wm Brent of Graie's Inn, Esq., & to Robt Carter in trust to sell & pay off the above mortgages. To my niece Kath. Warner at 21, the 1st dau. of my brother Sir John Warner, all the household goods as named in the Inventory da. 2 Oct. last, also 1 silver stand with cup & cover & my ring sett with 3 great diamonds & 4 sparkes which was my father's, also 1 sett with little sparkes which was Sir Tho. Hanmer's 1st ladie's, her grandmother. To Susan Warner at 21, the youngest dau. of my brother Sir John Warner, the goods as named in the Inventory & a silver skillett & cover, a great preserveing spoone, a silver porringer & spoon, & a ring sett with 13 pearls & diamonds which was my mother's wedding ring, also a ring with a table diamond between 2 rubies which was my sister Eliz. Warner's. To my good friend M[r] John Savage a clock watch & ring with a rubie between 2 diamonds. To W[m] Brent & Rob[t] Carter £10 each. To each servant £5. To my brother Sir John Warner a picture case sett with diamonds & a ring with a table diamond, & appoint him sole Ex'or, giving him all residue. If he do not come over within 2½ years & settle in England, or if he shall release that power of revocation reserved to him by deed of 15 Oct. 1664, then my brother Edmund to be in his place. W[m] Brent & Rob[t] Carter to be overseers. Witnessed by Robert Pilworth.

John Warner of London, Haberdasher. Will dated 24 March 1672; proved 2 April 1673. (51 Pye.) To be buried at S[t] Michael, Cornhill. My mother M[rs] Kath. Newman, widow, Ex'trix. My brother Thos. Warner now in Barbados. My sister Kath. Gonge at 21 or marriage. My niece Eliz[th] Warner, dau. of my said brother Thos. Warner. My cousin Ester Bromeley. My uncle M[r] Geo. Burkett. My master M[r] John Martyn with whom I live. My mistress M[rs] Rhoda Martyn.

Captain Renatus Enys, late Provost-Marshall of Antigua, died intestate. In one will he gave his estate to Colonel W. Byam, deceased, and Lieut.-Colonel Nathaniel Clerke his Ex'or, and in another he gave all his estate to Mrs. Mary Warner. Adm'on to Lieut.-Colonel N. Clerke and Mrs. Mary Warner (she under age) 5 May 1673 by Governor P. Warner.

John Warner of Sudbury, co. Suffolk, Esq., 1678. (105 Reeve.) Brothers Samuel, Henry, dec[d], Edmund Warner, son Samuel, etc.

Thomas Warner of Antigua, Esq. Will dated 27 Sep. 1695. By Indenture da. 3 Dec. 1691 between myself & my mother M[rs] Henrietta Warner I covenanted to pay all debts of my deceased father Col. Philip Warner to the value of his chattels, & to pay to my sisters Ann Barnes, Frances Tempest, Grace Pearn, Gertrude & Henrietta Warner, & to (? my) youngest son Ashton 100,000 lbs. each, & 24,000 lbs. yearly to my 1st son Edw[d] during my mother's life, & I gave her a bond of £5000 st., & to each of my sisters bonds of 200,000 lbs., & by Indenture of same date I let my plantations of Cobb's Cross, Savanna, & Folly to Esay Burges, D[r] of Physick, Major Edw[d] Byam, M[r] Edward Walrond, & Cap[t] John Roe for 99 years in Trust that they should pay yearly to my wife Jane 40,000 lbs., & the rest to perform the said covenants, & after that the lease to cease. I confirm all the said articles & after all debts are paid ⅓ of all profits to my wife Jane. I give her 7 negros. To my son Ashton 50,000 lbs. at 17. To my son Henry £500 at 17 & ½ of the Folly plantation, but the profits which accrue during my partnership with Chas. Lloyd to go for my debts. To my y[st] son Philip £500. To any future child £500. My 1st son & heir Edw[d] to have £50 a year till 21. To His Excell[cy] the Gen[l] a ring. To M[r] John Pearce my Barbuda horse, a negro boy, & maintenance. All residue to my son Edw[d], he to be sole Ex'or. My good friends Chr. Codrington, Esq., Capt.-Gen[l], Edw[d] Byam, Esq., John Palmer, Esq., Edw[d] Walrond, Esq., & my wife Jane, overseers & Guardians. If Edw[d] die then Ashton to be Ex'or. Several goods have come to me from the late Thos. Knapp's estate to which I administered. Edw[d] Byam & my brother-in-law Henry Pearne, G[t], to be Ex'ors for Knapp's estate. My 2 briganteens. To my goddau. Eliz[th] Sergent £20 c. Witnessed by Charles Webb, James Brodie, William Rumbold, John Forster. Before Christopher Codrington, Captain-General, were sworn Captain John Forster, William Rumbold, and Charles Webb 19 Nov. 1695. Recorded 27 Nov. 1695.

Henriatta Warner. Will dated 5 . . . . 1697. Jane Pearne. My nephew M[r] Edward . . . Warner Ex'trix. Witnessed by Jane Warner, George Harrison, Charles Lloyd, John Butler. By Christopher Codrington, Esq., were sworn Charles Lloyd and John Butler 4 Oct. 1697. Recorded 5 Oct. 1697. (Fragment only.)

Isiah Burgeois* *alias* Burges, Doctor of Physic, of Antegoa in America, now in England in the parish of Shoreditch. Will dated 21 April, proved 31 July 1707 by Thomas Mathews. (158 Poley.) My good friend M[r] Nath[l] Gale to defray funeral. My well beloved wife Mary Burges that part of my estate the law allows her. My Ex'or may recall all agreements of sale I was persuaded to consent to, or that were made by my wife by virtue of letters of attorney given to her while I was publicly known to be "non compos mentis," viz., sales of land to M[r] Nath[l] Samson, M[r] Cain Osborn, dec[d], & M[r] Barry Tankard, which tend to the ruin of my poor children. My son-in-law Capt. Tho. Mathews, Com[r] of H.M.S. Dover, sole Ex'or, & to make such a dividend amongst my children as he shall think fit. My affairs in very great disorder. Witnessed by Samuel Laferty, Stephen Duport, William Fletcher, John Cheeke.

Edward Warner of Antigua, now of Eltham, co. Kent, Esq. Will dated 27 Dec., proved 21 Feb. 1732 by William Tryon, Edwin Somers, and Francis Kirke, Esquires. £50 c. to the poor of St. Paul's Parish, Falmouth, Antigua, & £20 c. for church ornaments. £10 to Christ Church Parish, Barbados. £20 c. to my cousin Olive Lurting. £50 c. to my cousin Mary Anne Burges of Antigua. £10 each to my cousin Eliz. Dunbar & her husband Chas. Dunbar of Antigua, Esq. £10 c. to my godson Malham Pryn. £10 to the poor of Eltham. To be bur. with my dear son in Eltham church. £300 c. to my dear brother Ashton Warner, & £100 c. to his wife Eliz., also £10 to his son my godson Thos. Warner. My gold watch & seals to my dau. Grace. £200 to my sister-in-law Phillis Kirke for her care of my children and 20 gs., also £100 to her husband Cap[t] Francis Kirke & £10. "I give to my said brother Ashton Warner one diamond ring in the shape of a heart, supposed to be that which was given by Queen Elizabeth to the Earl of Essex." To my aunt M[rs] Anne Barnes, £10 a year & 10 gs. to my unhappy sister Jane Johnson *al's* Ker. My aunt-in-law M[rs] Mary Walrond of Greenwich, deceased, did by will give to my 2 daus. Grace & Eliz. Anne a legacy, my wife also their mother, deceased, did upon her marriage with me make over her estate in Barbados, charged with the payment of £500 c. to each of our younger children, I therefore charge the payment of the same on my estates. £50 to M[rs] Mary Chantrell. £5 each to my servants. £40 for funeral. My coach, chariott, plate, furniture, & horses to be sold. All residue to my 3 daus. Grace, Eliz. Anne, & Jane & appoint them Ex'trices. If they die without issue then to my brother Ashton Warner. I appoint him & my good friends Francis Carlisle & Geo. Lucas of Antigua, merch[ts], Jonathan Blenman of Barbados, Esq., & Messrs. W[m] & Tho. Tryon & Edwin Somers of London, merch[ts], & Francis Kirke, Guardians & Overseers. Witnessed by John Hallewill, William Hart, T. Smith. Recorded also at St. John's, but the copy there is partially destroyed.

* Testator was a trustee 1695 to Thomas Warner. Buried at St. John's "1725, June 4, Mad[m] Mary Burges." She was probably a daughter of Governor Philip Warner. See Ashton Warner's Will.

1733, Nov. 13. Elizabeth Warner, late of Eltham, deceased. Adm'on granted to Edward Somers, Francis Kirke, and Thomas Tryon, guardians appointed for Grace Warner, Elizabeth Anne Warner, and Jane Warner, children of Elizabeth, Edward Warner the husband dying without taking on him execution, and commission 1733, Nov. 16, to them to administer till Richard Scot's will is sent to England.

Ashton Warner. Will dated 6 July 1750. If I die in Antigua to be buried in St John's church yard in the same tomb as my wife Eliz^th^, & on the stone these words to be placed: "And under this same stone lyes the body of the said Ashton Warner who died . . . . day . . . . In the year of our Lord . . . . In the . . . . year of his age." To my dear dau. Eliz^th^ I confirm the gift made to her of her mother's watch, chain, & large crystal seal with my arms, crest, & cypher cut on 3 sides of it, also all clothes & ornaments. To my dau. Eliz^th^ my best Bible (except the great Bible which was my late brother Edw^ds^), & all religious books called her mother's, my best bed & bedstead, 2 pavillions or muskiter curtains, etc., & 50 heavy pistoles worth 30s. *4d.* each, a riding horse & sadlery, my large old fluted silver cup & cover which was my brother Henry's, & maintenance while single at my dwelling house called Clarkes, & if molested there by the owner to have £50 c. a year & use of the N.W. upper green room. I particularly make these provisions because her dear mother on her death bed tenderly recommended her as the only dau. she could not see provided for. £1000 st. at her marriage & £60 a year till then . . . . If my son Saml Henry study the law then I give him all my law books. The diamond ring I have commonly called Queen Elizabeth's ring & my great bible shall go to my son Thos. & descend for ever to my heirs-at-law as heirlooms. To my cousin Oliver Surting who is in distressed circumstances, not her fault, £14 c. yearly during her widowhood, charged on Clarkes, & I hereby declare by Clarkes I mean, not only 110 acres which was my late wife's inheritance, but the residence & 100 acres I bought of Saml Byam, Esq., & the lands called Hunts, now in dispute between Edwd Otto Baijer & myself. To my son W^m^ my gold watch, chain, & gilt seal. My plantation called Clarkes & 3 negros I drew from there & put on Staughtons (but none of the slaves bought with Staughtons, nor any of the plantations lately bought called Nantons or Dimsdales), all my plantations, cattle to John Tomlinson, Stephen Blizard, & Row^ld^ Oliver in trust for my son Thos. & his heirs male . . . . to each such son of the said Ashton Warner for life in tail male, & failing heirs male of my 1st son to my 2^d^, & so on. To my cousin Mary Ann Burgess £100 c. in discharge of deed of purchase made to me by Admiral Thos. Mathew & M. A. Burgess of a plantation called Staughtons or Burgess's or Mathews, also called Clarks, with all sums I have agreed to pay annually to my son Thos. by any marriage articles to be made on his marriage with Eliz^th^ his now wife, formerly Eliz^th^ Kerby, & empower him to charge s^d^ estate with the further yearly sum of £50 for his wife, & any son who shall hereafter hold Clarkes may charge it with jointure of £120 st. a year. As my daus. Barbara & Anne are already provided for I give them only small legacies. To my sons Joseph, Ashton, Daniel, Edwd, W^m^, & Saml Henry each £1000 st., & to the latter at 21. To all my sons & daus., my sons' wives, & my daus.' husbands £20 c. for mourning & a guinea ring, & a like ring to Jonas Langford & all his children, to each of my Ex'ors & to Chas. Dunbar, his wife & children, & to each of my brother Edward's daus. & their husbands. To His Excell^cy^ Wm Mathew a ring of 20 gs. To my son Thos. all my firearms, swords, daggers, & bayonets, cartouch boxes, slings, etc. As I have £2000 lying in partnership between my son W^m^ & Mr John Bannister at 6 °/~o~ I will that after my death only 5 °/~o~ be charged. To my dau.-in-law Eliz^th^ wife of Thos. all hogs & feathered stock & 6 sheep. To my son Thos. all my salt provisions & food for whites & blacks, wine, beer, & cordials, all pictures, coaches, chaises, & gear, & 2 draught horses, all old rum, & rum put up to be old, & so long as a son of mine hold Clarkes he supply his brothers with old rum in Antigua as I have done, & put up a quantity yearly for this purpose. My Ex'ors to buy 6 spare mourning rings & to give 2 to Mr John Bannister & his lady. To John Tomlinson, Stephen Blizard, & Rowland Oliver all my lands in Barbados, the estate called Staughtons in Antigua, & all my lands called Nantons or Dimsdales with cattle & slaves, formerly the estate of Richd Nanton, afterwards of W^m^ (Furnell's ?), all lands in St Mary's parish, & all other lands except Clarkes, all ready money, furniture, & plate in Trust to sell & to pay debts & legacies & to divide any surplus among all my sons (except Thos.) & my dau. Betsy, but as I apprehend a deficiency then my son holding Clarkes to take only £150 st. yearly till legacies be paid. My said trustees & my son Thos. Ex'ors & Guardians of Saml Henry & Eliz^th^ till 21, & to get for my said dau. moneys due on a bond by Mr Jas. Barter at Antigua to Saml Greaves, assigned to Jonas Langford, & by him assigned in trust for her. Witnessed by John Haycock, Charles Broomhall, Jonathan Chandler.

Codicil dated 24 Jan. 1752. To my son Thos., now in G^t^ Britain, all slaves purchased from Geo. Crump, administrator of the will of John Osborne, dec^d^, but he to pay to my Ex'ors £1933 c. which I paid for them on 21 Aug. 1751. Witnessed by Charles Broomhal, Jonathan Chandler. Before John Tomlinson, Esq., was sworn Jonathan Chandler 13 Feb. 1752. Recorded 15 Feb. 1752.

Daniel Warner of Antigua, merchant. Will dated 21 Jan. 1759; proved 12 Aug. 1760 by William Warner, Esq.; power reserved to Thomas, Joseph, Ashton, Edward, and Samuel Warner the brothers and Rebecca Warner the widow. (412 Cæsar.) To my dear wife Rebecca £2500 c., my chaise & harness, furniture, & plate in lieu of dower. All residue to be sold. My brothers Thos., Joseph, Ashton, Edwd, W^m^, & Saml Warner & my wife Rebecca Ex'ors, giving them 25s. each. All my estate equally to my children Rebecca, Eliz., Grace, Thos., Daniel, & Joseph at 21. Witnessed by John Rose. On 10 April 1760 before his Excellency Governor George Thomas were sworn John and Stephen Rose of Antigua, Gentlemen. Recorded 15 April 1760 by Nathaniel Gilbert, Secretary, William Atkinson, Deputy-Secretary. Recorded also in the Registrar's Office, St. John's, 8 May 1760.

Edward Warner of Austin Fryars, Esq. Will dated 28 Feb. 1771; proved 9 April 1772 by Joseph Warner, Esq., the brother and Godshall Johnson, Esq., the nephew; power reserved to Thomas Warner, Ashton Warner, and Samuel Henry Warner, Esquires, the brothers. (152 Taverner.) To my wife Cath. Warner £1200 & all my plate, furniture, jewels. To my brother Joseph Warner my gold watch & seals except the one on which my arms are quartered. To my friend Capt. Pyne £20. To my clerk Chas. Jones £10. To each of my servants £5. All residue to my brothers Tho., Joseph, Ashton, W^m^, & Saml Henry Warner, & my nephew Godshall Johnson in trust for my wife for her life, then to be divided into 3 portions. $\frac{1}{3}$ to my brother Joseph Warner, $\frac{1}{3}$ to the children of my brother Daniel Warner, deceased, $\frac{1}{3}$ to my nephew Ashton Warner, son of my brother Saml Henry Warner, at 21. My house in St John's town to be sold. My trustees to be Ex'ors, & give them each a guinea ring. Witnessed by Joseph Pickering, John Henckell, William Phelps.

1st Codicil dated 6 June 1771. Late of Austin Fryars, now of Hampstead. To my brother Joseph Warner my coach horses & a pipe of Madeira wine, now in the possession of my brother Wm Warner. I trust some friend of mine & my brother Saml Henry Warner will take care of little Ashton Warner his son. To my wife all my liquors as well as those at Mr Knowlys, cooper in Harp Lane. To my servants John & Thos. my old cloaths, & my fine linen to my brother Joseph. To my good friend Wm Gunthorpe, Esq., my blue snuffbox. My 2 swords & case of screw barrel pistols, goldheaded cane, & goldheaded bow stick to my brother Joseph. A mourning ring to Mr Ditcher, surgeon at Bath. Witnessed by Joseph Pickering, Bridgett Melsh.

2nd Codicil dated 14 Dec. 1771. My brother Wm Warner has dyed in Antigua & by his will dated 7 Dec. 1770, subject to certain contingencies, gave all the residue of his estate equally to his 5 brothers. I give my ⅕ share to my 2 brothers Joseph Warner of Hatton Street, surgeon, & Saml Henry Warner of Antigua. Witnessed by Joseph Pickering, William Phelps, Samuel Mander.

Dr. Ashton Warner. Will dated 5 April 1789. To my wife Rachel all jewels & plate left her by her aunt Kath. Tunkes & a silver epergne given her by Mrs Ann Athill & use of my plate in England for life. I give her also my gold watch by Ellicot which was her father's. To Mr Jas. Masset, son of Mary Ann Masset, widow, all my printed books (except medical ones & my father-in-law's family bible which latter I give my wife). To Mrs Mary Ann Masset absolutely all plate in Antigua, all furniture, linen, china, glass, & earthen ware called Wedgwood or Queen's ware, my best 2 wheeled chaise or whisky & 2 horses, all liquors in my house at St John's & on my estate called Belvidere except the rum reserved for the use of the estate, also after my wife's death all plate in England. Whereas by Indenture between my wife, myself, & my late brother Thos. Warner, dated 22 March 1774, I am empowered during her life to charge ⅙ of the plantation & slaves in Old North Sound Div^n & also a plantation I purchased of the late Valentine Morris Horne, Esq., called Hornes, but now Belvidere in St John's parish, with £2000 I do so charge the same & give it to Mrs Mary Ann Masset. Whereas an estate called Waterford devised to my wife by her aunt Mrs Kath. Tunkes is indebted to me I give all such sums to Mrs M. A. Massett, also all my lands in St John's Town. To Hon. Jas. Nibbs & Philip Hicks, Esq., barrister, all my plantations & slaves in Antigua & Barbados in Trust to sell & pay to my sister Eliz^th Dunbar, widow, £100 st. yearly, the interest of remainder to Mrs Massett. I do not wish Belvidere to be sold, but give it to Mrs Massett for life & after her death to my nephew Tho. Norbury Kerby, Esq., Jas. Nibbs, Philip Hicks, Tho. N. Kerby, & Mrs M. A. Massett, Ex'ors. Witnessed by Thomas H. Halloran, Henry Loving. Before Edward Byam, Esq., were sworn Thomas Turner Wise, Barrister, and Thomas Hanson Halloran 11 April 1789.

Codicil dated 5 April 1789. Whereas I directed Messrs. Tho. Daniel & son of Bristol to purchase a lottery ticket I give this to Mrs Massett. Witnessed by Thomas H. Halloran and Thomas Turner Wise.

Rachel Warner, widow of Hon. Ashton Warner, late of Antigua, Esq. Will dated 26 May 1803. To my dear nephew Rowland Otto-Baijer, Esq., & my niece Kath. Edwards all my plantation called Waterford in Barbados equally. To my s^d nephew ½ of my moiety of Pares estate in Old North Sound, Antigua, charged with £500 a year to my great-nephew Saml Otto-Baijer & with £2500 to my great-niece Rachel Pare Edwards for life, then to my great-nephew Saml Otto-Bayer & in default of issue to Rachel P. Edwards. To Kath. Edwards the other ½ of my moiety for life, then to her children Bryan Edwards, Eliza Edwards, Rachel Pare Edwards, Kath. Edwards, & Frances Edwards. To my great-niece Rachel Pare Edwards £5000 at 21. To Saml Otto Bayer £500 a year. To my nephews Rowl^d Otto Bayer, Saml Otto Bayer, & to Tho. Rogers, Esq., of Antigua, manager of Pares, my plantation called Belvidere in St John's div^n & parish on Trust to pay the following legacies, viz., to Mrs Barbara Dunbar, sister of my late husband Dr Warner, £100 a year. To Henry Fowke of Hawkesbury, co. Gloster, Esq., £1000. To my nephew Rowl^d Otto-Baijer £500. To my niece Kath. Edwards £500. To my great-nephew Bryan Edwards £2000. To my great-nieces Eliza Edwards, Kath. Edwards, & Frances Edwards £100. To Jane Charlotte Fowke, wife of Henry Fowke, £100. To Mrs Barbara Kennedy £600. To her sister Mrs Mary Walrond £200. To Mrs Mary Pringle £100. To Miss Wilhelmina Pringle, her dau., £50. To Mrs Sarah Fouks of Barbados £300. To my goddau. Anne Rachel Fowke £500. To Mrs Cath. Wilkinson £200, if she be dead to her dau. Rachel London. To Miss Wilgress, dau. of Rev. Dr Wilgress of Eltham, co. Kent, £200. To Mrs Barbara Grey, relict of John Grey, Esq., £200. To Miss Mary Pickering £200, & then the said plantation to my godson Ashton Warner, Junr, son of Wm Warner, Esq., dec^d, if he die without heirs then to his brother Joseph Thos. Warner. A marble monument with epitaph to be placed over the grave of my brother in the burial ground at Cochran's estate & £200 for it. To my niece Kath. Edwards my diamond ear rings, gold watch, a locket set with my brother & sister's hair, set of pearls, diamond picture bracelets of my sister & nephew, 4 diamond rings, etc. To my niece Eliza Edwards my grand piano. To my niece Rachel Edwards my harpsichord. To Rachel P. Edwards my gold watch & seals & bible. To my great-niece Kath. 3 pair of pearl ear rings & necklace. All plate to Saml Otto Baijer & Kath. Edwards. To Mrs Fowke a miniature of her dau. set with pearls. To Saml Otto Baijer a portrait of myself & another to Kath. Edwards. To my great-nephew Rowl^d P. Edwards the miniature of my great-nephew Saml Otto-Baijer, a wheatsheaf on brilliants, & diamond ear rings. All residue of jewels to the daus. of my niece Kath. Edwards. All residue to my nephew Rowl^d Otto-Baijer & my niece Kath. Edwards. Rowl^d Otto Baijer, Saml Otto-Baijer, Kath. Edwards, & Thos. Rogers, Ex'ors. Witnessed by John Townly, Devonshire Place, Barbara Stanley, Jane Edge, Inner Temple.

Codicil dated 29 Nov. 1805. One year's wages to my servants. Witnessed by James Edge. On 29 Nov. 1805 appeared Edward Fishwick of Lyon's Inn, Gent. Testatrix was of Devonshire Place. Sworn under £1500.

On 20 Dec. 1805 adm'on to Samuel Otto-Baijer, Esq., the great-nephew, one of the surviving Ex'ors; power reserved to Kath. Edwards, widow, the niece, & Thomas Rogers. Recorded 17 July 1807.

Close Roll, 11 Geo. III., Part 7, Nos. 6 and 7.

Indenture made 22nd March 1771 between William Fauquier of Stratton Street, Piccadilly, Esq., and Thomas Fauquier of the Horse Guards, Esq. (the only son of William Fauquier and Grace Fauquier his late wife, deceased), of the one part, and Joseph Pickering of Great Queen Street, Lincoln's Inn Fields, Gentleman, of the other part, witnesseth that in consideration of 5s. William and Thomas Fauquier grant to Joseph Pickering all that their one-third of two plantations, both lying in the parish of Falmouth, Antigua, *i.e.* the Folly containing 109 acres, bounded N. with William Young, E. with William Young and Main Sweet, Esq., and Edward Chester, Esq., formerly Barry Tankerd, Esq., and James Barter, S. with Sir William Codrington, deceased, and Francis Goss, W. with John Sawcolt and John Barton, deceased, now or late William Yeamans, Esq., and that other plantation called the Savannah (including the houses and lands called Cobb's Cross), containing 900 acres, bounded N. by the lands called Monks, now or late in the possession of Dr. Stephen Lavington, Archibald Cockran, deceased, Robert Christian, Esq., Edward Sutton, deceased, John Ince, merchant, and the sea in Willoughby Bay Harbour, E. with the lands of Benjamin Merchant which he formerly purchased out of the Savannah and the sea, S. with the lands of —— Stephenson, formerly purchased out of the Savannah, the sea in Indian Creek, several parcels of country or ten acre land, and the land heretofore given to His Majesty for the use of H.M.'s ships in English Harbour, and to the W. with part of English Harbour, the lands heretofore of Henry Blizard, deceased, Falmouth Harbour, Falmouth Town land, the land formerly of Main Sweet, deceased, late in the possession of Dr. Joseph Buckshorne, and land formerly Monks, now or late of Dr. Stephen Lavington, and all messuages and negros for one whole year yielding and the rent of one peppercorn that he may be in actual possession, etc. Tobias Pickering, Samuel Mander, witnesses.

No. 6.

Indenture tripartite made 23rd March 1771 between William Fauquier, of the 1st part, Thomas Fauquier, of the 2nd part, and Joseph Pickering, of the 3rd part, witnesseth that to the intent of barring all estates tail and reversions, and that Joseph Pickering may be able to reconvey the said plantations, William and Thomas Fauquier grant (as in previous Indenture) to the use of William Fauquier for life, and at his death to Thomas Fauquier and his heirs for ever, and they appoint Thomas Warner and William Warner, Esquires, both now residing in Antigua, their Attorneys.

Close Roll, 21 Geo. III., Part 2, Nos. 12 and 13.

Indenture made 27th April 1781 between the Hon. Ashton Warner of Antigua, Esq., but now residing in Barbados, and Rachel Warner his wife (niece of Katharine Tunckes, late of St. Michael's Parish, Barbados, widow, deceased), of the one part, and Joseph Pickering of Great Queen Street, near Lincoln's Inn Fields, Gentleman, of the other part, witnesseth that in consideration of 5s. Ashton and Rachel Warner grant, etc., to Joseph Pickering that plantation in the parish of St. Michael, Barbados, called Waterford Forestall and Tuckers, containing 319 acres, 2 roods, and 19 perches, butting on the lands now or late of Isaac Dopiza (?), on lands belonging to the parish of St. Michael, on lands now or late of Francis Ford, on the plantation called Turtons of which Katharine Tunckes died possessed, on lands now or late of John Robinson, on lands now or late of Edmund Dayrell, on the Belle Plantation, on lands now or late of William Robinson and of Samuel Carter and of Henry Peers, together with the mansion or dwelling-house and kitchen and buttery, windmill, watermill, and also 3 horses and 27 bulls, 15 oxen, 8 cows, 1 bull calf, and 1 cow calf, and all negro or other slaves (names given), about 180 men, women, and children, all which premises were in the occupation of Katharine Tunckes at the time of her decease, and now are in that of Ashton Warner, and became and are now vested in Rachel Warner in fee tail by virtue of the last will of Katharine Tunckes her late aunt deceased, to have and to hold for one whole year, paying therefore one peppercorn, etc., that Joseph Pickering may be in actual possession and thereby enabled to take and accept a grant and release of the reversion and inheritance thereof to the use of Joseph Pickering and his heirs for ever. Ashton Warner's name set and subscribed to the Indenture by Joseph Warner, Esq., the younger, by virtue of a Letter of Attorney dated Jan. 23rd last past.

No. 12.

Indenture made 28th April 1781 between the Hon. Ashton Warner, Rachel Warner his wife, of the one part, and Joseph Pickering, of the other part, witnesseth that for destroying and barring all estates tail and all remainders and reversions, and in consideration of 10s., Ashton and Rachel Warner grant to Joseph Pickering all those plantations (as in previous Indenture) that Joseph Pickering may be enabled to convey and settle, etc., them to such persons as Ashton and Rachel Warner shall appoint, and failing such direction in trust to the use of Rachel Warner and her heirs for ever.

Close Roll, 26 Geo. III., Part 21, Nos. 4 and 5.

Indenture made the 28th Nov. 1786 between Joseph Warner the elder of Hatton Street, Esq., of the one part, and Joseph Pickering the elder of Great Queen Street, Lincoln's Inn Fields, Esq., of the other part, witnesses that in consideration of 5s. Joseph Warner grants, etc., to Joseph Pickering all that plantation in Antigua called Clarkes or Clarke's Hill and the dwelling-house, and all slaves and cattle, as by schedule annexed, which were heretofore the estate of Ashton Warner, late of Antigua, Esq., deceased (father of Joseph), and all that parcel of ground adjoining the plantation containing 60 acres, which was some years ago purchased by Thomas Warner, late of Antigua, Esq., deceased (brother of Joseph), of John Hart, Esq., deceased, to have and to hold to Joseph Pickering for one whole year to the uses of an Indenture to bear date the day after these presents.

On Clarke's Hill Plantation—Negros (names given) 28, 29 cows, 13 oxen, 17 heifers, 7 young bulls, 6 bull calves, 7 cow calves, 5 steers, and 2 pasture bulls. Belonging to Clarke's Hill Plantation but removed and now on Hatton Garden Plantation, Dominica—Negros (names given) 96, cattle (names given), 10 oxen, 4 cows, and 4 calves.

No. 4.

Indenture made the 29th Nov. 1786 between Joseph Warner the elder and Elizabeth Warner his wife, of the 1st part, William Warner, late of Dominica, now residing in Devonshire Street, near Queen Square (eldest son and heir apparent of Joseph Warner the elder), of the 2nd part, Joseph Warner the younger of Hatton Street, Esq. (youngest son of Joseph Warner the elder), of the 3rd part, Elizabeth Thornton (wife of Edward (? Robert) Thornton of Hatton Street, Esq., only daughter now living of Joseph Warner the elder), of the 4th part, Joseph Pickering the elder, etc., of the 5th part, William Fauquier of Stratton Street, near Piccadilly, Esq., and Justinian Casamayor of Bond Court, near Walbrook, Esq., of the 6th part, Edward David Batson of Hatton Street, Esq., Tobias Pickering of New London Street, near the Tottenham Court Road, Gentleman, of the 7th part, and Richard Jones of East Wycombe, co. Kent, Esq., and the Rev. Joseph Pickering the younger of Fig Tree Court, Inner Temple, Clerk, of the 8th part. Whereas Joseph Warner the elder is entitled in possession to the freehold of the plantation, etc. (as in previous Indenture), for life, with power to charge it with the yearly sum of £120 as a provision for his now wife for life, and with the sum of £2000 for his younger children, and subject thereto William Warner his eldest son is entitled to an estate in remainder in fee tail (on the decease of Joseph) for his life; and whereas William Warner is indebted to his father in the sum of £1753 sterling. Now this Indenture witnesses that in consideration of the natural love and affection, etc., and also for docking and barring all estates tail and remainders, etc., and in consideration of 10s., Joseph Warner the elder and William Warner his eldest son grant to Joseph Pickering the elder all that Clarkes or Clarke's Hill Plantation to have and to hold to Joseph Pickering that he may be seised thereof in fee simple, and enabled to convey it to William

Fauquier and Justinian Casamayor to the uses and trusts following, to pay to Joseph Warner for life £1000 sterling a year free from all taxes, and subject to that in trust for 200 years for William Warner and Joseph Warner the younger as tenants in common and not joint tenants during the life of Joseph Warner the elder, and after his death to pay to Elizabeth Warner £120 a year for life, and immediately after the death of Joseph and Elizabeth Warner, if Elizabeth Thornton be then living, in further trust to Justinian Casamayor to receive during her life £60 a year for her sole and separate use, and on the determination of that estate, and immediately after the death of Joseph Warner the elder, to the use of Joseph Warner the younger for 500 years, subject to a provision for redemption on payment to him of £1000 within six months of the decease of Joseph Warner the elder with interest at 6 per cent., and subject to the said term to the use of Edward David Batson and Tobias Pickering for 1000 years in trust if Elizabeth Thornton be living and shall have a child or children that shall live to attain to 21, being sons or daughters, to raise £1000 to pay to such children in such proportions as Elizabeth Thornton shall appoint, and if at the decease of Elizabeth Thornton she has a daughter or daughters under 21 to raise money for the maintenance of such child or children not exceeding the interest of their portions, and on the determination of that term, etc., to the use of Richard Jones and Joseph Pickering the younger for 2000 years, to be void on the payment to Joseph Warner the elder and his Ex'ors of the sum of £1753 on the 29th Nov. 1787, and on the determination of that estate to the use of William Warner and his heirs for ever, and Joseph Warner, William Warner, and Joseph Pickering appoint Langford Lovell, Esq., and Thomas Warner, Esq., both of Antigua, their Attorneys.

Close Roll, 27 Geo. III., Part 2, No. 13.

Indenture of three parts made the 28th Feb. 1787 between Ashton Warner, late of Antigua, but now residing in Percy Street, Middlesex, Doctor of Physic, of the 1st part, Thomas Dunn of Lincoln's Inn, Gentleman, of the 2nd part, and Justinian Casamaijor of London, merchant, of the 3rd part. Whereas by Indentures made the 15th and 16th March 1754 between Ashton Warner and Rachel his wife, of the one part, and Thomas Warner, Esq., of the other part, duly recorded in Antigua, one undivided 3rd part of all that plantation in the division of Old North Sound in Antigua, which was late the estate of Rachel Pare, mother of Rachel Warner, containing 153 acres, and butted and bounded as therein described, stands limited in trust to Thomas Warner to preserve the contingent remainders from being destroyed to the use of Ashton Warner for life, with remainder to Rachel Warner for life, with remainder to the first and other of their sons in tail general, with remainders to their daughters as tenants in common, and for default to the right heirs of the survivor of Ashton Warner or Rachel; and whereas by Indentures made the 1st and 2nd May 1771 between Ashton Warner and Rachel his wife, of the one part, and Thomas Warner, of the other part, duly recorded, etc., after reciting the said Indentures, and that Mary Faibie, a sister of Rachel Warner, was dead without issue, so that one undivided 3rd part of the said plantation had descended to Rachel Warner and Elizabeth Otto (*sic*) as her sisters and heirs-at-law, and that Ashton Warner and Rachel his wife were desirous of settling, etc., the said 6th part to the uses thereinafter mentioned, it was by the release witnessed that for the considerations therein mentioned Ashton Warner and Rachel his wife did grant, etc., to Thomas Warner their one undivided 6th part in trust during their joint lives, and to the heirs and assigns of the survivor, but subject to the provisoes and agreements thereinafter mentioned, and it was further witnessed that for the considerations expressed Ashton Warner and Rachel did grant, etc., to Thomas Warner all that plantation of Ashton Warner lately purchased from Valentine Morris Horne, late of Antigua, but then of Grenada, Esq., in the division and parish of St. John, containing 247 acres, 3 roods, and 30 perches, butted and bounded as therein and hereinafter mentioned, and also the dwelling-house and all negros, slaves, cattle, and other things comprised in a schedule thereunto annexed, in trust as before and subject as before, and if Ashton Warner died first he might charge the 6th part so descended to Rachel and the said plantation purchased of Valentine Morris Horne or one of them with £2000 sterling to be paid as he should direct, and in the said Indentures was also a power of revocation: and whereas by Indentures made the 13th and 14th March 1774 between Ashton Warner and Rachel his wife, of the one part, and Justinian Casamaijor, of the other part, duly recorded, etc., it was witnessed that in consideration of £2352 18*s.* 10*d.* sterling Ashton Warner and Rachel did grant to Justinian Casamayor all that plantation lately purchased of Valentine Morris Horne and the slaves, etc., thereon, with provisoe of redemption by Ashton Warner or Rachel Warner; and whereas by other Indentures made the 21st and 22nd March 1774 between Ashton Warner and Rachel his wife, of the one part, and Thomas Warner, of the other part, duly recorded, etc., reciting the Indentures of the 15th and 16th March 1754, it was witnessed that for the considerations therein mentioned Ashton Warner and Rachel did grant to Thomas Warner the undivided 6th part and the plantation purchased from Valentine Morris Horne in trust for their joint lives and to the heirs of the survivor, subject to the provisoes and agreements, and in the said Indenture of release now in recital it is declared that Ashton Warner may charge the said 6th part and the said plantation with £2000 to be paid after his death if he should die before Rachel as he shall appoint; and whereas by Indentures made the 29th and 30th July 1784 between Justinian Casamaijor, of the one part, and the Rev. Daniel Debat, since deceased, John Casamaijor, Esq., Charles de Laet, Esq., and Thomas Dunn, Gentleman, of the other part, after reciting the said Indentures of mortgage for securing the £2352 18*s.* 10*d.*, it is witnessed that Justinian Casamayor did grant to Daniel Debat, John Casamayor, Charles de Laet, and Thomas Dunn the said plantation, etc., subject to redemption on payment of the money to them; and whereas the sum owing to John Casamaijor, Charles de Laet, and Thomas Dunn is still due, but all interest has been paid to the 26th April last past; and whereas Katharine Tunkes, late of the parish of St. Michael, Barbados, widow, made her will the 21st Nov. 1777 and ordered all her debts and legacies (except the legacy to Henry Fowke, jun., her grandnephew which would be otherwise appointed), to be paid from the ready money in her possession at death, but if insufficient from the profits of the plantation whereon she then lived called Waterford, Forestalles, or Tunkes's, and for those purposes she left in particular £1000 ready money, and she gave her plantation called Waterford together with the sugar works, cattle, horses, stock, and negro and mulatto slaves to Rachel Warner her niece for life and to the heirs of her body, subject to such debts as should remain unpaid and subject to the payment of the annuities therein mentioned, and among other legacies she gave to each of the children of Elizabeth Otto Baijer her niece as should be living £1000 currency, and to the heirs of their bodies for ever, and she gave to Anne Catharine Hothersall her great niece at 18 or marriage £500 currency, and if she died before gave it to Hester Hothersall her mother, and she gave to Ashton Warner £1000 currency, and appointed Edward Pare her nephew, Ashton Warner, Henry Fowke, Jonas Maynard, Henry Frere, and Thomas Hothersall, Esquires, her Ex'ors;

and whereas Katharine Tunkes soon after departed this life, and Ashton Warner alone proved the will in Barbados and took on him execution; and whereas by Indentures made the 27th and 28th April 1781 between Ashton Warner and Rachel his wife, of the one part, and Joseph Pickering, Gentleman, of the other part, and by other Indentures of of the 3rd and 4th May in the same year the release tripartite between Joseph Pickering, of the 1st part, Ashton Warner and Rachel his wife, of the 2nd part, and Justinian Casamaijor, of the 3rd part, all duly executed in Barbados as by the law is required for docking and destroying estates tail, the said plantation of Waterford or Forestalls or Tunkes's containing 319 acres 2 roods and 19 perches and all negros thereon were conveyed to Joseph Pickering in trust to the use of Ashton Warner for life, and after his death as Rachel Warner should appoint, and in default of her appointment to her heirs and assigns for ever; and whereas Ashton Warner hath applied the ready money in payment of testatrix's debts and legacies so far as it would extend, but there was not sufficient to pay all legacies and he has out of his own money paid to Rowland Otto-Baijer, Esq. (as one of the children of Elizabeth Otto Bayer) £1000 currency, and to Anne Catharine Hothersall (now Mrs. Harris) £500, and several small legacies, and therefore he is a creditor for those sums charged on the hereditaments and is also entitled to have raised from the premises £1000 currency his legacy; and whereas Ashton Warner has for some time past and now is indebted to Justinian Casamayor in the sum of £10,826 sterling, for which Justinian Casamayor has no security except a bond in the penal sum of £20,000, executed several years ago for securing £10,000 part of the said sum, and a warrant of attorney to confess and enter judgment on the bond; and whereas Ashton Warner hath agreed to give Justinian Casamaijor such further security as is hereinafter mentioned. Now this Indenture witnesseth that in pursuance and part performance of the agreement, and in consideration of £10,826 so owing, and for the better securing the payment, and in consideration of 10*s.*, Ashton Warner at the request and nomination of Justinian Casamayor grants to Thomas Dunn all those sums of £1000 and £500 bequeathed to Rowland Otto-Baijer and Anne Catherine Hothersall (now Mrs. Harris) and the interest due, and all other sums bequeathed by the said will which he has paid, and also all that sum of £1000 bequeathed to him Ashton Warner in trust, and further witnesseth that in pursuance and in consideration of 10*s.* at the request of Justinian Casamayor, Ashton Warner grants to Thomas Dunn all those plantations comprised in the said several Indentures of 1754, 1771, 1774, and 1784 and in the will of Katharine Tunkes and the Indentures of 1781 respectively in trust for 99 years if Ashton Warner so long lives, subject to the provisoes, and for 100 years if Ashton Warner and Rachel so long live, subject to the provisoes, and by the powers given Ashton Warner charges the 6th part which descended to Rachel Warner by the death of Mary Fahie and the plantation which he purchased from Valentine Morris Horne, but without prejudice to Justinian Casamayor, with the payment of £2000 three months after his death if he dies before Rachel, and so charged grants them to Thomas Dunn in trust for 1000 years to pay Justinian Casamayor, with provision of redemption by the persons to whom they shall descend, and in further pursuance and in consideration of 10*s.* Ashton Warner grants to Justinian Casamaijor all the plantations, etc., comprised in the said Indentures without prejudice to the Indentures of 1754 or 1771, Ashton Warner to possess and manage the said plantations for four years, and from time to time ship and consign to Justinian Casamayor all sugars and profits except the rum and part of the sugars necessary for the use of the managers and overseers, and at the end of four years if the debt is not paid Thomas Dunn with all convenient speed, with the consent of Justinian Casamaijor, with or without the concurrence of Ashton Warner, to sell the said plantations, provided always that though Ashton Warner is to have the management, yet as he will not reside in Barbados so that the plantation must be managed by attorneys residing there, it may be lawful for Justinian Casamaijor to join with Ashton Warner in appointing such attorneys, and no persons shall be legally appointed during the four years save by them jointly, Thomas Dunn to stand possessed in trust for the payment of Justinian Casamaijor and to sue, and Justinian Casamayor in trust to permit Ashton Warner to possess and manage the premises in Antigua and to transact all affairs as he shall think fit during the four years and to receive £500 a year free from all taxes, and in case he is not paid Justinian Casamayor at the end of the four years to enter upon and sell, and Ashton Warner during the four years may sell the rum to defray the necessary annual expenses and keep so much sugar either clayed or muscovadoed as shall be necessary for the use of his family, whether residing in Antigua or in England or elsewhere, and for the use of the managers, overseers, clerks, servants, and slaves according to the allowance usually made, and to the end these Indentures may be registered in Antigua and Barbados, Ashton Warner and Justinian Casamayor nominate, etc., Langford Lovell and Thomas Norbury Kirby of Antigua, Esquires, and Sir John Gay Alleyne, Bart., and James Shepherd, Esq., of Barbados their Attorneys.

Schedule 1. On Belvedere Plantation, men 44, women 73, children 30, mules 12 and 1 old; cattle, 9 oxen, 7 bulls, 11 cows, 5 calves.

Schedule 2. On Pare's Plantation, men 63, women 89, children 13 (all names given). John Lancaster, George Bramwell, Lincoln's Inn, witnesses.

Close Roll, 40 Geo. III., Part 7, Nos. 9 and 10.

Indenture made the 21st Aug. 1800 between Thomas Warner, of the one part, and William Manning, John Proctor Anderdon, and Charles Bosanquet, all within named, of the other part, witnesseth that Thomas Warner in consideration of 5*s.* bargains and sells to the others the within mentioned plantation, capital messuage, slaves, now in the occupation of him or his agents, for one whole year. William Percy Cooke, Thomas Grundy, witnesses.

No. 9.

Indenture made the 22nd Aug. 1800 between Thomas Warner, late of Antigua, but now of Bristol, Esq., and Dorothy his wife, of the one part, and William Manning, John Proctor Anderdon, and Charles Bosanquet, all of London, merchants and copartners, of the other part. Whereas Thomas Warner is seised and possessed of and entitled unto the plantation in Antigua with the negro slaves and live and dead stock thereon, hereinafter mentioned; and whereas he was indebted to William Manning, John Proctor Anderdon, and Charles Bosanquet on the 30th April last past on an account then stated and settled between them in the sum of £3911 which still remains unpaid, and they have since then advanced and paid certain further sums to and on account of him, and may hereafter have occasion to make further advances for him or to his use; and whereas he hath agreed to secure to them the repayment by a mortgage of his plantation, and Dorothy his wife hath agreed to join in order to bar her title to dower. Now this Indenture witnesseth that in pursuance of the agreement and for the considerations and purposes aforesaid and in consideration of 10*s.* Thomas Warner and Dorothy his wife grant to William Manning, John Proctor Anderdon, and Charles Bosanquet the freehold part in their actual possession being all that capital mansion or dwelling-house and all that plantation or sugar estate containing 149 acres, and all those several pieces of pasture ground thereto belonging or therewith occupied containing together 80 acres, all which messuage and plantation, etc., are in the parish of St. George, Antigua, and abutting and bounding E. on the lands of Thomas Brooke, Esq., S. on the lands of —— Grant and Joseph Warner, Esquires, W. on the lands of the said Joseph Warner, and N. on the lands of George Thomas, Esq., and are now in the occupation of Thomas Warner or his agents, and every the negro and other slaves being 170 in number, all those 11 mules and 40 head of cattle and all other live stock, provided always that if Thomas Warner on or before the 30th April 1801 pays the said £3911 and interest at 6 per cent. from the 30th April last past, William Manning, John Proctor Anderdon, and Charles Bosanquet shall at the cost of Thomas Warner reconvey and reassure the said plantation, and Thomas Warner is rightfully and lawfully seised in a good, sure, absolute, and indefeasible estate of inheritance in fee simple, and Thomas Warner is to cause to be made before the 30th April 1801 a list of all slaves and to deliver it to the others, and lastly Thomas Warner and Dorothy his wife, William Manning, John Proctor Anderdon, and Charles Bosanquet constitute, etc., Philip Hicks and Samuel Warner, Esquires, of Antigua, their Attorneys.

Close Roll, 54 Geo. III., Part 49, No. 21.

Indenture made the 21st Oct. 1814 between Thomas Warner, formerly of Antigua, but now of the parish of Clifton near Bristol, Esq., and Dorothy his wife, of the one part, and the Hon. Samuel Warner, one of the Members of His Majesty's Council in Antigua, of the other part. Whereas Thomas Warner is seised in his demesne as of fee in a plantation or sugar estate in the division of New North Sound and parish of St. George in Antigua, hereinafter mentioned, and also of sundry slaves, which plantation and slaves stand charged with £8000 currency to Elizabeth Byam, deceased, formerly wife of the Hon. William Warner, formerly of Antigua, deceased, under the last will of the said William Warner, and with sundry debts due from Thomas Warner, either on record in the Secretary or Marshall's Office in Antigua or due to persons residing there or in Great Britain, and hereinafter particularly mentioned; and whereas Thomas Warner did in Jan. 1812 contract and agree with Samuel Warner for the absolute sale to him of the plantation and slaves, but no conveyance hath yet been made, in consideration that Samuel Warner will well and truly pay and discharge all debts of Thomas Warner, namely, a debt due to the heirs of Elizabeth Byam, probably now about £3500 sterling, and also another due to Messrs. Rodie, Charles Shand, and William Shand of Liverpool, merchants and co-partners, on mortgage, amounting to £4167 5*s.* 3*d.* sterling, and also a debt due on a running account to them amounting to £4626 6*s.* 6*d.* sterling, and also a debt due to Rebecca Gray, late of Antigua (widow of the Hon. John Gray, deceased), but now residing in Great Britain, amounting to £2608 16*s.* 5½*d.* currency, equivalent to £1490 sterling, more or less, and also another debt on bond due to Elizabeth Mayer, formerly of Antigua, but now residing in Great Britain (widow of John Wickham Mayer, late of Antigua, Esq., deceased), amounting to £500 sterling, and in consideration also of £550 sterling to be paid to Thomas Warner on or before the execution of these presents, and in consideration of a clear annuity of £700 sterling for the life of Thomas Warner, to begin from the 1st Jan. 1812, and of another clear annuity of £400 sterling for the life of Dorothy Warner, if she survives her husband, and in further consideration that Samuel Warner saves harmless Thomas Warner from all debts, etc., on account of the plantation. Now this Indenture witnesseth that in pursuance of the agreement, and in consideration of the covenants hereinafter contained on the part of Samuel Warner, and of 10*s.*, Thomas Warner and Dorothy his wife grant and convey to Samuel Warner all that plantation in the division of New North Sound and parish of St. George called Stoney Hill or Belle Vue, containing 149 acres of cane land and 89 acres of pasture, in the whole 238 acres, bounded E. with the lands of Thomas Langford Brooke, S. with lands formerly of Lachlan Grant, Esq., deceased, and now of . . . , and the lands of the heirs of William Warner the younger, Esq., deceased, W. with the lands of the said heirs of William Warner, and N. with the lands of George Thomas, Esq., and all negro and other slaves reputed to be, amounting in number to 120, more or less, on the 21st Jan. 1812, and all mules, cattle, and other live stock, and all that capital mansion or dwelling-house on the said plantation, to Samuel Warner and his heirs and assigns for ever; and Samuel Warner covenants to pay the debts and annuities as above; and Thomas Warner and Dorothy his wife nominate the Hon. Thomas Norbury Kerby and Rowland Spencer Frye of Antigua, Esquires, to be their Attorneys. James Hartley King, James Peterken, clerks to Thomas Sermon of Gray's Inn, witnesses.

Edmund Warner, born 2 July 1610, entered Merchant Taylors' School 1618-19.

1627, July. Henry Warner, s. of Edmund, late of Parham, Suffolk, Esq. dec[d]; apprenticed to Rich[d] Aldsworth; Francis Warner, of the Inner Temple, being bound. (Merchant Taylors' Company in 'Misc. Gen. et Her.,' Second Series, vol. v., p. 372.)

Francis Warner, gen., held 6 Car. I. the Manor of Vicedelieu in Cransford, by half a Knight's Fee; which was Thomas Rickthorn's 30 Eliz. (Loder's 'History of the Manor of Framlingham,' p. 334.)

Among the copyholders were Edmund Warner, 20 Car. II.; John Warner, Esq., 1650; Francis Warner, 19 Eliz. (*Ibid.*, p. 348.)

Manor of Saxted copyholders:—Edmund Warner, gen., adm. 6 Oct. 1698 to 1 acre mag. ten. of the tenement Brothers', abutting upon Butnall-Mere: which was Edmund Warner's, esq., 21 Car. II.; Sir John Warner's, baronet, 16 Car. II.; Robert Warner's, gen., 1657. (*Ibid.*, p. 368.)

Edmund Warner, Esq., held 104 acres of freehold 1 Jac. I., which were Edmund Warner, Esq'res, 20 Car. II., and John Corrance, Esq'res, 11 W. III. (*Ibid.*, p. 379.)

Francis Warner, gent., was an Armour-Keeper of the Castle of Framlingham temp. Eliz. (*Ibid.*, p. 397), also a bailiff of Loes Hundred.

John Warner, Esq., and Henry Warner, Esq., each of £1000 per annum, both of Suffolk, qualified to be made Knights of the Royal Oak in 1660. (Collins's 'Peerage,' vol. v., p. 373.)

On 6 Oct. 1662 John Warner was admitted in fee to the copyhold of this estate holden of the manor of Framlingham ad Castrum, under the surrender and will of his father Francis Warner of Moulsey, co. Surrey, esq., deceased. ('History of Framlingham,' by Richard Green.)

The English Ladies of Pontoise, near Paris.

A token to y[e] com[ty] from Mrs. Susan Warner, when she entered to be Religious (at Dunkirk), wh[ch] was noe less a concurring Kyndness from her worthy Father, Revd Father Clare (Sir John Warner), and y[e] consent and goodwill of his other Dau'r Dame Agnes Warner.

128 livres 12 sous.

In the handwriting of Lady Abbess Neville who died 1689, æt. 84.

Lieut.-Colonel Sutton of Montserrat deposed in 1676 that when the French conquered that island in 1666 he escaped to the woods, and found "Henry Ashton, Esq., son of —— Ashton, formerly Govr of Antegoa and then a dweller there, lying desperately wounded," whom he carried into the house of Mr. Angus, which the Indians then burnt down, and the said Henry Ashton was also burnt alive.

1669, March 21. Wee, Philip Warner, Esq., and Dame Henrietta my wife, sole heiress to Henry Ashton, late of Antigua, Esq., her brother, deceased, Elizabeth Ashton, widow of the said Henry Ashton and administratrix, hath relinquished all claim, her release being dated one day before this, grant certain slaves to said Elizabeth Ashton. Witnessed by Nathaniel Reaves, Thomas Morgan, George Tirwhitt. Recorded 30 Jan. 1671.

1671, July 12. Sir Charles Wheeler, Bart., Captain in the Guards, appoints Colonel Philip Warner, President of H.M. Council, also Colonel of a regiment of foot in Antigua. Recorded 1 Nov. 1671.

1671, Jan. 13. Mr. Henry Warner, 161 acres in Nonsuch by Governor Philip Warner; surveyed 20 Feb.

1672, Feb. 1. Hon. Colonel Philip Warner for £900 st. sells to Owen Martyn, Esq., ye Savannah. Deed of partnership and inventory annexed.

1672, March 21. Letter of Attorney from Owen Martin of London, Esq., to William Barnes of Kingsaile, Ireland, Gent., to take possession of a plantation called the "Savannah," lately sold by ye Hon. Colonel Philip Warner to me by deed of sale dated 1 Feb. last.

1673, April 4. William Wainwright of Antigua, carpenter, leases 50 acres to Colonel Philip Warner.

1673, June 6. Thomas Compton of Antigua, Gent., for 5000 lbs. sells to Colonel Philip Warner, Governor, 68 acres near Falmouth Harbour.

1673. Colonel Philip Warner, Governor of Antigua, by commission from William Stapleton, Esq. I am authorized to appoint all Magistrates, both Military and Civil, in Antigua.

1674, Jan. 29. Simon Warner, 10 acres by Governor Warner; surveyed 18 Feb. 1674-5.

1675, Dec. 14. Colonel Phillip Warner, late Governor of Antigua. Appoint my wife Henrietta my Attorney.

1675, March 3. Mr. Thomas Warner, 12 acres by Colonel Rowland Williams; surveyed 7 March.

In 1675 Colonel Philip Warner was in the Tower, charged with the murder of his brother Indian Warner at Dominica. (See Vol. I. for full particulars.)

1676. Letter of Attorney from Colonel Philip Warner to his wife Dame Henrietta Warner.

On 2 Aug. 1676 appeared John Lachaisnaye, Deputy-Secretary of Antigua, and stated that Madam Henrietta Warner left Antigua on 26 July 1676 for Barbados, but had to return.

1678-9, Feb. 20. Colonel Philip Warner, 200 acres by Hon. Captain Paul Lee, Judge of Falmouth; surveyed June 1679.

1679, Sep. 23. William Wainwright, planter, sells a plot 120 feet by 80 feet at Falmouth Town to Philip Warner, Esq., for 12,500 lbs.

31 Charles II., 3 Nov. 1679. Colonel Philip Warner possesses ye Savana by pattent from William, Lord Willoughby, dated 11 April 1668, now confirmed by Sir W. Stapleton; the said freehold to be the mannor of Framingham, and to have all royalties, a full-grown Bore to be paid yearly to his Majestie.

1681, May 24. Colonel Philip Warner, 200 acres granted by Sir W. Stapleton.

1692, July 22. Colonel Thomas Warner, four proportions at St. John's Town, bounded east with Ebenesar Langford, and 107½ acres (late in possession of William Lloyd, who was convicted of murder) granted by Christopher Codrington.

Besse relates that: "Col. Philip Warner, as he was riding, his Horse stumbled and fell upon him, so that he died a few Days after of the Hurt he had received." ('Sufferings of the Quakers,' vol. ii., p. 371.)

Petition of Dame Ann March, widow, reciting that she was possest of a well settled plantation in Nevis left to her by her husband Sir Thomas Warner as her only support, which she was prevailed upon to surrender to her son Colonel Philip Warner of Antigua, now deceased, in consideration of £100 a year; eight years now past and nothing has been paid her. She is now of great age and infirm, and appeals for justice. Endorsed dead 27 June '92. Nothing done.

'The Life of the LADY WARNER, *of Parham, in Suffolk*, in Religion call'd Sister Clare of Jesus, 2nd edition, with Life of her Sister Mary Clare, written by a Catholic Gentleman (N.N.).' 1692.

1700. Samuel Warner of Parham was High Sheriff.

1711, April 5. Petition of Barry Tankard, Samuel Philips, and Francis Carlile on behalf of Edward Warner, Gent., for £584 for negros.

Memorial of Edward Warner to be of the Council, Antigua. He states that he has a considerable estate there which was his father's and grandfather's before him. His grandfather was Lieut-Governor and his father a Member of the Council. He is now bound over there with his wife and family, has had a liberal education in England, and was here during the Parke riot. Received 5 Feb. 1711-12. Mandamus dated 15 March following. (B. T. Leeward Islands, vol. 12.)

Division of the Folly Plantation between Henry Warner, Gent., and Edward Warner, Esq., 197 acres; surveyed 26 March 1714.

1714, Nov. 26. Henry Warner, Gent., and Philles his wife sell 100 acres called the Folly to William Codrington, Esq., for £110, part of a greater sum.

1715. Census of Barbados. Christ Church Parish. Hon. Richard Scot, æt. 61; Elizabeth his lady, æt. 60. His will was recorded at Barbados, and his daughter Elizabeth, wife of Edward Warner of Antigua and Eltham, Esq., was his sole Ex'trix and residuary legatee.

1715, Jan. 4. Hon. Edward Warner of Antigua, Esq., and Elizabeth his wife sell to Mr. Henry Blizard of Antigua, planter, 112 acres in St. Paul's for £784 c.

1715, Feb. 21. Edward Warner, Member of Council, sworn.

Letter from Edward Warner, dated 9 April 1728, saying that he has been in England two years after having spent thirteen or fourteen years at Antigua. His shattered health and young family. Asks for fifteen months' more leave.

1742, Feb. Thomas Warner, of Gray's Inn, Esq; to Miss Kerby. ('London Mag.,' p. 101.)

1749, Nov. 3. Deposition of Thomas Warner, Esq., æt. 33, and Ashton Warner, Esq., æt. 58. (B. T. Leeward Islands, vol. 29.)

1749, Oct. Attorney-General Warner laid up with a fit of the stone.

1750, April 18. Daniel Warner is sworn Member of Council. On 9 June 1756 he was appointed Treasurer *vice* William Horne.

1758, July 13. Thomas Warner appointed Attorney-General.

1760, March 27. William Warner to succeed Daniel Warner as Treasurer; and on 9 June 1756 he was returned for St. John's Town.

In Chancery. 1763, Feb. 25. Thomas Smith, Esq., Ex'or of Phillis Maria Kirke, *v.* Stephen Blizard, Rowland Oliver, and Thomas Warner, Esquires, Ex'ors of Ashton Warner, Esq., deceased, and Robert Christian and John Halliday, Ex'ors and Trustees of Henry Warner the younger, deceased, and Margaret Warner, and Ashton Warner, an infant, and Sarah Warner, an infant, defendants.

1771, Dec. Wm. Warner, Esq; Treasurer of the Island of Antigua. ('Gent. Mag.,' p. 570.)

In a copy of the 'Antigua Mercury, or St. John's Weekly

Advertizer,' of 20 Sep. 1777 (inserted in vol. ii. Colonial Correspondence) Thomas Warner, Esq., advertizes the sale of his plantation called Osborn's or Barter's.

1779, June 2. At Antigua, in his 63[d] year, the hon. Thomas Warren (*sic*), his Majesty's attorney general for the Leeward Islands. ('Gent. Mag., p. 423.)

1786, Dec. Lieut. Ashton Warner then of the 60th Regiment.

Rachel Warner was rated for St. Peter's, Parham, 1796 to 1813, and Samuel Warner 1796 to 1814.

Joseph Warner died at his house in Hatton Street on 24 July 1801, aged 85. From a long notice of him in 'Gent. Mag.' for 1801, pp. 768 and 956, it appears that he was born at Antigua 1717 on the family estate, entered at Westminster School, and remained there six or seven years, at the age of 16 was apprenticed to Samuel Sharpe, Surgeon, and resided with him seven years, was then admitted Joint Lecturer in Anatomy at St. Thomas's Hospital, and became Surgeon there in 1746, which appointment he held for 44 years. In 1756 he was elected F.R.S., and in 1771 an Examiner at College of Surgeons. He published several surgical cases. The celebrated Essex ring descended to him at the death of his elder brother Thomas, who left no issue.

1802, May 11. At St. Mary-la-Bonne, Joseph Warner, esq. of Sloane-street, to Miss Hoadly Ashe. ('Gent. Mag.,' p. 469.)

Joseph Warner writes from Lewes 20 June 1814 saying that the depot there is about to be abandoned, that he has a wife and six children, that his losses at St. Vincent in 1795 and the three succeeding years amounted to £70,500 st., on which he has since paid six per cent. interest, and applies to their lordships to be appointed to the office of Secretary or Registrar of Antigua. (Colonial Correspondence, vol. 59.)

1814, Sep. 1. At Kensington, Lieut.-col. E. B. Wynyard, 1st Guards, to Louisa, second dau. of Joseph Warner, esq. ('Gent. Mag.,' p. 288.)

1815, Nov. 30. At Grenada, in his 59th year, Sir Chas. Shipley, governor of that island . . . . a Major General and senior Col. of Engineers, etc., leaving a widow and 3 daus. (*Ibid.*, 1816, p. 276.)

H. N. Coleridge wrote in 1825: "The house of Mr. Warner, the President of the Council, is a very finished affair; he is a descendant of the person of the same name, who was the chief colonizer of this and some of the neighbouring islands: the original grant by Charles I. is framed and set over the door of his dining-room. ('Six Months in the West Indies,' p. 243.)

1825, Dec. 11. At Meopham, Kent, the wife of Rev. Daniel Francis Warner, a dau. ('Gent. Mag.,' p. 79.)

1826, Oct. 16. At Rochester, the wife of the Rev. D. F. Warner, a dau. (*Ibid.*, p. 365.)

1829, March 11. At Worcester, Chas. Wm. Warner, esq. son of Lieut.-Col. Warner, to Isabella, eldest dau. of — Carmichael, esq. of Bromwich-hill. (*Ibid.*, p. 365.)

1830, Sep. 4. At Trinidad, in his 50th year, Ashton Warner, Esq. Chief Justice of that Colony. (*Ibid.*, p. 645.)

1833, Nov. 1. At Ralf House, Eltham, in her 82d year, Mildred, relict of William Warner, esq. of Dominica. (*Ibid.*, p. 476.)

1836. Lately. At Bath, Laura, widow of Jos. Warner, esq. late of S[t] Vincent's. (*Ibid.*, p. 109.)

1839, June 11. On her passage to England from Trinidad, aged 20, Jane, wife of Thornton Warner, esq. of that island. (*Ibid.*, p. 438.)

1841, March 29. At S[t] John's Wood, Isabella, wife of C. W. Warner, esq. her Majesty's Solicitor-Gen. for Trinidad. (*Ibid.*, p. 553.)

1843, June 20. At Marylebone, Frederick, third son of the late Ashton Warner, esq. Chief Justice of Trinidad, to Jeannetta-Maria, third dau. of the late Rev. William Gunthorpe, of Antigua. ('Gent. Mag.,' p. 200.)

1843, July 25. In Jamaica, Henry Warner, esq. barrister-at-law, second son of the late Ashton Warner, esq. Chief Justice of Trinidad. (*Ibid.*, p. 446.)

1863, Aug. 4. In Stanhope-street, Gloucester-gate, Catherine Jane Mathew, widow of Col. Edward Warner, and eldest dau. of the late Major-Gen. Sir Charles Shipley. (*Ibid.*, p. 384.)

1864, Sep. 4. At Hoo St. Warburgh, near Rochester, aged 73, Sylviana Maria, wife of the Rev. Daniel Francis Warner, Vicar of the Parish. (*Ibid.*, p. 533.)

1866, Sep. 12. At Chaussée de Charleroi, Brussels, Augusta Mary, wife of James Alexander Manning, esq., and dau. of the late General Sir Charles Shipley, Governor of Grenada. (*Ibid.*, p. 563.)

The following Notes have been supplied to me by Dr. J. J. Muskett, Editor of 'Suffolk Manorial Families':—

Robert Appleard of Framlingham at the Castle, co. Suffolk, Esq. Will dated 10 Oct. 1558; proved 7 March 1558 at Norwich. Lands in Cratfield, Linstead, Wethersdale, Weybred, & Fressingfield in said co. to grds. Rob[t] Warner at 21, failing issue of the Warners to the children of my sister Daile of Shanfeld. Fra. Warner my son-in-law. Lands to Anne my wife for life, then to my grandchildren W[m], Francis, & Priscilla Warner in tail. Lands in co. Norfolk to nephew John Appleyard, Esq. My wife Ex'trix.

In Book No. 66, Vesye, fo. 57b, Norwich Consistory, testator is styled Appleton *alias* Appleyard.

Anthonie Warner of Stradbrook, co. Suffolk, Gent. Will dated 14 April 1601; proved 25 May 1601 by Edmond Warner at Norwich, fo. 289. Poor of Stradbrook £10. Lands in Stradbrook & Wingfield to Edmund Warner, Gent., my nephew, he to surrender dower to Eliz. my wife. Money to Dorothy Warner* my dau. the gift to Eliz. my said wife of Prudence Moyster her mother, also the gift of Tho. Tybenham, Gent., late deceased, her grandfather. Said Edmund Warner to pay legacies to Francis Asteley, wife of Tho. Asteley, Esq., & to Mary Soane her sister, my kindswomen, & £100 to Edward Warner, Gent., my nephew, & legacy to Rob[t] Warner, Gent., my kinsman. If Edmund Warner die without heirs male my lands to said Edward Warner, Rob[t] Warner my nephew, Dorothy Warner my dau. & her heirs for ever. Francis Warner, Gent., my brother. The wives of Edmund & Rob[t] Warner. Eliz. Covell my niece. Mary Asteley, wid. Francis Asteley my godson, s. & h. of said Tho. Asteley my kinsman. Cozen Augustine Blowe, his wife, & Mary Blowe her dau. M[rs] Mary Holland, wife of John Holland, Esq., my kinswoman. Rest of all my goods to Dorothy Warner my dau. at 21 or marriage.

Francis Warner of Parham, co. Suffolk, Gent. Will dated 5 Jan. 3 Jac.; proved 14 May 1606 by the Ex'ors. (28 Stafford.) To be buried at Parham. Wainefarthinge, where I was born. To Edmond Warner my son my mansion house, etc., in Parham & Framlingham, & lands in Stradbrooke, & his heirs male, in default to Edward Warner my son, Henry Warner my son, Robert Warner my grandson, John Warner my grandson. To Edward Warner my son lands in Leiston. Henry Warner my son lands in Crannesford & Great Glemham. Mary Girlinge my grandchild lands in Sutton, Hollisley, Shottisham, & Eyke. 30 acres in Framlingham park by lease to me by Thomas Colvill, Gent., my son-in-law. Anne Warner my dau.-in-law a chain of gold. To Edmond Warner my son plate,

* She married Edmund Poley of Badley, and died in 1625. (Le Neve's 'Knights.')

armor, seal at arms. Dan. Collvill £20. Dorothie Warner my neece; Ursula Warner, dau. of my son Edmond Warner; Frances Girlinge, dau. of Wm Girlinge, Gent.; Elizabeth Warner, wife of Robert Warner, Gent.; Eliz. Cocke, dau. of Robert Buxston, Esq.; Mistris Saunders of Bloxsall, Mistris Norton, my sister Hoo, cozen Shemynge his wife, Eliz. dau. of cozen Reynoldes, Ann Spalldinge, Kath. Hogge, Anne Manchepe, widow, Frances Holbeck wife, Francis Asteley my grandchild. Thos. Asteley my best horse. To Isaac Asteley & Dorothy Asteley, children of the said Thos., silver spoons. Wm Girling, Gent., a gelding. Cozen Robt Buxston, Esq., a cup. Cozen Calles wife 40s. Wife of John Reydon of Hacheston 20s. Francis Warner my grandchild. John Warner my grandchild £100 on condition he give up all right to any of my lands bequeathed by this will, & to Robt Warner my grandchild £100 on the same condition after his said brother John is paid. Francis Call, son of Anthony Call, 40s. Furniture, etc., to my 3 sons Edmond, Edward, & Henry equally. S.-in-law Tho. Colvill, Gent., £20. My 2 sons Edmond & Edward Ex'ors. Witnessed by Thomas Wythe, Thomas Stofer, Robert Northall, Edmund Jordane.

Anne Norton of Framlingham, co. Suffolk, widow. Will dated 24 Oct. 4 Jac.; proved 4 May 1607. (46 Hudleston.) To be buried in Baringham Chancel near my husband. My sister Hoo my seal ring of arms. Cozen John Cornewallis, neece Anne Warner, neece Marie Girlinge, rings. Nephew Tho. Colvill £20. Nephew Edmond Warner & neece Eliz. Colvill all linen. Nephew Henry Warner 40s. Mr John Bedingefeilde of Bedlingfeilde £40 & his wife. Nephew Edward Warner £10. Nephew Frances Warner. Neece Anne Dix 20s. Neece Frances Godfrey 20s. Nephew Edmund Warner the Younger £10. Neece Ursula Warner £10. Neece Eliz. Colvill £10 yearly. Cosen John Cornewallis, Esq., & nephew Edmond Warner Ex'ors. Witnessed by Anne Nortonne, John Raffe, Robert Cockerbold.

Mrs. Anne Warner. Will dated 24 May 1642; proved 28 June 1642 at Ipswich, no. 128, by Ursula Warner, Ex'trix. My mother. Brother Warner & his wife & their 3 children. Sister Alston. Sister Dorothy. Brothers Edward Warner & Robert Warner. Aunt Colville. All residue to my sisters Ursula & Dorothy.

Will of Dorothy Warner of the Parham family, proved P.C.C. 1696. (82 Noell.)

Robert Warner of Winfarthing, co. Norfolk, Gent. Inq. p.m. 33 Hen. VIII., no. 99, much defaced. Obiit 32 Hen. VIII. Wm Warner his s. & h., æt. 30. Settlement upon Anthony Warner, younger s. of the said Robt & Johanna. Francis Warner another son. Lands in Stradbrook, co. Suffolk.

In the parish church of St. Andrew Undershaft, London. On a monument:—

Edward Warner Esquire a worthy Citizen and Merchant of London, who departed this mortal life the 28 day of October 1628, he was the second son of Francis Warner of Parham in the County of Suffolk, Esquire by Mary his second wife Daughter & Coheire of Sir Edmund Rowse of the said County, Knight which Frances Warner was truely & lineally descended from the ancient and generous Family of the Warners who possessed a place of their own name at Warners hall in Great Waltham in the County of Essex.

He dyed without issue and made Francis Warner of Parham aforesaid, Esquire his Nephew and next heire in blood the Executor of his will and principall heire of his estate who out of duty & affection to the memory of his dear Uncle, hath dedicated this Monument.

He had to his first wife Mary, daughter of Master Aylmer of Bisden in Hartfordshire, and to his second, Margaret, daughter of Master John Cheynie.

(Stow's 'Survey of London,' pp. 153 and 824. Davy's 'Suffolk Collections.')

PARISH REGISTER OF ST. JOHN.

Baptized.

1733	Dec. 27	Henry Samuel the s. of Ashton Warner, Esqr, & Elizabeth his wife.
1735	June 23	Elizabeth the d. of Ashton Warner, Esqr, & Elizabeth his wife.
1747	July 22	Rebecca the D. of Daniel Warner and Rebecca his wife.
1750	Aug. 20	Ashton the s. of Daniel Warner and Rebecca his wife.
1751	Dec. 2	Grace the D. of Daniel Warner and Rebecca his wife.
1753	Dec. 17	Thomas the S. of Danl Warner and Rebecca his wife.
1755	Mar. 18	Daniel the S. of Danl Warner & Rebecca his wife.
1758	Nov. 23	Joseph the S. of Daniel Warner, Esqr, & his wife Rebecca; b. the 15th Febry. 1756.
1762	Jan. 6	Ashton S. of Samuel Warner and Frances his wife.
1770	April 26	Samuel the S. of Samuel Henry Warner and Ann his wife.
1774	May 28	William the S. of Wm Warner and Frances his wife.
1776	July 20	Thomas Francis the S. of Wm Warner & Frances his wife.
1778	July 16	John the S. of Ashton Warner and Sarah his wife.
(? 1785)	July 30	Margaret D. of Ashton Warner (Planter) and Sarah his wife.
1787	April 5	Agnes D. of Ashton Warner and Sarah his wife.
1790	Feb. 23	Elizabeth Anna D. of Ashton Warner and Sarah his wife. B. 9th November 1789.
1792	July 13	Charles James S. of Ashton Warner and Sarah his wife. B. the 25th May 1792.
1802	June 27	Elizabeth Warner D. of Ashton Warner and Jane Lovell. B. the 9th May 1802.
1806	Feb. 6	Charlotte Wilcox D. of Joseph Warner & Jean his wife. B. the 23d December last.
1826		Recd into Church Dec. 22. B. the 11th Inst. Thomas S. of Samuel Ashton & Mary Warner, St John's, Clerk, Rector of St George's; privately baptized 11th Inst.
1833	Dec. 6	Joseph Weston s. of Samuel Ashton & Mary Warner. Date Hill. Rector of St George's; b. 1 Nov. 1833.

Married.

1738	Nov. 30	William Dunbar & Barbara Warner. L.
1738	Jan. 2	Francis Byam & Jane Warner; married by ye Revd Mr Charles Rose.
1743	July 23	Thomas Parker & Henrietta Warner. L.
1746	May 13	Hamilton Kerby and Ann Warner.
1746	Sep. 8	Thomas Whitford and Mary Warner.
1753	Oct. 25	Richard Ottley and Elizabeth Warner.
1772	Nov. 26	William Warner, Junr, to Frances Tew. L.
1773	Mar. 18	Jonas Blizard (Surgeon) to Elizabeth Warner. L.

1773 July 28 Doctor John Dunbar to Sarah Warner. L.

1775 Nov. 2 Martin Byam to Elizabeth Warner, Widow. L.

1775 Dec. 5 John Gray to Rebeccah Warner. L.

1791 Nov. 15 Samuel Warner to Ann Hurst.

1798 Sep. 6 Thomas Blizard Moore to Eliza Frances Warner, Spinster. L.

1842 May 12 Edward Looby Warner, Bach., & Margaret Watson Barnard, S., of this parish. L.

Buried.

1691 June 28 Thomas Warner.

1723 Sep. 24 Philip-Ashton, Esq[r], & his wife (? Warner omitted).

1748 June 4 Elizabeth Warner, wife of Ashton Warner.

1752 Feb. 12 Ashton Warner, Esq[re].

1754 Sep. 6 Henry Warner.

1761 June 19 Elizabeth Warner.

1763 Aug. 15 Elizabeth Warner, C.P.

1765 Nov. 5 Margaret Warner, P.

1771 Oct. 12 William Warner.

1772 Nov. 9 Grace Warner.

1774 June 30 William Warner.

1779 Feb. 14 Samuel Henry Warner.

1779 June 3 Thomas Warner, senior.

1784 Nov. 20 Daniel Warner.

1786 Nov. 3 Henry Warner, Inf.

1787 April 21 Agnus Warner. Infant.

1789 April 7 The Honourable Ashton Warner, M.D., President of his Majesty's Council.

1795 Mar. 3 Eliza Grace Jane Warner, Infant.

1802 Dec. 22 Ann Warner.

1803 Sep. 14 Catherine Warner.

1833 Jan. 29 Joseph Warner. S[t] John's. 7.

1833 Sep. 9 Fergus Savage Ashton Warner. S[t] John's. Infant.

1834 Jan. 11 Joseph W. Warner. S[t] George's. Infant.

1838 April 9 Samuel Warner. President of H.M. Council. S[t] John's. 70.

1841 Feb. 28 Adam Warner. S[t] John's. 6.

1845 Dec. 8 Samuel Bott Warner. S[t] John's. 17.

1848 Nov. 18 Samuel Warner. S[t] John's. 47.

PARISH REGISTER OF ST. PAUL.

Baptized.

1726 Aug. 29 Anne the D. of Ashton Warner, Esq[r], and Elizabeth his wife.

1750 Feb. 21 Ashton S. of M[r] Henry Warner and Margaret his wife.

Married.

1748 Feb. 2 Henry Warner, Gent., and Margaret Marchant, Spinster; by L.

Buried.

1731 Sep. 8 Henry Warner, Esq[r].

PARISH REGISTER OF ST. GEORGE.

Baptized.

1774 Mar. 10 Joseph Thomas S. of William Warner, Esq[r], and Mildred his Wife.

1791 Feb. 12 Rebecca Dorothy D. of Thomas Warner & Dorothy his wife; b. Oct[r] 31st last. By M[r] A. Freeman.

1793 Aug. 21 Elizabeth Grace Jane D. of Thomas Warner and Dorothy his wife; b. Sept[r] 9th last.

Married.

1738 Jan. 2 Francis Byam & Jane Warner.

1754 Feb. 14 W[m] Warner, Gentleman, & Elizabeth Blizard, Spinster.

1755 Dec. 20 Samuel Henry Warner, Gentleman, & Ann Ash, Spinster.

PARISH REGISTER OF ST. PHILIP.

Married.

1748 Feb. 2 Henry Warner to Marg[t] Marchand; by the Rev[d] M[r] Davison.

1776 Sep. 5 Ashton Warner & Sarah Brown, spinster.

Buried.

1779 Sep. 30 Ashton Warner s. of Ash. & Sarah Warner. Willoughby Bay.

PARISH REGISTER OF ST. MARY.

Married the Rev[d] Samuel Ashton Warner to Mary Whitlock, Spinster; by L. from His Honor Samuel Athill. J[s] Curtin 18 . . June the 10; at the Valley Chapel of Ease.

PARISH REGISTER OF ST. MICHAEL, BARBADOS.

Buried.

1679 July 23 S[r] Thomas Warner, K[t].

PARISH REGISTER OF LEE, CO. KENT.

Married.

1739 Jan. 1 John Johnson of S[t] Lawrence, near Guildhall, London, and Elizabeth Ann Warner of East Greenwich.

1742 May 24 William Fauquier of S[t] Sepulchre, Esquire, and Grace Byham of Eltham, widow.

1746 Sep. 22 Edward Warner of S[t] Mary-le-Bow, London, and Katherine Johnson of Eltham; by M[r] Brian of Greenwich. (Mem. 18 May 1767: The name of the Clergyman who married the above-named parties was Francis Byham, as Mrs. Warner informs me. J. L., Rector.)

CAMBERWELL, CO. SURREY.

Buried.

1666-7 Jan. 2 Nathanael son of M[r] Alderman Warner.* Duke Str. chapel, Westm[r].

('Collect. Top. et. Gen.,' vol. iii., p. 383.)

ELTHAM, CO. KENT.

Buried.

1729 Sep. 2 Rich. Scott Warner s. of Col. Edw. Warner.

1732 Feb. 19 Col. Edw. Warner.

1772 Mar. 23 Edw. Warner, from Lond.

(Drake's 'History of Blackheath,' p. 213.)

ST. MARY'S CHURCH, CRATFIELD, CO. SUFFOLK.

Against the east end of the north aisle is a large escutcheon bearing the arms of Warner, of four coats; impaling Jernegan, of eight coats, viz.:—1, *Or, a bend engrailed between six roses gules, barbed vert* (WARNER); 2, *Azure, a chevron between three owls argent* (APPLEYARD); 3, *Argent, a lion rampant azure, debruised by a bend voided gules, his head resting upon a chief or* (THORNBURY); 4, *Gules, a fess nebulee between three etoiles argent* (COURTHOP): impaling, 1, *Argent, three buckles lozengy gules* (JERNEGAN);

* Francis Warner, Sheriff of London, 1659.

VIEW NEAR ENGLISH HARBOUR, SKETCHED ABOUT 1830.

2, *Gules, a cross engrailed argent* (INGLETHORP); 3, *Gules, three bars gemelles or, a canton argent* (FITZ-OSBERT); 4, *Argent, a unicorn erect sable, semée of fleurs-de-lis of second* (HARLING); 5, *Argent, on a chevron between cotises, outwardly engrailed sable, three escallops or* (GONVILLE); 6, *Sable, a pall reversed ermine* (KELVEDON); 7, *Sable, a lion rampant within an orle of cinquefoils argent* (CLYFTON); 8, (JERNEGAN).

On a monument:—

Hic jacet Robertus Warner, sen., Gen., vir prudens, pius, et honestus; filius et heres Gulielmi Warner, nuper de Cratfield, Gen., filii et heredis Francisci Warner, de Parham, Arm., et Margaretæ Jernegan, unius filiar. Georgii Jernegan, Arm., filii et heredis Johannis Jernegan, nuper de Somerle towne, militis, ætatis suæ 80, 1654, et Eliz. uxor ejus, filia Alexandri Courtop, de Cronbrook, in comitatu Cantuariensi, Armig. Robert Warner, jun., Gent., son and heir of Robert Warner, and Margaret his wife, died in August, 1641, aged 23 (? 29). (Suckling's 'Suffolk.')

PARISH CHURCH OF OLD ROAD, ST. CHRISTOPHER'S.

On a tomb:—

An Epitaph vpon The
Noble & Mvch Lamented Genr^{l} Sir
Tho. Warner, K^{t} Lievtenant
General of ye Carribee
Islands & Gover^{r} of y^{e}
Island of St Christopher
Who Departed This
Life the 10th of
March 1648.

First Read then weepe when thou art hereby taught,
That Warner lyes interr'd here, one that bought.
With losse of Noble bloud Illustrious Name.
Of A Comander Greate in Acts of Fame.
Trayn'd from his youth in Armes. his courage bold.
Attempted brave Exploites. and vncontrold
By fortunes fiercest Frownes. hee still gaue forth
Large Narratiues of Military worth.
Written with his sword's poynt. but what is man
In the midst of his glory. and who can
Secure this Life A moment since that hee
Both by Sea and Land, so longe kept free
at Mortal Strokes at length did yeeld
grace) to conquering Death the field.
fini Coronat.

(Copied in 1785. See Davy MSS.)

SAVANNAH ESTATE, NEAR ENGLISH HARBOUR.

On a large ledger in a small walled family burial-ground. The tomb which supported this ledger is broken up, and the whole place is neglected and forsaken:—

Here lyeth the Body of
Mr HENRY WARNER
who died on the 7 day of
September 1731
in the 39 Year of his Age
Much beloved and lamented
by all that knew him
in memory of whom his
affectionate Brothers EDWARD
and ASHTON WARNER
Erected this Monument.

On an adjoining ledger over a well-preserved tomb:—

ANTIGUA
Here Lyeth the Body of Mrs ELIZABETH WARNER
Late Wife of EDWARD WARNER
of this ISLAND ESQ^{R}.
She was a Woman of Exemplary Piety,
She was the Beft of Wifes;
The Tenderft of Mothers,
The Faithfulleft of Friends,
And of a moft Charitable compafsionate Difpofition
Whofe Death was Generally and defervedly lamented
by all good People that knew her
She departed this Life the Thirteenth day of Aug.
in the Year of Our LORD GOD One thoufand
Seven hundred Twenty & Three
In the 37th year of her Age.

ST. JOHN'S CHURCH.

On a monument which formerly stood in the church, but which is not now to be seen, having been destroyed by the earthquake:—

This monument
Is erected to the memory of
THE HONOURABLE WILLIAM WARNER ESQ.,
Who was a member of His Majesty's Council,
And Treasurer of this Island.
Honourable by his office of Counsellor,
But
More honourable as a man:
For if
Virtue alone is true nobility,
And if justice, moderation, temperance, meekness,
Consummate honesty, charity, generosity, and
Conjugal affection, are virtues that are held in any estimation
Among men,
This man,
Who lived in the exercise of them all
Was truly honourable.
He died on Friday, 11 October, 1771, in the forty-third year of his age, |
Universally regretted, and lamented by all orders and degrees among |
Us.
To commemorate her anguish for his loss, and as a public
Testimony of her love and duty, his disconsolate widow hath
Caused this memorial to be raised.
Gloria in excelsis Deo!

('Antigua and the Antiguans,' vol. i., p. 225.)

ST. JOHN'S CHURCHYARD.

On a large marble tomb, surmounted by a stone ledger:—

ASHTON WARNER ESQ.
depofited this Marble
In Memory of his dearly Beloved
and Tenderly Affectionate Wife
ELIZABETH
Whofe Body is here Interred
They were Marryed the 8 of April 1714
She died the 2^{d} of June 1748
In the 58th Year of Her Age
And vnder the same Stone lies
the Body of the said
ASHTON WARNER
who died the Eleaventh day of February
in the Year of Our Lord One thoufand
seven hundred and fifty two in the
Sixty firft Year of his Age
And under the fame Stone lies
the Body of ELIZABETH WARNER
late the Wife of THOMAS WARNER Esq.
who died the 15 of August, 1763
aged 40 Years.

BURIAL-GROUND OF ST. ANDREW, HOLBORN, LONDON.

On the ledger stone over the Warner Tomb:—

WILLIAM AND MARY WERE THE SON AND
DAUGHTER OF JOSEPH WARNER ESQ
MARY . . . . ELIZABETH HUNGERFORD
WERE THE DAUGHTERS OF
WILLIAM WARNER ESQ
THE INFANT MARY WAS THE GRANDDAUGHTER
OF JOSEPH WARNER ESQ
[Two lines of small undecipherable lettering here]
LIKEWISE ELIZABETH WARNER
WIFE OF JOSEPH WARNER ESQ
IN THIS VAULT ARE DEPOSITED THE REMAINS
OF ROBERT THORNTON ESQ OF KENSINGTON
HE DIED ON THE 29TH . . . .
IN THE 68TH YEAR OF HIS AGE
HE MARRIED THE YOUNGEST DAUGHTER OF
JOSEPH WARNER ESQ OF HATTON GARDEN
[Two lines of small undecipherable lettering here]
IN THIS VAULT ARE DEPOSITED THE REMAINS
OF MRS ELIZABETH THORNTON RELICT OF
ROBERT THORNTON ESQ WHO DIED
9 JANUARY 1817 AGED 63 YEARS
WITHIN THIS VAULT REST THE MORTAL
REMAINS OF ISABELLA ANN THE BELOVED
WIFE OF CHARLES WILLIAM WARNER
BARRISTER AT LAW SOLICITOR GENERAL
OF THE ISLAND OF TRINIDAD
IN THE WEST INDIES
SHE LEFT HER HUSBAND AND
FIVE CHILDREN TO DEPLORE HER LOSS
[One line of small lettering here]
BORN 6TH FEBRY 1802 DIED IN LONDON
29TH MARCH 1842.

At the north end of the tomb:—

MISS MARY PELHAM WARNER
. . . .

MISS ELIZA HUNGERFORD WARNER
. . . . .

At the south end:—

SACRED TO THE MEMORY OF
ELIZABETH WARNER WIFE OF
JOSEPH WARNER ESQ
. . . . . .
MARCH . . . . YEARS.

SACRED TO THE MEMORY OF
JOSEPH WARNER ESQ
. . . . . .
. . . . . .
JULY 180 . Æ 8 YEARS.

At the east side:—

WILLIAM WARNER ESQ
. . . . . . etc.

At the West side:—Nothing legible.

The whole of the tomb is in a bad condition on the surface from the flaking off of the stone, due to exposure to the weather and bad material.

Pedigree of Watkins.

JEREMIAH WATKINS, Speaker of Antigua 1669; J.P., Member of Council, and Judge of the Court of Common Pleas 1675; of Dickinson's Bay 1678; Serjeant-Major 1679; living 1688. =Joan . . . . living 1675.

Gyles Watkins, senior, of Cirencester, co. Gloucester, clothier, and of Antigua. Will dated 19 Jan. 1702; proved 14 Jan. 1706. (22 Poley.) =. . . .

Giles Watkins of Antigua, Esq., Manager of Blackman's 1703; Captain 1704; Member of Assembly for Dickinson's Bay 1712—16; J.P. 1721; Registrar 1728; Puisne Judge and incapacitated by old age 1736; bur. 13 Sep. 1744 at St. John's. =Elizabeth, dau. of Mrs. Grizell Morris and sister of Colonel Valentine Morris; bur. 13 July 1738 at St. John's.

Deborah Watkins, mar. . . . . Higgins; living 1702.

Mary Watkins, mar. William Freeman, senior, of Cirencester, grocer. His will proved 1738. (36 Brodrepp.)

Anne Watkins, mar. Thomas Heard of St. Margaret's, Westminster, by licence dated 19 Feb. 1684, she æt. 27.

John Watkins of Antigua, Esq., Deputy-Registrar 1730, later Registrar; Major 1745; Judge of Court of Common Pleas and æt. 37 in 1749; Member of Assembly for St. John's 1749 and 1757; Master and Examiner in Chancery 1759. Will dated 23 April 1760; sworn 5 Aug. 1762. =Ann, dau. of Hon. Colonel Richard Oliver; bapt. 11 July 1711 and mar. 30 Jan. 1741 at St. John's; living 1765. s.p.

Elizabeth Watkins, bur. 12 Oct. 1701.

Alice Watkins, bur. 12 Sep. 1703.

Frances Watkins, bur. 29 May 1708.

Elinor Watkins, bur. 13 Nov. 1733. Will dated 11 Nov. 1733; sworn 21 March 1736-7.

Alice Watkins, mar. 3 March 1725 Henry Knight.

Grizell Warner, mar. 10 Oct. 1726 Robert Martin.

Thomas Watkins, Esq., Member of Assembly for Popeshead 1727, 1734, and 1739; Member of Council 1739; Colonel; 1st son and heir 1743; died s.p.m.; bur. 8 Feb. 1745 at St. John's. Will sworn 20 Feb. 1745-6. =Elizabeth, 1st dau. and coheir of Jacob Morgan, Esq.; bapt. 16 July 1706, mar. 1 Sep. 1726, and bur. 10 July 1742 at St. John's.

Ellinor Watkins, bapt. 10 Aug. 1728; mar. . . . . Dunbar. (? bur. 26 Jan. 1773 at St. John's.) s.p.

Thomas Watkins, bur. 4 Dec. 1730.

Morgan Watkins, bapt. 26 May 1733; bur. 4 April 1738.

Elizabeth Watkins, mar. *circa* 1746 William Gunthorpe, Esq.; he died 1779.

Caroline Watkins, bapt. 9 May 1736; bur. 3 April 1738.

Margaret Watkins, bapt. 9 May 1736; bur. 19 July 1738.

Mary Watkins, bapt. 6 Jan. 1739; bur. 14 Aug. 1745.

Ann Watkins, coheir, bapt. 9 July 1738; owned "Watkins"* in Dickinson's Bay. =Byam Freeman, Esq., bapt. 1731. Will dated 1770. (See Vol. I., p. 261.)

* This estate passed to her only child Harriet Freeman, who married 1781 Thomas Oliver, Esq., Lieut.-Governor of Massachusetts, later of Bristol, and at her death it descended to her first daughter Harriet Watkins, who married Captain Henry Haynes, R.N. For further details see under Oliver.

George Watkins of Bristoll, cooper, now at Nevis. Will dated 16 Nov. 1672; proved 19 April 1673 by Joane Watkins the relict. (51 Pye.) Wife Joane Ex'trix. 3 sons Hugh, Geo., & Edw[d]. Friends Capt. Geo. Smyth & Tho. Elliott overseers. Witnessed by John Gosse, Stephen Stanley, clerk.

Phillip Watkins of Mercer's Creek Division, Antigua, planter. Will dated 26 March 1693. To my cosen Thos. Pearce, son of Francis Pearce, a negro girl. To Benj[n] Wickham, jun[r], son of Benj[n] Wickham of Antigua, all my estate & his heirs. Benj[n] Wickham, sen[r], & W[m] Linsey to be trustees & Ex'ors. Witnessed by William Lavington, John Martin, James Parke, William Steele. By the Deputy-Governor John Yeamans, Esq., were sworn William Lavington and William Steele 11 Sep. 1693. Recorded 23 Sep. 1693. Thomas Gatewood, Secretary.

Order dated 11 Sep. 1693 to empower William Lavington, Stephen Duer, and James Parkes to make inventory of goods. The value of the estate as shewn by Lieut. Benjamin Wickham was 30,352 lbs.

Antigua. Order to Abraham Swan and George Reynolds to appraise a negro now in the possession of Mrs. Benjamin Wickham and formerly Philip Watkins' 31 Oct. 1694. Signed by John Yeamans. Recorded 1 Nov. 1694.

By the Deputy-Governor. Philemon Bird, Esq., and William Lavington, Gent., both of Antigua, adm'ors of George Watkins, deceased, late agent on the plantation of Mr. Abraham Lloyd, petition for audit of account. Captain John Tankard, Captain David Martin, and Mr. Robert Amory to audit same 27 Feb. 1694. Thomas Poskins is now agent of ye estate of Mr. Abraham Lloyd* and Co. of Bristoll, and William Lavington is one of the adm'ors of late George Watkins. They find 3000 lbs. are due to the estate of latter, but six hogsheads of sugar and two bags of cotton to Lloyd and Co.

* Joseph Loyd of Nevis, merchant, in his will, proved 1690 (74 Dyke), named his brother Mr. Henry Loyd of Bristol, merchant. The will of a Captain John Lloyd of Nevis was proved 1696 (74 Bond) by Hannah his widow.

Gyles Watkyns the elder of Cirencester, co. Gloster, clothier. Will dated 19 Jan. 1702; proved 11 Jan. 1706 by Thomas Wilkins. (22 Poley.) To my dau. Deborah Higgins that portion of my tenement where I live in Abott al's Coxwell Str., *i.e.* the 4 street rooms where my son Thos. lives, with the chamber over them, & the cockloft over that, with free passage to the pump & to the brook, for life, then to my son Thos. All the rest of the house I give to him. I give her also the furniture of my best chamber, a silver goblett, 2 silver spoons, a pair of great andirons, etc., and the brass pewter to her & her dau. Alice Higgins. Her son Jas. Higgins. To my dau. Mary Freeman my silver punch bowl. To my son Joseph Wilkins my silver tea taster & the book which I last brought from Antigua. To my granddau. Alice Wilkins a bed, etc. To Mary & Ann Wilkins, daus. of my son Tho. Wilkins, a silver spoon each. To my grandson Tho. Heard £5 when he finishes his apprenticeship. All residue of my chattels here to my son Thos. & appoint him sole Ex'or for England. My sons-in-law W[m] Willkyns & W[m] Freeman, both of Cirencester, to be overseers, & I give them 10s. apiece. ½ of all my lands in Antego to my son Gyles Watkins, & ½ to my son Sam[l] Watkins, charged with the payment of £400 each to my son Thos. Watkins & my daus. Deborah Higgins & Mary Freeman, & £400 equally among John, Sarah, Alice, Ann, & Hester Wilkins, son & daus. of my son-in-law W[m] Wilkins. If my granddau. Alice Watkins shall not have the estate in Upton left her by her mother or £50, my Ex'or to pay her £50. My dau. Deborah Higgins is to pay to her son James & her dau. Alice £20 each. All residue in Antigua to my sons Giles & Sam[l] & appoint them Ex'ors for that Island, & M[r] Tho. Morris & M[r] Abraham Reddwood overseers, & I give them 100 lbs. apiece for gloves. Witnessed by James

[continued below.

Elinor (? Miss Griffin, niece of Lord Griffin), living 1709; bur. 5 Aug. 1727 at St. John's. 1st wife. = Samuel Watkins of Antigua, Esq., Provost-Marshal 1698; Member of Assembly for Dickinson's Bay 1699—1710; Captain and J.P. 1704; Colonel and æt. 38 in 1708; Chief Justice 1706, 1716-17, and 1739-40; of "Monteyroes" 1737; of very advanced age 1742-3; bur. 5 Feb. 1745 at St. John's. Will dated 4 April 1743. = Margaret, dau. of Colonel John Gamble; mar. 1 May 1728; mar. 2ndly, 1756—62, Charles Alexander, Esq.; sole heiress to her sister Mrs. Elizabeth Haddon 1762; owned "Dunnings" 1763. 2nd wife.

Thomas Watkins of Cirencester 1702.

(? Ann Watkins, mar. Samuel Eliot.)

Giles Watkins, bur. 13 Sep. 1703.

Elinor Watkins, mar. 9 Oct. 1707 Colonel James Parkes.

Mary Watkins, living 1743.

Elizabeth Watkins, mar. 21 March 1714 John Kerr, Col. of the 38th Regiment; living a widow 1743.

Jane Watkins, mar. John Eliot; living his widow 1743.

John Watkins, = . . . bapt. 9 Aug. 1729; owner of "Monteyroes" 1755, then of Brampton near Huntingdon.

(? Samuel Watkins.)

Margaret Watkins, bapt. 25 Aug. 1731; bur. 21 Nov. 1733.

Jane Watkins, bapt. 26 Dec. 1732; living 1746.

Mary Watkins, bapt. 5 March 1737; living 1746.

Samuel Watkins, 1st son and heir 1763; to inherit "Dunnings" 1780; of "Monteyroes" 1788; Member of Council 1794.

John Watkins, a minor 1763; living 1788.

George Watkins, living 1763.

Margaret Watkins, only dau. 1763.

Clutterbuck, William Clarke, Charles Holland. On 24 March 1814 adm'on of goods of Giles Watkins, late of Cirencester, yarnmaker, deceased, left unadministered by Thomas Watkins the son and Ex'or, deceased, granted to John Archdale Palmer of Cheapside, London, warehouseman, nominated by Letitia Wilkins, widow of John North Wilkins, and by the Rev. William Field the devisees in trust named in the will of the Rev. William Wilkins, late of Berry Field House, Bourton on the Water, co. Gloster, deceased, concerning only the tenement in Cirencester comprised in the term of 200 years assigned to the said Giles Watkins by Indenture quadrupartite dated 10 July 1701. The said Ex'or died intestate. Recorded at St. John's.

Elinor Watkins. Will dated 11 Nov. 1733. To my mother Elizth Watkins, my sisters Elizth & Mary Watkins each a negro. To my brother John Watkins all residue. Witnessed by Grizell Martin, Henry Knight. Before William Mathew, Esq., was sworn Grizell Martin 21 March 1736-7. Recorded 22 March 1736.

William Freeman, sen., of Cirencester, co. Gloucester, grocer, a Baptist. Will proved 1738. (36 Brodrepp.) My copyhold message in Coxwell Street, formerly in possession of Tho. Watkins & Deborah Higgins, widow, now of me & her my said sister. My son Wm £550, etc.

Samuel Watkins of Antigua, Esq. Will dated 4 . . . . 1743. My son Thos. Watkins to be my residuary legatee. My dau. Jane Watkins. My dau. Mary Watkins. Whereas . . . . Margt Watkins has thought proper to absent herself from me . . . . duty of a wife & breach of marriage vow I deprive her of all interest in my personal estate. To my dau. Jane Eliot, widow of John Eliot, £300 c. To my dau. Elizth Kerr, widow of John Kerr, £300 c. To my granddau. Ann wife of Joseph Davison £50 c. Jonas Langford, Stephen Blizard, & my son Thos. Ex'ors. Witnessed by Merrick Turnbull, John Hart, Thomas Warner. On 20 Feb. 1745 was sworn Thomas Warner. Recorded 29 May.

Thomas Watkins. Will (much mutilated). To Elizth & Mary each . . . . thousand pounds c. in addition to . . . . their mother. Having no male issue testator apparently leaves his plantation to be divided into lots, & the negros appropriated to each lot by the members of the Council & Assembly for reduced & honest families. 10 acres around the mansion to be kept as a residence for the Commander-in-chief. The works & 4 acres for common use. 2 acres for a school. Col. Stephen Blizard . . . . gford, Capt Wm Mackinen, Capt Robt Christian Ex'ors.

On a scrap. Thomas Watkins' will sworn to by Joseph Davison 20 Feb. 1745.

Samuel Watkins of Antigua, mariner. Will dated 7 May 1758. To my nephew Abraham Marshall a negro woman Mary & her son, also Hanah. If he die before 21 then to my dau. Rachel Jane Watkins. I give him also £100 c. to be paid at the expiration of his apprenticeship. To my wife Sarah Watkins my furniture & use of house. All residue to my said dau., & in default to my brother Jas. Watkins of Antigua, mariner, then ½ to the children of my sister Mary Challoway of Tortola, & ½ to my wife Sarah & nephew Abraham Marshall. My Ex'ors to sell vessell or boats. John Lesprainer Spencer Rossington, merch', Peter Gilliat, planter, Ex'ors. Witnessed by Christopher Ceely, James Davis. Before His Excellency George Thomas was sworn Christopher Ceely 19 Feb. 1759. Recorded 12 Jan. 1764.

John Watkins of Antigua, Esq. Will dated 23 April 1760. To be buried in the family burying place, late belonging to Henry Knight, & now in the possession of Saml Nibbs, in the grave with my sister Knight. To my nephew Wm Smith, Esq., of St Christopher's my gold watch & chain & seals. To Lucy Reynolds £25 c. To Mr Wm Atkinson all my linen & release him of payment of 4 guineas which I am charged with for him by Richd Oliver of London, Esq. If my present dear wife Ann be living at my death I give her all residue, but if she be dead then to my 2 nephews Richd Oliver the Younger of London, merch', & Wm Smith. Wm Smith, Rowld Oliver, Esq., & my wife Ann Ex'ors. Witnessed by George William Freeman.

1st Codicil. 27 Feb. 1762. Thos. Oliver, Esq., son of Robt Oliver of Boston, Esq., & Francis Farley of Antigua, Esq., also Ex'ors. Witnessed by George William Freeman.

2nd Codicil. 1 Aug. 1762. To my nephew John Martin £50 c. To my kinsman Jeremiah Watkins £50 c. & a negro boy. Witnessed by William Atkinson. Before Governor Thomas were sworn William Atkinson and William George Freeman of Antigua, both clerks to John Watkins, Esq., 5 Aug. 1762.

Richard Watkins, Esq. Will dated 18 May 1763; proved 23 April 1770 by Mary Watkins the relict. (167 Jenner.) Andrew Lessly (father of my wife Mary Watkins) has lately been obliged to sell his estate & is now reduced in circumstances, & will not be able to give his dau. the £1000 Antigua c. 6 months after my decease, pursuant to the marriage articles. The pensions of sea officers' widows are so small. My superannuation. Have no landed & but little personal estate. All my moneys, plate, furniture, etc., to my wife Mary, & if she die before me then all to my sister Winnifred Thomas, my sister Ann Thomas, my sister-in-law Judith Williams equally, & if all are dead to my nephew Reynold Thomas, my nephew John Deere Thomas, & my wife's niece Sarah Eliz. Williams, or such as may be surviving their mothers. Now at Youngsbury, near Wade's Mills in Hartfordshire. On 21 April 1770 appeared Margaret Smith, wife of John Smith of Princes Street, St. Christopher le Stocks, and James Sammes of Great Russell Street, cabinet maker, and swere they knew Richard Watkins, late of Kensington, Esq.

Joseph Freeman of Cirencester. Will dated 1771. (479 Trevor.) My cousin Wm Wilkins. Wife Ann £2000, dau. Mary Freeman. Sister Jane Overbury, etc.

Sarah Watkins, widow of Samuel Watkins. Will dated 28 Oct. 1791. My niece Ann Rosco, dau. of my niece Lydia Rosco. To the latter my house. All residue between my niece Lydia, my grandniece Ann Rosco, my nephew Moses Glover, & grand nephew Richd Rosco. Elias Ferris, planter, M. Glover, & Richd Glover Ex'ors. Witnessed by Elizabeth Fellais (*sic*), Elias Ferris. Before Edward Byam, Esq., was sworn Elizabeth Fellows 21 Dec. 1791. Recorded 9 March 1793.

Close Roll, 25 Geo. II., Part 4, No. 7.

Indenture made the 1st Nov. 1751 between John Watkins of Brampton, near Huntingdon, Esq. (son of the Hon. Samuel Watkins, formerly Chief Justice of the Court of Common Pleas, Antigua, deceased), of the one part, and Walter Tullideph of Antigua, Esq., Practiser in Physic, and Charles Alexander, now of Great Britain, but late of Antigua, Esq., Captain in H.M.'s Regiment of Foot quartered in the Leeward Islands, of the other part. Whereas Samuel Watkins by his last will, dated the 4th April 1743, did devise to John Watkins his son, party hereto, all his estate called Monteyros and all negro slaves, and for default of issue devised the same to Thomas Watkins his son; and whereas the said plantation so devised to John Watkins, party hereto, was by Samuel Watkins in his lifetime let on lease to John Watkins of Antigua, Esq., which lease will expire in October 1752, and it is imagined that John Watkins, party hereto, may become indebted to John Watkins of Antigua in a considerable sum of money upon a reappraisement of the slaves, works, buildings, cattle and horses, which he may be obliged to borrow; and whereas John Watkins, party hereto, hath already gotten 2 sons. Now this Indenture witnesseth that in consideration of 10s., and also in consideration of the natural love he beareth to his youngest son already born and may bear to other children to be born, and for making a reasonable provision for such younger children, and to the intent to barr and destroy all estates tail and remainders, John Watkins conveys to Walter Tullideph and Charles Alexander all that plantation called Monteyros and all negros, which said plantation is in the parish of St. Mary and in New Division in Antigua, and contains 250 acres, in trust to repay to themselves all moneys advanced, then to the use of John Watkins for life, and after his death to pay £40 sterling yearly for the maintenance and education of his eldest son till 14, and from 14 till of age £60 yearly, and £60 per annum for the maintenance and education of younger children, and as to the residue of the produce after payment of the dower of Margaret Watkins (mother of John Watkins) to keep the same in their hands till £2000 sterling shall be raised for younger children, if there shall be 3 or more, to be equally divided at 21 and not sooner, and if not more than one younger child, or two, then £1500 and no more to the said one younger child, or equally divided between the 2 at 21 and not sooner, and after raising the said sum to the use of the heirs of the body of John Watkins, and for default to his right heirs for ever, and John Watkins nominates James Doig, Joseph Dewberry, and George Lucas, all of Antigua, Esquires, his Attorneys. James Davis, Robert Merryfield, witnesses.

Close Roll, 29 Geo. II., Part 13, Nos. 2 and 3.

Indenture made the 12th June 1755 between John Watkins of Bampton, near Huntingdon in Huntingdonshire, Esq. (son of the Hon. Samuel Watkins, formerly Chief Justice of the Court of Common Pleas, Antigua, deceased), of the one part, and Walter Tullideph of Antigua, Esq., and Christopher Baldwin of Antigua, merchant, of the other part, witnesseth that in consideration of 5s. John Watkins grants, etc., to Walter Tullideph and Christopher Baldwin all that plantation called Monteyros, containing 250 acres, in the parish of St. Mary and in New Division, Antigua, and all negro and other slaves, horses, mares, mules, horned and other cattle, and stock live and dead for one whole year. Fras. Eyre, Richard Tompkins, witnesses.

No. 2.

Indenture tripartite made the 13th June 1755 between John Watkins of Brampton, near Huntingdon, of the 1st part, Charles Alexander of Antigua, Esq., of the 2nd part, and Walter Tullideph and Christopher Baldwin of the 3rd part. Whereas Samuel Watkins by his last will in 1743 (recited); and whereas by an Indenture made the 1st Nov. 1751 (recited); and whereas in pursuance of the said recited Indenture Charles Alexander, soon after the expiration of the lease in October 1752, did pay on such reappraisement several hundred pounds, and hath advanced several other considerable sums; and whereas since the execution of the said recited Indenture John Watkins hath contracted considerable debts in Great Britain, and the several creditors have threatened to distress John Watkins, who hath proposed to them to barr all estates tail and other uses created or limited by the said Indenture, and to secure such new contracted debts by the said plantation when so barred, if he may by law be enabled; and whereas on advising with Counsel from the inaccuracies of penning the abovementioned Indenture it is apprehended that John Watkins may be enabled to barr all or some of the estates, particularly the estate tail whereby the provision for his family may be defeated; and whereas Charles Alexander is desirous to preserve the plantation for the benefit of the family, subject to the charges hereinafter mentioned, and hath agreed to pay off all the creditors. Now therefore this Indenture witnesseth that in consideration of the several sums already advanced and of a further sum of £400 sterling paid by Charles Alexander, and in consideration of a provision for the children of John Watkins, and all other premises hereinbefore recited, John Watkins grants, etc., to Walter Tullideph and Christopher Baldwin, in their possession now being, all that plantation called Monteyros in trust to the use of Charles Alexander for 100 years, and on the determination of that term to the use of John Watkins for life, and to preserve the contingent remainders to his heirs for 500 years, to his first son and his heirs male, whom failing to the heirs of the body of John Watkins, whom failing to the heirs of John Watkins for ever, and as to the 100 years that Charles Alexander may enter in and receive the rents without rendering any account until all money advanced by him is repaid, and as to the 500 years to raise portions for younger children, if only one £1500, if two or more £2000 to be divided amongst them, to sons at 21, if John Watkins is then dead and the rents sufficient, and daughters at 21 or marriage, all portions to be considered vested interests at 21, and to raise money for the maintenance and education of an eldest or only son, and of all other children, for the eldest son till 14 not over £40 a year, and from then not over £60, and the maintenance for the younger children not to exceed in the whole £60 a year, and the said sums to be raised without prejudice to the money due to Charles Alexander, and the dower of Margaret Watkins, mother of John, and John Watkins constitutes James Doig, Werge Lucas, and Henry Alexander, all of Antigua, his Attorneys.

Close Roll, 3 Geo. III., Part 12, Nos. 11 and 12.

Indenture made the 10th June 1763 between Charles Alexander of London, merchant, and Margaret his wife (late Margaret Watkins, widow and relict of the Hon. Samuel Watkins, Esq., heretofore Chief Justice of the Court of Common Pleas, Antigua), of the one part, and Harry Alexander of Antigua and William Colcraft of London, merchant, of the other part, witnesseth that in consideration of 5s. the former grant, etc., to the latter all that plantation called Dunnings, containing 140 acres, lying in or near the parish of St. Mary, Antigua, and all negro and other slaves, horses, mares, mules, horned and other cattle, and stock live or dead whatsoever to have and to hold for one whole year, yielding therefore one peppercorn, to the intent that by virtue of these presents and by force of the statute for transferring uses into possession in that behalf made and provided, they may be in actual possession and enabled to accept a grant and release of the reversion and inheritance upon the several uses to be mentioned. John Alexander, Grocers' Hall, Samuel Tatlocke, his clerk, witnesses.

No. 11.

Indenture made the 11th June 1763 between Charles Alexander and Margaret his wife, etc., of the one part, and Harry Alexander and William Colcraft, etc., of the other part, witnesseth that in consideration of 10s. and for settling and assuring the plantation, etc., hereinafter described (purchased by Margaret Alexander during her widowhood), the former grant, etc., to the latter, all that plantation called Dunnings (as in No. 12), to have and to hold to the use of Charles Alexander and his assigns, for the joint lives of him and Margaret, and at his decease to her use and behoof for life, and then in trust for 500 years, out of the rents, etc., to pay to Lucy James, a black servant, now living with Margaret Alexander, £5 sterling a year for life, clear of all taxes, and to raise such sums of money for the portions of the 3 younger children of John Watkins (son of Margaret) as follows, that is to say, for John Watkin the younger £1000 at 21 or so soon after as it can be raised, Margaret Watkins only daughter £500 at 21 or marriage, George Watkins her younger brother £500 at 21 or so soon after, and in case John or George die before 21 the portion equally between the 2 survivors, and if 2 of the younger children die to the survivor, and if the 3 die the term of 500 years to be void on the decease of Lucy James, and immediately after the determination of the said term, and subject thereto, the plantation to the only use of Samuel Watkins (eldest son of John and grandson of Margaret Alexander) and to his heirs for ever, and Charles and Margaret Alexander reserve to themselves power by will or deed to revoke, and lastly they appoint John Lyons, Esq., and Edward Gamble, and William Alexander, Gentlemen, all of Antigua, their Attorneys.

Petition of Joan Watkins complaining that Joan Seagrave abuses her. Joan Watkins is the wife of Captain Jeremiah Watkins. Ordered that if it continue Joan Seagrave be banished the island. The said Joan Seagrave is the cause of the separation of conjugal union between Joan Watkins and her husband (1675).

Captain Jeremiah Watkins, 70 acres St. John's Division by Governor Warner; surveyed Jan. 1677.

Ye Hon. Major Jeremiah Watkins purchased 40 acres of William Bowen; surveyed 7 Nov. 1678.

1678, Nov. 20. William Bower, planter, sells a parcell of land in St. John's Division to Major Jeremiah Watkins.

1678, Jan. 24. John Quinby, planter, sells to Mr. Philip Watkins, planter, 20 acres.

1679, May 17. Evan Watkins, planter, for 900 lbs. sells 6 acres to George Robinson.

1679, July 8. Colonel James Vaughan sells to Major Jeremiah Watkins 100 acres in St. John's Division in exchange for 70 acres.

1683, May 25. Joseph Watkins, 145 acres granted by Sir W. Stapleton.

Samuel Watkins was Provost-Marshal of Antigua in 1698; he was Ex'or of Leonard Waller, and in his deposition of 1708 then aged 38. (B. T. Leeward Islands, vol. ii.)

1701, July 12. Captain Gyles Watkins, 70 acres granted by Christopher Codrington.

Indenture dated 16 March 1709 between Samuel Watkins of Antigua, Esq., of the one part, and Daniel Mackinen of Antigua, Esq., Elinor now wife of Samuel Watkins. He gives all his estate to Daniel Mackinen and Edward Perrie.

1711, Aug. 17. Giles and Samuel Watkins petition that their father Gyles Watkins, formerly of England, deceased, by his will dated 19 Jan. 1702 gave them a plantation; they wish to break the intail.

George French stated that Samuel Watkins murdered one Weatherhill in cold blood by a stab under the table. He was sent home a prisoner in 1712 for his action in the Parke riot.

John Kerr, sen., Esq., of Antigua, æt. 59 in Sep. 1713. (French's 'History,' p. 228.)

1714, March 1. By Indenture Valentine Morris of Antigua, planter, gives to his niece Grizell Watkins, daughter of his sister Elizabeth Watkins, a negro girl.

An Act to enable Giles Watkins and Samuel Watkins to aliene, grant, or devise a Plantation situate, lying, and being in the Parish of St. John's, in the Division of Dickenson's Bay: as also some Pieces of Land situate and being in the said Parish, and in the Division of Popeshead of this Island, or to charge the same with Portions for younger Children. Dated 29 March 1717. Antigua.

In Chancery. 1723, May 1. Giles Watkins, Esq., and wife *v.* Hon. Thomas Morris.

1728, Jan. Henry Blizard, guardian of the children of Samuel Watkins, deceased. (Minutes of Council.)

1730, Aug. 24. Petition of Giles Watkins, Esq., to have his son appointed Deputy-Registrar; granted. (*Ibid.*)

1737, July 18. Judge Watkins's windmill formerly Monteyros.

1739, Aug. 1. Thomas Watkins removed into Council. His seat in the Assembly vacant.

1743, Dec. 6. John Watkins elected for St. John's Division *vice* Ashton Warner.

1745, April 23. Colonel Thomas Watkins and Major John Watkins members of Court Marshall.

1746, March 26. John, Jane, and Mary Watkins, the infant children of the late Chief Judge, have entered three actions against the heirs-at-law of the late Hon. Thomas Watkins, Esq., and the guardians of his children for 60 slaves formerly belonging to the late judge. Thomas Watkins left the residue of his estate to the public.

1746, June 27. Thomas Watkins, member of Council for Antigua, being dead, Andrew Leslie is appointed in his place. (B. T. Leeward Islands, vol. 55.)

In 1747 John Watkins, Esq., was a member of vestry St. Mary's Parish.

Deposition of John Watkins, Esq., æt. 37, and has been a Judge of Court of Common Pleas ten years Nov. 1749.

1777. Rev. Mr William Watkins, at Antigua. ('Gent. Mag.,' p. 47.)

1777, Jan. The Rev. Mr. William Watkins, at Antigua, who held the livings of Landilo, Lanvihangel, and Langattock, in the county of Monmouth. ('Town and Country Mag.,' p. 55.)

In 1780 Samuel Watkins was rated on 231 acres and 70 slaves.

The Vicarage, Ashburton, Devon.
Oct. 28th 1895.

My Dear Sir,

I have copied the letter which my cousin Miss Dalzell sent me some time since containing her grandmother's recollections; from the way they are jotted down they are evidently the recollection of an old lady, and she may have made some mistake in certain names, but the main facts seem correct. The Judge had two wives you will see, but she says the second wife was Miss Morgan. As you have made researches I have no doubt you are correct . . . . I have a Griffin pedigree, but could find no trace of any niece of Lord Griffin of Braybrooke. As regards the Mayers I may mention that my cousin told me that many years ago Mr. Owen Pell purchased the Mayer estate, and with it he found a chest of old papers and MSS. which he kept . . . . I remember my brother, when he was Fort Adjutant of Antigua in 1847, telling me he had met a Mr. Lydiatt who had claimed him as a cousin, his father having married Mrs. Mayer . . . . My nephew John Grant Birch and my niece Ann Mayer Birch were both born in Antigua, and that is the last we have had to do with the Island.

"Copy of a letter written by Mrs Dalzell, dau. of John & Esther Mayer. Arrived in the reign of Queen Anne. Samuel Watkins appointed Chief Judge of Antigua W. I., he married Miss Griffin, niece of Lord Braybrooke, by whom he had one son Thomas and 3 girls.

"The eldest, Ann Watkins, married Mr Elliott of Antigua and had 3 or 4 children, the eldest, Samuel, married Miss Yeamans and had a son Samuel with others.

"The second daughter Elizabeth (Watkins) married Col. Kerr, 38th Regt, & had 5 children, Sarah (Kerr), the second married Joseph Wickham & had one daughter, Esther, who married John Mayer, Eleanor (Kerr), the second, married Mr Simon Farley & had 3 daughters & two sons, the eldest, Elizabeth,* married 1 Captain Archbold in the army, 2 Sir James Laroche, Bart.

"Thomas Watkins, the Judge's son, married in Antigua & left 3 daughters. The eldest, Eleanor, married Dunbar, no issue. The second married Mr John (William) Gunthorpe & had 2 sons John & George, the eldest married Miss Christian; his 3 daughters, one married Mr Byam & then Mr Stevens; the second married Mr ——, then Admiral Cosbie, no issue; Mary remained single.

"The Chief Judge married secondly Miss Morgan,† by whom he had 2 sons, one Samuel, one daughter married Mr Christopher Baldwin, the other died unmarried.

* This must be wrong. See the Laroche Pedigree, Vol. II., p. 161.

† It was the Judge's son Thomas who married Miss Morgan.

"Eleanor Watkins, by his 1st wife, married Mr Parke, nephew of General Park, her daughter married Mr Wallace, no issue; 2dly Colonel Farley & had 2 sons & 2 daughters, the eldest, James, married Miss Bird, dau. of Colonel Bird of Virginia, the other son died single. The eldest daughter Eleanor Farley, married Sir John Laforey, Bart., & had one son & one daughter, the present Sir Francis Laforey;* the daughter married Capt. Molloy, R.N., they had 3 children, the daughter married Sir John Beresford & had one son.

"Rebecca Farley, died single. James Farley, by Miss Bird, had 4 daughters, Mrs Izard, Mrs Corbet, Mrs Lightfoot, & Mrs Banister. Grandmother Kerr had 2 sons Samuel Watkins Kerr who married Miss Furlong, ? issue, 2 sons who died single & one daughter who married Mr Thomas Montgomery, an Irish Gentleman, no issue."

So far my great-aunt Mrs. Dalzell. I may add that my mother used to speak of her mother's cousins, the Laforeys, and that Mrs. Montgomery was her grandmother and curiously enough mine, hence my second name. She died an old lady when I was very young.

W. M. Birch.

Parish Register of St. John.

Baptized.

1693 . . . . . . Ellinor the daughter of Samuel Watkins & Ellinor his wife.

1706 Sep. 5 Franciss Daughter of Giles Watkins & Elizabeth his wife.

1709 Sep. 20 Alice Daughter of Mr Giles Watkins & Elizth his wife; born 17 April.

1712 May 12 Elinor Daughter of Giles Watkins & Elizth his wife.

1712 Nov. 13 Grizelle & Elizabeth Daughters of Samuel Watkins & Jane his wife.

1713 Nov. 9 John son of Giles Watkins & Elizth his wife.

1714 Jan. 4 Samuel son of Samuel Watkins & Jane his wife.

1716 Aug. 23 Elizth daughter of Giles Watkins & Elizth his wife.

1719 May 25 Mary Daughter of Giles Watkins & his wife.

1720 June 13 James & Mary son & Daughter of Saml Watkins and his wife.

1728 Aug. 10 Elinor the d. of Thomas Watkins and Elizth his wife.

1729 Aug. 9 John the s. of Samuel Watkins & Margaret his wife.

1729 Dec. 11 Thomas the son of Thos Watkins and Elizth his wife.

1731 Aug. 25 Margaret d. of the hon. Samuel Watkins & Mary his wife.

1732 Dec. 26 Jane D. of Samuel Watkins, Esqr, & Margarett his wife.

1733 May 26 Morgan the s. of Thos. Watkins & Elizth his wife.

1736 May 9 Caroline and Margaret the D's of Thomas Watkins & Elizth his wife.

1736 Jan. 30 Ann Crawford the D. of John Watkins and Elizabeth his wife.

1737 Mar. 5 Mary ye D. of Samuel Watkins & Margaret his wife.

1738 July 3 Giles ye s. of John Watkins & Elizabeth his wife.

1738 July 9 Ann ye D. of Thomas Watkins & Elizabeth his wife.

1739 Jan. 6 Mary ye D. of Thomas Watkins & Elizabeth his wife.

1744 Oct. 11 Sarah the D. of Samuel Watkins and Sarah his wife.

1745 Nov. 15 Margaret the D. of Philip Watkins and Elizabeth his wife.

1748 June 21 Elizabeth Hanson the D. of Philip Watkins and Elizabeth his wife.

1756 Oct. 14 Rachel Jane the D. of Saml Watkins & Sarah his wife; b. Sept. 26th last.

1835 April 24 Samuel George s. of Samuel & Maria Watkins. Donovans, parish of St George. Planter.

Married.

1707 . . . . 9 James Parkes and Ellinor Wattkins. L.

1710 April 13 Samuel Watkins & Jane June. L.

1714 (? Mar.) 21 John Kerr and Elizth Watkins. L.

1725 Mar. 3 Henry Knight and Alice Watkins. L.

1726 Sep. 1 Thomas Watkins and Elizabeth Morgan. L.

1726 Oct. 10 Robert Martin and Grizell Watkins. L.

1728 May 1 Samuel Watkins and Marg. Gamble. L.

1735 Aug. 28 Samuel Watkins and Sarah Cross. L.

1741 Jan. 30 John Watkins and Ann Oliver.

1743 May 14 Capt Richard Watkins and Mary Lessly.

1744 Feb. 10 Wm Watkins and Mary Phenix. L.

1746 Nov. 30 Isaac Anderson and Mary Watkins.

1747 Nov. 24 William Watkins and Mary Bowen.

1747 Jan. 30 James Watkins and Sarah Cross.

1805 June 19 Thomas Francis Weatherill to Mary Watkins, Spinster. L.

1805 Dec. 18 Richard Byam to Frances Watkins.

1809 Dec. 14 John Thibou to Jane Watkins.

Buried.

1691 Aug. 28 Joseph Watkins (?).

1691 Sep. 9 Richard s. of Joseph & Elizab. Watkins.

1701 Oct. 12 Eliz. d. of Giles Watkins & Eliz. his wife.

1701 Dec. 3 James Watkins, on bord ye Success from Guinea, Captn Sam. Peachey, Comdr.

1703 Sep. 13 Giles s. of Capt Sam. Watkins.

1703 . . . . 12 Alice D. of Giles Watkins & Eliz. his wife.

1705 Aug. 31 Elizabeth Watkins.

1708 May 29 Ffrancis D. of Giles Watkins & Eliz. his wife.

1724 May 3 Jane Watkins, w. of Samuel Watkins.

1724 Sep. 22 Mrs Ann Watkins.

1727 Aug. 5 Elinor wife of Samuel Watkins, Esq.

1730 Dec. 4 Thos s. of Thos Watkins.

1731 Nov. 18 Sarah Watkins, a child.

1733 Nov. 13 Mrs Elinor Watkins.

1733 Nov. 21 Margaret Watkins, a child.

1738 April 1 Morgan ye s. of Thomas Watkins.

1738 April 3 Caroline ye D. of Thomas Watkins.

1738 July 13 Elizabeth ye wife of Giles Watkins.

1738 July 19 Margaret ye D. of Thomas Watkins.

1741 Oct. 28 Elizabeth Watkins, w. of John Watkins.

1742 July 10 Elizabeth Watkins, w. of Thomas Watkins, Esqr.

1744 Sep. 13 Giles Watkins, Esq.

1745 Aug. 14 Mary Watkins, a child of Collo Thos Watkins.

1745 Dec. 16 Margt Watkins, a child.

1745 Feb. 5 The Honble. Samuel Watkins.

1745 Feb. 8 The Honble. Collo Thomas Watkins.

1746 April 18 Francis Watkins, a child.

1747 Sep. 20 Mary Watkins, w. of Wm Watkins.

1748 Jan. 12 Gabriel Watkins.

1751 Dec. 7 Mary Colley D. of Elizabeth Watkins.

1759 Feb. 11 Samuel Watkins. (Popeshead.)

* He succeeded in 1796 and died in 1835.

1763 Jan. 13 Rachael Watkins, in the Country.
1771 Oct. 13 James Watkins.
1774 Mar. 7 Elizabeth Watkins.
1775 April 12 George Watkins.
1786 Nov. 11 Rachel Watkins.
1791 Oct. 31 Sarah Watkins.

PARISH REGISTER OF ST. PHILIP.

Buried.

1694 Feb. 11 George Watkins.

1684-5, Feb. 19. Thomas Heard, of St Margaret's, Westminster, Bachr, abt 28, & Mrs Anne Watkins, of Cirencester, co. Glouc., Spr, abt 27, with consent of her father Mr Giles Watkins; at Cirencester or . . . .

ST. PAUL'S, FALMOUTH.

On a head-stone:—

SACRED | To the Memory of | Henry Herbert Watkins | who departed this life Nov. 16, 1833 | Aged | Two Years Two Months Three Days.

Pedigree of Watson.

ROBERT WATSON of Antigua. Will dated 8 Dec. 1734; sworn 22 Aug. 1754. = ...

Rachel, dau. of Thomas Elmes, senior; mar. 5 Sep. 1734 at St. Philip's. 1st wife. = James Watson, only son and heir, joined the Troop 1736. = Elizabeth . . . . 2nd wife.

Children of James Watson and Rachel:

James Watson, planter, bapt. 11 Feb. 1740 at St. Paul's; died s.p. legit. Will dated 26 Jan. and sworn 7 March 1799. = Winifred Ann Olton, widow, housekeeper, bur. 18 Sep. 1814 at St. Philip's.

Children of James Watson and Elizabeth:

John Watson, bapt. 1 Jan. 1745 at St. Paul's.

Elizabeth Watson, bapt. 6 Feb. 1742 at St. Paul's.

Children of James Watson and Winifred Ann Olton:

James Watson, Esq., died at sea 12 Aug. 1806, æt. 38.

Thomas Watson.

Francis Watson, Esq., of "Watsons" and the "Hope" 1852. = Jane Margaret, dau. of Thomas Johnson, Captain in the West India Trade, and sister of the wife of James Salmon; died March 1895, æt. 84, at East Ham, London; bur. at Ilford Cemetery.

Mary Eliza Ann Watson, mar. 31 Oct. 1860 Athill Harman; he was bur. 1867 at St. Philip's.

Robert Watson. Will dated 8 Dec. 1734 . . . . My son Jas. Watson's marriage with Rachel Elmes, dau. of Thos. Elmes, senr. All residue to my son James. Major Henry Lyons, Mr Francis Delap to assist my wife . . . . in executorship. Witnessed by Francis Delap, William Horton. By George Thomas, Esq., was sworn Francis Delap 22 Aug. 1754. Recorded 27 Aug. 1754.

George Watson, Gent., leaves all his estate to a mulatto. Will recorded 28 Jan. 1792.

James Watson, planter. Will dated 26 Jan. 1799. To my sister Elizth Harris £100 c., & to her son Dr Jas. Watson Roberts £20 st. for mourning. To my son Jas. Watson my chaise, horse, & 8 cows. To Winifred Ann Olton my housekeeper my furniture, 4 cows, & 6 sheep, my whisky, & horse, & £33 c. for mourning, also several negros, & after her death to my natural son Thos. Watson, & in default to his brother my natural son Francis Watson. All residue to Daniel Hill, senr, Wm Brinton, Jno Harris, Junr, & Dr Jas. Watson Roberts in trust to be sold & £350 c. to buy a house for Winifred Ann Olton & the residue to my natural children. My son Jas. Watson, Danl Hill Ex'ors. Witnessed by Aaron Jesse, Robert Bunthorn. Recorded 7 March 1799.

1682, Dec. 1. Mr. Peter Watson, 160 acres at Bermudian Valley granted by Sir W. Stapleton.

1806, Aug. 12. On board the Duke of Kent packet, on his passage to England, and in the 39th year of his age, James Watson, esq. of the island of Antigua; whose amiable manners and integrity rendered him a valuable and much-respected member of society. ('Gent. Mag.,' p. 876.)

1825, Nov. 6. William, an infant son of Mr. George Watson.

1825, Nov. 17. Mr. Robert T. Watson, aged 32. (Almanack of St. Christopher.)

At "East Ham," London, deeply lamented, JANE MARGARET WATSON, relict of the late FRANCIS WATSON of the Island of Antigua, in her 85th year, from Influenza and Bronchitis. Her remains lie in Ilford Cemetery, No. of grave 83,187. ('Antigua Standard,' 30 March 1895.)

PARISH REGISTER OF ST. JOHN.

Baptized.

1728 Mar. 2 John s. of Joseph Watson and Abigaile his wife.

PARISH REGISTER OF ST. PHILIP.

Married.

1704 Dec. 21 Roger Wattson to Sarah Bradshaw.
1734 Sep. 5 James Watson, Gent., to Rachel Elmes. L.
1735 Feb. 16 William Redhead, Surgeon, to Frances Watson.
1790 July 24 Pinkey Watson to Sarah Lynch, spinster. L.

Buried.

1814 Sep. 18 Ann Winifred Olton, Widow, Mother of Francis Watson, Esquire, at Willoughby Bay in the Church Yard near the grave of Mrs Willcox.

PARISH REGISTER OF ST. PAUL.

Baptized.

1740 Feb. 11 James S. of Mr James Watson and Elizabeth his wife.
1742 Feb. 6 Elizabeth D. of Mr James Watson & Elizabeth his wife.
1745 Jan. 1 John S. of Mr James Watson & Elizabeth his wife.

Buried.

1748 Oct. 3 Mr Thomas Watson.

"Watsons" is in St. Philip's Parish. In 1852 it contained 460 acres, and was owned by Francis Watson, who also had the "Hope" of 208 acres.

Pedigree of Weatherill.

JAMES WEATHERILL of Antigua, Captain of ye privateer "ye Charles" of Jamaica 1693; Member of Assembly for Popeshead 1700-1, and for St. John's May 1701; bur. *circa* 1702 at St. John's. ═ Mary .... of Popeshead 1707; owned 310 acres 1710; bur. 5 Aug. 1727 at St. John's.

Col. James Weatherill of "Popeshead" Plantation of 350 and of "Duncombe's Folly" of 575 acres in St. John's; joined the Troop 1712; Member for Popeshead 1716—23, and for Dickinson's Bay 1741-2; A.D.C. to Governor Hart 1723; brother-in-law of Mrs. Elizabeth Langford 1744; bur. 7 Jan. 1745 at St. John's. Will dated 6 Jan. 1745. ═ Margaret (? dau. of Governor Michael Lambert of St. Christopher's.) She and her son joined in the sale of ⅓ of the Lambert estate before 1747.

Major George Weatherill, joined the Troop 1716; he and his wife released her dower of "Dennings" 1724; bur. 24 Oct. 1727 at St. John's. ═ Catherine, dau. of Henry Lyons, Esq., and relict of William Denning; had dower of "Dennings" 1743; of St. John's 1753.

Children of Col. James Weatherill:

Michael Lambert Weatherill, Ensign 1742-3; 1st son and heir 1746; of Westminster 1767. ═ Elizabeth .... living 1767.

James Weatherill, bapt. 10 April 1722 at St. John's; bur. 28 Jan. 1770 at St. George's. Will dated 10 July 1769.

John Weatherill, bur. 19 June 1745 at St. John's.

Charles Pym Weatherill, living 1739; Member for Dickinson's Bay 1762; died 10 Dec. 1765; bur. at St. George's. Will dated 9 Dec. 1765; sworn 3 April 1766.

Colonel George Weatherill of "Duncombe's Folly" Estate; Student of Medicine at Leyden 1744; Member for Dickinson's Bay 1749—52; Member of Council for St. Kitts 1757; died 14 and bur. 15 Nov. 1765 at St. John's. ═ Louisa, dau. of Stephen Blizard, Esq.; bapt. 20 Oct. 1740 at St. John's; mar. 23 Feb. 1765 at St. George's. (? bur. 1 Sep. 1806.)

Thomas Weatherill, bur. 12 Oct. 1754 at St. John's.

Margaret Weatherill, mar. Drewry Ottley; she was bur. 20 Jan. 1746 at St. John's; he died *circa* 1751.

Children of Major George Weatherill:

James Weatherill, bapt. 24 July 1726.

Sarah Weatherill, bapt. 19 Nov. 1724 at St. John's.

Margaret Weatherill, bapt. 25 June 1728 at St. John's. (? mar. 23 Dec. 1745 Jos. King.)

Thomas Weatherill of Antigua. ═ Sarah Inglefield, mar. 21 April 1781 at St. John's.

Georgiana Weatherill, only child, posthumous, born 11 and bapt. 31 Jan., and bur. 1 Feb. 1766 at St. John's.

Children of Thomas Weatherill and Sarah Inglefield:

Thomas Francis Weatherill, bapt. 27 May 1782 at St. John's. ═ Mary Watkins, mar. 19 June 1805 at St. John's.

Joseph Francis Weatherill, bapt. 8 and bur. 29 Dec. 1783.

David Francis Weatherill, bapt. 16 Feb. 1785.

Samuel Harman Weatherill, born 8 Nov. 1792; bapt. 28 July 1794.

Charles Inglefield Weatherill, born 8 Feb. and bapt. 31 Aug. 1795.

Daniel Burnthorn Weatherill, born 7 Feb. 1799, and bapt. 29 Jan. 1800.

Judith Weatherill, born 9 Jan. and bap. 7 July 1802.

Children of Thomas Francis Weatherill and Mary Watkins:

Samuel Watkins Weatherill, born 28 April and bapt. 11 June 1806.

Louisa Jane Weatherill, born 21 May and bapt. 4 Aug. 1807.

Maria Ann Weatherill, born 22 Nov. 1808; bapt. 8 March 1809.

Sarah Inglefield Weatherill, born 8 Aug. 1812; bapt. 7 April 1813.

Elizabeth Blashford Weatherill, born 19 April 1814; bapt. 16 Nov. 1815.

John Wetherell of Westminster, Gent., Yeoman of the Guard. (99 Carr.)

Edward Weatherell of St. Botolph's, Bishopsgate. (67 Eure.) Buried there "1672, May 7, Richard Wetherell, 46." No other of the name and year.

Thomas Weatherill, fourth mate of the ship "King George," E.I.C.S., now at Bombay. (286 Bolton.) My sister Mrs Margaret Weatherill, sole Ex'trix, £1000. My niece Mrs Mary Langford. Testator died at Surrat. Sworn 6 Nov. 1723.

St. Christopher's. Charles Pym, Esq. Will dated 13 Dec. 1739; proved 16 April 1741 by the Right Hon. Priscilla, Lady Romney (formerly Priscilla Pym), the daughter, the wife of the Right Hon. Robert, Lord Romney. (132 Spurway.) To old Will his freedom & 2 barrels of beef yearly. To my mulatto girl Bussy her freedom & £300 c. at 21, & £20 c. per annum till then. To Mrs Jane Burt £500 c. if she be living in my house at my death. To Chas. Pym Weatherill, son of Jas. Weatherill, Esq., ... at 21. My godson Chas. Pym Burt, son of Wm Pym Burt, Esq., of St Christopher's, £500 .... at 21. My goddau. Frances Pym Douglas, dau. of John Douglas, Esq., of St Christopher's, £500 at 21 or marriage. My niece Mrs Eliz. Fox, widow, of Montserrat, £300 c. To the hospital for found children in Great Britain now about to be founded £100. To the poor of Old Road £100 c. To my dau. Priscilla Pym all residue & sole heir & Ex'trix, but to be in trust for her till 21 or marriage, & if she die under age & without issue then to my good friend Col. Vallentine Morris £1000 st., to Wm Pym Burt, Jas. Browne, & John Spooner, sen., Esq^res^, & Capt. Syer Allicocke £500 apiece, to Mrs Deborah Smith £100, & all residue to my nephew Wm Pym Burt & to Col. Valentine Morris equally. My good friends John Willet, sen., Jeremiah Browne, & Wm Pym Burt, of St Christopher's, Esq^res^, & Samuel Hawkes of Montserrat, merchant, Ex'ors in trust & £100 each. Witnessed by John Franck, William Panton, Thomas Pellet.

Mrs. Elizabeth Langford in 1744 names her brother-in-law James Weatherill and his wife.

James Weatheril. Will dated 6 Jan. 1745 . . . . Witnessed by Michael Lovell, Thomas Williams, Archibald Whyte.

Codicil, same date. To my wife Margaret certain negros. Annul legacy to my son James, & give him in lieu £100 a year & negros. I request my wife to make an allowance out of her thirds to my son George, who is now studying for physician, as the amount I left him is not sufficient for his studying till 23. Before George Lucas, Esq., Lieut.-Governor, was sworn Captain Thomas Williams. Recorded 2 April 1747. [The above is but a fragment of the will.]

Mrs. Mehetable Nibbs, daughter of Jonas and Elizabeth Langford, in her will dated 30 Oct. 1757, mentions certain gifts from her aunt Weatherill.

Charles Pym Weatherill of Antigua, Esq. Will dated 9 Dec. 1765. ½ my estate to my nephew Thos. Ottley & ½ to my niece Martha Ottley; if both die then to my nephew Jas. Ottley. Stephen Blizard, Thos. Warner, Wm Warner, & Edwd Byam the younger, all of Antigua, Ex'ors. Witnessed by Jeremiah Blizard, William Millar. Before Governor George Thomas were sworn Jeremiah Blizard of Antigua, Esq., and William Millar of Antigua, Physician, 3 April 1766. Recorded 25 March 1778.

James Weatherill of Antigua, Gent. Will dated 10 July 1769. To John Swinton Jarvis £50 c. To Henry Jarvis £50 c. All residue to my friend Mr Ebenezer Lovel, he to be Ex'or. Witnessed by Thomas Jarvis, King Pittman. By Edward Otto-Baijer, President, was sworn Hon. Thomas Jarvis, Esq., 29 March 1770. Recorded 10 July 1782.

Close Roll, 20 Geo. II., Part 18, Nos. 15 and 16.

Indenture made the 20th Jan. 1746 between Michael Lambert Weatherill, late of Antigua, but now of St. Martin's in the Fields, Esq. (eldest son and heir of James Weatherill, late of Antigua, Esq., deceased), of the one part, and Richard Oliver of East Greenwich, Esq., of the other part, witnesseth that in consideration of 5*s*. Michael Lambert Weatherill grants, etc., to Richard Oliver all that Popeshead Plantation, containing 350 acres, in the parish of St. John, Antigua, bounded E. with the lands of Jonas Langford, N. with the sea, S. with the lands of Samuel Nibbs, and W. with the sea, and also all slaves, horses, cows, oxen, sheep, and other cattle whatsoever, for one whole year, and he appoints Rowland Oliver, Michael Lovell, John Wise, and John Murray, all of Antigua, Esquires, his Attorneys. Matthew Christian, Charles W. Man, William Johnson, witnesses.

No. 15.

Indenture made the 21st Jan. 1746 between the above. Whereas Michael Lambert Weatherill is well entitled to an estate in fee tail in all that Popeshead Plantation, now in the possession of Margaret Weatherill his mother, widow and relict of James Weatherill, deceased, or of Stephen Blizard, John Douglas, Thomas Warner, and Drury Ottley, Esquires, trustees appointed by the last will of James Weatherill, all which plantation, together with another one called Duncombe's Folly in Antigua, are subject to dower during the life of Margaret Weatherill under her husband's will, and charged with his debts and divers legacies and annuities to the amount of very considerable sums of money; and whereas Michael Lambert Weatherill has agreed to bar all estates tail and remainders in the plantation, etc., hereinafter mentioned, and Richard Oliver has therefore contracted for the absolute purchase of all Michael Lambert Weatherill's interest for £500 sterling, and, in lieu of an annuity of £400 currency given him by his father's will, to pay him £100 sterling a year for life, in consideration whereof Michael Lambert Weatherill has agreed to assign the annuity, the full payment whereof is rendered doubtful by the many other incumbrances affecting the estate, to Richard Oliver. Now this Indenture witnesseth that in pursuance of the agreement, and in consideration of £500 and £100 sterling a year for life, and to the intent all estates tail and remainders may be effectually barred and destroyed, according to the laws of the Leeward Islands, Michael Lambert Weatherill grants to Richard Oliver all that Popeshead Plantation charged with the dower of Margaret Weatherill and the debts and legacies of James Weatherill, and further witnesseth that in consideration of the further sum of 10*s*. Michael Lambert Weatherill assigns to Richard Oliver the annuity of £400 currency.

Close Roll, 21 Geo. II., Part 9, Nos. 13 and 14.

Indenture made the 19th Jan. 1747 between Richard Oliver, heretofore of Antigua, now of East Greenwich, Esq., of the one part, and Michael Lovell and John Wise of Antigua, merchants, of the other part, witnesseth that in consideration of 5*s*. Richard Oliver grants, etc., to Michael Lovell and John Wise all that Popeshead Plantation, containing 350 acres, in the parish of St. John, Antigua, and 170 slaves, and all horses, cows, oxen, sheep, and other cattle whatsoever, for one whole year, and Richard Oliver appoints John Murray, Rowland Oliver, and Ashton Warner, all of Antigua, Esquires, his Attorneys.

No. 13.

Indenture tripartite made the 20th Jan. 1747 between Richard Oliver and Mary his wife, of the 1st part, Michael Lovell and John Wise (trustees named by Margaret Weatherill party hereto), of the 2nd part, and Margaret Weatherill of Antigua, widow, of the 3rd part, witnesseth that in consideration of £1000 sterling paid by Margaret Weatherill to Richard Oliver, Richard Oliver and Mary his wife grant, etc., to Michael Lovell and John Wise, in their actual possession being, all that Popeshead Plantation and the 170 negros, deceased, which were part of the estate of James Weatherill, deceased, husband of Margaret, and father of Michael Lambert Weatherill, and by Indentures of the 20th and 21st Jan. 1746 granted by Michael Lambert Weatherill to Richard Oliver, subject to the debts of James Weatherill, and also to diverse legacies and annuities in his will given, in trust that the said lands shall stand charged as by the will of James Weatherill, dated the 6th Jan. 1745, and duly proved and recorded, since his death, in Antigua, but not to ease or discharge any other estate of James Weatherill, particularly the plantation called Duncombe's Folly, or the reversion of it after the death of Margaret Weatherill, but all the said estates to be liable as if those Indentures had never been made; and whereas James Weatherill by his will gave to Margaret the property of all his plate, watches, jewels, furniture, pictures, etc., and all his dwelling houses in Popeshead for life and no longer, and gave all residue to John Douglas of St. Kitts, Stephen Blizard, Drewry Ottley, jun., and Thomas Warner of Antigua, Esquires, in trust to pay one third of his real estate to his wife for life in lieu and barr of dower, and diverse other trusts, and empowered them to allow to Lambert Weatherill his son £400 a year currency till the trusts should be performed, and then to convey to him all estate real and personal; and whereas by the said recited Indentures Michael Lambert Weatherill did grant the said £400 currency a year to Richard Oliver, who for securing the payment of £100 sterling a year entered into a penal bond of £500 sterling bearing even date; whereas it is agreed that Richard Oliver shall continue to pay the said annuity, and that as a compensation the premises shall stand charged with the payment to him of £100 a year during the life of Michael Lambert Weatherill, and Margaret Weatherill has given a bond for £1000 to Richard Oliver; now this Indenture further witnesseth that in consideration of all the premises and of 5*s*. Richard Oliver and Mary his wife grant to Margaret Weatherill all that annuity of £400 currency, subject to the trust following, and constitute Michael Lovell and John Wise their Attorneys in trust, to pay to them from the said annuity £100 sterling a year for the life of Michael Lambert Weatherill and then in trust for Margaret Weatherill and her heirs for ever.

Close Roll, 22 Geo. II., Part 19, Nos. 10 and 11.

Indenture made the 27th Sep. 1748 between Michael Lambert Weatherill, late of Antigua, but now of the parish of St. George, Southwark, Esq., of the one part, and Richard Holmes of May Fair, St. George's, Hanover Square, Esq., and George Weatherill of Antigua, Esq., of the other part, witnesseth that in consideration of 10*s*. Michael Lambert Weatherill grants, etc., to Richard Holmes and George Weatherill all that plantation or sugarwork called Duncombe's Folly, containing 575 acres, in the parish of St. John, Antigua, bounded E. with lands belonging to Edward Williams, Esq., S. with lands belonging to Richard Oliver, Esq., W. with lands belonging to Peter Thibou, Esq., and Samuel Martin, Esq., and N. by lands formerly belonging to and in the possession of Robert Chester, Esq., but now or late held by Colonel George Lucas, and those 107 negros and all cattle, horses, as such are or lately were in the possession or occupation of Michael Lambert Weatherill, subject to the estate for life of Margaret Weatherill, widow, his mother, for one whole year to the uses of an Indenture to be made. William George Douglas, Hugh Hamersley, witnesses.

No. 10.

Indenture tripartite made the 28th Sep. 1748 between Michael Lambert Weatherill, of the 1st part, Richard Holmes and George Weatherill, of the 2nd part, and Charles Pym Burt of Gray's Inn, Gentleman, of the 3rd part. Whereas by Articles of Agreement of the 1st Nov. 1746 between Michael Lambert Weatherill, late of Antigua, but then of St. Martin's in the Fields, Esq., of the one part, and Richard Holmes, then of Brook Street, Hanover Square, Esq., and George Weatherill of Antigua, Esq., of the other part, reciting that Michael Lambert Weatherill was entitled either in tail general or some other good estate, subject to the life estate of his mother of and in the plantation called Duncombe's Folly, as the same was then in the possession of Margaret Weatherill, and that Richard Holmes and George Weatherill had agreed for the absolute purchase of his interest for the price of £500 sterling and an annuity of £200 sterling to be effectually secured to him by them and charged on the plantation, but the annuity not to take effect till after the death of Margaret Weatherill; it was witnessed that in consideration thereof Michael Lambert Weatherill did agree to grant to Richard Holmes and George Weatherill, and to vest the said premises in them as tenants in common and not joint tenants, and give them a good estate of inheritance in fee simple; and whereas by an Indenture of Assignment made the 4th Sep. 1747 between Michael Lambert Weatherill, of the one part, and Charles Pym Burt of Southampton Buildings, of the other part, reciting as above, it was witnessed that Richard Lambert Weatherill had sold to Charles Pym Burt the said annuity of £200 for the price of £500; and whereas the said sums of £500 and £500 were paid, and Richard Holmes and George Weatherill have applied for the absolute conveyance of the said plantation, charged with the £200 a year to Charles Pym Burt for the life of Michael Lambert Weatherill. Now this Indenture witnesseth that for the above considerations Michael Lambert Weatherill grants to Richard Holmes and George Weatherill, in their actual possession being, all that plantation called Dnncombe's Folly, subject to the life estate of Margaret Weatherill, and to their heirs for ever, and Michael Lambert Weatherill appoints, etc., Thomas Warner, Edward Warner, and John Banister, Esquires, all of Antigua, his Attorneys.

No. 5.

Weatherill *v.* Holmes, as recited in Close Roll, 22 Geo. II., Part 19, No. 10, but Richard Holmes described as of Gaddesdon, Herts, and George Weatherill as of the Inner Temple.

Close Roll, 7 Geo. III., Part 14. No. 8.

Indenture made 24th March 1767 between Michael Lambert Weatherill, formerly of Antigua, but now of the parish of St. John, Westminster, Gentleman (brother and heir-at-law and also one of the next of kin to George Weatherill, late of Antigua, Esq., deceased), and Elizabeth Weatherill his wife, of the one part, and Stephen Blizard of Antigua, Esq., and William Warner of Antigua, Esq., of the other part (which said Stephen Blizard and William Warner are two of the Ex'ors of the said George Weatherill), witnesseth that in consideration of 5*s*. Michael Lambert Weatherill and Elizabeth his wife have bargained, etc., to Stephen Blizard and William Warner all that plantation in the parish of St. John, Antigua, called Duncombe's Folly, containing 574 acres, late in the possession of George Weatherill, deceased, and all negros and slaves now used on the plantation, and all horses, cows, oxen, sheep, and other cattle whatsoever, for one whole year, that they may be in actual possession, to the uses of an Indenture to be made. Michael Lambert Weatherill and Elizabeth his wife appoint, etc., Thomas Warner, Ashton Warner Byam, and Thomas Kidder, Esquires, all of Antigua, their Attorneys. Sherland Swanston, Thomas Berry, witnesses.

No. 7.

Indenture made 25th March 1767 between Michael Lambert Weatherill, etc., and Elizabeth Weatherill his wife, of the one part, and Stephen Blizard and William Warner, of the other part. Whereas George Weatherill died the 14th Nov. 1765 seised in fee simple of the plantation hereinafter described; and whereas a short time before his death he gave instructions to Thomas Warner and Edward Byam the younger to draw his will, by which he gave to Louisa Weatherill his wife all his estate for life and at her death to the child she went with in fee, or if more than one, equally, and if they died under age he gave his estate to Charles Weatherill his brother and his heirs, and appointed Stephen Blizard, Thomas Warner, William Warner, and Edward Byam his Ex'ors, and the said instructions were proved as his will before Sir George Thomas as he died before they were reduced to writing, and he left Louisa Weatherill his widow then with child; and whereas Charles Pym Weatherill (brother of George) soon after died, having duly made his last will 9th Dec. 1765, and thereby gave one undivided moiety of his estate to Thomas Ottley, Esq., in tail general, and the other moiety to Martha Ottley, spinster, in tail general, with cross remainders in tail, with a remainder in fee to James Ottley of St. Kitts, Esq., which will was duly proved; and whereas Louisa Weatherill was on the 11th Jan. 1766 delivered of a daughter, who died on the 27th of the same month, leaving Michael Lambert Weatherill her heir-at-law, who is also heir-at-law of George Weatherill, and on the death of the said daughter the remainder in fee of the estate of George Weatherill would have become vested in Charles Pym Weatherill, expectant on the death of Louisa had Charles Pym Weatherill survived the daughter of Louisa, and is now vested in Thomas Ottley and Martha Ottley according to the will of Charles Pym Weatherill; and whereas Louisa Weatherill by the marriage settlement, dated 27th Feb. 1765, made on her intermarriage with George Weatherill, is entitled to a jointure of £200 currency a year for life from a plantation of his called Duncombe's Folly, but in case she should elect dower out of his estate she is to be *dowable* thereof and has a right to waive the jointure: and whereas soon after the death of her husband Louisa Weatherill filed a Bill of Complaint in the Court of Chancery, Antigua, against the Ex'ors of George Weatherill and the devisees and Ex'ors of Charles Pym Weatherill, and against Michael Lambert Weatherill, as brother of the whole blood and heir-at-law of George, for an account and discovery of the estate real and personal of George Weatherill, that she may be capable of judging whether she shall adhere to the jointure or elect dower of her husband's manors; and whereas the Statute of Fraud is not in force in Antigua, and Louisa Weatherill and the devisees of Charles Pym Weatherill filed their Bill of Complaint against Michael Lambert Weatherill; and whereas William Ottley, Esq., and Richard Ottley, Esq., have, as creditors of George Weatherill, filed a Bill on behalf of themselves and of such other creditors as would contribute to the expense of a suit against Louisa Weatherill and Michael Lambert Weatherill and the Ex'ors of George Weatherill and the devisees and Ex'ors of Charles Pym Weatherill, and against Thomas Mills and John Mills of London, merchants, for an account and discovery, and in order that the creditors may be paid from the personal estate of George Weatherill, and subpœnas have been served on Michael Lambert Weatherill and Thomas and John Mills, but Michael Lambert Weatherill has not appeared; and whereas George Weatherill died in debt to divers persons to the amount of £57,000 currency of Antigua; and whereas Louisa Weatherill, Thomas Ottley, Martha Ottley, and James Ottley, and the creditors have for facilitating the sale of the real and personal estate of George Weatherill empowered Stephen Blizard and William Warner to treat with Michael Lambert Weatherill for the purchase of his right to all estate real, personal, and mixed of George Weatherill; and whereas it is doubtful whether the whole will be sufficient to pay all just debts, and if these shall be more than sufficient, yet if the instructions are established as the will of George Weatherill then Michael Lambert Weatherill can receive no benefit, therefore Michael Lambert Weatherill has proposed, as heir-at-law, to convey to Stephen Blizard and William Warner the said plantation and negros, and also as one of the next-of-kin all his right to the personal estate of George Weatherill, on the payment to him of £54 12*s.* a year for life, and Stephen Blizard and William Warner have agreed, and for securing the payment thereof Thomas Truman, Richard Neave, and John Willett of London, merchants and co-partners, have at the request of Stephen Blizard and William Warner executed a bond, bearing even date with these presents, and have become bound to Michael Lambert Weatherill in the penal sum of £1000. Now this Indenture witnesseth that in consideration of the said annuity Michael Lambert Weatherill and Elizabeth Weatherill his wife grant, etc., to Stephen Blizard and William Warner all that plantation to the only proper use of Stephen Blizard and William Warner; and by an Indenture of 26th Feb. 1767 between Louisa Weatherill, Thomas, Martha, and James Ottley, of the 1st part, the creditors of George Weatherill, of the 2nd part, Stephen Blizard and William Warner, of the 3rd part, and Michael Lambert Weatherill, of the 4th part. It was witnessed as above.

Edward Walrond, Esq., writes in 1697-8 that "James Weatherill, now an Inhabitant of Antigoa, about four years since being Com'ander of a Privateer Sloop called ye Charles of Jamaica," captured a large and valuable Spanish ship, but the Court refused to put him on triall for pyracy. (B. T. Leeward Islands, vol. 5.)

1714, March 30. John Weatherill has been gunner of Parham Platform three years.

1715, March 13. Mary Weatheril, widow, states that she owns 135 acres in St. John's, Dickinson's Bay Division, E. with the lands of her late husband Captain James Weatheril, deceased, and Jonas Langford, deceased, W. and N. with the sea, S. with Henry Graden, deceased; also 15 acres E. and N. with Captain James Weatheril, deceased, S. and W. with Christopher Knight, deceased. Prays for a patent.

James Weatheril, Gent., of St. John's in Popes Head, states that he owns 74 acres, N. with the sea, S. with Jonas Langford, deceased, and petitioner, E. with Samuel Boone and Mr. Callender, deceased, W. with Jonas Langford, deceased; also lands in Dickinson's Bay of 4 acres, N. and W. with petitioner, E. with Jonas Langford, deceased, S. with lands lately in possession of Margaret Hodge; also 11 acres, W. with his 4 acres, E. N. and S. with petitioner; also 96 acres, N. with Jonas Langford, deceased, and Henry Norton, S. with Colonel Samuel Watkins, Christopher Knight, Edward Makin, and Henry Graden, E. with Henry Norton and Jonas Langford, deceased, N. with William Crill (?), deceased. Prays for patent. (Minutes of Council and Assembly.)

1715, April 10. Mrs. Mary Weatherill, widow and relict of Captain Weatherill, sells 10 acres to Mr. Christopher Knight.

Indenture dated 6 July 1724 between George Weatherill of Antigua, Gent., and his wife Catherine, of the one part, and Edward Traut of Antigua, merchant. Grant of her thirds on Dunnings Plantation of 347 acres, St. Mary's Parish, for 18 years for £250 yearly.

1736, Jan. James Weatherell of the Folly and James Weatherell of Popeshead both named.

Weatherill, Georgius, Britannus, 6 Nov. 1744. Weatherill, Georgius, Anglus, 18 Maii 1745. (Graduates of Leyden University.)

1757, Feb. 25. Mr. George Weatherill has been appointed to the St. Christopher's Council by Governor George Thomas. (B. T. Leeward Islands, vol. 31.)

George Weatherill to be of the St. Kitts' Council. Mandamus dated 20 Feb. 1759 at St. James.

1766, Jan. 29. Governor G. Thomas announces the death of Colonel George Weatherill of St. Kitts.

Antigua. In Chancery. Conveyance of an estate in trust to Alexander Willock at the suit of William Ottley of Great Britain, Esq., and Richard Ottley of St. Vincent, Esq., reciting that on 19 June 1766 in the Court of Chancery, as Creditors of George Weatherill, deceased, against Stephen Blizard, William Warner and Thomas Warner, and Edward Byam of Antigua, Esquires, and Louisa Weatherill and Thomas Ottley of Antigua, Esq., and Martha Ottley of Great Britain, spinster, and James Ottley of Great Britain and Michael Lambart Weatherill of Great Britain, Esq., and John and Thomas Mills of Great Britain, Esquires. George Weatherill's bond of £5000 for payment of £2500, and bond dated 6 June 1762 of £2500 for £1500. He owed £60,000 c., and died 14 Nov. 1765, leaving his estate to his wife for life and then to his brother Charles Pym Weatherell, and appointed Stephen Blizard, Thomas Warner, William Warner, and Edward Byam, jun., of Antigua, Esquires, and his wife, and owned a plantation called Duncombe's Folly and personal estate of £40,000. Charles Pym Weatherell died 10 Dec. 1765, and by his will dated 9 Dec. he left half his estate to his nephew Thomas Ottley of St. Christopher's, Esq., and half to his niece Martha

Ottley, and on 11 Jan. 1766 Louisa Weatherill had a daughter called Georgiana which died 31 Jan. 1766. James Ottley and his sister Martha. Estate to be conveyed in Trust for payment of debts, etc. . . . . Michael Lambart Weatherill seems to have claimed the estate as heir male.

Antigua. In Chancery. Louisa Weatherill, widow and relict of George Weatherill, late of Antigua, Esq., deceased, complainant, *v.* the Ex'ors of said George Weatherill, Charles Pym Weatherill, and Michael Lambert Weatherill, etc., defendants. Publication to pass. 5 Sep. 1767. Ashton W. Byam, Counsell for complainant, and Thomas Warner for defendants.

Indenture dated 23 April 1770 between Edward Gamble of Antigua, Esq., Master in Chancery, of the 1st part, Hon. Stephen Blizard and William Warner of Antigua, Esquires, of the 2nd part, Louisa Weatherill, widow of George Weatherill of Antigua, Esq., deceased, of the 3rd part, Thomas Ottley of St. Vincent, Esq., and Martha Ottley of Great Britain, spinster, and James Ottley of Great Britain, Esq., of the 4th part, Alexander Willock of Antigua, Esq., of the 5th part, and Hon. Francis Farley of Antigua, Esq., of the 6th part. Lease for one year to Francis Farley of a plantation called Duncombe's Folly in St. John's Parish and Division of 456 acres, bounded W. with Olivers and Bendalls, N. with Briggins, S. with Hon. S. Martin, E. with Edward Williams, Esq. Schedule of negros and stock: 78 men, 51 women, 10 boys, 11 girls.

PARISH REGISTER OF ST. JOHN.

Baptized.

1722 April 10 James the s. of James Wetherill & Margaret his wife.
1724 Nov. 19 Sarah the d. of Geo. Wetherill and Cath. his wife.
1726 July 24 James the s. of George Wetherill & his wife.
1728 June 25 Margaret the d. of Geo. Wetherill and Catharine his wife.
1766 Jan. 31 Georgiana the D. of Geo. Wetherill and Louisa his wife.
1782 May 27 Thomas Francis the S. of Thomas Weatherill and Sarah his wife.
1783 Dec. 8 Joseph Francis the S. of Thomas Weatherill and Sarah his wife.
(? 1785) Feb. 16 David Francis the S. of Thomas Weatherill and Frances his wife.
1794 July 28 Samuel Harman S. of Thomas Weatherill and Sarah his wife; b. the 8th November 1792.
1795 Aug. 31 Charles Inglefield S. of Thomas Weatherill and Sarah his wife; b. the 8th February 1795.
1800 Jan. 29 Daniel Burnthorn S. of Thomas Weatherill and Sarah his wife. B. the 7th February 1799.
1802 July 7 Judith the D. of Thomas Weatherill and Sarah his wife. B. 9th Jan'ry 1802.
1806 June 11 Samuel Watkins S. of Thomas Francis Weatherill and Mary his wife. B. the 28 April last.
1807 Aug. 4 Louisa Jane D. of Thomas Francis Weatherill and Mary his wife. B. the 21st May last.
1809 Mar. 8 Maria Ann D. of Thomas F. Weatherill and Mary his wife. B. the 22d November last.
1813 April 7 Sarah Inglefield D. of Thomas F. Weatherill and Mary his wife. B. 8th August 1812.
1815 Nov. 16 Elizabeth Blashford D. of Thomas F. Weatherill and Mary his wife. B. the 19th April 1814.

Married.

1745 Dec. 23 Joseph King and Marg^t Weatherill.
1781 April 21 Thomas Weatherill to Sarah Inglefield. L.
1805 June 19 Thomas Francis Weatherill to Mary Watkins, Spinster. L.

Buried.

(? 1702-3) Capt James Weatherell.
1727 Aug. 5 Mad^m Mary Weatherill.
1727 Oct. 24 Maj^r George Weatherill.
1745 June 19 John Weatherill s. of Coll^o Weatherill.
1745 Jan. 7 Coll^o James Weatherill.
1751 Oct. 21 James Weatherill.
1751 Oct. 12 Thomas Weatherill.
1765 Nov. 15 George Weatherill, Esqr.
1766 Feb. 1 Georgiana Weatherill, C. Child.
1780 June 2 John Weatherell.
1783 Dec. 29 Joseph Francis Weatherill, an Infant.
1804 Feb. 13 Lucy Weatherill.
1804 July 7 Eliza Hill Weatherill, Inf^t.
1806 Sep. 1 Louisa Weatherill.
1809 Jan. 22 Thomas Weatherill.
1813 Oct. 24 Sarah Weatherill.

PARISH REGISTER OF ST. GEORGE.

Married.

1743 April 9 John Stevens and Sarah Weatherel, Spinster.
1765 Feb. 23 George Weatherill, Gentleman, from St Christopher's, & Louisa Blizard, Spinster.

Buried.

1766 . . . . . . Charles Weatherill.
1770 Jan. 28 James Weatherill; in the burying Ground on the Estate of Stephen Blizard, Esqr.

ST. JOHN'S CHURCHYARD.

On a ledger, the inscription very indistinct:—

Arms: *Three lions or leopards passant* (? WEATHERILL); impaling . . . . *a chevronel* . . . . *between three* (? *talbots*) . . . . *a chief* . . . . (? BLIZARD).

HERE LIES THE BODY OF GEORGE WEA . . . . ESQ
WHO DEPARTED THIS LIFE (month illegible) 14th 1765
AGED 40.

PARISH OF ST. THOMAS, MIDDLE ISLAND, ST. CHRISTOPHER'S.*

In the churchyard:—

Arms: *Per chevron* . . . . *three lambs* . . . .

Crest: *A griffin.*

Here lyeth the body of Michael Lambert, Esq. Maj^r General of the Leeward Islands and some time Lieut. Governor of St Christopher's. He died the 26th day of March 172¾ in the 70th year of his age. Here also lyeth the body of Frances his youngest daughter and wife of Charles Pym, Esq., who died the 9th day of Novr 1724 in the 20th year of her age.

"Weatherills" is in St. John's Parish. In 1852 it contained 300 acres, and was owned by John Tollemache, Esq. (formerly Delap-Halliday). It is now (1892) owned by Mr. Lane, who has rebuilt the dwelling-house and effected other improvements. There is an old family burial-ground here containing several brick vaults, but the top slabs with the M.I. were lost or destroyed before Mr. Lane's time. This burial-ground and the one at Mount Jarvis are the only two of all the plantation family burial-places that are still kept clean and cared for. Nearly all the others have been desecrated, and are used for mule-pens or dust-heaps. Langfords was full of old iron and other rubbish.

* This M.I. was copied some years ago and sent to me by Mr. N. Darnell Davis.

Pedigree of Webb.

NATHANIEL WEBB of Philips Norton, co. Somerset, died 1686╤. . . .

Robert Webb of Taunton, co. Somerset╤. . . .

Bethiah, dau. of William Gerrish, Esq.; bur. 27 Oct. 1728 at St. Anthony, Montserrat. 1st wife. ╤ Nathaniel Webb of Montserrat, merchant, Collector of Customs; Member of Council 1727; died Feb. 1741 at Taunton. Will dated 14 March 1739; proved 26 March 1741. (78 Spurway.) ╤ Jane . . . . living 1739. 2nd wife.

Ann Webb, mar. . . . . Stone.

Sarah Webb, mar. . . . . Smith.

Robert Webb of the Temple 1742; M.P. for Taunton; late of Wigmore Street, deceased, 1777; s.p.

Nathaniel Webb, M.P. for Taunton, bapt. 1726 at St. Anthony, Montserrat; sold his estate in Antigua 1777. ╤ Elizabeth . . . .

John Webb, bapt. 27 Oct. 1727 at St. Anthony, Montserrat; inherited 500 acres in Connecticut.

Ann Webb, bapt. 14 June 1723 at St. Anthony, Montserrat; mar. Aug. 1742 Andrew de Vismes of London, merchant; he was born 19 May 1718. Will dated 1761; proved 1779. (297 Warburton.)

Nathaniel Webb, bur. 8 Oct. 1748 at St. Paul's, Antigua.

Thomas Thompson of Montserrat. ╤ Amy, dau. of . . . . Symes of Antigua.

William Gerrish, Collector and J.P. of Montserrat 1704; lost £20,000 by damages at French Invasion 1712; æt. 44, 1718, then Member of Council; died 21 June 1741. ╤ Mary . . . .

James Thompson of Montserrat, 1st son and heir. 1st husband. ╤ Mary Gerrish ╤ David Stone. 2nd husband.

Bethiah Gerrish, mar. Nathaniel Webb of Montserrat, Esq., Collector of Customs; she was bur. 27 Oct. 1728 at St. Anthony's.

Henrietta Gerrish, mar. . . . . Douglas; living his widow 1765 at Witton Hall, co. Durham.

John Gerrish, bur. 18 Nov. 1729 at St. Anthony, Montserrat.

John Thompson, Lieut in the Army, dead 1763.

Amy Thompson. Henrietta Thompson. Ann Thompson. Spinsters 1763.

Nehemiah Webb of Bristol, grocer. Will dated 20 April, proved P.C.C. 1683. (78 Drax.) Wife Jone £600. S. Nath. £800. Daus. Hester & Eliz. £1000 apiece. Neph. Nehemiah s. of bro. Robt. Bros. Wm, Robt, & Ezekial. To be bur. at St Thos.

Thomas Webb. Will dated 7 July 1733. To my sister Ann Woodstock . . . . of Wm Woodstock, £40 c. To my sister Elizth Woodstock, another dau., £50 c. To my goddau. Susannah Russell, dau. of Wm Russell in Barbados, £20 c. to buy a negro. To my dear child Christian Webb all my estate, if she die then all equally to . . . . Woodstock & Elizth Woodstock, they paying £25 to . . . . & £25 to David . . . . of Barbados. My loving father . . . . Ex'or . . . . ugent . . . . Nibbs. Before Edward Byam were sworn 7 July 1733 Major Walter Nugent and Mr. William Nibbs. Recorded 31 July.

Nathaniel Webb of Mountserrat, merchant. Will dated 14 March 1739; proved 26 March 1741 by Robert Webb, Esq., the son; power reserved to the other Ex'ors. (78 Spurway.) My Ex'ors are to grant a lease to my wife Jane of all my negros on my plantation in St Anthony's called "Carolls" & my house in town, also all cattle on the Northward plantation, in lieu of dower, she to pay £250 a year. I give her also the use of $\frac{1}{2}$ my house in Taunton & all my furniture in Montserrat, & my Ex'ors are to lend her £300 on bond to be free of interest for 3 years. To my 1st son Robt all my estate in the co. of Somerset, formerly under lease to John & Richd Barber of Taunton at £140 per annum, & all my houses & lands in the town of Taunton, also £5000, & all plate & furniture in my house at Taunton. To my son Nathl my plantation in Montserrat now under lease to John Dyer, & my house & land in the town of Basseterre, St Christopher's. To my son John all my lands in the county of Connecticut, N.E., near the town of Seabrook, of 500 acres. To my brother John Webb of Abington £100 & forgive debts. To my brother Harry Webb 50 gs. To my Ex'ors 10 gs. each. To my sisters Anne Stone & Sarah Smith £20 apiece & rings. To my 5 children, viz., Robt, Ann, Ruth, Nathl, & John all residue equally, but all surplus of their shares over £5000 to my son Robt. All sums due to me in Montserrat & St Christopher's to be sent to Wm Gerrish, Esq., in London. Wm Gerrish, Esq., in London, Isaac Hobhouse of Bristol, mercht, John Paine of Taunton, mercer, Dominick Traut, Tho. Meade, Geo. French, & Peter Lee of Montserrat, Harry Webb of Antigua, & my son Robt Ex'ors & Guardians. Witnessed by William Harcum, Peter Hussey, James Fyffe.

Nathaniel Webb of Bristol, Gent. Will dated 3 Oct. 1740; proved P.C.C. 1744. (66 Seymer.) In 1738 I surrendered to the Lord of the Manor of Taunton Dean, co. Som., all my lands there for the use of my wife Sarah till my s. Jno Bowdidge Webb is 21, then to him.

John Webb = Mary, dau. and coheir of John Sweet of Taunton.
John Webb of Abingdon 1739.

Harry Webb of the Inner Temple; æt. 41 Nov. 1749; Attorney-General of the Leeward Islands 1754; sold "Lucas's" in Antigua 1777; bur. at Taunton. Will dated 12 Dec. 1783; proved 30 March 1786. (199 Norfolk.) = Margaret, dau. of Thomas Nicholas of Antigua, Esq.; mar. 1st, 29 Oct. 1745, at St. John's, Bastian Otto-Baijer, who was there bur. 3 Jan. 1745-6; remar. 4 Jan. 1746. (*Vide* Vol. I., p. 18.)

Ruth Webb, bapt. 20 Sep. 1724 at St. Anthony, Montserrat.

Mary Webb, bapt. 27 Oct. 1727 and bur. 1729 at St. Anthony, Montserrat.

William Webb, Member of Assembly and Assistant Judge of Montserrat; died 1793 at St. Christopher's. = ...

Francis Webb, born 18 Sep. 1735 at Taunton; at one time a minister, later a political writer; died 2 Aug. 1815, æt. 80, at Barrington, co. Somerset. = Hannah, dau. of William Milner of Poole, co. Dorset, Esq.; mar. 31 March 1764 at Wareham.
s.p. supers.

Henry Webb. Edward Webb. Mary Webb.

Andrew De Visme of St. Margaret Lothbury, merchant. Will dated 20 July 1761; proved 19 July 1779 by Anne De Visme the relict; power reserved to Nathaniel Webb the other surviving Ex'or. To my wife Anne plate, linen, furniture, horses, & carriages, lease of my house in Lothbury. My 2 clerks Cha. Christian Hoeitzer & Cha. Day £100 each. ⅓ of all my personal est. to my wife Anne. ⅓ to my son Philip Nathaniel De Visme at 22, but if he die to my brothers-in-law Rob[t] Webb & Nath. Webb, Esq[rs], & my brothers the Rev. Lewis De Visme & M[r] Stephen De Visme in Trust to pay the interest to my wife, & at her death to be sold & ½ as she shall appoint & ½ to my brothers Lewis, Stephen, Gerard, Leo, W[m], & my sister Amelia De Visme; the other ⅓ to my said 4 trustees to pay to my wife Anne for life, then to my son Philip. All residue both real & personal to my said wife & son equally. My trustees & wife Ex. Witnessed by John Tubb, William Mackey.

1763, May 11. Testamentary letter from Abraham Webb at Cobbs Cross Hospital in Antegoe, dated 7 June 1762, giving all prize money from H.M.S. "Tartar" to his father Edward Webb, who proved the will. (260 Cæsar.)

Josiah Webb of Stoney Hill, Nevis, Esq. Will dated 20 Feb., proved 1 Dec. 1767 by George Webbe, jun., and William Neeve. (468 Legard.) £500 to a free mulatto Geo. New, now at Bridgewater. To John Freeman of ditto £100. To my sister Mary Fenton £1000. To my sist. Fra. Lowman £500, & to her d[r] Marg[t] Lowman £1200. To Fanny Ross, d[r] of my late bro. Joseph Webbe, Esq., £600. To my neph. Geo. Lowman my sister's son £2500. To my niece Sarah Daniel, d[r] of my late sister Eliz. Daniel, £1200, & to my neph. Geo. Webbe Daniel my sister's son £2500 in 3 years. To my niece Ann Daniell £1200 in 5 years. To my niece Phœbe Daniell £1200 in 6 years. To my sister Ann Webb £10 a y[r]. To Hagar Chapman a free negro woman £40 c. & a barrel of sugar a y[r], also the house, 5 acres of land I lately purchased of Eliz[th] Edgerly & Joseph Herbert, Esq., at S[t] John's, Nevis, with the use of my slave Sophia, then to Geo. Webb, jun[r], son of my late bro. Joseph Webb. The wills of my late father & mother, dec[d]. All my lands & ½ the plantation I hold with my bro. Geo. Webb, Esq., to my neph. Geo. Webb, Esq. My s[d] neph. & W[m] Reeve of Bristol, merch[t], Ex'ors. Witnessed by Samuel Lawrence, jun., James Lawrence, William Tuckett.

1st Codicil. 9 April 1767. £60 c. a y[r], not £40 c., to my negro. Witnessed by James Chapman, John Tuckett, William Tuckett.

2nd Codicil. Annul legacy to my neph. Geo. Lowman, & give him a plantation I lately purchased of Jn[o] Latoysonere & 30 slaves & £1000 payable in 3 years. Witnessed by James Chapman, John Lytton Coram, John Tuckett. Before Hon. Joseph Herbert, President of Nevis, appeared William Tuckett, Attorney-at-Law, 14 April 1767, and John Tuckett, Gent. A. Henderson, Deputy-Secretary. Nevis, *vera copia* 15 July 1767.

1771, May 18. Nathaniel Webb of Bristol, widower, deceased. Adm'on to David Webb and Nathaniel Webb, uncles and guardians of Richard Webb the son, a minor.

Harry Webb, Esq. Will dated 12 Dec. 1783; proved 30 March 1786 by Philip Nathaniel de Visme and Harry Smith, Esquires. (199 Norfolk.) His body to be carried to Taunton & deposited in the Family Vault, pursuant to the Inscription on the marble part of a Stone Monument erected by him. Whereas his Annuity of £200 a year (charged on all the real Estate of Nathaniel Gilbert the elder, Esq., late of Antigua, dec., estimated at £30,000 ster. a few years ago), will end with his life, Ex'ors are to demand & receive all arrears then due, as was done in like case on his wife's Annuity of £200 a year charged on the said Estate. Whereas he is possessed of a joint Bond from John Halliday, Esq., since dec., & John Delap Halliday, Esq., his eldest son & heir, for payment of £6500 to his Ex'ors within 6 months after his decease, with interest at 5 per cent., & meantime for payment to himself of £162 10*s.* every 29th May & every 29th January (the original Bond is in a tin case with other original papers, & a duplicate of his will & an attested copy thereof by the Clerks of M[r] Wilmot, who drew the Bond for the sale of the Antigua Estate, is in another tin case in the hands of Henry Smith, nephew, one of his Ex'ors), gives the £6500 as follows: Anne Stone, sister, £600, but if she dies first Anne Dunsford her daughter £200 of it, & the remainder to Robert Stone & William

Stone her sons equally. Ex'ors £600 in trust to pay the interest to William Webb, nephew, for life, & at his death the principal to Harry Webb & Mary Webb his 2 children equally. Nephews Francis Webb, Joseph Jeffries, Robert Smith, & Henry Smith £600 apiece. Nieces Anne Tuckwell, Bethia Webb, Anne Dunsford, Sarah Stone, Anne Boon, & Jane Toulmin £300 apiece. Mary Arabella French, late wife's sister, £300. Elizabeth Whyte, late wife's half sister, £100. Elizabeth Anne Stone (daughter of George Stone, eldest son of sister Anne) £100. If any of these die in his life the Legacies void. Whereas he is possessed of another Bond from Robert Gray, late of Antigua, Esq., dec., for £1000, with interest at 6 per cent., which Testator lent him to complete the purchase of a settled Plantation in Antigua when Testator resided there (the original Bond is in the hands of George Savage, Esq., Testator's Attorney), & they are also to attend to the Letters between John Grey of Antigua, Esq., son & heir of the said Obligor, & Testator touching the said Bond, & to the case & opinion thereon by Mr Glanville that "the Father's Bond has a legal & adjudge of priority to any Mortgage by the Son or by the Trustees under the Father's Will," & that on the Sale of the said Plantation the Bond must be first paid, which Testator stated in writing to Messrs Boddington the Mortgagees of the said John Gray the son, which Mr Smith delivered to them with a copy of the said case & opinion, which Testator likewise sent to his said Attorney in Antigua for his direction. Whereas by the non-payment of Testator's said Annuity of £200 a year for 4½ years the 5th of the present month of December 1783, amounting with interest & penalties to £1200 or thereabouts, as stated in the accounts in the said tin cases, & by non-payment of the interest on the last recited Bond due 20th May now last past, & several losses by Colepeper & Gines (?), Testator has been obliged to sell out of the Government Annuities for 30 years, whereby he is now possessed of £100 per an. only therein & may probably be obliged to sell out more to supply further defaults. Ex'ors are to sell all his remaining property therein as soon as conveniently may be & apply the produce as follows: first, to pay all his debts & funeral expenses, then to retain £200 for their own care & trouble in keeping the accounts touching the Executorship, which are to be kept in a separate Book from the Partnership Book, for the inspection of any Legatee who shall require it, & then to pay to his servant Jeffry Snape £200. John Clarke, coachman, who has served Testator for 18 years, 45 guineas; horses jobbed at £103 a year since 1765. As to his personal Estate distinct & separate from the 2 Bonds, the Government Annuities, & the arrears of his own Annuity, as follows: Anne Stone, sister, his gold Watch, formerly a Lady's, & the Seals (except the one with wife's Arms quartered), but if she dies to Sarah Stone her daughter. Mary Arabella French, wife's sister, the said excepted Seal, & her sister's Silver Ink Stand, & the Silver Sugar & Tea Canisters with the like quartered Arms in a Shagreen case, & Testator's little Silver Saucepan, & 6 Table spoons. Jeffry Snape all wearing apparel, Shirts, Stocks, household & other Linen, & everything not otherwise bequeathed except Bank Notes, Cash, 2 gold snuff boxes (presented to Testator by Robert Webb Stone & William John Glanville, nephews aforesaid, to whom he was Guardian, when they came to age), & all papers of all kinds whatsoever. George Savage £100. All residue of personal Estate as follows: To Henry Smith, nephew, £400, & the rest to him in trust to divide equally between Mary Arabella French, wife's sister, Robert Smith & Robert Webb Stone, nephews, 2 reduced Captains of Foot, & William John Glanville, nephew, but to retain a fifth part for himself. Philip Nathaniel De Visme & Henry Smith, nephew, Ex'ors. Richard Jones, stationer, Temple, John Alrain, George Hall, at Mr. Jones's, witnesses.

Close Roll, 17 Geo. III., Part 3, Nos. 22 and 23.

Indenture made the 28th Jan. 1777 between Harry Webb of the parish of St. George's, Hanover Square, Esq., and Nathaniel Webb of Savile Row, St. James's, Westminster, Esq. (brother and heir-at-law and devisee of Robert Webb, late of Wigmore Street, St. Marylebone, Esq., deceased), of the one part, and John Halliday of Queen Anne Street, Cavendish Square, Esq., of the other part, witnesseth that in consideration of 5*s.* Harry Webb and Nathaniel Webb grant to John Halliday all that plantation in the parish of St. Paul and divisions of Willoughby Bay and Falmouth in Antigua, containing 321 acres 1 rood and 15 perches, bounded E. with the lands of Francis Delap, Esq., S. with the lands of Martin Blake, Esq., Colonel Valentine Morris, deceased, and Baptist Looby, deceased, W. with the lands of John Yeamans, Esq., deceased, and N. with the lands of the said John Yeamans, John Duer, Esq., and Francis Delap, and the two dwelling-houses as now in the occupation and possession of Harry and Nathaniel Webb, and all negros, slaves, cattle, and stock, which at the expiration of a lease on the 2nd Sep. last, formerly made to Simon Farley, Esq., were or now are on the plantation for one whole year, and Harry and Nathaniel Webb and John Halliday constitute the Hon. Thomas Warner, Esq., Attorney-General of Antigua, and George Savage and Bertie Entwisle, both of Antigua, Esquires, their Attorneys. John Blake, Essex Street, Gentleman, John Lancaster, Bloomsbury Square, Gentleman, witnesses.

No. 22.

Indenture made the 29th Jan. 1777 between Harry Webb and Nathaniel Webb and Elizabeth his wife, of the one part, and John Halliday, of the other part. Whereas Harry and Nathaniel Webb being seised in fee of a plantation called Rockhill otherwise Lucas's in Antigua, with the negros, in equal moieties as tenants in common, have lately by a memorandum in writing dated the 21st Nov. now last past agreed to sell the same to John Halliday for £13,000 sterling, with interest at 5 per cent. from the 2nd Sep. last, of which £6500, one moiety, was to be paid or secured to be paid to Harry Webb, and the like sum, the other moiety, to Nathaniel Webb as therein mentioned; but John Halliday and Nathaniel Webb have since come to an agreement that John Halliday shall pay at the execution of these presents the said sum of £6500 with interest to Nathaniel Webb; and whereas on the said treaty it was agreed that John Halliday should be entitled to the benefit of the produce and increase of the slaves from the 2nd Sep., he paying all taxes from that time and all incidental expenses for the supply of the plantation and subsistence of the slaves, and also all such supply for the plantation as has been since that time sent out to Antigua by Messrs. Devisme and Smith, merchants in London, to George Savage, Esq., and Harry Webb and Nathaniel Webb paying all up to the 2nd Sep. This Indenture therefore witnesseth that in pursuance of the agreement and in consideration of £6632 13*s.* 5*d.*, principal and interest from the 2nd Sep., secured to be paid to Harry Webb, and of the like sum paid to Nathaniel Webb in full for the absolute purchase, and for docking and destroying the estate of dower of Elizabeth, Harry Webb and Nathaniel Webb and Elizabeth his wife grant and confirm to John Halliday in his actual possession being all that plantation (as in No. 23) to the use of John Halliday and his heirs and assigns for ever.

1704-5, Feb. 6. Montserrat. Colonel John Johnson, Commander-in-Chief, has sworn in Mr. William Gerrish as a Member of the Council.

1724, July 20. Nevis. Josiah Webbe and George Webbe both Members of the Assembly.

1726-7, March 4. Montserrat. Nathaniel Webb then of the Council.

1729-30. Montserrat Census. Nathaniel Webb, Esq., Collector. 34 slaves, 7 in family, 40 acres of cane, 20 mules.

1736, Sep. 16. Montserrat. Governor Mathew writes that he has appointed John Webb as a Councillor there *vice* Nathaniel Webb, absent.

1741. Nevis. Josiah Webb, a proper person to fill a vacancy in the Council.

1741, Feb. At his Seat near Taunton, Nathaniel Webb, Esq; Collector of the Customs at Monserrat, in which Island he had a very plentiful Estate. His Death was occasion'd by a Fall from a Scaffold erected by the Workmen who were at work on some of his Out-houses, by which he fractur'd his Skull and broke one of his Thighs. He is succeeded in his Estate by his eldest Son, Robert Webb, Esq; of the Temple. ('Lond. Mag.,' p. 101.)

1741, June 21. William Garrish, Esq. an eminent West India Merchant, who never suffer'd his Name to be seen on the Debtor Side of Tradesmen's Books. ('Gent. Mag.,' p. 332.)

1742, Aug. Mr. Andrew Devisme, Merchant, to Miss Ann Webb, Sister to Robert Webb, of the Temple, Esq. ('Lond. Mag.,' p. 413.)

1744, June 5. Harry Webb has twelve months leave.

1745, March 21. His letter to the Assembly read, dated 30 Nov., saying convoy has been delayed, and asking for extension of leave.

1749, Nov. 2. Deposition of Harry Webb, Esq., then aged 41. (B. T. Leeward Islands, vol. 29.)

1754, June 21. Harry Webb, Esq., to be Attorney-General of the Leeward Islands *vice* Ashton Warner, Esq., deceased. (America and the West Indies, No. 103.)

1756, March 27. Harry Webb, who is going to reside in England, resigns his seat in the Assembly of Antigua.

1760. The proclamation of George III. was signed by Josiah Webbe, Speaker of Nevis.

1778, Jan. 6. Harry Webb recommended to be a Councillor of the Virgin Islands.

Joseph Webbe, son of George Webbe of Nevis, Esq., matriculated from Wadham College 17 Feb. 1770, aged 18, and was created M.A. 8 July 1773; he died 1779, æt. 27. M.I. at Stratford, near Salisbury. His sister married James Tobin of Nevis.

1786, March 17. Henry Webb, esq. of New Bond-street, formerly His Majesty's attorney-general, and judge-advocate of the Leeward Islands. ('Gent. Mag.,' p. 168.)

1804, June 22. At Bourne-house, co. Cambridge, where he had arrived only a few days, with an intention of residing there, Geo. Webb, sen. esq., late an opulent merchant of the island of Nevis in the West Indies.

1815, Aug. 2. At Barrington, co. Somerset, far advanced in years, F. Webb, esq., a gentleman well known for his literary acquirements; of whom more hereafter. On p. 563 is a long biographical account of him, with a list of his writings. ('Gent. Mag.,' p. 278.)

1817, July 2. P. N. De Visme, esq. of Notting-hill House, Kensington. (*Ibid.*, p. 90.)

Parish Register of St. John.

Baptized.

1742 Mar. 13 Elizabeth D. of Capt John Webb and Catherine his wife.

1749 Jan. 22 William the S. of Capt John Webb and Catherine his wife.

1751 June 25 Edward the S. of Capt John Webb and Catherine his wife.

Married.

1725 Mar. 12 Thomas Webb and Christian Woodstock. L.

1743 Sep. 11 James Webb and Mary Bendall. B.

1746 Jan. 4 Harry Webb, Esqr, and Margt Otto Bayer.

1747 Dec. 2 Nath. Sampson Webb and Eliz. Nanton.

1754 Aug. 6 John Gallway and Christian Webb.

Buried.

1724 May 7 Capt Wm Webb from Bristoll.

1727 Aug. 5 Christian the w. of Doct. Thomas Webb.

1733 April 18 Doctr Thomas Webb.

1751 Dec. 22 Capt John Webb.

Parish Register of St. Paul.

Buried.

1748 Oct. 8 Nathaniel S. of Nathaniel Web & Elizabeth his wife.

Parish Register of St. Anthony, Montserrat.

(B. T. Leeward Islands, vol. 21.)

Baptized.

1723 June 14 Anne D. of Mr Nathll Webb & Bethia his wife.

1724 Sep. 20 Ruth D. of Mr Nathll Webb & Bethia his wife.

1725 Aug. 21 Nathaniel S. of Mr Nathall Webb & Bethia his wife.

1728 Oct. 25 John & Mary S. & D. of Mr Nath. Webb & Bethia his wife.

Buried.

1728 Oct. 27 Bethia wife of Nathll Webb, Esq.

1729 (? May) Mary D. of Nathll Webb, Esqr.

1729 Nov. 18 John S. of Wm Gerrish, Esqr, & Mary his wife.

Somerset House Chapel, London.

Married.

1744-5 Nathaniel Webb, of Bristol, to Jane Man.

1676, May 6. Samuel Webb, of St James in Bristol, co. Somerset, Gent., Bachr, abt 22, & Anne Whitewood, of St John in Bristol afsd, Spr, abt 21, her parents dead; at Keinsham, co. Somerset, or Clifton or Harvell, co. Gloucester. (Marriage Allegations: L. A. C.)

1692, March 28. Nathaniell Webb, of Bristoll, Grocer, Bachr, abt 25, & Mrs Elizth Churchey, of Watcombe, Dorset, Spr, abt 22, with consent of her brother, her parents dead; alleged by Thos Hawkins, of Bristol; at Watcombe. (Marriage Licences: Vicar-General of the Archbishop of Canterbury.)

St. Paul's Churchyard.

There is a large granite slab, with the name:—

M FRANs WEBB.

Pedigree of Weir.

. . . . , WEIR, bur. with his wife and children in Elgin Cathedral ╤ . . . .

Captain John Weir of Antigua, merchant and planter, leased 350 acres for 21 years of Harvie Keynell, Esq., 1679; Member of Assembly 1686—89 and 1698; bur. 8 Nov. 1704 at St. John's. Will dated 9 July, and sworn 17 Nov. 1704. 1st husband. ╤ Ann . . . . remar. in England 1705—08; bur. 18 April 1717 at St. John's. ╤ John Vincens, formerly of Kensington, later of Antigua, Surgeon; bur. 13 Feb. 1726-27 at St. John's. Will dated 4 Feb. 1726; proved 18 March 1728. (91 Abbott.) 2nd husband.

Children of Captain John Weir and Ann:

- Colonel Robert Weir, only son and heir, sold "Little Zoar" of 223 acres in St. John's Division to Edward Chester 1704; Colonel of ye Forts 1731; bur. 11 April 1748 at St. John's. ╤ Mary . . . . living 1748.
- Frances Weir, mar. John Haddon; settlement dated 7 June 1716.
- Ann Weir, niece of Mrs. Frances Oliver 1705.
- Mary Weir, bur. 9 Sep. 1691 at St. John's.

Children of Colonel Robert Weir and Mary:

- Walter Weir, Manager and Storekeeper of Great George Fort 1742—46. Will dated 10 Oct. 1748.
- Frances Weir, bapt. 7 June 1711 at St. John's; living 1748.

John Dipford of Antigua, planter. Will dated 1 May 1703, 2 Anne. To my wife Sarah Dipford my horse, bedstead, etc. All residue to my dau. Eliz. Dipford, now an infant, but if she die all my estate to my sister Mary Dipford. My sd only dau. Eliz. Dipford Ex'trix. My loving uncle Capt. Jno Weir & Rob. Oliver of Antigua, Gent., overseers & adm'ors & guardians. Witnessed by James Nesbitt, Florence Crowlie, John Anderson, William Maekelmore.

Codicil. 8 May 1703. A negro girl to my wife. By Lieut.-Governor John Yeamans, 20 July 1703, appeared James Nesbitt and John Anderson and were sworn. Recorded 27 Sep. 1703.

John Weir of Antigua, planter. Will dated 9 July 1704. To my wife Ann & to my son Robt Weir all my estate equally, & after her death her share to my son. If he die without heirs then to my nephew Patrick Weir, son of my brother Robt Weir, then to the 1st son of my brother Geo. Weir. To my dau. Ann Weir £1500. To my dau. Frances Weir £1500, but if either marry a Roman Catholic to have but £100 c. To my brother Robt Weir £5 yearly, or if he come here lodging, etc. To my nephew Patrick Weir £150 st. to purchase medicine to sett up his trade at St John's. To my cousin Mary Dipford £100 c. 1 year after her marriage. £30 st. to ye church of Elgin in Murray to purchase a piece of plate for communion, & £10 for a bell for ye Grammar School at Elgin. £30 st. to ye Great Church of New Aberdeen for a piece of communion plate. £50 st. to Glasgow for a Cupp, a vessell of gold for ye City Hall as is proper at ye usual sollemnity of making Burgers, etc. £10 st. to build a tomb for my father & mother's Grave where they & their children are buried in the Cathedral Church of Elgin. My good friends Capt. Richd Oliver & his brother Robt Oliver of Antigua, also my brother Robt Weir, now of Bristol, to help my wife. Richd & Robt Oliver to have each £20 c. for mourning. My son Robt Weir not to have any claim on my estate while his mother lives than what she & they think right, & not to inherit after her death till he is 31, & if he marry before he is to settle on part of ye 100 acres. Witnessed by Robert Oliver, John Barnes. By Sir William Mathew was sworn John Barnes 17 Nov. 1704. Recorded 10 Nov. 1704.

Robert Weir of Antigua. Will dated 4 Feb. 1720. To my son Alexr a negro boy & horse. To my son James £30 c. To my son Thos. a negro boy at 16. To my son Walter £25 c. To my dau. Eleanor Weir a negro girl. To my dau. Elizth Weir a negro girl at 17. To my wife Cristobella all my estate. My wife, Mr Jas. Evans, & Walter Sydserfe of Antigua Ex'ors. Witnessed by Jonathan Keeling, Thomas Goulding, Henry Phillips. By Edward Byam, Esq., was sworn Jonathan Keeling 17 Feb. 1724-5.

Inventory of chattels of John Weir, £137 10s.

John Vincens of Antigua, Surgeon. Will dated 4 Feb. 1726. On 18 March 1728 commission to John Bap the Attorney of George Jennings and Phil. Reynolds. (91 Abbott.) To my wife Elizth the house & land in St John's Town where I dwell, & after her death to my neph. Cornwall Vincens & his heirs, with remainder to my neph. Jno Bap. To sd Cornwall Vincens half a proportion of land adjoining the house I rent of Mr Rich. Soanes. To my neph. Jno Bap the house where Joshua Gill & Lewis Meriday dwell. To my now wife her own plate, etc. All slaves, plate, furniture, & residue to my 2 nephews. All surgical appliances to my neph. Cornwall Vincens. £50 to the poor. Witnessed by John Haddon, John Price, Ed. Tyley.

My 3 riding horses. Annuities payable to me by the will of my brother Jno Jas. Vincens,* late of St Anne's in the Liberty of Westmr. Ashton Warner & Geo. Jennings of Antigua, Esqres, & Phil. Reynolds, mt, Ex'ors.

Codicil of same date as will. A £50 slave to my gods. Rich. Haddon, s. of Capt Jno Haddon. Before Hon. Edward Byam, Lieut.-Governor, appeared John Haddon, Esq., John Price, planter, and Ed. Tyley 18 Feb. 1726-7. Recorded at St. John's.

Cornwall Vincens, Surgeon. To my wife Martha £30 c. per annum, & after her death to the poor of the parish of St . . . . n's, Westmr, co. Midd., for ever, being the place of my nativity, & 2 negros. To my . . . . son Frazier Thibou, son of Lewis Thibou of St John's, shop-keeper, a negro. £20 c. to be used for the schooling of so many of the poor of St John's as my Ex'ors think fit. To Wm Levine, s. of Jno Levine, marr, £20 c. My Ex'ors to sell all my negros & residue of est. for the poor of the parish of St Anne's, Westmr. (Remainder of the will is missing.)

Elizabeth Vincens, widow. Will dated 1 Nov. 172– (? 1727). My negro to be free. To my dau. Mabetable Humphrys my plate, jewells, linen, etc., & to her heirs, & in default to my other 3 daus. Elizth Gillyat, Mary

* His will was proved P.C.C. 1724. (285 Bolton.)

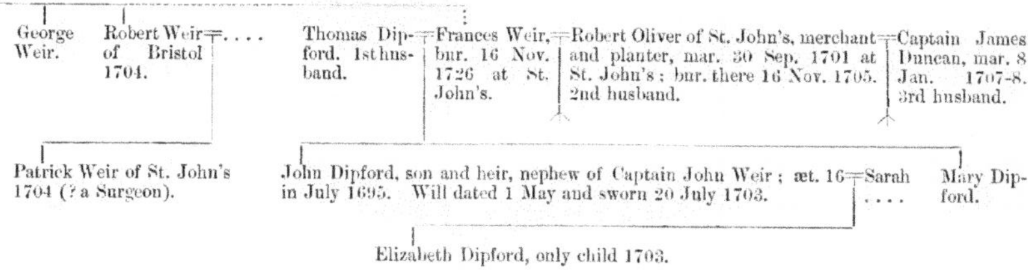

Knight, & Ann Delafons equally. To my said 3 daus. & my grds. Nath[l] Humphrys each a negro. To my dau. Mehitable Humphrys 8 negros & all residue at 21, or 18 if she marry. Tho. Stevens, m[t], Sam[l] Gillyat, pl[r], Ex'ors & guardians. Witnessed by Eb. Ricket, Elizabeth Keir. Before William Mathew, Esq., Governor-General, was sworn George White, the other witnesses being long since dead, 17 Dec. 1739. Recorded 20 May 1740.

Walter Weir, planter. Will dated 10 Oct. 1748. To my cousin Geo. Lucas Osborne all my estate in Antigua & elsewhere in trust for his son Rob[t], he to take the name of Rob[t] Weir Osborne, & in default of issue to his son Mathew Fraser Osborne, he also to take the name of Weir, then to Geo. Lucas Osborne in trust for his daughter Ann, then to his daus. Eliz[th] Pricilla Osborne, Mary Osborne, & Jane Frances Osborne. In case Geo. Lucas Osborne recover my estate called Glanville, now known as Weirs, the same to be in trust for his son Rob[t], & to each other of his children above mentioned £600 c., but if he also recover my estate called Zoars then to each such child £1000 c. If Weirs be recovered I leave to John Osborne, Edw[d] Osborne, Grace Osborne, & Eliz[th] Osborne, sons & daus. of my cousin John Osborne, dec[d], £500 c. each at 21, if also Zoar then £1000 c. each. To Humphry Osborne, son of my cousin John Osborne, £100 c., knowing he is well provided for by his uncle. To my sister Frances Weir £500 c. . . . . p[d] 3 years after my father's decease . . . . but if he recover Weirs £1000 c. To my mother Mary Weir £70 a year . . . . if Zoars be recovered £100 with use of my house & 4 slaves, with £30 c. yearly as per deed on account of Five Island estate for life, after to Rob[t] Osborne. To Ann d. of Geo. Lucas Osborne a cow, 3 heifers, & an ox. To Jane Frances Osborne all my silver plate. Witnessed by Frances Nicholson, John Johnson, John Peter Marchant. Before James Virchild, Commander-in-Chief of Antigua, was sworn John Johnson, jun.

1678, Feb. 7. Edward Dendy sells to Mr. John Weire, merchant, half a house.

1679, June 1. Harvie Keynell, Esq., leases for 21 years to John Weire, merchant, Little Lear (? Zoar) in St. John Division of 350 acres, he to pay 10,000 lbs. for the first year, 15,000 lbs. for the second, and 20,000 lbs. for the third year, and to pay off debts of 80,000 lbs. Schedule follows: 3 Christian servants, 20 negros, 30 sheep, 22 cattle, 2 horses.

1679, Dec. 5. John Weire of Antigua, Gent., sells to Edward Dendy two proportions of land in St. John's Town.

1699, Nov. 28. Captain John Weir, two proportions of land granted by John Yeamans; surveyed 20 Sep. 1699.

George Weare and Thomas Weare sign the Petition of the Bristol merchants in 1708 for the supersession of Governor Parke.

1708. Petition of Anne Vincent, formerly the wife of Captain John Weir of Antigua, deceased, stating that she is entitled to £120 a year, payable by Edward Chester since 1705. She went to England since then, and unfortunately married there one Mr. John Vincent, then and now of Kensington, barber-surgeon, who ill-used her, so she returned by the help of her friends to this island. Her husband has taken her £120 a year. Frances Weir, spinster, also deposes. Governor Parke makes an order for the money to be paid to her solely. (B. T. Leeward Islands, vol. 11.) Court of Chancery.

1711, Nov. 21. Robert Weir of Antigua, Gent., leases to Edward Chester, sen., of Antigua, Esq., 60 acres for £50 c. rent.

1713, July 27. Petition of John Forster and Mary his wife that John Weir, lately deceased, by Indenture of sale dated 18 . . . . ember 1702 sold to John Rayn of Antigua, deceased, for £100 c. certain land in St. John's, 53 feet in front and 80 feet backwards. John Rayn built a house and died. John Rayn was husband of ye petitioner Mary, John Forster having since married her. (Minutes of Council and Assembly.)

1746, Aug. 13. Petition of Robert Weir, Esq., for £20 a year for his son Walter Weir's services as manager and storekeeper under him from Nov. 1742; rejected.

1774, Jan. John Weir Esq; to be Commissary-gen. of the Stores in the Island of Dominica. ('Gent. Mag.,' p. 47.)

1776, Dec. John Weir Esq; His Majesty's Commissary General in Dominica, to Miss Elizabeth Bowman, daughter of John Grove, Esq. of Ashgrove. (*Ibid.*, p. 578.)

PARISH REGISTER OF ST. JOHN.

Baptized.

1711	June	7	Frances D. of Rob[t] Weir & his wife.
1759	May	6	William the S. of John Weir & Frances his wife.
1761	May	25	Elizabeth the D. of John Weir and Frances his wife.
1775	April	29	Lydia the D. of John Weir & Dorothy his wife.

Married.

1722	May	27	John Weir and Jane Waldrun. L.
1730	April	6	Henry Walten and Martha Vincens. L.
1731	Jan.	17	James Weir and Ann Nibbs.
1756	Jan.	22	Adam Smart and Frances Weir. L.
1758	May	27	John Weir and Frances Sherwood. L.

Buried.

1691 Sep. 9 Mary D. of John & Ann Weir.
1704 Nov. 8 Captn John Weir.
1717 April 18 Ann Vincens.
1726-7 Feb. 13 Dr John Vincens.
1730 Feb. 22 Dr Cornwall Vincens.
1738 June 30 Elizabeth Vincens, widow.
1743 July 26 James Wair.
1748 April 11 Col. Robert Weir.
1751 April 14 Mary Weir.
1756 May 1 James Weir.
1762 Aug. 28 Walter Weir. P.
1764 Nov. 14 Frances Weir. P.C.
1765 Nov. 5 William Weir, child.
1775 June 22 John Weir.
1805 May 17 Daniel Weir.
1819 June 17 Dorothy Weir.
1832 May 27 Robert Weir. St John's. 23.

PARISH REGISTER OF ST. GEORGE.

Buried.

1741 . . . . . . Ann Weir.

PARISH REGISTER OF ST. PHILIP.

Buried.

1757 Dec. 26 . . . . Weir.

Pedigree of Weston.

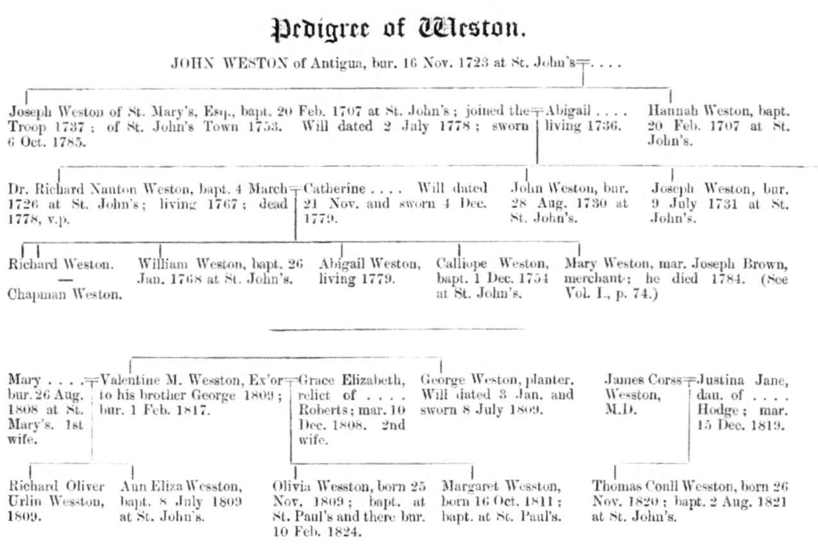
JOHN WESTON of Antigua, bur. 16 Nov. 1723 at St. John's = ...
Joseph Weston of St. Mary's, Esq., bapt. 20 Feb. 1707 at St. John's; joined the Troop 1737; of St. John's Town 1753. Will dated 2 July 1778; sworn 6 Oct. 1785.
= Abigail . . . . living 1736.
Hannah Weston, bapt. 20 Feb. 1707 at St. John's.
Dr. Richard Nanton Weston, bapt. 4 March 1726 at St. John's; living 1767; dead 1778, v.p.
= Catherine . . . . Will dated 21 Nov. and sworn 4 Dec. 1779.
John Weston, bur. 28 Aug. 1730 at St. John's.
Joseph Weston, bur. 9 July 1731 at St. John's.
Richard Weston.
Chapman Weston.
William Weston, bapt. 26 Jan. 1768 at St. John's.
Abigail Weston, living 1779.
Calliope Weston, bapt. 1 Dec. 1754 at St. John's.
Mary Weston, mar. Joseph Brown, merchant; he died 1784. (See Vol. I., p. 74.)
Mary . . . . bur. 26 Aug. 1808 at St. Mary's. 1st wife.
= Valentine M. Wesston, Ex'or to his brother George 1809; bur. 1 Feb. 1817.
= Grace Elizabeth, relict of . . . . Roberts; mar. 10 Dec. 1808. 2nd wife.
George Weston, planter. Will dated 3 Jan. and sworn 8 July 1809.
James Corss Wesston, M.D.
= Justina Jane, dau. of . . . . Hodge; mar. 15 Dec. 1819.
Richard Oliver Urlin Wesston, 1809.
Ann Eliza Wesston, bapt. 8 July 1809 at St. John's.
Olivia Wesston, born 25 Nov. 1809; bapt. at St. Paul's and there bur. 10 Feb. 1824.
Margaret Wesston, born 16 Oct. 1811; bapt. at St. Paul's.
Thomas Coull Wesston, born 26 Nov. 1820; bapt. 2 Aug. 1821 at St. John's.

Joseph Weston, Esq., of St. Mary's Parish. Will dated 2 July 1778. Freedom to my negro Betty & £5 c. yearly. To my granddau. Sophia dau. of Josiah Weston £30 st. for a negro out of the first ship from Guinea. All my furniture, plate, linen, equally between my granddaus. Abigail Weston, dau. of my son Richd Nanton Weston, Sophia dau. of my son Josiah Weston. To Rebecca Mackey £20. Of the residue, ¼ to my grandchildren Richd Weston, Chapman Weston, Wm Weston, & Abigail Weston, sons & dau. of my late son Dr Richd Nanton Weston, ¼ to my son Josiah Weston, ¼ to my son John Weston, ¼ to my son Saml Weston. My sons John & Saml Ex'ors. Witnessed by Daniel Hill, John Bawn, John Thibou. Before Thomas Jarvis, Esq., was sworn Daniel Hill 6 Oct. 1785. Recorded 12 Oct. 1785.

Catherine Weston of Antigua, widow. Will dated 21 Nov. 1779. To my dau. Abigail Weston 2 negros, my horse & chaise, & ½ furniture. To my son Richd Weston a negro & ½ furniture. To my son Chapman Weston a negro girl. To my son Wm Weston 4 negros & £500 c. To my grandson Richd Brown, son to Mr Joseph Brown of Antigua, mercht, 2 negros. To my granddaus. Cath. Brown & Rebecca Brown, daus. of said Jos. Brown, each a negro girl. To Margt Hurst of Antigua, widow, £33 c. To my kinswoman Sophia Weston, dau. of Rev. Josiah Weston of Antigua, £16 10s. c. To Geo. Wm Jordan of Antigua, Esq., 50 guineas. To Mr Joseph Brown & Mr Danl Hill, senr, 5 guineas each. All residue to my son Richd Weston, my son Chapman Weston, my son Wm Weston, & my dau. Abigail Weston equally. Jos. Brown, Danl Hill, & Geo. Wm Jordan Guardians & Ex'ors. Witnessed by William Smith, Thomas Stevenson, George William White. Before His Excellency William Mathew Burt were sworn Thomas Stevenson and George William White 4 Dec. 1779. Recorded 10 Sep. 1781.

Richard Weston of Antigua, Gent., Lieut. of 53rd Regiment. Will dated 4 Feb. 1802. All my estate to my (? mother) Mary widow of Rev. Josiah Weston of Antigua, she to be Ex'trix & Richd Lovely Nanton Ex'or.

George Weston of Antigua, planter. Will dated 3 Jan. 1809. To my nephew Richd Oliver Urlin Weston, & my niece Ann Eliza Weston, children of Valentine & Mary Weston, all my estate. My brother Valentine Weston of Antigua Ex'or. Witnessed by Charles Rowbotham and William Henry Livingston. Before Edward Byam, Esq., was sworn William Henry Livingston 8 July 1809.

In 1767 a Church Rate was levied in St. Mary's Parish.

	Slaves.	Acres.
Richard N. Wesston . . .	27	29
Joseph Wesston . . .	158	403
Samuel Wesston . . .	8	none
John Wesston . . .	32	139
In 1780 a similar Rate was raised.		
Joseph Wesston . . .	100	250
Samuel Wesston . . .	32	
Josiah Wesston . . .	20	
John Wesston . . .	60	139
Estate of Richard Wesston .	34	

Parish Register of St. Paul.

Baptized.

(? 1811) Olivia d. of Valentine and Grace Wesston; b. the 25th of Novr 1809.

(? 1811) Margaret d. of Valentine and Grace Wesston; b. the 16th of October 1811.

Married.

1822 May 4 Morris Nanton Weston, Batchelor, & Elizabeth Ann Jones, spinster. L.

1826 Jan. 19 Alfred Nanton, Bach., St John's, & Ann Eliza Weston, spinster. L.

Buried.

1817 Feb. 1 Valentine Weston in St Paul's Church Yard.

1824 Feb. 10 Olivia Weston in St Paul's church yard.

1827 Dec. 17 Margaret Weston of Country Pond, aged 16.

Rev. Josiah Weston, Rector of St. Mary's 1789 and 1807.=Margaret, dau. of . . . . Martin by Catherine his wife. (See her mother's will dated 1777 and her brother's 1787.) (? mar. 1st, 25 July 1757, Mary Ann, dau. of Nathaniel French and relict of William Dunning, and 3rdly, 11 Oct. 1794, Elizabeth Eleanor Nanton.) Dead 1812.

Samuel Weston, living 1778.

John Weston, living 1778; died 3 Feb. 1797, æt. 61.=Catherine . . . .

Children of Rev. Josiah Weston and Margaret:

- Martin Weston (? Rev., bur. 14 Nov. 1814).=Ann . . . . bur. at St. Mary's 1808, æt. 33.
- George Weston.
- Samuel Weston.
- Henry Weston.
- Margaret Weston.
- Mary Weston.
- Sophia Weston, living 1779.
- Rachell Weston, bapt. 19 March 1769 at St. John's.
- Rebecca Weston, bapt. 18 Feb. 1768 at St. John's; mar. 5 July 1784 Richard Nanton at St. John's; died Feb. 1845, æt. 77.

Children of John Weston and Catherine:

- Abigail Nanton Weston, born 18 May 1774; mar. 24 July 1793 William Blizard Jarvis, who died 1811; remar. 22 Aug. 1818 Thomas Hardman; she died 9 March 1820.
- Joseph French Weston, bapt. 26 Jan. 1768 at St. John's; joined the Troop 1794.=Honora, dau. of Callaghan McCarthy, Esq.; mar. 10 June 1793; she had ⅓ of "Forsters"; dead 1797.

Children of Joseph French Weston and Honora:

- John Weston, born 11 June and bapt. 27 Dec. 1795 at St. John's.
- John Weston, born 10 Feb. and bapt. 24 May 1797 at St. John's; inherited ⅓ of "Forsters" in 1797.

Parish Register of St. John.

Baptized.

1707 Feb. 20 Joseph & Hannah S. & D. of John Weston & his wife.

1726 Mar. 4 Richard Nanton the s. of Joseph Weston and Abigail his wife.

1754 Dec. 1 Calliope the D. of Docr Richd Weston & Cath. his wife.

1768 Jan. 26 Joseph French S. of John Weston and Cathrine his wife.

1768 Jan. 26 William S. of Richard Nanton Weston and Cathrine his wife.

1768 Feb. 18 Rebecca the D. of Joseph Weston, Junr, and Margrett his wife.

1769 Mar. 19 Rachell D. of Josiah Weston and Margaret his wife.

1795 Dec. 27 John S. of Joseph French Weston and Honora his wife. B. the 11 June 1795.

1797 May 24 John S. of Joseph French Weston and Honora his wife, both deceased. B. the 10th February 1797.

1804 Oct. 17 Edward* S. of Daniel Wesston* and Angelica his wife; b. 5th Octr 1804.

1807 Jan. 30 Jane D. of Daniel Wesston and Angelica his wife. B. the 7th December last.

1821 Aug. 2 Thomas Coull S. of Doctor James Corse Wesston and Justina Jane his wife. B. November 26, 1820.

Married.

1757 July 25 Josiah Weston and Mary Dening (Widow). L.

1784 July 5 Richard Nanton and Rebecca Weston, Spinster. L.

(1793?) June 10 Joseph French Wesston to Honora McCarthy, Spinster. L.

1794 Oct. 11 The Reverend Josiah Wesston to Elizabeth Eleanor Nanton, Spinster. L.

1802 May 31 Joseph Wesston to Mary Pew, Widow.

1808 Dec. 10 Valentine Wesston to Grace Elizabeth Roberts, Widow. L.

* Both coloured persons, and signed the Petition 1830.

1819 Dec. 15 James Corss Wesston, M.D., to Justina Jane Hodge, Spinster. L.

1824 July 20 Robert Wilkinson to Sophia Huyghne Wesston, Spinster. L.

Buried.

1723 Nov. 16 Mr John Weston.
1730 Aug. 28 John s. of Joseph Weston.
1731 July 9 Joseph s. of Jos. Weston.
1816 Jan. 7 Henry Weston.

PARISH REGISTER OF ST. MARY.

Baptized.

Ann Eliza D. of Valentine Wesston by Mary his Wife was baptized in St John's Parish by Josiah Wesston July 8, 180–.

Buried.

The Body of Ann Wife of the R . . . . Martin Wesston, was Interred . . . . Burial Ground, at the Valley Ch . . . . (aged 33 years) by the Revd James C . . . . 1808.

. . . . Catherine Hanson Wesston . . . . red in the Burial Ground . . . . Valley Chapel by Martin Wesston Sep. 18th, 1808.

The Body of Mary Wife of Valentine M. Wesston was Interred in the Burial Ground at the Valley Chapel by James Coull Aug. 26th, 1808.

The Body of George Martin Wesston was Interred in the Burial Ground at the Valley Chapel by James Coull Decr 22d, 1809.

Buried the Body of Alicia Wesston, aged abt 18 years, a White Lady, at Valley Chapel yard by J. C. Novr the . . . .

Buried The Body of Martin Wesston. Valley. Novr 14, 1814.

PARISH REGISTER OF ST. GEORGE.

Married.

1794 Dec. 11 Josiah Wesston, Clerk, to Elizabeth Eleanor Nanton, S.

1812 May 9 William Wardle, Merchant, to Grace Elizabeth Wesston, d. of the late Revd Jos. Wesston. L.

Buried.

1747 or 1748 Jan. 9 Mrs Ann White.

In 1852 Mary Wesston owned "Dark Valley" in St. Mary's Parish of 170 acres.

Pedigree of Wethered.

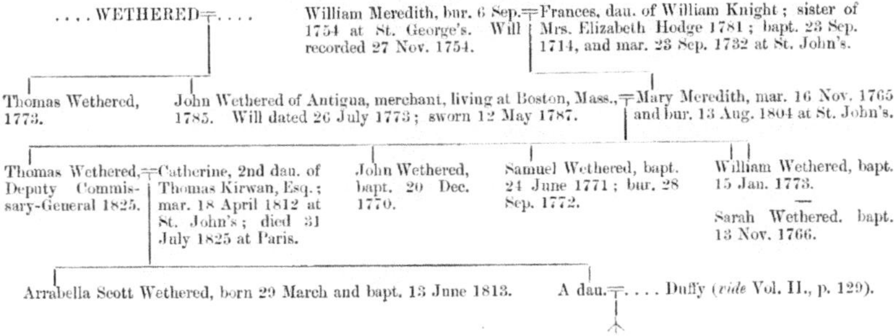

The will of William Meredith was recorded on 27 Nov. 1754, but does not now exist.

John Wethered of Antigua, merchant. Will dated 26 July 1773. To my friend Mark Ward £20 c. To my wife Mary the use of my house, plate, furniture, & 4 negros in lieu of dower. All other slaves to be leased out. After my wife's death all my Est. to be sold & divided equally among my children at 21, remainder to my brother Tho. Wethered & my sister-in-law Cath. Dickson. Mark Ward & Wm Pitts of Antigua, Esqres, Ex'ors & G. Witnessed by Fra. Claxton, Boyce Ledwell, Ab. Marshall. Before President Edward Byam was sworn Ab. Marshall 12 May 1787. Recorded 28 Nov. 1787.

Elizabeth Hodge, widow, in her will of 21 Nov. 1781 names her niece Mary Wethered, her sister Frances Meredith, and John Wethered, merchant. Lydia Meredith a witness.

1785, Nov. 30. John Burke, Esq., writes about the brig of John Wethered of Antigua, merchant, who had not resided here for many years, is in Boston, an avowed American, but his wife lived here.

1799, Sep. 29. At Stoke Newington, Mr Thomas Turner Wetherhed, to Miss Rigby. ('Gent. Mag.,' p. 900.)

1825, July 31. At Paris, Catharine, wife of Thomas Wethered, esq. Deputy Commissary General, and second daughter of the late T. Kirwan, esq. of co. Galway. (*Ibid.*, p. 190.)

PARISH REGISTER OF ST. JOHN.

Baptized.

1762 Feb. 16 Dorothy Bonnin the D. of Willm. Meredith and Frances his wife.

1766 Nov. 13 Sarah the D. of John Wethered & Mary his wife.

1770 May 30 Christian the D. of William Meredith and Frances his wife.

1770 Dec. 20 John the S. of John Wethered and Mary his wife.
1771 June 24 Samuel the S. of John Wethered and Mary his wife.
1772 Dec. 3 William the D. (*sic*) of W[m] Meredith, deceased, and Frances his Widow.
1773 Jan. 15 William the S. of John Wethered and Mary his wife.
1813 June 13 Arrabella Scott D. of Thomas Wethered and Catherine his wife. B. the 29th March last.

Married.

1732 Sep. 23 William Meredith and Frances Knight. L.
1758 May 13 Henry Blizard to Margaret Meredith, Spinster.
1765 Nov. 16 John Wethered to Mary Meredith; by Lic.
1787 Mar. 11 Francis Blizard (writing Clerk) to Sarah Meredith, Spinster. L.
1812 April 18 Thomas Wethered (Dep. Com. Gen[l]) to Catherine Kirwan, Spinster. Lic.
1815 June 27 John Burke, Esquire, to Dorothy Bonnen Meredith of the Town of Saint John's, Spinster. L.

Buried.

1723-4 Feb. 9 Joseph s. of Lewis Meredith.
1729 Dec. 16 Eliz. D. of Lewis Meredith, a child.
1734 Oct. 14 Rebecka D. of Lewis Meredith.
1772 Sep. 28 Samuel Wethered.
1804 Aug. 13 Mary Wethered.
1817 April 9 Frances Meredith.

PARISH REGISTER OF ST. ANTHONY, MONTSERRAT.
(B. T. Leeward Islands, vol. 28.)

Baptized.

1740 April 7 Mary y[e] D. of Thomas & Ann Weatherhead of y[e] P. of S[t] Anthony was christen'd.

PARISH REGISTER OF ST. GEORGE.

Baptized.

1752 Aug. 30 John S. of William Meredith & Frances his wife, about 10 years old.
1752 Oct. 4 Sarah d. of William Meredith & Frances his wife.
(? 1755 or 1756) Ann, Dorothy, ... night, Lydia, in all . . . . e. The S's & D's of W[m] Meredith, deceased, & Frances his surviving Widow.

Buried.

1754 Sep. 6 William Meredith.

PARISH REGISTER OF ST. PETER.

Buried.

1728 Aug. 28 Henry s. of William Meredith.

Family of White.

Susannah White. Will dated 31 Oct. 1732. To my son Joseph Taylor . . . . Chas. Jacob Ex'or. By Hon. Edward Byam was sworn Mr. James Browmley May 1733. Recorded 31 May 1733.

Patrick White, mason, of Antigua. Will dated 30 May 1765. To Ch[r] D . . . . x (? Devereux) & his sister Ann D. £200 st. To Tho. Parker, carp[tr], £200 st. for his unmarried dau. To P. White of Dublin his children, gardiner, £15 st. each. To Tho. Parker's eldest unmarried dau. £200 c. To Coleman Heyns of Antigua, planter, £200 st. To my mulatta Mary Ann her freedom & £60 c. yearly. To Sally her dau. her freedom, & her 2 sons Edmund & Jack their maintenance, to be procured by their supposed fathers Coleman Heyns & D[r] John Hurst. My mulatta Sally to be maintained. All residue to my heir-at-law. W[m] Murray, Esq., M[r] Rich[d] Reddy, M[r] Philip Heyns, & M[r] Coleman Heyns, planters, Ex'ors. Witnessed by James . . . . Parkinson, Thade Fitzpatrick. By His Excellency George Thomas was sworn James Parkinson 8 June 1765. Recorded 11 July 1765.

Mary Burke, widow, dau. of Robert Brown, Esq., of Bodkins, in her will dated 15 April 1774 names her nieces Mary Ann White and Antonetta White, under 16, daus. of her sister Elizabeth White. Her brother James Brown, Esq., by his will dated 27 Sep. 1797 left his estate to his sister Elizabeth White, widow of Christopher White, merchant, and to their children.

John White, late of St. Christopher's, now of the City of Chichester, Esq. Will dated 2 March 1775; proved 23 Feb. 1776 by George White, Esq., the son. (104 Bellas.) Own very considerable real & personal estate plantations in S[t] Christopher's & elsewhere. By my marriage settlement I agreed to pay my wife Marg[t] £200 a year which I confirm. I give her no more because her late father Sir Geo. Thomas, Bart., has made a provision for her. All my estates to my son Geo. White & his heirs, then to my nephew Michael White of Montserrat, Esq., & then to his 2[d] son Michael White, charged with £80 a year to my brother Nicholas White & £10 a year to 2 free mulattas. If my son Geo. die without issue then the following legacies to be paid, viz., £80 a year to my sister M[rs] Jane Bennett, widow, £1000 to my nephew her son Henry Bennett, £500 to my sister M[rs] Henrietta Alvarez, widow, £500 to my sister Martha, £1000 to my cousin W[m] Croke of S[t] Christopher's, Esq. . . . . to the grandson of my sister Jane Bennett, £1000 to my cousin Craister Greathead of S[t] Christopher's, Esq., £4000 each to the daus. of my late brother W[m], £400 to my niece Mary Brown, dau. of my sister M[rs] Alvarez by her former husband, £10 a year more to my 2 mulattas. The negros on my plantations not to be chattels but heirlooms. All the old slaves to be well cared for. My cottage at Pagham, co. Sussex, to my servant John Gray. All residue to my son Geo. & appoint him sole Ex'or. Witnessed by William Milton, G. Russell, jun., Thomas Voller.

Michael White, Esq. Will dated 1 Sep. 1784; proved 4 March 1785 by Robert White the son; power reserved to Mary White the widow, Michael White, Esq., the son, John Stanley, Esq., William Lee, Esq., Thomas Meade, Esq., Jacob Kladen, Esq., Charles Chambers, Esq., and William Manning. (164 Ducarel.) My wife Mary, my son Michael White, jun[r], Cha. Chambers of Montserrat, John Stanley of Queen Anne Str., Cavendish Sq., but lately departed for the West Indies, Alex^r Willock of Putney Park, merch^t, to settle all affairs with creditors, to sell or mortgage my property in St Vincent, Dominica, Montserrat, N. America, & to make provision for my family, & then to pay portions to my 5 daus., then to my 3 younger sons Mich^l, Robt, & John. All residue to my son W^m. To my wife Mary £600 a year in lieu of dower till debts are paid, then £900 a year more & liberty to live on one of my estates. To each dau. & son (except 1st son) £3000. To my friend Cha. Chambers, Esq., £200 a year for managing my estates. To my near & good relations Lydia Walsh, Jane, Eliz., & Alice Tomlinson of Richmond £20 each. To my friends Wm Lee of Dominica, Tho. Meade of Montserrat, & Jacob Kladen of St Vincent £20 each. My wife Mary, my sons Michael & Robt, John Stanley, Alex^r Willock, Wm Lee, Tho. Meade, Jacob Kladen, & Cha. Chambers Ex'ors. Witnessed by Jane Elizabeth Moone, Richard Jones, John Ridon.

Codicil. 8 Feb. 1785. Wm Manning of St Mary Axe, merch^t, to be Ex'or & trustee *vice* Alex^r Willock, & to receive sugars till debts are paid. To my son Robt 3500 stock instead of £3000. Witnessed by Mary Ross, William Miller.

Pedigree of White.

. . . . WHITE (? William White, senior, of Montserrat, who lost £5642 by the French Invasion of 1712, and was Member of Assembly and Captain 1692). = ... (? Mary, bur. 18 June 1724 at St. Anthony, Montserrat).

John White, Member of Council of Montserrat 1726; later of St. Kitts 1755, then of Chichester; died 6 and bur. 12 Feb. 1776, æt. 75, and M.I. at Yapton, co. Sussex. Will dated 2 March 1775; proved 23 Feb. 1776. (104 Bellas.) = Lydia, dau. of Sir George Thomas, Bart., Governor of the Leeward Islands, and of Yapton and Ratton, co. Sussex; mar. 25 Oct. 1744 at St. George's; died 14 and bur. 22 Aug. 1794, æt. 76, and M.I. at Yapton.

William White, dead 1775. = ...
Daus.

. . . . Crosbie = ...

George White-Thomas, M.P. for Chichester in seven Parliaments; took the name of Thomas on inheriting Yapton from his grandfather Sir George Thomas, Bart.; inherited Watergate through his wife; bur. 3 July 1821, æt. 71, and M.I. at Yapton. = Frances, dau. and coheir of John Page of Watergate House, near Chichester; died 15 Nov. at Watergate House and bur. 23 Nov. 1807, æt. 64, and M.I. at Yapton.

. . . . Crosbie (? Lieut.-Colonel William Crosbie of the 22nd Foot, Governor of Portsmouth, who died June 1798). Will dated 27 May 1790. = ...

John Crosbie of "Crosbies" in Popeshead, Antigua, Esq. Will dated 21 Jan. 1814; sworn 11 Jan. 1815. = Jane, dau. of . . . . Moore and widow of Dr. James Farley; mar. 1 July 1775, and bur. 24 Feb. 1778 at St. John's.

Frances Page Thomas of Watergate House, only child and heir, died there 27 Feb. 1835. = General Sir John Gustavus Crosbie, G.C.H., of Watergate House; died 24 Aug. 1843.

Rev. James Way, son of James Way of Thame, co. Oxford, Esq.; matriculated from Pembroke College, Oxford, 2 Nov. 1792, æt. 17; Exhibitioner 1793; B.A. 1796; M.A. 1799; Rector of Adwell, co. Oxford, and Curate of Lapworth, co. Warwick, 1803, till his death in 1816. = Elizabeth Garrett Ross Crosbie, only surviving child, bapt. 11 Dec. 1776 at St. John's; died 16 May 1810 at Lapworth, co. Warwick.

Sarah Crosbie, bapt. 6 July 1778 (? bur. 3 March 1779 at St. John's).

Charles Crosbie, D.L., of Watergate House, later of Northlands, near Chichester, born 1803; only son and heir 1832. = ...

Other issue.

John Stone of Long Grendon, co. Bucks, Esq., living 1832. = Sarah Frances Warner Way, sole heir to her grandfather John Crosbie in 1814, then a minor; living 1832.

John Gustavus Crosbie of Northlands, near Chichester, Captain 60th Rifles; born 1841.

Sarah Garrett by her will dated 5 Sep. 1789 bequeathed her estate in equal shares to her kinsman Joseph James Farley, only son of Dr. James Farley, deceased, and to Elizabeth Garrett Ross Crosbie his half-sister and dau. of John Crosbie, Esq., remainder to her kinswoman Mrs. Elizabeth White, widow of Mr. Christopher White, deceased, and her two children Antonetta and Robert.

John Crosbie of Antigua, Esq. Will dated 21 Jan. 1814. To my Manager Wm Crosbie £1000 c. All res. to Jno Gustavus Crosbie, a Maj^r Genl, Sam. Lightbourn Darrell, & Jno Burke of Antigua, Esq^{res}, & Tho. Rodie of Liverpool, m^t, on T. to pay the rents to my granddau. . . . . Way, dau. of my late dau. Eliz. Way, till 21, then all to be conveyed to her, & in default to my s^d neph. T. to be Ex'ors. Witnessed by Peter Murray, George Halstead, Jos. George Leech, planter. Before Sir James Leith, Governor and K.B. and Knt. Commander of the Portuguese Royal Order of the Tower and Sword, Lieut.-General and Colonel of the 4th West India Regiment, Commander of the Forces in the Leeward Islands, etc., sworn 11 Jan. 1815.

Close Roll, 3 Will. IV., Part 12, No. 11.

Indenture made the 4th Feb. 1832 between John Stone of Long Grendon, Bucks, Esq., and Sarah Frances Warner his wife (formerly Sarah Frances Warner Way, spinster, granddaughter and also a devisee and legatee named in the last will of John Crosbie, late of Antigua, Esq., deceased), of the 1st part, John Gustavus Crosbie of Watergate House, Sussex, a General in H.M. Army, and Charles Crosbie of the same place, Esq. (1st son and heir of John Gustavus Crosbie), of the 2nd part, and Edward Leigh Pemberton of Salisbury Square, Gentleman, of the 3rd part. Whereas John Crosbie duly made his will dated the 21st Jan. 1814

From Johnson's Account, 1830 (*reduced*).

and gave to his then present manager William Crosbie £1000 currency, and all residue real and personal to the said John Gustavus Crosbie his nephew, Samuel Lightbourne Darrell and John Burke and Thomas Rodie in trust to apply the yearly profits for the benefit of his granddaughter, then Sarah Frances Warner Way (daughter of Elizabeth Way his late daughter, deceased), till 21, and then to convey the said estate to her and the heirs of her body, and if she should die without issue the estate to John Gustavus Crosbie his nephew and his heirs and assigns for ever; and whereas John Crosbie died in 1814 without revoking; and whereas Sarah Frances Warner Stone hath attained the age of 21; and whereas John Crosbie was seised at his death of the estates hereinafter particularly mentioned and intended to be conveyed; and whereas the said plantations and slaves, etc., at the death of John Crosbie were subject, and so will continue subject, to the payment of certain debts due from him and charged on the bulk of the said plantations by way of mortgage; and whereas the said mortgage debts greatly exceed the value of the property disposed of by John Crosbie's will; and whereas John Gustavus Crosbie and Charles Crosbie are entitled to and interested in the said mortgage debts; and whereas John Stone and Sarah Frances Warner his wife being satisfied that their interest in the said hereditaments is by reason of such incumbrances of no value, an agreement has therefore been entered into between John Gustavus and Charles Crosbie and themselves for transferring to John Gustavus and Charles Crosbie the fee simple and equity of redemption, discharged of all their claims thereon, and in pursuance of the said arrangement

continued below.

Michael White of St. Anthony, Montserrat, Esq., Member of Council 1759; President 1764 till his death 15 Feb. 1785. Will dated 1 Sep. 1784; proved 4 March 1785. (164 Ducarel.) = Mary, only dau. of John Tomlinson, senior, of Antigua, Esq.; mar. 26 Feb. 1726 at St. John's; living 1785.

Nicholas White, living 1775.

William White, 1st son and heir, bapt. 11 Jan. 1727 at St. Anthony; Ex'or 1785.

Robert White, Ex'or 1785.

John White.

Mary (formerly Hussey), 1st wife. = Michael White of Montserrat, Esq., 1775; Ex'or 1785. = Mary (formerly Lee), 2nd wife.

Elizabeth White, bapt. 23 Nov. 1729 at St. Anthony; mar. George Molineux Montgomery; living 1802.

Alicia White, mar. Humphrey Butler, only son of John Butler, Esq., M.P., and grandson of Brinsley Butler, 1st Viscount Lanesborough.

Three other daus., living 1784.

William White of Antigua, Esq., heir to Penelope Tomlinson 1805.

Michael White, 2nd son 1775.

Robert White.

John White, under 15, 1802.

Lydia White, living 1802.

Elizabeth Hamilton White, living 1802.

they, John Stone and Sarah Frances Warner his wife, at the request of John Gustavus Crosbie and Charles Crosbie have agreed to bar the estate in tail by the said will limited to Sarah Frances Warner Stone, and to convey the same to Edward Leigh Pemberton in trust. Now this Indenture witnesseth that in consideration of 10s. John Stone and Sarah Frances Warner his wife convey to Edward Leigh Pemberton all that plantation in the parish of St. John and division of Popeshead in Antigua, containing 132 acres, bounded E. with the lands formerly of John Willcox and the heirs of Timothy Clarkeley, deceased, W. with the lands formerly of Samuel Martin, Esq., and John Delap Halliday, Esq., N. with the sea, and S. with land late of Barry Conyers Hart and the heirs of Jonas Langford Brooke, deceased, and also the dwelling-house, and also all that parcel of land of John Crosbie, deceased, called Hughes in the division of Popeshead, containing 75 acres, bounded N. by Boons and Crosbie's estates, E. by Langfords and Crosbies, S. by the High Road, and W. by Boons and Langfords, and all those negros and other slaves as set forth in a schedule annexed, in trust, subject to the debts of John Crosbie, but freed and discharged from the estates tail of Sarah Frances Warner Stone, for such persons as John Gustavus Crosbie and Charles Crosbie shall jointly appoint, and till then in trust for John Gustavus Crosbie for life, and after his death for such persons as Charles Crosbie shall appoint if he survives his father, and failing his appointment in trust for him and the heirs of his body, and for default to the 2nd and other sons of John Gustavus Crosbie and their heirs male, and for default to the daughters of John Gustavus Crosbie now living and hereafter to be born, equally as tenants in common, and to the heirs of their respective bodies, and to the survivors, and for default to Charles Crosbie and his heirs and assigns for ever, and John Gustavus Crosbie may charge the plantations, etc., with the payment to any wife of £600 a year for life, provided always and it is hereby agreed that in case any wife of John Gustavus Crosbie shall become entitled to any jointure by any appointment which has been made or shall be made by John Gustavus Crosbie, under the power of jointuring created and limited by the will of William Crosbie, Esq., a Lieut.-Colonel of H.M.'s 22nd Foot, deceased, dated the 27th May 1790, in such case such wife not to be entitled to any payment in respect of the power herein conveyed except so far as may be necessary to make up the £600 a year, Edward Leigh Pemberton with the consent of John Gustavus Crosbie may make leases not exceeding 21 years and not in reversion or by any way of future interest. Schedule: (name, sex, colour, age) 67 men, women, and children. Robert Jackson, 41 Salisbury Square, Donald Macdonald, clerk to Messrs. Green, Pemberton, Crawley, and Gardiner, Salisbury Square, London, George Annesly, 46 Salisbury Square (witnesses of the Crosbies' signatures). Mary Ann Sheldon, Stanton Street, John Oxon, William Welch Lea, solicitor, Henley in Arden (witnesses of the Stones').

1668. Captain Anthony White, 155 acres, Government grant.

1669, Jan. 6. Lieut. Christopher White and two others granted 500 acres by Colonel William Byam and Captain S. Winthrop, Deputy-Governors of Antigua, at New North Sound; surveyed 16 Jan. 1669.

1671, Jan. 11. John White, 10 acres by Governor Warner; surveyed 18 Feb. 1671.

1674, June 11. Ensign Anthony White, 40 acres by Governor Warner: surveyed 10 April 1675.

1677, March 27. John White, 10 acres by Governor Warner; surveyed Aug. 1677.

1692, March. Captain William White of the Assembly of Montserrat.

1712. William White, sen., of the Leeward Division of Montserrat, lost £5642 at the French Invasion.

1726, Aug. 9. Montserrat. John White to be of the Council.

Indenture of marriage settlement dated 26 Feb. 1726 between Michael White of Montserrat, Esq., John Tomlinson, sen., of Antigua, Esq., and Mary Tomlinson, spinster, sole daughter of latter. Whereas a marriage is shortly to take place between Michael White and Mary Tomlinson, in consideration of £2000 st. paid by John Tomlinson as a portion Michael White doth release to John Tomlinson two plantations in the Windward part of Montserrat in the parish of St. George, of about 100 acres each, commonly called Bangs, and one in St. Peter's Parish of 120 acres, with all slaves, etc., to pay to Mary Tomlinson if she survive Michael White £200 st. yearly for her life.

Hon. J. White in his letter of 21 June 1755 at Chichester informs their Lordships that he will not return to St. Kitts.

Michael White to be of the Montserrat Council 20 Feb. 1759, and on 30 May 1764 Governor G. Thomas appointed him President on the death of George Wyke.

John Bayly, Esq., of Debsborough, born 1755, married 1776 Catherine, 1st dau. and coheir of Lancelot Crosbie, Esq., of Tubbrid, co. Kerry. She also inherited the estates of her uncle John Gustavus Crosbie, Esq., M.P. (Burke's 'Landed Gentry' and 'Extinct Peerage,'—Earldom of Glandore.)

1785, Feb. 15. Hon. Michael White, Lieut. Gov. of Montserrat. ('Gent. Mag.,' p. 158.)

1793, Dec. Col. Wm Crosbie, appointed major-general on the continent of Europe only. (*Ibid.*, p. 1159.)

1796, Feb. 22. John White, esq. of the royal navy, to Miss Losack, only daughter of Richard H. L. esq. of St Kitt's, and lieutenant-general of the Leeward Islands. (*Ibid.*, p. 253.)

1798, June 16. Suddenly, at garrison, General Crosbie lieutenant-governor of Portsmouth, etc. (*Ibid.*, p. 543.)

1806. Michael White, Member of the Council of Montserrat, has been absent since 1795.

1807, Nov. 15. At Watergate-house, Sussex, the wife of George Thomas, esq. M.P. for Chichester. ('Gent. Mag.,' p. 1085.)

1810, April 12. At Antigua, aged 49, Capt. Charles White, R.N. Commissioner of the dockyard at St John's. (*Ibid.*, p. 90.)

1810, May 16. Suddenly at Lapworth, Warwickshire, Elizabeth Garrett Ross, the wife of Rev. John Way, M.A. rector of Adwell, Oxon, and only child of John Crosbie, esq. of the Island of Antigua. (*Ibid.*, p. 594.)

1811, Feb. 3. The wife of Capt. Whyte, R.N. of Yapton-place, Sussex. (*Ibid.*, p. 195.)

1814, Dec. 20. John Whyte, only son of Capt. W. R.N. of Yapton-place, Sussex. (*Ibid.*, 1815, p. 96.)

1835, Feb. 27. At Watergate, Frances-Page, wife of Gen. Crosbie, only child of the late G. W. Thomas, esq. (*Ibid.*, p. 445.)

1843, Aug. 24. At Watergate, his seat near Lewes, General Sir John Gustavus Crosbie, G.C.H. This gallant officer entered the army in June 1780, became Lieutenant 30th April 1781; Captain in the 67th Foot, 1st May 1783; Major 31st Dec. 1793; Lieutenant-Colonel in the 22^{d} Foot 28th Sept. 1794; Colonel in the army 1st Jan. 1800; Major-General, 25th April 1808; Lieutenant-General, 4th June, 1813; and General, 22d. July 1830. He was nominated a Grand Cross of the Hanoverian Guelphic Order in 1837. He married Frances, the sole daughter and heiress of George Thomas, esq.* of Watergate and Yapton-Place, Sussex, M.P. for Chichester, by Frances, daughter and heir of John Page, esq. also M.P. for Chichester. By that lady he had a numerous family, of whom Katherine Louisa, the youngest dau., was married in 1839 to the Hon. Henry Keppel, Capt. R.N. fourth surviving son of the Earl of Albemarle. (*Ibid.*, p. 544.)

1843, Nov. 6. At All Soul's, Langham-pl., William Jas. Jameson Higgens, esq. of Fairfield, Hambledon, to Charlotte-Mary, youngest dau. of the late Capt. John Whyte, R.N., of Yapton House, Sussex. (*Ibid.*, 1844, p. 87.)

Stoughton Parish, co. Sussex.

Watergate, the residence of Richard Christy, Esq., was occupied in the last century by the Drury family, and afterwards by the Pages of Donnington, from whom by marriage it passed to G. W. Thomas, Esq., and from him to his daughter Frances, who married General Crosbie. The estate is principally in Walderton (a part of Stoughton), but the mansion is in Up. Marden.

West or Up. Marden.

Watergate, the seat of Richard Christie, Esq., is situated partly in this parish and partly in Stoughton, the adjoining parish; the mansion was erected early in the seventeenth century by William Drury, and remained in the same family for many generations; it is a handsome and commodious residence, standing in a spacious and well-wooded park, a short distance from the road, surrounded by interesting scenery.

Parish Register of St. John.

Baptized.

1776	Dec. 11	Elizth Garrett Ross the d. of John Crosbie and Jane his wife.
1778	July 6	Sarah the d. of John Crosbie and his late wife Jane Crosbie.
1785 (? Aug.)	13	James the S. of James Crosby and Frances his wife.
1788	May 24	James French S. of George William White and Elizabeth his wife; b. 10th May 1788.

Married.

170$\frac{0}{1}$	Mar. 23	Willm Tileman and Alce Crosbey.
1705	May 16	Franciss Sanders & Sarah White. L.
1707	Feb. 8	Thomas White & Elizabeth Munck. B.
1726	Feb. 26	Michael White and Mary Tomlinson. L.
1729	May 6	William White and Catherine Paynter. L.
1729	Mar. 24	Richard White and Eliz^{a} White.
1732	May 20	Robert White and Susannah Browne. L.
1744	Aug. 18	Arch^{d} White and Marg^{t} Nicholas. L.
1757	Nov. 23	Robert Browne (Merch^{t}) and Lucy Crosby. L.
1775	July 1	John Crosbie to Jane Farley (Widow); by L.
1783	Nov. 11	George William White to Elizabeth French. L.

* Son of John White, esq. of Chichester, by Lydia, daughter of Sir George Thomas, the first Baronet of Yapton: Sir George, though he left male issue, bequeathed estates to his three nephews, Inigo Freeman, George Thomas Freeman, and George White, esquires, who each in consequence assumed the name of Thomas only. ('Gent. Mag.,' p. 544.)

Buried.

1731 Dec. 15 Mr Robert White.
1750-51 Mar. 5 William White S. of Michael White, Esqr.
1778 Feb. 24 Jane Crosbie.
1778 Oct. 28 Mary Humphry Crosbie.
1779 Mar. 3 Sarah Jane Crosbie.

PARISH REGISTER OF ST. GEORGE.

Married.

1744 Oct. 25 John White and Lydia Thomas, Spr.
1749 Sep. 2 William Antrobus & Mary White, Spr.

Buried.

1754 Sep. 11 Frances White.
1779 Nov. 21 Catharine White.

PARISH REGISTER OF ST. PAUL.

Married.

1732 . . mbr 18 Alexander Macpherson & Mary White; by B.

PARISH REGISTER OF ST. PHILIP.

Married.

1698 Oct. 16 Nathaniel Crump to Ann White.

YAPTON, SUSSEX.

Buried.

1776 Feb. 12 Mr White.
1794 Aug. 22 Mrs Lydia White.
1807 Nov. 23 Frances wife of Geo. White Thomas, Esquire.
1821 July 3 George Thomas, Esquire, Watergate House, 72 years.

ST. ANTHONY, MONTSERRAT.

Baptized.

1727 Jan. 11 William S. of Mr. Michael White & Mary his wife.
1729 Nov. 23 Elizabeth D. of Mr. Michael White & Mary his wife.

Buried.

1724 June 18 Mrs. Mary White, widdow.

ST. JOHN'S CHURCHYARD.

On a headstone:—

IN MEMORY OF THOMAS WHITE SON
OF GEORGE & SARAH WHITE
WHO DEPARTED THIS LIFE 25TH
FEBRUARY 1804 AGED 8 (?) YEARS.

On a brick ledger:—

RICHARD STARKIE
WHITE
Inscribes this faint memorial to the memory
of his attached and devoted Wife, the partner of
his Joys AND Sorrows for the lengthened period
of Seventeen years
MARIA KIRWAN WHITE
Who departed this life
in the certain hope of a glorious resurrection
on the 11th Decr 1848,
Aged 49 Years.
This Stone also records the removal from
this world of tribulation and distress to the
realms of bliss, of three beloved Infants
children of the above, VIZ!
RICHARD STARKIE,
Died 24th May 1833,
Aged 3 Months & 16 days.
JOHN ROBERT NIBBS,
Died 1st Septr 1836,
Aged 1 Month & 22 days.
FRANCIS HOLBER BROWN
Died 25th May 1838
Aged 18 Months & 21 days.
(Three lines follow.)

YAPTON, CO. SUSSEX.

North wall of chancel:—

TO THE MEMORY OF
GEORGE THOMAS, ESQUIRE,
OF THIS PARISH
AND OF WATERGATE HOUSE
IN THIS COUNTY;
ONE OF THE REPRESENTATIVES OF THE CITY OF CHICHESTER,
IN SEVEN SUCCESSIVE PARLIAMENTS:
WHO DEPARTED THIS LIFE ON THE 24TH DAY OF JUNE 1821,
IN THE 72D YEAR OF HIS AGE.

SACRED
TO THE MEMORY
of
JOHN WHITE ESQ
WHO DIED FEBY 6TH 1776
AGED 75 YEARS
ALSO OF
LYDIA HIS WIFE,
WHO DIED
AUGUST 14TH 1794
AGED
76 YEARS.

South wall:—

SACRED TO THE MEMORY
OF FRANCES THE WIFE OF GEORGE THOMAS
DAUGHTER AND COHEIRESS OF JOHN PAGE, ESQ;
OF WATERGATE HOUSE,
IN THIS COUNTY;
WHO DIED NOVEMBER 15TH 1807,
AGED 64 YEARS.

Pedigree of Whitehead.

WILLIAM WHITEHEAD of Antigua, Esq., 1758, later of Ormsby, near Appleby, co. Cumberland; died Dec. 1791 in England. = Jane Furnall, mar. 31 Dec. 1763 at St. John's; died 2 Sep. 1800 at Winchester.

- Rev. Robert Whitehead, educated at Tunbridge under Rev. Mr. Knox; of Queen's College, Oxon, matric. 6 Dec. 1785, æt. 18; B.A. 1789; M.A. 1792; in 1831 of Hensingham, co. Cumberland; died 31 May 1851 at Rochester. = ... niece of Mr. Children of Tunbridge; mar. in 1790.
  - A son, born in 1791.
- Jane Whitehead, 1st dau., bapt 16 Oct. 1764, and mar. 8 Sep. 1782, at St. John's, Thomas Jarvis, Esq., President of Council; she died 6 Feb. 1797, æt. 33.
- Jane Whitehead, bapt. 16 Oct. 1764 at St. John's; living 18 Sep. 1791.
- William Whitehead, bapt. 1 April 1766 and bur. 8 Aug. 1767 at St. John's.
- George Whitehead, bapt. 15 and bur. 30 Oct. 1772 at St. John's.
- Ann Whitehead, bapt. 28 Aug. 1769 at St. John's.

1758, Dec. 14. William Whitehead to join the Troop.

1791. Lately (Dec.). Wm. Whitehead, esq. of Antigua. ('Gent. Mag.,' p. 1235.)

1800, Sep. 2. At Winchester, Mrs. Whitehead, relict of Wm. W. esq. of Antigua. (*Ibid.*, p. 908.)

For further information about the Whiteheads see under Jarvis.

PARISH REGISTER OF ST. JOHN.

Baptized.

1764 Oct. 16 Jane the d. of Wm Whitehead and Jane his wife.

1766 April 1 William the S. of Wm Whitehead and Jane his wife.

1769 Aug. 28 Ann D. of William Whitehead and Jane his wife.

1772 Oct. 15 George the S. of Wm Whitehead and Jane his wife.

Married.

1763 Dec. 31 William Whitehead to Jane Furnall; by L.

1782 Sep. 8 Thomas Jarvis to Jane Whitehead. L.

1806 Dec. 11 Thomas Lynch to Eliza Whitehead, Spinster; L.

Buried.

1767 Aug. 8 William Whitehead (an Infant).

1772 Oct. 30 George Whitehead.

- William Wickham, matriculated from New College, Oxford, 24 Dec. 1725, æt. 18.
- Colonel John Wickham, Member of Assembly for Old North Sound 1738—41. Will dated 12 Sep. 1750; sworn 25 Feb. 1752. = Patience, dau. of Hon. Nathaniel Crump; sister of Dr. George Crump 1756; bur. 5 Aug. 1774 at St. George's.
  - Ann Wickham, coheir, mar. before 1753. Will dated 1 May 1795; sworn 14 Oct. 1797. = Thomas Freeman, Esq., who changed the name of "Wickhams" to "Upper Freemans;" died in or before 1785.
  - Sarah Wickham, coheir, mar. 4 Sep. 1746 at St. Philip's (? bur. there 11 Aug. 1747). = William Lyons of St. Philip's Parish, Esq.; died 1770.
    - s.p.
- Samuel Wickham, a minor 1716; living 1739; died s.p. = Sarah, dau. of Charles Lloyd, Esq.; mar. 2ndly, 6 Sep. 1750, John Blizard; 3rdly, William Murray. Her will dated 1 Dec. 1775.
  - s.p.

John Podivinns, Surgeon, in his will proved 1697 (125 Pyne), names his friend Nathaniel Wickham of London, Citizen and Surgeon.

Benjamin Wickham of St. Peter's, Parham, planter. Will dated 2 July 1705. To my 1st son Saml £500 c. & £20, & to his wife Rachell £20 c. To my 3d son Benjn Wickham £800 c. To my 4th son Nathl Wickham £800 c. at 22. To my 2 daus. Martha & Rachell Wickham £800 c. each at 22. To my 2d son John Wickham all residue & my plantation in St Peter's Parish & all negros, & to his heirs, then to my 3rd son Benjn. My son John Ex'or. Witnessed by John Buxton, Nathaniel Crump, Samuel Phillips, William Barclay, Joshua Jones. By John Yeamans, Esq., appeared Lieut. Samuel Phillips, Joshua Jones, Gent., and Nathaniel Crump 31 May 1706.

. . . . Wickham. Will dated . . . . To my wife Sarah Wickham her horse & . . . . My godson Wm Wickham . . . . my dau. Ann Wickham each £50 c. To my cousin John Wickham, Esq., & my brother in . . . . nan, Esq., £20 c. To my said dau. . . . ., all my estate . . . . the Body of my said dau. Sarah. Wm Wickham Sanderson, son of . . . . (This fragment I found among wills recorded in 1743.)

John Wickham, Esq. Will dated 12 Sep. 1750. To my wife Patience the furniture of her bedroom & £500 c. To my godson John Wickham Sanderson, son of Captn John Sanderson, £100 c.; the same to my goddau. Ann dau. of Mr Philip Crump, decd. To my goddau. Mary dau. of Saml Redhead £50 c. To my godson John son of Chr. Scandrett, decd, £50 c. . . . . All residue to my dau. Ann Wickham . . . . I give to my godson John Wickham Sanderson, provided he take the name of Wickham . . . . Geo. Crump, Joshua Crump, John Sanderson, Robt Brown, & . . . . Ex'ors. Witnessed by Oliver Burk. By John Tomlinson, Esq., was sworn Oliver Burke 25 Feb. 1752. Recorded 29 Feb. 1752.

Benjamin Wickham of Antigua, planter. Will dated 14 July 1759. Freedom to my mulattos Joe & Sally & Dicky (children of Phibba's), to Joe £36 a year. To my 2 negros Molly & Hannah their freedom & maintenance, & £7 a year to Molly. To my loving friend Joseph Tadman £200. All residue to my brother Joseph Wickham & his heirs male, then to his dau. Hester Wickham, then to my kinsman Saml Lavicount of Antigua, then to Philip Lavicount, son of my kinsman Peter Lavicount. My Brother Joseph Wickham & my kinsman Saml Lavicount Ex'ors. Witnessed by William Redhead, Andrew Martin, Alexander Sherriff. To my niece Hester Parker £200. By Governor George Thomas was sworn William Redhead 12 July 1760. Recorded 22 July 1760.

Pedigree of Wickham.

ARMS.—*Two chevrons between three roses.*
CREST.—*A bull's head erased, charged on the neck with two chevrons.*

BENJAMIN WICKHAM of St. Peter's Parish, Antigua (? removed from Barbados 1679); purchased 20 acres 1681; Coroner 1693. Will dated 2 July 1705; sworn 31 May 1706. = ...

Major Samuel Wickham, granted 100 acres 1701; served as Coroner; of Old North Sound 1707; Member of Assembly for Nonsuch 1707-8; dead 21 Nov. 1709. = Rachel . . . . mar. before 1705.

Major John Wickham of Old North Sound 1707; Capt. of the Carabiniers 1709; J.P. 1712; Member of Assembly 1717-18, and for Belfast 1721-2; æt. 30 in 1718; died 30 Nov. 1723, æt. 41. M.I. at "Wickhams." = Elizabeth . . . . æt. 25 in 1718.

Benjamin Wickham, sole heir to Philip Watkins 1693; of the Carabiniers 1708; Member of Assembly for Belfast 1714-15; of St. Philip's Parish and owner of 480 acres and 100 slaves 1720.

Nathaniel Wickham, merchant, under 22 in 1705; of the Carabiniers 1712-13; Member of Assembly 1717-18; æt. 25 in 1718, then of Parham Town. = Mary . . . . living 1718.

Martha Wickham, living 1705.

Rachel Wickham, mar. 11 July 1714 John Robinson.

Joseph Wickham, a minor 1739; of Belfast 1753 (? bur. 6 Feb. 1779 at St. Philip's). Probably son of Major Samuel or Nathaniel. = Sarah, 2nd dau. of Colonel John Ker of the 38th Regiment (he was aged 59 in 1713); mar. 31 Jan. 1739 at St. Philip's.

Benjamin Wickham of Belfast, planter, 1753; bur. 4 July 1761 [*sic*] at St. Philip's. Will dated 14 July 1759; sworn 12 July 1760.

Esther Wickham, only dau., mar. 13 Dec. 1759 at St. Philip's; remar. there 18 June 1779 John Ledeatt, and died 1801. = John Mayer of St. Philip's Parish.

Anne Mayer, mar. 1778; died 1796 at Antigua. Had fifteen children. = Charles Grant of The Adelphi, St. Vincent, and of Carron, N.B., died 1821 at Marseilles. (See Vol. II., p. 29.)

Ann Montgomery Grant, born 1789; mar. 1809 at St. Vincent; died 1868 at Clifton. = John Birch, Captain and Adjutant 90th Regiment, later Major 65th Regiment, died 1844 at Clifton.

Elizabeth Birch, born 1810.

Anne Mayer Birch, born 1815.

John Birch, died s.p. 1857 in Australia.

Charles Grant Birch, Ensign 1st West India Regiment, died s.p. 1840.

Colonel James Francis Birch, born 1821; Fort Adjutant of Antigua 1847. = Juliana Mary, dau. of Major Anderson of Nassau, Bahamas, and niece of Sir George Anderson; mar. there 1846.

Wickham Montgomery Birch, matric. from Trinity College, Oxford, 17 May 1850, æt. 19; B.A. 1854; M.A. 1857; Vicar of Launceston 1866—79 and of Ashburton, Devon, since 1879. = Jane Judith, 3rd dau. of Northmore H. P. Lawrence of Launceston, Cornwall. (*Vide* Vivian's 'Visitation of Cornwall.')

John Grant Birch, born 1847 in Antigua; Hon. Major 3rd Lancashire Volunteer Regiment. = Anne Isabella Turnbull of Hayden Bridge, Northumberland, mar. 1879.

Anne Mayer Birch, born 1849 in Antigua.

Mary Frances Birch, born in Jamaica; mar. 1887 Rev. A. R. Hudson. Issue.

Emily Birch, mar. 1887, at Liverpool, John Stuart Horner of Mells, co. Somerset. Issue.

James Kortright Birch, Magistrate Straits Settlements, born 1850 at Nassau. = Kate Renoldson, mar. 1890.

Charles Wykeham Male Birch, born at Liverpool. = Madge Wallace, niece of the American Bishop of Tokio, Japan; mar. 1896 in Japan.

John Kenneth Beaufoy Birch, born 1880 at Liverpool; Cadet R.N. 1897.

Alan Grant Birch, born 1882 at Liverpool; at Winchester School 1896.

Eric Wykeham Birch, born 1892 at Bedfont Lodge, co. Middlesex.

Dorothy Fetherston Birch, born 1894 at Singapore.

1638. Nathaniel Wickham then an inhabitant of Barbados. ('Memoirs of the First Settlement.')

May the 20th, 1679. Benja Wickham in the Barq. "Resolution" for Antegoa, John Inglebe, Comandr; security.

September the first 1679. Eliza Wickham in the Sloop "John & Francis" for Antegua, John Howard, Comander: time out.

October the 6th, 1679. Thomas Wickham in the Sloop "True freindship" for Antegoa, Charles Kallahane, Comandr; security. (Tickets from Barbados. Hotten's 'Lists of Emigrants.')

1681, April 19. John Murphey sells 20 acres to Benjamin Wickham.

1701, Oct. 10. Benjamin Wickham, Gent., 60 acres bounded E. with William Cochran, Gent., W. with Arthur Freeman, chirurgeon, in St. Peter's Parish. His son Samuel Wickham also 100 acres. Granted by Christopher Codrington.

Indenture dated 26 Feb. 1705-6. Captain Benjamin Wickham of St. Peter's Parish releases his son Benjamin Wickham of all debts.

1710, Nov. 17. Nathaniel Wickham is granted unimproved land in Parham Town, being E. and W. 60 feet, N. and S. 80 feet, bounded E. with the house and tenement of Thomas Martin, deceased, now in the possession of William Glanvile, W. with the house and tenement of Charles Tudway, deceased, S. with the Queen's land, N. with the street on which he wants to build. (Minutes of Assembly.)

Richard Wickham, son of Nathaniel Wickham of Wapping, co. Middlesex, M.D., matriculated from New College, Oxford, 9 July 1715, æt. 15.

1716, July 21. Catherine Newgent petitions the Assembly for a patent for 20 acres, which is opposed by Benjamin Wickham, Gent., who petitions that William, Lord Willoughby, of Parham, by patent dated 5 Nov. 1669 granted to Thomas Hicks 20 acres in Nonsuch Division on the N. side of the harbour, bounded E. with Francis Allen, N. with Henry Lory, W. with John Chard, and S. with the creek of Nonsuch Harbour. The said Thomas Hickes on 7 Jan. 1690 granted to John Cane the said 20 acres; it then passed to John Hall, deceased, and was forfeited. Samuel Martin by deed of 12 Oct. 1693 granted to William Thomas, Gent., a certain plantation of 80 acres, bounding on Henry Lory, Tim. St. John, and Thomas Lydia [sic], formerly John Hall's 80 acres, and including the said 20 acres in it; and William Thomas on 19 Jan. 1701 by deed granted to the Hon. Christopher Codrington the said 80 acres, and the latter by deed of 19 Oct. 1704 granted to John Duer, Gent., the said 80 acres and other lands; and the said John Duer on 3 Feb. 1707 leased to Tim. St. John 210 acres for 10 years from 1 Jan. preceding, and including the said 80 acres. John Duer on 4 May 1714 granted to petitioner the said 210 acres. Ordered that the 20 acres were never so included to Catherine Newgent, widow. (Minutes of Assembly.)

1717-18, Feb. 3. Mr. Nathaniel Wickham's house at Parham Town. Writ issued against Parker's wife for abusing Master John Wickham.

In B. T. Leeward Islands, vol. 15, are the original depositions of the following persons:—

Mrs. Mary Wickham, wife of Mr. Nathaniel Wickham of Parham Town in Antigua, merchant, 4 Feb. 1718.

Nathaniel Wickham, merchant, aged 25, 4 Feb. 1718.

John Wickham, Esq., J.P., aged 30, brother of Mr. Nathaniel Wickham, 5 Feb. 1718.

Madam Elizabeth Wickham, wife of John Wickham, Esq., aged 25, Feb. 1718.

Nathaniel Wickham, Doctor in Physic, presents a memorial in favour of Colonel Thomas Morris of Antigua on 1 April 1718.

1718-19, Feb. 18. Nathaniel Wickham petitions for land in St. John's Town E. with John Brett, W. with the sea, N. with a wharfe run out by Colonel Parke, S. with the street and the sea.

1719, Nov. 17. John Vickery of Parham Town petitions that Mr. Benjamin Wickham claims his grant.

1739, Aug. 7. Benjamin and Joseph Wickham to join Troop, and on Aug. 21 Samuel Wickham struck out.

1739, Oct. 30. Joseph Wickham's vote null, he being a minor.

1835. Richard S. Wickham then Superintendent of Police.

PARISH REGISTER OF ST. JOHN.

Married.

1714 July 11 John Robinson & Rachel Wickham.

PARISH REGISTER OF ST. PHILIP.

Married.

1720 July 2 Joseph Wickham & Eliza Waser: by Banns published.
1739 Jan. 31 Joseph Wickham to Sarah Kerr; by L.
1746 Sep. 4 William Lyons & Sarah Wickham.
1750 Sep. 6 John Blizard, junr, & Sarah Wickham, Spinster [*sic*].
1759 Dec. 19 John Mayers & Esther Wickham.

Buried.

1739 Oct. 23 Mrs Esther Wickham, Widow.
1761 July 4 Benjamin Wickham.
1779 Feb. 6 Joseph Wickham.

PARISH REGISTER OF ST. GEORGE.

Married.

1750 Sep. 6 John Blizard, Junior, of the Parish of St George's, Fitches, Widower, & Sarah Wickham of St Phillip's Parish, Widow; married September 6th.

UPPER FREEMAN'S PLANTATION.

At the family burial-ground, in a cane piece, and under a large bread fruit tree. On ledger, over stone vault:—

Arms: *Two chevrons between three roses, 2 and 1*; impaling [*blank*].

Crest: *A bull's head erased, charged on the neck with two chevrons over helmet.*

HERE LYETH INTERRED THE BODY OF
MAJOR IOHN WICKHAM
OF THIS ISLAND WHO DEPARTED THIS
LIFE NOVEMR THE XXXTH MDCCXXIII.
IN THE XLIID YEAR OF HIS AGE
MEMENTO.

On an adjoining ledger:—

ELIZABETH WICKHAM
Once the Comfort, the Joy, and the Pride of her Parents
The Delight of ALL who knew her,
The Admiration of ALL who saw Her
Was
Born XXVI Jan. MDCCXXXIII
Died 11 Feb. MDCCXLV.
(Twenty-seven eulogistic lines follow.)

Rowlandson gives the arms: *Argent, two chevrons Sable between three roses Gules, seeded Or, barbed Vert;* and Crest: *A bull's head Sable, armed Or, charged on the neck with two chevrons Argent,* as belonging to Wickham of Kent, Abingdon, co. Berks, and of Swalcliffe, co. Oxon.

"Wickhams" is in St. Philip's Parish. In 1852 it contained 216 acres and was owned by Burnthorn Musgrave.

Pedigree of Williams.

ARMS.—*Or, a winged griffin segreant gules.*
(Griggs's 'Examples of Armorial Bookplates.')

. . . . WILLIAMS, settled at the Old Road in St. Mary's Parish = ...

Colonel Rowland Williams,* the 1st male white child born on the Island, granted patent for 300 acres 1668; Lieut. 1669; Major 1671; Lieut.-Colonel 1676; Colonel 1677; Member of Council 1674; Deputy-Governor 1675-82; Clerk of the Navy 3 William and Mary; bur. 20 July 1713, æt. over 80, and M.I. at St. Mary's. Will dated 10 July 1713; proved 21 May 1714. (106 Aston.) = Elizabeth, 1st dau. of Samuel Winthrop, Deputy-Governor of Antigua, and relict of William Mildon of Nevis and of Francis St. John; named in her mother's will 1675 and brother's 1679.

Colonel Thomas Williams of Old Road, Antigua, and of Newlands in Thames Ditton, co. Surrey, living 1679; Member of Assembly for St. John's 1710; bur. 18 March 1733 at St. Mary's. Will recorded at Antigua. = Mary, dau. of Edward Byam, Esq., by Sarah, dau. of Samuel Winthrop, Deputy-Governor of Antigua; born 13 Oct. 1690; mar. 1705. Will dated 29 Aug. 1742; proved 4 May 1743. (182 Boycott.) To be bur. at Cheshunt, co. Herts.

Samuel Williams,† Gent.-Commoner of Christ College, Oxford, matriculated 14 April 1697, æt. 16; B.A. 12 March 1700-1; ob. s.p.

Ann Williams, only unmar. dau. 1713.

Frances Williams.

Elizabeth Williams living 1679.

A dau., probably mar. Hon. Colonel Rowland Oliver, whose son, Alderman Richard Oliver, M.P., was cousin of Edward Williams 1782.

Rowland Williams, bapt. 18 July 1707 at St. John's; matric. from Queen's College, Oxford, 26 May 1726, æt. 18; later a Physician; ob. s.p. in New York. Will dated 18 Feb. 1737; sworn 16 March 1738-9.

Edward Williams, sole heir to his brother Rowland, bapt. 30 April 1710 at St. John's; owner of 250 slaves and 1030 acres in St. Mary's 1780; died 6 April and bur. 15 April 1784, æt. 74, and M.I. at Thames Ditton. Will dated 10 April 1782; proved 16 April 1784. (238 Rockingham.) = Mary, dau. of . . . . Bennett of Penrith, co. Cumberland; dead 1806.

Samuel Williams, inherited "Horns" from his father; matric. from University College, Oxford, 27 Oct. 1737, æt. 17.

William Williams, a minor 1738; living 1742. (See his bookplate above.)

Thomas Williams, bapt. 14 Aug. 1713 at St. John's.

Sarah Williams, bapt. 14 Aug. 1713 at St. John's; died s.p.

Rowland Edward Williams of Antigua and of Thames Ditton, born 18 Dec. 1748; inherited from his father the "Road," "Tom Moores," and the "Cistern" plantations; died 28 Nov. and bur. 8 Dec. 1826, æt. 77, at Thames Ditton. = Mary, dau. of Robert Symes of Esher, co. Surrey, and Jamaica; marriage settlement dated 23 April 1783; died 18 June 1827.

Samuel Williams, Barrister-at-Law, inherited the "Body" plantation from his father; died 1825 and bur. at Lyndhurst, co. Hants.

Rowland Edward Louis Charles Williams, Member of Council and Puisne Baron of Exchequer, Antigua; Captain 10th Hussars; born April 1784; bur. 2 June 1852, æt. 68, at St. Mary's. He called his ancestral estate "Claremont." = Clara Susanna, 2nd dau. of Major-General Sir Patrick Ross, G.C.B., Governor of the Leeward Islands, and of Craigie, N.B.; died 28 and bur. 30 March 1840, æt. 32, and M.I. at St. Mary's.

Samuel Harry Williams, æt. 9 in 1806; Lieut. R.N. 1825.

Maria Williams.

Elizabeth Williams.

Harriet Williams.

Rowland Edward Louis Henry Williams of Antigua and of Newlands in Thames Ditton, only son and heir, of the 32nd Foot, born 17 Oct. and bapt. 30 Nov. 1828 at St. John's; died 3 Oct. 1867, æt. 38, at Upper Norwood. M.I. at Thames Ditton.

* Mrs. Mary Frye, who died 1769, æt. 81, and Mrs. Frances Lucie Blackman, who died *circa* 1758, æt. 71, were apparently also his daughters. (See Vol. I.)

† Joseph Winthrop in his will 1679 names his nephew Samuel Williams.

.... Williams. [Lieut. Charles Williams of Nevis granted 300 acres in Antigua 1681, and Mrs. Elizabeth Williams 200 acres.] = Martha, sister of Captain Thomas Oesterman of Antigua: named in his will 1724.

William Mead, Member of Council of St. Kitts 1689; President 1698—1701. Will dated 23 July 1702, late of Nevis, then of London, Esq.; proved 26 July 1704. (36 Ash.) See *ante*, p. 90. = Penelope, dau. of Sergeant-Major Michael Smith of Nevis. Will dated 31 Aug. 1733; proved 23 March 1735. (106 Ducie.)

Colonel John Williams of Antigua, heir to his uncle Thomas Oesterman, Esq., 1724 (? nephew of Mrs. Penelope Mead 1733): died 30 Nov. and bur. 1 Dec. 1736, æt. 52, and M.I. at St. John's. Will dated 29 Nov. and sworn 11 Dec. 1736. = Mary ...., remar. 4 July 1738, at St. John's, Dr. David Parvianee, and died 5 Jan. 1738-9, æt. 32, and M.I. there.

Thomas Williams of Nevis, heir to his brother Jacob 1736. = ...

Jacob Williams of Nevis, bur. 14 Dec. 1736 at St. John's. Will dated 10 Dec. and sworn 16 Dec. 1736.

Martha Williams, mar. .... Woodward.

Elizabeth Williams, mar. George Saunders.

Hon. Col. Michael Williams of Nevis, nephew of Mrs. Penelope Mead 1733. Will dated 13 Oct. 1740; proved 16 June 1741. (168 Spurway.) = Anne ...., living 1733.

Thomas Oesterman Williams, sole heir to his father; bur. 9 Jan. 1742 at St. John's.

Martha Williams, bapt. 28 Oct. 1729 at St. John's; living 1736.

Mary Williams, living 1736.

Elizabeth Williams, bapt. 1 Feb. 1734 at St. John's; living 1736.

Sarah Williams. = Hon. John Williams, Member of Council of Nevis 1743 till his death there May 1785, æt. 80.

Michael Williams, Ex'or to his father 1741 (? died 6 Feb. 1758 at Bath).

Elizabeth Williams, mar. William Peterson* before 1733, and had issue.

Anne Williams.

Sarah Williams.

Frances Williams.

Penelope Williams.

Henrietta Williams.

Mary Williams.

All single 1740.

John Williams, son and heir 1766; of Whitton, co. Middlesex. = Charlotte Mary Thornhill More, a minor, legatee in the will of Charles, Duke of Bolton.

This Pedigree is very doubtful, and requires proof.

* See Peterson in the Dasent Pedigree.

John Williams of Antigua, planter. Will dated 31 May 1672. To Morris Lee 200 lbs. To my friend Timothy Swining 1500 lbs. due from Howell Jones, latter to be Ex'or. My goddau. Kath. Jones his dau. Witnessed by John Barry, John Carney, Daniel Pello. On 4 June 1672 were sworn John Carney and Daniel Pello. Recorded 5 June 1672.

Edward Williams of Antigua, planter, died intestate. Adm'on to Lewis Garnish as next-of-kin granted by Philip Warner 25 June 1673. Recorded same date. Inventory by warrant on 28th June to Anthony White, Robert Oxford, and William Kerby, 12,500 lbs.

Ann Williams, æt. 16, daughter and heir of Arthur Williams of Antigua, deceased, hath chosen Captain John Roe as guardian 17 Jan. 1695. Inventory to be taken.

Elliner Williams of Antigua, relict and executrix of William Williams. Will dated 22 Jan. 1696-7. To my godson Tho. Stevenson, s. of Wm Stevenson, 2000 lbs. To my friend Darby Cahand all my estate, he to be Ex'or. Witnessed by John Cochran, Edward Laver, Adam Martin. By the Deputy-Governor appeared Adam Martin and John Cochran 11 Feb. 1696. Recorded 22 Feb. 1696.

Roger Willims (or Williams) of London, merchant. Will dated 11 June 1711; proved 17 Nov. 1721 by William Gregson; power reserved to Allen Smith. (213 Buckingham.) All my plantation & slaves in Antigua to my friends Allen Smith of Battersea, sugar baker, & Wm Gregson of London, gent., to sell for my son Thomas Willims at 21; if he die £100 to the dau. of my brother Edward Willims & all residue to the sons of my brother Hugh Willims. All residue to my said son Thomas. Trustees to be Ex'ors. Witnessed by Samuel Blunt, William Tothall, Phil. Traheran.

He was of St. John's Town in 1707, and for further information about his estate see *ante*, p. 170.

Rowland Williams of Antigua, Esq. Will dated 10 July 1713; proved 21 May 1714 by Colonel Edward Byam and Colonel John Frye. (106 Aston.) To each of my daus. now married £50 apiece, their portions having been already paid. To each of my grandchildren by name Rowland £50. To my unmarried dau. Ann Williams £1000 at day of marriage & handsome maintenance till then. To my naturall dau. Frances Williams £250 at marriage & maintenance, also 6 negros which are to be given to her mother Mrs Mary Magaskey & 12,000 lbs. of sugar & £100 to her said mother. To Ceazor Williams his freedom & 2 negro boys. To Mr Tho. Trant 50 gs. To my Ex'ors £100 apiece. All residue to my loving son Tho. Williams. I appoint my trusty friends Col. Edwd Byam & Col. John Frye Ex'ors. Witnessed by Thomas Reston, William Bradshaw, William Freeman. By His Excellency Walter Douglas, Esq., Captain-General of H.M. Leeward Islands, were sworn Thomas Reston and William Freeman. Recorded in Secretary's Office in libro "M," fos. 286 and 287, 24 July 1713, John Booth, clerk, Secretary. Recorded in the Registrar's Office in libro "M," fo. 127, 25 July 1713. Examined per Henry Symes, Registrar, and copy sworn to also by Thomas Ward, Ra. Williamson, John Swettenham, and Benjamin Cowell.

Colonel Thomas Williams. Will (nearly destroyed). My beloved son E .... my plantation in St John's, all slaves & cattle .... To my son Saml .... my upper plantation by name of Horns, also 50 acres adjoining .... My son Wil .... 150 acres .... name of the Cisterns ginger ground .... also £300 c. charged on my Road plantation. My son Wm Williams. To my dau. Sarah Williams £2000 c., ½ charged on my Road & ½ on my Body plantation .... To my beloved .... ary Williams a negro girl .... My wife to have a good room & all my plate. To .... etta Jefferson, d. of Eliz^th Jefferson, £ .... c. yearly. All residue to my son Rowland Williams. Appoint Tho. Freeman ....

John Williams, Esq. Will dated 29 Nov. 1736. To my son Tho. Oesterman Williams £50 st. To my wife Mary all furniture. To my brother Thos. Williams of Nevis my pistols & swords. To my brother Jacob Williams of Nevis my silver spurs & gold headed cane. All clothing to my cousin Wm Oesterman of Antigua. To my Ex'ors each a ring of a moydore in value. 26 slaves to my wife & daus. Martha, Mary, & Elizabeth Williams. All residue to my son Tho. O. Williams. Rowl^d Oliver of Antigua, planter, Walter Tullideph, Surgeon, & my wife Mary during her widowhood Ex'ors. Witnessed by David Purviance, Elizabeth Wragg, William Wyne. And I also give my wife my saddle horse. Before William Mathew, Esq., were sworn William Wyne, Gent., and David Purviance, Surgeon, 11 Dec. 1736. Recorded 28 July 1737.

Jacob Williams, planter, of Nevis. Will dated 10 Dec. 1736. To my nephew Tho. Oesterman Williams my gold headed cane & a pair of spurs lately left me by his father. To my sisters Eliz^th Saunders & Martha Woodward £2 rings. To Eliz^th d. of Geo. Saunders a negro. To my nephew Jac. Williams Saunders £25 st. All residue especially the land left me by my uncle Tho. Oysterman, Esq., to my brother Thos., he to pay to my nieces Martha & Eliz^th daus. of my late brother John Williams £400 st. each at 21. My brother Thos. & Rowl^d Oliver, Esq., Ex'ors. Witnessed by Francis Herbert, William Osterman, David Purviance. Before William Mathew, Esq., was sworn William Osterman 16 Dec. 1736. Recorded 24 Dec. 1736.

Rowland Williams. Will dated 18 Feb. 1737. To my brother Wm Williams £200 c. at 21 over & above the money my father left him, also £500 c. at 23. All residue to my brother Edwd, & if he die without male issue to my bro. W^m, & should he try to cut off W^m then £8000 to W^m at Edward's death. My bro. Edwd sole Ex'or. Witnessed by William Young, Thomas Balderston, James Bolitho.

Codicil dated 3 Dec. 1738. Freedom to 2 slaves. To John Yeamans, jun^r, £50 for a ring. To Rev. Geo. Homes £50 c. To Robt Freeman & Edwd Byam, late of Antigua, & Stephen Bayard of this city, merch^t, Ex'ors in New York to see me decently buried. Witnessed by Henry Cuyler, jun., George Lurting, Elias Desbrosses. Before William Mathew, Esq., was sworn Henry Cuyler, jun., 16 March 1738-9. Recorded 12 April 1739.

John Williams, mariner. My wife Elinor, my dau. Joan, my 1st s. John, my 2^d s. Alex^r, my 3^d s. Gratrick. Recorded 5 May 1737.

Michael Williams of Nevis, Esq. Will dated 13 Oct. 1740; proved 16 June 1741 by Michael Williams the son; power reserved to John Williams. (168 Spurway.) To my dau. Eliz. Peterson £5 for a ring. To each of my 6 daus. Anne, Sarah, Frances, Penelope, Henrietta, & Mary Williams £400 c. apiece & all my plate. To my granddaus. Eliz., Anne, & Elenor Peterson, daus. of my dau. Eliz. Peterson, £100 c. each & £100 I lent their father Wm Peterson, Gent. To my son John Williams my parcell of land in the mountains purchased of John Fawcett, planter, & Mary his wife. All residue to my 2 sons Michael & John whom I appoint Ex'ors & Guardians of my grandchildren. Witnessed by William Kitt, George Jones, Edmund Parris.

Mary Williams, widow of Colonel Thomas Williams, late of Antigua, now of Hadley, co. Middlesex. Will dated 29 Aug. 1742; proved 4 May 1743 by William Byam, Esq.; power reserved to Elizabeth Carlile. (182 Boycott.) To be buried at Cheshunt, co. Herts, near my 2 children already buried there. To St Geo.'s Hospital, Hyde Park Corner, 30 gs. to be p^d to Mr Joseph Hudson the Treasurer. 10 gs. to 5 poor families in Hadley, & 20 gs. to the charity school now founded there, to be paid to Mr Pennant the Minister. To Mrs Prudence Morgan, now living with my mother, 20 gs., & 10 gs. more for Anne Thomas, dau. of Crook Thomas. 5 gs. & my clothes to my maid. To my good friend Mrs Eliz. Carlile & my dear brother Wm Byam, Esq., 10 gs. each. To my 1st son Edwd Williams all my plate, furniture, linen, in my house at Hadley & 30 gs. Rings to my mother, brothers, & sisters. To my youngest son Wm Williams all sums due from my son Edwd Williams or in the hands of Messrs. Frye, merch^ts. My dear brother Wm Byam, Esq., & my cousin Eliz. Carlile Ex'ors. Witnessed by John Middleton, Bristol.

1st Codicil. My body not to be buried till offensive. N.B. I have left in my plate trunk inside my silver tea kettle 100 guineas. Guinea rings to my mother & sister Freeman, my brother & sister Wm Byam, my brother & sister Francis Byam, my brother & sister Edwd Byam, my sister Byam at Edmonton, my brother George's widow. To Mrs Anne Hill 5 gs. On 29 April 1743 was sworn Steven Venn of Mark Lane, Gent., and on 3 May 1743 Samuel Frye of London, merchant, Steven Venn, and William Byam of St. Clement Danes, Esq.

Arthur Williams of Antigua, planter. Will dated 3 March 1756. To my d. Marg^t £100 c. To my 2 sons W^m & John £100 c. each at 21. To my d. Marg^t £20 c. yearly, & to W^m & John £15 c. yearly. To my nephew John Boudinot £40 c. All residue to my 2 sons. Mathew Williams, sen., John Richardson, Barry Nibbs, and Jeremiah Blizard, jun., Ex'ors. Witnessed by George Powell, Edward Gamble. (See Richardson Pedigree.)

Edward Williams, formerly of Antigua, now of Thames Ditton, co. Surry, Esq. Will dated 10 April 1782; proved 16 April 1784 by Thomas Oliver, Esq., and Rowland Edward Williams, Esq., the son; power reserved to Richard Oliver, Esq., Michael Lovell, Esq., and Samuel Williams the son. (238 Rockingham.) To my beloved wife Mary all my plate, jewells, linen, pictures, china, & £800 a year for life (£600 charged on my "Road" estates & £200 on my "Body" ones), also my dwelling house, garden, & 16 acres at Weston Green in the parish of Thames Ditton for life, & £500. I have a bond da. 16 March 1775 for £400 for the payment of £200 & interest owing by Jas. Chalmers, formerly of Angel Gardens, St Geo. in the East, co. Midd., now of Mile End, farmer, I give this to Richd Oliver, late one of the Alderman of London, but now residing in the island of Grenada, Esq., to Tho. Oliver of London, merch^t, & to Mich^l Lovell of London, merch^t, in trust for Ann Chalmers (my wife's niece) who is wife of said Jas. Chalmers. To the same trustees all my "Body" plantation in St John's parish in trust for Saml Williams, now residing in Antigua, Esq., barrister, & his heirs, then to Rowl^d Edwd Williams, then to Richd Oliver. To Miss Dorothy Bennett my wife's niece now residing with me £100 & 20 gs. To Mrs Jane Giles, widow, my wife's sister, £25 a year & 20 gs. To my servants John Kervill & Wm Hunter £50 each, & to each of my women servants £10. To my trustees my 3 plantations called the "Road," the "Upper" or "Tom Mores," & the "Cistern," all in St Mary's parish, in trust for Rowl^d Edwd Williams his heirs, then to Saml Williams his heirs, then to Richd Oliver. All residue of my real estate to Rowl^d Edwd Williams, & in default to my cousin Richd Oliver. All residue of my personal estate in trust for Rowl^d Edwd Williams. I appoint Richd Oliver, Tho. Oliver, Michael Lovell, Saml Williams, & Rowl^d Edwd Williams, Esq^res, Ex'ors. Witnessed by A. Wynne, W. Thorn, Richard Nicholl, jun. Recorded at St. John's 29 June 1784.

John Williams, carpenter. My wife Eliz^th, my daus. Eleanor Lindsay, Hester Hall, & Mary Williams, & my sons Alex^r & Wm Williams. Recorded 8 June 1789.

James Williams, planter. Will dated 16 Jan. 1795. All my estate to John son of Robt French & W^m son of Philip Hall equally & to be Ex'ors. Witnessed by John Haycock, John Lindsay, John Pett. Recorded 29 July 1796.

Thomas Williams of Massachusetts. Will dated 7 Oct. 1809 at Gustavia, Island of St. Bartholomew. To my heirs the lawful children of my parents all my estate. I appoint Robt M. R. Ashley of the town of Lee in Mass. my Ex'or. Witnessed by Elijah Warfield, Dr. George R. Porter of Tortola. Before Andrew Bergsted, Justice of St. Bartholomew, one of His Majesty's Secretaries, appeared F. W. and W. Israel, merchants, 22 March 1810.

Close Roll, 18 Geo. III., Part 3, Nos. 12 and 13.

Indenture made the 24th March 1778 between Watkin Williams of Pembordro, co. Denbigh, Esq., and Elizabeth Williams his wife, of the one part, and the Rev. Philip Puleston of Pickill, co. Flint, Clerk, of the other part, witnesses that in consideration of 5*s.* apiece Watkin and Elizabeth Williams grant, etc., to Philip Puleston all that undivided 8th part of their share of the Fountain Plantation in St. Kitts, and all their undivided 4th part of another 8th part of the said plantation, and all their undivided 4th part in the plantation called Russell's Rest in Nevis, and all their undivided 4th part in that other plantation in the Old Windward Passage in Nevis called the River Plantation, and all their parts in negros and other slaves, etc., to have and to hold for one whole year, etc.

No. 12.

Indenture tripartite made the 25th March 1778 between Watkin Williams, Esq., and Elizabeth Williams his wife, of the 1st part, Catharine Stapleton of Bodriddan, co. Flint, spinster, of the 2nd part, and the Rev. Philip Puleston, of the 3rd part. Whereas Watkin Williams and Elizabeth his wife (in right of Elizabeth) are seised in fee simple and entitled to the parts of several plantations (as in No. 13), subject to a debt due by them, or one of them, to Messrs. Richard Neave and John Willett of London, merchants, to the amount of £1745 14*s.* 8*d.*, and to a further sum of £2800 being the proportion of Watkin Williams and Elizabeth, of and in a debt due from them together with the rest of the proprietors of the said plantations, and also subject to the proportion of Watkin Williams and Elizabeth; and whereas Catherine Stapleton has contracted with Watkin Williams and Elizabeth his wife for the absolute purchase of their parts of the said plantations for the sum of £14,000, was agreed that £11,000 should be secured to Watkin Williams and interest at 4½ per cent. till all should be paid. Now this Indenture witnesses that in pursuance of the agreement and in consideration of £3000 paid by Catharine Stapleton, Watkin and Elizabeth Williams grant, etc., to Philip Puleston all their parts (as in No. 13) in trust, and it may be lawful to Catharine Stapleton to pay off the £11,000 before the expiry of the 8 years.

Close Roll, 46 Geo. III., Part 12, Nos. 3 and 4.

Indenture made the 27th June 1806 between Richard Oliver of Low Layton, Essex, Esq. (eldest son and heir-at-law, and also an Ex'or of the last will of Thomas Oliver, late of London, merchant, deceased), Rowland Edward Williams of Weston Green, Thames Ditton, Surrey, Esq., and Rowland Edward Louis Charles Williams in H.M.'s 10th Light Dragoons (eldest son of Rowland Edward Williams), of the one part, and Isaac Rogers of Little Bell Alley, Coleman Street, Esq., and William Healing of Lawrence Lane, Gentleman, of the other part, witnesses that in consideration of 5*s.* the former grant to the latter all that plantation, etc., called Tom Moore's, in Antigua, containing 170 acres, bounded as follows, E. with land formerly belonging to Colonel John Burton, now or late to Mr. Yeamans, S. with land now or late of William Williams, W. partly with other lands of Rowland Edward Williams and partly with land now or late of Colonel John Huyghue, N. partly with land now or late in the possession of James Salmond, partly with land now or late of Ashton Warner, Esq., and partly with land formerly of William Young, deceased, and also all the Road Plantation in Antigua, containing 700 acres, bounded E. with the lands now or late of John Farley and James Doig, S. with the lands now or late of Major Edward Horne, W. partly with the broad path and partly with the river and partly with land now or late of Colonel John Huighue, N. partly with the estate formerly of Samuel Williams, deceased, now in the possession of Rowland Edward Williams, and partly with land now or late of William Williams, and all that other plantation called the Cistern Estate in Antigua, containing 120 acres, butted and bounded on the side by the lands called Tom Moore's, on the side by the Road Plantation, on the side by a plantation called Gardiners, in the possession of Mrs. Rachel Russell, and on the side by and all messuages, etc., and all negros and other slaves (names given), about 52 men, 9 children, 70 women, 9 children, and all horses for one whole year, yielding therefore a peppercorn, that they may be in actual possession and enabled to accept, and take, and grant, and release to the uses of an Indenture to bear date the day after these presents.

No. 3.

Indenture of seven parts made the 28th June 1806 between Richard Oliver, of the 1st part, Rowland Edward Williams, of the 2nd part, Rowland Edward Louis Charles Williams, etc., of the 3rd part, Mary Williams (wife of Rowland Edward Williams), of the 4th part, Isaac Rogers and William Healing, of the 5th part, Robert Farquhar of Portland Place, Marylebone, Esq., and Christopher Terry of Kingston-upon-Thames, Esq., of the 6th part, and the Hon. Samuel Athill of Antigua and George Betts of Antigua, planter, of the 7th part. Whereas by Indenture dated 23rd April 1783 between Edward Williams of the parish of Thames Ditton, Surrey, Esq., and Rowland Edward Williams (his eldest son), of the one part, and Robert Symes of the parish of Esher, Esq., and Mary Williams (then Mary Symes, spinster), one of the daughters of Robert Symes, of the other part, being the settlement previous to a marriage between Rowland Edward Williams and Mary Symes, it was witnessed that for the considerations therein mentioned Edward Williams and Rowland Edward Williams granted, etc., to Mary Williams, then Mary Symes, £500 a year from all those plantations called Old Road, Tom Moore's, and the Cisterns, in the parish of St. Mary and division of Old Road, Antigua, for life from the day of the death of Rowland Edward Williams, if she survived him, in full of jointure; and whereas the said Indenture was not registered in the Island as by the Laws, etc.; and whereas Edward Williams made his will 10th April 1782 (recited), and departed this life the 6th April 1784, and Thomas Oliver and Rowland Edward Williams alone proved the will; and whereas Mary Williams (widow of Edward) has departed this life, and it is alleged that all arrears of her annuity have been paid; and whereas Richard Oliver and Michael Lovell departed this life leaving Thomas Oliver surviving, and he has since departed this life intestate as to the real estate of which he was a trustee leaving Richard Oliver party hereto, eldest son and heir-at-law, him surviving, and did make his will 8th June 1797 and therein mentioned Richard Oliver one of his Ex'ors, and he and the others proved the will 5th Feb. 1803; and whereas no conveyance or assignment has ever been made of the estates of Edward Williams, deceased, pursuant to the trusts; and whereas it is alleged to Richard Oliver that all debts and legacies, etc., have been fully paid; and whereas Rowland Edward Williams and Mary Williams his wife have issue Rowland Edward Louis Charles Williams their eldest son who hath attained to 21, Samuel Harry Williams their younger son now 9 years of age, and Maria Williams, Elizabeth Williams, and Harriet Williams their three daughters all infants under 21. Now this Indenture witnesses that in consideration Richard Oliver and the others grant to Robert Farquhar and Christopher Terry all the aforesaid plantations, etc., in trust for 200 years for Rowland Edward Louis Charles Williams and his heirs, whom failing for Samuel Harry Williams and his heirs, whom failing for any other sons of Rowland Edward Williams, whom failing for his daughters as tenants in common, whom failing for Samuel Williams (brother of Rowland Edward Williams) and his heirs, and they appoint Samuel Athill and George Betts, both of Antigua, their Attorneys.

Serjeant Robert Williams of Five Islands has 10 acres (before 1667) granted by Governor Carden.

1667, March 2. Robert Williams, 9 acres granted by Governor Winthrop; surveyed 18 July 1668.

1668. Rowland Williams granted a patent for 300 acres.

1668, March 11. Edward Williams, 10 acres granted by Governor Winthrop; surveyed 15 April 1668.

1669, July 6. Mr. Thomas Skleyser and Lieut. Ro. Williams, deed of partnership for five years *re* plantation at Carlile Road.

Deposition of Roger Williams, æt. c. 25, 7 March 1670.

1671, Jan. 13. Major Rowland Williams, 11 acres by Governor Philip Warner; surveyed 20 Feb. 1671.

1676, July 15. Lieut.-Colonel Williams, parcell of land granted by Sir W. Stapleton.

1676, Jan. 26. William Williams, 10 acres granted by Governor Warner; surveyed 8 Feb. 1676.

1677, April 9. Colonel Rowland Williams, 360 acres in Road Division by Colonel Philip Warner; surveyed 12 July 1679.

1677, Aug. 7. James Williams, 100 acres by Governor Warner; surveyed 15 Jan. 1678.

1677, Aug. 13. Edward Williams, 30 acres granted by Governor Warner; surveyed Sep. 1677.

1678, Aug. 26. Arthur Williams, 30 acres by Colonel James Vaughan; surveyed 2 June 1680.

Novembr ye 7th, 1679. Arthur Williams in the Sloop "Hopewell" for Antegua, Wm Murphy, Comandr; time out. (Ticket from Barbados. Hotten's 'Lists.')

1680, April 23. Colonel Rowland Williams sells to John Pynchon and Samuel Willis, Esq., and Mr. Richard Lord of New England his Cabadge Tree Plantation, formerly Colonel William Byam's, in Willoughby Bay Division, also 25 acres.

1680, May 15. Arthur Williams, planter, sells 100 acres in Leeward Division to Ed. Norton, planter.

1680, May 26. Colonel Rowland Williams, patent for 300, 260, and 360 acres with all Royalties at rent of an ear of Indian corn by Sir W. Stapleton 32 Charles II.

1680, July 7. Lieut. Charles Williams, 300 acres granted by Sir W. Stapleton; surveyed 12 Oct. 1680.

1681, May 13. Mrs. Elizabeth Williams of Nevis, 200 acres by Sir W. Stapleton.

1681, May 23. Lieut. Charles Williams of Nevis, 300 acres by Sir W. Stapleton.

1682, May 4. Serjeant James Williams, 100 acres by Sir W. Stapleton.

1682, May 23. Colonel Rowland Williams and Mr. Stephen Lawler, 300 acres by Sir W. Stapleton.

In 1690 Antego furnished a whole Regiment of 400 Men, who were commanded by the Deputy-Governor, Col. Rowland Williams, whose Son, Mr Samuel Williams, was some Time after a Gentleman Commoner of Christ-Church in Oxford, and a great Lover of the Studies of Humanity; in which he made a good Proficiency in a short Time. The Author owes this Justice to the Memory of his Friend, and the Reader will therefore excuse this Digression. (Oldmixon's 'British Empire in America,' vol. ii., p. 201.)

Anne Reg. William and Mary by Letters Patent 4 June 3rd of their reign appointed Rowland Williams, Esq., Clerk of the Navy. We do now revoke the same and do re-appoint him for the islands of Nevis, St. Christopher's, Montserrat, Antigua, 4 Aug. 1 Anne. Recorded 27 April 1703.

1707-8. Nevis Census. Michael Williams. 1 man, 6 women (white); 12 men and 21 women slaves.

1709, April 23. Colonel Rowland Williams, Member of the Council, was never sworn.

1718. Colonel Thomas Williams then churchwarden of St. Mary's. (Vestry Book.)

1723, Dec. 12. Michael Williams, Esq., Member of Council of Nevis.

1726. Old Road Town or Carlile Town. Colonel Rowland Williams's house and proportions of land laid out.

1735, Sep. 19. "John Williams, Senr, having been recommended to us as A Person everyway qualified to serve His Majesty in that Station; We Humbly take leave to propose that the said John Williams, Senr, may be appointed of His Majesty's Council in the said Island of St X'opher's in the room of the above mentioned Peter Soulegre." To the Queen. Signed by five Lord Commissioners of Trade, etc. (B. T. Leeward Islands, vol. 55.)

1735, Nov. 26. John Williams, sen., to be of the Council of St. Christopher's *vice* Peter Soulegre, resigned; he was still acting 1738.

1735, Jan. 12. Dr. Rowland Williams then a Member of St. Mary's Vestry.

1738, April 21. Edward Williams, Esq., returned Member of Assembly for St. John's Division.

1738, July 24. Rowland Williams granted twelve month's leave.

1738, Oct. 21. Governor Mathew writes that he has sworn John Williams, jun., to the Council of Nevis.

1739, March 29. Rowland Williams is dead (before the 15th).

1742, Jan. 21. Edward Williams resigns his seat in the Assembly.

In 1743 John Williams, Esq., was a Member of Council for Nevis.

Edward Williams, Esq., at Road Division, Tom Moore's Plantation of 120 acres and 50 acres. The Cistern Plantation of 150 acres and the Road Plantation of 954½ acres. Surveyed 19 Sep. 1743.

1758, Feb. 6. Mich. Williams of Nevis, Esq; at Bath. ('Gent. Mag.,' p. 94.)

In 1780 Edward Williams was taxed on 250 slaves and 1030 acres in St. Mary's Parish. (Church Rate, Vestry Book.)

1785, May. Aged 80, John Williams, esq. of Nevis, son of Col. W. of St Kitts. He was the oldest planter in the old sugar islands, and had been senior member of the council above 40 years. ('Gent. Mag.,' p. 489.)

1824, Oct. 19. At the palace, Corfu, Capt. Holmes, 90th Light Inf. to Amelia, dau. of Maj.-Gen. Sir Patrick Ross. (*Ibid.*, p. 560.)

1826, Nov. 28. Surrey. Aged 77, R. E. Williams, esq. of Weston-green, and of Antigua. (*Ibid.*, p. 573.)

1827, June 18. Mary, relict of R. E. Williams, Esq. of Thames Ditton. (*Ibid.*, p. 647.)

1840, March 20. Surrey. The wife of Rowland Edward Williams, esq. of Weston-grove, second daughter of Major-Gen. Sir Patrick Ross. (*Ibid.*, p. 667.)

1840, March 28. At Antigua, Clara Susanna, wife of

Rowland E. Williams, esq. of Weston Grove, Surrey, second dau. of Major-Gen. Sir Patrick Ross. ('Gent. Mag.,' p. 333.)

1867, Oct. 3. At Upper Norwood, aged 38, Rowland Edward Williams, esq. late 32nd Regt., eldest son of the late Rowland E. Williams, esq., of Claremont, Antigua, and of Weston Grove, Thames Ditton, and grandson of the late Major-Gen. Sir Patrick Ross, G.C M.G. (*Ibid.*, p. 688.)

Parish Register of St. John.

Baptized.

169 . . . . Mary the d. of James Williams & Mary his wife.
1690 July 19 Benjamin the s. of Richd Williams & Mary his wife.
1707 July 18 Rowland S. of Thomas Williams & Mary his wife.
1710 April 30 . . . . ye . . . . of Thomas Williams & Mary his wife.
1713 Aug. 14 Thomas & Sarah S. & D. of Coll. Thos. Williams & Mary his wife.
1714 July 18 John S. of Richard Williams & Frances his wife.
1714-15 Jan. 23 Katherine D. of Arthur Williams, Junr, & Anna his wife.
1722 Jan. 22 John s. of John Williams & Ann his wife.
1727 Aug. 4 . . . . d. of John Williams and Elinor his wife.
1729 Oct. 28 Martha the d. of Coll. John Williams and Mary his wife.
1729 Dec. 21 Alexander the s. of John Williams and Elinor his wife.
1734 Dec. 19 Crediek the s. of John Williams & Elinor his wife.
1734-5 Feb. 1 Eliz. the D. of Coll. John Williams & Mary his wife.
1736 June 27 Herbert the s. of Herbert Williams and Martha his wife.
1748 July 31 Elinor the D. of John Williams and Elinor his wife.
1748 Dec. 18 Edward the s. of Arthur Williams and . . . . his wife.
1750 April 22 Esther the D. of John Williams and Esther his wife.
1755 . . . . . . David the S. of John Williams, Merch^{t}, & Eliz. his wife.
1773 Mar. 24 Anna Eliza the D. of Capt Wm Peere Williams and Henrietta his wife.
1828 Nov. 30 Rowland Edward Louis Henry s. of the hon^{ble} Rowland Edward Louis Charles & Clara Susanna Williams. Claremont in the Parish of St Mary. Puisne Baron of the exchequer & Captain in Horse Marines. Born 17 Oct. 1828.

Married.

1733 Oct. 31 William Williams and Ann Pritchard. L.
1733 Nov. 16 Herbert Williams and Martha Franckling. B.
1738 July 1 David Purviance & Mary Williams.
1751 June 11 Alexander Williams and Sarah Hanson. L.
1758 June . . Joseph Greenway and Marg^{t} Williams, Spinster. L.
1758 Dec. 11 Mathew Williams to Patience Crab. L.
1767 Nov. 2 Joseph Bodkin to Ester Williams. L.
1779 Oct. 23 John Williams to Sarah Nibbs. L.
1788 April 24 James Williams (of Grenada) to Dorothy Elmes, Spinster. L.

Buried.

1702 July . . Mr Roger Williams from Duncomb's.
1704 Oct. 29 Mr Sam^{ll} Williams.
1708 Sep. 16 Cap^{tn} Robt Williams, Com^{dr} of the Hanover Frigott.
1718 May 24 John Williams.
1718 June 18 George Williams.
1719 April 28 Francis Williams.
1720 May 29 Elizth Williams.
1727 Sep. 22 Elinor Williams.
1727 Sep. 24 John Williams.
1727 Nov. 2 Mad^{m} Frances Williams.
1732 Feb. 28 Credick Williams, a child.
1733 Nov. 18 Honour Williams.
1736 Nov. 2 Capt John Williams of this Island.
1736 Dec. 1 Coll^{e} John Williams of this Island.
1736 Dec. 14 Mr Jacob Williams of Nevis.
1737 Dec. 13 Herbert ye S. of Herbert Williams.
1737 Dec. 30 Herbert ye S. of Herbert Williams.
1737 Dec. 30 Martha ye wife of Herbert Williams.
1738 May 12 Joan ye D. of John Williams, deceased.
1742 Jan. 9 Thomas Oesterman Williams.
1745 June 21 John Williams, a child.
1746 Oct. 7 Elinor Williams, widow.
1749 April 5 Benoin Williams.
1749 June 4 John Williams; in the country.
1749 June 18 Grace Williams, a child.
1749-50 Jan. 11 William Williams.
1754 Feb. 3 Meredith Williams.
1760 (? Jan.) . . Elizabeth Williams.
1772 Nov. 1 Samuel Williams.
1775 Feb. 3 Patience Williams.
1830 July 2 Ann Williams. St John's. 75.
1833 Mar. 7 Sarah Williams. St John's. 46.

Parish Register of St. George.

Baptized.

1734 Mar. 9 Mathew ye S. of Arthur Williams & Sosina his wife.
(? 1735) . . . . 4 Thomas ye S. of Arthur Williams & Sosina his wife.
(? 1738) . . . . . . Elizabeth the D. of Arthur Williams and Susannah his wife.
1744 Dec. 16 John the S. of Arthur Williams & Susannah his wife.
1749-50 Feb. 25 . . . . Arthur Williams & Susannah his wife; b. Feb. 1st, 1749-50.
1752 June 22 Catharine D. of Arthur Williams & Susannah his wife.

Married.

1743 Sep. 1 John Greenway and Ann Williams, S.

Buried.

1735 Aug. 14 Abigail Williams.
1739 Sep. 21 Arthur Williams, Senr.
1743 Nov. 17 John the S. of Arthur Williams and Susannah his wife.
1744 Mar. 18 Elizabeth Williams.
1744-5 Mar. 29 John Williams.
1745 April 5 Arthur Williams.
1746 April 27 Elizabeth Williams.
1748-9 Feb. 1 Annie the D. of Arthur Williams & Susannah his wife.
1748-9 Feb. 5 Edward the S. of Arthur Williams & Susannah his wife.
1752 July 1 Susannah Williams.
1755 Sep. 18 Katherine Williams d. of Arthur Williams.
1756 Mar. 11 Arthur Williams.
1758 Jan. 21 Mary the D. of Arthur Williams & Margaret his wife.

1758 Dec. 20 Arthur the S. of Tho. Williams & Maryan his wife.
1758 Dec. 22 Maryan the Wife of Thos Williams.
1771 Jan. 1 Mrs Susanna Williams, Widow, in the family Private Burying-Ground.
1779 Jan. 3 John Richardson Williams, in the family burying ground.

PARISH REGISTER OF ST. PHILIP.

Married.

1748 Dec. 29 John Williams to Elizabeth Symes.

Buried.

1696-7 Mar. 24 Amy Williams.
1728 Dec. 26 Edward Williams.

PARISH REGISTER OF ST. PAUL.

Baptized.

1757 Jan. 25 Anne D. of Williams Arthur (*sic*), Esqr, and Henrietta his wife.

PARISH REGISTER OF ST. MARY.

Buried.

1733* Mar. 18 Coll. Thomas Williams, buried at the Road.
1840 Mar. 30 Clara S. Williams wife of Rowland Williams, daughr of Sir Patrick Ross; at Parish Church St Mary's from Claremont. 32 years.
1852 June 2 The Honble Rowland E. Williams, Member of H.M. Council. Claremont Estate. 68 yrs. & 2 mos.

THAMES DITTON, CO. SURREY.

Buried.

1784 April 15 Edward Williams, Esqr.
1826 Dec. 8 Rowland Edward Williams. Weston Green, Thames Ditton.

ST. JOHN'S CHURCHYARD.

On a large ledger:—

Here Lies ye Body of
Coll: IOHN WILLIAMS of Antigua
& Family. he departed this life Novr 30.
in the Year of our Lord 1736
Aged 52 Years.

On a white marble panel, on south side of Colonel John Williams's tomb:—

Here lies the Body of
MARY PURVIANCE
late Wife of Dr DAVID PURVIANCE
and Relict of Coll: JOHN WILLIAMS,
who Died the 5th of *Junwry* 173$\frac{8}{9}$
in the thirty third Year of her Age
This Tomb was Erected by the said
PURVIANCE.

On an altar tomb:—

Here lieth the Body of
MRS FRANCES WILLIAMS
the Wife of
MR JOHN WILLIAMS
who departed this life Novemr y 2. 1727
Aged 37 Years.

PARHAM NEW CHURCHYARD.

On a white marble headstone:—

IN | MEMORY | OF | CAPTAIN | GRIFFITH WILLIAMS | OF CARRECYRO, PORTMADOC, | NORTH WALES; | DIED 16TH AUGUST 1882. | AGED 33 YEARS.

* This entry is from a copy for that year in B. T. Leeward Islands, vol. 24.

ST. MARY'S CHURCH, OLD ROAD, ANTIGUA.

On a marble ledger in the chancel:—

M.S.
Hic securè jacent Maternâ in terra,
Terrenæ ROLLANDI WILLIAMS reliquiæ.
Pulvis et umbra sumus.
Primus Europæorum Mafculus infans,
Qui in infulâ hac natus est, Verus
Sic Pater huic patriæ.
Quum Virerafit, Vinum fe præftitit
Tam Marte, quam Mercurio, Decus
Tuni fibi, tumq suis
in Campo, audax Militum Præfectus,
in Curia, Sagax rerum Senator. Quid
Vis fine Confilio?
Regi subditus Patriæ patronus, Liberis Pater,
Hofpitibus hofpes, amicis amicus, Verbo,
Omnibus Omniscerat, æquus
in Omni Vitâ mentis sanæ in Corpore sano
Summæ indolis, honestæ curæ, dives opum Morti
Victima tarda ruit
Annos plufquam octoginta Natus,
Vicefimo jul die 1713 Sepultus,
Quum certò moriendum est,
Quam cito refipifcendum est!

On a marble tablet on north wall of chancel:—

Arms: *Quarterly*, 1, *Or, a winged griffin segreant gules* (WILLIAMS); 2, *Gules, a man's head proper, bearded affrontée*; 3, *Argent, two wolves counter courant gules*; 4, *Argent, a lion rampant sable, langued gules*; impaling, *Or, a fess chequy sable and argent between three water-bougets of the first* (ROSS).

Motto: *Per Aspera Virtus.*

SACRED TO THE MEMORY OF
CLARA SUSANNA,
DAUGHTER OF GENERAL SIR PATRICK ROSS
KNIGHT GRAND CROSS OF
THE MOST DISTINGUISHED ORDERS OF
ST MICHAEL AND ST GEORGE,
SOMETIME GOVERNOR OF THESE ISLANDS,
THE WIFE OF ROWLAND EDWD WILLIAMS, ESQRE
OF CLAREMONT, IN THIS PARISH.
SHE EXCHANGED AN EARTHLY FOR A HEAVENLY ABODE
AT CLAREMONT, ON THE 28TH DAY OF MARCH 1840
AGED 32 YEARS.

(Three lines follow.)

THAMES DITTON, CO. SURREY.

In the north aisle, over the family pew:—

SACRED
TO THE MEMORY OF
ROWLAND EDWARD LOUIS
HENRY WILLIAMS,
OF WESTON GROVE
AND LATE OF THE 32ND LIGHT INFANTRY,
WHO DIED AT UPPER NORWOOD,
ON THE 3RD OCTOBER 1867,
AGED 38 YEARS.

On a ledger formerly existing on the north side of Thames Ditton Churchyard, but which has been destroyed (Manning and Bray, vol. i., p. 468):—

Here lies the Body of EDWARD WILLIAMS Esquire, of the Island of Antigua, who departed this life the 6th of April 1784, aged 74 years.

"Claremont" and "Mountain" are in St. Mary's Parish. In 1852 they contained 938 acres, and were owned by Rowland E. Williams.

Pedigree of Willock.

CREST.—*Out of a ducal coronet an eagle's head erased.* (Monogram, A. W.) From an impression of a seal affixed to some papers by Alexander Willock in 1772.

ALEXANDER WILLOCK of Antigua, merchant, also of Putney Park, co. Middlesex, and Broad Street Buildings, London (? mar. Fanny Atkinson, as 2nd wife, in 1777); bankrupt in 1793; Willock and Morson were partners; died Dec. 1801. Will dated 19 Oct. 1790, codicil 20 Feb. 1796. = Rebeccah . . . . named in the will of Mathew Christian 1757.

Francis Willock, 1st son and heir, bapt. 21 April 1759 at St. John's; of Hill, Southampton; died there 1 Jan. 1829, æt. 69. = F . . . . dau. of . . . . Gore; mar. 2 Aug. 1785.

Alexander Willock, bapt. 13 Aug. 1760 and bur. 7 Oct. 1761 at St. John's.

Archibald Willock, bapt. 19 April 1764 at St. John's.

John Willock, bapt. 9 Oct. 1765 and bur. 5 April 1766 at St. John's.

James Willock, bapt. 31 March 1770 at St. John's.

Frank Gore Willock, 1st son and heir, æt. 21 on 24 June 1808; Captain R.N.; died at sea 18 Jan. 1834, æt. 47. M.I. at All Saints, Southampton.

Alexander Charles Willock, Lieut. R.A., died 6 April 1821, æt. 31, at Woolwich. M.I. = Harriet Maria, only dau. of John Dawes of Highbury, co. Middlesex.

Frederick Willock, Lieut. Madras Artillery, died 28 March 1815, æt. 24, at St. Thomas's Mount. M.I.

Arthur Willock of the Madras Civil Service, died 18 Sep. 1824, æt. 25, at Madras. M.I.

Edward Hulse Willock, Major Bombay Artillery, died 8 July 1839, æt. 45, at Ahmednuggar. M.I.

Rev. Charles William Willock, only son, matric. from Balliol College, Oxford, 22 March 1839, æt. 18; B.A. 1843; M.A. 1847; of Barton Hill, Sussex; assumed the additional name of *Dawes* by Royal Licence 1870 under the will of his maternal uncle. = Maria, dau. of R. Gosling of North Cray; mar. there 22 June 1847.

Close Roll, 33 Geo. III., Part 1. No. 7.

Indenture made the 14th March 1793 between Randle Ford and John Calthorp Gough, Esquires, and Peter Still, Gentleman, Commissioners of Bankruptcy, against Alexander Willock and Francis Willock of Broad Street Buildings, merchants and partners, of the one part, and William Curtis of London, Esq., Alderman James Daniell of Herbert Lodge, Surrey, Esq., and John Sowerby of Hatton Garden, Esq., of the other part. Whereas by a Commission of Bankruptcy issued the 14th March 1793 and directed to Randle Ford, John Calthorp Gough, Henry Joddrell, Esquires, and Peter Still, Gentleman, on examination of witnesses it is found that Alexander and Francis Willock for three years and upwards traded as West Indian merchants, and became justly indebted to Timothy Curtis, William Curtis, and Richard Henry Clarke of Wapping, merchants and partners, in £100 and upwards, and were become bankrupts. Now this Indenture witnesseth that in consideration of 5*s.* the Commissioners convey to William Curtis, James Daniell, and John Sowerby as trustees all plantations, etc., and real and personal estate of Alexander and Francis Willock whatsoever and wheresoever in trust for its immediate preservation for the benefit of the creditors.

No. 4.

Indenture made the 27th March 1793 between William Curtis of London, Esq., Alderman James Daniell of Herbert Lodge, Surrey, Esq., and John Sowerby of Hatton Garden, Esq., of the one part, and James Weston of Fenchurch Street, Gentleman, of the other part, witnesseth that in consideration of 10*s.* William Curtis, James Daniell, and John Sowerby convey to James Weston all plantations of Alexander and Francis Willock for one whole year, and enabled to reconvey, and they appoint, etc., Henry Benskin Lightfoot and Daniel Hill, sen., of Antigua, Thomas Tuckett, James Stephen, and John Fearnhead of St. Kitts, Walter Maynard, Josiah Maynard, and Andrew Hamilton of Nevis, Samuel Martin Irish and Edward Byam Wyke of Montserrat, Griffin Curtis and John Robinson of Dominica, Duncan Campbell and James Taylor of St. Vincent's, and John Miller, Thomas Wilson, and William Bruce of Tobago (all Esquires), to be their Attorneys.

No. 3.

Indenture made the 27th March 1793 between James Weston, of the 1st part, Randle Ford and John Bowles, Esquires, and Peter Still, of the 2nd part, and William Curtis, Alderman James Baillie of London, Esq., James Daniell, and John Sowerby, of the 3rd part, the reconveyance by James Weston (the Commissioners joining) to William Curtis and the others.

Close Roll, 49 Geo. III., Part 18, No. 10.

Indenture made the 20th Oct. 1808 between Francis Willock of Baker Street, Portman Square, Esq. (eldest son and heir-at-law of Alexander Willock, formerly of Antigua, but afterwards of London, Esq., deceased), and Frank Gore Willock, Lieut. R.N., but at present residing in Baker Street (eldest son and heir apparent of Francis Willock), of the one part, and James Weston of Fenchurch Street, Gentleman, of the other part. Whereas Alexander Willock being at the time of making his will and at his decease lawfully seised of the plantations hereinafter described, did publish his last will dated the 19th Oct. 1790, and gave all his plantations, negro and other slaves, cattle, etc., in the Island of Tobago, and all other real estate in the West Indies or Great Britain or wheresoever else to his trustees and Ex'ors, in trust to preserve the contingent uses and estates, and subject to several provisions, to the use of Francis Willock his eldest son and his assigns for life, and immediately after his decease to the use of his first son and to his heirs male, and in default upon several further trusts therein mentioned; and whereas Alexander Willock by a codicil dated the 20th Feb. 1796 revoked the appointment of the trustees and Ex'ors contained in his will, and appointed Langford Lovell, Esq., his friend, then of Antigua, Robert Johnson his nephew, and also his friends Thomas Coles of London, broker, and Ambrose Weston of Fenchurch Street, Gentleman, trustees and Ex'ors in their stead, and gave to them all his estate real and personal in trust (as before); and whereas Alexander Willock departed this life in Dec. 1801 without having altered his will so far as relates to the hereinbefore recited trusts in favour of Francis Willock and his first son, and without having altered the codicil; and

William Willock, bapt. 14 Oct. 1772 at St. John's; bur. 10 Aug. 1812 at St. George's. = Octavia Payne, dau. of Anthony Wyke of Montserrat and Antigua; mar. 10 Sep. 1799 at Southampton; she mar. 2ndly, 24 Aug. 1816, at St. John's, John Kentish.

Arthur Morson Willock, bapt. 26 Aug. 1776 at St. John's.

—

Jane Willock, bapt. 1 Dec. 1756 and bur. 6 Dec. 1757 at St. John's.

Mary Willock, bapt. 16 Feb. 1758 and bur. 9 July 1759 at St. John's.

—

Elenor Willock, bapt. 10 Oct. 1761 and bur. 26 Aug. 1763 at St. John's.

Elizabeth Willock, bapt. 8 Feb. 1767 at St. John's. (? mar. Captain Cuthbert, R.N., 6 July 1803.)

—

Rebeccah Willock, bapt. 31 March 1770 at St. John's.

Stephen Rose Willock. = ...

Ralph Lavington Willock, born 4 Feb. and bapt. 9 April 1805 at St. John's.

William Andrew Ross Willock, born 31 Jan. 1808 and bapt. 21 Dec. 1809 at St. John's; died 2 June 1833. M.I. at St. George's.

Louisa Wyke Willock, 1st dau., born 16 March 1800; died 24 Dec. 1876. M.I. at St. George's.

—

Rebecca Farley Willock, born 21 Nov. 1800; bapt. 25 March 1801 at St. George's.

Ann Byam Wyke Willock, born 14 Aug. 1806; bapt. 21 Dec. 1809 at St. John's; mar. 26 March 1828, at St. George's, Thomas Anderson, M.D.

Alicia Henrica Willock, youngest dau., born 25 Sep. 1811 and bapt. 3 July 1816 at St. John's; died 4 Oct. 1851. M.I. at St. George's.

Mary Willock, only surviving dau., mar. 10 June 1824, at St. Mary's, Rev. Samuel Ashton Warner, Rector of St. George's.

whereas Langford Lovell died in testator's lifetime, and Robert Johnson, Thomas Coles, and Ambrose Weston refused to take upon them execution of the trusts, and in due form of law disclaimed the devises and bequests; and whereas Frank Gore Willock, who as eldest son of Francis Willock is first tenant in tail under the will, attained his age of 21 on the 24th June now last past, and the Ex'ors having also renounced, probate administration of the personal estate has been granted to Francis Willock in the P.C.C. and in the West Indies. Now this Indenture witnesseth that for barring and destroying the estates tail created by the will, and all other estates tail and remainders, and all conditions and collateral limitations, and in consideration of 10s. each Francis Willock and Frank Gore Willock grant and confirm to James Weston all those four estates or plantations called the Folly Estate, Mount Pleasant, Blizards, and Samuel Byam's in Antigua with all appurtenances whatsoever, and also all that plantation called Brodericks and Basses, containing 200 acres of cane and 100 acres of pasture and provision land, in the parish of St. Anthony in Montserrat, bounded N. with the bottom of Basses Gut, W. with the lands now or late of Bridget Blake, Owen Sullivan, deceased, Bodingfield Bramley, Esq., the land late of John Carroll, deceased, and the lands now or late of Edward Sankey, S. with the lands now or late of the said Bodingfield Bramley and Reed's Gut, and E. with the mountains, and a parcel of land part of the said plantation, bounded W. with the sea, N. with the land now or late of Robert Dyott, E. with the lands of the said Bodingfield Bramley, and S. with the lands now or late of . . . . Hodgskin, and also all that plantation called the Windward Plantation, containing 100 acres of cane and 100 acres of pasture and provision land, in the parish of St. George, Montserrat, bounded N. with Saunder's Gut, E. with the lands now or late of Richard Tuite, S. with the cliff and the lands now or late of . . . . Potter and William Irish, Esq., and W. with the lands now or late of the said William Irish and the mountains, and also that plantation called Tarr River Plantation, containing together 70 acres of cane and 180 of pasture and provision land, in the parishes of St. George and St. Patrick in Montserrat, bounded as follows, that is to say, one part of the said premises which lie in St. George's Parish is bounded N. with the bottom of Tarr River Gut, E. with the said Tarr River Gut, S. with the lands now or late of William Irish, Esq., and the lands now or late of William Teague, and W. with the mountains, one other part in St. George's Parish called Potter's Lands is bounded N. with the lands now or late of William Irish, E. with the highway, and S. and W. with Tarr River Gut, and also one other part in St. George's Parish called Sweenys is bounded N. with the lands now or late of Michael Vest and the lands of William Teague, E. with the sea, S. with the lands now or late of John Long, deceased, and W. with the bottom of Bitter Water Gut, one other part in St. George's Parish is bounded N. with the lands now or late of John Long, deceased, E. with the top of Cowhill, S. with the lands now or late of William Irish, and W. with the mountains, and one other part in St. George's Parish is bounded N. with the lands now or late of William Irish, E. and S. with Scott River, and W. with Billey's Gut, and one other part in St. Patrick's Parish is bounded N. with the bottom of Scott River and Billey's Gut, E. with the sea, S. with the lands now or late of William Trench and Gutma (?) Trancy (?), and W. with the mountains, and also that plantation called the Northward Plantation, containing 85 acres of cane and 60 acres of pasture and provision land, in the parish of St. Peter in Montserrat, bounded N. with the lands now or late of Edward Sweeny, W. with the lands now or late of Thomas Burrey, Esq., and S. and E. with the lands now or late of Patrick Blake, Esq., and also all that plantation in the parish of St. Anthony in Montserrat, and also all that plantation in the said island called the Northward Plantation, which said two last mentioned plantations are bounded at the end thereof with the lands called Harts, now or late in the possession of Thomas Mead, Esq., at the foot thereof with the road leading to the estate now or late of the said Edward Parsons, and S. with the high road and the lands now or late of Earl Daniell, Esq., and also all that other plantation late belonging to Alexander Willock called Orange Valley in Tobago in the West Indies, containing 300 acres or thereabouts, and all negros and other slaves, etc., belonging to the plantations, in trust that James Weston immediately after the execution of these presents by Indentures of Lease and Release already prepared, the lease to bear date the day next after these presents, and the release the day next after the lease, may join with Frank Gore Willock in conveying and assuring the said plantations and slaves, etc., to the use of Francis Willock and his heirs and assigns for ever upon the trusts to be expressed, and Francis Willock and Frank Gore Willock constitute the Hon. John Burke and Thomas Norbury Kerby and John Harvey, Esquires, of Antigua, John Queely Fagan and Nicholas Hill of Montserrat, Esquires, and John Balfour of Tobago, Esq., their Attorneys. John Francis, Charles Derrick, 38 Fenchurch Street, witnesses.

1777, March 16. Mr Willock, merchant, of Antigua, to Miss Fanny Atkinson of Lancaster. ('Gent. Mag.,' p. 147.)

1785, Aug. 2. Francis Willock, esq: to Miss F. Gore. (*Ibid.*, p. 664.)

1788, Dec. 18. In her 16th year, Miss Willock, eldest daughter of Mr. W. of Golden-square. (*Ibid.*, p. 1131.)

Dr. Adair of Antigua in 1788—91 refers to "Mrs. Crawford, mother of the Colonel. Mrs. Alexander Willock her sister."

1791, Nov. At Hendon, in her 68th year, Mrs. Patience Willock, wife of Mr John W. of that place, and mother of Mr W. of Golden-square. ('Gent. Mag.,' p. 1235.)

1799, Aug. 22. James Willock to be of the Council of Montserrat. He was still such in 1806.

1799, Sep. 10. At Southampton, William Willock, esq. to Miss Octavia Payne Wyke. ('Gent. Mag., p. 812.)

1803, July 6. Capt. Cuthbert, of the royal navy, to the eldest daughter of the late Alexander Willock, esq. of Bedford-square. (*Ibid.*, p. 690.)

1805, March 25. Charles F. Broadley, esq. merchant, of Hull, to Miss Willock, daughter of the late Alexander W. esq. of Bedford-square. (*Ibid.*, p. 1235.)

1806, Aug. 25. At his house at Brompton, in his 73d year, Francis Grojan, esq. an eminent attorney in Vine-street, Piccadilly, clerk to the Commissioners of the Court of Requests, and many years deputy high bailiff of the city and liberty of Westminster. (*Ibid.*, p. 783.)

1807, April 23. Jn. Willock, esq. of Golden-square, to Miss Grojan, daughter of the late Francis G. esq. of Brompton-grove. (*Ibid.*, p. 375.)

1808, Sep. 27. At her house at Brompton-grove, aged 71, Mrs. Grojan, widow of the late Francis G. esq. and mother of Mrs. Willock, of Golden-square. (*Ibid.*, p. 955.)

1810, Aug. Resignation of Colonel Willock of Montserrat referred to.

1821, April 6. At Woolwich Common, Lieut. A. C. Willock, R.A. son of Francis Willock, esq. of Hill, Southampton. ('Gent. Mag.,' p. 382.)

1829, Jan. 1. At Southampton, aged 69, Francis Willock, esq. (*Ibid.*, p. 93.)

1831, Jan. 18. At sea, on his voyage from Bombay, to Bushire, of a fever taken at Muscat, aged 47, Captain Frank Gore Willock, R.N. (*Ibid.*, p. 335.)

1831, Feb. 18. At Bushire, Frank Gore Willock, esq. Capt. R.N. This officer was a native of the West Indies. He first entered the service under the auspices of Sir Joseph Yorke, and was present in the capacity of Midshipman in the battle of Trafalgar. He subsequently served in the Northumberland 74, in the action off St Domingo; and in 1807 was appointed Lieutenant of the Osprey, which was cast away in Bayo Honda, and it being found necessary to fire her, to prevent her falling into the enemys hands, he received Lord Mulgrave's approbation for his conduct on that occasion. At the reduction of Martinique he performed the duty of First Lieutenant of the Abercrombie; he served subsequently on board the Dragon, and from her was appointed to command the Wanderer. In 1811 in command of the Spider he for some time protected the trade of Tortola and the adjacent islands, for his "very judicious and officer-like conduct" in which service he received the "fullest approbation" of Rear-Adm. Sir F. Laforey. In 1814 he removed into the Fox, in which he served during the American war, and was promoted to Post Rank Nov. 25, 1815. After this he was not employed again afloat: though he actually offered to fit out a ship at his own expense, if the First Lord of the Admiralty would honour him by nomination to a command. Impatient of repose, he gave exercise to the activity of his mind in travel. Russia, the Caucasus, Georgia, Persia, parts of Arabia, and the wide territories of British India, were all visited by him; and he was about to return to his native country, when he took his fatal fever at the cove of Muscat, where the Arab vessel touched in which he was sailing from Bombay to Bushire. Capt. Willock was characterised by the genuine virtues of an ocean son,—frank, enthusiastic, brave and humane; these noble and generous qualities, accompanied by occasional eccentricities, gave a warmth and colouring to the most trifling action of his life. ('Gent. Mag.,' 1835, p. 335.)

1847, June 22. At North Cray, the Rev. C. W. Willock, of Baliol coll: Oxf. son of the late A. C. Willock, esq. R. Art. to Maria, dau. of R. Gosling, esq. of North Cray. (*Ibid.*, p. 312.)

PARISH REGISTER OF ST. JOHN.

Baptized.

1756	Dec.	1	Jane the D. of Alex^r^ Willock & Rebeccah his wife.
1758	Feb.	16	Mary the D. of Alex^r^ Willock and Rebecca his wife.
1759	April	24	Francis the S. of Alexander Willock and Rebecca his wife.
1760	Aug.	13	Alexander the S. of Alexander Willock and Rebecca his wife.
1761	Oct.	10	Elenor the D. of Alexander Willock and Rebecca his wife.
1764	April	19	Archibald the S. of Alexaader Willock and Rebecca his wife.
1765	Oct.	9	John the S. of Alexander Willock and Rebecca his wife.
1767	Feb.	8	Elizabeth Willock D. of Alexander Willock & Rebecca his wife.
1770	Mar.	31	Rebeccah the D. of Alex^r^ Willock and Rebeccah his wife.
1770	Mar.	31	James the S. of Alex^r^ Willock and Rebeccah his wife.
1772	Oct.	14	William the S. of Alex^r^ Willock & Rebecca his wife.
1776	Aug.	26	Arthur Morson the S. of Alex^r^ Willock & Rebeccah his wife.
1805	April	9	Ralph Lavington S. of William Willock and Octavia his wife. B. the 4th February 1805.
1809	Dec.	21	Ann Byam Wyke. B. 11th Augt 1806. William Andrew Ross. B. 31 Jany. 1808. } D. & S. of William Willock & Octavia his wife.
1816	July	3	Alicia Henrica D. of William Willock, deceased, and Octavia his late wife. B. the 25th September 1811.

Married.

1816	Aug.	24	John Kentish to Octavia Willock, Widow. L.
1823	Oct.	21	George Savage Martin to Anne Willock, Spinster. L.

Buried.

1757 Dec. 6 Jane Willock, a Child.
1759 July 9 Miss Mary Willock (a Child).
1761 Oct. 7 Alexander Willock, junr.
1763 Aug. 26 Elenor Willock, a Child.
1766 April 5 John Willock, Child.

PARISH REGISTER OF ST. GEORGE.

Baptized.

1801 Mar. 25 Rebecca Farley D. of William Willock and Octavia his wife; b. Novr 21st last.

Married.

1828 Mar. 26 At the Parish Church, Thomas Anderson, M.D., & Anne Byam Wyke Willock, Spinster, the former of St John's Parish in this Island of Antigua, the latter of this Parish; by L.

Buried.

1812 Aug. 10 William Willock from St John's; in the same Burying Ground at Fitche's Church-yard. (The Wykes' vault).

ST. GEORGE'S CHURCHYARD, FITCHE'S CREEK.

On a stone ledger:—

SACRED
TO THE MEMORY
OF
WILLIAM ANDREW ROSS WILLOCK
youngest son of the late
WILLIAM WILLOCK Esquire
Born
31 January 1808
Died
2nd June 1833.

On a ledger:—

SACRED
TO THE MEMORY
OF
ALLICIA HENRICA WILLOCK
youngest daughter of the late
WILLIAM WILLOCK Esquire
Born
6 September 1811
Died
14 October 1851.

On a headstone:—

SACRED
TO THE MEMORY
OF
LOUISA WYKE WILLOCK
ELDEST DAUGHTER OF THE LATE
WILLIAM WILLOCK ESQR
BORN 16TH MARCH 1800
DIED 24TH DECEMBER 1876.

On a ledger adjoining preceding:—

SACRED
TO THE MEMORY OF
MRS OCTAVIA KENTISH
RELICT OF THE LATE
JOHN KENTISH ESQ
WHO DIED 29 SEPTEMBER 1832
AGED 56 YEARS
A TRIBUTE OF RESPECT
TO A BELOVED MOTHER BY HER
AFFECTIONATE CHILDREN.

ALL SAINTS' CHURCH, SOUTHAMPTON.

On the north wall of the nave, on a white marble tablet:—

SACRED TO THE MEMORIES OF ALEXANDER CHARLES WILLOCK, |
LIEUTENANT OF THE ROYAL ARTILLERY, WHO DIED
AT WOOLWICH APRIL 6TH 1821, AGED 31 YEARS.
OF FREDERICK WILLOCK, LIEUTENANT OF THE MADRAS |
ARTILLERY, WHO DIED AT ST THOMAS'S MOUNT
MARCH 28TH, 1815, AGED 24 YEARS.
OF ARTHUR WILLOCK, OF THE MADRAS CIVIL SERVICE,
WHO DIED AT MADRAS |
SEPTEMBER 18TH 1824, AGED 25 YEARS.
OF EDWARD HULSE WILLOCK, MAJOR OF THE
BOMBAY ARTILLERY, WHO DIED AT AHMEDNUGGUR
JULY 8TH 1839, AGED 45 YEARS
THIS MONUMENT IS PLACED BY THEIR
SURVIVING BROTHERS AND SISTERS.

SACRED TO THE MEMORY OF
FRANK GORE WILLOCK,
CAPTAIN IN THE ROYAL NAVY,
WHO DIED AT SEA OF A FEVER CAUGHT AT MUSCAT,
ON HIS PASSAGE FROM BOMBAY TO BUSHIRE
ON THE 18TH OF JANUARY 1834,
AGED 47.
HE WAS THE ELDEST SON OF THE LATE
FRANCIS WILLOCK ESQR OF SOUTHAMPTON,
THIS TABLET IS ERECTED BY HIS
SURVIVING BROTHERS AND SISTERS
WHO DEEPLY MOURN HIS LOSS.

IN THE CATACOMBS
BENEATH THIS CHURCH ARE DEPOSITED
THE REMAINS OF
FRANCIS WILLOCK ESQRE
WHO DIED AT SOUTHAMPTON
JANUARY 1ST 1829
AGED 69 YEARS.
THIS TABLET IS DEDICATED
TO THE MEMORY OF AN EXCELLENT PARENT
BY HIS GRATEFUL CHILDREN.

"Willocks" is in St. Mary's Parish. In 1852 it contained 368 acres, and was owned by Mrs. Ann Willock.

Family of Willoughby.

Francis, Lord Willoughby of Parham. Will dated 17 July 1666: proved 10 May 1678; commission to Elizabeth, Countess of Ranelaigh, the daughter, and to Frances Brereton, wife of William Brereton, the daughter, the Ex'ors renouncing. (55 Reeve.) All my debts to be first paid, particularly £700 owing to Lucas Lucie, mercht, to whom I have made an assignment out of £3000 due to me from His Majesty. I also owe Dr Peeter La Rouse 188 Mexico pieces of eight. To my dear daus. Frances Brereton, wife of Wm, Lord Brereton, and to Eliz. Jones, wife of Richd Jones, Esq., 1st son of Lord Viscount Rannalaigh, all my moiety & the revenue of the Islands of Barbados, St Christopher's, Nevis, Mont Serrat, Antigua, & other the Charibbee Islands, except 100,000 lbs. of sugar yearly to be paid to my beloved nephew Henry Willoughby, Esq., during his stay in Barbados. If my daus. die before the expiration of the lease His Majesty granted me then all to their younger children equally. To my said 2 daus. ⅔ of my whole moiety of lands in the Province of Willoughby Land with all the proprietory & dominion thereof, the other ⅓ to my beloved nephew Henry Willoughby, Esq., & his heirs male, & in default to my nephew Wm Willoughby, Esq. To my said 2 daus. ⅔ of my plantation called Parham Hill on the river of Surinam, & ⅓ to my nephew Henry Willoughby. All residue of lands in Willoughby Land to my 2 daus. To my nephew Wm Willoughby, Esq., £200 a year for life to be paid in England or during his stay in the Indes in sugar at 10*s*. per 100. To my good friend Dr Peeter La Rouse 50,000 lbs. of Muscovado sugar I formerly lent him & charged upon Major Wm Bate to pay. To my Ex'ors 20,000 lbs. of sugar each. To Mrs Jane Frith, wife of Mr Wm Frith Clarke, for her care of my family in Barbados, 20,000 lbs. & £20 a year. To my servant John Fowles £20. To Dixon my porter 2000 lbs. yearly so long as he remain in the service of my nephews Henry or Wm Willoughby. To my servant Robt Stoakes £10 a year. To my page Edwd Sprag £10 a year. To my servant Dodsworth 2000 lbs. yearly. To my servants Nicholas Walker & Richd Wills £10 yearly. My nephew Henry Willoughby, Tho. Wardall, & Saml Barwicke, Esqres, & Dr Peeter La Rouse, & my secretary Henry Haughton to be Ex'ors, the latter to take accounts & to have £100 a year. My brother Wm Willoughby, Esq., Sir Bolstrod Whitelocke, Kt, & Sir Chas. Pim, Kt & Bart., to be overseers & to have £20 each. All produce of my plantations to be consigned to John Champantie of London, mercht, he to have £100 a year. Witnessed by William Frith, Jo. Fowles, Robert Stoakes.

William, Lord Willoughby of Parham. Will dated 18 May 1672; proved 27 Nov. 1673. (157 Pye.) About to proceed to my Governorship on the island of Barbados. Have given orders for mortgage of certain lands to raise £3000, Sir Robt Clayton & John Morris holding the instructions, as a portion for my dau. Anne Willoughby in case a convenient match may be found for her with consent of my honoured brother John Cary, Esq., & my loving friends Sir Wm Hickman & Sir Robt Clayton. To my dau. Kath. Willoughby £2000. I owe at Sir Robt Clayton's shop £4000 upon Knaith, & to Sir Wm Ellis £1200 upon mortgage of Warsopp, Mr Lister £1000 upon Burton & Brampton, Mr Brewer £600 upon Salterfield & Sansom Woods, also to Mr Edwd Token £200, Lady Foster £350, Mr Hen. Andrewes £500, Mr Johnson of Lincolne £200, Mr Fothergill £200, Mr Farmery of Lincolne £50, & Watkinson £40, Mr Tufton of Nottingham £200, Mr John Hall £100, Sir Wm Turner £100, Hen. Andrewes £110 for horses, John Hall £16 for horse & mare, Hawkins my saddler £33; all these on bond. To my trustees John Hall, Gt, John Bainbrigg, Gt, Henry Andrewes, Gt, my manor of Stowe in Stowe Sturton, Willingham Kerby, Upton Burton, Newton & Knaith in Martin Brampton, Fenton, Laughterton, & Kettlethorpe, co. Lincoln, except the part settled on my son George at his marriage, & except Stowe Lea purchased by me in the names of Sir Robt Clayton & John Morris of the Ex'ors of Mr Godfrey of Thunnock, co. Lincoln, Esq., also except my manors of Washopp & Salterfield, co. Notts, & Bestwood Park, co. Notts. My son George to sell Thorpe, co. Lincoln. To my grandchild John Willoughby all my household goods at Knaith. To my 3 sons John, Cary, & Chas. all those at Bestwood. My 2 daus. to have £150 per annum till their portions are paid. To Jas. Halsey, Esq., my best horse. To my Ex'ors John Hall, John Bainbrigg, & Henry Andrewes £20 each. Witnessed by Robert Clayton, Henry Darell, William Belke, Peter Clayton. To my friend Sir Robt Holmes a horse.

Memorandum that on 23 Dec. 1673 the Hon. Carew Willoughby, Esq., deceased, late son of the late Right Hon. William, Lord Willoughby of Parham, lying sick made his will nuncupative. All my estate left me by the will of my late father to my sister Kath. Willoughby, my mare to Sir John Harpur only excepted. Witnessed by German Parker, Anne Hawet. Proved 19 Dec. 1676; commission to the Hon. Catherine Willoughby the sister. (158 Bence.)

Antigua. By ye Governor. Adm'on to Colonel John Willoughby and Charles Willoughby, Esq., sons and Ex'ors of William, Lord Willoughby of Parham, 16 March 1674.

1678, Feb. 15. John, Baron Willoughby of Parham. Adm'on to Sir William Hickman, Bart., guardian of Elizabeth Willoughby, a minor, sister of John, Lord Willoughby, late of the City of Winchester, deceased, Lady Jane ffynes and Dorothy ffynes consenting.

Barbados. John, Lord Willoughby of Parham. Will dated 10 June 1678: published 28 Sep. 1678, testator having died at Stanwell, co. Middlesex, in the presence of James Smith, Daniel Bruce, Abraham Langford, sen., Thomas Griffin, Samuel Judd; proved 7 Nov. 1678 by Lady Ann Willoughby the widow, and on 19 Nov. 1678 by Charles, Lord Willoughby of Parham, Sir William Hickman, Bart., Sir John Harper, Knt., and John Cary, Esq. (134 Reeve.) To be buried at Knaith, co. Lincoln, among my ancestors. To my wife Anne all my estate in Barbados, Antegoa, & America, & after her death to my brother Chas. Willoughby. I give him also my manors in England & his heirs, & in default ½ to his right heirs & the other ½ to my 3 loving sisters Lady Frances Harper, Lady Ann Harper, & Mrs Kath. Willoughby. To my brother Chas. all my plate & household stuff in my manor house of Knayth. To my sister Kath. £1000, & to the Ladys Frances & Ann Harper £50 each for rings. To Rebekah Judd, wife of Saml Judd, £20 payable out of my Barbados estate. To Dr Richd Laford £50. To the poor of Stansted, co. Herts, £50. To Mr Chas. Collins £20. To my sister Kath. Willoughby my hoop ring of gold which was my mother's wedding ring, also my ring with a blewe stone & a diamond on either side, formerly my brother Henry's. To my good friends the Hon. Henry Walrond, senr, Esq., & Tho. Coliton, Esq., £50 each. To John Hallett, Esq., Francis Bond, & John Goring, merchts, £25 each for mourning. My wife Anne to be sole Ex'trix for Barbados & Antigua. My dear uncle John Cary, Esq., my brother Chas. Willoughby, Esq., Sir Wm Hickman, Bart., Sir John Harper of Swarkiston, Kt,

Ex'ors for England & £50 each. To my good friend the Hon. John Wytham, Esq., £100. To my wife Ann £1000. To my friend Capt. Joseph Buckley £25. Witnessed by Jer. Cooke, Abraham Langford, John Harris.

Ellis Crispe, Esq., of Wimbledon, in his will of 1684 refers to his grandfather Rowland Wilson, who bought lands of £200 a year by Indenture of 2 Oct. 1639 between Lady Sophia, Viscountess Wimbleton, the Right Hon. Francis, Lord Willoughby of Parham, and Elizabeth his wife (one of the daughters and coheirs of the late Lord Cecill, Baron of Putney and Viscount Wimbleton), James Fines, son and heir of Viscount Say and Seale and Frances his wife, Sir Charles Wray, Knt., and Albinia his wife, and Dorothy Cecill, two other daughters and coheirs of the said Viscount Wimbleton.

1685, Feb. 19. Adm'on to George Willoughby, Esq., second cousin to Elizabeth Willoughby, late of Bantam in the East Indies, spinster, deceased.

John Cary, son of Sir Philip Cary, by his will dated 1686 bequeathed his estate (and among them Stanwell, co. Middlesex, which he had inherited from Thomas, Lord Knyvet) to his great-niece Elizabeth only surviving daughter of George, Lord Willoughby of Parham, son of William, Lord Willoughby, by Anne daughter of Sir Philip Cary, provided that she should within three years of his decease marry Lord Guildford, in failure of which condition to the Falkland family. She, however, married the Hon. James Bertie, but a decree of the House of Lords in 1697 determined in favour of her life interest in the manor of Stanwell, adjudging the reversion to be vested in Lucius Henry, Lord Falkland. Mrs. Bertie died in 1715. (Lysons's 'Environs of London,' vol. v., p. 252.)

Phillip Willoughby of Antigua, Gent. Will dated 20 April 1691. Bound to New England. To my mother Jane Willoughby of Ireland £6 yearly. To my brother Jonas Willoughby £10. To Eliz^th wid. of Joseph Willoughby my brother £5. All residue to my dau. Eliz^th Willoughby. My wife Bazill to have her thirds. If she have a son, being now with child, I give to such son all my estate & to my said dau. 30,000 lbs. at 21, but if it be a dau. then all estate to my said 2 dans. Mr Jno Lucas my loving friend guardian. He & my wife Ex'ors. I give her 3000 lbs. for mourning & to my Ex'or 1000 lbs. Witnessed by Thomas Johnston, James Reade, Thomas Skerrett, Pierce Lynch. If my child die before 21 without issue then all estate to my wife for life, & then to the heirs general of the Willoughbys. On 23 May 1694 appeared Thomas Skerrett and Pierce Lynch before Christopher Codrington, Esq. Recorded 24 May 1694.

Pedigree of Willoughby.

ARMS.—*Fretty azure.*

SIR ROBERT WILLOUGHBY, Knt. His pedigree entered in the 'Visitation of co. Notts.' = Cecily, cousin and coheir of Lyonell, Lord Wells.

Sir Christopher Willoughby, Knt., Lord Willoughby of Eresby = Margaret, dau. of Sir William Jenny of Knottishall, co. Suffolk, Knt.

William, Lord Willoughby of Eresby. | Sir Christopher Willoughby. = ... | Sir Thomas Willoughby, Knt., Lord Chief Justice of the Common Pleas. = Bridgett, dau. and coheir of Sir Robert Read, Knt., Chief Justice of the Common Pleas, by Margaret, dau. and coheir of John Alphew of Bore Place, co. Kent.

Christopher Willoughby, 2nd son. = Elizabeth, dau. of Sir George Talboys and sister and coheir of Gilbert, Lord Talboys of Kyne.

Elizabeth, dau. and heir of Sir Thomas Heneage,* Knt., of Hainton and Knaith. 1st wife. = Sir William Willoughby, Knt., son and heir; created Baron Willoughby of Parham by patent 1 Edward VI. (20 Feb. 1547); appointed Governor of Calais 4 Edward VI., but removed by Mary; died 1574. Will made at Doncaster 10 Dec. 1573, 16 Elizabeth. To be bur. at Parham, co. Suffolk. = ... widow of Walter, Viscount Hereford; died s.p. 2nd wife.

Charles, 2nd Lord Willoughby of Parham, died 1603. = Lady Margaret Clinton, dau. of Edward, 9th Lord and 1st Earl of Lincoln, K.G., Lord High Admiral 1584-5. A

Mary Willoughby, mar. William Metham of Bullington, co. Lincoln, Esq.

* Edward VI. by indenture in the second year of his reign granted the manors of Whitfield and Little Pysing to Sir Thomas Heneage, Knt., and William, Lord Willoughbye, who seem to have sold their joint interest to James Hales, whose heirs possessed them at the latter end of the reign of Queen Elizabeth. (Hasted's 'Kent,' vol. iv., p. 16.)

A

William Willoughby of Cots, Esq., 1st son, died v.p. = Elizabeth, dau. and heir of Sir Christopher Hildyard, Knt., of Winestead, co. York.

See PEDIGREE A.

Sir Ambrose Willoughby, 2nd son. = Susan, dau. of . . . . Brooke.

Edward Willoughby, 3rd son. = Elizabeth Manby.

Edward Willoughby, only son = Rebecca, dau. of Henry Draper.

Robert Willoughby, died young.

Edward Willoughby, died an infant.

Henry Willoughby of Virginia, died 1685. = Mary . . . .

Richard Willoughby = . . . Waldron.

Sarah Willoughby, mar. . . . . Birt.

Rebecca Willoughby, mar. Richard Hull.

Henry Willoughby, died 1720 or 1722. = Elizabeth, dau. of William Pidgeon of Stepney.

Edward Willoughby, died s.p.

Ambrose Willoughby, died s.p.

Susan Willoughby, died a spinster.

Henry Willoughby, 16th Baron, succeeded Hugh. Will dated 3 Aug. 1754; proved 5 July 1775. (295 Alexander.) = Susanna, dau. of Robert Greswell.

William Willoughby, 2nd son. = Elizabeth, dau. of . . . . Knochton.

Edward Willoughby, 3rd son, died s.p.

Joseph Willoughby, 4th son, living 1754; died s.p.

Fortune Willoughby, 5th son, dead 1766. = Hannah, dau. of Thomas Barrow and widow of Cook Tollet of Swanscombe, co. Kent; sole heir to her son; died Nov. 1796.

Elizabeth Willoughby, died s.p.

Mary Willoughby, died s.p.

Henry Willoughby.

Henry Willoughby.

Ambrose Willoughby. Died infants.

Elizabeth Willoughby, mar. 1st John Halsey and 2ndly Edward Argles, and died 1763.

Susan Willoughby, died infant.

William Willoughby, died 1754—66, s.p.m.

Other issue, s.p.

George Willoughby, 17th and last Baron, born 1748; succeeded his uncle Henry 4 July 1775; died s.p. 29 Oct. 1779; title extinct. Will dated 23 June 1778; proved 25 Nov. 1779. (481 Warburton.)

PEDIGREE A.

William Willoughby = Elizabeth Hildyard.

William, 3rd Lord Willoughby of Parham. Inq. p.m. 12-14 Elizabeth. = Lady Frances Manners, 2nd dau. of John, 4th Earl of Rutland; mar. licence dated 4 Feb. 1602 at Lincoln.

Katherine Willoughby, mar. Joseph Godfrey of Thorock, co. Lincoln, Esq., who died *circa* 1631; she died 15 Aug. 1658, æt. 75. M.I. at Drifield, co. York.

Henry, 4th Lord Willoughby of Parham, died an infant.

Francis, 5th Lord Willoughby of Parham, Lord Lieut. of co. Lincoln 1642; Governor of Barbados and the Leeward Islands; drowned 4 Aug. 1666. Will dated 17 July 1666; proved 10 May 1678. (55 Reeve.) = Lady Elizabeth Cecil, 2nd dau. and coheir of Edward, Viscount Wimbledon; mar. 16 Nov. 1638.

William Willoughby, died young, v.p.

Elizabeth Willoughby, mar. Richard, 3rd Viscount Ranelaigh; she was bur. 3 Aug. 1695 in Westminster Abbey; he died 1711, s.p.m.

Diana Willoughby, mar. Heneage, 2nd Earl of Winchilsea; he died 1689, s.p. superst.

Frances Willoughby, mar. William, 3rd Lord Brereton; he was born 4 May 1631 and died 1679.

George, 7th Lord Willoughby of Parham, born 18 March 1638 at Belvoir Castle, co. Lincoln; died 1674 and bur. at Snaith. = Elizabeth, dau. and coheir of Henry Fienes *alias* Clinton of Kirksted Abbey, co. Lincoln; mar. 9 Oct. 1666; dead 1677.

Henry Willoughby, Lieut.-General and Governor of Antigua 1668; died a bachelor, v.p., *circa* 1670.

William Willoughby, died a bachelor, v.p.

James Willoughby, died a bachelor, v.p., at Antigua *circa* 1670.

Cary Willoughby, died a bachelor. Will dated 23 Dec. 1673; proved 19 Dec. 1676. (158 Bence.)

John, 9th Lord Willoughby of Parham, Member of Council and Colonel of Militia of Barbados 1673; died s.p. Sep. 1678 at Stanwell; bur. at Knaith. Will dated 10 June, proved 7 Nov. 1678. (134 Reeve.) = Ann . . . . sold her estates in Antigua in 1679. s.p.

John, 8th Lord Willoughby of Parham, only son and heir, born 16 July 1669 at Knaith; baptism registered at Stanwell; died 1677 at Winchester. Adm'on 15 Feb. 1678 to his sister Elizabeth.

Elizabeth Willoughby, sole and eventual heir of the Carys, carried Stanwell to the Berties; born 29 April 1673; mar. 5 Jan. 1691-2; died 26 Sep. and bur. 2 Oct. 1715 at Stanwell. = James Bertie of Westminster, 2nd son of James, 1st Earl of Abingdon; born 13 March 1673; died 1734.

Anne Willoughby, died young.

Charles Willoughby, 4th son, died s.p.

Sir Thomas Willoughby, 5th and youngest son. = Mary, dau. of . . . . Thorney.

Anne Willoughby, mar. Sir William Pelham, Knt.

Mary Willoughby, mar. . . . . Erle of Corpsey, Esq.

Catherine Willoughby, mar. Sir John Savile, Knt.

Thomas Willoughby, 11th Baron, succeeded Charles, 10th Baron; summoned by writ 19 May 1685; died 1691, æt. 89. Had seven sons and four daus. = Eleanor, dau. of Hugh Whittle of Horwath, co. Lancaster, Esq.

William Willoughby, a Romish Priest.

Mary Willoughby, mar. 1st Augustine Wingfield and 2ndly . . . . Saul.

Anne, dau. of Lawrence Halliwell of Tockwold, co. Lancaster, Esq. 1st wife. = Hugh Willoughby, 12th Baron, æt. 40, 1692; died s.p. Aug. 1712. = Honora, dau. of Sir Thomas Leigh, son and heir of Thomas, Lord Leigh, of Stoneleigh, co. Warwick, and widow of Sir William Egerton, K.B.; mar. licence dated 5 Oct. 1692, then æt. 25. 2nd wife.

Thomas Willoughby and Edward Willoughby, both died young.

Jonathan Willoughby.

Francis Willoughby, 4th son. = Eleanor Rothwell.

Mary Willoughby, mar. Samuel Greenhalgh of Adlington, co. Lancaster.

Sarah Willoughby.

Abigail Willoughby.

Thomas Willoughby, died young 1682.

Thomas Willoughby, died a bachelor.

Edward Willoughby, 13th Baron, a private in the Army; died a bachelor April or May 1713.

Charles Willoughby, 14th Baron, succeeded his brother Edward; died 12 June 1715 in co. Lancaster. = Hester, dau. of Henry Davenport, Esq., of Darcy Lever, co. Lincoln; died 11 Sep. 1730 at Kensington. Adm'on 10 Feb. 1731 to Sir Walter Bagot, Bart.

Hugh Willoughby, died a bachelor.

Eleanor Willoughby.

Alice Willoughby.

Margaret Willoughby.

Hannah Willoughby.

Mary Willoughby.

Sarah Willoughby.

Rebecca Willoughby.

Hugh Willoughby, 15th Baron, P.S.A. and F.R.S., at one time in the Army; died a bachelor 21 Jan. 1765, æt. 55. Adm'on granted March 1765 to his two sisters.

Hellena Willoughby, wife of Baxter Roscow 1765.

Elizabeth Willoughby, widow of . . . . Shaw 1765.

William, 6th Lord Willoughby of Parham, Governor of Barbados, where he died 10 April 1673; bur. at Knaith, co. Lincoln. Will dated 18 May 1672; proved 27 Nov. 1673. (157 Pye.) The dates and places of birth of his fourteen children are recorded at Hunsdon, co. Herts. = Anne, dau. of Sir Philip Cary* of Stanwell, co. Middlesex; bapt. 20 June 1615; bur. 12 Jan. 1671 at Aldenham.

Frances Willoughby, mar. Sir Bulstrode Whitlock of Fawley Court, co. Bucks, Knt.; he died 1675.

Charles,† 10th Lord Willoughby of Parham, 7th and youngest son, died s.p. 9 Dec. 1679; bur. at Knaith. Left his estate to his niece Elizabeth Bertie. = Mary, dau. of Sir B. Dixie, Bart.

s.p.

Frances Willoughby, mar. 1st, by licence dated 3 June 1661, Sir John Harper, Knt., of Swarkeston, co. Derby; 2ndly, Charles, Earl of Bellomont; 3rdly, Henry Heveningham; she died 25 May 1714, æt. 71; bur. and M.I. at Swarkeston.

Elizabeth Willoughby, died v.p.

Anne Willoughby, born 15 Dec. 1652 at Stansteadbury, co. Herts; mar. Sir John Harpur, Bart., of Calke, co. Derby; she was living 1679; he died 1681.

Katherine Willoughby, born 14 May 1655 at Stansteadbury, co. Herts; mar. *circa* 1679 Charles, 3rd Viscount Cullen; he was bur. 3 Jan., æt. 30, and she 13 Feb. 1688-9 at Rushton, co. Northants.

Mary Willoughby, born and bapt. July 1656 at Hunsdon.

* For a good Pedigree of Cary see the 'Herald and Genealogist,' vol. iii., p. 42.

† On his death the title should have gone to Henry grandson of Sir Ambrose, but he was in Virginia, and Thomas son of Thomas, fifth son of Charles the second Lord, assumed it.

1731, Feb. 10. Dowager Lady Willoughby of Parham. Commission to Sir Walter Wagstaff Bagot, Bart., the guardian of Egerton Bagot, Esq., a minor, the nepos and next-of-kin.

Henry Willoughby of the Precinct of the Tower, Esq. Will dated 3 Aug. 1754; adm'on 5 July 1775 to the Right Hon. George, Lord Willoughby of Parham, of all the estate of the Right Hon. Henry, Lord Willoughby of Parham, deceased. (295 Alexander.) To my nephew Wm Willoughby £200. My nephew Geo. Willoughby £300 at 21. My sisters-in-law Hannah Willoughby & Eliz. Cogan £10 each, & to Hannah Willoughby & Mr Edward Argles £10 a year on trust for my brother Joseph Willoughby. To said Edwd Argles £100. All residue to Miles Halsey, late of Ludgate Hill, Esq., & Alex. Whitchurch of Copthall Court, Gent., on trust for my dau. Eliz. Argles & her children, remainders equally to my nephews Geo. & Wm Willoughby. Witnessed by R. Wilson, Granville Sharp.

1st Codicil. 3 Nov. 1766. My dau. & only surviving child Eliz. Argles is dead, also my nephew Wm Willoughby, s. of my late brother W^m, & I have now no nephew nor niece except only my nephew Geo. Willoughby, s. of my youngest brother Fortune Willoughby, deceased, & all my other brothers & sisters, viz., W^m, Edward, Joseph, Fortune, & my sisters Eliz. & Mary are dead s.p. Confirm gift of residue & my leasehold estate to my said nephew Geo. Willoughby who is my heir general, to be placed in trust by my sister-in-law Hannah Willoughby & Ex'trix (instead of Miles Halsey) & by Alex. Whitchurch till he is 21. Revoke £100 to M^r Ed. Argles & give him £20. To my said sister-in-law £20 a year. To Alex. Whitchurch £100. Witnessed by Charles Shuter, John Peight.

2nd Codicil. 18 Feb. 1767. My friend Mr Mathew Dove £20.

3rd Codicil. 10 Dec. 1768. My friends Hugh, Earl of Marchmont, & John, Lord Berkeley of Stratton, & Daniel Booth, Esq., overseers, & a 20 g. ring each.

4th Codicil. 25 May 1771. £30 to my servant.

1765. March 23. Adm'on of Right Hon. Hugh, Lord Willoughby of Parham, bachelor, deceased, granted to Hon. Hellena Roscow, wife of Baxter Roscow, and Elizabeth Shaw, widow, the sisters.

George, Lord Willoughby of Parham. Will dated 23 June 1778. On 25 Nov. 1779 adm'on to Hannah Willoughby the mother. (481 Warburton.) All my estate to my honoured mother Hannah Willoughby. Witnessed by Alexander Whitchurch, C. Shuter, Thomas Shuter.

See Vol. I. for information about the Lords Willoughby.

In 1642 Francis, Lord Willoughby of Parham, was Lord Lieut. of the county of Lincoln under Parliament. (See Rushworth's 'Historical Collections,' vol. iv., p. 676, for the letters which passed between him and the King relative to the Militia.)

1648. Francis, Lord Willoughby of Parham. The goods at his house in Charterhouse Yard and in Lincolnshire ordered to be sequestrated and £1700 due to him, he being Vice-Admiral of the revolted ships. ('Calendar of the Committee for Compounding Royalist Estates,' p. 941.)

LORD WILLOUGHBY* TO LADY WILLOUGHBY.

My dearest Friend,

I did, not above a fortnight ago, write at large to thee by the way of Holland, by my governess Cateline, the carpenter's wife, whom upon her earnest importunity, I gave leave to go home. She performed her trust very carefully and honestly in keeping all things under her charge, but for anything else she was loth to trouble herself. Honest Mary is all my stay now, and I hope will do as well as she can. I have entertained another coarse wench to be under her, allowing her help enough of negroes, which are the best servants in these countries, if well tutored, and cost little, only a canvass petticoat once a year, and there is no more trouble with them.

Mrs. Chavve, this bearer, who hath promised me to deliver this with her own hand, is one who challenged acquaintance of me upon your score, which caused me to give her pass for her sugar, custom free: she tells me, she waited upon you when you lay in of little Dosey. I do not remember her, nor would not have believed her, but she gave me such a token by naming the child. If I be deceived, if this letter come safe to you, I shall not be much troubled at the cheat, for it is frequent here to have tricks put upon one of such kind.

My Lord Charles Paulet's daughter, I writ to you of, proves no such thing, for she is run quite away, and I think out of the island, for I cannot hear of her, which makes her appear a cheat: she knowing that I had writ into England about her, made her not dare to stay a return of my letter. I did by Cateline write so large, giving thee an account of myself, and the state of the island, by some papers, acquainting thee what we had done in order to our self-preservation against that storm which was threatened us from England, by their printed declaration calling us rebels, so as I shall touch no more upon anything of that, only what we have further added since: which is, to make ourselves strong in men, as well as in words; and to that end have raised forces, both of horse and foot, which the country pays, and are constantly to be kept in a body to resist any forces that shall come against us. It was occasioned by Mr. Arnold, who came at the time of the Assembly's meeting: he is a very honest man. By him I received two letters, and three from my children; one more which was superscribed to Mr. Rich. We had a fine passage, being but five weeks upon the way. I could wish to my heart thou hadst been with him; but I know not how I should be so happy, though thy goodness to me, in saying thou wilt come, puts me in some comfort: for which kind resolution of thine, God in heaven reward thee. He came in a very opportune time, for the terror of his news, that so many ships were coming with men to reduce the island, stirred up the spirits of the Assembly, caused them to desire me to put the island in a posture of war, occasioned the raising of horse and foot, so as we shall be very able to resist them, and send them home again, shewing them the island is not so easily to be won as they are made to imagine it.

And I hope they will reward those runaway bankrupt rogues, who durst stay no longer here, for fear of a gaol, whereof learned Mr. Bayes is one; having by their villany, done what in them lies to ruin one of the best and sweetest islands in the English possession, or in any others, except the Spaniards, with whom we hear they have made a league, offensive and defensive; and if that be their planting the Gospel, I hope God will never prosper it.

I thank God we are all in good health and good heart, wanting nothing, but those things I so long agone writ for; of which I have now so much want as I would give double what they were worth for to have them. I might have been as much beholding to my friends as to have done me that courtesy to have furnished those things; I writing that it was not to be upon my particular account, any merchant would have done it; if not out of England, yet out of Holland, from whence ships come daily in to us. I sent a list to you by two conveyances, which I hope failed not: but however thy letters put me out of hopes of having any return of my desires in that particular.

I thank thee for having a care of my credit in Mr. Read's business, in which thou didst me a very great kindness. I am very sorry it was forced to fall upon thy particular; it was none of my meaning it should have done so; for poor soul, to hear of the sadness of thy condition, to be brought to so low a stipend, cuts my heart: but I hope God, who has hitherto kept us up, will still preserve us, and though cruel men may rob, oppress, and steal away what I have, yet I shall find a way to live: and since they began so deeply with me, as to take away all at one clap, and without any cause given on my part, I am resolved not to sit down a loser, and be content to see thee, my children, and self ruined.

There was wont reparation to be allowed to those that were injured by the contrary party; and being it is in my own power to help myself, shall I not do it, but sit still, like an ass, seeing the meat torn out of thine and my children's mouths? No! I will not do it: and therefore, dear heart, let me entreat thee to leave off thy persuasions to submit to them, who so unjustly, so wickedly, have ruined thee and me and mine.

If ever they get the island, it shall cost them more than it is worth before they have it. And be not frighted with their power and success: God is above all.

There is an inclosed note directed "the Gentleman," which I am confident, if you will, you may make use of, praying you not to omit the opportunity. I shall send him as much in sugar, when I hear from you that you have made use of this. Be not frightened nor perplexed for me; I am confident yet God will bring us together into

* There are several original letters of his in Egerton MS. 2395, Brit. Mus.

these parts, according to my former petitions to him, that we may end our days together in happiness; for I have had a return of my discovery of Guiana, which I writ to you formerly of: and the gentleman which I sent hath brought with him to me two of the Indian Kings, having spoke with divers of them, who are all willing to receive our nation, and that we shall settle amongst them; for which end I am sending hence a hundred men to take possession, and doubt not but in a few years to have many thousands there.

It is commended, by all that went, for the sweetest place that ever was seen; delicate rivers, brave land, fine timber. They were out almost five months; and amongst forty persons, not one of them had so much as their head ache. They commend the air to be so pure, and the water so good, as they had never such stomachs in their lives, eating five times a day plenty of fish and fowl, partridges and pheasants innumerable; brave savanas, where you may, in coach or on horseback, ride thirty or forty miles.

God bless me into life. And if England will be a friend, or that we make them so by tiring them out, either their seamen by the tedious voyages, or the state by the great expense they must be at, which I am very confident we shall, being all so well-resolved to stand by one another to the last man, then I shall make thee a brave being there: for since all is gone at home, it is time to provide elsewhere for a being.

I am very much troubled for honest Jo. Ward, that we should suffer so much for his honesty and kindness to me. Pray you, send for him, and commend my kind love to him, and tell him, that if he will come to me, he shall never want as long as I have it.

Though God is at present pleased to afflict us, and that justly for my sins, yet so long as he gives us health, let us not despair, but do our best; for who knows what a day may bring forth? Do thy best where thou art, playing the game as well as thou canst, and I will do the like here, and when the fleet shall return, and the gentlemen see how they are abused, you may perchance find them more charitable, at least in a more calm humour to be spoke with.

One comfort we have, they can neither starve us with cold, nor famish us for hunger; and why should they think so easily to put us to it then? If a qualm should come, I thank God I have some of thy cordial water left still; but I thank my God, I never was more healthy in my life, I want nothing but thy sweet company: that would make time short, and all things easy to me. When once this expected storm is over, and this place settled, so as no more trouble may disquiet it, then shall I with all violence pursue thee with my humble suit and desire for thy company. God keep thee in health. Puil up a good heart, and yet all may be well.

I have no tokens to send my poor children for their kind letters. Mr. Arnold commends Will much, and relates a great deal of discourse he had with him one day, when you were from home. My best of blessings to them all.

For Mrs. Betty, if there be such an inclination in the young lord you mention, let not the present want of portion discourage; I have known unhandsomer than she married as well for nothing; but I shall hope however in a few years to be able to give a portion, though as yet it goes out apace.

As for Frank, I hope you will be careful for her health, in preventing what you fear. What I mentioned to you concerning my Lord Callender, be not so averse, out of an opinion of our too much good fellowship, for he is a noble lord, and an honest man! I had a letter lately from him, and he is resolved to come and plant in these parts of the world.

This enclosed engagement I sent by another conveyance, and renew it again, because I would have it with you, to satisfy your fear of my being delivered up. God but preserve thee, and I cannot do amiss. Farewell, my dearest joy.

The account Mr. Knowles gives me, by his letter, concerning the improvement of Will in his learning, is a great comfort to me; but the consideration of the loss of it again by his leaving of him is as great a cross. He expresseth to me, that because you could not continue his allowance to him, is the cause of his leaving him: if that be all, I should not doubt but, by God's blessing, I may be able to procure that, and shall spare it out of my own belly, if you can procure him to come to you again upon any reasonable terms; for I fear change of masters may do by him as it did by me. Prythee, dear heart, let me hear from thee. If there be any hopes of getting him to thee again, I will strain hard to procure means for the good of my boy. When you have read this letter, pray you seal it, and convey it to my lo—— by my brother, to whom I forbear to write, because I will not endanger him more than I have.

(Schomburgk's 'History of Barbados,' pp. 273—276.)

[From Barbados, 1651.]

In 1660 William Contset of Barbados made over his estate to one Turner in trust for himself and wife for their lives. Afterwards the writer of this letter coming to Barbados in 1672, was informed that Contset had been prevailed on to make another deed of trust to Christopher Codrington, Deputy-Governor, and Judge Sharpe who drew the deeds had, to please Codrington, instead of a trust for Contset and his heirs, conveyed the estate to Codrington after the death of Contset and his wife, who were very old, who learning it after the registration made great clamour and complaint of fraud. Codrington said, "I know the violent humour of Contset's wife & she had made the poore man out of his witts." Codrington gave Lord Willoughby £4000 for the title Lord Willoughby's son had to the estate by Contset's will, said he was ashamed, he had been purely frightened by Mr. Knight about a mouth after William, Lord Willoughby, arrived.

1669. Contset had one of the best estates in the island . . . . he and his wife were very illiterate people . . . . Mrs. Contset, who died last, left it by will to Lieut.-General Henry Willoughby, who on his arrival presently after her death, and intending to sue Codrington, was invited by him to supper, went from Codrington's at nine at night, fell after he came into his lodging into a violent burning fever of his stomach, and died next morning by seven of the clock. (P.R.O.—Mrs. V. T. C. Smith.)

Letter from Sir Bulstrode Whitelock to his brother-in law Lord Willoughby of Parham, dated 18 Aug. 1660, as to the duties and office of Constable of Windsor who "may constitute a Steward or Deputy (which your nephew Will. now is)." ('Annals of Windsor,' vol. ii., p. 295.)

1668. Antigua. Henry Willoughby, 600 acres granted by his father William, Lord Willoughby.

Henry Willoughbie, 600 acres by grant from Right Hon. Lieut.-General Henry Willoughby; surveyed 10 Nov. 1668.

1668, Dec. 18. Captain Jo. Lee sells his ¼ of Barbuda to Lieut.-General Henry Willoughby.

Antigua. I Elizabeth Ashton, widow, surrender to the Lieut.-General Henry Willoughby, Governor of Antigua and Berbuda, all the said land by him to me formerly granted, this 2 April 1669. Witnessed by Nathaniell Clerke, George Terwhitt, Joseph Hodgkin.

Harry Willoughby retook the colony of Surinam on 7 Oct. 1667. He was living on 27 April 1669 at Antigua, and dead before 10 Jan. 1670.

In 1670 William Byam, Governor of Antigua, wrote to William, Lord Willoughby of Parham, acquainting him with the death of the Lieut.-General (Henry Willoughby), and with the manner of death of James Willoughby in that island.

1670, Jan. 20. John Willoughby was appointed deputy to Lord Ashley, one of the Lords' Proprietors of Carolina. On 30 May 1673 he was sent home from Barbadoes with despatches by his father.

1670, March 23. Nicholas Blake writes, "believes it is no news in England that the two sons Lord Willoughby left behind him are dead; these parts have been nothing smiling or fortunate to that noble gentleman."

1673, April 2. He was sworn in by his father as a Member of Council and Colonel of a Regiment of Foot *vice* Christopher Codrington superseded. May 27, John and Charles Willoughby Ex'ors to the late Lord Willoughby. May 28, a list of the most eminent planters in Barbados, Colonel John Willoughby, 450 acres; and one of the Council. Sir Peter Colleton, President, wrote the same day, "On 10th of last month died Lord Willoughby." On 4 March 1674 John Willoughby was still of the Council.

Lieut.-Colonel Nathaniel Clarke and Samuel Winthrop, Attorneys to William, Lord Willoughby, the purchaser of the estate of Lieut.-General Henry Willoughby, deceased, appoint John Mitchell their Attorney 6 April 1672. Proved and recorded 7 May 1672.

1672, June 10. His Majesty charged with a debt of £6000 to the late Lord Francis Willoughby's daughters for so much used of their moiety of the 4½ per cent. duty.

William, Lord Willoughby, arrived at his government of Barbados on 13 Oct. 1672 after eleven weeks voyage, and spent £3000 st. for necessary outlay. (Egerton MS. 2395.)

About June 1673 the body of William, Lord Willoughby, was sent to England in H.M.S. the "St. David," Captain Poole, which was the same ship which brought him out.

1673, July. Warrant for payment of £8397 to Richard, Lord Ranelagh, and William, Lord Brereton, in right of their wives being daughters and coheirs of the late Francis, Lord Willoughby, for their moiety of H.M.'s 4½ per cent. revenue at Barbados, some having been employed in H.M.'s service in the war against the Dutch.

Charter of ship the "Friendship" of London, John Thompson, Commander, to Hon. John Willoughby, Esq., of Barbados, at £40 per month, with crew of eight men and one boy; to voyage between Barbados and Antigua. Recorded 10 Nov. 1676.

1676, Feb. 6. Colonel Willoughby, Parham, 1000 acres granted by Governor Warner. By the Act of 10 April 1668 no plantation is to be given over 600 acres, yet Colonel Henry Willoughby obtained a patent from William, Lord Willoughby, of all Parham . . . . and several islands, reputed 8 or 10,000 acres, and held by his heirs since, all lying waste . . . . do you therefore measure to Colonel John Willoughby and Charles Willoughby, Esq., Ex'ors to William, Lord Willoughby, 1000 and 3 acres at Parham; surveyed Feb. 1676.

1677, June 23. Indenture of apprenticeship between Richard Duckworth of St. Michael's, Barbados, blacksmith, of the one part, and Hon. John Willoughby of St. George's, Barbados, of the other, for meat, drink, and apparel for three years, and 2000 lbs. of sugar yearly, and 10 acres in fee simple.

"Antigua Division. Part 2. Of the Lands taken up on the West side of the Creeke.

2000 acres. Taken upp for the use of the Right Honble Frauncis, Lord Willughbye, of Parham by Mr Nathaniel Clarke. One Tract of Land in Seryno Creeke beginning some Twenty Cheine below the present landing place of Comacabo Towne, and running in breadth along the Creeke one hundred and sixty chaine. Contayning Two Thousand Acres part Savanna and part Woodlands; with power to sett up Mills or any other thing in any Creeke or Creekes in the aforesaid Tract. Recorded the 10th of January 1653 per Robert Sanford, Sec^ry^.

Not brought into ye office till 2 Dec. 1678."

[This deed refers to His Lordship's settlement at Surinam.—V. L. O.]

Indenture dated 2 June, 31 Charles II., 1679, between the Right Hon. Charles, Lord Willoughby, Baron of Parham, of the one part, and the Right Hon. Ann, Lady Willoughby, widow and Ex'trix of Right Hon. John, late Lord Willoughby, deceased, of the other part, for £1600 st. sale to her of all the estate in Barbados, Antigua, Berbuda, etc., and the plantation that was settled by her in reversion after her decease on her late husband John, Lord Willoughby, in Barbados, and all the stock and lands of his formerly belonging to Henry Willoughby, Esq., and George, Lord Willoughby, brothers of the said Charles, Lord Willoughby, or to William, Lord Willoughby, father of the said Charles, in Antigua, Berbuda, or elsewhere, free of all claims against Charles, Lord Willoughby, William, Lord Willoughby, George, Lord Willoughby, John, Lord Willoughby, Henry Willoughby, Lady Ann Harper, Mrs. Katherine Cockayn, sisters of the said Charles, Lord Willoughby. Witnessed by Abraham Langford, William Buckley, Thomas Mascham, John, William, and Edward Thornburgh, Charles Modyford, John Harding, Richard Worsam.

Indenture dated 10 Dec. 1679, 31 Charles II., between the Right Hon. Ann, Lady Willoughby, widow of John, Lord Willoughby, eldest son and heir of William, Lord Willoughby, and brother and heir of George, Lord Willoughby, who was brother and heir of Henry Willoughby, Esq., deceased, of the one part, and Clement Tudway and George Turney of London, merchants, of the other, for £600 st. paid and £1200 st. secured, she sells to them her plantation called Parham Hill of 1000 acres, also her moiety of Long Island, and ¼ of Berbuda, ⅛ to each of them. Witnessed by Thomas Yate, Charles Modyford, William Thorn, James Bowman, John Sampson, Jonathan Francis, William Barnes, Joseph Lawrence, Abraham Langford, John Pratt, Hugh Everard, Bastian Bayer. By Valentine Russell, President, appeared James Bowman, Commander of the ship "Owners Adventure" of London, and John Sampson of London, merchant.

1680, April 5. On 12 April 1680 possession was given. Schedule of 45 negro men and women, 36 children, 33 cattle, 2 horses, 20 sheep, 12 hogs, 1 cattle mill, coppers, still, etc. Clement Tudway and George Turney. Letter of Attorney to William Barnes to take possession of the estate.

1684, Feb. 18. Phillipp Willoughby, 90 acres. Government Grant.

1715, June 12. Dy'd Charles Willoughby, Lord Willoughby of Parham, and was succeeded in Honour and Estate, by his Son Hugh Willoughby, Esq. ('Historical Register.')

1730, Sep. 11. Dy'd at her Lodgings at Kensington, the Right Honourable Eleanor, Dowager Lady Willoughby, of Parham, whose jointure was 300*l.* per Annum. (*Ibid.*, p. 59.)

1765, Jan. 21. R^t^ Hon. Lord Willoughby of Parham, president of the society of antiquarians, & F.R.S. ('Gent. Mag.,' p. 47.)

1775, June 27. Right Hon. Henry Lord Willoughby, of Parham. He took his seat in the H. of Peers, in consequence of their Lordships order on the hearing of his claim to the title, in March, 1767; his honours and fortune devolve on his only nephew, George Willoughby, Esq; late of Queen's College, Cambridge. (*Ibid.*, p. 451.)

1779, Oct. 29. George Lord Willoughby of Parham; who was born about 1748, educated at Warrington academy, and admitted pensioner of Queen's College, Cambridge, about May 1770, where he resided till about July 1772, and was distinguished for his amiable disposition, for his integrity, steadiness in his friendships, and that beautiful philanthropy for which his friends and acquaintance so much esteemed him. Upon the death of that venerable old man, Henry Lord Willoughby of Parham, July 4, 1775, he succeeded to the title; which is now extinct. (*Ibid.*, p. 566.)

1784, Nov. 24. By special licence, at Birdsall, one of the seats of the right hon. Lord Middleton, Richard Langley, of Wykeham-Abbey, esq; to the hon. Miss Willoughby, Lord W's eldest daughter. (*Ibid.*, p. 955.)

1796, Nov. At Knightsbridge, Mrs Willoughby, mother to the late Lord Willoughby, of Parham. Her husband, Fortune, 5th son of Henry W. having died, 1720, before the title came into the family, his son, the late lord, succeeded to it; in consequence of which his mother was never dignified with the peerage. She was Hannah, dau. of Thomas Barrow, and widow of Cook Tollet, of Swanscomb, Kent. (*Ibid.*, p. 968.)

"Willoughby of Parham, seated at Knath, neare Gainsborough, in Lindsey coast; hath parted with all, to W. Willoughby his brother, under value, who hath gott an estate of nere 3000*l.*" Knaith was originally the property of the Darcy family. The present chapel is believed to have been the church of the priory of Heynings, which was granted at the dissolution to Sir Thomas Heneage. By an heiress of Heneage, Knaith came to the Willoughbys, and from them to the Berties, etc. ('Herald and Genealogist,' vol. ii., p. 119.)

Knaith, a very small village on the east bank of the Trent, three miles south from Gainsborough, fourteen miles north-west of Lincoln, once the property and residence of the Barons Darcey, and after of the Lords Willoughby of Parham. The chapel of the ancient nunnery is now the parish church. The manor house stands near the church. ('History of Lincoln,' vol. ii., p. 48.)

In one of the east windows of Viscount Wimbledon's Chapel at Wimbledon Parish Church there is a shield of: *Or, fretty azure* (WILLOUGHBY); impaling, *Barruly of ten, argent and azure, six escutcheons, three, two, and one, sable, each charged with a lion rampant argent* (CECIL); and on a tablet "The Lo. Frances Willoughby of Parrom and his wife Elizabeth Cecill." (Manning and Bray's 'Surrey,' and Lysons's 'Environs of London,' vol. i., p. 533.)

PARISH REGISTER OF ST. PHILIP.

Baptized.

1833	April 18	Henrietta Emma Eresby Startle d. of John & Eliza Margaret Willoughby. Parham. Officer of H.M. Customs.

Married.

1686	Nov. 18	Phillip Willoughby to Bazel Bagwell.

Buried.

1686	April 2	Bridget Willoughby.
1693	Dec. 29	Phillip Willoughby.
1694	June 11	Ye sd Willoughby's Child.

1602, Feb. 4. Wm Willowby, son of Wm Willowby, late of Cots, Esqr, decd, & Lady ffrances Manners, dau. of the Earl of Rutland [at Wolstrop Church]. (Lincoln Marriage Licences.)

1623, Jan. 27. Sir Thos Willoughby, sen., of Newton juxta Trent, Knight, & Letticia Nevell, of Thorney, co. Notts, wid.; Appln. by Chas. Kemp, of Lea, yeom. [at Newton Church]. (Lincoln Marriage Licences.)

1691-2, Jan. 4. The Hon. James Bertie, of St Margaret's Westmr, Gent., Bachr, abt 19 (with consent of his father the Rt Hon. James Earl of Abington), & Mrs Elizabeth Willoughby of St Martin's in the Fields, Spr, abt 18, with consent of her guardian, her parents being dead; alleged by Roddon Trowe, of St Margts afsd, Gent.; also attested by Francis Jackman of St Martin's, Ludgate, Lond., Distiller; at St Martin's in the Fields. (Marriage Licences: Vicar-General of the Archbishop of Canterbury.)

1692, Oct. 5. Rt Hon. Hugh Lord Willoughby, of Parham, abt 40, & the Hon. Honora Egerton, Spr, abt 25; alleged by Ben. Barnett, of St Martin's in the Fields, Midd., Clerk; at St Martin's afsd, or St Paul's, Covent Garden, Midd. (*Ibid.*)

IN DRIFIELD CHURCH IN YORKSHIRE.

(Brit. Mus. Add. MS. 19,155.)

Here lyeth buried the Body of Katherine the daughter of Will. Willoughby Esq
eldest son of Charles Ld Willoughby, Baron
of Parham, wife to Joseph Godfrey of Thorock
in the County of Lincolne Esq 27 years
1 month and 21 dayes his Widow: dyed 15
Aug. Ao Dom. 1658 aged about 75 yeares. Willoughby Godfrey of Edethorpe second son
to her, having decently seen her inter'd
did erect this, as his last duty, with her
due Armories.

(Le Neve's 'Mon. Angl.,' vol. ii., p. 62.)

Pedigree of Winthrop.

ARMS.—*Argent, three chevrons gules crénelé, over all a lion rampant sable armed and langued azure* (WINTHROP).
CREST.—*A hare proper running on a mount vert.* Confirmed 24 June 1592 by William Detheck, Garter.

The early portion of the following Pedigree has been taken from the very complete ones published in Dr. Muskett's 'Suffolk Manorial Families,' Part I., pp. 1—33. The Antiguan portion on page 28 of that work appears to have been drawn up, without acknowledgment, from information supplied by me to Mr. Winthrop and Mr. Lyons.

ADAM WINTHROP of Lavenham, co. Suffolk, 1498. 1st husband. ═ Joane Burton, living 1520. ═ John Ponder of Lavenham, clothworker. Will dated 1520. (30 Aylofle.) 2nd husband.

Alice Henny, mar. 16 Nov. 1527; died 25 June 1533. 1st wife. ═ Adam Winthrop, son and heir, born 9 Oct. 1498 at Lavenham; free of the City of London 1526; purchased Groton Manor 1544; Master of Clothworkers' 1551; died 9 Nov. 1562. M.I. at Groton. Will dated 20 Sep. 1562; proved 15 Jan. 1563. (2 Chayre.) His portrait by (?) Holbein is in U.S.A. ═ Agnes, dau. of Robert Sharpe of Islington; mar. 20 July 1534, then æt. 18; remar. 1563 William Mildmay of Springfield Barnes, co. Essex, and died 13 May 1565. 2nd wife.

A B

A

William Winthrop, born 12 Nov. 1529; died 1 and bur. 2 March 1581-2 at St. Michael's, Cornhill. = Elizabeth, dau. of .... Norwood of co. Kent; died 2 June 1578 in Kent.

Issue.

Thomas, Christopher, Thomas, and Bridget Winthrop, died infants.

B

John Winthrop, born 20 Jan. 1546; of Groton Manor; later of Aghadowne, co. Cork, where he died 26 July 1613; conveyed Groton to his brother Adam 1594. Will dated 28 March 1613; proved 31 Jan. 1613-14. (Dublin Record Office.) = Elizabeth, dau. of Robert Risby of Thorpe Morieux, co. Suffolk; mar. 6 Feb. 1566-7; remar. Reynold Brauneh (licence dated 8 July 1617); she died 1637 at Southwark.

s.p.s.

Mary, only child and heir of John Forth of Great Stambridge, co. Essex, Esq.; born 1 Jan. 1583; mar. 16 March 1605 at Great Stambridge; bur. 26 June 1615 at Groton. 1st wife. = John Winthrop, only son and heir, born 12 Jan. 1587 in Edwardston; entered Trinity College, Cambridge, 2 Dec. 1602; removed to Mass. 1630, where he was many years its distinguished Governor; sold Groton 1631; died 26 March and bur. 3 April 1649 at Boston, Mass. = Thomasine, dau. of William Clopton of Castleins, Esq.; mar. 6 Dec. 1615; died in childbed 8 and bur. 11 Dec. 1616 at Groton. 2nd wife. s.p. = Margaret, dau. of Sir John Tyndal, Knt., of Great Maplestead, co. Essex; mar. there 29 April 1618; died 14 June 1647, æt. 56, at Boston, Mass. 3rd wife. = Martha, dau. of Captain William Rainsborough, R.N., and widow of Thomas Cotymore of Boston; mar. Gov. Winthrop Dec. 1647; remar. 1652 John Coggan of Boston. 4th wife. s.p.s.

John Winthrop, born 12 Feb. 1606-7 at Groton; of Trinity College, Dublin, 1622; of Inner Temple 1624; Governor of Connecticut; ancestor of present American family. = Martha Fones, mar. 8 Feb. 1631.

Issue.

Henry Winthrop, born 20 Jan. 1607 at Groton; was planting at Barbados 1627-8; drowned 2 July 1630 at Salem, Mass. = Elizabeth Fones, mar. 25 April 1629; remar. twice.

s.p.m.

Forth Winthrop, born 30 Dec. 1609; of Emmanuel College, Cambridge; bur. 28 Nov. 1630 at Groton, bachelor.

Mary Winthrop, born 1612; mar. *circa* 1632 Rev. Samuel Dudley, son of Governor Thomas Dudley; she died 12 April 1643.

Henry Winthrop, born 1649 at Rotterdam; educated in New England; Captain of Militia, Antigua; owned 240 acres in St. Peter's; living 1709-10. = Henrietta, dau. and coheir of Captain William King (her sister Mary mar. John Frye, senior); conveyed her 190 acres to her husband 1677.

Joseph Winthrop, born before 1653; educated in New England; Captain of Militia, Antigua; owned "Cinnamon Valley" of 300 acres. Will dated 13 Oct. and sworn 12 Nov. 1679. = Catherine .... in 1679 intailed "Cinnamon Valley" on her dau.; remar. 1680 Richard Slicer,* Gent. (*Vide* Vol. I., p. 261.)

Samuel Winthrop, æt. 8 in 1700; his trustees sold his 240 acres in 1701; living in St. Mary's Parish 1716—1767. = Abigail .... living 1755 and 1759 (? bur. 13 Dec. 1773). She may have been Abigail Lavington, sister of Major William Lavington.

Mary Winthrop, spinster 1704; mar. Major William Lavington; postnuptial settlement dated 3 March 1709-10 (? bur. 15 Aug. 1753 at St. Philip's).

Sarah Winthrop, stated to have mar. Colonel George Thomas; he died 1707.

Elizabeth Winthrop, living 1725 and 1758. = Captain Jacob Huyghue of St. Paul's. His will was dated 1758.

Mary Winthorpe. Will dated 6 Sep. 1759; sworn 26 Feb. 1760.

William Winthrop, Gent., in 1765 witness to will of Robert Gray, Overseer, perhaps son of Samuel and Abigail Winthrop.

Robert Winthrop, bur. 27 June 1779 at St. John's.

Henrietta Huyghue, in a deed of 1774 styled ad'trix of Samuel Winthrop, Gent. Will dated 1781.

Mary Huyghue, bapt. 30 Sep. 1753 at St. John's; niece of Mary Winthorpe 1759.

Other issue (see Huyghue Pedigree).

* The estate of Thomas Slicer, merchant, was appraised by warrant from Governor Philip Warner dated 7 Dec. 1671. Thomas Compton and Samuel Tristo valued it at 372,203 lbs. Recorded 30 Jan. 1671.

William Mildon of Bristoll, merchant. Will dated 17 June 1669; proved 23 Aug. 1669 by John Wathen, and on 7 March 1675 by John Trevers the surviving Ex'or. (97 Coke and 32 Bence.) To the children of my well beloved friend Capt Saml Winthrope of Antegua 20,000 lbs. of sugar. To the children of Mr Richd Hill of Nevis, planter, 20,000 lbs. To his son Jacob Hill ½ of my plantation called "Paul's" in Antegua, lately purchased from the widow Ellinr Paull, together with 12 or 13 negros. To my friend John Trevers the other ½ of my plantation also my moiety of the sloop "Martha," & ⅓ of the ship "Charles" of Nevis. To my servant John Ithill 12,000 lbs. Concerning a will of mine past to Mr John Wathen of Bristoll, I give ⅓ of all my estate to see the same duly performed, ⅓ to my espoused wife Mrs Eliz. Winthorpe, dau. of the said Capt Saml Winthorp, & of the remaining ⅓, ½ for building a hospital for the poore in Nevis, & ½ for the same purpose in Antegua. I appoint Capt Saml Winthorp of Antegua, Gent., Mr Richd Hill of Nevis, planter, & Mr John Trevers of Nevis, mercht, Ex'ors. Witnessed by Joseph Jorijs, John Mallett, William Welcome, Thomas Hughes. Proved with a codicil dated 21 Nov. 1666.

Alice, dau. of William Still of Grantham, and sister of Dr. John Still, Bishop of Bath and Wells; mar. 16 Dec. 1574; died 24 Dec. 1579 in childbed; bur. at Hadley. 1st wife. =

Adam Winthrop, born 10 Aug. 1548 in St. Peter's, Gracechurch; succeeded to Groton 1594, then of the Temple; died 1623, æt. 75; bur. and M.I. at Groton. s.p. =

Anne, dau. of Henry Browne of Edwardston, clothier; mar. 20 Feb. 1579; died 19 April 1629; bur. and M.I. at Groton. 2nd wife.

Alice Winthrop, born 15 Nov. 1539; mar. Sir Thomas Mildmay, son of William Mildmay above; died 8 Nov. 1607.

Bridget Winthrop, born 3 May 1543; mar. Roger Alabaster of Hadleigh, and died 4 Nov. 1614 at Tharfield, co. Hereford.

Mary Winthrop, born 1 March 1544; mar. 1st William Celie of London, and 2ndly Abraham Veysie of Ipswich.

Catherine Winthrop, born 17 May 1550.

Susanna Winthrop, born 10 Dec. 1552; mar. Dr. John Cotta; died 9 Aug. 1604 at Coventry.

Anne Winthrop, born 16 Jan. 1585; mar. 25 Feb. 1604 Thomas Fones; died 16 May 1619.

Jane Winthrop, born 14 June 1592; mar. 3 Jan. 1612 Thomas Gostling of Groton, clothier; she died 16 May 1616.

Lucy Winthrop, born 9 Jan. 1600; mar. 10 April 1622 Emanuel Downing of the Inner Temple, and later of New England; she died 19 April 1679.

Stephen Winthrop, born 24 March 1618 at Groton; one of Cromwell's Colonels and M.P.; died 1658 at London; mar. and left issue. Will (418 Wootton).

Adam Winthrop, born 7 April 1620 at Groton; died 1652, æt. 32, at Boston; mar. and left issue.

Deane Winthrop, died 16 March 1704, æt. 81, at Boston, Mass.; mar. and left issue.

Nathaniel, William, Ann, and Sarah Winthrop, died infants.

Samuel Winthrop, youngest son, a Quaker, born 28 Aug. 1627 at Groton; planter of St. Christopher's, later of Antigua; Deputy-Governor of latter 1667—1669; Registrar 1669—1671; died 1674 at Antigua. Will dated 18 Dec. 1672, but not on record. His plantation was called "Groton Hall." =

Elizabeth .... mar. June 1648 at Rotterdam. Will dated 11 Dec. 1675; sworn 5 Jan. 1675-6.

Samuel Winthrop, Junior, born before 1657; styled Lieut. 1678; granted 237 acres 1682; died in or before 1701. =

.... stated to have been a dau. of Governor Philip Warner. (No proof.)

John Winthrop, born before 1657 at St. Christopher's; twin with Samuel.

Thomas Winthrop, born Feb. 1660 at St. Christopher's; died young.

Stephen Winthrop, under 17 in 1675; living 1679; died young.

Elizabeth Winthrop, born before 1654 at St. Christopher's; mar. 1st, 1 Nov. 1666, William Mildon of Bristol and Nevis, merchant; his will dated 17 June, proved 23 Aug. 1669 (32 Bence); s.p.; mar. 2ndly Captain Francis St. John, Secretary of Antigua, who died 1670; mar. 3rdly, 1672—1675, Colonel Rowland Williams.

Sarah Winthrop, born *circa* 1655 at St. Christopher's; mar., before 1675, Colonel Samuel Jones; by his will dated 15 June 1684 he left her over 1000 acres; s.p. by him; mar. 2ndly Edward Byam, youngest son of General William Byam.

Rebecca Winthrop, born in Antigua; under 16 in 1675; mar. *circa* 1679 Col. Willoughby Byam. His will dated 25 May 1690; sworn 31 March 1692.

Sarah Winthrop, mar. 24 Aug. 1690 Colonel Henry Lyons of Antigua. His will dated 24 April 1714; sworn 21 June 1715. He owned "Groton Hall" plantation in North Sound, apparently through his wife.

Elizabeth Winthrop of Antigua, widdow. Will dated 11 Dec. 1675. To my son Henry Winthrop my part of Barbuda & all the stock there. To my son Sam[l] Winthrop all monies in Urope [*sic*], also Long Island, & my land & storehouses at S[t] John's, & my gray Barbuda horse. To my dau. Eliz[th] Williams £6 st. for a tankard. To my dau. Sarah Jones 10,000 lbs. & my own silver tankard. To my dau. Rebecca Winthrop 40,000 lbs. at 16, my side saddle, & 2 negros, my silver coadile cup & cover, my silver porringer, & all clothing. To Jonas Langford for his care in looking after me in my sickness 4000 lbs. & my great bible. To my son Stephen Winthrop my part of Groaten Hall plantation by my dear husband Sam[l] Winthrop, dec[d], by his will given to me, he to pay legacies. If Stephen die single then to my son Sam[l], but if he marry & die without male issue then to my son Sam[l], & he to pay 60,000 lbs. to Stephen's widow. My son Sam[l] to manage till my son Stephen be 17. My 3 friends Sam[l] Jones, Jonas Langford, & Edmund Hull, overseers & guardians of my 2 children Rebecca & Stephen, "y[e] true ministers of y[e] gospell whom y[e] world in scorn call quakers bee intertained and accomodated freely and assisted in what business or occassions y[t] have from time to time with all Curtesie possible. Lastly, my deare Children, I commend you all to y[e] true feare of the Lord and y[e] Instruction and Guidance of Christ y[e] Light, who alone is God's salvation to y[e] ends of y[e] earth, farewell." Witnessed by William Barnes, Francis Carlile. St. John's, 5 Jan. 1675 appeared Mr. William Barnes and Mr. Francis Carlile. Signed by Rowland Williams. Recorded fo. 134 in Book of Protests, Secretary's Office, 8 Aug. 1679.

Joseph Winthrop. Will dated 13 Oct. 1679, 31 Charles II. My wife Kath. & my dear dau. Sarah Winthrop, Ex'trices, & to have all my estate equally, & after my wife's death all to my dau., & if she die without issue all my real estate to the issue male of my brother Sam[l] Winthrop, then to the 1st son of my brother Henry Winthrop, & whoever of my brother's sons shall inherit to pay to Sam[l] & Tho. Williams my nephews, sons of Col. Rowland Williams, 100,000 lbs.

each, & to my niece Eliz^th Williams 60,000 lbs., to my niece Frances St Johns 50,000 lbs. To my sister Eliz^th Williams, my sister Sarah Jones, & my sister Rebecca Byam £10 st. each for a piece of plate. Major Wm Barnes & Capt Saml Jones to assist my Ex'trices. Witnessed by John Vernon, William Barnes, Samuel Winthrop. Before ye Judge of ye Precincts of St. John's, Jeremiah Watkins, on 12 Nov. 1679, appeared Major William Barnes and Mr. Samuel Winthrop. Recorded in ye Book of Protests, fos. 141 and 142, Secretary's Office, St. John's, 12 Nov. 1679.

Mary Winthorpe, spinster. Will dated 6 Sep. 1759. To my mother a negro girl & then to my niece Mary Hayghue. Jas. Brebner to be Ex'or. Witnessed by Patrick Grant. By His Excellency George Thomas was sworn Patrick Grant 26 Feb. 1760. Recorded 2 April 1760.

Samuel Winthrop, youngest son, by his 3^d marriage, of Gov. John Winthrop of Mass., was b. at Groton Manor, Aug. 28, 1627, came to N.E. with his mother in 1631, & was subsequently a student at Harvard Coll., near Boston.

His father's property became much impaired by the dishonesty of his agent in England, and Samuel left Boston at an early age to seek his fortune. In 1645 he is known to have been in London, in 1645-6 in Teneriffe, in 1647 in Barbados & St Kitts, in 1648 in Fayal & in Holland. In June 1648 he is stated to have mar. in Rotterdam, a Dutch lady, Elizabeth . . . . About 1650 he established himself as a planter in Antigua, but subsequently removed to St Kitts, where he resided several years, & then re-established himself in Antigua, where he died, it is believed in 1674, though the precise date has not yet been ascertained. About ten years previously he became a Quaker, under the influence of his particular friend, the celebrated Geo. Fox, during the latter's stay in the West Indies.

Wm Coddington of Rhode-Island, writing to Gov. John Winthrop of Connecticut in 1672, mentions a report that the latter's brother Samuel was to be named Gov. of Antigua, & there are other reasons for thinking he might have received this appointment had he desired it but for his death in the prime of life. Some 25 of his letters to his father & brother John are still preserved in Boston, & most of them have been printed in Winthrop Papers, part iv. (Mass. Hist. Soc. Coll., series 5, vol. viii.). They give a very pleasing impression of his character, & abound in references to West Indian affairs. I have never seen an abstract of his will, but it is stated that he devised his estate in New North Sound, Antigua, commonly known as "Groton Hall Plantation," jointly to his 3 elder sons (Henry, Joseph, & Samuel) & his wife Eliz^th, & that the latter devised her ¼ to her y^st son Stephen. The said Eliz^th, wid. of Samuel, is believed to have died in the latter part of Dec. 1675, or early in 1676. Her will is dated Dec. 11, 1675. (Communicated by R. C. Winthrop, jun., of Boston.)

Geo. Heathcote, writing to his kinsman Gov. John Winthrop of Connecticut, under date of New York, March 21, 1667-8, speaks of having recently heard from his (Heathcote's) parents in Antigua, and adds, "I heard thy brother Samuel was Commander-in-chief, and that he said he did intend to give up his Commission, for it was a thing as it were in a manner forced upon him." Geo. Heathcote's father was agent to Col. Middleton at Antigua. (See 2 Proceedings, Mass. Hist. Soc., vol. v., p. 105.) (*Ibid.*)

SAMUEL WINTHROP TO HIS FATHER.

S^t X^tpors, August : 30 : 1647.

Hono^rd Father

S^r,—My laste vnto you was from the Barbados, where I advized of my health and purpose of coming downe to this Island wth a parcell of wines, wch is now put in execution, &, blessed bee God, well sold. I thought to have remained at the Barbados, but want of a passage hath diverted my minde. I must now p'foarce see London or Holland, I must not lie still and begge. Sir Thomas Warner hath used me verry kindely here and showne me a great deale of favor both in advice & assistance, being a stranger, & like wise his Lady interteyned me wth a great deale of courtesy, who is now gon for Holland. Pray S^r be not unmindfull in yor next letters to returne him thankes.

('Life and Letters of John Winthrop,' vol. ii., p. 368.)

The following letter of his is recorded in an old book of deeds at St. John's *circa* 1670—72:—

Governor Warner,

By the Commission thou hast given out to Merchants for View of the Estate of Daniel Ely,* deceased, I perceive that thou hast taken a very Commendable care for prevention of all imbezzellments and for preservation of such intrustm^ts as were in his hands of other persons, Now in regard some Marchants in Barbadoes, Major John Hallett, Francis Bend, and Richard Forstall have Considerable Efects in his hands, and are persons who imployed him by my recomendation I request in their behalfes that what the Comissioners have found to belong to the s'd Marchants, and the invoices Letters, &^c, may be delivered to me for their use, that I may cause the orders formerly given to the deceased to be performed for which I shall be accountable, & remain thy assured real friend,

SAMUEL WINTHROPE.

COLL^O PHILLIPE WARNER, Governor of Antigua.

Recorded & Exam^d p' WILL. BARNES, Dep. Sec^ry.

(For other Letters, see Vol. I.)

Samuel Winthrop signs land warrants as Deputy-Governor of Antigua during 1667 and 1668.

1669, Jan. 6 and March 10. He signs with Colonel William Byam as joint Deputy-Governor.

1669, Feb. 14. His name appears as Register.

1668. Sarah Winthrop, spinster, grant of Maiden Island.

1668. Barbuda granted to Captain Samuel Winthrop, Captain Joseph Lee, William Milden, and Francis Sampson, and their heirs, for 32 years, subject to 4½ per cent. on the produce.

1669, Sep. 1. Jonas Langford, Administrator of Francis Sampson, deceased, for 66,000 lbs., sells to Samuel Winthrop of Antigua, planter, a moiety of 200 acres in New North Sound.

1670, July. Collonel Samuel Winthrop signs as President of ye Council.

1670, Aug. 23. The death of Captain Francis St. John the Secretary announced. (Minutes of Council.)

Sir Charles Wheeler, Bart., Captain-General, superseded Winthrop because he was a Quaker, and the latter records this in the following terms: "Heere ends ye Commission of Samuel Winthrop, Register for all Records in this Booke, delivered to Majo^r Rowland Williams, now Register by ye Commission & appointm^t of Coll^o Phillip Warner, dep^y Govern^r of this Island, Antigua, as witnes ye hands of both ye said Registers this sixteenth day of January 1671."

1671, April 3. The Council met at Captain Samuel Winthrope's house.

1672, April 6. Samuel Winthrop of Antigua, planter, and late Registrar; Letter of Attorney to John Muhell (?).

1672, June 1. Elizabeth St. John of Antigua, widow of Francis St. John, leases to her brother Henry Winthrop the estate given her by her father Samuel Winthrop.

* Daniel Ely of Antigua, deceased. Adm'on 14 Oct. 1674 to Daniel Ely the father. (P.C.C.)

1673, Feb. 15. Sixty-four acres are surveyed for Mr. Samuel Jones which he purchased of Colonel Samuel Winthrop.

1675, Sep. 28. Mr. Joseph Winthrop, 40 feet by 50 feet in Bridge Town by Governor Williams; surveyed 8 Oct. 1675.

1677, March 10. Surveyed for Mr. Henry Winthrop 190 acres in Bermudian Valley, in right of his wife Heneretta (*sic*), part of the lands formerly in the possession of Captain William Kyn.

An Act to enable Mr Henry Winthrop, Capt Jos. Winthrop, & Lieut. Sam. Winthrop to sell the late Capt Sam. Winthrop's plantation in New North Sound, called Grooton Hall (*sic*), wh he gave by his Will equally to his said three sons & to his wife Eliz. She at her death gave her ¼ to Steph. Winthrop, yst s. of Capt. Sam. Winthrop—There are debts of 350,000 lbs.—Power granted to sell their share after 26 July 1678. Signed by Governor James Vaughan and William Barnes, Speaker.

1678, Jan. 25. Captain Joseph Winthrop and Samuel Winthrop of Antigua, Gentlemen, for 5125 lbs. of sugar sell to Major William Barnes 150 acres in New North Sound.

1679, May 23. Captain Joseph Winthrop and Samuel Winthrop of Antigua, Gentlemen, for 15,125 lbs., and for our brother Stephen Winthrop, sell to Mr. John Nibbes 20 acres in New North Sound.

1679, July 10. By Indenture Henry Winthrop, son of Captain Samuel Winthrop, deceased, who owns ⅛ of Berbuda ($\frac{1}{16}$ from his father and $\frac{1}{16}$ from his mother), sells this for six negros and 20,000 lbs. of sugar.

Indenture of same date between Samuel Winthrop, jun., son of Captain Samuel Winthrop, deceased, of the one part, and Colonel Philip Warner, Attorney of Colonel Christopher Codrington, and Lieut.-Colonel John Codrington of Barbados, of ye other part. Whereas the said Captain Samuel Winthrop with Joseph Lee, Francis Sampson, and William Mildred (*sic*), obtained a lease of Berbuda for 32 years from William, Lord Willoughby, dated 1 Oct. 1668, and Captain Samuel Winthrop by will dated 18 Dec. 1672 gave his ¼ to Elizabeth his wife and to his three sons Henry, Joseph, and Samuel, the said Samuel Winthrop, jun., has $\frac{1}{16}$ which he now sells for six negros.

1679. Indenture of Agreement between Henry Winthrop, Gent., and Robert Carden,* Gent., deed of partnership for seven years. Each to put eight negros on Winthrop's plantation.

1679, Oct. 19. Peter Welch, planter, and Jane his wife, widow of Thomas Moses, deceased, sell 30 acres at Bermuda Valley to Henry Winthorp, Gent.

1679, Jan. 22. Catherine Winthrop, widow of Captain Joseph Winthrop, conveys her plantation of Synamon Valley of 300 acres to Major William Barnes in trust for her use for life, then for her daughter Sarah and her heirs, remainder to the first son of Samuel Winthrop, Gent., and to first son of Mr. Henry Winthrop.

1680, June 30, 31 Charles II. Indenture between Richard Slicer of Antigua, planter, and Katherine his wife, relict and Ex'trix of Captain Joseph Winthrop, son of Captain Samuel Winthrop, both of Antigua, deceased, of the one part, and Colonel Philip Warner, Attorney to Colonel Christopher Codrington, and Lieut.-Colonel John Codrington of Barbados, of the other, reciting that Samuel Winthrop, Joseph Lee, Francis Sampson, and William Milden obtained a lease of Burbooda for 32 years from William, Lord Willoughby. Samuel Winthrop's will was dated 18 Dec. 1672, and he gave his ¼ to his wife Elizabeth and to his three sons Henry, Joseph, and Samuel. Joseph Winthrop had $\frac{1}{16}$, and sold it on 10 July 1679 to Colonel Philip Warner as Attorney for the Codringtons for six negros. Richard Slicer and Katherine his wife now quit claim for one negro.

* Half-brother to Henry Winthrop's wife.

1682, Aug. 4. Samuel Winthrop, Esq., patent for 237 acres by Sir William Stapleton.

1688. Henry Winthorpe was rated on 26 slaves and 250 acres at Bermuda Valley. (St. Mary's Vestry Book.)

1692. . . . . Winthorp was rated on 31 slaves and 250 acres. (*Ibid.*)

1696. Mr. Henry Winthorpe was rated on 32 slaves and 250 acres. (*Ibid.*)

1700, Oct. Draught of Winthrop Act reciting that Hen. Winthrop, ye father & guardian of his son Saml, has a plantation of 240 acres of waste & no other estate, owes ½ the value of the land to St Peter's Parish for taxes. Said Sam. is now 8 years of age. (Minutes of Assembly.)

Act. No. 120. Private. An Act to enable John Frye, junior, and George Thomas, or either of them, to sell 240 Acres of Land, situate & lying in the Division of New North Sound, for Payment of the Publick & Parish Taxes, & selling the Surplussage for the Maintenance & Advancement of Samuel Winthrop, a Minor. Dated the 12th day of April, 1701.

1704, Sep. 19. Henry Winthorp of Antigua, Gent. Deed of gift of negro to his daughter Mary Winthorp.

1706, June 7. Mr. Henry Winthorpe was rated on 38 slaves and 190 acres. (St. Mary's Vestry Book.)

In 1684, 1685, and 1686 he was one of the Gentlemen of the Vestry.

1709-10, March 3. I Henry Winthrope of Antigua in consideration of a marriage lately solemnized between William Lavington of Antigua, Gent., and Mary Winthrop my daughter, and in lieu of a portion, have granted to him 12 negros.

1710, Dec. 26. Henry Winthrop leases to Charles Jacob of Antigua, planter, 10 acres for five years at £6 currency per annum.

1716, April 26. At a Vestry Meeting in St. Mary's Parish, Pew 26 was alloted to Mr. Samuel Winthorpe.

1738. Thomas Winthorp described as a free mulatto.

1767. St. Mary's Vestry. Samuel Winthorpe taxed on 11 slaves (no land).

PARISH REGISTER OF ST. JOHN.

Buried.

1779 June 27 Robert Winthorpe.

PARISH REGISTER OF ST. PAUL.

Buried.

1773 Dec. 13 Mrs Winthrope.

PARISH REGISTER OF ST. PHILIP.

Married.

1690 Aug. 24 Henry Lyons to Sarah Winthrop.

"Winthorpe's" of 231 acres is in St. George's Parish. In 1852 Inigo Thomas was the proprietor. Winthorpe's Bay and Winthorpe's Village are adjoining.

Pedigree of Wise.

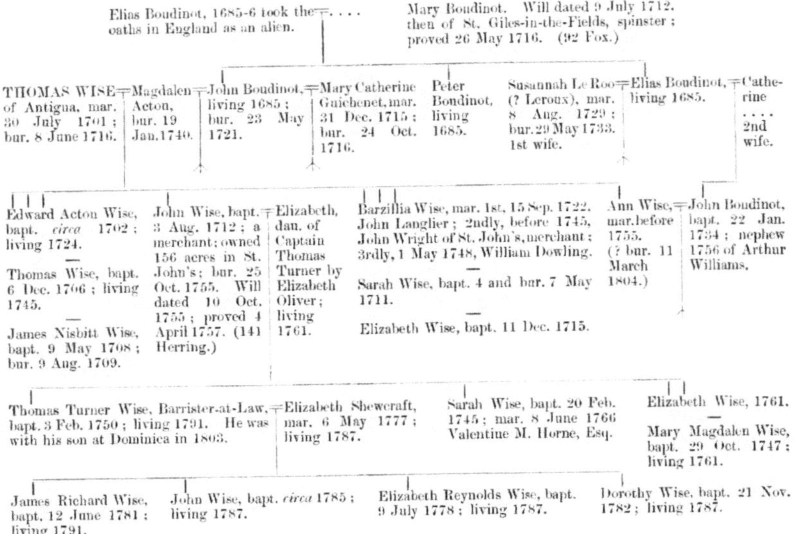

Mary Boudinot of St. Giles in the fields, spinster. Will dated 9 July 1712; proved 26 May 1716 by Mary Belin. (92 Fox.) To the poor of the French Ch. 1 guinea. My neph. Elias Boudinot, living in New York, 1 g[a], & to all his brothers & sisters 1 g[a] each. To John Belin my neph. & to his dau. at Rotterdam 1 g[a] each. To my niece the wife of Isaac Vaillant 1 g[a]. To Jas. Belin, s. of Allard Belin, my neph., dec[d], 1 g[a]. To Mary Belin my gr'dniece, dau. of M[r] Jas. Belin & Jane Montague, the rent of 38 livres Tournois on a house at Maran's Boat in the province of Xaintonge in France. To my grdneph. Allard Belin, merch[t] in Lond., & to his sister Jane Mary Belin, £60 each. All res. to my s[d] gr'dniece Mary Belin & Ex'trix. Witnessed by Stephen Brigand, Anthony Sion, Isaac Delpech, Notary Public. Translated from the French by latter.

Henry Guichenet of London, Gent. Will dated 1 July 1724; proved 20 March 1730 by Timothy Motteux. (66 Isham.) Bound beyond the Seas. To my sist. Eliza & bro. Peter £5 ea. To M[r] Timothy Motteux & his wife & M[r] Paul Breton a guinea ring each. To my loving bro. Gideon Guichenet, apprenticed to a haberdasher in Barbekin, all res. either here, in the Orphans' Court of Rotterdam, or the West Indies. M[r] Timothy Motteux of Leadenhall Str., merch[t], Ex'or. Witnessed by John Perkins, Samuel Dupuy, Notary Public, C. Thompson.

John Wise of Antigua, merchant. Will dated 10 Oct. 1755; proved 4 April 1757 by John Watkins, Esq.; power reserved to Elizabeth Wise the widow, Ann Boudinot, Rowland Oliver, and Francis Farley. (141 Herring.) £10 for funeral. To be buried in a deal coffin, lamblacked, without any covering or ornament. Some time ago I purchased in fee simple from my brother-in-law Tho. Turner a plantation in Five Islands Division, subject to 2 mortgages made by Tho. Turner to Rich[d] Oliver, Esq., of London, merch[t], & to a lease (expiring in 1759) to John Murray, Esq., at £280 a year, & by him assigned to Ephraim Jordin, in which lease £30 a year of the rent is payable to Tho. Turner, & the remainder to Rich[d] Oliver, & further if the former die during the term his wife Eliz. Turner is to have £50 a year. The lease is duly recorded in the Register's Office. Since the above purchase I mortgaged the equity of redemption to Rich[d] Oliver for £600. To prevent his foreclosing my Ex'ors are to sell all my land in S[t] John's Town to pay him. To my wife Eliz. all furnitnre, plate. To my daus. Sarah & Mary Magdalen Wise £1000 c. each at 21, & £40 c. a year till 15 then £50 till 21. To my friend M[r] Henry Livingston of London a 2 g. ring. All my estate to my son Tho. Turner Wise, & in default of issue to my said 2 daus., then to my wife, she paying to my sister Ann Boudinot £2000 c. My good friends . . . . & my wife Eliz. during her widowhood & my sister Ann Boudinot whilst single Ex'ors & Guardians. The Hon. Rowl[d] Oliver, Esq., John Watkins, Esq., & Francis Farley, Esq., to be also Ex'ors. Witnessed by John Sheriffe, John Boudinot. On 25 Nov. 1755 before George Thomas, Esq., Captain-General and Governor-in-Chief. were sworn John Sheriffe and John Boudinot before John Webb, Notary Public. Recorded also at S[t] John's.

Arthur Williams, planter, in his will, dated 3 March 1756, bequeathed his nephew John Boudinot £40.

Richard Oliver, Esq., by his will dated 17 Sep. 1761, bequeathed an annuity of £35 c. to his niece Elizabeth Wise and a negro to each of her daughters Sarah and Elizabeth Wise.

Christian Sheweraft, spinster. Will dated 28 Oct. 1787. About to take a voyage. To my sister, the wife of Thos. Turner Wise, all my plate & furniture except my press which I give to my niece Dorothy 2[d] dau. of my sister Eliz[th] Wise.

To my nephew Richd James, 1st son of my said sister Elizth, negros. To my niece Elizth Wise negros. To John Wise negros. Thos. T. Wise, Ex'or. Witnessed by J. N. Gilbert, Elizabeth Royall, George Wyke. By Hon. John Stanley, Commander-in-Chief for the time being, was sworn John Gilbert 8 Oct. 1793. Recorded 2 Nov. 1793.

Close Roll, 12 Geo. III., Part 3, Nos. 21 and 22.

Indenture tripartite made the 2nd June 1772 between Thomas Turner Wise, Esq. (son and heir and residuary devisee and legatee of John Wise, late of Antigua, merchant, deceased), of the 1st part, William Livingston of Antigua, Esq., of the 2nd part, and the Hon. Francis Farley of Antigua, Esq., of the 3rd part, witnesseth that in consideration of 5*s.* paid to each Thomas Turner Wise and William Livingston grant to Francis Farley all that plantation, late of John Wise, deceased, containing 156 acres, in the parish of St. John, Antigua, bounded E. with the lands heretofore of John Haddon, and late of John Weeks, deceased, but now of James Nibbs, Esq., N. with land late of John Weeks, deceased, but now of James Nibbs, and the lands late of Henry James, but now of Giles Blizard, Esq., S. with the lands of the Hon. Edward Otto-Bayer, Esq., and W. with Flashes, and also the dwelling-house, and all slaves, etc., described in a schedule, and all horned cattle and living stock whatsoever, for one whole year, that Francis Farley may be in actual possession. Benjamin Cook, David Gibbs, witnesses.

Schedule (names given): 29 men, 8 boys, 4 children, 30 women, 12 girls.

No. 21.

Indenture tripartite made the 3rd June 1772 between the above. Whereas John Wise made his last Will the 10th Oct. 1755 (recited), and whereas some doubts have arisen whether the estate limited to Thomas Turner Wise his son is an estate in fee simple or tail; and whereas the legal estate in fee simple of and in the said plantation, slaves, etc., is standing out in William Livingston as assignee of Richard Oliver, late of Antigua, but late of Great Britain, Esq., who was mortgagee of the plantation. Now this Indenture witnesseth that to obviate all doubts touching the nature of the estate claimed by Thomas Turner Wise under the Will of his father, Thomas Turner Wise and William Livingston, in order to dock and bar all estates tail and remainders, and in consideration of 5*s.* paid to each, grant, etc., to Francis Farley all that plantation (as in No. 22) to have and to hold to the use of Thomas Turner Wise and his heirs for ever, and to no other use, etc., and they appoint, etc., Francis Farley, Esq., and Langford Lovell, Esq., of Antigua, their Attorneys.

1685-6, March 5. Elias Boudinot, Peter, Elias, John, and Mary, his children, aliens born, made free denizens of England.

1687, April 9. Also Francis Vaillant, Jaqueline his wife, Paul, Francis, Isaac, Susanna, and Mary their children, and on Dec. 16, Ozee Belin, Ozee his son. ('Lists of Aliens,' Camden Society.)

1699, March 24. Henry Guichenet, French, born in Province of Guienne, took the oaths at Antigua as an alien.

Edward Perrie, writing 20 June 1710, names the briganteen "Antigua," Captain Gideon Guischinett, Commander, for Bristol.

1714. Mr. Thomas Wise, five proportions of land in St. John's Town, granted 15th instant, surveyed 10 March.

1724, May 16. Indenture between Edward Acton Wise of Antigua, Gent., and Magdalen Boudinot, widow and relict of John Boudinot of Antigua, merchant: sale of seven negros.

PARISH REGISTER OF ST. JOHN.

Baptized.

170– (? 1702) Feb. 4 Edwd Acton s. of Thomas Wise & Magdalen his wife.
1706 Dec. 6 Thomas S. of Thomas Wise & Magdalen his wife.
1708 May 9 James Nisbet Wise S. of Thomas Wise & Magdalen his wife.
1709 Jan. 28 Gideon S. of Henry Guichenet & Catherine his wife.
1711 May 4 Sarah d. of Thomas & Magdalen Wise. B. 4 March.
1711 Dec. 23 Benjamin Buex s. of Henry Guichenet & his wife.
1712 Aug. 3 John s. of Thomas Wise & Magdalen his wife.
1715 Dec. 11 Elizth D. of Thos Wise & Magdalen his wife.
1734 Jan. 22 John the s. of Elias Boudinott & Catherine his wife.
1745 Feb. 20 Sarah the D. of John Wise and Elizth his wife.
1747 Oct. 29 Mary Magdalen the D. of John Wise and Elizabeth his wife.
1750 Feb. 3 Thomas Turner the S. of John Wise and Elizabeth his wife.
1778 July 9 Elizabeth Reynolds the d. of Tho. Turner Wise and Elizabeth his wife.
1781 June 12 James Richard the s. of Tho. Turner Wise & Eliz. his wife.
1782 Nov. 21 Dorothy the D. of Thomas Turner Wise and Elizabeth his wife.
(? 1785, Feb.) 22 John Infant S. of Thomas Turner Wise and Elizabeth his wife.

Married.

1701 July 30 Thomas Wise & Magdalen Acton.
1715 Dec. 31 John Buddinott and Mary Catharine Guichenett. L.
1722 Sep. 15 John Langelier and Barzillia Wise. L.
1729 Aug. 8 Elias Boudinott and Susannah Le Roo.
1733 Oct. 29 Peter Guichinett and Susannah Strong. L.
1739 May 24 John Litch & Mary Bondinott. L.
1747 Nov. 21 Henry Guichenet and Sarah Scandret.
1766 June 8 Valentine Morris Horne to Sarah Wise. L.
1777 May 6 Thomas Turner Wise to Elizabeth Shewcraft. L.

Buried.

1701 April 8 John Francis Guichenet s. of Henry Guichenet & Catherain his wife.
1709 Aug. 9 James Nisbitt Wise S. of Thomas Wise & Magdalen his wife.
1711 May 7 . . . . Wise D. of Thos. Wise.
1712 Aug. 5 Mrs Guichenett.
1715 Feb. 4 Eliz. Wise.
1715 Sep. 28 Adrianetta Guichenett.
1716 June 8 Thomas Wise.
1716 Sep. 19 Benj. Guichenett.
1716 Oct. 24 Mary Catherine Buddinot.
1719 Nov. 15 John Acton Bondinett, a child.
1721 May 23 John Boudinett.
1733 May 29 Mrs Susannah Boudinett.
1739 Oct. 9 Susanna ye w. of Peter Guichenet.
1740 Jan. 19 Magdalene Boudinet.
1754 May 10 Sarah Guichenet the wife of Hen. Guichenet.
1755 Oct. 25 John Wise.
1757 Nov. 25 Peter Guichenet.
1773 May 7 Henry Guichenett.
1779 Sep. 29 Richard Oliver Wise.
1804 Mar. 11 Ann Boudinot.

Pedigree of Woodley.

ARMS.—*Sable, a chevron between three owls argent.**
CREST.—*An owl argent.*

WILLIAM WOODLEY of Nevis. Had two children living 1678. ═ . . . .

. . . . Wall. [Lieut. Jasper Wall a Member of Assembly of Nevis 1687.] Arms: *Argent, a bend between three wolves' heads, couped sable.* ═ . . . .

William Woodley of St. Christopher's, Esq., partner with Mathew Mills 1707, then æt. 32; took up French lands 1718; living 1733; dead 1743. ═ Bridget Wall, 2nd dau., born 1682. Will dated 9 Feb. 1756, then of Little Parndon, co. Essex; proved 1 April 1756. (125 Glazier.)

Jasper Wall of Nevis, died 1714.

Tobias Wall, heir to his elder brother Jasper 1714; of Nevis 1722, then of St. Christopher's 1733; died 1744. Will dated 2 July 1743, then of Southampton, Esq.; proved 11 July 1747. ═ . . . . s.p.

William Woodley, living 1756. ═ . . . . Payne.

John Woodley of the "Profit" Plantation, St. Kitts, of 195 acres (? entered Gray's Inn 1742). Will dated 8 July 1767, then of Cork Street; proved 2 Dec. 1767. (468 Legard.)

Jasper Woodley, matric. from Oriel College, Oxford, 4 Feb. 1724-5, æt. 16.

William Woodley, matric. from Queen's College, Oxford, 21 April 1738, æt. 16; inherited the "Profit" Plantation; Governor and Captain-General of the Leeward Islands 1766 and 1792; died June 1793 at St. Christopher's. ═ Frances, only surviving dau. and heir of Abraham Payne of St. Christopher's; mar. 30 March 1758 at St. George's, Hanover Square; died 29 March 1813, æt. 75, at Bloxworth, co. Dorset.

Edward Parson, Junior, 1st son and heir 1771; Member of Council 1786 and 1798. ═ . . . . Eight children 1798.

Rachael, dau. of William Yeamans of Antigua; bapt. 1731; mar. 1st, 13 July 1749, James Emra, Esq., of Nevis and Antigua, and 3rdly Major Lockhart Russell of Antigua. ═ William Woodley Parson of Great Marlborough Street and of St. Christopher's. Will dated 4 Nov. 1766; proved 7 Aug. 1770. (307 Jenner.) ═ . . . . dau. of . . . . Newth; mar. 25 Jan. 1749

William Woodley, 1st son 1767; President of St. Christopher's 1807; Lieut.-Governor of Berbice 1808; died 1810. ═ . . . .

John Woodley, living 1767; Member of Council and Solicitor-General of St. Christopher's 1807; Attorney-General 1826. ═ Catherine, dau. of Rev. Dr. Horne of Chiswick; died 15 July 1818, æt. 38, at St. Kitts.

Mary Woodley, 1st dau., mar. 1st, 7 Sep. 1815, Hon. Frederick Noel, Captain R.N., who died 27 Aug. 1833; 2ndly, in 1838, Lieut.-General Sir Thomas Hawker, K.C.H., who died June 1858; she died 24 Jan. 1867, æt. 74, in Kensington.

Eliza Woodley, mar. 13 Feb. 1817 Captain Willows.

* The above arms have been reproduced from a bookplate which *may* have belonged to John Woodley of St. Kitts; they are also identical with those borne by Woodley of Halshanger, co. Devon, of which family there is a good pedigree in Vivian's 'Visitations,' p. 858.

Mathew Mills of St. Christopher's, æt. 36 in 1707.╤. . . .
(See next page.)

William Mills,╤. . . . Member of Council of Nevis 1754.

John Mills of Great St. Helen's, merchant, died 1 Sep. 1769. Will dated 8 Sep. 1768; proved 6 Oct. 1769. (346 Bogg.)

Mary Mills, mar. Mathew Towgood of Clement's Lane, banker. His will dated 13 Jan. and proved 19 Feb. 1791. (102 Bevor.)

Thomas Mills of Nevis,╤Frances . . . . of St. Eustatia. Esq., 1753, later of London, merchant (? of Great St. Helen's in 1767).

Elizabeth Mills.

Ann Mills.

John Mills, Esq., died╤Sarah . . . . born 21 Sep. 1743; died 19 Sep. 1819. M.I. at Hitchin. 15 Aug. 1781, æt. 42, at Grenada. M.I. at Hitchin, co. Herts.

Thomas Milliken Mills of Bishopshul, co. Somerset, Esq. Will dated 15 Jan. and proved 3 Nov. 1774. (400 Bargrave.)

William Maynard Mills.

Mathew Mills.

John Colhoun Mills, President of╤. . . . Nevis, died at sea 15 July 1828, æt. 56. M.I. at Hitchin.

Henry Roper Mills, born 25 March 1784; died 14 Feb. 1790. M.I. at Hitchin.

Elizabeth Mills, born 14 Jan. 1770; died 19 May 1811. M.I. at Hitchin.

Sarah Pittman Mills, born 19 Oct. 1774; died 11 July 1827. M.I. at Hitchin.

John Mills, lost at sea in 1825, æt. 18. M.I. at Hitchin.

Thomas Mills╤Margaret, 2nd dau. of John Blanchard, Commander E.I.C.S.; mar. 16 Sep. 1845 at St. Pancras.

Edward Parson, Esq., Secretary-General of the Leeward╤. . . . Islands; Member of the Council of Montserrat 1693; dead 1701.

Lucretia Wall, 1st dau., mar. John Mills of St. Christopher's, Esq.; he died 1739; she was dead 1747.

Anne Wall, youngest dau., a spinster 1714; mar. . . . . Newth; living at Hunsdon, co. Herts, a widow, 1747.

(? Edward) Parson, Member╤Grace, cousin of William Frye of Montserrat, Esq., 1730. Will dated 14 May and proved 10 Oct. 1735. (214 Ducie.) of Council of Montserrat, died 1723-4.

Mary Woodley╤Edward Parson of Little Parndon, co. Essex, Esq., and of St. Christopher's. Will dated 1 June 1771; proved 17 July 1780. (374 Collins.)

Henrietta Parson, mar. John Dasent of Nevis; he was born 8 Sep. 1712, removed to Antigua, Member of Assembly 1742, and died 10 April 1747.

Read Parson, matric. from Christ Church, Oxford, 20 May 1731, æt. 18; of St. Kitts 1733.

James Parson of Montserrat, mar. Anne Mills; she remar. Nicholas Gallwey, who died 1736.

John Parson, 3rd son, living 1756 and 1771.

James Parson, living 1756 and 1771.

Jasper Parson, 5th son, living 1756 and 1771.

Read Parson, living 1756 and 1771.

Mary Parson.

Lucretia Parson.

Bridget Parson.

Frances Parson, born after 1756.

Grace Parson, a minor 1756.

Frances Woodley, 1st dau. 1767; mar. 11 Aug. 1784 Henry Bankes, Esq., M.P. of Kingston Lacy; she died 22 Nov. 1823, æt. 62, in Old Palace Yard; he died 1835. (See Hutchins' 'Dorset.')

Harriet Woodley, 2nd dau. 1767; mar. 11 Jan. 1788, at St. George's, Hanover Square, Thomas Pickard, Esq., of Bloxworth, co. Dorset; he died s.p. 1830.

. . . . youngest dau., mar. P. L. Fletcher of Gwerabeyled, Wales; she died 15 Dec. 1808.

Frances Anne Woodley, mar. 27 Oct. 1819 Frederick White, Esq., of Parham.

Caroline Woodley, died 29 Dec. 1815, æt. 10.

Amelia Woodley, mar. 6 June 1818 John Wright, Esq.

John Mills of St. Christopher's, Esq., Member of Council; his death announced 8 May 1739. ═ Lucretia, sister of Tobias Wall of St. Christopher's; dead 1747.

Mathew Mills of St. Christopher's, æt. 36 in 1707; Chief Justice temp. Governor Hamilton; bur. 4 July 1744 at St. George's Parish.

. . . . 1st wife. ═ John Mills of St. Christopher's, Esq., Member of Council 1739; resigned 1742; living at Exeter 1743; of Twyford, co. Southants, 1747. Will dated 13 Jan. and proved 8 Nov. 1758. (339 Hutton.) ═ . . . . mar. settlement dated 9 March 1753. 2nd wife.

Anne Mills, mar. 1st James Parson; 2ndly Nicholas Gallway of St. Kitts, whose will was dated 14 May 1736 and proved 9 Feb. 1736-7. (25 Wake.) She was named 1743 in the will of Tobias Wall.

Lucretia Mills, mar. Nathaniel Parson.

Frances Mills, mar. . . . . Colhoun.

Mathew Mills, living 1746.

Lucretia Mills, mar. 28 Jan. 1747, at St. George's, Hanover Square, Henry Compton of Bistern, co. Southampton. (See Burke's 'Landed Gentry.')

Elizabeth Mills, mar. Sir John Pole of Shute, co. Devon, Bart.; she died 13 Aug. 1758 and he 19 Feb. 1766.

Mathew Mills, Citizen and Goldsmith of London. Will dated 1664. (84 Bruce.) Dau. Alice, son Thos, wife Frances.

Mountserratt. Grace Parson, widow. Will dated 14 May and proved 10 Oct. 1735 by Anthony Hodges, Esq.; power reserved to Nathaniel Webb, Esq. (214 Ducie.) My sister-in-law Mrs Sarah Parson, son-in-law John Dasent, Henrietta Dasent, & my dau. Jane Parson & granddau. Grace Dasent each a suit of mourning. My son Edward Parson £20 for a suit & £20 for a ring. Granddau. Grace Dasent £300 at 21. My dau. Jane Parson 2 riding horses. My daus. Henrietta Dasent & Jane Parson all negros, mules, cattle in schedule annexed to lease by me made to Wm Fenton, Esq., dated 1 Sep. 1731; also all money with Mr Wm Coleman, merchant in London, & all residue. Nathl Webb of this Island, Esq., & Anthony Hodges, Esq., merchant in London, Ex'ors. Witnessed by John Molineux, Simeon Bouveron, Harry Ross. By Hon. William Frye, Esq., President and Deputy-Ordinary, appeared John Molinenx, Esq. Henry Parker, Deputy-Secretary. On 10 Oct. 1735 appeared Anthony Hodges of London, merchant, and George French, late of Montserrat, now of London, Esq., Secretary of the said Island.

Tobias Wall of Southampton, widower. Will dated 2 July 1743; proved 11 July 1747. To my sister Anne Newth £5000, her dau. Lucretia Newth. To my nephew John Mills who now lives in or by Exeter £2000. To my nephew Wm Woodley £2000, t'is the said Wm that is now married to Mrs Paine. To my nephew John Woodley £2000, brother to the said Wm. To my sister Woodley £100 a year. To Mrs Eliz. Weekes who now lives at my house £500 & the house I now live in. To her sister Weekes that is now married to Capt. John Wise £100. To Ann Gallwey, widow of Nichs Gallwey, £500. All residue here, in Nevis & St Kitts, with my sugar house to Mathew Mills, Esq., of Abchurch Lane, London. Bridgett Woodley, widow, & Ann Newth, widow, sisters, appealed as next-of-kin against the will.

1744, Aug. Tobias Wall of Southampton, Esq., deceased. Adm'on to John Mills of Exeter, Esq., the nephew, pending the suit between Mathew Mills, Esq., the nephew and residuary legatee who propounds the will, and Bridget Woodley, the sister of deceased.

Mathew Mills, late of St. Christopher's, now of Soho Square, Esq. Will dated 30 July 1746; proved P.C.C. 18 Jan. 1753 by Cornelia Mills the relict, Peter Soulegre, Esq., and John Mills; power reserved to Thomas Mills. (23 Searle.) All my estate to my 4 trustees & Exor's. To my wife Cornelia all jewels, use of plate, the interest of £10,000 st., & ½ the nett profits of my estate. Trustees to invest all residue of my personal est. till my 1st child Peter Mathew Mills, born 23 March 1743, be 21, then to divide it among all my children equally, with remainder to my nephew Math. Mills (son of my dear brother John Mills) & my other neph. Math. Mills Gallwey (son of my sister Ann Gallwey). As to my real estate, all my plantations & negros to my Trustees for my s. at 21 in tail, & in default of issue ½ the rents to my wife & all my est. to my sd 2 nephews, but if the latter ever inherit they shall pay £5000 st. to my other neph. Henry Parson (son of my sister Lucretia Parson). My wife, my father-in-law Peter Soulegre, Esq., my cousin Tho. Mills of St Christopher's, Esq., & my cousin John Mills of Abchurch Lane, London, Trustees, Ex'ors, & Guardians. Witnessed by Richard Phillips, Jonathon Popham, Henry Cock.

Peter Loubier, the Elder, of Christ Church, co. Middlesex, weaver. Will dated 19 Dec. 1749; adm'on 1 Feb. to Mary Loobier the relict. (49 Greenly.) To my son John £300 at 24. To my son Peter £300 at 24. To my wife Mary all residue. Witnessed by Abraham Bluzee, John Keen, William Carter.

Bridget Woodley of Little Parndon, co. Essex, widow. Will dated 9 Feb. and proved 1 April 1756 by John Woodley the son, Edward Parson, Esq., and William Woodley, Esq.; power reserved to William Woodley the son and William Woodley the grandson. (125 Glazier.) My 2 sons Wm & John, my son-in-law Edwd Parson of Little Parndon, Esq., my kinsman Wm Woodley of Rougham, co. Suffolk, Esq., & my grandson Wm Woodley, Ex'ors. To my grandson Wm Woodley £50. To my grandson Edwd Parson, junr, 1st son of my Ex'or, & to my grandson Wm Woodley Parson £50 each. £1000 & my silver plate to my granddau. Grace Parson, dau. of Edwd Parson & Mary his wife, if she die under 21 then to their next surviving 1st dau., then to their younger sons. My late husband Wm Woodley's will. All my furniture, linen, & pictures to my dau. Mary Parson & £2000. All residue in Gt B., Nevis, St X'phers, to my Ex'ors on trust to sell & the proceeds to my 4 grandchildren John, Jas., Jasper, & Read Parson, sons of Edwd & Mary Parson, at 21, then to their daus., then to their 2d son Wm Woodley Parson. Witnessed by Henry Wilmot, H. Osborn, J. Price.

Codicil dated 9 Feb. 1756. To my son Wm Woodley £2000. All estate to accumulate for my said 4 grandsons at 21.

Colonel Peter Soulegre of St. Christopher's, settled there 1702; a native of Languedoc; æt. 30 in 1707; Member of Council 1722—1728; died 12 March 1760 in London. Will dated 16 Dec. 1758; proved 28 March 1760. (124 Lynch.) ═ . . . .

Mathew Mills, Junior, of St. Christopher's, Esq., Speaker 1727; Member of Council 1738; of St. Anne's, Soho, 1747; murdered 19 Nov. 1752. Will dated 30 July 1746; proved 18 Jan. 1753. (23 Searle.) ═ Cornelia Soulegre, mar. 23 June 1743 at St. George's, Hanover Square; died 19 Dec. 1757 at Richmond.

Catherine Soulegre, mar. 13 Dec. 1750, at St. George's, Hanover Square, Sir Stephen Theodore Janssen, 3rd Bart., Lord Mayor and Chamberlain of London; she died 25 Oct. 1757 and he 8 April 1777. His will dated 1 Oct. 1776; proved 22 April 1777.

Peter Mathew Mills, born 23 March 1743-4; heir to his grandfather Peter Soulegre 1758. Will dated 20 April 1791, then of Twickenham, Esq.; proved 17 July 1792. (390 Fountain.) ═ Catherine . . . .

Mary Mills, living 1776 and 1792.

Lucretia Mills, 2nd dau., mar. 9 Aug. 1764 John Smith Budgen* of Dorking, co. Surrey, Esq.; he was born 28 June 1741 and died 25 May 1805; she died 8 Nov. 1798; both bur. in Dorking Chancel.

George Galway Mills, M.P. for Wallingford and Winchelsea; friend of the Prince Regent and cousin of Lord Lavington; Member of Council for St. Christopher's 1800. ═ . . . .

Charles Andrew Mills, youngest son 1791.

Charles Hamilton Mills, 1st son and heir. ═ Frances Jane, 1st dau. of Benjamin Brown Davis, Esq., of Antigua and St. Christopher's; mar. 21 July 1820 at the latter place.

Charles Andrew Mills, drowned at St. Christopher's; s.p.

* Only son and heir of Thomas Budgen, M.P. for Surrey in the two last Parliaments of George II., by Penelope dau. of Daniel Smith, Governor of Nevis. (Berry's 'Surrey.')

John Mills of Woodford Bridge, co. Essex, Esq. Will dated 13 Jan. 1758; proved 8 Nov. 1758 by John Mills and Henry Compton, Esquires. (339 Hutton.) To my 1st dau. Lucretia wife of Henry Compton, Esq., £100. To my yst dau. Eliz. wife of Sir John Pole, Bart., £100. To my good friends John Woodley of London, Esq., John Mills & Thos. Mills of Gt St Helen's, London, merchts, & Steven Payne of St X'ophers, Esq., £50 each. To John Woodley £200. On my marriage with my present wife, by Indenture of 9 & 10 March 1753, I settled £300 a year on her, which I confirm. To John Woodley & Tho. Mills all residue of my real estate in St X'ophers, Nevis, or Gt Britain, in trust ⅓ to any 1st son by my present wife, & in default ½ to my grandson Henry Compton, 1st son of Henry Compton of Bisterne, co. Southampton, Esq., then to his 2d son John & 3d son Chas. Langley, etc., then to the beirs of Henry Compton, then to the sons of my dau. Lucretia by any other husband, then to my grandson John Pole, Esq., son of Sir John Pole, Bart., then to his other sons, then to the sons of my dau. Eliz. by any other husband, then to my nephew Peter Mathew Mills, son of my late brother Mathew Mills, deceased, then to my nephew Mathew Mills Gallaway, son of my sister Anne Gallaway, then to my nephew Henry Parsons, son of my sister Mrs Lucretia Parsons, then to my nephew Wm Colhoune of St X'ophers, Esq. The other moiety of the ⅓ to my grandson John Pole, etc. One other third in trust for my grandson Henry Compton, etc. The other ⅓ to my grandson John Pole, etc. To any younger children I may have £5000 & £200 a year. To my wife £100 a year. To my grandson John Compton (not yet 21) £100 a year. Trustees to be Ex'ors. To Eliz. Mills, dau. of Mathew Mills of Bridgewater, £100. Freedom to my mulatto Jas. Seaton, £15 a year, & £100 in 2 years. Witnessed by Mark Noble, Thomas Clark, Samuel Jones, servants to Mr Mills.

1st Codicil dated 13 Jan. 1758. To my godson John Creake, son of Mr John Creake of Alresford, co. Southampton, £40 a year till 21, then £400. To Sarah Betty Webb dau. of Mr John Webb of Winchester, £100.

2nd Codicil dated 25 Sep. 1758. Out of the ⅓ given to John Pole, Esq., £5000 is to be paid for the younger children of Henry Compton. My dau. Eliz. has died since I made my will. Witnessed by Samuel Figgale Reade, Thomas Guillaume, Mark Noble.

Peter Soulegre of Dean Street, Soho, co. Middlesex, Esq. Will dated 16 December 1758; proved 28 March 1760 by Catherine Durban, spinster, Ralph Willett, and Timothy Waldo, Esquires; power reserved to Peter Papon. (124 Lynch.) £300 to the directors of the French Church Hospital "La Providence." £100 to the managers of the French Charity for bread. £50 to the poor of Richmond. £200 to my late wife's niece Mrs Cath. Durban. £10 each to the Rev. Messieurs Marchandis & Misson, Ministers of the French Hospital, commonly called the Greek Church, for 20 poor people. £20,000 on trust to Ralph Willett of Shooter's Hall, Esq., my kinsman Peter Papon of London, merchᵗ, & Timothy Waldo of Salter's Hall, London, Esq., for my granddau. Henrietta Janssen, dau. of my son-in-law Steph. Theodore Janssen, Esq., Alderman of London, at 21 or marriage with her father's consent, & in default to my grandson Peter Mills (son of my late dau. Cornelia Mills) & his 2 sisters Mary Mills & Lucretia Mills. £12,000 to the said trustees for my said granddau. Mary Mills at 21 or marriage, then to her sister Lucretia Mills at 21. £12,000 to same trustees for my granddau. Lucretia Mills at 21 or marriage, then to her sister Mary Mills. £300 a year to my son-in-law Steph. Theod. Janssen, charged on my plantation in St Christopher's. £31 10*s*. yearly to my brother-in-law John Brozet of Southampton during the joint lives of him & his wife. £25 a year to my nephew Mr Peter Papon for managing my plantation. £100 a year to my niece Cath. Durban, she to take charge of my 2 granddans. Mary & L[illegible]'s, also plate & furniture to the value of £400, £2000 for her own use. £21 yearly to Mrs Viala, widow of Mr Viala, late of France. All my plantations in or near St Christopher's to my trustees for my grandson Peter Mills

& his heirs at 21, then to my 2 granddaus. Mary & Lucretia Mills equally. £300 to my cousin Stephen Cabibel & £50 to each of his 2 daus. £100 to Mrs Louisa Papon. £50 to my sister Mrs Mary Loubier of Province of Languedoc. £50 each to my 2 nephews Jas. & Peter Loubier of same place. £50 to my nephew Peter Soulegre of same place. £50 to my niece Susannah Allatby of Castres in said Province. £50 to Mr Lewis Brozet. £50 each to the 3 sons of the late Mr Jas. Brozet,* now at St Christopher's. £50 to Mr Moses Castas of Piccadilly. £200 to each of my Ex'ors. £100 to Mr Francis Guichard of St Christopher's. £50 to Stephen Payne, Esq., & to Mrs Mary Payne his wife £100. £50 to Louis Boisniel, son of Jas. Bosniel of Mazanet in France. £50 to Lieut. Stephen Papon, now in foreign parts in H.M. service. £15 to each of my godsons Peter Graciense, son of John Graciense, & Peter Viala. £15 to the son of Mr Ardesoif of the Strand, jeweller. £15 to Mr Benezet, engraver. A year's wages to my servants. All residue to my grandson Peter Mills. My kinsman Peter Papon, Mrs Cath. Durban, Ralph Willett, & Timothy Waldo, Ex'ors. Witnessed by Thomas Bennett, John Stanley, Samuel Groom.

Captain Stephen Papon of H.M. 22nd Regiment of Foot. Will dated at Bristol July and proved 13 Aug. 1763 by Peter Papon, Esq., the brother. (398 Cæsar.) A bond for £100, due since 1753, to Mr Baily of Dublin. £50 to my sister Lucy Guinard. £30 to my cousin Peter Brozet & £30 to his bro. Lewis. I owe £14 to Mr Nightingall & £40 to my uncle John Brozet at Southampton. All sums due in the agent Mr Calcraft's hands to my dear bro. Mr Peter Papon of Leicester Fields, he sole Ex'or. Sums owing me by the heirs of Archd Cathcart to be cancelled if they pay Mr Cottingham, mercer, £14, & £10 to a taylor Mr Hamilton knows. On 10 Aug. 1763 John Palairet of St. James, Westminster, and Eleanor Carpenter of Bristol, spinster, swore that they knew testator.

William Woodley Parson of Great Marlborough Street, Esq. Will dated 4 Nov. 1766; proved 7 Aug. 1770 by Rachel Parson the relict; power reserved to Edward Parson, Esq., the father, and William Maxwell. (307 Jenner.) All my estate to my wife Rachel, but if she die before me then £500 to Wm Maxwell of Carredon in Scotland, Esq., £100 each to Mrs Mary Udny, widow of Mr Ernest Udney, Mr Tho. Yeamans Elliott, & Mr Cha. Yeamans Martin, all these nephews & nieces of my wife. £100 also to Mrs Grace Patterson, her particular friend, & all residue to my sisters Lucretia, Bridget, & Frances at 21. If my negros & plantations should be sold after my death Mr Wm Maxwell to have the refusal. My wife Rachel, my father Edwd Parson, & Wm Maxwell Ex'ors. Witnessed by Henry Wilmot, John Lancaster, Valentine Henry Allott.

John Woodley of Cork Street, Burlington Gardens, St. James, Westminster, Esq. Will dated 8 July 1767; proved 2 Dec. 1767 by William Woodley, Esq., the nephew, and William Woodley, Esq. (468 Legard.) To be buried anywhere but in the vault belonging to Edwd Parson, Esq., in the parish church of Little Parndon, co. Essex. Interest of £500 for my sister Mary Parson his wife, then to her dau. Frances Parson at 21, who was born after the death of my mother Mrs Bridget Woodley & was not provided for by her. To my neph. John Parson, my sister's 3d son, £60 a year on account of his ill-health. To Jasper Parson, my sister's 5th son, £200. To my niece Frances wife of my nephew Wm Woodley 100 gs. To my great-nephew Wm Woodley, 1st son of my nephew Wm Woodley of Hill Str., Berkeley Sq., Esq., £100, & to his bro. John, the 2d son, £1000 & all my silver plate & 3 gold seals with my coat of arms. To my great-niece & goddau. Frances Woodley, 1st dau. of my said neph., £1000 at 18, & to Harriet, his yr dau., £1000 at 18. To my 2 very good friends Mr John Mills & Mr Tho. Mills, merchts in Great St Helen's, 20 gs. each. To my godson Mr John Mills, jun., 1st son of latter, £100. To my godson John Woodley, natural son of Wm Woodley of Eccles, co. Norf., £100. To Mr Walter Charles of Morden College, co. Kent, 20 gs. a year. To Mr Cha. Hancock of Little Parndon 10 gs. To Mr Henry Freelove of Hendon, co. Midd., 20 gs., he to be employed to bury me. To my servant John Frost £20. To my servant Francis Oakley £50. To Jane Woodley, a negro woman, 20 gs. & 10 pistoles a year. My bond to Mary Spencer, spr, for £100 a year. My negro Andrew Woodley, living on my plantation called the Profit in St Christopher's, to be free if the estate pass from our family. To my neph. Wm Woodley £100 for a ring. To Wm Woodley of Eccles £1000. All residue to my neph. Wm Woodley & his heirs male, then to Wm Woodley of Eccles Hall, they 2 Ex'ors. Witnessed by John Hogarth, Glasshouse Street, Thomas Penstone in Cork Street, James Hart, Cork Street, Ab. Charles Adye of Lincoln's Inn.

John Mills of Great St. Helen's, merchant. Will dated 8 Sep. 1768; proved 6 Oct. 1769 by Mathew Towgood and Sherland Swanston; power reserved to William Mills, Esq., the brother. (346 Bogg.) To my aunt Sarah Legg of Bristol £25 a year. To my aunt Sarah Bretland of Exeter £20 a year. My sister-in-law Sarah Mills £50 a year. John Brooks £10 a year & £200 at the termination of his apprenticeship, & to his sister Sarah Brooks £15 a year & £200 at 21. My cousin Elinor Harvey of Axminster £10 a year, & to her sister Eliz. Harvey the same. John Mills Player, my clerk, £20. Samuel Charles, my clerk, £10. Mr Wm Stead, treasurer of the Baptist fund, £50. Mr Sherland Swanston, my clerk, £500. My brother Wm Mills £100 & £1000 on trust for his daus. Eliz. & Ann Mills at 21, they so well provided for. To my said brother & Mr Sherland Swanston £12,000 on trust for my sister Eliz. Towgood & her children. My brother-in-law Mathew Towgood, her husband, who is in business. To Mathew & Mary Towgood £2500 in trust for their 5 children, John, Wm, Mathew, Eliz., & Mary, at 21. To the said trustees £12,000 in trust for my nephew Thos. Mills, son of my brother Thos. Mills, deceased, at 21, & if he die £5000 to his sister Sarah Mills at 21. £5000 to my trustees for her. All residue to my said nephew Thos. Mills, & if he die for all my nephews & nieces. Trustees to be Ex'ors. My nephews Thos. Mills & John Towgood to succeed in my business.

Codicil. My cousin Mr John Mills & Mr John Warrington, my partners, 5 gs. each. Mr Sherland Swanston, formerly my clerk, now my partner, so give him only £200. My ⅜ of the business.

On 29 Sep. 1769 appeared Leaver Legg of Cornhill, woollen-draper, and John Danvers of New Court, Broad Street, hosier.

On 5 Oct. 1769 appeared Mathew Towgood of Great St. Helen's, Esq., and John Mills of ditto, Esq., and swore that testator died 1 Sep. last.

On 2 Aug. 1837 adm'on of estate left unadministered by Mathew Towgood and Sherland Swanston, deceased, was granted to John Towgood and Samuel Towgood, the sons and Ex'ors of John Towgood, deceased, the nephew. William Mills, the brother, died without proving the will. Sherland Swanston survived Mathew Towgood, and appointed his wife Frances Swanston and his son Sherland Hill Swanston his Ex'ors. Frances Swanston died, and Sherland Hill Swanston proved it and died intestate, and Thomas Mills the nephew died under 21.

* See Archer's 'M.I. in the West Indies,' p. 420, and under Payne, *ante*, p. 7.

Edward Parson of Little Parndon, co. Essex, Esq. Will dated 1 June 1771; proved 17 July 1780 by Edward Parson, Esq.; power reserved to Mary Parson the relict and William Woodley, Esq. (374 Collins.) To be buried in the parish church. By the articles on the marriage with my wife Mary she is entitled to the interest on £8000, & £2000 was to be for her own use, but in lieu thereof I give her my mansion house & 40 acres for life, & the use of all furniture, coaches, & horses, also £1000 & £700 a year. To each of my 4 sons, John, James, Jasper, & Read, & to each of my 4 daus., Mary, Lucretia, Bridget, & Frances Parson, £1500 at 21. My sister M[rs] Jane Osborn £250, & her sons Humphry Osborn & John Husband Osborn £100 each. My friend W[m] Woodley of Eccles, co. Norfolk, Esq., £20. All residue to my 1st son Edward. Legacies to be in lieu of marriage articles. My wife, W[m] Woodley, & my son Edward to be Guardians & Ex'ors. Witnessed by Charles Freeman, William Sewell, Philip Martin.

Thomas Milliken Mills of Bishopshul, co. Somerset, Esq. Will dated 15 Jan. and proved 3 Nov. 1774 by Judith Butler Dunbar, sole Ex'trix. (400 Bargrave.) All my messuages, mills, etc., of the customary manor of Taunton Dene, co. Somerset, all my negros, cattle, coppers, & my share of the negroes & crops, which were my late father's, Tho. Mills, in Nevis, & all residue to M[rs] Judith Butler Dunbar, wid., of Bishopshul, & sole Ex'trix. Witnessed by Richard Escott, W. P. Thomas, Proekter Thomas.

Peter Leheup of Albemarle Street, Esq., in his will dated 24 Nov. 1774 (224 Collier), refers to his mortgage of £7000 charged on the estates of the late John Mills, Esq., of St. Christopher's.

Sir Stephen Theodore Janssen, Bart., by his will dated 1 Oct. 1776 and proved 22 April 1777, bequeathed £500 to his nephew Peter Mathew Mills, Esq., and £300 each to his nieces Miss Mary Mills and L. Budgen. John Smith Budgen, Esq., of Dorking, was one of his Ex'ors.

Mathew Towgood of Clement's Lane, banker. Will dated 13 Jan. and proved 19 Feb. 1791 by John Towgood. (102 Bevor.) To my wife Mary £200 a year. To my son John the interest & arrears of £6800 in respect to a legacy of £12,000 bequeathed to my said wife by the will of her late brother John Mills the Elder, Esq. To each of my other children, W[m] Towgood, Mathew Towgood, Eliz. Kemble, & Mary Savery, £100. To my father & sister £50 each. All residue to my son John, he to deduct £4000 for said annuity, & residue to be divided into 5 parts, $\frac{1}{5}$ to him, $\frac{1}{5}$ to W[m], $\frac{1}{5}$ to Mathew, $\frac{1}{5}$ to Fra. Kemble, Esq., husb[d] of my dau. Eliz. Kemble, $\frac{1}{5}$ to John Savery, Esq., husb[d] of my dau. Mary Savery. My son John Towgood sole Ex'or.

Peter Mathew Mills of Twickenham, co. Middlesex, Esq. Will dated 20 April 1791; proved 17 July 1792 by the two Ex'ors; power reserved to Mary Mills, spinster. (390 Fountain.) I confirm the deed of trust to W[m] Colhoun of Wretham, co. Norfolk, Esq., one of my Ex'ors. All my real estate in S[t] Christopher's to my 1st son George Galway Mills, subject to the trusts of the said deed & the payment of legacies. To my youngest son Chas. Andrew Mills £2000 over & above the £8000 payable to him by the said deed. To Cosmo Merigi, who lives with me, £300 & £50 a year. W[m] Colhoun, John Smith Budgen of Twickenham, Esq., & my sister Miss Mary Mills of the same place Ex'ors. Witnessed by T. Simpson, T. Marshall, John Smith.

Codicil. 20 Sep. 1791. To Cosimo Louis Merrigi of Florence all my personal estate abroad. £50 rings to my Ex'ors. Witnessed by Charles North Hunt, No. 8 Featherstone Buildings, Holborn, Thomas Pycroft, clerk to Mr. Hunt, John De Lannoy at Mr. Moore's, Holborn.

Close Roll, 21 Geo. II., Part 7, No. 34.

Indenture quinquepartite made the 11th April 20 Geo. II., 1747, between John Mills of Twyford, co. Southampton, Esq., eldest son and heir-at-law of Lucretia Mills his late mother, deceased, who was the eldest sister of Tobias Wall, late of the town and county of Southampton, Esq., deceased, and as such is the nephew and one of the three coheirs of the said Tobias Wall, of the 1st part, Bridget Woodley of Hunsdon, co. Herts, widow, eldest surviving sister of Tobias Wall, one other of the coheirs, of the 2nd part, Anne Newth of Hunsdon, widow, youngest surviving sister of Tobias Wall, one other coheir, of the 3rd part, Mathew Mills of St. Ann, Soho, in the Liberty of Westminster, Esq., younger son of the said Lucretia Mills, who claimed to be the sole residuary legatee in the will of Tobias Wall, of the 4th part, and Drewry Ottley, late of the island of St. Christopher, now of Redlyon Street, Holborn, Esq., and Samuel Martin of Berry Street, St. James, Westminster, Esq., of the 5th part. Since the death of Tobias Wall there have been suits-at-law, but terms have been now come to, and by an agreement of 22 and 23 Jan. 1745 the residual estate was to be shared as to $\frac{1}{4}$ to John Mills, $\frac{1}{4}$ to Bridget Woodley, $\frac{1}{4}$ to Ann Newth, and $\frac{1}{4}$ to Mathew Mills, as tenants in common, and it was conveyed to Drewry Ottley and Samuel Martin on trust. Whereas the said Tobias Wall had an estate at Nevis, with mills, etc., heretofore the estate of Jasper Wall his elder brother, and he had worked it with his own estate from 1714, when Jasper died, till 1744, when he himself died, and a will of Jasper Wall has just been produced whereby he gave his lands for want of heirs to his brother Tobias, to his three sisters Lucretia Mills, Bridget Woodley, and Ann Wall now Newth. Now this estate shall be considered as part of that of Tobias Wall, and in consideration of £480 paid to Bridget Woodley by John Mills and Mathew Mills, and of 5s. paid to Drewry Ottley and Samuel Martin, all parties are satisfied, and they convey the estate to the said two trustees for one year, deed to be enrolled in Chancery Court and recorded in America, and they appoint Ralph Payne, Thomas Mills, and Charles Molineux, all of St. Christopher's, Esquires, and Joseph Herbert and Richard Lytcott, both of Nevis, Esquires, their Attorneys.

[There was a previous Indenture 19 Geo. II., Part 17, No. 3.]

Close Roll, 2 Geo. III., Part 20, Nos. 16 and 17.

Indenture made the 20th Oct. 1762 between William Woodeley of Hill Street, St. George's, Hanover Square, Esq., and Frances Woodeley his wife (only surviving daughter and heir-at-law of Abraham Payne, late of St. Kitts, deceased), of the one part, and John Audain of St. Kitts, Surgeon, of the other part, witnesses that in consideration of 5s. paid to each, William and Frances Woodley grant, etc., to John Audain all that plantation in the parish of St. Paul, Capisterre, late the estate of Abraham Payne, abutting and bounding N. on the lands of Lewis Brotherson, Esq., E. on the King's Road leading round the island, S. on a path that divides the plantation of the heirs of John Franks, Esq., and other lands of John Franks, leading to White Flagg Bay, and W. on the sea, containing 79a. 3r. 8p., and the dwelling-house, etc., for one whole year, yielding therefore one peppercorn, etc. Abraham Audain, Jonathan Price, witnesses.

No. 16.

Indenture made the 21st Oct. 1762 between William Woodley and Frances his wife, of the one part, and John Audain, of the other part. Whereas John Audain hath contracted with William and Frances Woodley for the complete purchase in fee simple of the above plantation and negros for £7100 sterling, William and Frances Woodley grant, etc., to John Audain (as above), it is further witnessed that they grant to him and his heirs all those 56 negro and other slaves (names given), etc., on the plantation.

Close Roll, 7 Geo. III., Part 16, Nos. 1 and 2.

Indenture made the 21st Dec. 1767 between His Excellency William Woodley, Captain-General and Commander-in-Chief over all H.M.'s Leeward Caribbee Islands, of the one part, and Henry Wilmot of Bloomsbury Square, Esq., of the other part, witnesseth that in consideration of 5*s.* William Woodley grants, etc., to Henry Wilmot all that plantation called the Profit in the parish of St. John, Capisterre, St. Kitts, late the estate of John Woodley, Esq., deceased, containing 195 acres, and all negros, bounded to the E. by the lands of Edward Parson, Esq., to the N. by the lands of .... Millard, Esq., W. by the lands now or late belonging to Herbert Guichard, Esq., and S. by the mountain, for one whole year, yielding therefore one peppercorn, to the uses of an Indenture to be made, etc., and William Woodley appoints Stephen Payne, Esq., and George Irvine, Esq., both of St. Kitts, his Attorneys.

No. 1.

Indenture made the 22nd Dec. 1767 between His Excellency William Woodley, etc., of the one part, and Henry Wilmot, etc., of the other part, witnesseth that for barring and extinguishing all estates tail and remainders, etc., and in consideration of 5*s.*, William Woodley grants, etc., to Henry Wilmot, in his actual possession being, all that plantation, etc. (as above), to the use of William Woodley and his heirs for ever, and to no other use. John Lancaster, Valentine Henry Allott, witnesses.

1678. Nevis. William Woodley, 1 white man, 1 white woman, and 2 white children: 2 negro women and 2 negro children.

1687, March. Nevis. Lieut. Jasper Wall a Member of the Assembly.

1693, May 8. Montserrat. Edward Parson a Member of the Council.

1700. Montserrat. The death of Colonel Thomas Delavall, the Lieut.-Governor, announced. Mr. Parsons, the senior Member of Council, being factor of the Royal African Company, cannot serve.

1704, Aug. 24. Montserrat. Edward Parsons appointed an Assistant to the Chief Justice of the Court of Common Pleas.

1705. St. Christopher's. List of Militia—Cornett Soulegre.

1707-8. Nevis. Jasper Wall, 1 white male, 16 negro males, 25 negro females.

1707-8. St. Christopher's. William Woodley, aged 32, in his household 1 man, 1 woman, and 1 boy; and in partnership with Mathew Mills, 57 slaves, viz., 21 men, 24 women, 4 boys, and 8 girls.

Peter Soulegre, aged 30, in his household 2 men, 1 woman, 1 boy, and 1 girl; and 36 negros, viz., 19 men, 11 women, 1 boy, and 5 girls.

Mathew Mills, aged 36, in his household 1 man, 1 woman, 2 boys, and 1 girl; and in partnership with William Woodley 57 slaves, as above.

1711. St. Christopher's. Mr. Mathew Mills, 1 man, 2 women, 6 children, and 37 negros.

St. Ann's, Sandy Point. Captain Peter Soulegre, 2 men, 1 woman, 1 boy, and 42 negros.

William Woodley, 1 man, 2 women, 3 children, and 28 negros.

1712. Montserrat. Losses from the French attack. Edward Parson £11,096.

1717. Memorial of Peter Cabibil, sen., of London, merchant, dated 22 Aug. 1717, that on 23 June 1702 he entered into partnership with Peter Soulegre, and the latter a few days after sailed to settle at St. Christopher's. They could not get any plantation there, so embarked their money in merchandize, which they lost to the amount of £1000 st. by the French Invasion of 1705. Later, Peter Soulegre obtained a grant of 150 acres on 30 March 13 Anne, and from 160 to 200 acres on 10 Sep. 1715, all French lands, which they have settled, and for which they desire a title.

1718. List of the 97 Grantees of French Lands at St. Christopher's. "Mr. Wm. Woodley. He is an industrious, honest Man, has a large family, but no land of his own in that or any of these Islands saving what he possesses by these Grants." (B. T. Leeward Islands, vol. 15.)

1718. Nevis. John Woodley, Member of Assembly, also in 1724 and 1730-31.

1721, Feb. 5. Antigua. In Chancery. Lawford Coles, Esq., *v.* Mathew Mills, Esq.

1722, May 12. St. Christopher's. Major Peter Soulegre appointed Member of Council.

1723-4. Montserrat. Death announced of Edward Parsons, a Member of the Council.

1727, Oct. 24. St. Christopher's. Mathew Mills elected Member of Assembly for Christ Church, Nichola Town; served as Speaker.

1728-9, March 24. Major Peter Soulegre writes from London resigning his seat at the Council of St. Christopher's.

1729-30. Montserrat. Mrs. Grace Parson, planter. 1 windmill, 1 cattle-mill, 1 man, 2 women, 2 girls under 14, 1 boy under 19, 119 slaves, 6 in family, 100 acres of cane, 30 cattle, 17 mules. (B. T. Leeward Islands, vol. 21.)

1733. St. Christopher's. Read Parsons then of St. John, Capisterre. (Act, No. 89.)

1735, Sep. 19. St. Christopher's. Peter Soulegre, Esq., has resigned his seat on the Council. (B. T. Leeward Islands, vol. 55, fo. 32.)

Governor Hamilton appointed Mathew Mills, Esq., Chief Justice of St. Christopher's in the place of Clement Crook (Oldmixon, vol. ii., p. 295). Oldmixon further states (second edition, 1741) that 53 years ago he himself went with Mr. Mills when he was to embark at Gravesend for Nevis.

1738, May 18. Edward Mann, Esq., of the Council of St. Christopher's, is about to resign, and Mathew Mills, jun., Esq., is proposed in his place. (B. T. Leeward Islands, vol. 55, fo. 139.)

1738, Nov. 27. The Governour writes that Peter Soulegre, Esq., of the Council, has been absent for many years, he supposes on H.M. leave. (*Ibid.*, vol. 26, fo. 19.)

1739, May 8. John Mills of the Council of St. Christopher's is dead. John Mills, Esq., is appointed to fill the vacancy. (*Ibid.*, vol. 55, fo. 160.)

1739, June 12. John Mills, Esq., to be of the Council of St. Christopher's *vice* John Williams, Esq.

1741, May 15. Mathew Mills, jun., then of the Council of St. Christopher's.

1742, March 23. Samuel Crooke, Esq., is appointed to the Council of St. Christopher's *vice* John Mills, who does not intend to return to the island, but wishes to resign. At the Court of St. James. (B. T. Leeward Islands, vol. 27.)

1743, Nov. 8. Mathew Mills, jun., Esq., of the Council of St. Christopher's, is in England, and John Mills, Esq., another Member, is also absent. (*Ibid.*, fo. 69.)

1752. In the 'London Magazine,' pp. 347—350, is a long account of the murder of Mathew Mills, Esq., of St. Kitts, by John Barbot, an Attorney. Mr. Mills was shot dead on 19 Nov.

1754, Aug. 6. At the Court of Kensington. William Mills, Esq., to be of the Council of Nevis *vice* William Jones, Esq., deceased.

About the latter half of the eighteenth century Mrs. Frances Mills of Enfield, co. Middlesex, and of St. Eustatia, left four sons, John, Thomas Milliken, William Maynard, and Mathew.

1761, May 28. Mr. Mills had leave to lay a flat stone over the grave of a relation. ('Annals of St. Helen's, Bishopgate.')

1767, June 18. On the application of Mr. Mills to be allowed to pay the sum of £18 to be excused serving the office of Church Warden, the Vestry, considering that his election into that office may be some years hence, agreed to accept thereof. (*Ibid.*, pp. 166 and 172.)

1786. The mandamus for Edward Parson to be of the Council of St. Christopher's was dated 24 July.

1798. April 5. Edward Parson, Member of the Council, writes to their Lordships that he has ten brothers and sisters, a wife and eight children of his own, and much business to settle, and desires extension of leave. Heraldic seal obliterated. ('Colonial Correspondence,' vol. 33.)

1800, Oct. George Galway Mills to be of the Council of St. Christopher's.

1807. President William Woodley writes 13 Aug. that he has appointed John Woodley, Esq., a Member of Council of St. Christopher's; and on 8 Sep. that he has nominated him Solicitor and Proctor-General *vice* W. A. Mardenbrough, deceased.

1807, Dec. It is stated that Mr. Woodley of St. Kitts has three estates there, producing 300 hogsheads yearly.

1808. President Woodley on 15 Nov. acknowledges the receipt of his appointment as Governor of Berbice.

1810. Charles Mills has been appointed Collector at Point à Pitre.

1823. Hon. John Woodley, Attorney and Advocate-General, Member of Council, A.D.C. to His Excellency with the rank of Lieut.-Colonel.

Hon. Charles Woodley, Member of Council, Assistant Justice of the Court of King's Bench and Common Pleas, Assistant Baron of the Court of Exchequer, and Collector at Basseterre.

Hon. William Woodley, Assistant Baron of the Court of Exchequer, Assistant Justice of the Court of King's Bench and Common Pleas. (St. Kitts Almanac.)

EXTRACTS FROM THE 'GENTLEMAN'S MAGAZINE.'

1749, Jan. 25. Wm. Woodley of Little Parndon, Essex, Esq;—to Miss Newth of Hertfordshire (p. 44).

1757, Dec. 19. Relict of Mat. Mills, Esq; at Richmond (1758, p. 46).

1758, March 30. Wm. Woodley of Hill Street, Esq;—to Miss Payne of Hanover-square (p. 196).

1760, March 12. Col. Soulagre aged 94 (p. 154).

1762, Jan. 23. Lady of Wm. Woodley, Esq. M.P. G[t] Bedwyn, a son (p. 44).

1763, July 26. Capt. Stephen Papon; he served as adjutant in the expedition against Louisbourgh, Quebec, Montreal, Martinico, and the Havannah (p. 415).

1764, Aug. 9. John Smith Budgen, Esq; of Surrey—to Miss Mills (p. 397).

1764, Nov. 6. J. Woodley, Esq; lately arrived from Carolina (p. 546).

1766, Nov. Lately. William Woodley, Esq; Gov. of the Leeward Islands in the room of Gov. Thomas (p. 496).

1784, Aug. 11. Henry Bankes, esq. of Kingston-hall, Dorset, to Miss Woodley, daughter of William Woodley, esq. ('Town and Country Mag.', p. 448.)

1788, Jan. 11. T. Pickard, esq. of Bloxworth, co. Dorset, to Miss Harriet Woodley, second daughter of Wm. W. esq. of Stratford-place (p. 81).

1791, Sep. Wm. Woodley, esq. appointed captain-general and governor in chief of his Majesty's Leeward Caribbee Islands, *vice* Shirley resigned (p. 878).

1792. Rev. W. Woodley, M.A. appointed to Swanbourne V. co. Bucks (p. 486).

1793, Feb. 3. The Lady of Wm. Woodley, esq. of Bury S[t] Edmunds, a son and heir (p. 184).

1793, June. At S[t] Christopher's, General Woodley, governor of the Leeward Islands (p. 768).

1798, Nov. 15. George Cerjat,* esq. of the royal cinque-port dragoons, and aid-du-camp to General Garth, to Miss Woodley, only daughter of Wm. W. esq. of Eccles, co. Norfolk (p. 1150).

1802, Oct. 7. At St. James' Church, Cha. Woodley, esq. to Miss Sophia Law (p. 973).

1805, May 25. At his house in Montpelier-row, Twickenham, co. Middlesex, in his 65th year, John Smith Budgen, esq. . . . . He has left one son a captain in the Surrey militia, and three daughters, who are unmarried. His father possessed a good estate in Surrey; and was invited to represent that county in 1751, on the death of Ld. Baltimore, and again at the general election 1754 (p. 495).

1807, Jan. In her 92d year, Mrs. Hannah Woodley, of Abingdon (p. 180).

1808, Oct. 8. William Woodley, esq. to be lieutenant-governor of Berbice (p. 1183).

1808, Dec. 15. Mrs. Fletcher, wife of P. L. F. esq. of Gweraheyled, Wales, and youngest daughter of the late Governor Woodley (p. 1191).

1810, May. Lately. At Beeche, Herts, Thomas Woodley, esq. At Berbice, Wm. Woodley, esq. lieut.-governor of Berbice (p. 500).

1813, March 29. At Bloxworth, co. Dorset, aged 75, Mrs. Woodley, widow of the late W. W. esq. Governor of the Leeward Islands (p. 393).

1815, Sep. 7. Hon. Capt. Noel, R.N. son of Sir G. Noel, of Exton, to the eldest dau. of the late William Woodley, esq. Governor of Berbice (p. 370).

1815, Dec. 29. At Kensington, aged 10 years, Caroline Woodley, fourth daughter of Governor Woodley, of the Island of Berbice (1816, p. 88).

1817, Feb. 13. Capt. Willows, East India Company's Military Service, to Eliza, second dau. of the late William Woodley, esq. Governor of Berbice (p. 274).

1818, June 6. John Wright, esq. of Montagu-street, Portman-square, to Amelia dau. of the late Governor Woodley, of Berbice (p. 562).

1818, July 15. In the Island of S[t] Christopher, aged 38, Catherine, wife of Hon. John Woodley, member of the Council of that island, and daughter of Rev. D[r] Horne of Chiswick (p. 374).

1819, Sep. 19. In her 76th year, at Roxley-house, Willian, Sarah, relict of John Mills, esq. late of Hitchin, Herts, etc. (p. 472).

1819, Oct. 27. Fred. White, esq. of Parham, to Frances-Anne, third daughter of the late Wm. Woodley, esq. Governor of Berbice (p. 458).

1820, July 21. At S[t] Christopher's, West Indies, C. Hamilton Mills, esq. eldest son of G. Galway Mills, esq. to Frances-Jane daughter of the Hon. B. Brown Davis, esq. of that island (p. 272).

* He was born 1755 and died 1801. They had an only son William Woodley Frederick Cerjat, born 1800. (See Pedigree of Cerjat in 'Misc. Gen. et Her.,' New Series, vol. iv., p. 223.)

1828, July 15. On his passage from the West Indies John Colhoun Mills, esq. late president of the island of Nevis. (Annual Register.)

1838, Oct. Lately. At Nice, William Woodley, esq. Commander R.N. etc. (p. 454).

1845, Sep. 16. At St Pancras, Thomas Mills, esq. of the island of Nevis, West Indies, second son of the late John Colhoun Mills, esq. President of the Legislative Council there, to Margaret, second dau. of the late John Blanchard, esq. Com. East India Co. Naval Serv. (p. 524).

1847, Jan. 13. At Bath, Cornelia, dau. of the late John Smith Budgen, esq. (p. 332).

1867, Jan. 24. At 23 Kensington-gate, aged 74, Mary, relict of the late General Sir Thomas Hawker. She was the eldest dau. of William Woodley, esq., and married first, in 1815, Capt. the Hon. Frederick Noel, R.N. (brother of Charles 1st Earl of Gainsborough), who died Dec. 1833; and secondly, in 1838, Gen. Sir T. Hawker, and was again left a widow in June 1858 (p. 396).

PARISH REGISTER OF ST. JOHN, ANTIGUA.

Baptized.

1738 June 29 John the s. of William Mills & Rebecka his wife.

1751 Mar. 30 John the s. of William Mills and Eleanor his wife.

1760 Feb. 12 Frances, Edward, & Ann, the children of William Mills and Elinor his wife.

Married.

1744 July 27 William Mills and Elinor Gibson.

Buried.

1737 June 16 James Mills, brother of William Mills of this Island.

1738 Mar. 30 Sarah ye D. of William Mills.

1738 June 30 John ye S. of William Mills.

1742-3 Mar. 22 Mary Mills, a child.

PARISH REGISTER OF ST. PAUL.

Baptized.

1746 Aug. 20 John S. of William and Rebecca Mills.

1747 Mar. 20 Samuel a Posthumous S. of William Mills, Deceased, and Rebecca his Widow.

Buried.

1817 Dec. 1 John Mills.

ST. MARY CAYON, ST. CHRISTOPHER'S.

Baptized.

1728 June 27 Wm S. of W^m & Ann Woodley.

1728-9 Mar. 16 James s. of James & Ann Brozet.

CHRIST CHURCH, NICHOLA TOWN.

Buried.

1729 May 14 Eliz. D. of James & Ann Brozet.

PARISH REGISTER OF ST. GEORGE, ST. CHRISTOPHER'S.

Baptized.

1742-3 Jan. 6 Thomas Mills, Esqr, his son Thomas.

1744 Dec. 27 Thomas Mills, Esqr, his son William.

Buried.

1744 July 1 Mathew Mills, Esqr.

RICHMOND, CO. SURREY.

Baptized.

1737-8 Mar. 13 Joseph, a Black of riper years, Servt of Tobias Wall, Esqr.

PARISH REGISTER OF ST. GEORGE, HANOVER SQUARE.

Married.

1743 June 23 Mathew Mills, of St Nicholas Acon, London, B., & Cornelia Soulogre [*sic*], of St Ann, Westminster, S. L.A.C.

1747 Jan. 28 Henry Compton, of Bistern, co. Southamp., Esq., B., & Lucretia Mills, of Kilmaston in the s^d county, S., a minor. L.A.C.

1750 Dec. 13 Stephen Theodore Janssen, Esqr, one of the Aldermen of the City of London, B., & Catherine Soulegre, of St Ann, Westminster, S. L.A.C.

1758 Mar. 30 William Woodley, B., & Frances Payne, S. Lic.

ST. PAUL'S, FALMOUTH, ANTIGUA.

Here Lieth | THE BODY OF | MARY MILLS | WIFE OF | JOHN MILLS WHO DEPARTED THIS LIFE | 5TH AUGUST 1809 AGED 17 YEARS | SHE WAS AN AFFECTIONATE WIFE A TENDER | MOTHER AND A SINCERE FRIEND | ALSO TO THE ABOVE JOHN MILLS | LATE FOREMAN OF SAILMAKERS IN H.M. NAVAL | YARD IN THIS ISLAND AND WHO DEPARTED THIS LIFE | 30 NOV. 1817 AGED 53 YEARS | HE WAS BORN IN DEVONSHIRE IN THE YEAR 1764 | SERVED HIS APPRENTICESHIP IN H.M. DOCKYARD | AT PLYMOUTH AND THROUGH HIS GOOD CONDUCT | etc.

LITTLE PARNDON, CO. ESSEX.

On the north wall:—

Arms: *Sable, a cheveron between three owls argent;* impaling, *Argent, a bend between three wolves' heads, couped sable, langued gules.*

In the family vault of her son-in-law, Edward Parson, of this parish, esq. are deposited the remains of Mrs Bridget Woodley, widow of William Woodley, esq. of the island of St Christopher, where he is interred. She departed this life the 13th day of February, 1756, aged 74 years, eminently distinguished by every conjugal, social, and Christian virtue, and most justly meriting this last testimony of filial duty and respect, from her affectionate son John Woodley, who erected this to the best of parents, MDCCLXVI.

(Wright's 'Essex,' vol. ii., p. 304.)

HITCHIN, CO. HERTS.

On the wall of the south aisle of the nave:—

In a vault near this spot are deposited the remains of Sarah, relict of John Mills, Esq; who was born September 21st, 1743, O.S., and died September 19th, 1819. Also of three of their children, Elizabeth, born January 14th, 1770; died May 19th, 1811: Sarah Pittman, born October 19th, 1774; died July 11th, 1827: Henry Roper, born March 25th, 1784; died February 14th, 1790. The above named John Mills, Esq. died at Grenada, in the West Indies, August 15th, 1784, in the 43rd year of his age. This tablet also records the death of his eldest son John Colhoun Mills, who died on his passage from Nevis, July 15th, 1828, in the 57th year of his age; and of his eldest son John Mills, who was lost at sea in his passage from America to Nevis the latter part of the year 1825, in the 19th year of his age.

(Cussans' 'Herts,' vol. ii., p. 70.)

IN BLOXWORTH CHURCH, CO. DORSET.

To the memory of FRANCES WOODLEY, widow of William | Woodley, esq. this monument was erected by Hariot Pickard, as | a token of duty and affection to her beloved and lamented | mother, who died March 29, 1813, aged 75 years. (Hutchins' 'Dorset,' vol. i., p. 182.)

Pedigree of Wyke.

GEORGE WYKE of the "Waterwork" Plantation of 600 acres, Montserrat; Chief Justice 1704; Member of Council 1704-5; President 1739; Colonel of Militia; bur. 18 Aug. 1742 at St. Anthony's. ═ . . . .

Edward Wyke, Lieut.-Governor of Montserrat. ═ . . . .

George Wyke, junior, Member of Council 1734 (? President 1755, till his death in 1764).

. . . . Wyke ═ . . . .

William Irish, Esq., mar. 7 March 1722 at St. George's, Montserrat; bur. there 1 Dec. 1725. 1st husband. ═ Sarah Wyke ═ Colonel Samuel Martin of Antigua, died 1776, æt. 83. 2nd husband.

Anthony Wyke of Montserrat, appointed Member of Council May 1764; Lieut.-Colonel of Carabineers; Judge of Court of Vice-Admiralty; died March 1778. ═ Ann, 1st dau. of Colonel William Byam of Antigua; born 27 Sep. 1744 at Barley's, Exeter; mar. 13 Jan. 1763 at St. John's, Antigua; died 18 June 1814 at Bath.

William Byam Wyke, R.N., of Antigua, bapt. 23 Nov. 1763 at St. George's; Member of Council of Montserrat 1806. ═ Sophia, dau. of Daniel Hill, senior; mar. 29 Dec. 1806 at St. John's.

Edward Byam Wyke of Antigua, Barrister-at-Law, appointed Member of Council of Montserrat 1797; bur. 7 Aug. 1812 at St. George's. ═ Sarah . . . .

Anthony Wyke, Barrister-at-Law, mar. 19 March 1814 at St. Peter's; bur. 10 Jan. 1820 at St. George's. Will dated 12 Dec. 1819; sworn 26 Jan. 1820. ═ Elizabeth Mary Langford, dau. of Dr. William Crowe; mar. 2ndly, 18 Feb. 1830, at St. Peter's, Dr. Thomas Coull.

William Byam Wyke, born 24 April and bapt. 28 Sep. 1808 at St. John's.

Henry Martin Wyke, born 28 Dec. 1809 and bapt. 20 Jan. 1810 at St. John's.

Edward Byam Wyke, born 17 Jan. 1811 and bapt. 5 April 1812 at St. John's.

William Byam Wyke, born 19 Jan. and bapt. 20 Feb. 1806 at St. John's.

Charles Dilke Wyke, born 7 Sep. 1808 and bapt. 1 July 1809 at St. John's.

George Wyke, Captain in the Guards.

Charles Dilke Wyke, living 1820.

Eliza Wyke, bapt. 22 Sep. 1769 at St. George's (? mar. 1812 Hugh Mackay of Bighouse, N.B.).

Louisa Sarah Rebecca Weatherill Wyke, bapt. 2 Nov. 1779 at St. John's; mar. there, 3 Nov. 1796, Captain Henry Mitford, R.N., son of Colonel William Mitford of Exbury, Hants, and nephew of Lord Redesdale.

Octavia Payne Wyke, mar. 1st, 10 Sep. 1799, at Southampton, William Willock; 2ndly, 24 Aug. 1816, at St. John's, John Kentish.

Alicia Wyke, mar. Captain William Henry Byam, R.N.; died s.p. 26 Nov. 1838.

Anne Byam Wyke, mar. 12 March 1789, at St. George's, Daniel Hill, jun., Esq. His will was dated 1811.

Anthony Wyke of Antigua, Barrister. Will dated 12 Dec. 1819. To my wife Eliz[th] Mary Langford Wyke all my estate. Thos. Rogers & W[m] Lee, Esq., of Antigua, Ex'ors. Witnessed by John Osborn, jun. Before John Horsford, Esq., was sworn John Osborn 26 Jan. 1820.

Codicil dated 5 Jan. and sworn 26 Jan. 1820. On a voyage to Bermudas with my wife. In case she die before she takes profits of my estate all to my brother Chas. Dilke Wyke & my sister Octavia Wyke.

1688, Nov. Roger Wyke then a Member of Assembly of Montserrat.

1704, Aug. 24. George Wyke appointed Chief Justice of Common Pleas at Montserrat.

1704-5, Feb. 6. President John Johnson writes that he has sworn in as a Councillor of Montserrat Mr. George Wike, the late Chief Justice.

George Wyke of the Leeward Division of Montserrat lost £4021 at the French Invasion of 1712.

Census of Montserrat. George Wyke, Esq., planter, 2 windmills, 1 cattle mill, 7 men, 6 women, 3 children, 223 slaves, 16 in family, 300 acres of cane, 40 cattle, etc.

1726-7, March 4. George Wyke then Member of Council.

1727, Sep. 26. George Wyke, jun., signs address to George II.

1734. George Wyke and George Wyke, jun., both sign the address from the Council of Montserrat.

In vol. 26 B. T. Leeward Islands is a long letter from George Wyke, President of Montserrat, dated Dec. 1739, giving a descriptive account of the Virgin Islands.

1748, Jan. 1. George Wyke to be Member of Council for Montserrat, and John Bramley, his brother-in-law, was also a Member about that time.

1748-9, Jan. 19. George Wyke to be of the Council of Montserrat.

1755. George Wyke then President of Montserrat, also in 1760.

1764, May 30. Governor George Thomas writes announcing the death of Mr. Wyke, the President of Montserrat, and that he has appointed Anthony Wyke to succeed his uncle in the Council. On Dec. 24 he had appointed George Wyke to be also of the Council.

1776, Dec. 10. Anthony Wyke recommended to be of the Council of Montserrat.

1778, Feb. The Hon. Anthony Wyke, at Montserrat, lieutenant-colonel of the troop of Carabineers, and Judge of the Court of Vice Admiralty of that island. ('Gent. Mag.,' p. 167.)

1790, Nov. 19. Samuel Martin Irish to be of the Council of Montserrat.

1797, Jan. Edward B. Wyke to be of the Montserrat Council. On 27 Oct. 1796 President J. J. Thomas had appointed him Master and Examiner in Chancery there.

1806. William Byam Wyke then of the Council of Montserrat.

1807, Nov. Warrant to be prepared for Edward Byam Wyke to be of the Council of Montserrat.

1810, Aug. 23. Hon. Mr. Wyke of Montserrat is now settled at Antigua.

PARISH REGISTER OF ST. JOHN.

Baptized.

1806 Feb. 20 William Byam S. of Edward Byam Wyke and Sarah his wife. B. the 19th January last.

1808 Sep. 28 William Byam S. of William Byam Wyke and Sophia his wife. B. the 24th April last.

1809 July 1 Charles Dilkes S. of Edward Byam Wyke and Sarah his wife. B. the 7th September 1808.

1810 Jan. 20 Henry Martin S. of William Byam Wyke and Sophia his wife. B. the 28th December last.

1812 April 5 Edward Byam S. of William Byam Wyke and Sophia his wife. B. the 17th January 1811.

Married.

1763 Jan. 13 Antony Wyke to Ann Byam. L.

1806 Dec. 29 William Byam Wyke to Sophia Hill.

1812 . . . . . . Hugh Mackay, Merchant, to Eliza Wyke, Spinster. L.

1815 Mar. 25 Thomas Dickson Foote to Margaret Wyke, Spinster. L.

PARISH REGISTER OF ST. PAUL.

Married.

1813 Oct. 9 Lieutenant Joseph Steele of the Navy to Ann Byam Wyke, Spinster; by L.

1815 Sep. 11 Lieutenant Thomas Cunningham Pilkington of H.M. 4th W.I. Regt to Elizabeth Harcum Wyke, Spinster; pr L. from Honble Edwd Byam.

1824 Oct. 18 Thomas Clark, Junr, & Octavia Wyke. L.

PARISH REGISTER OF ST. GEORGE.

Baptized.

1763 Nov. 23 William Byam the S. of Anthony Wyke and Ann his wife.

1769 Sep. 22 Eliza the D. of Anthony Wyke of Montserrat & Ann his wife.

1779 Nov. 2 Louisa Sarah Rebecca Weatherill the D. of Anthony Wyke, decd, and Ann his Widow.

1791 . . . . D. of William Wyke, Esqr, of Montserrat, & his wife.

Married.

1789 Mar. 12 Daniel Hill, Junr, Merch., and Ann Wyke. Spinster.

1796 Nov. 3 Henry Mitford & Louisa Sarah Rebecca Weatherill Wyke, Spinster.

Buried.

1812 Aug. 7 Edward Wyke, Barrister at Law, from St John's; in the Family Burying Ground in Fitche's Churchyard.

1820 Jan. 10 Anthony Wyke, Barrister, from St John's.

PARISH REGISTER OF ST. PETER.

Married.

1814 Mar. 19 Anthony Wyke, Esqr, Barrister at Law, to Elizabeth Mary Langford Crowe, Spinster; by L. at Cedar Hill.

1830 Feb. 18 Thomas Coull of this Parish, Physician, and Elizabeth Mary Langford Wyke of the Parish of St John's, Widow; by L.

ST. ANTHONY, MONTSERRAT.

Buried.

1726 June 26 Martha wife of Collo Wyke.

1742 Aug. 18 The Honble George Wyke, Esqr, of ye parish of St Anthony.

ST. GEORGE'S, MONTSERRAT.

Married.

1722 Mar. 7 Wm Irish, Esqr, & Sarah Wyke; by L.

Buried.

1725 Dec. 1 Wm Irish, Esqr.

BATH ABBEY.

On the floor of the south transept:—

To the Memory
of
HESTER ANN WYKE
Died 2nd Jan. 1813
Aged
3 Years & 9 Months.

Buried.

1813 Jan. 9 Hester Ann Wyke. Stanhope Str, Walcot. 3 yrs & 8 mths.

Family of Yeamans.

Edith Yemans, singlewoman, the daughter of Richard Yemans of Henburye, co. Gloster. Will dated 10 March and proved 21 April 1593. To be bur. at Henbury. To Wm Nelme 10s. To my brother Wm Yemans 40s. To my sister Joan Shipman £3 at 18, but if she die ½ to my brother Wm Yemans, & ½ to Richd Jayne, s. of my brother-in-law Richd Jayne. To my sister Joan Shipman my best partlett, Kercher, my mother's wedding ring, a pair of tachokes, & a silver pin. To Tho. Yemans, s. of John Yemans, 10s. To Julyan Jayne 5s. To Agnes Shipman my 3d petticote. To my brother Richd Shipman a kercher. To my sister Charity Shipman a double kercher & my best smocke. To Wm Ames, my brother-in-law's kyne, 12d. All residue to my brother-in-law Wm Jayne, he to be sole Ex'or. My brother-in-law Richd Jayne & John Yemans, overseers, & 6d each. Witnessed by Richard Jo'sonne, Clerke, Richard Jayne, John Yemans, William Collins, William Amis. Endorsed Henbury. Recorded at Bristol.

John Yeman of Bristoll, grocer. Will dated 5 July 1600. To be bur. in the church of our Ladye at Reklyefe. To my dau. Cath. Yeman my fether bed, etc. My dau. Mary. To my 2 sons Tho. & Wm Yeman my house in the p'sh of St Mary's in Cardiff in Wales. My wife Ales their mother during their Minoritie to have the profitts. My youngest s. Wm. My wife Ex'trix. John Tanner & David Low of Cardiff, overseers, & Jas. Bigton, minister of St Thomas. Endorsed "my father's last wyell & testamentte 1560" (?). Recorded at Bristol.

Alice Yeomans of Bristol, widow, late wife of John Yeomans of Bristol, merchant. Will dated 14 Feb. 1603; proved 15 Dec. 1604. To my dau. Alice my best fether bed, etc. To my dau. Christian my 2[d] bed. To Morgan B . . . . my gold ring which was his father's. My dau. Collis. To my s. Rob[t] a bed. To Thos. a bed. To my sister Julyan my best apron. To my sister Jane my new sylke apron. My sister Julyan's dau. Marie. Marian Heybrooke. My brother-in-law W[m] Higgins & coz. John Stubbins. My husband's dau. Kath. Witnessed by Roger Coocke, Thomas Hall, John C . . . ., Hellen R . . . ., Elizabeth Usher. Recorded at Bristol.

Nuncupative will of William Yeman of St. Peeter, Bristoll, grocer, dated 18 July 1616; proved 28 Nov. 1616 by John Yeman the son. (P.C.C., 116 Cope.) His late wife. £120 to Edw[d] Cox out of the profits of the Castle Mills. All leases, etc., to son John Yeman. Witnessed by Humphrey Brynte, Lettice Carye, Susan Northall.

George Yemans of the parish of St. Augustine's, co. Gloster, husbandman. Will dated 31 Dec. and proved 7 Feb. 1620. To my godd. Joane Skrine, d. of W[m] Skrine, £10 at 21. To the ch[n] of Hen. Whippie. To Jn[o] Whippie my best doublett. To the poor of Henbarie 20*s*., & to the poor of S[t] Augustine's 20*s*. To my kinswoman the d. of Hen. Creene, late of Barton hundred, £10 at 21. To W[m] Skrine's servants 12[d] apiece. All res. to W[m] Skrine & sole Ex'or. Rob[t] Phillipes oweth me 40*s*. W[m] Dy . . . . of Elberton, blacksmith, oweth me 40*s*. Appoint Jn[o] Hooper & Geo. Langston of Augustine's, overseers. To M[r] Owen for writing this will 3[s] 4[d]. Witnessed by John Owen, William Owen, William Skrine, etc. Recorded at Bristol.

1633, Oct. 26. Nuncupative will of Mr. William Yemans, Prebendary of the Cathedral Church of Bristol, and Vicar of St. Philipp's, Bristol. To now wife all goods & household stuff, & after her death ½ to Gervase Yeoman my son. Witnessed by Susanna Northall, Mary Kemp. Adm'on 3 Jan. 1633 to Catherine Yemans the relict. Recorded at Bristol.

1633, Nov. 28. Adm'on of goods of John Yemans of St. James, Bristol, granted to Joanna the relict. (P.C.C.)

Katherine Yemans of Bristol, widow. Will dated 12 Nov. and proved 9 Dec. 1641. To be bur. in S[t] Philipp's churchyard in the grave of my dec[d] husb[d]. Goods to be delivered to my son W[m] Yemans by his grandfather Yeamans, viz., 4 great candlesticks of brass, 1 great brass chafing dish of the old pattern, 1 Arras carpet, 1 silver beare boule, 1 silver beaker, 1 great broad gilt wine boule, & after his death they are to go to my grandson his s. W[m] Yemans. To my d. Mary Kempe & to her daus. 15 pair of flaxen sheetes. To my grandd. Mary d. of my s[d] d. Mary Kempe 1 spruce chest. To my s.-in-l. W[m] Kempe 20*s*. To W[m] Yemans, s. of my s. Gervase Yemans, my great silver salt sellar. To Mary the d. of my s. Gervase my suite of damaske & bed, etc., in parlour. All res. to s. Gervase Yemans & he sole Ex'or. Witnessed by Richard Standfast, Cleric, and Robart Willson. Seal.—A three-masted ship. Recorded at Bristol.

John Yeamans, brewer. Will dated 12 June 1645; proved 7 Nov. 1645 by Blanche Yeamans the relict. To the poor of Redcliffe £10. To my sons-in-l. Jas. Wathen,* Tho. Warren, Jn[o] Woory, & Jn[o] Pope, & Jn[o] Tomlinson £40 apeece as a token for their wives. To my d. Eliz[th] Ditty £40. To my s. Geo. Yeamans £40. To my s. Jn[o] Yeamans £40. To my s. W[m] Yeamans £140. To my s. Rob[t] Yeamans £40. To my s. Rich[d] Yeamans £40. To my s. Joseph £200. My brewhouse, viz., 2 houses which are Redcliffe Church Lands, & a tenem[t] n[r] it which I purchased of Henry Pitt in fee, & a tenement adjoining, late in the holding of Jas. Hobbs, dec[d], I give to my wife Blanche, & after her death to my son Joseph. To Edw[d], Mary, Sarah, Eliz., Alice, Walt[r], Jn[o], & Tho., ch[n] of my bro. Edw[d] Yeamans, dec[d], £5 apeece. I forgive my kinsman Francis Yeamans all debts. My wife Ex'trix & all residue. To my son-in-l. Peter Hiley 40*s*. My bros. Jn[o] Yeamans & W[m] Yeamans, overseers, & 40*s*. apeece. To my serv[ts] Jn[o] Hall & Jn[o] Buttler 40*s*. apeece. Witnessed by Frauncis Yeamans, John Woorye, John Pope. Recorded at Bristol.

* 1663. (101 Juxon.) James Wathen, pinmaker, Bristol.

William Yeamans, late of Bristoll, now of Stapleton, co. Gloucester, Gent. Will dated 23 Jan. 1646; proved 18 Feb. 1647 by Anne Yeamans the relict. (17 Essex.) My wife Anne Ex'trix. My brother John Yeamans & my sons-in-law Math. Warren & John Haggatt overseers & £5 each. To my s. W[m] Yeamans & my dau. Anne Yeamans & my kinsman Fra. Yeamans £5 each. To my 2 daus. Eliz. Haggatt & Joyce Warren & my sist. Blanche Yeamans, wid., 40*s*. each. To my mother Tomlinson & all my wife's brethren & sisters & my loving friends M[r] John Price & M[r] Gyles Earle 20*s*. each. To Alice sister of s[d] Fra. Yeamans £10, having already given some portion to all the rest of her brothers & sisters. To my grandch[n] Anne Yeamans, dau. of my s. W[m] Yeamans, John, Marie, & Nath. Haggatt, Math., W[m], & Joice Warren £10 each. My wife to receive the profits of my tenement at Stapleton, & after her death to my s. W[m] Yeamans. To my dau. Sarah £300 at 21. All my law books to my s. Haggatt. All my messuages in longe Rowe, S[t] Thos. P'sh in Bristoll, to my wife. To the 9 children of my dau. Anne Yeamans £200. All residue to my wife. Witnessed by Mathew Warren, Francis Yeamans, John Till-Adam.

Codicil. 16 March 1646. £5 to the poor of T . . . . & X[t] Ch., Bristol.

John Yeamans of Tortworth, co. Gloucester, yeoman. Will dated 3 Feb. 1646; proved 18 Feb. 1647 by William Yeamans and Francis Yeamans. (16 Essex.) Wife Alice £25, furniture, & 3 kine. Bro. W[m]'s children £3 each. Bro. John's children £3 each. Bro. Edw[d]'s children. To my kinsmen W[m] & Fra. Yeamans all rest of goods, they to be Ex'ors.

Alderman Hugh Browne of Bristol, Esq. Will not dated. (P.C.C., 490 Alchin.) My wife Eliz. A house to the Merchant Adventurers for 2 poor men. My brother-in-law John Tomlinson, merch[t]. My uncle Rob[t] Tomlinson, clothier. My s. Hugh Browne. My dau. Eliz. Creswick. My aunt Yeamans. My coz. Warren.

Codicil dated 1653.

Anne Woolfe of Bristol, widow. Will dated 18 Dec. 1653. (326 Alchin.) To be buried at Christ Church, near my late husband. To my grandchildren Francis, Robert, John, Isaack, & Anne Yeamans, children of Francis Yeamans by Anne his late wife, deceased, £30 each at 21. My two sisters Dorothy & Margaret 20*s*. rings. Kinswoman Marie Hurle & my sister Gale 20*s*. My cozen Marie Woolfe. Marie dau. of my son-in-law Francis Yeamans 22*s*. Cozen Mathew Woolfe 40*s*. All residue to Francis Yeamans & Ex'or. Cozens Miles Woolfe & Mathew Woolfe overseers. Witnessed by Dorothy Childe, Mathew Woolfe, Jo. Hellier.

Codicil. 22 Jan. 1653. My dau. Yeamans a 40*s*. ring, & cozen Miles Woolfe 20*s*. Witnessed by Mathew Wolfe.

No record of Probate, but the volume belongs to the year 1653.

Pedigree of Yeamans.

Arms.—*Sable, a chevron between three cronels of spears argent.*

John Yeman, living 1573 = ...

William Yeman, senior, of Bristol, glover. = Joan . . . . Will dated 21 Dec. 1573; proved 5 April 1574. Recorded at Bristol.

William Yeman, junior, of All Saints, Bristol, grocer. = ... Will dated 14 Nov. 1580; proved 7 Jan. 1580-81. Recorded at Bristol. Relations at Cardiff in Wales.

William Yeman. — Alice Yeman.

Margery Yeman. — Katherine Yeman. — Joan Yeman.

John Yeman of St. Mary Redcliff, Bristol, grocer, bur. there 13 July 1600. Will dated 5 July 1600. Recorded at Bristol. Property at Cardiff in Wales. = Alice . . . . bur. 15 Feb. 1603 at St. Mary Redcliffe. Will dated 14 Feb. 1603; proved 15 Dec. 1604. Recorded at Bristol.

William Yeman (? of St. Peter's, grocer, 1587, and will 1616. 116 Cope).

Thomas Yeman.

William Yeman, bur. 28 Jan. 1603 at St. Mary Redcliffe.

Catherine Yeman.

Mary Yeman.

Frances Yeman, bur. 17 Jan. 1603 at St. Mary Redcliffe.

. . . . YEAMANS = ...

John Yeamans of St. Mary Redcliffe, Bristol, brewer. Will dated 12 June and proved 7 Nov. 1645. = Blanche Germain, mar. 29 June 1610 at St. Mary Redcliffe; proved her husband's will; named in the will of her brother-in-law William Yeamans 1646, then widow.

See Pedigree A.

John Yeamans, overseer to his brother John 1645, likewise to his brother William 1646. (? of Tortworth, co. Gloucester, yeoman, and will dated 3 Feb. 1646; proved 18 Feb. 1647. 16 Essex.)

William Yeamans of Bristol, merchant, living 1643. Will proved 1673. (52 Pye.) = Mary, dau. of Mrs. Frances Pinney of Bristol; her will proved 1665. (65 Hyde.) Will dated June 1677; proved 7 May 1678. (55 Reeve.)

Robert Yeamans, Sheriff of Bristol 1642; hanged by the Parliament Party 30 May 1643; bur. in Christ Church. (See Rushworth.) = Anne . . . . her nine children were living 1646; she remar., before 1646, Robert Speed, merchant and Quaker. ('Bristol Past and Present,' vol. iii., p. 26.)

Anne Yeamans, named in her father's will 1646. (? mar. . . . . Ducie. Will dated 9 Dec. 1684. 3 Ent.)

Ann Yeamans, living 1646; mar. William Whittington.

Mary Yeamans, 1684.

John Yeamans, merchant of Bristol 1684.

A dau. of . . . . Limp. 1st wife. = Sir John Yeamans, Bart., created 12 Jan. 1664-5; settled in Barbados; Governor of South Carolina till 1680, where he had a grant of 48,000 acres; dead 1686. = Margaret, dau. of Rev. John Forster of Barbados. 2nd wife.

Sir William Yeamans. = Willoughby, dau. of Sir James Browne, Knt. She was of St. Lucy's and St. Peter's Parishes 1676—80.

Robert Yeamans of Barbados, heir to his uncle Sir Robert Yeamans 1686. = Elizabeth, dau. of Elisha Mellows, Esq.

Sir John Yeamans. = Margaret, dau. of Philip Gibbes* of Barbados, Esq.; æt. 45 and of St. Peter's 1715; remar. William Foster, Esq.

Colonel Robert Yeamans (? of St. James Parish 1715). = Sarah, dau. of John Trent, Esq., of Barbados; remar. Rev. William Dowding.

John Yeamans. = Mary, dau. of Alexander Walker, a Judge of Barbados.

Philip Yeamans. = Mary, dau. of Joseph Gibbs, Esq., of Barbados.

Sir John Yeamans, æt. 26 in 1715. = Anne, dau. of Mr. Seantlebury; mar. in Barbados; æt. 26, 1715.

A son, æt. 13, 1715. — A dau., æt. 18 in 1715.

Robert Yeamans, only son, died 7 Nov. 1740, æt. 10.

Walker Yeamans.

Sir John Yeamans, only son, living in Barbados 1771 = ...

Rev. Sir Robert Yeamans, died s.p. 19 Feb. 1788. Title extinct.

* This Philip Gibbes had a second wife Willoughby, dau. of . . . . Yeamans, and widow of . . . . Smith, who was his Ex'trix in 1697. (Betham's 'Baronetage.')

John Drayton of Bristol, merchant. Will dated 26 June 1659. (235 Nabbs.) Mr Wm Yeamans overseer.

The same year Arthur King of Bristol names Francis Yeaman, scrivener, overseer. (199 May.)

1660. (103 Nabbs.) Mathew Wolfe of Bristol names his kinsmen Francis Yeomans, sen., Francis Yeamans, jun., and Anne Yeamans, dau. of the said Francis Yeamans, and gives his law books to Francis Yeamans, jun.; latter's brother Robt Yeamans.

Frances Pinney of Bristoll, widow. Will proved 14 June 1665. (65 Hyde.) To be buried near my husband in St Thos. ch.-yd. My 2 daus. Anne Deane, widow, & Mary Yeomans, wife of Mr Wm Yeomans of Bristoll, merchant, all my lands.

William Payne of Bristoll. Will dated 20 March 1667; proved 15 May 1669 by Mary Payne. (60 Coke.) Now aged 71. Born at St Earth, near St Ives, Cornwall, 20 April 1597. Poor of St Stephen's 50s. Sister Jane Dun of St Earth 50s. S.-in-law Mr Joseph Yeomans my gold ring with the armes of my ancestors. S.-in-l. Jas. Whitwood. Son John Payne in Ireland £5, having spent his portion. Dau. Mary Payne my house in Marsh str. Dau. Mary my house in the Key. Brother Mr John Payne of St Ives. Dau. Mary Ex'trix.

Ann Yeamans of St. Stephen's, Bristol, widow. Will dated 1668. (132 and 162 Hene.) Sons Robert & Wm.

William Yeamans the Elder of Bristoll, merchant. Will proved P.C.C. 1673. (52 Pye.) Wife Mary. Dau. Anne wife of Wm Whittington. Kinsman Wm Yeamans of Bristoll, merchant, Ex'or. Witnessed by Thomas Yeamans.

William Yeamans of Bristoll, merchant, now residing in St. Dunstan's in the East, London. Will dated 13 March 1674; proved 23 Oct. 1675 by Thomas Yoakley. (105 Dycer.) A considerable sum due to me from the King, & I owe a large sum to Tho. Yoakley, whom I appoint sole Ex'or, he paying debts, etc., all residue to my wife & children. Witnessed by Ed. Hillyard, John Boucher.

Mary Yeamans* of Bristol, widow of William Yeamans of Bristol, merchant. Will dated June 1677; proved 7 May 1678 by Anne Deane the sister. (55 Reeve.) Rev. Richd Towgood, Dean of this Cathedral, & my kinsman Nath. Haggatt, Esq., are my Trustees for lands in Tedstone & Rosemoore, co. Heref., which my husbd gave me power to will away. They shall continue to hold them & pay £12 a yr. to my sister Ann Deane for life, then to her 2 sons Rob. & John Deane; also £4 a year to my sister Joane Hucks for life, then to her 4 daus. All residue of lands to my sister Hester Phelps. £3 to the poor of St Thos. My dau.-in-l. Ann Whittington. My sister-in-l. Elinor Eliott 10s. Suzan Spencer 10s. My cozens Wm Cox & John Hicks 20s. each. To my cozen Nath. Haggat the legacy left me by my late mother-in-law, his grandmother. All residue to my sister Ann Deane, she to be Ex'trix. Witnessed by Suzanna Northen, Mary Northen, William Hassell.

* See the will of her mother Frances Pinney.

William Yeamans of Bristol, Gent., overseer to his brother John 1645. Will dated 23 Jan. 1646, then of Stapleton, co. Gloucester; proved 18 Feb. 1647. (17 Essex.) = Anne, dau. of .... Tomlinson; sole Ex'trix to her husband 1647.

Edward Yeamans, named in the will of his brother John in 1645 as "deceased." His eight children were then living. = ...

Sarah Yeamans, a minor 1646.

Elizabeth Yeamans, mar. John Haggatt; he living 1643, 1646, and 1668.

Joyce Yeamans, mar. Mathew Warren, Mayor of Bristol 1633; he bur. 1654 in St. Thomas's Church. See his father's will (33 Sadler). Her will dated 26 May 1668; proved 12 April 1671. (53 Duke.)

Margaret Yeamans, mar. William Cann, Mayor of Bristol 1648. Their son Robert was created a Baronet 1662.

Edward Yeamans. — Walter Yeamans. — John Yeamans. — Thomas Yeamans.

Mary Yeamans. — Sarah Yeamans. — Elizabeth Yeamans. — Alice Yeamans.

.... bur. at St. Mary Redcliffe. 1st wife. = Sir Robert Yeamans, Knt. and Bart., of Bristol; created Bart. 1666; Mayor 1669; D.L. 1670, 1674, and 1685; bur. 7 Feb. 1686 at St. Mary Redcliffe. Will dated 24 Jan. 1686; proved 11 May 1687. (71 Foot.) = Abigail .... living 1716. 2nd wife.

s.p. s.p.

Joseph Yeamans. = ...

John Yeamans, brewer, 1st son, 1686. Robert Yeamans, 2nd son, 1686. George Yeamans, 3rd son, 1686.

Frances Yeamans of Clifton, co. Gloucester, widow. Will dated 17 June and proved 22 July 1678 by Lanrence Hodges, sen. (81 Reeve.) Aged. To my sister Amy Pickerne £4 a year. To the poor Widows of Clifton 50s. To Frances dau. of my cousin Lanr. Hodges the Elder my silver tankard & 6 spoons. To the wife of Mr John Whittington my prayer-book with gilded covers. To Mrs Canne, wife of Mr John Canne, mercht, my silver salt, & to his dau., my goddau., 2 guineas. To my servant 30s. £10 for my funeral. All residue to my cousin Laur. Hodges of Bedminster, co. Som., Gent., he Ex'or. Mr James & Mr Addyes of Bristol, mercht, overseers. Witnessed by John Knight, Dorothy Horwood.

Elizabeth Yeamans of Bristol, widow and ad'trix of Joseph Yeamans, brewer. Will dated 27 Feb. 1682; proved 5 Jan. 1683 by John and George Yeamans the sons. (10 Hare.) To be bur. at St Mary Redcliffe near my husbd. £10 to the poor. I have already pd the portions of my sons & daus., except that of Patience which is £300, & is to be pd to her husbd. To my s. Geo. the mess. I purch. of Mr Fra. Yeamans the Elder in Wine Str., Xt Ch. To my s. Richd the mess. I purch. of Mr Wm Hobson on St James' back in the Suburbs & £50 left him by his bro. Jos. I have pd all 7 of his brothers & sisters their £50 each. My son Morgan. My cousin David Dorvill. The house on the Key, lately in the tenure of Richd Jones, taylor, to my s.

John, he to pay to my sist. Joan Wittwood 25s. quarterly, & to the lord (Wm Balding) £5 a yr., & the residue to his sist. Ann Morgan. To my sist. Wittwood £10. My farm at Bisford I hold for the lives of my sons Geo. & Richd is to go to Geo. first, he to pay to his sist. Ann Morgan, my s. John & wife, my s. Robt & wife, my s. Morgan & wife, my s. Steph. & wife, £6 a year each. My sons Geo. & Richd £3 each. To each gr'dchild 20s. My daus. Ann Eliz. Yeamans & Patience. To my s. Geo. my wedding ring, silver tankard, porringer, & spoons. To my s. Richd my silver beer bowle marked J. Y. E., & a wine bowle H. W. B., & 2 spoons T. N. E. P. To my s. Robt the house in the marshe. My s. Richd under age. 40s. in bread to the poor. My sons John & Geo. Ex'ors. My loving friend Mr John Cooke, chamberlain, & Mr Jas. Millard, mercer, overseers & 20s. each. Witnessed by Elizabeth Yeamans, Edmund Durban, Mathew Micklebrooke, Elizabeth Hayter.

PEDIGREE A.

John Yeamans ═ Blanche Germain.

- John Yeamans, bapt. 28 Feb. 1611 at St. Mary Redcliffe; named in his father's will 1645.
- Anthony Yeamans, bapt. 17 Feb. 1615.
- William Yeamans, named in his father's will 1645.
- Robert Yeamans, bapt. 19 April 1617 at St. Mary Redcliffe; named in his father's will 1645.
- Joseph Yeamans, bapt. 27 Sep. 1619 at St. Mary Redcliffe; named in his father's will 1645; inherited the brewhouse; died intestate before his wife. ═ Elizabeth, dau. of William Payne of Bristol, whose will (60 Coke) see; bur. 9 Dec. 1683. Will dated 27 Feb. 1682; proved 5 Jan. 1683. (10 Hare.)

Children of Joseph Yeamans and Elizabeth:

- Joseph Yeamans, bapt. 31 Oct. 1651 at St. Mary Redcliffe; died 18 March 1672, æt. 21 years and 5 months. M.I. By his will he bequeathed £50 to his 8 brothers and sisters.
- William Yeamans, bapt. 13 Feb. 1656 at St. Mary Redcliffe; died 17 Sep. 1680. M.I.
- John Yeamans, proved his mother's will 1683. ═ . . . . living 1682.
- Robert Yeamans, bapt. 22 March 1657 at St. Mary Redcliffe. ═ . . . . living 1682.
- George Yeamans, bapt. 30 Aug. . . . . at St. Mary Redcliffe; proved his mother's will 1683. Will dated 2 Feb. and proved 14 Feb. 1686. (35 Foot.) ═ . . . .

William Yeamans of London, merchant, leased Colonel Middleton's plantation in Antigua in 1668. ═ . . . . survived her husband, and enjoyed his plantation.

John Yeamans, Esq. (? born in St. Margaret, Lothbury, and aged 12 in 1661-2), of Antigua 1668; Speaker 1683 and 1684; Member of Council 1684; Deputy-Governor 1698—1711; owned 400 acres at Old North Sound. Will dated 15 Dec. 1717; proved 12 April 1718. (71 Tenison.) ═ Elizabeth Nichols, living 1717.

- William Yeamans, Barrister-at-Law, inherited a plantation of 400 acres from his father; died 1753. Will dated 9 Aug. 1750; proved 29 Dec. 1755. (332 Paul.) ═ Mary . . . .
- John Halliday Yeamans, bapt. 28 Nov. 1703 at St. John's.
- Frances Yeamans, living 1717 (? mar. Samuel Martin, Esq.; he died 1777, æt. 81, if so; she was dead 1729).
- Mary Yeamans, mar. 1st Nathaniel Sampson; 2ndly, 30 Oct. 1701, Colonel William Byam.
- Henrietta Yeamans, goddau. of Governor Christopher Codrington 1698; wife of Richard Ash 1717.
- Rachel Yeamans, died a spinster.
- A dau., ux. . . . . Freeman.

Children of William Yeamans and Mary:

- Frances Yeamans, mar., 9 April 1741, at St. Paul's, Nicholas Collins, Esq. (They had a dau. Mary, who mar. 4 Sep. 1759, at St. Philip's, Nicholas Lynch, and had a dau. Mary, who mar. Samuel Athill, who bought out the other heirs.)
- Sarah Yeamans, mar. 1st William Thomas, who died 1728; 2ndly, Dr. Joshua Archbold, who died 1758; 3rdly, 21 June 1759, at St. John's, Ernest Udney.
- John Yeamans, junior, living 1750. ═ Elizabeth Anne Kerr, mar. 4 Sep. 1737 at St. Philip's; died at Clifton, Bristol. Adm'on granted 11 May 1765 to her dau.
- Rachel Yeamans, bur. 20 April 1729 at St. Paul's.
- Elizabeth Yeamans, mar. 1st, 1737, at St. Paul's, Samuel Eliot, Esq.; 2ndly, in 1746, Dr. William Maxwell.
- Charity Yeamans, mar. William Mackinen, Esq.; he died 8 Oct. 1767.
- Mary Yeamans, mar. 8 May 1735, at St. Paul's, Josiah Martin, President of Antigua.
- Rachel Yeamans, bapt. 22 Aug. 1731 at St. Paul's; mar. there 1st, 13 July 1749, James Emra, Esq., of Nevis and Antigua; he died 28 Dec. 1759, æt. 37; M.I. at Parham; 2ndly, William Woodley Parson, Esq., who died 1770 (307 Jenner); 3rdly, Major Lockhart Russell of Antigua.

Children of John Yeamans, junior, and Elizabeth Anne Kerr:

- William Yeamans, junior, joins Troop 1742; coheir to his grandfather William Yeamans 1750. Adm'on 30 Sep. 1757 to his mother.
- Mary Yeamans, bur. 1742, infant.
- Elizabeth Rachel Anne Yeamans, bapt. 25 March 1746-7 at St. John's; sole surviving child and heir; owned 233 acres in St. Paul's and 180 acres at the Old Road; mar. 1st William Yeamans Archbould, Esq., who died 1763, s.p.; 2ndly, Sir James Laroche, Bart.; bur. at Stapleton, co. Gloucester.
- Frances McKinnon Yeamans, bapt. 18 June 1749 at St. John's. Adm'on granted 30 Sep. 1757 to her mother.

John Yeamans of Bristol, merchant. Will dated 26 Sep. 1682; proved 22 Jan. 1699 by Thomazin Yeamans the relict. (17 Noel.) My sister Sarah Meacock, wife of Sam. Meacock, £5. All residue to my wife Thomazin Yeamans & the child she now goes with, & sole Ex'trix. Witnessed by George Williamson, jun., William Wallis, Fra. Carrington.

1686. (9 Lloyd.) Thomas Weare of Bristol, ropemaker. My niece Thomasine Yeamans, dau. of my brother John Weare, & her son Weare Yeamans; my nephew John Yeamans.

Ann Ducie, late of Bristol, now of Saston, co. Gloucester, widow. Will dated 9 Dec. 1684. (3 Ent.) To be buried at Saston, near my late husband. My cozen Robert Yeomans, son of my cozen Robert Yeomans, merchant, deceased, £100 at 21. My cozen Mary dau. of my late brother Wm Yeomans, merchant, deceased, & all residue to his son, my cozen, John Yeamans of Bristol, merchant.

Codicil. 20 Aug. 1685 and 4 Oct. 1686. Cozen Robert Yeamans, son of my cozen Robert Yeamans, now a trooper in Sir Richd Bassett's troop.

Richard Yeamans, bapt. 13 March 1624; named in his father's will 1645.

George Yeamans, named in his father's will 1645 (? bur. 11 Feb. 1653).

Patience Yeamans, bapt. 26 Feb. 1614 at St. Mary Redcliffe.

Sarah Yeamans, bapt. 16 June 1618 at St. Mary Redcliffe.

Martha Yeamans, bapt. 3 Oct. 1620 at St. Mary Redcliffe.

Jone Yeamans, bapt. 29 May 1623 at St. Mary Redcliffe.

Richard Yeamans, bapt. 20 Jan. 1663 at St. Mary Redcliffe; named in his mother's will 1682.

Stephen Yeamans, named in his mother's will 1682. = ... living 1682.

Ann Yeamans, mar. . . . . Morgan; named in her mother's will 1682.

Elizabeth Yeamans, bapt. 20 Nov. 1649 at St. Mary Redcliffe.

Elizabeth Yeamans, bapt. 29 May 1653 at St. Mary Redcliffe; named in her mother's will 1682, then single.

Patience Yeamans, mar. . . . . Read; mentioned in her mother's will 1682; living 1686.

Eliakim Hutchinson, 7th son of Richard Hutchinson of Boston, Mass.; bapt. 1640; æt. 73 in Jan. 1712-13. = A sister of Colonel Shrimpton of Boston, Mass.

Thirteen children.

Colonel Samuel Shrimpton, mar. in England. Will dated 5 June 1697, then of Boston, New England, Esq.; proved 3 June 1700. (89 Noel.) = Elizabeth Beadon, dau. of Mrs. Elizabeth Roberts; mar. 2ndly Simeon Stoddard.

Elizabeth Yeamans, wife of Colonel John Sawcolt 1717; she died 1741; he died 1748.

Henry Yeamans of Enfield, co. Middlesex, 1697; died v.p. = Mary, dau. of Benjamin Shute* of London, dyer, and sister of 1st Viscount Barrington; bur. 30 March 1697 at St. Peter's, Cornhill.

Samuel Shrimpton, only child, born in America; mar. 7 May 1696. = Elizabeth Richardson, mar. 2ndly David Stoddard, son of the above Simeon Stoddard by a former wife.

A dau., died a spinster.

. . . . Smith of St. Thomas. 1st husband. = Elizabeth Yeamans. (See Sumner's 'History of East Boston,' p. 231.) = ... Flocke of St. Eustatius. 2nd husband.

. . . . dau. of . . . . Stoddard of Boston. 1st wife. = John Yeamans, senior, Member of Council of Antigua 1718—1730; Agent 1727—1743; reappointed Member of Council 1743; died at Richmond, co. Surrey. Will dated Feb. 1747, then of St. James, Westminster, Esq.; proved 27 June 1750. (219 Greenly.) = Elizabeth Shrimpton, only child and heir, born 26 Aug. 1702; died 4 Dec. 1721, æt. 19. 2nd wife.

A dau.

A dau., mar. probably John Duvind.

Shute Shrimpton Yeamans, only son and heir, born 20 Aug. 1721; Member of Council 1748; æt. 28, Nov. 1749; died 10 and bur. 18 Sep. 1769 at Richmond, co. Surrey. Will dated 4 Aug. 1768, then of Richmond, co. Surrey, Esq.; proved 30 Sep. 1769. (330 Bogg.) = Matilda, dau. of Hon. Colonel John Gunthorpe of Antigua; mar. 17 April 1746 at St. George's; dead 1768.

Daniel Duvind.

John Yeamans, born 1 and bapt. 19 Dec. 1749 at St. George's.

Shute Yeamans, bapt. 16 Nov. 1754 at Richmond; died at sea. Will dated 28 April and proved 5 Oct. 1774. (383 Bargrave.)

Ann Yeamans, bapt. 12 March 1752 at Richmond.

John Duvind, born in St. Thomas's, as was his father, an alien incapable of inheriting.

* See the printed 'Registers of St. Peter's, Cornhill,' for many entries relating to this family.

1689. (73 Ent.) Joseph Yeoman of co. Gloucester, Gent. Brother Geo., bro. Saml, bro. John, decd.

Sir Robert Yeamans of Redland, co. Gloucester, Knt. and Bart. Will dated 24 Jan. 1686; proved 11 May 1687 by Dame Abigail Yeamans the relict. (71 Foot.) To be bur. in the Church of St Mary Redcliffe, near my 1st wife. £50 to the poor there, the interest for bread every week. To the poor of Westbury super Trym £20 in like manner. To my loving wife Abigaile Yeamans all my lands in Glostershire for life. My farme in Redland, now in the possession of Joyce Beavin, spr., which I purch. of Ralph Sadler, Esq., decd, & Lord Aston, decd, to my kinsman Robt Stafford, Esq. My 3 houses in Redland in the tenancy of Anthony Elseworth, Gent., ... Wyke, cordwainer, & myself, to my loving friends Rowld Thrupp, Esq., Richd Lane, & Edw. Freeman, Gent., all of Bristoll, for 99 years in Trust for my loving kinsman Robt Yeamans, now resident in Barbados, s. of my late brother Sir John Yeamans, decd, & his heirs; remainder to my kinsman John Yeamans of Bristoll, brewer, 1st s. of my bro. Jos. Yeamans, decd, then to Robt Yeamans his 2d s. & Geo. Yeamans his 3d s. To Robt Stafford £40 a yr. & £500 due fr. . . . . Tomson, Esq., & 5 guineas. All residue to my wife Abigaile, & appoint her sole Ex'trix, & my 3 Trustees to be overseers. Witnessed by John Goldingham, Mary Wynne, Mary Aston, George Freeman.

George Yeamans of Bristol, Gent. Will dated 2 and proved 14 Feb. 1686 by Benjamin Warren. (35 Foot.) To be bur. in St Mary Redcliffe, near my late wife. Small worldly estate. My sisters Joane Hiley & Patience Reade 20s. each. My kinsman Fra. Yeamans £5. To my cousin Hen. Compton one of my rings, the other to the s. of Tho. Porter, mariner, with whom I lodge, & to latter's wife Frances my leasehold house in Froglane. To my kinsman Benj. Warren my house in Christmas Str. & my tenement in St James P'sh, & I ratify the conveyance of the said houses to my kinsman Fra. Yeamans & Sam. Hunt, distiller, to the uses therein declared. All residue to my kinsman Benj. Warren, he Ex'or. Witnessed by John Avery, Giles Gough, Ambrose Shirley.

1686, Feb. 24. (71 Foot.) William Yeamans of St. Giles in the Fields, yeoman. Brother Chr. Yeamans of Madman's Necke, Queen's County, Long Island, New York. Wife Eliz. Sister Ann Bakewell, wid.

Mary Yeamans of Bristoll, widow. Will dated 19 July and proved 26 Sep. 1687 by William Pope, and on 18 Feb. 1687 James Pope sworn. To my bro. Wm Pope of Bristol, maulster, my signett ring. To my bro.-in-l. Jno Yeamans a gold ring, & to his s. John 5s. peece of gold & release debts. To my bro.-in-l. Robt Yeamans my mourning ring. To my sist.-in-l. Patience Steevens, wife of Tho. Steevens of Bristoll, sopeboyler, my wedding ring formerly my husband's mother's. All clothing to my 2 sisters Eleanor Crispe & Anne Pope equally. I discharge my bro.-in-l. Richd Yeamans of all debts. To my sister Sarah Pope 1 small gold ring. All res. to Ex'ors in Trust for my son lately born, at 21, but if he die then $\frac{1}{2}$ to my sister Elianor Crispe, & $\frac{1}{2}$ in Trust for my sister Ann Pope. I appoint Mr Jas. Pope of Bristoll, soap boyler, & my sd bro. Wm Pope, Ex'ors in Trust. Witnessed by Mary Smithwick, George Fownes. Recorded at Bristol.

Joseph Yeamans of Newport in Bearkley, co. Gloucester, Gent. Will dated 2 Nov. 1688; proved 14 May 1689 by the three Ex'ors. (73 Ent.) To my friends Ed. Mors of Dursley, co. Glouc., Gent., Jas. Thatcher of Froome Selwood, Wm Alway of Hawkesbury, co. Glouc., Gent., & Honor Yeamans my sister, my mansion house called the Chantry in Newport, purch. of the Ex'ors of Cap. Cam', etc., in Trust for my 2 daus. Gertrude Yeamans & Ann Yeamans at 21. My brother Geo. Yeamans, my brother Sam. Yeamans & his wife, my sister Mary Williams, my sister Honor, my cozen Mary Yeamans, dau. of my bro. John Yeamans, decd, my coz. Tho. Rich & his wife, my coz. Jos. Rich & his wife, 10s. apiece. All res. to my 2 daus. Trustees to be Ex'ors & 40s. each. Witnessed by Thomas Davies, James Wickham, John Nele, Mary Wickham.

Edward Yeamans of St. Mary Redclift, marriner. Will dated 2 Feb. 1690; proved 27 June 1695. To my loving wife Eliz. Yeamans all lands in Bristol & Bedminster, she sole Ex'trix, & all res. Witnessed by William Cording, Samuell Whibben, Robert Jones, Charles Spicer, William Littler. Recorded at Bristol.

William Redman of Antigua. Will dated 5 March 1697. All my estate to my wife Elizth & my 2 sons Wm & John Redman, they to be Ex'ors, my sons not 21. If she marry, then Capt Jas. Wetherley [Wetherell] & Dr Danl McKenney [Mackinen] to be Guardians & Ex'ors in trust. Witnessed by John Weston, Alexander Coal, Charles Harper. Sworn before John Yeamans by John Weston and Alexander Coal 7 April 1698. Recorded 21 April 1698.

Order by John Yeamans dated 5 Nov. 1698 to appraise the goods of Captain William Redmond, deceased. Elizabeth Redmond his widow and Ex'trix. To Mr. Thomas Long, Mr. Edward Taylor, and Mr. David Rutherford. Inventory of goods valued at £48. Recorded 21 Nov. 1698.

Samuel Shrimpton of Boston in Suffolk County, Massachusetts Bay, New England, Esq. Will dated 5 June 1697. On 3 June 1700 commission to Elizabeth Roberts, the mother and attorney of Elizabeth Shrimpton the relict. (89 Noel.) To my son Saml Shrimpton my brick messuage called the Exchange taverne in Boston, also my brick warehouse nr the town dock, & my parcel of land at the North end of the town. To my kinswomen Abigail & Eliz. Bourne of London £300 apiece besides the legacies left them by their grandfather Shrimpton, deceased. To my beloved wife Eliz. all residue with liberty to dispose of £1000 by will, & the remainder to my relations, & I appoint her sole Ex'trix. Witnessed by Lydia Watts, Ursula Cooles, Eliezer Moody. True Copy per Isa. Addington, Registrar for the Probate of Wills in co. Suffolk. (See Savage's 'Genealogical Dictionary.')

Richard Yeamans of Bristol, Gent. Will dated 21 May and proved 13 Nov. 1701. To my sister Ann Cox £10. To my brother Fra. Yeamans £60. $\frac{2}{3}$ of residue to my brother Tho. Durbin & $\frac{1}{3}$ to my brother John Yeamans & Ex'ors. Witnessed by Thomas Bushell, William Lewis, Ri. Macie. Recorded at Bristol.

John Yeamans of Bristol, merchant. Will dated 28 June 1709; proved 12 Dec. 1710 by Sarah Yeamans the daughter and only surviving Ex'trix. (278 Smith.) To my wife £50 & our furniture from the fort. I give my dau. £50 in lieu of the £30 her grandfather Woolfe left her. To my son £5 in lieu of 40s. from his grandfather Woolfe, & to his wife & dau. each 1 gs, & to his son a small gold signet coat of arms. My servant Eliz. Burges 1 ga. My sister Cox £5. All residue to my wife & my dau. equally & Ex'trices. Cozen Mr John Hipsly to assist.

Sarah Yeamans of Bristol, widow. Will dated 29 July and proved 12 Dec. 1710 by Sarah Yeamans the daughter. (278 Smith.) My son John & his wife Sarah & 3 children 1 ga. All residue to my dau. Sarah Yeamans, spinster, of Bristol, & Ex'trix. 3 gas to my sister-in-law Ann Cox, widow. Witnessed by Elizabeth Burges, John Hipsly.

Robert Yeamans of Bristol, Gent. Will dated 17 Feb. 1714; proved 3 Aug. 1715 by Elizabeth Yeamans the relict. (168 Fagg.) To my 2 daus. Henrietta & Eliz. Yeamans 20 guineas each. All residue to my wife Eliz. & Ex'trix. Witnessed by William Logan, Abraham Jones, servant.

Charles Yeamans of Bristol, marriner. Will dated 8 Aug. 1716; proved 6 July 1717 by Mary and Joyce Yeamans. (161 Whitfield.) To the 2 children of my brother Robt Yeamans £20 each at 21. To my brother & sister Hole £10 each, & to her children £20 each. All residue to my sisters Mary & Joyce Yeamans & Ex'ors. Witnessed by Rowland Thruppe, William Besley.

Antego. John Yeamans, Esq. Will dated 15 Dec. 1717; proved 12 April 1718 by William Parrott the Attorney of William Yeamans the son, and on 10 April 1718 by John Yeamans the grandson. (71 Tenison.) To my wife Eliz. Yeamans 25,000 lbs. of sugar yearly, a horse & velvet side saddle, ½ my silver plate, 2 beds, 7 negros, & ½ my linen & household stuff, & such portion of my house as she may choose to dwell in, & £200 c. To my dau. Mary now wife of Col. Wm Byam £100 c., I give them also a suit of mourning & a 30s. ring apiece, likewise £30 c. to each of their children at 10. To my dau. Eliz. now wife of Lieut.-Col. John Sawcolt £300. I give them each a suite of mourning & a 30s. ring, & £30 c. to each of their children at 10. To my dau. Henrietta & to her husband Mr Richd Ash mourning & 30s. rings, & to each of their children £30 c. at 10. To my dau. Frances & her husband each a mourning suite & a 30s. ring, having been very generous to her in her marriage portion. To Eliz. Symes, the dau. of my wife's sister, £50 c. To my cousin Saml Parry a 20s. ring & forgive him all the wrongs he hath done me, & to his son John Parry £20 c. To my wife ½ my live stock. My sister-in-law Jane Nickols by her will gave to my son Wm Yeamans 2 or 3 negros who have been brought up in my household, & it being unadvisable to part them, he is to give up all claim to them. To my son Wm Yeamans ⅔ & to my grandson John Yeamans ⅓ of all my remaining live stock & household stuff. The other part of my linen to my son Wm & my dau. Sawcolt. To the daus. of my son Wm Yeamans £30 apiece. To Frankey son of Sabel his freedom, to be kept at school till 13, & for 4 years after to have £10 c. yearly. To my wife £100 more. If my estate should be damaged by the enemy then all legacies to be lessened. All my lands & residue to my son Wm Yeamans & to my grandson John Yeamans equally. If John die without male issue his share to my son Wm. My son Wm's sister never to inherit. If my son Wm die without male issue the estate to his daus., but in such case they are to pay to each of their aunts £200 & to my dau. Sawcolt's 5 elder children £60 apiece. My grandson Wm Sawcolt shall be decently maintained in England till his father can send him to the university. To Mr Paul Parry £5. I confirm the gift of glebe land at the Road parish. I appoint my wife Eliz., my son Wm Yeamans, & my grandson John Yeamans, Ex'ors. Witnessed by John Wickham, Elizabeth Wickham, John Killick. Before His Excellency Walter Hamilton, Esq., Governor-in-Chief, were sworn John Wickham of Antigua, Esq., and Elizabeth his wife, and Mr. John Killick, 28 Dec. 1717. Recorded also at St. John's.

Recorded in the Secretary's office at Antigua in Libro O, fos. 39—45, 28 Dec. 1717, Charles Hedges, Secretary, and in the Register's office in Libro O, fo. 201. Examined by Giles Watkins, Register, *vera copia*. Before the Governor appeared Charles Hedges, Esq., and Giles Watkins, Esq., and swore to the copy, 6 Jan. 1717, 4 Geo.

John Yeamans of London, merchant. Will dated 26 Jan. 1718; proved 11 Aug. 1719 by Sarah Yeamans; power reserved to Henry Palmer. (155 Browning.) To my wife Sarah my 2 tenements in the old church-yard in Bridge Town, Barbados. To my 2 daus. Barbara & Sarah Yeamans £1000 each at 21. My sister Sarah Lewellyn, widow, £20 a year. My friend Mr Henry Palmer of London, merchant, Ex'or. All residue to my wife Sarah & Ex'trix. Witnessed by Thomas Abbis, William Hinton, Thomas Hopkins, ser.

Codicil. 26 Jan. 1718. £300 for John Cole *alias* Yeamans.

George Yeamans of Bristol, clothier. Will dated 15 May 1722; proved 12 Oct. 1727 by Elizabeth Yeamans the relict. (246 Farrant.) 1st s. Geo. at 21 my house in Temple Street where John Evans, brewer, dwelleth. To my 2d s. Frederick & youngest son Joseph joyntly my house in Redcliffe Street where my mother-in-law Mary Orchard now dwelleth. To my wife Eliz. & 3 daus., Mary, Eliz., & Blanch, £360 as a common stock. To my s. Geo. a silver porringer marked I. Y. All residue to my wife & Ex'trix. Witnessed by William Blackmore, Bernard Pyne, George Webb.

Sir William Daines of Bristol, Knt. Will dated 1723. (205 Bolton.) Son-in-law John, Viscount Barrington, & Ann his wife, my dau., etc.

Sarah Yeamans of St. Michael's, Barbados, widow. Will dated 11 Dec. 1724; entered at Barbados 22 Dec. 1725; proved 30 May 1727; commission to Henry Palmer the Attorney of Burch Hothersall and George Howe. (128 Farrant.) To my dau. Sarah 3 negros, & in default of issue to my dau. Barbara, then to my kinsman Wm Wheeler Skeet. To my dau. Sarah at 21 £720 c. £100 to my niece Sarah Walwin at 21. All my remaining slaves to be sold, & all residue to my 2 daus. equally. My friends Burch Hothersall, Esq., & Geo. Howe, mercht, Ex'ors & Guardians. Witnessed by Thomas Harrison, James Hasel, John Tyache. Barbados. By Henry Worsley, Esq., Governor, etc., appeared William Webster, Esq., Deputy-Secretary, and swore to the copy.

John, Viscount Barrington. Will dated 1726. (142 Brodrepp.) My wife's late father Sir Wm Daines of Bristol, Kt. My brother Saml Shute, Esq., now Governor of New England. Nephew John Yeamans, Esq., £20 & Guardian.

Elizabeth Yeamans of Bristol, widow. Will dated 28 Sep. and proved 15 Dec. 1727 by the Ex'ors. (313 Farrant.) My 3 daus. Mary, Eliz., & Blanch at 21, & my 2 sons Geo. & Fred. on being put out apprentice, £30 each. My good friends John Shuter & Wm Calcott, clothiers, Ex'ors in Trust. Witnessed by John Hart, Nl Careless.

Richard Yeamans of Redland, co. Gloucester, deceased. Adm'on 12 March 1733 to Susannah Yeamans the relict.

Jarret Yeamans of St. Philip and St. Jacob, co. Gloster, brass-maker. Will dated 10 Oct. and proved 9 Nov. 1734 by Margery Yeamans the relict. All my goods to my wife Margery & Ex'trix. Mr Nehemiah Champion & Mr Moses Slade overseers. Witnessed by Walter Parker, William Shartman. Recorded at Bristol. Seal: . . . . *a chevron or between three garbs . . . .* (? *cronels of spears*).

Mary Yeamans of Bristol, spinster. Will dated 9 June 1744; proved 16 March 1744 by John Hipsly and Richard Parker, Mary Willoughby renouncing. (101 Seymer.) Of advanced age. Am seised of the mess. in St Michael's parish given to John Hipsly of Bristol, Gent., & Richd Parker, Gent., in Trust for my niece Mary Willoughby, wife of Tho. Willoughby of Bristol, merch[t]. Release all bonds of my neph. Cha. Hood of Lond., stuff-printer. Mary Willoughby sole Ex'trix. Trustees to be overseers. To my sister Odey, sister Yeamans, cousin Skinner, & cousin Arthur, his wife, & children, each a piece of gold. Witnessed by Edward Kendrick, Samuel Adey, Jo. Harris.

John Yeamans of St. James, Westminster, Esq. Will dated Feb. 1747; proved 27 June 1750 by Shute Shrimpton Yeamans the son. (249 Greenly.) All my real & personal estate to my only son Shute Shrimpton Yeamans, he to pay following legacies. To my niece Sarah Black, wife of M[r] Johannis Windt of S[t] Thomas, £400. To M[rs] Eliz. Stoddard of Boston £20 a year, she being the mother of my late wife. £10 a year each to M[rs] Mary Stoddard, M[rs] Sarah Stoddard, & M[rs] Mehitabel Stoddard, all of Boston, & sisters of my late dear wife. My son to be sole Ex'or. If he die before me then £200 a year to my dau. Matilda my son's wife, charged on my estate in Antigua. All my real estate on that Island I give to Geo. Thomas, Esq., Sam[l] Martin, Esq., & Sam[l] Martin the Younger, Esq., all now or late of Antigua, in Trust for the heirs male of my son, charged with the payment of £800 to M[rs] Mary Black, £40 a year to M[rs] Eliz. Stoddard, £20 a year each to M[rs] Mary, M[rs] Sarah, & M[rs] Mary Stoddard, all these legacies in lieu of the ones above given. If my son die before me without heirs, then all my real estate in Antigua & my personalty in England in trust for M[rs] Mary Black & her heirs, & all that in New England for Eliz., Mary, Sarah, & Mehitabel Stoddard & their heirs, & in default to Eliakim Hutchinson, Esq., of Boston. My trustees to be Ex'ors if my son die before me, & I give them £50 apiece. Witnessed by H. Maria Byam, Lydia Byam, Elizabeth Mackinen.

Elizabeth Yeamans.* Will . . . . To Eliz[th] Yeamans, dau. of my son John Yeamans, late of Rhode Island, dec[d], my plate & furniture. To Eliz[th] Kidd & Ann Redmond, daus. of my son W[m] Redmond, dec[d], £10 c. each yearly for 7 years. To my nephew Cæsar s. of my sister Mary Roach all residue, he to be Ex'or. Before Governor John Tomlinson was sworn John Martin 31 Aug. 1750.

William Yeamans of Antigua, Gent. Will dated 9 Aug. 1750; proved 29 Dec. 1755 by William Mackinen and William Maxwell, Esquires. (332 Paul.) To Wm Mackinen, Esq., & D[r] W[m] Maxwell all my estate real & personal in trust for the maintenance of my son John Yeamans, his wife & children, & all residue to my grandson W[m] Yeamans [to the 1st son of my son John with remainder to my grandson Thos. Yeamans Eliot]. To my granddau. Eliz. Rachel Ann Yeamans £500 c. at 21. The like sum to my granddau. Frances Mackinen. [To my dau. Mary Martin £500 c. if she survive her husband Josiah Martin; to my dau. Eliz. Maxwell the reversion of 20 acres given by me to my son for his life & scandalously sold for his debts, & now in possession of Harry Webb.] I appoint W[m] Mackinen & W[m] Maxwell [my son John] Ex'ors. Witnessed by James Kittrick, James Craik, Nathaniel Webb. By the Hon. John Tomlinson, Esq., Lieut.-Governor of Antigua, were sworn on 20 March 1753 Nathaniel Webb, planter, James McKittrick, Surgeon, Rev. Charles Rose, Doctor of Laws, and Samuel Martin of St. John's, merchant, all of Antigua. Testator after the christening of his grandson William Yeamans, son of his son John, altered his will in his favour.

N.B.—The portions placed in brackets have been all drawn through in the will.

* Daughter of William Halliday. Captain William Redman or Redmond was her first husband and Joseph Yeamans her second. Her sister Mary married 1708 Major John Roach.

Frances Mackennin Yeamans of Bristol, spinster, and William Yeamans of ditto, bachelor, deceased. Adm'on 30 Sep. 1757 to Elizabeth Ann Yeamans the mother.

1765, May 11. Adm'on of Elizabeth Ann Yeamans, late of Clifton, co. Gloucester, widow, deceased, granted to Elizabeth Rachel Ann Laroche the daughter.

Shute Shrimpton Yeamans of Richmond, co. Surrey, Esq. Will dated 4 Aug. 1768; proved 30 Sep. 1769 by William Gunthorpe and Samuel Mercer, Esquires; power reserved to William Berners, Esq., and Thomas Greenough. (330 Bogg.) £50 for funeral. To my son John my watch & rings. To my son Shute Yeamans my silver tureen, large cup, 3 cases of knives & forks, & bread casket. The remainder of my plate, jewels, books, to my son John. The lease of my house on Richmond Green to be sold. To my son Shute £4000 at 21. To my servant Sarah Walton £21 for her care of my late wife & dau. in their illnesses. £5 to each other servant. I give my son Shute the Chelsea farm, n[r] Boston, N.E., now let to Rob[t] Temple, Esq., at £40 a year. All my lands in Antigua, in N.E., & N. Hampshire to W[m] Berners, Esq., of Wolverston Park, co. Suffolk, W[m] Gunthorpe of Antigua, Esq., Sam[l] Mercer of London, Esq., & M[r] Tho. Greenough of Boston, on trust for my son John at 21, & his heirs, then to my son Shute, then to my aunts Mary Chauncy, Sarah Greenough, & Mehetable Hyslop of Boston. All residue to my son John at 21, then to my son Shute. Trustees to be Ex'ors & Guardians, & I give them each £50. Witnessed by Godfrey Kettle, Basinghall Street, London, Timothy Thornhill, clerk to Mr. Kettle, Howell Powell, servant to Mr. Kettle.

Shute Yeamans, now residing in South Audley Street, Grosvenor Square, Esq. Will dated 28 April and proved 5 Oct. 1774 by William Davis; power reserved to Henry Perkins Weston. (383 Bargrave.) All sums I owe to Joseph Dallaway of Old North Str., Red Lion Sq., tailor, to be p[d]. To my servant Tho. Dear £200. All residue to my friends Henry Perkins Weston of West Horsley, co. Surrey, Esq., & W[m] Davis of Buckingham Str., York Buildings, Surgeon, & Ex'ors. Witnessed by William Harborne. On 5 Sep. 1774 appeared Charles Harman of Queen Corner, Christ Church, London, Gent., who well knew testator, who was formerly of Richmond, co. Surrey, late of St. George, Hanover Square, but at sea, Esq., deceased.

John Walcot, Esq., in his will proved 1776 names his late wife Mary Yeamans and his son Edmund Walcot, who was largely provided for by the will of his late grandfather John Yeamans, Esq.

Extracts from the Great Orphan Book of Wills, Bristol.

1564. James Dowle, grocer. Witnessed by William Yeman.

1565. Michael Colstonne, draper. William Yemanns an overseer.

William Yeman, glover, of the cytie of Bristoll. Will dated 21 Dec. 1573; proved 5 April 1574. To my son William 2 houses in S[t] Peter's & one in S[t] James's parish in Brodemede, also £20 & best goblett. W[m] Yeman the Y[r], grocer, to have custody of this son W[m]. My daus. Alice, Margery, Kath., & Joan £20 apiece, & base dau. Kath. £5, paid at 20. My father John Yeman a silver spoon. Wife Joan to have the residue & Ex'trix. Recorded at Bristol.

1575. John Boydell, vintner. Tenement in the High Street in the occupation of Wm Yeman the elder.

William Yeman of Bristowe. Will dated 14 Nov. and proved 7 Jan. 1580. To be buried in All Saints' Church. Mr Haslyn the Vicar there 3*s.* 4*d.*, & a preacher at my burial 6*s.* 8*d.* 6 poor men to have 6 gowns. My son Wm 2 goblets, the best ring of gold with a seal in him, etc. Susan Yeman £3 6*s.* 8*d.* at day of marriage; the same to her sister Mary Yeman. My dau. Joan Hunt £6 13*s.* 4*d.*, etc. Joan dau. of Ed. Evenet £3 6*s.* 8*d.* at day of marriage; the same to her sisters Florence and Alice Evenet. 20*s.* to Joan dau. of John Yeman, shoemaker, at her marriage; the same to her sister Annis Yeman & the same to Grace Yeman their sister in Cardiff. 20*s.* to cousin Joan dau. of Stephen Tanner at marriage. Legacies also to Agnes dau. of Arthur Yeman in Cardiff & her sisters Mary & Joan Yeman. All residue to my s. Wm & Ex'or. Mr Tho. Colston & Tho. Fawkett overseers.

1587. Thomas Pollington, merchant. William Yemans, grocer, an overseer.

1589. Philip Scapulis, stationer. Alice and Elizabeth Yeomans testator's maids.

BRISTOL WILLS PROVED P.C.C.

1659. John Drayton. Mr Wm Yeamans overseer. (235 Nabbs.)

1659. Arthur King. Fra. Yeaman, scrivener, overseer. (199 May.)

1663. Ann Edson, widow of Robert Edson, dyer. Kinsman Fra. Yeamans, Sr, Gent., overseer. (79 Juxon.)

1666. Robert Sheward. Witnessed by Francis Yeamans, sen. and jun. (64 Mico.)

1667. Henry Gibbs. Witnessed by Thomas Yeamans.

John Tomlinson of Bristoll, Gent. Will dated 22 Nov. 1667; proved 26 July 1673 by Mary Tomlinson the relict. (96 Pye.) Wife Mary Ex'trix. Brother Peasley's 3 children £20 each. Brother Bickham's 2 children £20 each. Sister Sarah Tomlinson £100. Brother Joseph Tomlinson houses. Cousin John Haggat, Esq., & uncle Robt Vickris, Esq., father-in-law Walter Clements, Gent., overseers.

1668. John Leaver of Barbados, merchant. Goddau. Rachel Yeomans £25. Mr Edwd Yeomans & his wife 1000 lbs. of sugar. (6 Hene.)

1669. Richard Vickris, merchant, Alderman of Bristol. Wife Alice. Grandchn John, Joseph, & Sarah Tomlinson. Brother-in-law Mr Fra. Yeomans overseer. Witnessed by Isaac Yeomans. (26 Coke.) Testator had married Alice, second daughter, and Frances Yeamans Jane, fifth daughter of Richard Cary of Bristol.

1669. Edward Morgan, sen. Marriage of my son Edward Morgan to his now wife Eliz. dau. to Joseph Yeomans. (126 Coke.)

1670. Thomas Yate. Witnessed by Thomas Yeamans. (144 Penn.)

Anna Winniatt, widow. Witnessed by Francis Yeomans, jun. (183 Penn.)

1672. Benjamin Snacknell. Witnessed by Francis Yeamans. (94 Eure.)

1673. John Willoughby. Witnessed by Thomas Yeamans. (40 Pye.)

1673. Christopher Brinsden. Witnessed by Francis Yeamans, jun.

1675. John Higginbottom. Witnessed by Thomas Yeamans. (83 Dycer.)

1678. Richard Baugh, glover. Francis Yeamans, junr, & Richd Yeamans. (1 Reeve.)

1681. Alexander James, Esq. Friend Fra. Yeamans, senr. (45 North.)

1687. Philip Tyler, merchant. Francis Yeamans, my friend & attorney. Estate at Nevis. (14 Foot.)

1687. William Pope. Messuage to Geo. Yeamans, son of sister Mary Yeamans, decd. (155 Foot.)

1688. Mathew Kelly of London, merchant. Brother Abell Kelly of Bristol, grocer. Brother-in-law John Tomlinson. Sister Martha Tomlinson. Late father Abell Kelly of Bristol, grocer. (108 Exton.)

1690. Margaret Stoakes, widow. Gods. John Yeomans, jun., s. of John Yeomans, merchant. Said John Yeomans, his wife, their son & dau. (116 Dyke.)

1690. Edward Tilly. Friend John Yeamans of St Michael's parish, merchant, Ex'or. (160 Dyke.)

1696. Thomas Jenkins. Will of Hugh Brown, Esq. Brother-in-law Joseph Tomlinson of Hawksbrooke, co. Glouc. (160 Bond.)

1697. Edmund Arundell, Esq. Friend John Yeamans, jun., merchant. (45 Pyne.)

Close Roll, 33 Geo. II., Part 14, No. 22.

Indenture made the 6th July 1759 between Shute Shrimpton Yeamans, late of Antigua, but now of Richmond, Surrey, Esq., and Matilda his wife, of the one part, and John Harvey of Antigua, planter, of the other part, witnesseth that in consideration of £1050 sterling Shute Shrimpton Yeamans and Matilda grant and confirm to John Harvey and his heirs for ever, in his actual possession being, all that plantation in the division of Old Road and parish of St. Mary, Antigua, containing 193 acres, bounded E. with the lands late of Henry Douglass, Esq., deceased, W., with the glebe land and lands late of William Furlong, deceased, N. with the mountains, and S. with the sea, to the only proper use of John Harvey and his heirs and Ex'ors for ever, but subject nevertheless to a lease thereof made by Shute Shrimpton Yeamans to Robert Lovie of Antigua, planter, for twenty-three years, by an Indenture dated the 7th Nov. 1749, and they constitute, etc., Thomas Warner, Daniel Warner, and Samuel Martin of Antigua, Esquires, their Attorneys. Michael Lovell, A. Wynne, witnesses.

Close Roll, 8 Geo. III., Part 22, Nos. 11 and 12.

Indenture made the 20th Nov. 1768 between James Laroche the younger of Clifton, co. Gloucester, Esq., and Elizabeth Rachel Ann his wife, late Elizabeth Rachel Ann Archbould, widow, and heretofore Elizabeth Rachel Ann Yeamans, spinster (sole surviving child and heir of John Yeamans, late of Antigua, Gentleman, deceased, who was eldest son of William Yeamans, heretofore of Antigua, Gentleman, deceased, and sole surviving sister and heir of William Yeamans the younger, deceased, who was grandson of William Yeamans the elder), of the one part, and James Laroche the elder of Bristol, Esq., and one of the Alderman of the City, Henry Casamaijor of Tockington in the parish of Olvestone, Gloucester, Esq., and the Rev. Daniel Debat, late of Portishead, co. Somerset, but now of the City of Bristol, Clerk, of the other part, witnesseth that in consideration of 5*s.* James Laroche the younger and Elizabeth Rachel Ann his wife grant, etc., to James Laroche the elder, Henry Casamaijor, and Daniel Debat all that plantation containing 233 acres and 20 perches in the parish of St. Paul and division of Falmouth, Antigua, bounded E. by the plantation now or late of Robin Browne, and the plantation now or late of Shute Yeamans, W. with the plantation now or late of John Burke, and the plantation now or late of . . . . N. by the plantation now or late of John Duer, and S. by the plantation now or late of Bendict Willis, and the plantation now or late of the said Robin Browne, and all that other plantation in the division of Old Road, containing 180 acres, bounded N. with the land now or late of

John Sawcolt, Esq., and Francis Burton heretofore of Antigua, Gentleman, deceased, W. with the land now or late of Ashton Warner, Esq., Thomas Williams, heretofore of Antigua, deceased, and John Franklyn, planter, S. with the land heretofore of the said Thomas Williams, and E. with the land heretofore of Edward Warner, heretofore of Antigua, Esq., deceased, and the land now or late of Samuel Redhead, Gentleman, and Frances Goss, spinster, and all negros and other slaves, and all cattle and stock of which they are seised in right of Elizabeth Rachel Ann for one whole year. Samuel Worrall. William Davids, Thomas Morgan, witnesses.

No. 11.

Indenture made the 21st Nov. 1768 as before. Whereas James Laroche the younger and Elizabeth Rachel Ann his wife, in right of her, are seised of the plantation and slaves in the parish of St. Paul and division of Falmouth, and entitled to the reversion and remainder in fee simple of the plantation and slaves in the division of Old Road. Now this Indenture witnesseth that for settling and assuring the said premises to the several uses hereinafter mentioned, and in consideration of 5*s*. James Laroche and Elizabeth Rachel Ann his wife grant, etc., to James Laroche, Henry Casamaijor, and Daniel Debat, in their possession being, all that plantation (as in No. 12) in trust to the use of James Laroche for life, and after his death to Elizabeth Rachel Ann for life if she survives him, and from the death of the survivor to preserve the contingent remainders to their children as they shall appoint, and if there are no children to such persons as Elizabeth Rachel Ann shall appoint, and if she shall survive James Laroche, and marry again, she may demise to any person in trust for such husband for life one undivided moiety, and if there are children of such other marriage they are to share equally with the others, and if James Laroche and Elizabeth Rachel Ann his wife are minded to sell the plantations, etc., they may do so, but the money to be in trust as aforesaid to purchase lands, etc., in fee simple in England.

One of the earliest and most respectable settlers in Antigua, named Yeamans, says an account of that island, was carried off by the Caribs . . . . He, however, returned to Antigua after an absence of several years, at the felicitous moment when his wife was about giving her hand to another husband. (The 'West India Sketch Book,' vol. ii., p. 253.)

Francis Yeamans, s. of F., of Bristol, Gent., matric. from Queen's Coll. 5 April 1682, aged 16. (Foster's 'Alumni Oxonienses.')

Robt Yeamans, Pleb., matric. from Magd. Hall 10 March 1656-7, Demy 1657—62, B.A. 12 Feb. 1658-9, M.A. 3 Dec. 1661, Fellow 1662—5. M.I. in North Aston Church, Oxon, to Robert s. of Francis Yeamans of Bristol, d. 28 June 1665, æt. 23. (*Ibid.*)

Weare Yeamans, s. of John, of Bristol, Gent., matric. from Balliol Coll. 2 March 1699-1700, aged 16, B.A. 1703, M.A. 1708. (*Ibid.*)

Wm Yeaman of Bristol, Pleb., matric. from Balliol Coll. 8 Nov. 1594, aged 16, B.A. 4 May 1598, M.A. from Gloucester Hall 10 July 1601 (as Yemans), Vicar of St Philip's, Bristol, 1603, Preb. 1622. (*Ibid.*)

Gervase Yeoman, s. of Wm. of Bristol, Sacerd., matric. from Magd. Hall 23 May 1628, aged 19 (as Yeman), B.A. 5 Feb. 1628-9, M.A. 20 Oct. 1631, Vicar of Weare, co. Som., 1632. (*Ibid.*)

1638. John Yeomons, Thomas Yeomans, and Robert Yeamans inhabitants of Barbados.

In a pamphlet printed in 1643, styled 'The two state martyrs or The Murther of Master Robert Yeomans, and Master George Bowcher, Citizens of Bristoll,' it is stated that the said Robert Yeomans had served as Sheriff of Bristol the previous year, and that he had H.M. Commission to raise a Regiment of Foot. Reference is also made to William Yeomans his brother, John Haggat his brother-in-law, Mistress Hazard his sister, and Master Yeomans his father-in-law. He was buried the night of his execution at Christ Church. He left a widow great with child, and eight small children, the eldest not able to put on its clothes. His estate was confiscated, but his widow was enabled to redeem the residue of it for £500.

Jane, fifth daughter of Richard Cary of Bristol, who died 1644, by Mary Shershaw, married Francis Yeomans of Bristol, Gent.

Book of Burgesses, Bristol.

1647, April 1. George Yeamans, merchant, son of John Yeamans, brewer, admitted to freedom.

1647, April 1. Joseph Yeamans, brewer, son of John Yeamans, brewer, admitted to freedom.

1647, Nov. 10. Edmund Yeamans, merchant, son of William Yeamans, merchant, admitted to freedom.

1649, Aug. 31. John Yeamans, merchant, son of John Yeamans, brewer, admitted to freedom.

Register of Mr. Dugard's Private School, London, 1661-2. John Yeamans, eldest son of William, merchant, b. in St. Margaret, Lothbury, aged 12. (See 'Misc. Gen. et Her.,' New Series, vol. iv., p. 345.)

1665. John Yeamans, a respectable planter of Barbados, sailed from that island with a party of emigrants to establish a colony on the south side of Cape Fear in America. (Southey, vol. ii., p. 59.)

1668, Dec. 23. Indenture of lease. Colonel Thomas Middleton of London, Esq., leases to William Yeamans of London, merchant, the plantation of Captain Fletcher of 1050 acres. Witnessed by John Yeamans.

1676—1680. Barbados Census. St. James's Parish. Elizabeth Yeamans.

St. Lucy's Parish. Dame Willoughby Yeamans.

St. Peter's Parish. The Lady Willoughby Yeamans.

1678, Dec. 14. Henry Nicols, Gent., sells 10 acres in the Road Division to John Yeamans, Gent.

1678, Jan. 8. John Yeamans leases 145 acres to Henry Nicoles.

"That this day being ye Eight of January 1678 wee under written was prsent and did see ye within mentioned John Yeamans give Liverie and seisien unto ye within named Henry Nicoles turfe and twig uttering these words following, vizt: here I deliver speaking to ye said Henry Nicoles and delivering him turf and twig to your seisien of this Land in ye name of all ye Land contained in this deed according to ye forme and effect of ye deed, to you dureing yor naturall Life; and likewise ye said John Yeamans speaking then to ye said Henry Nicoles holding ye latch of ye doore belonging unto his now dwelling house I deliver you seisein of this house in ye name of all ye houses, Tenements, and what els is Contained in this deed to you dureing your naturall Life. Row. Williams."

1681, Dec. 10. Captain John Yeamans, 155 acres. Patent by Sir W. Stapleton.

1682, May 21. Captain John Yeamans, 100 acres. Patent by Sir W. Stapleton.

1682-3. Sir W. Stapleton writes that Thomas Middleton, Esq., before his death sold his great settlement called Middleton and Fletcher to one Yeomans of London, who enjoyed it since the war, also Mr. Yeamans' relict and successors.

1688. In an Indenture of this year John Yeamans is described as "late Governor of Antigua."

1697, Dec. 7. John Yeamans, Esq., Deputy-Governor and Escheator, 28 acres granted by patent from Governor Christopher Codrington.

1701. Joseph Yeamans, Master of the sloop "Charles." (Royal African Accounts.)

1704, July 12. John Yeamans, Esq., 80 acres. Patent by Governor Christopher Codrington.

1705. John Yeamans applies for payment of his salary of £200 a year as Lieut.-Governor of Antigua. (Calendar of Treasury Papers, p. 360.)

1707, Dec. Joseph Yeamans of St. John's Town petitions that he was lately employed as Master, Lieut., and Pilot on the sloop "Anne," and claims 6s. per diem for 36 days. (Minutes of Assembly.)

1709, Nov. 17. Lieut.-Governor John Yeamans was bred to law, and is not a soldier. (B. T. Leeward Islands, vol. 49.)

1710, Sep. 23. Petition of John Yeamans, Esq., of Parham, to build a wharf near his house; granted. (Minutes of Council.)

1711, July 2. Joseph Yeamans, Master of the sloop the "Delight," Mr. Edward Chester's. (*Ibid.*)

1713, Dec. 16. Elizabeth Yeamans, widow, petitions that William Redman, her former husband, for £40 paid to Thomas Balaam, by deed dated 14 Aug. 1694, purchased four parcells of land on the N. side of St. John's, and built two houses on the S. side of the street and on the W. side of the Queen's highway. Abigail widow of Thomas Balaam claims them. Elizabeth Yeamans has four poor fatherless children.

1713, Feb. 12. Elizabeth Yeamans, widow, her former husband William Redman, *re* four proportions of land; surveyed.

1715. Barbados Census. St. Peter's Parish. Dame Margaret Yeamans 45, a son 13, and a daughter 18; a servant maid 23, and child 6. Sir John Yeamans 26, his Lady 26, and servants, a boy 14, a girl 13.

St. Michael's Parish. Mrs. Sarah Yeamans, 2 women, 40, 24, a boy 18, a girl 4 months.

St. James's Parish. Colonel Robert Yeamans, 3 men, 30, 45, 48; 2 women, 30, 40; 3 boys, 9, 10, 12; 2 girls, 4, 6.

1715, July 30. William Redman of Antigua, mariner, sells one proportion of land in St. John's Town to his mother Mrs. Elizabeth Yeamans of Antigua, widow, formerly wife of Captain William Redman of Antigua, deceased.

1715, Dec. 13. Petition of William Redmond of St. John's Town for land N. with the street, S. with Elizabeth Yeamans, E. with Mrs. Balaam, W. with Ric. Mercer.

1716, June 16. Yeamans, Joannes, Anglo-Britannus. (Leyden University.)

In the parish church of Westbury-upon-Trym (Redland being part of the parish) there is an old alms-dish, which bears this inscription:—"Dame Abigail Yeamans, Relict of Sr Robert Yeamans, late of Redland, K^t Bar^t, gave this Silver Basin to ye Parish Church of Westbury upon Trim for Collecting ye Charity money at ye Comunion there, Octr 7, 1716 R Y A." ('Gloucester Notes and Queries,' vol. ii., p. 95.)

1716-17, Feb. 4. William Yeamans petitions for 30 acres between the lands late of Powells, now possessed by John Yeamans, Esq., and one Bishop; granted.

Michael Harvey, M.P. for Weymouth, married secondly Agnes daughter of Thomas Yeoman (Yeman or Yeamans). She was born *circa* 1648, married 1664, and died 1716-17. Arms: *Gules, a chevron between three spear-heads argent.* (See Harvey Pedigree in 'Misc. Gen. et Her.,' Second Series, vol. iii., p. 362.)

1717-18, March 2. At Vestry Meeting, St. Mary's Parish. By Indenture dated 11 July 1717 between Hon. John Yeamans of Antigua, Esq., and Elizabeth his wife, and Rev. John Simpson of Antigua, Clerk, 60 acres for glebe were given, bounded N. with John Yeamans and the top of Dildo Hill, and W. with Charles Jacobs, and S. with the sea.

1718, June 23. John Barrington of Tofts, co. Essex, Esq., writes to Mr. Popple: "My Nephew Mr Yeamans, who will have the pleasure to deliver this to you, being ready to Embark for Antego, where he has a considerable Plantation, I beg the favor of you to procure him a Mandamus to be One of the Councill of that Island." Received 25 June 1718.

1718, July 4. Mr. Barrington writes a second letter on hearing there is no vacancy.

1718, Oct. 4. Also a third one from Beckett House, near Farrington, co. Berks, about his nephew Mr. John Yeamans, who had not been appointed as he was led to expect. The seal has the Barrington arms. (B. T. Leeward Islands, vol. 15.)

Petition of William Yeamans, Esq.; his plantation, formerly that of John Yeamans, Esq., of 100 acres at Old North Sound; surveyed 26 Nov. 1718.

1719, July 6. John Yeamans, Esq., took the oaths and his seat at the Council Board, having been appointed *vice* Colonel William Thomas, deceased. His mandamus was dated 6 Dec. 1718.

1719, Aug. 12. An Act was presented to enable John Yeamans, Esq., to sell his moiety of a certain plantation and negros. William Yeamans, Esq., opposes it, with Edward Shilfe, Esq., and William Hinde, Esq., his Council. John Yeamans was heard by Michael Arnald, his Council, and the Bill was rejected. On the previous 7th Aug. he had petitioned that he held his plantation in fee tail, and had a wife and relations he wanted to provide for, and wished to dock the intail.

1725, Aug. 14. William Yeamans of Antigua, Esq., and Mary his wife sell 50 acres to Thomas Bishop.

1727, Dec. 15. John Yeamans, Esq., now in London, to be Agent.

1732, Feb. 4. William Yeamans, Esq., resigns his seat as Member for Old North Sound.

1735, July 10. William Yeamans gives 20 acres to his son John Yeamans.

1735, Dec. 12. An Act for continuing John Yeamans, Esq., as Agent for three years. (B. T. Leeward Islands, vol. 55.)

1742, Sep. 6. William Yeamans, jun., joins the Troop.

1742, Dec. 15. John Yeamans, Agent, given six months' leave to visit Antigua.

1742-3, Feb. 16. John Yeamans, Esq., appointed Member of Council *vice* Valentine Morris, deceased. (B. T. Leeward Islands, vol. 55, p. 235.)

1743, May 10. Long letter from John Yeamans to the Lords Commissioners of the Board of Trade. He had just been appointed Member of H.M. Council of Antigua on 27 April 1743 *vice* Valentine Morris, deceased, and applies for his proper seniority, stating that he was first appointed Member of H.M. Council in 1719, served till 1730, when he resigned, and has been Agent from 1730 till the present time. The Governor is later instructed to inform him that he cannot take his former rank. (*Ibid.*, vol. 27, p. 55.)

1743, March 21. Letter read from John Yeamans, Agent, dated at Boston, New England, 9 and 10 Feb. 1743, notifying his resignation as Agent.

1744, June 1. William Yeamans, Esq., struck off Troop as being infirm.

1748, Sep. 1. Shute Shrimpton Yeamans present at the Council Board for the first time. In a deposition of 2 Nov. 1749 his age was given as 28. (B. T. Leeward Islands, vol. 29.)

1760. The Proclamation of George III. at Montserrat was signed, among others of the Council and Assembly, by John Yeamans.

A Shute Shrimpton Yeamans was rated for St. Peter's Parish 1800—1815, but was apparently dead in 1816. (Vestry Book.)

There is a short pedigree of Shrimpton, Stoddard, and Yeomans in the 'New England Historical and Genealogical Register' for 1854.

PARISH REGISTER OF ST. JOHN.

Baptized.

1703 Nov. 28 John Halliday Yeamans, s. of John (? Joseph) Yeamans & Elizabeth his wife.

1706 Feb. 16 Elizabeth D. of Joseph Yeamans & Elizabeth his wife.

1708 Feb. 13 Joseph S. of Joseph Yeamans & Elizabeth his wife.

1712 Oct. 20 Ann D. of Joseph Yeamans & Elizabeth his wife.

(?1731) .... 28 John and Eliz^th^ s. and d. of Jo .... Yeamans & Margaret his wife.

1745 June 9 Richard William the s. of William & Dorothy Yeamans.

1746-7 Mar. 25 Eliz. Rachel the D. of John Yeamans & Eliz^th^ Ann his wife.

1749 June 18 Frances M^c^Kennin the D. of John Yeamans, Jn^r^, and Ann his wife.

1760 Jan. 29 Mary the D. of John Yeamans and Ann his wife.

1761 May 2 Elizabeth the D. of John Yeamans and Ann his wife.

Married.

1701-2 .... 28 Joseph Yeamans & Eliz. Redman.

Buried.

1691 June 13 John Youman.
1712 Oct. 25 Ann D. of Joseph Yeamans.
1715 Jan. 13 Eliz. Yeamans.
1715-16 Mar. 20 Joseph Yeamans.
1731 Oct. 5 John s. of Jno Yeamans.
1750 Aug. 18 Elizabeth Yeamans.
1781 May 5 Ann Yeamans.
1787 Aug. 21 Joseph Yeamans.

PARISH REGISTER OF ST. PHILIP.

Married.

1737 Sep. 4 John Yeamans, Esqr, to Elizabeth Ann Kerr.

Buried.

1724 Dec. 24 John Yeamons.
1742 (? Aug.) 2 Mary Infant D. of John Yeamons.

PARISH REGISTER OF ST. PAUL.

Baptized.

1731 Aug. 22 Rachel D. of William Yeamons, Esqr, & Mary his wife.

Married.

1735 May 8 Mr Josiah Martin & Mrs Mary Yeamons.

1737 .... ot (Samuel Eliot) & Mrs Elizabeth Yeamons.

1741 April 9 Mr Nicholas Collins & Mrs Frances Yeamons; by L.

1749 July 13 James Em ...., Esqr, and Mrs Rachael Yeamons; by L.

Buried.

1729 April 20 Rachael D. of William and Mary Yeamons.

PARISH REGISTER OF ST. GEORGE.

Baptized.

1749 Dec. 19 Jno the S. of Shute Shrimpton Yeamans & Matilda his wife. B. Dec. 1st.

Married.

1746 April 17 Shute S^n^ Yeamans & Mathilda Gunthorpe, spinster.

RICHMOND, SURREY.

Baptized.

1752 Mar. 12 Ann d. of Shute Shrimpton Yeamans, Esqre, & Matilda his wife.

1754 Nov. 16 Shute s. of Shute Shrimpton Yeamans, Esqre, & Matilda his wife.

Buried.

1769 Sep. 18 Shute Shrimpton Yeamans, Esq.

ST. PETER'S, CORNHILL.

(Harl. Soc. Pub., vol. xiv.)

Buried.

1697 Mar. 30 Mary wife of Henry Yeomans of Enfield, Gent., in the South Chappell, near her ffather Benjamin Shute.

ST. MARY REDCLIFFE, BRISTOL.

Baptized.

1611 Feb. 28 John the sonne of John Yeomans.
1614 Feb. 26 Patience the daughter of John Yeomans.
1615 Feb. 17 Anthony the sonne of John Yeomans.
1617 April 19 Robert the sonne of John Yeomans, Brewer.
1618 June 16 Sara Yeomans, the daughter of John Yeomans.
1619 Sep. 27 Joseph the sonne of John Yeomans.
1620 Oct. 3 Martha Yeomans, the daughter of John Yeomans.
1623 May 29 Jone Yeomans, the daughter of John Yeomans.
1624 Mar. 13 Richard Yeomans, the sonne of John Yeomans.
1649 Nov. 20 Elizabeth da. to Joseph Yeomans & wyfe.
1651 Oct. 31 Joseph sonn to Mr Joseph Yeomans.
1653 May 29 Elizabeth da. to Mr Joseph Yeomans.
1656 Feb. 13 William son to Mr Joseph Yeamans.
1657 Mar. 22 Robert son to Mr Joseph Yeamans.
* Aug. 30 Georg son to Joseph Yeamanes.
1663 Jan. 20 Richard sonn to Mr Joseph Yeamans.

Married.

1610 John Yeomans and Blanche Germain; wedded June the 29th.

Buried.

1600 July 13 John Yemans.
1603 Jan. 17 Frances d. to Alice Yemans, widdo.
1603 Jan. 28 Wm Yemans s. to Alice Yemans.
1603 Feb. 15 Alice Yemans, widdo.
1653 Feb. 10 Mr Gordge Yemanes, Juner. Bured In the curch.
1653 Feb. 11 Mr Gordge Yemanes, seneor. Bured In the curch.
1653 July 28 Mary da. to Joseph Yeamans.
1683 Dec. 9 Mrs Elesabeth Yemanes.
1685 Jan. 9 John son to Mr John Yeamanes. In the Church.
1686 Feb. 7 Sr Robert Yemanes, night & Barron night. Bured In the Curch.

ST. STEPHEN'S, BRISTOL.

Baptized.

1627 June 20 Ann the d. of William Yeamans.
1635 Aug. 24 Robert the s. of William Yeamans and Anne his wife.
1639 April 17 Richard the s. of William Yeamans & Anne ux.

* The year was accidentally omitted from my extracts.

1641 May 9 Thomas the s. of William Yeamans & Anne ux.
1641 Feb. 8 Edward the s. of Edward Yeamans & Barbara ux.
1643 Sep. 14 Sarah the d. of William Yeamans & Anne ux.
1646 June 12 John s. of William Yeamans & . . . .

In 1640 William Yeamans was churchwarden.

Married.

1647 April 26 Thomas Yeamans & Mary Hathaway.
1647 Sep. 16 Joseph Yeamans & Elizabeth Payne.
1650 Jan. 1 Thomas Yeamanes & hanah Hames.
1670 April 20 Jossua Powell & Sarah Yeamans. Lifence.

St. Werburg's, Bristol.

Baptized.

1644 Anne the d. of William Yeomans and Anne his wife the 31 daie of May.
1684 Elizabeth d. of Robt Yeomans 30th November.
1686 Mary d. of Robert Yeamans and of Mary his wife 28th of March.

Redcliffe Church, Bristol.

On the floor of the tower, on a flat stone:—

Arms: *A chevron between three cronels of spears.*

HERE LYETH THE BODY OF JOSEPH
THE SONN OF MR JOSEPH YEAMANS
OF THIS P'ISH BREWER WHO DECEASED
MARCH YE 18 ANN DOMINI 1672
AGED 21 YEARES AND 5 MONTHS.
ALSO HERE LYETH YE BODY
OF WILLIAM YE SON OF MR JOSEPH
YEAMANS SENIOR HEE DIED YE 17
OF SEPTEMBER ANNO 1680
AGED 2 YEARS & 8 MONETHS.

On a second flat stone, adjoining the above:—

At the top are the arms of Yeamans impaling . . . . *a bend cotised* . . . . the name YEAMANS can be read, but the other lines are worn away so as to be illegible.

Hanging on the wall is a wooden representation of a mayor's mace on a board, with the following inscription beneath it:—

1686 Sr Robert Yeamans Knight
& Baronet, Mayor of this Citty
1669 And Borne in this Parish
1617, gave £50 the Proffit
thereof to the poor of this
Parish in Bread on every
Lords day for ever.
1729 Rd from the eftate of
Lady Yeamans £13 17s. 6*d.* the
Intereft to the poor f . . ever.

St. Peter's Church, Antigua.

South wall, black and white tablet:—

This Monument | Was erected by RACHEL EMRA | To the Memory of | her beloved Husband | JAMES EMRA* *ESQRE.* | Who departed this Life | December 28 1759 | Aged 37 Years.

"Yeamans" is in St. Peter's Parish. In 1852 it contained 120 acres, and was owned by Messrs. R. and H. Jefferson. "Mill Hill" is in St. Mary's Parish, and in 1852 contained 333 acres, and was in the possession of Edward Lipscombe.

* 1746. Thomas Emra, Esq; of the Island of Nevis, to Miss Elizabeth Hudson, of Roscommon in Ireland. ('Lond. Mag.,' p. 647.)

Pedigree of Yorke.

AMBROSE YORKE, Esq., of Dickson's Bay, Antigua, 1678. Will dated 2 March 1716; sworn 25 May 1717. = Margaret . . . . living 1725. Will recorded at St. John's before 1753.

Children:

- John Yorke, 1st son.
- Ambrose Perrie Yorke of Antigua, planter, 2nd son and heir, joins the Troop 1718; mortgaged his estates to Valentine Morris, Esq. Will dated 5 June 1731; sworn 12 Oct. 1738. = Rachel . . . .
- William Yorke, witness to the will of his brother Perrie 1731.
- Elizabeth Yorke, mar. 20 Feb. 1724, at St. John's, Robert Dunning. His will dated 6 Feb. 1734.
- A dau., mar. Thomas Hanson.

Children of Ambrose Perrie Yorke and Rachel:

- Ambrose Yorke (? bur. 5 Jan. 1766 at St. John's).
- Perrie Yorke, a minor 1731.
- Ann Yorke, bapt. 22 Dec. 1728 at St. John's; bur. there 18 June 1732.
- Margaret Yorke, bapt. *circa* 1731 at St. John's.
- Ambrose Yorke, bur. 4 Oct. 1728 at St. John's.
- Samuel Yorke, bur. 18 Nov. 1726 at St. Peter's.

Ambrose Yorke, Esq., of Antigua. Will dated 2 March 1716. To my 2d son Perrie Yorke all my estate, he to pay all legacies. To my 1st son John Yorke £60 c. yearly for 7 years. To my wife Margt 2 negros in addition to her thirds. To my son Ambrose Perrie £400 c. at 21 & maintenance. To my son Wm Yorke £400 c. at 21. To my dau. Elizth Yorke £400 c. at 21. To my son Wm Yorke my land in New Division now leased to my son-in-law Thos. Hanson. Mr Geo. Leonard & Thos. Hanson Ex'ors & Guardians. Witnessed by Robert Delamer, Charles McReily, William Hinde. Before Edward Byam were sworn Robert Delamer and Charles McReily 25 May 1717.

Margaret Yorke, widow. Will dated 9 Jan. . . . . Witnessed by Elizabeth Yorke, Margaret Yorke, James Millar. Before Hon. John Tomlinson appeared James . . . . yeoman of Antigua. Recorded before 1753.

Perrie Yorke, planter. Will dated 5 June 1731. To my son Perrie Yorke £500 c. at 21. To my dau. Ann Yorke £500 c. at 19. To my dau. Margt £500 c. at 21, & to each of them & to my son Ambrose maintenance. To any future child £500 c. To Ashton Warner £42 c. My estate to be charged with my debts & those of my late father. All residue to my son Ambrose, Ashton Warner,

Tho. Stevens, & Dr Wm Young, Ex'ors & Guardians. Witnessed by Richard Baker, John Hixon, William Yorke. Before William Mathew, Ashton Warner renounced execution and legacy 12 Oct. 1738, and Ashton Warner, Esq., Robert Addison, merchant, James Hanson, coppersmith, and Robert James, book-keeper, swore to handwriting, all the witnesses being now dead. Recorded 18 Oct. 1738.

1672, Nov. 2. John Everard of Antigua, planter, sells to Thomas Yorke of Antigua, planter, 10 acres.

1674. Thomas Yorke, patent for 10 acres 26 Jan. 1673 by Governor Warner; surveyed 1 Nov.

1677. Thomas Yorke, grant of Tropic Bird Island 23 June 1676 by Governor Williams, and 20 acres 27 March 1677 by Governor Warner; surveyed Sep.

1678. Mr. Thomas Yorke, 20 acres from the Governor; surveyed 4 Dec.

1679, July 22. William Hill, planter, sells to Ambrose Yorke, planter, 30 acres in St. John's Division, bounded N. and W. with Thomas Oliver, N. with Christopher Reed, E. and S. with Edmund Hull.

1679, Sep. 29. Thomas Yorke, planter, sells to Philip Lile, planter, 20 acres at Nonsuch.

1680, May 25. Dennis Crawley, planter, sells 10 acres to Thomas Yorke.

Ambrose Yorke, Gent., 35 acres and 15 acres and 30 acres in Dickinson's Bay, bounded N. and W. with Thomas Oliver, and two proportions at St. John's Town; patent granted 21 Jan. 1684 by Sir W. Stapleton.

1688. Ambrose York was rated on 6 slaves and 20 acres in 1692, on 13 slaves and 220 acres in 1696, on 12 slaves and 152 acres; and 7 June 1706 on 56 slaves and 138 acres. (St. Mary's Vestry Book.)

1706. Captain Ambrose Yorke, 6 acres on 9 July 1706 by John Johnson, Esq.

Indenture dated 18 Sep. 1724 between Margaret Yorke, widow, and her son Ambrose Yorke, merchant; sale of house in St. John's Town to James Hanson.

1735, Jan. 12. Mr. Perrie Yorke was then a Member of Vestry, St. Mary's Parish.

PARISH REGISTER OF ST. JOHN.

Baptized.

1728 Dec. 22 Ann the d. of Ambrose York and his wife.
(?1731) ...... Margaret the d. of Ambrose York & Rachell his wife.

Married.

1724 Feb. 20 Robert Dunning and Eliz^a Yorke. L.
1743 July 17 William Yorke and Ann Jones.

Buried.

1728 Oct. 4 Ambrose S. of Ambrose Yorke.
1732 June 18 Ann D. of Ambrose Yorke.
1766 Jan. 5 Ambrose Yorke. C.P.

PARISH REGISTER OF ST. PAUL.

Married.

1748 Aug. 16 William Yorke and Anne Hicks, Widow; by B.

PARISH REGISTER OF ST. PETER.

(B. T. Leeward Islands, vol. 19.)

Buried.

1726 Nov. 18 Samuel S. of Ambrose York.

Family of Young.

Sir William Young of Delaford, co. Bucks, Bart. Will dated 21 March 1784. To be buried at Chartham, co. Kent, near Canterbury. By the articles on my marriage with my now wife £14,200 was agreed to be laid out by trustees for our use for our lives, & then to our 1st & other sons successively, & was invested in an estate at Standlinch in Wilts, but by an Act of Parliament 4 present reign this estate was vested in Geo. Montgomery, since decd, & Richd Maitland of London, Mercht, in trust to sell, & with £1000 I agreed to add in the purchase of other lands, & whereas I have purchased of Geo. Tash, Esq., the manor of Delaford in the parish of Iver, co. Bucks, the conveyance dated 30 July 1768, for £18,300 & part thereof £15,200 is settled to the use of my marriage articles, & I have added £400, making a total of £15,600, & while in the office of Receiver of monies for the sale of lands in the Ceded & Neutral Islands I purchased several estates on those islands, & a large debt became due from me to the Crown to satisfy which I have delivered up all my West Indian estate in trust, & I was to be paid thereout £1600 a year. All debts are to be charged on my Tobago estate, £400 to be raised to make my marriage settlement up to £16,000. The annuity due to my sister Nanton & interest due to my dau. Sarah Elizth Ottley have been provided for by the said trust deed charged on my Antigua & Calliaqua estate. To my dear wife whatever she is entitled to by settlement besides the legacy left her by her aunt Mrs Mary Taylor, also £300 yearly, jewels, carriages, horses, use of plate, furniture here & at my house in Newman Str., then to my 1st son Wm & £200 st. I covenanted by my marriage settlement to give to my 1st son £4000 or £400 a year, & I have settled on him, his wife, & their issue £400 a year in satisfaction. Whereas by my marriage settlement I covenanted to pay to my dau. Sarah Elizth Young, now widow of Richd Ottley, Esq., decd, £2000, the provision of £10,000 I made on her marriage is in full discharge of same. I also covenanted to pay £2000 to each of my younger children. To John my son & Elizth Hartley, Portia, Mary, & Olivia Young, my 4 daus., £100 yearly each as interest. To my uncle Thos. Young £50 a year as usual, & to his son Henry Young £40 a year. To my old servant Mrs Cath. Kentzill £20 a year. £33 c. yearly to Sally Bishop, a free mustee. I free also my mustee Betsy Nanton & her children. To my son-in-law Jas. Hartley £100. To Mrs Mary Hartley £50 c. To Drewry Ottley, Esq., £50 c. To my sisters Mary Hartman of St Croix & Margt Nanton of Antigua £50 c. each. To my niece Mrs Martha James of St Croix £50 c. My mulatto John to be free. To my negros on each plantation 10 barrels of good herrings & a holiday. Mourning rings to all my relations, Ex'ors & Managers of my plantations. To my son Wm £200 a year. To my son John & my 4 daus. Elizth wife of Jas. Hartley, Esq., Portia, Mary, & Olivia Young £100 a year each if possible. All residue to my son Wm. My wife, my son Wm, my dau. Sarah Elizth Ottley, & my friends Richd Hawkshaw Losack, Robt Wynne, & John Stanley, Esqres, Ex'ors. My sister Margt Nanton & my friends John Laforey, Geo. Savage, & Lachlan Grant, Esqres, Ex'ors in Antigua only. My son-in-law Jas. Hartley, Drewry Ottley, & Jas. Fraser, Esqres, Ex'ors in St Vincent & Bequia, & Jas. Hartley, Drewry Ottley, & my friends John Hamilton & Wm Bruce, Esqres, Ex'ors in Tobago. Witnessed by Ant. Richardson of Powis Place, Great Ormond Street, Peter Francklyn, late of Tobago, now of Welbeck Street, Cavendish Square, Thomas Millar of

Richmond, Yorkshire, now at Sir William Young's. Republished at St. Vincent 6 April 1788; witnessed by George Young, William Glenn, Amos Thorne.

1st Codicil dated 13 Dec. 1784. Whereas my son John hath married Miss Jane Blizard, late of Antigua, if he die before me £100 a year to his widow & £2000 to their children, & the further sum I have given him also to his 1st child. Witnessed by Ed. Pauncefort, N. Pauncefort, F. Thorne. Affidavit of Hon. George Young, Member of Council of St. Vincent 11 April 1788, before Governor James Seton. Recorded at St. Vincent 11 April 1788. Tobago recorded 8 July 1788.

2nd Codicil. St. Vincent, 7 June 1783. Mourning rings as follows to Mr Drewry Ottley, son of Mr Richd Ottley, & his wife, Mr & Mrs Joe Warner, Senr, Mr & Mrs Joe Warner, Junr, Polly Ottley, Alice Ottley. To each of my children & godchildren, Mrs & Miss Lawrence, my sister Hartman at St Croix, my sister Nanton, my nieces & nephews in St Croix, & to my niece Mrs James the ring with her sister's hair, Mrs Hartley the old lady, my uncle Mr Tho. Young, Mr Henry Young, Capt David Young, Capt Geo. Young, Govr Smart, & Capt Scott, Mr Wm Smith, Mr & Mrs Gordon, Mr & Mrs Losack, Mr Elliot of Old Road, & Mrs Ives of Old Road, my brother-in-law Sir Wm Fagg & his wife, Mr & Miss Fagg, Revd Mr Edwd Taylor, Mr & Mrs Paunceforth, to each Ex'or, attorney, & manager, to Mr John Sim & Capt. Sim, to Graney Ruthey at the Old Road, Mr Abel, Mr Horne, Mr Brunias, Mr Godschall Jackson, Mr B. & T. Boddington, Mr Manning. Confirmed 22 May 1784.

St. Vincent, 7 June 1783. To my wife my diamond mourning ring with my 1st wife's hair, my diamond heart buckle, miniature picture of my son Brook, my 1st wife's portrait. To Mrs Ottley my gold watch & enamelled picture of my 1st & present wife, & miniature of my wife by Humphrys. To Billy my silver grace cup, my father's picture of the Amorons Boy & Girl, my silver mounted hanger given to Harry by Billy. To Mrs Young a set of Johnson's poems. To Mrs Hartley a portrait of myself & wife. To Mr Hartley the measuring wheel. To Portia my gold fountain pen given me by Lord Dartmouth & Jack Young's miniature. To Mary my gold case of instruments, the picture in miniature of my 1st wife by Soldi, my large book of prints & cartoons given me by my uncle Taylor. To Jack the portrait of my brother Nanton, a case of pistols by Wogden. To Olivia 2 shells in relief set in silver from Sicily & my piano. To Billy Young my grandson my family picture at the Old Road on the death of my sister Nanton. To Wm Young Ottley my diamond mourning ring with Mr Richd Ottley's hair & Mrs Ottley's miniature. To Govr Stewart the case of pistols he gave me. Confirmed 22 May 1784. St. Vincent, before Governor James Seton appeared Henry Sharpe and Richard James Whytele, Bart., 30 April 1788. Recorded at St. Vincent 30 April 1788.

3rd Codicil dated 6 April 1788 at St. Vincent. By the Treaty of peace at Versailles 3 Sep. 1783 Tobago was ceded to France. Notice of claims should have been sent in, and at the High Court of Chancery at St Louis on 10 Sep. past under His Excelly Count Arthur Dillon my trust deed relating to Tobago was cancelled, & the Government of Tobago have very generously vested the estate in me in fee simple free of the trust deed. The said additional pro rata sums to my children to be absolute. To my wife £100 a year more. To Mrs Mary Hartley £50 c. yearly. To my dau. Elizth Sarah Ottley 100 guineas. To my son-in-law Jas. Hartley £100 c. To my friends Gilbert Hillock, Esq., & Susannah his wife £50 c. each. To Mr John Sim £50. To Capt Geo. Young of the ship Delaford now in St Vincent £50 c. To Mr Augustine Brunias £50 c. My son-in-law Jas. Hartley to be Ex'or. Lachlan Grant is since dead. Dr Fairbane, Ex'or for Antigua, & Jas. Hartley, Ex'or for St Vincent & Bequia. Tho. Wilson of Montpelier in Tobago, Esq., & Alexr Gordon of Tobago, Esq., also Ex'ors. Witnessed by George Young, William Glenn, Amos Thorne. Affidavit of Hon. George Young 11 April 1788 before Governor James Seton. St. Vincent recorded 11 April 1788; Tobago recorded 8 July 1788. Recorded at Antigua 13 Sep. 1788.

Pedigree of Young.

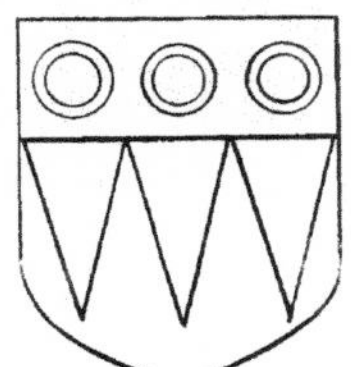

ARMS.—*Or, three piles sable, on a chief of the first three annulets of the second.*
CREST.—*A cubit arm erect, the hand grasping an arrow, all proper.*
MOTTO.—*Press through.*

SIR JOHN YOUNG of Leny in Scotland, Knt.,=. . . .
Chamberlain to Mary Queen of Scots 1561.

Sir John Young of Leny, Knt., temp. Jac. I., born 1605=. . . .

David Young, born 1623=Lady Jane Grey.

David Young, only son,=Catherine, dau. of Sir Andrew Toshaw of Monavedt by Catherine, dau. of born 1646. | Duncan Campbell, Earl of Breadalbane; mar. 1679.

A

A

David Young of Leny: his estates confiscated in 1715; eighth in direct descent from Sir John. = ...

William Young of Antigua, Surgeon, only son and heir, born 14 Nov. 1687; living Feb. 1735-6; dead 1740. = Margaret, relict of . . . . Nanton of Antigua; mar. 1720.

Thomas Young, living 1784. = ...

William Young, 2nd son, born 27 Aug. 1761 at Borrowstouness, N.B.; Vice-Admiral of the Blue 1846; died 11 Feb. 1847 at Denmark Hill, Camberwell. (See O'Byrne's 'Naval Biog. Dict.') = Ann Spencer, 1st dau. of Robert Curling of Camberwell.

Sarah, dau. of Charles Fagg of Mystole, co. Kent, Esq., granddau. of Sir John the 1st Bart.; died 1746, æt. 18. M.I. at Chartham. 1st wife. = Sir William Young, 1st Bart., only son and heir, born 1725; Member of Council for Antigua 1761; Lieut.-Governor of Dominica 1768—1774; purchased Delaford Manor in Iver, co. Bucks, 1768; created Bart. 3 May 1769; died 8 April 1788, æt. 62, at St. Vincent. Will dated 21 March 1784; sworn 11 April 1788. = Elizabeth, only child of Brook Taylor of Bifrons, co. Kent, D.C.L., F.R.S.; born 1729; bapt. 25 March 1730; mar. 1747; died 12 July 1801 at Chertsey, co. Surrey; bur. at Patrixbourne, co. Kent. 2nd wife.

s.p.

Henry Young, living 1784.

William Hall Young, 1st son, Midshipman R.N., died Oct. 1809 at Plymouth.

George Frederick Young, merchant and shipowner, M.P. for Tynemouth and Scarborough; Vice-President Board of Trade 1852; J.P. and D.L. for Middlesex; died 23 Feb. 1870 at Reigate, Surrey. = Mary, dau. of John Abbott of Brompton House, Thanet; mar. 1814.

Sarah, dau. and coheir of Charles Lawrence, Esq.; mar. Aug. 1777; died 6 Jan. 1791 in Westminster. 1st wife. = Sir William Young, 2nd Bart., F.R.S., F.S.A., born Feb. 1750; M.P. for St. Mawes 1806; Governor of Tobago, where he died 10 Jan. 1815. = Barbara, dau. of Col. Richard Talbot and Baroness Talbot de Malahide; mar. 22 April 1793 at St. George's, Hanover Square. 2nd wife.

s.p.

Sir William Lawrence Young, 3rd Bart., matric. from Brasenose College, Oxon, 15 Nov. 1794, æt. 16; Lieut.-Colonel Bucks Militia; died 3 Nov. 1824, æt. 46. = Anna Louisa, 2nd dau. of William Tufnell of Langleys, co. Essex, Esq.; mar. 21 Dec. 1805.

Brook Harry Young, Lieut.-Colonel in the Army, died 1813.

Charles Young, Lieut. R.N., died 1815.

Sir William Lawrence Young, 4th Bart., of Hughenden House, born 29 Sep. 1806; M.P. for co. Bucks; died 27 June 1842, æt. 36. = Caroline, dau. and coheir of John Norris of Hughenden House, co. Bucks, Esq.; mar. 27 March 1832; died 15 Feb. 1871.

Rev. Henry Tuffnel Young, born 9 Oct. 1810; matric. from Balliol College, Oxford, 24 Jan. 1828, æt. 17; Vicar of Steeple with Stangate, co. Essex, 1836. Has issue. = Josephine Isabella, only surviving dau. of Joseph Saville of Waltham Lodge, Essex; mar. 6 July 1841 at Springfield.

Sir William Norris Young, 5th Bart., born 15 Jan. 1833; of the 23rd Fusiliers; killed at Alma 20 Sep. 1854. = Florence, 2nd dau. of E. Clarke, Esq., of Efford Manor, co. Devon; mar. 10 March 1854; remar. 10 April 1860 John Soltau, Esq.

s.p.

Sir George John Young, 6th Bart., born 1 March 1835; died 22 Oct. 1854 in the Crimea.

1887.—The late Sir Charles Young. Probate has been granted of the will (dated the 3rd of August 1871), with one codicil, of Sir Charles Lawrence Young of Hatfield Priory, Essex, and 5 Ashbourn Place, who died on the 11th of September last, aged 48 years, and appoints as executors his wife, Dame Margaret Alice Young, and his son, Sir William Lawrence Young, the present baronet. The testator gives to his wife for her life, if she so long remains his widow, the income of all his property, including his plays, stories, copyright stories, and writings, and his share and interest therein, and on her decease or remarriage devises and bequeaths all his property, real and personal, in equal shares to his sons Sir William L. Young and Charles Alban Young, with the option to the former to buy the lease of the house, No. 5 Ashbourn Place, for £5000, the value of the testator's personalty being declared at £9330 12*s.* 5*d.*

1685, March 26. Sarah Young, widow, and her children (she was Ex'trix of Mr. George Fletcher) granted 200 acres.

1724, Sep. 18. Margaret Young, widow, by deed, gives a negro girl to her niece Ann Gamble.

1724, Feb. 3. John Farley and his wife Rebecca sell to William Young of Antigua, Surgeon, 32 acres at Falmouth for £500 c.

Letters of agreement between Thomas Bishop and the late Dr. William Young, deceased, dated 6 March 1740. Recorded 12 Oct. 1743.

1756, July 21. William Young, Esq., has twelve months' leave.

Governor George Thomas writes 3 June 1761 that he has appointed to the Council William Young, "who is a Gentleman of a polite Education, and is possessed of a very considerable Landed Estate in this Island," *vice* Colonel Nath. Gilbert, deceased. On 21 Oct. 1762 he further says that Mr. Young has gone to England.

1767. The Hon. William Young rated on 233 slaves and 460 acres in St. Mary's Parish. (Vestry Book.)

1768. W. Young, Esq; Lieut. gov. of Dominica, *vice* Geo. Scott, Esq; dec. ('Gent. Mag.,' p. 143.)

1774. Thos. Shirley appointed Govr of Dominica *vice* Sir Wm. Young resigned. (*Ibid.*, p. 47.)

1777, Aug. Wm Young, Esq; eldest son of Sir Wm Young, Bart.—to Miss Lawrence, of Red-lion-square. (*Ibid.*, p. 403.)

1780. The estate of Sir William Young, Bart., rated on 325 slaves and 655 acres. (St. Mary's Vestry Book.)

1787, Feb. Sir William Young, on whom I had waited in Antigua previously to my present visit, has a large estate in this island (St. Vincent's), not far from the residence of Mr. Otley. By Sir William Young I was received with the greatest politeness. (Dr. Coke's 'History of the West Indies.')

1788, April 8. In the island of St Vincent, aged 62, Sir Wm. Young, bart. ('Gent. Mag.,' p. 562.)

1791, Jan. 6. In Great George-street, Westminster, after a fortnight's illness, Lady Young, wife of Sir Wm. Y. bart. M.P. (*Ibid.*, p. 92.)

1791. Wm Young (later Bart.) travelled in Italy in 1772. Only 10 copies of his journal were printed at a private press. (*Ibid.*, p. 742.)

In Bryan Edwards' 'Historical Survey of St. Domingo' is an account of the Tour made by Sir William Young, Bart., in 1791 and 1792 to the West Indies. Sir W. Young's plantations at St. Vincent consisted of the Calliaqua one about half a mile from the shore, and the Pembroke Estate of 3000 acres in the Valley of Buccament three miles from Kingston. In Antigua he owned the Old Road Plantation half a mile from Old Road Bay. In Tobago the Louis d'or Estate at Queen's Bay.

1793, April 25. By special licence, at the house of the Marquis of Buckingham, Sir Wm. Young, bart. M.P. to Miss Barbara Talbot, daughter of the late Col. T. and a near relative of the Marchioness. ('Gent. Mag.,' p. 373.)

1798, Sep. 24. At his house in Margaret-street, Cavendish-square, James Hartley, esq. late of the island of St Vincent. (*Ibid.*, p. 995.)

John Young, bapt. 10 Sep. 1761 at St. John's, Antigua; sold his estate there 1802; of Brock Street, Bath, 1823; died there 24 March 1834. ═ Jane, dau. of Jeremiah Blizard of Antigua; bapt. 14 Aug. 1760 at St. George's; mar. before 1788; died 3 Dec. 1838, very aged, at Bath.

Sarah Elizabeth Young, mar. 12 June 1770, at Iver, co. Bucks, Richard Ottley, Esq.; he died 20 Oct. 1775, æt. 45, and she 17 March 1825, æt. 77; bur. at St. Anne's, Soho.

Elizabeth Young, mar. James Hartley of St. Vincent, Esq.; he died 24 Sep. 1798 in London.

Portia Young, died 9 May 1832, very aged.

Mary Young.

Olivia Young, died Jan. 1815 at Chertsey, co. Surrey.

George Young, Major in the Army. Left issue. ═ Mary, dau. of John Harris of Derby, Esq.

Sarah Elizabeth Young, mar. Nov. 1803, at Hartwell, co. Bucks, Sir Richard Ottley, Knt., Chief Justice of Grenada; he born 1782 and died Aug. 1845; she died 16 Nov. 1849.

Caroline Young, mar. Thomas Robson of Holtby, Yorkshire, Esq.

Brook Young, born 16 Aug. 1813; died 23 Feb. 1879.

George Augustus Young, born 28 April 1822. Has issue ═ . . . .

Three daus.

Mary Florence, youngest dau. of H. H. Toulmin, Esq., of Childwickbury, co. Herts; born 14 Jan. 1845; mar. 11 Aug. 1863; died 21 July 1870. M.I. at St. Michael's, St. Albans. 1st wife. ═ Sir Charles Lawrence Young, 7th Bart., born 31 Oct. 1839; matric. from New College, Oxford, 23 March 1858, æt. 18; B.A. 1862; Barrister-at-Law Inner Temple 1865; died 12 Sep. 1887. ═ Margaret A. M., 1st dau. of Rev. W. S. Wade, Vicar of Redbourn, co. Herts; mar. 3 Aug. 1871. 2nd wife.

Two daus.

Sir William Lawrence Young, 8th Bart., born 3 Aug. 1864. ═ Helen Mary, dau. of Hon. Henry William Petre; mar. 12 April 1887.

Charles Alban Young, born 18 Nov. 1865.

Mary Agnes Young, born 18 Sep. 1868.

1801, July 12. At the Abbey-house, Chertsey, Surrey, the relict of Sir William Young, bart. Her remains were interred in the family-vault of the Taylors, at Patrixbourne, Kent. ('Gent. Mag.,' p. 677.)

1811. Lately, July. At Tobago, in the West Indies, Sir William Young, bart. formerly M.P. for St Mawe's, Cornwall, and agent for the island of Dominica. He was the son of Sir W. Young, Lieutenant-governor of Dominica, and was born in 1742. In 1806 he was appointed Governor of Tobago. Sir William Young was a man of considerable talent and knowledge, and was well known in the first literary and political circles. In Parliament he generally supported the Whig Interest; although his principles may be better known to our readers by informing them that he voted for the Union with Ireland, against the abolition of the Slave Trade, and supported Mr Whitbread in the affair of Lord Melville. Sir William Young has appeared as an author in the following publications:—

1. 'The Spirit of Athens,' 8vo, 1777.
2. 'The History of Athens,' 4to, 1785.
3. 'A Pamphlet on the Amendment of the Poor Laws,' 8vo, 1788.
4. 'The Rights of Englishmen.'
5. 'Letter to Mr Pitt, on the Poor, and Workhouses.'
6. 'Speech on the Slave Trade,' 8vo, 1791.
7. 'Life of Dr Brook Taylor (Sir William Young's grandfather),' prefixed to his 'Contemplatio Philosophica,' 8vo, 1793, printed only for his private friends. (See also 'Gent. Mag.,' 1798, p. 1089.)
8. 'The West India Common Place Book.'

(*Ibid.*, p. 90.)

The late Sir Wm. Young, bart. was born in February 1750 (not 1742, as we have before stated); and was nominated governor of the Leeward Islands, etc., during the late Grenville administration. He lately sat in Parliament for Buckingham. He was twice married. Besides the publications we have already noticed, he was the author of a statistical account of the West Indies, and several pieces of fugitive Poetry. ('Gent. Mag.,' p. 294.)

We have much pleasure in contradicting the report of the death of Sir William Young, bart. Governor of Tobago, who was in good health, as appears by letters from himself to his family, at a later date than the unaccountable, and, to them, alarming report, alluded to. (*Ibid.*, p. 494.)

1815, Jan. At Chertsey, Mrs. Oliver Young, sister of Sir Wm. Young, bart. (*Ibid.*, p. 89.)

1815, Jan. 10. At Government house, Tobago, his Excellency Governor Sir Wm. Young, bart. F.R.S. and F.S.A. He was born in 1749, and succeeded his father Sir William in 1788. He married first, in 1777, Sarah, daughter of Chas. Laurence, esq. by whom he had issue, 1, William; 2, Brook Henry; 3, Charles; 4, Sarah; 5, Caroline; and 6, George. Sir William married secondly, in 1792, Barbara, daughter of Richard Talbot, of Malahide Castle, Ireland, esq. by whom he had no issue. He represented the borough of St Mawes in four parliaments. (*Ibid.*, p. 373.)

1816. The Father of Sir Wm. Young, the first baronet, was lieutenant-governor of Dominica, where he possessed considerable estates: and his mother was the daughter of Dr Brook Taylor, secretary to the Royal Society. Sir William first obtained a seat in Parliament in 1784, for the borough of St Mawes, for which he was re-elected in 1790, 1796, and 1802, and was returned for Buckingham in 1806. In the following year, he was appointed Governor of Tobago, where he has ever since resided. He was author of a 'History of Athens' and various pamphlets and the 'West India Common Place Book,' etc. (*Ibid.*, p. 632.)

1824, Nov. 3. At Hastings, in his 47th year, Sir William Lawrence Young, bart. He was eldest son of Sir William, second Bart. by his first wife, dau. of Charles Lawrence, esq. On the 21st of Dec. 1805, he married Louisa, 2d dau. of Wm. Tuffnell, esq. of Langley, co. Essex, and had issue. On the death of his father, in Nov. 1811, he succeeded to the baronetcy. ('Gent. Mag.,' p. 573.)

1832, May 9. At an advanced age, Mrs. Portia Young, sister of Sir W. Young, Bart., late Governor of the island of Tobago, and dau. of the late Sir W. Young, Bart. of Delaford, near Iver, in the county of Bucks. (*Ibid.*, p. 475.)

1834, March 24. At Bath, John Young, esq. son of Sir Wm. Young, Bart., of Delaford, Bucks. (*Ibid.*, p. 566.)

1838, Dec. 3. At Bath at an advanced age, the relict of John Young, esq., youngest son of the late Sir William Young, of Delaford, Bucks. (*Ibid.*, 1839, p. 108.)

1841, July 6. At Springfield, the Rev. H. T. Young, second son of the late Sir W. L. Young, Bart., to Josephine-Isabella, only surviving dau. of the late Joseph Savill, esq. of Waltham Lodge, Essex. (*Ibid.*, p. 313.)

1842, June 27. At his seat Hughenden House, Buckinghamshire, aged 36, Sir William Lawrence Young, the fourth Bart. (1769); one of the three Members of Parliament for that county, etc. (*Ibid.*, p. 425.)

1870. George Frederick Young, who died 23 Feb. 1870 at Reigate, was first son of the late Vice-Admiral William Young by Ann Spencer his wife, daughter of Robert Curling. He was of the family of Sir Charles Lawrence Young, Bart.; represented Tynemouth and Scarborough in Parliament; was a merchant and ship owner; Vice-President of the Board of Trade 1852; J.P. and D.L. for Middlesex; married in 1814 Mary daughter of John Abbott of Brompton House, Thanet, by whom he leaves three sons and two daughters surviving. ('Illustrated London News,' 1870, p. 283.)

PARISH REGISTER OF ST. JOHN.

Baptized.

1761 Sep. 10 John the S. of William Young and Elizabeth his wife.

Married.

1700 Aug. 28 Robert Young of Miston parish, Nottinghamshier, and Mary Sompleat of St Dunstan's in ye west London, England.

Buried.

1749-50 Mar. 24 Jane Young, a child of Anthony Young.

ST. GEORGE, HANOVER SQUARE.

Married.

1793 April 22 Sir William Young of Huntercombe, co. Bucks, W., & Barbara Talbot of Malahide Castle, co. Dublin, S. Special Licence.

HUNTINGDON CHAPEL, BATH.

In the burial-ground:—

In Memory of
WILLIAM JOHN YOUNG 2nd Son of
GEORGE & MARY YOUNG
of Grosvenor Place
Grandson of Sir WILL^M YOUNG Bart
Formerly of *Delaford* Bucks
Decessit May 10th 1843
Aged 16 Years.
(Seven lines follow.)

Also of SAMUEL YOUNG
His Brother Who fell Asleep
In Jesus Novr 30th 1846
Aged 11 Years p. s. s.
Also of HENRY YOUNG
Who departed this life
Feby 20th 1847, Aged 17 Years.
Also of DAVID YOUNG
obiit June 17th 1849 Aged 10 Years.

CHARTERHOUSE CHAPEL.*

On the cloister walls:—

Arms: YOUNG; impaling, *Ermine, on a chief gules a leopard's head between two cross-crosslets argent.*
Crest: YOUNG.

Lieutenant
Sir WILL'M NORRIS YOUNG Bart.
Of the Twenty Third Royal Welsh
Fusileers on the tenth
of March 1854 was married
to Florence the second
Daughter of Ewing
Clarke Esqr of Efford
Manor in the County
of Devon and was killed
in the Battle of the Alma
on the 21st of September. He was born
Jan'y 15th 1833 and died aged 21
Without issue.

"Young's," Old Road, is in St. Mary's Parish. In 1852 it contained 573 acres, and was owned by John Dawson.

* Harleian Society's Publications, vol. xviii., p. 98.

Appendix.

Among the Records preserved in the Registrar's Office at St. John's is an ancient book, bound with parchment, styled "The Book of Claims," dating from about 1667. The first twenty-one folios are missing. The early portion consists of folios 22 to 43 inclusive, so that about half is missing. All the earlier records appear to have been lost. It will be remembered that Antigua was devastated by the French in 1666, when many of its inhabitants were driven off, and re-settled in 1667 by William, Lord Willoughby.

FIVE-ISLANDS.

Roger Trottman, son and heir of Roger Trottman, deceased, possesses 95 acres in Hawksneast Valley, granted to the said Trottman, deceased, by Governor Austin, bounded E. with Colonel Robert Carden, N. with waste of 5 acres, W. with the sea, S. with Richard Warnebey. He is also possessed of 5 acres, bounded N. with the sea, E. with William Hemmong, W. with William Hemmong, formerly John Harvey's, S. with the mountain.

Hey. Renders owns 45 acres, formerly David Thomas's, and purchased by the said Hey. Renders of Colonel Robert Carden, deceased; also 10 acres at Pinchin's Hill, purchased of George Hoomes, and he of John Longmaid.

Henry Ball, in his own right and in right of Mary Ranger, daughter of William Ranger, deceased, owns 12 acres, purchased of William Gritt who had it with his wife, the widow of Fra. Carew, deceased, and he of Thomas Pollard, and he of Serjeant John King, deceased, and he of Governor Austin in Hawksneast Valley.

William Cooper, in right of his wife Elizabeth and her children, she being the widow of Robert Howell, deceased, owns half of 30 mens land, purchased of Christopher Wingfeild on 2 Oct. last 1661, the other half his own, which he purchased of Henry Croydon, John Adlin, Steven Sexton, John Marshall, and Samuel Taylor.

Serjeant Robert Williams has 10 acres granted by Governor Carden.

James Belcher has 30 mens* land purchased of Robert Roe, and he of Patrick Rickards and John Fullerton, and they of John Williams and John Hillman, and they of Nicholas Isaacks, and he was granted it by patent from Governor Austin bearing date ye .... year of this Collony Anno 1645.

David Wollerton, half of 20 mens land purchased of Katherine Knowles, wife of Nicholas Isaak, deceased, who left ye same and ye other half to his daughter, who was carried away by ye Indians twenty years since.

Robert Cooke, in right of his wife Mary, widow of John Marshall, deceased, has 30 mens land.

John Fullerton, 15 acres at Pension *alias* David's Hill, granted by Governor Carden.

William Hemmons, who married the widow and relict of John Marshall, deceased, 100 acres granted to the said Marshall by patent from Governor Ashton, dated 6 April 1645; also 25 acres at Hawksneast Valley, being half of 50 acres purchased of James Harvey on 12 May 1656, and he of John Longwood on 27 Nov. 1655, and he of John King, and he had a grant of Governor Austin; also 12½ acres he purchased of John Harvey on 15 Oct. 1664, and he of Henry Ball 5 Aug. 1661, and he of James Harvey.

William Hill, who married Ann, daughter and heir of Edward Newman, deceased, is in her right possessed of 50 mens land, and in her right of 21 acres being a moiety of 42 acres in partnership with John Blackwell, 30 acres were granted by patent to the said Newman and Blackwell by Governor Austin, and 12 by Governor Bunckle to the said Blackwell and William Hill.

John Blackwell has a moiety of 42 acres in partnership with William Hill.

Edmond Johnson, 40 acres, purchased of Hermon Clanson Bisterfeilt on 29 May 1665.

Richard Glanfeild (ye son of Katherine ye widow of Nicholas Isaaks, deceased), has a moiety of 20 mens land; ye other moiety was sold by the said Katherine to Claviel David Wollerton.

Garret Garretson van viana (son and heir to Garret Garretson van viana, deceased), 17 acres called David's Hill, purchased of China Knight, deceased, 10 Nov. 1663.

Robert Carden (son and heir to Colonel Robert Carden, deceased), by his mother, Mrs. Mary Carden, has 360 acres.

George Muggh, a moiety of 60 acres purchased of Mathew Madley 17 Feb. 1665.

Robert Cooke, in right of his wife the relict of Patrick Rickards, deceased, owns quarter of 30 mens land.

FALMOUTH.

Lieut. Obadiah Bradshaw has 48 acres, purchased of James Everden, and he had it of Percivall Inocent, and he bought it of Captain Benjamin Langham in May 1647, and he had it by patent of Governor Ashton; also 70 acres (in right of his wife Martha, sole daughter and heir of Thomas Deereman, deceased), being 40 mens land, granted to the said Deereman by patent from Governor Austin of 4 Jan. .... and in her right of 200 acres.

Edmond Ellis, 50 acres in right of his wife Ann the relict of Samuel Welborne, deceased, who enjoyed it in right of Prudence his second wife, ye relict of Hugh Evans, deceased, who bought it of John Winter, and he of Abraham Knowles, and he by grant of Governor Austin.

Lieut. William Prockter, 50 acres by patent from Governor Austin dated 18 Feb. 1646; also 72 acres formerly William Pike's, and by him mortgaged to Cloies Abrahamson *alias* Baker, whose heirs entrusted it to Colonel Bastian Boyer, which latter sold it to said Lieut. William Prockter; also 5 acres by the nuncupative will of Peter Thornhill, a parcel of William Pike's land sold to George Noble, and from him to said Thornhill.

John Bradshaw (by Obadiah Bradshaw his father), 15 acres by gift from Governor Bunckle his godfather.

Edward Cole, a moiety of 25 acres by his marriage with Elizabeth the relict of Hugh Cheesewood.

* There is no clue as to the extent of a "man's land."

Sarah Cheesewood (daughter of Hugh Cheesewood, deceased) is possessed, by Edward Cole her father-in-law, of 10 acres.

William Gilliard and Thomas Butler, 104 acres by bill of sale from Edmond Ellis.

Mathew Gillingwater, 10 acres by sale from William Connell, and he of Michael Stodder, and he by deed of gift dated 1 Aug. 1650.

William Wainewright, 100 acres by patent from Governor Austin, dated 16 Feb. 1646, to Captain Simon Turfrey and Serjeant Richard Buck, and by bill of sale to said Wainewright.

Charles Baldwin (son and heir of Christopher Baldwin, deceased), by Walter Refford his father-in-law and Guardian, 5 acres, being a moiety of 10 acres bought by the said Christopher Baldwin of Robert Myles.

Renalder Barter, 14 acres bought of Lieut. Obadiah Bradshaw.

Captain Joseph Lee, one plantation of 990 acres by patent of Governor Austin dated 4 Nov. 1648; also another of 510 acres by the will of Captain Benjamin Laugham, deceased, called Michaell's Mount, by patent from Governor Austin dated 2 March 1648; also 19 acres (late Captain Benjamin Langham's), granted by patent from Governor Keynell on 20 May 1654.

Ellenour Myles (widow of Robert Myles, deceased), 20 mens land by sale from William Morris and Fra. Nayle, who bought it from Thomas Deereman, and he of Captain Samuel Winthrop, Attorney to Major William Byam, who married ye daughter of Dame Alice Huncks, formerly possessor of this plantation.

George Rawlins, 12½ acres, being a moiety of 25 acres from the sale of Lieut. Obadiah Bradshaw, 12 May 1666, who had it in right of his wife Martha, daughter and heir of Thomas Deereman, deceased, to whom it was given by Danell ô Crynn by will.

Mr. Thomas Compton, 68 acres by sale from Hester Buckingham (late widow of Richard Buckingham, deceased), 20 May 1666, formerly in the possession of Robert (?) Buckingham, deceased, who had a patent from Governor Austin, deceased.

John Philpot, a moiety of 15 mens land bought of Samuel Welborne 9 June 1661, and he bought it of Captain Turphrey, and he of Ralph Ottaver.

Samuel Irish, 170 acres by patent from Governor Buncle 6 Feb. 1662.

Edmond Ellis (in right of his wife ye widow of Samuel Welborne, deceased), 60 acres.

John Ellis, by gift from his father Edmond Ellis, deceased, 50 acres. "This land is by y[e] will of y[e] s'd Jn[o] Ellis, made y[e] 11th of Jan[y] 1668, & proved before y[e] L[t] Generall y[e] 17th of March 1668, bequeathed unto his brother Edmond Ellis."

George Rawlins, in right of his wife Margaret, 25 acres, being a moiety of 50 acres by sale to them from Edward Snow dated 20 Sep. 1656.

Captain Joseph Lee. The boundaries of his plantation are recorded in a later hand in 1668 "per me Gilbert Gregory, Surveyor."

Antigoa. I Elizabeth Ashton of Antigoa, widow, surrender to the Lieut.-General Henry Willoughby, Governor of Antigoa and Berbuda, all the said land by him to me formerly granted this 2 April 1669. Witnessed by Nathaniell Clerke, George Terwhitt, Joseph Hodgkin.

This 16 Aug. 1669 appeared Edmond Ellis and produced ye will of his brother John Ellis, deceased, proved before Lieut.-General Henry Willoughby, Governor of Antigoa, in which testament he gave to the said Edmond Ellis his plantation of Figtree Pond of 50 acres.

Signed "Samuel Winthrop, Register."

WILLOUGHBY BAY.

John Ellis, 50 acres by gift from his brother Edmond Ellis 10 Nov. 1666, and he possessed it in right of his wife Ann, relict of Samuel Welborne, deceased, who enjoyed it in right of his first wife Margaret, relict of William Stimpson, who had a grant from Governor Austin.

Major Richard Burreston, 200 acres by grant from His Excellency Francis, Lord Willoughby, of Parham, 16 May 1664.

Robert Chesham, 20 acres by assignment of patent for 40 acres, granted by Governor Ashton to Hugh Cheswood, and from the latter to the said Robert Chesham; also 5 acres by grant from Governor Keynell.

Mathew Gillingwater, 20 acres, being the moiety of 40 acres granted by Governor Austin to Hugh Cheswood, who assigned it to John Partington, and he to Mathew Gillingwater on 5 Oct. 1658; also 50 acres by sale from Christopher Towler to Mathew Gillingwater and Richard Zancby, and the latter sold his share to Mathew Gillingwater.

John Russell, 20 acres, bought of John Partington, who had it by assignment of Thomas Good, and he by warrant of Governor Keynell.

John Gratridge, 30 acres, being a moiety of 60 by patent to him and his partner (who shortly after died), from Governor Austin, 11 June 1649.

Richard Smart, 30 acres, being a moiety of 60 by bill of sale from William Line.

John Partington, 65 acres, ½ by bill of sale from John Barton, senior, on 14 May 1659, and ½ by his marriage with the widow of John Barton, junior.

John Nichols, 22 acres by bill of sale from William Kington, deceased, as attorney to William Biffin, late ye land of James Prevoe.

John Cole, 10 acres by assignment from John Russel.

Thomas Dawson, 35 acres by bill of sale from David Harrison; also 100 acres (in right of Lucretia, daughter and heir of John Robinson, deceased), by patent to Michael Stodder, deceased, 80 of which was assigned by Henry Stodder to the said John Robinson, 30 acres in his said right were a moiety of 60 acres near Cynamon Valley, sold to John Robinson by Pharaoh Lavamore, and 20 acres in his said right, being ⅓ of 60, were bought of William Davies by the said John Robinson.

John Ellis, 20 acres by bill of sale from Thomas Dawson.

John Baan, 15 acres by bill of sale from Charles Bernard.

William Quinbee, 23⅓ acres bought of Thomas Peck, part of 35 acres.

Minos Ross, 11¾ acres, remainder of the said 35 acres.

John Keelharne, 30 acres plantation, being a moiety of 60 acres sold by Lieut. Mark Brenster to John Palmer, and by him sold to Edward Clufton, who by gift of 17 Feb. 1666 gave it to the said John Keelharne.

Mrs. Joan Hall, for self and children, 40 acres by sale from John Barton to Colonel Christopher Keynell on 16 Nov. 1659.

Joseph Northeast (son and heir of Morgan Northeast, deceased), 200 acres by his guardian Captain Joseph Lee by patent from Governor Austin to Nathaniel Clarke 14 May 1649.

Mr. Thomas Compton, 200 acres by sale from Hester Buckingham, the relict of Richard Buckingham, deceased, 20 May 1660, formerly Robert Buckingham's, deceased, by patent from Captain Henry Austin, Governor of Antigoa.

Edward Mayle, 20 acres.

Thomas ap Thomas, 10 acres in right of his wife, being ⅙ of 60 acres granted to William Gettings and John Rowland, and sold by the said Gettings to Samuel Neal, predecessor of ye said Thomas ap Thomas.

Derrick Brounehurst, 20 acres, granted from Colonel Carden 30 Oct. 1660.

John Church, 20 acres by grant from Governor Carden 30 Oct. 1660.

John Nicolls, 10 acres, 30 Aug. 1661, bought of Henry Stodder, being a moiety of 20 granted by patent from Governor Austin to Richard Buckingham and Deirmon Hogan, and the said Buckingham sold to James Praevoe his moiety of the said 20 acres 10 Oct. 1649. One Pharaoh Loachland sold 10 acres of the said land to Ensign Morgan Northeast 16 Oct. 1649. Christian, relict of the said Morgan Northeast, George Blanchard, and Steven Martin, feofees in trust of the last will of the said Morgan Northeast, deceased, sold 10 acres of the said land to James Praevoe in 1653. George Williams sold to John Russell 10 acres of the said land 6 Aug. 1663, and the said John Russel assigned over the same to John Cole 19 March 1665. The said patent was dated 11 June 1649.

Dennis MacCharty, 30 acres bought of John Barton, junior, who had it by marriage with the relict and ex'trix of Thomas Macham, deceased, and he by grant from Governor Keynell 2 Sep. 1653.

Francis Gifford, junior (son of Sergeant Francis Gifford), 20 acres by the will of Edward Winclevour, part of 40 acres granted to Robert Bristoll, deceased, by Governor Austin, ye other 20 acres given by the said Winclevour by will to Mary Bristoll, daughter of the said Robert Bristoll, deceased, by his will dated in Antigoa 21 Jan. 1667.

William Brummell, married Sarah, daughter of William Maile, deceased, and in right of his said wife, and in right of his two brothers William Maile and Robert Maile (the land by their father's will was given to the said three), claims 25 acres bought by the said William Maile from John Andrener 18 Nov. 1662, a moiety of 50 acres of which Jacob van der veild had ½.

Richard Brown, 45 acres (administrator of George Mould, deceased, in right of his wife Barbery Mould, sister by the whole blood of the said deceased), ½ bought of William Tyler 18 Nov. 1662, and ½ of Henry Stodder 11 June 1661; also 60 acres bought of Steven Martin 26 June 1660, who had a patent from Governor Austin 14 May 1649.

John Waters (son and heir of William Waters, deceased), by his friend Barbery Brown claims 60 acres, granted to his father by patent from Governor Austin 11 June 1649.

James Townsend (son of James Townsend, deceased), 52 acres, viz., 26 in his own right and 26 in the right of his sister Jean, being ½ of 104 acres bought by the said James Townsend, deceased, of Willoughby Orton, and he of Lieut. William Proctor and Edmund Ellis, ye attorneys of Lieut. Henry Graves, and he by patent of Governor Austin 11 June 1649.

Roger Thomas, 13 acres bought of Mary Townsend, ye daughter of James Townsend, deceased; also 13 acres as administrator to his partner George Williams, deceased, who bought it of the said Mary Townsend 8 July 1665, ¼ of the said 104 acres above entered.

John Sharpe, 26 acres in right of his wife Anne, daughter of James Townsend, deceased (¼ of the said 104 acres). The said 104 acres was by his will given to his son James and his three daughters.

Lieut. William Proctor, 30 acres by gift from Thomas Withered by his will, who bought 10 acres from Richard Bartlet 20 Feb. 1650.

RENDEVOUS BAY.

Benjamin Blanchard (son and heir of George Blanchard, deceased), 30 mens land by his guardian Major Richard Burreston, and by patent from Governor Austin 22 Jan. 1644 "ye 10th year of ye Collony"; also 20 mens land by patent granted by Governor Austin to John Winter and Thomas Thompson 6 Jan. 1645, which they sold to George Blanchard, deceased, by grant from Governor Keynell.

Richard Fisher (son of Richard Fisher), 10 acres by Major Richard Burreston his Guardian, granted by Governor Austin.

Ensign Robert Smith, 20 mens land by grant from Governor Austin.

Thomas and Grace Tiphany (coheirs of Robert Tiphany, deceased), 20¾ acres by Ensign Robert Smith their Guardian, being ¼ of 83 acres granted to Henry Elliott and John Stanwarth, by patent 20 Jan. 1650 from Governor Austin. The said Elliott sold his moiety to Ensign John Hall, who died s.p., and left it to his wife Grace, who married Robert Tiffany, ye father of these orphans, and so became their mother.

Ann Armitage (relict of Thomas Armitage, deceased), 25 mens land.

Richard Burreston, 11 acres by patent from Governor Ashton.

Henry Walton, 21 acres by sale dated 23 Oct. 1647 from William Stewart, and he bought of Richard Snow, who derived from the first patent of Governor Ashton.

Robert Oxford, 23 acres, part of the patent next before bought of Mr. John England of Bristoll, who was administrator of Mr. John Newberry, deceased.

Thomas Ellis (son of Edmund Ellis, deceased), 30 mens land by William Wainewright his father-in-law, 15 granted by Governor Austin to the said Edmund Ellis by patent of 20 Jan. 1644, and 15 granted by Governor Austin to Thomas Scott and William Stimson. The said Thomas Scott gave his interest to Hugh Cheswood, and from him to the present orphans.

Joseph Northeast (son and heir of Morgan Northeast, deceased), 100 acres by his guardian Captain Joseph Lee, granted to Governor Austin to the said Morgan for 1000 years.

Edward Cole, 30 acres.

"Lieut John ffrye in ye Right of Katherine his wife layes Clayme unto tweenty acrees of Land Given her by her father Captain Thomas Tuck, deceased, Lyeing and being behind Rendevons Bay Mountaines, being in breadth 25 Chaines upon ye Points East & west, and in lengthe Eighty Chaines upon ye Points North & south; Bounded to ye East with ye Land of Capt Benjamin Langham, to ye south with ye topp of Rendevous Bay Mountaines. To ye North and west with land untaken upp. Granted by Warr. from Go. Keynell."

Benjamin Tuck, by patent granted by Governor Austin to Lieut. Thomas Tuck his father on 10 Dec. 1647, land in Rendevous Bay, 160 paces.

Joan Elliott (daughter of Henry Elliott, deceased), 20¾ acres by her father's will, dated 9 Oct. 1654, being ¼ of 83 acres as in entry of Thomas and Grace Tiffany who have ¼, and the following Robert Smith has ½.

Robert Smith, junior, by gift of his father Ensign Robert Smith claims ½ of 83 acres by the will of John Stanworth.

Captain John Cade, 110 acres in right of his wife by patent from Governor Bouncle to Thomas White, who sold to Governor Bouncle, and the latter gave it to his niece ye wife of ye said Captain Cade.

Thomas Akhurst, deceased, 233 acres. His heirs have the right to 233 acres, now in the occupation of John Roberts, 50 mens land granted by Captain Rowland Thompson, then Governor, and the residue by Governor Henry Austin. Measured 2 May 1654.

ROAD.

Thomas Cleruck, 21 mens land by sale from Richard Tanckred 18 Oct. 1639, purchased of John Lapthorne, and he by patent from Governor Huncks; also 33 mens land purchased of Richard Tanckred, and more land bought of Richard Daniell and John Masters, dated 21 March 1639, by patent from the said Hunckes; also 13 acres by sale of Isaack Holland, granted by Governor Thompson.

Lieut. William Chune, 267 acres called Betties Nook, bought of James Portingall 20 June 1665.

William Hill, 30 mens land bought of James Portingall by patent from Governor Henry Austin 20 March 1644.

Mrs. Joan Hall, for selfe and children, a parcel of land, 20 Jan. 1644, by patent from Governor Austin, 13 acres belongeth to Mr. Thomas Clerick and part to Captain John Lint; also 30 mens land by sale from Mr. Henry Austin 17 Jan. 1664; also 42 acres by patent from Governor Austin to Clement Allen and George Rawlins 27 Feb. 1656, and confirmed by Clement Allen to Colonel Christopher Keynell by sale 11 May 1657; also 74 mens land bought by Colonel Christopher Keynell her former husband.

Mr. Thomas Compton, 20 mens land bought of Samuel Hinde 7 Oct. 1656; also 10 mens land.

Nathaniel Monke, 16½ mens land formerly belonging to Thomas Thompson Cooke by patent from Captain Henry Austin, late Governor, 5 June 1645, and by sale from George Richardson 6 Dec. 1648; also 19 mens land formerly in possession of John Smyth and John Watkins, by sale 23 Aug. 1651, and ye other ye 8 April 1654.

Mrs. Joan Hall, 20½ mens land formerly belonging to Rowland Smyth, Humphries Randoll, and Peter Jones; also 41 mens land by sale from Lieut. Colonel Boyer, as Attorney for the heirs of Captain Abraham Baker.

Thomas Taylor (son and heir of Thomas Taylor, deceased), 30 mens land by his mother Mrs. Margery Taylor.

Mrs. Margery Taylor, 22 mens land by sale from Mrs. Joan Hall.

Ann Jolly, an infant by Mrs. Joan Hall, 45 mens land.

Mr. Alexander Pollington, 32 mens land bought of Gowin Hill; also 22½ mens land formerly belonging to John Collinson by bill of sale from the said John Collinson to the said Mr. Pollington.

Lieut. Mark Brewster, 210 acres by deed of sale from Colonel Christopher Keynell 9 Jan. 1657.

Captain John Cade, 39 mens land in right of his wife, by gift of Colonel John Bunele, deceased, he purchased of Mr. James Holliday and Katherine his wife, the Executors of Major Richard Lisle; also 25 acres bought by the said Bunele of Mr. Thomas Taylor.

Captain Henry Nicolls, 50 mens land by deed of sale and patent granted by Major Henry Huncks to William Chune and Trustram Fletcher.

Captain John Cade, 25 mens land in right of his wife, by deed of gift from Governor John Bunele, and he of Colonel Charles Ghest; also 30 mens land bought by the said Colonel Bunele of Mr. Samuel Irish.

Evan Griffin, 15 mens land bought of John Morris.

Captain John Cade, 35 mens land in right of his wife by gift of Colonel John Bunele, deceased, he bought of Mrs. Ann Warrington.

Benjamin Steel, 40 mens land granted by Colonel Carden; also 6 mens land bought of Dennis Hicks.

Robert Oxford, 6 mens land.

Lewis Bryan, 30 acres.

Roger Elsmore, 30 mens land. He married the widow of John Butler, deceased, and by the will of the said deceased, dated 23 July 1666, the said John Butler bought of William Barloe and William More, and they from John Roberts and Robert Kirke, and Robert Kirke by patent from Governor Austin 28 Jan. 1644.

William Allen, 100 acres. He married the relict of William Joslin, deceased, and he bought of Isaack Holland 2 last of Oct. 1664; the first grant was by patent to Isaack Holland and William Kaynell; Bagnell, Attorney to Simon Bowers, sold his ½ to Isaack Holland ye 13 Sep. 1662.

John Greire, 66 mens land bought of William Joslin and his wife, ye relict of William Shingleton.

Captain Harvey Keynell, on 2 May 1668, entered claim to the plantation of Thomas Mudd at Crabb Valley, and presented his petition to William, Lord Willoughby of Parham, on 11 May 1668, which was referred to the Lieut.-General Henry Willoughby, Governor, and was read 19 May; claim not allowed, claim not timely made.

BERMUDIAN VALLEY.

Luke Norton, 13 acres in right of his wife Margaret and Jane Spitlee, coheirs to Alexander Spittle, deceased, by sale from William Jones, deceased, 5 Feb. 1654.

"30 Mœland. Lt John ffrye stands Possessed of 30 mens Land. Bounded to ye southward with ye land of Andrew Curteens & to ye Northward with ye ld. of Hugh Crane & Lewis Owen, Extending in Longitude from ye sea side to ye top of ye Next Adjacent Hill, & there to take ye Breadth of fifety men or 160 Geom. Paces unto ye top of ye next high Mountaine East & by North. And ye greater part of it Purchased of Mr Allexand. Pollington of London by virtue of a deed of sale under his hand dated in Lond. Octob. ye 19th, 1661, ye other Part as shall be made appeare by other deeds of sale from John Claus."

"More he is Possessed of twelve acres of Land Purchased from Andrew Curteen by virtue of his deed of sale dated ye 29th day of May 1666, and to him Confirmed by Pattent from Capt. Henry Austin, sometime Govern^r of this Island. Bounded to ye North-ward with ye land of ye s^d ffry: to ye South-ward with ye land of Coll. Robert Carden, dec^d, Extending in Longitude from the Mangroves to ye little hill upon ye Point East."

"More also nine acrees of Land Bounded to ye North with ye Land of Robert Nanton, to ye south with ye land of ye sd. ffrye, to ye East with ye land of Jasper Griggs & John Nowling, & to ye west with ye land of Anthony Morrell and ye land of ye s^d L^t ffrye."

Captain Richard Ayres, 33 acres granted by Colonel Carden.

George Nanton, 12 acres by his guardian Captain Henry Nicolls.

Ruth Courteene, 15 acres by patent from Colonel Henry Austin.

Joseph Richardson claims half of the above 15 acres by purchase of Edward Clifton, which is left for him to prosecute before Governor Winthroppe.

Anthony Morrell, 20 mens land, being half of 40 bought of Robert Clapper 31 May 1648.

George Hawkins, 67 acres by several deeds of sale to Francis Petean, Thomas Wright; also 100 feet square bought of William Byat 4 May 1650.

Captain John Lint, 132 acres by patent (and deeds destroyed by ye Indians).

Thomas Price, 10 acres as administrator of Lewis Owen.

Phylom ô Brandon, 40 acres bought of Ralph More, and 20 he has sold to John Shaw, and sold by the latter to William Sharpe, and is now claimed by Daniel Pelloe, who married the widow of the said William Sharpe; also 10 acres, ½ of 20, bought of Lieut. Mark Brewster 20 Sep. 1662.

Sarah Fisher, 15 acres bought of Katherine Johnson; she

THE COURT HOUSE

Saint John's, Antigua.

relinquished the said land in Court 28 July 1668, and it was granted to John Nanton.

Daniel Pelloe, 20 acres in right of his wife (ye widow of William Sharpe, deceased).

Edward Johnson, 20 acres in right of his wife Katherine by deed of sale from William Summers and Owen Kennedy 31 Aug. 1649.

Luke Norton, 20 acres by deed of sale from William Banger.

William Wainewright, 30 acres in right of Robert Harwood, who, going to England, willed it to Sarah Wainewright. He bought it of William Banger, and he had a grant from Governor Austin.

George Hawkins, 50 acres bought of Chany Knight 19 Sep. 1664, and by him conveyed from Joan Rowles, widdow, dated 22 Jan. 1662, and to her conveyed by patent from Colonel Henry Austin (now lost).

Frances Smithwick, deceased, 20 acres bought of Anthony Kenedy 10 Feb. 1665.

Henretta Mary Kin (heir of Captain William Kin, deceased), 380 acres bought of Henry Stoot, and he by grant from Governor Austin.

Thomas Halfhead, deceased, 200 acres.

By Commission from William, Lord Willoughby of Parham, dated 13 April 1668, for lessening and bounding Colonel Philip Warner's lands at ye Savanna and that of James Hollijday. In Blubber Valley have bounded him.

Hollyday's two parcells of 1400 acres, one in Blubber Valley of 1100 acres for sugar and 300 at Musketa Cove for cattle. (? if said 1400 is not too great for one man.)

Signed Bastian Boyer.
Nath. Clarke.

Antego. By His Excellency ordered to Lieut.-General Henry Willoughby 11 May 1668.

Fra. Sampson, Secretary.

Antego. By Henry Willoughby, Esq., 19 May 1668, ye lands of said James Holliday be reduced to 800 acres.

ST. JOHN'S DIVISION.

Anthony Rierson, 50 acres bought of Hugh Gambell 26 March 1666, and he by patent from Colonel Keynell.

Lieut.-Colonel Charles Ghest, deceased, his heirs, his two daughters Arabella and Caralina, 500 acres now in the possession of their mother Ann Ghest, deceased's widow. The first grant by William, Lord Willoughby of Parham, and his Governor Henry Ashton, deceased, to Sir Nicholas Pointz, Knt., deceased. Charles Ghest was the Ex'or to Sir N. Pointz, and the lands were confirmed by Governor Christopher Keynell 18 May 1658; also an island of 6 acres in St. John's Harbour.

Benjamin Tuck, 200 acres granted by Governor Austin to Lieut. Charles Tuck ye father.

Lieut. Robert Clarke and Susan (only daughter of Henry Clark, deceased), 570 acres bought by the said Robert and Henry Clark from Captain John Noye, who bought 175 acres of Henry Knight and one Jones and the rest of George Mugh, and he of Captain George Sterrell and William Joslin, who had a grant from Governor Austin. Confirmed to the said Robert and Henry Clarke by patent from John Buncle March 1661.

Captain Harvey Keynell, 100 acres by grant from Colonel Carden to Henry Clarke, deceased, 1661.

John Boschmann of ye Citty of Amsterdam, merchant, 100 acres by his agent Henry Mayer, ½ of 200 acres bought of Lewis Chivirier of Captain Robert Points, deceased, and sold to John Boschmann 15 Feb. 1663.

Lewis Chivirier, 100 acres, half of 200 bought of Captain Robert Points 8 Sep. 1659; the other half sold to John Boschmann.

Lieut.-Colonel Bastian Boyer, 500 acres by grant and purchase. In St. John's Division 728 acres and in Popeshead 140 acres; total 868. The 500 acres in St. John's granted by Governor Austin; also 18 acres by grant from Governor Keynell; also 50 acres bought of Robert Hollingworth, and he had grant from Governor Austin; also 30 acres as Ex'or to John Miller, deceased; also 40 acres bought of John Swan and his wife, she was the relict of Thomas Boer; the first grant by Austin to William Lawrence, and by him sold; also 50 acres granted by Governor Austin to Edward Powell, deceased, and by him left to his wife and successor William Roe, and from him to Robert Jessop as administrator, and so to Colonel Bastian Boyer; also 20 acres bought of John Jenkin and Patrick Richards granted by Governor Austin to John Thurland; also 20 acres granted by Governor Austin to Edward Pittman, deceased, and by his successor William Joslin sold by Egbert Johnson, deceased, and so by letters of administration to the said Colonel Boyer; also 100 acres in Popeshead bought of John Howell and William Joslin, granted by Governor Keynell to the said Howell and partners; also 40 acres bought of Thomas Mudd, deceased, granted by Governor Buncle. Rudolphus Johnson bought of Colonel Boyer 300 acres, by the said Colonel Boyer bought of Jacob Moulton and others, granted by Governor Henry Austin, mortgaged by the said Johnson to Peter Coene and John Otto, and now in possession of the said Colonel Boyer on their behalf as their Attorney.

Captain George Mugh, 430 acres by patent from Francis, Lord Willoughby, deceased; also 85 acres granted by Governor John Buncle.

Michael Fræmoet, 200 acres bought, 100 granted by Governor Henry Austin to Samuel Jolly, deceased, and by his heirs sold to Jacob Moulson, and by the latter sold to Colonel Boyer, and so to the said Michael Fræmoet, and 100 acres granted by Governor Henry Austin to Thomas Hobbs, deceased, and by his widow and heir sold to Thomas More and William Peete, and from them to Jacob Moulson, then to Colonel Boyer, and from him to Captain Mugh, and 20 acres to Michael Fræmoet.

Michael Lock, deceased, 50 acres claimed by his heirs by Serjeant William Carefoot, who married Katherine ye widow of Michael Lock, granted by patent from Governor Keynell 1 Feb. 1653.

Joseph Birtch, 20 acres bought of John Thurland granted to Joseph Birtch by Governor Austin.

Richard Belcher, 300 acres in right of his wife Abigall, widow of Robert Poynts, deceased, 24 Aug. 1668, by agreement between Lieut. Robert Clarke and Captain Harvey Keynell *re* said lands.

"RECORD

"Of y[e] returnes of such warrants as have been directed to y[e] Surveyo[rs] for laying out of lands since y[e] 10th of ffeb. 1667.
"By authority from his Ex[cy], W[m], Lord Willoughby of Parham."

	Acres.		Name of Dep. Governor.	Date of Gov.'s Warrant.	Date of Survey.	Name of Surveyor.
Tho. Gregory	50	Nonsuch Div[n]	Cap. Sam. Winthrop	29 June 1668	20 Sep. 1668	H. N.* & G. G.†
Jn[o] Dowgan	20	"	" "	14 Mar. last	18 May "	H. N.
W[m] Johnson	10	"	" "	—	2 Oct. "	"
Rob[t] Gilbert	10	"	" "	15 Mar. 1667	2 Sep. "	G. G.
W[m] & Geo. Lockwood	—		" "	25 April 1668	20 " "	"
Thos. Hill	10		" "	15 Mar. 1667	3 " "	"
Francis Mason	10		" "	25 " "	4 " "	"
" Gifford	40		" "	23 April last	26 Aug. "	H. N.
Samuel Mann	20		" "	" "	" "	"
John Ward	20		" "	5 Mar. 1667	22 April "	"
Hen. Soaper & Francis Bonnier	30	Nonsuch	" "	18 May 1668	9 Sep. "	"
John Carney	30	Willoughby Bay	" "	30 April "	19 Oct. "	"
Cap. Rich. Ayres	40	Nonsuch	" "	—	21 April "	"
W[m] Trappin	15	"	" "	—	—	G. G.
" "	10		" "	—	8 Oct. 1668	H. N.
Stephen Harper & Vall. Peirce	—		" "	27 April 1668	30 Sep. "	"
John Howard	35		" "	30 April last	1 June "	"
John Evans & Walter Howell	30		" "	—	22 April "	"
W[m] Ellis	10		" "	2 Mar. 1667	7 Oct. "	"
Tege Matthby (?)	10		" "	—	15 June "	"
Andrew Davidson	13		" "	2 Mar. 1667	30 April "	G. G.
John Sparkes	40		" "	" "	28 Mar. "	"
Rice Morgan, Gent.	180	Bermudian Valley	" "	17 April last	10 Sep. "	H. N.
M[rs] Eliz. Collison	200		L[t] G[l] Hen. Willoughby	21 May "	20 Nov. "	"
Cap. Tho. Strutt	100		Cap. Sam. Winthrop	14 April 1668	16 June "	G. G.
Geo. Hawkins	126		" "	4 Mar. 1667	10 Nov. "	H. N.
Francis Hawys, Fra. Peterson, & Hen. Hackney	60			3 " "	30 Mar. "	G. G.
					31 " "	"
Rob. Taylor	15			—	—	—
Hendrick Clanson, Jn[o] Moon, & Merian Perret	40			2 Mar. 1667	2 April 1668	G. G.
L[t] W[m] Thomas	100	Old North Sound		24 " "	4 Aug. "	H. N.
Hugh Gamble	50			—	18 July "	"
Howell Jones, Tho. Elmes, Jn[o] Williams, Tho. Lloyd, & W[m] Combes	65			4 Mar. last	5 June "	"
Renaldus Barter	14			—	3 " "	G. G.
James Ward	14			—	25 " "	"
Geo. Stewart	70			—	9 July "	H. N.
Rich[d] Burraston	233			—	28 April "	"
Jn[o] Bradshaw	150			—	2 Sep. "	G. G.
" "	150			—	13 June "	"
James Noone	20		Gov[r] Sam. Winthrop	—	15 " "	H. N.
Tho. Dawson	10		Col. Henry Willoughby	5 Sep. 1668	2 Oct. "	G. G.
Cha. Harrison	1 6/25		Gov[r] Winthrop	—	26 " "	"
" "	20		" "	—	27 " "	"
Benj. Steele	30		" "	18 Mar. 1667	29 Aug. "	H. N.
Rob[t] Elliot	150		" "	2 " "	15 May "	G. G.
Thos. Gregory	50		" "	29 June 1668	2 Sep. "	"
John Harley	100		" "	—	6 Aug. "	"
Pat. Mathews	15		" "	—	20 Nov. "	"
Roger Keneday	20		" "	—	22 Oct. "	H. N.
Rich[d] Abrahall	20		" "	—	18 July "	"
Hen. Willoughbie	600		by R[t] Hon. L[t] Gov[r] Hen. Willoughbie	—	10 Nov. "	G. G.
Roger Clarke & Wife & Jn[o] Keneday	20 10		Sam. Winthrop	2 Mar. 1667	27 May "	"
Rob. Poole & Tho. Wildgoose	10 10			—	7 " "	"
Dennis Maiala	10		Gov[r] Winthrop	1667	28 " "	"
Nich. Fowler & John Barry	20 10		" " " "	12 Mar. last	28 " "	"
Peter Meyer	20		" "	2 Mar. 1667	29 " "	"
Thos. Stakes & Wife	20		" "	" "	29 " "	"
James Nicoles	10		" "	" "	29 " "	"
W[m] Hunt & Walt. Phillips	10 10		" "	—	16 Oct. "	H. N.
Jn[o] Masters	40		" "	2 Mar. 1667	30 July "	G. G.
Jn[o] Burrows	10		" "	4 May 1668	" "	"
Derby Naylan	10		" "	10 April "	16 Oct. "	"
Terrence M[c]Shee	—		" "	10 Aug. "	" "	"
Chr. Rymer	20		" "	20 June "	" "	"
Tho. Hicks	20		" "	20 April "	6 Sep. "	"
Francis Allen	10		" "	15 " "	" "	"
James Connell	10		" "	8 Mar. 1667	" "	"
W[m] Duncan	15		" "	16 April 1668	3 July "	"
Tho. Robinson	20		" "	20 " "	2 " "	"
Phil. Upshott	10		" "	9 July 1668	7 " "	"
Tho. Granger, Sen., & Tho. Heath, & Thos. Granger, Jun[r], & Timothy Watson	10 10 10 —		" "	2 Mar. 1667	7 Sep. "	"
Tho. Hardwick	10		" "	20 April 1668	3 July "	"
Teig Mahone & Wife Mary, Minos Moxon, & Jn[o] Campbell	20 10 10		" "	2 Mar. 1667	19 June "	"
Rob[t] Cook	30		" "	29 April 1668	18 June "	"
Jn[o] Evans	30		" "	2 Mar. 1667	" "	"
George Foster	30		" "	20 April 1668	3 July 1668	"

* Henry Nicholls. † Gilbert Gregory.

	Acres.		Name of Dep. Governor.	Date of Gov.'s Warrant.	Date of Survey.	Name of Surveyor.
Rob. Tate & his mate Edwd Malin	10 10		Govr Winthrop	20 April 1668	3 July 1668	G. G.
Wm Drowne & Tomasen his wife	20		,, ,,	2 Mar. 1667	7 Sep. ,,	,,
Wm & Eliz. Knightly	150		,, ,,	—	7 Aug. ,,	,,
Tho. Liddy	20		,, ,,	20 Mar. 1667	—	,,
Martin Spicer	20		,, ,,	10 ,, ,,	16 Oct. 1668	,,
Leonard Hamme	100		Govr Hen. Willoughby	—	3 ,, ,,	,,
Tho. Pike	200		,, ,, ,,	—	2 ,, ,,	,,
Antony Ryerson	55		,, Sam. Winthrop	17 April 1668	24 June ,,	,,
Mr Jno Barnes, Mr Nath. Thornton, Mr Rob. Stevens	600		,, ,, ,,	12 this inst. April	16 April ,,	,,
Jno Brittaine & Jno Norton	100 sq. ft.		,, ,, ,,	—	17 Mar. ,,	,,
Tho. Turner & Jno Bridge	266⅔		,, ,, ,,	2 Mar. 1667	8 July ,,	H. N.
Jno Atkins & Jno Murphy	20		,, ,, ,,	,, ,,	—	G. G.
Robt Cook	40 ft.		,, ,, ,,	20 April 1668	4 June 1668	,,
Math. Maudlin & Rich. Mathewes	50 ft.		,, ,, ,,	,, ,,	,, ,,	,,
Chr. Ramsay	10		,, ,, ,,	5 Mar. 1667	13 Oct. ,,	,,
Tho. Chatborne	10		,, ,, ,,	23 ,, ,,	10 ,, ,,	,,
Edwd Cooke	10		,, ,, ,,	28 April 1668	10 ,, ,,	,,
Andrew Donne	30		,, ,, ,,	—	18 July ,,	,,
Wm Wood	—	hath more than is entered		—	—	,,
. . . . Byam	200	land formerly granted to Rich. Wilkin of London, in Willoughby Bay, 20 Mar. 1664		—	—	H. N.
Ellenour Miles	5			—	7 1668	G. G.
Chas. Baldwin, son of Chr. Baldwin	5	At request of Walt. Refford & Jane his Wife, ye Relict of Chr. Baldwin		—	27 July ,,	,,
Peter Lander	10			—	16 Nov. ,,	,,
. . . .	300	Formerly Cap. Wm Boucheir		—	2 Sep. ,,	H. N.
. . . . Cade	500	lately possessed of Cap. Jno Cade, ye ½ of 1000 called Cynamon Valley		—	16 Oct. ,,	,,
Garret Sherwood	30			—	22 April ,,	,,
Nath. Juice	30		from the Govr	—	15 June ,,	,,
Anthony Senlthrop	20		,, ,, ,,	—	,, ,,	,,
Abra. Cabbat	100		Winthrop	—	2 Mar. 1667	G. G.
Robt Key	30		,,	11 Mar. past	15 April 1668	H. N.
Tho. Daniel	10		,,	,, ,,	,, ,,	,,
Edwd Williams	10		,,	,, ,,	,, ,,	,,
Nath. Clarke	400	from Lt Col. Chamman & Arundell : 200 by patent from Govr Ashton		—	28 April ,,	,,
Lt Wm Burdeu	240		Winthrop	—	6 Aug. ,,	G. G.
Richd Pew	25		Lt Genl Hen. Willoughby	—	25 Jan. ,,	A. C.*
Dennis Hicks & Wife	20		Winthrop	—	—	G. G.
John Cable	20		,,	2 Mar. 1667	22 Jan. 1668	,,
Phil. Winter & Wife & James Robinson	20		,,	—	23 ,, ,,	,,
Wm Wainwright	19		,,	12 June 1668	5 Feb. ,,	H. N.
,, ,,	50		Lt Genl Hen. Willoughby	27 Jan. last	,, ,,	,,
Lewis Garrish & Joseph Hester	20		Winthrop	9 Mar. 1667	23 Jan. ,,	,,
John Todd	20		,,	1 April 1668	27 ,, ,,	G. G.
Rich. Rolph	25		,,	25 May ,,	5 Mar. ,,	H. N.
Willoughby Orton	20		,,	—	23 July ,,	G. G.
Roger Jones	10		,,	14 Mar. 1667	28 Jan. ,,	,,
Tho. Gibson	10		,,	,, ,,	,, ,,	,,
Wm Jones	10		,,	,, ,,	,, ,,	,,
Walt. Douglas	10		,,	—	,, ,,	,,
Tho. Dawson	20	formerly Cap. Mich. Stodder's		—	—	—
Tho. Connoway	100	at Musqueto Cove		—	3 April 1669	H. N.
Domingo Fardinando	10		Winthrop	30 Mar. 1667	23 Feb. 1668	,,
Deirmon Dehortie	20		,,	14 ,, ,,	15 Oct. ,,	,,
Fra. Scelton	10		Hen. Willoughby	27 Sep. 1668	21 May 1669	A. C.
Robt Harwood	30	nr Bermudian Valley		—	12 Mar. 1668	H. N.
Owen McCartie	10		Hen. Willoughby	17 inst.	25 ,, 1669	,,
Geo. Sergeant	10	On 27 Mar. last granted patent to Jno Hamlin for 10, assigned on 17 Oct. to Geo. Sergeant	Sam. Winthrop	27 Mar. last	28 Nov. 1668	,,
,, ,,	20		Lt Genl Hen. Willoughby	14 May	,, ,,	,,
Teigó Rene	10		Winthrop	2 Mar. 1667	17 Jan. ,,	G. G.
Jno Russel	20	by sale from Jno Partington		—	5 Mar. ,,	H. N.
Tho. Dawson	20	formerly Cap. Mich. Stodder's		—	8 ,, ,,	,,
Tho. Seagrave	15		Winthrop	2 Mar. 1667	1 May 1669	,,
Jno Groves	10		,,	,, ,,	16 Mar. 1668	,,
Rob. Ainge	10			—	15 ,, ,,	G. G.
Robt Williams	9		Winthrop	,, 1667	18 July ,,	,,
Rob. Ainge & Wife	20		,,	—	20 ,, ,,	,,
Edmund Ellis	20		Hen. Willoughby	22 May 1668	5 April 1669	,,
Tho. Gregory	20		,, ,,	,, ,,	12 Jan. 1668	,,
Wm Roe, Corn. Lawson, Rob. Robinson & wives, & Derby How	70		Sam. Winthrop	4 Mar. 1667	16 Mar. ,,	,,
Danl Minahan	10		Govr	14 Mar. 1667	12 Oct. ,,	H. N.
Edwd Cames & Deirmon Matross	20			2 ,, ,,	18 July ,,	G. G.
Humph. Freind	20		Winthrop	—	22 Jan. ,,	,,
Rich. Gill & Abra. Brittaine	50		,,	17 April 1668	14 Mar. ,,	,,
Rich. Freeman	100	Old North Sound	,,	2 Mar. 1667	2 April ,,	,,
Jno Casie	20		Sam. ,,	3 ,, ,,	27 Mar. 1669	H. N.
Wm Jarsey	20			—	1 April ,,	G. G.
Tho. Moses & Cado. Fogatee	20		Sam. ,,	28 July 1668	27 Mar. ,,	H. N.
Col. Clement Everard	200	at Pondridge	Hen. Willoughby	—	24 April ,,	,,
Math. Holmes	20		,, ,,	—	4 ,, ,,	A. C.
Wm Quinby	20	granted by late Fra., Lord Willoughby		—	3 May 1668	G. G.
,, ,,	17	purch. of . . . . 5 given to his son Jno Quinby by warrt from S. Winthrop 17 Mar. 1667		—	—	—

* Archibald Cochran.

	Acres.	Name of Dep. Governor.	Date of Gov.'s Warrant.	Date of Survey.	Name of Surveyor.
Wm Quinby	36	also 14 from Hen. Willoughby	—	12 Oct. 1668	G. G.
Teig Hare	10	Sam. Winthrop	—	26 July 1669	H. N.
Jno Blundell & Wm Goodale	20		—	21 June ,,	,,
Deirmon Doherty & Teig Mather	40	Fra., Lord Willoughby	—	—	,,
Wm Atkison	12	bought of Jno Swan	—	1 Sep. 1669	A. C.
Minos Ross	12½	owns	—	23 Oct. 1668	H. N.
Rob. Magoa	20	Winthrop	—	18 May 1669	,,
Jno Cane	20	,,	—	,, ,,	,,
Tho. Price	19	Hen. Willoughby	22 Sep. inst.	27 Sep. ,,	,,
Lt Mark Breuster	12	,, ,,	16 Feb. 1668	4 ,, ,,	,,
Cap. Jno Lint	104½	July 14, 1660, claims 100; 50 granted by Col. Rob. Carden & 50 given by his kinsman Wm Playstead, decd, for Jno Lint, Junr	—	19 Feb. 1667	,,
. . . .	4		—	1 Sep. 1668	,,
Jno Nibbs	15	New North Sound Division	—	Sep. 1669	A. C.
Chr. Marsh	10		—	—	,,
Nich. Collins	16½		—	—	,,
Mr Jn Fitz Randolph	400	in Falmouth, formerly in possession of Mrs Eliz. Ashton Hen. Willoughby	24 June 1669	7 Aug. 1669	,,
Jno Atkinson & Wife & Phil. Lisle & Wife	40	Sam. Winthrop	—	12 Oct. ,,	,,
Richd Crabb	100	Hen. Willoughby Governor of Antego, Barbuda, & Anguilla	—	20 ,, ,,	,,
Jno Thurland	6		—	10 Jan. ,,	,,
Mr Tho. Dunning	500	New Division Winthrop	—	13 June ,,	G. G.
Mr Edmd Hull	5		—	8 Jan. ,,	A. C.
Jonas Langford	45	Pope's Head Divn, purchased of Hannah Jefferies, Wid. of Eustace Jefferries, decd	—	7 ,, ,,	,,
Rich. Belcher	45		—	8 Jan. ,,	,,
Wm Wainewright	60′ × 40′	in Falmouth Hen. Willoughby	—	16 May ,,	G. G.
Benjn Steele	40	,, ,,	25 Jan. 1668	27 Mar. ,,	H. N.
Corn. Paw	20		—	16 Jan. ,,	A. C.
Mr Rich. Belcher	11½		—	18 Feb. ,,	,,
Cap. Archd Henderson, David Arnutt, & Lt Chr. White	500	by Warrant from Col. Wm Byam & Cap. Sam. Winthrop, Dep. Govrs of A., at New North Sound	6 Jan. 1669	16 Jan. ,,	,,
Dan. Dalley	10	purchased of Jonas Langford	—	15 Mar. ,,	,,
Jno Humphreys	98	New North Sound Govr Winthrop	20 Mar. 1667	4 Feb. ,,	,,
,, ,,	61¾	Hen. Willoughby	8 Nov. 1669	3 ,, ,,	,,
Jno Roe	20	,, ,,	19 Mar. 1668	3 Mar. ,,	,,
Wm Walton	10	Sam. Winthrop	17 ,, 1667	4 ,, ,,	,,
Harvey Keynell	—	Storehouse, St John's Town ,, ,,	10 ,, 1669	10 ,, ,,	,,
Morgan Jones	—	,, ,, ,, ,,	10 ,, ,,	10 ,, ,,	,,
Hugh Gammell	—	,, ,, ,, ,,	10 ,, ,,	10 ,, ,,	,,
Jno Bridges	—	,, ,, ,, ,,	10 ,, ,,	10 ,, ,,	,,
Edmd Hull & Jno Atkins	—	,, ,, ,, ,,	28 Feb. ,,	10 ,, ,,	,,
Danl Marloe	10	,, ,,	—	29 June 1670	G. G.
Corn. Cornelison	—	Hen. Willoughby	—	9 ,, 1669	,,
Tho. Villroy & Wm Summers	—	Govr	26 May last	22 Oct. 1668	H. N.
Edmd Hull	100	Sam. Winthrop	—	29 April ,,	G. G.
Jno Humphreys	20	Purchased of Jno Jenkins	—	12 Mar. 1669	A. C.
Mr Wm Wainewright	40	Col. Wm Byam, Dep. Govr	—	8 ,, ,,	G. G.
Cap. Harvey Keynell	140	by Col. Wm Byam & Cap. S. Winthrop, Dep. Govrs	10 Mar. 1669	14 April 1670	A. C.
Capt Giles Blizard	155	At request of Dr Hen. Stodder have surveyed ye plantation lately belonging to Cap. Giles Blizard & now in possession of his children	—	27 ,, ,,	G. G. & A. C.
Serjt Mark Jackson	60	Sam. Winthrop	—	15 ,, ,,	G. G.
Nath. Monke	30½	,, ,,	28 Mar. 1668	14 ,, ,,	H. N.
Lt Brian Cansfield	—	land for storehouse in St John's T. ,, ,,	10 April ,,	15 ,, ,,	G. G.
Tho. Stakes	20	Hen. Willoughby	—	14 Feb. 1669	H. Wby.
Lucrecia Parson	78	Orphan Mr Tho. Dawson, adm'or of Jno Robinson, decd	—	8 April 1670	A. C.
Henry Carr	10	Sam. Winthrop	6 Mar. 1667	19 Feb. 1669	,,
Dr John Clark	200	by Col. Wm Byam's Warrt for 200	—	16 Aug. 1670	,,
Edmond Johnston	32	Hen. Willoughby	27 July 1669	16 July ,,	,,
John Evans, Senr	10	Sam. Winthrop	Mar. 1667	20 Aug. ,,	,,
Edmond Jonston	28	,, ,,	9 July 1668	16 July ,,	,,
Lt Col. Bast. Byares	70	New Divn by the Govr	7 May ,,	22 Aug. ,,	,,
Henry Mayer	—	land for storehouse, St John's T. Hen. Willoughby	12 Aug. 1669	1 ,, ,,	,,
Cornelius Pow	20	by the Govr	—	22 ,, ,,	,,
John Evans, Jun.	50	Sam. Winthrop	11 Mar. 1667	Aug. ,,	,,
Roger Foulser	70	,, ,,	—	23 June 1671	H. N.
Garret Sherwood	12		—	15 ,, ,,	,,

"Heere ends ye Commission of Sam. Winthrop, Register for all Records in this Booke delivered to Major Rowland Williams now Register by ye Commission & appointmt of Collo Phillip Warner, depy Governor of this Island Antigua, as witnes ye hands of both ye said Registers this sixteenth day of January 1671."

Dermott Adams	10	by Col. Philip Warner, President of ye Council	29 Aug. last	4 Jan. 1671-2	H. N.
Henry Bine	10	bequeathed by Lawr. Jones	—	18 Oct. 1671	A. C.
Jacob Hill	40	by Col. Wm Byam, Govr	3 June 1670	6 Aug. 1670	,,

"RECORD

"Of the Returne of such warrants as have been directed to ye surveyors for laying out of lands since ye 10th of January 1671-2.

"By authority from his Excy, Sr Charles Wheeler, Barronet."

Nath. Monke	40	Col. Philip Warner	11th inst.	19 Jan. 1671-2	H. N.
James Garland	10	,, ,,	,,	,, ,,	,,
Henry Pellick	10	,, ,,	,,	,, ,,	,,
Wm Bowden	10	,, ,,	,,	,, ,,	,,
Ralph Steele	10	,, ,,	—	22 Jan. ,,	,,
Chr. Quick	10	,, ,,	—	22 ,, ,,	,,
Rich. Kitchin	5	,, ,,	—	2 ,, ,,	,,
Rob. Mounsly	10	,, ,,	—	15 ,, ,,	,,
Wm Lee	10	,, ,,	—	15 ,, ,,	,,
Dr Jones	30	,, ,,	—	15 ,, ,,	,,

	Acres.		Name of Dep. Governor.	Date of Gov.'s Warrant.	Date of Survey.	Name of Surveyor.
Tho. Syms	20		Col. Philip Warner	—	16 Jan. 1671-2	H. N.
Jno Pheby	10		" "	—	16 " "	"
Ann Ofe	5		" "	—	18 " "	"
John Parry	150		" "	11 Jan. 1671	20 " "	"
Rob. Hughes	30		" "	12 " "	22 " "	"
Rob. Oswell	10		" "	11 " "	22 " "	"
Peter Engham	10	Old North Sound, west with Robt Olliver	Col. Philip Warner	13 " "	—	—
Rob. Taffe	10		Govr Philip Warner	11 " "	27 " "	A. C.
Robert Olliver	10	Old North Sound	" "	12 " 1671-2	27 " "	"
Cyprian Rogers	10		" "	12 " "	28 " "	"
Martin Morton	10		" "	11 " "	3 Feb. "	"
James Butterworth	10		" "	13 " "	3 " "	"
Mark Benn	10		" "	13 " "	6 " "	"
Chr. King	20		" "	13 " "	5 " "	"
Tho. Lodge	10		" "	19 " "	8 " "	"
Daniel Gording	10		" "	19 " "	10 " "	"
Ralph Steede	10		" "	11 " "	22 " "	"
Wm Whitingham	10		" "	13 " "	23 " "	"
George Gerrish	10		" "	11 " "	24 " "	"
Tho. Brookes	10		" "	19 " "	24 " "	"
Majr Rowld Williams	14		" "	13 " "	20 " "	"
Mathew Bryan	10		" "	11 " "	20 " "	"
Tho. Litman	10		" "	15 " "	20 " "	"
Edward Ralph	10		" "	11 " "	20 " "	"
Mr Henry Warner	161	Nonsuch	" "	11 " "	20 " "	"
Lt John Fry	19	Bermudian Valley	" "	13 " "	20 " "	"
" "	9	" "	" "	23 " "	20 " "	"
John Palmer, Jr	35		" "	—	20 Mar. "	"
Benj. King	10		" "	11 " "	17 Feb. "	"
John White	10		" "	11 " "	17 " "	"
James Nibbes	15		" "	11 " "	19 " "	"
Rich. Masters	10		" "	11 " "	6 Mar. "	"
Tho. Poole	10		" "	11 " "	26 Feb. "	"
John Marshall	30		" "	15 " "	26 " "	"
Rich. Kitchin	10		" "	11 " "	27 " "	"
Archd Cochran	30		" "	11 " "	2 Mar. "	"
Col. Nath. Clarke	50		" "	11 " "	3 " "	"
Edward Leaver	30		" "	11 " "	3 " "	"
Wm Whipham	30		" "	14 " "	6 " "	"
Tho. Seagrave	3		" "	14 Feb. "	18 " "	"
Edward Leaver	20		" "	7 Mar. "	8 " "	"
Wm Atkinson	10		Col. Philip Warner	7 " 1671	8 " 1671	"
John Beck	30			27 Feb. "	20 " "	"
Nath. Milner, Mercht	200			5 Mar. "	20 " "	"
Geo. Smith	40			Jan. "	20 " "	"
Geo. Tower	50			" "	29 " 1672	"
Tho. Bartlet	10			12 Mar. "	20 " 1671	"
John Austine	40			—	12 April 1672	"
Jonas Watts	300			30 Aug. last	2 Sep. "	H. N.
Ralph Hoskins	40			11 Mar. 1671	10 Oct. "	"
John Woofe	18			11 Jan. "	" "	"
Edward Williams	10			7 April 1673	—	A. C.
Wm Purtford (?)	15		Cap. Sam. Winthrop	18 " 1668	18 Sep. 1673	H. N.
Wm Therland	20			14 May	20 May "	A. C.
Col. Row. Williams & Cap. Ob. Bradshaw	160′ × 60′	Indigo work, etc.		13 Jan. 1671	16 Aug. 1672	"
Ralph Hoskins	40			2 April 1672	23 Oct. "	Rich. Harris.
Jonas Watts	800	Blubber Valley		17 Feb. inst.	20 Feb. 1672-3	H. N.
Rob. Sutton	10			7 Oct. 1672	16 Oct. 1672	A. C.
Peter Lavicount	36			12 April 1673	3 Jan. 1673	"
John Grayhues	10			1 Jan. 1671	" "	"
Wm Shaw	18			29 May 1673	" "	"
Ben. Tuck	—			4 Mar. last	1 April "	H. N.
John Perry	—			23 Dec. 1672	4 Feb. 1672	A. C.
Rich. Rogers	60′ × 80′			21 Oct. "	23 Oct. "	"
Rob. Oxford	60′ × 40′			1 Jan. "	1 Feb. "	"
Wm Jonston	10			6 " "	4 " "	"
Roger Complaine	50′ × 80′			—	4 " "	"
Morris Lee	10			29 Oct. 1672	14 Oct. "	"
Chr. Reyner	10			" "	14 " "	"
Wm Windwright	40′ × 60′	Falmouth		" "	23 " "	"
Tho. Graswell, Jr	10			—	27 Aug. "	"
Wm Kerby	20			20 July 1672	20 " "	"
John Berry	10			29 Oct. "	15 Oct. "	"
Tho. Crawfield	60′ × 40′	Falmouth Town		14 Aug. "	29 " "	"
Rob. Huse	10		Philip Warner	2 Oct. "	14 " "	"
John Ellson	10		" "	—	—	"
John Evans	50′ × 80′	St John's Town	Col. Sam. Winthrop, President	July 1670	8 July 1670	"
John Masters	15		Philip Warner	29 Oct. 1672	15 Oct. 1672	"
Daniel Pello	20		" "	" "	14 Nov. "	"
Edward Cooke	10		" "	" "	14 " "	"
Rob. Key	5		" "	9 Nov. "	16 " "	"
John Foster	10		" "	13 Jan. 1671	20 Aug. "	"
John Hopton	10		" "	29 Nov. 1672	14 Nov. "	"
Patrick Hurdy	10		" "	" "	15 " "	"

"The 20th of octobr 1674."

"Here begineth the Entry and Recording of the Surveyors' returnes of warrants to them directed for the Laying out and admeasuring of Lands to the persons following,

"by WILL. BARNES, dept Register."

Cap. Rich. Ayres	26	Green Island, Nonsuch	Col. Philip Warner	Feb. 1673-4	14 Mar. 1673-4	A. C.
Edward Cooke	10		" "	29 Oct. 1672	15 Nov. 1672	"
Lt George Turney	93	New North Sound	" "	—	24 Sep. 1673	"
Cap. Edward Maynard	—		" "	24 Dec. 1673	26 Feb. "	"
Anthony Ryerson	—		" "	16 Mar. 1673-4	1 April 1674	"
John Wills (?)	50′ × 80′	St John's Town	" "	" "	" "	"
Jonas Watts	50′ × 80′	" "	" "	21 Oct.	20 Dec. 1673	"
Cap. Ob. Bradshaw	10		" "	29 Nov. 1673	20 Jan. "	"
Tho. Edwards	10		" "	19 " "	" "	"

	Acres.		Name of Dep. Governor.	Date of Gov.'s Warrant.	Date of Survey.	Name of Surveyor.
Owen Sullivant	20		Col. Philip Warner	7 April 1674	16 July 1674	A. C.
Francis Carlile	50′ × 80′	St John's Town	,, ,,	28 June 1673	20 Feb. 1673	,,
Wm Williams	50′ × 80′	,, ,,	,, ,,	3 Mar. 1673-4	1 April 1674	,,
Roger Complaine	50′ × 80′	,, ,,	,, ,,	26 Feb. ,,	,, ,,	,,
Chr. Nicholls	10		,, ,,	8 Oct. 1673	18 Oct. 1673	,,
Rich. Allen	50′ × 80′	St John's Town	,, ,,	10 Mar. 1673-4	April 1674	,,
Cap. Edward Maynard	50′ × 80′	,, ,,	,, ,,	17 Oct. 1673	4 Nov. 1673	,,
Wm Bitely	10		,, ,,	7 July ,,	30 Mar. 1674	,,
John Liskum	10		,, ,,	18 Sep. ,,	17 Oct. 1673	,,
John Elmore	10		,, ,,	30 May ,,	16 Sep. ,,	,,
Francis Hawyes	50′ × 80′	St John's Town	,, ,,	2 Sep. ,,	4 —ber ,,	,,
Derby Collins	10		,, ,,	13 ,, ,,	18 Oct. ,,	,,
John Dexee	10		,, ,,	12 Oct. ,,	16 ,, ,,	,,
Nath. Garrett	50		,, ,,	11 Jan. 1671-2	10 Jan. ,,	,,
Mr Sam. Jones	64	bought of Col. Sam. Winthrop		—	15 Feb. ,,	,,
Mich. McDaniell	20		by the Govr	—	12 Oct. 1668	H. N.
Sam. Irish	—	30 mens land	Col. Philip Warner	28 Nov. last	8 Dec. 1674	,,
Mr John Vernone	60	Old North Sound	,, ,,	30 April 1673	22 Feb. 1674-5	A. C.
Geo. Tower	60′ × 80′		,, ,,	5 June ,,	12 July 1673	,,
Philip Lile	10		,, ,,	11 Oct. 1674	19 Oct. 1674	,,
John Murphey	10		,, ,,	4 Nov. ,,	18 Nov. ,,	,,
Edward McShedy	10		,, ,,	9 ,, ,,	16 ,, ,,	,,
Edward Ricketts	10		,, ,,	3 Sep. 1672	9 Nov. ,,	,,
Simon Warner	10		,, ,,	29 Jan. 1674	18 Feb. 1674-5	,,
Phillem. McCarty	10		,, ,,	15 Oct. ,,	4 Nov. 1674	,,
John Lace	10		,, ,,	16 ,, ,,	30 Oct. ,,	,,
Tim. Murphy	10		,, ,,	15 ,, ,,	4 Nov. ,,	,,
Francis Hawyes	50′ × 80′	St John's Town	,, ,,	—	12 Jan. ,,	,,
Tho. Moore	50′ × 80′	,, ,,	,, ,,	—	,, ,,	,,
Edward Wiltshire	50′ × 80′	,, ,,	,, ,,	16 Oct. 1674	23 Oct. ,,	,,
John Thompson	10		,, ,,	15 ,, ,,	10 Feb. ,,	,,
Andrew Hamilton	30		,, ,,	18 May ,,	12 July ,,	,,
Tho. Yorke	10		,, ,,	26 Jan. 1673	1 Nov. ,,	,,
Wm Taxter	20		,, ,,	18 May 1674	12 July ,,	,,
Jaxe Ixeson	20		,, ,,	2 Nov. ,,	18 Nov. ,,	,,
John Browne	—		,, ,,	20 July ,,	19 ,, ,,	,,
Sam. Man	50		,, ,,	8 Mar. ,,	4 ,, ,,	,,
John Stratton	50		,, ,,	29 Jan. ,,	14 Feb. ,,	,,
Sam. Jones	500	New North Sound	,, ,,	18 Dec. ,,	13 Jan. ,,	,,
Tho. Haynes	20		,, ,,	—	16 ,, ,,	,,
Francis Ashwell	10		,, ,,	Aug. 1671	10 April 1675	,,
Lt Wm Procter	10		,, ,,	17 Oct. 1672	,, ,,	,,
Owen Bramwell	—		,, ,,	—	17 May ,,	,,
Francis Ashwell	10		,, ,,	8 Nov. 1674	26 June ,,	,,
Mr Nich. Clarke	166		,, ,,	28 June 1675	6 ,, ,,	,,
Col. Cha. Guest, dec^d	—	for the equal Division of his estate of 364 a. in St John's Divⁿ. To go to his 2 daus., Arabella Guest & Caroline Guest, & to his Wid., now ye wife of Tho. Hutton, therefore :—		7 ,, ,,	June ,,	,,
	121	Mr Tho. Moor, in right of his Wife Arabella Guest				
	121	Tho. Hutton				
	121	Mr Tho. Moor & Cap. Harvey Keynell as Guardians of Caroline Guest				
Ensign Anthony White	40		Col. Ph. Warner	11 June 1674	10 April 1675	,,
Walt. Williamson	20		,, ,,	10 Feb. 1672	,, ,,	,,
John Dowgan	10		,, ,,	Oct. 1675	8 Oct. ,,	,,
Edmond Hill	50′ × 80′	St John's Town	,, ,,	22 June 1675	8 Aug. ,,	,,
James Barton	40		,, ,,	23 ,, ,,	20 July ,,	,,
Tho. Cochran	30		Col. Rowland Williams	16 July ,,	18 Oct. ,,	,,
John Heydon	10		,, ,,	,, ,,	30 ,, ,,	,,
Jer. Thistletwaite	4		Govr Ph. Warner	14 June ,,	—	,,
Wm Norris	10		Govr Row. Williams	13 Sep. ,,	28 Oct. 1675	,,
Roger Massie	10		,, ,,	12 July ,,	24 July ,,	,,
Francis Vencolo	20		,, ,,	11 Sep. ,,	30 Oct. ,,	,,
John Knight	10		,, ,,	,, ,,	28 ,, ,,	,,
Edmond Hull	50′ × 80′		Ph. Warner	—	8 Aug. ,,	,,
Cap. Wm Thomas	25	Bird Island delivered according to ye ancient custom of Eng. with turff & twig		11 April 1675	12 June ,,	,,
Daniel Hayes	6½		Row. Williams	14 July ,,	22 July ,,	,,
Tho. Shelton	10		Ph. Warner	30 Nov. 1674	9 Mar. 1674	,,
Lt Edward Cooke	14		,, ,,	2 Mar. ,,	8 Nov. 1675	,,
Philip Everdon	50′ × 80′	St John's Town	,, ,,	6 April 1675	20 April ,,	,,
Edward Lawrance	10		Row. Williams	11 Sep. ,,	28 Oct. ,,	,,
Wm Knightly	100		,, ,,	9 July ,,	12 Aug. ,,	,,
Patrick Long	20			Dec. 1674	8 Mar. 1674	,,
Wm Taylor	50′ × 80′		Row. Williams	16 July 1675	6 Aug. 1675	,,
Digory Cole	10		Col. Row. Williams	12 ,, ,,	24 July ,,	,,
Lt Wm Procter	60′ × 40′	Falmouth T.	Col. Ph. Warner	17 Feb. 1674	24 Feb. 1674	,,
Rich. Buraston	10	son of Tho. B., dec^d	,, ,,	12 ,, ,,	3 July 1675	,,
Widow Gambell	38		,, ,,	7 Mar. ,,	23 April ,,	,,
Sarah Barton	100	Her husband Ch^r B., dec^d	,, ,,	18 Dec. ,,	25 ,, ,,	H. N.
Cap. Henry Hunt	915	Have bounded 430, formerly Mugg's	Cap. Geo. Rynerson Col. Ph. Warner	—	5 June ,,	A. C.
Tho. Andersuch	10		Col. Row. Williams	2 Feb. 1675-6	22 Feb. ,,	,,
Wm Dadson	10		,, ,,	—	13 Sep. ,,	,,
Roger Binin	10		,, ,,	2 Sep. 1675	,, ,,	,,
Mr Tho. Warner	12		,, ,,	3 Mar. ,,	7 Mar. ,,	,,
Roger Thomas	10	bought of Col. Nath. Clarke	,, ,,	—	10 July 1674	,,
Tho. Haynes	10	,, ,,	,, ,,	—	,, ,,	,,
Arch. Cochran	—	Seadinell, now Goat Island	Col. Ph. Warner	28 June 1675	7 Mar. 1675	R. H.
John Knight	10		,, ,,	1 April ,,	Sep. ,,	A. C.
Wm Bourke	100	At request of Lt Col. Jno Mayer, Agent to John, Ld Willoughby of Parham		—	20 Jan. ,,	,,
John Carde	70	,, ,,	,,	—	20 ,, ,,	,,
Rob. Fruod	20	,, ,,	,,	—	22 ,, ,,	,,
Owen Sullavan	20	,, ,,	,,	—	24 ,, ,,	,,
James Conell	20	,, ,,	,,	—	24 ,, ,,	,,
John White & Garret Browne	—	,, ,,	,,	—	26 ,, ,,	,,
Mr Fra. Carlile	100	St John's Divⁿ	Lt Col. Row. Williams	20 Dec. 1675	4 ,, ,,	,,
Mr Joseph Winthrop	40′ × 50′	Bridge Town	,, ,,	—	8 Oct. ,,	,,
Cap. Rich. Ayres	,,	,, ,,	,, ,,	—	,, ,,	,,
Wm Barnes	,,	,, ,,	,, ,,	—	,, ,,	,,

	Acres.		Name of Dep. Governor.	Date of Gov.'s Warrant.	Date of Survey.	Name of Surveyor.
Chr. Rymer	40′ × 50′	Bridge Town	Lt Col. Row. Williams	—	8 Oct. 1675	A. C.
Lt Daniel Pelloe	"	" "	" "	—	" "	"
Philip Upshot	"	" "	" "	—	" "	"
Mr Fra. Carlile	"	" "	" "	28 Sep. 1675	" "	"
Lt Edward Cooke	"	" "	" "	" "	" "	"
Mr Anthony Maynard	"	" "	" "	" "	" "	"
Symon Gubbins	"	" "	" "	" "	" "	"
Public	3 & 3½	near Willoughby Bay, for a town	Col. Ph. Warner	—	28 June "	"
Henry Soper & Francis Bonnor	40′ × 50′	Bridge Town	Col. Row. Williams	28 Sep. 1675	8 Oct. "	"
John Marshall	"	" "	" "	—	" "	"
Domingo Fardinando	"	" "	" "	—	" "	"
John Marchant	"	" "	" "	—	" "	"
John Dowgan	"	" "	" "	—	" "	"
Howell Jones & John Carney	"	" "	" "	—	" "	"
Mr Rich. Roggers	"	" "	" "	—	" "	"
John Bacon	"	" "	" "	—	" "	"
Mr Wm Barnes	"	" "	" "	—	" "	"
Geo. Mathews	"	" "	" "	—	" "	"
John Hall	"	" "	" "	—	" "	"
Cap. Ob. Bradshaw	"	" "	" "	—	" "	"
Nath. Garrett	"	" "	" "	—	" "	"
Rich. Sphier	"	" "	" "	—	" "	"
Cap. Roger Jones	"	" "	" "	—	" "	"
Geo. Bisse	80		Govr Wm Byam	19 June 1671	Aug. 1676	"
Mrs Joan Hall	—			—	17 Nov. 1676	"
Public	—	Goat's Hill	Col. Ph. Warner	15 Nov. last	Nov. 1676	"
Henry Sharpe	40		Col. Ro. Williams	18 Sep. last	14 Nov. 1676	H. N
Lt John Fry	632¼	Bermudian Valley	by the Govr	6 Mar. 1674-5	27 Aug. 1675	"
Majr Tho. Malet	—	At his request have bounded ½ of Bettys hope, being 362½ acres purch. by Ensign John Hall		—	22 June 1676	A. C.
Flew Ellin Rice	20		Col. Ph. Warner	10 May 1674	14 Mar. 1675-6	"
Jane Ward	20		" "	26 Mar. 1675	20 May 1676	"
Mr Steven Lawler, Mercht, & Mr Tho. Webb	—	St John's T.	Col. Row. Williams	11 Nov. 1676	18 Dec. "	"
Mr Jno Hamilton	50′ × 80′	St John's T.	Col. Ph. Warner	11 Nov. 1676	18 Dec. "	"
John Ennis	"	" "	Col. Row. Williams	14 Aug. "	20 Sep. "	"
Edwd Wiltshire	"	" "	" "	24 Mar. 1675-6	6 April "	"
Cap. John Vernon	"	" "	" "	30 " 1676	" "	"
Mr Fra. Carlile	"	St John's Town	" "	30 April "	" "	"
Lt Jacob Hill	"	" "	" "	27 " "	24 Sep. "	"
James Pheby	"	" "	" "	27 " "	July "	"
Mr Anthony Regerson	10′ × 80′	" "	Col. Phil. Warner	—	6 Feb. "	"
Oliver Alldwin	50′ × 80′	" "	Col. Row. Williams	16 Dec. 1675	July "	"
Mrs Eliz. Morgan	"	" "	" "	29 Mar. 1676	20 July "	"
Geo. Phillips	"	" "	" "	29 Aug. "	24 Sep. "	"
John Evans	"	" "	" "	30 " "	Sep. "	"
John Masters	—		" "	—	16 Mar. 1675	"
James Glass	—		Col. Phil. Warner	15 Mar. 1674	14 " "	"
George Mackrow (?)	—		"	28 Jan. 1675	14 " "	"
Hon. Lt Col. Randolph Russell	511		"	16 " 1676	—	—
Nath. Monk	47 & 37½		"	15 Dec. "	19 Feb. 1676	A. C.
John Rider	10		Row. Williams	—	17 Mar. 1675-6	"
Wm Williams	10		Ph. Warner	26 Jan. 1676	8 Feb. 1676	"
Rob. Stanley	20		Row. Williams	—	9 Jan. 1675-6	"
Dr Tho. Gatter	—		Ph. Warner	6 Dec. 1676	—	"
Hugh Evans	10		"	—	20 Jan. 1676	"
Lt Jacob Hill	88		Row. Williams	Sep. 1676	30 Sep. "	"
Henry Pellum	3		Ph. Warner	25 June 1675	14 Mar. 1675	"
Robt Hastings & Sam. Harper	20		Row. Williams	13 Jan. "	20 April 1676	"
Wm Richardson	20		" "	—	15 Mar. 1675	"
Tho. Robison	50′ × 80′	St John's T.	" "	30 Aug. 1676	24 Sep. 1676	"
Tho. Middleton	"	" "	" "	10 April "	July "	"
David Bell	"	" "	" "	" "	" "	"
Seath Marlo	"	" "	" "	29 Mar. "	" "	"
Roger Compline	"	" "	" "	16 April "	20 July "	"
John Evans	"	" "	" "	29 Mar. "	" "	"
John Mooue	"	" "	" "	—	6 April "	"
John Heely	"	" "	" "	31 Aug. 1676	6 Sep. "	"
Wm Bowden	"	" "	" "	21 July "	" "	"
Lt Jacob Hill	"	" "	" "	27 April "	24 " "	"
John Sewell	"	" "	" "	21 Aug. "	11 " "	"
Joseph Harvie & Rich. Heely	1 prop.	(1 proportion) St John's T.		9 Jan. "	12 Jan. "	"
Cap. John Pogshon	"	St John's T.	Col. Ph. Warner	25 Nov. "	9 " "	"
Tho. Lydiott	"	"		14 Aug. "	20 Sep. "	"
Bettys Hope	725	Old North Sound (its boundaries given)		—	—	"
Col. Willoughby	1000	Parham. By Ph. Warner. By Act da. 10 April 1668 no plantation was to be granted over 600 acres, yet Col. Hen. Willoughby obtained a patent from Wm, Ld Willoughby, of all Parham & several islands, reputed 8 or 10,000 acres, & held by his heirs since, & is waste. Do you therefore measure to Col. John Willoughby & Cha. Willoughby, Esq., Ex'ors to Wm, Ld Willoughby, decd, 1000 & 3 acres at Parham		6 Feb. 1676	Feb. 1676	"
John .... & Margt his Wife	—	St John's T.	Col. Row. Williams	10 April 1676	July 1676	"
John Michell & Tho. Dedford	50′ × 80′	Merchts of St John's T.	" "	" "	26 Mar. 1676	"
Rich. Jenkins	"	St John's T.	" "	—	July 1676	"
Mr Tho. Becke	200		Ph. Warner	3 April 1677	April 1677	"
Wm Garrett, Peter Garrett, & Cornelius Garrett	102		" "	19 Mar. 1676	26 April 1677	"
Tho. Jones, Jr	50		" "	13 Jan. "	" "	"
Wm Bowden	50′ × 80′	St John's T.	" "	—	" "	"
John Fry	180	On the N. side of Rendevous Bay Mountains	Ph. Warner	14 Nov. 1676	" "	"
Ensign Rob. Parker	100		"	9 Mar. 1676	26 Mar. 1677	"
Randolph Booker	60		"	—	—	—

	Acres.	Name of Dep. Governor.	Date of Gov.'s Warrant.	Date of Survey.	Name of Surveyor.
George Robinson	180	Ph. Warner	3 April 1677	27 April 1677	A. C.
Mr Rich. Haddon	250	„	20 Feb. 1676	24 Feb. 1676	„
Ralph Pigott (?)	9½	„	28 „ „	20 April 1677	„
Tho. Jones	30	„	27 Mar. 1677	—	„
Wm Browne	15	„	—	5 June 1677	„
Majr Wm Mussinden	500	„	—	7 Aug. „	„
Mr Tho. Pike of Nevis	200	Col. Ph. Warner	23 April 1677	12 May „	„
Mr Lenard Ham of Nevis	200	„	„ „	„ „	„
J . . . . J . . . . eson	—	Col. Row. Williams	1675	23 Aug. „	„
Mr Henry Mayer	50	formerly part of 100 of Lewis Chenevy's, & now belonging to Ens. Ben. Jefferies in right of his wife Anna Chenery Col. Row. Williams	—	Oct. „	„
Mr Henry Winthrop	190	Bermudian Valley, in right of his Wife Heneretta; part of land formerly in the possession of Cap. Wm Kyn Col. Row. Williams	—	10 Mar. „	„
Lt John Fry	190	Bermudian Valley, in right of his Wife Mary; formerly land in the possession of Cap. Wm Kyn Col. Row. Williams	—	„ „	„
Cap. Sam. Painter	75		—	1676	„
Mr George Dickby	75		—	„	„
Jno Palmer	50	Col. Ph. Warner	27 Mar. 1677	April 1677	„
Edward Williams	30	„	13 Aug. „	Sep. „	„
Darby Collins	10	„	—	29 Aug. 1677	„
Timothy Singin	20	„	16 Jan. 1676	June 1677	„
Cap. John Vernon	260	1st Warrt da. 1674 for 60 by Col. Ph. Warner; a 2d for 100 da. 5 Sep. 1675 by Col. Row. Williams; & a 3d for 100 da. 11 Oct. 1677 by Col. Ph. Warner in Old North Sound	—	4 Oct. „	„
Rob. Howard	26	Col. Ph. Warner	27 Mar. 1677	June „	„
Mr John Lasheny	50	„	„ „	Aug. „	„
John White	10	„	„ „	„ „	„
Walter Burke	20	„	„ „	„ „	„
Edward Bourke, Jr	35	„	„ „	„ „	„
Tho. Hawes	100	„	„ „	„ „	„
Philip Lile	20	„	„ „	„ „	„
Peter Lavicount	30	„	„ „	„ „	„
Garratt Browne	10	„	„ „	„ „	„
John Carde	50	„	„ „	„ „	„
Teag Sullivan	14	„	„ „	18 Sep. „	„
Owen McCarty	28	„	„ „	June „	„
Thos. Nanton & Rob. Nanton	20	„	20 Sep. „	Nov. „	„
Rob. Sutton	30	„	29 May „	21 Aug. 1677	„
Joshua Leech	100	„	„ „	14 June „	„
John Stratton	60	„	9 Oct. „	Nov. 1677	„
Rich. Pitts	40	„	27 Mar. „	June „	„
James Farrill	20	„	24 Jan. 1676	July „	„
Edward Thomas	50	„	27 Mar. 1677	Aug. „	„
Wm Browne	15	„	„ „	„ „	„
John Hatherly	20	„	„ „	„ „	„
Tho. Cummins	20	„	„ „	20 July 1677	„
Teage Callahan	10	„	26 June „	Aug. 1677	„
Lt Col. John Mayers	60	„	14 Aug. „	„ „	„
Emaniuel Desilier	10	„	15 Sep. „	Sep. „	„
Nicholas Fowler	20	„	26 June „	Aug. „	„
Rich. Bowin	10	„	27 Mar. „	„ „	„
Wm Bourke	100	„	„ „	„ „	„
Lt Sam. Jeafferson	30	„	„ „	— „	„
John Pearse	35	„	„ „	— „	„
Paulle Maynard	60	„	„ „	Aug. „	„
James Connell	20	„	„ „	„ „	„
Edward Rawly	20	„	„ „	„ „	„
Mich. McDaniell	20	„	„ „	„ „	„
Edmond Connorico (?)	10	„	7 Aug. „	„ „	„
Daniel Dally	10	„	27 Mar. „	„ „	„
Tho. Jones	35	„	„ „	„ „	„
John Hill	15	„	„ „	„ „	„
Philom McCarty	15	„	„ „	„ „	„
Mr Tho. Lowell	50	„	„ „	April „	„
Torlogh McShee	20	„	„ „	May „	„
Wm Thompson	20	„	„ „	„ „	„
Darby McCarty	10	„	„ „	„ „	„
Wm Warrin	15	„	„ „	April „	„
Denis Crawly	10	„	„ „	Sep. „	„
Tho. Yorke	—	Tropic Bird Island Col. Row. Williams	23 June 1676	—	—
„ „	20	Col. Ph. Warner	27 Mar. 1677	Sep. 1677	A. C.
Timothy Burton	10	„ „	„ „	Aug. „	„
Teage Wollaghan	20	„ „	„ „	—	„
James Cavan	10	„ „	„ „	Aug. 1677	„
Public	30	For Mercers Creek Guard House „ „	„ „	„ „	„
Rich. Gill	30	„ „	„ „	„ „	„
John Bowden	25	„ „	„ „	„ „	„
Simon Warner	10	„ „	„ „	„ „	„
Owen Sullivan, Jr	20	„ „	„ „	July „	„
Mr Fra. Carlile	50	„ „	„ „	„ „	„
John Bedford	13		—	Aug. 26 1678	Mordecay Rogers, Surveyr.
John Ennis	10		—	„ „	„
Cap. John Pogson	200	Govr Wm Stapleton	—	24 June 1676	A. C.
„ Hamilton	180	Govr Col. James Vaughan	7 Oct. 1678.	9 Oct. 1678	„
Lt John Hall	123	Col. Ph. Warner	27 Mar. 1677	Aug. „	„
Cap. John Frye	40	Govr Col. Jas. Vaughan	2 Oct. inst.	24 Oct. „	H. N.
Mr Joshua Brewster & Mr John Ker	2 prop. 80f × 60f	Falmouth T. „ „	—	25 „ „	M. R.
. . . .	—	Cap. Paul Lee, Judge of ye precincts of Falmouth, his Warrt to appraise ye plantn of Nath. Garrett in Nonsuch. We value it at 2000 lbs. of sugar or tobacco yearly. (Signed) Tho. Malet, Joseph Winthropp, Danll Pelloe, Jno Hall. Col. Ph. Warner	—	Nov. 1677	A. C.
John Levicount	100	Belfast	—	30 July 1678	M. R.
Cap. Jer. Watkins	70	St John's Divn, ye Hon. Majr Jer. Watkins purchased 40 of Wm Bowen Col. Ph. Warner	—	Jan. 1677 7 Nov. 1678	A. C. M. R.

	Acres.		Name of Dep. Governor.	Date of Gov.'s Warrant.	Date of Survey.	Name of Surveyor.
Mr Joseph Downham	2 prop. 100f × 80f	St John's Town opposite Lt Sam. Winthrop's house		— —	14 Nov. 1678 —	M. R. —
Wm Browne	50		Col. Jas. Vaughan	15 Oct. last.	26 Nov. 1678	H. N.
Peter Welsh	128	Bermudian Valley		—	27 „ „	„
Nath. Hoare & Geo. Philips	20		Col. Sam. Winthrop	—	11 Mar. 1668 (*sic*)	G. G.
Teige Mahone & Wife	20			2 Mar. 1667	13 „ „	„
Darby How	13½	from Wm Roe, decd		—	15 „ „	„
„ „	7		Cap. Sam. Winthrop	4 Mar. 1668	15 „ „	„
Rob. Robinson & Wife	18½		„ „	„ „	16 „ „	„

"Division. Part 2. Of the Lands taken up on the West side of the Creeke.

"Taken upp for the use of the Right Honble Frauncis, Lord Willughbye of Parrham, by Mr Nathaniel Clarke. One Tract of Land in Seryno Creeke, beginning some Twenty cheine below the present landing place of Comacabo Towne, and running in breadth along the Creeke one hundred and sixty chaine. Contayning Two Thousand Acres, part Savanna and part Woodlands; with power to sett up Mills or any other thing in any Creeke or Creekes in the aforesaid Tract. Recorded the 10th of January 1653.

"per ROBERT SANFORD, Secy."

[The above probably applies to Surinam.]

Cornelius Lawson	23		Cap. Sam. Winthrop	4 Mar. 1677	16 Mar. 1668-9	G. G.

N.B. 2 Dec. 1678. "The Six foregoing Records und' the Hand of Gilbert Gregory were not brought into ye office untill this present day as above.

"per ROWLAND WILLIAMS, Regr."

James Roach	20		Col. Jas. Vaughan	—	15 Nov. 1678	A. C.
Mr Edward Dendy	1 prop.	St John's Town	„ „	—	—	M. R.
Lt Wm Tramill	300		„ „	20 Aug. 1678	6 Sep. 1678	A. C.
John Tyer	100		„ „	„ „	8 „ „	„
Edward Panly	200		„ „	„ „	10 „ „	„
Edward Dune	100		Col. Ph. Warner	27 Mar. 1677	12 „ „	„
James Williams	100		„ „	7 Aug. „	15 Jan. 1678	„
John Lucas	2 prop.	St John's Town 100f × 80f	Col. Jas. Vaughan	—	15 Oct. „	M. R.
Mr Tho. Inett	200			—	28 Nov. „	„
Mr Corn. Hafferin	100		Wm Stapleton	29 April 1678	20 June „	A. C.
Joseph Daniell	20			—	—	M. R.
Joseph Heath	50			—	29 Aug. 1678	„
Rob. Stanley	40			—	8 Sep. „	„
Tho. Cooper	20			—	9 „ „	„
Constant Cleaghly	20			—	25 „ „	„
Owen Cartye	20			—	27 „ „	„
Mr Tho. Inett	1 prop.	Falmouth Town		—	28 „ „	„
Tim. Murphy	30			—	—	„
Seth Marley	1 prop.	St John's Town		—	15 Oct. 1678	„
Mr Giles Hill	„	Falmouth Town		—	20 Nov. „	„
Geo. Norcutt	„			—	20 „ „	„
Mr Joshua Brewster & Mr John Ker	2 prop.	Falmouth Town		—	20 „ „	„
Mr Nath. Mouke	50			—	23 „ „	„
John Hambleton	15			—	27 „ „	„
Mr Geo. Smith	—	Exchange Island	Hon. Paul Lee, Esq. from Govr	—	2 Dec. „	„
Mr Tho. Yorke	20			—	4 „ „	„
Martin Spicer	10			—	6 „ „	„
Mr John Knight	20			—	12 „ „	„
Lt Peter Willcox	—	To Govr Stapleton. Petition of Peter Wilcox, an inhabitant 29 years, has only 20 acres for his Wife, 6 children, & 5 servants, & asks for late Roger Seldon's land by his Will da. 1672. Warrant accordingly, da. 30 Jan. 1678.		—	7 Feb. „	„
Ensign Sam. Martin	20		Col. Jas. Vaughan	17 Sep. 1678	20 Sep. „	„
John Campbell	10		Cap. Sam. Winthrop	—	20 Feb. „	„
Tho. Searvill	20			—	3 Oct. „	„
Cap. Arch. Cochran	80		Col. Ph. Warner	27 Mar. 1677	—	H. N.
Jas. Stapleton & Wm Stapleton, Jr, Esqres	1025		Col. Jas. Vaughan	20 Sep. 1678	7 Mar. 1678	A. C.
Mr Rob. Winstarley	1 prop.	St John's Town	„ „	25 Feb. 1678	3 „ „	M. R.
Wm Taylor	„	„ „	„ „	1 inst. Nov.	4 Nov. „	„
Serjt Maj. Wm Barnes	250		Wm Stapleton	—	13 May 1679	A. C.
Dr Isack Edye	60		Hon. Maj. Jer. Watkins, Judge of St J. Precincts	—	18 „ „	„
Mr Tho. Vaughan & Gov. Col. Jas. „	600 328		Col. Jas. Vaughan	26 Mar. 1679	22 April „	„
Wm Burke, decd		Warrt by Paul Lee, Judge of Falmouth Precincts, to Messrs. Lt Jno Hall, Edmd Cole, Pet. Lavicount, Jno Cane, to appraise, da. 25 June 1679. Returned at 10 acres, worth 975 lbs., 27 June 1679.		—	—	—
Sargt Maj. Wm Barnes	237	Warrt from Hon. Sarj. Maj. Jer. Watkins & Hon. Cap. Paul Lee, Judges		16 July	20 July 1679	A. C.
Col. Row. Williams	360	Road Divn	Col. Ph. Warner	9 April 1677	12 „ „	„
Cap. John Hamilton	250		Hon. Maj. Jer. Watkins, Judge of St John's	June 1679	19 „ „	„
M. Rogers (myself)	150		„ „ „	July „	13 „ „	M. R.
Col. Ph. Warner	200		Hon. Cap. Paul Lee, Judge	20 Feb.	June „	A. C.
Abra. Vascom	1 prop.		Hon. Maj. Jer. Watkins	21 July 1679	5 Aug. „	M. R.
Wm Hill	5	purchased of Sam. Vines		—	9 Oct. „	„
Ben. Jefferies	150		Jer. Watkins	3 May „	9 June „	„
Rob. Winstanley	200		Col. Jas. Vaughan	26 Sep. 1678 & 23 July 1679	26 July „	„
Morgan Tooles	100		„ „	22 July 1678	24 „ „	„
Tho. Edwards	20		„ „	—	2 Mar. 1678	„
Rob. Harris	1 prop.	St John's Town	Jer. Watkins	—	12 June 1679	„
John Nibs	20		Mr Sam. Winthrop	—	—	A. C.
Mr Edward Horne	400	Body Divn	Jer. Watkins	27 May & 10 Aug. 1679	14 Aug. 1679	M. R.
Cap. John Vernon & Cap. Arch. Cochran	200	St John's Divn	Wm Stapleton	Feb. 1678	7 June „	R. T.*

* Robert Tremills.

	Acres.		Name of Dep. Governor.	Date of Gov.'s Warrant.	Date of Survey.	Name of Surveyor.
Cap. Sam. Gardiner & Ens. John "	300		Wm Stapleton	7 Feb. 1679	25 July 1679	M. R.
Mr John Lucas & Mr Rich. Traveis	600		Hon. Maj. Jer. Watkins	16 June "	30 Aug. "	"
Lt Wm Waynwright	50		Cap. Paul Lee	11 Jan. 1677	20 April "	A. C.
Marton Spicer	10			—	6 Dec. 1678	M. R.
John Bushoone	87		Jer. Watkins	25 July 1679	1 " 1679	R. T.
Howell Jones	20		Col. Ph. Warner	1677	1678	A. C.
" "	9		Col. Jas. Vaughan	13 Sep. 1678	Feb. 1678	"
Pharaoh Laramore	20		Col. Ph. Warner	1677	9 Jan. 1679	"
Cha. Kallahane	110		Jer. Watkins	1679	Jan. "	"
Wm Hughes	20			—	15 Sep. 1678	M. R.
Lt John Morrisse	511		Jer. Watkins	22 Feb. 1677	1679	A. C.
Ensign Sam Martin	—	Island in Five Islands' Harbour		22 Jan. 1679	6 Feb. 1679	"
Mr Rob. Phillips	20			18 Oct. 1676	20 July 1677	"
Cap. Edmond Bridgewater & Mr Cha. Goss	300		Hon. Cap. Paul Lee, Judge	10 Feb. 1679	20 Feb. 1679	R. T.
Mr Rob. Phillips	5		" "	—	20 July 1678	A. C.
Edward Pawly	200	former Warrt from Col. Jas. Vaughan, & one now from Col. Val. Russel, Presidt		—	29 Mar. 1680	H. N.
John Parry, Esq.	10			1678	—	A. C.
Mr Watts	200		Wm Stapleton	1 Feb.	16 Mar. 1679	R. T.
Mr John Otto	20		Hon. Maj. Jer. Watkins, Judge	5 July 1679	4 Aug. "	"
Francis Morell	50		" "	9 Aug. "	—	—
Wm Oliver	100	Body Divn	" "	" "	7 Dec. 1679	R. T.
Wm Taylor	100		" "	Dec.	" "	"
John Richardson	100		" "	18 Mar. "	" "	"
Wm Poatten	50		" "	27 " "	24 May "	"
James Grimes	30		" "	18 " "	21 Dec. "	"
Mr John Bruning	142		Hon. Cap. Paul Lee, Judge	27 " "	1 Aug. "	"
Sarah Hughes	30	dau. of Rob. H., decd	Col. Ph. Warner	15 Jan. 1676	20 Feb. "	"
Mr John Moone & Mr Henry Walden	150		Hon. Maj. Jer. Watkins	23 May 1679	Aug. "	"
Cap. Moyle Jonson	75		Hon. Val. Russel, Govr	—	18 Aug. 1680	H. N.
Wm Harris	100		Col. Ph. Warner	23 April 1677	—	A. C.
John Mayo	20			7 Aug. "	7 July 1680	H. N.
Derby Newgent	—	In Right of his Wife Margaret, dau. of Cap. John Lintt, decd. Warrt to divide 132 acres now in possession of Cap. Jno Fry, ½ to Fry & ½ to Newgent. By Val. Russell		—	31 Aug. "	"
Col. Chr. Codrington & Col. Jno "	380 600	Old North Sound Guiana Island	Col. Ph. Warner	1677	27 Sep. "	A. C.
Cornett Fra. Burton	300	called Crabb Hall	Sr Wm Stapleton	7 July 1680	10 Oct. "	R. M.*
Lt Cha. Williams	300			" "	12 " "	"
Mr Tho. Beck	28		Hon. Val. Russell, Presidt	18 Mar.	19 1679-80	R. T.
Maj. Wm Mussenden	9		Hon. Cap. Paul Lee	10 Nov.		—
John Sharpe	26	¼ of 104, called Pickadilly		—	7 Feb. 16 . .	G. G.
John Chard	50		Col. Ph. Warner	27 Mar. 1677	Aug. 1677	A. C.
Tho. Brookes	1 prop.	St John's Town	Col. Jas. Vaughan	—	13 Oct. 1678	M. R.
Mr Geo. Robinson	28		" "	11 Nov. 1678	12 Feb. "	"
Mr Edward Dendy	1 prop.	St John's Town	Jer. Watkins	" 1679	20 " 1679	"
Arthur Williams	30	Measured in 1677 10 for Ralph Steele	Col. Jas. Vaughan	26 Aug. 1678	2 June 1680 17 Mar. 1677	R. T. A. C.
Lt John Morrise	160		Col. Ph. Warner	5 July 1677	1679	"
Jonas Baker	70		Hon. Maj. Jer. Watkins, Judge	1677	20 Nov. 1679	"
Edmond Painter	4		Col. Ph. Warner	7 Aug. 1677	12 Mar. "	"
Edward Thomas	180		Col. Jas. Vaughan	4 Nov. 1678	April 1680	"
Mr Edward Leaver	32			16 Dec. "	1679	"
Mr Rich. Lord	118		Hon. Cap. Paul Lee, Judge	18 Feb. 1679	April 1680	"
Sam. Willis, Maj. John Pinckett, & Mr Rich. Lord	261		Wm Stapleton	26 " 1677	Mar. "	"
Tho. Duncom	150		Hon. Cap. Paul Lee	Feb.	21 July 1680	R. M.
Steph. Lawler & Mr Cha. Smith	1 prop.	St John's Town	Hon. Val. Russel, Govr	2 July 1680	2 Aug. "	"
Mr Geo. Fletcher	3 prop.	" "	" "	24 Aug. "	30 " "	"
Rich. Duckworth, blacksmith	10	Warrt by Col. Row. Williams & Cap. John Vernon, attorney of Lady Ann Willoughby, & granted to him by Hon. John. Lord Willoughby, by deed da. 23 June 1677		1 Jan. 1679	11 Oct. "	A. C.
Mr Stephen Duer	70		Col. Val. Russel	11 Oct.	19 Oct. "	"
Tho. Elmes	50			—	20 " "	H. N.
Mr Geo Craft	100		Sr Wm Stapleton	29 June 1680	21 " "	R. M.
Cap. Moyle Johnson	60			11 inst.	15 Sep. "	H. N.
Mr James Rolt *als* Devell	—		Sr Wm Stapleton	8 June 1680	30 Oct. "	R. M.
Tho. Everard	40½			2 Oct. past	8 Nov. "	H. N.
Mr Rich. Sheares	230			—	5 Oct. "	"
John Evans	30		Govr Winthrop	2 Mar.	13 Mar. 1668	G. G.
Edward Dun	50		Hon. Val. Russel	1 Sep.	20 Jan. 1680	R. M.
Morgan Toole	86			12 Feb. 1679	22 Feb. "	"
Cap. John Hamilton	46	New North Sound	Hon. Maj. Jer. Watkins, Judge	—	Sep. "	A. C.
Lt Wm Wainwright	1 prop.	Falmouth Town		22 Sep. 1680	17 Feb. "	R. M.
Cap. Tho. Foreman	2 prop.	" "	from the Govr	17 Feb. "	" "	A. C.
Sr James Russell & Nich. Rainsford, Esq.	1050		Sr Wm Stapleton formerly Col. Tho. Middleton's	3 Mar. "	8 Mar. "	"
Cap. John Edy	240	Warrt to Mr Hen. Syms, Prov. Mar., to give up the said plantn of 240 a., called Irish's plantn. Recorded in Sec. Office 8 Mar. 1680 at Falmouth, by Aqu. Stoughton, Dep. Sec.	Sr Wm Stapleton	3 1680	9 " "	"
Mr John Ley	70		Sr Wm Stapleton	—	15 Feb. "	"
Mr Geo. Dewitt	2 prop.	St John's Town		14 Feb. 1680	23 " "	R. M.
Mr Jno Blackleach	47		Hon. Val. Russell, Presidt	8 April 1681	14 April 1681	"
Mr Edward Dendy	—		Hon. Val. Russell, re-surveyed	—	9 " "	"
Lt Roger Complain & Wm Mould	100	In Hockley's Hole	Hon. Maj. Jer. Watkins, Judge	24 June 1679 & 17 July "	18 Aug. 1679	R. T.
Tho. Turton	10		Hon. Val. Russel, Presidt	15 Mar. 1680	10 Dec. 1681	R. M.

* Robert Martin.

VOL. 2.

Surveyor Genls book from 12 April 1688 to 2 Oct. 1750.

			Govrs Name.	Date of Grant.	Date of Survey.
Mr Nath. Barnes	2 prop.	St John's Town	Sr N. Johnson	28 June 1688	7 July 1688.
Cap. Fra. Carlile	20		"	—	12 Sep. "
Col. Tho. Hill	130		Chr. Codrington	26 Sep. 1689	23 Nov. 1689.
Mr Chr. Kirton	2 prop.		Sr N. Johnson	26 Oct. 1688	8 " 1688.
Jac. Le Roux	1 prop.	St John's Town, West with Mr Rich. Oliver	Chr. Codrington	—	4 May 1692.
Mr Wm Munroe	2 prop.		—	—	1 Jan. 1691.
Nath. Barnes	1 prop.	Parham Town	Jno Yeamans	1693	6 June 1693.
Maj. Philemon Bird	2 prop.		Chr. Codrington	17 Aug. 1693	19 Aug. "
Dr D. McKinen	—	2 places for wharf	—	1693	27 Jan. 1691.
Mr Rich. Oliver	1 prop.	St John's Town, 50′ × 80′	Chr. Codrington	3 Nov. 1693	15 Nov. 1693.
Mr Jno Blackleach, S	145	His plantation re-surveyed	—	—	29 June 1697.
Mr Robt Oliver	1 prop.	St John's Town	Chr. Codrington	12 Aug. 1697	13 Aug. "
Cap. Jno Weir	2 prop.		Jno Yeamans	28 Nov. 1699	20 Sep. 1699.
Gust. Adolp. Christian	"	St John's Town	"	27 Aug. 1700	29 Aug. 1700.
Mr Robt Oliver	—		Chr. Codrington	25 Sep. 1701	25 Oct. 1701.
Rich. Cheshire	10		—	—	7 Mar. 1704.
Chr. Stoodly	2 prop.	St John's Town	—	20 Aug. 1705	3 Sep. 1705.
Jno Lucie Blackman	6	plashes, W. side of Fitche's Creek	Jno Johnson	—	30 Mar. "
Capt Main Swete	337	Plan of his plantation at Falmouth	—	—	15 July 1701.
Mr Giles Blizard, Jr	30	Belfast	—	—	9 Sep. 1706.
Mr Geo. Lucas, Hon. Jno Yeamans, Jno Lucas, Esq.	380	Have divided their Est. by Jno Yeamans & Jno Lucas possessed as tenants in common over 20 years past; Jno Lucas has given his ½ to his son	—	—	22 April 1707.
Jno Burt, Chirurgeon	10		—	—	21 May 1707.
Mr Hopetor Bendall	1 prop.	St John's Town	—	1 Mar. 1708	23 " 1708.
Rich. Oliver, Esq.	3 prop.	& 1 prop. bought	—	—	17 Jan. 1709.
Hen. Symes, Jr	10		—	17 Nov. 1710	12 " 1710.
Hon. Jno Hamilton	1 prop.	St John's Town	—	2 Sep. last	15 Nov. 1711.
Mr Sam. Laferty, clk.	"	" "	—	3 May 1710	11 May 1712.
Mr Jervas Turton, deceased	260	Bermudian Valley	—	—	23 Dec. "
Mr Baldwin Johnson	—	St John's Town	—	22 Dec. 1712	17 Feb. 1713.
Mrs Ann Laferty & Abr. Laferty	2 prop.	" "	—	—	1 June "
Eliz. Yeamans, Wid.	4 prop.	Her former husb. Wm Redman	—	—	12 Feb. "
Col. Jno Frye	100	Willoughby Bay	—	—	22 Aug. "
Hen. Warner, Gent., & Edwd Warner, Esq.	197	Division of the Folly plantn	—	—	26 Mar. 1714.
Mr Rich. Cochran & Mr Arch. Cochran, Gtm	327	Mr Wm C., decd. Division of Est. Plan appended	—	—	25 Aug. "
Cap. Hen. Symes	20	with consent of Mrs Henrietta S., Wid. of Cap. Hen. S., decd	—	—	23 Sep. "
Mr Tho. Wise	5 prop.	St John's Town	—	—	10 Mar. "
Mr Hen. Blizard	$100\frac{3}{4}$	Savanna. At request of Hon. Ed. Warner	—	—	9 Dec. 1715.
Jno L. Blackman	—	Petitions that since 9 July 1706 he hath had 6 acres of plashes by pat. fr. Gov. J. Johnson	—	—	—
Mr Tho. Jarvis	38	fr. Rob. Martin, Esq., decd	—	—	4 . . . . 1717.
Josh. Archbould, chir.	—		—	25 Sep. 1718	1 Oct. 1718.
Mr Jno Bezune	1 prop.	St John's Town	—	—	18 Sep. "
Wm Yeamans, Esq.	100	Old N. Sound, formerly Jno Y., Esq., re-surveyed	—	—	26 Nov. "

On 15 Jan. 1719 laid out the Town of Willoughby Bay, & the streets, lanes, & Market-place. East Str., West Str., King Str., Maiden Lane, Church Str., 80′ × 60′ for market, N. Str., Market Str., Exchange Alley, Princes Str., Rosemary Lane.

Cap. Hen. Symes	1 prop.	Willoughby Bay	—	13 inst.	30 April 1720.
Mr Row. Hamilton	250	given him by Cap. Ed. Horn	—	—	13 Jan. 1719.
Hen. Douglas, Esq.	150	Road Mountains	—	—	12 " 1720.
Mr Rich. Oliver	—	parcell at St John's Town	Walt. Hamilton	4 inst.	9 Mar. "
" "	2 prop.	St John's Town, 100′ × 80′	Jno Hart	—	31 Dec. 1722.
" "	—	2 parcells at do.	—	—	11 Mar. "
Cap. Jno Huyghue	186	Road Divn	Jno Hart	—	11 May 1724.

Old Road Town or Carlile Town.

1. Colln Rowld Williams. House & prop.
2. Cap. Cæsar Rodeney. Houses.
3. Cap. Cha. Gost, prop.
4. Wm Blackburn, house & prop.
5. Morgan Tool's prop.
6. Mr Jno Sampson's proportions.
7. Rich. Fisher's "
8. Jno Terry's "
9. The Streets.
10. Mrs Felt's proportions.
11. Mr Jno Smith's proportions.
12. Mary Davis' proportion.

Voghen's spring on the Est. of Majr Bayer Otto Bayer ¾ acre for public pond. Appraised at £50 c. May 1726.

Cobb's Cross Pond of 3 acres, Col. Ed. Warner's. 6 July 1726.
Molasses Gutt in Dr Buckshorn's $\frac{1}{15}$ acre. Falmouth.
Man of War Pond at Eng. Harbour, ¼ acre on Tho. Bodkin's.
Spring at Rendesvous Bay of Mrs Ann & Franklyn. ¾ acre.
Spring in Mr Sam. Brooke's Plantn at Old Road Divn, $1\frac{3}{15}$ acres.
Spring on Hon. Jno Yeaman's Road Divn est., $\frac{2}{15}$ acre.
Spring at Col. Tho. William's, ¼ acre.

Cap. Walt. Nugent	2 prop.	St John's Town	23 May 1724.
Dr Walt. Sydserfe	32	Belfast	25 June 1731
Mr Barry Nibbs	2 prop.		15 May "
Cæsar Rodeney, Gent.	2 prop.	St John's Town	1731
Ashton Warner, Speaker	—		1733
Cap. Paul Horseford	61, 3, 17	Falmouth, sold to Dr Buckshorne's plantation	18 July 1734.
Mrs Mary Blizard		petitions for a path 1 Dec. 1730	3 Dec. "
	1½	for cisterns at Eng. Harbour, bought of Mr Tho. Bodkin of Ireld, Gent.	25 Oct. "
		To lay out Winthrop's pond, near the high road, fr. Barnacles Pt or Byam Ft to St John's Town	5 June 1736.
	1	Public pond on Gale's plantn, Falmouth	12 April 1737.
Mr Sam. Lyons	2 prop.	Willoughby Bay	12 " "
Francis Delap, Esq.	205	2 parcells, Willoughby Bay Div., bought of Hon. Geo. Lucas	20 Feb. "
Barbara Cook, Wid.		her former husbd Geo. Collins	1738
Dr Slingsby Cressy	10	St John's Town	1 Aug. 1740.
Steph. Blizard, Speaker	—		20 Sep. 1742.

Geo. Jennings, Esq., dec^d	330	Plan of plantation	7 July 1743.
Col. Jno Barton	11¼	To his son Fra. B., plan attached. Letters of agreement betw. Tho. Bishop & the late Dr Wm Young, dec^d, da. 6 Mar. 1740	12 Oct. ,,
Col. Jno Hughues Est.	174		
Edwd Williams, Esq.	170	Tom. Moore's plant^n at Road Div^n	—
	150	Cistern plant^n	19 Sep. 1743.
	254¼	Road ,,	
Jonas Langford, Esq.	319½	Formerly Tho. Morris, Esqr's, in Old Road Div^n & Old N. Sound, St Peter's P'sh, &c.	10 May 1742.
Sam. Bogle	2 prop.	St John's T	6 Mar. 1745.
Mr Jno Knight	—	land for Wharf of Parham T. Mariner	10 Oct. 1746.
	1¼	Public pond, St Philip's P'sh, Nonsuch Div^n, land of Tho. Melcher	15 ,, ,,
	1 a. 12 p.	Public Pond in Roomes, St W. Codrington	

BOOK OF PATENTS OR GOVERNMENT GRANTS OF LAND, 1668—1713.

Note.—The first page is marked "fo. 28" and the last "fo. 260." A clause is inserted at the commencement by Sam. Winthrop, Register, stating that the Island having been reconquered from the French by the King, and the Representatives having acknowledged His Majesty's said title by conquest, William, Lord Willoughby of Parham, has commanded the inhabitants to take out and record fresh grants of land.

A^o 1668.

To	Acres	
David Bowen	16½	
John Marshall	32½	
Christopher Read	50	at Popes Head, bounded E. with James Mold, and W. with Thomas Oliver.
Symon Osberston	76	
Roger Trottman	100	
William Allen	297	
Richard Glanfeild	10	and 10 mens land.
Martyn Payne	15	
Richard Veale	15	
John Keeley	48	
John Church	30	
Anthony Gilliat	38	
Thomas Daniell	10	
David James	10	
Elinor Glanfeild and Posthuma Glanfeild her dau.	25	(William Glanfeild being deceased.)
Christopher and John Knight	73	
Jean Monroe	147½	
Henrietta and Mary Kinn	380	Daus. of Captain William Kinn.
William Reynolds	20	
John Lucas	25	son and heir of John Lucas, deceased.
Elizabeth Greenland	30	
Roger Seldon	30	
William Price	15	
John and Elizabeth Richards	70	
John Collins	10	
Robert Powell	20	
Franciscoe Baldrey	25	
Ensign Peter Wilcocks	50	
Edmond Eustace	30	
John Warde	60	
John Morris	15	
Bartholomew and John Applegate	25	
Lieut. Richard Ball	300	in St. John's Division.
Captain Richard Ayres	158½	
Lieut. John Campbell	50	
Mary Floyd, Jean Floyd, and Elizabeth March	20	
James Belchare	30	Mens land.
Robert Elliatt	150	

To	Acres	
John Atkins and John Morphey	40	
John Moone, Hendrick Clauson, and Merrian Garrett	40	
Robert Carden	360	son and heir of Colonel Robert Carden, deceased, Five Island Division.
Hugh Trotter	65	
William Cooper	30	mens land
Captain George Mugg	553	called Ceadr Ridge, St. John's Division.
William Hemmens	137	
John Depie	7½	
John Nibbs	24	New North Sound.
Lewis Brian	45	
John Cobb	10	
Mathew Madline	10	
Darbie Minsham	40	New North Sound Division, W. with land formerly Sir Sydenham Poynts.
John Sanders	60	
William Hinde	7½	
Alexander Pollington	54	mens land.
Henry Soaper	17½	
Teigue Mathew	30	
John Williams and William Comis	70	Nonsuch.
John Sparkes	40	St. John's.
William Lockwood and George Lockwood	20	Nonsuch.
Ann Halfhide	200	Bermudian Valley.
Clement Everard, Gent., junior	160	Popeshead.
Anthony Browne	105	Willoughby Bay.
Andrew Davidson	20½	St. John's.
Thomas Hill	10	Nonsuch.
John Howard	55	,,
Robert Gilbert	10	,,
David Morgan and Price Morgan	180	Bermudian Valley.
Henry Cooke	130	Nonsuch.
Nathaniel Juce (? Ince)	55	,,
John Lynt ye Elder	240½	Bermudian Valley.
Thomas Lloyde	10	
Reynaldus Barter	28	
Charles Harrison	36	Nonsuch.
Samuel Man	20	,,

To	Acres	
James Warde	14	Falmouth.
Francis Mason	10	Nonsuch.
William Hill	172	and 86, mens land, Popeshead.
John Humphries	150	Popeshead and North Sound.
Lieut.-Colonel Proctor	157	
Thomas Elmes and Howell Jones	50	
Robert Poole and Thomas Wildgoose	20	
Lieut. William Barden	500	
John Fullerton	15	
John Bridges and Thomas Turner	266⅔	St. John's.
Lieut. William Thomas	122½	Old North Sound.
Hugh Gamble	50	
Robert Lynt	100	Nonsuch Gutt.
Benjamin Steele	30	and 6 mens land.
Francis Gifford	60	
Thomas Ellis	30	mens land.
John Bacon	45	and 100 square feet, Nonsuch.
Captain Anthony White	155	
Joshua FitzRandolph	300	Old North Sound.
Toby Buttler	25	
Rowland Williams	300	
Dennis Molala	10	
Roger Clarke	20	
Roger Kennida	20	
William Knightly and Elizabeth Knight	150	
Henry Willoughby	600	"my well beloved son."
Daniel Mitchell	50	
Captain Gilbert Gregory	189	
George Hawkins	243½	and 100 square feet.
John Chard	80	
Mathew Gillingwater	140	
William Drowne	16	
Robert Clarke	375	
Henry Soaper and Francis Bonner	47½	
William Gilliard	52	
Robert Parker	30	
Mary Burdett	10	
Cornelius Cornelison	14	
William Trappin	32½	
Thomas Liddy	20	
Thomas Beck	70	
Jane Forde	30	dau. and heir of William Ford, deceased.
Nicholas Fowler and John Barry	30	
Susanna Clarke	300	dau. and heir of Henry Clarke, deceased.
Elizabeth Collinson, widow	200	
William Wood	42½	
John Barnett	190	
Martyn Spicer	20	
Thomas Chatborn	10	
Charles Barnett, Teague Haye, and Thomas Chatborn	200	
Patrick Hardy	25	
Henry Smith	100	
Mr. John Parry and Mrs. Anne Washington	325	
Willoughby Orton	30	
Richard Belchare	100	
John Moss	45	

To	Acres	
William Fullham	150	
John Carney	40	
William Ennis and Austine Michellson	20	
Symon Gubbins	20	
Henry Lory	140	
Katherine Knight	10	dau. and heir of China Knight, deceased.
Thomas Dawson	45	
Thomas Gregory	70	
John Harley	100	
William Johnson	20	
Thomas Pike	200	
Daniel Pellot	58	
John Bradshaw	165	
John Russell	20	
Lenard Hamme	100	
Anthony Riarsom	179	
John Doegon	57	
James Noone	20	
Sarah Winthrop, spinster	—	Maiden Island.

Barbuda granted to Captain Samuel Winthrop, Captain Joseph Lee, William Milden, and Francis Sampson, and their heirs for 32 years, subject to 4½ per cent. on the produce, dated 1 Oct. 20 Charles II.

To	Acres	
Benjamin Steele	40	and 6 mens land.
Lieut.-Colonel Bastian Boyare	100	Five Islands' Division.
Anne Johnson	40	

A° 1669.

To	Acres	
Anne Johnson	40	
Robert and Mark Noble	52½	
Captain Symon Turphrey	100	
Thomas Reighnolds	15	
George Serjant	30	
Francis Couterier	20	
Thomas Hicks	20	
Thomas Price	19	
Francis Haines	20	
John Partington	65	
Daniel Duncing	15	
William Jarsey	—	
Mames Ross	11⅔	
Thomas Garraway	10	
John Brittana	20	and 50 feet.
Edmond Ellis	120	
Jonas Baker	10	
Roger Foulsher	50	
Robert Tate	20	
Colonel Everard	200	St. John's.
Thomas Kenniston	25	
Thomas Seagrove	35	
William Duncan	31	
Anthony Sculthrop	20	
Teigue McCarte and Thomas Huckle, son and heir of James Huckle, deceased	30	
George Griggs	9	
John Norton	25	and ½ of 100′ square.
Robert Ainge	30	
William Goodale and John Blunden	—	
Rudyerd Hanham	40	
Stephen Harper and John Ellis	20	
Owen McCarty	17½	

To		Acres	
William Quinby	. .	56	
Domingo Fardinando	.	20	
Thomas Hardwick	. .	10	
William Wainwright	. .	182	and 100′ square.
John Woodhouse	. .	10	

"Here Ends the entrys of Pattents Recorded by Samuel Winthrop, Register. Recorded in the Booke and delivered to ye new Register, Major Rowland Williams, by commission and appointment of Coll. Phillip Warner, depty Governor of this Island, the Sixteenth day of January Anno Domini one Thousand Six hundred Seaventy one, as wittss the hands of Both the sd Regrs the day and yeare above written."

GRANTS BY SIR WILLIAM STAPLETON.

Lieut.-Colonel Williams, parcell of land. 15 July 1676. Robert Phillips, Deputy-Register.

Captain Henry Hunt, Nevis, 130, St. John's Division. 20 Aug. 1675.

Moyle Johnson, 200. 16 Aug. 1676.

Captain Harvey Keynell, 350.

Captain Samuel Jones, 126, 500. 18 Oct. 1676.

Captain John Pogson, 200. Late Lieut. of a Foot Company in Sir Tobias Bridge's Regiment. 20 Aug. 1677. Signed at Nevis. Valentine Russell, Secretary. James Phipps, Provost-Marshal of Antigoa.

Vallentine Russell, Gent. and Secretary of Nevis, 511 in Falmouth at an ear of Indian corn rent. 1 Aug. 1678.

Captain John Bell, 62½. 2 May 1679.

Colonel Phillip Warner possesses ye Savana from William, Lord Willoughby's patent, dated 11 April 1668, which is hereby confirmed as a freehold and to be known as the Mannor of Framlingham, and to be a Royaltie, the holder to pay a full-grown Bore yearly to His Majestie. Dated 31 Charles II. and 3 Nov. 1679.

Colonel James Vaughan, 600 for ever at yearly rent of an ear of Indian corn. 26 April 1679.

Walter Simons, Esq., 600. 26 April 1680.

Colonel Rowland Williams, 300, and 260, and 360, with all Royalties, at the yearly rent of an ear of Indian corn. 26 May 1680, 32 Charles II.

Richard Lord, 344 at yearly rent of an ear of Indian corn. 12 June 1680.

Ceasar Rodney, 213. 17 Oct. 1680.

John Gilliott, 40. 14 Oct. 1680. Ebenezer Kyrtland, sen., Secretary.

Katherine Watts, 1200 at yearly rent of an ear of Indian corn. 10 Feb. 1672.

James Rolt, 200. 10 Feb. 1680.

Captain Archibald Cochran, 372. 17 Feb. 1680.

Major William Barnes, 237. 28 Feb. 1680.

Captain John Hamilton, 283. 28 Feb. 1680.

Major William Barnes and Captain Fra. Carlile, 117. 28 Feb. 1680.

Mr. William Barnes, jun., 230 at yearly rent of an ear of Indian corn. Mr. William Yeamans being deceased.

Mr. Thomas and Mary Earskins, 140. 10 Feb. 1680.

Jonas Langford, 126. Popeshead Division. 8 March 1680.

Captain John Vernon, 84.

Cornett Fra. Burton, 300. 2 May 1681, 33 Charles II. G. Cruft, Secretary-General.

Colonel Philip Warner, 200. 24 May 1681.

Mr. Edward Dendy, 184. 1 July 1681.

William Tremill, 300. 22 Aug. 1681.

Colonel Christopher and Lieut.-Colonel John Codrington, 380. 4 Oct. 1681.

Captain Edward Bridgwater and Mr. Charles Goss, 325. 30 Sep. 1681.

Captain John Yeamans, 155. 10 Dec. 1681.

Fra. Eddins, a mason, 40. 30 Jan. 1681.

Robert Carden, Gent., 150. 10 Dec. 1681.

Captain Willoughby Byam, 80, and 2 proportions of land. 17 Jan. 1681.

John Straton, 2 proportions of land. 15 Jan. 1681.

Edward Pawley, Gent., 200. 10 Nov. 1681.

John Parry, parcel of land. 28 Feb. 1680.

Major William Thomas, Gent., 25, and 12½ mens land, and 4 proportions. 24 Oct. 1681.

Sir James Russell, Knt., and Nicholas Raynsford, Esq., 1050. 28 Nov. 1681.

William Barnes, jun., Gent., 230. 8 Dec. 1681.

Captain Fra. Carlile, 150. 4 March 1680.

Mrs. Elizabeth Williams of Nevis, 200. 13 May 1681.

Peter Welch, 120. 1 Feb. 1681.

Morgan Toole, 216. 10 Dec. 1681.

James Boyd, 64 mens land or 150 acres given to Jane his wife (late wife of Captain John Cade, deceased). 21 March 1682.

Jane and Mary Cade, daughters and coheirs of Captain John Cade, deceased, 500. 25 March 1682.

Mr. Jacob Lucy and Co., 529. 18 May 1682.

Colonel Rowland Williams and Mr. Steven Lawler, 300. 23 May 1682.

Captain John Yeamans, 100. 21 May 1682.

Captain John Eady, 240. 9 Aug. 1681.

John Lingham, Gent. Confirm to him 1200, formerly Katherine Watts's and her husband the said John Lingham. Sold to Colonel Rowland Williams 10 Aug. 1681, and sold back 13 Aug. 1681. 10 Nov. 1681.

Henry Hackney, 30. 24 May 1681.

Lieut. Charles Williams of Nevis, 300. 23 May 1681.

John Gunthrop, 500. New North Sound. Confirmed 10 Jan. 1681.

Samuel Willis, Esq., and Richard Lord and John Pincham, merchants. 29 Nov. 1681.

Captain John Lingham, 50. 1 March 1681.

Mr. Henry Symes, 100. 8 May 1682.

Serjeant James Williams, 100. 4 May 1682.

John Parry, 10, and a proportion. 22 May 1682.

Mary Humphreys, 50. 22 May 1682.

John Ware, 91, and a proportion. 24 May 1682.

John Lucas, 511. 27 May 1682.

Captain John Fry, 532. 12 May 1682.

Edward Leaver, 100. 23 May 1682.

Fra. Eddins, 54⅔. 22 July 1682.

Thomas Jones, 50. 20 April 1677.

John Ennis, 10. 30 Aug. 1678.

Edmond Painter, 123½. 23 Jan. 1681.

Elinor Mallham, widow, to Edward Horn, carpenter, 200 for 74,000 lbs. released by her 1 June 1682. 30 Nov. 1682.

Edward Horne, carpenter, 400. 29 May 1682.

Lieut. Roger Compton and William Moule, 250. 19 June 1682.

Thomas Beck, 230. 25 May 1678.

Samuel Martin, 226, and 30 mens land, 1 island, and 1 proportion. 22 May 1682.

Anthony Darcy, 25. 27 May 1682.

Thomas Everet, 45. 1 Jan. 1681.

Robert Winstandly, 70. 27 May 1682.

John Moor and Carolina his wife, 52. 27 May 1682.

Samuel Winthrop, Esq., 237. 4 Aug. 1682.

Elinor, Susanna, and Sara Tyer, 100. 20 May 1682.

Geoffry Shackerly, Esq., 200. 15 June 1682.

Lieut. George Symes, 260. 23 May 1681.

Edward Dun, 150. 15 May 1683.

William Oliver, 100. Body Division. 27 May 1682.

Major Charles Pym of Nevis, Gent., 260, and paid 20,000 lbs. to Mr. Thomas Belchamber and Mr. Richard Cary of Antigua, merchants, 20 March 1682. 22 June 1682.

Peter and William Garret, 102. 22 Nov. 1678.

Thomas Duncomb, Esq., 250, and 2 proportions. 8 Sep. 1682.

Thomas Duncomb, Esq., 650. 8 Sep. 1682.

Richard Green, 60.

James Boyd, Gent., parcell of land given to his wife Jane, late wife of Captain John Cade, 150, and 64 mens land. 21 March 1682.

Mr. Peter Watson, 160. Bermudian Valley. 1 Dec. 1682.

Lieut. Samuel Hilder, 127. 13 Sep. 1683.

Mr. Peter Bosiman, 257. 13 Sep. 1683.

Jasper Joyce, merchant, 100. 30 Dec. 1681.

Captain John Morris, 500. Old North Sound. 24 May 1682.

William Mussenden, 180. 28 April 1682.

Richard Haddon, 250. 23 Jan. 1681.

George Dewit, 200. 23 Jan. 1681.

George Cruft of Nevis, 100. St. John's. 10 June 1683.

Colonel Edward Powell, 380. 17 Sep. 1683.

Benjamin Ravencroft, 130. 22 May 1682.

Constant Cleaghly, 20. 23 May 1683.

Redmond Stapleton, Esq., 1025, to pay a yearly rent of an ear of Indian corn for the said Mannor and Royalties. 1 Jan. 1679. Redmond Stapleton sells to Sir William Stapleton for 100,000 lbs. Dated at Montserrat 6 July 1682. Witnessed by Nicholas Meade, etc.

Phillip Hall, 192. 21 Jan. 1683.

Mr. John Light, parcel in St. John's Town. 21 Jan. 168–.

James Davenport, 43 mens land. 3 March 1683.

Robert Nanton, 20. 7 March 1683.

Edward Burke, 15 and 35. 22 March 1683.

Elizabeth Lisle, 100 at yearly rent of an ear of Indian corn. 22 May 1681.

William Abraham, 50 at yearly rent of an ear of Indian corn. 22 May 1681.

Thomas Bankes, 40. 1 April 1684.

Joan Hall, 350. 4 March 1683.

Ambrose Yorke, Gent., 35, and 15, and 30, in Dickinson's Bay, north and west with Thomas Oliver; also 2 proportions. 21 Jan. 1684. Henry Symes, Register.

John Ravenscroft, Gent., 80, and 210. 30 June 1684.

John Robinson, Gent., parcell of 3 acres. St. John's Town. 26 Sep. 1684.

Christopher and John Codrington, Esquires. Charles Rex and William, Lord Willoughby, on 1 Oct. 20 Charles II., gave Barbuda for 32 years to four persons, who have since assigned to Christopher and John Codrington, Clement Tudway and George Turney, Gent. A lease for 50 years is now granted to the four last named, with power to hold a Court of franke-Pledge, a Court of Pypowder, etc., to have all wrecks, and erect markets, and to pay one horse yearly. These present letters pattent dated 29 Jan. 35 Charles II.

George Cruft of Nevis, 75. 31 Aug. 1680.

John Light, 125. 26 Dec. 1684.

Lieut. Fra. Burton and Mr. John Roe, parcell of land. St. John's Town. 3 Sep. 1684.

George Cruft, 2 proportions. 20 Oct. 1684.

Peter Boschman, 18, and 20. 26 Dec. 1684.

Benjamin Jefferes, 30. 24 Dec. 1684.

Captain John Hamilton, 317, and 4 proportions. 10 Jan. 1684.

Henry Steenman, 140. Nonsuch. 10 Jan. 1684.

Walter Phillips, 20, and 10, and 90, and 50. 18 Feb. 1684.

Frances, Mary, and Susannah Browning, daughters and coheirs of Mr. John Browning, deceased, 442 in Falmonth. 18 Feb. 1684.

Thomas Beck, 36. 18 Feb. 1684.

Thomas Bitten, 40. 14 Feb. 1684.

Thomas McCaffry, 100. Nonsuch. 17 March 1683.

Henry Symes, parcell. St. John's Town. 20 Feb. 1684.

Edward Thomas, 180. 18 Feb. 1684.

Mr. Charles Callahan, 140. Old North Sound. 18 Feb. 1684.

Phillipp Willoughby, 90. 18 Feb. 1684.

William Greere, 32. 28 Feb. 1684.

Mrs. Elizabeth Dewitt and her sons, George, Thomas, and John Dewitt, 81. 18 Feb. 1684.

Captain Thomas Bartlett and John Terry, 200. 18 Feb. 1684.

Mr. John Mascoll, merchant, 170. Belfast. 28 Feb. 1684.

Sarah Yongue, widow (Ex'trix of Mr. George Fletcher), and her children, 200. 26 March 1685.

Colonel Edward Powell, Governor, 380. St. John's Division. "Paul" Plantation, now "Golden Grove." 27 Dec. 1684.

Benjamin Ravenscroft, 50. 16 Feb. 1684.

Nathaniel Monck, Gent., 37½, and 50, and 49. 21 Jan. 35 Charles II.

Major Richard Borraston, Gent., 200, called "Dimsdales" or "Michaell's Mount," also 100 feet square, and 10 and 2½ acres. 20 Jan. 1684.

Mr. Thomas Belchamber of Nevis, merchant, 2 proportions. St. John's Town. 1 Dec. 1684.

Henry Symes, Gent., 65. 6 Feb. 1684.

Isaack Johnson, 10, and 20, and 10. 2 Jan. 1684.

Sir James Russell, Knt., and Nicholas Raynsford, Esq., 100, of flashes. 15 March 1684.

Mr. Henry Walden, 59. 18 Feb. 1684.

James Boyd, parcell of land. 30 March 1685.

Thomas Oliver, 20, in Popeshead north with Mr. Nicholas Bayer, also 20. 2 Feb. 1684.

John Robinson, 30, and 3½, and 1 proportion. 22 Dec. 1684.

Mr. Garret Powell, 6. St. John's Town. 30 March 1685.

Colonel Samuel Jones, Esq., 230, and 126, and 17. 6 May 1682.

Joseph Daniell, blacksmith, 2 proportions. St. John's Town. 24 Dec. 1684.

Marcus Kirwan, 50. 30 May 1685.

Samuel Jeaffreson, planter, 30. 21 Feb. 1684.

Major Archibald Cockran, Gent., 20. 14 Feb. 1684.

Captain Cæsar Rodney and Mr. John Sampson, 200, called "Rodney Stoak." 27 March 1684.

George Turney, 152. 3 Nov. 1686. By Sir James Russell, Knt., Governor and Commander-in-Chief of Nevis and the Caribbee Leeward Islands. In ye event of ye decease of ye Captain-General, ye Governor of Nevis is to take on the government, and William Stapleton made me Deputy-Governor of Nevis.

James Grimes, 45. St. John's. 28 Feb. 36 Charles II.

Sir Samuel Foxon, 150. 18 Feb. 1684.

Mr. Benjamin Jefferes, half of 133, 87. 24 March 1683.

Joseph Clarke of Nevis, merchant, 125. 22 Jan. 1684.

Thomas Hill, Esq., of St. Christopher's, late our Lieut.-Governor. Grant of a moiety of a plantation of 300 acres in St. John's Parish, late in the possession of John Drew, planter, and by him left to his wife Ann Drew, and forfeited by her attainder for murder. 28 Nov. 1 William and Mary. Joseph Clarke, Deputy-Register. By Christopher Codrington, Lieut.-General and Commander-in-Chief.

Richard Powell, joyner, 70. 17 June 1 William and Mary. By Sir Nathaniel Johnson, Captain-General.

Lieut. Roger Complin and Mr. Thomas Turner, planter, 90, late in the possession of Lieut. Roger Complin, deceased; also 4 proportions at 1*s*. currency rent. 8 July 1689. By Sir N. Johnson. Thomas Oesterman, Deputy-Register.

John Browne, planter, 144. 13 July 1689. By Sir N. Johnson.

George Gamble, merchant, 127, and 4 proportions. St. John's Town. 2 July 1689. By Sir N. Johnson.

Lieut.-General Thomas Hill, half of Drew's. No date, duplicate of former.

Colonel Fra. Carlile, Esq., 18. 20 March 1688, 5 James II. By Sir N. Johnson.

Colonel Thomas Warner, 4 proportions, St. John's Town, east with Ebenesar Langford; also 107½, lately William Lloyd's, who was convicted of murder. 22 July 1692, 4 William and Mary. By Christopher Codrington.

Captain Samuel Horn, parcell. St. John's Town. 3 William and Mary, 3 Sep. Christopher Codrington.

Thomas Long, parcell. St. John's Town. 1 March 1692-3, 5 William and Mary. By Christopher Codrington.

William Thaxter, planter, 18¾. St. John's Division. 1 Sep. 3 William and Mary. By Christopher Codrington.

Samuel Horn, 114. 10 Jan. 1683. By Sir W. Stapleton.

Edward Acton of St. John's Town, merchant, 1 proportion. 12 Dec. 1693, 5 William and Mary. By Christopher Codrington.

Major William Mussenden, 47. 26 Dec. 1680. Sir W. Stapleton.

Thomas Long of St. John's Town, merchant, 2 proportions. 27 July 1694, 6 William and Mary. By Christopher Codrington.

Petition of Daniel Mackinen that he has bought 50 acres of Captain John Gamble and 30 of Jonathan Squire, formerly ye land of Thomas Oliver, deceased, also 45 acres, and desires a patent. Patent accordingly, dated 26 Nov. 1695, 7 William and Mary, by Christopher Codrington. William, not Thomas Oliver named in the patent.

Edward Thomas, planter, 50. 18 Feb. 1684. W. Stapleton.

Captain Henry Lyons, 100. Willoughby Bay. 6 Oct. 1696, 8 William III. By Christopher Codrington.

Joseph Watkins, 145. 25 May 1683. By W. Stapleton.

Robert Jeaffreson, planter, 20. 15 April, 9 William. By Christopher Codrington.

Petition of John Blackleach, sen., Gent., dated 10 Aug. 1697. Patent granted for 145 acres 10 Aug. 1697, 9 William. By Christopher Codrington.

John Martin, vintner, 1 proportion, St. John's Town. 11 Nov. 1697. By Christopher Codrington.

Leonard Waller, chirurgeon, and Robert Erving, planter, 18, and 16½, and 27. 1697, 9 William III. By Christopher Codrington.

Captain John Tankerd, planter, land formerly belonging to George Gray and his wife, and Mary Weale, George Gray's mother, and the late Lieut. William Burden, deceased, a former husband to the said Mary Weale, 235 acres. Roger Jones was also a former husband of the said Mary Weale. Also 165 acres bought of Marcus Kirwan and Mary Weale. 6 Aug. 1697, 9 William III. By Christopher Codrington.

Cornelius Hollerin, planter, and Ann his wife. 11 April 1698, 10 William. By Christopher Codrington.

Captain James Porter, Esq., 2 proportions, Captain Charles Tudway being deceased. 1 June 1698. By Christopher Codrington.

Petition of Captain Peter Lee for patent for 65 acres. Granted 4 Feb. 1697. By Christopher Codrington.

Lieut. John Saunderson, Gent., 2 proportions at Parham Town. Patent granted 30 Jan. 1698, and signed by the President and Council of Nevis.

Samuel Phillips, Gent., 37. 1 June 1700. By Edward Foxe, Lieut.-General and Governor-in-Chief.

Robert Thornton, Gent., 60. 29 July 1701, 13 William. By Christopher Codrington.

Edward Perrie of St. John's Town, merchant, 1 proportion. 29 July 1701. By Christopher Codrington.

Barry Tankerd, Gent., 590½. St. Paul's Parish, north with Kean Osborn, Gent. 10 Sep. 1701. By Christopher Codrington.

William Glanvile, merchant. 23. 10 Sep. 1701. By Christopher Codrington.

Charles Kallahan, Gent., 3 proportions. 10 Sep. 1701. By Christopher Codrington.

Benjamin Wickham, Gent., 60, east with William Cochran, Gent., west with Arthur Freeman, chirurgeon. In St. Peter's Parish. Benjamin Wickham's son, Samuel Wickham, also 100 acres. 10 Oct. 1701. By Christopher Codrington.

John Perrie, Esq., Provost-Marshal-General, parcel St. John's Town. 10 Oct. 1701. By Christopher Codrington.

Jacob Le Reux, planter, 206 (east with Cassada Garden, now in the possession of Abraham Redwood). 7 Feb. 1701. By Christopher Codrington. Patent signed by John Yeamans, Ed. Byam, John Hamilton, Henry Pearne, and James Thynne, all of H.M.'s Council.

William Codrington, Esq., 80. Road Division. 27 June 1702. By Christopher Codrington.

Stephen Duer, 70, Old North Sound. 22 May 1682. By W. Stapleton.

Petition of Barry Tankerd, who was granted 590½, formerly Colonel Valentine Russel, deceased. 10 Sep. 1701.

Daniel Mackenin of St. John's Town, chirurgeon, 3 proportions. 1694, 6 William and Mary. By Christopher Codrington.

Edward Horn, 750, east with Richard Cary, south with "Sedge-hill," now in the possession of Sir Thomas Cooke of London, Knt. Signed by the Council, Ed. Byam, John Hamilton, William Codrington, Richard Oliver, and Henry Lyons. 20 Jan. 1703, 2 Ann. By Christopher Codrington.

Samuel Phillips, Gent., 45. 26 Jan. 1703. By Christopher Codrington.

John Halloran, planter, 40. 22 Jan. 4 James II. By N. Johnson. Robert Lucas of Antigua, Gent., and Lucia his wife, late widow of John Halloran, deceased, release 40 acres to Nicholas Collins, Gent.

John King, planter, 50. 28 June 1703. By Christopher Codrington. Signed by the Council, Peter Lee, Thomas Morris, etc.

John Yeamans, Esq., 80. 12 July 1704. By Christopher Codrington.

Thomas Francis, planter, 11. 16 April 1702. By Christopher Codrington.

Captain Gyles Watkins, 70. 12 July 1704. By Christopher Codrington.

James Browne, 10. 3 Feb. 1704. By Christopher Codrington.

Captain George Leonard of Anguilla and Charles Kallahan of Antigua, lands lately possessed by Richard Gallwey of Anguilla. 4 Jan. 1700. By Christopher Codrington.

William Codrington, Esq., 100. St. Mary's Parish. 9 July 1706. Hon. John Johnson, Lieut.-Governor and Commander-in-Chief.

John Lucie Blackman, Gent., 6. 9 July 1706. Hon. John Johnson.

Captain Ambrose Yorke, 6. 9 July 1706. Hon. John Johnson.

William Harman, Gent., parcell St. John's Town. 12 July 1704. Christopher Codrington.

Giles Blizard, jun., planter, and his wife Elizabeth, 24. Belfast. 24 May 1707. By Daniel Parke.

John Butler, planter, 80. Old Road. 20 May 1707. By Daniel Parke.

Henry and Robert Martin, 42, sons of Robert Martin, Esq., deceased. 28 July 1707. By Daniel Parke.

John Burton, planter, 180. 21 Oct. 1708. By Daniel Parke.

Edward Chester, sen., Esq., 1 proportion, St. John's Town, 87 feet by 50 feet. 18 Aug. 1707. By Daniel Parke.

Richard Oliver, Esq., 150 feet by 160 feet in St. John's Town, adjoining his house. 8 Jan. 1707, 7 Anne. By Daniel Parke.

Dr. Thomas Roome of Belfast, 20, and 20, and 10, and 50. 4 Feb. 1708. By Daniel Parke.

Peter Martin, planter, 84. 29 Jan. 1707. By Daniel Parke.

Sarah Morgan, in Anguilla, 15,000 feet by 5000 feet, and 2000 feet by 500 feet. Michael Ayon, Secretary to ye General. 23 March 1708. By Daniel Parke.

John Brady, Esq. Salt ponds in Anguilla. 24 Jan. 1708. By Daniel Parke. Which he assigns to Martin French 21 April 1709.

Martin French granted "Nixon's Hill" plantation of 145 at Montserrat. 21 April 1709. By Daniel Parke.

Robert Sheres, planter, 90, in Bermudian Valley, south and west with Samuel Frye, Gent. 19 Jan. 1707. By Daniel Parke.

John Tomlinson, Esq., 264. Joseph French, Esq., Escheator. 3 June 1709. By Daniel Parke.

William Stiler, planter, 50, north with Thomas Lovel, deceased. 17 Feb. 1684. W. Stapleton.

William Hamilton, planter, 40. 20 Jan. 1707. Daniel Parke.

Humphry Osborne, Gent., 40. 20 Aug. 1709. Daniel Parke.

Thomas Skerret, planter, 214. Nonsuch, St. Philip's Parish. 17 Feb. 1707. Daniel Parke.

John Wright, 20. 25 Aug. 1709. Daniel Parke.

Colonel Thomas Hill, land in St. Christopher's, called Brimstone Hill. 1 Feb. 1684. W. Stapleton.

Andrew Boull, Esq., 53. 17 Jan. 1709. Daniel Parke.

Thomas Long, Esq. Ratt Island. Feb. 1709. Daniel Parke.

Jer. Blizard, planter, 149, New North Sound, bought by him, and 12 acres left him by his father. 27 June 1710. Daniel Parke.

William Horton, a minor and orphan, 20. 31 July 1707. Daniel Parke.

George Gamble, Esq., 30. 19 Jan. 1707. Daniel Parke.

Michael Ayon, Esq., parcell, which he assigns to Governor Parke 11 Oct. 1710. Henry Symes, Register. 28 Sep. 1710. Daniel Parke.

George Gamble, Esq., of St. John's, merchant, plot. 6 July 5 Anne. John Johnson.

George Gamble, Esq., of St. John's, merchant, plot. 25 Aug. 1707. Daniel Parke.

William Glanvile, merchant, 160. New North Sound. 17 Nov. 1710. Daniel Parke.

John Fisher, planter, 10. 23 Feb. 1709. Daniel Parke.

Richard Oliver, 180 feet by 80 feet. 28 Sep. 1710. Daniel Parke.

John Perrie, Esq., 100. 18 May 1704. By Christopher Codrington.

John Yeamans, Esq., Deputy-Governor and Escheator, 28. 7 Dec. 1697. By Christopher Codrington.

Jonas Langford, planter, 286, some years in the possession of his ancestors in St. John's Division; desires a patent. Granted. 19 March 1712. By Walter Douglas.

Edward Sutton, planter, a parcel. Old Road. 12 March 1711. By Walter Douglas.

John Barton, planter, 35. 20 March 1711. By Walter Douglas.

Richard Soanes, vintner, 1 proportion. 6 May 1712. By Walter Douglas.

Thomas Breton, Esq., Attorney-General of St. Kitts, 100, east with Captain Tob. Lisle. 10 Oct. 1711. By Walter Douglas.

William Franklin, merchant-taylor, 1 proportion. St. John's Town. 13 July 1706. John Johnson.

Isaac Royall, Esq., 6. Popeshead. 5 Jan. 1712. Walter Douglas.

John Greenway, 50. Guana Island. Bought of William Codrington. 22 Jan. 1712. Walter Douglas.

John Fry and Thomas Williams, Esquires, 28, in St. Mary's Parish, for the use of the Rectors. 11 Feb. 1712. Walter Douglas.

Thomas Roome, 20. 8 July 1713. Walter Douglas.

ACCOUNTS OF SLAVE COMPENSATION CLAIMS FOR THE COLONY OF ANTIGUA.

UNCONTESTED CLAIMS

ORDERED BY THE HOUSE OF COMMONS TO BE PRINTED 16TH MARCH 1838. PAPER 215.

LIST A.

Date of Award.	Number of Claim.	Name of Party to whom the Payment is awarded.	Number of Slaves.	Sum. £	s.	d.
	1	Litigated Claim, amount deposited with Accountant General	100	—		
12 Oct. 1835	2	Henry Sam. Eyre, Esq., & John Willing Warren	56	852	0	3
19 Oct. 1835	3	William Shand, Esq.	98	1450	7	7
5 Oct. 1835	4	Elizabeth Lynch	5	104	19	8
	5	(No Claim or Return)	—	—		
14 Dec. 1835	6	Darius Davy	20	292	10	8
	7	(No Claim or Return)	—	—		
5 Oct. 1835	8	George Rickards	21	281	2	6
19 Oct. 1835	9	William Shand, Esq.	198	2746	7	2
14 Dec. 1835	10	Darius Davy	9	142	14	0
	11	(Litigated Claim)	112	—		
14 Dec. 1835	12	Thomas Clark	2	20	18	7
	13	(No Claim or Return)	—	—		
5 Oct. 1835	14	Mary Harris Doig	10	183	1	1
15 Feb. 1836	15	George Monk, Edward Monk, & Charles Jones Barnard	55	800	8	7
	16	(Litigated Claim)	22	—		
5 Oct. 1835	17	John Proctor Anderdon	180	2491	16	1
16 Nov. 1835	18	Ralph Peters	240	3804	14	2
5 Oct. 1835	19	Sir H. W. Martin, Bart.	319	4454	2	6
—	20	Robert and Henry Jefferson	146	2342	2	0
	21	(Litigated Claim)	66	—		
19 Oct. 1835	22	William Shand, Esq.	107	1563	4	8
	23	(Litigated Claim)	13	—		
	24	(Litigated Claim)	124	—		

Date of Award.	Number of Claim.	Name of Party to whom the Payment is awarded.	Number of Slaves.	Sum. £	s.	d.
5 Oct. 1835	25	Langford Lovell Hodge	201	2756	7	6
—	26	Gen. John Gustavus Crosbie	55	772	1	7
—	27	John Harris	26	426	8	4
—	28	Peter Langford Brooke	305	3701	14	4
—	29	John Horsford, Jun.	2	25	0	8
	30	(Litigated Claim)	333	—		
29 Feb. 1836	31	David Barnes	6	100	10	1
5 Oct. 1835	32	Mary Cable	4	55	8	7
16 Nov. 1835	33	Richd. Burroughs Eldridge	2	25	0	8
—	34	Richd. Burroughs Eldridge	3	32	15	10
	35	(Litigated Claim)	276	—		
19 Oct. 1835	36	William Shand, Esq.	131	2135	6	11
23 Nov. 1835	37	Lucy Tobin, John Cave, & Chas. Anthony Partridge	137	1984	16	10
	38	(Litigated Claim)	199	—		
	39	(Litigated Claim)	119	—		
	40	(Litigated Claim)	108	—		
5 Oct. 1835	41	William B. Lavicount	3	52	17	6
	42	(Litigated Claim)	235	—		
5 Oct. 1835	43	Ann Pierson	14	212	3	1
—	44	Eliza Drew	5	74	12	5
—	45	Eliza Drew & Ann Pierson	5	77	17	9
	46	(Litigated Claim)	152	—		
	47	(Litigated Claim)	46	—		
5 Oct. 1835	48	George W. W. Ledeatt	1	13	0	2
—	49	George W. W. Ledeatt	1	22	12	9
—	50	George W. W. Ledeatt	4	35	3	9
	51	(Litigated Claim)	24	—		
	52	(Litigated Claim)	127	—		
5 Oct. 1835	53	Robert Grant	7	130	4	5
—	54	Mrs A. M. Bethell, widow, Sir E. Codrington, Bart., & Bethell Walrond, Esq.	190	2588	6	6
14 Dec. 1835	55	James O'Connor	3	54	8	1
5 Oct. 1835	56	John Samuel Bayley	9	135	16	11
—	57	Josiah Martin	150	2121	14	8
	58	(Litigated Claim)	106	—		
	59	(Litigated Claim)	101	—		
5 Oct. 1835	60	Thomas Speucer Edwards	172	2468	11	2
—	61	Robert Jefferson & Henry Jefferson	309	4549	5	10
—	62	Samuel G. Watkins	8	143	13	11
11 Jan. 1836	63	Margaret Thibou	6	107	5	3
	64	(No Claim or Return)	—	—		
5 Oct. 1835	65	Darius Davey	12	151	7	4
31 July 1837	65A	Darius Davey	—	9	11	3
	66	(Litigated Claim)	160	—		
28 Nov. 1835	67	John Adams Wood	110	1601	15	3
5 Oct. 1835	68	John Ramsay	1	22	12	9
—	69	Elizabeth Frances Spencer	208	3251	0	10
—	70	Thomas Coull	107	1620	5	5
—	71	Samuel Pearson	8	138	1	11
—	72	Anne Jones	2	22	4	2
—	73	Ann C. Powell	4	65	12	11
—	74	Frances Lynch	3	64	11	5
	75	(Litigated Claim)	114	—		
5 Oct. 1835	76	Sarah C. Garland	11	199	0	4
23 Jan. 1836	77	Eliza Grant	3	39	0	7
5 Oct. 1835	78	Edm. and Car. Hayward	1	19	16	3
2 Nov. 1835	79	Charles John Manning & the Earl of Rosslyn	233	3626	12	1
5 Oct. 1835	80	James M. Hodges	11	162	14	1
—	81	George Francis Redhead	86	1499	10	11
	82	(Litigated Claim)	268	—		
	83	(Litigated Claim)	106	—		
	84	(Litigated Claim)	125	—		
5 Oct. 1835	85	George Samuel Bladen	6	83	8	9
—	86	John Ewart, William Myers, William Taylor, & Joseph Christopher Ewart	213	2790	8	8
	87	(Litigated Claim)	58	—		
	88	(Litigated Claim)	157	—		
5 Oct. 1835	89	James Salmon	3	42	0	5
7 Jan. 1836	90	James Salmon	1	21	11	7
	91	(Litigated Claim)	102	—		
	92	(Litigated Claim)	133	—		
5 Oct. 1835	93	John Adams Wood	63	989	19	1
	94	(Litigated Claim)	116	—		
	95	(Litigated Claim)	225	—		
16 Nov. 1835	96	Ralph Peters	156	2363	5	9
	97	(Litigated Claim)	254	—		
	98	(Litigated Claim)	235	—		
5 Oct. 1835	99	William Thomas Gore	9	129	0	10
—	100	Josiah M. Horton	4	55	3	10
—	101	Sir C. B. Codrington, Bart.	296	4442	2	0
	102	(Litigated Claim)	199	—		
	103	(Litigated Claim)	197	—		
5 Oct. 1835	104	Langford Redwood, Esq.	33	636	16	10
—	105	Peter Langford Brooke	190	2461	7	7
	106	(Paid into Court)	41	—		
	107	(Litigated Claim)	81	—		
5 Oct. 1835	108	Langford Lovell	175	2549	6	1
—	109	Thomas Prizgar, Esq.	2	26	0	5
—	110	Amy Clark Prizgar, spinster	3	35	4	4
	111	(Litigated Claim)	145	—		
5 Oct. 1835	112	John J. Mascall	9	107	8	6
—	113	Mary Hawes	2	39	12	6
	114	(Litigated Claim)	144	—		
5 Oct. 1835	115	Rowland Eward Williams	62	1004	6	9
	116	(Litigated Claim)	56	—		
5 Oct. 1835	117	J. Trecothick the younr, John Henry Roper, William Coles, & Francis Thwaites, Esq.	34	622	15	1
11 April 1836	118	Mary Gregory, Anna Jane Gregory, George Murray Gregory, Thomas Smith, & Eliza Gregory	49	731	5	9
5 Oct. 1835	119	Langford Lovell, Esq.	33	434	8	2
	120	(Litigated Claim)	42	—		
5 Oct. 1835	121	John Gray	10	125	16	6
—	122	Jane Maria Gilchrist & Elizabeth Grace Gilchrist	12	161	17	5
	123	(Litigated Claim)	115	—		
5 Oct. 1835	124	Robert Augustus Hyndman	4	90	9	5

Date of Award.	Number of Claim.	Name of Party to whom the Payment is awarded.	Number of Slaves.	Sum. £	s.	d.
	125	(Litigated Claim)	184	—		
5 Oct. 1835	126	Samuel Athill Turner	63	932	4	2
	127	(Litigated Claim)	3	—		
	128	(Litigated Claim)	160	—		
5 Oct. 1835	129	Joseph Taylor	1	13	0	2
—	130	John Alexander Trott	1	19	16	3
	131	(Litigated Claim)	159	—		
5 Oct. 1835	132	Samuel G. Dow	1	19	16	3
—	133	William Walkingshaw	1	21	11	7
21 Dec. 1835	134	Ann C. Gamble Hunt	1	19	16	3
—	135	Rachel S. Russel Hunt	3	42	0	5
5 Oct. 1835	136	James Athill	17	171	7	7
	137	(Litigated Claim)	99	—		
	138	(No Claim or Return)	—	—		
5 Oct. 1835	139	Ann Eliza Edwards	4	60	10	4
—	140	Eliza Mary Ann Edwards	5	113	1	9
	141	(No Claim. Return for one aged Slave)	1	—		
5 Oct. 1835	142	Elias A. Brown	1	13	0	2
—	143	Maria Chalmers	2	26	0	5
—	144	Eliza Parnell	1	13	0	2
	145	(Litigated Claim	2	—		
5 Oct. 1835	146	Grace W. Hinson & Elvira Morson	1	13	0	2
—	147	Richard Morgan	2	26	6	10
—	148	David Cranstoun	1	13	0	2
9 July 1836	149	George Blaney	1	16	19	11
5 Oct. 1835	150	Mary T. Symes	2	26	0	5
	151	(No Return)	—	—		
5 Oct. 1835	152	Mary Freeman Barton	4	43	0	6
—	153	Joseph P. Lake	1	13	0	2
—	154	Robert Shaw	1	13	0	2
—	155	Elizabeth Christian	1	13	0	2
	156	(No Claim or Return)	—	—		
5 Oct. 1835	157	David Cranstoun	9	173	19	8
—	158	Isaac Joseph Carlisle	1	13	0	2
	159	(Double Return by error. See No. 1043)	1	—		
14 Dec. 1835	160	John Bradshaw & Samuel M. Richards	1	13	0	2
5 Oct. 1835	161	John Wells Allaway	9	123	11	3
—	162	Mary Allaway	4	30	16	3
—	163	Catherine Allaway	2	15	8	1
—	164	Margaret Allaway	1	13	0	2
—	165	Jeremia Wells Allaway	2	51	11	3
—	166	Eliza Goddard	5	54	8	9
—	167	John Wells Allaway	1	25	15	7
—	168	Mary Dow	25	332	9	1
—	169	Michael Saturnin Bouisson	2	15	8	1
—	170	Charles S. Bouisson	1	25	15	7
—	171	Charles S. Bouisson	5	67	4	2
—	172	Frances Broadbridge	6	60	16	5
16 Nov. 1835	173	Owen Pell	1	13	0	2
5 Oct. 1835	174	William Boyd	6	72	3	3
—	175	Jane Boyd	7	82	15	8
—	176	Mary Garret Clarke	28	354	15	3
—	177	Ann Donaldson, widow	6	61	13	7
—	178	Sarah Martha Blair	4	52	0	10
—	179	William Brinton	5	67	4	2
—	180	James Curtin	17	178	14	4
19 Oct. 1835	181	Edward Corbett	21	343	9	10
	182	(Double Return by error. See No. 907)	2	—		
	183	(Remains for Adjudication)	1	—		
5 Oct. 1835	184	Janet Hall Byrne	1	25	15	7
—	185	Eliza Crawford	4	52	0	10
—	186	Richard Austin Farmer	1	13	0	2
—	187	John Adams Wood	1	13	0	2
—	188	Charlotte Bean	1	13	0	2
—	189	Grace Elyatt	2	13	0	3
—	190	Catharine Brown	12	138	17	8
—	191	George Betts	4	56	0	7
—	192	Charlotte French	5	45	5	7
—	193	Louisa Audain	3	39	0	7
—	194	William Fairclough	19	313	2	10
—	195	Ann Bailey	1	13	14	9
	196	(Litigated Claim)	7	—		
5 Oct. 1835	197	Hugh Edwards	3	59	8	9
—	198	William Wardle	9	107	4	1
	199	(Double Return by error. See No. 1055)	2	—		
5 Oct. 1835	200	Charles Barnard	1	13	0	2
12 Oct. 1835	201	Jane Carville	15	176	16	9
—	202	George Athill	3	47	12	0
—	203	George Beare	1	13	0	2
—	204	Eliza Burnthorn	1	13	0	2
—	205	John Ashford	3	55	15	9
—	206	James Barton	2	26	0	5
—	207	Dorothy Bonnin Burke	2	26	0	5
—	208	Samuel Crawford	2	15	8	1
—	209	Anne Anderson	2	15	8	1
—	210	Captain James Scott	1	25	15	7
	211	(Remains for Adjudication)	1	—		
12 Oct. 1835	212	Margaret Mackie	6	80	4	11
—	213	Mary Halliday	8	121	3	4
—	214	Gratian Hart	1	13	0	2
28 Mar. 1836	215	Robert Carr Brown	1	13	0	2
12 Oct. 1835	216	James T. Keeling	11	122	7	7
—	217	Lewis J. Butler	2	26	0	5
—	218	Mary Appleby	1	13	0	2
—	219	Ann Charles	1	13	0	2
	220	(Remains for Adjudication)	1	—		
12 Oct. 1835	221	Charles Benjamin Eudelle	1	13	0	2
16 Nov. 1835	222	Owen Pell	1	13	0	2
12 Oct. 1835	223	Margaret Fairbairn	6	82	15	7
—	224	Elizabeth Allers	2	33	19	11
—	225	Henry Titus Jones & Mary Nicholls his wife	9	95	17	3
	226	(Double Return by error. See No. 827)	3	—		
12 Oct. 1835	227	Elizabeth Broadbridge	3	43	0	4
—	228	Margaret M'Millan	2	38	15	10
—	229	Eliza Biffin	3	17	16	0

Date of Award.	Number of Claim.	Name of Party to whom the Payment is awarded.	Number of Slaves.	Sum. £	s.	d.
12 Oct. 1835	230	Richard Rogers Ferris	1	16	19	11
—	231	Henry Este	6	86	15	4
	232	(Litigated Claim)	2	—		
12 Oct. 1835	233	Ann H. Petrie	1	13	0	2
—	234	Ann McGuire	4	52	15	4
—	235	Francis G. Tucker	1	13	0	2
—	236	Samuel Brown	1	13	0	2
—	237	Mary Este	10	138	9	8
—	238	Edward Eliot	2	26	0	5
—	239	Richard E. Leecatt	8	104	16	2
—	240	Mary Loury	6	57	11	2
—	241	John Adams Wood	5	67	4	2
—	242	Isabella Hill	5	65	15	7
—	243	Elizabeth Ann Ferris	2	13	0	3
	244	(Remains for Adjudication)	3	—		
12 Oct. 1835	245	Ann Carty	1	16	19	11
—	246	John Adams Wood	2	26	14	11
—	247	Elias Adams Brown	1	13	14	9
	248	(No Claim or Return)	—	—		
12 Oct. 1835	249	James Gilchrist	3	28	8	4
—	250	John Adams Wood	2	38	15	10
—	251	Ann Hamilton	3	39	0	7
—	252	Alice Ferris	8	116	17	1
—	253	Ann Harris Brinton	2	26	0	5
—	254	Samuel Crawford	1	13	0	2
—	255	Mary Ann Shires	4	52	0	10
	256	(Litigated Claim)	17	—		
	257	(Litigated Claim)	73	—		
19 Oct. 1835	258	James Douglass & Eliza Douglass his wife	40	541	15	8
—	259	Sir William Abdy, Bart., Sir Thomas Fellowes, Knt., The Rev. G. Caldwell, Clk., and James A. Gordon, Esq.	152	2289	14	8
	260	(Litigated Claim)	54	—		
	261	(Litigated Claim)	40	—		
12 Oct. 1835	262	Francis Watson	17	185	5	9
—	263	John Adams Wood	168	2230	14	9
25 Jan. 1836	264	Thomas Fitt Tucker	1	19	16	3
	265	(Litigated Claim)	331	—		
	266	(Litigated Claim)	274	—		
	267	(Litigated Claim)	178	—		
	268	(Litigated Claim)	213	—		
	269	(Litigated Claim)	97	—		
	270	(Litigated Claim)	146	—		
	271	(Litigated Claim)	69	—		
12 Oct. 1835	272	Mary Harman	3	24	12	1
—	273	Ann Harman	1	19	16	3
16 Nov. 1835	274	Owen Pell	3	52	12	9
	275	(Litigated Claim)	103	—		
12 Oct. 1835	276	Mary Ann Buntin	2	47	7	3
—	277	George Buntin	2	22	4	2
—	278	Nathaniel Gilbert	48	889	1	5
	279	(Litigated Claim)	101	—		
14 Dec. 1835	280	Eliza Leicatt	12	204	15	0
	281	(Litigated Claim)	161	—		
	282	(Litigated Claim)	114	—		
	283	(Litigated Claim)	199	—		
12 Oct. 1835	284	Robert Farquhar	420	5498	14	3
	285	(Litigated Claim)	71	—		
26 Oct. 1835	286	John Adams Wood	124	1763	6	5
	287	(Litigated Claim)	22	—		
12 Oct. 1835	288	Mary Harney Marchant	9	72	9	11
—	289	Mary Richards	10	179	7	11
—	290	Margaret Taylor	3	22	18	5
—	291	Caroline Thwaites	1	13	0	2
—	292	Jane Mathews	2	30	7	11
—	293	Mary Gilchrist	1	25	15	7
—	294	Elizabeth Gilchrist	2	33	11	0
—	295	Janet Gilchrist	2	33	11	0
21 Dec. 1835	296	Elizabeth Austin & Sarah Austin	1	19	16	3
—	297	Ann Halloran	1	21	11	7
13 Nov. 1837	298	Henry Spencer Papps, Ann Papps, & George Snook Papps	2	32	16	5
12 Oct. 1835	299	Jarvis Turner	9	160	14	6
—	300	Catherine Bigsby	3	67	17	0
19 Oct. 1835	301	William Francis Hall	4	65	12	11
—	302	Thomas Coull, M.D., & William Byam	180	2638	7	11
—	303	William Shand	142	2123	1	9
—	304	John Freeland	1	19	16	3
—	305	William Willis, senior	5	92	5	3
—	306	Horatio N. Richardson	3	42	0	5
	307	(Litigated Claim)	4	—		
19 Oct. 1835	308	Peter Langford Brooke	134	1935	13	3
—	309	Ann Robson	2	34	11	10
	310	(Litigated Claim)	167	—		
14 Dec. 1835	311	Francis Smyth	1	13	0	2
—	312	John Bradshaw & Samuel M. Richards	12	175	11	2
29 Feb. 1836	313	Rachel Coates Sones, widow	3	52	12	9
19 Oct. 1835	314	Lydia Byam	6	63	12	8
—	315	John Adams Wood	5	50	12	6
—	316	William Byam	123	1967	12	4
—	317	Elizabeth Sedgwick	25	441	1	7
—	318	William Byam	133	2149	3	10
—	319	Samuel Sedgwick, Doctor of Physic	20	333	17	5
	320	(Remains for Adjudication)	2	—		
19 Oct. 1835	321	William Shand	170	2539	7	6
—	322	Isaac Krutho	5	50	12	6
—	323	John Lideatt	2	39	12	6
	324	(Litigated Claim)	329	—		
19 Oct. 1835	325	William W. Dow	2	32	16	5
—	326	Eliz. Harcum Pilkington	2	39	12	6
—	327	Robert Charles Tudway	182	2869	14	5
—	328	Robert Chas. Tudway, Esq.	181	2689	6	11
—	329	Sir C. B. Codrington, Bart.	169	2468	10	2
—	330	Robert C. Tudway, Esq.	194	3001	7	10
	331	(Litigated Claim)	72	—		
19 Oct. 1835	332	Sir C. B. Codrington, Bart.	137	2078	1	7
	333	(Litigated Claim)	144	—		

Date of Award.	Number of Claim.	Name of Party to whom the Payment is awarded.	Number of Slaves.	Sum. £	s.	d.
19 Oct. 1835	334	Sir C. B. Codrington, Bart.	299	4920	9	10
—	335	Samuel Otto Baijer	170	2551	18	4
9 Nov. 1835	336	The Hon. John Brodick	122	2019	1	3
	337	(Litigated Claim)	43	—		
19 Oct. 1835	338	Sir C. B. Codrington, Bart.	146	2227	13	8
	339	(Litigated Claim)	161	—		
19 Oct. 1835	340	J. Watson Borradaile & Joseph Edlman	99	1554	5	5
—	341	Francis Ifrye Brown	11	223	7	0
—	342	Sir William Abdy, Bart., Sir Thomas Fellowes, Knt., The Rev. G. Caldwell, Clk., & James Adam Gordon, Esq.	314	4677	11	11
	343	(Litigated Claim)	244	—		
19 Oct. 1835	344	Christopher Ronan	1	19	16	3
	345	(No Claim or Return)	—	—		
	346	(Litigated Claim)	162	—		
19 Oct. 1835	347	James Hancock Donovan	1	22	12	9
—	348	W. H. Rowland Irby, Esq.	130	2043	7	10
	349	(Litigated Claim)	187	—		
	350	(Litigated Claim)	297	—		
	351	(Litigated Claim)	246	—		
19 Oct. 1835	352	Alexander Millar, Esq.	196	3156	2	2
	353	(Litigated Claim)	395	—		
	354	(Litigated Claim)	264	—		
	355	(Litigated Claim)	303	—		
19 Oct. 1835	356	Kean B. Osborn	94	1405	6	8
16 Nov. 1835	357	Ralph Peters	58	908	14	6
23 Nov. 1835	358	Freeman Thomas, Esq.	162	1937	19	8
	359	(Litigated Claim)	171	—		
	360	(Litigated Claim)	135	—		
19 Oct. 1835	361	Clement T. Swanston & William Clarke	46	891	5	11
	362	(Litigated Claim)	159	—		
	363	(Litigated Claim)	217	—		
19 Oct. 1835	364	John S. Jarvis	29	337	19	8
	365	(Litigated Claim)	81	—		
19 Oct. 1835	366	John Keen	2	26	0	5
—	367	Sarah Ann Buckley & John Edward Buckley	1	13	0	2
—	368	David Cranstoun	7	123	6	10
—	369	Elizabeth Furlong	2	30	0	2
—	370	Eliza C. Nibbs	13	199	18	0
—	371	Jane Prudden	4	72	9	0
	372	(No Claim or Return)	—	—		
14 Dec. 1835	373	Francis Crichton	2	22	4	2
19 Oct. 1835	374	Amelia James	2	30	7	11
—	375	George James	1	22	12	9
—	376	Francis Byam	4	88	3	2
	377	(Litigated Claim)	73	—		
19 Oct. 1835	378	James Barrett	1	25	15	7
—	379	Kean Osborn Barrett	2	39	10	4
—	380	Mary E. Rundle	1	22	12	9
—	381	Kean Osborn Barrett	7	125	1	9
—	382	Dorothy Martin	4	40	11	1
—	383	Eliza A. T. Ash	3	32	15	10
—	384	Charles J. Barnard	9	131	2	2
14 Dec. 1835	385	John W. Gallwey	1	19	16	3
	386	(No Claim or Return)	—	—		
	387	(Litigated Claim)	264	—		
19 Oct. 1835	388	Rebecca Bailey	1	13	0	2
—	389	Charles Parmenus Hosier	9	107	11	1
	390	(Litigated Claim)	158	—		
	391	(Litigated Claim)	153	—		
	392	(Litigated Claim)	159	—		
19 Oct. 1835	393	Henry Tucker Pigot	12	182	10	4
—	394	Hardman Earle & John H. Turner, Esq.	237	3604	8	9
—	395	Robert Sutton	114	1736	9	7
2 Nov. 1835	396	James Foster Groom	111	1650	17	6
	397	(Litigated Claim)	325	—		
19 Oct. 1835	398	Rebecca Maria Harriet Gilchrist	32	331	3	9
—	399	Eliza Ottley	5	98	6	2
—	400	Barbara Jarvis Fitch	17	273	6	2
	401	(Litigated Claim)	42	—		
26 Oct. 1835	402	Sarah Dow, Ann Wager, Lydia Dow, & Eliza Dow	1	19	16	3
—	403	Henry R. Nanton	1	21	11	7
—	404	Henry R. Nanton	2	33	11	0
—	405	Henry R. Nanton	3	56	3	6
—	406	Rebecca Athill	3	24	12	1
30 Jan. 1836	407	Sarah Stephenson	1	19	16	3
26 Oct. 1835	408	John Burke Righton	10	164	16	11
11 Jan. 1836	409	Nancy Mills	1	19	16	3
26 Oct. 1835	410	James Johnston	5	74	16	11
—	411	Margaret Brooks	1	13	0	2
—	412	William Cutting Brooks	7	121	16	5
—	413	Jos. Lyons Walrond Brooks	2	32	16	5
30 Jan. 1836	414	William Cutting Brooks	1	13	0	2
15 Aug. 1836	415	Jane Williamson	1	25	15	7
26 Oct. 1835	416	John Crawford	10	135	17	0
16 Nov. 1835	417	Owen Pell	4	37	12	3
26 Oct. 1835	418	Thomas W. Richardson	2	32	16	5
—	419	Catherine Hamm	14	178	18	8
7 May 1836	420	Thomas N. Scholar	1	19	16	3
26 Oct. 1835	421	Thomas B. Ragin	5	78	13	2
—	422	Francis Ann Barton	1	13	0	2
	423	(Litigated Claim)	3	—		
26 Oct. 1835	424	Samuel Barton	11	145	5	8
—	425	Elizabeth Barton	1	13	0	2
—	426	Lieut. Richard S. Wickham	1	19	16	3
—	427	William Killikelly	4	65	12	11
—	428	Lizette Deselles	3	52	12	9
—	429	Edmon Grant Barton	10	149	13	10
—	430	John Atkinson	2	22	4	2
—	431	Martha Cole	3	52	12	9
13 June 1836	432A	John Black	4	68	19	0
—	432B	George Wakefield	2	33	11	0
26 Oct. 1835	433	Peter Martin	4	55	0	8
—	434	Elizabeth McCarty	2	39	12	6
—	435	Benjamin Blake	2	39	12	6
—	436	John Latimer	8	118	5	9

Date of Award.	Number of Claim.	Name of Party to whom the Payment is awarded.	Number of Slaves.	Sum. £	s.	d.
26 Oct. 1835	437	George Byron Figerilla	10	149	10	5
—	438	Ann Shipley Nanton	9	151	2	2
—	439	Elizabeth Parker	1	19	16	3
—	440	James Barker	1	16	19	11
—	441	Joseph N. Hart	4	85	18	10
—	442	Joseph N. Hart	10	129	0	2
—	443	James William Barton	4	55	0	8
—	444	Robert Henry Grant Barton	16	202	1	10
14 Dec. 1835	445	Thomas W. Bladen	12	182	7	10
30 Jan. 1836	446	Margaret Francs Scholar	17	241	12	4
26 Oct. 1835	447	Eleanor M. Chambers	2	22	4	2
—	448	John R. Chambers	8	110	12	3
—	449	Mary Nanton	2	41	7	11
—	450	Henry Elliott	1	19	16	3
—	451	Petoney Burke	7	105	5	7
—	452	Mary Harris	5	85	9	2
—	453	Luke Cole	2	32	16	5
—	454	Jane Payne	1	19	16	3
—	455	Zabeth Dick	2	32	16	5
—	456	Pamela Steer	2	26	0	5
—	457	Pamela Steer	6	53	0	5
—	458	William Jacobs	12	190	11	5
—	459	Mary Seaman	1	19	16	3
—	460	Catharine Fox	3	52	12	9
—	461	Joseph Donowa	2	32	16	5
4 April 1836	462	George Black	13	227	14	4
26 Oct. 1835	463	Samuel Elliott	7	125	1	9
—	464	Rebecca Webster, widow	1	19	16	3
—	465	Ann Robertson	1	13	0	2
	466	(Litigated Claim)	8	—		
26 Oct. 1835	467	John Samuel Bayley	8	103	5	3
—	468	John Samuel Bayley, Peter Bayley, & William Edward Bayley	4	65	10	9
16 Nov. 1835	469	Richard Burroughs Eldridge	4	69	3	8
26 Oct. 1835	470	Lucy Mortimer	3	52	12	9
—	471	Eleanor M'Carty Donowa	1	19	16	3
—	472	Jane Pringle Nanton	1	13	0	2
26 Oct. 1835	473	Henrietta Leston Nanton	2	32	16	5
—	474	Christian B. Geiger	4	14	8	4
—	475	Ann M'Carty	1	19	16	3
15 Aug. 1836	476	Elizabeth Jane Williams	1	13	0	2
26 Oct. 1835	477	Sarah Graham Lyons	2	32	16	5
—	478	Elizabeth J. W. Donowa	1	13	0	2
—	479	Joseph N. Hart	1	19	16	3
27 Feb. 1836	480	George William Foord	3	54	8	1
26 Oct. 1835	481	Eliza Thibou	1	19	16	3
—	482	William Petrie	3	35	4	4
—	483	Joseph B. Lavicount	8	104	9	0
—	484	Andrew Lyons	1	25	15	7
	485	(Double Return by Error. See No. 1053)	2	—		
	486	(Litigated Claim)	105	—		
	487	(Litigated Claim)	176	—		
26 Oct. 1835	488	Owen Pell	2	45	11	10
—	489	John J. Mascall	18	294	15	2
—	490	Joseph Donowa	1	13	0	2
—	491	Thomas Dickson Foote	4	52	15	4
—	492	Eleanor Crichton	7	63	4	4
—	493	Margaret Dunlop Nicolls	2	26	0	5
—	494	Margaret Dunlop Nicolls	5	84	6	1
—	495	Charity Barnes	3	39	0	7
—	496	Elizabeth Boyd	4	51	16	1
—	497	John Crawford	10	181	18	3
	498	(Litigated Claim)	25	—		
26 Oct. 1835	499	Jane O'Loughlin	1	13	0	2
23 Jan. 1836	500	James & Sarah Walling	10	145	10	6
2 Nov. 1835	501	John J. Mascall	1	13	0	2
—	502	Thomas Wethered	3	40	9	9
—	503	Elizabeth Winthorpe	1	13	0	2
—	504	Margaret Smith	5	54	8	9
—	505	Hugh Thompson	2	38	15	10
—	506	Hugh Thompson	2	35	6	5
—	507	William Harvey Thompson	2	33	19	11
—	508	John Adams Wood	10	185	3	6
11 July 1836	509	Hugh Cunningham	1	13	14	9
2 Nov. 1835	510	John Joseph Ronan & Hugh Thompson	9	176	9	2
—	511	Anna Scotland	6	68	3	6
—	512	Ann Margaret Scotland	1	13	0	2
11 Jan. 1836	513	Penelope Pew	2	26	0	5
2 Nov. 1835	514	Mary Anna Scotland	3	39	15	2
16 Nov. 1835	515	Owen Pell	2	26	14	11
	516	(Litigated Claim)	4	—		
4 April 1836	517	Susannah Stocker, Elizabeth Parry Stocker, & Mary Gregory	3	39	0	7
2 Nov. 1835	518	Sarah J. Symes	3	28	8	4
	519	(Remains for Adjudication)	2	—		
2 Nov. 1835	520	John Bradshaw & Samuel Misson Richards	1	25	15	7
14 Dec. 1835	521	John Bradshaw & Samuel M. Richards	6	68	3	6
2 Nov. 1835	522	John Bradshaw & Samuel M. Richards	1	13	0	2
—	523	John Bradshaw & Samuel M. Richards	5	73	0	7
—	524	Samuel Bott Johnson, Sarah Rebecca Johnson, & Cecilia Margaret Johnson	1	16	19	11
	525	(No Claim or Return)	—	—		
2 Nov. 1835	526	Robert Tait	3	39	15	2
—	527	Anthony Musgrave	1	13	0	2
—	528	Anthony Musgrave	5	65	1	0
—	529	Eleanor Dickman	10	122	7	5
	530	(No Claim or Return)	—	—		
2 Nov. 1835	531	Henrietta B. Cable	4	52	0	10
—	532	Charlotte M'Connell	1	2	7	11
—	533	Richard Joshua Blizard	1	13	0	2
—	534	Eliza Sophia Blizard	1	16	19	11
—	535	Sophia Grace Blizard	9	121	1	7
—	536	David Cranstoun	1	25	19	5
14 Dec. 1835	537	David Cranstoun	1	22	12	9
2 Nov. 1835	538A	John Bradshaw & Samuel M. Richards	1	13	0	2
—	538B	Sarah Wolff	1	13	0	2
—	539	Daniel Hill & Nathaniel Hill	2	26	0	5

Date of Award.	Number of Claim.	Name of Party to whom the Payment is awarded	Number of Slaves.	Sum. £	s.	d.
14 Dec. 1835	540	John Thibon	2	26	14	11
2 Nov. 1835	541	John Bradshaw & Samuel M. Richards	1	13	0	2
—	542	David Cranstoun	4	70	6	2
—	543	Margaret H. Symes	10	130	10	7
11 Jan. 1836	544	Elizabeth Lydia Jackson	13	166	9	11
14 Dec. 1835	545	John Henry Jones	4	51	1	1
16 Nov. 1835	546	Owen Pell	3	51	16	0
18 Jan. 1836	547	Ann Melligham & Mary Chapman	4	41	8	6
2 Nov. 1835	548A	Mary Eliza Manderston	1	13	0	2
—	548B	Mary Eliza Manderston & Marg. Lewis Manderston	1	13	0	2
	549	(Double Return by Error. See No. 1023)	1	—		
	550	(No Claim or Return)	—	—		
2 Nov. 1835	551	Eliza Teresa Stepney	1	13	0	2
	552	(No Claim or Return)	—	—		
	553	(Litigated Claim)	3	—		
	554	(Litigated Claim)	35	—		
15 Feb. 1836	555	Eliza Brown	3	39	0	7
2 Nov. 1835	556	Rebecca O'Shaughnessy	1	13	0	2
—	557	John Bradshaw & Samuel M. Richards	1	13	0	2
—	558	Sir C. B. Codrington, Bart.	492	6286	18	11
—	559	Robert Carr Brown	1	13	0	2
	560	(Litigated Claim)	8	—		
2 Nov. 1835	561	Sarah Jeffry	3	39	0	7
21 Jan. 1837	562	Brodie George M'Nish	1	13	0	2
2 Nov. 1835	563	Ann Dowrich	1	13	0	2
	564	(Remains for Adjudication)	2	—		
2 Nov. 1835	565	James Graham Rennie & Elizabeth his wife	11	164	11	9
—	566	Margaret Pearson	14	225	3	6
—	567	George Nelson	8	168	13	3
—	568	Esther G. Willock	1	13	0	2
—	569	Ann Barnes	2	26	0	5
—	570	Sophia Carlisle	5	54	8	9
—	571	William Bertie	1	2	7	11
—	572	John Bradshaw & Samuel M. Richards	1	22	12	9
—	573	Sarah Taylor	5	77	16	5
—	574	Rebecca Carlisle	1	25	15	7
7 May 1836	575	Samuel Lightburn Darrell	3	39	0	7
2 Nov. 1835	576	John Bradshaw & Samuel M. Richards	1	13	0	2
16 Nov. 1835	577	Richard Burroughs Eldridge	4	77	11	8
2 Nov. 1835	578	John Bradshaw & Samuel M. Richards	3	39	0	7
	579	(No Claim or Return)	—	—		
2 Nov. 1835	580	George Dawson	2	26	0	5
—	581	John Bradshaw & Samuel M. Richards	1	13	0	2
—	582	Jane Fraser	1	13	0	2
14 Dec. 1835	583	John Bradshaw & Samuel M. Richards	2	30	0	2
2 Nov. 1835	584	Mary Johnstone Browne	6	78	1	3
—	585	George Diamond	1	16	19	11
16 Nov. 1835	586	Owen Pell	3	47	0	2
2 Nov. 1835	587	Thomas Burton	1	25	15	7
—	588	Sarah Brand	2	20	15	5
—	589	Chris. Columbus Blizard	1	13	0	2
—	590	Elizabeth Emerson	1	13	0	2
14 Dec. 1835	591	Peter Abrahams	1	13	0	2
	592	(Litigated Claim)	7	—		
2 Nov. 1835	593	John Bradshaw	1	13	0	2
—	594	Joseph Leaver Bindon	1	13	0	2
16 Nov. 1835	595	Owen Pell	5	33	4	2
2 Nov. 1835	596	Joseph Leaver Bindon	1	13	0	2
—	597	John Brooke Donaldson	8	94	3	11
16 Nov. 1835	598	Owen Pell	2	26	0	5
2 Nov. 1835	599	The Hon. John Berkeley	2	26	0	5
—	600	William Boyd	3	39	0	7
9 Nov. 1835	601	Mary Bruce	3	39	0	7
—	602	Mary Jane Craig	1	13	0	2
—	603	James Brinton & Jane Brinton	1	13	0	2
—	604	Henry Donovan	3	39	0	7
—	605	Maria Clegg	2	15	8	1
—	606	Charles Bradfute	1	16	19	11
	607	(Litigated Claim)	11	—		
9 Nov. 1835	608	Robert Claxton	1	13	0	2
—	609	Lydia Weir	1	13	0	2
14 Dec. 1835	610	John Bradshaw & Samuel M. Richards	9	119	19	6
9 Nov. 1835	611	John Dover	2	15	8	1
—	612	William Closs	8	93	9	4
—	613	Mary Ailhaud	3	26	0	6
—	614	John Allan	4	46	15	10
—	615	Joseph Ablett	2	26	0	5
—	616	Jane E. Donovan	6	82	15	7
14 Dec. 1835	617	Joshua Kentish	34	550	8	8
9 Nov. 1835	618	Rachel Winston Rose	1	13	0	2
—	619	Lucy A. Kippen Partridge	1	13	0	2
—	620	William Musgrave	1	13	0	2
25 Jan. 1836	621	John Hicks & James Tait	3	39	0	7
14 Dec. 1835	622	Joshua Bradshaw & Samuel M. Richards	4	52	15	4
9 Nov. 1835	623	Richard Musgrave	1	13	0	2
	624	(Remains for Adjudication)	1	—		
16 Nov. 1835	625	William Jenkins	3	39	0	7
9 Nov. 1835	626	Peter Johnston	2	39	10	4
	627	(Litigated Claim)	18	—		
9 Nov. 1835	628	Barnice Joseph	1	13	0	2
—	629	Henry John Glover	6	81	13	6
	630	(Remains for Adjudication)	1	—		
9 Nov. 1835	631	Mary Gregory, Anna Jane Gregory, Eliza Gregory, John Troup, George Murray Gregory, & Thomas Smith	5	86	3	6
14 Dec. 1835	632	John Bradshaw & Samuel M. Richards	2	26	0	5
23 Jan. 1836	633	Thomas Ward	1	13	14	9
14 Dec. 1835	634	Thomas Ward	5	55	3	3
—	635	Thomas Ward	2	26	14	11
—	636	Mary Ann Horsford	3	28	8	4
—	637	John Bradshaw & Samuel M. Richards	1	13	0	2
—	638	Ann Harris	1	13	0	2
—	639	Catherine Lynch	1	13	0	2
11 Jan. 1836	640	Henry Hill	8	122	19	11
9 Nov. 1835	641	John Gaynes	2	26	0	5
—	642	William Lee	3	39	0	7

Date of Award.	Number of Claim.	Name of Party to whom the Payment is awarded.	Number of Slaves.	Sum. £	s.	d.
9 Nov. 1835	643	William Harris	2	26	0	5
	644	(Litigated Claim)	2	—		
9 Nov. 1835	645	Eliza Hodge	6	78	15	9
—	646	William Wickham Harman	10	133	11	9
—	647	Charles Parmenus Hozier	21	267	8	2
—	648	Henry Edward Gale	4	28	8	5
—	649	Elizabeth Gregory, widow	6	67	8	11
—	650	Sarah Davis	3	28	8	4
—	651	Sus. Williams Greenway	12	181	13	4
—	652	Eliz. Williams Greenway	12	126	2	11
	653	(Litigated Claim)	14	—		
9 Nov. 1835	654	Mary Kirkwood	1	13	0	2
—	655	Eleanor Hillhouse	3	39	0	7
—	656	John Harris	16	288	8	1
	657	(Remains for Adjudication)	1	—		
9 Nov. 1835	658	Evan Jack, junior	5	103	7	3
—	659	Christina Luke & Mary Ann Luke	8	93	9	4
15 Feb. 1836	660	Mathew Lowry	1	25	15	7
14 Dec. 1835	661A	Elizabeth Lee	2	26	0	5
—	661B	Henry Loving	1	13	0	2
9 Nov. 1835	662	Joseph Shervington	7	103	16	10
14 Dec. 1835	663	John Bradshaw & Samuel M. Richards	2	38	15	10
9 Nov. 1835	664	Sarah Tait	2	26	0	5
—	665	Joseph Shervington	1	52	15	4
—	666	Tyrrell Shervington	2	26	14	11
—	667	Lydia Weir & Mary Wethered	14	221	1	7
14 Dec. 1835	668	William Bladen Pigot	1	13	0	2
9 Nov. 1835	669	Grace Ann Hodge	1	13	0	2
23 Jan. 1836	670	Joseph Leaver Bindon	5	78	11	0
9 Nov. 1835	671	Jane Thibou	2	30	0	2
—	672	Mary E. Ravely, widow	3	47	0	2
14 Dec. 1835	673	Eliza Adams, Joseph Samuel Sheriff, & Sarah Thompson	4	52	0	10
9 Nov. 1835	674	Louisa Wyke Willock	2	26	0	5
—	675	Ann Ward	8	118	6	2
—	676	Peter Wheatland	2	26	14	11
—	677	Martha Thomas	1	13	0	2
—	678	Jacob D. Walker	2	26	0	5
16 Nov. 1835	679	Owen Pell	4	52	0	10
9 Nov. 1835	680	Thomas Lane	1	13	0	2
—	681	John Gore, Esquire	51	667	2	7
—	682	Thomas John Fuller	1	13	0	2
—	683	Richard Rogers Ferris	1	13	0	2
—	684	Frances Carrington	3	28	8	4
—	685A	Alexander Murrain	—	13	0	2
—	685B	John Bradshaw & Samuel M. Richards	2	25	15	7
—	686	Sarah Hill	1	13	0	2
—	687	James Grenville Hicks	3	39	0	7
—	688	Catherine Hardcastle	6	57	11	2
15 Feb. 1836	689	John M'Hugo, jun.	1	16	19	11
14 Dec. 1835	690	Coleman H. Lamitt	2	26	0	5
9 Nov. 1835	691	Ann Nibbs	1	13	0	2
—	692	Anna Jane Gregory	5	58	8	6
—	693	John Joseph Ronan	2	30	0	2
16 Nov. 1835	694	William Greenidge	4	81	19	1
9 Nov. 1835	695	William Thomas Lorven	2	26	0	5
—	696	John Bradshaw & Samuel M. Richards	1	13	0	2
—	697	John Lloyd	1	25	15	7
14 Dec. 1835	698	The Hon. Paul Horsford	1	13	0	2
9 Nov. 1835	699	Nathaniel Humphreys	5	54	8	9
—	700	John Davis	8	93	9	4
16 Nov. 1835	701	Mary Haycock & Jane Juliana Hall	3	51	19	7
—	702	William Alexander Horne	7	89	3	3
—	703	Ann Hunt	5	44	11	0
—	704	John Adams Wood	1	13	0	2
23 Nov. 1835	705	Anthony Musgrave	11	182	17	8
16 Nov. 1835	706	Elizabeth Looby	3	39	15	2
—	707	Charlotte Nicholson	4	41	8	6
11 Jan. 1836	708	Sarah Ruddock	4	56	15	2
16 Nov. 1835	709	James Nibbs Brown	2	26	0	5
—	710	John Hicks	1	25	15	7
—	711	William Burnthorn	7	108	11	2
—	712	Owen Pell	1	13	0	2
—	713	Frances Herbert	3	28	8	4
—	714	Richard Burroughs Eldridge	7	111	16	5
—	715	Richard Burroughs Eldridge	1	13	0	2
—	716	Owen Pell	4	41	8	6
14 Dec. 1835	717	William A. Ross Willock, Louisa Wyke Willock, & Alicia Henrica Willock	10	146	13	0
—	718	John Bradshaw & Samuel M. Richards	2	26	14	11
16 Nov. 1835	719	Frederick Camm	1	16	19	11
—	720	Harriet Rose	12	141	18	2
—	721	Jane Spencer	2	26	0	5
—	722	Samuel H. Wills	1	13	14	9
—	723	Henry Thomas Gallery	1	25	15	7
—	724	Adam White	3	15	8	2
—	725	Robert Jait	16	155	1	10
23 Jan. 1836	726	Samuel Williams & Grace Williams	1	13	0	2
16 Nov. 1835	727A	Lydia Weir	—	20	3	11
—	727B	John Bradshaw & Samuel M. Richards	6	26	0	5
	728	(Litigated Claim)	10	—		
16 Nov. 1835	729	John Bradshaw & Samuel M. Richards	1	25	15	7
25 Jan. 1836	730	Eliza Waite	1	13	0	2
16 Nov. 1835	731	Ann Smith	8	119	0	9
—	732	Richard H. Mason	3	51	16	0
—	733	John Bradshaw & Samuel M. Richards	1	13	0	2
—	734	Catherine A. Thomas	7	63	4	4
14 Dec. 1835	735	Richard H. Mason & Stephen Mason	1	13	14	9
16 Nov. 1835	736	Richard H. Mason	4	39	15	3
—	737	Richard S. White	1	25	15	7
—	738	Stephen Mason	7	81	3	8
—	739	Richard S. White	4	30	16	3
—	740	Dorothy Nibbs	2	15	8	1
—	741	Barbara Grant	1	13	0	2
—	742	John Jacobs, senior	1	25	15	7
—	743	William Williams	5	78	11	0

Date of Award.	Number of Claim.	Name of Party to whom the Payment is awarded.	Number of Slaves.	Sum. £	s.	d.
16 Nov. 1835	744	Elizabeth Worlock	2	26	0	5
—	745	William Irish Wyke	1	13	0	2
—	746	William Irish Wyke	2	47	7	3
	747	(Litigated Claim)	11	—		
16 Nov. 1835	748	Amelia Sheriff	1	13	0	2
—	749	David Yetts	5	55	3	3
—	750	William Jenkins	9	61	12	7
—	751	Owen Pell	3	28	8	4
—	752	John Athill	1	13	0	2
—	753	John Buckley, Richard Thos. Buckley, & Rachel Jones	3	26	0	6
	754	(No Claim or Return)	—	—		
16 Nov. 1835	755	Maria Athill	4	30	16	3
—	756	John Athill & Mary Athill	4	41	8	6
—	757	Anthony Browne	2	32	16	5
	758	(Litigated Claim)	4	—		
16 Nov. 1835	759	James Simmons	1	21	11	7
14 Dec. 1835	760	John Bradshaw & Samuel M. Richards	2	26	0	5
16 Nov. 1835	761	John Adams Wood	4	41	8	6
	762	(Remains for Adjudication)	11	—		
16 Nov. 1835	763	Rachel Scholes	1	13	0	2
—	764	Grace Bruce	2	26	0	5
—	765	James Armstrong	6	79	10	4
—	766	Mary Lowry	1	13	0	2
—	767	Mary Eleanor Prynne	3	39	0	7
30 Jan. 1836	768	Mary Ann West	1	13	0	2
16 Nov. 1835	769	Daniel W. Scarville	1	13	0	2
5 Mar. 1836	770	William Beech, Robert Peddie, & John Billinghurst	15	198	15	11
16 Nov. 1835	771	Jane Elizabeth Edden	22	279	17	0
—	772	Ann Bean Walter	12	222	3	3
—	773	Samuel Thibon	3	29	2	10
—	774	Ann Hamilton Proudfoot	17	199	18	11
—	775	Ann Florrie Taylor	1	13	0	2
—	776	Ann Robb	1	13	0	2
—	777	Baptist Looby Slaney	2	38	15	10
—	778	Thomas F. Weatherill	3	43	0	4
—	779	Penelope Ward	2	26	0	5
—	780	William M'Connochie	3	29	2	10
—	781	William Davis	1	13	0	2
—	782	Ann Weatherill	1	13	0	2
—	783	Ashton Warner	1	13	0	2
4 Dec. 1837	784	John Hart Moor	1	13	0	2
16 Nov. 1835	785	Jane Arbuthnot, Robert Keane, Ann Keane, & Maria Keane	1	13	0	2
—	786	John Wilson	2	26	0	5
—	787	Mary Young	11	100	13	1
—	788	John Wilson	9	74	12	8
—	789	Eliza Lyne	5	65	1	0
11 Jan. 1836	790	William Gell Collins	1	13	14	9
16 Nov. 1835	791	Richard Starke	1	13	0	2
—	792	Mary Walker	1	13	0	2
—	793	Stephen Murray O'Brien	1	13	0	2
—	794	Richard Starke	1	13	0	2
—	795	Grace Elizabeth Wesston	4	52	0	10
—	796	Ann Smith	7	59	4	7
—	797	Richard Wesston Nanton	3	39	0	7
—	798	Ann Dyett	5	65	1	0
—	799	Mary Athill	24	357	0	0
	800	(No Claim or Return)	—	—		
23 Nov. 1835	801	Maria Wheeler	1	13	0	2
—	802	Eliz. M. Langford Coull	6	78	1	3
—	803	John Furlonge	16	161	17	11
—	804	Mary Watkins Green & Frances Margaret Green	3	17	16	0
—	805	Margaret Hamson	5	65	15	7
—	806	William Wyke & Edward Byam Wyke	5	67	19	3
4 April 1836	807	Sarah Taylor	7	80	9	2
23 Nov. 1835	808	Hester Macsween & Catherine Macsween	2	26	0	5
—	809	John Shiell	3	39	0	7
—	810	Rebecca Bean	5	43	16	5
21 Dec. 1835	811	Daniel Wesston	1	13	0	2
31 July 1837	812	The Hon. Ann Byam Stapleton, widow	12	156	2	6
	813	(Double Return by Error. See No. 798)	5	—		
23 Nov. 1835	814	Jane Bruce	1	25	15	7
—	815	Anne Armstrong, widow	2	26	0	5
—	816	Letitia Scarville	1	13	0	2
—	817	Owen Pell	6	60	16	5
—	818	Mary Ann West	2	15	8	1
18 Jan. 1836	819	Martha Maria Harman	5	81	16	2
	820	(Litigated Claim)	6	—		
23 Nov. 1835	821	Thomas Kippin	10	98	5	2
10 Dec. 1835	822	Margaret Watts	3	39	0	7
	823	(Remains for Adjudication)	2	—		
1 Feb. 1836	824	Thomas Kippin	6	56	16	8
23 Nov. 1835	825	Thomas Kippin	1	13	0	2
3 Dec. 1836	826	Daniel H. O. Gordon	8	104	1	8
23 Nov. 1835	827	Elizabeth Craig	3	39	0	7
—	828	George Scotland	4	64	16	3
14 Dec. 1835	829	Maria Hughes	1	13	0	2
23 Nov. 1835	830	John Adams Wood	2	26	0	5
	831	(Litigated Claim)	11	—		
7 May 1836	832	Samuel Lucas Bourne	5	65	1	0
23 Nov. 1835	833	Mary H. Nibbs	6	69	8	8
—	834	Margaret Baily	4	28	8	5
	835	(Litigated Claim)	7	—		
14 Dec. 1835	836	Sarah Bertie	2	26	0	5
23 Nov. 1835	837	Jessie Thwaites	1	26	0	7
23 Jan. 1836	838	Rose Philips	2	26	0	4
23 Nov. 1835	839	Mary Este & Charlotte Este	1	13	0	2
—	840	William Patterson	2	27	9	6
	841	(No Claim or Return)	—	—		
23 Nov. 1835	842	Caroline Augusta M'Intosh	10	108	17	6
—	843	Sophia Otto Norman	7	93	19	1
—	844	Charlotte M'Carthy	1	13	0	2
—	845	William Este	7	59	4	7
—	846	Jane M'Kie	1	13	0	2
—	847	Nathaniel S. Wood	3	39	0	7
—	848	Nathaniel S. Wood & Mary Ann Wood	3	28	8	4

Date of Award.	Number of Claim.	Name of Party to whom the Payment is awarded.	Number of Slaves.	Sum. £	s.	d.
23 Nov. 1835	849	Rebecca Jackson	1	13	0	2
—	850	James M Kie	4	64	16	3
—	851	Eliza Lynch	2	15	8	1
18 Jan. 1836	852	Regan Higgins	5	55	17	10
23 Nov. 1835	853	William Robinson	1	25	15	7
—	854	Ann Sherman	4	52	0	10
—	855	William Lynch	4	52	0	10
—	856	Thomas Warwick Hyndman	5	107	2	10
—	857	Mary Aird	5	31	10	11
—	858	Mary Cumming, widow	4	52	15	4
—	859	Francis Crichton	1	16	19	11
16 Jan. 1836	860	Peter Ferris Mercier & Ferris Ferris Mercier	1	13	0	2
23 Nov. 1835	861	Sophia F. Mercier	1	13	0	2
—	862	William Johnstone	4	64	16	3
—	863	Geo. Wright Mardenborough	3	17	16	0
—	864	John Richardson	1	16	19	11
15 Feb. 1836	865	John Fleming & Ann Fleming his wife	3	43	14	11
23 Nov. 1835	866	Mary Dorothy Mainwaring	2	26	0	5
—	867	Robert Peddie	2	26	0	5
—	868	John Adams Wood	1	13	0	2
—	869	John Adams Wood	2	26	0	5
—	870	Catherine Pyle	4	52	15	4
—	871	John Adams Wood	3	39	0	7
—	872	John Adams Wood	6	57	11	2
—	873	Ann Jackson Rosco	2	26	0	5
16 Jan. 1836	874	Thomas Smith	7	103	0	9
23 Nov. 1836	875	Frances S. Pitt	4	60	0	4
—	876	Margaret Pearson	6	93	14	4
	877	(Litigated Claim)	12	—		
16 April 1836	878	Thomas Pratt & Eliza Pratt	8	135	15	11
23 Nov. 1835	879	Thomas Pratt	1	13	0	2
—	880	Eliza Pratt	1	13	0	2
—	881	Sarah Trusted Reynolds	2	15	8	1
—	882	Elizabeth Lynch & Mary Lynch	1	13	0	2
—	883	Edward Wesston	5	54	8	9
29 Feb. 1836	884	Edward Wesston	1	16	19	11
23 Nov. 1835	885	Mary Mackie	4	52	0	10
—	886	Ann Sarah Ryan	4	52	0	10
—	887	John Robert M'Guire	7	78	15	11
15 Feb. 1836	888	Francis W. Robinson	1	13	0	2
	889	Francis W. Robinson	3	47	0	2
14 Dec. 1836	890	Thomas Bunch	1	13	0	2
	891	(No Claim or Return)	—	—		
	892	(No Claim or Return)	—	—		
	893	(Double Return by Error. See No. 213)	8	—		
23 Nov. 1835	894	John Halliday	1	13	0	2
—	895	John Bradshaw & Samuel M. Richards	1	25	15	7
11 Jan. 1836	896	Julia Kysh & Margaret Haruey Kysh	3	39	15	2
	897	(No Claim or Return)	—	—		
23 Nov. 1836	898	Sophia Playfair	3	39	0	7
1 Feb. 1836	899	Giles S. Musson	5	81	16	2
23 Nov. 1836	900	William R. Jones	1	13	0	2
14 Dec. 1835	901	Giles S. Musson	1	13	0	2
30 Nov. 1835	902	Ann M'Causland	5	54	8	9
—	903	Francis J. Jones	1	13	0	2
—	904	Abraham Roach	4	52	15	4
—	905	Grace Rolland	3	28	8	4
—	906	Jane Mackay	8	97	9	1
—	907	The Rev. John Cox Collins	2	15	8	1
—	908	William Roberts	5	54	8	9
14 Dec. 1835	909	Aspasia Merrick	7	104	11	5
—	910	John Bradshaw & Samuel M. Richards	4	56	0	7
30 Nov. 1835	911	Robert M'Donald	1	13	0	2
—	912	Mary Ann Nelson	3	39	0	7
—	913	Thomas Sanderson	1	13	0	2
—	914	Elizabeth Millett	4	53	9	11
—	915	Samuel Gore	10	113	11	10
—	916	John O'Brien	1	13	14	9
—	917	William B. Pigott	11	127	9	5
—	918	Edward Morgan	6	70	7	2
—	919	Alexander M'Dowal	1	13	0	2
—	920	John Page	7	80	9	2
—	921	Otho Hamilton Wemyss	2	15	8	1
14 Dec. 1835	922	Mary Ann Thibou *alias* Mary Ann Marchant	6	57	11	2
14 Mar. 1836	923	John Rose	13	126	13	6
30 Nov. 1835	924	Charlotte M'Connell	8	104	1	8
15 Feb. 1836	925	Walter Price	14	152	9	2
30 Nov. 1835	926	Charles Robertson	1	13	0	2
14 Dec. 1835	927	John Bradshaw & Samuel M. Richards	8	72	19	4
30 Nov. 1835	928	Charles Robertson	4	20	3	11
—	929A	Rebecca Nanton	8	69	17	0
—	929B	John Bradshaw & Samuel M. Richards	5	82	4	2
	930	(Litigated Claim)	16	—		
30 Nov. 1835	931	Anna Stevens Royall	6	91	11	2
—	932	John Adams Wood	2	26	0	5
—	933	Hannah Clark	8	88	5	11
—	934	Eleanor D. Robinson, widow	1	13	0	2
—	935	Charles Robertson	6	80	18	11
—	936	Mary Ann Leonard Rochester	5	67	4	8
—	937	William Boyd, jun.	1	13	0	2
—	938	Joseph E. Philip	8	72	4	9
—	939	Paul Horsford Malone	7	91	1	5
—	940	James Douglass	14	159	19	7
—	941	William Morrin	1	13	0	2
—	942	Thomas W. Martin	1	13	0	2
—	943	Eliza Seaton	3	28	8	4
—	944	Frances Jane Symes	7	91	1	5
—	945	James Bird	3	28	8	4
—	946	James Thibou	9	184	18	8
—	947	John Hurst	1	13	0	2
—	948	Jane Tyley	3	39	0	7
—	949	Jane Middleton	1	13	0	2
—	950	Rich. Burroughs Eldridge	6	68	3	6
	951	(No Claim or Return)	—	—		
30 Nov. 1835	952	Rachel Wilkinson	1	13	0	2

Date of Award.	Number of Claim.	Name of Party to whom the Payment is awarded.	Number of Slaves.	Sum. £	s.	d.
30 Nov. 1835	953	Rachel Wilkinson	2	13	0	3
—	954	John Adams Wood	4	52	15	4
—	955	Sarah Moore	2	26	0	5
20 Aug. 1836	956	Sarah Blizard Phillips	1	13	0	2
30 Nov. 1835	957	Rich. Burroughs Eldridge	1	13	0	2
—	958	Rich. Burroughs Eldridge	3	51	16	0
—	959	James Pritchard	1	16	19	11
—	960	John M'Guire	5	33	4	2
—	961	George T. Metcalfe	5	43	16	5
—	962	Eliza Grace Amelia Williams	1	13	0	2
—	963	Sarah Bailey Williams	10	108	17	6
—	964	James John M'Nemara	3	43	14	11
—	965	Sarah M'Carty	2	33	19	11
—	966	Rachel M'Carty	1	13	0	2
—	967	Robert Orr	1	13	0	2
27 June 1836	968	William Macnish, A. Colquhoun Macnish, & Jane Macnish	3	39	0	7
30 Nov. 1835	969	Elizabeth Pittman	7	73	16	7
—	970	Eliza Ann Ronan	13	166	12	2
—	971	John Adams Wood	1	16	19	11
—	972	John Joseph Ronan	7	63	4	4
—	973	John Joseph Ronan	12	185	15	11
—	974	Mary Donovan	2	26	0	5
—	975	Pinkey M'Dougall	2	15	8	1
—	976	Elvira Rolland	4	52	0	10
—	977	Charles Russell Martin	1	13	0	2
—	978	Charles Murray	2	51	11	3
—	979	Margaret Watson	1	13	0	2
—	980A	Sophia Nanton	6	56	0	10
—	980B	John Bradshaw & Samuel M. Richards	3	49	7	8
—	981	Margaret Roach	1	13	0	2
—	982	Jane Roach	4	54	3	11
—	983	John Adams Wood	1	16	19	11
—	984	Elizabeth Thibou	3	28	8	4
—	985	William Steel	13	233	11	4
—	986	Maria Scotland	2	15	8	1
—	987	Thomas M'Coard	12	288	13	8
	988	(Double Return by error. See No. 849)	1	—		
30 Nov. 1835	989	John M'Hugo	4	30	16	3
—	990	Anna Underwood	1	13	14	9
—	991	Mary Mulcare	2	26	14	11
—	992	Margaret Maynard	1	13	0	2
—	993	John Robertson	1	25	15	7
—	994	Richard Pigott	1	16	19	11
—	995	Ann M'Connell	1	13	0	2
—	996	Jane Tenant	4	64	16	3
—	997	Jane Hart	5	58	8	6
—	998	Samuel M. Richards	3	39	0	7
—	999	Ann Robins	11	187	18	2
—	1000	Thomas Hoggard	7	141	18	5
7 Dec. 1835	1001	John Hoggard	5	43	16	5
	1002	(Litigated Claim)	5	—		
7 Dec. 1835	1003	John Hoggard	20	232	1	10
—	1004	Mary Sandiford Richards	4	52	0	10
—	1005	William Harney	4	60	0	4
—	1006	John Adams Wood	8	143	17	6
—	1007	John Tibner	3	39	0	7
—	1008	John H. Brinn	4	41	8	6
—	1009	Alexander William M'Nish, John M'Nish, & Brodie George M'Nish	15	143	10	9
—	1010	Hannah Whitlock	8	102	2	2
—	1011	Francis Byam Ottley	13	184	5	4
—	1012	John Bradshaw & Samuel M. Richards	1	13	0	2
—	1013	Brodie George M'Nish	1	25	15	7
—	1014	Arthur Rogers	1	16	19	11
—	1015	Mary Ann Allan	19	212	6	9
23 Jan. 1836	1016	Walter Cox	5	39	15	4
7 Dec. 1835	1017	Walter Cox	5	65	1	0
—	1018	Sarah Aska	2	26	0	5
—	1019	James Boyd	2	15	8	1
—	1020	Elizabeth Hodge	2	33	19	11
—	1021	Catherine Boyd	9	129	17	3
—	1022	Owen Pell	1	25	15	7
—	1023	Elizabeth Adney	1	13	0	2
—	1024	Rebecca Chatfield	16	235	17	0
14 Dec. 1835	1025	Elizabeth Symes	3	39	0	7
7 Dec. 1835	1026	Eleanor Sarah Bascome	2	26	0	5
—	1027	George R. Burn, Margaret Burn, Eliza Burn, & Isabella Burn	1	25	15	7
—	1028	Eleanor Sarah Bascome	5	116	2	8
—	1029	Eliza Murray	8	130	7	0
—	1030	Mary M'Lellan & Francis M'Lellan	9	108	12	8
	1031	(Paid into Court)	184	—		
7 Dec. 1835	1032	Mary Osbiston & Grace Sheriff	17	199	2	0
	1033	Mary Manning	3	53	0	8
	1034					
	1035					
	1036					
	1037	(No Claims or Returns)	—	—		
	1038					
	1039					
	1040					
7 Dec. 1835	1041	John Billinghurst	59	1085	1	5
—	1042	Freeman Thomas	180	2535	8	9
11 July 1836	1043	Eliza M. Donaldson	1	19	16	3
	1044	(Litigated Claim)	250	—		
	1045	(Litigated Claim)	113	—		
7 Dec. 1835	1046	John Adams Wood	18	352	2	3
—	1047	Rowland Edward Williams	183	2565	1	3
—	1048	Susannah Glover	6	68	3	6
—	1049	John Bradshaw & Samuel Misson Richards	2	26	0	5
—	1050	William Burnthorn, Esq., & The Hon. G. Savage Martin	11	190	19	8
	1051	(Litigated Claim)	24	—		
7 Dec. 1835	1052	John Bradshaw & Samuel M. Richards	1	25	5	7
—	1053	Grace Nanton	2	26	0	5
—	1054	Joseph Bailey Wilkinson	2	39	12	6
—	1055	Lucy Elscoe	2	26	0	5

Date of Award.	Number of Claim.	Name of Party to whom the Payment is awarded.	Number of Slaves.	Sum. £ s. d.
7 Dec. 1835	1056	William N. Eldridge	2	30 0 2
	1057	(Litigated Claim)	8	—
7 Dec. 1835	1058	John Ogilvie	4	65 12 11
—	1059	Anne Murray	6	116 6 9
—	1060	Henry Nanton Murray	1	21 11 7
—	1061	Elsey Bagnold	1	19 16 3
—	1062	William Ronan	5	85 9 2
—	1063	Mary Benjamin	2	22 4 2
14 Dec. 1835	1064	Anna Maria Bladen	6	61 4 11
7 Dec. 1835	1065	Christiana Ann Keen	7	95 16 8
—	1066	Eliza Murray	15	240 4 4
—	1067	William Eyre Odlum	8	144 18 0
—	1068	William B. Wyke	2	57 4 4
—	1069	Thomas Sinister	1	13 0 2
—	1070	Langford Lovell Hodge	42	711 8 0
—	1071	Ann Daniell	5	55 8 9
—	1072	William Bertie Wolseley	11	159 3 3
11 June 1836	1073	James H. Donovan	1	13 0 2
7 Dec. 1835	1074	Charles Cheshire	4	64 16 3
19 Dec. 1835	1075	Thomas Osborn	2	45 11 10
29 Feb. 1835	1076	Robert Brereton	2	39 12 6

LITIGATED CLAIMS

Ordered by the House of Commons to be Printed 16th March 1838. Paper 215.

List C.

Date of Adjudication and Award.	Number of Claim.	Name of Party to whom the Payment is awarded.	£ s. d.	Sum. £ s. d.	Number of Slaves.
2 May 1836	1	Kean Brown Osborn		1803 0 8	100
10 Oct. 1836	11A	Rich. Trench & R. E. Williams	926 1 11		
27 Nov. 1837	11B	J. Thompson	713 7 5		
		J. Thompson, the interest on £496 5*s.* 3*d.*, & James Cavan & J. M'Kellar the principal sum of	496 5 3	2135 14 7	112
16 Jan. 1837	21	William Dunbar & Charles Henry O'Key	861 18 7	861 18 7	66
	23	James Hammer Baker		327 19 5	13
10 Oct. 1836	24	George Savage Martin		1842 17 7	124
		C. Richardson	1082 3 7		
24 Oct. 1836	30	Thomas Ward, John Athill, The Rev. Alex. Scott, & Thos. Redding	2666 13 4		
		Hard. Earle & J. H. Turner	445 15 8		
		With the interest on the whole.		4194 12 7	276
10 Oct. 1836	35	Samuel Boddington	450 0 0		
		Sam. Boddington & Rich. Davis	1164 0 8		
		George Cotsford Call & William Alex. Mackinnon	2307 13 7		
		Edward Thomas Cardale	20 7 10		
		And the interest on the whole.		3942 2 1	276
	38	Benjamin Travers, Joseph Travers, William King, & Henry Jonas Barton		2482 16 2	199
6 Feb. 1837	42	Robert Grant		3353 12 4	235
23 Jan. 1836	46	John Adams Wood		2075 15 9	152
10 Oct. 1836	47	Ann Bean Walter, Jacob Daniel Walter, & Peter Philip Walter		738 7 1	46
1 May 1837	52	William Shand, and the interest thereon	527 2 0		
		Sarah W. Ledeatt	573 0 3		
		Chris. Owens	640 1 8		
		And the interest thereon; and also the interest on the above-mentioned sum of £573 0*s.* 3*d.*		1740 3 11	127
7 Aug. 1837	59	Owen Pell		1648 16 8	101
28 Nov. 1836	66	Henry Moreton Dyer		2272 8 4	160
26 June 1837	75A	Rob. Peddie	1043 15 6		
—	75B	S. Boddington, R. Davis, & T. Boddington the younger	707 11 1		
		And the interest on the whole.		1751 6 7	114
10 Oct. 1836	84	Sarah Masterson		1830 1 2	125
28 Nov. 1836	87	Joseph Liggins	64 17 5		
		Hardman Earle & J. H. Turner	943 15 2		
		And the interest on the whole.		1008 12 7	58
28 Mar. 1836	88	Robert Grant		2322 12 0	157
16 May 1836	91	John H. Doyle		1704 16 11	102
28 Nov. 1836	92	Henry Moreton Dyer		2238 2 3	133
28 Nov. 1836	94	Thomas Brown		1877 19 3	116
7 Aug. 1837	95A	Nich. Kirwan	951 12 2		
—	95B	George Betts	1031 4 4		
—	95C	S. Boddington, Rich. Davis, & T. Boddington, junior	872 0 0	2854 16 6	225
17 Oct. 1836	102	Ann Bean Walter, Jacob Daniel Walter, & Peter Philip Walter		2980 6 2	199
13 Feb. 1836	103	J. Trecothick, junior, & J. H. Roper	1428 9 5½		
28 Mar. 1836	103	Lang Redwood	1428 9 5½	2856 18 11	197
21 Nov. 1836	111	Michael White	190 14 0		
		E. Montgomerie	278 10 0		
		C. M. Montgomerie & T. M. Montgomerie	1751 4 11		
		And the interest on the whole.		2220 8 11	145
24 Oct. 1836	114	Mary Weston	2159 14 1	2159 14 1	144
28 Mar. 1836	116	William Buruthorn		1137 15 6	56
23 Jan. 1836	120	John Adams Wood		716 13 10	42
1 May 1837	125	Thos. F. Nibbs	624 11 8		
		Hen. M. Dyer	2349 4 3	2973 15 11	184
31 Oct. 1836	127	Mary Weston		40 0 6	3
28 Nov. 1836	128	C. Wollaston	769 12 7		
		Wm Shand	828 10 8		
		Wm Musgrave	787 19 1	2386 2 4	160

Date of Adjudication and Award.	Number of Claim.	Name of Party to whom the Payment is awarded.	£ s. d.	Sum. £ s. d.	Number of Slaves.
13 June 1836	131	Nathaniel Gilbert		2401 2 11	159
28 Mar. 1836	145	John Bradshaw & Sam. Misson Richards		30 0 2	2
28 Nov. 1836	196	James Gilchrist		91 1 5	7
—	232	Margaret Dunlop Nicolls		26 14 11	2
27 Feb. 1837	256	Sarah Gillan		219 11 7	17
—	257	Nevile Reid & John Dixon		889 10 1	73
1 May 1837	260	John Jameson		391 6 2	54
23 Jan. 1836	265	Hard. Earle & J. H. Turner	2373 12 7½		
		Charles Turner	2373 12 7½		
				4747 5 3	331
28 Mar. 1836	266	Norborne Thompson & Henry Shepherd Pearson		4236 3 7	274
27 Feb. 1837	268	Thomas Daniel & John Daniel		3171 3 4	213
27 Feb. 1837	270	Ab. F. Favey	48 2 7		
		Sam. Nelson	29 0 4		
		R. H. Mason	22 9 0		
		John M'Kie, W. Graham, & W. Croil	252 2 1		
		John Ahile	372 17 10		
		John Jones	32 6 5		
		J. Jamieson & John Ramsey	37 10 4		
		Wm Shand	565 13 2		
		E. Y. Walcott & G. L. Wilder	678 0 3		
		And the interest on the whole.		2038 2 0	146
4 April 1836	281	Mary Russell		2301 15 3	161
9 May 1836	282	John Hoggard		1691 11 10	114
1 May 1837	283	Anne Byam Hill		2753 17 10	199
27 Feb. 1837	285	Geo. Horsford	523 9 6		
		Sam. Nelson	252 0 10		
		John Athile	168 1 5		
				943 11 9	71
6 Nov. 1837	287A	H. S. Papps, C. G. Gloyne, & Geo. S. Papps	167 16 10		
—	287B	Mathew Lowry	39 17 0		
—	287C	Frances M'Kie	61 0 10		
		And the interest on the whole.		268 14 8	22
13 June 1836	307	Wm. H. Slater	13 14 9		
		Wm. H. Slater	59 8 10		
				73 3 7	4
23 Jan. 1836	310	Thomas Daniel & John Daniel		2728 15 9	
13 Nov. 1837	324	J. C. Strode, W. A. Johnson, The Rev. J. Kirby, & The Rev. H. Kirby	2226 5 0		
		C. H. Strode	726 5 0		
		John Vernon	1953 15 5		
		And the interest on the whole.		4906 5 5	329
13 Feb. 1836	331	Andrew Colville & Alexander Seton		1115 2 9	72
27 Jan. 1836	333	Æneas Barkly, Henry Davidson, & William Davidson		2087 18 6	144
4 July 1836	337	Tryphania White		779 13 7	43
1 May 1837	350	Hard. Earle & J. H. Turner	3000 0 0		
		A. Gunthorpe & J. Gunthorpe	922 3 0		
		And the interest on the whole.		3922 3 0	297
5 June 1837	351	Wm. Shand	3336 13 10		
		Sam. Warner	337 19 3		
				3674 13 1	246
27 Feb. 1837	353	Nevile Reid & John Dixon		5168 19 4	395
5 June 1836	354	William Shand		4128 14 6	264
23 Jan. 1836	355	Marmaduke Robinson		4303 3 1	303
28 Mar. 1836	359	Hugh O'Connor & Edward Moore		2399 1 4	171
15 May 1837	360	James Tresothick, jun., William Kelso, jun., William Martin, & Archibald Kelso		2063 10 5	135
14 Nov. 1836	362	Hardman Earle & John H. Turner		2158 12 0	159
24 April 1837	363	The Hon. Anne Byam Stapleton & The Right Hon. Lord James O'Bryen, The Hon. Hercules Robert Pakenham, Robert Hitchens, & William Hitchens		2919 14 8	217
10 Oct. 1836	365	George Savage Martin		1246 18 11	81
12 Mar. 1836	377A	William Shand	470 19 10		
20 June 1836	377B	John Allen	613 19 10		
				1084 19 8	73
15 May 1837	387	J. V. Purrier, E. Purrier, & Thos. Purrier, and the interest thereon	346 3 9		
		Mary Johnson	665 0 0		
		J. B. Darvall & Hen. V. Tebbs	2450 13 9		
		And the interest thereon; and also the interest on the above £665.		3461 17 6	264
27 Feb. 1837	391	Samuel Nelson		2866 11 9	153
28 Mar. 1837	392	Henry Raper, Peter Laugford Brooke, & Thos. D. Broughton		2306 18 3	159
27 Feb. 1837	397	J. Liggins	642 1 8		
		N. S. Chauncey	3883 6 0		
		And the interest on the whole.		4525 7 8	325
9 May 1836	423	Barnard Alexander		35 4 4	3
26 June 1837	466	Joseph Ablett		111 5 0	8
27 Nov. 1837	486	J. Bradshaw & S. M. Richards	45 9 4		
		Ann Latham	1192 18 10		
		And the interest thereon, together with the interest on the above sum of £45 9*s.* 4*d.*			
		R. B. Eldridge, and the interest thereon	66 17 9		
		J. Liggins, and the interest thereon	147 11 6		
				1452 17 5	105
27 Nov. 1837	487A	John Bradshaw & Samuel Misson Richards		85 11 6	176
28 Mar. 1836	498	Mary Weston		497 16 8	25
26 June 1837	516	Mary Weston, widow		79 0 9	4
18 April 1836	553	Montague Main. Cumming		39 0 7	3
5 June 1837	554	Samuel Watts & Robert Horsford, one moiety; Samuel Watts & Margaret his wife, the other moiety		498 9 3	35
— Jan. 1836	560	Wm. Southey & Rich. Molineux	142 17 8		
		Steph. Lewis & John M'Rae	15 9 4		
		And the interest on the whole.		158 7 0	8
—	592	John Bradshaw		91 16 0	7
26 June 1837	627	Paul Horsford		224 6 0	18
28 Mar. 1836	644	John R. Harvey		15 8 1	2
23 Jan. 1836	653	Ann Byam Hill		175 14 0	14
—	728	Henrietta Dallas		193 19 2	10
26 June 1837	747	Robert Tait		100 13 1	11
24 Oct. 1836	820	James Gilchrist		56 16 8	6
26 June 1837	831	James Gilchrist		144 11 5	11
12 Mar. 1836	835	William Shand		118 19 10	7
9 May 1836	877	Mary Scotland		149 2 5	12
4 April 1836	930	Martin Nanton		200 8 8	16

Date of Adjudication and Award.	Number of Claim.	Name of Party to whom the Payment is awarded.	Sum. £	s.	d.	Number of Slaves.
28 Mar. 1836	1002	John Bradshaw & Samuel Misson Richards	43	16	5	5
23 Jan. 1836	1004	Marmaduke Robinson	3589	15	1	250
26 June 1837	1045	William Fraser, William Maxwell Alexander, Claud Neilson, & Boyd Alexander	1681	4	1	113
16 Jan. 1837	1051	Mary Grant Gordon	412	7	6	24

LIST D.

Date of Adjudication and Award.	Number of Claim.	Name of Party to whom the Payment is awarded.	Sum. £	s.	d.	Number of Slaves.
28 Mar. 1836	97	Pulsford v. Elwin	4103	18	7	254
	98		3483	2	11	235
8 Feb. 1836	106	Lyne v. Thompson	702	5	2	41
11 Jan. 1836	1031	Ravenscroft v. Frisby	2918	2	9	184

LIST E.

Date of Adjudication and Award.	Number of Claim.	Name of Party to whom the Payment is awarded.	Sum. £	s.	d.	Number of Slaves.
	339	Samuel Warner	1832	9	7	—
	349	Samuel Warner	2834	18	7	—

CAPTAINS-GENERAL AND GOVERNORS-IN-CHIEF OF ALL THE CARIBBEE ISLANDS OF THE PROVINCE OF CARLIOLA.

Sir Thomas Warner, Knt.; commission dated 13 Sep. 1625; knighted 21 Sep. 1629; appointed sole Governor of St. Kitts under the Earl of Carlile 29 Sep. 1629; re-commissioned by the Earl of Warwick 24 Nov. 1643; died at St. Kitts 10 March 1648.

Francis, Lord Willoughby of Parham; received a patent from the Earl of Carlile for 21 years from 17 Feb. 1646-7; removed by Parliament 1651-2; re-commissioned by Charles II. 23 June 1660; drowned at sea 4 Aug. 1666. Portrait in 'England's Champions.'

William, Lord Willoughby of Parham, younger brother of Francis; commissioned 3 Jan. 1666-7; on the subdivision of the Government in 1670 became Governor of the Windward Group, and died at Barbados 10 April 1673.

CAPTAINS-GENERAL AND GOVERNORS-IN-CHIEF OF THE LEEWARD CARIBBEE ISLANDS.

General Sir Charles Wheler, 2nd Bart.; commissioned 25 Jan. 1670-71; of Martin Hussingtree, co. Worcester; Colonel of a regiment of foot; M.P. for Cambridge University, and died 26 Aug. 1686.

General Sir William Stapleton, Bart.; commissioned 10 Feb. 1671-2 *vice* Wheler recalled; was re-appointed Deputy-Governor of Montserrat 24 Feb. 1670-71; created Bart. 20 Dec. 1679; died at Paris Aug. 1686.

Sir Nathaniel Johnson, Knt.; appointed 7 Aug. 1686 *vice* Stapleton deceased; had been knighted 28 Dec. 1680; Governor of South Carolina 1705.

Lieut.-General Christopher Codrington; appointed about Aug. 1689 *vice* Johnson; had been President of Barbados 1668—72, and was still a Member of Council there in 1688, aged 48; died at Antigua 20 July 1698.

Colonel Christopher Codrington, son and heir of the preceding; appointed 25 March 1698-9; Colonel of the 1st Guards; recalled 3 Dec. 1703; born 1668 at Barbados, where he died 7 April 1710. Portrait at All Souls', Oxon.

Sir William Mathew, Knt.; patent dated 26 Jan. 1703-4 *vice* Codrington recalled; served at the siege of Namur 1695; Colonel of Monk's Regiment and Brigadier-General of the Guards 1702; knighted 23 March 1703-4; died at Antigua 4 Dec. 1704.

Colonel Daniel Parke; appointed 25 April 1705 *vice* Mathew deceased; had been M.P. for Whitechurch, co. Hants; served as A.D.C. to the Duke of Marlborough in 1704; killed at St. John's 7 Dec. 1710, aged 41. Portraits in Virginia.

Major Walter Douglas; appointed 29 March 1711 *vice* Parke deceased; recalled 1714. Governor Douglas had been tried by the Court of Queen's Bench and found guilty of bribery and extortion, having exacted £10,000 from the Island of Antigua before publishing the Queen's pardon. He was sentenced to a £500 fine and five years' imprisonment, and was then in the King's Bench Prison. His fine was remitted. (Treasury Papers, 1718, June 19.)

Lieut.-General Walter Hamilton; appointed 23 Aug. 1715 *vice* Douglas superseded; served as a Captain in Sir T. Thornhill's Barbados Regiment in 1689; will dated 16 April 1722, and proved 22 Feb. following.

Colonel John Hart; appointed 9 May 1721 *vice* Hamilton; had been Governor of Maryland 1714—20; Governor of Fort St. George, and died Dec. 1740.

Thomas Pitt, Earl of Londonderry, second son of Governor Thomas Pitt; appointed 2 June 1727 *vice* Hart (? recalled); Colonel of Horse 1714; created Baron of Londonderry 1719 and Earl 1726; died at St. Kitts 12 Sep. 1729.

[Colonel William Cosby's appointment was published 29 April 1731, but it was subsequently cancelled on his being made Governor of New York Jan. 1732.]

Lieut.-General William Mathew, third son of Sir William Mathew, who was Governor in 1704; appointed 13 Sep. 1732; Colonel of the Coldstreams and Brigadier-General; served as second in command under Lord Peterborough in the Peninsula; had been appointed Lieut.-Governor of Nevis and St. Kitts 19 Dec. 1721; died 14 Aug. 1752 at Antigua.

Sir George Thomas, Bart., a native of Antigua; appointed 25 Jan. 1752-3 *vice* Mathew deceased; had previously served nine years as Governor of Pennsylvania; created Bart. 6 Sep. 1766; resigned 18 Dec. 1766; died in London 31 Dec. 1773, aged 79. Portrait at Ratton.

William Woodley, a native of St. Kitts; appointed Oct. 1766 *vice* Thomas, resigned.

Sir Ralph Payne, K.B., a native of St. Kitts; appointed 10 May 1771 *vice* Woodley; resigned 17 Feb. 1776; M.P. for Plympton 1762 and Shaftesbury 1769; K.B. 1771; created an Irish Peer as Baron Lavington of Lavington 1 Oct. 1795; Privy Councillor 1799. See later.

William Mathew Burt; appointed 31 Oct. 1776 *vice* Payne resigned; was a Member of Council of his native island St. Kitts 1755; died 27 Jan. 1781 at St. John's.

General Sir Thomas Shirley, Bart.; appointed 4 April 1781 *vice* Burt, deceased; had been Lieut.-Governor of Dominica; created Bart. 27 June 1786; resigned about May 1791; died at Bath 1800, aged 72.

William Woodley; re-appointed 21 Sep. 1791 *vice* Shirley resigned; died at St. Kitts 2 June 1793. (See 'Gent. Mag.,' p. 768.)

Major-General Charles Leigh; appointed about Sep. 1794; quitted the island on 3 July 1796.

Sir Ralph Payne, Lord Lavington; re-appointed 20 Jan. 1799 *vice* Leigh; died at Antigua 3 Aug. 1807, aged 68.

Hugh Elliot; appointed Sep. 1808; formerly Minister to Sicily; recalled about Nov. 1813.

General Sir James Leith, K.B.; appointed Feb. 1814 *vice* Elliot, K.B., 1813; died 16 Oct. 1816.

Lieut.-General George W. Ramsay; appointed March 1816 Governor of Antigua, Barbuda, and Montserrat only; died 1 Nov. 1819, and was buried on the 4th at St. John's, aged 57.

Major-General Sir Benjamin D'Urban, K.C.B., K.C.H., and C.T.S.; appointed 22 Jan. 1820 *vice* Ramsay deceased; recalled 1826; Governor of British Guiana 1831.

Major-General Sir Patrick Ross, K.C.M.G.; born 26 Jan. 1778; appointed 1826 *vice* D'Urban. He was Governor 1 July 1832. [See his pedigree in Burke's 'Landed Gentry.']

Sir Evan John Murray McGregor, Bart., C.B., K.C.H.; appointed about 1832 over Antigua, Barbuda, Montserrat, and Dominica; Governor 1833-4.

Sir William McBean George Colebrooke; appointed about 1837; returned to England 1840; Governor of Barbados 1852.

Lieut.-Colonel Sir Charles Augustus Fitzroy, K.C.B., K.C.H., second son of Charles, 3rd Duke of Grafton; appointed 1842; later Governor of New South Wales; born 10 June 1796; died 16 Feb. 1858.

Sir James Macaulay Higginson, K.C.B., 1846—50; Governor of Mauritius 1851—7; died 1885; married secondly, 1854, Olivia Nichola, first daughter of Conway Richard Dobbs of Castle Dobbs, Antrim, who survives.

Robert James Mackintosh, 1850.

Ker Baillie Hamilton, C.B., 1855.

Colonel Sir Stephen John Hill, K.C.M.G., C.B., 1863—9; Captain 2nd West India Regiment 1842; Governor of Gold Coast 1851—4; Governor of Sierra Leone 1854—62; of Newfoundland 1869—76; C.B. 1860; K.C.M.G. 1874; born 10 June 1809 and died 20 Oct. 1891 in Sutherland Avenue, Maida Vale, aged 82. He married firstly, 30 Nov. 1829, Sarah Anne, daughter of William Vesey Munnings, Chief Justice of the Bahamas, and secondly, 3 Aug. 1871, Louisa Gordon, daughter of Chief Justice Shiell of Antigua.

Sir Benjamin Chilly Campbell Pine, K.C.M.G., son of Benjamin C. Pine of Tunbridge Wells, 1869—73; B.A. Trinity College, Cambridge, 1834; Barrister-at-Law Gray's Inn 1841; Lieut.-Governor Natal 1849—56; Governor Gold Coast 1856—9; Lieut.-Governor St. Kitts 1859—68; Governor West Australia 1868-9; Lieut.-Governor Natal 1873—5; knighted 1856; K.C.M.G. 1871; born 1813; died in London 25 Feb. 1891; married firstly, in 1841, Elizabeth (died 1847), daughter of John Campbell of Lochhead, co. Argyll; secondly, 1859, Margaretta Anne, daughter of Colonel John Simpson.

Sir George Berkeley, K.C.M.G., first son of General Sackville H. Berkeley, Oct. 1874—81; Colonial Secretary of Honduras 1845; Lieut.-Governor of St. Vincent 1864; Governor of West Africa Settlements 1873, etc.; born at Barbados 2 Nov. 1819; B.A. Trinity College, Dublin, 1842; living 1894, a bachelor.

Captain Sir John Hawley Glover, R.N., G.C.M.G., 1881—3; entered the Navy 1841; Captain 1878; Colonial Secretary Lagos 1864; G.C.M.G. 1874 for service at Ashanti; Governor Newfoundland 1875—81 and again 1883; died 1885; married, 1876, Elizabeth Rosetta, first daughter of William James Butler Scott of Anns Grove Abbey, Queen's County, who survives.

Sir Charles Cameron Lees, K.C.M.G., 1883—5, son of Sir John Campbell Lees, Chief Justice of the Bahamas; born 1837; entered the Army 1854 and retired 1866; Governor of Labuan 1879; the Bahamas 1881—3; Barbados 1885—9; Mauritius 1889—93; and of British Guiana since 1893; married, 1875, Maria, daughter of Sir Oliver Nugent of Antigua.

Viscount Gormanston, 1885—8; born 1837; succeeded his father as 14th Viscount 1876; Governor of British Guiana 1888—93, and of Tasmania since 1893.

Sir William Frederick Haynes Smith, LL.D., K.C.M.G.; appointed 8 Nov. 1888; son of John Lucie Smith, LL.D.; Barrister-at-Law Middle Temple 1863; Solicitor-General of British Guiana 1865—74; Attorney-General 1874—7; K.C.M.G. 1890; transferred to Bahamas 6 Feb. 1895.

Sir Francis Fleming, K.C.M.G., 6 Feb. 1895.

COMMANDERS-IN-CHIEF OF THE LEEWARD ISLANDS DURING THE ABSENCE OF THE CAPTAIN-GENERAL AND GOVERNOR-IN-CHIEF.

NOTE.—With the exception of the first two, who were Presidents of Nevis, the following were all Presidents of St. Kitts.

James Virchild, 1 June 1766, on departure of Governor Thomas.

Richard Hawkshaw Losack, 3 July 1770, on departure of Governor William Woodley.

Major John Johnson,* Brevet-Colonel of the Enniskillings 4 Dec. 1704—14 July 1706.

Daniel Smith, Esq., Dec. 1713.

Craister Greatheed, July 1775-6.

Anthony Johnson, 27 Jan. 1781, on death of Governor W. M. Burt.

John Nugent, 18 June 1788, on departure of Sir Thomas Shirley.

John Stanley, 2 June 1793, on death of Governor William Woodley.

Archibald Esdail, 3 July 1796, on departure of Major-General Charles Leigh; died 25 Sep. 1796, aged 61.

John S. Thomas, succeeded President Esdail; died 15 April 1797.

Robert Thompson, succeeded President Thomas; he was dismissed from the Council of St. Kitts 1 July 1802.

William Woodley, 1 Aug. 1807, on death of Lord Lavington.

James Tyson, 15 March 1809, on departure of William Woodley; died 7 Sep. 1809.

John Julius, Sep. 1809, on death of Tyson; also in Jan. 1814.

Henry Rawlins, 1815, during absence of Sir James Leith and President Julius.

* Treasury Papers 1702—7, C.I. No. 73, 1707, March 25. Report of Mr. William Blathwayt to Lord High Treasurer on the petition of Colonel Thomas Whetham for Mary the widow and relict of Major John Johnson, late Governor of Nevis, and sometime Commander-in-Chief of the Leeward Islands, praying for payment of his salary. He was Chief Governor of those Islands from 4 Dec. 1704 (the day of the death of Sir William Mathew) to 14 July 1706 (the day of the arrival of Governor Park), and was barbarously murdered while these islands were invaded by the French, and his affairs left in the utmost distraction.

B. T. Montserrat, No. 1, 1706, Nov. 23. John Pogson, Esq., Member of Council for St. Christopher's, had been tried for the death of Colonel John Johnson, Esq., Lieut.-Governor of Nevis, and Commander-in-Chief of the Leeward Islands. He was acquitted by the Jury, but fled from the island. His wife petitioned the Governor on his behalf. [He had killed Johnson in a duel.]

LIEUT.-GOVERNORS AND PRESIDENTS OF THE COUNCIL.

NOTE.—The Lieut.-Governor was appointed by patent and drew £200 a year; the President was only the senior Member of Council, and unpaid till later times.

Captain Edward Warner, 1635, is stated to have founded the colony under his father Sir Thomas.
Major Henry Huncks, 1638, the fourth year of the colony; appointed by the Earl of Carlile; Governor of Barbados 1640.
Captain Rowland Thompson, 1641.
Captain Henry Ashton,* 1644—50. See Colonel H. Tillyer's will of 1649.
Sir Sydenham Poyntz, 1650.
Colonel Christopher Keynell; appointed 1653 by Sir George Ayscue under Parliament; displaced 1660.
Colonel Robert Carden, 1660.
Colonel John Buncle, 1661; killed 1667 in the attack on St. Christopher's.
Colonel Robert Carden, 1664, *vice* Buncle, dismissed; killed 1666-7.
Colonel Daniel Fitch, Dec. 1666, under Lieut.-General Henry Willoughby *vice* Carden, a French prisoner.
Lieut.-General Henry Willoughby, 1666—9, Governor of Antigua, Barbuda, and Anguilla, for his uncle Lord Willoughby; died about 1670.
Captain Samuel Winthrop, 1668; displaced by Sir Charles Wheeler 1671 for being a Quaker.
Colonel William Byam, 1669-70. Perhaps acting only during the absence of Warner; died between 7 June 1670 and 3 Jan. following.
Colonel Philip Warner, 1669—77; dismissed by the King 1677; died 23 Oct. 1689.
Colonel Rowland Williams, *pro tem.* 1674-5-6; Deputy-Governor in 1690-91; died July 1713.
Colonel James Vaughan, 1678-9.
Colonel Valentine Russell, 1680.
Paul Lee, 10 Oct. 1682.
Colonel Edward Powell, June 1683, Lieut.-Governor.
John Parry, 1692.
John Yeamans,† Lieut.-Governor, 1698—1711.
Colonel John Hamilton, 1709.
Edward Byam, Lieut.-Governor, *vice* Yeamans, 1711—37 or later.
Nathaniel Crump, 1735.
Lieut.-Colonel George Lucas, Lieut.-Governor 9 Nov. 1743; died a prisoner at Brest 11 Jan. 1747.
Josiah Martin, April 1743—8.
David Monroe, Lieut.-Governor; died Nov. 1749 (see 'Gent. Mag.').
Charles Dunbar, 12 April 1750.
Colonel John Gunthorpe, *circa* 1750; died 26 Nov. 1754.
Colonel John Tomlinson, March 1753; died 20 Sep. 1753.
Andrew Lessly, April 1753—9—60.
Rt. Hon. Francis, 3rd Lord Hawley, Lieut.-Governor, 1755; died Sep. 1772.
Lieut.-General Sir James Adolphus Oughton, K.C.B., Lieut.-Governor 18 Dec. 1772 *vice* Hawley, deceased.
Thomas Jarvis, 1770-1—6—83.
Edward Otto-Baijer, 1776.
Edward Byam, 7 April 1789—1804.
Thomas Norbury Kerby; died 1819.
Samuel Warner, *pro tem.*, 1831-3-4-5.
Home Meade Daniell, M.D., 1842—52.
Sir William Byam, 1853; knighted 1859; died 1869.

* Colonel Ashton, a Royalist, was hanged, drawn, and quartered in London 7 July 1658. (Smith's 'Obituary,' p. 47.)

† Treasury Papers, XCV., 1705, July 4. Report of Mr. William Blathwayt to the Lord High Treasurer on the petition of John Yeamans, Esq., that he is entitled to his salary of £200 a year as Lieut.-Governor of Antigua by his patent dated 1 Anne, 7 Sep. 1702.

SPEAKERS OF ANTIGUA.

Thomas Compton, 11 April 1668, 1687-8, 1688.
Jeremiah Watkins, 15 Sep. 1668, 28 Oct. 1669.
Samuel Irish, 14 Aug. 1672.
Thomas Mallett, May 1674.
Richard Borraston, 1675, 9 Feb. 1676.
William Barnes, 6 Nov. 1678.
Philip Warner, 15 July 1679.
John Vernon, 24 May 1682.
John Yeamans, 1683.
Cæsar Rodney, 28 Oct. 1684.
Richard Ayres, 7 April 1687.
George Symes, 1688.
Samuel Martin, 13 Feb. 1689.
John Lucas, 21 July 1692, 10 Oct. 1696.
William Barnes, 1693, 10 May 1694.
George Gamble, 1 Sep. 1697, 22 Dec. 1698, 1699, 1700-1, 28 June 1704.
Peter Lee, 28 June 1702.
Richard Oliver, 14 March 1704-5, 1706, 1707.
Nathaniel Crump, 1708, 1710, 1711.
Samuel Watkins, 1711.
George Lucas, 17 July 1712, 1713, 1714, 1715.
Archibald Cochran, 12 Nov. 1715.
Ashton Warner, 3 May 1716, 1717, 1718, 1719, 1721-22, 1723, 1724, 1725, 1726, 1729, 1730, 1732.
Samuel Martin, 27 Aug. 1728.
George Thomas, 11 Dec. 1728.
Thomas Kerby, 1734, 1736.
Stephen Blizard, 1738 to 1750.
Samuel Martin, 1750 to 1763.
Nathaniel Gilbert, 1763 to 1769.
Thomas Warner, 1769 to 1777.
Rowland Burton, 1777 to 1785.
John Burke, 1785 to 1788.
Thomas Freeman, 1788 to 1793.
James Athill, 1793 to 1803.
John Taylor, 1803 to 1810.
Samuel Warner, 1810.
Paul Horsford, 1814.
T. Sanderson, 1842.
Dr. Nicholas Nugent, 1831, 1835; died 1843.
James Watson Sheriff, 1845.
Sir Oliver Nugent, 1858.
Thomas D. Foot.
Henry Ogilvie Bennett.

The following served as Deputy-Speakers *pro tem.*

Thomas Warner, 1760.
John Lyons, 1773.
George Leonard, 1775 and 1778.
Thomas Daniell, 1780.
Philip Hicks, 1785.
John Taylor, 1795.
John Burke, 1798.
Oliver Yeamans Ash, June 1803.

CHIEF JUSTICES OF THE COURT OF KING'S BENCH AND COMMON PLEAS.

This Court was established by Act of March 1689. It consisted of a Chief Justice and four Assistant-Justices.

John Yeamans, 1699-1700.
Peter Lee, 1702.
Colonel George Gamble, 1703-4.
John Lucas, Dec. 1705.
Samuel Watkins, 13 Sep. 1706.
Lieut.-Governor John Yeamans, 16 Feb. 1708-9.
John Gamble, 25 Feb. 1715-16.
Samuel Watkins, 20 Feb. 1716-17, *vice* Gamble, resigned.

Samuel Watkins, 15 Feb. 1739-40.

William Lavington, 26 Jan. 1745-6.

Stephen Blizard, 29 May 1750, *vice* Lavington, resigned.

Thomas Jarvis, about 1776, *vice* Blizard, deceased; died 18 Dec. 1785.

Rowland Burton, 7 June 1786; called to the Bar 1772.

James Athill, 28 April 1814, *vice* Burton, deceased: patent dated 7 Aug.

Paul Horsford.

Richard Weston Nanton, 1842; died May 1844, æt. 60.

John Sheil, March 1846; died 6 Sep. 1847.

Sir Robert Marsh Horsford, K.C.B., March 1848—56; died May 1875, æt. 76.

Sir William Snagg, 1856—68, *vice* Horsford, retired: son of William Snagg of St. Vincent: called to the Bar by Middle Temple 1829; Attorney-General of Grenada 1847: knighted July 1859; Chief Justice of British Guiana 1868—78; died 17 April 1878, aged 71, at Clevelands, Demerara; married firstly, in 1838, Ann, daughter of John Turner, who died 1861; secondly, in 1865, Adeline, daughter of Charles H. Okey, Puisne Judge of Antigua; thirdly, in 1876, Constance Marian, daughter of late Major John Larkins of the Bengal Artillery.

Arthur Peel, M.A. Oxford 1852; of the Inner Temple 1852; died 15 Oct. 1873, æt. 46.

Sir William Doyle *vice* Peel, *circa* 1876.

Sir George Anderson *vice* Doyle.

Sir John Gorrie, Knt., 1885-6, *vice* Anderson; Chief Justice of Trinidad 1888; dead.

Sir Henry Ludlow, D.C.L., Knt., 1887-8, *vice* Gorrie.

Sir Henry Thomas Wrenfordsley, Knt., 1892, *vice* Ludlow.

JUDGES OF THE COURT OF VICE-ADMIRALTY.

Ashton Warner, 1727.

Robert Arbuthnot, 26 April 1729.

Stephen Blizard, 26 Nov. 1729.

Benjamin King, 27 May 1748.

Robert Christian.

Edward Byam, 30 Sep. 1776, *vice* Robert Christian, deceased: still acting 1809.

R. W. Nanton, 1842.

REGISTRARS OF THE SAME COURT OR NAVAL OFFICERS.

Colonel Rowland Williams, May 1691, "clerk of the navy."

John Brett, 6 June 1704.

John Floyer, 20 Dec. 1717. John Booth, Deputy.

Edward Perrie, 23 July 1744.

Captain Anthony James Pye Molloy, R.N.; died 25 July 1814, æt. 68. Hastings Elwin, Deputy.

John William Molloy, Barrister-at-Law, succeeded his father Oct. 1814.

S. Harman, 1842.

MASTERS AND EXAMINERS IN COURT OF CHANCERY.

Walter Quarme, appointed 29 Nov. 1703.

Charles Daly, sworn 8 June 1708.

Thomas Gateward, sworn 27 Nov. 1710.

George Jennings, sworn 14 Jan. 1711.

William Johnson, sworn 3 Jan. 1725-6.

George Jennings, sworn 25 March 1729.

John Watkins, sworn 26 Feb. 1759.

James Scotland.

John Gray, 1787—92.

James Athill, 1809.

Hon. John Gray and R. B. Eldridge, 1852.

Octavius Humphrys, 1891.

TREASURERS AND COLLECTORS OF THE IMPOST.

This office was established on 15 Sep. 1668.

Richard Belcher. In April 1673 styled "late treasurer of St John's precincts."

Samuel Martin, 1693.

Colonel George Gamble, 1705.

Joseph French, 1706.

Nathaniel Crump, 2 July 1711, *vice* French.

George Lucas, 3 March 1717-18, *vice* Crump.

Thomas Kerby, 1723.

George Byam, 20 Sep. 1726, *vice* Kerby, resigned.

William Byam, 20 Dec. 1734, *vice* Byam, deceased.

Ashton Warner, 1743.

William Horne, resigns 9 June 1756.

Daniel Warner, 9 June 1756, *vice* Horne, resigned.

William Warner, 17 April 1760, *vice* Warner.

Edward Byam, 31 Oct. 1771—92, *vice* Warner, deceased.

Thomas Norbury Kerby, 1809—16.

Anthony Musgrave, M.D., 1825—52.

Henry Berkeley, 1871—76, or later.

SECRETARY-GENERALS OF THE LEEWARD ISLANDS.

NOTE.—This office was held by patent from the Crown.

Thomas Weaver, 1691.

Thomas Fernley.

John Palmer, patent dated 11 Jan. 3 Mary, *vice* Fernley, deceased; dismissed 11 Feb. 1696-7.

Edward Parsons, patent dated 22 Feb. 9 William III. during pleasure, *vice* Palmer.

Henry Carpenter of Nevis, appointed 27 Nov. 1701, 13 William III., *vice* Parsons, deceased.

George Larkin, 1703.

Hon. Charles Finch, 31 March 1704, *vice* Larkin.

Charles Hedges, Jan. 1714-15, *vice* Finch.

John Knight of Gosfield, co. Essex, Dec. 1718, *vice* Hedges, resigned.

Wavell Smith, Oct. 1722, *vice* Knight, resigned; died 1756.

Robert Aberdein, before 1809.

Samuel Bates Ferris, June 1815, *vice* Aberdein, dismissed.

James Le Marchant, April 1814; dismissed same year. "Mr. Oswald the late patentee."

Thomas Lane, 1842—52; he signed as Secretary in 1833.

Edwin Donald Baines, superannuated Feb. 1883 after many years' service.

Neale Porter, C.M.G., 1883—87, or later.

Frederick Evans, C.M.G., 1889—95; transferred Feb. 1895 to Jamaica.

George Melville, C.M.G., 1895.

SECRETARIES OF ANTIGUA.

NOTE.—This office was sublet by the Secretary-General for an annual sum.

Benjamin Langham, 1649.

Francis Sampson, 1668.

Captain Francis St. John, 1669.

John Parry, 1671.

Edward Maynard, styled 15 Dec. 1674 the "late secretary."

George Towes, Deputy-Secretary 1673.

William Barnes, Deputy-Secretary 1673.

William Blakey, 1674—76; gave receipt to Barnes for records 30 Jan. 1674.

John Lachaisnaye, 1676.

Lewis Mayon, 1677; named in the will of Roger Jones.

John Ley, 1680.

Acquila Stoughton, 1680; signs on 8 March.

Ebenezer Kyrtland, sen., 1680; signs patent on 14 Oct.

Thomas Gateward, 1693-4.
Robert Amory, 1695.
Francis Sampson, 1700.
. . . . Cherret, 1705-6.
Thomas Kerby, 1707—10.
Nathaniel Browne, 1713.
Giles Thayer of Gray's Inn, 8 Feb. 1714-15.
Gilbert Fleming, 1719 and 1726.
James Smith, 1723.
Patrick Wilson, 1733-4.
Delacourt Walsh, 1738.
Edward Gamble, 1740.
Nathaniel Gilbert, 1744; attests will of John Goodall.
Thomas Oliver, 1760.
William Atkinson, 1764—72.
John Wilkins, 1773-4.
George William Jordan, 1776—79.
John Hardcastle, 1780—89.
William Mathews, 1789—1804, or later.
R. W. Nanton, 1809.

ATTORNEY-GENERALS OF THE LEEWARD ISLANDS.

Archibald Hutchison, 1687-8, of the Middle Temple, Barrister-at-Law, later M.P., aged 61 in 1722. Will dated 22 July and proved 15 Aug. 1740. (227 Browne.)
William Brodrick, 16 Jan. 1704.
Nicholas Nicholls, patent dated 9 Aug. 1704.
Herbert Pember, 1706—10.
Thomas Bretton, 12 July 1711.
Ashton Warner, 1716-17.
Harry Webb, 21 June 1754.
Thomas Walker, 16 Feb. 1757, *vice* Webb, resigned.
Thomas Warner, 6 Nov. 1758, *vice* Walker, deceased; died 1779, æt. 63.
William Leslie Hamilton, 3 June 1779, *vice* Warner, deceased.
John Stanley, 4 April 1781, *vice* Hamilton, deceased; later M.P.
John Burke, 11 June 1799, *vice* Stanley, deceased; of Gray's Inn, Barrister-at-Law 28 Jan. 1765; Solicitor-General 14 years; died Oct. 1821, aged 75.
Paul Horsford, 1815—20, or later.
Richard Musgrave, 1824.
William Lee, 1842.
Robert Marsh Horsford, 1846-7.
Hon. James Watson Sheriff, 1848—56; resigned 1856.
Robert ffrench Sheriff, 1874—77; called to the Bar, Inner Temple, 1862.
Sir Henry Burford-Hancock, 1877.
John Tankerville Goldney.
C. R. Tyser, 1877—79.
Stephen Herbert Gatty, 1885—87; ditto of Trinidad, 1888.
Thomas Baines, 1889, *vice* Tyser, retired.
Sir Charles George Walpole, M.A., *vice* Baines; born 7 Sep. 1848; called to the Bar, Inner Temple, 1873; only son of late Charles Walpole, C.B.

SOLICITOR-GENERALS OF THE LEEWARD ISLANDS.

T. Cottle, 20 March 1761.
. . . . Joddrell.
John Stanley, 11 May 1771, *vice* Joddrell, deceased.
Charles Winstone, 4 Oct. 1781.
John Burke, 9 April 1785.
Thomas Tuckett, 11 June 1799, *vice* Burke.
John Stephen, 17 Oct. 1800, *vice* Tuckett, deceased; born 1770; later Judge of Supreme Court, N.S. Wales; died in Sydney 21 Dec. 1833.
William Anthony Mardenbrough, 1803.
John Woodley, 8 Sep. 1807, *vice* Mardenbrough, deceased; Barrister-at-Law.
Sir Robert Marsh Horsford, 1825—46.
James Watson Sheriff, 1846—48.
John Rawlins Semper.
Thomas Woodcock, 1871.
Henry Spencer Berkeley, June 1878, 1886, 1887.
M. Berkeley, 1886-7.
Thomas Baines, 1888-9, *vice* Berkeley.
Charles Halman Beard, 1889, *vice* Baines.

PROVOST-MARSHAL-GENERALS OF THE LEEWARD ISLANDS.

This office was held by patent from the Crown.

Garret Cotter,* patent for three lives dated 9 March 28 Charles II.; confirmed 2 Aug. 31 Charles II.
Thomas Belchamber. Will dated 23 May and sworn 12 Aug. 1693.
William Barnes, patent dated 27 Jan. 1693-4, *vice* Belchamber, deceased, during pleasure.
John Perrie, patent dated 16 April 8 William III., *vice* Barnes, deceased, during pleasure; confirmed 1 Anne; still acting March 1710-11.
Henry Douglas, presents his patent 3 Feb. 1711-12.
Patrick Crawford, commission dated 29 July 1723.
William Janssen,† Nov. 1736, *vice* Crawford, resigned.
Richard Phelps, 1768.
John Pownall, patent dated 7 June 1771, 11 George III., for him and his two sons J. L. Pownall and G. Pownall, *vice* Phelps. He was born 1720, eldest son and heir of William Pownall, and elder brother of Thomas Pownall, Governor of Massachusetts.
John Lillingston Pownall, 1809; succeeded his father.
Sir George Pownall, Knt., succeeded his brother; died at Brighton 17 Oct. 1834, aged 79.
O. Wood, 1842.

PROVOST-MARSHALS OF ANTIGUA.

This office was held under the Provost-Marshal-General.

Captain Renatus Enys, took the oaths 13 Sep. 1671; died intestate. Adm'on 5 May 1673.
George Towes, died intestate. Adm'on 4 Dec. 1674.
James Phipps, 1677.
Henry Symes, 8 March 1680.
John Gunthorp, 1680.
Geffry Duncombe, Jan. 1703—June 1705.
Richard Oglethorpe, 1708—April 1711.
John Parke, appointed 8 March 1710-11.
Arthur Dabron, Feb. 1712-13—1723.
Colonel Edward Jessup, 1731.
Alexander Crawford, 1750.
Edward Warner, 15 Jan. 1754.
Samuel H. Warner, 1764—71.
John Rose, 1778—86.
Robert Clogstown, 1786—98.
John Roberts, 1798—1802 and 1809.

* On 11 Nov. 1689 was read the opinion of H.M. Attorney-General of England that Charles II., in 1679, granted to Garrett Cotter the office of Secretary and Marshal of the Leeward Islands during the lives of Captain James Cotter and Mary his wife, and James Cotter his nephew. Mary Cotter, and James Cotter the nephew, and Garrett Cotter are dead. Captain James Cotter is a papist and a rebel, and the patent may be revoked.

† Younger brother of Sir Stephen Theodore Janssen, Bart., Lord Mayor and Chamberlain of London.

William Collins, 1802—1804.
Martin Nanton, Deputy-Provost-Marshal, 1831.
Captain George Lowen, died 4 Jan. 1838.
Oswald Charles Wood, M.D., died 5 Nov. 1842.
Joseph L. Bindon, 1852.
Octavius Humphrys, since Dec. 1873.

REGISTRARS.

This office was established by Local Act of 13 April 1668.

Samuel Winthrop, 1667.
Colonel Rowland Williams, 16 Jan. 1671, *vice* Winthrop.
Robert Phillips, Deputy-Registrar, July 1676.
Edward Perrie, 1704.
John Booth, 14 Jan. 1711.
Captain Henry Symes.
Giles Watkins, 16 July 1714, *vice* Symes, deceased.
John Watkins, Deputy-Registrar, 24 Aug. 1730.
Edward Gamble, 19 Aug. 1762, *vice* Watkins, deceased.
Rowland Burton, 7 June 1786—1809, or later.
Thomas Scotland, 1825.
John Furlonge, M.D., 1852.
Octavius Humphrys, since Dec. 1873.

RECEIVERS AND COLLECTORS OF THE 4½ PER CENT. DUTY.

Colonel John Strode, Governor of Dover Castle, was granted 7 years' lease by patent dated 9 Sep. 22 Charles II., and appointed as his deputy :
Joseph Martin of London, 19 Dec. 1672, who appointed as his sub-collector :
Major Thomas Mallet of Antigua, 11 Feb. 1673-4.
Henry Bolton, 1697.
Richard Buckeridge, 1705.* The codicil to his will dated 19 Dec. 1715 and sworn 9 March following.
Hopefor Bendall, 25 Feb. 1715-16 ; died 28 Oct. 1728.
James Arbuthnot, 10 Jan. 1729-30, *vice* H. Bendall, deceased. ('Historical Register,' p. 8.)
James Gregory, Jan. 1743, *vice* Arbuthnot, deceased.
Henry Eyre, Feb. 1746, *vice* Gregory.
Hon. Charles Dunbar was probably patentee.
William Patterson, 1750, *vice* Dunbar, deprived.
John Halliday, 1759.
Samuel Martin, 1777, *vice* Halliday, resigned.
Josiah Martin, July 1795, *vice* Martin, superannuated; born 1772 ; died 1849.
Samuel Auchinleck, died 1808, æt. 76.
H. Trew, 1842 ; Collector of the Customs.

COLONIAL AGENTS IN LONDON.

This office was settled by Act of 22 Dec. 1698.

William Barnes, appointed Feb. 1683-4.
Richard Cary, merchant ; one of the four Commissioners for the Leeward Islands 1691—93 ; Agent 1702 ; died 25 Jan. 1726, aged 78.
Sir John St. Leger, Knt., 1712, 1713.
Archibald Hutchison, Barrister-at-Law, M.P., *vice* St. Leger. He was Attorney-General 1687-8.
Nathaniel Carpenter, jun., 8 Nov. 1715 for two years by Local Act.
William Nevine, 11 July 1716.
Ashton Warner, 10 March 1719-20, *vice* Nevine.
John Yeamans, 15 Dec. 1727 ; resigned in 1743 after 16 years' service.
Thomas Kerby of Mincing Lane, merchant, 10 April 1744, *vice* Yeamans. Will proved 14 April 1748.

* 1710-11. Jan. 26. Richard Buckeridge, Collector of the Customs, petitions for leave to go to London. Mr. James Fayerweather as his deputy. Edward Perrie, Esq., Surveyor of the Customs, is expected from Barbados.

John Sharpe of Lincoln's Inn, Solicitor to the Treasury, M.P. Callington, co. Cornwall, was paid £800 as four years' salary 22 July 1754 ; died 18 Oct. 1756. Will dated 29 Sep. 1756. (311 Glazier.)
Henry Wilmot of Gray's Inn, Solicitor, 4 Jan. 1757, *vice* Sharpe, deceased ; died 3 Aug. 1794, aged 84 (see Morris Pedigree). Was still Agent in 1765.
William Salmond, 1775-6.
Alexander Willock, merchant, and John Burton, jointly, 1784.
William Hutchinson, 5 June 1786, *vice* Willock, resigned. He was a nephew of Governor Sir Thomas Shirley, Bart.
Anthony Brown, 1833.
Nicholas Nugent, M.D., 1842 ; Devonshire Street, Portland Place.

SURVEYOR-GENERALS.

Captain Henry Nicholls.
Captain Gilbert Garrett.
Captain Archibald Cochran.
Gilbert Gregory.
Richard Harris.
Mordecay Rogers.
Robert Tremills.
Robert Martin, 1688. S.G.
Captain James Porter, 1708. S.G.
William Grear.
Edward Perrie, 25 July 1716.
John Teatte, 26 July 1717. S.G.
Gabriel Gamble, 1723. S.G.
Robert Baker, 1743 ; died 1756. S.G.
Samuel Byam.
John Rose, 16 Nov. 1786, *vice* Byam, deceased.
John Nicholas Beck, 1789.
Charles Chalmers, 1809.

CORONERS.

This officer had no salary, but was paid a certain sum for each inquest.

Benjamin Wickham, } 1693.
Samuel Hilder, }
Robert Oliver, died 1705.
Major Samuel Wickham, 1708.
Colonel Jeremiah Blizard, 1722.
Major William Grear, 1724.
Henry Symes, 1735—41.
Robert Baker, died 1756.
John Dick, 1769.
John Smith, jun., 28 July 1774.
Richard Bowman, 1784—92.
Paul Horsford, 1809—12.
Nathaniel Donaldson, 1812.
John Somers Martin, died 25 Aug. 1865, æt. 48.

POWDER OFFICERS OR COLLECTORS OF THE POWDER DUTY.

This office was established by Act of 9 Jan. 1676, which imposed a duty of 1 lb. of gunpowder per ton of shipping.

Major Philemon Bird, 30 Aug. 1693.
Captain Samuel Watkins, 9 Aug. 1704.
Major Thomas Long, 19 Aug. 1708, *vice* Watkins, deceased.
John Brett, 20 Oct. 1710, *vice* Long, deceased.
Colonel Samuel Watkins, acting as such 5 April 1711, and has charge of the forts.
Colonel George Lucas.
Main Swete, 21 Nov. 1715, *vice* Lucas.
George Thomas, 5 Nov. 1716.

Henry Warner, 10 Jan. 1722.
William Smith, 9 Oct. 1731.
Hon. John Gunthorpe, 10 Nov. 1752.
George Thomas, 22 Oct. 1753, *vice* Gunthorpe, deceased.
Hon. James Emra, 19 March 1753.
Samuel Byam.
John Rose, 16 Nov. 1786, *vice* Samuel Byam, deceased.
Edward Jones, 1809.

Close Roll, 25 Geo. II., Part 5, No. 6.

Indenture made the 10th Oct. 1751 between John Forster (son and heir of Samuel Forster of North Seaton, Northumberland, yeoman, deceased, who was brother of the whole blood and heir-at-law to John Forster, late of the town of St. John, Antigua, carpenter, deceased, which said John Forster, party hereto, is residuary devisee and legatee of the said John Forster, deceased), of the one part, and Thomas Warner, late of Antigua, but now of Great Britain, Esq., of the other part. Whereas John Forster, deceased, made his will the 28th June 1733, and gave to his eldest son living at his death all his estate, real and personal, in Antigua, Great Britain, or elsewhere, and if no son to his eldest daughter, and if no daughter, gave to his dear and loving wife Helena Forster his house and wharfs in Wapping Street in the town of St. John wherein he then dwelt, and the use of his household furniture for life, if his widow, and gave her dower from all residue, and at her death or marriage gave the said legacies and all his houses, etc., in St. Mary's Street in the town of St. John, then in the tenure and occupation of Mr. William Gerrish, merchant, and all residue, to his loving brother Samuel Forster of the town of Widdrington in the parish of Woodburn, Northumberland, Gentleman, for life, together with all negro slaves, cattle, and horses, and at the death of Samuel gave all to John and Joseph Forster (two sons of Samuel) equally for ever, or to the survivors; and whereas John Forster, deceased, left no issue, so that Samuel Forster became entitled to the real estate, and Samuel Forster is now dead, and John Forster is become entitled to the real estate in tail general, and by survivor of his brother Joseph, and he is desirous of barring all estates tail and remainders. Now this Indenture witnesseth that in pursuance thereof, and in consideration of 5s., John Forster grants, etc., to Thomas Warner all plantations, etc., of which John Forster, deceased, his uncle, was seised and possessed, to have and to hold to the use of John Forster.

Close Roll, 10 Geo. III.

Indenture tripartite made the 14th March 1770 between William Wood and John Trevanion of London, merchants, of the 1st part, Charles Payne Sharpe, late of St. Vincent's, but now of Bloomsbury Square, Esq., and Paulina Joddrell Sharpe his wife, of the 2nd part, and George Hooper of Rotherhithe, merchant, of the 3rd part. Whereas by Indentures of Lease and Release in St. Vincent's dated the beginning of the year 1766 between Charles Payne Sharpe, of the one part, and William Wood and John Trevanion, of the other part, the former conveyed to the latter and their heirs for ever the several plantations, etc., hereinafter mentioned for securing payment of £1000, and of all other moneys that might be advanced by William Wood and John Trevanion for his use, with interest at 6 per cent., on the 1st June 1768 (the said Indentures supposed to be now in the hands of Thomas Warner of Antigua, Esq.); and whereas the £1000 was not paid, whereby the said premises became absolutely theirs in law; and whereas they have since advanced and paid for Charles Payne Sharpe £4000 more, so that £5000 are due to them, all interest having been paid; and whereas George Hooper hath agreed to pay to William Wood and John Trevanion the said £5000. Now this Indenture witnesseth that in consideration of £5000 paid to William Wood and John Trevanion, and of £500 paid to Charles Payne Sharpe and Paulina Joddrell Sharpe his wife, they grant, etc., to George Hooper, in his actual possession now being, all that plantation in the parish of St. Andrew in St. Vincent's called Camden Park, containing 240 acres, and all that other plantation in the same parish, containing 150 acres, called Ladoux Plantation, adjoining to Camden Park, all which lands abutt N. on the lands of John Hunt, Esq., and Monsieur Guetelle, S. on the lands of Charles Payne Sharpe and of Thomas Ottley, Esq., and by the barracks, E. on the lands of Messrs. Payne and Burton and of Harry Alexander, Esq., and by impracticable mountains, and W. by the sea, together with 200 negros, etc., to George Hooper and his heirs for ever, but with the proviso that if Charles Payne Sharpe pays to George Hooper the £5000 on or before the 14th March 1771 the Indentures shall be void; and Charles Payne Sharpe appoints, etc., Harry Alexander of St. Vincent's, Esq., and Daniel Hooper, now going to Antigua, mariner, his Attorneys.

Close Roll, 11 Geo. III., Part 9, No. 2.

Indenture made the 17th May 1771 between William Peckham, late of Antigua, but now of London, Gentleman, and Sarah his wife (formerly wife and afterwards widow of John Rule, late of Antigua, shop-keeper, deceased), of the one part, and John Carruthers of Antigua, merchant, of the other part, witnesseth that in consideration of £122 2s. currency William Peckham and Sarah his wife grant to John Carruthers all that piece of land in the town of St. John, Antigua, E. and W. 55 feet and N. and S. 47 feet, bounded E. with the land of David Rainy, W. with a cross street leading from the east end of the Court House to Otto's pasture, N. with the land late of Margaret Bolan, widow, and S. with the land late of Thomas Shepherd, deceased, to have and to hold to John Carruthers and his heirs and assigns for ever; and lastly William Peckham and Sarah his wife constitute, etc., Thomas Warner of Antigua, Esq., and David Rainy and Edward Carlile of Antigua, merchants, their Attorneys. Hugh Wylie, Robert Martin, Thomas Scott, George Lowden, Elm Court, Middle Temple, witnesses.

Close Roll, 18 Geo. III., Part 8, No. 3.

Indenture made the 21st Oct. 1778 between William Tyssen of Cheshunt, Herts, Esq. (eldest and only surviving son and heir-at-law of Samuel Tyssen,* late of Hackney, Middlesex, Esq., by Sarah his wife, both deceased), of the one part, and Godfrey Kettle of Basinghall Street, Gentleman, of the other part. Whereas by virtue of the last will of Samuel Tyssen dated the 12th Aug. 1743 William Tyssen is seised to him and the heirs of his body of the plantation and lands, etc., hereinafter mentioned, remainder to testator's two daughters, Sarah, now Sarah Boddicott, widow, and Anna Maria Tyssen, in fee, and William Tyssen is desirous to bar the said estate tail and remainder or reversion expectant dependent thereon, and to settle the reversion and inheritance in fee simple in himself and his heirs. Now this Indenture witnesseth that for the purposes aforesaid, and in consideration of 10s., William Tyssen conveys to Godfrey Kettle all that plantation in the parish of Falmouth in Antigua, containing 250 acres, bounded N. by the lands now or late of Barry Tankard, Esq., E. by the lands now or late of Nathaniel Gale, S. by the lands now or late of Captain Isaac Horsford, and W. by the lands late of Mr. Thomas Kirby, and all slaves and cattle, in trust, to the use of William Tyssen and his heirs and assigns for ever; and he appoints Langford Lovell and James Athill of Antigua, Esquires, his Attorneys. Daniel Waldron of Basinghall Street, Samuel Moberly, clerk to Mr. Kettle, witnesses.

* 1776, May 17. Samuel Tyssen, Esq; at Hackney. ('Gent. Mag.,' p. 240.)

Close Roll, 26 Geo. III., Part 21, Nos. 13 and 14.

Indenture made the 20th Nov. 1786 between Joseph Hawkins, late of Antigua, but now of Belmont, near Uxbridge, Esq., and Elizabeth Hawkins his wife, of the one part, and John Long and Alexander Brodie of St. John's, Antigua, merchants, of the other part, witnesseth that in consideration of 5s. Joseph and Elizabeth Hawkins have bargained to John Long and Alexander Brodie all those several messuages or tenements, lands, etc., of Joseph Hawkins in the town of St. John's and elsewhere in Antigua, and all negros and other slaves whatsoever, to have and to hold for one whole year, etc., to the uses of an Indenture to bear date the day after these presents. Richard Hughes, Lincoln's Inn, I. J. Way, witnesses.

No. 13.

Indenture made the 21st Nov. 1786 between Joseph and Elizabeth Hawkins (as above), of the one part, and John Long and Alexander Bredie (as above), of the other part. Whereas Joseph Hawkins is seised of the inheritance in fee simple of several messuages, etc. (as above), and John Long and Alexander Brodie are his Attorneys for his real estate, but the general power already given them not being sufficient to enable them to act in and manage his estate, and he and Elizabeth being desirous that the negros should be sold, and that the messuages, etc., should be settled, in pursuance of their desire and in consideration of 10s. Joseph and Elizabeth Hawkins grant, etc., to John Long and Alexander Brodie (as above) in trust as to the real estate for Joseph Hawkins and his heirs, and as to the negros, etc., to sell, hire, or lett them out and to account for all the moneys to Joseph Hawkins.

Close Roll, 37 Geo. III., Part 10, No. 11.

Indenture made the 23rd Dec. 1797 between John Long of Crutched Friars, London, Esq., and Lidia his wife, of the one part, and Alexander Brodie of Antigua, planter, and William Gregory of Antigua, watchmaker, of the other part, witnesseth that to bar the right of dower of Lidia in the hereditaments hereinafter mentioned, and to enable John Long to dispose of them with greater facility and in consideration of 10s., John Long and Lidia his wife grant, etc., to Alexander Brodie and William Gregory all messuages, lands, etc., of John Long in the town of St. John, Antigua, in trust for John Long and his heirs and assigns for ever, and John Long constitutes Alexander Brodie and William Gregory his Attorneys for the absolute sale, and John Long and Lidia his wife constitute Robert McNish of Antigua, Esq., and John Troup of Antigua, Gentleman, their Attorneys to appear before the Secretary, etc. Ja. Cooper, Gray's Inn, Benjamin James Cooke, Commander of the ship "John and Thomas," of London, witnesses.

Close Roll, 41 Geo. III., Part 2, No. 12.

Indenture made the 6th Feb. 1801 between Henry Mitford of the town and county of Southampton, Captain R.N., and Louisa his wife, of the one part, and John Roberts, Gentleman, Deputy-Provost-Marshal of Antigua, of the other part, witnesseth that in consideration of £800 currency Henry Mitford and Louisa his wife grant to John Roberts and his heirs all that piece of land in St. George's Street in the town of St. John, Antigua, bounded E. by the lands of the heirs of John Buckley, deceased, W. by the lands of James Hay, deceased, N. by St. George's Street, and S. by the lands of John McConnell and Mrs. Jane Collins, together with the dwelling-house, and Henry Mitford and Louisa his wife constitute Daniel Hill the younger, merchant, and Oliver Yeomans Ash of Antigua, Esq., their Attorneys. John Woodcock, Lincoln's Inn, Charles Shadwell, his clerk, witnesses.

Close Roll, 47 Geo. III., Part 35, No. 13.

Indenture made the 16th Nov. 1807 between William Cook of the New Road in the parish of St. George's in the East, master mariner, and Elizabeth his wife, of the one part, and Margaret Pearson of Antigua, widow, of the other part, witnesseth that in consideration of £160 currency the former grant to the latter a negro slave Louisa and her mulatto child William, and they constitute Hugh Prackey (?) and Edward Rigg of Antigua their Attorneys.

Close Roll, 53 Geo. III., Part 6, No. 13.

Indenture made the 6th April 1813 between Lazarus Jones Venables, Esq., Alexander Forrest, and Richard Radcliffe, Gentlemen, all of Liverpool, Lancashire, of the one part, and John Tobin of Liverpool, merchant, and Henry Hunt of the same place, linendraper, of the other part. Whereas His Majesty's Commission made the 12th Feb. last past hath been issued against Isaac Thompson of Keeble Grove, near Whitehaven, Cumberland, merchant, carrying on business together with Joseph Thompson of Antigua, merchant, his co-partner in trade, directed to Lazarus Jones Venables, Alexander Forrest, and Richard Radcliffe, together with Henry Laurence, Esq., and John Litherland, Gentleman, and on due examination of witnesses, the said Commissioners have found that Isaac Thompson for several years past did follow the trade and business of a merchant in Antigua in co-partnership, and during all such time did endeavour to get his living as others of the same trade and business do, and the said Isaac Thompson did become indebted in £100 and upwards to Elizabeth Thompson of Liverpool, widow, and being so indebted did become a bankrupt to all intents and purposes before the date of the said Commission, and at a meeting to choose assignees the major part of the creditors did nominate John Tobin and Henry Hunt, and it was found that Isaac and Joseph Thompson were seised to them and their heirs or otherwise interested in or entitled to certain freehold estates in Antigua and other estate. Now this Indenture witnesseth that in consideration of 5s. the said Commissioners grant and set over to John Tobin and Henry Hunt all those freehold messuages, lands, tenements, etc., in Antigua or elsewhere, subject to such mortgages and incumbrances as may be thereon, in trust for the benefit of the creditors. J. Parry, clerk to Mr. Dawson, solicitor, Liverpool.

The following extracts have been made from such of the records of the earlier wills, etc., as now exist. Most of the old books of wills, etc., are in a deplorable condition; they have as a rule lost their covers, hundreds of pages are missing, and even some folios which are legible are so fragile from former exposure to damp that the paper falls to pieces on being turned over. The early records were always badly housed and kept, as may be seen by the Report made by a Committee of the Legislature in 1777. The later ones are at the present time well preserved, and are bound in volumes which stand in two large iron safes in the Court House.

I have endeavoured to tabulate the earliest series as follows:—

Liber A. 10 June 1668—1674; fos. 15—228.
B. 1674—1677; fos. 17—117 and 150—272.
C. 21 March 1678—4 Jan. 1680; fos. 1—318, complete.
D. 12 Feb. 1680—May 1681; fo. 8.
E. 1684—1686.
F. 1686—1696-7.
G. 21 June 1693—8 Dec. 1698; fos. 25—336.
H. 1699—1701.
I, J. 1702—1704; fo. 12.
K. 1704—1709.

Liber L. 1709—1711.
M. 1712—1714.
N. 1714—1716.
O. 1716—1718.
P. 1718—1719.
Q. 1719—1721.
R. 1721—1722.
S. Missing. This vol. existed in 1777.
T. 1724—1726.
U, V. 1724—1728.
W., X. } Missing. These vols. existed in 1777.
Y. 1729—1730.
Z. 1730; fos. 57—68.

The second series commenced with Liber A, 1732, B, 1733, etc.

In the succeeding series whole volumes are missing, and I could only discover wills for the following years:—

Feb. 1734—8 Feb. 1737, fos. 88—153; 1738—1741 and 1743, a few folios only; Sep. 1746, fos. 59—64; April 1747, fo. 71; March 1749-50, fo. 131; 1751—53; Book of Wills C, bound in parchment, 20 April 1756—25 April 1766, fos. 1—229; 1759, fo. 46 and 80—89; 1768, fo. 35; 1769, 1770, and 1775; 28 May 1781—24 April 1784, fos. 46—167; 5 May 1785, fo. 17; 1788, fos. 71 and 158—193; 1792, fos. 254—367; 1795, fo. 361; 22 May 1797—Dec. 1801, fos. 16—152; 1805, fo. 29; 4 Oct. 1806—1 March 1820, fos. 47—344; 1822, fos. 362—98; Dec. 1824.

Of the Chancery records there are some suits between 1717 and 1767, fos. 21—210.

William Ruinby. Will dated 10 Oct. 1670. To my son Jn° all Est., he to be Ex'or if my son W^m come to enjoy part of the Est. To my dau. Eliz. Griffin 20 acres in N. Sound near Betty's Hope Plantation. To Tho. Burgess as much land as he can manure for 6 years in the ground Pet. Ingram had, if he will instruct my son Jn° for that time. Thomas Dawson & Manns Ross Griffin, & tutors of my son Jn° till 21. To Richd Libburin 100 lbs. of tobacco for making this will. Witnessed by Peter Ingram, Jos. Parker. At a Court held by Hon. Colonel Philip Warner, Serjeant-Major, was sworn Peter Ingram 3 Jan. 1670.

Deposition of William Trappin, aged about 35, 7 March 1670, that John Phillpot said his wife should have his estate and then his children, and ye poor lame child to have 5000 lbs. extra. Recorded 9 March 1670. By Philip Warner, Nathaniel Clarke, and Rowland Williams.

Thomas Dawson of Antigua. Will dated 3 April 1671. To my wife Dorothy, my dau. Eliz. Dawson, & ye child my wife goes with, all my plantation & stock. To my mother-in-law Eliz. Cropper sufficient land to manure for 12 years, as also to my 2 brothers-in-law Robt & Jn° Jacob. To Stephen Cropper, son of Edward Cropper, 500 lbs. of tobacco if he go to school. To my friend Jn° Russell 1000 lbs. of tobacco. Towards building ye church in Falmouth 1000 lbs. of tobacco. To my sister-in-law Susannah Jacobs 1000 lbs. of tobacco. To my sister Eliz. Jacobs 500 lbs. of tobacco at her marriage. All residue to my wife Dorothy & appoint her sole Ex'trix. Jn° Parry & Wm Holland, Overseers & Guardians, & 200 lbs. of tobacco each. Witnessed by Thomas Cranfeild, Edward . . . ., John Parry. Sworn 12 April 1671. Recorded 26 April 1671.

1670, April 12. (P.C.C.) Mary Reade, widow and administratrix of Christopher Reade, late of Bristol, but in foreign parts defunct. Letter of Attorney appointing her friend James Knight of Bristol, cooper, to act for her. Deposition of Edward Cook, jun., before Roland Williams, Esq., J.P., 22 Dec. 1670, annexed.

1671, April 3. Warrant to Paul Lee and William Wainwright to value the estate of Captain Gilbert Gregory, deceased. Inventory = 16,779 lbs.

William Allin of Nevis, merchant. Letter of Attorney to Balthazer Mercer of Nevis, merchant, 8 Oct. 1670.

1670, Dec. 7. William Wrene of Cork, Chyrurgeon, Jane Morris of Cork, widow, Robert and George Rogers of Cork, merchants, their Letter of Attorney to Jonas Langford of Antigua, merchant, and John Berry of Cork, Chyrurgeon, to obtain sums from many debtors.

Thomas Griffin of Antigua, mason. Will dated 18 July 1671. All my estate to Mr Tho. Garrett & Dr Wm Jones. Witnessed by John FitzRandolph, Thomas Watres, who were sworn before Philip Warner on 27 July 1671.

On 11 Sep. 1671 Mr. Philip Steward, of the ship "Neptune" of Bristoll, makes his "protest against the seas and stormes for all damages, Prejudices, and Losses" incurred by the late storm in Falmouth Harbour on 9 Sep. last, when his said ship was forced ashore.

Letter of Attorney from John FitzRandolph, Gent., to John Parry, Gent., 27 June 1671.

George Rawlins of Antigua, planter. Will dated 25 Oct. 1671. To my godson Jas. Sharpe, son of Jn° Sharpe, 1000 lbs. of tobacco. All my plantation & negros to my friend & namesake Ann Rawlins, whom I appoint sole Ex'trix. To my friend M^r Jn° Parry 1000 lbs. of tobacco. Witnessed by John Parry, Thomas Parker, Roger Richard, who were sworn by ye Governor Philip Warner 13 Dec. 1671.

Letter of Attorney from David Arnett (partner with Abraham Henderson 1669) to Colonel Philip Warner and John Parry, Esq., 19 Dec. 1671. Witnessed by William Cornish, Edward Smith. Recorded 3 Feb. 1671.

Nuncupative will of Thomas Millier 6 Oct. 1671. All estate to Wm Townsend.

On 1 Feb. 1671 before John Parry, Chief Secretary of Antigua, Nathaniel Pyne, merchant, and Mr. John Warron, Master of the ship the "Patience" of Bridgewater, record the occurrence of a bad storm during their voyage from Madeira to Virginia. Recorded 3 Feb. 1671.

Captain Walter Leavens of Antigua, died intestate. Adm'on to Mrs. Catherine Leavens the widow 13 March 1671 by Governor Warner.

Nathaniel Jugne. Will dated 1 June 1670. Appoint my son Jn° Bacon & my friend Jn° Vorgan Ex'ors in Trust for my children. To my 2nd dau. Anne 30 acres in Nonsuch. All my household stuff to Anne, Rachel, & Sarah. To Anne ⅓ of the produce. To my 2 ys^t daus. Rachel & Sarah my dwelling house. My dau. Eliz^th. To my grandchild Nath. Bacon 1000 lbs. of tobacco. Witnessed by Richard Carter, Edmond Kennell. Sworn before William Byam, Esq., 25 June 1670. Recorded 20 March 1671.

Warrant from Colonel Philip Warner, Governor, dated 14th instant 21 March 1671, to audit the accounts between Jonas Langford and Daniel Ely, trustees to the estate of Robert Elliatt, deceased, and Captain James Carter and Mr. John Hall, now adm'ors of ye said estate. They find that 8000 lbs. of sugar are due to Jonas Langford and Daniel Ely. Signed by Nicholas Bayer, Henry Meyer, Edmund Hull. Recorded 28 March 1672.

Delamon Arundell of Plymouth, co. Devon, mercer. Letter of Attorney to Richard Kingston of Plymouth, mariner of the ship "Mary" of Plymouth, to receive all sums due from P. Jeff and Katherine Everdon, dated 24 Jan. 1661; proved 7 May 1672. Witnessed 3 Jan. 1671 by Edward Houper, Thomas Allen, John Webb, Nathaniel (?) Publicus, John Blake.

Thomas Short of Plymouth, co. Devon, mercer. Letter of Attorney for a bond dated 6 Oct. 1661, to seize lands under Brimstone Hill, St. Christopher's, which P. Jeff bought of Lieut. Thomas Hancock, Gent.

John Burill. Will dated 23 Feb. 1671. To my son Benj. my plantation & 1 negro. My wife Jane. To my dau. Sarah 1000 lbs. of Tobacco. My friend M^r Jn° Howard fefie in Trust. My dau. Rachel. All residue to my wife.

Witnessed by Christopher Rymer, John Bacon, who were sworn 4 May 1672 before Governor Philip Warner.

On 5 Aug. 1671 Archibald Cochran, Henry Newman, and William Atkinson appraise the estate of Thomas Griffin, deceased, by Warrant dated 4 Aug. They value it at 1655 lbs., as shewn by Mr. Thomas Garrett and Dr. William Joans the adm'ors.

1672, March 18. Warrant from Governor Philip Warner to appraise the estate of Captain Walter Lewins, deceased. Value returned 23,359 lbs. Signed by Lieut. Daniel Pello, Lieut. Daniel Michell, and Ensign John Austin. Sworn 2 July 1672.

1672, July 2. Debts due to Captain Richard Cowes and Co. from Mr. Roger Jones, 2158 lbs. Mr. William Procter 100 lbs. Mr. George Dowe (or Done) 280 lbs. Mr. Robert Link 100 lbs.

James Attkins, carpenter. Will dated 16 June 1672. To my mate Howell Jones 2000 lbs. All residue to Mr Jno Parry & appoint him Ex'or. Witnessed by William Coomes, William Walten. Recorded 20 July 1672.

Letter of Attorney from Nathaniel Pyne to Roger Jones 7 July 1672. Recorded 20 July 1672.

1666, April 3. Bond of Daniel Fitch to Robert Ruick, Gent., for 2000 lbs. of sugar. Witnessed by Christopher Ruick, William Johnson. Recorded 13 Aug. 1672.

Austin Miallson of Antigua. Will dated 19 Aug. 1672. All estate to W. Winifritt & appoint him Ex'or. Clothing & 1 homacco to my son Michell Miallson. Witnessed by Nicholas Brooke, Nathaniel Pello, who were sworn on 23 Sep. 1672 before Governor Philip Warner. Recorded 7 Sep. 1672.

Roger Seldon. Will dated 18 July 1672. To my son Rich. Seldon 10 acres in North Sound. To my daus. Eliz. Seldon & Mary Seldon 7 acres apiece. To my wife her thirds. Lt Peter Willcocks Ex'or. I sold 6 acres to Tho. Ledeatt. Witnessed by James Jones, John Mone, Math. Sulavan. By the Governor sworn 3 Sep. 1672. Recorded 7 Sep. 1672.

Mickell Bulger of Antigua. Will dated 19 Aug. 1672. To my wife Marg^t ½ my estate, the other ½ to my friend Tobias Buttler. To Wm Richards a suit of clothes, & my silver buttons to Teague Mathews. Tobias Buttler Ex'or. Witnessed by John Carney, Teague Mathews, Daniel Pellow. By Governor P. Warner sworn 3 Sep. 1672. Debts 260 lbs. Credits owing 703 lbs. Recorded 7 Sep. 1672.

William Townsing of Antigua. Will dated 17 Aug. 1672. To Rich. Ralph 1000 lbs. All residue to Jno Ward. Witnessed by Daniel Addams, William Hunt, Richard Rolfe. By Governor P. Warner sworn 20 Sep. 1672. Recorded 28 Sep. 1672.

1672, Sep. Teaggy Mocarty of Ireland. Letter of Attorney to John Ward. Witnessed by Richard Barrett, William Barrett, John Blundon. Before Governor P. Warner appeared John Blunden 20 Sep. 1672.

John Bandry (or Baudry) of Antigua, died intestate. Adm'on to Samuel Man 11 Oct. 1672 by Governor P. Warner. Recorded 15 Oct. 1672.

Demon Dehoidea of Antigua, died intestate. Adm'on to Daniel Minahan the greatest creditor by Governor P. Warner 15 Oct. 1672. Recorded same day.

Edward Bishpoole of Antigua, died intestate. Adm'on to Thomas Jones the greatest creditor 15 Oct. 1672 by Governor P. Warner. Recorded 15 Oct. 1672.

Warrant from Governor Warner 11 Oct. 1672 for the valuation of the estate of John Bandry, deceased. On 14 Oct. 1672 Tavernor Langford and Francis Gifford return the value as 1536 lbs. Recorded 22 Oct. 1672.

Warrant from Governor Warner 15 Oct. 1672 for the valuation of the estate of Dearman Dehorden, deceased. Returned as 30 acres, worth 7333 lbs. Recorded 22 Oct. 1672.

Captain Dunkin Campbell and Margaret his wife chose Captain Jeremiah Watkins, and Mr. Rise Morgan chose Nicholas Bayard, to decide their disputed accounts 10 Sep. 1672. Recorded 22 Oct. 1672.

John Stephens of Chipping Barenet, co. Bettford, churrergeon. Letter of Attorney to Mr. John Parry, merchant, 27 Jan. 1672. Witnessed by George Warde, Nicholas Clerke. Before Governor P. Warner 11 Nov. 1672 appeared Mr. Nicholas Clerke.

John Roane of Antigua, chirgion. Letter of Attorney to John Parry, Esq., 29 Aug. 1672 re 2100 lbs. Witnessed by Jane Knight, Ralph Gordges. Recorded in the Secretary's office. Sworn before Governor Warner. Recorded 16 Nov. 1672.

Francis Knollis of Antigua. Letter of Attorney to Mr. John Parry 6 July 1672. Witnessed by Roger Jones, John Roane. On 25 Nov. 1672 appeared Mr. Francis Knollis before Governor P. Warner. Recorded 28 Nov. 1672.

Warrant from Governor P. Warner for appraising the estate of Colonel Daniel Fitch, deceased, as shewn by Mr. Thomas Seagrove, chirurgeon. Thomas Turner and John Moore return the estate as one diseased negro woman worth 2500 lbs. of sugar 25 Sep. 1672. Recorded 30 Nov. 1672.

Warrant from Governor P. Warner for appraising the estate of Edward Bishpoole, deceased, as shewn by Thomas Jones the adm'or. Total value 1740 lbs., reported by Archibald Cochran. Recorded 30 Nov. 1672. John Parry, Secretary.

1672. The following done by George Towes, Deputy to Mr. Edward Maynard, Secretary:—

Nuncupative will of Richard Rolph 21 March 1672. All estate to my wife Martha during my son's nonage. Recorded 21 March 1672.

1673, April 8. Mr. Richard Belcher died intestate. Adm'on to Mrs. Mary Belcher the widow and Rachel Belcher the daughter by Governor P. Warner.

Letter from Sir W. Stapleton complaining that ships leave England and do not always give bond for their return, and refers to the Acts of Navigation of 12, 15, and 23 of His Majesty's reign.

Andrew Norwood of Barbados, merchant, says that he freighted a ketch called the "Willing Minde" of Boston in New England, from Boston to Carolina and back, that she was taken by the Dutch, but the crew re-captured her and brought her to Montserrat. Letter of Attorney to Daniel Ely of Antigua, merchant, and Thomas Cail of Montserrat 7 April 1672.

John Jersey of Antigua, planter. Will dated 12 Feb. 1672. All estate to Geo. Garnett of Antigua, planter. Witnessed by Christopher Quick, William Atkinson, William Whittingham, Jos. Richardson. Sworn 20 Feb. 1672 before Governor P. Warner.

1672, Nov. 18. William Boone of Antigua, planter, leases 10 acres of Ralph Hoskins of Antigua, planter.

Francis Goutririer (?). Will dated 25 March 1672. All estate to Rob. Noble & his brother Mark Noble. To Mary Brouncroft 2 gold rings, 1 here & 1 in Holland. To Cap. Jno Jacob 11½ lbs. of pewter. To Eve Jenkins my bed. To my maid Marg^t 1 year of her time & my late wife's linen. Derrick Brouncroft Ex'or in Trust "till ye children my sons-in-law be of age." Witnessed by William Thomas, Seith Marloe, Thomas Turner. At a Court at Falmouth 1 April 1673 appeared William Thomas and Seith Marloe.

Thomas Vittory of Nonsuch. Will dated 26 Feb. 1671. To my wife Eliz. all my estate for her life, then to my 3 sons, viz., my 1st son Thos., Robt, & ye youngest equally. My wife Ex'trix, & Jno Moss & Daniel Dening after her death. Witnessed by Richard Steal, John Tuce, John Ward. Before Governor P. Warner sworn 19 April 1673.

Major Thomas Mallet, agent to William, Lord Willoughby

of Parham. Letter of Attorney to John Michel 25 March 1673. Witnessed by Francis Manning and John Edwards. At a Court at Falmouth 1 April 1673 before Governor P. Warner appeared John Edwards.

Edward Conedy. Will dated 21 March 1672. All estate to Codeah Fonkecon. Witnessed by Thomas Moises, W. Grace. Before Governor P. Warner sworn 23 April 1673.

Jeremiah Hall of Antigua, died intestate. Adm'on granted by Governor Warner 29 April 1673 to Mr. Thomas Compton the greatest creditor. Warrant issued 29 April 1673 to Samuel Irish and Marke Boensta (? Brenster). Recorded 1 July 1673.

Richard Rogers of Antigua, planter, sells his house in Falmouth to James Pearsey of Antigua 5 July 1673. James Peirsey of Antigua, Gent., for 6600 lbs. of tobacco bought the said house.

Warrant of 10 April 1673 from Governor P. Warner to audit the accounts of Mr. Richard Belcher, Treasurer of St. John's precincts. Debts due to the Treasury 58,000 lbs. Signed by Jeremiah Watkins, Naha. Bayer, John Vernon, and John Axton the valuers.

Warrant dated 7 May 1673 for appraising the two negros of the late Henry Chanceller, deceased—5000 lbs. Signed by William Prester, William Wainwright, Robert Oxford.

Montserrat. Sir W. Stapleton's letter *re* a complaint of Captain Archibald Henderson, his estate damaged during his exile in England. By the King's letter of 12 June 1672 his said estate is to be restored. Order you Serjeant-Major Rowland Williams, Captain Jeremiah Watkins, Mr. Nicholas Bayer, Lieut. George Attorney (Turney), and Mr. John Vernon to meet at the plantation of Captain Archibald Henderson and inquire into the losses. Dated 16 Jan. 1672. On 28 March 1673 the appraisers met at the house of Nicholas Bayer, Esq., in St. John's Division and returned the damage at 20,000 lbs.

John Baine. Will dated 27 April 1673. To my 1st dau. Eliz. Baine 26 acres at Willoughby Bay. To the child my wife now goes with 15 acres at Nonsuch, but if a girl then all my 56 acres to the 2 equally. My wife Ex'trix & all residue, & after her death Cha. Barnard & Walter Phillipes Ex'ors. Witnessed by John Cox, John Mosse, Thomas Frastwell, John I . . . . Sworn 19 May 1673.

Letter from Colonel John Strode, Governor of Dover Castle, Esq. Whereas by Letters Pattent under the great seal, dated 9 Sep. 22 Charles II., between Charles II. of the one part, and myself of the other, I was granted the duty of 4½ per cent. on dead commodities at Nevis, Antegoa, Montserrat, and St. Christopher's as per the Act of 1663 for seven years, and I hereby appoint Joseph Martin of London, Gent., to be my Chief Collector 19 Dec. 1672.

1673, Aug. 2. Daniel Pelloe gives a receipt for 3093 lbs. of Mr. Peter Jeffries, Master of ye "William Edmond" of Kingsale, for the use of Mr. William Greble of Kingsale, merchant.

1673, July 30. The estate of Mr. Thomas Baker, chyrurgeon, deceased, valued at 3800 lbs.

1673, Aug. 16. Philip Taylor of Antigua, died intestate. Adm'on by Governor Warner granted 7 Aug. 1673 to Katherine Taylor his relict. Inventory. Total value 7796 lbs.

1673, May 20. Inventory of the estate of Captain Renatus Enys, deceased. Long list of bills due. Done by Ob. Bradshaw, Taverner Langford, Roger Jones, John Austin.

James Hesters of Nevis, merchant, died intestate. Adm'on to Charles Obeets, merchant, partner and creditor, 19 Jan. 1673 by Governor P. Warner.

1673, Feb. 2. Mr. Samuel Gachell, Master, and three mariners of the ketch "Saul and Margaret," sailed 11 Nov. 1673 from Cape Cod for Maryland in Virginia, and owing to a storm bore up to Antigua.

James Persy of Antigua, Gent., died intestate. Adm'on to Sarah Persy his relict 18 Feb. 1673. George Towes, Deputy-Secretary.

Jos. Crisp of Antigua, merchant. Letter of Attorney to Colonel P. Warner 1673. William Barnes, Deputy-Secretary.

1673, Mar. 2. Inventory of estate of James Persey, deceased. 190 acres at Crabb Valley valued at 27,168 lbs. Long list of names.

1673-4, Feb. 11. Joseph Martin appoints Major Thomas Mallet sub-collector of the 4½ per cent.

1673, Feb. 19. A galliotte lately wrecked in Falmouth Harbour. Rigging and sailes worth 8000 lbs.

George Bisse. Will dated 2 Sep. 1673. To my wife Cath. Bisse & Frances Bisse my dau. ⅔ of all goods. To my son Jnº Bisse ⅓ & all residue. I appoint him Ex'or. Witnessed by John Loshanay and Petter Gunnige. Sworn 16 March 1673 by Governor P. Warner.

Charles Abeels. Letter of Attorney to William Barnes, Gent., and Mr. Francis Carlile, merchant, 17 March 1673-4. Witnessed by John Ely, William Barnes, jun. Sworn 28 March 1674 before Governor P. Warner.

1674, April 17. Charles Farren of Corke, Ex'or of his son-in-law Thomas Bickford of Corke, merchant, deceased. Letter of Attorney to Daniel Pellowes of Antigua, merchant.

1674, July 18. Philip Taylor of Antigua, died intestate. Adm'on by Governor Warner to Catherine Taylor the widow. George Towes, Gent., Provost-Marshal.

Warrant from Governor P. Warner, dated 13 Sep. last, to take into custody and apprehend ye ship ye "Charles of Colerayne." James Hurd, Thomas Moore, and Richard Smith return its value as 38,750 lbs.

John Howard. Will undated. My wife Margery Howard Ex'trix, & my friends Jnº Martiall & Jnº Bacon fefes in Trust. To my son Jnº Howard all my Estate. To my 1st dau. Jone Howard 4000 lbs., & my yst. one Mary Howard 4000 lbs., & to both maintenance. To my wife her thirds. (1674.)

Inventory of goods in possession of Mr. Edward Laylige, agent to Mr. Thomas Rise of Bristoll, made by Daniel Pellow and Charles Rymer. (1674.)

1674, Nov. 14. Thomas Cranfeild of Antigua, cooper, died intestate. Adm'on refused by his widow, granted therefore to James Ward, planter, greatest creditor.

John Connor. Will dated 27 Aug. 1674. To Jnº Snigg 1000 lbs. to be shipped to him, likewise to Geo. White 500 lbs. To Philip Upshott & Morris Laham 600 lbs. All residue to Mr Jnº Dougan & Wm Shaw. Witnessed by William Shaw, Winfrit Upshot, Elizabeth O'Laham. Sworn before Governor P. Warner 12 Nov. 1674.

Peter Hancock of Barbados, merchant and Esq. Letter of Attorney to Colonel P. Warner 24 Dec. 1673.

Mr. George Towes, late Provost-Marshal, died intestate, and without heirs. Adm'on to Mr. William Barnes in trust for the next of kin, 4 Dec. 1674. Before Governor P. Warner.

William Whipham of Antigua, died intestate. Adm'on to Robert Stanley, in right of his wife Johana, formerly wife of the said William Whipham, 8 Dec. 1674.

Various receipts for goods received by Lieut. Daniel Pelloe, 18 Nov. 1674; also list of goods due to Mr. William Gisble of Kinsale, merchant.

Inventory of debts due to estate of Thomas Cranfeild, deceased.

Anthony Maynard of Antigua, Gent. Administrator of his brother Edward Maynard, deceased, late Secretary of Antigua. 32,686 lbs. are due to his said brother's estate. Letter of Attorney to Mr. William Barnes of Antigua 15 Dec. 1674.

Ye ship ye "Blessing" of Ceuras was seized here for trading contrary to the Act of Parliament of 12 Charles II. She has been sold for £74 st. to Serjeant-Major Rowland Williams, Captain Jeremiah Watkins, Lieut. George Torney, and Mr. Francis Carlile, her former owners. No date. (1674.)

Thomas Burgis of Antigua, died intestate. His widow Katherine refuses to administer. Adm'on to Lieut.-Colonel John Mayer 11 Dec. 1674, by Governor P. Warner.

Inventory of George Towes, by warrant, dated 4 Dec. 1674—45,450 lbs.

Inventory of Thomas Burgis. Long list of debts due to him.

1674, Jan. 18. Inventory of Mr. Edward Maynard's estate—110,965 lbs.

Inventory of William Whipham, of small amount.

There being a difference between John Trevers, only surviving Ex'or of Mr. William Milden, merchant, deceased, and Mr. Samuel Jones and Mr. Joseph Winthrop, Attorneys to James Ely, the administrator of Daniel Ely of Antigua, merchant, deceased, a warrant was issued, 22 March 1674, to Mr. Henry Mayer, Mr. Philip Everdone, Mr. James Cass, to settle ye same. A like difference in the accounts between John Trevers, agent to Mr. Thomas Wathen, Christopher Stephens and Co. of Bristoll, merchants, and Captain William Thomas and Jonas Langford, overseers of the will of John Bridges of Antigua, deceased. 20 March 1674.

The plantation of Colonel Thomas Middleton owes Margaret Heathcoat, in right of her husband Thomas Heathcoat, a balance of £36 10s. Thomas Heathcoat was manager, and was to be paid £25 st. yearly salary for five years from 7 Dec. 1661. (See her letter in Vol. I.)

Thomas Bisse of Bristoll, merchant. Letter of Attorney to Philip Tyler of Bristoll, merchant, and James Bisse of Nevis, merchant, for debts in Nevis, and in case of their death to Nathaniel King of Nevis, merchant. Referred to Edward Bisse. Witnessed by Philip Bisse and three others 6 March 1673.

Captain John Welch, died intestate. His estate, as shewn by Lieut. Daniel Pellow, the administrator, was appraised at 14,065 lbs. 26 June 1675, done by William Allin and William Fallam.

Petition of Caroline Guest, dau. and coheir of Lieut.-Colonel Charles Guest, deceased, praying that Captain Harvey Kennell and Mr. Thomas Moore be her guardians, and for division of the estate. Granted 8 April 1675.

William Comes of Antigua, merchant. Letter of Attorney to his wife Frances Comes and Daniel Pellam of Antigua, planter, 14 April 1675.

William Gribble of Kingsale, co. Cork, merchant. Letter of Attorney to Daniel Pelloe of Antigua, storehouse-keeper, 19 March 1674.

Leonard Powden of Boston, New England, merchant. Letter of Attorney to Charles Rymer, planter, and John Rule, mariner, 2 April 1675.

Petition of Samuel Irish for remission of fine. Remitted 16 April 1675.

1674, July 18. Governor P. Warner appoints Captain Paul Lee Judge of the Court of Common Pleas at Falmouth, and Captain Richard Ayres, Captain John Cade, and John Parry, Esq., his assistants.

1675, June 24. Inventory of the estate of Mr. George Towes, deceased.

1675, June 29. Protest by Robert Barker, Master, *re* ye Bark "Fortune of Kingsale," for damages by the sea.

John Cox of Nonsuch. Will dated 14 Aug. 1675. To Cha. Bernard 500 lbs. for a sword. To Eleanor Bernard 100 lbs. for a pair of gloves. To Jno. Ward my rapier & carbine. To Fra. Ashwell a suit. Jno. Inch & Tho. Adder. To Ann Mosse my cow & turkies. All residue to Anthony Brown my son-in-law (a child). Cha. Barnard & Jno. Mosse, Ex'ors. Nath. Monck to be paid a bill of sale for 50 acres. Sworn 20 Aug. 1675 before Rowland Williams.

Richard Howell and Richard Gay, Esquires, Francis Bond, and Richard Forestall, merchants, all of Barbados. Letter of Attorney to Lieut.-Colonel John Meares, 2 Aug. 1675.

1675, Aug. 31. Inventory of John Cox, deceased, Cr. 21,147 lbs.; Dr. 7,904 lbs.

Lewis Bryant of Antigua, planter, died intestate. Adm'on to Owen Bramwell for John Bryant, son of deceased, 20 Nov. 1675. Valued 2590 lbs. Governor Rowland Williams.

James Garland of Antigua, died intestate. Adm'on to James Davenport, chief creditor, 20 Sep. 1675. Value of estate 1636 lbs. By Governor R. Williams.

Joan Bradly of Antigua, widow. Will dated 21 Feb. 1674. To my friend Jno. Dugan, Jun., all estate of 37 acres. Witnessed by Henry Soper, Daniel Macharty, Corn. O'Brian. Sworn 28 Nov. 1675 before Governor R. Williams.

John Dapre. Will dated 19 Aug. 1675. All estate to my wife Eliz., she to be Ex'trix. Witnessed by John Cobb, Luke Forster, William Douglas. Sworn 28 Sep. 1675 before Governor Rowland Williams.

Robert Parker. Will dated 25 Feb. 1676. Cap. Rich. Ayres, & Ensign Henry Lorry to be Ex'ors for my wife & child. To my wife Sarah all my estate till my dau. Jone Parker be 15 or marry. Witnessed by John Tuce, Walter Lane. On 29 July 1676 appeared John Tuce and Walter Lane, and were sworn before Colonel Rowland Williams.

List of books and records of the Secretary's Office delivered to Mr. William Blakey 30 Jan. 1674. Mr. Blakey acknowledges to have received them all from Mr. William Barnes. The list is a long one, and includes a bag of papers of Tho. Bisse of Bristoll left by ye wife of Edward Lappage.

Elizabeth Rogers, widow of Richard Rogers of Nonsuch, deceased. Will dated 5 June 1676. To my 3 children John, Rich[d], & W[m] my house & 2 negros. Signed William Blakey, Secretary, J. Lachaisnaye.

1675, Jan. 10. I, Antoney Reyerson, of Antigua, agree to pay to Richard Alford 2133 lbs. at the house of Samuel Jones, Esq., and Co., at St. John's Town. Witnessed by John Bisse, Richard Mathews.

On behalf of Christoffle Canales, widower, at Antigua, Mr. Peter Colne of Amsterdam, in his affidavit, swore that he had orders from Mr. Canales to pay to Colonel Thomas Middleton at London 1311 guilders, dated 12 Feb. 1662. On 23 March 1674, before Nicholas Hayward, Notary Public in London, in the presence of Colonel Bastian Beyer and Mr. Jacob Lucie of London, merchants. Some dispute seems to have arisen in reference to the account with the late Lucas Lucie and Co.

Will of Daniel Minehan. My friends Dermott Nonan & Jn[o] Dugan to be Guardians of my 2 children. Witnessed by Robert French, Anton. D . . . .

1676, Dec. 1. Letter of Attorney from Samuel Farmer of Barbados, Esq., to Richard Peirson of Barbados, Gent., to receive from Joseph Crisp, merchant, and from ye Ex'ors of Colonel Samuel Winthrop, late of Antigua, deceased, all sums due.

Nuncupative will of William Righten, deceased, late of Antigua, planter, in the presence of Walter Phillip, John Gunter, and Charles Barnard, who were sworn on 31 Jan. 1676, that in Dec. last at Nonsuch William Righten gave all his estate to his wife Elizabeth for life and then to his dau. Mary. By Colonel Philip Warner.

Nuncupative will of Roger Beevin of Antigua, planter, made at Nonsuch in Dec. last, in the presence of Charles Barnard, Thomas Yorke, and Edward Cooke. Sworn 31 Jan. 1676 before Colonel P. Warner.

1676, May 10. Letter of Attorney of Edward Herbert of Bristoll, merchant, to William Barke of Montserrat, merchant. Before Paul Lee, Esq.

1675, Oct. 7. Charles Abeckes of Nevis, merchant, died intestate. Adm'on to Richard Slycer, principal creditor. By Governor R. Williams.

1674, July 22. At Parham Plantation with Colonel John Willoughby two or three days before he left the Island, May 1674, dispute about a negro.

Warrant, dated 11 Dec. 1675, for valuing the estate of Thomas Vittry, deceased, Cr. 1296 lbs.; Dr. 1170 lbs. *Re* the fly-boat the "St. Nicholas" of Galway, bound for Maryland 19 Jan. 1675.

1675, Jan. Robert Price of Antigua. Letter of Attorney to his father Edward Williams. Edward Williams of Barbados, planter. Letter of Attorney to Robert Price his son-in-law.

1675. Nov. 10. Thomas Burrowes and John Smalldridge of Kinsaill, co. Cork, merchants, and Ann Summergelt of ditto, widow. Letter of Attorney to George Beaker and Arthur Keefe of ditto.

Thomas Reynolds. Will dated 8 Jan. 1675. All estate to my wife Eliz. Sworn 4 Feb. 1675.

Henry Care of Antigua, planter. Will dated 28 Jan. 1675. To my wife Blanche Carre 20 acres. Witnessed by John Green, Thomas Shelton. Sworn 7 March 1675 before Governor R. Williams.

John Woodliffe of Nonsuch, planter. Will dated 12 Feb. 1675. All my plantation to Hugh Tratton, he to be Ex'or. Sworn 7 March 1675 before Governor R. Williams.

1675, June 23. Captain John Welsh, Commander of ye ship "Henry & Mary" of Swansy, died intestate. Adm'on to Lieut. Daniel Pelloe, agent to Mr. William Grible of Kingsale, merchant, principal creditor.

1675. William Styler, aged 57, and Edward Leaver, aged 31, sign affidavits.

1676, April 7. Letter of partnership between John Blendall and Walter Layne.

1676, April 27. Inventory of John Bacon, deceased—7434 lbs.

Richard Rogers. Will dated 24 April 1676. All estate to my wife Eliz. My 1st son John. My sons Rich[d] & W[m]. My wife Ex'trix. Witnessed by Teige Mathew, John Waglin. Sworn 29 April 1676.

Thomas Foster, carpenter, formerly of Barbados, now of Antigua. Will dated 22 April 1677. To my wife Martha all my estate. My son Thos. Foster to enjoy my plantation in Barbados at 21 & £30 st. Witnessed by Samuel Irish, Owen Brambelt, who were sworn on 1 May 1677 before Colonel Philip Warner.

1678, May 17. John White, planter, sells 10 acres to Mr. William Burke, planter.

1678, June 19. Lieut. William Proctor, planter, deed of sale to Mr. Thomas Inett, merchant.

1678, Aug. 21. Roger Compline, victualer, to Robert Winstanley, smyth.

1678, Oct. 6. Thomas Brookes, planter, and Catherine his wife, formerly ye widow of Clement Casbrooke, deceased, for 2000 lbs. sells 10 acres to George Robinson.

1678. Richard Abrahall sells 60 acres in St. John's Division to Dr. Thomas Gates, chyrurgeon.

30 Charles II., Dec. 24. John Saunders sells land to John Haydon.

1678, Dec. 28. Paul Lee, Gent. Mr. Thomas Eastchurch, deceased. Mrs. Anna Eastchurch, widow, now residing here. Mr. Nicholas Clarke, deceased. Grant of a plantation back to her.

1678, Nov. 26. Lewelling Rice, planter, sells 10 acres to Captain Paul Lee, and gives 6 acres to his son Richard Rice, planter.

1679, May 24. Edward Cooke, planter, and Catherine his wife sell a parcell of land at Falmouth Harbour to Anthony Maynard, planter, and Margery his wife.

1679, March 27. Philip Kenneday, planter, and Martha his wife sell to Lieut. Richard Slicer.

1679. July 8. Roger Trotman, planter, sells 25 acres to Captain Henry Fearnes . . . . ye Corke mariner.

1679, Aug. 7. Timothy Solevane, planter, sells 20 acres to James Maule, Minister of Belfast.

1679, Sep. 5. Thomas Compton, planter, sells his 200 acres held by patent from William, Lord Willoughby, in Willoughby Bay Division to Richard Lord.

1679, Aug. 31. Captain Samuel Jones of Antigua, Attorney, to Captain James Ely of Barbados, adm'or of Daniel Ely, late of Antigua, merchant, deceased, sells a parcell of land in St. John's Town for 1500 lbs. to Major William Barnes.

1679, Sep. 25. William Coomes, planter, sells his house at Bridge Town to James Maynard and Henry Cooke. Katherine Cooke, widow of ye said Henry Cooke, assigns it back 29 April 1680.

1679, July 12. William Chamberlaine, John Loftey, and Thomas Cox, planters, for 8000 lbs. sell 12½ acres in New North Sound to Francis Carlile and George Turney, merchants.

1679, Oct. 24. Edmond Connell, planter, sells 10 acres in Belfast to James Maule, Minister.

1679, Dec. 22. Philip Godfry, planter, sells to John Macaming.

1681, May 1. William Steele leases 80 acres, also 20 acres in the Leaward Division (formerly leased to said William Steele by Elizabeth Harris, widow of Richard Harris, deceased), to Owen Bramble for 700 lbs. payable yearly to the said Elizabeth Harris. The lease to be for 4 years 9 months 8 days.

1679, Feb. 20. Owen Sullivene for 13,500 lbs. sells 20 acres in Belfast.

1680, April 29. William Coomes, planter, sells his house in Bridge Town to John Birmingham, merchant.

1680, May 1. John Quinby of Antigua sells for 10,000 lbs. 36 acres (being all the land granted 1 Nov. 1669 to his father by William, Lord Willoughby) to Richard Lord of New England, merchant.

1680, May 21. James Almond sells 10 acres at Willoughby Bay.

1680, March 29. Thomas Beck, Gent., for 12 negros gives 128 acres in Five Islands Division to George Robinson, planter.

1680, May 17. Peter Walch, planter, by deed of gift grants ⅓ of his estate to his son Peter Walch.

1680, June 2. Emanuell Fera. Da Silva, planter, sells 10 acres for 3000 lbs. to John Hatherly, planter.

1680, March 27. Mr. John Ley, Secretary of Antigua, grants to Mr. William Wainwright the right to cut wood on 50 acres.

1680, June 8. William Harton, Attorney to William Chard of Nevis, sells 50 acres in Belfast Division to Arundell Thomas.

William Stevens of Popeshead. Will dated 18 June 1679. To my friend Walter Scott 500 lbs. To my goddau. Eliz. Roberts 500 lbs. To Mary England, dau. of Thos. England, a negro woman. All residue to my wife Jone, she to be Ex'trix. Witnessed by Jos. Heath, James Jones. Before Paul Lee sworn 10 June 1680.

1680, May 1. Jonathan Wilson and Cuthbert Jameson, late of Nevis, now of Antigua, merchants, sell 60 acres to Edward Dendy.

1680, June 11. Samuel Sizemore leases 10 acres and 2 negros to Bartholomew Avenell.

1680, June 18. Thomas Inett, Gent., for 17,000 lbs. sells to William Hollyman, Gent., the moiety of a plantation of 200 acres in the whole, and deed of partnership follows.

1680, June 27. Peter Dutton of Antigua leases 10 acres to Robert Browne and William Howard.

1680, July 2. Roger Fowler, planter, to William Reynolds, sen., planter.

At a Court of Common Pleas at St. John's 8 June 1680 Captain Samuel Jones, sen., assistant, and Captain John Vernon. Lieut. Roger Complin, plaintiff, v. Thomas Pew, defendant, re Soldier's Gutt. Verdict for plaintiff and possession.

1680. John Maskoll, merchant, has a right to the moiety of 170 acres at Belfast. Deed of partnership with Joshua Leach of Antigua.

1680, July 20. Grissell Deane, widow and relict of Mr. John Deane, deceased, and formerly widow and relict of William Allin, deceased, sells 100 acres to Joshua Brewster, carpenter.

1680. Agreement between Mr. James Davenport and Ann his wife with Mr. Henry Downes of Barbados. Deed of partnership re the former's plantation.

1680, Sep. 13. John Lachaisnaye, planter, gives 40 acres to John Murphy, and on 6 Oct. 10 acres to Thomas Lodge.

1680. Colonel James Vaughan to the King, 25 acres called St. John's Point.

1680, Feb. 12. Lucy Almonds, late wife of John Russell, deceased.

1680, Feb. 16. John Ravens, deed of sale to Cornelius Conner.

1680. William Coomes of Nonsuch, planter, sells 3 proportions at Bridge Town to William Creech, mariner.

1680. Philip Upshot of Nonsuch, planter, by the consent of Winifred Upshott, Ex'trix of Austin Nicholson, now his wife, sells 10 acres to William Coomes.

1680, Feb. 16. Ann Ellis, widow of Edmond Ellis, deceased, confirms the sale of an estate by her late husband to Obadiah Bradshaw in 1670.

1680, Feb. 15. John Atkinson of Antigua, planter, sells 20 acres to Michael McDaniel.

1680, Feb. 17. Daniel Morartee and Katherine his wife of Antigua sell 20 acres to George Robinson. Deed also between John Murphy and Daniel Morartee.

1680, Feb. 17. Richard Carter sells to Alexander Rollo.

1680, March 19. Sarah Phillips, widow of Robert Phillips, deceased, sells to Thomas Ellis.

1680, March 11. Walter Halfyard, planter, sells to Henry Walden.

1680, June 16. Edward Dendy sells to John Prynn.

1680, Oct. 16. Peter Delanoy to Peter Soaper and Walter Halfyard.

1680, Dec. 21. Rowland Gill and Charity (? his wife) of Barbados sell to Captain Daniel Hensley of Antigua, Gent.

1680, Jan. 21. Captain Daniel Hensley sells to Colonel Rowland Williams and Mr. Samuel Winthrop.

1681, March 28. John Shaw of Antigua sells to John Machoomine.

1680, Feb. 9. George Robinson sells to Henry Brograve.

1681, Mar. 31. Thomas Austin to Edward Robinson.

1681, April 4. John June to Luke Norton.

1681, April 1. Captain James Phipps sells 300 acres to Mr. Thomas Erskin.

1681, April 14. Thurlo Macshee to John Howard and to Cornelius Keneday.

1680, Dec. 29. William Barker, sen., gives 10 acres to his son William Barker, jun.

1681, April 18. Thomas Yorke to Edward Thomas.

1680, Oct. 6. John Hull to Owen Bramble.

1681, Feb. 11. Abraham Cames to Philip Chapman.

1681, April 23. Thomas Aldersuch to Michael McDaniel.

1681, April 23. Edward Ricket to Elias Carter.

1681, April 23. John Gunter to Walter Phillips.

1681, April 25. William Wharton to Lewis Garnish.

1681, April 9. Laurence Turton and Ann (? his wife) to Robert Blither, carpenter.

1681, May 11. Pharo Laramore to Robert Howard.

1692, April 29. Order by President John Parry to appraise the goods of Henry Sharp as shewn by his widow Cisley, directed to Captain Philip Willoughby, Thomas Nanton, Michael Bennett, and William Williams. On 2 May return made of one negro valued at 4000 lbs.

Nuncupative will of Captain William Rokby. To my wife Jane all Est. In presence of Thomas Pratt and John Ware 27 Feb. 1692. Recorded 5 April 1693.

1692, Sep. 19. Appointment made by Christopher Codrington, Esq., of Major Philemon Bird and Captain Peter Lee to be guardians to the two sons James and John of George Cruft, deceased. Recorded 23 April 1693.

The estate of George Grief, deceased, appraised by John Light at 22,737 lbs. Recorded 23 April 1693.

(On a scrap.) To Anthony Montyro a 30s. ring. Witnessed by James Junn, Thomas Everett, and Anthony Montyroe. Recorded 19 May 1693.

1693, Aug. 4. Goods of John Bellwood, deceased, appraised at 45,951 lbs.

Robert Strode, late of co. Dorset, now of Antigua, Gent. Will dated 5 April 1693. All goods, etc., to Nath. Barnes of Antigua for his care of me in my sickness, & appoint him sole Ex'or. Witnessed by George Wright, Charles Powell his mark, Charles Chambers, Charles Pearce. Sworn before His Excellency 21 June 1693. Recorded 21 June 1693. Thomas Gateward, Deputy-Secretary.

Thomas Walters of Boston, New England, now at Antigua, merchant. Will dated 8 July 1693. All estate to my wife & children equally. Richd Oliver of Antigua, merch^t, Ex'or. Witnessed by Thomas Tyler, Jonathan Woodberry, Thomas Gatewood. Sworn before Deputy-Governor Yeamans 15 July 1693.

John Belwood of Antigua, merchant. Will dated 20 April 1693. All estate to my wife Rebecca living in Ratcliffe, near Lyne House, near London. My s^d wife, Wm Jordam, & Mr Edward Acton Ex'ors. Witnessed by Alexander Coall his mark, Issabell Gilchrist, Thomas Gatewood. Sworn 18 July 1693 before Christopher Codrington, Governor.

Mathew Thorne of Antigua. Will dated 27 March 1693. "Now myself going upon the Expedition to Martinico." All my estate to be distributed at the discretion of my friend Wm Browne. To my wife E. Thorne 25 acres bounding on Fra. Crisham & Peter Martin to the S., Sr Sam. Ffox (? Foxon) to the W., Fra. Crisham & Hen. Sharpe, dec^d, to the E., & to the N. part of my said land not gadged (? mortgaged) to Jno Howard; also my Negro woman. In case she die without issue by me I give the land, etc., to Wm Browne. Witnessed by Richard Dashwood, John Rowllor, Charity Martin. Sworn 29 May 1693. Recorded by Richard Dashwood 25 July 1693.

Archibald Michaelroy of Antigua, joyner. Will dated 20 Jan. 1692. All my estate to my brother Wm Johnson of Antigua, planter, he to be sole Ex'or. Witnessed by William Jardine, Roger Dooley, Thomas Gatewood. Sworn 24 March 1692 before President John Yeamans. Recorded 25 July 1693.

1693, June 24. By His Excellency. Order to appraise all the negros, chattels, and credits of Thomas Cook, Surgeon, late of Antigua, deceased, as shewn you by Elizabeth Cook the relict, Jonas Langford, George Gamble, and Joseph Watkins the Ex'ors, within twenty days, and to make return to the Secretary's Office on oath. To Thomas Oysterman, Samuel Watkins, John Burton. Valued accordingly at 62,198 lbs. of sugar. Recorded 18 July 1693.

1693, July 20. A like order for appraising the estate of John Belwood as shewn by William Jurdan and Edward Acton the Ex'ors. To Captain John Weir, Lieut. John Wright, Thomas Turner, and William Mathews.

1693, March 27. By His Excellency. Order to appraise the goods of Archibald Michaelson of Antigua, joyner, as shewn by William Johnson. To Mr. Thomas Long, Captain John Perley, Mr. Nathaniel Sampson, Mr. John Balokloek, Mr. John Bellwood, Mr. Edward Acton. Valued at 12,710 lbs. 3 May 1693.

1693, Aug. 23. Thomas Banbury, aged 14, son of Joseph Banbury, late of Antigua, deceased, appeared before me, Christopher Codrington, and of his own free will elected Christopher Chapman as his guardian during his minority. Recorded 30 Aug. 1693.

Richard Pugh, late Commander of H.M.S. "Norwich," died intestate. Adm'on to Thomas Weaver, Esq., and inventory to be exhibited within twenty days in the Secretary's Office, by Christopher Codrington. Recorded 24 Nov. 1693 by Thomas Gatewood, Deputy-Secretary.

Jonah Bateman, late of London, merchant. Will dated 3 Nov. 1693. The whole of my effects & cargo, together with debts accruing therefrom, lately in possession of Mr Tho. Knap, dec^d^, in partnership with me (to whose estate I have administered), are to be taken care of by my Ex'ors, & to be disposed of towards satisfying my creditors, as well as other effects in this Island, likewise in New England in Andrew Belcher's hands, in Lisbon in Jno Cleak's & Daniel Denny's possession, in Leghorn in Tuscany in company with Rigby & Shepheard, & in other parts of Europe. Mr Tho. Weaver sole Ex'or, to whom I give £200 st. Witnessed by James Brodie, Dennis Mackelmore, Richard Buckeridge. Sworn Nov. 1693. Recorded 4 Dec. 1693.

Nevis. Thomas Belchamber of Nevis, Gent. Will dated 9 Feb. 1692-3. To my sister Eliz. Pennington's children now living £50 st. each. To my sister Moriam Shelberry's children £10 each. To my sister Augustin's children £10 each. To my goddau. Eliz. Holt 1000 lbs. of Muscovado sugar per annum till the age of 21 or day of marriage, charged on my Antigua plantation. To my beloved friend Col. Cha. Pym my ordering horse, saddle, pistolls, sword, & belt. To the parish of Charles Town in this Island a piece of plate of £20 st. for the service of the communion table. To Silvanus Taylor & Henry Bolton £100 c. for settling the books of account in my partnership with Hen. Carpenter, Esq., dec^d^, as we were concerned for the customers of the R. African Co. Our debts to Mr Carr. Col. Row. Williams, Cap. Sam. Horne, & Mr Alex. Crafford to manage my Antigua plantation & to ship the sugar to Rich. Cary, to each of whom a beaver hat. My well beloved friend the said Rich. Cary of London, merch^t^, sole Ex'or & heir. Col. Cha. Pym, Aaron Chapman, Esq., Mr Phil. Brown, & Silvanus Taylor, overseers, & to each a beaver hat. Witnessed by Thornton Jones, Bridgett Rogers, Dinah Munde, Martha Moore, Henry Bolton. Exemplification sent out by P.C.C. signed by Thomas Welham, Deputy-Registrar. Recorded 3 Jan. 1693. (See the P.C.C., 179 Coker.)

Darby Noonan of Nonsuch Division, planter. Will dated 30 July 1691. To my 2 daus. Ellinor & Mary Noonan all my estate, & to the survivor, & if both die all to my wife Joane. To my wife the use of my estate during the minority of my daus. & appoint her sole Ex'trix. Witnessed by James Ceman, Anthony Browne, Nathan Bradford his mark, William Stephanson. Sworn 4 Feb. 1691-2 before Christopher Codrington.

1693, July 1. The goods of Thomas Knap of London, merchant, deceased, as shewn by Colonel Thomas Warner were valued by us Nathan Stanbury, John White, and John Amory at £2061 c.

1693, July 1. Inventory of the rigging, sayles, yards, etc., on board the brigantine the "Swan," Samuel Willard, Commander, as shewn by Colonel Thomas Warner, administrator of Mr. Thomas Knap's estate. The hull and all belonging is valued at £300 c.

George Baker and Susanna his wife request adm'on of goods of John Maccamount, deceased; granted 9 April 1694 by Christopher Codrington.

William Munroe. Will not dated. To my wife her thirds. All residue to my dau. Jane Munroe, whom I appoint sole Ex'trix. Maj. Sam. Martin & Jno Perrie Ex'ors during her minority. Witnessed by Richard Buckley, Patrick Ronane. Sworn 9 March 1693. Recorded 20 March 1694.

By His Excellency the General. Timothy Cokely, late of Antigua, died intestate. Adm'on to Jonathan Wells and his wife 3 May 1694. On 8 May Thomas Tanner, Darby Nugent, and Dominick Bodkin value the effects at 4790½ lbs. of sugar.

By His Excellency the General. John Pen of Antigua, planter, died intestate. Adm'on to Edward Pen the brother 18 May 1694. Recorded 29 May 1694. Thomas Gateward, Deputy-Secretary.

Stephen Bath of Antigua, planter. Will undated. All estate to my wife Mary. To Steph. Le Roux, son of Jacob Le Roux, 1000 lbs. of sugar. To Abigail Le Roux, dau. of Jacob Le Roux & sister of Steph., 1000 lbs. To Chas. Ward, jun., son of Chas. Ward, sen., 1000 lbs. My wife Ex'trix. Jonas Langford, planter, Nath. Humphreys, planter, Dr Tho. Coocke, & Erastus Reyerson of Antigua Trustees. On 9 May 1692 appeared William Peck and Thomas Byshop and were sworn. Recorded 16 June 1694 and 13 May 1699.

By His Excellency Christopher Codrington, Esq. Samuel Harris of Antigua, died intestate. Adm'on 16 July 1694 to Walter Quarme the chief creditor. Recorded 18 July 1694.

John Woode of Antigua, taylor. 13 March 6 William and Mary. Codicil to my will which is in the hands of Mr. Abraham Blush and Jos. Billings of Boston in New England, merchants. My friends Sam. Proctor & Nathan Stanbury, merch^ts^ in Antigua, to gather in all debts here. Witnessed by Edward Taylor, Thomas Gateward. Before the Deputy-Governor John Yeamans sworn 25 July 1694. Recorded 20 Aug. 1694.

Richard Liddall recites a Contract of Charter between Mr. Rowland St. John of London, merchant, in behalf of self, and the owners of the ship "Fellowship" of London, and appoints Joseph Corbett, chief mate, to succeed him in the command of the said ship, or John Salkeld if Joseph Corbett die. Witnessed by Michael White, Martin Creagh, William Treekill, and Edward Perrie 25 Aug. 1694. On 6 Sep. 1694 was sworn Captain Michael White. Recorded 6 Sep. 1694.

John Hull of Antigua, carpenter. Will dated 8 July 1689. Bound to St Christopher's in military service. All my 20 acres in the Road Div^n^ & 7 negros & all residue to my dau. Mary Hull, & if she die to Cap. Jno Yeamans & Cha. Goss. To my goddau. Eliz. Chapman 1500 lbs. Cap. Jno Yeamans & Chas. Goss Ex'ors & Guardians till she be 18, & I give them 6000 lbs. apiece. Witnessed by William Buckle, Andrew Cule (his mark), Thomas Bartelott. Sworn 14 Aug. 1691. Recorded 14 Jan. 1694.

William Halliman of Antigua, planter. Will dated 26 July 1694. To my dau. Rueth 9 acres next to Popeshead path, with the house thereon, & a negro woman. To my wife Eliz. & my dau. all my goods, etc., they to be Ex'trices. Witnessed by Adam Martin, Elizabeth Cowell. Sworn 21 Dec. 1694. Recorded 16 Feb. 1694.

J. Hyrandus of Five Islands Division, Antigua. Will dated 10 May 1692. To Cornelius Lawson 2 negros. To Jno Bell 2 negros. Sarah to be free. To Ralph Pengilly all my bedding & 600 lbs. My friends Corn. Lawson & Jno Bell Ex'ors. Witnessed by Edward Mall, James Waight. Sworn by Edward Mall before Deputy-Governor John Yeamans 15 May 1695. Recorded 15 May 1695.

Anthony Maynard of Antigua, planter. Will dated 29 March 1693. Bound upon this present Expedition for Martinico. To my son W^m^ (not 21) ½ my estate. To my wife Margery ½. Cap. Jn° Prynn & Mr Ben. King Trustees. Witnessed by David Dekarter, Edward Cooke, James Lennan. Before Deputy-Governor Yeamans were sworn Edward Cooke and James Lennan 5 March 1694.

Mr. Pasco Lapp. Will dated 12 March .... The ship "Endeavour" to my mother. The ship "Blessing" to my sister Baker, the Master Rob. Addison to get in debts. All residue to my sister Baker. Witnessed by Robert Addison, A. Freeman, Thomas Barry. Recorded 12 June 1695.

1695, July 16. By His Excellency Mary Barry, orphan of John Barry, late of Antigua, deceased, has chosen Thomas Cap and John Eliot of Antigua, planters, her Guardians. Thomas Bartelot, Deputy-Secretary.

Lewis Garnish of Antigua, planter. Will dated 8 Nov. 1690. To my wife Agnes all my Estate. My gun & sword to Mark Monk, son of Nath. Monk. To my godchild Mark Monk, son of Mark Monk, a heifer. My kinswoman Bridget Bryand, wife of Jn° Bryand. Witnessed by John Deane, David Decoster, John Chambers. Sworn 1 Dec. 1690.

Francis Iddins of Antigua. Will dated 2 June 1693. To my wife Eliz. all my Estate. To my brother Geo. Iddins' 1st son £100. To my sisters Eliz. & Hannah £100. To Jn° Perrie my silver-hilted sword. My wife Eliz. Ex'trix. Witnessed by .... Edgecombe, ... Pearce, ... Hutchinson. On 26 Sep. 1695 was sworn John Perrie. Recorded 30 Sep. 1695. Robert Amory, Deputy-Secretary.

Osbert Hougham of Antigua died intestate. Adm'on 3 Sep. 1695 to Robert Amory. Recorded 3 Oct. 1695.

By His Excellency General Codrington. John Rawlings, late of Antigua, died intestate, and has no kindred here. Adm'on to Edward Parsons of Montserrat, Esq., for all the Leeward Islands 9 Nov. 1695. Recorded 13 Nov. 1695.

Walter Scot of Antigua, planter. Will dated 14 Oct. 1684. To my dau. Joan Scot, my son Joseph Scott, my son Martial Scot, & my dau. Henrietta Scott all my estate equally at 18. My wife to manage my estate, but if she marry then my good friend Majr Jn° Vernon to do so, & I appoint them Ex'ors. Witnessed by Henry Brograve, James Porter, James Harper. On 19 Nov. 1695 was sworn James Porter. Recorded 2 Dec. 1695.

1695, Dec. 10. Joseph Scott, aged 15, son and heir of Walter Scott, late of Antigua, deceased, has chosen John Howard, Gent., as his Guardian. Recorded 11 Dec. 1695.

John Keetch, merchant, late of Boston, New England, died intestate. Adm'on 4 Oct. 1695 to William Abraham of Antigua, Gent., for the wife and child of deceased.

Adam Martin, on behalf of his correspondant Mr. William Gordon, merchant in London, who had supplied goods to James Mordoch, deceased, was granted on 22 Jan. 1695 adm'on of the latter's estate. An inventory was prepared and an appraisement made by Mr. Richard Buckridge, Mr. William Fenton, Mr. Anthony Montiroe, and Mr. Nathaniel Sampson, and the estate sworn under £200 on 14 Feb. 1695. Recorded 22 Dec. 1695.

William Palmer of Antigua, butcher. Will dated 5 July 1695. All estate to my wife Eliz. Witnessed by James Bayley, John Smith, George Wilkinson (all marks). Sworn 26 Feb. 1695. Recorded 2 March 1695-6.

Codicil to will of George Erwin dated 17 Sep. 1695-6 [*sic*]. To my mother Mary Erwin, widow, in London, in St Ollive's, Hart Street, all residue. Mr Joseph Watkins Ex'or. Witnessed by Daniel Mackinen, James Feild, Thomas Long, Lawrence Morphy. Sworn 11 March 1695-6. Recorded 11 March 1695-6.

Thomas Bartelot of Antigua. Will dated 29 Feb. 1695-6. To my mother 5000 lbs. To my 2 sons 3000 lbs. equally. To my kinsman Hen. Tilson, jun., 1000 lbs. My friend Jn° Lucas Ex'or. To my friend Amory a 30s. ring. Witnessed by Robert Amory, John Campbell, Elizabeth Laramore. Sworn 11 March 1695-6 by Robert Amory. Recorded 12 March 1695-6.

Henry Chearnley. Will dated 28 Dec. 1695. To my wife Frances all my estate, she to be sole Ex'trix. My good friends Mr Geo. Gamble & Mr Anthony Monteyro Trustees. Witnessed by John Martin, Nathaniel Sampson. Sworn 11 March 1695-6.

(On a fragment.) (Signed) Alexander .... Witnessed by Nathaniel Crump, Thomas Banes, Robert Amory, 1695. Recorded at the request of Leagh Marrel 26 March 1696.

David Kallahan of Antigua died intestate. Adm'on 12 March 1695-6 to David Rutterford. Recorded 28 March 1696. Robert Amory, Deputy-Secretary.

Antigua. Order to Captain William Frye and Captain Jos. Lettel to inventory the goods of John Rawlinson, late of Antigua, deceased, as shewn by Edward Parsons of Montserrat, Esq., administrator of the deceased, 9 Nov. 1695. Montserrat. William Frye and James Pilson value the goods at 17,914 lbs. Mr. David Lloyd sends in an inventory of the goods at Spanish Town. Total value £213. Signed at St. Christopher's 17 Feb. 1695 by Lieut.-General Thomas Hill. Signed also by John Panton, John Bourryane, William Hamilton. Recorded at St. Christopher's 20 Feb. 1695. Recorded at Antigua 22 May 1696 by Robert Amory.

Antigua. By His Excellency Christopher Codrington, Esq. Captain William Waller, Commander of ye Barbados forces, and late of Antigua, died and left a will which Thomas Ruben the Ex'or refuses to prove, so Captain Samuel Horne is hereby granted adm'on 31 Dec. 1695. Warrant dated 31 Dec. 1696 [*sic*] to Mr. George Gamble, Mr. Thomas Long, and Mr. Jos. James to appraise, who on 15 Jan. 1695 return the value of estate at £51.

By John Yeamans, Esq. John Singleday of Antigua died intestate. Adm'on 10 May 1696 to Richard Buckeridge. Recorded 22 May 1696. Warrant for inventory directed to Mr. Nathaniel Sampson, Mr. Adam Martin, and Mr. William Hawkes. Total £21. Recorded 22 May 1696.

Inventory of the estate of Osbert Hougham taken 24 May 1696. Dominick Bodkin and Richard Buckridge value the goods, as shewn by Mr. Robert Amory the administrator, at £14. Recorded 11 June 1696.

James Maule, Minister of Antigua. Will dated 27 March 1693-4. My son Wm Maule, now at Edinburgh, to be heir to all my lands & my house in that city, & my houses & lands in the city of Pearth called St Johnston, & my houses on ye N. side of the lower gate, Patrick Threeplam now possessor, once my brother Wm Maule's, decd, also all my plantation of 50 acres & 6 negros in Bellfast, Antigua, he paying to my 1st dau. Katrin Maule 20,000 lbs. & to my youngest dau. Masse Maule 20,000 lbs. My brother Mr Rob. Maule, Minister in Killinliah, co. Down, & his children. My friends Lt Wm Wainwright & Dennis Kine of Antigua Ex'ors in Trust. Witnessed by Cuthbert Black, Rosseman Brown. Sworn 9 June 1696. Recorded 11 June 1696.

Francis Pearce. Will not dated. To my wife Alice, besides her thirds, a negro girl. My buckaneer gunn, ye silver tankard, my trooping saddle, & pistolls to be sold for my son Francis Pearce. All estate to my wife & son equally. When my time is out with Mr Tho. Archer. My friends Mr Nath. Sampson, Steph. Duer, Sam. Lowyer, & my wife Alice Pearce Ex'ors & 25s. rings. Witnessed by James Porter, Roger Dooly, Edward Laver. Sworn 13 May 1696. Recorded 16 June 1696.

Fremant Miller of Antigua died intestate. Adm'on to Hon. Colonel Rowland Williams for his widow and children 11 June 1696. Recorded 24 June 1696. Christopher Chapman, William Devereux, John Bramball appraise the estate at £44. Recorded 16 July 1696.

Robert Everitt of Antigua, planter, died intestate. Adm'on to Mary Everitt the relict 16 July 1696. Recorded 18 July 1696.

John Terry of Antigua, carpenter. Will dated 29 Sep. 1683. To my wife Anne Terry all my estate for life, then equally to my children, viz., John, Marg', Basil, David, & Benjn Terry. Witnessed by Thomas Bartelott. Sworn 17 Aug. 1696. Recorded 8 Sep. 1696.

Susanna Ewen, aged 16, daughter of John Ewen of Antigua, hath a right to four negros, and hath chosen David Rutherford and Sarah Turner, widow, her Guardians. Confirmed 6 Sep. 1696. Recorded 9 Sep. 1696.

John Chambers of St. Paul's, Falmouth, Antigua. Will dated 24 July 1696. To my wife Hannah all my Estate. Witnessed by Charles Lowe, Richard Buckeridge, William Wainwright. Before Christopher Codrington, Esq., were sworn Lieut.-Colonel Wainwright and Mr. Charles Lowe 14 Aug. 1696. Recorded 10 Sep. 1696.

Walter Quarme, John Brett, and Thomas Banks on 7 Aug. 1696 value the estate of John Kingsley of London at £131. Recorded 21 Sep. 1696.

By warrant dated 16 July 1696 John Roe, Henry Winthrop, and Laurence Turton value the goods of Thomas Everitt of Antigua, planter, deceased, as shewn by his widow Mary, his administratrix, at £37, 28 July 1696. Recorded 21 Sep. 1696.

Nathaniel Humphry and Gawen Roe, acting by warrant, value the goods of Gilbert Taylor, deceased, as shewn by his widow Florance Taylor, at £78. Recorded 6 Oct. 1696.

Daniel Dawley of St. Phillip's. Will dated 17 April 1696. To my son Humphrey Dawley a negro at 18. To my son George Dawley all my Estate at 21, with remainder to Humphry, & to pay my son Jno Dawley 2000 lbs. of tobacco. My wife to manage my estate. My friends Mr Jno Parry & Geo. Baker Trustees & Guardians. Witnessed by Philip Ledeatt, Daniel McCharty. Sworn 4 Aug. 1696. Recorded 9 Oct. 1696.

Thomas Phillipes of Antigua, planter. Will dated 17 Aug. 1696. To my wife Mary 10 acres I bought of Robt Jefferson for life, then to my dau. Mary Phillipes. To my dau.-in-law Ann Salter 5 acres. To my dau. Mary Phillipes 10 acres where I now live & a negro woman. My friends Lt Nath. Crump & Geo. Baker Trustees & Guardians. Witnessed by Elizabeth Garrett, George Baker. Sworn 17 Sep. 1696. Recorded 9 Oct. 1696.

Whereas Henry Chearnly, late of Antigua, widow, desired George Gamble, merchant, to administer his estate in right of his wife Frances Chearnly, whom he named his Ex'trix. Adm'on was granted 11 March last. George Gamble wishes to be discharged of the trust, and Barry Tankerd, merchant, is on 2 Oct. 1696 appointed in his place. Recorded 12 Oct. 1696.

1696, Oct. 11. Antigua. By Christopher Codrington, Esq., to Hon. John Yeamans, Esq. My presence required at the other isles, you are to prevent all pressing of marriners by H.M. ships. Recorded 12 Oct. 1696.

Elizabeth Jenkings of Antigua. Will dated 17 Oct. 1695. All my estate to Jas. Bayly & his wife Jane. Witnessed by John King, Thomas Balam. Sworn 30 Oct. 1696. Recorded 31 Oct. 1696.

1696, Nov. 17. By the Deputy-Governor. Henrietta Scot, daughter of Walter Scot, deceased, has chosen Mr. James Sparkes of Antigua her Guardian. Inventory required. Recorded 3 Dec. 1696.

Captain Ferditick Weghman, Commander of H.M.S. "Colechester," died intestate. Adm'on to Jacob Poulton 22 Feb. 1696. Nathaniel Sampson, William Hawkes, and Thomas Banks value his effects at £102. Recorded 22 Feb. 1696.

George Erwin, deceased. Dr. Daniel Mackinen and Mr. George Gamble appraise his estate, as shewn by Mr. Joseph Watkins the Ex'or, at £244, 2 Oct. 1696. Recorded 9 March 1696-7.

Thomas Comins of Antigua died intestate. Adm'on to Mary his widow 3 March 1696. Recorded 12 March 1696.

Captain John Mountford of Antigua died intestate. Adm'on to Mary (? his widow) 26 March 1696-7. By warrant Mr. John Wright, Mr. John Martin, and Captain John Ker appraise his effects at £15, 26 March 1697. Recorded 7 April 1697.

William Tudor of London, merchant. Will dated 28 Dec. 1696. To my wife Mary all my Estate for life, then to my 3 children W^{m}, Jos., & Mary Tudor. Mr Jos. Martin of Love Lane, merch^{t}, Mr Rich. Tudway, merch^{t} in London, Maj. Edw. Byam, & Jas. Porter of Antigua, Ex'ors. Witnessed by Samuel Phillips, Arthur Freeman, Richard Cochran, William Glanvile. Sworn 16 Jan. 1696-7. By the Governor. Warrant to Mr. William Glanvile, Mr. Samuel Lowger, Mr. Thomas Lasher, and Mr. Samuel Phillips to appraise, 18 Jan. 1696-7. They return an inventory 22 Jan. 1696-7, and give total value of estate as £761, also £315 due, 29 Jan. 1696-7. Recorded 28 May 1697.

Amongst those owing money in the schedule are :—

Mr. Samuel Lewgar.	Mr. John Eliott.
Richard Dashwood.	Mr. John Bradshaw.
Mr. John Painter.	Daniel McCarty.
Henry Lowry.	Owen McCarty.
Colonel Vernon.	Florence McCarty.
Mr. William Brown.	Mr. Nathaniel Gilbert.
Mark Kerwan.	Mr. William Cochran.
Cornelius Hallerin.	Mr. John Cochran.
Mr. John Duer.	Mr. John Martin.
Peter Garrett.	Mr. John Crachroad.
Dr. Toby.	Mr. David Sweegle.
Mr. Howard.	Mr. Josh. Barsham.
James Fallow.	Mr. Samuel Phillips.
Mr. John Lucas.	Mr. Robert Nanton.
Mr. Arthur Freeman.	Lieut. John Lyons.
John Bullock.	Mr. Derby Nugent.
Mr. Porter.	Mr. John C . . . .
Mr. Glanvile.	Samuel Thomson.
Hester Glanvile.	Mrs. Patience Thomas.
William Miles.	Mr. Baker.
Mr. Jeremiah Blizard.	Captain Thomas Oysterman.
Mr. Richard Cochran.	Thomas Barry.
Mr. James Parke.	Mr. George Reynolds.
Mr. Samuel Parry.	Mr. Thomas Martin.
Mr. Francis Christian.	Anthony Quiwart.
Mr. Henry Smedmore, agent to Colonel Byam.	Mr. James Porter.
Mrs. Jane Cochran.	Mr. Laurence Crabb.
Captain John Tankerd.	Captain John Yeamans, Esq.
	Mrs. Grissell Morris.

Joshua Leach of Antigua, planter. Will dated 16 April 1697. To my dau. Mary Mumford 10 acres in Belfast, formerly Dennis Keef's, & a negro girl. All residue to my wife Mary for life, then to my s^{d} dau. To my goddaus. Eliz. Spencer & Kath. Keef 500 lbs. of tobacco each. To my poor friend Tho. Callaway 20s. If my wife & dau. both die then all my estate to the poor of Belfast Div^{n}. My loving friends Cap. Jno Ker & Nath. Crump Ex'ors. Witnessed by Samuel Mayer, Dennis Keef, George Hyde. Sworn and recorded 29 June 1697.

1697, July 1. Elizabeth Rice, daughter of Elisha Rice of Antigua, deceased, has chosen Thomas Duncombe, Esq., and Colonel Edward Byam Guardians. Recorded 1 July 1697.

Mark Hall of Antigua, planter. Will dated 4 June 1690. About to serve my country in this present Expedition against ye French & rebell Irish. To my brother-in-law Jno Sonds 5 acres. To my brother Danl Sonds 5 acres. To Jno Stanly, son of Terence Stanly, 5 acres. To Math. Nelmor 500 lbs. of tobacco. All my household stuff to Jno

Sonds, Danl Sonds, & Jno Stanly. Jno Bowdon, Tho. Burke, & Jno Martin Ex'ors in Trust & 30*s.* rings. Witnessed by Robert Burn, Jeffrey Dowling. Recorded 5 July 1697.

John Julius, Commander of ye shallop privateer "Fancie," bound on the Expedition against the French. Will dated 19 June 1697. To Mrs Eliz. Smith, dau.-in-law of Jno Wright, all my Estate. Witnessed by George Roach, Francis Cox, John Wright. Sworn and recorded 29 July 1697.

Robert Ceassam of Antigua, mason. Will dated 18 April 1697. To my sister Passent Thomas all my Estate & 14 acres in Willoughby Bay Div^{n}, she Ex'trix. My mare to my niece Ann Thomas. Witnessed by John Glasgoe, Walter Barnet, James Darcy (their marks). Sworn 22 July and recorded 19 Aug. 1697.

John Harbert of Antigua died intestate. Adm'on to Elizabeth Smith, widow.

Before Christopher Codrington, Esq., appeared Darby Cahane, John Cochran, and Charles Harrison, and swore that they saw testator Edward Leaver sign his will. Recorded 18 Sep. 1697.

Witnessed by Thomas Clerk, Antho. Monteyro, Jos. Monteyro. On 1 Oct. 1697 Captain Thomas Clerk and Mr. Antho. Monteyro swore they saw the testator Captain William Henry O'Bryan sign his will. Recorded 4 Oct. 1697.

Warrant, dated 8 Sep. 1697, to appraise the goods of Laughlin Guin of Antigua, deceased, as shewn by Sarah Guin his administratrix, directed to Mr. Francis Christian, Mr. William Stephenson, and Mr. George Reynolds.

1696, Dec. 31. John Mitchell and Cuthbert Black, witnesses to the will of David Hartnoll, were sworn. Recorded 27 Nov. 1697.

Order to appraise the goods of Mrs. Kath. Fenton of Antigua, deceased, as shewn by Benjamin Anderson her administrator, directed 7 Dec. 1697 to Mr. Richard Oliver and Mr. John Martin, Nathaniel Gateward, and Nathaniel Sampson. Inventory, £13, made 24 Dec. and recorded 30 Dec. 1697.

Order to appraise the goods of William Burne, deceased, as shewn by John Cozen, administrator, directed 27 Jan. 1697 to Captain Isaack Horsford, Mr. Thomas Franklin, and Mr. Cuthbert Black. Inventory made 29 Jan. and recorded 7 Feb. 1697.

Jonathan Wells of Antigua. Will dated 21 Nov. 1696. To my wife Eliz. all my Estate, she to be Ex'trix. Witnessed by Robert Broughton, Jonathan Squire, John Bartt. Sworn 4 Feb. and recorded 7 Feb. 1697.

John Ellstoub of Antigua. Will dated 1 March 1697. My wife Mary. I owe Jno Aling 15 pieces of 8, Mr Breat 5 do., Mr Banks 3*s.*, Mrs Susana Kerley 20 pieces. Witnessed by (Mr.) Charles Montjoy, Susanna Kearley. Sworn 7 March and recorded 10 March 1697.

Ellinor Cahan of Antigua, late of Nevis. Will dated 24 Feb. 1697. To my brother Ambrose Wheeler & my sister Jane Chahan a negro & $\frac{1}{2}$ of a plantation in Nevis left me by the will of my father Derman Cahan. All residue to my s^{d} brother, he sole Ex'or. Witnessed by Jonathan Squire, John Evans, Charles Harper, and John Davis. Sworn and recorded 10 March 1697.

John Blacklock of Antigua, merchant. Will dated 10 March 1697. To my half-sister Mrs Mary Blakely of Pasely in Scotland all my Estate. Wm Hawkes & Mr Nath. Sampson, merchants, of Antigua, Ex'ors in Trust. Witnessed by John Butler, Tho. Wise. Sworn and recorded 16 March 1697-8. Order to appraise goods directed 16 March 1697 to James Nisbitt, Edward Acton, and Robert Oliver—£62. Recorded 28 March 1698.

John Howard of Antigua. Will dated 25 Jan. 1697. All Estate to my 2 sons W^{m} & Jno Howard equally at 21, & in default to my 2 daus. Mary & Sarah Howard at 21. To my 1st dau. Mary Howard 30,000 lbs., & to my dau. Sarah Howard 50,000 lbs. at 17. To my youngest dau. Alice Howard 10,000 lbs. at 15. Wm Glanvile, Rich. Hughes, & Tho. Nanton, overseers. Witnessed by Thomas Devvie, Peter Lucas, Margaret Almond. Sworn 13 March and recorded 29 March 1698.

John Hewson of Antigua died intestate. Adm'on to Archibald Johnston 4 April 1698. Order passed 4 April 1698 by Governor Yeamans to Mr. Nathaniel Sampson, Mr. Robert Olliver, and Mr. William Hawkes to appraise. Recorded 11 April 1698.

Daniel Mackdanill of Antigua, planter. Will dated 2 April 1698. All Estate to my friend Mr Jas. Nisbet. Witnessed by William Hawkes, David Nicholsone.

All my Estate to my friend Mr Wm Gordon, merch^{t} in London, he to be Ex'or. Cap. Rob. Martin & Mr Jno Hume Ex'ors in Trust.

1698, May 21. 94,439 lbs. from Justice Duncombe and Mr. Richard Oliver, *re* plantation of Mr. Christopher Chapman, deceased, Mrs. Catherine Chapman his administratrix. Recorded 2 June 1698.

Adam Kenedy, merchant. Will dated 22 June 1698. To my friends Jno Martin, Cap. Rob. Martin, & Mr Jno Hume, each a beaver hat. The dau. of Cap. Rob. Martin called Jean. Witnessed by William Moll, Robert Donaldson. Sworn 24 June 1698.

Order, dated 1 June 1698, to Mr. William Lavington, Mr. Nathaniel Gilbert, and Mr. John Durer to appraise the estate of Samuel Hathorne, deceased, as shewn by Margaret Hathorne the widow and administratrix. Returned at £176 14 June 1698. Recorded 29 June 1698.

1698, May 27. William, Rex to Colonel Edward Byam and Captain John Ker the guardians of George, John, Rachell, Isakaell, Benjamin, James and Phillitor Reynolds, the sons and daughters of William Reynolds, deceased, to divide two negro women and five boys. Inventory £209. Recorded 8 July 1698.

Thomas Capps of Antigua, planter. Will dated 17 Dec. 1696. To my dau. Eliz. Capps all my Estate, if she die $\frac{1}{2}$ to my son-in-law Mr Steph. Maine & to Mr Abr. Swan, & $\frac{1}{2}$ to Mrs Annaker. Ste. Maine & Ab. Swan Ex'ors in Trust. Witnessed by Nathaniel Crump, Susannah Baker, Ellinor Goold. Sworn 13 Feb. 1696-7. Recorded 8 July 1698.

1698, June 25. Order to Mr. Nathaniel Sampson and Mr. William Hawkes and Mr. Francis Browne to appraise the goods of Adam Keneday, deceased, as shewn by the Ex'ors Captain Robert Martin and John Hume. Inventory £315. Recorded 20 Aug. 1698.

1697, March 16. John Blacklock, deceased. Adm'on to the Ex'ors in trust William Hawkes and Nathaniel Sampson. Recorded 22 Aug. 1698.

Nicholas Lawson of St. John's in Five Islands Division, planter. Will undated. To my dau. Kath. Lawson £100 c. at 18. To my 2 godchildren Jno & Mary Soward 500 lbs. each. To my son Cornelius Lawson all my Estate, he to be Ex'or, remainder to my dau. Kath., remainder as to $\frac{1}{2}$ to my 2 godchildren, & $\frac{1}{2}$ to my wife's sister Marg^{t} Chapman of Antigua. Mr Wm Walters, Mr Steph. Main, & Tho. Turner Ex'ors in Trust. Witnessed by (Captain) Robert Martin, Robert Broughton. Sworn 22 and recorded 24 Sep. 1698.

Peter Delanoy of Antigua. Will dated 8 Feb. 1696. To my 5 children Jno, Peter, Tho., Ann, & Mary Delanoy 17 acres in New North Sound Div^{n} equally. My wife Mary Delanoy Ex'trix. My brother-in-law Wm Johnson & friend Wm Mole Trustees. Witnessed by Thomas Darlow, jun., James Jones. Sworn 12 Nov. 1697. Recorded 10 Oct. 1698.

John Howard of St. John's, freeholder. Will dated 10 April 1698. To my wife Elizth all my goods, she to pay to Maj^{r} Bird, Wm Browne, Jonathan Squires, Marg^{t} Ray, & Gillien Ward 40*s.* each. To Ben. Pepper, son of Wm Pepper £5 st. To Jos. Allen £5 st. Witnessed by William

Howard, William Bonworth. Sworn 20 Oct. and recorded 21 Oct. 1698. Adm'on to Elizabeth Howard 20 Oct. 1698. Order to appraise to Mr. Thomas Stevens, Mr. John Jairden, Mr. William Edwards. Inventory £25.

John Sulevan of Antigua, cooper. Will dated 26 May 1698. To my wife Kath. & my dau. Eliz. Sulevan all Estate, they to be Ex'trices. Witnessed by Benjamin Machin, Richard Davis, Thomas Skerret. Sworn 3 and recorded 7 Nov. 1698.

Codicil of John Carruthers of Antigua, merchant, dated 20 Nov. 1698. My will was drawn up in London in 1698, & is in the hands of Mr Robert Fade, mercht, near Threadneedle Street. All goods here to be shipt to Engld. Cap. Rob. Martin & Mr Adam Martin of Antigua, Gentn, Ex'ors. Witnessed by James Martin, John Chamberlain, Charles Harper. My goods to be sent to Mr Rob. Fade & Mr Jno Carruthers, linendraper, at the 3 pigeons in Cheapside at the corner of Gutter Lane. Jno Somerwall's effects to go to Mr Geo. Cunin in Corbett's Court, near Gratia Str. Mr David Guilein, Mr Alex. Gordon, & Mr Mungoe Somerwall. Sworn 29 and recorded 30 Nov. 1698.

Joseph Pallmer of the town of Gospeth. Will dated 22 Nov. 1698. To my mother Jane £29 st. To Mrs Ann Waid a ring. To Palmer Nobbs & James Pallmer my clothing. To my mother all wages from the ship "Fame." Mr James Bowden Ex'or in Trust. Witnessed by John Pottwine, James Parkins, Gabriel Racey. Sworn 29 Nov. 1698.

Francis Boadelott of Antigua. Will dated 1 Nov. 1698. All Estate to my partner John Foster, he to be Ex'or, & to discharge the rents & obligations jointly given to Rich. Oliver for the use of Jno Huse, a minor. Witnessed by Nicholas Maw, William Howard. Sworn 24 Nov. and recorded 5 Dec. 1698.

1698, Oct. Robert Martin and John Haddon appraise the goods of Nicholas Lawson at £243. The Ex'ors to be Guardians. 29 Nov. Recorded 8 Dec. 1698.

Peter Cames, son of Edward Cames, deceased, has chosen Mr. Thomas Turner for his Guardian, 29 Nov., and recorded 8 Dec. 1698.

Here follow some Hutcheson papers and correspondence:—

Affidavit of Archibald Hutcheson, dated 8 Jan. 1690-91, that he has not carried off any pillage from St. Christopher's. Witnessed by J. Legard, William Mead, and William Ritt.

He also gave his account of affairs ye 8 Jan. 1690-91 to the Commissioners of the Army at St. Christopher's, stated that the prisoners were all embarqued for St. Domingo. Recorded by John Smargin, Secretary. In a long letter to General Codrington he says that he has been accused of receiving bribes and taking goods and of being a Papist, 20 Feb. 1690-91.

Christopher Codrington issued a Proclamation, 23 Feb. 1690-91, at St. Christopher's, after the receipt of the letter from Archibald Hutcheson, Esq., late Attorney-General of the Leeward Islands.

At a General Council and Assembly of the Leeward Islands, held at Antigua 28 March 1691, the following Members sign a declaration that none have appeared to accuse Mr. Hutcheson, and further state that he hath been falsely calumniated and grant him 20,000 lbs. for his services. Signed by—

Anthony Hodges, Speaker.	Samuell Winthrope.
John Gunthorpe.	John Yeamans.
Edward Byam.	Walter Simmonds.
Phillip Dewitt.	William Helme.
Robert Brodbelt.	Thomas Symmons.
John Scott.	William Fox.

Mr. Archibald Hutcheson writes on 21 April 1691 asking General Codrington for a share of St. Christopher's pillage from Their M.S. ye "Mary," near Guadaloupe. The General refers this to ye Field Officers of ye Army 28 April 1691, "from ye camp at Guadaloupe."

The field officers by letter agree to give him £200. Signed by—

Richard Kirby.	John Dowly.
A. Hamilton.	Edward Nott.
John Hamilton.	Rowland Williams.
Anthony Hodges.	Nathaniel Blackiston.
Charles Pym.	Philemon Bird.
John Stanley.	

Archibald Hutcheson writes again on 21 Aug. 1691 to the Governor Thomas Weaver, Esq., Secretary of Warrants and Secretary-General of the Leeward Islands, certifies that it was publicly read before a Council of War in St. John's Town, when there were present:—

His Excellency the General.	Commissary-General.
Lieut.-General Hill.	Colonel Hamilton.
Colonel Williams.	Colonel Gardner.
Colonel Blackiston.	Major Gunthorpe.
Master of Ordnance.	Major Kitt.
Esay Burges, Esq.	Sworn 9 July 1692.

Mr. Hutcheson wrote again 11 July 1692 to the General, in answer to which the Governor and Assembly agree to sign a certificate of Mr. Hutcheson's honourable conduct, clearing him of all aspersions. Signed by—

John Lucas, Speaker.	Robert Freeman.
Esay Burges.	John Tankerd.
William Abram.	Christopher Codrington,
Charles Tudway.	Captain-General.
Thomas Edgecombe.	J. Parry.
David Martin.	John Frye.
Ed. Horne.	John Yeamans.
Ed. Byam.	Thomas Duncombe.
Robert Martin.	Francis Carlile.
Christopher Knight.	Thomas Warner.
Samuel Horne.	

(On a fragment.) To my dau. Mary a negro woman, 10 acres, & a colt. To my son Sam. 15,000 lbs. & a mulatto boy at 21. To my son Wm 15,000 lbs. & a negro. To my son Jas. 15,000 lbs. & a boy. All residue to my son John. My wife Jane sole Ex'trix, but if she marry then my good friends Mr Jno & Mr Wm Lynine (?), & Mr Rich. Oliver to be Ex'ors. No name.

Antigua. Before Hon. Stephen Blizard, Esq., Chief Judge of the Court of Common Pleas, appeared John Wilkins, Deputy-Secretary and Clerk of ye Crown of Antigua, and swore that the preceding writings from fo. 1 to fo. 336 were transcribed from an original book of records in the Secretary's office that was damaged in the late hurricane on 31 Aug. 1772, which he received authority from the Legislature of Antigua to get copied. Sworn 20 Aug. 1774. (N.B.—The first 24 folios are missing.—V. L. O.)

Will of Daniel Mackdanill. Before John Yeamans, Deputy-Governor, were sworn William Hanker and David Nicholson 11 April 1698. Recorded 12 April 1698.

Darby Cabane, planter. Will dated 13 Oct. 1697. To Tho. Lasher, Mr, 20 acres & a negro. To my godson Tim. Fowler, son of Nich. Fowler, a horse. To Dan. Cartee, Sr, a roan mare. My negro Jack his freedom. All res. to Tho. Lasher whom I appoint Ex'or. Witnessed by John Willson, Isabell Sangster, Owen Cartee, Sen. Recorded 12 April 1698.

Roger Complaint died intestate. Adm'on 12 April 1697 to David Rutherford, value £103. Recorded 15 April 1698.

John Cozens. Will dated 14 Jan. 1697. All Est. to my wife Sarah, she to be Ex'trix. Denis Miachelmore sworn 26 April 1698 by Christopher Codrington, Esq.

1698, April 26. Soloman Dun died intestate. Adm'on to Ann his widow. Appraised tobacco 528 lbs., cotton 286 lbs.

The estate of Mr. Christopher Chapman, deceased, as shewn by his widow Katherine, 94,439 lbs.

1701, Feb. 12. Letter of Attorney from William Humphry, citizen and ironmonger, of London, reciting will of John Sampson of Antigua, planter. "My 1st son Jno to be heir of all my lands & negros in Barbados."

Anne Reg. Commission to Colonel Thomas Wotham to be Colonel of Brigadier Tiffine's Regiment of Foot, deceased, and to act for the Governor-in-Chief in his death or absence. At our Court at the Bathe 5 Sep. 1702. Recorded Feb. 1702-3.

Thomas Haliman of Long Hamborowe, co. Oxon, yeoman, only surviving son of Anthony Haliman, late of ditto, yeoman, deceased, and only surviving brother and heir of William Haliman, late of Antigua, planter, deceased. Letter of Attorney to Colonel George Gamble and James Read of Antigua, merchants.

1702, April 30. Deposition of Ann Cornett of St. Saviour's, Southwark, wife of Henry Cornett, vintner, that Thomas Haliman is aged about 50, etc., 30 April 1702. Endorsed by Sir William Gore, Knt., Lord Mayor of London.

1700, Jan. 4. Mr. Thomas Ashburn of Jamaica, merchant, now in London, revokes Letter of Attorney formerly given to John Wright and James Browne, merchants of Antigua, against Laurence Crabb, and now gives the same to William Thomas.

1702, Oct. 14. William Telfeir, hammerman (? blacksmith), of Glasgow. Letter of Attorney to Mr. John Anderson of Antigua, merchant taylor, to recover sums of Mr. William Haulks, merchant in Antigua, and the representatives of Mr. Nathaniel Sampson, merchant, deceased, for assisting Mary Blacklock, half-sister and heir, and Ex'trix to her brother Mr. John Blacklock, merchant, deceased, now my spouse according to his will dated 10 March 1698.

Leonard Walter, chyrurgeon of Antigua. Will dated 1 Feb. 1702-3. To my wife Kath. £100 c. To my 2 daus. Mary & Jemima all Estate. To the poor of Newport Pagnell, co. Bucks, £10 c. To the poor of St. John's £10 c. Cap. Sam. Watkins & Jas. Feild, clk., of Antigua, Ex'ors. Witnessed by William Hamilton, Robert Irving. Sworn 27 and recorded 30 May 1703.

By John Dove, Esq., Commissioner for Recovery of Rights and Perquisites of the Admiralty. H.R.H. Prince George of Denmark, Lord High Admiral of England, Ireland, and all the plantations, appoints Sigismond Cooper, Esq., his agent, to seize all prizes and pirates taken by uncommissioned vessells, and to receive for his trouble one-tenth of all such. At Yorke Buildings 1 Jan. 1702. Recorded 12 June 1703.

Henry Smedmore of Antigua, planter. Will dated 16 Jan. 1702-3. To my mother Susanna Horsnaile of London 4 negros, 2 mares, & the profits of my plantation, & in case of her death to my brother Cha. Smedmore. To Mr Corn. Vaughan £10 c. & my large silver handled cane. To Cap. Jno Paynter my ring. To Mr David Ervin a gold pistole. To Dr Jno Burt all residue. Hon. Ed. Byam, Esq., Cap. Isaac Horsford, & Dr Jno Burt, Ex'ors. Witnessed by Dennis Mackelmore, Simon Ervin. Sworn before Deputy-Governor John Yeamans 11 June and recorded 13 July 1703.

Appointment of Walter Quarme, Esq., Master in Chancery, 29 Nov. 1703, by Christopher Codrington, Esq. Recorded 1 Dec. 1703.

List of payments made to the officers and men of Colonel Henry Holt's Regiment. In 1693 Henry Lyons, Piggot, Delavall, David Ganspole, Thompson, and Garth were Captains.

On 22 May 1703 appeared Daniel Jones, Gent., of Antigua, and produced the charter paper dated 12 Feb. 1701 between John Wild of London, mariner, master of the Barbuda galley of 100 tons, and Vavasor Cage of London, Gent., part owner, of the one part, and Arthur Freeman of London, merchant, of the other part, to fetch from Parham 20 hogsheads of sugar at 6s. per cwt.

Abraham Lloyd, Isabel Lloyd, and Caleb Lloyd of Bristol, merchants. Letter of Attorney to James Reed of Antigua, merchant, with the advice of Captain John Perrie, Major John Lyons, and Captain Edward Byam, 9 Jan. 1702.

James June of Antigua, planter. Letter of Attorney to his wife Jane, John Paynter, Gent., and Benjamin Felton, Gent., 9 July 1702.

Mary Lingham of St. Dunstan in the West, spinster, Thomas Elliott of London, gardener, and Elizabeth his wife, and John Earle of Middlewich, co. Chester, cooper, which said Mary, Elizabeth, and Sarah are the sisters and coheirs of John Lingham of Antigua, Gent., deceased, their Letter of Attorney to John Wetham of London, merchant, to take possession of land called Blubber Valley, and Muskito Cove and Green Island, 1 April 1703.

Thomas Coles of Antigua, planter. Will dated 9 March 1703-4. To my brother Jno Coles, grocer in London, all my negros. To my friend Tho. Chitton £15 c. To Eliz. Chitton my clothes. To my friend Rich. Gosney £30 c. To Roger Chilton, son of Tho. Chilton, £30 c. All residue to Jno Burt of Antigua, Surgeon. Cap. Isaac Horsford, Mr Tho. Nanton, & the sd Burt Ex'ors. Witnessed by William Howard, John Howard, William Grear. Sworn 10 May and recorded 2 June 1704.

Sir Samuel Garrard, Bart. Letter of Attorney to Edward Perrie of Antigua, merchant.

David Swigle of Antigua, chirurgeon. Letter of Attorney to James Brown, Richard Pick, and Richard Cockran of Antigua 23 July 1704.

William Stevenson and Jane his wife, Ex'trix of Robert Jones *alias* Sutton of Antigua, deceased, recite a sale of negros to Marcus Kirwan FitzRichard on 25 May 1689. Recorded 29 Sep. 1704.

George Hide of St. Philip's Parish. Will dated 9 May 1704. To my dau. Eliz. Hide a negro girl. To my son Geo. Hide all my estate, he to allow maintenance for my children John, Tho., & Mary Hide. My wife Mary & my friends Tho. Rome & Ben. Steele Ex'ors & Guardians. Witnessed by John Sutherly, John Witts. Sworn 27 Sep. and recorded 6 Oct. 1704.

James Morian of Antigua, merchant. Will dated 13 Dec. 1704. All estate to my aunt Eliz. Morian of Bristoll, wid. My friend Ed. Taylor of Antigua, carpenter, Ex'or. Witnessed by John Lucas, Elias Jamain, Ed. Taylor. Sworn 20 and recorded 21 Dec. 1704.

Ed. Willson of St. Michael's Town, Barbados, Administrator of Ed. Morris of Barbados, deceased. Letter of Attorney to Mr. Richard Peck of Antigua, merchant, 15 Sep. 1704. Recorded 15 Feb. 1704-5.

Anne Reg. Appointment of William Brodrick, Esq., Attorney-General for Nevis, St. Christopher's, Montserrat, Antigua, Barbuda, and Anguilla, 16 Jan. 1704, by John Johnson, Esq. Recorded 12 Feb. 1704.

Samuel Lilley and Co., *i.e.* Samuel Lilley, David Jeffries, and Francis Clarke of Boston in New England, merchants. Letter of Attorney to Isaac Royall of Boston, merchant, 13 Dec. 1704. Recorded 1 March 1704-5.

Abraham Elton of Bristoll, merchant, for self and Co., owners of the ship "George and Grace." Letter of Attorney to Captain Stephen Duer of Antigua 5 Jan. 1704. Recorded 7 April 1705.

James June of Antigua, planter. Will dated 9 July 1702. Going to Jamaica. To my children Jane, Eliz., Jno, & Jas. June all Estate. Wife Jane to manage it, but if she marry my friends Jno Painter & Ben. Felton to be Ex'ors in Trust. Witnessed by Philip Pursgrout (?), Richard

Bamton, Thomas Gateward. Sworn 22 and recorded 24 May 1705.

Michael Bennett of New Division, carpenter. Will undated. My wife Mary. My dau. Mary. All residue to my son Michael. My dau. Susannah.

Edward Burrish of Antigua, merchant. Will dated 4 May 1703. All Estate to my wife Anne, she to be Ex'trix. Witnessed by Anthony Monteyro, A. Redwood, Thomas Kerby. Sworn 27 April and recorded 31 May 1705.

John Tully of Boston, mariner. Will dated 7 Nov. 1702. To my brother Wm Tully of Seabrook in New England the land his house is on. To Wm Christopher of Antigua 100 acres, part of 1000 left my father as a legacy by Joshua, the Indian King, next to Connecticut River. To my wife all residue, she to be Ex'trix. Witnessed by Cæsar Rodeny, Thomas Kerby, Edward Morgan. Sworn 29 and recorded 31 May 1705.

Nathan Staubury of Philadelphia, merchant. Letter of Attorney to Isaac Royall of Antigua, merchant, 14 April 1705. Recorded 9 June 1705.

By Governor Yeamans. Robert Thornton of Antigua, Esq., died intestate. Adm'on 9 May 1705 to Mary ye widow. Inventory £1149. Recorded 18 July 1705.

Mark Robison of Antigua, merchant. Will dated 6 June 1705. All Estate to my wife Mary. £3 c. to Rob. Donaldson & his wife for a ring. My clothes to Dav. Gullin, Wm Pawling, & Jas. Cruickshank. My wife Ex'trix. Majr Rob. Nanton & Rob. Donaldson of Antigua, Gentn, Ex'ors in Trust. Witnessed by John Magorman, David Gullin, James Cruckshank. Sworn 16 and recorded 20 July 1705.

Arthur Wharfe of Antigua. Will dated 5 Aug. 1705. To my brother Nathl Wharfe £60 c. for his children. To my brother Jno Wharfe £50 c., to be left in the hands of my brother Fra. Holmes of Boston for his maintenance. To my wife Mary all residue, she & my friend Tho. Trant to be Ex'ors. Witnessed by Ann Burrish, Nathaniel Hinton, Thomas Kerby. Sworn 6 and recorded 10 Sep. 1705.

Inventory of estate of Nicholas Nicholls, Esq. John Yeamans administrator. A small library of books taken 5 Feb. 1705.

By Sir Bevill Granville, Governor of Barbados, at Pilgrim 24 Aug. 1705. On 25 May 1705 was proved the will of Charles Thomas, Esq., and the Hon. William Holder and Benjamin Bullard, Esq., two of the Ex'ors resident in Barbados, were granted adm'on exclusive of Sir Dalby Thomas, Thomas Pindar, merchant, and Thomas Stewart, merchant (Joseph Hole, merchant, renouncing). Will forwarded as follows:—

Charles Thomas* of St. Michael, Barbados, Esq. Will dated 14 March 1704. To my dau. Susannah Thomas all my Estate, but if she die under 18 a spinster, then all to my brother Sr Dalby Thomas, Knt, & after his death to the heirs male of my Neph. Dalby Thomas his son, remainder as to ½ to Susannah Thomas, dau. of the sd Sr Dalby Thomas, & ½ to my sister Mrs Susanna Penny. My sd brother, my loving friend Tho. Pinder of London, mt, Mr Tho. Stewart of London, mt, Guardians of my dau. My interest in several vessels to be sold. After my dau. shall have received £6000 from the Estate I give to my niece Susanna Thomas, dau. of my sd brother Sr Dalby Thomas, £1000 st. If my dau. die £1000 st. to my sister Susanna Penny. To apprentice Leonard Hancock my clothes. To my brother Sr Dalby Thomas & Dorothy his wife, my nephew Dalby Thomas & my niece Susanna Thomas £100 between them for mourning. To my sister Susanna Penny £50. Mr Tho. Pinder £20. Mr Tho. Stewart £20. Hon. Wm Holder, Esq., £20. Col. Ben. Bullard £20. Jos. Hole, mt, £20. Sr Dalby Thomas, Tho. Pinder, Tho. Stewart, mts, Hon. Wm Holder, Esq., Ben. Bullard, Esq., & Joseph Hole, mt, Ex'ors. Witnessed by Thomas Lynch, Francis De Laet, Joseph Windmills. To Cap. Jno Trotter, Comr of H.M.S. "Warwick," £20. To the poor of St Michael £20 c. To my goddau. Eliz. Rust, dau. of Cap. Walt. Rust, £25 c. My Brigandeen "Larke," Math. Harman, Comr. To Jane Reynolds my nurse £10 c. Sworn 25 May 1705 before Sir B. Granville. Recorded at Antigua 20 Oct. 1705.

* This will was recorded in 1711 (P.C.C., 94 Young), and that of Sir Dalby Thomas, Knt. (116 Young).

Aron Ruberds of St. Phillip's Parish. Will dated 25 Dec. 1700. To my grandchildren Tabitha Phillpot 2 negros, Rebecca Phillpot a negro woman, Jno Phillpot a mare & £6000 c., Wm Phillpot a negro, Sabia Phillpot a negro woman, Frances Phillpot 7 goats, the children of Sam. Phillpot. My friends Phil. Ledeatt & Saml Phillpot Ex'ors. Witnessed by Thomas Ledeatt, Ab. Swan, Thomas Ledeatt. By Christopher Codrington appeared Thomas Ledeatt, senior, Ab. Swan, and Thomas Ledeatt, junior, 7 July 1701. Recorded 17 Dec. . . . .

Richard Buckeridge, Collector of Antigua, bound to England. Letter of Attorney to Hon. Colonel George Gamble, Esq., Mr. James Browne, Mr. Thomas Wise, and Mr. John Brett, 13 Aug. 1705. By Hon. John Lucas, Chief Justice. Sworn 10 Dec. 1705.

By Hon. Stephen Blizard, Esq., Chief Justice of the Court of Common Pleas, appeared John Wilkins, Deputy-Secretary and Clerk of the Crown, and swore that the preceding folios 11 to 288 have been transcribed from an original Book of Records in the Secretary's Office that sustained considerable damage in the late hurricane on 31 Aug. 1772. Sworn 20 Aug. 1774.

Circa 1710. Philemon Bird of Antigua, Gent. Letter of Attorney to Samuel Proctor of St. John's, merchant, and Thomas Turner and Henry Symes of Antigua, Gentlemen.

Robert Shares of Antigua, planter. Will dated 2 Oct. 1711. To my kinsmen & friends, the 2 sons & 2 daus. of my brother & sister John & Mary Love, £300 c. between them. My wife's dau. Sarah Laughland. All residue to Shares Stevens, son of Jno Stevens. My kinsman Jno Stevens Ex'or. Witnessed by John Mayo, Thomas Laughland, Robert Tremills, who were sworn 7 Nov. 1711 before Lieut.-Governor John Yeamans.

1711, Sep. 21. Henry Soper to William Soper.

Walter Long of Antigua. Will not dated. To my wife Anne Long a proportion of land, house, & furniture, & after her death to Wm Mould & his children. To my friend Jas. Nisbit & Wm Mould a proportion of land & house equally. All residue to Jas. Nisbitt, Wm Mould, & Wm Kennedey equally, & Ex'ors. Witnessed by John Jairchen, William Pauling. Sworn 20 Feb. 1708 before Governor Parke.

Rebecca Heiferman of Antigua, widow. Will dated 26 March 1705. To my niece Cath. Hargust, now Clifton, all my Estate in Nevis. To Eliz. McCarty, dau. of Owen McCarty, a negro girl. To Cath. McCarty her sister a negro girl, & to Margt McCarty her sister £12 c. & a gold ring. To Peter my godson, son of Martin Levicount, £6 c. To Cath. dau. of Dennis Sulivan £6 c. To Mrs Mary Urlin a gold ring. To Mrs Ann Burton, wife of Jno Burton, a negro boy. To Mr Owen McCarty & Jno Burton all residue, they to be Ex'ors. Witnessed by John Hutchinson, James Newland, Thomas Skerrett. Sworn 12 April 1705.

Aliens.	Date of taking the Oaths.
Samuel Nelson, Dutch, born in Zealand	9 Dec. 1699.
Peter Burchell, born in the Province of Rochell	7 Feb. 1700.
John Decoster, Dutch, born in the Province of Amsterdam . . .	9 Dec. 1699.
James Burtell, French, born in the Province of Donee	30 Nov. 1699.
Peter Fontagnu, French, born in the Province of Languedock . .	30 Nov. 1699.

Aliens.	Date of taking the Oaths.
Elias Jamain, French, born in the Province of Rochell . . .	15 June 1700.
James Morrin, French, born in the Province of Poiton . . .	11 Dec. 1704.
Francis Pouch, French, De perigord in Guienne	5 Sep. 1704.

Thomas Laughland, Chirurgeon, of St. Mary's Parish. Will dated 4 Jan. 1713. To my son Jn° Laughland 40s. c. for a ring. All Estate to my wife Sarah & my dau. Mary Laughland. Sam. Frye of Bermudian Valley, Gent., Ex'or. Witnessed by John Haynes, Catherine Reid, Robert Tremills. Sworn 20 July 1714.

Timothy Bryan of Antigua, planter. Will dated 30 Sep. 1713. To my wife Mary 2 negro women & all my Estate, then to M[rs] Eliz. Terry. My wife & friend Cha. Jacob Ex'ors. Witnessed by Thomas Hues, Francis Franklyn. Sworn 22 Jan. 1713.

John Ewen of Antigua, planter. Will dated 11 July 1706. To my 3 grandchildren Eliz., Marg[t], & Jas. Johnson, children of my dau. Susanna Johnson, sen[r], wife of Tho. Johnson of Antigua, planter, as following:—To my 1st grandchild Eliz. $\frac{1}{3}$ of all my Estate at 18 or day of marriage. To the 2[d] sister Marg[t] $\frac{1}{3}$ at 16 or marriage, & to Jas. Johnson $\frac{1}{3}$ at 21. Tho. Johnson & Susanna his wife Ex'ors & Guardians. Witnessed by John Darlowe, William Brown, Thomas Bliss, Jo. Barry.

Peter Vallard of Antigua, goldsmith. Will dated 24 July 1714. To my 3 children Jn°, Mary, & Hanna Vallard $\frac{2}{3}$ of all my Estate at 21. To my wife Jean her thirds, & appoint her Ex'trix and Guardian with M[r] Tho. Wise, sen[r]. Witnessed by William Graer, William Franklyn, John Chamberlain, William Lynch. Sworn 10 March 1714.

Simon Turfrey, sen. Will dated 16 Nov. 168–. To my dau. Annaker 30 acres. To my wife 70 acres & all residue, she to be Ex'trix, & after her death to my 2 sons Simon & George. Witnessed by William Wallace, John Batho, Cuthbert Jameson. On 15 Nov. 1689 before Lieut.-General Christopher Codrington appeared Cuthbert Jameson. Recorded *circa* 1715.

1716, April 11. Timothy Singin, planter, and Henrietta his wife for £500 c. sell 30 acres at Belfast to Charles Golden of Antigua, planter.

James Howey of Antigua, planter. Will dated 1 Dec. 1708. To my wife Mary £30 & a mare. To my dau. Eliz. Howey £150 at 16. To my sons Tho. & Jas. all residue at 18. To M[r] W[m] Steele & M[r] Jn° Ker £5 each, they to be Ex'ors. To Francis Phillips £5. Witnessed by Francis Powe. By Governor Daniel Parke sworn 17 Sep. 1709.

William Wollam of St. Philip's. Will dated 18 July 1698. To my wife Grace 10 acres, & then to Peter Hadgit & his sister Eliz. Hadgit. To Martha Hadgit a colt. M[r] Jas. Parker & Martin Levicount Ex'ors. Witnessed by Samuel Mayers, John Spencer. Sworn 16 Aug. 1699.

John Poulton of Antigua, mason. Will dated 4 June 1716. To my sister Mary Darlow 20 acres & all residue. Dan[l] Mackinen, Esq., M[r] Tho. Johnson, planter, & M[r] Sam. Mitchell Trustees & Guardians. Witnessed by John Byne, John McGrigory, Peter Keins, Joseph Thwayte. Sworn 26 June 1716 before Walter Hamilton, Esq.

John Ford of St. John's, mariner. Will dated 13 Oct. 1719. All my Estate to Jn° Vincens, Chirurgeon.

Richard Buckeridge of Antigua, now in London, Gent. Will dated 5 March 1714. In consideration of the marriage portion of £500 secured to be p[d] with Anne my now wife, dau. of Jn° Jackson, sen., of London, haberdasher, I have been bound by deed dated 15 April 1706 to the s[d] Jn° Jackson in the sum of £1500 in trust for the use of my s[d] wife. If she accept this £1500 in lieu of dower, & have no children, then I give her £500 in addition. To my sister Grydesweed Buckeridge £50 only as she disobliged me in her marriage. To my niece Eliz. Buckeridge, dau. of my brother Seabourne Buckeridge, dec[d], £100, now living with Jos. Pember in Billiter Sq. To each dau. of my brother Edmond Buckeridge, now living in Rotterdam in Holland, £100. To my brother Arthur Buckeridge £100. These 3 last legacies payable only if I die childless. All residue to any children I may have, with remainder to the issue male of my brother Edmond equally. Tho. Jackson & Jas. Fairweather of Antigua Ex'ors & £50 c. each, & Micajah Perry of London, Esq., & his son Rich[d] Perry, Gent., Ex'ors, & to each £50 st. Witnessed by William Parrott, W. Plaxton, John Hicks, Drawer at the Fountaine Taverne in Bartholomew Lane, London.

Codicil. 19 Dec. 1715. Revoke Jas. Fairweather as Trustee & appoint Jn° Booth. Witnessed by Francis Delap, Richard Baker, William Seabrooke. Before Walter Hamilton, Esq., were sworn Francis Delap and William Seabroke 9 March 1715-16. Recorded 1716 (P.C.C., 201 Fox).

Nicholas Fowler, planter. Will dated 12 May 1705. To my wife Jennett my Estate for life, then to my sons Jn° & Timothy equally, & in default equally to my daus. Marg[t], Susannah, & Eliz. My wife, Tho. Ledeat, & M[r] Tho. Rome Ex'ors. Before Hon. John Yeamans was sworn William Steele 10 July 1705.

Walter Shelly. Will dated 17 Dec. 1715. All my Estate to my wife Jane, she to be Ex'trix. £400 c. to M[r] Ben. Wickham, he to be Ex'or. Sworn 19 Dec. 1716.

James Cridelanze. Will dated 9 Dec. 1717. All Estate to my friend Jn° Langelier. Richard Baker sworn 12 March 1717.

John Bayley, butcher. Will dated 6 May 1717.

Mathew Andrews of St. Peter's Parish, Antigua, now residing in Philadelphia. Will dated 6 Sep. 1717. All Estate to my son Edmond & my dau. Eliz. Harry Hodge & Tho. Chawkly, both of Philadelphia, m[ts], Jn° Lightfoot, & Rich. Cochran & Arch[d] Cochran of Antigua, Ex'ors & Guardians of my children. Witnessed by Isaac Marryott, Mary Thorp, John Cadwalader. Before Peter Evans at Philadelphia appeared J. Maryott and J. Cadwalader and were sworn 14 Nov. 1717.

Edward Leaver of St. Peter's Parish, planter. Will dated 19 May 1685. To my wife $\frac{1}{2}$ of my Estate during her widowhood, but if she marry only her thirds. To my daus. Mary & Hannah Leaver 20,000 lbs. of sugar or tobacco each on their marriage, & in default to my son Edw[d] Leaver, remainder to my brother Geo. Leaver. To my trustees a 25s. gold ring each. My wife & son Ex'ors. Maj. Arch. Cochran, Cap. Fra. Carlile, & L[t] Steph. Duer Trustees. Witnessed by Richard Kitchin, Digby Coll. Before J. Parry, Esq., sworn. (No date.)

1713, Dec. 30. Robert Dillsworth of St. Phillip's Parish, mason.

John Brand married to relict of John Barton.

Alice widow of William Milman.

Nickles Lawson, planter. Will dated 13 Sep. 1698. To my dau. Kathrin £400 c. To my godchildren Jn° & Mary Soward 500 lbs. each. To my son Cornelius Lawson all my Estate, remainder to my dau. Kath., then $\frac{1}{2}$ to my 2 s[d] godchildren & $\frac{1}{2}$ to my wife's sister Marg[t] Chapman. M[r] W[m] Walters, M[r] Steph. Main, & Tho. Turner Ex'ors. Witnessed by Robert Martin, Robert Broughton. Captain Robert Martin sworn 22 Sep. 1698.

Captain Charles Pinkerhunan of Liverpool, mariner. Will dated 21 June 1717. To my dau. Mary Pinkerhunan of Liverpool all Estate, she to be Ex'trix.

1724, April 15. Arthur Skelton of Antigua, carpenter, and Mary his wife; sale to John Prynn of Antigua, Gent.

1724, April 22. James Crow of St. John's Town, Gent., and Mary his wife; sale to Mathew Coningham, shopkeeper.

James Proctor,* late of Finchley, co. Middlesex, now of Antigua, merchant. Will dated 1 April 1721. To my wife Eliz. all real Estate for life, then to my right heirs. My copyhold lands in Midd. & use of plate & furniture. All residue of personalty to my right heirs. My wife Ex'trix. & my friend Mr Tho. Clarke of London, mt, Ex'or in Gt Britain, & Mr Amb. Lynch & Mr Wm Lynch James of St John's Town, mts, Ex'ors in Trust for Antigua. Witnessed by Henry Symes, Mark Monk, William Hinde. Sworn 25 May 1724. Ambrose Lynch refused the execution.

1724. Arthur Dabron, Gent., and Agnes his wife.

John Earle. Will dated 6 June 1723. To my mother Alice Chambers £10 c. To my sister Jane Cunningham £10 c. To my bro. Hen. Earle £10 c. All residue to my bro. Tho. Earle, he & Mr Hen. Osborn Ex'ors. Witnessed by Thomas Skerrett, George Hewit, George Skerrett. Sworn 12 Dec. 1724 before Governor Hart.

1724, Dec. 28. Daniel Pelloe of Antigua, planter, and Grace his wife. Deed of gift of 4 acres.

1724. Will of Robert Hunt of Antigua, carpenter. Wife Margaret.

1724. Will of John Byrne of Antigua, mason.

Israell Desilva. Will dated 27 Dec. 1724. All Estate to my dau. Eliz. at 17 or marriage; she is to be bred a seemstress; if she die to my sister Eliz. Desilva & my sister Dinah Desilva, then to the 1st s. of my bro. Paul Desilva. Jno Goble & Jonath. Martin Ex'ors. Witnessed by John Ronan, John Scarvill, John Dawley. Sworn 26 Feb. 1724.

1724. Wills of John Libert and Daniel Minchan recorded, but missing.

William Riddell of Antigua, merchant. Will dated 1 Feb. 1724. To my wife Lustina Riddell all my goods & negros. To my father David Riddell & my mother Mary Riddell of Newtown, Leam Mady, Irel^{d}, £30 c. My wife & Jas. White & Mr Wm Lynch James of St John's Town, mts, Ex'ors. Witnessed by James Godsell, Joseph Caddy, Joseph Wright.

Timothy Singen. Will dated 5 Sep. 1705. To my wife Jane her thirds & a horse. To my dau. Kath. £100 c. To my dau. Jane £100 c. at 21. To my dau. Elinor wife of Ochtrey Campbell certain negros. To my brother Dennis Sweeny, his 2 sons, & his dau. Elinor £50 c. each. To my sister Honour wife of Timothy Connor £50 c. To Jane dau. of Ochtrey & Elinor Campbell £100 c. at marriage. All residue to my son Timothy, he & Cap. Jno Ker Ex'ors. Witnessed by Thomas Rome (?), John Ker, jun. Sworn 26 June 1725.

Herbert Pember, Esq. Will dated 9 Dec. 1725. All Estate to my wife Mary, she to be Ex'trix. Witnessed by Elizabeth Theyer, Walter Sydserfe, William Wyne. Sworn 12 Feb. 1725.

Hazael Reynolds. Will dated 23 April 1726. To my dau. Rebecca Reynolds £200 c., my dau. Rachell Reynolds £100 c., my dau. Ann Reynolds £200 c. at 21 or marriage. To my wife Ann all Estate for life, then to my youngest dau. Eliz. Reynolds, my son Jno Reynolds, my dau. Rachel, my dau. Ann. My wife & Isaac Royall, Esqr, Ex'ors. Witnessed by William Meredith, Sarah Jordan. Sworn 25 May 1726.

Henry Norton, planter. Will dated 10 Aug. 1724. My son John & his son, my grandson, Henry. My son Wm. My son Laurence certain negros. To my dau. Jane £250 c. To my dau. Ann negros & furniture & £250 c. My son Ben. My wife Ann negros. To each son a horse & cow. All residue equally to my sons Jno, Wm, Laur., Ben. at my wife's death. My son Jno to work the Estate & to pay my son Ben. £100 c. at 24, also the maintenance of Ben. & Ann till 21. My wife, my son John, & Wm Samuel Ex'ors. Witnessed by Richard Downing, William Boole, Colonel MacMahon. Before Francis Phipps sworn 20 Nov. 1724.

* See the wills of Samuel Proctor and of his wife Elizabeth later, 1726 (P.C.C., 150 Plymouth).

Return Wodell, Gent., planter. Will dated 12 Oct. 1708. To my wife Abigail negros & furniture. To my 1st son Richd a house & 10 acres at English Harbour. To my youngest son Gershom (?) & my dau. Mary negros. Cap. Barry Tankard, Cap. Baijer Otto-Baijer, Cap. Jas Burcher, & Mr Jno Hughes Ex'ors. Witnessed by William Anderton, Elizabeth Anderton, John Millnor. Sworn 6 May 1724.

James Verdon. Will dated 21 May 1725. To my wife Ann 3 negros & a horse. To my son Wm, my son Geo., & my dau. Eliz. negros. To my brother Jno my silver-hilted sword.

Will of Archibald Muckewen, carpenter, dated 29 Sep. 1724.

Will of John Bawn, planter, dated 1 Jan. 1728-9.

Will of John Stevens, planter, dated 23 Sep. 1726.

Will of Edward Perkins, planter. (Half destroyed.) My dau. Cath. Perkins. My dau. Mary & £50 . . . . in recompense of dower. Maudlein Perkins a negro. To my son . . . . whole estate. My 3 daus. . . . . Wm Gear & Mr Wm Pike . . . . Aug. 1712. Witnessed by . . . . Skerrett, ... Martin.

Codicil. Gift to my wife . . . . Aug. 1712. Witnessed by Thomas Skerrit, Peter Martin. Sworn before the Hon. John Yeamans 10 May 1714. H. Hill, Deputy-Secretary. Recorded 6 March 1733.

Will of Peter Aggett dated . . . . To my son Sam. Aggett. My son Peter Aggett. My son Jno Aggett. My son Rowld 2 negros. My son Aron. My wife Sabra . . . . household goods. To my son Francis Aggett all residue & maintenance till the age of 14. Witnessed by Thomas Toft, Benjamin Wickham, James Howey. Recorded April 1733. Before the Hon. William . . . . was sworn Benjamin . . . . 15 Aug. 1730. Recorded 15 Aug. 1730. H. Hill, Deputy-Secretary. Recorded in Register's Office 2 . . . . 1733.

Will of John Walters. My wife Sarah. My son John. My bro.-in-law Geo. Nicholls. Recorded 17 Dec. 1733.

Will of John Stewart, Gent. All Estate to Pat. Wilson of St John's, goldsmith. Recorded 15 April 1735.

John Gosse. Will dated 1 June 1725. All Estate to my sister Frances Gosse. To Mrs Eliz. Trelawny a negro & £100 c. to be at once sent home to her. To Mr Tho. Edgcumb my English targett gun. Col. Jno Burton, Jas. Barter, Fra. Burton, & Mr Wm Horne Ex'ors. Witnessed by John Butler, Thomas Edgcumb. Sworn 4 Oct. 1725. Recorded 7 May 1735.

Peter Fontaine. Will dated 10 Dec. 1709. All Estate to my wife Eliz. Witnessed by John Martin, Perre Martineau, Nicholas Weeks. Sworn 27 April 1725. Recorded 19 June 1735.

John Partis, merchant. Will dated 4 May 1735. I ratify a former will made before my last departure from England. Wines to be shipt home. To Hon. Val. Morris, Dr Wm Young, & Mr Jno Dun, jr, £70 each for mourning, & appoint them also Ex'ors. Witnessed by Walter Sydserfe, Walter Tullideph, Robert James. Sworn 11 June 1735 before Edward Byam, Esq. Recorded 1 July 1735.

Philemon Bird of Bristol, Esq. Will dated 9 Oct. 1699. To Mrs Sarah Porter of Bristol £200 st. to be pd by my Ex'ors in Trust Mr Richd Oliver, Mr Nath. Sampson, & Cap. Hen. Symes. To my sister Mrs Anna Hulet £50 st., & ratify a will left in the hands of my Ex'ors in Antigua touching the disposal of my Estate. Witnessed by Robert Baskervile, Samuel Jacob, Thomas Cary. Sworn before Lyonell Lyde, Mayor of Bristol, 4 Nov. 1735. Recorded in Antigua 26 March 1736. Probate granted to Ashton Warner for Antigua.

Hugh Hugas. Will dated March 1735-6. To my wife Susanna all my Estate for life, & after her death to my grandson Peter Hugas 2 negros. To my grandson Jno Hugas 2 negros. My granddau. Jane Darlow & my grandson, her brother, Jno Darlow, each a negro. To the latter after my wife's death 3 negros & my house at St John's.

To my son Jno Hugas 1s., & never to enjoy any portion of my Estate. Rich. Oliver, Esq., & Mr Ebenezer Hughes Ex'ors, & a ring of a pistole to each of them. Witnessed by W. Shorter, Robert White, James Prideaux. Sworn 5 June and recorded 1 July 1736.

William Griffith, mariner. Will dated 9 April 1730. All Estate to my sons W^{m}, Jas., & Thos. My wife Mary, Jno Wilkinson, & Mr Josiah Newfiald Ex'ors. Witnessed by John Forster, Louis Thibou. Recorded 12 July 1736.

Will of Chappell Fowler, carpenter, recorded 23 July 1736.

Will of John Ripsley, mariner. All Estate to my wife Eliz. Recorded 29 July 1736.

Thomas Mountain. Will dated 13 July 1736. To my wife Rebecca £200 c., negros, & my house in St John's for ever. Debt due from Ed. Jessap, Esq. To Jno Spencer, a soldier, my clothing. To my goddau. Sarah dau. of Jno Cox, taylor, dec^{d}, & his wife Carolina all the land in St John's I purchased of her s^{d} father, with maintenance for 3 years, but if her mother or aunt Mrs Mary Reynolds take her from my wife's protection such allowance to cease. My wife Ex'trix. Witnessed by Hugh Peard, William Norton, William Harrox. Sworn 7 and recorded 8 Dec. 1736.

Will of John Green, mariner. All to wife Frances. Recorded 5 Feb. 1736.

William Wyne, Gent. Will dated 17 March 1736. All my Estate to my Ex'ors in Trust for my wife Sarah. Cæsar Rodney to remit all sums owing to me, & I give him £14 c. To my brother-in-law Wm Harrox a ring of a moidore. My cousin Jno Wyne* of London, Cæsar Rodney, & Ed. Trant of Antigua, m^{ts}, & my wife Ex'ors. All residue to my wife & son Madira Wyne equally. To my cousin Jno Wyne, Esq., £10 st. If my son die then all to my wife, except £100 st. to my s^{d} brother. Witnessed by Lydia Trant, Agl. Osborn, Mary Nowell. Sworn 18 March 1736-7. Recorded 28 March 1737.

Henry Ross. Will dated 21 Oct. 1724. To my natural wife & child several negros to be kept by my own wife till of age to possess them. To Jno Reynolds, son of my wife, a negro. To my 1st son Thos. 2 negros. To my godson Tho. Carmoch £5 c. To Henry son of Jonath. Martin by Ann his wife £5 c. Cap. Jno Goble & Mr Rob. Glover, s^{r}, Ex'ors. Witnessed by Thomas Jemitt, John Duncan. Sworn 25 April 1735. Recorded 6 April 1737.

William Bawn, planter. Will dated 30 Sep. 1736. To my wife Mary £70 c. yearly & £30 c. for mourning, my best horse & side-saddle, & a cow, the use of my house, & all furniture. To my godson Rob. Thomas £25 c. To my goddau. Arabella Spencer £25 c. To my Ex'ors rings of a moydore in value. All residue to my dau. Barbara Bawn. Robt Christian, Jno Kerr, Jno Francis, & Peter Bawn Ex'ors. Sworn 13 and recorded 28 Oct. 1737.

Catherine Crofts, widow. Will dated 22 Jan. 1737. To my son Francis a negro. To my dau. Sarah Crofts a negro. All residue to them. Walt. Sydserfe & Geo. Nicholds Ex'ors. Witnessed by William Hall, Thomas Teague, John Hall. Sworn 4 and recorded 8 Feb. 1737-8.

John Price,† Gent. Will dated 28 Nov. 1733. To my wife Christian certain negros & the use of plate & furniture, & after her death to my dau. Christian Price. To Edwd son of Edwd Monteigue of St John's, my godchild Christian dau. of Hen. Knight, Lucy dau. of Ben. Arty, Mary dau. of David Davis, & Joseph son of Jos. Jaggers, & any other godchildren £5 c. each. Whereas by Indenture dated 10 March 1721 between me & my wife Christian & Joshua Jones, Esq. (since dec^{d}), I covenanted to pay Joshua Jones £200 c. for Christian & Cha. Knight at 18, & having p^{d} Christian Knight his part I desire Cha. Knight's portion may be p^{d}. I give them also £60 c. & £30 c. respectively when the negros I have in Jamaica are delivered. To Frances Pott a negro. My lands called Spring Garden & houses in St John's to be rented out, & the proceeds p^{d} to my wife. All residue to my dau., & in default of issue to the children of my brothers Tho. & David Price, now living in the parish of Nantgwulle, High Talfarm Green, in Cardiganshire, S. Wales, commonly called Ap. Rice, & to the children of my 4 sisters Mary, Cath., Marg^{t}, & Eleanor. Hon. Geo. Thomas, Wm Yeamans, & Wm Mackinnen, & my wife & dau. Ex'ors. My dau. not 17. Witnessed by John Lillie, Edward Monteigue.

1st Codicil. Certain negros to my wife for ever.

2nd Codicil. 17 Jan. 1733. Chr. Knight to be an Ex'or. Sworn 8 March 1733. Recorded 5 Aug. 1738.

Will of Robert Denman, carpenter, dated 10 May 1738. Recorded 1739.

James Tweedy of Antigua. Will dated 27 Nov. 1734. To my 1st son W^{m} 5 negros at 21. To my dau. Rachel Tweedy my house in Long Street, St John's Town, & 3 negros at 21. All residue to my son Jas. Tweedy. Witnessed by Anthony Fletcher, Ralph Hatchett. Sworn 13 Jan. 1740. Recorded 20 Jan. 1741.

Henry Wallace. Will dated 10 March 1739. To my cousin Jane Wallace of Dublin £50 & £25 st. a year. To my cousin Geo. Knox £25 st. & £100 st. a year. All residue to my wife Elinor, she & Jno Keith, m^{t}, & Tho. Stephens & Harry Webb of Antigua, Esq^{rs}, Ex'ors, to whom I give 25 gs. each for a ring. Witnessed by Lydia Glover, Elizabeth Wilson, George Crump, Esq. Sworn 17 Feb. 1740-1. Recorded 25 May 1741.

Richard Brookes, planter. Will dated 8 July 1740. To my bro. Ben. Brookes my gold buckle & a guinea ring. To my bro. Robt Brookes my shoe-buckles & a ring. To my cousin Tho. Bostock a ring. To Ed. Looby £5. To Rob. Symes 2 guineas. All residue to my wife Frances Brookes, & remainder to my s^{d} 2 brothers. Ed. Looby & Robt Symes Ex'ors. Witnessed by Dr. B. Bernourd, Alexander Dow. Sworn 29 Aug. 1740. Recorded 25 May 1741.

Robert Hillman. Will dated 4 Aug. 1713. To my children Ambrose, Robt, Eliz., all my Estate, remainder to my son-in-law Jno Hutchins. To my wife Eliz. a negro. My mother to be maintained. To my s^{d} son-in-l. Jno Hutchins £20 c. at 21. Col. Sam. Parry, Cap. Nath. Crump, & Mr Cornelius Holloran Ex'ors. Witnessed by George Hilton, John Weatherill. Sworn 30 March 1713. Recorded 27 May 1741.

Roger Adams, Surgeon. Will dated 4 Oct. 1737. To Mrs Ann Chauncey of Bristol, mother of Mary Parsons of Antigua, dec^{d}, £20 st. a year. To Jno Player Adams, son of Jno Player of Winterborn, Bristol, blacksmith, by Ann my niece, maintenance till 21. My wife Frances. Witnessed by Isabella Storey, Richard Oliver, Hugh Holmes. Recorded 3 June 1741.

George Hewitt, planter. Will dated Jan. 1729. To my daus. Rachel, Elinor, Cath., Ann, Sarah, & Jane £200 each at 21. To my wife Elinor £100 & 2 negros. To my son George all my Estate in Nonsuch, & in default of issue to my s^{d} 6 daus. equally. Mr Fra. Delap & J. Mathews & my wife Ex'ors. The Ex'ors all refuse to act, and adm'on was granted. Sworn 17 Nov. 1730. Recorded 9 June 1741.

Will of William Ballenten, shop-keeper, recorded 16 June 1741.

James Mastin. Will dated 24 . . . . 1746. To Jos. Woodyatt my mare & silver ½ pint cup. To Nath. Sampson Webb all residue. Isaac Sampson, s^{d} Nath. S. Webb, & Jos. Woodyatt Ex'ors. Witnessed by John Coleman. Before Hon. Josiah Martin sworn by John Coleman, Gent., 19 Dec. 1746.

* See his will later, 1736 (P.C.C., 45 Wake).

† Testator married 23 Oct. 1718 Mrs. Christian Knight, widow (Vol. II., p. 132).

Will of Thomas Colley, planter. Wife Anna, dau. Mary. 9 Sep. 1746

Jane Ashley, widow. Will dated 21 March 1747. All Estate to my dau. Ann Montague Ashley, she to be Ex'trix; in case she die without issue then to my .... ther Jn° Doyle at 21, & in default to my Ex'ors & Mrs. Eliz. Allicocke, dau. of my dec[d] friend Cap. Syer Allicock. Jn° Frye, jun., Walt. Nugent, & Edw[d] Horne Ex'ors. Witnessed by Mary Horne, Henrietta Looby. Before Josiah Martin, Esq., was sworn Henrietta Looby 1 April, and recorded 2 May 1747.

Will of Joseph Heale. His wife Eliz. Recorded 11 June 1747.

Alexander Allaire, Gent. Will dated 28 April 1748. To my wife Ann £300 c. To my 4 sisters Sarah Crispin, Rachel Allaire, Jane wife of Tho. Martin, & Cath. Allaire £20 c. each. All residue to my dau. Ann, but if she die before 21 then £50 c. more to each of my s[d] sisters & all residue to my wife. Jas. Alihand, planter, & Tho. Martin, m[t], Ex'ors. Witnessed by Wiseman Clagett, W. Richards. Sworn 19 May 1748.

Will of Roger Eeterlony. All Estate to wife Eliz. Recorded 25 June 1748.

James Mitchelson, Surgeon. Will dated 23 July 1748. To Eliz. dau. of Hen. Symes £200 c. To my godchildren Sarah Lyons, Mary Elmes, & Eliz. Parry £30 c. each. To Mary dau. of Joshua Crump negros. To my godson Nich. Taylor a negro. To Joshua Crump a horse. To Hen. Symes a horse. To Tho. Elmes my books. To my wife Henrietta all my furniture. All residue to my wife & my sisters Eupheme & Lilias. Tho. Elmes, J. Crump, & H. Symes Ex'ors. Witnessed by William Hunt, Robert Yuille, John Grant.

William Barclay, Physician. Will dated 31 March 1744. To Ashton Warner £60 c. To my cousin Hugh Barclay, watchmaker at Edinburgh, £200 st. To my cousin W[m] Barclay, glass-grinder at Edinburgh, £200 st. To my cousin Cha. Irving, Surgeon at Jamaica, £300 st. To my cousin Geo. Barclay the elder in England £200. To my cousin Geo. Ellis, m[t] at Philadelphia, £100 st. To M[r] Row. Frye, m[t] in London, £20 st. To M[r] Sam[l] Frye, m[t] in London, £20 st. All Estate, negros, etc., to M[r] Pat. Grant of Antigua, Surgeon. Asht. Warner, Sam. Frye, & Pat. Grant Ex'ors. Sworn 22 Feb. 1744.

Will of Simon Sevin recorded 17 Feb. 1752.

Will of Eleanor Higgins recorded 29 Feb. 1752.

Samuel Foster of North Seaton, Northumberland. Will dated 13 Jan. 1747. To Steph. Watson of do. & Ed. Wilson .... all my plantation & negros in Trust for my wife Marg[t] to pay her £4 a year, & $\frac{1}{3}$ of residue to my son Jn°, & residue eq. to W[m], Sam., Geo., Mary, Marg[t], Margery Foster. Recorded 29 Feb. 1752.

Will of John Vickery. To my wife Eleanor .... sister of my wife £100 st., Sam. Lightfoot, viz., Sarah Barton £100 .... & to Ann Lightfoot. All residue .... Witnessed by .... ary Gilbert, j[r], ... ice Bryant, ... Hilton. Recorded 3 March 1752.

Robert Lovie, planter. Will dated 14 May 1752. To Frances Bishop my house at Baileys & 40 acres for life or till marriage, also 10 negros, £100, 5 cows, & 40 sheep for what she suffered in reputation for me which she never deserved, & God forgive them, for she was quite clear of what was said. To .... Murray, Mary Murray, & Ann Murray, children of Chas. Murray, dec[d], £30 c. each. To my Ex'ors & to M[rs] Eliz. Horsford £2 rings. All residue to my sister Mary Lovie's children in Scotland. Hon. And. Lessley, Cap. Jn° Dunn, M[r] Pet. Guichinet, & M[r] Tho. Bishop, Ex'ors. Witnessed by Samuel Franklyn, John Terry, Elizabeth Horsford. Sworn before President John Tomlinson 17 Aug. and recorded 18 Aug. 1752.

Will of John Coleman recorded 25 Aug. 1752.

Sarah Welch. Will dated 4 Feb. 1753. To my son Edw[d] £5 c. To my son Francis a negro, he to pay £3 to my son W[m]. To my dau. Sarah Wilson my house in Bishopgate Str., S[t] John's. All residue to my children. Alex. Crawford, Esq., Sam. Watkins, & M[r] Jn° Leaycraft Ex'ors. Witnessed by John Yeamans, Jeremiah Blizard, Thomas Chaplin. Sworn 13 and recorded 15 Feb. 1753.

Thomas Lewis, Surgeon. Will dated 28 April 1753. To M[r] Jas. Muer & M[r] Jn° Dun & .... Blane mourning rings. All estate to M[r] Jas. Tannet of Glasgow, m[t]. Jn° Dun & Jn° Blane Ex'ors. Witnessed by William Campbell, Thomas Robinson, William Evans. Sworn 10 May 1753. Recorded ....

(Fragment.) My wife Mary Lambert. My niece Eliz. Lambert, dau. of my s[d] brother, and the children of my sister Marg[t] Lambert. 1755. Witnessed by Thomas Lynch, Charles Crouch, George Glover.

Will of Thomas Moore. My daus. Jane & Ann. My wife .... Sworn by James Brebner & John Hillhouse 29 Nov. 1754. Recorded 10 Jan. 1755.

Isaac Bayly of St. Paul's, planter. Will dated 25 Aug. 1755. To my 3 sons Rich. Fisher Bayly, Jn° Bayly, & Peter Bayly all my Estate. To my son Rich[d] F. Bayly $33\frac{1}{2}$ acres I bought of the Ex'ors of Ashton Warner, Esq. To my son Jn° Bayly $33\frac{1}{2}$ acres bought as aforesaid, & bounding lands of Bladen & Bodkin & N.W. on the lands I have given to my son Rich[d] Bayly. To my son Peter Bayly the rest of my land, viz., 40 acres bounded W. with my son Rich. Bayly & E. with the lands given to my son Jn° Bayly, also the house & chattles. To my son W[m] Bayly 1s. My loving friend Jn° B .... & Jn° Dunn, Esq., both of Antigua, Ex'ors. Witnessed by Daniel Le Tellier, Gent., Roger Astley. Sworn and recorded 20 April 1756.

Will of William Williamson of Antigua. To my wife Mary the use of my furniture. To my dau. Mary Tudhope, wid. of Jn° Tudhope, lately dec[d], £300 c. To my dau. Eliz. Williamson £200 c. To my dau. Rebecca Judith Williamson £400 c. at 21. To my niece Mary Williamson, dau. of my late bro. Jn° Williamson, ... at 21. To my son W[m] Williamson, now in the care of Rich. Boddicott, Esq., all residue, remainder to my s[d] 3 daus. & my dau. Ann Brunsell, wife of W[m] Brunsell. Leases of 2 estates 1 rent. My wife Mary Ex'trix, & Pat. Cusack, Jn° Jeaffer .... Merrifield, all of Antigua, & Rich. Boddicott & Son, m[ts] of London, Ex'ors. On 18 .... 1756 was sworn Richard Southwell of Antigua, planter. Recorded 18 Oct. 1756.

Will of Joseph Young missing.

James Figg. Will dated 11 Sep. 1753. To my dear friend W[m] Byam, Esq., all my Estate & house in the West of S[t] John's & land bounded E. with waste, W. with Tho. Symmonds, N. with S[t] George's, S. with Gust. Hamilton, provided he procure my wife (?) Molly Page & my children by her, viz., Jas. Figg, Rich. Figg, & Sam. Figg their freedom; he to be sole Ex'or, or if he be absent then the Rev. Fra. Byam. Witnessed by Francis Byam, John Williams, carpenter. Sworn 6 April and recorded 25 May 1757.

John Haslewood of Antigua, staymaker. Will dated 21 April 1757. To Sam. Gunthorpe of Antigua, m[t], & Tho. Bridges of Antigua, carpenter, all my Estate in Trust for my 2 sons Geo. & Jn° Haslewood equally. Witnessed by Edmond Griffith, Jos. Baker, staymaker. Sworn 26 April and recorded 14 July 1757.

Frances James of Antigua, widow. Will dated 16 Aug. 1757. By Indenture tripartite of 5 Feb. 1756 between W[m] Dickinson of Antigua, m[t], of the 1st, & me Frances James, wid. of Laughlin Ramsay, late of Antigua, planter, & after wife & wid. of Hen. James, late of Antigua, planter, dec[d], of the 2[d], & Jn° Dunn of Antigua, merch[t], of the 3[d] part, a messuage in S[t] John's & 3 slaves were vested in the s[d] Trust. He is to sell the same & all other lands, & to pay $\frac{1}{2}$

to my son Wm Ramsay, ⅕ to my son Jas. Ramsay, ⅕ to my son Evan Ramsay, ⅕ to my dau. Ann Pellew, wid. of Alexr Pellew, overseer, but now married to Jas. St . . . . taylor, & ⅕ to my dau. Jane de Young, wife of Jno de Young of Essequibo, planter. To my dau. Ann Herrick all furniture. All residue to my sd 5 children. Jno Dunn Ex'or. Witnessed by James Butler, book-keeper, John Gloyne. Sworn and recorded 25 July 1757.

William Griffiths of Antigua, Gent. Will dated 2 Oct. 1755. To my godson Pat. Williams, son of Jno Williams, late of Antigua, mariner, decd, £40 c. at 21. To my friend Jas. Dewar of Antigua, Surgeon, £50 c. To Mrs Abigail Winthorpe, wife of Sam. Winthorpe of Antigua, Gent., £10 c. All residue to Hon. Dan. Warner of Antigua, Esq., & Jas. Dewar & Nath. Gilbert, jun., of Antigua, Esq., on Trust to pay all profits to my bro. Hen. Griffiths & his children, & remainder as to ⅓ to . . . . Williams, ⅓ to Eleanor Williams, dau. of Jno Williams of Antigua, carpenter, & ⅓ to Jas. Dewar. Witnessed by Cornelius Sherman, John Jacob, Mathew White. Sworn 13 Nov. 1755. Recorded 26 July 1757.

Mary Brennan of Antigua, spinster. Will dated 1 Nov. 1754. To Mrs Ann Pillow £10 c., & to her & Miss Cath. Ricketts all my clothing. My negro Bathe to be free. To Hen. Bonnin of Antigua, mt, 2 years' service of my negro Willey, then to be free, he to be Ex'or. Witnessed by Edward Monteigne, John Smith, jun., James Cooke. Sworn 21 June 1757.

(On a scrap *circa* 1758.) My wife Eliz. To each child £1200 st. My sd 6 children. My son Wm. My 5 daus. all under 14. My dau. Mary.

James Walker of Antigua, Gent. Will dated 15 March 1758. To my wife Mary all my Estate, she & Rob. Bannister of Parham Town & Sam. Martin of St John's, mts, Ex'ors. Witnessed by Ann Seymour, James Webb Ferris, Charles Martin, jun. Sworn and recorded 8 May 1758.

William Reynolds of Antigua, carpenter. Will dated 8 June 1758. All Estate to my wife Eliz. & my sons Ambrose & Wm & dau. Margt Reynolds. My wife, Fra. Farley, Esq., Mr Mich. Haslom Ex'ors & Guardians. Witnessed by Edward Paynter, Benjamin Keyzar. Sworn and recorded 15 June 1758.

Charles Wager Man. Will dated 23 Jan. 1759. My green ring to Dr Ashton Warner. My horse, saddle, pivillion, & furniture to Mr Wm Warner. All residue to my brother Cap. Rob. Man, he to be Ex'or in England & Wm Warner in Antigua. If my brother be dead all residue & 2 slaves to my cousin Jane, wife of Hen. Hall, Esq., Barrister. John Webb and John Sherrif swore to the writing 1 March 1759. Recorded 5 March 1759.

Thomas Malcher, planter. Will dated 4 March 1759. To my wife Guarthrud all Estate. She & Jno Dunn, mt, Ex'ors. Witnessed by William Wallis, William Fordyce, Ambrose Merchant. Sworn and recorded 4 April 1759.

Thomas German of Antigna, mariner. Will dated 9 Nov. 1758. To Mrs Ann Hayton all lands, etc., & 2 negro boys for life, then 1 negro to Miss Frances Ellyatt, dau. of Hen. Ellyatt, & 1 negro to Miss Ann Ellyatt, & all residue to his son Jno German Ellyatt. Mr Jno Smith, mt, & Ann Hayton Ex'ors. Witnessed by James Watson, William Moore, Ann Hall. Sworn 4 and recorded 14 April 1759.

Will of Robert Wilkins, tavern-keeper, 7 June 1759.

Will of Edward Wilson. Mr Sam. Lyons sole heir & Ex'or, & to pay £36 c., now in the hands of Mr Geo. Hurst, to the wife of Dr Rob. Meares, also to purchase the freedom of a mulatto boy, son to Betty, a slave belonging to Chr. Codrington, Esq., & place £10 for her use. My old clothes to the white servants on the Estate. Witnessed by William Sherrington, John Jones.

Sarah Scandrett. Will dated . . . . 1746. To my daus. Anna, Eliz., & Sarah Scandrett 2 negros apiece. To my dau. Rebecca 3 negros. To my son Jno Scandrett a negro. Whereas there are now in the hands of Nath. Gilbert £95 c., placed by my brother Tho. Martin, mt, for freeing 4 negros, mortgaged to Mr Slingsby Bethell of London, mt, by my late husbd Chr. Scandrett, the sd negros are to be sold & the profits divided among my children. If not redeemed then the £95 c. to be divided as follows: To my son Jno Scandrett £50, & the residue to my son Henry. £20 to my dau. Ann. £20 to Eliz. . . . . Hen. Scandrett, Mr Mich. Lovell, & my brother . . . . Witnessed by Henry Ginchenet, Benjamin Ramsay. Sworn 13 July 1758. Recorded 30 Aug. 1758.

Elizabeth McSweeny, spinster. Will dated 19 June 1756. 4 negros to Jno Haycock, Gent., he to be Ex'or. Witnessed by John Devereux Murphy, Thomas Hanson. Sworn 14 and recorded 20 Dec. 1758.

Will of William Wilson. Rev. Mr Rob. Davidson & Mr Nath. Marchant Ex'ors. All Estate to purchase the freedom of my mulatto dau. Jane. Witnessed by James Tweedy, merchant, Samuel Ince Marchant. Sworn 23 April and recorded 5 Sep. 1759.

James Boag, Surgeon. Will dated 1750. All my Estate to be sold for my mother Margt Boag. To my bro. Wm Boag £100 st. after her death. All residue to Jno Boag. Jas. Brebner, Rob. Gray, Harry Alexander, & Alex. Crawford Ex'ors. Sworn 2 Feb. and recorded 14 Sep. 1759.

Will of Margaret Arty, spinster. Negros to my son & dau. & my grandson Wm Salmon. Witnessed by John Nibbs, Jonathan Nibbs, Catherine Nibbs, John Hillian. Recorded 25 September 1759.

Will of Frances Gors, spinster, recorded 20 Nov. 1759.

William Pringle, Surgeon. Will dated 8 June 1762. To my mulatto Geo. Brown £100 at 21. My 2 negro women to be free; all other slaves to be sold. To Robt the son of Rob. Bannister £30 c. Mr Rob. Bannister, Dr Pat. Grant, & Dr Willoughby Byam Ex'ors, & £30 c. each. All residue to my brother Rob. Pringle, Attorney at Kelso, & remainder as to ½ to my cousin Jno Jamison, mt at Leith, & ½ to my cousins Jas., Adam, & Jno Waldie, tailors in London. Witnessed by John Reid, Henry Ronan. Dr. William Redhead and Mr. John Addis swore to the will, John Reid being dead and Henry Ronan off the Island, 20 Oct. 1758. Recorded 25 July 1760.

Robert Mallorins. Will dated 25 June 1758. My saddle, horse, & furniture to my wife. To my son Cornelius 3 negros & £200 c. at 21. To my dau. Eliz. 3 negros & £200 c. at 21. To my dau. Harriet 2 negros & £200 c. To my dau. Jane 2 negros & £200 c. All residue to my son Robt. Frances Farley, Jno Jefferson, & my son Robt when 21, Ex'ors. Witnessed by Thomas Downs, Thomas Phillipps. Sworn 13 and recorded 16 Oct. 1758.

Nuncupative will of Henrietta Arty, spinster. Benjamin Salmond, planter, swore that she died 21 March 1751, and two days previous sent for him to her dwelling-house called Needsmust, St. George's Parish. She gave to her mother two negros for her life, to go after her death to her sister Margaret. Recorded 7 Nov. 1758.

John Robinson of English Harbour. Will dated 8 July 1758. To my dau. Kitty a negro woman I bought of Maxwell & Udney, mts in St John's. To my dau. Anne a negro woman. Witnessed by William Sloan, William Barton, Theobald Barrell of Antigua, Gent. Sworn before Governor Thomas 28 April and recorded 5 May 1760.

John Colburn of St. Phillip's Parish. Will dated 15 June 1756. To my son Wm Colburn, my dau. Ann Colburn, my son Jas. Colburn, my son Daniel Colburn, & my son Jno Colburn a negro each. My wife a bed. All residue to my son Wm. Rowld Hamilton, Esq., Mr Corn. Minchan, & Mr Wm Sheriff Ex'ors. Witnessed by George Hopson, John

Edward Hamilton. Sworn 29 April and recorded 15 May 1760.

Thomas Bartlett of Antigua, planter. Will dated 18 July 1759. To my son Jn° Bartlett 2 negros. To my dau. Eliz. Ellyat a negro. Mr Jo. Martin, Mr Rich. Jones Ex'ors. Witnessed by Charles Hosier, Grace Mayo Hamilton. Sworn 11 and recorded 15 July 1760.

William Wallis of Antigua, planter. Will dated 17 July 1751. To my dau. Eliz. Wallis £500 c. at 21. To my dau. Rachel Wallis £500 c. at 21. To my wife £100 c., maintenance, & the use of my house. All residue to my son Wm Wallis. My trusty friends Tho. Elmes, Esq., Rob. Christian, Esq., & my son Wm & my wife Rachel Ex'ors.

Codicil dated 16 Sep. 1758. To my daus. Eliz. & Rachel Wallis each £500 c. more. On 2 Jan. 1761 John Watkins of Antigua, Esq., and Samuel Gunthorpe of Antigua, merchant, swore they knew testator, who was a carpenter. Recorded 5 Jan. 1761.

Elizabeth Reiley of Antigua, widow. Will dated 2 Jan. 1761. All Estate to my negro Sarah Pasquall. My friend Anthony Savage of Antigua Ex'or. Witnessed by Richard Hosier, jun., Thomas Page, sen. Sworn 7 and recorded 22 Jan. 1761.

Margaret Dawley of Antigua, widow. Will dated 21 July 1759. To my sist. Mary Dawley 3 negros. To Robt Martin, son of Mr Jn° Martin of Antigua, 3 negros, & to his sister Ann Allen Martin a negro, & to his brother Jn° Martin a negro. Mr Jn° Martin Ex'or. Witnessed by Robert Allen, jun., Alexander McAlister. Sworn 23 Feb. 1761.

James Stone of Antigua, blacksmith. Will dated 20 Nov. 1759. All Estate to be sold except my negros, which are to be leased out for my infant daus. Susanna & Ann. Rowld Oliver, Danl Warner, & Richd Kirwan, Esqres, & Dr Neill Campbell Ex'ors. Witnessed by Thomas Hicks, Thomas Bishop. By President Thomas Jarvis was sworn Thomas Bishop, and recorded 17 March 1761.

Peter McAdam, tailor. Will dated 21 Sep. 1760. To my negro Chloe, late of Mr Glanville's Estate, £10 c. All residue to my bro. Jn° of N. B. & my friend Rich. Barrow of Antigua, mt, equally. Dr Wm Campbell, late of Antigua, now of N. B., Wm Evans of Antigua Ex'ors. Witnessed by George Roberts, Charles Carr. Sworn 26 Sep. 1760. Recorded 29 May 1761.

William Lithgow of London, merchant. Will dated 4 June 1740. To my wife all furniture. To my mother Barbara Lithgow £20 st. To my bro. Dav. Lithgow £50. To my 3 sisters Janet, Eliz., & Ann £10 apiece. To my dau.-in-law Eliz. Masters £10. To my Ex'ors £10 each. If I have no children $\frac{1}{4}$ of all residue to my wife Mary, & $\frac{3}{4}$ to my dau. by my former wife Mary Lithgow. If I shall have any child by my now wife, then I give to my wife $\frac{1}{4}$, & $\frac{3}{4}$ to my sd dau. Mary & any child unborn. Mr Nath. Fletcher of London, mt, Mr Job. Pearson of Clapham, Gent., Mr Pet. Thompson of London, mt, Ex'ors & Guardians & Trustees. Witnessed by Mary Browne, William Daman, George Augustus Prosser, Attorney-at-Law at Portsmouth. Proved at London 9 March 1747 by Nathaniel Fletcher; power reserved to Job. Pearson and Peter Thomson. Recorded at Antigua 5 June 1761.

Thomas Hudson of Antigua, mariner. Will dated 11 Dec. 1760. To Isabella Rolland, dau. of Alex. Rolland, £200 c. of Barbados & 1 negro. All residue to my s. Rich. Hudson. Jn° Luke, Dav. Benson of Barbados, my bro.-in-law Alexr Rolland of Antigua, mariner, Ex'ors. Witnessed by John Wills, mariner, James Dealy, William Evans. Sworn 18 May and recorded 17 June 1761.

William Storton of St. Phillip's Parish in the Old Market of the City of Bristol, but now of Antigua. Will dated 5 Dec. 1751. To my dear friend Jn° Gallway of Antigua, town agent, 600 gals. of old rum now at Painters, with my gun, gold watch, pistols, spy-glass, & clothing. My 4 negros to be sold, & the freedom of old Nanny & her mulatto children purchased & £50 c. to her. All residue to my sist. Eliz. Maney living in the Old Market near Lawford's Gate, Bristol. Mr Jas. Scot, Jn° Gallwey Ex'ors. Witnessed by John Bisbey, Isaac Manwaring, Christian Gallwey. Before Governor Thomas appeared James Knewstub, Thomas Winterflood of Antigua, Gentlemen, Samuel Dring of Antigua, Gent., and Joseph Manwaring of Antigua, Gent. (brother of Isaac Manwaring, since deceased), 13 June 1761.

Isaac Jacob of Antigua, Gent. Will dated 18 Jan. 1761. To Sarah Looby, dau. of my friend Jn° Brooke of Antigua, Esq., £50 c. To the sd Jn° Brooke my fowling-piece & pair of pistols. All residue to my wife Mary Cath. Jacobs, she & Jn° Brooke Ex'ors. Witnessed by John Harvey, Gent., Samuel Weston, Walter Colquhoun, planter. Sworn 30 April and 23 June and recorded 13 July 1761.

Samuel Hoskins of Antigua, vendue-master. Will dated 10 June 1761. To my wife Anne a horse & the use of my furniture, linen, & plate for life, then to my 3 children Ann Huggins & my 2 sons Rob. & Geo. All residue to my friend Wm Warner, Jn° Stevens, & Langford Lovell, Esqres, on Trust to pay $\frac{1}{3}$ to my dau. Ann during the life of her husbd Hill Huggins & $\frac{2}{3}$ for my 2 sons. Trustees & my wife Ex'ors & Guardians. Witnessed by S. Lovely, William Atkinson. Rev. Samuel Lovely sworn 4 July. Recorded 31 July 1761.

Peter Delanoy of St. John's, Antigua, mariner. Will dated 8 April 1760. All Estate to my friends Tho. Nicholls of Antigua, butcher, & Wm Lesly of Antigua, mariner, in Trust, $\frac{1}{3}$ for my wife Frances and $\frac{2}{3}$ for my children Jane Nicholls Delanoy, Tho. Nicholls Delanoy, & Ann Nicholls Delanoy at 21; remainder to my wife & the children of my bro. Robt Delanoy. Trustees, Ex'ors & Guardians. Witnessed by Morgan William Mullins, William McLean, Joseph Grainger. Sworn 11 June 1760. Recorded 2 Sep. 1761.

William McLean of Antigua. Will dated 18 June 1761. To my mother Christy McLean of Glasgow £100 st.; if dead to the 1st child of my sist. Margt McLean of Glasgow, remainder to my friend Euphany Taylor of Antigua, sempstress, also a negro & £50 c. to the latter. To Geo. Lingar of Antigua, writing clerk, £20. To Edw. Horn, Tho. Nicholls all residue, they to be Ex'ors. Witnessed by David Key, Michael Kelly, mariner. Sworn 27 June and recorded 2 Sep. 1761.

John Hall of Antigua, carpenter. Will dated 4 Sep. 1761. To my good friend Rob. Bannister, Esq., all my Estate here, including 5 negros. To my mother all Estate in England for life, then to my neph. Tho. Willson. Rob. Bannister, Esq., Ex'or here, & Fra. Warrick, Esq., at Warrick Hall, co. Cumb., Ex'or for England. Witnessed by John Renshaw, Patrick Ogilvy. Sworn 1 and recorded 5 Oct. 1761.

Prudence Gregory, widow and relict of Edward Gregory of Antigua, deceased. Will dated 28 March 1761. To my dau.-in-law Susannah Sutcliffe, wid. of my late son Robt Sutcliffe, a bond from Hon. Jn° Tomlinson the elder, decd, of the penal sum of £425, conditioned for the payment of £212. My dau. Mary Walker to remit the money. To Sarah Martin, dau. of Sam. Martin of St John's Town, £50 c. All residue to my sd dau. Apollo to be free after her death. My sd dau. sole Ex'trix, but Mr Rob. Bannister, sen., & Mr Sam. Martin of St John's Town to advise her. Sworn by Samuel Martin 26 June and recorded 12 Oct. 1761.

Jane Rule of Antigua. Will dated 9 May 1758. Whereas my present husbd Jn° Rule by Indenture of Assignment made over to Rich. Oliver, Esq., mt in London, £400 st., I give it to my dau. Margt Wilson, & in case of her death to my dau. Ann Rule. Richd Oliver, Esq., of London,

M[r] Rich. Pearce, now of Antigua, Gent., & my husb[d] Jn[o] Rule Ex'ors. Witnessed by Alexander Shipton, Gent., John Inglise. Sworn and recorded 1 April 1762.

Thomas Williamson of Antigua, mason. Will dated 27 Aug. 1760. All Estate to my friend Rob. Dunning, he to be sole Ex'or. Witnessed by Peter Norton, book-keeper, Elizabeth Johnson. Sworn 1 April and recorded 8 April 1762.

John Leacraft of Antigua, mariner. Will dated 22 Oct. 1761. My large Bermuda-built boat & my 4 negros to be sold. To my wife Jane my mulatto girl & 10 negros, & then to the children of my brothers W[m] Leacraft & Viner Leacraft. To my wife £200 c. & furniture & all residue. To Jas. Hanson my mulatto girl. My watch & seals to M[r] Jn[o] Haycock. M[r] Jn[o] Smith, j[r], m[t], D[r] Neill Campbell, & my wife Ex'ors. Witnessed by Alexander Williams, Gent., Gratick Williams, Noell Brown. Sworn 1 April and recorded 3 May 1762.

John Conyers of Antigua, Esq. Will dated 1 March 1760. To Tho. Kidder of Antigua, m[t], & Joshua Snook of Nevis, Esq., all Estate in Antigua in Trust to sell for my adopted boy called Jn[o] Conyers. My Trustees Ex'ors. On 10 March 1762 was sworn Edward Barnes of Antigua, Gent., clerk to John Conyers, Esq. Recorded 13 May 1762.

Quinton Kenedy, Captain of the 17th Regiment. Will dated 27 April 1762. To my good friend Hen. Hamilton of the 15th Reg[t] £100 st. To Cap. Jn[o] Ross of the 95th £50 st. All residue to my bro. Primrose Kenedy. Rob. Christie of the 38th Ex'or, & give him £100 & all my horses & mules in Martinico. Witnessed by James Jewers, Edmond Comberbach, Andrew McMurtrie. On 2 June 1762 was sworn James Jewers, Serjeant of the 38th. Recorded 2 June 1762.

Edward Reed of Antigua, carpenter. Will dated 19 Feb. 1763. To Bess Smith a mulatto, £30 c. & 2 negros, & a row of negro-houses to the S. of country pond for her life. To the 1st dau. of my sister Susannah Sheldon, wife of Jos. Sheldon, carpenter in Hungerford Market, co. Midd., £40 st. All residue to my mother Ann Shaksphere. My friends Mr Tho. Tew, Mr Cæsar Roach, & Mr Rob. Killingly Ex'ors. Witnessed by John Richardson, John Robertson, Benjamin Ailhand. Sworn 24 and recorded 25 Feb. 1763.

William Walker, sen., of Antigua, shop-keeper. Will dated 15 Nov. 1762. All my Estate to be remitted to Scotland & divided between my mother Marg[t] Walker & my sist. Eliz. Walker. W[m] Walker, j[r], & Geo. Fitzgerald, m[ts], Ex'ors. Witnessed by Robert Beatty, James Robb. Sworn 27 Jan. and recorded 14 April 1763.

Thomas Biggins, house-carpenter of H.M. yard at English Harbour. Will dated 27 June 1762. To my friend Anthony Ruth, shipwright of H.M. yard, £10 c. To my dear sister Agnes Fox, relict of the late Rob. Fox, carpenter in the town of Lancaster, England, & to their surviving children, all the profits from the sale of my goods. Anth[o] Ruth to be Ex'or. Witnessed by James Thomas, William Gibson, John Gordon. Sworn 18 March and recorded 14 April 1763.

William Wordsworth of Antigua, carpenter. Will dated 21 Nov. 1762. To my housekeeper Ann Martin my negros & furniture. All residue to be sold, & ½ to her & ½ to my parents W[m] & Ann Wordsworth of the Borough of Southwark. Jn[o] Yeamans of Antigua, Esq., Tho. Barnes, & W[m] Atkinson of Antigua, Gent[n], Ex'ors. Witnessed by William Carter, Robert Anderson, Gent. Sworn 18 Dec. 1762 and recorded 30 May 1763.

Samuel Philpott of Antigua. Will dated 17 May 1763. To my brothers W[m], Steph., & Jn[o] Philpott £15 c. each. To Ed. Gratrix £15. To W[m] Lynch all residue, he to be sole Ex'or. Witnessed by James Athill, John Ledeatt, William George Crabb. Sworn 19 May and recorded 7 July 1763.

Sarah Ward *alias* Adams of Antigua. Will dated 19 April 1761. To my son W[m] Ward 1*s*. To my son Sam. Ward 2 negros & all residue, & in default to Ann Barke, dau. of Walt. Barke of Limerick, but now of Antigua. Walter Burke & M[r] Jas. Austin of S[t] John's Ex'ors. Witnessed by Mathew Meech, John Cullen.

Codicil. 9 Jan. 1762. If my son Sam. Ward die without issue then to the s[d] Ann Burke & her brother Jn[o] Burke each a negro woman. John Cullen sworn 19 May 1763. Recorded 1 Sep. 1763.

William Topham,* Clerk. Will dated 27 July 1756. To Rev. W[m] Shervington my books. To M[r] Sam. Martin, m[t] in S[t] John's, my books of Philosophical Transactions. All residue to my wife Sarah, she sole Ex'trix. Witnessed by Samuel Martin, William Shervington Denbow. Sworn 4 May and recorded 21 Sep. 1763.

William Evans of Antigua, book-keeper. Will not dated. My negro Radnor to be sold, but his silver ticket & all residue to be sent to my sister Cath. Evans of Brecon, Brecknockshire, for her care of my old mother, & in default to my sisters Eliz. Evans, Marg[t] Meredith, Ann Harris, & Rachel Gonow. M[r] Jn[o] Pooley, Edm[o] Hill, M[r] Alex. Willock Ex'ors. Witnessed by Francis Loder, Robert Anderson. Sworn 3 and recorded 4 Nov. 1763.

Isaac Gethins of Antigua, mariner. Will dated 2 Nov. 1763. All goods, etc., to David Keys, he to be sole Ex'or. Witnessed by James Hanson, jun., Robert Gibbons. Sworn 24 Nov. and recorded 6 Dec. 1763.

Robert Marshal of Dunfarline, Fife, now of Antigua. Will dated 25 Sep. 1763. All Estate to my son W[m] Marshal of Dunfarline. Jas. Stewart, planter, Ex'or. Witnessed by James Goggins, Thomas Nugent, Evan Edwards. Sworn 11 Oct. and recorded 13 Dec. 1763.

Thomas Blackey of Antigua, overseer. Will dated 2 Jan. 1764. All Estate to Mary Whitell, particularly the wages due for 7 years from the Estate of William Yeamans Archbold, deceased, of £45. Witnessed by Mansfield Ord, James Manwaring. Sworn 12 and recorded 26 Jan. 1764.

James Cosgrave of Antigua, mariner. Will dated 9 Jan. 1763. All goods to my wife Leah, she sole Ex'trix. Witnessed by Daniel Livingston, William Evans. Sworn 1 March and recorded 13 April 1764.

George Dixon of Antigua, now of Bristol, mariner. Will dated 16 Sep. 1760. To my wife Mary my ½ share of the house, lands, & negros of my late grandmother Jane Ben in S[t] John's, Parham, or elsewhere, she to be Ex'trix. Witnessed by James Rees, Ann Sprode, William Farr. From P.C.C. Recorded 27 April 1764.

Thomas Caddell of Parham, victualler. Will dated 15 Dec. 1762. All Estate to my wife Elinor, she to be sole Ex'trix. Witnessed by Samuel Massett, Thomas Nugent, Gent., Benjamin Bannerman. Sworn 24 Jan. 1763 and recorded 26 May 1764.

Ann Gateley, wife of John Gateley, merchant. Will dated 14 Aug. 1764. To Mary Chena of Antigua, spinster, & Sarah M[c]Allister, wife of Jn[o] M[c]Allister of Antigua, Gent., & Mary Lions, wife of Jn[o] Lions, Esq., my 6 slaves jointly. Jn[o] Bannister, Esq., & Jn[o] Smith, j[r], m[t], Ex'ors. Witnessed by Richard Topping, Thomas Winstone, Gent. Sworn 26 and recorded 27 Sep. 1764.

William Kipps of Antigua, Gent. Will dated 12 July 1764. To my brother Ben. Ozbaston my apparel. To my wife Rachell my furniture & goods, she, Jn[o] Godfrey, & Jn[o] Jackson Ex'ors. Witnessed by Jos. Norden, Jos. Green. Sworn 5 Sep. and recorded 2 Oct. 1764.

John Christie of Stirling, N.B., now of Antigua. Will dated 6 Oct. 1764. To my bro. W[m] Jas. Christie of Stirling all the estate bequeathed me by my late father. To my bro. Rob. Christie £50 st. To my bro. Alex[r] Christie all residue. Mainswete Walrond, Esq., & M[r] W[m] Alexander, m[t], Ex'ors. Witnessed by Kenneth Macdonald,

* He was appointed Rector of St. George's, Fitche's Creek, in 1748.

John Hosier. £50 c. interest to be paid ½ y'rly for life to my mulatto boy Alexr on the estate of Cha. Tudway, Esq. Alexander Macdonald sworn 19 Nov. 1764. Recorded 13 Dec. 1764.

Mary Strong, spinster. Will dated 6 Aug. 1762. To my sist. Eliz. Strong 3 slaves. All residue to my sist. Sarah Denit, wid. of Tho. Denit, Gent. Sarah Denit & Eliz. Strong Ex'trices. Witnessed by Mary Murrain, Nathaniel Gilbert. Sworn 15 Jan. 1765.

Ann Wilkinson, widow. Will dated 29 July 1758. To my s. Ph. Wilkinsen 1s. To my son John & my daus. Antonetta, Ann, & Elinor Wilkinson, 4 negro women. Furniture to my daus. Mr Jno Le S. Rossington & Mr Hen. West, mts, Ex'ors. Witnessed by Abraham Osborn, Richard Manwaring, Thomas Osborn, Gent. Sworn 23 and recorded 24 April 1765.

Thomas Austin of Antigua, merchant. Will dated 4 Feb. 1764. To my bro. Jno Austin of Dublin, Wm Livingston, Esq., & Jas. Alley, mt of Antigua, & my wife Judith in trust all my Estate to sell, & ¼ of the proceeds to my wife. To my child at 21 an equal share of residue. Rob. White & Jas. Alley Guardians. To my wife 2 slaves. Trustees to be Ex'ors. Witnessed by Robert Nixon, William Johnson. Sworn and recorded 25 April 1765.

Mansfield Ord, cooper. Will dated 25 Jan. 1761. My mulatto woman to be free. All residue in Trust to Samuel Warner, Esq., Sam. Martin, sr, mt, & Sam. Clapham to divide eq. among my relations Tho. Caldwell, mariner, Jas. Ord *al's* Manwaring, apprentice to the sd Clapham, & my mulatto Mary. Trustees Ex'ors. Witnessed by James Watson, John Meredith. Sworn 9 April 1764. Codicil 16 March 1764. Recorded 27 Nov. 1765.

Carter Stevens, merchant. Will dated 14 July 1762. Now bound for Martinico. All Estate to my wife Anne, trusting she will devise the same to my sisters & their children. She & Jno Jenkins Ex'ors. Witnessed by Becher Crawfield. George Harney, Gent., and Dorothy Harney, widow, swore to the handwriting, B. Crawfield having left the Island, 19 Dec. Recorded 20 Dec. 1765.

George Pinkerton, planter. Will dated 7 Feb. 1766. To my bro. Jas. Pinkerton, son of Geo. Pinkerton of Antrim in Irel'd, £100 st. To Wm Pinkerton, bro. to Jas. Pinkerton, £100 st. To Geo. Pinkerton, son to Wm Pinkerton, £100. To my sist. Martha Pinkerton £50. To my sist. Eliz. Pinkerton £50. To Sarah, Janett, & Margt Pinkerton £50. To Tho. Osborne, s. of Mr Kean Osborne of Antigua, planter, £100 & a mulatto. To Sarah Lyons Walrond, dau. of Mainswete Walrond, Esq., £50 st. To Eliz., Jane, Abigail, & Margt Osborne, daus. of Mr Kean Osborne of Antigua, £50 st. ea. To Mr Jo Hosier of Antigua, planter, £6. Residue if any to legatees. Mr Kean Osborne & Mainswete Walrond, Esq., Ex'ors. Witnessed by Charles Gordon, Andrew McLintock, overseer. Sworn 17 Feb. and recorded 4 April 1766.

1766, May 10. In Court of . . . . Rev. David Hopkins of Antigua, Clerk, and Martha his wife against Ralph Willet, Esq., Ex'or of Walter Griffiths, mariner.

1767, July 6. Indenture between James Parkinson of Antigua, Surgeon, and James Shewell of Antigua, Gent.

John Mutch of Antigua, planter. Will dated 26 Oct. 1768. All my Estate to be sold. The interest of £700 to my father Alexr Mutch in the parish of New Machere, co. Aberdeen, then to my bro. Alexr & sisters Jane & Christian. £100 to my neph. Jno Mutch, son of my bro. Alexr Mutch. Dav. Cuthbert, Esq., Commissioner of the Customs at Edinburgh, & Teige More of Scotstoun, Ex'ors in Scotland, & Pat. Grant, Jas. Simms, & Gavin Montgomerie, Ex'ors in Antigua. Witnessed by Patrick Malcolm, Richard Davies. Sworn 3 Nov. 1768. Recorded 1 April 1769.

Mary Pritchard of Antigua, spinster. Will dated 6 Dec. 1762. My negro woman Sippy to be free. To Mrs Sarah Waldron, ye wife of Mainswete Waldron of Antigua, Esq., £100 c. To my sister Eliz. Pritchard all residue for life, then to Mrs Sarah Waldron. My sd sist. & Mainswete Waldron Ex'ors. Witnessed by William Walter Rossington, Elizabeth Step. Rossington.

1st Codicil. 30 Dec. 1762. Revoke the £100 to Mrs Sarah Waldron.

2nd Codicil. 15 March 1763. M. Waldron not to be Ex'or, & to my sd sister all my estate for ever. Mr Geo. Savage of St John's Town, mt, & Dr Jno Achill of St John's Town Ex'ors. Sworn 16 March 1769 by W. W. Rossington, mt.

Richard Davies. (Fragment.) Will dated 13 Jan. 1779. To Sarah Lyons £20 c. If my wife Dorothy have any children, then my estate to her & them equally. Wm Wickham Harman, John Bright, & Rev. John Bowen Ex'ors. Witnessed by John Bell, John Marshall, Thomas Browne. Before Hon. Otto Baijer, President, was sworn J. Marshall.

1778, Dec. 5. Indenture of Sale. David Grewer of Antigua, shipwright, Ex'or of the will of Robert Grant, cabinet maker, dated 3 Dec. 1774, sells a negro boy for £88 10s. to Barbara Anderson.

1773, July 15. John Boyd of Antigua, Gent., sells a negro woman to William Eales of Antigua, Esq.

Robert James of Antigua, writing clerk. Will dated 12 June 1779. To my mother Jane James of Antigua 5 negros, then to my sist. Mary Taylor, wife of Jno Taylor, writing clerk, & to their dau. Jane Taylor 2 negros. To my neph. Rob. Jas. Taylor a negro. To my neph. Jno Taylor a negro at 21. My negro Jack to be free after my mother's death. All residue to my sd mother, whom with Boyce Ledwell of Antigua, mt, Elias Ferris of Antigua, planter, & Jno Robertson, Surg., I appoint Ex'ors. Witnessed by Robert Darnell, gent., Elenor Salkreig, Mary Darnell. Sworn 16 July and recorded 1 Aug. 1781.

James Cockley of Antigua, Gent. Will dated 5 March 1766. To my son Laurence Cockley my house at Falmouth & 10 acres at Indian Creek & 5 negros & ⅓ of my cattle. To my son Hen. Cockley a proportion of land at Falmouth & 4 negros & ⅓ of my cattle. To my son Geo. Cockley a proportion at Falmouth, 5 negros, & ⅓ of my cattle. To my wife Margt Cockley the lease of my house, 2 negros, & all residue. Jas. Irwin Ex'or. Witnessed by George Blower, James Gaul, sen. Sworn 9 Sep. 1773. Recorded 14 Sep. 1781.

Richard Harrison of Antigua, Gent. Will dated 30 March 1781. To Eliz. Winkworth, dau. of Mrs Ann Winkworth, a negro. To my negro woman called Francky all my furniture. Mr Sam. Webb of Antigua, Gent., Ex'or. Witnessed by Robert Barton, William Tweedy. Sworn 27 April 1782.

Mary, wife of Robert Milne of Antigua. Will dated 26 April 1774. All Estate to my husbd, he to be Ex'or. Witnessed by Coleman Heyns, William Scheviz. Sworn 6 June 1782 by John Staunton, the witnesses having been away for years.

Arthur Cormick of Antigua, planter. Will dated 7 June 1782. To Mrs Eliz. Hughes a negro. All residue to my dau. Sarah Cormick. My wife Anne & Mr Tho. Powell Ex'ors. Witnessed by Daniel Ross, Diana Dealy. Sworn 27 July 1782.

Alexander Reid of Antigua, planter. Will dated 30 Nov. 1774. All Estate to my brother-german Pat. Reid late of Antigua, now of Dominica, planter, he paying to my father Tho. Reid & my mother Rachel Farquharson £20 a year & £20 c. to my friend Jno Scot, now manager of ye Folly. Pat. Reid, Jno Scot, & Dr Jas. Gilchrist Ex'ors. Signed at Mr Kerby's Estate called Parrys. Jas. McNaught, planter. Sworn 7 Jan. 1782.

Ann Pitts of Antigua, widow. Will dated . . . . 1781. To my dau. Mary Pitts plate. All land in Nevis Str.,

St John's Town, to be sold for my children Thos. Pitts & Mary Pitts at 21. To my son Jno Pitts 1s. Betty to be free. Jno Bott, wheelwright, Ex'or. Witnessed by Richard Topping, Edward Tyrrel Murphy, Susanna Braham. Sworn 12 Jan. 1782.

Ann Taylor of Antigua, spinster. Will dated 10 Nov. 1777. All Estate to my neph. Jno Taylor, he to be Ex'or. Witnessed by Thomas Kenyon, Benjamin Steel, George Harney, Gent. Sworn and recorded 26 Aug. 1782.

Elizabeth Fontaneau of Antigua, spinster. Will dated 1 Oct. 1779. To my 2 nieces Ann & Mary, daus. of my bro. Wm Fontaneau, my house. Sarah & Phillis & their children to be free. Tho. T. Wise, Esq., & Mrs Ann Boudinott Ex'ors. Witnessed by Sarah Powell, Elizabeth Wise, John Bridges. Sworn and recorded 26 Sep. 1782.

Mary Reynolds, widow of George Reynolds, cooper. Will dated 17 June 1779. To my son Geo. my books. To my sons Jno & Ben. £3 6s. 0*d*. c. My granddau. Mary Reynolds, dau. of Ben. & Mary Reynolds. To my dau. Louisa Wilson *al's* Hodges 1s. To my dear friend & benefactress Eliz. Dunbar of Antigua, wid., all residue, she to be Ex'trix. Witnessed by John Nugent, writing clerk, William Buckland, William Catow. Sworn 1 Nov. 1781.

Will of Jac. Ernst of Antigua, sailmaker. All Estate to Eliz. Ernst (my dau. by Henrietta Marchant now Ramsay). Mr Jonath. Ramsay & Mr Tho. Powell, writing cl'k, Ex'ors & Guardians. Witnessed by John Cuthbert, planter, Samuel White. Sworn 2 Dec. 1782.

Will of Jonathan Broadbridge, blacksmith.

Will of John Hope of St. Paul, Shadwell. Copy from P.C.C. Recorded 1782.

Charles Crouch of Antigua, Gent. Will dated 2 March 1783. Ben. & Tho. Boddington of London, m^{ts}, & Mr Wm Brinton & Mr Sam. Rigg of Antigua, m^{ts}, Exors. All Estate to my son Chas. My house at Spring Gardens, Antigua, to my dau.-in-law Eliz. Ryder. Witnessed by Jonas Langford Blizard, William Dickinson, Edward Horne, Esq. Sworn 13 March 1783.

Richard Harris, Rector of St. Mary. Will dated 7 Aug. 1774. To my wife Jane all Estate, she to be Ex'trix. Witnessed by John Ives, Gent., Sachariah Bishop. Sworn 16 Jan. and recorded 22 March 1783.

James Hogan of Antigua, planter. Will dated 8 Feb. 1783. All Estate to my father Dennis Hogan of Anah in the parish of Cloughpraior, Irel^{d}, then to my bro. Jno Hogan & my sister Mary Hogan. My friends Pat. Cummins of Antigua, planter, Jno Larmer, shopkeeper, & Mary Burke of Antigua, wid., Ex'ors. Witnessed by Richard Staunton, Alexander Grant. Sworn 24 and recorded 25 March 1783.

Mary Salnarve of Antigua, widow. Will dated 29 Sep. 1781. To my niece Mary Maria Cuthbert, wife of Mr Jno Cuthbert, & her inf^{t} dau. Ann Dingwell Cuthbert 7 negros, & all residue to her. Mr Jno Cuthbert, planter, Ex'or. Witnessed by Eliz. Huyghue, spinster, Jos. Shillott. Sworn 17 and recorded 22 May 1783.

Michael Moran of St. John's Town, Gent. Will dated 16 March 1782. To my brother Dan. Moran of Roscrea, co. Tipp., whitesmith, my house in St John's Town & £1000 st. To my father Martin Moran of Tinoe, co. Tipp., £15 a yr. My late wife Susanna. All residue to my bro. Witnessed by Thomas French, John Egan, John Cleare. Copy from P.C. of Dublin.

Mary Stanly of Falmouth, widow. Will dated 4 May 1771. All Estate to my son Jno Diggs Stanly at 21, & in default to my dau. Mary Stanly. Rob. Christian, Esq., Pet. Alsop, Esq., & Mr Jas. Irvin Ex'ors. Witnessed by James Tweedy, Finlay Martin, John Martin. Sworn and recorded July 1783.

George Hazlewood of Antigua, planter. Will dated 25 June 1783. All furniture to my bro. Rich^{d} of England, £50 c. to Mr Jas. Hill, 2^{d} son of Dan. Hill, s^{r}, Esq., & £10 each to Messrs. Math. Crawford, Tho. Fraser, & Alex. Keith of Antigua, planters. All residue to them. D. Hill, s^{r}, Esq., Math. Crawford, & Alex. Keith Ex'ors. Witnessed by Francis Lynch, Barry C. Hart. Sworn 3 July 1783.

Will of John Hodson of Antigua, carpenter. Recorded 1783.

James Stilling of St. John's Town, merchant. Will dated 10 Oct. 1783. To my Ex'ors all my Estate in Trust to sell, & $\frac{1}{3}$ to my wife Anne & $\frac{2}{3}$ to my daus. Mary Anne & Louisa. To my sister-in-law Jane Roberts £50. My wife, Dan. Hill, S^{r}, of Antigua, Esq., Boyce Ledwell, & Ed. Rigg, m^{ts}, of Antigua, Ex'ors & Guardians. Witnessed by Dr Francis Brown, John Barke. Sworn 17 and recorded 25 Oct. 1783.

Will of James Davis, foreman of H.M. yard.

Will of John Ord of Antigua, mariner. Alex. Livingston of Antigua, Gent. Sworn 3 Dec. 1783.

Mary McClintock of St. John's Town, widow. Will dated 16 July 1780. All Estate to my friend Cath. Thibou of St John's Town, spinster, she & Alex. Coates of St John's, shipwright, Ex'ors. Witnessed by Joel Sangster, John McDavid, Mary Hamilton. Sworn 28 Aug. 1783. Recorded 27 Jan. 1784.

Richard Battyson of Antigua, Gent. Will dated 24 June 1782. To my wife Eleanor Denbow Battyson £100 c. All residue to Leonard Stout & Is^{c} Eccleston, m^{ts} of Antigua, on Trust for my wife & to any child, remainder to my father & mother Jno & Marg^{t} Battyson of Kerby Lonsdale, co. West. Trustees to be Ex'ors. Witnessed by William Pigott, Samuel Sayer, writing clerk, John Cuthbert. Sworn 1 Dec. 1783. Recorded 2 Feb. 1784.

Will of Edward Hall, Master of H.M.S. "Cornwall." All Estate to my wife Christiana Hall, living in New York. Jos. Blake Higgins & Wm Whitehead of St John's, m^{ts}. Sworn 1784.

Richard Southwell of Antigua, Gent. Will dated 5 April 1784. To Phil. Tudhope Winterflood & Wm Winterflood of Antigua, sons of Tho. Winterflood & Eliz. his wife, £100 c. each. To Mary Meredith, 1st dau. of Wm Meredith, late of Antigua, dec^{d}, & Frances his wife, £100 c. To Rebecca Blizard, a free mulatto, 4 negros. Nine negros to be sold & the proceeds given to Jane Bruce for Alex., Alice, Jane, Mary, & Sarah Bruce, her children by Alex^{r} Bruce her husb^{d}, dec^{d}. All residue to Rebecca Blizard. Tho. Winterflood of Antigua, Gent., & Tho. Goolsby of Antigua, silversmith, Ex'ors. To be bur. at St John's. Witnessed by Hugh Chalmers, John Henderson, David Cuffe. Sworn 10 April 1784.

Will of Margaret Robinson of Antigua, widow. Recorded 1784.

Will of Elizabeth Carnegie of Antigua, widow. My bro. Jos. Allicocke. Recorded 1784.

Edward Tyrrell Murphy. Will dated 26 June 1783. To my mother Susanna Haycock 4 negros & my $\frac{1}{3}$ of the 11 negros I became possessed of on the death of my grandmother Eliz. Haycock as heir-at-law of Rebecca Devereux Murphy, 1 of the devisees of my uncle Sam. Murphy, dec^{d}. To my natural bro. Chr. Murphy £20 c. All residue to my bro. Jno Devereux Murphy. Alex^{r} Scott, Boyce Ledwell, Esq., Ex'ors. Witnessed by Mary Shony (?), James Delap, Chistian Haycock. Sworn 5 April and recorded 9 May 1785.

Ann Chapman, freewoman. Will dated 12 Nov. 1784. All estate to my dau. Fra. Johnston, now of Dominica, except £200 c. due by Miss Grace Bryant, to be used to free my son Jas. Nich. Lynch, Rich. Page Ex'ors. Witnessed by Ed. Tyley, Samuel McCarty. Sworn May and recorded 22 June 1785.

William Clearkly, carpenter. Will dated 4 Jan. 1785. My bro. & sist. Recorded 18 June 1785.

James McNight, coppersmith. Will dated 17 May 1785.

All Estate to my son Jas., remainder to my bro. Pat. McNight. Mr Alex. Petrie, Mr Jno Blair Ex'ors. Witnessed by Alexander Stewart, William Thompson. Sworn 5 and recorded 9 July 1785.

Patrick Malcolm, Surgeon. Will dated 16 Aug. 1785. To Janet Malcolm, dau. of Geo. Malcolm, decd, of Tullibarden, & niece of Wm Malcolm, decd, surveyor of the Excise in London, who lives at Bowlie (?), near Breas, wife to Duncan McKenzie, the interest of £1000 st. for life, then to the 3 sons & dau. of her bro. Jno Malcolm, who is said to have died 8 years since, & her son Daniel McKenzie. To the 3 sons & dau. of Jno Malcolm, decd, & Danl McKenzie £500 st. Wm Sharpe, Surgeon, Jno Scotland, mt, & Sam. Martin, collector, Ex'ors. Before President Thomas Jarvis was sworn Robert Anderson 24 Aug. 1785. Recorded 30 Aug.

John Scott, book-keeper. Will dated 2 March 1783. To my mother Ann Gale a negro woman. I free my friend & companion Zaide Scott & give her 5 negros, & after her death a negro to John Hart, son of Barry C. Hart. Becky to be free. To my cousin & goddau. Lucy, wife of Nich. Lynch, 2 negro women, also all my lands & tenem'ts in Nevis Str., & all residue, charged with £30 c. yearly to Zaide Scott, & £6 12s. yearly to my mother, & £5 yearly each to my aunts Frances Gale, Hester Gale, & Eliz. Earle. My furniture, horse, etc., to Zaide. Barry Conyers Hart & Nich. Lynch Ex'ors. Witnessed by John Daniel Bean, Mark Tyley. Sworn 23 and recorded 28 Nov. 1785.

Will of John Ives, planter. To Cha. Kerr & Dan. Hill in Trust for my dau. Sarah Mascall 4 negros & all my estate, except what I hereafter set apart for my wife Frances Ives. John Thibou sworn 3 Nov., and recorded 17 Dec. 1785.

Barbara Carson of Elk River, Maryland. Will dated 13 May 1782. To my son Robt £200. To Jas. Murray, Lieut. & Quarter-Master of the 9th British Regt, £50. To Zachariah Lorrel in France £50. To Col. Paul Cox of Philadelphia £100. To my son-in-law Tho. Huggins £500. To my son Robt my plate & furniture. All residue to my grandson Sam. Carson Huggins at 21. Another £500 & all residue to the sd Robt Carson, he & Col. Paul Cox Ex'ors. Witnessed by William Sharpe, Robert Gray.

1783, Dec. 24. Paul Cox renounced execution before George Campbell, Registrar at Philadelphia. Recorded 9 Jan. 1786.

Jacob Woolf of Rotherhith, Surrey, master mariner. Will dated 18 Jan. 1769. All my land in Surrey to my wife Eliz. for life, then to my 6 children Ann, Jacob, Ephraim, Eliz., Sarah, & Rebecca. All residue to my wife, & appoint her sole Ex'trix. Witnessed by Elizabeth Hutchinson, John Greir, Thomas Patterson. Copy sent from P.C.C.

Petition of Sarah Summers, sister to Samuel Summers, that the following writing may be proved as his will, viz.:—

To my sister Sarah Summers £30 st. To Richd son of Tho. Hodges £50 c. To Ann dau. of Jno & Mary Wall £50 c. All residue to Hon. Steph. Blizard & his heirs. Steph. Blizard, Tho. Hodges, & Jno Wall Ex'ors. Samuel Summers died about 1784, having survived the residuary legatee and the Ex'ors. In 1784 the Hon. Ed. Byam applied for letters of adm'on which your Excellency granted. On 28 May 1785, as natural heir and next-of-kin, petitioner obtained letters of adm'on from the Archbishop of C.C. Sarah Summers, by deed poll of 1 May 1785, appointed James Richards Maud and John Burk her Attornies in Antigua; and petitioner understands that the Hon. Ed. Byam is willing to renounce claim to adm'on. Consented to by Thomas Shirley, Governor, etc., 30 March 1786. Claim revoked by Ed. Byam in favour of petitioner 31 March 1786.

Will of John Houlton Warlock, planter. All Estate to my mother & wife Christian. Recorded 31 Jan. 1787.

Will of Benjamin Ailhaud, shopkeeper. My sisters Ann Margt Allair, Eliz. Marchant, & Anne Hamilton. Recorded 25 April 1787.

Will of John Macher, planter, recorded 25 April 1787.

Will of Francis Booth of Tottenham Court Road, London. Property from my bro. Alexr Dean of Antigua to my grandchildren. From P.C.C. Recorded 18 June 1787.

Letter from James Nibbs dated 16 July 1788. Mr. Horsford, the gentleman appointed by the Court, has found a codicil to the will your brother made and left in England, which codicil I transcribe. I have given a retainer to the Council your brother has employed of ten johannies (£20); he recommends not taking letters of adm'on as it would enable Mr. Hyde to continue his prosecution in Chancery against the estate. He appears to have owed in 1782 to Richard Adney, sen., £10,699, and the partnership of Deane and Adney appear to be indebted to Mr. Alexander Deane £10,360. Mr. Hicks, the gentleman retained, accompanies me to your brother's estate. I need not observe how necessary it will be for you to send the will as soon as proved. Mrs. Nibbs writes compliments and family love to my relations and family at Beauchamp.

P.S.—Samuel Byam the Ex'or is dead.

Codicil. 13 Feb. 1780. Whereas I, Richd Adney, on leaving England at the end of 1768, made a will and left certain matters to be adjusted by my Ex'ors Richd Adney, Gent., Ann Adney, spinster, & Rev. Jno Adney, being anxious to add an Ex'or here, do now appoint Sam. Byam, Esq. If they distress the Estate of Deane & Adney by a suit at law, my Ex'or Sam. Byam shall dispose of such negros as Richd Adney hath bought in his own name. The overseer to pay £29 for my funeral. 2 jo'es to Mary Byam *al's* Franklyn for her services. To Matty & her children all the dollars & 6 jo'es. Witnessed by Ann Brown, John Ausiter, Hugh Eggleson. Recorded 22 Dec. 1788. On 26 Sep. 1788 appeared the Rev. John Adney of Alplowman in Devon, Clerk, and swore to being the brother and surviving Ex'or of the will of Richard Adney, formerly of the parish of St. Bride's, London, but late of Antigua, dated 31 Dec. 1768, and that about the end of 1770 Richard Adney went to live at Antigua, and that he received the enclosed letter from James Nibbs saying his brother died 28 June last.

John Pyne. Will dated 12 Nov. 1788. All Estate to my sons Jno Battyson Pyne & Geo. Pyne. Jos. Desilvia Ex'or. Recorded 25 March 1789.

Will of James McMillan. All Estate to my father, & after his death to my sisters Griswell Johnson, Jean McNish, & Sarah Jolly. Recorded 25 Oct. 1790.

Benjamin Graham, merchant, of London, now of Dominica. Will dated 6 July 1782. Jno Robinson, Tho. Rainy of Dominica, Esq., & Isaac Walker & Jno Freeman of London, linendraper. . . . . Recorded 21 Dec. 1790.

Will of Jos. Blake Higgins, 2 Nov. 1789.

Here follow extracts from folios 126—361, 27 Oct. 1787 to 8 Oct. 1795.

Alexander Scott, Esq. Will dated at Antigua 10 Aug. 1780, and subscribed 8 Jan. 1787 John Robertson, Nathaniel Marchant, James Gillan. Before Major-General Sir Thomas Shirley, Bart., appeared James Gillan of Antigua, Gent., John Robertson and Nathaniel Marchant, both Practitioners in Physic. Recorded 27 Oct. 1787.

John Scott of Antigua, planter. Will dated 7 Oct. 1787. To my neph. Wm Scott my gold watch & chain with my seal with the Scotts' coat of arms. To my brother Walter Scott, farmer at Monks Lee, near Carlisle, co. Cumb., the interest of all my Estate for life, then to his 8d son Wm Scott. Walt. Scott, with Rob. Anderson, mt, Wm Entwisle, Esq., & Hon. Tho. Jarvis, Esq., of Antigua, Ex'ors. Witnessed by John Malcolm, Walter Scott, James Malcolm. Sworn and recorded 17 Nov. 1787.

William Scheviz of Antigua, accountant. Will dated 30 Dec. 1779. To my brother Geo. Scheviz of Antigua, planter, a suit of mourning. To my brother Kenneth Scheviz of Inverness all residue. Kenneth Scheviz and Geo. Scheviz, with Mr Lachlan Grant & Mr Jas. Gillan of Antigua, planters, Ex'ors. Witnessed by John Watson, Timothy Allen. Sworn 1 and recorded 2 Nov. 1787.

James Hutchinson of Antigua, Esq. Will dated 26 Feb. 1788. All Estate to my sister Margt Hutchinson* of Paisley in Scotland, & appoint her sole Ex'trix. Witnessed by Archibald Gloster, Isaac Field Thibou, Robert Wilson. Before Sir Thomas Shirley appeared Robert Wilson of Antigua, taylor, Archd Gloster, Barrister, and Dr. Isaac F. Thibou 3 March 1788. Recorded 2 March 1788.

James Wallace of Antigua, planter. Will dated 25 Aug. 1787. Names only mulatto issue.

Richard Davies of Antigua, Gent. Will dated 26 Oct. 1786. To my bro. the Rev. Mr Wm Davies of Wantage, co. Berks, £300 st. To my 3 sisters Margt, Ann, & Eliz. Davies £200 st. each. To my friend Pet. Alsop of Antigua, Esq., £200. To my friend Mr Rob. Barton of Antigua 8 new shirts. All residue to my bro. & sisters. Pet. Alsop Ex'or. Witnessed by James Irvin, Laver Martin, Edward Gamble.

Codicil. 7 Dec. 1786. £20 & my live stock to my nurse Corunna Hurst. Witnessed by S. Murray, Robert Barton. Before Sir T. Shirley, Bart., appeared Laver Martin, Surgeon, and James Irvin, Esq., Edward Gamble, Esq., and Robert Barton, Gent., 17 Feb. 1787. Recorded 14 May 1788.

Before President Byam, 18 Nov. 1789, Frederick William Fisher of Antigua, Gent., swore that he saw James Simms, planter, deceased, sign his will. Recorded 18 Nov. 1789.

Will of Mary Gloyne, widow. My sist. Eliz. Berry.

Will of Antonio Villion of Port of Spain. All residue to Eliz. Villion (my Legitima Muger y por Dona Albana). Will part in French and part in Spanish. By Sir Thomas Shirley, 1 Sep. 1790, appeared John Lindsay of St. John's Town, vintner, and swore that Antonio Villion was late of London but last of St. John's Town, merchant. Recorded 3 Sep. 1790.

Will of John Ralm of St. P., shipwright.

William McDowall of Antigua, merchant. Will dated 4 Sep. 1789. To Robt & Nancy, s. & dau. of David King of Antigua, mt, $\frac{1}{2}$ of all the profits of my estate & the stock in hand. To my mother £200 c. To my wife & any child she might have all residue. Mr David King, & Mr Pat. Reid of Ayr & my wife Ann Ex'ors. Witnessed by George Potter, ship master, John Wyllie, clerk, and Robert Lyons, clerk. Sworn and recorded 25 Sep. 1790.

Will of John Richards Maud of Antigua, merchant. All my real estate in Great Britain to Sr Jas. Laroche, Bart., & Walt. Jacks of Bristol, mt, in Trust . . . . etc.

Note.—Folios 217 to 231 are missing.

Before Sir T. Shirley, Bart., appeared Thomas B. Powell of Antigua, writing clerk, *re* the will of William Thomson. George Bladen was also a witness. Sworn and recorded 7 April 1791.

Elizabeth Croswell of Antigua, spinster. Will dated 2 May 1790. All Estate to my mother Sarah Croswell of Antigua. Witnessed by Elizabeth Grant, Sarah Worlock. Elizabeth Grant, spinster, sworn 9 April. Recorded 12 April 1791.

Christian Shelton of Antigua, widow. Will dated 10 Dec. 1789. Castillo to be free in a year. All my Estate to my Ex'ors in Trust to pay the rents to my dau. Eliz. McKaile of Antigua, wid., & after her death to my nephew Dr Jas. Irvin of St Croix. My brother-in-law Jas. Irvin, sen., & my neph. Jas. Irvin, jun., Ex'ors. Witnessed by Edward Gamble, Stephen Parker, gunner R.A. Sworn 7 April and recorded 7 May 1791.

Frances Ives, widow. Will dated 1 June 1789. To my dau. Sarah Mascall 3 negros. To my grandson Edmond Osborn Mascall 2 negros. To my grandson Jno Ives Mascall a negro. To my grandson Wm Mascall 2 negros. Filloret to be free. My son-in-law Jno Mascall Ex'or & my dau. Sarah Mascall Ex'trix. Witnessed by J. Elliott, junr, S. Marchant. Sworn 21 Sep. 1790.

Henry Topham of Charlotte Street. Will dated 8 April 1786. Mr Jno Read of Old Jewry, mt, & Mrs Anne Topham my wife Ex'ors in Trust. To my children Anne & Charlotte Topham £1000 apiece. To my sist. Margt Stockdill £25 a year. All residue to my wife Anne Topham. On 4 Feb. 1790 appeared Charles Barber of Old Jewry, Gent., and Nathan Meteyard of Sunbury, co. Middlesex, servant. The testator was formerly of Antigua but late of Sunbury, Esq., decd. From P.C.C. On 9 Feb. 1790 adm'on to Anne Topham the relict.

Jeremiah Willcox, writing clerk. Will dated 28 Oct. 1785. My dau. Jean Willcox. My son Jer. Willcox. My wife Charlotte. My sist. Margt Rogers. My mother Lonisa Rogers £10. My sist. Eliz. Clark. My brother Robt £5. All effects to be sold, & $\frac{1}{3}$ to my wife & $\frac{2}{3}$ to my children. Witnessed by John Willcockes, Benjamin Hughes, Edmund Paul. On 25 Jan. 1791 was sworn Benjamin Hughes, writing clerk. Recorded 25 Jan. 1791.

Ezra Whipple, harbour master. Will dated 15 Jan. 1791. To Sarah Murray, dau. of Mrs Rebecca Murray, a negro. To Edwd Barnes, pilot, my boat. To Rob. & Anne King, son & dau. of David King, all residue. Witnessed by Robert Lyons, John Wyllie. Sworn and recorded 19 May 1791.

Sarah Steele, widow of Benjamin Steele of Antigua, planter. Will dated 2 Jan. 1790. All Estate to my son Jno Steele. Dr Tho. Kirwan, Ex'or. Witnessed by Ed. Horne, Samuel Gunthorpe, John Hodges. Sworn and recorded 12 Nov. 1791.

Hannah Anderton, wife of William Anderton, now of Antigua, Gent. Will dated 1 Nov. 1779. Four negros to Alex. Willock & Jos. Brown of Antigua, Esqres, in Trust for my husband, & after his death to be freed. Witnessed by Margt Barter, Ulick Burke. Montserrat. Before President Samuel Martin Irish was sworn Ulick Burke, Esq., 10 Nov. 1791. Recorded 17 Nov. 1791.

Mary Webley of Antigua, widow. Will dated 24 Oct. 1789. All Estate to Cha. Yeamans Martin, Esq., Dr Jno Robinson, & Langford Lovell, Esq., in Trust. Polydore to be free & to have £10 c. a year. To Chas. Yeamans Martin my book case & diamond ring. To Arch. Shannon, Esq., my emerald & diamond ring. All residue for my mother Mary Steele, & after her death 1 negro to Frances Merrefield Atwater, dau. of Cap. Luman Atwater, & $\frac{1}{2}$ of the residue to Eliz. Merrefield, late wife of my son Robarts Merrefield, & $\frac{1}{2}$ to my cousin Edward Powe, senr, of St Croix, then to his dau. Mary Powe or his 2 sons Geo. & Ed. Powe. My Trustees to be Ex'ors. Witnessed by Henry McDavid, Benjamin B. Davis, Luman Atwater.

Codicil. 17 Nov. 1789. All my Estate to be sold & the interest given to my dau.-in-law Eliz. Merrefield, then to my mother Mrs Mary Steele. My dau.-in-law Justina Merrifield. Witnessed by Louisa Stevens, Elias Ferris, Archibald Grover Dow. Before Governor Woodley was sworn Henry McDavid, writing clerk, 4 Jan. 1792 and Louisa Stevens, spinster. Recorded 4 Jan. 1792.

Ann Stilling, widow. Will dated 4 Jan. 1792. All my Estate to Arch. Dow, Jno Taylor, & Jno Burke, Esqr, in Trust for my daus. Mary Ann & Louisa Stilling. To Miss Ann Clark who lives with me all sums due to me from her late father's estate. Trustees Ex'ors. Witnessed by Arthur

* She died in 1795, aged 69, and was stated to have inherited a fortune of £300,000 from her brother James. (See 'Gent. Mag.')

Robertson, Nathaniel Marchant. Sworn and recorded 16 Feb. 1792.

Ann Stevens. Will dated 3 July 1791. To my niece Eliz. Mathews of Antigua, wid., negros. To Ann Stevens Green, wife of Geo. Green, negros. All residue to Jn° Taylor, Esq., late of Antigua, now of England. Jn° Taylor & Wm Mathews, Esq^{rs}, Ex'ors. Witnessed by A. Brown, Ebenezer Hughes. Recorded 16 Feb. 1792.

Joseph Hawkins. Will dated 30 Nov. 1786. . . . . to pay the annuity of £200 to my wife, & on further Trust that they the s^d Eliz. Hawkins my wife, Jn° Hume, & Alex^r Learmonth hold all residue for my children. Witnessed by Richard Hughes, Lincoln's Inn, Thomas Spencer, Rathbone Place, D. C. Fabian, Temple. Copy from P.C.C. Recorded 26 April 1792.

Will of John Bawn recorded 17 July 1792.

Will of John Martin, joiner, recorded 14 Aug. 1792.

James Corss, planter. Will dated 23 Jan. 1793. To my sist. Jane Grant (formerly Corss) all residue & to her son Jn° Grant. Witnessed by Henry Jarvis. Sworn 26 Jan. 1793.

Catherine Philpott, widow. Will dated 7 Jan. 1792. My 1st dau. Sarah, & my daus. Frances & Eleunus & my s. Ben. negros. My dau. Martha. To my sons Sam., Francis, & Tho. my wooden tenement. My 3 y^{st} sons Fra., Tho., & Ben. all residue equally. Mr Geo. Gore & M^r Jn° Bawn Ex'ors. Witnessed by William Johnson, wheelwright, Judith Johnson. Sworn 16 and recorded 18 Feb. 1793.

Will of Benjamin Keyzser, coppersmith, recorded 27 March 1793.

Thomas Montgomery. Will dated 19 Dec. 1792. All Estate to my wife Eliz. Ann for life, then to my sist. Mary Ann Montgomery. Recorded 18 April 1793.

Richard Chapman, Gent. Will dated 13 Dec. 1792. To my children Sarah Fletcher Chapman, Wm Redhead Chapman, Grace Redhead Austin, Eleanor Justina Chapman, Rich. Jos. Chapman, & Euphemia Chapman all estate equally. To my granddau. Maria Barbara Austin £33 c., her "detestable & most horrid father Fra. Edwin Austin." The share of my unfortunate dau. Grace R. Austin to be on Trust. Is^c Eccleston, Wm Shervington, & Jn° Scholes, Esq^{res}, Ex'ors. Sworn 15 April 1793.

Edmund Wendell, merchant. Will dated 2 June 1787. All Estate to my wife Marg^t, she Ex'trix, & Wm Gamble Denbow, Sam. Watts, Jn° Kelsick, & Walter Jacks, Esq., in England, Ex'ors. Witnessed by Isaac Eccleston, Ann Donaldson. Recorded 25 April 1793.

Elizabeth Topping, widow. Will dated 5 Jan. 1792. To my cousins Marg^t dau. of my late uncle-in-law Peter Tho. Tyson, her sist. Eliz. Tyson, Mary wife of Cap. Jn° Skelton, Wm Tyson of St Christopher's, Esq., Jas. Tyson of do., Danl Tyson, Geo. Tyson, barrister, Cath. wife of Mr Jas. Morgan, negros. To Mrs Sarah Peyton of Antigua, wid., £100 c. All residue to my cousin Jn° Tyson, Esq., of St Christopher's, he & Tho. Turner Ex'ors. Witnessed by William Shervington, Hugh Flin, Langford Lovell Hodge. Sworn and recorded 8 May 1793.

Will of James Robb. Only mentions negros. Recorded 6 July 1793.

Elizabeth Ailhaud, widow of Jacob Ailhaud. Will dated 16 July 1790. All Estate to Elias Ferris in Trust for my niece Eliz. Coates, wife of Mr Alex^r Coates, shipwright. Recorded 13 Sep. 1793.

Will of Robert Bennett, planter, recorded 1793.

Will of John Bott, wheelwright, sworn 12 Jan. 1794.

Will of John Long dated 9 Oct. 1793. Recorded.

Will of Alexander Nicholls, planter, recorded 9 Nov. 1793.

Will of Stephen Hubbard. All Estate between my father Wm Hubbard & my wife Henrietta Leyburne Hubbard equally. Witnessed by Nathaniel Gilbert, John Gilbert. Recorded 5 March 1794.

Will of Richard Suton, shipwright, recorded 15 March 1794.

Will of Archibald Smith, tavern-keeper, recorded 29 March 1794.

Will of Adam Watson, hairdresser, dated 2 Dec. 1793. Recorded 1794.

Wills of Thomas Byshopp recorded 1 March 1794, and of Frances his wife recorded 6 June 1794.

Will of Thomas Hinson Prizzar, master mariner, recorded 13 Nov. 1793.

Will of Dorothy Constant. All Estate to my daus. Sarah Rolland, Ann Creese, & Eliz. Constant equally. Recorded 23 July 1794.

Will of William Biddle, planter, recorded 18 Sep. 1794.

John Daniel Bean, Gent. Will dated 30 Sep. 1793. My mulatto children. To my sist. Eliz. Askengreen of Stockholme £200 c., & to her son Peber £200 c. Witnessed by James Langford Nibbs, jun., William Heywood. Sworn and recorded 8 Dec. 1794.

Benjamin William Keyzar, Gent. Will dated 10 Nov. 1794. All Estate to my mother Eliz. Keyzar, & after her death to Mrs Eliz. Burnet. Cha. Kerr, Is^c Eccleston, Wm Shervington, & Ph. Hicks & Mr Sam. Burnet Ex'ors. Thomas Winterflood and Margaret Keiling, widow, sworn 19 and recorded 29 Jan. 1795.

Will of John Ailhaud. All Estate to Sarah Jennings & our 3 children. Recorded 12 May 1795.

Sarah Bowyer, widow of Joseph Bowyer of Antigua. Will dated 30 April 1792. To Hon. Jn° Burke all Estate in Trust for my sons Erasmus & Jas. Graydon till 21. Witnessed by John Walker, Ebenezer Ferguson, Robert James Taylor. Sworn and recorded 3 Sep. 1795.

James Irwin. Will dated 13 Aug. 1794. Martha wife of Arch. Dow. All residue to my sisters & to my bro. W^m's children. Pet. Alsop, Arch. Dow, & Dr Ste. Murray Ex'ors. Witnessed by T. Hanson, Daniel Roberts. Sworn and recorded 11 Sep. 1795.

Will of Elizabeth Bowman, spinster. All Estate to my father Richd Bowman. Recorded 5 Nov. 1795.

Richard Gowan. Will dated 26 Aug. 1795. All Estate in Great Britain to my bro. Ph. Gowan of Ireland, & all in the West Indies to Danl Allt (?) of Antigua, m^t. All my real estate to Arch. Campbell Hawkesley & Jn° Rutherford of Dublin, m^{ts}, in Trust to pay $\frac{1}{3}$ to my bro. Ph. Gowan, $\frac{1}{3}$ to my half-blood sisters Eliza & Martha Nicholson equally, & $\frac{1}{3}$ to my cousin Peter s. of Dr Hen. Roe of Gorey, Wexford, Ireland. Witnessed by George J. Furnace, George W. White. Sworn and recorded 21 Dec. 1795.

Will of John Walker, shop-keeper, recorded 29 Dec. 1795.

Richard Adney, merchant of London. Will dated 31 Dec. 1768. All my Estate in Trust to my uncle Rich. Adney of Addle Str., London, Gent., & my bro. the Rev. Jn° Adney to sell, & apply $\frac{1}{5}$ of the proceeds to my s^d uncle Rich^d, $\frac{1}{5}$ to the 2 children of my bro. Ben., $\frac{1}{5}$ to my sister Anna Adney, $\frac{1}{5}$ to my brother Jn° Adney, & $\frac{1}{5}$ to Jn° Bragge, Esq., husb^d of my sist. Eliz. My uncle Rich^d & my bro. Jn° Ex'ors. Witnessed by Robert Greenway, John Greenway, Middle Temple, David Davies, servant to Messrs. Greenway. A letter is appended, dated from Antigua 29 June 1788, saying: "Your brother died last night at 12 o'clock, being laid up from the result of a carriage accident; unable to give further particulars . . . . but believe he has died without a will."

Joseph Carpenter, planter. Will dated 11 Dec. 1784. Negros to my sister Ann Manderstone, & all residue to my mother Arabella Carpenter, she to be Ex'trix. Witnessed by John Martin, Thomas Powell. Recorded 9 May 1789.

Will of Ann Bird, widow of John Bird. All Estate to my sons Jn° & Chr. Recorded 29 April 1789.

Will of John Nicholas Beck. All Estate to my wife Jenet & my dau. Mary Anna. Recorded 9 June 1789.

Mary Ann Massett. Will dated 16 Sep. 1789. All Estate to my son Jas. Rev. Fra. Massett & Alex. Dover, Esq., Ex'ors. Witnessed by Thomas Turner Wise. Sworn and recorded 8 Oct. 1789.

George Pettierew. Will dated 3 April 1797. To my brothers Math. & Hugh Pettierew, & my sisters Eleanor wife of Wm White, Jean wife of Jno Blair, Grace wife of Sam. Gordon, & Mary wife of Jas. Egger, £50 c. each. To my sister Jeannette & my mother Jane £100 c. each. To Wm Bird £300 c. All residue to my bro. Sam., he with Mr Wm Shervington & Rob. Hyndman of Antigua Ex'ors. Witnessed by Alexander McPherson, James Croile, John Hawkseye. Sworn and recorded 25 April 1797.

Will of John Marquis recorded 11 July 1797.

Will of Alexander McLellan, planter. All Estate to my father Adam McLellan. Recorded 17 April 1797.

Mary Owens. Will dated 4 Nov. 1793. All Estate to my mother & sister Jane Carr. Witnessed by Elizabeth Oliver, Hugh Crawford. Recorded 9 Sep. 1797.

Will of Margaret Wendall, widow. All Estate to my niece Jane Bowers. Sworn 20 Sep. 1797. Recorded 1797 or 1798.

George Burford, planter. Will dated 8 Nov. 1797. All my Estate to my sist. Barbara Ann Burford. Tho. Wm Bladen & Jno Whitwell Ex'ors. Recorded 18 Nov. 1797.

Will of Marie Marguerite Angelique Desjardin Salon of Guadaloupe. All to my dau. Mary. Recorded 14 March 1798.

Peter Alsop. Will dated 16 April 1795. All my property in Antigua to be sold, & to be held by my Ex'ors in Trust. Interest of £600 c. to my mulatto. To my sist. Mary Smith £50 st. To my brothers Tho. & Joseph £50 st. each. To my bro. Chas. £100 st. To the children of my sist. Eliz. Davidson £100 st. equally. All residue to my dau. Mary wife of Edwd O'Brien, Esq., Capt. R.N., she & her husband & Osborne Standart, Esq., of the Navy Office, Great Britain, with Cha. Kerr, Arch. Dow, & Dr Steph. Murray of Antigua, Ex'ors, & to each £20 c. Witnessed by W. Bates, T. Hanson.

Codicil. Interest of £900 c., not £600, to my mulatto. Sworn and recorded 21 April 1798.

Elizabeth Sherwood, late of Antigua, Gentlewoman, and now of Glasgow, N.B. Will dated 9 June 1795. To my niece Eliz. Weir Vere of Glasgow, wid. of Hallen Bowman, Esq., & dau. of Jno Weir Vere, Commissary of Dominica, dec^d, ½ my Estate, the other ½ to Eliz. Walker, dau. of Wm Weir, Commissary of St Vincent, & to Thos. his son, a Capt. in the 60th Reg^t, they to be Ex'ors. Witnessed by William Wanley, John Walker. Copy sent from Glasgow. Recorded 25 May 1798.

John Garside, Lieut. 59th Foot, on board the "Friendship" troopship at sea. Will dated 25 June 1794. All Estate to the wife of Serj^t Baker of the 59th. Witnessed by Robert Haldon, Ensign, and William Moorhead, Quartermaster. Recorded 30 June 1798.

Will of William Bailey, planter. To Becky Jackson, dau. of Tho. Jackson, formerly of Antigua, belonging to the trust estate of Jas. Parke Farley, £100 c. to redeem herself. To Myrtella *al's* Charlotte Farley several negros & all household furniture & £10 c.; in case of her death my slaves to Mrs Ann Hosier. Recorded 8 Sep. 1798.

Richard Bailey, planter. Will dated 3 Aug. 1798. To Tho. Kirwan, Esq., £200 c. To my sister Rebecca £50 c. To Tho. Kirwan, Esq., £100 c. on the recovery of a legacy left by Jno Ledeatt, Esq., dec^d, to his son Cha. Manning Ledeatt, dec^d, by my late brother Wm Bailey, dec^d. My lands in St Paul's P'sh to my mother Rebecca, & after her death to my sister Mary Ann. £200 c. to free my mustee son called Richard. Of the residue ⅓ to my mother Rebecca, ⅓ for my sist. Mary Ann, & ⅓ to my s^d son Rich^d. Tho. Kirwan & Hon. Sam. Byam Athill Ex'ors. Witnessed by Alexander McCarthy, Nicholas Ryan. To my sist. Mary Ann £600 c., horse, & furniture. Sworn and recorded 17 Nov. 1798.

Alexander Dover, Esq. Will dated 17 Aug. 1798. To the 1st dau. of my brother Jno Dover my diamond ring. To Mrs Jane Scott my horse & whiskey & £100 c. All residue between my bro. Jno Dover, my sister Agnes McCraken, & Eliz. Bowie. Campbell Brown, Rob. Clogstown, Esq., of Antigua, Ex'ors. Witnessed by John McConnel, Archibald Douglas, Frances Meredith. Sworn and recorded 27 Aug. 1798.

Will of George Love, bachelor, shopkeeper, recorded 2 Nov. 1798.

Will of Henrietta Ireland, widow, recorded 5 Dec. 1799.

Will of Domingo Figerella, Gent., recorded 30 Dec. 1799.

Will of Henry Thomas, auctioneer. My wife Sarah. Recorded Dec. 1799.

Richard Flint of Boston, co. Lincoln, Gent. Will dated 21 April 1798. To my wife Hannah all my estate in co. Linc., & after her death to my niece Sarah dau. of my bro. Tho. Flint my farms & land, etc., in Boston, & to my nephew Blanchard Flint, son of my s^d brother, my farm & lands in Sutterton, & after his death to his son Rich^d. The cottage & land in Frieston, co. Linc., to Rich^d son of my neph. Richd Flint, dec^d, remainder to his bro. W^m. To my brother Francis Flint my cottage in Boston, purch. of Jno Watson, for life, & after to my niece Mary dau. of my brother Tho. Flint. To my wife all furniture, plate. To my bro. Fra. Flint £200. To my nieces Sarah & Mary £100 each. To Sarah dau. of my niece Ann wife of Tho. Hell £100 at 21. All residue to my wife, including my lands in St John's Parish, Antigua. Wm Brockett & Tho. Waite (of Boston) Ex'ors. Witnessed by Jane Waite, John Waite, Thomas Nelsey. Copy sent out from P.C.C. Recorded 17 Oct. 1799.

Thomas Pooley, planter. Will dated 3 Nov. 1794. To my Ex'ors Messrs. Wm Hubbard, Jno Compton, Jno Croome, & Geo. Buck, planters, £20 c. for mourning. To Wm Hubbard a negro. To my mulatto son Jas. Pooley £20 c. To my godson Geo. Tho. Fisher, son of Fred. Wm Fisher, £50 c. All residue to my neph. Sam. & niece Rachel Pooley, children of Sam. & Hannah Pooley of New York, together with the legacy from my late brother Jno Pooley of Norfolk. Witnessed by Robert Freeman, Samuel Harris, John Swain. If my s^d neph. & niece be not found then to my sister Mary Bec. of Gillingham, Norfolk. Sworn and recorded 17 March 1800.

Sarah Peyton, widow of Thomas Peyton of Antigua, master mariner. Will dated 30 March 1798. To my relation Miss Hester Scandrett a negro. My friend Mrs Mary Symes, wife of Nich. Symes of Antigua, Esq. My friend Mrs Mary Havereum, wife of Jas. Havereum of Antigua, Esq. To my old friend Mrs Fra. Kenyon £33 c. To Hugh Lyons of Antigua, Esq., £60 c., & to his sister Miss Louisa Lyons £20 c. All residue to Nich. Symes, Esq., Wm Shervington, & Fra. Bott of Antigua, Esq^res, Ex'ors. Sworn 10 April 1804.

John Aska, planter. Will dated 15 March 1800. All my Estate to Alex. Petrie, Gent., in Trust for my mother late Mary Aska, now Mary Bowyer, & after her death to my 1st cousin Tho. Aska Fellows of Antigua, writing-clerk. Alex. Petrie & T. A. Fellows Ex'ors. Witnessed by Lovell Warden, Richard Boraston. Sworn and recorded 19 May 1800.

Will of Elizabeth Fricker, widow of Edward Fricker, trader, recorded 6 Aug. 1800.

Elizabeth McKaile. Will dated 4 Sep. 1796. To Eliz. wife of Jno Martin. To Ann Barton. To the 1st dau. of

Rich. & Mary Pigott. To Wm son of Geo. & Christian Bladen. To Anna Maria their dau. To Eliz. Dow, sr. To Martha dau. of Arch. & Martha Dow. To the children of the late Robt Barton certain negros. All residue to Arch. Dow, sr, he & Alexr Dow, sr, Ex'ors. Witnessed by T. Hanson, Alexander W. Bruce, Peter Alsop. Sworn 13 and recorded 20 Sep. 1800.

Alexander Proctor of Antigua, Gent. Will dated 30 Nov. 1793. To my wife Grace all Estate. Sworn 7 March 1795. Recorded 29 Oct. 1800.

Will of John Robinson, mariner. Stephen Rose of Antigua, Gent., sworn 2 Feb. 1801.

Mary Catherine Jacobs of Antigua, relict of Isaac Jacobs of Antigua. Will dated 21 Nov. 1799. All pers. Estate to my niece Eliz. Coates, wife of Alexr Coates, Esq., she to be Ex'trix. Witnessed by Stephen Rose, auctioneer, M. T. French. Sworn 29 March 1800. Recorded 1 April 1801.

Will of Robert Carr, tavern-keeper. Nicholas Lynch of St. John's, merchant, sworn.

Margaret Braxton of Antigua, spinster. Will dated 15 Aug. 1801. To my cousin Eliz. Grant 2 negros. My friend Donald Grant Ex'or. Sworn 6 Nov. and recorded 1 Dec. 1801.

Ophelia Pattinson of St. John's. Will dated 5 Dec. 1795. My house to Rich. Oliver Athill of Antigua, Esq., in Trust for my dau. Eliz. Pattinson of Scotland, he to be Ex'or. My late Master's sister Mrs . . . . of Scotland. Thomas Blizard Moore, writing clerk, and Henry Adney sworn 21 June 1799.

Will of Jane Stoney, spinster. George Powell, Esq., and Sarah Powell, spinster, sworn.

Will of Catherine Irwin was dated 3 Nov. 1802.

Christopher Baldwin, formerly of London, now of Bentley Green near Farnham, Surrey, Esq. Will dated 15 Jan. 1805. To my wife Jane all my real estate in Antigua & Dominica on Trust, to reserve for herself £500 a year, & to pay to her sist. Mrs Mary Watkins £200 a yr., & to Mrs Mary Drinkwater, formerly wife of my son Chr. Baldwin, decd, & now wife of Rich. Drinkwater of Farnham, Surgeon, £200 a yr. All residue to my wife whom I appoint sole Ex'trix. Witnessed by James Bogue, clerk to Messrs. Weston of Fenchurch Street, London, John F. Butterfield of Bentley Green, Gent., Mary Miller of do., Spinster.

Codicil. 15 Jan. 1805. To my wife Jane all sums due from the Estate of Jno Dunbar of Antigua, Esq., decd. Sworn 31 Jan. 1806. Copy from P.C.C. Recorded at Antigua *circa* 1806.

Elizabeth Urlin of Antigua, spinster. Will dated 19 Feb. 1806. To my friend Mrs Mascall, wid. of Edmond Moore Mascall, decd, a negro girl. Sampson & Lucinda to be free. To my 3 godchildren Antho Robertson, dau. of Arthur Robertson of Trinidad, Oliver Weston, son of Valentine Weston, & Sam. Downing, son of Jno Downing of St Croix, all my lands in St John's Town, & my furniture equally. To Mrs Mary Downing, wife of sd Jno Downing of St Croix, a negro. To Mrs Mary Weston, wife of Valentine Weston, a negro. All residue to my nearest relations. My friends Dan. Hill, sr, & Oliver Yeamans Ash Ex'ors. Witnessed by Nathaniel Baptist Donaldson, writing clerk. Sworn 20 Feb. 1807 before Lord Lavington. Recorded 1807.

William Carr, R.N. Will dated 8 April 1807. To Chas. Cheshire, Master Attendant of H.M. yard, the sword voted by the Patriotic Fund. To Mrs Sarah Cheshire a box of plate. To Hugh McKay, mt of St John's, 2 pistoles. To Geo. Carr, planter, my friend & namesake, a spy-glass. All residue to Grace Jarvis & my 2 children Mary & Cesilia by her. Witnessed by William Collins, sen., Thomas Gillan. Recorded 1807.

Lazarus Pritchard of Antigua, Gent. Will dated 23 Oct. 1807. To Jno Bird & Sarah his wife of Cardiff in South Wales £10, & to his dau. Sarah Roberts, widow, £10. To Ann Taylor, sist. of Edwd Pritchard of Wick, £20. To Sarah Llewellin of Wick £5. To Eliz. Mathews of Sondernes £5. To the churchwarden of Wick £10. All residue to Edwd Pritchard, organist of Colridge, S. Wales, he & Dan. Hill, jr, of Antigua, Ex'ors. Witnessed by William Gregory, jun., writing clerk, James Shaw. Sworn before President Byam 9 Nov. 1807.

Ralph Cuming of Antigua, M.D. (? R.N.). Will dated 20 June 1808. To my 3 surviving children Ralph Wm, Lavinia Sarah, & Jno all my Estate, remainder to my bro. Wm Cuming & my 2 sisters Judith Sarah & Ann, then to Miss Ann Sherlock, then to the family of my late father Wm Cuming, decd. My children while here to be under the protection of Mr Tho. Alexander, ordnance store-keeper, Mr Jno Gilbert, Mr Clarke, & Mr Cheshire. On their return to England they are to be under the care of Mr Bonnet, Dissenting Minister of Romsey, co. Hants. Mr Williams, Minister of the Church of England, Messrs. Coleman & Sharpy, & family of Tho. Coowley (?), & Rev. Mr Julian of the Church of England at Water in Suffolk near Landguard Fort, with Capt. Kennedy of the Volunteer Force & Capt. McFarlane, R.N. My sons to be educated under Mr Britain at the Dean's Church House, co. Durham, where I was educated. Ralph to be brought up for a Physician & John for Divinity. Dr Harness, Rev. Julian, & Mr Coleman, Surgeon of Ramsay, Ex'ors. Witnessed by Robert Johnston, J. B. Douglass. On 11 July 1808 was sworn John Bouke Douglass of Antigua, Dispenser. Recorded 1808.

Will of Hester Brenner, free coloured woman. Nicholas Jos. Lynch, writing clerk, sworn 1809.

John Wall of Antigua. Will dated 11 March 1809. To my father Tho. Wall of the Barony of Ath . . . , co. Galway, all Estate. Pat. Lamer of Antigua, planter, & Jno Lamer, store-keeper, Ex'ors. Witnessed by Francis E. Austin. E. B. F. Edwin of Antigua sworn 29 April 1809. Recorded 1809.

Mary Hunt of Parham Town, spinster. Will dated 23 Dec. 1808. Free 5 negros (named) & give them each £3 6s. c. yearly. To my godson Cha. Campbell Gordon, son of Chas. Gordon of Carton House in Parham, 3 negros & £1000 c. & £250. To Edwd Hunt, ye son of Wm Hunt, jr, decd, £40 c. To Wm Hunt's 1st dau. Ann Hunt £100 c. To Wm Edmond Krogman, son of Joachim Krogman, decd, £66 c. To Jno Drew, son of Jno & Eliz. Drew, £66 c. To Cha. Gordon of Parham £100 c. My house in Parham Town I bought of Dr Kean Brown Osborn to Ed. Gamble of Antigua, Esq., & Cha. Gordon on Trust, to pay the rents to Mrs Sarah Ryce, wife of Jno Ryce of Antigua, planter. All residue to my godson Cha. Campbell Gordon. Trustees to be Ex'ors. Witnessed by F. Hallet, Methodist Minister. Sworn 5 May 1809. Recorded 1809.

Jos. Beckford Besouth of Antigua, merchant. Will dated 15 June 1809. To Maria Turner, a free coloured woman, my house in Newgate Str., St John's Town. To my reputed dau. Eliz. Besouth £3000 c. All residue to my father Jos. Besouth. Tho. Latham of London, mt, Jno James of Barbuda, & Jno Taylor of Antigua, mt, Ex'ors. Witnessed by Patrick Doig, Robert Tait, Thomas Coull, Surgeons. Sworn 23 June 1809.

Codicil. 15 June 1809. To my dau. Eliz. £2000, not £3000. Witnessed by Gilbert Bradley, Gent. Recorded 1809.

Samuel Petticrew of St. John's Town. Will dated 22 Aug. 1809. All my Estate in Ireld to my bro. Math. Petticrew. All Estate in Antigua to be sold. To my mother Jane Petticrew £2000 st., & all residue to my 5 sisters Elinor wife of Wm White, Mary wife of Jas. Egger, Jane wife of Jno Blair, Grace wife of Sam. Gordon, & Jennett wife of Sam. Calbreath, & my sd bro. Math. Petticrew equally, he & Rob. Hyndman & Jas. Crichton of

Antigua, mts, Ex'ors. Witnessed by Robert Pearce, John Robertson, writing clerk. Sworn 1 Sep. 1809. Recorded 1809. (See the will of his brother George in 1797.)

Hugh Cameron, Esq., Captain of H.M.S. "Hazard." Will dated 31 Nov. 1809. To my wife Sarah all my pers. Estate & prize money for the capture of the "Abercromby." In the event of my father's death please assist my sister Cath., who will then be dependent on her bro. Archd. Witnessed by Stephen Branch, purser, Hugh Mackay of Antigua, merchant. Sworn 4 April 1810. Recorded 1810.

Lewis Barbier of Antigua. Will dated 8 March 1810. To my niece Agnes Barbier all my landed estate in Guadaloup. To my friend Fred. Deprier, planter there, all my slaves, he & Jno Gavanon, Esq., Ex'ors. Witnessed by William G. Bowyer, John Stephen Pizamy. Sworn 5 April 1811 (? 1810). Recorded 1811 (? 1810).

James Thompson of Antigua. Will dated 12 Nov. 1807. To my bro. Wm Thompson £200. All residue to my 2 sisters in Scotland. Jas. Crichton, Hugh Chalmers, & Pet. Playfair Ex'ors. Witnessed by George Crichton, William Crichton, merchant. Sworn 4 July 1810.

William Johnston of Antigua, carpenter. Will dated 17 June 1810. My house at St John's. To my sister Mary Johnston of Dumfries in Scotland £1000. To my brothers Geo. Johnston & Walt. Johnston £500 st. each.

David Kennedy of Antigua, surgeon. Will dated 1 June 1809. All Estate to my wife Eliz., then to our 4 children, Jean wife of Alex. Bott of Antigua, Esq., & Gilbt Kennedy, Phœbe Kennedy, & Helen Kennedy. My wife, Alex. Bott, Jos. S. Darrell, & Rob. McNish of Antigua, Esqres, Ex'ors & Guardians. Witnessed by James Farley, Charles Willett. Sworn 29 May 1810. Recorded 1810.

John Smith Tracey, on the "Belisle" at sea. Will dated 20 Sep. 1808. I confirm my wife's marriage settlement of £4000 on her & our children. My father to have £40 st. yearly. To my sister Agnes £40 a year. To my bro. Geo. £20 a year. All plate to my wife Anna, she & Hen. Abbott, Esq., of Essex Street, Strand, Guardians.

Codicil. 11 April 1809. Going into action. To my sist. Agnes £500 & my bro. Geo. £200. Kean Osborn of Antigua was sworn 18 May 1811. Recorded 1811.

"1811. At Barbadoes, on his passage to England, John Smith Tracey, esq., Secretary to his Excellency Sir A. Cochrane." ('Gent. Mag.,' p. 299.)

Robert Shaw, planter. Will dated 13 Dec. 1809. To Dr Jas. Coull my gold watch & plate. Sworn 22 Dec. 1810.

Will of James Wilson Hatrick, writing clerk. Byam Kirwan, cordwainer, sworn 1812.

Edward Rigg of Antigua, Esq. Will dated 12 Jan. 1813. All my real Estate in England to my 2 sisters Isabel Rigg & Grace Rigg for life, then to my neph. Wm Rigg & my nieces Ellen Rigg & Isab. Rigg equally. Of my pers. estate ⅓ to my sist. Isabel Rigg, ⅓ to my sist. Grace Rigg, & ⅓ to my sd neph. & 2 nieces. Wm Brinton & Wm Collins of Antigua, Esqres, & Tho. Sanderson of Antigua, mt, Ex'ors. Witnessed by William Scholes, James Curtin, Edward Gamble. Sworn 19 Jan. 1813. Recorded 1813.

John Boyd, sen., of Antigua, merchant. Will dated 26 March 1808. All Estate to Jno Boyd & Polly White's children, viz., Eliz., Isabel, Mary, Jane, Sarah, Cath., Ann, Margt, & Grace. To my neph. Wm Boyd £100 c. £100 c. to Elizabeth's child Jas., & £5 st. to my brothers & sisters if living. My neph. Jno Boyd Ex'or. £50 c. to Ann dau. of Tho. Kirwan, & £25 c. to each of Mary's children Eliza & Jane. On 6 Oct. 1813 appeared Robert McNish, Esq., and Patrick Kirwan, Esq., and swore testator died 16 Sep. last. Recorded 1813.

Thomas Hyde of Antigua, planter. Will dated 2 July 1809. To my father Jno Hyde, late of Antigua, now of Westminster, Jno Yeates of Antigua, planter, Rob. Farquhar, late of Antigua, planter, now of London, & Sam. Mortimer Marchant of Antigua, planter, all my Estate in Trust, to pay £150 c. a year to Ann McConnell, a black woman, & £100 c. a year to Anna B[illegible]lesteyn, spinster, of Harp Lane, Tower Str., London. Trustees to be Ex'ors. To my father what is due as my share of the estate called "Body Ponds," then to my mother Mary. Witnessed by Robert Briggs, planter, Michael O'Brien. Sworn 27 Jan. 1810. Recorded 1813.

From P.C.C. *re* the will of John Hyde of North Street, St. John's Parish, Westminster, Esq., of which adm'on was granted to Mary Hyde the widow and relict on 31 March 1813; power reserved to Samuel Mortimer, John Yeates, and Isaac Blydistine.

John Hyde of North Street, Westminster, Esq. Will dated 9 Feb. 1813. To my bro. Wm Hyde £20. To my neph. Wm Hyde. To my bro. Sam. Hyde £20. My share of ye Body Ponds estate in Antigua to Sam. Mortimer Merchant & Jno Yeates of Antigua in Trust, to pay to my wife £100 a year, & to my sist. Alice Hyde £50 a year. All real estate in Antigua to my dau. Mary Hyde & Mary Miller. If Mary Miller die under 21 her ½ to my sd dau. Mary Doyle. All negros, etc., to my wife Mary Hyde, my sd dau. Mary Doyle, & Mary Miller equally. All residue to my wife. Sam. Mortimer Merchant, Jno Yates, & Isaac Blydistine of London, mt, & my wife Ex'ors. Witnessed by Leonard Tunney, Millbank Street, Westminster, Samuel Pryor, Gray's Inn, John Barber, Gray's Inn.

Re will of Henry Coates, formerly of Antigua, late of . . . . Hill, Hampstead Ponds, co. Midd., Esq., dated 22 June 1810. Adm'on to Margaret Charlotte Stewart Coates the widow and Ex'trix; power reserved to Hon. Thomas N. Kerby, Hon. John Burke, William Brinton, Esq., and Robert Hyndman, Esq. (P.C.C.)

Will of Henry Coates, late of Antigua, now of Eberstock Hill, Hampstead Road, Esq. £100 to each Ex'or. To Sophia Harris of Southampton, wid., £100. All residue of pers. estate to my wife Margt Charlotte Stewart Coates. All my real estate in Antigua to her. Hon. Tho. N. Kerby, Treasr of Antigua, Hon. Jno Burke, Solicitor-General of the Leeward Islands, & Wm Brinton of Antigua, Esq., Rob. Hyndman of Antigua, Esq., & my wife Ex'ors. Witnessed by Harry Courtney Wharton, John Holden, clerk to Mr. Dickinson Craft, jun., H. Jenkinson Sayer, Charter House Square. Sworn 5 July 1810. Recorded 1813. (For a long notice of Henry Coates see 'Gent. Mag.')

John McConnell. Will dated 24 April 1814. As 1st son am entitled to lands in Galloway as heir-at-law to my father Alexr McConnell, decd, which sd lands were lately in the possession of my brother Wm McConnell. I give them to my wife Anne, as also all my Estate in Antigua, she, my son Hen. McConnell, & my friend Wm Collins, printer, Ex'ors. Witnessed by Dr. Patrick Doig, Dr. Thomas Coull, R. King. Sworn 10 May 1814.

Will of Henry Glover, gunsmith and cutler.

Joseph Darrell of Antigua, Esq. Will dated 3 Nov. 1815. All Estate to my bro. Sam. Lightbourn Darrell, Tho. Sanderson, & Jno Billinghurst of Antigua, Esqres, in Trust to sell & to be divided into 8 parts, & I give 2/8 to my wife & my 2 children by her, Jno Elliston Darrell & Wm Perot Darrell, & 6/8 to my children by my former wife Mary Darrell, viz., Francis Perot Darrell, Sam. Jos. Darrell, Mary Angelina Darrell, & Jas. Perot Darrell at 21. My 3 Trustees & wife Ex'ors. Witnessed by Fortunatus Gibbons, Josiah Dickinson, merchant. Sworn 9 Nov. 1815.

John Graham of Antigua, writing clerk. Will dated 27 Oct. 1815. To my 2 daus. Ann Graham & Mary Graham my 2 negros & house. To Ann Eliot a negro. All residue to my sd 2 daus. at 21. Ann Eliot to be Guardian, & with Tho. Franklyn Nibbs & Jno Rose, Esqres, of Antigua, Ex'ors. Witnessed by Walter Oliver. Sworn 3 Nov. 1815.

James Potter of Brentford, New Haven, Connecticut,

U.S., now residing in Antigua. Will dated 17 July 1816. To my wife Pamelia of Brenford & our 3 children Pamelia, Mary Ann Minerva, & Polly Jirome all my Estate. M[r] Asa Morris of New Haven, now in Antigua, & Jn[o] Potter of Brentford, my dear father, & Ralph Foote of New Haven Ex'ors. Witnessed by Daniel B. Garling, Owen Williams, cordwainer. Sworn 10 Aug. 1816 before Major-General Governor George Ramsay.

Will of Thomas Harrison Webster of Antigua, planter.

Peter Nicolls of Antigua, merchant. Will dated 22 Nov. 1818. To be bur. in Fitche's Creek churchyard. If I die in Scotland, in the parish of Eastwood, n[r] Pollockshaws. To my 3 natural mestee daus. all my Estate. Should my father & mother survive me I give them £30 a year. My son Rob[t]. brother of my s[d] 3 daus. To my bro. Rob[t] Nicolls £10. My bro. Jas. Irvine Ex'or & my 3 daus. The birthday of my 1st dau. aged 13 years. Before the Hon. John Horsford, Esq., Commander-in-Chief, was sworn Adam Gordon of Antigua, merchant, 23 Nov. 1819.

Henry McConnell of Antigua. Will dated 9 Dec. 1819. All Estate to my mother Ann McConnell. My bro. Ed. McConnell, W[m] Collins, j[r], printer, & my mother Ex'ors. Witnessed by Thomas Coull, James C. Wesston. Sworn 31 Dec. 1819.

Will of William Cruse of Antigua, master mariner.

Will of William Gilbert Bowyer, shipwright.

P.C.C. 18 Feb. 1820. Adm'on to Colin Robertson, Esq., the surviving Ex'or of the will of Major-General George William Ramsay, Governor of Antigua and Montserratt, now residing at Wigmore Street, co. Middlesex, dated 27 Feb. 1816. To my wife Jean Charlotte Ramsay my copyhold tenement at Cheltenham, formerly my father's, Geo. Ramsay, Esq., dec[d], & all other my real estate for life, then to my son Cap. Geo. Antoine Ramsay. All residue to Dav. Milligan & Colin Robertson of Fenchurch Str., m[ts], on Trust to sell for my wife & then to my son. Trustees to be Ex'ors. Witnessed by Theodore Gwinnett of Cheltenham, Solicitor, Henry Taplin, Hugh Pople, both of Wills' coffee house, Serle Street, Lincoln's Inn Fields.

Various Fragments.

Will of John Bishop, planter. To my sister Frances Bishop my negros. Recorded 13 May 1752.

Thomas Lynch was an attesting witness to the will of Mathew Towers.

My s. Tho. Rushbrook. My dau. Mary Thompson .... Martin wife of M[r] John Ma .... My dau. Jane Martin .... To my s[d] 2 daus. my house & land in S[t] John's ....

Will of John Branan 1752. My s. Jas. Branan. My grds. Morgan Branan. .... Barry Tankard .... Church of S[t] John's Parish .... My sister Rose Murphy ....

My beloved 2 children John Chapman & Rebecca Chapman. My sister Eliz. Murphy, wife of Edward ....

Will of David Haycock. *Codicil.* Two children born named John .... July 1740. To Eliz. Haycock all residue to .... my wife now goes with .... Hester & Eliz. .... & Tho. Hanson, jun[r].

To my wife Grace Hadgit all my estate, but if she remarry only her thirds. To my son Peter all my estate after his mother's death, remainder to my 2 daus. Martha & Eliz. Hadgit.

Before William Mathews, Esq., William Dening swore to the will of James Brochett 16 June 1743.

Will of Robert Towers. My wife Sarah Towers all estate.

Philip Quears, son of Robert & Ann Wears, ... son of Joshua Crump, son-in-law .... Geo. Crump, son of Joshua Crump, grandson Thos. Fr. .... son John William. Residue to my granddau. Ann ffreeman. June 17 ....

Patt. Wilson. Residue to my s. Patrick .... Ogilvy & Mary Marg[t] Tullideph, dau. of Hon. Walter .... I appoint Hon. Walter Tullideph, Jas. Doig, D[r] .... Capt. Tho. Tew Ex'ors. 1755. Witnessed by James Russell, Richard Clark.

Anthony Fletcher. All estate to my wife Eliz., & after her death to my nephew W[m] Howison. 11 July 1755.

Indenture tripartite dated 20 Feb. 1710 between Edward Taylor, jun., of St. John's, son and heir apparent to Edward Taylor, sen., merchant, and only son and heir of Rebecca, deceased, late wife of the said Edward Taylor, sen., of the first part, Nathaniel Humphry of Antigua, planter, of the second part, Edward Taylor, sen., of the third part.

TICKETS GRANTED OUT OF THE SECRETARY'S OFFICE OF BARBADOS FOR EMIGRANTS TO ANTEGOA. (HOTTEN'S 'LISTS.')

1678	Feb.	17	Rachaell Brown, in the Barq "Adventure," Chr. Berrow, Com[r]; security.
„	„	„	Nich[s] Lynch & Alice his wife, in ditto; time out.
„	„	21	Rich[d] Travis, in the Ship "Fellowship," Tho. Pim, Com[r]; time out.
„	Mar.	5	James Bilford, in the "Pink Seaventure," Geo. Battersby, Com[r]; time out.
„	„	10	Anthony Viner, in the Ship "James," Paul Crean, Com[r]; time out.
„	„	„	Rich[d] Cary, in the "Pink Seaventure," Geo. Battersby, Com[r]; security.
„	„	12	Alex[r] Robinson, in the Ship "Ann & Mary," John Johnson, Com[r]; security.
„	„	13	Oliver Enderbee, in ditto; security.
„	„	14	W[m] Jaceson, in ditto; time out.
„	„	„	Timothy Melony, in ditto; security.
„	„	21	Owen Parris, in the Barq "Joseph," for Saltertudos, Stephen Clay, Com[r]; security.
1679	April	9	John Daniell, in the Barq "John's Adventure," John Welch, Com[r]; time out.
„	„	17	W[m] Bushell, in the Ship "Pearle," Rich[d] Williams, Com[r]; time out.
„	„	19 (& Sep. 13)	Nath. Johnson, in the "Friend's Adventure," John Long, Com[r]; time out.
„	„	28	Daniell Mahony, in ditto; time out.
„	„	29	Ann Armstrong, in the Ship "Francis," Peter Jefferys, Com[r]; time out.
„	May	10	Pearce Stanton, in the Barq "Resolution," John Inglebee, Com[r]; time out.
„	„	20	Benj. Wickham, in ditto; security.
„	July	29	Jacob Leroux, in the Ketch "Dove," John Grafton, Com[r]; security.
„	„	„	Miles Poor, in ditto; time out.
„	„	„	Maren Dran, a servant belonging to Jacob Leroux, in ditto.
„	Sep.	1	Eliz. Wickham, in the Sloop "John & Francis," John Howard; time out.
„	„	2	Jas. Cole, in ditto; security.
„	„	„	Dennis Griffin, in ditto.
„	„	3	Mary Watlington, in ditto; time out.
„	„	16	Rich[d] Lynch, in the Sloop "True Friendship," for Nevis, Chas. Kallahane, Com[r]; time out.
„	Oct.	1	Patrick Maden, in ditto; time out.
„	Oct.	2	Henry Elliott, in ditto; time out.
„	„	„	Tho. Clovan, in ditto; security.
„	„	4	James Belfour, in ditto; time out.
„	„	„	Rich[d] Banister, in ditto; time out.
„	„	„	John Butcher, in ditto; security.
„	„	6	Chas. Evan, in ditto; time out.
„	„	„	Tho. Wickham, in ditto; security.

1679	Oct.	7	Sam. Wall, in the Sloop "True Friendship," for Nevis, Chas. Kallahane, Comr; security.
,,	,,	,,	Wm Jennings, in ditto; security.
,,	,,	,,	John Mountaine, in ditto; security.
,,	,,	,,	Tho. Swinny, in ditto; security.
,,	,,	,,	Tho. Greenslatt, in ditto; security.
,,	,,	,,	John Hilk, in ditto; security.
,,	,,	,,	Alexr Hancock, in ditto; security.
,,	,,	29	Hale Barnaby & Tho. How, Servts belonging to Collo Chr. Codrington, in the Barq "Dove," for Nevis, Anthо Jenoux, Comr.
,,	,,	,,	Joseph Holt, in the Sloop "Hopewell," John Ayres, Comr; time out.
,,	Nov.	6	Wm Corbett, in the Sloop "Katherine," Andrew Gall, Comr; time out.
,,	,,	7	Wm Jones & Hector Jones, in the Sloop "Hopewell," Wm Murphy, Comr; time out.
,,	,,	,,	Geo. Salter, in ditto; time out.
,,	,,	,,	Wm Tremills, in ditto; time out.
,,	,,	,,	Arthur Williams, in ditto; time out.
,,	,,	8	Alexr Urquhart, in ditto; time out.
,,	,,	10	Abell Oldridge, in ditto; time out.
,,	,,	15	Stephen Dewer, in the Barq "Resolution," Tho. Gilbert, Comr; time out.
,,	,,	21	Nath. Manerick, in ditto; security.
,,	,,	25	Sarah Are, in the Sloop "Katherine," Andrew Gall, Comr; security.
,,	,,	25	Rowland Gidion, in the Ketch "Phœnix," Robt Flexny, Comr; security.
,,	,,	25	Abraham Abudient, in the Barq "Resolution," Tho. Gilbert, Comr; security.
,,	,,	26	Roger Farrell, in the Sloop "Katherine," Andrew Gall, Comr; security.
,,	,,	27	Kath. Alsop, in ditto; security.
,,	,,	,,	Wm Corbett, in ditto; time out.
,,	,,	,,	Owen Parris, in the Barq "Resolution," Tho. Gilbert, Comr; time out.
,,	,,	29	Nichs Kew, in ditto; security.
,,	,,	,,	Morgan Lynch, in ditto, the said Lynch being a Servt to John Codrington, Esqr.
,,	,,	,,	Robt Spittle, in the Sloop "Katherine," Andrew Gall, Comr; time out.
,,	Dec.	22	John Downing, in the Ship "Lawrell," for Nevis, Robt Ox, Comr; time out.
,,	,,	24	Roger Holeman, in the Sloop "True Friendship," Chas. Kallahane, Comr; time out.
,,	,,	30	Jeoffery Burke, in ditto; time out.

ST. JOHN'S PARISH.

17,953 Acres.

The following List of Plantations and their owners is taken from Luffman's 'Map of Antigua,' 1787-8, Johnson's Account, 1829, and the Antigua Almanacks for 1852, 1871, and 1878. See also Moll's Map of 1732 in Vol. II., which gives the names of the owners. Some Estates have changed names so often that their identification is difficult:—

1. ALLEN'S, 239 acres. Thomas Allen, 1788. Robert McNish, 81 slaves, 1829. Heirs of Robert McNish, 1852.
2. BATH LODGE, 456 acres. Fryers Concrete Co., 1878.
3. BELLE VUE or STONEY HILL, 527 acres. Samuel Warner, 261 slaves, 1829. S. W. Shand, 1852. Francis Shand, 1871. 70 acres in St. George's Parish.
4. BELVIDERE, formerly called HORNES, 361 acres. Hon. Ashton Warner, 1788. Messrs. Hyndman, 125 slaves, 1829. Heirs of T. Sanderson, 1852. With Green Castle, 1388 acres, Fryers Concrete Co., 1871.
5. BENDALL'S, 503 acres. Thomas Oliver, 1788. Messrs. Hyndman, 249 slaves, 1829. W. P. Hyndman, 1852. Fryers Concrete Co., 1878.
6. BODY PONDS, 210 acres. Thomas Oliver, 1788. Lieut. William Grant sold this in 1803 to John William Dow. George Doyle, 102 slaves, 1829. John H. Doyle, 1852. Heirs of J. H. Doyle, deceased, 1871.
7. BOONS, 85 acres. John Delap-Halliday, 1788. Admiral John Halliday Tollemache, 101 slaves, 1829. J. Tollemache, 1852. G. J. Crosbie, 1878.
8. BRECKNOCK'S, 220 acres. Peter Gaynor's in 1738. Sir George Colebrooke, Bart., 1788. Messrs. Turner, 234 slaves, 1829. John Bennett, 1852. Estate of John Bennett, deceased, 1871.
9. BRIGGINS, 440 acres. Harvie Keynell in 1679 leased to John Weir his plantation called Little Zoar of 350 acres, 203 acres of which in 1704 was conveyed to Edward Chester. The latter also purchased in 1704 and 1706 233 acres of Dr. Daniel Mackinen. Robert Chester purchased in 1724 423 acres for £16,092 c., and called the plantation "Briggins" after his estate in Hertfordshire. In 1788 this estate was in the possession of Benjamin Ireland. William Gregory, 50 slaves, 1829. Heirs of W. Gregory, 1852. Dr. Jesse W. Thibou, M.R.C.S. England, 1871. Antonio J. Comacho, 1878.
10. BUCKLEYS, 98 acres. Daniel Hill, 1788. David Cranstoun, 1852. W. B. Nibbs, 1871. Rev. Tho. B. Nibbs, 1878.
11. GEORGE BYAM'S, 366 acres, 132 slaves. Heirs of James Athill, 1829. John Foreman, 1852. Fryers Concrete Co., 1878.
12. CASSADA GARDEN, 600 acres. In 1679 the Sampsons conveyed to Jonas Langford a moiety of 1000 acres called Cassava Garden. The latter by his will dated 1709 bequeathed his Cassava or Cassada Garden plantation of 570 acres to his grandson J. L. Redwood, and it was still in the possession of the Redwoods in 1852. Messrs. A. and L. Redwood, 204 slaves, 1829. Francis Shand, 1871. 40 acres in St. George's Parish.
13. CEDAR VALLEY, 218 acres. In 1781 this contained 200 acres and was in possession of Nathaniel Bogle-French. W. and F. Shand, 1852. Francis Shand, 1871. 40 acres in St. George's Parish.
14. CLARE HALL or SKERRETTS, 613 acres, formerly "Nugents." Sir B. Codrington, Bart., 322 slaves, 1829. Sir W. C. Codrington, Bart., 1852. Henry Liggins, 1871.
15. CLARKE'S HILL. Joseph Warner, 1788. The name of this estate has been probably changed.
16. COOKS, 604 acres. John Otto-Baijer by his will dated 1722 bequeathed the plantation he had purchased of Lady Elizabeth Cooke and John Cooke, Esq., of 536 acres, to his son Edward, who by will of 1779 gave it to his son Captain John Otto-Baijer. Sir Thomas Cooke, Knt., of London, had it from . . . . Horne. Heirs of L. L. Hodge, 253 slaves, 1829. L. L. Hodge was owner in 1852. J. E. Anthonyson, 1871. Isaac C. Anthonyson, 1878.
17. CREEK SIDE or THIBOUS, 396 acres. Walter Thibou, 1788. Messrs. F. Nibbs, 187 slaves, 1829. Thomas F. Nibbs, 1852. John Hart Moore, 1871. 180 acres in St. Mary's Parish.

18. CROSBIE'S, 240 acres. In 1788 called Mount Prospect, and John Crosbie then owner. General Crosbie, 67 slaves, 1829. John Crosbie, 1852. Charles Crosbie, 1871. G. J. Crosbie, 1878.

19. DREW'S GIFT of 175 acres belonged to Captain Andrew Murray, at whose death in 1720 it passed to his son John, who was owner in 1751.

20. DREW'S HILL, 253 acres. Governor W. Mathew in 1752 bequeathed it to his grandson William Mathew. John Conyers, 1788. Heirs of A. Bott, 403 acres, 160 slaves, 1829. Burnthorne Musgrave, 1852. Herberts and Drew's Hill, 788 acres, Mrs. Emma Purves, 1871. Charles J. Manning, 1878.

21. DUNBAR'S, 165 acres. Dr. Dunbar, 1788. Sir George Thomas, Bart., 215 slaves, 1829. W. Dunbar, 62 slaves, 1829. W. Dunbar, 1852. Purchased by the late Mr. Langford-Brooke. 188 acres sold lately to Mr. Comache. C. H. Okey, 1871.

22. FIVE ISLANDS (Upper and Lower), 703 acres. President Edward Otto-Baijer inherited from his father the Five Islands plantation of 215 acres, which descended to his son the Hon. John Otto-Baijer, who died 1817. In 1852 Sir George Thomas, Bart., was the owner. Colonel Stephen J. Hill, C.B., 1871.

23. FOLLY. John J. Walter, with 255 slaves, 1829. Heirs of John J. Walter, 1852.

24. FRENCH'S, 128 acres, 139 slaves. Richard Musgrave.

25. FRIARS HILL, 327 acres. In 1679 Dorothy Clarke sold to Francis Carlile her 96 acres called Fryer's Hill in Popeshead. Captain Haynes, R.N., 166 slaves, 1829. Mary Thomas, 1852. Colonel Stephen J. Hill, C.B., 1871. Montagu W. White, 1878.

26. GAMBLES, 300 acres. In 1710 contained 316 acres, and was sold by Hon. George Gamble to Governor Parke for £6000 c. Edward Chester owned it in 1720. John Halliday, 300 acres in 1771. John Delap Halliday, 1788. Rear-Admiral J. H. Tollemache, 145 slaves, 1829. J. Tollemache, 1852. Lord Combermere, 1871.

27. GOLDEN GROVE, 254 acres. In 1684 Governor Edward Powell had a patent for "Pauls," now (1864) "Golden Grove," of 380 acres, also "Road" *alias* Rakes Bay. Dr. Daniel Mackinen had a lease of this in 1702 for 99 years at £200 a year. Callaghan McCarthy, Esq., had purchased this before 1792 of William Mackinen. B. Entwisle leased to Shand and Co., with 458 slaves, 1829. Heirs of B. Entwisle, 1852. Thomas Peters, 1871. Rev. Thomas Peters, 1878.

28. GREEN CASTLE (with Belvidere), 1388 acres. Fryers Concrete Co., 1871.

29. GULLY BAY, 447 acres. Heirs of George T. Thomas, deceased, 168 slaves, 1829. Inigo Thomas, 1852. Heirs of F. Thomas, 1871.

30. HADDONS or WEEKES was left by Mr. John Weekes to James Nibbs in 1750. James L. Nibbs, 1788, then of 294 acres; his in 1760.

31. HARTS and ROYALS, 206 acres. Harts in 1788 belonged to Barry C. Hart. John Furlonge, 123 slaves, 1829. W. and F. Shand, 1852. Thomas Jarvis, 1871. Charles J. Manning, 1878.

32. HAWKS HILL, 180 acres. John Billinghurst, 62 slaves, 1829. John W. Allaway, 1852. Sarah Elizabeth Farr, 1871. Rev. Peter Malone, 1878.

33. HERBERTS, 305 acres. William Burnthorn, 197 slaves, 1829. Anthony Musgrave, M.D., 1852. Charles J. Manning, 1878.

34. HILL HOUSE, 167 acres. James H. Baker, 1852. Heirs of Samuel Williams, 1871.

35. HODGES, 200 acres. Henry Hodge, 1788. Mrs. Hodge, 180 slaves, 1829. L. L. Hodge, 1852. F. Garraway, 1871. Was sold in 188– by Rev. William O'B. Hodge to Oliver Nugent.

36. LANGFORDS, 494 acres. T. L. Brooke, 1852. Langford's Popeshead plantation was sold in 188– by the Langford-Brooke trustees to Mr. Comache. Langfords and Mount Pleasant, P. L. Brooke, 494 acres, 288 slaves, 1829. Thomas L. Brooke, 621 acres, 1871.

37. LANGFORD'S WOOD, 280 acres. In 1816 styled the Body or Wood plantation. P. L. Brooke, 184 slaves, 1829. Thomas L. Brooke, 1852 and 1871. Sold in 188– by Langford-Brooke trustees to Mr. Comache, a Portuguese.

38. McKINNONS, 830 acres. Hon. William McKinnon, 1788. Messrs. McKinnon, 271 slaves, 1829. McKinnon, 1852. Edward Beckett, 1871 and 1878.

39. MARBLE HILL, 172 acres. Hon. James Nibbs, 1788. Bertie E. Jarvis, 201 slaves, 1829. B. E. Jarvis, 1852. Mrs. Jarvis, 1871.

40. MATHEWS, 315 acres. Luckie Brothers and Co., 1871. Omitted from the Almanack for 1879.

41. MOUNT PLEASANT. Alexander Willock, 1788. Francis Willock, 192 slaves, 1829. Mrs. G. S. Martin, 1852. Sold in 188– by the Langford-Brooke trustees to Mr. Comache.

42. MURRAYS or BELMONT, 276 acres. In 1788 this was known as Murrays, and was owned by Sir John Laforey, Bart. M. H. Daniell, 165 slaves, 1829. W. and Francis Shand, 1852. Belmont and Brodies, Mrs. Emma Purves, 1871. Charles J. Manning, 1878.

43. OLIVERS, 313 acres. Thomas Langford Brooke, 1871.

44. OTTOS, 678 acres. John Otto-Baijer, 1788. B. Otto-Baijer, 165 slaves, 1829. L. Lovell, 1852. F. Garraway, 673 acres, 1871. Samuel Dobee and Sons, 1878.

45. POTTERS, 77 acres. Hon. William Gunthorpe, 1788. R. McDonald, 1852. McDonald and Co.

46. RENFREW, 17 acres. Edward Emerson. J. S. W. Watkins, 1871.

47. ROSE HILL and HAMMERSFIELD, 63 acres. James Thibou. Thomas Adamson, 1871. F. J. Edwards, 1878.

48. ST. CLARE, 384 acres. Rowland E. Williams, 1829 and 1852. James B. Thibou, 1871.

49. THIBOUS, 368 acres. B. E. Jarvis. Hon. Tho. Jarvis, 1788. B. E. Jarvis, 319 acres and 159 slaves, 1829. Thomas Jarvis, 1871.

50. TOMLINSON'S, 600 acres. Heirs of John Tomlinson, 1788. John Osborne, 149 slaves, 1829. Francis Shand, 1871.

51. TURNBULL'S or GRAYS, 100 acres. John Gray, 48 slaves, 1829, 1852, and 1871.

52. UNION, 514 acres. Heirs of L. L. Hodge, 208 slaves, 1829. L. L. Hodge, 1852. Robert Dobson, 1871.

53. VILLA or DANIELS, 290 acres. Samuel Morgan sold it *circa* 1742 to William Lindsey, father of John Lindsey. Called MORGANS in 1777, and then bequeathed by John Lindsey, Esq., to his son William, who conveyed it to Thomas Daniel in 1779. Thomas Daniel, 1788. Heirs of T. Blackburn, deceased, 42 slaves, 1829. Heirs of T. Blackburn, 1852. F. Garr, 1871. Lord Combermere, 1878.

54. WATKINS, afterwards known as FREEMANS, was bequeathed by Byam Freeman by will dated 1770 to the heirs of his only child Harriet, who married Thomas Oliver, Deputy-Governor of Massachusetts, and in 1814 was in the possession of Harriet Watkins Oliver, their elder daughter and heir, who married Captain Haynes, R.N.

55. WEATHERILLS, 300 acres. John Halliday purchased before 1776 of Provost-Marshal, formerly Charles P. Weatherells. Francis D. Halliday, 1788. Rear-

Admiral John Halliday Tollemache, 129 slaves, 1829. John Tollemache, 1852. Lord Combermere, 1871.

56. WILLIAM'S FARM and MOUNT RURAL, 50 acres. William Williams, 1852. Heirs of William G. Grant, deceased, 1871. Edward H. McGuire, 1878.

57. YAPTON FARM, 343 acres. Messrs. Hyndman, 111 slaves, 1829. Ra. L. Baxter, 1852. Mrs. Sheil, 1871.

BISHOPS OF ANTIGUA.

The Diocese of Antigua was formed in 1842, and includes Antigua, St. Christopher's, Nevis, Montserrat, Dominica, Barbuda, Anguilla, and the Virgin Islands. There are two Archdeaconries of Antigua and St. Christopher's. Antigua was originally included in the Diocese of Barbados, founded in 1824, which extended from Guiana to the Virgin Islands, with three Archdeaconries of Barbados, Guiana, and Antigua. Dr. William Hart Coleridge was the first Bishop, after whose resignation each of the Archdeaconries was made a separate See.

DANIEL GATEWARD DAVIS, 1842—1857.

He was the son of the Rev. William Davis of St. Christopher's, matriculated from Pembroke College, Oxford, 17 May 1808, aged 20; B.A. 1814; M.A. 1823; D.D. by decree of convocation 9 July 1842; died 1857 in London. (See Foster's 'Alumni Oxon.')

His first son, Gateward Coleridge Davis, matriculated from Merton College, Oxford, 20 Jan. 1853, aged 18; Barrister-at-Law Inner Temple 1860; died at Sydney, N.S.W., 13 April 1882, having married Miss Elizabeth Gordon Jackson, a daughter of Bishop Jackson of Antigua; she died in London 29 March 1892, aged 49.

His second son, Robert Claxton Davis, matriculated from Exeter College, Oxford, 21 April 1855, aged 19, and died at Sydney, N.S.W., 13 Nov. 1866, aged 31. (See 'Gent. Mag.')

Another member of this family, the Rev. Thomas Gateward Davis, only son of Thomas Davis of St. Christopher's, matriculated from Brasenose College, Oxford, 16 June 1857, aged 18; B.A. 1861; M.A. 1871; Vicar of Batley, Yorkshire, 1874.

STEPHEN JORDAN RIGAUD, 1857—1859.

First son of Stephen Peter Rigaud of Westminster, Esq., matriculated from Exeter College, Oxford, 23 Jan. 1834, aged 17; Fellow 1838—41; B.A. 1841; M.A. 1842; B. and D.D. 1854; Mathematical Master 1840; Select Preacher 1856; F.R.A.S., Under Master Westminster School 1846—50; Head Master Queen Elizabeth's School, Ipswich, 1850—7; died 17 May 1859 of yellow fever.

WILLIAM WALROND JACKSON, 1860—1895.

Born 9 Jan. 1811 in Barbados; was educated at Codrington College; 1st Scholar 1830; Deacon 1834; Priest 1835; D.D. 1860 by the Archbishop of Canterbury; Hon. D.D. Durham 1876; Curate-in-Charge of St. Lucy, Barbados, 1834—6; ditto of Holy Trinity, Trinidad, 1836—9; Rector of Charlotte Parish, St. Vincent, 1839—42; Minister of St. Paul's, Bridgetown, 1842—60; Chaplain to the Forces 1846—60; consecrated Bishop of Antigua on Ascension Day 1860; retired 1879; died 25 Nov. 1895 at Fulbrook House, Grange Road, Ealing.

His son, the Rev. W. W. Jackson, is Warden of Exeter College, Oxford. A daughter, Elizabeth Gordon Jackson, married Gateward Coleridge Davis; she died in London 29 March 1892, aged 49. Another daughter lives at Ealing unmarried.

CHARLES JAMES BRANCH, 1895—1896.

Born 7 Oct. 1834 in Barbados; educated at Codrington College; Scholar, Deacon 1857; Priest 1859; Curate of St. Simon's, Barbados, 1857—64; Rector of St. Andrew's Grenada, 1864—6; Rector of St. John's, St. Croix, 1866—79; Archdeacon of Antigua 1879; Rector of St. John's, Antigua, 1880; D.D. Durham 1882; consecrated Bishop Co-adjutor of Antigua on St. James's Day 1882; died at St. Christopher's 31 Aug. 1896.

His son, Rev. Edmund S. Branch, B.A. Durham; Deacon 1884; Priest 1886; Curate of St. John's Cathedral and Head Master of the Grammar School 1884.

RECTORS OF ST. JOHN'S.

1679. Rev. . . . . Lambert. (See Besse.)

1690. Rev. William Leaders, Priest. (See Besse.)

1679, 1684, and 1698. Rev. William Jones. Gave the Communion Plate in 1698. He left a son William, who was dead 1706. (See J. Langford's Tract.)

[Rev. James Denby, "minister," was buried Aug. 1693 and John Howlett, "clergyman," 14 Nov. 1706.]

1692. Rev. James Field. In 1716 stated he had been Minister of St. John's 24 years; living 1688; also Rector of St. Mary's; died 1728 at Windsor.

[Rev. Henry Husband, "minister" of St. John's, was buried in 1729.]

[In 1741 Rev. . . . . Mackey and James Berrie officiated.]

Rev. Philip Darby. Will dated 2 May 1740.

1745. Rev. Thomas Whitford, "minister."

1755. Rev. Francis Byam, M.A., entered Trinity College, Cambridge, 3 July 1728, æt. 19; signed Registers 1733; "minister" 1741; died July 1757.

1758, Jan. 4. Rev. Henry Byam, D.D., by patent from Governor George Thomas; died 1760.

1760, Oct. 7. Rev. David Hopkins, by patent from Governor George Thomas, *vice* Byam, deceased; buried 25 Jan. 1767.

1767, Jan. 28. Rev. John Bowen, by patent from Hon. James Virchild, *vice* Hopkins, deceased.

1783, July 1. Rev. James Lindsay, by patent from Governor Shirley, *vice* Bowen resigned; died 23 April 1801.

1801, Sep. 1. Rev. Henry Campbell, by patent from Governor Lord Lavington, *vice* Lindsay, deceased.

1802, July 17. Rev. Samuel Lyons, by patent, *vice* Campbell, resigned; lost at sea 1827.

1803, Aug. 20. Rev. Samuel Wickham Harman, by patent, *vice* Lyons, resigned; buried 21 May 1827, æt. 58.

1827, Aug. 1. Rev. Robert Holberton, M.A., by patent from Governor Sir Patrick Ross, *vice* Harman, deceased. Became the first Archdeacon of Antigua in 1842.

1852. Rev. Samuel Ashton Warner, born 1799; Rector of St. George's 1826.

1871. Rev. Edwin Elliott.

1880. Bishop Branch, till his death 1896.

Old St. John's Church was a brick edifice erected in 1719; its length 130 feet and breadth 50 feet, with north and south porches 23 feet by 20½ feet. The tower, 50 feet high with cupola, was built in 1789. The altar-piece, originally intended for a church in Jamaica, was bought of the master of a vessel, and the lead cast images of St. John the Evangelist and St. John the Baptist were taken from a Martinique ship during the Seven Years War, 1756—63. "The Organ was put up in 1760, the sum of £261 st. being raised by Subscription, and the Vestry making up the difference. Mr Oliver, a Merchant in London, Proprietor of an Estate in this Island bearing his name, was directed not to exceed the sum of £450 on the purchase of it." The brass chandelier was the gift of the Rev. Philip Darby, who, by his will dated 22 May 1740, directed his Ex'ors "to lay out the sum of £30 st. in the purchase of a brass Branch, to hold 32 Candles, which I give to the Parish Church of St. John, to be hung up in the middle Aisle thereof."

VESTRY MINUTES.

The first volume of the records of Vestry Meetings commences A° 1741. The first 28 folios are missing.

1741, April 18. Rev. Fra. Byam, Minister, & Wm Furnell & Jonas Langford, Churchwardens. Richd Oliver, Merrick Turnbull, Tho. Watkins, Jacob Morgan, Tho. Hanson, & Geo. Crump present.

1740-41, Jan. 9. All the above & Walter Nugent & John Murray present.

1741, Jan. 9. Thos. Shephard present.

1741, Jan. 22. Rowld & Richd Oliver present. The charitable bequests of the Hon. Edwd Byam referred to.

1742-3. March 8. Richd Oliver, churchwarden.

1743, Jan. 9. Andrew Lessly present.

1744, May 3. Col. Jas. Weatherill, J.P. A roof is ordered to be put over the bell tree. The rector receives £200 a year & £50 a year for a house.

1744. Rowld Oliver present, & on Jan. 7 John Wise, Esq., & Edwd Gamble. Theophilus Field's legacy is discussed.

1745, Aug. 22. Rev. Tho. Whitford, minister.

1745, Jan. 13. John Otto-Baijer present.

1746. Jonas Langford, a churchwarden.

1746-7, Jan. 10. John Murray, Esq., J.P. John Dunn & Jas. Barton present.

1746-7, Feb. 5. John Tomlinson present. Dr. Slingsby Cressy.

1747, March 17. Bellfry to be altered & rebuilt to 47 feet above the body of the church for a ring of bells, a spire of 35 feet to be added. The churchwardens are to remit Mr Nisbit Darby's bill of exchange to Richd Oliver, Esq., to purchase a brass branch, the gift of Mr Philip Darby.

1748, Jan. 9. Danl Warner & Walt. Tullideph, J.P., present.

1748, Feb. 20. Major Oliver has sent over a brass branch.

1749, Jan. 6. Chas. Alexander present.

1750, Nov. 7. Jno Gatley present.

1750, Jan. 7. Saml Nibbs & Edwd Horne, J.P., present.

1751, Oct. 15. Jno Dearmon Nanton, Saml Martin, & Hen. Douglas present.

1752. Jan. 11. Jno Halliday & Jas. Doig present. Dr Jas. Dewar as Surgeon of the Hospital is to be pd £42 a year.

1752. Mrs Charity Jarvis keeps a boarding school.

1752, April 23. Jno Watkins present.

1753, Jan. 8. Tho. Lessly present.

1753, Jan. 22. Jno Tomlinson present.

1754, Jan. 7. Nathl Gilbert, Junr, present.

1755, Jan. 10. Tho. Jarvis present.

1756, Jan. 10. Cæsar Roach present.

1757, Jan. 29. Extract of the Jury's Return made Oct. 28, 1719:—"The Burying place now laid out at the Point for Christians to be 400′ E. & W. & 300′ N. & S., & to the Northward of the said place a Burying place for Negros E. & W. 400′ N. & S. 200′ upon the S. side of the said Burying places a lane of 30′ wide to extend 400′ E. & W. to be called Forster's Lane. On the E. side of the said Burying places a Lane of 30′ wide to extend from Forster's Lane to Dickinson's Bay Street, which is the bounds of the said Burying places."

1758, Jan. 5. Wm Allyn present. The Rector being dead, a patent da. 4 Janr 1758 is presented from Govr Geo. Thomas appointing Rev. Hen. Byam.

1760, May 24. Cap. Tho. Tew present. Rev. Mr Bowen, minister.

1760, Oct. 8. Death of Rev. Henry Byam is announced.

1760, Oct. 7. Patent from Govr Thomas appointing Rev. David Hopkins Rector, later he appears to have been a J.P.

1761, Jan. 8. Saml Gunthorpe & Wm Anderton present.

1762, Jan. 12. Francis Farley present.

1763, Jan. 8. Jno Yeamans present. Wm Buckley.

1764, Jan. 16. Jno Braham present.

1764, May 5. Jno Smith, Junr, present. Wm Warner.

1765, Feb. 18. Battlements to be placed on the church.

1766, Sep. 19. Harry Alexander, Esq.

1767, Jan. 9. Henry Livingston, Esq.

1767, Jan. 27. The Rector, Rev. David Hopkins, is dead. By Hon. Jas. Virchild, Commander-in-Chief, Rev. Jno Bowen is appointed Rector by patent 28 Jan. 1767.

1768, Jan. 20. Wm Livingston, Baptist Looby, Elias Ferris, present.

1769, Jan. 5. Alexr Willock, Tho. Martin, present.

[The second volume commences 9 Jan. 1770.]

MEMBERS OF VESTRY.

Rev. Jno Bowen, Rector.	Saml Gunthorpe.
Tho. Jarvis.	Francis Farley.
Edwd Byam.	Baptist Looby.
Wm Livingston.	Elias Ferris.
Jno Smith, Junr.	Jas. Furlong.
Edwd Gamble.	Alexr Willock.

1770, May 31. £150 voted for church & altar cloths. Subscriptions invited for clock & steeple.

1771, Jan. 19. The Rector receives £300 a year. Dr Farley is surgeon of the parish Hospital, & is paid £42 a year and the nurse £30 a year. £6 a year to be paid for keeping clean the Burial ground at the Point.

1771, Jan. 24. 100,000 bricks ordered from England & America, & a tower to be erected close to the W. end of the church. Wm Whitehead, churchwarden.

1772, Jan. 20. Stephen Rose & Oliver Birch present.

1772, Feb. 8. £100 st. a year as salary to organist=£165 c. Mr Geo. Harland Hartley appointed.

1772. Nov. 17. The present hospital is to be pulled down & a new one built.

1773, Jan. 8. Hon. Francis Farley, J.P., & Rev. Jno Bowen, J.P. Mr Green is offered the organist's place. Dr. Farley, surgeon, to be pd £66 a year.

1773, Feb. 25. The old parish hospital was blown down by a Hurricane on 31 Aug. last.

1775, April 25. Thos. Halloran & Tho. Hughes present.

May 23. The tower which was to be 60′ is to be 48′, & to be surmounted by an octagon spire of wood.

1776, Jan. 5. Thos. T. Wise present.

1776, Jan. 23. 13 pews are granted.

1777, Jan. 7. Geo. Savage, Esq., J.P.

Jan. 21. Tho. Hanson Halloran present. The clerk is to be pd £140 a year for burying the poor, etc.

1778, Feb. 3., Mrs Lessly, Jas. Nibbs, Esq., & lady do sit in Pew No. 64.

1778, Feb. 11. Rev. Mr Bowen has leave of absence for 18 mos.

1778, June 3. John Rose present.

1780, Jan. 12. Hon. T. Jarvis, J.P.

1781, Jan. 15. The Rector to be pd £350 a year. Dr. Awsiter, surgeon of the Hospital, to be pd £65 a year.

1781, May 22. John Dunbar, Esq., present.

1783, June 2. Will of Giles Blizard, Esq., deceased, referred to.

1783, July 4. Rector has resigned. Sir Thos. Shirley's patent to Rev. Jas. Lindsey is da. 1 July 1783.

1784, Jan. 20. Hon. Jas. Nibbs, Danl Hill, Senr, Boyce Ledwell, & Jno Smith, Esqres, present.

1785, Feb. 15. Jno Taylor, Esq., present.

1786, Jan. 10. Hon. Ashton Warner, Hon. Jno Gray, Philip Hicks, Esq., present.

1786, March 21. Richd Manning has the contract to finish the tower & to repair the church for £1280 (viz.,

£500 for tower & £780 for church), & Wm Whitehead, Esq., £1150 for mason's work.

1787, Jan. 9. Hon. W^m McKinen present.

1787, March 23. List of Pews as following:—

1. The Lieut. Govr, President, Council, & Assembly.
2. The Minister.
3. Thos. Oliver, Friers Hill, Thomas Oliver, Bendals, Walter Thibou, Russel Gloster, Archibald Gloster, Philip Hicks, Thos. Daniel.
4. Mrs Walsh, Miss Tomlinsons, John Laforey, Jonas L. Brooke, Jonas Blizard.
5. Jno Dunbar, David King, Saml Williams, John R. Herbert, Wm Bowie, Mich^l Branthwaite, David Kennedy.
6. Mrs Hodge, Chas. Kerr, Tho. H. Halloran, Mrs Rice.
7. Sir Geo. Colebrooke, Jas. Hutchison, Danl Brice, Richd Adney.
8. Geo. Byam, Saml Martin, Dewits, Ann Stilling, Francis Grant Gording.
9. Jno Scotland, Revd Mr Coull, Hester Martin, Mary Hurst, Eliz. Dunbar.
10. Tho. Bridges, Sarah Bridges, Jno Bridges, Mary Wethered.
11. Wm M. Hughes, Tho. Goolsby, Wm Birch, Sirviah Harris.
12. Sir Geo. Thomas, Bertie Entwisle, Richd Wright, Jas. Robinson, Wm Entwisle.
13. Mrs Hodges, Mrs Brice, Jno Payne, Lieut. Jno Burke.
14. Wm Smith, Ann Stevens, Richd Martin, Wm Reese.
15. Jno Fletcher, Frances Meredith, Mrs Royal, Mrs Rose.
16. Ann Clinch, Jas. Wallace.
17. Strangers.
18. Churchwardens.
19. Alex^r Proctor, Lucy Carlile, Mrs Kennell, Jno Johnson.
20. Francis Pitman, Jane Grant, Jas. Gillan.
21. Wm Jardine, Rob. Reid, Rob. McNish, Mrs Massett.
22. Jno Bott, Jno Lynch, Dr Tho. Lynch, Thos. Austin.
23. Mrs Croswell, Mrs Byrne, Mrs Montigue, Mrs Murray.
24. Richd Kirwan, Isab. Rossington, Thos. Kirwan, Sarah Watkins.
25. Wm Whitehead, Mrs Furnell, Hen. Thomas.
26. Alex^r Coats, Richd Bowman, Geo. Glenny, Wm Brinton.
27. Richd Topping, Jno Aird, Dr Byam, Mrs Mearns.
28. Wm Eales, Miss Garretts, Mrs Evanson, Mrs Alex^r Scott.
29. Jos^h Greenway, Jos^h Bowyer, M^rs McNabb, Tho. Hughes, Junr.
30. Elias Ferris, Danl Hill, Mrs Braham, Wm Mathews, Mrs Mathews.
31. Tho. T. Wise, Hon. Jno Burke, Mrs Fergusson, Isaac Eccleston.
32. Jno Otto-Baijer, Senr, Jno Otto Baijer, Junr, Langford Lovell, Jno Taylor, Saml Martin, Collector, Geo. Savage.
33. Ashton Warner, Rowl^d Burton, Abraham Redwood, Sir Peter Parker, Ann Gamble, Wm Gunthorpe.
34. Alex^r Willock, Jno D. Halliday, Jno Gray, Mrs Lindsey, Wm Mackinnen.
35. Mrs Mackins, Gilb^t McConnell, Geo. Dalzell.
36. [*blank*.]
37. Benjn Keyzar, Susannah Haycock.
38. Tho. Dickman, Jas. Thomson.
39. Jas. Buchanan, Monica Kirwan, Jas. Haverkam, Alex^r Dover.
40. Jno Long, Miss Humphreys, Miss E. Humphreys, Ebenezar Lovell, Mrs Humphreys.
41. Mrs Bonnin, Ann Boudinott, Mrs Lyons, Miss A. Stevens.
42. Jno Haycock, Jno Williams, Sarah Williams.
43. Alex^r Livingston, Alex^r Bowyer, Mrs Steele, Miss Wilkinson.
44. Mrs Dewit, Mary Bowers, Eliz^h Strong, Christopher Hewetson.
45. Jno Boyd, Jas. Tenant, Rob. McNish, Jun.
46. Jno Lindsay, Edwd Payne, Wm Anderson, Jno Sawcolt.
47. Wm B. Thomas, Tho. Duncan.
48. Mrs Keeling, Mrs Scandrett, Aldrich Leeder, Jas. Burley.
49. Marg^t Toole, Mary Hodgson, Jno Scholes, Richd Joseph.
50. Tho. Kays, Jno Malcolm, Jos^h Patterson.
51. Geo. White, Edwd Barnes, Jno Bawn, Tho. Winterflood.
52. Jane Malloun, Eliz. Perrott, Ann Massey.
53. Wm Cramp, Hen. Glover, Wm Foard, Alex^r Troup.
54. Jno Taylor, Sen., Richd Maning, Hen. Gabb, Jno Stanton.
55. Benjn Ireland, Tho. Winter, Wm Gregory.
56. Jno Smith, Mrs Muir, Jas. Smith, Jno Willding.
57. Tho. Jarvis, Jacob Jarvis, Miss Salmon, Jno Crosbie.

58, 59, 60, 61, 62, 63. Free people of Colour.

64. Edwd Byam, Eliza Byam, Jas. Nibbs, Anne Lesslie, Mrs Saml Warner.
65. Jno Wilkins, Jno Buckley, Dr Marchant, Robt Clogstoun.
66. Eliz. Jones, Mary Webley, Marg^t Osborne, Lucy Brown.
67. Jno Ireland, Jas. Knenstub, Mrs Shewcraft.
68. Miss Sanderson, David Ross, Wm Butler, Tho. Kentish.
69. Jno Rose, Eliz. Rosington, Jno Robertson, Arthur Robertson.
70. Mrs Atkinson, Alex^r Brodie, Mrs Shervington, Richd Shervington.
71. Eliz. Roberts, Henry Symes.
72. Ann Crosier, Archibald Smith.
73. Wm Hamilton, Jos^h Aska.
74. Jno Daniel Bean.

S. Corner of the Organ Loft. Parish Children.

Corner Pew, S. Gallery. Jno Barry, Peter McDonough.

The next Pew. Miss Richardson and Schollars.

The next Pew. Mrs Higgins and Schollars.

N. Gallery. H.M. Troops Stationed here.

1789, Jan. 6. Hon. Jno Gray & Rev. Jas. Lindsey, both J.P.'s.

1789, Jan. 22. Jno Lindsay, Esq., present.

1789, May 17. Jno Delap Halliday, Esq., gives a clock & bell. The iron gates have arrived.

1790, June 22. Admiral Sir Jno Laforey, Bart., to sit in pew 34. Eliz. Nibbs, who has 3 dau's, is allowed £20 a year. Dr Robt Reid, Surgeon of Hospital.

1793, Jan. 8. Philip Hicks, Esq., J.P., Mr Clogstoun, & Dr Athill present.

1794, Jan. 27. Rev. Coull to officiate during Rector's absence of 12 mos.

1794, May 15. "That it appears to the Vestry that Captain Samuel Oliver, Master of the Ship Brooke, arrived in this Island about the month of April or May last year, and that he imported in the said Ship and another Ship called the Pinics (?), whereof Thomas Kidd was Master, certain Goods, Wares, and Merchandizes, and it further appears to the Vestry that the said Samuel Oliver was at the time of importation aforesaid a Transient-trader, and departed this Island without paying the Transient-trader tax and without giving any Account upon Oath before the Acting Church-Warden of the Goods, Wares, and Merchandizes by him imported, it is therefore Ordered that the said Samuel Oliver do appear before the Acting Church-Warden and take the Oaths prescribed by Law, respecting the Goods, Wares, and Merchandizes imported by him as aforesaid, and that he do pay the Tax that shall be assessed him for the same, and in failure thereof it is further Ordered that the said Acting Church-Warden do enter an Action of Debt against the said Samuel Oliver for one hundred pounds, the Penalty which he has incurred by departing this Island without giving an account as aforesaid."

1795, Jan. 8. Baijer Otto-Baijer present.

1795, March 2. New List of Pews.

1796, Jan. 8. Jno Otto-Baijer present.

1796, Feb. 29. Clarks Hill, the property of Joseph Warner, Esq.; Dicky's Hill, of Thos. Oliver, Esq.; Old Plantation, Tho. L. Brooke, Esq.; Potters, Wm Gunthorpe, Esq.; Bawns Land, in the possession of Robt McNish, Esq.; Ledwell & Scotts, Sawcolts, Jno Horseford, Esq.; Blizards, heirs of Giles Blizard; Renfrew, Jno Otto-Baijer, Esq.; Mount Rural, Jno Kilean, Esq. (The above is a list of estates paying rates, etc.)

1799, Jan. 22. Dr Kean B. Osborn to be Sargeon.

1800. Walter Colquhoun present. Lord Lavington lived at the Parsonage House as Govt House by permission of the Rector.

1801, Sep. 8. Letter from Lord Lavington appointing Rev. Hen. Campbell to be Rector *vice* Rev. Jas. Lindsay, decd, who died 23 April last, da. 1 Sep. 1801.

1801, Sep. 26. Not the duty of Rector to bury slaves. The church is to be used by the Govr for investing Lieut.-Genl Trigg & Rear-Admiral Duckworth with the Order of the Bath. Throne to be erected in front of the altar & pews in the chancel to be removed. David King, Esq., Ch. Warden.

1802, July 17. Warrant from Lord Lavington. Rev. H. Campbell has resigned. Rev. Saml Lyons is presented as Rector.

1803, Jan. 7. Paul Horseford present.

1803, May 25. The burial ground at the Point to be cleaned & put in good order. Free people of colour were buried there.

1803, Aug. 31. Warrant from Lord Lavington. Revd Saml Lyons has resigned. Presentation of Rev. Saml Wickham Harman da. 20 Aug. 1803.

1805. Dr Jas. Athill present.

1806, Jan. 8. Langford L. Hodge present, & John Otto-Baijer.

1806, Feb. 27. Following pew list:—

1. Lieut Govr, President, Council, Assembly.
2. Minister.
3. Walter Thibou & family, Jno Scholes & family, Wm B. Jarvis & family.
4. Miss Tomlinson, Robt Hyndman & family, Josh Dyett & family, Wm Lenaghan & family.
5. David King & family, David Kennedy & family, Robt McNish & family, Jno Hyde.
6. Ann Halloran & family, Jno Buntin & family, Jno Troup & family.
7. Jno McConnell & family, Jos. S. Darrell & family, Rach. Martin, Frances Worlock, Richd Wright, Miss Livingston, Wm Collins.
8. Geo. W. White & family, Jas. Curtin & family, Robt French & family, Harriot L. Hubbard, Miss Hurst, Miss French.
9. Mrs Scotland, Sen., & family, Rev. Jas. Coull & family, Jno Lyons & family, Jno McCormick & family, Miss Mary Hurst, Miss Weathered.
10. Jas. Smith, Geo. Pratt & family, Tho. Browning, Wm M. Hughes.
11. Benjn Scotland & family, Mrs Sherman, Philip Hall Harris, Wm Turner & family.
12. Mrs Jas. Robinson, Jno Proudfoot & family.
13. Mrs Coates, Jno Scotland & family, Alexr Petrie & family.
14. Chas. McComb, Capt Bunch & family, Andrew Marshall, Hen. Keeling, Jno J. Walters.
15. Mrs Stephen Rose, Wm Park & family.
16. Warmick Pearson, Tho. F. Nibbs.

17 & 18. Strangers.

19. Mrs Proctor, Miss Urlin, Jas. Hill.
20. Jas. Wilson, Jas. Johnson, Jas. Weir.
21. Henry Glover & family, Robt Mason & family.
22. Mrs Harney, Isaac Newton & family.
23. Mrs Croswell & family, Mrs Montague, Jno Shires, Wm Waring.
24. Dr Kirwan, Jno Harris, Saml Auchinleck & family.
25. Tho. B. Mackie, Mrs Jesse, Sen., Tho. Clark, Isaac De Forest & family.
26. Alexr Coates, Geo. Glenny, Amy Clark, Mrs Willding & family, Mrs Nugent.
27. Mrs Hughes, Stephen Rose & family, Wm Burnthorn & family, Saml Sheriff & family.
28. Saml Bott & family, Margt Eales & family, Wm Johnson & family, Tho. Hyndman & family, Mrs McNish, Sen.
29. Mrs Greenway & family, Jno Wm Dow & family, Philip Hall, Archibald G. Dow & family, Andrew Sawers & family.
30. Mrs Doig, Eleanor Montegue, Mrs Nanton, Geo. McNish & family.
31. Jno Burke, Mrs Eccleston & family, Mrs Robinson & family, Mrs Kelsick & family, Mrs Hardcastle & family.
32. Jno Otto-Baijer, Mrs Savage, Miss Lovells, Mrs Ledwell & family, Jno Hall & family, Mrs Mathews & family.
33. Jno Taylor & family, Wm Gunthorpe & family, Edwd B. Wyke & family, Tho. Jarvis, Tho. Rogers & family, Margt Pearson, Miss Stillings.
34. Rowland Burton & family, Mrs Gray, Eliza Doig, Oliver Y. Ash & family, Danl Hill, Jun., & family.
35. Wm Jervis, Jno Crosbie, Hugh Mackay, Patrick Lenaghan.
36. Clementina Smith & family, Robt Heynes & family, Ann Thomas.
37. Richd Pigott & family, Jno B. Hamilton.
38. Mrs Dickinson & family, Mrs Atwater & family, Mrs Humphreys, Miss Humphreys.
39. Mrs Buchanan & family, Mrs Haverkam & family, Jno Hill & family, Mrs Merrifield, Miss Underwood, Miss Iles.

40 & 41. Langford Hodge & family, Jas. Athill, Paul Horsford & family, Hastings Elwin & family.

42. Mrs Mary Lee, Mrs Williams, Anna Stevens, Mrs Baker.
43. Miss Wilkinson, Mrs Braham, Mrs Brice, Mrs Perrott.
44. Mrs Potter, Edwd Gore & family, Judith Broockbank, Mrs Crawfield.
45. Jno Boyd, Mrs Can & family, Mrs Desilvia & family.
46. Jno Smith, Wm Gregory & family, Wm Hamilton & family.
57. Church Wardens.
64. Edwd Byam & family, Richd S. Byam, Tho. N. Kerby & family.
65. Mrs Marchant, Martha Dow & family.
66. F. G. Robinson & family, Jno Laviconnt & family, Jno L. Elson & family.
67. Francis Meredith & family, Jas. Crichton, Duncan Dow & family.
68. Mrs Wm Butler & family, Tho. Kentish & family, Richd Oliver & family, Wm Lee.
69. Tho. Scotland & family, Wm Scholes & family, Saml Warner.
70. Danl Hill & family, Jno Harney & family.
71. Tho. Osborn, Eliz. Osborn, Miss Ann Williams.

72. Jeremiah Nibbs, Wm Laidlaw & family, Henry Donovan, Abrah. Marshall & family.

73. Andrew Edwards, Sen., & family, Dr Daniel & family, Dr Osborn, Tho. Kirwan & family.

74. Wm Brinton, Edwd Rigg, Henry Hodge, Campbell Brown.

47 & 56. Parish Poor.

E. Pew, S. Gallery. Jno Rose & family, Miss Rose, Miss E. Rose, Jno Roberts & family, Jas. Watson & family, Jno Rose & family, Mrs J. Rose, Sen., & family, Mrs Crump.

Next Pew. Miss Richardson & Schollars.

S. Corner Organ Gallery. Parish Children.

N. Gallery. H.M. Troops Stationed here.

48, 49, 50, 51, 52, 53, 54, 55, 58, 59, 60, 61, 62, & 63. Free People of Colour.

1807. M. H. Daniell, Doctor for the hospital, & to have £125 a year.

1813. Dr Coull present, & Joshua Dyett.

1815. Mr Geo. Green the organist is dead. Mrs Jane Troop succeeds him. Francis B. Ottley present.

1819, March 19. Rev. Saml Wickham Harman, Rector. Messrs. Horsford, Nibbs, Dyett, French, Ottley, Sanderson, & Darrell, members of the vestry.

1819, Dec. 1. Hon. & Rev. S. W. Harman, Rector, Hon. Saml Warner, Hon. Meade H. Daniell, Hon. Henry Hodge, Mr Dyett, Mr Ottley, Mr Sanderson, Mr Darrell, Mr Nibbs, present.

1820, Jan. 26. £330 c. voted as a present to the Rector S. W. Harman.

1820, Feb. 15. Paul Horsford, Tho. Coull, Hen. Hodge, Fra. B. Ottley, Tho. Sanderson, Robt Grant, Joshua Dyett, & Tho. F. Nibbs, present.

1821, Jan. 24. Dr Coull, Dr Saml F. Daniell, present. Dr Anthony Musgrave, surgeon of the hospital.

1822, Feb. 11. Allotment of pews as following :—

1. Rector.

2. Councill & Assembly.

3. Miss French, Nathl Humphry, Saml Darrell & family.

4. Joshua Dyett & family, Wm & John Harman.

5. Mrs Kennedy & family, Robt McNish, Junr, & family.

6. Jno Halloran & family, Joseph Z. Huison & family, Mrs Mary Halloran & family.

7. Geo. McConnell & family, Wm Collins & family, C. Robertson & family.

8. Robt Grant & family, C. P. Hosier & family, Jno French.

9. Miss Scotland, M. Cummings & family, Wm Scotland & family.

10. Tho. B. Sears & Sons.

11. Wm Turner (?), Jno Allaway & family.

12. Mrs Proudfoot & family, Cha. Chatfield & family.

13. Mrs Petrie & family.

14. Cap. Bunch & family, Andrew Marshall, Jno J. Walter.

15. Cha. Steel & Bros., Jno Stewart & family.

16. Jno W. Hall & family.

17. Strangers.

18. Churchwardens.

19. Saml Philpott.

20. Mrs Green & daughter.

21. Henry Glover, Jas. Bland, Jno McNiell.

22. Isaac Newton, Jas. Penny & family.

23. Miss Croswell, Jno Shires & family, Wm Warring & family.

24. Jno Harris, R. Jaggard & family, Wm Closs.

25. Tho. W. Clark, Mrs De Forest.

26. Mrs Wilding & family, G. S. Musson & family.

27. Mrs Hughes, Jas. Allers & family, Jno Harvey, Walter McFarlane & family.

28. Mrs W. Johnson & family, Robt McNish, Senr, & family, F. J. Jones & family, Wm R. Jones & family, W. C. Tymes & family.

29. Miss Greenway, Jas. S. Pruden & family, Jno Gow & family, Mrs Sears, Miss Davis.

30. Mrs Doig, Mrs Martin & family, Mrs Nugent, Jno H. Jones.

31. Mrs Robinson & family, Abiah H. Adams & family, C. H. Lamitt & family, Mrs Scholes, Senr.

32. Miss Lovell, Mrs Dow & family, Mrs Hardcastle & family, Dr Weston & family.

33. Margt Pearson, Mrs Wyke, Mrs Edden & dau's, Mrs Kirwan, Mrs Richardson, Mrs Simpson & family.

34. Mrs Hill & family, Mrs Musgrave & family, Mrs McKay, Francis Ottly & family, Hon. S. Warner, Jno Furlonge & family, Anthony Musgrave & family, Mrs Kentish & family, Joshua Kentish & family.

35. Jno Haggard & family, Jno Farr & family, Jno Bradshaw.

36. Miss Heyness & family, Wm Williams & family.

37. Richd Piggott & family, Jno Crawford & family, W. B. Pigott, Mrs Baker & family.

38. Mrs Humphrys, Capt Lindsay & family, Mrs Burke, Geo. Clark & family.

39. Mrs Haverkam & family, Mrs Merrifield, Mrs Geo. White & family, Nathl Donaldson & family, Mrs Ablett.

40. Hon. Jas. Athill, Hon. Paul Horsford & family, Hon. Wm Gunthorp & family, Hon. M. H. Daniell & family, Richd Musgrave & family.

41. [*Blank.*]

42. Tho. Kippan, Mrs Bruce, Mrs Perrott, Jas. Brown, Jas. Mason.

43. Wm Gregory & family, Wm Hamilton & family.

44. Parish Poor.

45 to 52. Free people of color.

53. Parish Poor.

54. Tho. S. Trott & family, Jno A. Wood & family.

55 to 60. Free people of color.

61. Dr Coull & family, Tho. Sanderson & family, Warwick Hyndman, Tho. W. Hyndman.

62. Martha Dow & family, Wm Gilchrist & family, Dr West & family.

63. Jno L. Elson & family, Geo. Blaney & family, Tho. Underwood & family, Wm Wyke & family, Henry Gow & family.

64. Jas. Irwin & family, Jas. Greenidge & daughters.

65. Lewis Butler, W. Lee, Jno Boyd & brothers, Mrs Oliver, Wm Kelly & family.

66. Tho. Scotland & family, Wm Nicholas & family, Richd L. Nanton & family.

67. Mrs Hall & family, Saml Sheriff & family, Duncan Dow & family.

68. Eliz. Osborn & family, Miss Ann Williams, Tho. F. Nibbs & family, W. Burthorne & family.

69. Henry Donovan & family, Miss Wethered, Mrs Muir, C. J. Barnard & family.

70. Hugh Edwards & family, Dr Osborne, Cha. Taylor & family.

71. Hon. Henry Hodge, Mrs Michael L. Hodge, Margt Eales, Peter Murray & family.

E. Pew, S. Gallery. Joseph Rose & family, John Rose, Mrs Crump, Han . . . Whitlock & family, Richd Hodges, Geo. Pratt & family.

2nd Pew, S. Gallery. Geo. Metcalf & family, Mrs Cummings, Senr.

3rd Pew, S. Gallery. [*Blank.*]

4th Pew, S. Gallery. Robt Wilkinson, Edwd Bascome, Saml J. Darrell.

S. Corner, Organ Gallery. Parish Children.

N. Gallery. His M. Troops stationed here.

1823, Jan. 8. Paul Horsford, Saml Warner, Meade H. Daniell, Henry Hodge, Joshua Dyett, Saml L. Darrell, Tho. F. Nibbs, Tho. Coull, Fra. B. Ottley, Tho. Sanderson, Robt Grant.

1825, Dec. 31. Richd L. Nanton, Esqr, Dep. Provost Marshall.

1827, Jan. 10. Robt Horsford present.

1827. The Rev. S. W. Harman being deceased after 24 years' service.

1827, Aug. 1. Presentation of living to Rev. Robt Holberton by His Excelly Sir Patrick Ross.

1827, Dec. The burial ground at the Point having become unfit for use owing to floods, the glebe land attached to the Rectory to be used as a burial ground for black & coloured people.

1829. Giles L. Masson, C. P. Hosier, Jas. Scotland, Junr, Saml Darrel, & Rev. Wm Harman, present.

1830, Jan. 9. Bertie E. Jarvis, K. B. Osborn, present.

1831, Jan. 8. L. L. Hodge, Kean B. Osborn, present.

1832, Sep. 15. The 1st color'd person buried in the churchyard. In future that & the glebe ground to be considered open for all free persons.

1833, Jan. 11. Hugh Edwards present.

1833, Nov. 12. Church to be thoroughly repaired.

1834, Jan. 8. Jno Athill present.

1835, Jan. 7. Anthony Musgrave present.

1836, Jan. 11. Francis Shand, Richd H. Mason, & Tho. Fergusson, present.

1838, Feb. 21. "That the Rector having shewn to the Vestry the Vessel used for a flagon at the Sacrament of the Lord's supper, & it having appeared to be quite out of Character with the rest of the Plate, be authorised to sell it in the Island, or send it to England as old silver, & to obtain in lieu thereof two flagons suited for Sacred use."

[Vol. 3.]

1840, Jan. 9. Jno Bradshaw, Wm Thibou, Wm Boyd, Tyrrel Shervington, present.

1841, Jan. 9. Rowland Williams, Geo. S. Martin, Jas. W. Sherriff, present.

1841, March 1. Fee of 25$ for every metallic coffin interred in the churchyard unless in a vault, & £50 st. if deposited in the church without a vault.

1841. New burial ground consecrated.

1843.

Memorandum of the Awful Earthquake.*

On Wednesday 8th February 1843, the very day after the meeting of the Vestry, as before recorded, this Island was visited by a most terrific and destructive Earthquake. At 20 minutes before 11 o'clock in the forenoon, while the Bell was ringing for Prayers and the Venerable Robt Holberton was in the Vestry room awaiting the arrival of persons to have their Marriage solemnized before the commencement of the morning Service, the whole Edifice from one end to the other was suddenly and violently agitated. Every one within the Church after the first shock was compelled to escape for their lives. The Tower was rent from the top to the bottom, the North dial of the Clock precipitated to the ground beneath with a dreadful crash, and the East parapet Wall of the Tower thrown upon the Roof of the Church. Almost the whole of the North West Wall of the North Gallery fell out in a mass. The North East Wall was protruded beyond the perpendicular; the Alter piece, the Public Monument erected to the Memory of Lord Lavington, and the private Monuments bearing the names of Kelsick, Warner, Ottley, and Atkinson fell down piece meal inside. A large portion of the top of the East Wall fell, and the whole of the South East Wall was precipitated into the Church Yard, carrying along with it two of the East Iron Windows, while the other 6 remained projecting from the Walls in which they had been originally inserted. A large pile of heavy cut stones and masses of Brick fell down at the South and at the North Doors. Seven of the large front Pipes of the Organ were thrown out by the violence of the Shocks, and many of the metal and wooden Pipes within displaced; the massive Basin of the Font was tossed from the pedestal on which it rested and pitched upon the pavement beneath uninjured. Thus within the space of 3 minutes the church was reduced to a pile of crumbling ruins. The Walls that were left standing being rent in every part, the main roof only remaining sound, being supported by the hard wood pillars. Having been constituted a Cathedral Church and Episcopal See by the Mandate of Her Most Gracious Sovereign Queen Victoria, as announced in the Official letter of His Excellency the Governor in Chief, Sir C. H. Fitz Roy, K.H., dated 10th Nov. 1842, it was the intention of the Members of the Vestry at their next meeting, proposed to be held on the 27th inst., to have entered into a Contract for improving the Chancel and elevating the Stone work of the Tower, completing the same with four Minarets in a manner suitable for a Cathedral. The said Vestry of St John's holding now their next meeting this 24th day of February 1843 under a Tent, and beholding the destruction of the Cathedral and Parish Church by the late Calamitous Earthquake (which indeed has either rent or laid waste all the stone Buildings in the Island), at the same time gratefully acknowledging the merciful interposition of the Most High in the remarkable preservation of human life, have agreed to have this Record made of the appawlling Earthquake of the 8th inst. for their own instruction and for that of future generations.

"Come, behold the works of the Lord, what desolations he hath made in the earth." "Be still, and know that I am God." Psalm xlvi., v. 8, 10. R. Holberton, Archdeacon of Antigua and Rector of St John's.

T. F. Nibbs, } Churchwardens.
J. Bradshaw, }

[Vol. 4.]

1843. Rt Rev. Daniel Gateward Davis, D.D., 1st Bishop of Antigua. Installed 12 May 1843. Patent dated 21 Aug. 1842 by V. Reg., & to establish archdeacon of Antigua & St Kitts. A former patent was da. 24 July 1824, Geo. IV.

1844. Members of Vestry:—

Hon. Paul Horsford.	Geo. Athill, Esq.
,, Tho. Sanderson.	Peter P. Walter, Esq.
,, Hugh Edwards.	Hon. T. Shervington. } City.
John Bradshaw, Esq.	
Anthony Musgrave, M.D.	Wm Thibou, Esq. } City.
John Martin, Esq.	Jas. Wm Sheriff, Esq. } City.

The rector, Rev. Archdeacon Holberton.

Rev. Saml A. Warner (? curate 1846). His son died 1845.

The new Cathedral* was opened for service 10 Oct. 1847, having cost nearly 40,000 *l*. The rector is pd £400 st. yearly.

1850. Great disputes arose because the clergy wore a surplice in the pulpit; the curate's salary was stopped in consequence.

1825. 28 sq. miles, 12,300 inhabitants, S. W. Harman, rector; A. W. McNish, curate; 1 church, 800 sittings. (Bishop Coleridge's charges.)

1834. R. Holberton, M.A., rector; J. Grant, curate; 1 church, 1400 sittings. St Luke's & St James' chapels, 600 sittings. (*Ibid.*)

* See a pamphlet on the Earthquake at Antigua February 8, 1843, printed at the 'Weekly Register' Office.

* The corner-stone of the Cathedral was laid in 1845, and the building was completed in 1848. (Church Calendar for Diocese of Antigua.)

CHURCH PLATE.

On a large silver salver there is a representation of our Lord and the twelve Apostles at supper. The marks give the English Hall mark, the date of 1715-16, and the mark of the silversmith John Fawdony. The following inscription runs around the plate:—

Donum Domini Johannis Otto
Bayer ad Templum Divi
Johannis in Antigua.

There are also two silver cups and small plates all dated 1698-9, and inscribed:—

In usum Templi Divi Johannis in Antigua
Gulielmus Jones Parochiæ hujus olim Rector Donum Dedit.

OLD WEST INDIAN CHURCHES.

SIR,—I read with the interest of an old West Indian, and which may be shared by Canadian Churchmen, the following reference to the Cathedral in my old island of Antigua, in that excellent repertory of colonial news *The Colonies and India*, of the 1st January.

"*Old Cathedral Candlesticks.*—A most interesting relic of antiquity has just been restored to the Cathedral of St. John (Antigua). There are probably very few churches in the West Indies which possess any silver nearly two hundred years old. Two very massive candlesticks were given to St. John's Church somewhere about the beginning of the last century, for the giver of them, Mr. Peter Lee, died in the year 1704. They bear the inscription "Donum domini Petri Lee ad Templum Divi Johannis in Antigua." The candlesticks continued in the possession of the church till 1848. They were seen by Mrs. Lanaghan, and are mentioned in her book "Antigua and the Antiguans," vol. i., p.p. 220, 221. In January 1848 the vestry ordered the silver candlesticks and the large brass chandelier to be sold and the proceeds applied to the organ; there is no further record in connection with them."

It is fortunate the utilitarian ideas of the churchwardens of 1848 did not result in their destruction. Referring to the above work "Antigua and the Antiguans," a copy of which is in my library, it is further stated in describing the cathedral "the communion service plate is very handsome, the large salver measuring eighteen inches in diameter, was presented to the church by John Otto Baijer, Esq., about the year 1724. It displays a representation of the Lord's Supper, the figures in beautiful basso relievo, and bears the following inscription: 'Donum domini Johannis Otto Baijer, ad Templum Divi Johannis in Antigua.' The two smaller salvers and the cup are inscribed as follows: 'In usum Templi Divi Johannis in Antigua Gulielmus Jones Parochialis hujus olim Rector Donum Dedit.'"

It is now many years since I left the West Indies to become a resident in Canada, but I am reminded by the above of several old churches there, the service books of which were impressed with the royal arms and inscriptions signifying that they were the gift of Queen Anne, in whose reign, 1704 to 1714, the relics alluded to were presented by old Mr. Lee, whose descendants were in Antigua in my early days, and I believe are still residing in the old colony.

Yours truly,
SAMUEL B. HARMAN.

Toronto, 25th January 1866.

Parish Registers.*

Baptized.

1689 9-ber 16 Frances d. of William War . . . . & Frances his wife.

170– (? 1702) Feb. 14 Margaret d. of Rich[d] Prichard & his wife.

1706 . . . . 5 W[m] S. of John Nicholson & Joan his wife.

* Baptisms and Burials commenced in 1689. Marriages in 1690.

1708 June 20 Mary D. of John Hugas & his wife.

1709 Mar. 5 Jane & Mary d's of Bryan & Margaret Hollgan, dec.

1710 April 8 John ye s. of John Henry & Margaret Bryan.

1712 Sep. 28 Thomas s. of Thomas Murrel & Mary his wife.

1715 Sep. 25 Katherine d. of Arch[d] Shear & his wife.

1716 Mar. 30 Philip Watkins, Ann, & Lucy, s. & d's of Patrick Bryan & Mary his wife.

1716 June 3 William Francis s. of Thos. Murrell & Mary his wife.

1716 Oct. 9 John s. of John Bryan & Sarah his wife.

1717 Dec. 22 Mary D. of Thomas Bishop & Mary his wife.

1718 April 7 Robert s. of Samuel Bryan & Mary his wife.

1718 July 27 John Bishop of Riper years.

1718 Oct. 6 Nathaniel s. of John Booth & Rebecca his wife.

1718 Oct. 23 Samuel s. of Christopher Scandrett & Sarah his wife.

1719 Sep. 25 Ann D. of Samuel Bryant & Mary his wife.

1719 Feb. 9 Ann son (*sic*) of Christopher Scandrett and Sarah his wife.

1721 Jan. 14 Elizabeth D. of John Jenkins & Cristian his wife.

1722 April 29 Jane the D. of David Haycock & Eliz[th] his wife.

1722 July 1 Elizabeth the D. of Christopher Scandrett & Sarah his wife.

1723 Oct. 2 Henry Baker s. of Christopher Scandrett & Sarah his wife.

1724 May 10 Mary the D. of John Jenkins & Christian his wife.

1724 June 21 Rebecca D. of William Thorne & Joanna his wife.

1724 Feb. 21 Mary the d. of David Haycock and Eliz[th] his wife.

1725 April 9 James the s. of Patrick Bryan & Mary his wife.

1725 June 27 James the s. of James Tweedy and his wife.

1725 . . . . . . Sarah the d. of Christopher Scandrett and Sarah his wife.

1726 (? 1725-6) Jan. 26 Peter the s. of John Hugus and Margaret his wife.

1726 Mar. 9 John the s. of John Bishop & Eliz[th] his wife.

1726 April 10 David the s. of John Skerry & Elinor his wife.

1726 July 6 Hester D. of David Haycock & Eliz[th] his wife.

1727 Feb. 22 Susannah the d. of Thos. Austin and Jane his wife.

1727 July 14 William the s. of John Skerry and Eliner his wife.

1728 Aug. 17 W[m] the s. of William Thurston and Eliz[th] his wife.

1728 Sep. 8 Thos. the s. of John Bishop and Eliz[th] his wife.

1729 Nov. 20 David the s. of David Haycock & his wife.

1730 July 5 Madera the s. of William Wyne and Sarah his wife.

1730 Sep. 6 Richard the s. of John Skerry and Eliner his wife.

1731 April 19 Elizabeth the d. of David Haycock and Eliz[th] his wife.

1733 June 10 John the s. of David Haycock & Eliz[th] his wife.

1733 Mar. 23 Wm Vaughan the s. of William Ewens & his wife.

1734 Aug. 28 Christian D. of John Jenkins & Christian his wife.

1734 Sep. 29 Lacey D. of Capt John Green & Frances his wife.

1737 July 12 Edward Morre ye s. of David Haycock & Elizabeth his wife.

1738-9 Feb. 23 William Coddington of Rhode Island, of riper years.

1739 Nov. 20 Catherine ye D. of William Dickenson & Ann his wife.

1739-40 Mar. 6 Ann Mary ye D. of William Ewens & Catherine his wife.

1741 Oct. 23 Elizabeth the D. of Dr William Boyle & Mary his wife.

1741-2 Mar. 14 William the s. of William Dickenson & Ann his wife.

1742 Aug. 28 William the s. of Philip Lambert & his wife.

1743 Dec. 10 Sarah the D. of Arch^{d} Johnston and Sarah his wife.

1744 July 7 Ann the D. of Capt James Hall and Ann his wife.

1744-5 Feb. 9 John the s. of Arch^{d} Johnston and Sarah his wife.

1745 Aug. 11 Charles the s. of William Dickinson and Ann his wife.

1746 June 24 Mary the D. of William Graham and Mary his wife.

1747 Sep. 23 Richard the s. of Rev. Mr Thomas Whitford & Mary his wife; born 19 August last.

1749 Aug. 31 Christopher the s. of Capt Henry Bowers and Mary his wife; born 20 July 1747.

1749 Jan. 7 Philip the s. of Philip Hall and Ann his wife.

1750 Dec. 16 W^{m} the s. of Wm Antrobus and Mary his wife.

1752 June 8 Sarah the D. of Capt Saml Curle and Elizabeth his wife.

1753 Jan. 25 Philip the S. of Doc^{r} Robert Mears and Ann his wife.

1754 Aug. 5 Robert the s. of John Langley and Penelope his wife.

1754 Oct. 8 James Alexander the S. of Capt Jam. Stewart & Eliz. his wife.

1755 May 25 Horatio Sharp the s. of Capt Hen. Cowell & Ann his wife.

1756 Dec. 12 Robert Spencer the S. of Pet^{r} Blachford & Marg^{t} his wife.

1757 Oct. 31 Nathan Flinn, of riper years, Patrick his Father's name & Mahew his Mother's; born in Boston, and condemn'd for Plundering a Spanish Ship.

1757 Nov. 6 James the S. of Capt James Connor & Bridget his wife.

1758 July 20 Elizabeth D. of Capt James Stewart and Elizabeth his wife.

1758 Oct. 29 Rebecca the D. of Capt George Green by Elizabeth his wife.

1760 Sep. 18 George the S. of Earnest Udny and Sarah his wife.

1761 Jan. 24 Christopher the S. of Christopher Ceily and Margaret his wife.

1761 Aug. 25 Thomas Hazlewood the S. of Robert Delanoy and Ann his wife; b. 8^{br} 25, 1760.

1761 Nov. 8 John Melvil s. of Capt William Hadlam and Ann his wife.

1762 May 6 Elizabeth Nugent D. of William McIntosh and Ann his wife.

1763 Mar. 15 Robert Skerrit the S. of Coleman Heyns and his wife.

1767 Jan. 10 Sarah the D. of Robert Towers and Sarah his wife.

1767 Sep. 27 Edward Holleway S. of Thomas Beech and Ann his wife.

1768 Mar. 17 Christian the D. of Coleman Hains and Sarah his wife.

1770 Mar. 21 Elizabeth the D. of James Hay and Mary his wife; b. Jan'ry 27th, 1769.

1770 Mar. 21 James the S. of James Hay and Mary his wife.

1770 May 7 Gilbert Shuckburgh the S. of Capt James Stewart of His Maj$^{ty's}$ 68 Reg^{t} & Eliz^{a} his wife.

1770 May 9 Ann the D. of John Taylor (Merch^{t}) and Grace his wife.

1771 April 28 Ann Mary Gravenor the D. of Thomas Beech and Ann his wife.

1772 Jan. 15 Sarah the D. of James Ramsay and Sarah his wife.

1772 July 6 Henrietta the D. of Doc^{r} John Robertson and Eliz^{a} his wife.

1772 Oct. 14 George the S. of James Hay (Merch^{t}) and Mary his wife.

1772 Oct. 17 Sophia the D. of John Taylor (Merchant) and Grace his wife.

1773 Jan. 2 Francis the S. of Philip Hall, Junr, & Anne his wife.

1773 Jan. 2 Thos Afflick Wade the S. of Philip Hall, Junr, & Anne his wife.

1774 Feb. 10 John Duncombe the S. of John Taylor (Merch^{t}) & Grace his wife.

1775 Oct. 25 Grace the D. of John Taylor (Merchant), and Grace his wife.

1775 Dec. 19 Sarah Rachel the D. of Coleman Heyns & Sarah his wife.

1776 Jan. 2 Mary the D. of Robert Milne & Mary his wife.

1776 Jan. 20 Jennet the D. of Doc^{r} John Aird and Isabella his wife.

1776 June 5 Mary Johnson the D. of James Hay (Merchant) & Mary his wife, who was b. the 8th of March 1774.

1776 June 5 Robert the S. of James Hay (Merchant) and Mary his wife, who was b. the 20th of August 1775.

1776 Sep. 9 Lewis Hansford the S. of John Taylor (Merch^{t}) and Grace his wife.

1778 Feb. 12 Eliz. the d. of Doc^{r} Wm Bowie & Marg^{t} his wife.

1778 May 28 Frances the d. of Robt Milne & Mary his wife.

1779 Jan. 13 David the S. of Doc^{r} John Aird & Isabella his wife.

1780 Nov. 12 Ann the d. of Capt Jno Robinson and Ann his wife.

1783 Mar. 23 Ann Laforey the D. of John Mascal and Sarah his wife.

1784 Nov. 4 William Clark and Richard S's of Richard Joseph (Merch^{t}) and Rebecca his Wife.

(?1785) July 6 Jackman Infant S. of John Wilkins, Esqr, & Rachel his wife.

(?1785 Aug.) . . . . beth Anne D. of Philip Hall and Hester his wife.

1785 May 15 Eliza D. of David Scott (Merchant) and Christian his wife.

1785 Sep. 9 Thomas John Panton Infant S. of John Myddelton & Mary his wife.

1786 April 30 Alexander Infant S. of David Scott and Christian his wife.

1786 June 22 Henrietta the D. of Doctor Arthur Grant Robertson and Elizabeth his wife. B. 22 April 1786.

1786 Aug. 3 Jane D. of Doctor David Kennedy and Elizabeth his wife. B. 23 July 1786.

1787 May 20 Judith Lesslie D. of Christopher Hewetson and Judith his wife. B. the 11th March 1787.

1788 Feb. 3 James Hutchison S. of Robert Wilson and Ann his wife. B. 24th December 1787.

1788 Feb. 23 Louisa Elizabeth D. of John Taylor, Merchant, and Lillias his wife. B. 20th June 1787.

1788 May 12 Jean D. of Doctor William Bowie and Margaret his wife. B. 31st December 1787.

1788 May 17 Thomas D. [sic] of Doctor David Kennedy and Elizabeth his wife. B. 18th January 1788.

1788 Dec. 10 Elizabeth D. of Christina Sperkin and Sarah his wife; b. the 4th July 1788.

1789 Mar. 25 Mary Sawcolt d. of Captain John Robinson and Elenor Denbow his wife. B. the 14th August 1788.

1789 July 8 Lillias Mary D. of John Taylor and Lillias his wife. B. the 22nd March 1789.

1789 Aug. 2 James Delap S. of John Whitlock and Margaret his wife. B. the 23rd July 1789.

1789 Aug. 3 Gilbert McClure S. of Doctor David Kennedy and Elizabeth his wife. B. the 9th July 1789.

1790 Aug. 4 Frances Merrefield D. of Luman Attwater and Harriet his wife; b. the 5th September 1789.

1791 Jan. 7 Gilbert McClure s. of David Kennedy and Elizabeth his wife. B. the 29th December 1790.

1791 May 5 William Stevenson S. of Luman Attwater and Harriett his wife. B. the 21st January 1791.

1792 Nov. 19 Maria Ray D. of Luman Attwater and Harriett Nash his wife. B. the 9th Septer. 1792.

1793 June 1 Phœbe Branthwaite D. of David Kennedy and Elizabeth his wife. B. the 6th May 1793.

1794 Aug. 12 George Attkinson S. of Alexander McPherson and Margaret his wife; b. the 16th May 1793.

1795 Jan. 7 Eliza D. of Captain John Robertson and Elenor his wife. B. the 18th December 1793.

1795 July 23 Robert S. of Doctor David Kennedy and Elizabeth his wife. B. the 4th February 1794.

1795 Aug. 15 John Smith S. of Robert Mason and Margaret his wife. B. the 3rd April 1795.

1796 Jan. 1 Edward Gamble S. of William Hunt, deceased, and Rachel his wife. B. the 5th March 1793.

1796 Dec. 31 Mary Ann Atkinson D. of Alexr McPherson and Margarett his wife. B. the 11th June 1796.

1797 July 9 William S. of Robert Mason and Margaret his wife. B. the 15th December 1796.

1797 Aug. 21 David S. of David Kennedy and Elizabeth his wife. B. the 14th Instant.

1797 Oct. 10 Ann Charlotte D. of Sebastian Chevalier de Duret, late Commander of the French part of St Martin's, and Lady Ann Desmont his Wife. B. in this Island the 29th July last.

1797 Oct. 19 Betsey D. of Capt John Robinson and Eleanor his wife. B. the 12th September 1797.

1799 Nov. 7 Richard Hoare S. of Robert Mason and Margaret his wife. B. the 26th June 1799.

1800 July 3 Frances D. of Captain John Shaw and Frances his wife. B. the 27th April 1800.

1801 July 14 Helen William D. of David Kennedy and Elizabeth his wife. B. the 3d April 1801.

1802 July 1 Stephen S. of Robert Mason and Margaret his wife. B. the 14th November 1801.

1803 Aug. 20 John Elliott S. of John Gore, Junr, & Elizabeth Ann Rebecca his wife; b. the 20th November 1801.

1804 Feb. 14 Ann Lynch D. of Stephen Rose Whitlock, decd, and Hannah his Widow; b. 3d Instant.

1805 Jan. 19 George Pigott S. of John Gore and Elizabeth Ann Rebecca his Wife; b. the 22d Decr 1804.

1805 Feb. 21 Elizabeth Amelia D. of Abiah H. Adams and Sarah his wife. B. the 18th January last.

1805 Sep. 19 Lavinia D. of Lieut George Skipton of 3d W. I. Reg. and Catherine his wife. B. 22d August last.

1807 Jan. 1 Eliza Catherine D. of John Gore and Elizabeth Ann Rebecca his wife. B. the 26th Septe'r last.

1808 Nov. 9 Sarah Elizabeth Chester D. of Charles Chester Fitch and Eliza Tilson his wife. B. 28th October last.

1809 June 1 Charlotta Elizabeth Joanna D. of Frederick Charles Petrie, Lieut. of H.M. Batt. 60th Reg., and Catherina Elizabetha Simonetta his wife. B. the 8th April last.

1809 July 28 Grace Claxton D. of The Revd Francis Hallett and Fanny his wife. B. the 4th April last.

1810 April 24 Thomas Coke S. of The Revd Thomas Isham and Alice Creque his wife. B. the 7th Feb'ry 1809.

1810 June 13 William Sinclair Cathcart Infant S. of Lt Col. George Mackie, 3d Battn 60th Reg., and Catherine Ceely his wife.

1810 Aug. 31 Ann McConnell D. of Abraham Lewis Hebert, Lieu. York L.I.V., and Arabella Patten his wife.

1811 June 12 Edwin Fulton S. of John Gore and Elizabeth Ann his wife. B. the 23d May last.

1812 Mar. 14 Georgiana Perrot D. of The Reverend Evan Beaven and Catherine Plaxton his late wife, dec'ed. B. 15th July.

1813 Oct. 19 Henrietta D. of William Newman, Lieut Y.L.I. Volrs, and Eunice his wife. B. the 7th Instant.

[Second Book.]

1814 July 8 Emily. B. the 28th June 1812. Amy Jane. B. the 24th March 1814. } D's of William Butts (Captain Royal Artillery) and Victoria Elizabeth his wife.

1815 July 17 Eleanor Adeline Frances D. of Lieut Thomas Farrer, late of W.I. Regt, & Elizabeth his wife (both deceased). B. the 10th February 1809.

1816 Feb. 24 Sophia D. of George Allan, Captain 4th W.I. Regt, and Lucy his wife. B. 7th January last.

1816 July 17 Thomas S. of Thomas Jones, Lieut in the 4th W.I. Regt, and Elizabeth his wife. B. the 28th December last.

1816 July 17 Charles S. of Charles Miller, Lieut in the 4th W.I. Regt, and Fanny his wife. B. the 25th May last.

1816 July 17 George S. of Thomas Cuningham Pilkington and Elizabeth Harcum his wife. B. the 30th June last.

1816 Aug. 2 James S. of The Reverend James Curtin and Lucy his wife. B. the 12th Feb'ry last.

1816 Oct. 6 William Leith S. of William Butts, Captain Royal Artillery, and Victoire Elizabeth his wife.

1816 Oct. 15 Eliza Ann D. of Stephen Pell and Susannah his wife. B. the 20th July last.

1817 May 5 Eliza Antonietta D. of The Reverend William Chaderton and Mary Rachel his wife. B. the 16th March last.

1818 Feb. 15 William Manning S. of Revd James Curtin and Lucy his wife. B. the 19th Nover. last.

1826 Sep. 8 B. 7 July last. George William Clarke S. of Charles & Eliza Robertson, St John's, Esquire.

[Third Book, 1827—1840.]

1829 Jan. 25 Eliza Harriet D. of Thomas & Elizabeth Lane. St John's. Colonial Secretary.

1829 Oct. 30 Charlotte Louisa D. of Rev. Thomas & Louisa Parry. Clare Hall. Archdeacon of Antigua.

1830 June 11 John S. of Thomas & Elizabeth Lane. St John's. Colonial Secretary.

1831 Jan. 1 Amelia Louisa D. of Thomas & Louisa Parry. Clare Hall. Archdeacon of Antigua.

1834 Aug. 22 George Robert Ottley s. of Robert & Georgiana Holberton. Rectory House, St John's. Rector of this parish.

1839 Mar. 1 Georgiana Jane D. of Robert & Georgiana Holberton. Rectory House, St John's. Rector of this parish.

1853 Feb. 2 Thomas (b. 5 Jan. 1853) s. of Adam and Caroline Sophia Nicholson. St John's. Medicine Doctor.

Married.

[First Book.]

1691 Nov. 17 Nicholas Lawson & Mary D. of Philip and Margret Chapman.

1695 Oct. 1 Arther Wharf and Mary Wright, Widdow.

1697 April 15 Thomas Ashton and Mary Quick.

1700 8-ber 12 Joseph Langley of Stanford parish, Lincolnshier, and Sarah Mersser.

1700 9-ber 14 Edward Barrish & Ann Ashton, Widdow.

1700 x-ber 10 Mark Roberson & Mary Farington, Widdow.

1700 x-ber — James P . . . . e and Elizabeth ye d. of Stephen Rise.

1700 Jan. 6 Tho. Mahoney & Ann Bell, Widdow.

1700 Jan. 19 Oliver Jeaking and Elizabeth Phillipes, Maid.

1700 Feb. 19 Saml Ashbourn & Hanna Howard, Wid.

1700 Mar. 9 Henry Sherman & Mary Summers, Widdow.

1701 Feb. 10 David Sweegle & Eliz. Shuder.

1701 July 17 Walter Long and Ann Raynolds, Spinster.

1702 June 6 Michael Mason & Grace Dewberry.

After 1703 nearly all persons were married by licence granted by the Governor or his Deputy.

1705 Aug. 18 John Brenan & Catherine Jacobson.

1705-6 . . . . . . James Synnegot & Catharine Fraise.

1706 . . . . . . John Coduer & Elizabeth Erwin.

1706 . . . . 14 William Dyatt (?) & Elizabeth Jennings.

1707 Feb. 19 William Moss & Ann Long. B.

1708 April 22 Woolston Harvy & Mary Laurence. Banns.

1708 May 27 Nicolo Kofo & Ann Curteene. Banns pub.

1709 April 10 Charles Cook & Elliz. Lane.

1709 Sep. 24 Mr John Bradston & Anne Browning.

1709 Feb. 10 Edward Ricket & Catherine Brenan.

1710 May 11 George Whitwell & Alice Mather.

1714 Aug. — Levey Guichard & Caroline Le . . . .

1715 . . . . 18 Thomas Peirce and Rebecka Jeffries.

1715 Oct. 3 James Senegatt and Margarett Beaulieu.

1719 Mar. 31 Nathaniel Mason and Mary Coolullen.

1720 July 21 Jasper Oaks and Mary Crisp.

1721 Sep. 24 Willm Fitch and Phillis Nicholls.

1722 May 13 Henry Long and Sarah Ward. B.

1723 July 16 Darby Toole and Elizabeth Chandrois.

1724 April 5 Christopher Comberlidge and Elizª Price.

1725 Mar. 13 Joseph Allison and Mary Long. B.

1730 Sep. 5 John Reynolds and Mary Sweegle; by L.

1732 Sep. 9 William Dickenson and Ann Chaloner.

1736 May 31 Thomas Murrell and Frances Willis.

1737 . . . . 13 Daniel Pelloe & Ann Ramsay.

1738 Jan. 6 Alexander Wilson & Elizabeth Coppin.

1738 Jan. 22 John Chapman & Rebeckah Taylor.

1740 Sep. 24 George Washington to Elinor Thornton.

1743 July 11 William Mercer and Lucy Burroughs.

1743 Jan. 21 Thomas Towers & Eliz. Gallaspy.

1744 April 14 Archibald Campbell & Ann Cargill.

1744 Feb. 23 Carter Stevens and Ann Coppinger.

On a scrap, no date:—

. . . . John Machokall & Mary Welch.

. . . . 30 Vincent Loveday & Elizabeth Thompson.

1752 May 21 Henry Cooke and Frances Heathen.

1754 April 14 Mansfeild Ord and Elizabeth Brenan.

1754 Oct. 6 William Adlam and Sarah Dickinson.

1756 Sep. 28 Richard Pelham (Surgeon) and Helena Thomson.

1756 Oct. 23 James Storrack and Ann Pellow.

1757 Jan. 13 Wm Walker (Mercht) and Russell Sherwood.

1757 Nov. 19 Capt John Galston and Mary Lambert.

1758 Feb. — Capt Nathl Milberry to Elianor Gorman.

1758 April 15 Capt John Price to Sarah Addison.

1758 July 1 Aron Ward to Catherine Conn.

1759 Oct. 20 John Dearnon Fletcher to Catherine Dickinson.

1764 April 12 Doctr Rice to Martha Blunt.

1771 July 24 Revd Richard Harris to Jane Forrest.

1779 June 10 Capt Daniel Bruce to Martha Swand.

1786 Jan. 21 Jean Achille Joseph Breckwell, Chevalier Seigneur de larive, to Rosalba Elizabeth de Forceville, Spinster.

(? 1788) May 14 Alexander Macpherson (Practitioner in Physic) to Margaret Mackins.

1790 May 22 John Bremner to Margaret Rogers.

1796 Oct. 15 Thomas Rogerson to Mary Adney.

1799 Sep. 4 William Gray Polson, Capt in the 59th Regt to Charlotte Sarah McConnell.

1801 Aug. 31 James Thomas Light (Missionary) to Maria Reichel, Widow.
1802 July 8 Nathaniel Bascome, Merchant, to Elizabeth Corbusier, Spr.
1803 Jan. 2 Revd James Curtin to Sarah Deubow Richards, Spr.
1804 Sep. 24 John Baecker (Missionary) to Susanna Walters; banns.
1807 Aug. 17 William Croil, Merchant, to Dorothy Eliza Gocking, Spr.
1813 April 20 Joseph Ablett, Planter, to Harriet Hubbard, Widow.
1813 Aug. 31 Peter Bailey (Planter) to Isett Hencock.

[Second Book, 1814—1826.]

1814 June 28 Frederick William Kysh, Captain in the York Light Infantry Volunteers, to Julia Harney, Spr.
1815 Jan. 3 Richard Douse (Hospital Assistant Surgeon to the Forces) to Margaret Curran, Widow.
1815 Mar. 17 Richard Spratt, Lieut. 4th W.I. Regt, to Catherine Elizabeth Orphanic Okaga.
1819 July 29 Henry Richard Cassin, M.D., of the Island of Nevis, to Catherine Watts, Widow.
1824 Sep. 13 The Reverend James Curtin to Catherine Hardcastle, Spr.
1826 Mar. 6 Arthur Teagle, Planter, and Eliza Petrie, Spr.

[From a book, 1837—1840.]

1837 Mar. 9 Rev. Thos. Clarke of Trinity Chapel in the parish of St Philip's, Barbados, to Julia Bennett of this parish, Spr.
1838 Mar. 23 Alex. John Williams & Marion Irvin, both of this Parish.

[From a book, 1840—1853.]

1841 Mar. 30 Henry St John Clements, Officer of H.M. 1st W.I. Reg., & Helen D'Urban Burton Taylor of this Parish.
1850 Feb. 5 John Jeffery, native of Tunbridge Wells, Bach., & Adelaide Matilda Donaldson Nugent of this Parish.

Buried.

The words "The body of" so and so have been omitted in the following extracts.

1689 Mar. 5 Nathan Ransford of . . . .
1689 Mar. 15 Jacob Skelton of this Island, Mariner.
1689 Mar. 19 Elizabeth the wife of Anthony Royersson of this Island, Gent.
1690 Mar. 31 Anthony Royersson, Senr, of this Island.
1690 May 11 Catherine the wife of Robert Bronton.
1690 Sep. 25 Henry Thorn, born in Plymouth in England.
1690 Sep. 22 John the son of Jurien . . . . decesed.
1690 Oct. 14 Mr Hugh Rankon.
1690 Nov. 26 Elizabeth the wife of Thomas Burows.
1690 Mar. 18 Ruth the wife of John Robinson.
1691 May 28 Mr Epaphroditus Haughton.
1691 May 29 Joseph Wilcox.
1691 June 6 John Ditty.
1691 July 5 Thomas Moore.
1691 July 11 Lancelot Stepney, Gent.
1691 July 25 Edward Beane.
1691 July 28 Margaret the wife of William Kersey.
1691 Aug. 8 John Compton of Bristol.
1691 Sep. 4 Richard Deane.
1691 Sep. 7 Thomas Dyot (?).
1691 Sep. 7 R . . . . D. of William and Elizabeth Thurlan l—to say Hannah [*sic*].
1691 Oct. 6 Peter Carrove of New England.
1691 Sep. 11 John Stafford, Commander of the Satisfaction of Liverpool.
1691 Sep. 14 John Sutton of Prescot in Lancashire.
1691 Sep. 15 John Murch of Plymouth.
1691 Sep. 20 John Baker of Bristol.
1691 Sep. 29 James Hornby.
1691 Oct. 24 William Jobling, Mariner, born in Bristol, belonging to the Sucses of London.
1691 Oct. 30 Joseph Hacker, Commander the Sucses of London.
1691 Nov. 13 Joseph Prior.
1691 Nov. 27 Charles Biss, belonging to the Hopewel of Bristol.
1691 Dec. 29 Thomas Watts of Bristol.
1691 Mar. 14 Thomas Penington, born in London, nefeu to Thos. Belshamber, Esqr.
1692 April 26 Philip Hall.
1692 July 12 Erastus Reyerson.
1692 July 12 Mathew Barnett.
1692 Oct. 6 Thomas Cook.
1693 Aug. — Mr James Denby, Minister.
1693 Jan. 5 Captn Henry Cock.
1693 Jan. 30 John Poole of Boston in New England.
1694 June 4 Elizabeth the wife of Jno Evans.
1694 June 5 Charles Nelson.
1694 June 27 James Skinner, Commandr of the Mary of Liverpool.
1694 June 4 Richard Hyde of the Restoration, Saml Clavel, Comd.
1694 July 9 Richd Kindrick of London, Marcht.
1694 Aug. 12 John Kelly of Boston in New England.
1694 Aug. 26 Richard Liddall, Comand of the Fellowship of London.
1694 Oct. 27 William Mathis, Planter.
1694 Oct. 30 Samuel Jewitt of Ipswich.
1695 May 9 Hannah the wife of Thomas Stephens.
1695 Aug. 9 James the son of Archibald Markowen & Joan his wife.
1695 Sep. 3 Georg Ervin, Gent.
1695 Dec. 27 Humphrie Turel.
1696 April 20 Richd Loxley of the Bacon, Comand.

[Entries between July 1696 and Aug. 1700 are missing.]

1700 Feb. 20 Thomas Procter.
1701 May 29 Robert Collingwood, Major of his Majties Rijment of foot in ye Wt Indies.
1701 June 5 Richard s. of Lieut Thornton.
1701 June 11 John Fook, Marchat, from Mark Robersons.
1701 June 18 Robert Simson, Marchant.
1701 June 20 Robert Dove, Marchant with Mr How.
1701 June 25 Barbary Stutley, by Mr Pirce linch bury [*sic*].
1701 July 8 Captn Hays, Comd of the [*blank*].
1701 July 20 John Wilson, Mercht, belonging to Captn Wm Danviss, Comndr of ye Industry from Pensilvania.
1701 Aug. 11 Peter Dupin from New York, Surgeon.
1701 Aug. 23 Katherine at Dr Sweegles.
1701 Aug. 25 James Moore, on bord ye Oak, Captn John Searsbrick, from Liverpool.
1701 Sep. 14 Jasper s. of Peter Saverman and Eliz. his wife.
1701 Oct. 15 Mr Samll Lockwood, Apothecary.
1701 Jan. 1 Wm Beckquith, Dr.
1701 Jan. 17 Samll Hallier.
1701 Mar. 4 Sarah d. of Abraham Griffin & Eliz. his wife.
1701 Mar. 19 Captn John Bredgan, Comdr of ye Bridgwater, Frigot, from Guinea.

1702 Mar. 29 John Kaneer, Mercht.
1702 April 9 Captn John Cernish of ye betty, Sloop.
1702 April 25 Mr Gabriel Coxs, Mercht.
1702 April 25 Mr James Glassell of Dumfreese in Scotland, Mercht.
1702 June 4 Capt Abraham Evans, Comd of ye Humphrey, gally, of Bristoll, late from Guinea.
1702 June 5 Mr Richd Waller, gent. from Mr Duncombs.
1702 July .. Mr John Cook, Gentleman.
1702 July .. Mr William Walters, Surgeon on bord ye W . . . dston, Frigot, Capt Wm Fairbow, Comdr.
1702 July 28 Mr Jonah Jackson.
1702 July 28 Mr Archibald Campbell.
(? 1702 or 1703) Sep. 5 Eliz. wife of Capt Charles Kallahan.
(? 1702 or 1703) . . . . 31 Mr John Noble, Mercht.
(? 1702 or 1703) . . . . 10 Capt Philip Baryer . . . . from Boston.
(? 1702 or 1703) . . . . — Frederick s. of Dr David Sweegle.
(? 1702 or 1703) Mr Wm Biskers, Mercht.
James s. of John Rayne & Mary his wife.
Adrian Bennett, Genr.
Joseph s. of Samll Prossar & blanch his wife.
Mr Edwd Burrish.
Wm Murphy.
William Stripley, Genr.
Mr Benjamin . . . . oth.
James Thynne, Esqr.
Lawrence Murph . . . .
Edwd s. of Herculus Murphy & Ellinor his wife.
Robt Sear, Mercht.
Wm Childs, Planter.
1704 May 12 Ambrose Minchen, Gentleman.
1704 May 23 Mr Wm Christophers.
1704 Nov. 6 Mrs Bazill Buckeridge.
1704 Nov. 10 Mr Page Robinson.
1704 Nov. 23 Elizabeth D. of David Sweegle & Elizabeth his wife.
1704 Dec. 28 Captn Charles Bredgar.
1705 (? April) Mr Thomas Cox.
1705 June 20 Theophilus Bridger.
1705 July 4 Mr Thomas Hebbs.
1705 July 8 Sarah Hebbs.
1705 July 9 Mrs Mary Moore.
1705 July 19 John Dove.
1705 Aug. 3 Johannes Van Westhoven.
1705 Sep. 18 Mr Richard Tremain, Purser of ye Sheerness.
1705 Jan. 15 Mr Andrew Lundy.
1705 Jan. 16 Richd Glasson.
. . . . Feb. 22 Mr William Charter.
. . . . Aug. 18 Edward Cox.
. . . . Sep. 17 Mrs Rachell Philipps.
. . . . Nov. 14 John Howlett, Clergyman.
. . . . Feb. 2 Henry Hall, Mercht, belonging to ye Wm, Gally, Captn Parker, Comdr.
1706 Feb. 15 Walter Long.
1707 May 1 Hugh Bellass, a child.
1708 Oct. 15 Stephen Mummery, Comd of the Satisfaction.

(Rev. Philip Darby signs in margin.)

1709 Aug. 6 Mr John S. Plowman.
1709 Oct. 11 Mrs Bowless, buried out of this parish.
1709 Nov. 28 Martha Thorn.
1710 May 3 Margaret Raynesford.
1710 Oct. 14 Thomas Long.
1711 Aug. 26 Thomas Newell.
1711 Sep. 15 Samuel Walker.
1711 Oct. 1 Mary Cox.
1711 Nov. 20 Redmund Barrett.
1712 Aug. 23 Thomas Webster.
1712 Sep. 8 Mr Alea's Daughter.
1712 Jan. 1 Captn Watlington.
1713 June 16 Gertrude D. of Thos Fletcher.
1713 . . . . 24 Elizabeth Booth.
1714 Aug. 24 John Draken, Esq.
1714 Oct. 20 Mr Frampton.
1714 Dec. 4 Captn William Beard.
1714 Dec. 7 Captn Reav (?) Comd of the South river, merchant.
1714 Dec. 14 Captn Willm Skelton.
1714 Jan. 23 Captn Richd Jon . . . ., comd of the Grayhound.
1714 Mar. 15 Captn Gloster, whose ship was condemn'd here.
1715 Mar. 30 Captn Richd Dodge.
1715 June 30 Captn Wm Addison.
1715 Aug. 18 Mary Fitz Patrick, kill'd by the Indians.
1716 May 24 Captn Wm Cooke.
1716 Aug. 8 Mary Mercer.
1717 May 2 Nicholas Hillgrove.
1717 June 9 Caleb Lasher.
1717 July 1 Captn Stephen Curling.
1717 Aug. 9 Captn John Hamlin.
1717 Aug. 10 Captn John Vickerry.
1717 Oct. 6 Captn Jas. Clayton.
1717 Dec. 6 William Mascall.
1717 Mar. 14 William Wake.
1717 Mar. 27 Quintin Kenedy.
1718 Mar. 31 Captn Andrew Mitchell.
1718 April 19 Captn Josiah Harrison.
1718 May 1 Captn John Nennard.
1718 May 26 David Johnston.
1718 June 4 Jonathan Howard.
1718 July 19 Captn Richd Holland.
1718 Feb. 12 Mary Scott.
1719 April 26 Eliz. Stanton.
1720 July 17 Robert Watt (?).
1720 Sep. 19 John Murphy.
1720 Nov. 18 Henry Thornton.
1720 Dec. 2 Saml Brenan.
1720 Dec. 29 Henry James.
1720 Feb. 22 Eliz. Murphy, a child.
1721 Sep. 11 Captn Samuel Galpine.
1722 Mar. 30 Anthony Austin.
1722 April 21 Mr John Hewsen.
1722 April 24 Mrs Elizabeth Hastings.
1722 May 8 Mr Robert Toll.
1722 May 10 Mr John Dark, Mercht, of Captn Adam Clerke.
1722 June 5 Mr John Hoskins.
1722 July 23 Ensigne Peter Rupill.
1722 Sep. 18 Thomas Delamere.
1722 Sep. 24 Captn Thomas Watts.
1722 Sep. 30 Mr Obadiah Westmiucoate.
1722 Oct. 5 Rebecka Magan.
1722 Oct. 11 Capt. Samuel Hollyman, from Philadelphia.
1722 Nov. 6 Captn William Francis.
1722 Nov. 26 Mr Robert Milliken, a Waiter.
1722 Jan. 24 Dr Benjamin Rawleigh.
1722 Jan. 31 Mr John Fox.
1723 April 9 Mr James Rawleigh.
1723 May 28 [*blank*] wife of Mr Anthony Underwood.
1723 June 4 Capt John Done of Boston in New England.
1723 June 28 Mr Benjamin Bryant.

1723 July 25 Joan the wife of Christopher Comberlidge.
1723 Nov. 5 Mr Richard Harris.
1723 Nov. 7 Mr John Launder.
1723 Nov. 20 Erasmus s. of James Evans.
1723 Dec. 1 Mr William Hinde.
1723 Dec. 20 Mr Samuel Bryant.
1723 Jan. 10 Thomas Wallice.
1723 Jan. 23 James Lowe, late of this Island, Merct.
1723 Jan. 27 Capt John Bevan, from Bristoll.
1723 Feb. 26 Benjamin Flint.
1723 Mar. 13 Capt Peter Peters, from Philadelphia.
1723 Mar. 17 Mr Thomas Stevens, searchr.
1723 Mar. 24 Capt John Hews.
1724 April 23 Mrs Ann Gates.
1724 April 3 [*blank*] wife of Rev. Mr Connell Orr.
1724 June 26 Capt John Bowman, from London.
1724 July 16 Mr Thomas Raynolds.
1724 July 19 Mr Roger Legge.
1724 Aug. 9 Joseph Bryant, from Bristoll.
1724 Aug. 19 Hannah the wife of Capt John Harris.
1724 Aug. 20 Eliz. D. of John Jenkins.
1724 Aug. 21 Mrs Mary Chapman.
1724 Aug. 28 Mrs Jane Molls.
1724 Sep. 24 Joanna wife of Wm Thorne.
1724 Oct. 12 Mr John Stronge.
1724 Oct. 14 Capt Thomas Jackson, from London.
1724 Oct. 26 Sarah wife of Peter Walker.
1724 Nov. 15 Sarah Nicholson.
1724 Nov. 19 Drury Harris, one of the Duke of Montagu's servts.
1724 Dec. 7 Elizth wife of Philip Raynolds.
1724 Dec. 13 Eliz. D. of Samuel Bryant.
1724 Dec. 19 Eliz. the wife of Mr John Fyffe.
1724 Dec. 19 William Newell.
1724 Dec. 21 Mrs Mary Tofft.
1724 Jan. 21 Elizabeth Newell.
1724 Feb. 15 Wm s. of Wm Scott.
1724 Feb. 26 Capt John Moulton.
1724 Mar. 17 David Hews & his D.
1725 April 24 Mary the wife of John Stanton.
1725 Sep. 27 Thomas Rawleigh.
1725 Oct. 25 Margt D. of Margaret Bryant.
1725 Nov. 7 Doctr David Sweegle.
1725 Dec. 28 Ann Graham.
1725 Dec. 29 Bisse the D. of Mr Richard Sherwood.
1725 Jan. 20 Elizabeth widdow of Benjamin Rawleigh.
1725 Jan. 25 John Murphy.
1725 Feb. 3 Honour Sweeny.
1725 Feb. 16 Mrs Penelope Hassell.
1725 Feb. 18 Mrs Cadner, widdow
1725 Feb. 26 Mr William Kennedy.
1725 Mar. 12 Mr Thomas Pratchard, from Liverpool.
1725 Mar. 12 Capt Edward Houghton, from Guinea.
1726 May 5 Hazael Reynolds.
1726 Jan. . . Samuel s. of Cornelius Lawson.
1726 Feb. 8 Mrs Eliz. Theyer.
1727 April 21 Jane Hedges, a child.
1727 May 15 Jane D. of George Jenkins.
1727 May 24 James s. of Capt Ben. Hester.
1727 May 24 Alexander Green, formerly Commander of the Earl Gally.
1727 Aug. 16 Mr Rich. Burroughs.
1727 Oct. 24 Mary the D. of David Haycock.
1727 Nov. 13 Eliz. Sweegle, widow.
1727 Dec. 9 Jane the D. of David Haycock.
1727 Dec. 18 Mary D. of Mr Arthur Wilkinson.
1727 Dec. 29 Mr Patrick West of this Island, Merchant.
1727 Jan. 31 James s. of Thomas Reynolds.
1727 Mar. 9 Mary D. of Mr Philip Abram.
1728 May 10 Capt John Bush, from Bristoll.
1728 May 12 Capt John Ruggles, from Boston.
1728 May 17 Mrs Dorothy Wilson.
1728 Aug. 3 Mr Peter Hassell.
1728 Aug. 31 Mr John Beaty.
1728 Oct. 4 Mrs Mary Crow, widow
1728 Nov. 1 Mr Laurence Gregan.
1728 Nov. 7 Mr Edward Leigh, Comptroller of His Majesty's Customs in this Island.
1728 Nov. 9 Capt Richard Staples of London.
1728 Nov. 13 Mr William Barlow, belonging to the Lenox man of war.
1728 Nov. 21 Mr Benjamin Jeffries.
1728 Nov. 25 Margaret the wife of Mr James Falloone.
1728 Dec. 1 Mrs Lydia Steevens, widow.
1728 Dec. 10 Charlotte wife of Levey Guichard.
1728 Dec. 18 Mr Victor Chateneauf, Steward to the Earle of Londonderry.
1728 Jan. 2 Mr Thomas Ainsworth of this parish.
1728 Jan. 10 Barnabas Brabazon of this parish.
1728 Jan. 12 Thomas s. of Thomas Pierce.
1728 Feb. 14 Sarah wife of Emanuell Desilva.
1728 Feb. 16 Mr Thomas Pierce of this Island.
1728 Mar. 18 Mr Flann Ward, from Liverpoole.
1728 Mar. 27 Mr John Mortrue of London.
1729 April 18 Mrs Ann Bullock.
1729 May 5 Mrs Ann Burnash of this Island, widow.
1729 May 30 Mr John Cooper, from London.
1729 June 10 Mrs Catherine Kennedy, widow.
1729 June 2 Mr Thos Storey.
1729 July 12 Mary the D. of Mr Richd Sherwood.
1729 July 16 John Thompson, Bro. to the Lieu. of the Pearle.
1729 Aug. 8 The Reverend Mr Henry Husband, Minister of this Parish.
1729 Oct. 18 Francis Pierce.
1729 Nov. 12 Mary Scott.
1729 Nov. 15 Bartholomew Murphy.
1729 Nov. 24 William Thorne.
1729 Jan. 10 Mr Philip Reynolds.
1729 Jan. 20 Capt John Cowapp of Liverpool.
1729 Mar. 6 Mrs Eliz. Combes, who Dyed at St Eustatia.
1729 Mar. 9 Mary Austin.
1730 Mar. 31 Lydia Scarisbrick, widow.
1730 April 16 Mr William Lodge.
1730 May 26 Mr John Liott.
1730 June 11 Mrs Ann Storeye.
1730 June 28 Frances Goldsby, a child.
1730 Sep. 11 Mr James Evans.
1730 Oct. 13 Ann Anderton.
1730 Oct. 27 Mr Robert Henley.
1730 Oct. 28 Mrs Mary Brigg.
1730 Oct. 28 James Jenkins.
1730 Nov. 19 William Henry Spranger.
1730 Dec. 21 Charles Stanton.
1730 Jan. 24 Thomas Austin.
1730 Jan. 28 Capt Thomas Boyd.
1730 Feb. 1 Mr Thomas Core, from Liverpool.
1730 Mar. 25 Wm Jenkins, sould (*sic*, for "soldier").
1731 July 4 Mr Thomas Hancock, from Barbadoes.
1731 July 21 John Kennedy.
1731 July 30 Mr Arthur Dabron.
1731 Oct. 14 Peter Biggs.
1731 Nov. 16 Mr John Draper.
1731 Nov. 22 Thomas Rawleigh.
1731 Feb. 25 Mr Thos. Bullen.
1731 Mar. 26 Penelope Christophers.
1732 April 5 Mr John Shocknesses.
1732 July 9 Wm s. of Fran. Raines.
1732 Oct. 28 John Williamson.
1732 Nov. 25 Capt Daniell Beckman.
1732 Dec. 29 Mrs Sarah Bryne, widow.

1732	Feb.	7	Capt Edward Peyer (?).
1732	Mar.	9	Capt John Harlow.
1732	Mar.	14	James Arthur.
1732	Mar.	16	James Murphy.
1732	Mar.	27	Capt James Blair.
1733	May	3	Mr Peter Martinoe.
1733	May	29	Capt Robert Aulkins.
1733	Aug.	27	Mr Richard Baker.
1733	Sep.	9	Fanny Murphy, a child.
1733	Oct.	25	Mr John George.
1733	Nov.	8	Mrs Mary Tweedy.
1733	Nov.	27	Marianne Mascall, a child.
1733	Nov.	28	Mrs Anne Ridge.
[The Rev. Francis Byam first signs as Rector this year.]			
1733	Dec.	20	Mr Ernest Brincast.
1733	Jan.	28	Bryan McSweeny.
1733	Feb.	14	Mrs Eliz. Coppinger.
1733	Mar.	4	Mrs John Price.
1733	Mar.	8	Mr Willm Withington.
1733	Mar.	10	Rebecka wife of John Hugas.
1734	June	11	Capt Stephen Coffin.
1734	June	27	Capt John Wales.
1734	Sep.	2	Mr Thomas Benn.
1734	Sep.	18	Mr Edward Ragg.
1734	Sep.	25	Mr James Tyler.
1734	Oct.	2	John Kennedy.
1734	Oct.	9	Mr Thomas Clarke Daner.
1734	Oct.	15	Mr Robert Carrington.
1734	Oct.	19	Ensigne John Stewart.
1734	Nov.	24	Ann Murphy.
1734	Dec.	20	Edward Tankard Murphy, a child.
1734	Jan.	4	Mr James Crawley.
1734	....	8	Robert Laverack.
1734	Mar.	17	Eliz. Thompson, a child.
1735	April	6	Capt John Deshield.
1735	May	10	Mrs Catherine Lyell.
1735	May	12	Capt Phillip Grafferd.
1735	May	13	Mrs Jane Godsell.
1735	June	4	Capt John Partis.
1735	June	9	Mr Moses Cross.
1735	July	2	Mr John June.
1735	July	19	Mr James Evans.
1735	July	24	Catherine Rawleigh.
1735	Aug.	9	Mr Benjamin Harrold.
1735	Oct.	14	Capt Isaac Dickenson.
1735	Nov.	9	Capt Daniel Barber.
1735	Nov.	14	Mr John Wilkinson.
1735	....	19	Mr John Fogo, Merct.
1735	....	19	Mr Joseph Fruin.
1735	Dec.	21	Lawrence Scarsbrick.
1735	Mar.	26	Mr John Hugas of the Island.
1736	April	8	Capt Edward Kirk, from Cork.
1736	June	..	Capt. Mathew Shaw, Comd of the Ellen, from Bristoll.
1736	June	29	Mr William Chalmers, Merct, from Dublin.
1736	July	17	Capt Abraham Havely, from Waterford.
1736	July	22	Capt Jacob Wane, from Philadelphia.
1736	Oct.	14	Christian the D. of John Jenkins, decd.
1736	Oct.	23	Lydia the D. of Capt Syer Alicock.
1736	Dec.	14	Mr John Booth of this Island.
1736	Jan.	12	Capt William Belcher, from Maryland.
1736	Jan.	18	Mrs Sarah Strong of this Island, widow.
1736	Jan.	23	Ann D. of Hugh Peard.
1736	Jan.	31	Capt James Adean of Saint Christopher's.
1736	Mar.	12	Mrs Elizabeth Crawley, widow.
1736	Mar.	12	Capt Owen Arnald of Bristoll.
1736	Mar.	18	William Wyne, Esqr, of this Island.
1736	Mar.	22	Mr Upton Hassell of this Island.
1737	April	1	Elizabeth wife of Mr Michael Devereux.
1737	Aug.	31	Mary Murphy of this Island.
1737	Nov.	12	Robert Bryant of this Island.
1737	Dec.	9	Capt Benjamin Horskins, from Philadelphia.
1737	Feb.	10	Capt John Prentice.
1737	Mar.	24	John ye s. of Capt John Baker, from Boston.
....	Mar.	25	Capt John Baker, from Boston.
1738	April	10	Capt Henry Macmorraine, from Dublin.
1738	April	14	Russell Tankerd ye D. of Edward Murphy.
1738	April	19	Elias Dumaresque, Nephew to Capt Pipon.
1738	April	27	Capt John Chapman, consigned to Thomas Shephard.
1738	May	3	Capt Daniel Parsons, from Cape Ann.
1738	June	15	James ye S. of Capt James Flucker, from Boston.
1738	June	25	Capt Richard Carling, from London.
1738	June	29	Edward Loyd, Merchant, from Philadelphia.
1738	July	13	Margaret ye D. of William Dickenson.
1738	Aug.	3	Capt Allan Farrington, from Liverpool.
1738	Aug.	9	Capt James Hall, from Glasgow.
1738	Sep.	26	Sweegle s. of John Reynolds.
1738	Dec.	17	James Mackie, merchant.
1738	Nov.	12	Capt Richard Bowen, from Corke.
1738	Mar.	14	William Bird, Mercht, of this Island.
1739	May	7	Capt Robert McCombe, from Dublin.
1739	June	25	Alexander Findlay, merchant, from Dublin.
1739	July	9	Andrew Moncrief, from New England.
1739	July	12	Margaret ye wife of Cap. Bouchier.
1739	July	22	David Haycock, Pilot, of this Island.
1739	July	30	James Lowther, Marchant, from Glascow.
1739	Aug.	19	James Ashley, Ensign of the Regiment.
1739	Sep.	6	Capt Isaiah Townsend.
1739	Oct.	27	Capt John Robertson, from South Carolina.
1739	Dec.	17	Capt. Edwin Steevens, master of ye General's Sloop.
1740	Mar.	30	Rebecka Reynolds, widow.
1740	April	8	Robert Menzies, Surgeon of Capt Richard Nichols, from Guinea.
1740	April	8	Capt. John Scott, whose ship was cast away on ye reefe.
1740	Sep.	14	Capt James FitzPatrick, from Ireland.
1740	Oct.	16	Peter Lyott of this Island.
1740	Dec.	31	Henry Laine.
1740	Jan.	2	Capt James England.
1740	Jan.	19	Christian Jenkins.
1740	Jan.	25	Samuel Mascall s. of Thos. Mascall.
1740	Feb.	28	Thomas Benson.
1741	July	20	Thomas Stephens, Mercht.
1741	Oct.	25	Capt Boucher.
1742	July	21	Christopher Scandret.
1742	Jan.	3	Francis Woodward, Doctor of Capt Edward Coulter.
1742	Feb.	6	Strong Michael Grigore s. of Capt Thomas Grigore.
1743	May	29	Capt Richard Crispin.
1743	June	5	Capt James McAlpin.
1743	June	25	Capt William Trimble.
1743	July	20	John Bertles, a lawyer.
1743	July	28	Capt Zachariah Parratt.
1743	Oct.	21	William Ewin.
1743	Nov.	8	Elizabeth Jenkins, a child.
1743	Dec.	29	Leonard Turnbull, a child.
1743	Jan.	29	Ann England, a child.
1744	April	7	Robert Bryant.
1744	April	23	Capt James Hastey.
1744	May	30	Mr John Tysse.
1744	July	18	Capt Paul De Lafrale.
1744	Dec.	12	Ann Stanton.
1744	Dec.	19	Capt William Blinn, from Boston.

1745, April 15, Here Rev. Mr Whitford, Rector, began.

1745 May 27 John Thomas Booth, a child.
1745 July 6 Capt Moses Prince.
1745 Aug. 18 Capt Henry Dixon.
1745 Oct. 3 Thomas Mascall.
1745 Nov. 14 Samuel Liott, a child.
1745 Nov. 14 Mary Hugas, widow.
1745 Nov. 27 Ann Mascall, a child.
1745 Jan. 15 John Christophers.
1745 Jan. 23 Thomas Dickenson.
1746 July 27 Joanna Stanton.
1746 Aug. 2 Capt Edward Evans.
1746 Oct. 29 Capt John Gibbs.
1746 Nov. 13 Christopher Seely.
1746 Jan. 29 Mary Reynolds.
1746 Feb. 4 Lieut Francis Ruffane.
1747 April 14 Capt . . . . Morrison.
1747 May 5 . . . . Jenkins, a child.
1747 May 14 Capt Cornelius McNamarra.
1747 May 19 Capt Stephen Maylor.
1747 May 28 Capt Tho. Barrow.
1747 June 1 Capt Richard Leigh.
1747 June 19 Capt Benjamin Holmes.
1747 July 11 James Bolitho, in the country.
1747 July 27 Eliz. Mears, wife of Docr Mears.
1747 Nov. 11 Capt Edward Hubbard.
1747 Dec. 18 The Revd Mr James Berry.
1747 Dec. 14 . . . . Bowers D. of Capt Henry Bowers.
1748 May 23 Capt Richard Ball.
1748 Nov. 18 Capt Elias Shipman.
1748 Dec. 16 Capt Thomas Perkins.
1748 Jan. 11 Mrs . . . . Medcalf.
1749 April 12 John Dickinson.
1749 June 10 Capt John Ditchburn.
1749 June 30 Capt Abraham Trissior.
1749 Dec. 3 Marian Jenkins, a child.
1749 Jan. 11 Capt Thos. Fell.
1749 Jan. 26 Edwd Hubberd, s. of Capt Edwd Hubberd.
1749 Jan. 27 Albert Marance, a sailor of Capt Ellary's.
1750 July 31 William Bruce, Ensign of his Majty's Regt.
1750 Aug. 24 Joseph Langley, a child.
1750 Aug. 31 John Jeffries, a child of Docr Jeffries.
1750 Sep. 4 William Graham, Mercht.
1750 Oct. 20 William Jenkins.
1750 Nov. 29 Margt Senegat, wife of James Senegat.
(?1751) Feb. 1 Capt William Round.
(?1751) Mar. 11 Capt John Strong.
(?1751) Mar. 18 Charles Alley, Merchant.
1751 Sep. 28 Israel Desilvia.
1752 Feb. 23 Mary Delamare.
1752 May 1 John Tomlins.
1752 June 12 Benjamin Ramsey.
1752 July 12 Sarah Byrne, wife of Patrick Byrne's.
1752 Aug. 29 John Brenan.
1754 June 23 Capt John Baker.
1754 June 28 Edward Reily.
1754 Sep. 26 Geo. Frederick Nassau Piers.
1754 Oct. 1 John Tudhope (Carpr).
1754 Dec. 16 Lieut Samuel Baker.
1754 Dec. 21 Docr Duncan Campbell.
1755 May 19 Joseph Baptist De Piers.
1755 June 29 Thomas Burges.
1755 Aug. 14 Capt John Hoult.
1755 Sep. 6 Thos Mascall.
1755 Oct. 2 Frances Ramsay, a Child.
1755 Nov. 28 Elizabeth Cumberbatch, a Child.
1756 Feb. 13 John Langley.
1756 Feb. 24 Ancey Warlock, a Child.

[The burials of 50 or 60 French are recorded in March and April.]

1756 Aug. 1 Capt John Peisly.
1756 Aug. 22 Revd Wm. Topham.
1756 Sep. 14 William Washington.
1756 Oct. 12 Lieut. Thomas Crooke.
1756 Oct. 12 Capt Wm Fanchion.
1756 Nov. 20 Docr Richard Chancellor.
1756 Nov. 24 John Chalmers.
1756 Nov. 28 Charles St Ledger.
1757 Mar. 15 Capt Philip Styth.
1757 Mar. 16 Capt Taylor.
1757 Aug. 8 Capt Wm. Ball.
1757 Sep. 4 Capt Wm Cop.
1757 Sep. 19 Christopher Fawcet, late of Bowden in the County of Durham, Esqr, and Barrister at Law.
1757 Nov. 3 Capt Alexr Duchar.
1757 Nov. 16 Capt Wm. Venning.
1758 Feb. 15 Doctr Nilme Randall.
1758 Mar. 1 Jno Campbell, servt to Thos Jarvis, Esqr.
1758 April 24 Mr Kirkby, King's Hospl.
1758 April . . Capt Nicholas Southworth of the Pompadour, from Guinea.
1758 May 24 Capt Huyliger, a Dutch Man.
1758 June 11 Capt Edmund Agars.
1758 June 27 Capt Wills.
1758 June 29 Capt Goud Appell (Dutchman).
1758 July 8 Scott, Brother to Capt Scott (Chester).
1758 Aug. 2 Mrs Wilkinson, Relict of Arthr Wilkinson.
1758 Sep. 30 Ensign Kincade in ye Barrack Ground.
1758 Oct. 16 William Keagle, Surgeon of the Weasell.
1758 Oct. 20 Mrs Gibson.
1758 Oct. 25 Thomas Stevens, an Officer.
1758 Nov. 26 Mr Winterburn, Mastr of ye Buckingham.
1758 Dec. 14 Capt House.
1758 Dec. 26 Capt Alexr Campbell of H.M.S. Rye, from the Coast of Guinea.
1759 Jan. 1 Capt John Winchester.
1759 Feb. 18 Mrs Bowers.
1759 Feb. 21 Doctr James Boag.
1759 Feb. 26 Capt R. Jack (at the Barrack Ground).
1759 Mar. 2 Lieutenant Walker (at ye Barrack Grd).
1759 May 29 Capt Hugh Stevens.
1759 May 29 Lieut George Sinclair (Barracks).
1759 June 25 Mr McCombes.
1759 . . . . . . Capt Champion.
1759 June 27 Madera Wyne.
1759 Aug. 14 Doctor Robert Nicholson in the Barrk Ground.
1759 Sep. 5 Doctor Renton.
1759 Sep. 10 Doctor Roar.
1759 Sep. 30 Doctor Thompson.
1759 Oct. 4 Ann Dickinson. C.
1759 Oct. 16 Harry Alexander (a Child of E. Oisterman's).
1759 Nov. 27 Capt William Murphy.
1760 Feb. 18 Capt John Garraway.
1760 Mar. 12 Thomas Barry.
1760 April 8 Capt Elligood.
1760 May 27 Capt James Barratt.
1760 June 21 Thomas Shout (Surgeon).

1760, Nov. 10, Rev. Mr Hopkins begins here.

1760 Nov. 24 Mrs Guichard. P.
1760 Nov. 29 Capt Edward Thompson.
1760 Dec. 28 Mrs Benson.
1761 June 2 Jos. Downs, Lieut of the Lancaster.
1761 Aug. 17 Capt John Dickinson.
1761 Oct. 30 Capt John Leacraft.
1762 June 1 Capt Blanch.
1762 June 9 Capt John Boyd. P.
1762 June 18 Capt Rothery. G. P.
1762 July 11 An officer (Robert McCray). G.

1763 Nov. 1 An officer, Isaac Githin. P.G.
1763 Oct. 7 Doct^{r} Neil Campbell.
1763 Dec. 12 Lieu^{t} John Hardy. G.
1764 Feb. 12 Margarett Mascall.
1764 Feb. 18 George Mercer.
1764 April 1 Capt Andrew McCrae. G.P.
1764 April 6 Mansfeild Ord.
1764 July 23 Lieu^{t} Stafford. G.P.
1764 Aug. 16 Lieu^{t} Wm Melvile. G.P.
1764 Oct. 11 Capt Kilgore.
1764 Nov. 1 Capt James Somervile.
1764 Nov. 5 Lieu^{t} James Munro. G.P.
1765 Feb. 25 Captn Edmund Jenny. P.
1765 April 14 Ensign John Loyd.
1765 May 20 Capt Richard Navill. P.G.
1765 May 21 Capt David Caldwell. P.
1765 June 4 Capt William Dean. P.G.

1765, July 8, Rev. Mr John Gately begins here.

1765 Nov. 7 Doc^{r} James Thomson. P.
1766 Jan. 17 Capt Seth Chapman.
1766 Feb. 1 Capt James Berry. C.P.
1766 Mar. 20 Capt Richard Leacraft. P.
1766 May 21 Lieu^{t} Parks of the 68th Regiment. P.
1766 June 15 Argaile Dalrumple, Officer of the 68th Regiment.
1766 July 13 Cap^{n} Pullens. P.G.
1766 Sep. 28 Capt Loyd.
1766 Oct. 5 Capt John McFarlane. G.P.
1767 Jan. 25 Revd Mr David Hopkins, Rector.

1767, Feb. 7, Rev. Mr Bowen begins here.

1767 July 6 Henry Kirby, Lieut. in the 68th Reg^{t}. P.
1767 Oct. 5 John Turnbull, Lieut. in the 68th Regiment. P.
1767 Nov. 5 Alexander Duncan, a Guinea Surgeon.
1767 Nov. 15 Dominick Quinn.
1767 Dec. 15 Capt Joseph West.
1767 Dec. 20 Peter Sabsanl, a Guinea Doct^{r}. C^{y}.P.
1768 Feb. 3 Capt James Strangways. P.C^{y}.
1768 Feb. 26 Simon Branskum, a Capt. C^{y}.
1768 Mar. 23 Capt Thomas Watts. C^{y}.
1768 June 19 Capt James Clinton. C^{y}.P.
1768 July 8 John Price, a Capt.
1768 Oct. 31 Sarah Irvin, Widdow. C.P.
1768 Nov. 7 Capt Thos Dennison. C^{y}.P.
1768 Nov. 11 Samuel Welch, an Officer in the 68th Regim^{t}. P.
1768 Dec. 19 Rebecca Booth. Ag^{d} 96 Years. C.P.
1769 Jan. 4 Susanah Murrain. Ag^{d} 82. C.P.
1769 Feb. 6 Watkin Loyd, Ensign in the 68th Reg^{t}. P.
1769 May 3 Capt Edward Tew. P.
1769 Sep. 22 Aron Ward. Aged 95 Years. P.
1769 Nov. 23 Capt Joseph Poole.
1770 Jan. 28 Joseph Proctor.
1770 Jan. 30 Lodowick Lisle.
1770 April 19 William Oliver, a Sailor.
1770 Nov. 30 Ann Massey.
1771 Feb. 27 Mary Crook.
1772 Jan. 18 Ann Byrne.
1772 Jan. 23 . . . . Ramsay.
1772 Oct. 2 Nicholas Adser.
1772 July 17 Joseph Frewen.
1773 Jan. 27 Simon Long.
1773 April 19 Thomas Alfleck Wade Hall.
1773 April 24 Sarah Ramsay.
1774 June 3 William Ryley.
1774 June 4 Richard Reily.
1774 July 28 Robert Lowther.
1774 Oct. 18 Mary Tudhope.
1775 Feb. 16 Benjamin Ailhaud.
1775 April 2 Julian Grandidier.
1775 Aug. 25 Elizabeth Brennan.
1775 Sep. 13 John Walsh.
1775 Nov. 4 Sarah Pellow.
1776 Feb. 10 Capt William Gillies.
1776 Feb. 25 Capt Thomas Tew.
1776 Mar. 7 Sarah Buckley Beech.
1776 Aug. 21 Capt John Gillston.
1776 Oct. 10 Rachel Dam.
1776 Oct. 20 Capt Samuel Green.
1777 Jan. 30 Capt John Hall.
1777 April 1 Eliz. Blizard Keyzar.
1777 Dec. 20 Capt William Robinson.
1778 April 28 Capt Arthur Hollett.
1778 Aug. 14 James Rogers.
1778 Nov. 26 John Crispe.
1778 Dec. 18 Rev. James Somerville.
1779 Jan. 12 Capt David Kinnear.
1779 May 1 Capt John Campbell.
1779 Aug. 16 George Massey.
1779 Oct. 18 Capt James Taplay.
1779 Dec. 19 Samuel Bradstreet, Maj^{r} of 40th Regiment.
1779 Dec. 28 Capt Thomas Stable.
1780 Jan. 5 William Garnier.
1780 Jan. 15 Capt John Bennett.
1780 Jan. 28 Ann Beech.
1780 April 7 John Revel.
1780 April 30 Capt John Corrigall.
1780 Aug. 15 Archibald Campbell.
1781 Jan. 1 Penelope Crispe.
1781 Feb. 20 Claud Henderson.
1781 April 3 Thomas Cater, Lieu^{t} of his Maj$^{ty's}$ 40th Regim^{t}.
1781 April 3 William Dickinson, Senior.
1781 May 1 Capt Duncan Campbell.
1781 Aug. 2 David Jennings (Surgeon).
1781 Aug. 6 Benjamin Griffin (Surgeon).
1781 Aug. 11 Capt William Robinson.
1781 Sep. 1 Capt Francis Daunt.
1781 Sep. 16 Richd Forster, Ensign of his Maj$^{ty's}$ 28th Reg^{t}.
1781 Sep. 21 Capt William Mackie.
1781 Dec. 1 Capt John Cathcart of his Maj$^{ty's}$ 28th Regiment.
1781 Dec. 7 Lieu^{t} John Campbell, Lieu^{t} of his Maj$^{ty's}$ 55 Reg^{t}.
1781 Dec. 8 Lieu^{t} Thomas Irvin.
1781 Dec. 21 Samuel Newell.
1781 Dec. 28 Christiana Ross.
1782 Jan. 4 James Hay (Merchant).
1782 June 4 Richard Thomas, first Lieutenant of His Majesty's Ship Lizard.
1782 July 10 Lieutenant Babbinton of the 55th Regiment.
1782 July 10 Doctor Archibald Ramsay.
1782 July 18 William Hay the Infant S. of James Hay, deceas'd.
1782 Aug. 10 Owen Connor.
1782 Aug. 17 Thomas Regan, first Lieutenant to his Majesty's Ship Magicienne.
1782 Sep. 29 Captain Rutherford.
1783 Jan. 24 Captain Portins.
1783 Mar. 14 Thomas Hogan.
1783 Mar. 20 William Ewing the Merchant.
1783 July 8 Lauchland Ramsay Warlock.
1783 Aug. 3 Jane McConnell, an Infant.
1783 Aug. 8 Gilbert McConnell, an Infant.
1783 Aug. 10 Mrs Jane McConnell.
1783 Aug. 20 M^{rs} McCray.
1783 Aug. 29 Captain Hugh Curthbert.
1784 Jan. 1 Hugh McPherson.

1784 Jan. 16 Henrietta Ross the Infant D. of David Ross, Merch^{t}.

1784 April 17 Samuel Thompson (Planter).

1784 April 29 Mr Thomas Beardsley (Planter).

1784 Oct. 25 George Ross, Infant S. of George Ross.

1784 Dec. 3 Joseph Higgins, Infant.

1785 Mar. 3 Anne Laforey Mascall (Infant).

1785 June 22 Ann Ripingale.

1785 Aug. 5 John Bird (planter).

1785 Oct. 21 George Ross, Inf.

1786 June 20 Edmund M. Mascall.

1786 Oct. 5 George Simpson (Capt).

1786 Oct. 11 John Wade (Captain Engineers).

1786 Dec. 29 Captain Conner. P.C.

1787 Jan. 25 John Holton Warlock (Planter).

1787 Jan. 26 Aaron Jesse (Planter).

1787 Mar. 25 Thomas Mercer.

1787 Nov. 13 John Glanfield.

1788 Sep. 23 Doctor Corse.

(? 1789) April 25 Doctor Francis.

(? 1789) June 16 Capt John Moore.

1790 April 19 Andrew M^{c}pherson.

1790 May 25 Mary M^{c}pherson.

1794 July 30 Mad^{le} De Braglogne.

1794 Aug. 9 Edmund Bower, Lieut. 30th Reg.

1794 Aug. 11 George Gowan, Merchant.

1794 Aug. 15 Capt John Townsend.

1794 Sep. 29 Madam Marie M. C. St Luce.

1794 Oct. 10 Madam St Rose.

1794 Nov. 4 Michael Creigh, Lieu. 39th Reg.

1794 Nov. 25 Capt. John Hinson.

1794 Dec. 3 Jean Mathieu De Calmetz.

1794 Dec. 4 Magdelain Lucrece Barreau De Muratel De Calmetz.

1794 Dec. 10 Barret De Nazaris.

1794 Dec. 15 Alexandre Rene Fremon Duboussay.

1794 Dec. 15 Lewis Benjamin De Calmetz.

1794 Dec. 15 Charles Ross, Merchant.

1794 Dec. 16 Etienne David De Calmetz.

1795 Feb. 23 Elizabeth Walsh, Infant. P.P.

1796 Oct. 26 David Conyers.

1797 June 12 John Robertson, M.D.

1797 June 15 Edmund Osborne Mascall.

1797 Aug. 16 James Hay.

1798 June 18 John Garside, Capt 59th Reg.

1798 July 16 James Hannah, Lieu^{t} 59th Reg.

1798 Aug. 19 Alexander Dover (Col^{o} of Artillery).

1799 Mar. 15 Elizabeth Keyzar.

1799 Dec. 28 Robert McKinlay, Merchant.

1800 July 3 George Bowen, Mid. H.M. Ship Gaitie.

1802 Oct. 15 Samuel Pigott Gore, Infant.

1802 Nov. 13 Bernard Lenaghan.

1803 Aug. 20 Nathaniel Welch (at Dickinson's Bay).

1804 Mar. 30 Joseph Bolton, Surg^{n} Prince Ernest Packett.

1804 May 22 William Kion, L^{t} 7th Reg^{t}.

1804 June 18 Alexander Macpherson.

1804 Aug. 23 Doctor Evans, 70th Reg^{t}.

1804 Oct. 27 Joseph Nicoll, L^{t} 70 Reg^{t}.

1805 Mar. 15 Henry Byrne. P.P.

1805 Mar. 17 Mary Byrne.

1805 May 31 Mathew Quin.

1805 Sep. 12 David Kennedy, Jun.

1805 Oct. 26 William Spaight (Capt 70th Reg.).

1806 Jan. 7 Caleb F. Wood (Capt 70th Reg.).

1806 Jan. 9 James Pritchard.

1807 Sep. 28 John Desilvia.

(? 1808) July 31 Samuel Darrell, Sen.

(? 1808) Aug. 1 The Revd Francis Massett.

(? 1808) April 7 Margaret McPherson.

1808 Nov. 23 Archibald Campbell, Lieut. 60th Reg.

1808 Nov. 26 Francis Madeheim, Ass^{t} Surgeon 60th Reg.

1808 Dec. 19 Mary Darrell.

1809 Jan. 9 Ann Lynch Whitlock, Infant.

1809 Aug. 30 Samuel Pettierew.

1810 Aug. 13 Avis Hardenbrook.

1810 Aug. 15 Susannah Hardenbrook.

1810 Aug. 28 Thomas Hardenbrook.

1810 Sep. 13 Patrick Barry. P.P.

1811 . . . . . . Charles Chester Fitch, Infant.

(? 1813) Oct. 15 Amaza Thayer.

8 June 1814 this Register Book closed.

On a loose half-sheet :—

. . . . Doc^{r} John Grahame.

. . . . Jan. 10 Capt Thomas Adams.

[The second Book is a narrow, thick one, containing baptisms, marriages, and funerals, 1814 to 1826.]

1815 Oct. 19 John Ledger, Merchant.

1815 Oct. 30 John Hall, Merchant.

1815 Nov. 5 Joseph Darrell, Merchant.

1816 July 31 David Craige, Surgeon.

1816 Aug. 17 Revd John Lewis (Methodist Missionary).

1819 Nov. 4 His Excellency Lieutenant General George William Ramsay, late Captain General and Governor in Chief over His Majesty's Islands Antigua, Montserrat, Berbuda, etc.

[The third Book commences 1827 and ends 1849.]

On 2 Jan. 1828 was interred the first body in the new burial-ground attached to the glebe.

Monumental Inscriptions.

St. John's Cathedral.

On the north wall, plain marble tablet :—TO THE MEMORY OF | THE REV^{D} WILLIAM THOMAS BERNARD, A.B. | OF TRINITY COLLEGE DUBLIN, | LATE CURATE OF THIS PARISH, | WHERE AFTER A SHORT RESIDENCE OF FOUR MONTHS | IN THE FAITHFUL EXERCISE OF HIS MINISTRY, AND | THE MANIFESTATION OF MUCH PRIVATE WORTH, | HE DIED OF FEVER NOV. 2ND 1835 | IN THE 26TH YEAR OF HIS AGE, | MOST DEEPLY AND GENERALLY REGRETTED | THIS TRIBUTE OF ESTEEM AND AFFECTION | IS ERECTED | PARTLY BY HIS MUCH AFFLICTED SISTER | ELLEN M. BAYLY, | AND PARTLY BY THE RIGHT REVEREND WILLIAM HART COLERIDGE D.D. | LORD BISHOP OF THIS DIOCESE | THE CLERGY OF ANTIGUA AND OTHER FRIENDS IN THE | ISLAND, WHO MOURN OVER HIS EARLY REMOVAL.

On a shield beneath the above :—

Arms : Quarterly, in the first, ... *a bear rampant, collared.*

Motto : [*Bear an*]*d forbear.* (Part broken off.)

On the east wall of north transept, plain marble tablet :—IN MEMORY | OF | JOSEPH LIGGINS,* ESQ^{RE} | THE PROPRIETOR OF CLARE HALL, | LYONS AND FFRYES ESTATES IN THIS ISLAND | AND FOR NEARLY FORTY YEARS | A MERCHANT CONNECTED WITH THE COLONY. | HE DIED AT HIS RESIDENCE AT KENSINGTON, | GREATLY RESPECTED, | ON THE 22ND JUNE 1860, | AGED 69 YEARS. | HIS REMAINS | LIE IN KENSAL GREEN CEMETERY, LONDON.

Above is a shield bearing (see the duplicate M.I. in St. Philip's Church) :

Crest : *A demi-lion rampant, couped.*

Motto : *Be just and fear not.*

* Eliza dau. of Henry Liggins, Esq., of 3 Ladbroke Square and Antigua, mar. 1881 Francis E. Clayton, and died 1882 ('Baronetage').

In south transept, on a marble scroll:—To the Memory of | Agnes Morrison, | the beloved wife of | Donald McK Morison, | Merchant of this City. | Born at Edinr 14th June, 1822, | And died here 18th May, 1853. (Six lines follow.)

In south transept, on south wall, on a white marble tablet:—TO | THE MEMORY OF | ROBERT PEDDIE, | SURGEON, | NATIVE OF KELSO IN ROXBURGHSHIRE, N.B. | WHO DIED IN THIS ISLAND | ON THE XVI DAY OF NOVEMBER A.D. MDCCCXLI, | AT THE AGE OF XLI YEARS.

(Sixteen lines follow.)

Below on a shield:—

Arms: *Quarterly: 1 and 4, Argent, three martlets . . . . ; 2 and 3, a lion rampant . . . .*

Crest: *On a cap of maintenance, turned up with ermine, a lion's head erased.*

Motto: *True to the end.*

IN MEMORY OF | ARTHUR TEAGLE | WHO DEPARTED THIS LIFE | ON THE 20TH NOVEMBER 1839. | AGED 43 YEARS.

On a loose shield lying in the church:—

Arms: *A chevron sable between three birds (? choughs) . . . .*

Crest: *A bird.*

Motto: *Fidelis usque ad mortem.*

Below the central east window:—

THIS WINDOW IS PLACED BY A FEW FRIENDS WITH RESPECT AND AFFECTION TO THE MEMORY OF THE RIGHT REVD D. G. DAVIS FIRST BISHOP OF ANTIGUA.

On a shield are apparently his arms:—*Or, two crossed shank-bones between four eagles displayed.* On the north window are the Episcopal Arms:—*On a chief gules a key and pastoral staff crossed, surmounted by a crown.* On the sinister side:—*Argent, a cross gules between a serpent and dove.*

St. John's Churchyard.

On a headstone:—SACRED | TO | THE MEMORY OF | CHARLES ALEXANDER | A NATIVE OF SCOTLAND | AND LATE | A MERCHANT IN THIS CITY | WHO DEPARTED THIS LIFE | ON THE 11TH DECEMBER 1860 | AGED 38 YEARS | LEAVING A WIDOW AND INFANT CHILD | TO LAMENT HIS LOSS | AND SINCERELY REGRETTED BY HIS | NUMEROUS FRIENDS AND | ACQUAINTANCES.

On a white marble headstone:—SACRED | To the memory of | ANN JANE | The beloved Wife of PAUL AUSTIN | of the City of Bath and of this | Island Planter and eldest daughter | of the late G. W. H. GREGORY ESQR. | She departed this Life July 20th 1841 | Aged 27 Years.

On a headstone:—*In Memory | of | William Baird | who died the 26 July | 1779 | Aged 35 years.*

On a ledger:—Here lies Interred the Body of | MR THOMAS BARRY Merchant | who departed this Life March the | 12, 1760, Aged 38 Years.

On a stone altar-tomb:—SACRED | TO THE MEMORY OF | GEORGE BEARE, ESQ | LATE COLLECTOR OF HER MAJESTYS CUSTOMS | OF THE ISLAND OF ANTIGUA | DIED JULY 31, 1867 | AGED 56 YEARS.

Here lies the Body of Mathew | Bernard late a Merchant of | London who departed this life | January ye 23rd 1775 Aged 58 Years.

On a ledger:—SACRED | TO THE MEMORY OF | CHARLOTTE WALTER BENNETT | who died 11th Oct. 1835, of Yellow fever | aged 24 after a residence of | only 10 months in this Island | She was third daughter of the | late JOHN BENNETT, Secretary of | LLoyds, and Sister of John Bennett | Merchant of this Island.

On an altar tomb:—Here lyeth the Body of the Reverend | MR JAMES BERRY a Younger Son | of a Reputable and Genteel Family | in the County of Kildare | in the Kingdom of Ireland | Edvcated in the Vniversity of Dublin | and for Nine Years preceding his Death | Rector of Saint *George's* Parish | in this Ifland (fifteen lines follow) and Died Greatly lamented by all that | knew him on the Eleventh of December 1747 | in the 39th Year of his Age. | He married MARGARET Eldeft Daughter | of RICHARD SHERWOOD Efqr | who . . . . | Hath Erected this Monument.

On a ledger near north door:—Here Lyeth the Body of | Captn James Berry of Liver . . . . | who Died in the 34th Year of his | Age 1766.

On a headstone:—Here Lieth the Body of | James Bowyer | *departed this Life* | the 8 of October 1772 | Aged 36 years.

On a headstone:—SACRED | TO THE MEMORY OF | ELIZA ANN | ALLAWAY BILLINGHURST | WHO DIED | ON THE 5TH OF FEBRUARY 1861 AGED 18 YEARS.

(Five lines follow.)

On a headstone:—IN MEMORY | OF | ALEXR T. BILLINGHURST | WHO DEPARTED THIS LIFE ON | 12 FEBRUARY 1859 | AGED 21 YEARS.

On a ledger:—In Memory of Capt THOMAS BOYD | Mariner Late of Ratcliff in the | Parifh of Stepney LONDON in old | England he Died ye 27 : of Jany | 1730-31 Aged 69 Years. (Four lines follow.)

On a headstone:—In Memory of | an affectionate Brother | JOHN THOMAS BRAND | Interr'd beneath this stone | Octr 26th 1856 | Aged 44 Years.

On a headstone:—Here Lies the Body | of IAMES and IOHN | BRENNAN Born in ye | County of CARLO in | IRELAND IAMES Died | Sepr ye 24th 1743 Aged | 48.

(Remainder buried in earth.)

On a headstone:—IN MEMORY | OF | ELIZA BUNCH | . . . . | DEPAR . . . . LIFE | AUGU . . . . 95 | AGD . . . .

On a brick tomb:—Sacred to the Memory of | Mrs Elizabeth Buntin | Wife of John Buntin Esquire | who departed this life the 17th Sept 1866 | Aged 26 years.

(Eight lines follow.)

On a headstone:—MILLICENT BURNS | DIED 23TH DECEMBER 1859 | AGED 21 YEARS.

ELIZ. C. CARTER | *WIDOW* | OF LIEUT. COL. W. CARTER | . . . . INDIA REGT | DIED 27 JUNE 1807 | AGED 36 YEARS.

SACRED | TO | THE MEMORY OF THE | REVD JOHN CHILDE | CURATE OF ST LUKE'S . | RESPECTED, ADMIRED, BELOVED . | HE WAS CUT OFF IN THE MIDST OF A LIFE OF | INCREASING USEFULNESS AND ACCEPTANCE, | AFTER ONE DAYS ILLNESS, DECR 26TH 1866, | AGED 34 YEARS.

On a large ledger:—SACRED TO THE MEMORY OF | THOMAS CHAMBERS ESQR | MANY YEARS BARRISTER AT LAW | IN THE ISLAND OF MONTSERRAT | WHO DEPARTED THIS LIFE THE 20TH JULY 1828, | IN THE 87TH YEAR OF HIS AGE, | DEEPLY LAMENTED BY HIS NUMEROUS PROGENY | AND UNIVERSALLY REGRETTED | BY HIS ACQUAINTANCES. | THIS MONUMENT WAS ERECTED BY | HIS AFFECTIONATE AND ONLY SURVIVING CHILD | ELIZA ROBERTSON.

(Eighteen lines follow.)

On a headstone:—IN MEMORY of | Jonathan Eldeft Son | of Mr Jonathan Chefe- | brough and B . . . d . . . . t | his Wife who d . . . . | Febry 10th 1761 A . . . . | 30th Year of h . . . . (Four lines follow.)

On a ledger :—*SACRED* to the Memory of | Mrs DOROTHY COATES late Wife | of ALEXANDER COATES | of this Ifland Shipwright | She departed this Life | the 25th of November 1777 | And near to this Place | Lies interred the Bodies of | their Six Children THOMAS, | ALEXANDER, FRANCIS, RHODA, | DOROTHY and REBECCA, | who all died in their Infancy | This Stone is dedicated | to her Memory | by her faid Hufband | in grateful Remembrance | of her many Virtues.

SACRED | TO THE MEMORY | OF EDWARD COMMERFORD LATE | COLOUR SERGEANT LIGHT COMPANY | 36 REGIMENT WHO DEPARTED THIS | LIFE ON THE 21 (?) DAY OF JUNE 1835 | AT THE AGE OF 27 | YEARS | THIS STONE IS ERECTED BY HIS AFFECT | IONATE AND DISCONSOLATE WIDOW.

. . . . memory of | . . . . SON of MARGARET | . . . . D COMMERFORD Colov. | . . . . 36th Regt | Departed this LIFE 30th . . . . | 1831 AGED 5 Years 6 months.

(Three lines follow.)

On a headstone :—Here Lyeth . . . . | Body of ANDREW | DEAISEX COOPER | who died y 18 of | May 1743 Aged 77 | Years | Also Part of His | Family.

On a ledger :—Sacred to the Memory | of Mrs MARY DARRELL | who departed this life at Antigua | on the eighth day of December | in the year of our Lord | one thousand eight hundred and eight | Aged | thirty six years two months and eight days. (Eight lines follow.) This tribute of respect is paid | by her affectionate husband | JOSEPH . S. DARRELL.

On a marble altar-tomb within railings :—SACRED | TO THE MEMORY OF | ELEANOR SARAH, | THE ESTIMABLE WIFE OF | DARIUS DAVEY Esqr | WHO DEPARTED THIS LIFE | JULY 16 1832 (?) | IN THE 59TH YEAR OF HER AGE.

(Sixteen lines follow.)

On a marble altar-tomb :—SACRED | TO THE MEMORY OF | HENRY SYMES DAVEY | *SECOND SURVIVING SON OF* | DARIUS DAVEY Esq. | BOTH MERCHANTS OF THIS ISLAND, | DIED ON THE 24 FEBRUARY 1860 | IN THE 38 YEAR OF HIS AGE | AFTER A BRIEF ILLNESS OF SIX DAYS.

(Seven lines follow.)

On a large stone altar-tomb :—SACRED TO THE MEMORY | OF | BARBARA JANE | THE WIFE OF DARIUS DAVEY | WHO DEPARTED THIS LIFE DECEMBER 6TH | 1865 IN THE 56TH YEAR OF HER AGE. (Three lines follow.)

SACRED | To the Memory of | ROBERT THOMAS DEAKINS ESQ | *Staff Assistant Surgeon,* | who died in this Island, | on the 8th of June 1853, | Aged 28 Years.

On a marble altar-tomb within iron railings :—IN MEMORY | OF | TRYPHENA | WIFE OF | RICHARD BURROUGHES ELDRIDGE | of this Island | Who departed this life | on the 24th day of January | in the year of our Lord 1826 | AGED 29 YEARS | Not lost but gone before | ALSO OF | RICHARD BURROUGHS ELDRIDGE | who departed this Life | on the 13th day of September 1852 | AGED 57 YEARS | Born in Yarmouth Norfolk | on the 30th day of March 1795.

On a ledger :—To the Memory | of | *Mifs* JESSIE FORBES | Who died December 10 . 1778.

(Four lines follow.)

On a headstone :—**Erected** BY | WILLIAM FORREST MERCHANT | IN **Memory** OF HIS BELOVED WIFE | EDITH ELIZABETH, | WHO DIED 19th NOVR 1865 AGED 24 YEARS | ALSO IN MEMORY OF THEIR CHILD | EDITH MAUD, WHO DIED 3RD NOVR 1865 | AGED 22 MONTHS. | ALSO IN MEMORY OF HIS BROTHER | JAMES REID FORREST | WHO DIED 5TH DECR 1865 AGED 24 YEARS | ALSO OF HIS MOTHER-IN-LAW | SAPAH HUMPLEBY BACKER | WHO DIED 28TH FEBY 1865 | AGED 57 YEARS.

(Four lines follow.)

On a headstone :—**In** MEMORY OF | MICHAEL FURLONG . | A NATIVE OF THE ISLAND OF | MONTSERRAT ; | DIED IN ANTIGUA | 16TH MARCH 1861 | AGED 19 YEARS.

(Two lines follow.)

On a large slate headstone :—**Sacred** | TO THE MEMORY OF | ANNE HESTER GORE : | LADY OF SAMUEL GORE ESQUIRE, | WHO DEPARTED THIS LIFE | ON THE 7TH OF NOVEMBER 1838 | AGED 43 YEARS.

(Four lines follow.)

On a large ledger stone :—*Here lieth interred* | *the* Body *of* | Capt SAMUEL GREEN | *Commander of the Ship Charlotte of* N. Providence | *Diftinguifhed* | *by his* Virtue and Humanity | A Dutiful Son | A Kind and Affectionate Hufband | A Tender and indulgent Parent | A Firm and warm Friend | and | an eafy and agreeable Companion | He *departed this* Life *the* 20 *day of* Oct. 1776 . | Aged 28 Years | *Universally Regretted* | *but particularly by his afflicted Widow* | *and only Daughter.*

(Three lines follow.)

On a slate ledger stone :—SACRED | to the memory of | GEORGE GREEN | He was Organist of this Parish | 42 Years | and departed this life | the 5th Day of November | 1815.

Here lies the Body of | PRUDENCE GREGORY | who Died 2d of April 1761 | Aged 75 Years | to whose Memory | this Stone is Dedicated, | by her Daughter | MARY WALKER.

SACRED | TO THE MEMORY OF | MARY HARNEY, | WHO DEPARTED THIS LIFE | in the faith of Our Lord Jesus Christ | January 19th 1854 : Aged 80 Years | This stone is chiefly erected by | Marcus E. Sheriff, as a last token | in memory of the body that lies | BENEATH IT.

On a headstone :—ERECTED BY | CATHERINE HARVIE | IN MEMORY OF | HER BELOVED BROTHER | WILLIAM HARVIE | MERCHANT | WHO DIED 31ST JULY 1859.

On a headstone :—Here Lieth | the Body of | Abigl Higginf | Wife of Jacob | . . . . (Rest missing.)

On a headstone :—ERECTED | IN MEMORY OF | JOHN HORNEL ESQR, MERCHANT | of the House of Hornel and Coltart, | respected generally and greatly | regretted by many Friends, | Aged 34 Years. | This Stone is Erected by his Parents in | KIRKUDBRIGHT SCOTLAND.

On a headstone :—ERECTED BY LOUISA KERCHESNEY | TO THE | **Memory** OF | her late husband | JAMES HORNER, | who died here on the 15th | of August 1852, | Aged 30 Years.

On a large altar-tomb within iron railings :—IN MEMORY | OF | MARY ANN HOSIER | THE BELOVED WIFE OF | CHARLES P. HOSIER ESQ. | WHO DEPARTED THIS LIFE | ON THE | 11TH DAY OF JUNE 1838 | AGED 62 YEARS. | OF | CHARLES P. HOSIER ESQ. | MERCHANT OF THIS CITY | WHO DEPARTED THIS LIFE | ON THE | 22ND DAY OF OCTOBER 1847 | AGED 70 YEARS. | AND OF | JOHN HOSIER ESQ | SON OF THE ABOVE NAMED | MERCHANT OF THIS CITY | WHO DEPARTED THIS LIFE | ON THE | 3RD DAY OF SEPTEMBER 1868 | AGED 67 YEARS.

On a ledger stone:—HERE LYES INTERRED | SAMUEL HOSKINS SEN | WHO DEPARTED THIS LIFE | THE 25TH DAY OF JUNE 1761 | ON WEDNESDAY MORNING AT 8 O'CLOCK | IN THE 18TH YEAR OF HIS AGE. (Four lines follow.)

AND UNDER THIS TOMB LYES | HIS BELOVED SON GEORGE | WHO DEPARTED THIS LIFE | THE 11TH OF JANUARY 1763 | AGED 8 YEARS.

This Stone Was placed | . . . . by | *Margaret Hutchefon* | in memory of her Brother | *James Hutchefon* | Efq Son of | *John Hutchefon* of | Denfield in the *Parifh* of | GOVAN *County* of . . . . | **North Britain** | Who died in this ISLAND | *the 27 of Feby 17 . .* | *the 37 year of his age.*

On a ledger stone:—**Sacred** | *To the MEMORY of* | MARY A. H. ISHAM | *Daughter of* | THOMAS & A. C. ISHAM | *Who Died* | Novr *the* 30th 1809 | *Aged* | TEN YEARS SIX MONTHS | FOUR DAYS.

On a headstone:—ERECTED | BY | ALEXANDER JACK, JR. | Merchant of this City | IN | Memory of his Uncle | ALEXANDER JACK | who died Sep: 1st 1845.

On a ledger stone:—ERECTED | To the Memory | *of* | CHARLES JACK | *MERCHANT ANTIGUA,* | Who died 31st of December 1844, | Aged 39 Years. | And His Daughter | ISABELLA CHARLES JACK, | Who died 12th of May 1845, | Aged 5 Months. | This tribute of affection is placed here | By his Widow | JANE MCRITCHIE.

On a stone grave, surmounted by a cross:—ANNA LOUISA JACKSON, YOUNGEST CHILD OF | THE BISHOP OF ANTIGUA: | DIED 28TH FEBRUARY 1863 | AGED 12 | "*PATIENT IN TRIBULATION*" | ROM. XII. 12.

On a stone ledger:—SACRED | to the Memory of | JOHN JAMES ESQR | who departed this life | July the 31st 1826 | Aged 52 Years.

A large ledger stone on a brick tomb:—SACRED TO THE MEMORY OF | ELEANOR MARY | DAUGHTER OF | JOSHUA AND ELEANOR KENTISH, | *OF THIS ISLAND* | WHO DEPARTED THIS LIFE | ON THE 15TH JANUARY 1830 | AGED 18 MONTHS.

On a ledger stone within railings:—SACRED | TO THE MEMORY OF | ENSIGN GEORGE DANIEL KINAHAN | OF HER MAJESTY'S 54TH REGIMENT | WHO DIED ON THE 11TH OF DECR. | 1849 | AT SAINT JOHNS OF YELLOW FEVER | AGED 21 YEARS | THIS STONE WAS ERECTED | BY HIS BROTHER OFFICERS | OF THE 54TH REGIMENT | OUT OF AFFECTIONATE REGARD | TO HIS MEMORY.

On a ledger stone:—MARY LOUISA FRANCES | ONLY DAUGHTER OF | CAPT E. T. LLOYD R E. | DIED 3RD DEC. 1849 | AGED 18 YEARS.

Sacred | *to* | *the memory of* | George Lowen Esq | *formerly a Captn in H.M. 93* | *Regiment of Foot and late* | *Provost Marshal General* | *of this Island who departed* | *this life 4th January 1838* | *aged 57 years.*

On a monument, surmounted by an urn:—IN | SACRED MEMORY | OF | JOHN BELL LOWRY | DIED 13 AUGUST 1863 | ALSO OF EMILY | HIS WIFE | DIED 22ND JUNE 1860.

On a ledger stone:—In Memory of JOHN LYON | who departed this Life March the | 19th 1808 in the 37th Year of his Age. (Four lines follow.)

Also of | DANIEL DOUGLASS and MARGARET KIRK | who lie Interred here. He died on the 5th | January 1825 Aged 12 Years | The same Month Aged 28 Years | Dedicated by ELIZA DOUGLASS and | WILLIAM KIRK as a token of their Affection.

On a large white marble ledger stone near south-west gateway:—SACRED | TO THE MEMORY OF | MARGARET MACKIE | DAUGHTER OF THOMAS AND ANNE MACKIE | A NATIVE OF THIS ISLAND | BORN ON THE 12TH OF DECEMBER 1775 | EDUCATED AS THE DAUGHTER OF A WEALTHY MERCHANT | SHE LIVED TO EXPERIENCE THE TRIALS | BOTH OF PRIVATION AND WEALTH. (Five lines follow.) SHE DEPARTED THIS LIFE | ON THE 18TH OF MARCH 1851 | AT THE ADVANCED AGE | OF 76 YEARS. (Five lines follow.)

In Memory | of JANE wife of Gillt McConnell | who departed this Life on the | 9th August 1783 | And | of their three infant Children | JOHN, GILBERT and JANE | the first died on the 20th September | 1778 | And the two last in the | Same week with their | Amiable Mother. (Four Latin lines follow.)

SACRED | To the Memory | of | WILLIAM MCKENZIE | Who departed this Life | On the 28th day of Novr | 1784 | Aged 36 Years.

On a large granite slab, resting on four pillars:—SACRED | TO THE MEMORY OF | MARY SIMS GRAVESTOCK | WIFE OF | ROBERT MCKENZIE | MERCHANT | BORN JUNE 1825 | DIED 28TH DECEMBER 1865.

On a headstone:—SACRED | TO THE MEMORY OF | ROBERT MCKENZIE ESQ | NATIVE OF | GREENOCK SCOTLAND | AND LATE MERCHANT OF THIS ISLAND | WHO DIED JUNE 25TH 1868 | AGED 56 YEARS.

On a headstone:—**Sacred** | TO THE MEMORY OF | JOHN MCKNIGHT | CAPTN OF THE SHIP *PHOENIX* | WHO DEPARTED THIS LIFE AUGUST | 22ND 1853 | IN THE 43RD YEAR OF HIS AGE.

"Thy Brother shall rise again."—JOHN xi. C. 23 v.

On a headstone:—ERECTED | IN MEMORY OF | CAPT ADAM S. MCMINN | of the Brig CAMPBELL of Whitehaven | who died August 3rd 1839 | AGED 32 YEARS.

On a broken ledger stone:— . . . . the body of | . . . . PHERSON | . . . . life 4 Sept | . . . . his age | . . . . ody of | . . . . H SON to | . . . . SMIT . .

On a headstone:—SACRED | TO THE MEMORY OF | GEORGE MADGWICK WHO | DEPARTED THIS LIFE 26TH | MAY 1831 AGED 42 YEARS.

Here lies the Body of | MR GEORGE MAOVEY | who Died the 23rd Day of March 1773 | Aged Twenty Nine Years | He was the Only Brother | of STEWART MAOVEY of Tobago | who from the great affection | he had for him hath Caused this | Monument to be erected | to his Memory.

On a large ledger stone over tomb:—SACRED | TO THE MEMORY OF | ARABELLA MARTAIN | WHO DEPARTED THIS LIFE ON | THE 28TH OF JULY ANNO DOMINI 1809 | AGED 61 YEARS | Of | JOHN TAYLOR | WHO DEPARTED THIS LIFE ON | THE 6TH OF SEPTEMBER 1811 | AGED 17 YEARS | AND OF | ANN ARABELLA LLOYD | WHO LEFT THIS SCENE OF WOE ON | THE MORNING OF THE 20TH OF DEC 1820 | AGED 11 YEARS. (Twelve lines follow.)

On a slate slab on six pillars within railings:—SACRED | To the memory of Margaret Mason | Relict of Robert Mason who departed | this life on 25 Augt 1831, Aged 71 years | Also of | William King Mason Son of the said | Robt & Margt Mason, who departed this life | on 22nd October 1829 Aged 33 years | And | William Milford Mason Son of Richard H. | and Mary Ann Mason Aged 4 years. (Four lines follow.)

On a white marble altar-tomb:—STEPHEN MASON | BORN | NOVEMBER 13 1801 | DIED | AUGUST 24 1852.

On a ledger stone:—Beneath this stone lies the Body of | *GEORGE MASSEY* | Who departed this life the 14th day of | August 1779 | In the 48th Year of his Age | This stone is dedicated | To his Memory | By his disconsolate Widow | *ANN MASSEY* | Also | Near this Stone | Lays the Remains | of | the above Named | *ANN MASSEY* | Who departed this life | The 9th day of February | 1796 | In the 79th Year of her Age.

On a headstone:—MARY ANNA H. MERCER | FEB: 28TH 1859 | ÆT: XXVI YEARS.

On a headstone:—**In Memory of** | WILLIAM JOHN MERCER | Decr 25th 1861 Aged 60 | AND OF | DOROTHY HIS WIFE | June 25th 1864 Aged 54 Years.

(Two lines follow.)

On a large altar-tomb:—SACRED | to the Memory of | CHRISTIAN MEREDITH | who died February 2d Anno 1810.

On a headstone:—To the Memory of | WILLIAM MITCHELL | who Departed this Life | on the 4 Day of January | (?) 1819 AGED 38 years | And of | CHARLES SEYTON | MITCHELL | his son Who Departed | this life on the 28th day | of Sepr 1835 AGED 22.

On a large ledger stone:—In Memory of | MR THOMAS MOORE of this Ifland | Gent., who Departed this life July | the 22nd 1754 Aged 44 Years.

On the south side of tomb. On the ledger are cut a wreath and urn:—SACRED | TO THE MEMORY OF | GILES S. MUSSON, ESQUIRE, | MERCHANT, | WHO DEPARTED THIS LIFE ON THE 7TH MARCH 1855 | AT HIS RESIDENCE IN THE CITY OF ST JOHNS | ISLAND OF ANTIGUA | AGED 68 YEARS.

On a broken headstone:—SACRED | TO THE MEMORY | OF MURDOC MUNROE | OF MARYBURGH ROSS IN SCOTLAND | WHO DEPARTED THIS LIFE THE 28TH DAY | OF OCTOBER 1853 | AGED 28 YEARS | THIS STONE IS ERECTED TO HIS MEMORY | BY A FEW FRIENDS.

.... | .... MYLES son of | .... MYLES his .... | .... | .... | Placed at the request | of his affectionate Mother.

On a stone altar-tomb within railings:—BENEATH THIS STONE | REST THE REMAINS OF | MARY | THE BELOVED WIFE OF | THOMAS NICHOLSON M.D. | WHO DEPARTED THIS LIFE | ON THE 8TH DAY OF JULY 1854 | AGED 34 YEARS | (Eight lines follow) | BY HER SIDE LIE THE REMAINS OF | HER INFANT GRANDSON | THOMAS | WHO DIED ON THE 19TH DAY OF APRIL 1858 (?) | AGED 3 MONTHS AND 14 DAYS. | IN LOVING REMEMBRANCE OF | ADAM NICHOLSON M.D., | WHO DIED JUNE 6TH 1868; | AGED 49 YEARS | AND OF CAROLINE HIS WIFE | WHO DIED THE 19TH OF MAY 1862 | AGED 29 YEARS.

On a ledger stone:—SACRED | TO THE MEMORY OF | MRS ANN HYATT NORMAN | WIFE OF | JAMES NORMAN ESQRE | SEARCHER | OF HIS MAJESTYS CUSTOMS | ANTIGUA: | WHO DEPARTED THIS LIFE | APRIL 6TH 1826 | AGED 35 YEARS. (Four lines follow.)

On a headstone:—ERECTED | BY MICHAEL O'BRIEN, IN THE MEMORY OF | MARY, | his beloved wife, who died, Dec: 11th, 1869, | AGED 32 YEARS. | ALSO TWO INFANT DAUGHTERS: | CAROLINE | who died April 1st, 1853, Aged 2 Years | CATHERINE | who died Feb 18th 1856 Aged 2 Years. (Four lines follow.)

On a marble slab over brick tomb:—Underneath this Marble | are deposited the Remains of | MARY PEARSON | *late Wife of* HENRY PEARSON | *of* LONDON *Merchant*, | Whose conjugal affection induced her to | accompany during a temporary Visit to the | Weft Indies, her now difconfolate Hufband | (Five lines follow) | She was born at PERRY BARR | in STAFFORDSHIRE (27th May 1749) | And died in this Island | the 17th January 1785.

M.S. | SANDERS & SAMUEL PESHALL | fram & Fil Tho de Hawn | in Agro Salop Bar | Plofluvii nece bie præ proper accidere | SAM 18 Nov. 1753 | SANDERS 10 Sep. 1754.

On a ledger stone:—.... | GEORGE PETTIGREW .... of this | Island Merchant who departed | this life on the 19th day of August | 1797 in the 37th year of his age.

On a headstone:—SACRED TO | MEMORY OF | MICHAEL PHIL | LIPS | WHO DEPARTED | THIS LIFE | SEP. 10, 1836 | AGED 27 YRS.

On a headstone:—ERECTED | BY | JOSEPH PICKENS, | IN MEMORY OF HIS BROTHER | JOHN PICKINS, | *A NATIVE OF IRELAND* | who died, October 20th, 1860, Aged 22 Years | ALSO | JOHN WM. PICKINS, | SON OF JOSEPH PICKINS | who died, Nov. 20th, 1860, Aged 9 Months. | IN MEMORY OF | JANE ANN, | *A native of Ireland* | the beloved wife of JOSEPH PICKINS, | who died, Oct. 29th, 1865. Aged 27 Yrs.

On a headstone:—Sacred to the Memory of | Lieut THOMAS PILKINGTON | of the 4th West India Regiment | who died 10th July 1821 | Aged 30 Years.

On a marble headstone:—**Sacred** | TO THE MEMORY OF | ROSINA C. PIRIE, | WHO DEPARTED THIS LIFE | 5TH MAY 1868 | AGED 66.

On a slate ledger in pathway leading to south door of Cathedral:—Hic jacet | in spem Beatæ Refurrectionis depofitum | Reverendi THOMÆ POWERS Socii Collegii | Sacro-Sanctæ Trinitatis in Academia | Cantabrigenfi; Quondam Parochiæ | Beatæ Mariæ in Infulâ hac, altimo Parochiæ Divi | Iohannis in Infulâ Nevis, Rectoris. Vir universalis | Scientiis egregie doctus omnibus virtutibus | præclarè inftructus: In vitâ Summe | dilectus, in morte flebiliter deploritus. | Hanc vitam depofuit Decimo Quarto | die Decemb. Anno Domini 1698.

On a broken headstone:—SACRED | TO THE MEMORY | OF THE LATE | JAMES H. PRUDDEM ESQRE | A NATIVE OF BERMUDA | WHO DEPARTED THIS LIFE | ON 13TH AUGUST 1866 | AGED 72 YEARS.

On a headstone:—SACRED | TO THE MEMORY OF | DAVID QUIN | WHO DIED NOVEMBER 8TH 1865 | AGED 54 YEARS.

ERECTED | IN MEMORY OF | JOSE DE QUINTAL | A NATIVE OF MADEIRA | WHO DIED JULY 8TH 1865 | AGED XL YEARS. (Four lines follow.)

On a ledger stone lying loose on the ground:—SACRED | *to the memory of* | ABRAHAM RAVENA | *who departed this life* | NOV. 6. 1844 | Æ 80.

On a slab, surmounted by a sarcophagus, adjoining Sir W. Snagg's tomb:—STEPHEN JORDAN RIGAUD D.D. LATE FELLOW OF EXETER COLLEGE OXFORD AND SECOND BISHOP OF THIS DIOCESE | DIED MAY 17, 1859, AGED 43.

(One line follows.)

SACRED | TO THE MEMORY OF | MISS ANN ROBERTSON | ELDEST DAUGHTER OF | CHARLES ROBERTSON ESQ. | AGED 17 YEARS. | THIS YOUNG LADY HAD ONLY BEEN 21 DAYS IN | THE ISLAND AFTER AN ABSENCE OF NINE YEARS | IN ENGLAND FOR EDUCATION SHE WAS HURRIED | TO THE GRAVE BY A VIOLENT FEVER TO THE | GREAT GRIEF OF HER PARENTS & RELATIVES.

(Twelve lines follow.)

ALSO | OF SARAH CHAMBERS ROBERTSON | HIS YOUNGEST DAUGHTER AGED 11 MONTHS | 1821.

On a headstone:—Sacred | to the Memory of | M. CHRISTIAN SCHULTZ | who departed this Life | Sep. 15, 1765, Aged 50 Years | I. GEO. ENGLER | who dep^t June 2nd | 1775.

On a stone tomb within railings:—SACRED | to the Memory of | HENRY TATHAM RODIE | Son of | THOMAS RODIE ESQ^r | of Liverpool, | who died in this Island | on the 3rd day of Feb^ry 1817 | in the 20th Year of his Age | and whose Remains are here | Interred.

On a headstone:—*IN MEMORY OF | CAP. WILLIAM ROLLAN | WHO DEPARTED THIS LIFE | SEPT. 15TH 1789 | AGED 44 YEARS.*

Here lieth th . . . . | of WILLIAM . . . . | Infant Son of | GEORGE and | SUSANNA SCOTT | who departed this | life Nov. 18th 1798 | Aged 5 years 5 Mo^s.

On a ledger stone:—Beneath this Stone | are depofited the remains of | ALEXANDER SCOTT, *Efq.* | He was Born at Ochtergaven | Near Perth North Britain July 22^d 1746 | As an Affectionate Hufband and a | Steady Friend He has left few Equals, | As an upright Merchant, Humane | Planter, and worthy Magiftrate | He lived an Honor to this Ifland | and died univerfally lamented | on the 13th Day of January 1787 | Aged 40 Years | Near to this place | are also deposited the remains of | CHRISTIANA ROSS | Sister to the above named | ALEXANDER SCOTT | and wife of | DAVID ROSS | She died after a lingering illness | which she bore with Christian fortitude | on the 27th day of Dec. | 1781 Aged 33 years.

On a headstone:—SACRED | *To the Memory of* | PETER SHARPLES | Son of | THOMAS SHARPLES of *Liverpool* | who died on the 13th of March 1849 | Aged 17 Years. (Four lines follow.)

On a ledger stone:—SACRED | TO THE MEMORY OF | LOUISA G. SIMPSON, | WHO DEPARTED THIS LIFE | 6TH DAY OF JANUARY 1836.

On a slab, surmounted by a sarcophagus:—SACRED TO THE MEMORY OF | ANN | THE WIFE OF SIR WILLIAM SNAGG | MARRIED | 27 JAN. 1838 | DIED 10 FEBRUARY 1861.

(Two lines follow.)

[The Snagg and Rigaud graves are enclosed in the angle formed by the chancel and south transept.]

SACRED TO THE MEMORY OF | HENRY SOUTHWELL | *A NATIVE OF DUBLIN* | WHO DEPARTED THIS LIFE | AFTER A VERY SHORT ILLNESS | AT S^T JOHNS IN THIS ISLAND | ON THE 13 DAY OF DECEMBER 1831 | AGED 30 YEARS. | *HIS DISCONSOLATE WIDOW | HAS ERECTED THIS TABLET.* (Six lines follow.)

On a broken ledger stone:—SACRED | . . . . memory of | . . . . JAM STEELE | . . . . IVE of Scotland | . . . . departed this life | the 7th of May 1838 | *Aged 44 Years.*

On a headstone:—HERE LYES THE BODY OF | IOHN STEVENSON | Born IN THE COUNTY | OF YORK NEARE | WHITBY DIED THE 12TH | OF MARCH 1736 | AGED 40.

Arms:—. . . . *a chevron between three mallets, each surmounted by a fleur-de-lis.*

SACRED | *to the Memory of* | JAMES STRANACK | late Commander of the | Peggy of London who died | in this Island 29th May 1810 | Aged 49 Years | universally respected.

On a stone altar-tomb:—Sacred | to the Memory of | M^RS GRACE TAYLOR | the late Wife of | MR JOHN TAYLOR | of this Island Merchant | who died in Child Bed | the 9th of Sep^t 1776 | aged 29 Years | AND | of their three Children | ANN died the 12th Feby 1774 | Aged 5 Years | SOPHIA the 14th Feb. 1774 | Aged 4 Years | and LEWIS the 9th Sep^t 1776 | Aged 2 Days.

On a headstone:—HERE . LIES . THE | BODY . OF . JAMES . A. | TAYLOR . WHO . DEPA | RTED . THIS . LIFE . 18 | *February* 1820 *aged* 28 | YEARS.

On a headstone:—**Sacred** | *To the Memory of* | M^RS ELIZABETH Wife of | MR GEORGE TELFER | of the City of Rochester | in the County of Kent | who departed this Life | the 17th day of November 1805 | AGED 48 Years.

On a headstone:—ERECTED | BY | SAM^L M. JAMES | IN REMEMBRANCE | OF | HIS FATHER IN LAW | SOLOMAN THOMAS | DEPARTED THIS LIFE | JUNE 16TH . . . . RS.

On a ledger stone:—Sacred to the Memory | of Mrs Frances M. Tucker | the wife of John Tucker of Alexandria | in Virginia who Departed this Life | the 7th day of Decr 1806 | Aged 41 Years and 10 Months.

(Eight lines follow.)

On a ledger stone within railings:—SACRED | TO THE MEMORY OF | M^RS ANN UNDERWOOD | OF *MONTSERRAT* | WHO DIED IN THIS *ISLAND* | AUGUST 9TH 1807 AGED 55 YEARS.

On a ledger stone:—SACRED TO THE MEMORY | OF ANTHONY VILLIONE . . . . FORM | ERLY AN EMINENT MERCHANT IN | LONDON WHO DEPARTED THIS LIFE | ON THE 23 DAY OF JUNE | ANNO DOMINI 1790 | IN THE 67 YEAR OF HIS AGE.

On a ledger stone:—THIS MONUMENT | IS ERECTED TO THE MEMORY OF A | TENDER AND AFFECTIONATE HUSBAND | JAMES HENRY WALL | WHO DIED THE 24TH DAY OF MAY 1795 | AGED 46 YEARS | ALSO IN COMMEMORATION | OF AN ONLY AND BELOV'D CHILD | JAMES GEORGE WALL | WHO DIED THE 27TH DAY OF DECEMBER 1794 | AGED 22 MONTHS & EIGHT DAYS | BY A TRULY GRIEV'D AND FEELING | WIFE AND MOTHER | ANNA WALL.

(Two lines follow.)

On a headstone lying loose:—IN MEMORY OF | *GRACE ELIZABETH WARDLE* | the faithful affectionate Wife of | WILLIAM WARDLE | who departed this | life July 2nd 1833 | Aged 37 Years.

On a slate ledger:—HERE LIE | The Remains of | RACHEL | the wife of | James Whitworth | Minister of the Gospel | (Two lines) | She died in the Lord Novr 29th 1820 | Aged 33 Years | (Two lines) | ALSO | Mary Elizabeth | Daughter of | James and Rachel Whitworth | who died Decr 18th 1820 Aged 11 Months. (Four lines follow.)

On a stone slab on stone pillars:—IN MEMORY OF | ROBERT CHARLES | SON OF H. K. & E. S. L. WIGHT | BORN IN S^T CROIX 13 MARCH 1849 | DIED IN THIS ISLAND 30 AUGUST 1850 | IN MEMORY OF | ELIZABETH SARAH LOUISA | THE BELOVED WIFE OF H. K. WIGHT | BORN IN S^T CROIX 28TH SEPTEMBER 1828 | DIED IN THIS ISLAND 17 OCTOBER 1853. (Two lines follow.)

On a large brick tomb:—SACRED | TO THE MEMORY OF | OSWALD CHARLES WOOD | M.D. | LATE PROVOST MARSHALL | GENERAL OF THIS ISLAND | WHO DEPARTED THIS LIFE | 5 NOV. 1842 | AGED 37 YEARS | ALSO JOHANNA HIS WIFE | ON THE 30TH OCTR 1842 | AGED 31 YEARS | AND MRS ADAM | HER MOTHER | ON THE 15TH OCTR 1842 | AGED 66 YEARS.

On a broken ledger:—In Memory . . . . | Daughter of | . . . . UEL POOLE WOOLEY | . . . . *thodist Mifsionary* | & Mary his Wife | . . . . arted this life Nov. the . . . . | . . . . ed Six Y & Six Wee . . . . (Five lines follow.)

On a ledger:—Here Lyeth the body of | Allan . . . . ton* Commander | of the Ship Valentine of Livepool | Who Departed this Life the 2 Auguft | 1738.

On a much decayed headstone:—SACRED | TO THE MEMORY OF | MARY ANN ELIZABETH | . . . . OF | ISAAC GEORGE. (Six obliterated lines follow.)

On a headstone:— . . . . | 11TH MARCH 18 . 7 | Aged . . . . years | She was a Kind frend | an Affectionate Wife | and a true Christian.

There are several gravestones without any inscriptions.

1. A very large vault, adjacent to James Athill's tomb.
2. A large flat stone, near Mr. Thomas Barry's.
3. A small headstone, near the Otto-Baijer vault, buried in the earth.
4. A large flat concreted space, enclosed within iron railings, adjoining the Burton vault, is stated to have been the place of sepulture of Langford Lovell Hodge, Esq.
5. A large stone altar-tomb with naval emblems carved on it was stated to have been the vault of John Scarville, whose brother Daniel Ward Scarville lived near the church.
6. A large brick tomb, next to George Pettigrew's.
7. A large vault within iron railings, close to Lieut. Thomas Pilkington's.
8. A large ledger stone, close to R. T. Deakins' obliterated M.I.
9. A small headstone. M.I. obliterated.

ST. PETER'S PARISH.

8310 ACRES.

1. BETTY'S HOPE, COTTON (New Work), COTTON (Old Work), GARDEN, 1689 acres. Sir W. C. Codrington, Bart., 1852. Cotton Works, Christopher Codrington, 1788. Betty's Hope and Garden, Colonel Valentine Morris, 1788. 785 slaves, 1829. Betty's Hope, Garden, Cotton Old and New, 1420 acres, Sir William Codrington, 1871.

   1676. Ensign John Hall purchased half of Betty's Hope=362½ acres of Major Thomas Malet (see Keynell pedigree). Dame Joan Keynell, widow of Governor Christopher Keynell, was owner in 1667, but in 1668 her estate was forcibly given to Colonel Christopher Codrington.
2. CEDAR HILL (Upper and Lower), 452 acres. Edward Byam, 1788. William Byam, 266 slaves, 1829. William Byam, 1852. Captain Byam, 1871. Thomas Berkeley, 1878.
3. COCHRAN and PARES, 328 acres. . . . . Cochran, 1788. Heirs of Pare, 1788. Samuel Otto Baijer, 306 slaves, 1829. Owen Pell, 1852. Mrs. Owen Pell, 1871. William E. M. Pell, 1878.

   Cochrans in 1819 contained 170 acres, and with 135 slaves was sold by Daniel Byam Mathew as Ex'or of Colonel Archibald Cochran to Samuel Otto-Baijer, Esq., for £18,060.
4. COCOANUT HALL, 247 acres. Crumps Windward estate in 1769 contained 300 acres. Called CRUMPS in 1788 and in possession of Davis and Edwards. J. D. Edwards, 145 slaves, 1829. John Edwards, 1852. William Geddes, 1871.
5. CRABB'S, 400 acres. Valentine Morris sold this and Martins of 126 acres for £11,500 st. to James Gowan, who had leased them for 26 years from 1738 for £1100 c. a year. James Coull, 273 acres, 1829. Thomas Coull, M.D., 1852. W. J. Johnson, 1871.
6. DIAMOND, 131 acres. Francis Martin, 1790. Heirs of F. B. Ottley, 1852. Francis Shand, 1871.
7. GREAT DUERS, 339 acres. Heirs of John Duer, deceased, 219 slaves, 1829. Manning and Anderdon, 1852. Thomas D. Foote, 1871. W. A. Parker and Co., 1878.
8. LITTLE DUERS, 140 acres. Heirs of John Duer, deceased, 69 slaves, 1829. William Lee, 1852. Estate of William Lee, deceased, 1871. W. A Parker and Co., 1878. 44 acres in St. Philip's Parish.
9. EVANSONS 1788. Heirs of W. Martin, deceased, 134 acres, 84 slaves, 1829.
10. LOWER FREEMANS, 365 acres. Inigo Thomas, 127 slaves, 1829. Inigo Thomas, 1852. Louisa M. Peter, 1871. W. A. Parker and Co., 1878.
11. UPPER FREEMANS, 214 acres. T. I. W. Freeman, 160 slaves, 1829. T. I. W. Freeman, 1852. W. K. Martin, 1871. Thomas Daniell and Co., 1878.
12. GILBERT'S, 313 acres. Rev. Nathaniel Gilbert, 1788. N. Gilbert, 158 slaves, 1829. Mrs. N. Gilbert, 1852. Grace Gilbert, 1871. James and Robert Maginley, 1878.
13. GUANO ISLAND, 374 acres. George Holborow, 1871. 82 acres in St. Philip's Parish.
14. HAWES' and MERCER'S CREEK, 311 acres. Heirs of Thomas Rogers, 191 slaves, 1829. William Coull, 1852. W. A. Parker and Co., 1871—78.
15. JONAS', 325 acres. In 1779 styled Langfords MORRIS'S plantation, and was left by Jonas Langford to his grandson J. L. Brooke. In 1817 styled Morris's or North Sound. P. L. Brooke, 150 slaves, 1829. T. L. Brooke, 1852 and 1871.
16. MARTINS in 1799 contained 126 acres, and was owned by Trustees of James Brebner-Gordon. Valentine Morris sold this to James Gordon in 1767, who had held it by lease since 1738.
17. PARHAM HILL (Old and New Work), PARHAM LODGE or CRAWFORD'S, 1096 acres. Clement Tudway, 1788. John P. Tudway, 587 slaves, 1829. Robert C. Tudway, 1852. C. C. Tudway, 1871.
18. PARRYS, 222 acres. Ham. Kerby, 1765. Hon. T. N. Kerby, 1788. Heirs of T. Kerby, deceased, 161 slaves, 1829. George W. Ottley, 1852. F. Garraway, 1871. Thomas D. Foote, 1878.
19. SANDERSON'S and OSBORNES, 528 acres. James Gordon, 1788. Osbornes, Dr. Thomas Fairbairn, 1788. James Adam Gordon, 319 slaves, 1829. James Adam Gordon, 1852. W. K. Martin, 1871.
20. VERNON'S, 416 acres. J. J. J. Vernon, 1788. Major Vernon, 368 slaves, 1829. Major Vernon, 1852. Herbert Mayo, 1871, and his heirs, 1878. Sold 186 acres in Enc. Est. Court.
21. YEAMAN'S, 120 acres. Hyslop and Greenough, 1788. Messrs. Ruckers and Co., 210 acres, 110 slaves, 1829. R. and H. Jefferson, 1852 and 1871. 32 acres in St. Paul's Parish.

* Buried Aug. 3 Capt Allan Farrington from Liverpool.

RECTORS.

John Buxton, cited 3 May, 1711.

Samuel Saunders signs as Rector 1727; M.A. Oxon; matriculated 1690, æt. 16. (See *ante*, p. 70.)

Charles Rowe, LL.D., signs as Rector 1745; living 1750.

Francis Masset signs as Rector 1789; died 1808.

James Coull, 1809—28.

Alexander B. McNish, B.A.; died 16 March 1837.

Francis B. Grant, M.A., 1837—52.

Robert Ralston Abbott, 1855—85.

Richard Duncan King, inducted 1885; B.A. Trinity College, Dublin; resigned 1896.

The present Church was built in 1840, the old one having been burnt. The old churchyard is nearly two miles distant.

1825. Thirteen square miles, 1660 inhabitants. J. Coull, Rector of the united parishes of St. Peter and St. George. N. Gilbert, M.A., officiating at St. Peter's on his own estate. S. A. Warner, assistant Curate for both parishes. One church, 250 sittings. N. Gilbert's chapel, 350 sittings.

1834. A. W. McNish, Rector of St. Peter's, N. Gilbert officiating as before. One church, 300 sittings. N. Gilbert's chapel, 450 sittings. (Bishop Coleridge's Charges.)

The following names occur in the Journal for 1846:—

Rev. Francis B. Grant.
Sir C. W. Codrington.
Robt Chas. Tudway.
Hon. Wm. Byam.
James A. Gordon.
Trust Est., Jno Vernon.
Jno Duer.
Thos. D. Foote.
Thos. L. Brooke.
Thos. Rogers.
Thos. Coull, M.D.
Inigo Thomas.
Jno D. Edwards.
Revd Nathl Gilbert.
Thos. J. W. Freeman.
Hon. Geo. W. Ottley.
Hon. Wm. Lee.
Francis B. Ottley.
Prop. of Yeamans.
Wm. Este.
Jacob W. Fonseca.
Danl W. Searville, book-keeper.
Robt McLea, cl'k.
C. W. & F. Shand.
Saml Sedgwick.
Robt Hughes, cl'k.

In 1850 Owen Pell was rated on 323 acres.

The following names occur in an earlier ledger:—

	Years accounts were outstanding.			
Julia Crump	1810	1816	1821	
Dr Saml Lynch	1796	1798		
Ann Crump	1810	1820		
Justinian Casamajor	1796	1817	1824	
Eliza Redhead	1811			
Alicia Redhead	1811	1812		
Edward Gamble	1814	1815		
Sarah Fletcher Gamble	1818	1825		
Val. Morris, decd	1796	1818		
Tho. Ottley	1796	1805		
A. Cochran	1796	1814	1823	
Rowld Duer, decd	1796	1815		
Jno Duer, decd	1796	1815		
Tho. N. Kerby	1796	1818	1824	1831
Nathl Crump	1796	1803		
Ann Ledeatt	1813	1816	1818	
Nathl Gilbert, Senr, decd	1796	1814		
Ebenezer Lovell	1796	1815		
Clemt Tudway	1796	1814 to 1825		
Rachel Warner & Rowld Otto-Baijer	1796 to 1813			
Saml Warner	1796	1814		
Elizth Gilbert	1815	1818		
E. Crawford & Lindsay	1815	1822		
Dr Kean Osborn	1799	1810		
Shute S. Yeamans	1800	1815	decd in 1816	
Hen. Benskin Lightfoot	1801	1816		
Kean Brown Osborn	1811	1828		
Jno Duer, R.N.	1814	1824		
Julia Lightfoot	1815	1821		
Saml Otto-Baijer	1821	1832		
Rowld S. Frye	1821	1827		
Jno P. Tudway	1821	1828		
Tho. Coull	1821	1831		
J. J. Vernon	1822	1832		
Nath. Gilbert	1827	1832		

Total: 4500 slaves & 7293 acres.

Parish Registers.*

Baptized.

1773	Jan.	6	Mary the D. of William Masset & Mary Ann his Wife.
1823	June	5	Edward S. of Edward Corbet, Esquire, and Sophia his Wife, at Vernon's Estate; private baptism only.
1824	May	—	Sophia D. of Edward Corbet, Esquire, and Sophia his wife, at Vernons.
1827	Feb.	18	George Thornton S. of George Thornton and Christiana Frederica Metcalfe of Mount Vernon, planter.
1827	May	13	Edward Osborn s. of Stephen William & Christiana Ann Kean of The Garden. Planter.
1828	Nov.	9	Benjamin Coewry S. of Thomas Kerby & Mary Ann Leonard Rochester. Parham Plantation.
1828	Mar.	8	Charlotte D. of Thomas & Charlotte Tanner, Pares Plantation, & William S. of do.
1829	Oct.	11	Martha Byam D. of Joseph George & Maria Gore. Cedar Hill. Planter.
1829	Nov.	25	Margaret Elizabeth D. of John Samuel & Mary Elizabeth Bayley. Yeamans'. Planter.
1831	June	26	Julia Maria D. of Joseph George & Mary Gore. 'Hawes'. Planter.
1831	Aug.	21	Lewis S. of Thomas & Charlotte Tanner, Pares. Planter, & Elizabeth D. of do. Privately Baptized by The Revd Nath. Gilbert, A.M., 1826, & received this day.
1831	Aug.	28	Richard Edward S. of Richard Austin & Mary Farmer. Cotton New Work. Planter.
1836	Mar.	19	James Brown s. of John & Frances Isaac. Pares. Doctor.
1837	May	21	Charlotte Leslie D. of William Henry & Margaret Wendall Gale. Retreat. Planter.
1837	Nov.	7	Margaret Helen d. of Joseph G. & Maria Rhodes of Sir G. Thomas' North Sound. Planter.
1837	Dec.	17	John Nathaniel D . . . . S. of Thomas & Charlotte Tanner. Pares Estate. Planter.
1837	Dec.	27	Alicia Mary Ann d. of Thomas & Octavia Clark. Crabbs Estate. Planter.
1838	Oct.	1	William Byam S. of George & Elizabeth Margaret Pilkington. Vernons Estate. Planter.
1838	Nov.	18	Ann d. of William & Eliza Willis, Junr. Parham. Planter.

* Baptisms commenced in 1770, Marriages in 1771, and Burials in 1764.

1839 April 7 James Edward Laviscount s. of Joseph & Matilda Cheek. ? Freemans. Planter.
1839 June 1 George Henry s. of Joseph G. & Maria Rhodes. Gunthorpes. Planter.
1839 June 1 Francis Octavius s. of Thomas & Octavia Clarke. Tyrells Estate. Planter.
1841 April 13 Thomas Dixon S. of Joseph G. & Maria Rhodes. Gunthorpes. Planter.
1845 June 7 William Oliver S. of Robert & Elizabeth Rudd. Corton Old Work. Planter.

Married.

1774 April 21 John Liot & Louisa Masset.

1826, Alexr Wm McNish signs as Rector.

1826 April 5 William Farrant & Elizabeth Fauset.
1827 Sep. 22 Andrew Perrie of St John's, Merchant, & Rosina Catherina Glaser, Spr.
1834 July 17 John Dogan of St Peter's, planter, & Alethia Elizabeth Bochimlar Favey of St Philips, Spr.; by L.
1834 Sep. 7 Francis Smyth of St Peter's, Planter, & Sarah Pearsey of do.

Buried.

1728 Sep. 8 Anne Bell. (From B. T. Leeward Islands, vol. 19.)

1767 to 1770 and 1779 to 1808 missing.

1773 Jan. 10 Mary Masset.
1773 Sep. 9 Hugh Montgomery.
1773 May 31 John Masset.
1774 Sep. 26 William Masset.
1808 Aug. 1 Francis Masset, Rector of this Parish, died in St John's and was buried there.
1823 Dec. 24 Jane Janion D. of Chas. Janion, Methodist Missionary, in Parham Church Yard.

1825, Tho. Parry & Rob. Agasiz, officiating Ministers.

Monumental Inscriptions.

PARHAM OLD BURIAL-GROUND.

On a ledger over stone tomb:—*SACRED to the* | *MEMORY of* | Edmund Carter | Who departed this life | the 2 day of Oct | Anno Domini 1804 | at | Vernons Estate | Aged . . Years.

On a small loose stone:—SACRED | To the Memory | of | Jane Janion | Who departed this . . . . | the 23rd of Decemb . . . . | 1823 Aged 2 Years.

On a white marble headstone:—THIS STONE | is placed to mark the grave of | ROBERT KNOX | Born in the County of Tyrone, Ireland | 20th June 1827, | Died at St Johns, Antigua, | 7th March 1856. (Six lines follow.)

ERECTED | In Memory of | GEORGE KNOX | who departed this life | August the 31st 1844 | Aged 43 years.

On a large ledger inside iron railings:—SACRED | To the Memory of | ROBERT JARRITT ESQ | died December 30th 1835 | Aged 51 | Alfo | T. JARRITT ESQ | who died April 1831 | Aged 38.

On a large ledger lying on its edge near remains of sculptured slabs:—Here lye the Remains of | DOCTOR GAVIN MONTGOMERIE | of the Family of Barrager | in the County of Renfrew Scotland | and died, | on the 30th day of Auguft 1772 | in the 45 Year of his Age.

(Four lines follow.)

This Monument | *DEDICATED* | By his Mournfull Relations in Scotland | As a Small Tribute to the Memory of | AN *AFFECTIONATE BROTHER* | 1773.

On a headstone surmounted by an iron cross:—In | Memory of | Charles William | eldest son of | Thomas & Esther Owen | who died October 7th 1861 | aged 6 years and 4 months.

On a headstone:—To | The Memory | of | HARRIOT & MARGRETT LUKE | HARRIOT Died | 22d October | 1784 | Aged 4 Years | And | MARGRETT Died | 1st November | 1784 | Aged 2 Years.

On a small headstone:—In Memory | of | Mary Ann Haris | daughter of | Wm & Sarah Haris | who departed | this life Dec. ye 1st 1763 | Aged six yrs.

On a ledger over stone vault:—*SACRED* | to the Memory of | *JOSHUA WATERS* | Thirty four years | an highly respected, | and much efteemed member | of this Community; | who departed this life | fincerely lamented, | on the 17th April 1847, | Aged 50 Years.

(Six lines follow.)

On a ledger:—Here Lyeth Interred the Body of | Cap. *THOMAS ROBINSON* | who Departed this Life the 8th day | of December 1751 in the 36th | Year of his Age.

On a marble headstone:—SACRED | TO THE MEMORY OF | THOMAS CONRAD WALTER | *WHO DEPARTED THIS LIFE* | NOV 18TH 1856, | Æ 46. | *A tribute of affection from his* | *sorrowing Widow AMELIA.*

PARHAM NEW CHURCHYARD.

On a wooden cross:—IN MEMORY | of | BENONI . W . ARMSTRONG | Died Sept 28th 1885.

On a headstone:—**In** | FOND MEMORY OF | **Jane Maria** | THE MUCH LOVED WIFE OF | JOHN BELL ESQ . PLANTER, | BORN AT MOUNT SHANNON, | DROMOD, LEITRIM, IRELAND, | 19TH FEBRUARY 1866, | DIED AT ANTIGUA | SEPTEMBER 28TH 1885.

On a headstone:—IN MEMORY OF | JOHN ENGLISH | WHO DIED OCT 3RD | 1810.

On a headstone:—ERECTED IN | MEMORY OF | **our** | BELOVED | FATHER | **John Francis** | PROPRIETOR OF THE | **Hermitage Est** | A MEMBER OF THE | **St. Peters** | CHURCH COUNCIL | AND A FAITHFUL SABBATH | SCHOOL TEACHER | MUCH RESPECTED | BY ALL WHO KNEW | **him** | WHO DIED AUG 9TH 1882 | AGED 60 YEARS.

At this spot Lieth | the | Mortal | Remains of | JOHN IRVINE, who | Died June 4th 1849 aged | 52 Years, On his Right | are the Remains of his | son SAMUEL IRVINE who | Died Nov. 14th 1848 aged 19 | yrs: And also the Remains | of ALECIA A . BLACKWELL | Who Died Jan . 26 . 1846 . Aged | . 0 Years.

(Eight partially obliterated lines follow.)

SAM . W . B . . . . 1849.

SACRED | TO THE | MEMORY | OF | REBECCA JAMES | WHO DEPARTED THIS | LIFE 2ND OF JUNE | 1879.

On a large vault. Crest: *A dolphin on a wreath*:—IN | MEMORY | OF | ELSINA JERE . . . . | Who entered into rest the . . . . | of February 1864 in her thirty . . . . | Year.

On a headstone:—IN MEMORY OF | AMELIA ELIZABETH PITT | BORN MAY THE 11TH 1840 | DIED JULY 20TH 1882.

On a wooden cross:—IN MEMORY OF | CHRISTOPHER SETON | WHO DIED JUN . 8 . 1885.

On a headstone:—IN AFFECTIONATE REMEMBRANCE | OF ANN ELIZA | BELOVED WIFE OF | WILLIAM HENRY SHOREY | *OF CHATHAM, KENT, ENGLAND.* | WHO DEPARTED THIS LIFE, | ON SUNDAY 15TH FEBRUARY 1885 | AGED 29 YEARS. (Five lines follow.)

In the church on the south wall:—This Monument | Was erected by RACHEL EMRA | To the Memory of | her beloved Husband | JAMES EMRA *Esqr* | Who departed this Life | December 28 1759 | Aged 37 Years.

MOUNT WILLIAM ESTATE.

On a mutilated headstone:—ELIZABETH | HOWARD | Aged . . . Years | dep . Life | . . . . 177 .

On two fragments of white marble:—. . . . RD . E . OWEN R . N | . . . . UARY 13TH 1838 | . . . . ECTED | . . . . IONATESON, | . . . . MOTHER. (See his M.I. in St. Paul's Church, Falmouth.)

ST. GEORGE'S PARISH.

6000 ACRES.

1. BARNACLE POINT, 64 acres. Jeremiah Nibbs, 1788. B. Entwisle leased to Shand and Co., 1829. Heirs of B. Entwisle, 1852. Francis Shand, 1871.
2. BARNES HILL, 172 acres. Estate of James Law, deceased, 1871. John Freeland, 1878.
3. BLACKMANS or MOUNT LUCIE, 230 acres. In 1788 styled Mount Lucie and owned by heirs of . . . . Blackman. Hon. W. H. Irby, 330 acres, 138 slaves, 1829. W. and F. Shand, 1852. Frederick Garraway, 337 acres, 1871. Samuel Dobee and Sons, 1878.
4. GILES BLIZARDS, 162 acres. B. E. Jarvis, 1829 and 1852. Thomas Jarvis, 1871, and his heirs, 1878.
5. JUDGE BLIZARDS, 422 acres. Heirs of Byam, 219 slaves, 1829. Heirs of Stephen Blizard, 1852. Mrs. Stapleton, 1871 (? now John Jarvis').
6. WILL BLIZARDS, 90 acres. Francis Willock, 1829.
7. CARLISLE'S, 388 acres. In 1711 Francis Carlisle had a patent for this his estate of 350 acres, and bequeathed 500 acres to his son William, who died 1742, and left it to his mother Alice, who married secondly John Gray. In 1752 Mr. and Mrs. Gray settled the estate after their deaths on her grandson Lord Lavington. Lady Lavington, 365 slaves, 1829. K. B. Osborne, M.D., 1852. James Barrett, 1871. Charles J. Manning, 1878.
8. DATE HILL, 132 acres. Heirs of Samuel Byam, 1788. Samuel Martin, lessee of C. Robertson, 1829. Heirs of Charles Robertson, 1852. Thomas Jarvis, 1871.
9. DONOVANS, 247 acres. In 1736 styled VAUGHANS of 266 acres, and in possession of Baijer Otto-Baijer, who left it to his son Rowland, who died 1762 and bequeathed it to his son Rowland, who sold it in 1785 to James Donovan for £18,000 st. John H. Donovan, 154 slaves, 1829. Heirs of J. Donovan, 1852. Francis Shand, 1871, and his heirs, 1878.
10. FITCHE'S CREEK or MARTIN BYAMS, 517 acres. Hon. Martin Byam, 1788. William Byam, 260 slaves, 1829. W. and F. Shand, 1852. Francis Shand, 1871, and his heirs, 1878.
11. GRAVENOR'S, 83 acres. William Gravenor, 1788. Swanston and Clarke, 53 slaves, 1829. Heirs of John Freeland 1852 and 1871. 113 acres in St. John's Parish.
12. GROVE, 570 acres. Henry J. Cassin, 1878.
13. GUNTHORPES, 690 acres. Heirs of Gunthorpe, 280 slaves, 1829. Heirs of W. Gunthorpe, 1852. Francis Shand, 1871, and his heirs, 1878.
14. HIGH POINT, 212 acres. Samuel Martin, 1788. Hight Point and Nibbs, 268 acres, 163 slaves, Samuel Martin, 1829. Heirs of Samuel Martin, 1852 and 1871. George W. Bennett, 1878. 77 acres in St. John's Parish.
15. LIGHTFOOTS, 460 acres. Benjamin H. Edwards, 1871.
16. LONG ISLAND, 300 acres. Heirs of T. Jarvis, 1878.
17. MILLARS, 106 acres. Alexander Millar, 297 slaves, 1829. Alexander Millar, 1852. Horace Turner, 1871—78.
18. NIBBS, 131 acres. James L. Nibbs, 1788. Samuel Martin, 140 slaves, 1829. Heirs of Samuel Martin, 1852 and 1871.
19. NORTH SOUND, 602 acres. Sir George Thomas, Bart., 662 acres, 295 slaves, 1829. Sir George Thomas, Bart., 1852. George Estridge, 1871. Estridge now.
20. PAYNTER'S, 272 acres. Hon. William Gunthorpe, 1788. K. B. Osborne, 94 slaves, 1829. K. B. Osborn, M.D., 1852. Francis Shand, 1871, and his heirs, 1878.
21. SHERWOOD, 360 acres. Thomas Freeman, 1878.
22. WEIR'S, 136 acres. Hon. T. N. Kerby, 1788. Heirs of Kerby, 122 acres, 184 slaves, 1829. Miss Ottley, 1852. Samuel Sedgwick, 1871.
23. WINTHORPE'S, 231 acres. Heirs of George T. Thomas, deceased, 153 slaves, 1829. In 183– William Grant sold this to John William Dow. Inigo Thomas, 1852. Freeman Thomas, 1871.

RECTORS.

Henry Husband, 1728; M.A. Oxon; matriculated 1714, æt. 15.

James Berry, 1738, till his death 11 Dec. 1747, aged 38. M.I. at St. John's.

William Topham, 1748-52. Will dated 27 July 1756; sworn 4 May and recorded 21 Sep. 1763. (See *ante*, p. 345.)

George Holmes, 1753.

James Somerville, signs as Rector in 1775.

Arthur Freeman, 1791, died 6 July 1814; buried at St. Peter's.

James Coull, signed as Rector 1789 and 1818.

Samuel Ashton Warner, 1826-34 and later; Curate in 1825.

N. G. Hall, 1844.

George Jemmett, B.A., 1865.

Manoah James Drinkwater, 1872, till his death in 1888; Deacon 1864; Curate of St. Mary's 1864; Priest 1865 by the Bishop of Antigua.

The Church was built in 1735. There are no Vestry Records.

1825. 10 square miles, 3580 inhabitants. United in 1825 with St. Peter's. J. Coull, Rector of both. One church, 300 sittings. (Bishop Coleridge's Charges.)

1834. S. A. Warner, Rector. N. R. Callender, Curate of both. One church, 350 sittings.

Parish Registers.*

Baptized.

1754	Mar. 18	. . . . S. of Rowland . . . . eth his wife; b. Feb. 13, 1754.
1755	Aug. 9	Ann Nichols d. of Peter Delanoy & Frances his wife.

* Baptisms, Marriages, and Burials commenced in 1734.

1781 Nov. 6 Sarah Dyet the D. of John Desilvia and Mary his wife.

1784 April 4 Anthony Wyke the S. of John Desilvia and Mary his wife.

1797 Nov. 3 Frances D. of Capt Henry Mitford and Louisa his wife; b. Aug. 9 last.

1799 May 23 Louisa D. of Capt Henry Mitford and Louisa his wife; b. Dec. 22 last.

Married.

1742 Aug. 17 Carlisle Read and Mary Quinby, Widow. 1748. Rev. Mr Whitford signs.

1753 Mar. 31 John Tudhop & Mary Williamson, Spr.; by Revd Wm Topham for the Rev. Geo. Holmes.

1757 Nov. 11 George Skerrett Stephenson & Elizabeth Wilcox, Spr.

[Gap to 1764.]

1796 Dec. 10 Robert Cummings, Planter, & Rachel Marshal, Spr.

1799 April 25 Arthur Ormsby, Planter, & Elizabeth Gylliat Gore, Spr.

1807 April 21 Edward Harris Longstaff, Lieutenant in the Sixth West India Regt, and Elizabeth Gonnachaud, Spinster; by Lic. from General Brockton at St Lucia.

1808 Oct. 13 William Goddard, Planter, and Elizabeth Butts, Spr.; at Cedar Hill by L.

1810 Jan. 20 David Allan, Esqr, and Mary Ann Stilling, Spr.; by Lic. at Cedar Hill.

1818 April 13 Married at St Lucia by Licence from Colonel O'Hara, Commandant, John Cummings, late Captain in the 8th West India Regiment, & Deputy Assist Quarter Master & Barrick Master General, to Judith de Britton, Baroness, they having been married before in Jany 26th (1813?) in Guadalupe by a Roman Catholic Priest.

1818 April 27 John McKenzie, Lieutenant in the 1st West India Regiment, and Caroline Bisset, Spr.; by Licence from Colonel O'Hara, Commandant at the Morne, St Lucia.

1831 April 23 Robert Peddie, Esqr, M.D. of St John, & Louisa Frances Allan of St John. Lic.

1848 Jan. 13 William Edwards & Eliza Nash, spr. Lic.

1849 Sep. 11 Charles Andrew Scott Holberton, Widr, & Amelia Sarson of St John, spr. Lic.

1854 Nov. 23 George Hastings Dunn & Catherine Eaton, wid. Lic.

1865 April 11 Cheesman Moe Brathwaite, of St John, & Mary Jane Norman Gordon of St John. Lic.

1879 Oct. 9 George Stephenson Hobson of St John's, B., & Annie Alice Henrietta Harman of St Philip's, Spr. Lic.

Buried.

1734 June 15 Richard Terry, Colll William Paynter's overseer.

1735-6 Mar. 14 William Pellow.

1737 Oct. 9 Patrick Read.

1737 Feb. 28 The Revd Mr John Hinkesman.

1738 April 1 John Hinkesman, infant.

1741 Jan. 24 John Hinksman.

1743 Sep. 10 Oliver Bassett.

1746 May 5 Fretwell Spencer.

1747 Dec. 12 Revd Mr James Berrey.

1748 Sep. 24 Grace Foster D. of John Foster and Grace his wife.

1750 Oct. 31 Mrs Eliz. Dapwell, at Mr Todman's at Belfast.

1755 Nov. 25 Mrs Adams, from the Honble Rowland Ash's Estate.

1757 May 24 Doctor Zachary Fancins. Buried from the Estate of the late John Gunthorpe, deceased.

1758 Feb. 16 Doctor Willm Bell: buried from Mr Gray's Estate, com'only call'd Carlisles.

1759 Sep. 11 Mrs Arty, Widow, the Elder, of needs must.

1770 Feb. 6 John S. of John Gore & his wife; in Mr James Watson's Plantation.

1770 May 18 Margaret the Wife of John Desilvia.

1773 Nov. 15 Doctor William Reid.

1773 Dec. 22 Joshua Birkit.

1779 Feb. 27 Elizabeth Thurston; in the family burying ground.

1779 Sep. 29 Joseph the Infant S. of John Gore; in the family burying ground.

1780 Jan. 31 Elizabeth Birket; in the family Burying Ground.

1780 May 20 John the Infant S. of John Wilkins; in the family burying Ground of Thomas Jarvis, Esqr.

1782 Aug. 28 Ann Williams Gore the Infant D. of John Gore & Susannah his wife.

1787 Jan. 7 Elizabeth Philips.

1795 May 17 Ann Lydia Rogers, a Child from Belvidere.

1802 Sep. 8 Thomas Rogers, an Overseer from Lord Lavington's Estate.

1805 Jan. 2 John Gore, Senr, Clerk of this Parish; in the Family Burying Ground by Licence.

1810 Jan. 19 Ann Bird; in the Family Burying Ground at Barnacle Point.

1810 Aug. 18 Edwin Greenway Gore Infant Son of John Gore from Cassada Garden.

1818 Dec. 9 Anthony Beauman from Town; in the Family Vault of the Thomas's at Gillyatts, High Point.

1818 Sep. 16 Anthony Munton Rogers from Crabbs; in the Family Burying Place.

Monumental Inscriptions.

FITCHE'S CREEK.

In | **Memory** | **of** | BERTIE ENTWISLE BERTIE | Died 19 July 1825 | *Aged* 10 *Months* and 12 *days*.

On a large ledger:—Sacred to the Memory of | MRS MARGERY BUNTIN | Wife of IOHN BUNTIN ESQR | She was born the 26th May 1748 | And died Sincerely lamented | The 9th Febry 1813 Aged 64 Years | 8 Months and 14 Days. (Eight lines follow.)

On a white marble ledger:—**Sacred** | TO THE MEMORY OF | JOHN ALLAN ESQR | WHO DIED THE 21ST OF SEPTEMBER 1836 | AGED 75 YEARS.

On a headstone:—*In Memory of* | Iohn Lewis Favey | Died Octr 25 1801 Aged | 32 years.

On a headstone inside railings:—**To the memory** | OF | A BELOVED AND ONLY SON, | RICHARD HENRY CORFIELD, | OF *LIVERPOOL*, | AND LATELY | AN *OVERSEER* ON THE *ESTATE* | OF *FITCHES CREEK*, | IN THIS ISLAND, | WHO DIED 18TH APRIL 1864, | AGED 24 YEARS.

On a white marble slab over stone vault:—**Sacred** | TO THE MEMORY OF | THOMAS PEARSON, | MASTER MARINER LATE OF WHITBY | IN THE COUNTY OF YORK, | AGED 53 YEARS | WHOSE DEATH WAS CAUSED BY | THE UPSETTING OF A BOAT | ON THE 29TH OF MARCH 1829.

On a headstone:—Sacred | to the Memory | of | REBECCA SOUTHWELL | Who Departed this Life | On the 13 October 1815 | Aged 80 Years.

Three large brick vaults without M.I.

Over a large stone vault:—SACRED | To the memory of | James Barrett Esq^{RE} | Born 2nd October 1814 | Died 7th May 1872.

On a small wooden cross:—MARY . E. BERKELEY | DIED FEBRUARY 26 1856 | AGED 63 YEARS.

Sacred | To the memory of Mary | Elizabeth Green | who departed this | life on the fifteenth | of November 1861 | Aged 27 years.

ST. PAUL'S PARISH.

11,941 ACRES.

1. BARTERS, 193 acres. Before 1766 James Gordon purchased 180 acres of Edward Barter and heirs of Wickham, heretofore (1799) called Barters and Wickhams. Hon. R. W. Mara, LL.D., 1871. James Ackermann, 1878.
2. BLAKE'S, 276 acres. Martin Blake, 1788. Sarah Masterson, 259 acres, 98 slaves, 1829. Countess Masterson, 1852. Mrs. Millar, 1871. Mrs. Lucy Miller, 598 acres, 1878.
3. BODKIN'S, 412 acres. Messrs. Turner, 492 acres, 216 slaves, 1829. K. B. Osborn, M.D., 1852. Fryers Concrete Co., 494 acres, 1871.
4. BUCKSHORN'S, 200 acres. Mrs. Mary Willis, 1788. In 1815 Sir John Tyrrell, Bart., of co. Essex, sold this estate (then out of cultivation) to Charles Cheshire for £1500. Heirs of Mrs. Gilchrist, 1852. Teeheira Domingo, 100 acres, 1871.
5. BURKE'S, 364 acres. This was owned by John Burke in 1745, and then contained 450 acres. Burke's and Gable Hill, 585 acres, Samuel Nelson, 374 acres, 170 slaves, 1829 and 1852. James Maginlay, 1871.
6. COCHRAN'S, 545 acres. Arch. Cochran, 1788. Heirs of R. French, deceased, 147 slaves, 1829. Heirs of R. French, 1852. R. F. Sheriff, 1871. Heirs of A. W. Sheriff, 1878.
7. DELAP'S, 240 acres. John Delap-Halliday, 1788. Lucas' and Delap's, 560 acres, Rear-Admiral John H. Tollemache, 250 slaves, 1829. John Tollemache, 1852. Lord Combermere, 1871.
8. DIMSDALES, 407 acres. In 1648 this was called MICHAELLS MOUNT. In 1679 it was styled Michaells Mount or Deemesdales, and contained 275 acres, and had passed from Captain Benjamin Langham to Captain Joseph Lee, and by the latter's will of 1669 went to his son-in-law Major Richard Borraston. Was owned by Hon. Samuel Otto-Baijer, who died 1835. It cost him £7000, but was sold by him for only £300.
9. DOIGS. Walter Riddell, 1788.
10. FFRYE'S PASTURE, 100 acres. Henry Liggins, 1871.
11. FOLLY BYAM'S, 1931 acres [*sic*]. Godschall Johnson, 1788. Folly Byam's and Piccadilly, 2036 acres, 243 slaves, Godschal Johnson, 1829. Ditto 1852.
12. GALES. In 1716 contained 300 acres and was in possession of R. Rigby. James Gordon in 1766 devised this in trust for his nephew Captain F. Grant-Gordon, whose son Colonel J. W. Gordon owned it in 1806, called Gales or Table Hill.
13. HORSFORDS, Falmouth, 204 acres. John Horsford, 1829.
14. LA ROCHE'S, 231 acres. Sir James Laroche, 1788. In 1814 Thomas L. Brooke purchased this for £20,000, subject to £500 a year. Thomas L. Brooke, 174 slaves, 1829. Thomas L. Brooke, 1852 and 1871.
15. LOOBY'S, 286 acres. Valentine Morris, 1788. Heirs of Morris, 167 slaves, 1829. Assignees of J. Bullmer, 1852. Victor Guffrey, 1878.
16. MATHEWS' or CONSTITUTION HILL, 888 acres, 315 of these in St. John's Parish. In 1752 Ashton Warner owned this plantation, called Staughtons, or Burgess's, or Mathews. Mathews', heirs of Lachlan Grant, 1788. William Grant sold this 1803 to John William Dow. Warwick P. Hyndman, 1852. Luckie Brothers and Co., 1871. Heirs of Mr. Maginley, 1878.
17. MONKS HILL, 213 acres, formerly the Gordon's. Sir William Ably, Bart., 1871. F. B. Harman, 1878.
18. PATTERSONS and HORSFORDS, 407 acres. Horace Turner, 1852 and 1871. William H. Moore, 1878.
19. PICCADILLY, 1634 acres. C. M. Eldridge, 1871. Victor Guffry, 530 acres, 1878. Government, 1100 acres, 1878.
20. RED HILL, 400 acres. In 1775 contained 410 acres and belonged to Mathew Christian, from whom it passed to his sister and heir Margaret wife of William Gunthorpe, Esq. Ledwell and Scott were owners 1788. Mrs. Eudora Adlam, 1871—78.
21. RENDEZVOUS BAY, 171 acres. Thomas Woodcock, 1871. James Ackermann, 1878. Heirs of Ann Hamilton, 342 acres, 1878.
22. RICHMONDS and HOWARDS, 461 acres. William Maxwell at date of his will in 1768 owned Richmonds of 175 acres, Chapmans and Howards, which in 1820 were in possession of his son William. James Maxwell, 1788. Mrs. N. Gilbert, 1852. Mrs. Grace Gilbert, 1871. Miss M. McDonald, 365 acres, 1878.
23. ROCK HILL or LUCAS'S, 320 acres. In 1777 Nathaniel and Harry Webb sold this to John Halliday for £13,000 st. John Delap Halliday, 1788. Rear-Admiral John H. Tollemache, 110 slaves, 1829. John Tollemache, 1852.
24. THOMAS', 520 acres. Heirs of Gillan, deceased, 90 slaves, 1829. James W. Sheriff, 1852.
25. TYRRELS, 625 acres. Heirs of Admiral Tyrrel, 1788. Heirs of Tyrrel, 112 slaves, 1829. Heirs of A. Tyrrel, 1852. Thomas D. Foote, 1871.
26. WILLIS FREEMANS, 430 acres. In 1728 this was only 300 acres, and owned by Robert Freeman, and passed to his daughter Mary wife of B. Willis, and his two sons, and was also called Fig Tree Hill or Freeman's Rest, Benjamin and Joseph Willis. Mrs. Sutton, 122 slaves, 1829. Robert Sutton, 1852.
27. YEAMANS, 209 acres. R. and H. Jefferson, 1871.

RECTORS.

Simon Smith, M.A., was licensed by the Bishop of London 12 Dec. 1694, and was Rector in 1703. On 23 Sep. 1708 he was accused of bigamy and forgery. Buried at St. John's 19 May 1728 as Doc^{t} S. S.

. . . . Balneaves, 1713.

Charles Porter, 1716; presented by Governor Hamilton.

. . . . Leslie, 1719; presented by Governor Hamilton.

Richard Ridge, Minister of Falmouth. Buried at St. John's 8 Jan. 1725.

Thomas Allen, 1725—27.

Thomas Wilson, 1730—42.

Robert Davidson, 1743—70.

Richard Palmer, B.A., 1771—85; B.A. Oxon; matriculated 10 July 1761, æt. 21.

Samuel Lovely.

Arthur Freeman, 1795—1813.

Samuel W. Harman, M.A., *locum tenens* 1813—16.

Nathaniel Gilbert, 1815.

William Chaderton, 1816—22. Had previously been Rector of St. Mary's 1814—15. His patent from Sir James Leith was dated 10 Dec. 1815.

Thomas Fahie Horsford, M.A., 1822—28; son of Valentine Horsford, Esq., of Antigua; matriculated from Wadham College, Oxford, 12 May 1815, æt. 18; B.A. 1819; M.A. 1821; died 22 Aug. 1872.

Samuel Ashton Warner.

William Collins.

Joseph Bailey Wilkinson, 1831—50; was inducted 4 Jan. 1831 by the Bishop of Barbados; had previously acted as Curate 1828—31.

Darius Davey, Curate 1841—45.

E. O. Roach, 1850—53.

A. Berkeley, Priest-in-Charge 1853—54.

A. H. P. Culpepper, 1854—60.

Robert Holberton Bindon, 1860—88, resigned.

L. G. Richardson, Priest-in-Charge 1878-79, and Rev. G. Holman in 1882.

William James McConney died 1884.

J. Emrey, 1895.

The present Church was built in 1843, the year after the great earthquake.

1825. 18½ square miles, 4050 inhabitants. T. F. Horsford, M.A., Rector. One church, 350 sittings.

1834. J. B. Wilkinson, Rector. One church, 410 sittings; one temporary place of worship of 230 sittings.

There are no Vestry Records.

On an old silver flagon with the London hall-marks and date letter for 1699:—

This is Dedicated to our ever
Blefsed Saviour Jefus Christ
And ye Memory of William Wainwright
of Antigoa Esqe July ye 8th 1699.

On two alms dishes with the London hall-marks and date letter for 1724:—

In Usum Ecclefiæ Sancti Pauli, Parochiâ Falmouth in Antigua, Patina haec Elomofynæ et Euchariftiæ Gratiâ Humillimè Devota et Dicata est Anno Domini 1724.

Parish Registers.*

Baptized.

1729 Oct. 19 Robert S. of Joseph & Ann Carpenter.

1730 Jan. 17 John S. of John Riply & Elizabeth his wife.

1730 Jan. 30 Elizabeth D. of William Greatrix & Christian his wife.

1731 June 20 Barbara D. of William Bawn & his wife.

1733 June 3 Daniel S. of John Brenan & Margarett his wife.

1734 Aug. 26 Hamlin S. of John Brenan.

1734 Dec. 22 James S. of Alexander Macpherson and Mary his wife.

1734 Dec. 31 Theophilus William S. of William Greatrix & Christian his wife.

1735 Dec. 17 Elizabeth D. of John Brenan and Margarett his wife.

1736 Mar. 13 John S. of Benjamin Bawn.

1737 June 25 William S. of Alexander and Mary Macpherson.

1738 July 31 Elizabeth D. of Alexander McPherson and Mary his wife.

1744 June 10 William George Lucas S. of Mr Henry Parr & Amelia his wife.

1756 April 25 James Morison S. of Mr William Mackaile and Elizabeth his wife.

[1758—1770 gap.]

1771 May 26 Mary Ann D. of Doctor Joseph Steevens.

1772, Rev. Richd Palmer signs as Rector.

1784 Feb. 20 George s. of Geo. Walker, Lieu. 82 Regt. £1 18s. 0*d*.

1785 Dec. 4 Peter s. of Capt John Goldsmith Wade and Louisa his wife: b. 17th April 1785. 3s. 6*d*.

Circa 1810 William Sershall Sutton s. of Doctor William Eyre Odlum and Avis Justice Clapham Odlum; b. 21st day of last July.

1813 April 17 William Hynde s. of Cap. Foxton of Store ship Hyena & his wife; b. 7 weeks agone.

1813 Sep. 14 Walter Odlum s. of John S. Scholar of H.M. Dockyard & Margaret Frances his wife; b. 24th Decem. 1812.

1813 Nov. 26 Alfred Thomas Antonie Phillip s. of Phillip De Grasse, Ensign in Y.L.I. Volunteers & Charlotte his wife; b. 13 Nov. 1813.

1813 Dec. 16 James Alexander s. of John S. Scholar of H.M. Dockyard & Margaret Frances his wife; b. 14th Nov. 1813.

1814 Jan. 9 George Lindsey s. of Major George Bennett & Mary his wife; b. 22d Nov. 1813.

1814 Sep. 14 Sophia d. of Lieut. Alexr Smyth, Y.L.I. Vol., & Elizabeth his wife; b. 9th Aug. last.

1816 July 4 Mary Ann Gilbert D. of John S. Scholar & Margaret Frances his wife was baptized at English Harbour, aged 14 months.

1817 Jan. 6 Anne Campbell D. of William Eyre Odlum, M.D., & Avis Justice Clapham his wife was baptized at Jessamine Hill, aged 2 years, & Mary Clift D. of do., aged 14 months.

1817 May 5 Eliza Antoinetta D. of the Revd William Chaderton & Mary Rachel his wife was baptized at the Parsonage, St John's. B. 16 Mar. 1817.

1817 Aug. 12 Thomas William S. of Michael Vicary, Lieut. in the 63d Regiment, & Eliza his wife was baptized at Monks Hill; b. the 8th inst.

1818 May 7 William S. of Robert Hartle, Esqr, Senior Medical Officer, & Elizabeth his wife was baptized at the Detatchment Hospital. B. May 1st, 1818.

1818 July 27 Edward Boehmler S. of Capt William Butts of the R. Artillery & Victoria Elizabeth his wife was baptized at the Ridge. B. July 10th, 1818.

1818 Sep. 7 Rose Wilhelmina d. of the Rev. William Chaderton & Mary Rachel his wife was baptized at St. Paul's Parsonage. B. Aug. 24, 1818.

1821 Feb. 26 Henrietta Anna D. of Robert Hartle, Esqr, Senior Medical Officer, & Eliza his wife was Baptized; born on the evening of the 14 Feb. same year. Sponsors, Lady D'Urban & Miss D'Urban, Sir Benj. D'Urban & Walter D'Urban, Esq.

* Baptisms and Marriages commenced in 1725, Burials in 1726.

1822 April 14 Eliz. Ann d. of do.; b. on the 6th Ap. Sponsors Miss Eliz. Smith, Miss Mary Willoughby, Capt James Smith, & Sam. Marchant, Esq.

1823 Dec. 21 William s. of William Munro, Surgeon in the 35th Reg., & Charlotte Maria his wife was baptized; b. on the 30th of Nov. Godfathers, Major Sutherland & Dr Hartle. Godmother, Mrs Odlum.

1833 Mar. 27 Joseph Bayley s. of Joseph Bayley & Ann Campbell Wilkinson. St Paul's Rectory. Rector of this Parish. B. Jan. 29.

1835 . . . . . . William Eyre Odlum s. of Joseph Bayly & Ann C. Wilkinson. St Paul's Rectory.

1837 April 14 Charlotte St John D. of Joseph Bayly & Ann Campbell Wilkinson. St Paul's Rectory. Rector of this Parish. B. Feb. 10.

1840 May 20 Ann Campbell D. of Joseph B. & Ann C. Wilkinson. St Paul's Rectory. Rector of this Parish. B. 11 July 1839.

1844 Jan. 17 Admitted into church, bap. 15 May 1843, B. 9 Mar. 1843, Jonas s. of Joseph B. & A. C. Wilkinson. St Paul's Rectory. Rector of this parish.

1846 Mar. 25 William Eyre Lindsey s. of William S. S. & Anne Jarvis Odlum. Buckshorns. Practitioner of Physic.

1846 Nov. 11 Georgiana Maria Grace D. of William Eyre & Elizabeth Grace Odlum. Clarence House. Practitioner of Physic.

1848 Feb. 3 Louisa Avis D. of William Sershall Sutton & Ann Jarvis Odlum. Mount William. Practitioner of Physic.

1848 May 3 Avis Jane D. of Joseph B. & Ann C. Wilkinson. St Paul's Rectory. Rector of this parish.

1850 Feb. 25 Robert Wolsey s. of William S. S. & Ann J. Odlum. Mount William. Practitioner of Physic.

1850, Nov. 15, E. O. Roach signs as Rector.

1851 Sep. 30 Miriam de Courcy D. of William S. S. & Ann J. Odlum. English Harbour. Practitioner of Physic.

1853 June 21 Edwin William s. of Edwin Osmond & Mary Roach. The Parsonage. Rector of St Paul's & Garrison Chaplain at Antigua.

Married.

1726 April 10 Daniel Pellow and Mary Ely. P. Banns.

1726 May 21 John Reed and Jane Pellow. P. Banns.

1727, Tho. Allen signs as Rector.

1729, Jno Lister signs as Curate.

1730, Tho. Willson signs as Rector.

1730 June 14 William Greatrix & Christian Anderton; by Banns.

1730 Feb. 27 Thomas Mascall & Margaret Barry; by L.

1731, Robt Davidson signs as Minister, also in 1737 & 1743.

1736 May 22 Joseph Parker and Anne Todman.

1739 Feb. 21 Mr Benjamin Renouard & Mrs Jane Sutton; by L.

1743 July 28 Richard Saull and Mary Bawn; by L.

1772 Aug. 16 Mr Joseph Aska to Miss Mary Evans Bickford; per L.

1774 Mar. 8 James Worth, Esqr, Captain of His Majesty's ship the Chatham, to Miss Margaret Yunnie; pr L.

1799 Oct. 19 Robert Christie, surgeon of his Majesty's ship Hydra, to Ann Dingwall, Spr; pr L.

1809 Jan. 27 Henry Peirce, Capt in the Royal Artillery, to Helen Pringle, Spr.; by L.

1809 April 5 John Fitzgerald, gentleman, to Frances Campbell, widow.

1809 Oct. 19 William Eyre Odlum, doctor of his Majesty's ship Abercrombie, to Avis Justice Clapham Sutton, spinr.

1811, Arth. Freeman signs as Rector.

1811 Aug. 26 Charles Church, first Lieutenant of his Majesty's Ship Gloire, to Elizabeth Lemmon, d. of Wm Lemmon, Master Builder at English Harbour.

1814, Rev. Sam. Wm Harman signs.

1815, Rev. Nath. Gilbert signs.

1818, Wm Chaderton signs as Rector.

1822, Tho. Fahie Horsford signs as Rector.

1822 Dec. 2 Thomas Hall, Batchelor, and Mary Ann Willoughby, Spr.; by L.

1831 Jan. 26 Joseph Bayley Wilkinson, Rector, & Anne Campbell Odlum; by L.

Buried.

1729 Nov. 23 Captn Wright.

1730 Jan. 13 Mr Thomas Edgcombe.

1730, July 25. Tho. Wilson, Rector, signs.

1731 Sep. 22 Dr Ralph Jackson; at St Peter's, Parham.

1731 Dec. 12 Mary D. of William Bawn.

1733 Aug. 17 Frances Bawn.

1733 Nov. 4 Elizabeth Anderton, Widow.

1733 Feb. 2 Dr Thomas Grigg.

1734 Aug. 27 Hamlin S. of John Brenan.

1734 Sep. 2 Mary Edgcombe.

1734 Oct. 1 Thomas Fort, Lieutenant of his Majesty's Ship Newcastle.

1734 Sep. 19 Anne D. of Joseph Carpenter and Anne his wife.

1735 Nov. 24 John Ripley.

1735 Dec. 25 Mrs Martha Edgcombe.

1736 Oct. 26 William Bawn.

1736 Jan. 4 Margaret Wife of John Brenan.

1737 July 1 Jacob Ailhaud.

1738 Mar. 18 Hannah Greatrix.

1740 Aug. 18 Mr George Monro, Midshipman on Board his Majestie's Ship Anglesea.

1740 Dec. 27 Jane Wife of Mr Benjamin Renouard.

1742 Oct. 31 John Platers, Lieutenant of his Majestie's Ship the Pembroke Price.

1743 June 14 Richard Prater, Midshipman on Board his Majestie's Ship the Suffolk.

1743 July 1 Mr Andrew Home, Surgeon.

1743 Aug. 1 John Gage, Captain of his Majestie's Ship the Lively.

1743 Aug. 10 James Ralph, Midshipman of his Majestie's Ship the Lynn.

1743 Sep. 25 John Balderstown, Midshipman on Board his Majestie's Ship the Severn.

1743 Oct. 10 Benjamin Bawn.

1743 Nov. 29 Elizabeth Brenan D. of John & Margaret Brenan.

1743 Dec. 5 William Monteith, Surgeon on Board his Majestie's Ship the Lynn.

1743 Dec. 30 Thomas Rogers, Surgeon on Board one of his Majestie's Store Ships.

1744 July 23 Mr George Hammond, Midshipman on Board his Majestie's Ship the Severn.

1744 Mar. 19 William Holden, Midshipman on Board his Majestie's Ship the Deal Castle.

1745 July 22 Edward Willoughby, Midshipman on Board his Majestie's Ship the Superbe.

1746 Jan. 14 Seth Cocks, Lieutenant of Marines on Board his Majestie's Ship the Dreadnought.

1747 July 29 Jacob Wayman, S. of Jacob Wayman of Weymouth and Melcomb Regis in the County of Dorset.

1747 July 31 Mr William Moon, Lieutenant on Board his Majestie's Ship the Ludlow Castle.

1747 Oct. 18 Mr Joseph Clements, Lieutenant of Marines on Board his Majestie's Ship the Dragon.

1747 Dec. 14 Halsey Warner, an Officer of the Artillery.

1747 Jan. 19 Mr Newenman Herbert, Clerk to Dr Irwin.

1748 May 28 Mr Henry Parr of Liverpool.

1748 June 2 William Skinner, Midshipman on Board his Majestie's Ship Sunderland.

1748 Aug. 2 George Geddis, Midshipman on Board his Majestie's Ship the Captain.

1748 Feb. 18 Barbara D. of Mr John Taylor and Elizabeth his wife.

1749 May 14 Mr Peter Aliere.

1750 May 19 Eleanor Stevenson, Widow. Buried in Mr Elmes Windward Plantation.

1750 May 30 John Haggitt, Commander of the Store Ship in English Harbour, the Beckford.

1750 July 13 William Potter, Commander of the Ship the New Triton; buried in St Philip's Church Yard.

1752 Aug. 23 Richard Herbert Rower S. of Doctr Alexander Rower, Deceased, and Mary his Widow.

[Here New Style.]

1753 Sep. 10 Edmund Foster, Midshipman on Board his Majestie's Sloop the Badger.

1754 Feb. 19 Richard Walkup, a Midshipman on board the Advice.

1755 Feb. 10 Anna Maria D. of Mrs Mary Rower, Widow.

1756 Sep. 24 William Biggs, Lieutenant of Marines on board his Majestie's Ship the Stirling Castle.

1756 Oct. 6 Robert Baker, Coroner of this Island, and Surveyor.

1756 Nov. 14 Essex Roach, Surgeon of his Majestie's Ship the Saltash.

[1758—1767 gap.]

1769 Feb. 19 John Bodledge, Lieutenant . . . .

1769 May 26 Doctor Thom . . . .

1770 Jan. . . Doctor Andrew Manderston, Surgeon to the King's Hospital.

1770 Jan. 25 D. of Capt Garnier.

1770 April 4 Doctor Robert Salter.

1770 May 21 George Falconer, Surgeon to the Jason.

1770 Nov. 6 Maria Amelia D. of Mr Watts.

1772 Aug. 23 Mr James Hawthorne, Manager.

1772 Oct. 1 Doctor Joseph Steevens.

1773 Nov. 15 Mr Hen. Pell, Mid.

1777 Feb. 13 Thomas Wilkinson, Esq., Cap. of the Pearl Frigate.

1777 Mar. 17 Peter Man, Mid.

1777 Aug. 30 Alexander Boyd (Surgeon of the Cygnet).

1779 May 20 . . . . O'Hara, Lieut of Marines.

1779 . . . . 23 . . . . Broughton (Capt. of the Sphinx).

1779 May 15 . . . . Callaway (Surgeon).

1779 Sep. 30 Willm Cann (Surgeon).

1780 Jan. 3 . . . . McLawrin (Surgeon).

1780 Nov. 30 Honble James Charles P . . . .

1784 Oct. 16 Lieutenant Elliot. £1 13*s.* 0*d.*

1786 Jan. 13 Frederick Mowatt, Lieut of Marines on Bd Latona £3 6*s.* 0*d.*

1795 Dec. 27 Lieutenant Willsford of the Fury. £1 13*s.* 0*d.*

1795 Aug. 18 Mr Pittman, Lieut. of Marines.

1795 Aug. 22 Dor Papworth of the Perdrix.

1795 Aug. 29 Lieut Clerk.

1795 Aug. 30 Lieut Fox of the 59th Reg.

[The entries between 1795 and 1816 are missing.]

1816 June 6 Mrs Avis Sutton was buried in St Paul's Church Yard.

1816 Aug. 30 Doct Dawling, R. Arty. etc.

1816 Dec. 11 Serj. Maj. Ure of the 4th W.I. Reg., etc.

1816 Dec. 15 Mary Ure, etc.

1816 Dec. 16 George William Robinson, Ensign in the 63rd Reg., etc.

1817 Feb. 6 William Lennox, Serj. Maj. 63rd Reg., etc.

1817 Feb. 15 Lieut. Bell, 1st W.I. Reg., etc.

1818 Jan. 17 Serj. McLeod of the 1st W.I. Reg., etc.

1818 Nov. 1 Ensign Thomas Lovel Jinks, 1st W.I. Reg., etc.

1819 Mar. 11 John Davis McKonichie, Ensign in the R.W.I. Rangers, etc.

1819 Dec. 21 Diego Dunn Felix, Infant s. of William Dunn Fields & Rocelia his wife, etc.

1820 Oct. 10 Mrs Eliz. Johnstone, etc.

1821 Oct. 24 William s. of Dec. Robert Hartle, etc.

1821 Nov. 2 William Cathcart, Esqr, Purveyor to the Forces, etc.

1821 Dec. . . Augusta Farr, Infant D. of John Farr, Esq., etc.

1822 Mar. 11 Major Loftus of the 9th Reg., etc.

1822 Mar. 23 Thomas B. Powell, etc.

1824 Aug. 6 Ann Hartle, Mother of Dr Hartle, etc.

1825 Jan. 24 Thomas Gillan was buried in the private Burial ground at Red Hill; late Practitioner of Physic in this Island.

1825 May 21 Maria Davey, Infant D. of Mr Darius Davey, etc.

1825, Tho. Fahie Horsford signs as Rector.

1827 June 24 James Ireland, Lieu. & Adjutant of 93d Highlanders. Ridge. 52.

1834 Jan. 18 William Wilkinson (In Military ground, Ridge). Ridge. 24.

1835 June 8 Charles M. Burrows, Lieu. 36 Reg. Ridge. 32.

Monumental Inscriptions.

On a headstone:—SACRED | to | the memory of | ANN ANDERSON | late Wife of | WM ANDERSON Jr | who departed this life | the 8th December 1819 | Aged 24 Years.

On a ledger:—In Memory | of | CHARLES ANTROBUS ESQr | Commander | of His Majesty's Ship | Jafon | Who departed this Life | Nov. the 3d 1769 | Aged 44.

Buried 1769, Nov. 3, Charles Antrobus, Commander of the "Jason."

On a headstone:—I.H.S. | SACRED | TO THE MEMORY | OF . . . . A . . . . BA . RET.

On a headstone:—SACRED | to the Memory of | MR BENJN BENJAMIN | who DEparted this Life | March 19. 1827 | Aged 68 Years.

On a headstone:—**I.H.S.** | **Sacred** | to the memory of | ANN ELIZABETH BLACK | who died the 6th day | of December 1820 | *in the Twelfth Year* | *of her Age.*

Sacred to the | Memory of | SOPHIA CAMPBELL | who departed this | Life 25th Nov. 1798 | Aged 68 years.

On a large stone slab over stone vault:—I.H.S. | SACRED | to the Memory of | JOHN CUTHBERT who departed | this Life 14th of May 1805 aged | Sixty six years. | **Sacred** | to the Memory of | JOHN CUTHBERT McKELLAR | Son of | JOHN and ANNE McKELLAR | who departed this Life | . . . . May 1808 | . . . . Months | . . . . Days.

On a headstone:—SACRED | to the memory of | MARY DARTON | . . . . this life | . . . . | . . . . Age.

On a large stone tomb falling to pieces:—**Sacred** | To the Memory of | Mrs ELIZA DAVEY | who departed this life | January 8th 1838 | Aged 36 Years | Leaving the recollection of | her many Virtues deeply | enshrined in the hearts of her | Sorrowing Husband and Children.

On a ledger:—**Sacred** | To the Memory of | SARAH DIVINE | late Wife of | SERJT JAMES DIVINE | ROYALL ARTILLERY | who departed this Life | 17 October 1803 | Aged 32 Years. (Four lines follow.)

On a stone pedestal within railings on the north side is the following:—

TO | THE MEMORY | OF | BRIGADE MAJOR | ROBERT VANS AGNEW | A Lieutenant of the 1 Regt of Guards | and eldest Son of Robert Vans Agnew | Esquire of Barnbarrow in the County of | Wigton by his Wife Frances Dunlop Sister | to the General whose remains are also | here deposited | ob. 17 Aug. 1804 æt. 25.

(Eleven lines follow.)

Arms: 1 *and* 4 (*Argent*) . . . . *a bend* (*Gules*) . . . . ; 2 *and* 3, *a chevron, between in chief two cinquefoils* (*Gules*), *with a cross-crosslet fitchée* (*Sable*) *in centre, and in base a saltier couped.*

Crest: *A lion rampant, holding in its dexter paw a pair of scales over helmet.*

Motto, above: *Be faithful.*

Motto, below: *Consilio non impetu.*

(*Vide* pedigree of Vans Agnew of Barnbarroch in Burke's 'Landed Gentry,' where no mention is made of the above-mentioned Robert.)

TO | THE MEMORY | OF | BRIGADIER GENERAL | ANDREW DUNLOP | Who in the 48th Year of his Age while Commandant in | the Ifland of Antigua died of the Yellow Fever on the | 24th Day of August | MDCCCIV | THIS MONUMENT | Is erected as a Tribute of Respect due to his Talents | and Virtues by his mourning Relations. | General Dunlop was the Son of John Dunlop of | Dunlop in North Britain and became the Representative | of that ancient Family. | By his Mother he was descended | From the Elder Branch of the Family of the illustrious | Wallace the great Defender of Scottish Liberty | He early embraced a Military Life & in the progressive | Stages of Rank distinguished himself during War by | his Professional abilities Residing upon his Estate | during peace he there displayed the Energy of a Zealous | and upwright Magistrate tempered by the habits and | Accomplisiments of a Gentleman and endeared to | those it more immediately affected by the Qualities | of a benevolent & judicious Landlord. Nothing however | prevented his Listening to the Call of his Country as often | as she became involved in War | Promoted by his Soveraign in the Year 1803 to the | Rank of Brigadier General in the West Indies | where for | some time he held the Chief Command. It was his lot to see | the Troops under his immediate order subjected to the | dreadful Ravages of Pestilence. Amidst the Dead and | dying unrestrained by any fear of infection his indefatigable | endeavours to alleviate their suffering proved that he needed | not the Stimulus of Military Fame to induce him to lay down | his Life in the Service of his Country. Worn out at length | by his endeavour to check the Progress Calamity | despairing of Success after closing the Eyes of a beloved | Nephew the last surviving Member of the European | Part of his Family he submitted a resigned and unresisting | Victim to that Fate which his active benevolence had so | ardently struggled to avert from others.

Arms: *Within a bordure a double-headed eagle displayed* . . . .

Crest: *A dexter hand holding a short sword over helmet.*

Motto: *Merito.*

The shield backed by military trophies.

On a headstone:—. . . . lies the . . . . | BRIGADIER | VANDELEUR | who departed this Life | . . . . 1806 | . . . . the Country . . . . (Remainder obliterated.)

On a broken urn:—Robt FANS . . . . Died 5 July . . . . 1804 | . . . . WSHAW.

On a flat stone:—SACRED TO THE MEMORY | OF MRS JAMES FAVEY | *Wife of* CHARLES C. FAVEY | who departed this Life | the 3rd of February 1815 | Aged 23 Years. (Two lines follow.)

On a headstone:—**Sacred** | to the memory of | MR THOMAS FORD | *Late Citizen of London* | who departed this Life | 14th December 1815 | *Aged* 53 *Years* | *also* | His Son THOMAS | died 19th November 1816 | *AGED* 9 *YEARS.*

On a ledger:—**Sacred** | To the memory of | MR FRANCIS FOX | late Boatswain of | His Majestys NAVAL YARD | Who departed this Life | 11 October 1823 | Aged 49 Years | Forty of which were Spent in | His MAJESTYS SERVICE | He was an affectionate Husband | a loving Father and | a sincere Friend. (Four lines follow.)

On a large marble ledger:—**Sacred to the memory of** | JANE | *THE BELOVED WIFE OF* CHARLES JAMES FOX WHO DEPARTED THIS LIFE MARCH 14TH 1856 | AGED 46 YEARS. | **And of** | ROWENA FREDERICA | *THEIR ELDEST DAUGHTER* | WHO DEPARTED THIS LIFE MARCH 26, 1856 | AGED 26 YEARS | **And of** | LOUISA LEITH | *THEIR SECOND DAUGHTER* | WHO DEPARTED THIS LIFE APRIL 13, 1856 | AGED 15 YEARS.

(Five lines follow.)

Sacred | to the | memory of | ARTHUR W. ISAAC | who died 15 June | 1824 | Aged 42 Years.

Sacred | To the Memory of | EDWARD KELLY | *Quarter Master* | of the 4 (or the Kings Own) Regt | Died 5th March 1824 | Aged 18 years. (Eleven lines follow.)

Also | his Infant Daughter | AMELIA | who departed this Life | on the 27 May 1824 | Aged 8 Months.

Sacred | . . . . THE | MEMORY | of | AMELIA DAUGHTER | . . . . the late QR MR Kelly | 4th or Kings Own Regt. (Six lines follow.)

On a large stone slab resting on granite pedestals:—Sacred | To the Memory of | JOHN MAC CAUSLAND Esqr | Commander of H.M.S. Cruizer | Son of the | Revd OLIVER MAC. CAUSLAND | County of Derry IRELAND. | He died at Sea on the 7th of Oct. 1835. | Honored beloved and deeply regretted | by all who knew him | His mortal remains were deposited here | by the officers and crew of the Ship who | had ever considered him as their guide | their Guardian and friend. | Also | JOHN MAC. CAUSLAND. Esqr | Capt 89th Foot Died the 4th June 1839 | Aged 47 Years.

Buried 1835, Oct. 8, John Macausland, Commander H.M.S. "Cruizer." 46.

Buried 1839, June 4, John McCausland, Lieut. 89th Regiment. Ridge. 50.

On a ledger:—SACRED | *TO THE MEMORY OF* | HARRIET C. M^C DOWALL | WHO DEPARTED THIS LIFE | THE 14TH (or 11th ?) AUGUST 1842 | AGED 28 YEARS.

Sacred | to the memory of | MARIA MACNAMAR . who departed | this life the 2 day | of Sep. 1815 | Aged 75 Years.

On a marble cross:—SACRED | TO THE MEMORY OF | HENRY NETTERVILLE | CAMPBELL ODLUM.

Inside the church, on a small marble tablet on the north wall:—LIEU^T EDWARD . E . OWEN . R.N. | DIED JANUARY 13TH 1838, | AGED 40 YEARS.

(Erected by his mother.)

Buried 1838, Jan. 14, Edward E. Owen, Lieut.-Commander H.M.S. "Carron." English Harbour. 42.

SACRED | *TO THE MEMORY OF* | RAVELY THOMAS PARKER | *Aged 22 Years 3 Months* | *Born 23rd Nov^r* 1850 | *Died 25th Feb^ry* 1872.

On a flat stone:—Underneath are interred the remains | of the | Honb^le JAMES CHARLES PITT | Son of | The EARL of CHATHAM | Commander of his *MAJESTY'S* ship *HORNET* | Who departed this life at English Harbour | On the 13th of November 1780 | Aged 20 Years | The Genius that inspired | And the Virtues that adorned the | PARENT | Were revived in the | SON | Whose dawning Merit | Bespoke a meridian Splendor | Worthy of the Name of | PITT.

Sacred | To the memory of | DAVID REES, ESQ^R | Surgeon to the Forces | Who departed this life | the 1st August 1843 | Aged 52.

(Erected by his widow.) The tomb is similar to the McCauslands, and both were made at Dublin.

On a flat stone:—SACRED to the MEMORY of | JANE SAYER Wife of SAMUEL SAYER | who departed this Life February the 26 | in the Year of Our Lord One Thousand | Seven hundred and Seventy Nine in the | 39th Year of her Age. (Four lines follow.)

Also of her Infant Son SAMUELL who | departed this Life February the 21st in | the Year of Our Lord One thousand Seven | hundred and Seventy Nine.

of the above named SAMUELL SAYER | who departed this Life December 11th | in the Year of Our Lord One thousand eight | hundred and three in the 63rd Year of | his Age. (Four lines follow.)

To the Memory of | MR DANIEL SCARVILL | Who was fourteen Years Mafter | Shipwright of his Majeftys Dock | Yard of Antigua who departed this | Life at Antigua on the 16th day of | September 1797 Aged 63 Years.

On a ledger:—**Sacred** | To the Memory | of | WILLIAM SERSHALL | died 1st January 1793 | aged 30 Years | Richard Sutton | died the 8th of March 1794 | Aged 38 Years | William Serfhall Sutton | Son of the above | Richard Sutton | died 13th December 1808 | Aged 16 Years | AVIS SUTTON died the 5th June | 1816 Aged 49 Years | MARY RAMSAY Died 18th February | 1828 Aged 90 Years | AVIS JUSTICE CLAPHAM ODLUM | Died the 14th October 1841 | Aged 52 Years.

George M . . . . | Shoom . . . . | The 22 of October | Aged 2 . . . . Years | 1724.

On a ledger:—**Sacred** | To the Memory of | M^RS HANNAH SLOSS | *Wife of MR JOHN SLOSS* | who departed this Life Sep. 17. 1813 | in the 16th Year of her Age. (Nine lines follow.)

Alfo the above MR JOHN SLOSS | who departed this Life Feb. 19. 1811. | Aged 16 Years. (Several lines follow.)

On a ledger:—SACRED | to the Memory | *of* | JAMES D. WALKER | Late of *Glasgow* who died at | *English Harbour* of | Yellow Fever | Twenty seventh October MDCCCXXXV | Aged Eighteen Years.

SACRED | . . *the Memory of* | . . os WALKER Esqr | storekeeper of his | . . y's Ordnance in | . . is Island | . . . . parted this Life. (Fragment only.)

SACRED | To the Memory | of Mr William Woodcock | of his Majesty's Dock Yard | Antigua | Who departed this life June 23, 1827 | Aged 52 Years. (Two lines follow.)

On a marble slab lying on the ground:—Erected | to the | Memory | of | GEORGE WEBSTER ESQ^R | Ordnance Store-keeper | ANTIGUA, | Who died 17 Jany 1834 Aged 47 . | by his | afflicted Widow, REBECCA GIBSON, | in | testimony of her sincere | Esteem and Regard.

A stone tomb with no M.I.

A large stone tomb with no M.I., inside iron railings.

A large stone tomb broken down.

SHIRLEY HEIGHTS MILITARY BURIAL-GROUND.

ELIZABETH | The Beloved Wife of Philip Crofton | Royal Artillery Who Departed this | Life On the 20th Day of October 1851 | AGED 28 YEARS.

Sacred | TO THE MEMORY OF | CHARLES DAWSON M.D | SURGEON OF H . M . 54^R REGIMENT | WHO DIED THE 14TH OF NOVEMBER | 1849 | AGED 35 YEARS. (Nine lines follow.)

(Placed by his wife Jane Marian Dawson.)

On a stone tomb within iron railings:—SACRED | TO THE MEMORY OF | MOLINEUX MARSTON | CAPTAIN ROYAL ARTILLERY | AND | CHARLOTTE HIS WIFE | WHO DIED HERE | JANUARY 1854 | THIS TRIBUTE | TO THEIR MEMORY | IS ERECTED BY | G. F. C. PETER.

On a stone obelisk:—S^T KITTS S^T LUCIA | DOMINICA ANTIGUA.

Followed by lists of killed, which include Ensign George Daniel Kinahan of Antigua.

ST. PHILIP'S PARISH.

10,881 ACRES.

1. ARCHBOLD'S and BROWNS, 398 acres. Charles Robertson, 239 slaves, 1829. Thomas Daniell and Co., 1852 and 1871. Browns, Nicholas Brown, 1788.
2. COLEBROOKES, 356 acres. Formerly called Gaynor's Windward Estate; at death of Peter Gaynor in 1738 this passed to his daughter and heir Lady Colebrooke, whose son Sir James sold the Gaynor Estate in 1835 for £10,000. Messrs. Turner, 1829. Heirs of John T. Wood, 1852. James Goodwin, 1871, and his heirs, 1878.
3. COLLINS, 92 acres. W. and F. Shand, 1852. William Goodwin, 1871.
4. COMFORT HALL or THOMAS', 514 acres. Thomas S. Edwards, 1688 acres, 1829. Crumps Mercers Creek Estate in 1771 contained 240 acres.* Heirs of T. S. Edwards, 1852. McDonalds and Co., 1871. James Maginley, 1878.

* In 1802 Sir G. Thomas, Bart., for £22,000 sold to Thomas Edwards his estate of 286 acres in Belfast, with negros and stock.

5. ELLIOTS, 192 acres. Heirs of R. French, deceased, 226 slaves, 1829. Heirs of R. French, 1852. Estate of George and Henry French, 1871. Heirs of G. W. French, 1878.

6. ELMES, 158 acres. In 1775 Elme's Creek Estate contained 149 acres, and Windward ditto 180 acres, both owned by Mathew Christian. Messrs. Hyndman, 106 slaves, 1829. Philip Lyne, 1852. Francis Shand, 1871.

7. FFRYES, 320 acres. George Redhead, 130 slaves, 1829. Joseph Liggins, 1852. Dr. John Freeland, 1871. Charles J. Manning, 1878.

8. GAYNORS, 67 acres. Sir George Colebrooke, 1788 (? if this was the Creek or Mangrove plantation, formerly Peter Gaynor's in 1738). Heirs of Nicholas Symes, deceased, 117 acres, 71 slaves, 1829. B. Musgrave, 1852. Francis Shand, 1871.

9. GILBERTS and THE MANGROVE, 513 acres. Mrs. Gilbert, 1871.

10. GLANVILLE'S, 296 acres. Rear-Admiral J. H. Tollemache, 111 slaves, 1829. John Tollemache, 1852. Lord Combermere, 453 acres, 1871—78.

11. GOBLES, 210 acres. After the death of John Richardson, Esq., in 1705, John Goble purchased his 145 acres for £4000 c. Stephen Lynch, Esq., bequeathed this, 1771. Gobles 210 acres, and Montpelier 75 acres, 212 slaves, heirs of William Harman, 1829. Thomas R. Jones, 1852. Francis Shand, 1871. Gobles, Gaynors, and Elmes, 427 acres, William Goodwin, 1878.

12. GRANTS, 296 acres. John Lake, 1852. Grants and Jefferson's or Sion Hill, 112 acres, 272 slaves, John D. Taylor, 1829.

13. GRAY'S BELFAST, 230 acres. John Gray and William Gilchrist, 146 slaves, 1829. Heirs of Mrs. Gilchrist, 1852. McDonalds and Co., 1871. D. C. Odlum, 1878.

14. HARMANS. 148 slaves, S. B. Harman, 1852. Harmans and Walronds, 369 acres, Frederick B. Harman, 1871. Harmans, Upper Walronds, Montpelier, and Hope, 674 acres, F. B. Harman, 1878.

15. HARRY HARDINGS, 150 acres. Samuel Harman, 139 slaves, 1829. Samuel B. Harman, 1871.

16. HOPE, 208 acres. Richard Garland, 119 slaves, 1829. Francis Watson, 1852.

17. LAVINGTONS, 185 acres. James Adam Gordon, 150 slaves, 1829. James Adam Gordon, 1852. James McGinley, 1871—78.

18. LONG LANE and LITTLE DELAPS, 469 acres. John Lavicount, 1788. John Lavicount, 204 slaves, 1829. Heirs of John Lavicount, 1852. F. Kennington, 1871. James Maginley, 1878.

19. LYNCH'S, 596 acres. Samuel B. Athill, 368 slaves, 1829. Heirs of S. A. Turner, 1852. Horace Turner, 1871. Charles Turner, 1878.

20. LYONS (Upper and Lower), 562 acres. Captain John Lyons, R.N., 271 slaves, 1829. Heirs of John Lyons, 1852. F. Kennington, 1871. T. Kennington, 1871. James Maginley, 1878.

21. MANNINGS, 173 acres. W. E. Ledeatt, 68 slaves, 1829. W. E. Ledeatt, 1852. W. H. Harper, 1871. John F. Foote, 1878.

22. MAYER'S, 300 acres. Joseph W. Mayer, 1788. Owen Pell, or Benlomond, 100 slaves, 1829. Joseph G. Gore, 1852. Mrs. Owen Pell, 1871. Mrs. E. M. Pell, 1878.

23. MONTPELIER, 75 acres. Heirs of William Harman, 1852. Montpelier and The Hope, 318 acres, F. B. Harman, 1871.

24 PARSON MAULE'S and COLLINS, 179 acres. George L. Ledeatt, 152 slaves, 1829. George W. W. Ledeatt, 1852. Edward Becket, 1871.

25. RETREAT or MONTGOMERY, 166 acres. John J. Walter, 100 acres, 1829. Heirs of John J. Walter, 1852 and 1871.

26. ROOM'S, 318 acres. Christopher Bethell, 1788. W. I. Bethell, Sir Edward Cod, and B. Walrond, 168 slaves, 1829. K. B. Osborn, M.D., 1852. Robert Dobson, lessee, 1871. W. H. Edwards, 1878.

27. SHERIFF'S, 220 acres. William Sheriff, 1788. James W. Sheriff, 1852. F. B. Harman, 1871—78.

28. SION HILL or JEFFERSONS, 288 acres. John Lake, 1852. Mrs. Owen Pell, 1871. Mrs. E. M. Pell, 1878.

29. SKERRETT'S, 314 acres. Before 1750 Stephen Lynch, Esq., purchased this of William Skerret for £20,704 c. John Lynch, 1788. Nicholas Nugent, 170 slaves, 1829. Oliver Nugent, 1852 and 1871.

30. THOMAS', 170 acres. Heirs of J. W. Sheriff, 1878.

31. WALRONDS, Upper, 222 acres; Lower, 154 acres. Mainswete Walrond, 1788. Lieut. William Grant sold this in 1803 to John William Dow. Bethell Walrond, 246 slaves, 1829. Bethel Walrond, 1852. Lower Walronds, 150 acres, Henry Bowne, 1871.

32. WATSON'S, 460 acres. Francis Watson, 55 slaves, 1829. Francis Watson, 1852. Thomas T. Sword, 1871.

33. WICKHAMS, 216 acres. Joseph Martin, 131 slaves, 1829. B. Musgrave, 1852. J. E. Anthonyson, 1871.

RECTORS.

La Croix, 1681.

Isaac Grace, signs as Rector 1716.

Samuel Orr, signs as Rector 1727; M.A. Glasgow; ordained 1710 at Fulham. His death announced April 1729.

John Bernonville, 1733—46.

Dr. Mathew Towers, 1747—52.

Robert Moncreiff, 1753—67.

Richard Davies, 1767—78.

John Shepherd, 1778—81.

William Humphrys, 1781—88.

Theophilus Nugent, 1788—1803.

George Collins, 1803—25.

Thomas Parry, M.A., 1825—27 (? Archdeacon 1824—40). (See 'Alumni Oxonienses.')

John Ince Jones, 1828—63. He was born 26 Jan. 1801; ob. 28 April 1863. M.I. at St. Philip's Churchyard.

George Jemmet, 1863—65.

Darius Davey, 1865.

Thomas G. Connell, 1866—76.

The Venerable James Clark, M.A., Ph.D. University of Gottingen, F.R.A.S.; Deacon 1863; Priest 1864 by the Bishop of Ripon; Curate of Lindley; Curate of South Shields; Senior Curate of Rotherham; Curate of Middlesborough; British Chaplain at Memel 1869—74; Archdeacon of Antigna 1885; Rector 1876, till his death lately.

The old Church at Willoughby Bay was thrown down by the earthquake in 1842, and the present one was built on the top of the hill in 1850.

1825. 17 square miles, 1320 inhabitants. W. Collins, Rector. One church, 250 sittings. St. Stephen's Chapel, 120 sittings. (Bishop Coleridge's Charges.)

1834. J. I. Jones, Rector. One church, one chapel. Recently 340 sittings, rebuilt 220 sittings.

The Vestry Records appear to have been lost.

Parish Registers.*

Baptized.

1767	Oct. 4	George s. of Peter & Catherine Wilcox; b. 6 Aug. 1767.
1768	Oct. 11	Frances d. of William & Frances Hubbard; b. 10 Oct.
1768	Dec. 5	Rachael d. of John & Ann Hosier; b. 3 Oct.
1768	Dec. 11	Ann d. of Stephen & . . . . Constant; b. 6 Nov.
1770	Jan. 6	Sarah Cochran d. of Peter & Martha Wilcox.
1770	Nov. 17	Sarah Benedicta d. of Robert & Sarah Henville; b. 13th.
1772	Aug. 17	William s. of James Seaton.
1774	Jan. 30	Edward s. of Peter Wilcox.
1778	Jan. 6	Peter s. of Peter Wilcox & Ann Osbeston.
1780	Mar. 11	John s. of John & Sarah Storey.
1782	Jan. 1	William Sherriffe s. of John & Rachel Colburn.
1782	Jan. 1	William Burke s. of William & Rachel Hunt.
1788	Mar. . .	Sarah Colehurst d. of Richard & Sarah Hunt; b. 15 Mar. 1787.
1797	Nov. 2	Mary Martin d. of William S. & Arabella Waite.
1797	Nov. 19	Mary Ann Edington d. of J. V. & Mary Ann Champion; b. 1 July.
1801	June 14	Mary Athill d. of Thomas & Sarah Gillan; b. 17 Jan.; & Margaret Spencer d. of do. Omitted in 1798 [*sic*].
1809	April 18	Sarah Allen d. of John Ledwell & Ann Elson; b. 23 Feb.
1810	Feb. 20	John Nibbs s. of Richard & Sarah Coleburn Garland; b. 25 Jan.
1813	Aug. 13	Samuel Sneyd s. of Samuel Sneyd & Mary Durnford Lamb; bap. at English Harbour, Parish of St Paul.
1817	Jan. 12	Robert Hyndman s. of Richard & Sarah C. Garland; b. 12 Dec. 1816.
1832	Sep. 18	Mary Susannah d. of Joseph George & Maria Gore. Hawes. Planter.
1832	Sep. 28	Sarah Eliza d. of James & Catherine Garland O'Connor. Mount Vernon. Planter.
1832	Nov. 24	Mary Ann d. of Robert & Maria Jarritt. Bettys Hope. Planter.
1834	Jan. 14	Amelia d. of Thomas & Carlotte Tanner. Pares. Planter.
1834	April 13	William Henry s. of William Henry & Margaret Wendall Gale. The Garden. Planter.
1834	June 22	Margaret Eliza d. of Robert Maria Jarritt. Bettys Hope. Planter.
1834	Oct. 5	Sarah Elizabeth d. of . . . . Gore. Hawes.

Married.

1688	May 31	John Dougan to Rosamond Dowley.
1688	Aug. 20	Cornelius Cornelison to Ann Foux.
1702	April 27	Thomas Roome to Susannah Baker *al's* Howell.
1703	. . . . . .	James Read to Catherine Keife.
1714	Feb. 10	William Newell & Mary Gratrix.
1781	. . . . . .	Andrew Manderston to . . . .
1793	Dec. 8	William Sanderson Waite to Arabella Ann Dickman.

* Baptisms commenced in 1767, Marriages in 1683, Burials in 1685.

Buried.

1686	Feb. 10	John Mascnoll.
1688	May 28	Thomas Middleton.
1696	Nov. 1	John Howard.
1697	July 2	John Cracherode.
1697	Sep. 1	Leghlan Quin.
1697	Nov. 14	Elizth D. of Edwd Cook.
1697	Dec. 28	Margaret Quin.
1697	Feb. 9	Elizth Macnamarain.
1698	June 3	Sarah Quin.
1700	Nov. 20	Abraham Howard.
1704	May 8	Mingo Farthinando.
1704	Nov. 11	Edward Cooke.
1722	Oct. 20	Capt John Richards.
1722	Oct. 28	Edward Cooke.
1726	Aug. 9	Richard Delanoy.
1726	Jan. 7	Vallentine Keefe.
1728	April 7	Doctr Mosse Jacocks.
1728	Aug. 26	Peter Tarpy.
1728	Jan. 31	Mary Tarpy.
1732	April 17	The Rev. Mr La Croix.
1740	Mar. 18	Mr Thomas Vears.
1740	Mar. 25	Mr John Fletcher.
1743	April 19	William Rice, Infant S. of James Verdon.
1744	May 11	Dr William Barclay.

1747, Math. Towers, LL.D., now signs.

1758	July 15	Dr Thomas Downes.
1758	Aug. 2	Dr George Hopson.
1765	Nov. 26	Mr George Reynolds, junr.
1766	. . . . . .	Mrs Todman, Senr.
1766	Mar. 22	Rachael d. of Mr Thadee fitz Patrick.
1767	Nov. 2	William Bishop.
1768	April 14	John Wilkinson.
1768	April 28	Thomas Hariot.
1768	Aug. 12	John Todman.
1768	Aug. 22	John Heydon.
1768	Oct. 11	Frances Hubbard.
1768	Dec. 3	Henry Myln.
1768	Dec. 5	Adam Jackson.
1769	Feb. 18	John Shingles.
1769	May 18	Thomas Ried.
1769	July 10	Rachael Wallace.
1769	Dec. 4	Jacob Dooby.
1771	May 14	Robert Crookshank.
1771	June 30	Mary Dillon.
1771	July 26	Duncan McCartor.
1772	Aug. 16	William Seaton.
1773	Oct. 29	Daniel Colbarn.
1773	Nov. 19	Mrs Charles Hosier.
1773	Nov. 22	Rachel Hosier.
1773	Nov. 24	John Pearson.
1773	Dec. 19	Susannah Hubbard.
1774	Mar. 29	William Monroe.
1775	Mar. 12	James Seaton.
1775	Nov. 18	Charles Hosier.
1781	Dec. 23	Margaret Wilcox.
1781	Dec. 23	George Barclay.
1789	. . . . . .	John Colbourn. (Family burying place.)
1792	Dec. 23	Thomas Montgomery. Fam. B. G.
1793	Feb. 22	Mrs Seaton.
1793	Sep. . .	. . . . McKenzie.
1797	Nov. 23	Benjamin Ozbaldistone.
1798	Jan. 9	Ann Colburne.
1814	Jan. 8	John Blair, Esquire; at Willoughby Bay.
1832	Feb. 19	John William Tanner. Pares. Infant.
1833	Dec. 19	Martha Byam Gore. Hawes. 4.
1835	Dec. 31	Robert Jarritt. Bettys Hope. 51.
1839	Jan. 15	Sophia Mackenzie. Parham. 84.
1843	Feb. 28	Elizabeth Gore. Parham. 34.

Monumental Inscriptions.

ST. PHILIP'S CHURCH.

On a white marble tablet on north wall near the chancel. Crest: *A demi lion.* Motto: *Be just and fear not*:—IN MEMORY OF | JOSEPH LIGGINS ESQRE | THE PROPRIETOR OF CLARE HALL, | LYONS AND FFRYES ESTATES IN THIS ISLAND, | AND FOR NEARLY 40 YEARS | A MERCHANT CONNECTED WITH THE COLONY . | HE DIED AT HIS RESIDENCE AT KENSINGTON, | GREATLY RESPECTED | ON THE 22ND JUNE 1860. | AGED 69 YEARS | HIS REMAINS | LIE IN KENSAL GREEN CEMETERY, LONDON.

WILLOUGHBY BAY CHURCHYARD.

On a headstone:—To THE | Memory of ANN HUNT | Late Mother to THOS RYCE | Who in token of his sincere affec | tion caused the following lines to | be inscribed to her memory. (Eighteen lines follow.)

On a marble headstone:—SACRED | to the memory of | MRS ANN QUINLAN | who departed this Life | 10th June 1817 | Aged 66 Years.

ST. PHILIP'S CHURCHYARD, NEW GROUND.

On a granite headstone within railings:—SACRED TO THE MEMORY | OF ALFRED ARMEL GOODWIN | BORN MAY 6TH 1865 | DIED AUGUST 14TH 1885.

(One line follows.)

On a headstone:—TO | THE MEMORY OF | ISABELLA ELIZABETH FORBES | MCINTOSH | WHO DIED | ON THE 11TH OF JUNE 1844 | AGED 68 YEARS.

There are two arched stone vaults without M.I.

ST. STEPHEN'S CHAPEL, BELFAST BURIAL GROUND.

On a fragment of headstone:—Here . . . . | Body . . . . | . . . . WILL | etc.

On a headstone:—To | The Memory of | FRANCES | The WIFE OF Wm HUBBARD | Who Departed this Life Octr ye 16, 1768 | AGED 33 YEARS | Whose AFFABILITY | AFFECTION & DUTIFUL Conduct | For TWELVE Years; | As well in Adversity as Prosperity | Made her Death Justly Lamented.

On a flat stone over brick vault:—Here lieth the Body of | An Jackson late Wife of | John Jackson of this Parish | She departed this Life | the 24th day of November | 1765 Aged 24 years. (Four lines follow.)

Inside the Chapel:—Here lies interred | the Body of | Edward Barrow (?) | Died Nov. 8 . 1762 (?) Aged 3.

Here lies interr'd | the Body of | Elizabeth Borroughs | died Dec. 1st 1762 | Aged 54 years.

ST. MARY'S PARISH.

14,190 ACRES.

1. BIFFINS, 200 acres. Mathew Christian, 1775, then to his brother-in-law William Gunthorpe, Esq. Ledwell and Scott, 1788.
2. BLUBBER VALLEY and ROSE VALLEY. This estate in 1743 contained 1200 acres and was owned by Robert Pearne, Esq. (whose father and grandfather before him possessed it); he also held Musqueto Cove Estate of 600 acres. Shand and Co., lessees of P. T. Shaw, 1164 acres, 240 slaves, 1829. Heirs of F. T. Shaw, 1852. Dr. W. H. Edwards, 1871. G. W. Bennett, 664 acres, 1878.
3. BOLANS, 73 acres. Heirs of T. Watkins, 38 acres. Christopher Codrington, 1788. Heirs of G. Byam, 1878.
4. BROOKES and MORRIS', 744 acres. Heirs of John Brooke, 207 slaves, 1829. Henry Hill, 1852. Morris' of 100 acres had been purchased by John Brooke of Valentine Morris (see Looby Pedigree). Mrs. Tucker, 1871. Francis Tucker, 1878.
5. CADES BAY, 703 acres. John Brooke owned 350 acres, 1777. Frederick Garraway, 1871. William Sherridan, 1878.
6. CHRISTIAN'S VALLEY, 500 acres. Sydney Stead, 1871. His heirs, 1878.
7. CLAREMONT, 849 acres. Rowland E. Williams, 252 slaves, 1829. Rowland E. Williams, 1852. Charles Shand, 1871. G. W. Bennett, 1878.
8. COVE, 500 acres. Rev. J. McGuire, 1871.
9. CRABB VALLEY or COURAGES, 110 acres. Hon. Andrew Lessly, 1763; his other of 450 acres; all which he sold for £24,000 to William Livingson.
10. DALZELL'S, 186 acres. Dr. Jesse W. Thibou, 1871—78.
11. DARBYS, 59 acres. Heirs of Anna Doig. George A. Lardy, 96 acres, 1878. Contained 150 acres in 1774.
12. DARK VALLEY, 170 acres. Heirs of Joseph Weston, 159 slaves, 1829. Mary Wesston, 1852. Maria Jane Lowe, 1871.
13. DUNNINGS or PROVIDENCE, 170 acres. In 1680 Captain Thomas Philp sold Dunnings of 230 acres to Colonel Rowland Williams, part of 500 acres owned by Mr. Thomas Dunning. In 1743 it contained 346 acres, and was mortgaged by William Dunning to John Bolan. John Weston, 1788. P. P. Walter, 1852. Dunnings and Gilliards, 240 acres, heirs of F. Kennington, 1878.
14. FARLEYS GARDEN. Sir John Laforey, Bart., 1788.
15. FFRY'S, 543 acres. Henry L. Spencer, 203 slaves, 1829. Eliza F. Spencer, 1852.
16. FISHERS (with Nantons), 300 acres. Sir W. Young, Bart., 1788. Heirs of James Scotland, 1871. Mr. Taylor, 1878.
17. FURLONGS. William Livingson, 1788.
18. GARDNERS. Hon. Lockhart Russell, 1788.
19. GREEN CASTLE, 605 acres. Sir Henry Martin, Bart., 1788. Sir Henry W. Martin, Bart., 895 acres, 315 slaves, 1829. Sir W. Martin, 1852. Fryers Concrete Co., 1871.
20. HALLORANS. Dr. John Frye, 1788. Rowland Frye, 1788.
21. HARVEY'S, 703 acres. Robert Harvey, 1788, after whose death in 1791 it passed to . . . . Alexander and Robert Harvey in 1788 conveyed to trustees a plantation of 356 acres, formerly called Yeoman's Old Road Estate, at Cades Bay. Robert Farquhar, 399 slaves, 1829. Lady Shaw Stewart, 1852.
22. HERMITAGE, 117 acres. George Leonard, 1788. Heirs of J. Coull, 1829. Thomas Coull, M.D., 1852. W. A. Coull, 1871. John Francis, 98 acres, 1878.
23. HUYGHUE'S, 166 acres. Mathew Christian, 1775. Ledwell and Scott, 1788. James Green and James Kirwan, 1871. Thomas B. Kirwan, 1878.
24. JENNINGS, 316 acres. Heirs of E. Codrington, 1788. Hugh Thompson and heir of J. J. Ronan, 1852. Heirs of Darius Davey, 288 acres, 1871—78.
25. JOLLY HILL, 708 acres. B. Entwisle, 1788. B. Entwisle leased to Shand and Co., 1829. Heirs of B. Entwisle, 1852. Thomas Peters, 1871—78.
26. McGREGORS, 63 acres. William Thibou and others, 1852. H. C. Nanton, 1871, and his heirs, 1878.
27. McNISH MOUNTAIN, 159 acres. John Dobson, 1871—78. 42 acres of this in St. John's Parish.
28. MILL HILL, 392 acres. Hon. Lockhart Russell, 1788. Francis Russell, 1803, nephew of Lockhart.

Mrs. Mary Russell, 178 slaves, 1829. Edward Lipscombe, 1852. Heirs of Joseph F. Smith, 1871. Thomas B. Kirwan, 1878.

29. MONTEROS, 283 acres. The Hon. Samuel Watkins in 1743 left this estate of 250 acres to his son John. Samuel Watkins, 1788. Thomas Clarke, 115 slaves, 1829. Messrs. Shand, 1852. Dr. W. H. Edwards, 1871—78.

30. THE MOUNTAIN, 437 acres. Charles Shand, 1871. Thomas W. W. Shand, 1878.

31. NANTONS, 76 acres. Sir William Young, Bart., 63 slaves, 1829. Heir of James Scotland, 1852.

32. NEW DIVISION or TULLIDEPHS, 243 acres. Sir John Ogilvie, Bart., 1788. Heirs of Sir W. Ogilvie, Bart., 1852. Robert Dobson, 1871.

33. ORANGE VALLEY, 735 acres. K. B. Osborn, 98 slaves, 1829. K. B. Osborn, M.D., 1852. Orange Valley and Lower Fryes, 1293 acres, James Barrett, 1871. C. J. Manning, 1878.

34. PICARTS, 131 acres. Heirs of Picart, 109 slaves, 1829. Heirs of A. Picart, 1852. Estate of Gervais Picart, 1871.

35. RAVENSCROFTS. Benjamin Ravenscroft was granted 180 acres 1682—84. Sir James Douglas, Bart., 1788.

36. RIGBY'S, 263 acres. In 1759 James Doig left this to his second son James, whose son James was owner 1788. William H. Doig, 295 acres, 110 slaves, 1829. Sir W. Martin, 1852. Estate of James Law, 1871.

37. RIVER. Sir W. Young, Bart., 1788. Halliday and Taylor, 1871. River and Finlays, 140 acres, heirs of Margaret Taylor, 1878.

38. SAGE HILL, 162 acres. William Gilchrist, 1788. James Gilchrist, 103 slaves, 1829. W. E. Odlum, M.D., and Jane Gilchrist, 1852. E. Odlam, 1871. D. C. Odlum, 1878.

39. SAWCOLTS, 234 acres. Colonel John Sawcolt owned "Sawcolts Road" and died 1746 when it passed to his heirs, whose shares his son-in-law Mr. George Horsford purchased. Hon. John Horsford, 1788. Messrs. Hyndman, 72 slaves, 1829. Sir R. Horsford, 1852. Water Works Co., 1871.

40. SEAFORTHS, 622 acres. Just. Casamajor, 1788. Heirs of Just. Casamajor, deceased, 163 slaves, 1829. Edgar H. Lane, 1878.

41. SMITHS, 170 acres. R. W. Nanton, 64 slaves, 1829. W. and F. Shand, 1852. Archibald C. Fonseca, 1871.

42. TRANQUIL VALE, 109 acres. John Rose, 1788. Joseph W. Rose, 57 slaves, 1829. F. Crichton, 1852. George Black, 67 acres, 1871. Richard Hill, 20 acres, 1871.

43. TUCKS, 147 acres. John Laforey, 1788. William Ackerman, 1871. William Dougall, 1878.

44. VALLEY, 350 acres. Mathew Christian, 1775.

45. WILLOCKS, 368 acres. Mrs. Ann Willock, 102 slaves, 1829. Mrs. Ann Willock, 1852, and Upper Fryes, 513 acres. Heirs of Richard Abbott, 1871.

46. WINDY HILL. Alexander Brodie, 1788.

47. YORKS, 325 acres. R. H. McGuire. Heirs of Sir William Ogilvie, Bart., 404 slaves, 1829. Mrs. Margaret McGuire, 1878.

48. YOUNGS, Old Road, 573 acres. Sir W. Young, Bart., 1788. Sir W. Young, Bart., 97 slaves, 1829. John Dawson, 1852.

RECTORS.

William Leader, 1684.

Thomas Power, inducted Jan. 1695; Fellow of Trinity College, Cambridge; apparently resigned, as he was afterwards Rector of St. John's, Nevis; died 14 Dec. 1698. M.I. at St. John's, Antigua.

Richard Brocas, expelled 12 Jan. 1698.

Abraham Slade, June 1699.

Samuel Picart de Laferty, Oct. 1699.

James Whitfield, July 1700.

. . . . Moreane.

James Field, B.A., presented 17 May 1706; was later Rector of St. John's.

Frederick Woodside, "minister" 1708—10.

James Grigg, presented as Rector 18 Aug. 1711.

John Simpson (? M.A. Oxon 1709), inducted 26 May 1715; killed himself 1717.

James Knox, M.A. Glasgow; licensed by the Bishop of London 1715; presented 21 Aug. 1718; signed as Rector in 1727. Will dated 1729; proved 1741. (P.C.C., 128 Spurway.)

George Holme, presented as Rector 21 Sep. 1730; resigned 18 Jan. 1758.

David Hopkins, presented 15 May 1760; resigned 4 Nov. following.

. . . . Secum, presented 4 Nov. 1760.

John Frew, presented by Governor Thomas 20 Nov. 1760. Left Antigua in 1762.

Richard Harris, *circa* 1767. Will dated 7 Aug. 1774; sworn 16 Jan. and recorded 22 March 1783. (See Vol. III., p. 347.)

Josiah Weston, 1789—1804, or later.

Martin Weston, 1808.

James Coull, 1808—9.

William Chaderton, 1814—15; transferred to St. Paul's.

James Curtin, signs as Rector 1824 and 1847.

William James Reid, M.A., signs as Rector 1860; Archdeacon 1860—76.

J. A. Marshall, M.A., 1877.

. . . . Shephard.

Henry Hughes.

. . . . Richard.

Kenneth McKenzie Gillie, 1885.

The Church was built about 1685. The early Registers are stated to have been destroyed in the great hurricane of 1848.

1825. 22 square miles, 1430 inhabitants. J. Curtin, Rector. One church, 370 sittings; one chapel, 320 sittings.

1834. J. Curtin, Rector; J. Clinckett, Curate. One church, 400 sittings; one chapel, 350 sittings.

(Bishop Coleridge's Charges.)

The Chapel of Ease at "The Valley" was also built about 1685. Baptisms commenced in 1841, Marriages and Burials about 1839. James S. Crickett signs as Curate in 1840 and Theophilus Saulex in 1842.

EXTRACTS FROM THE OLD VESTRY BOOK.

A° 1684. Commission from ye Govr Edward Powell da. 9 June 1684 to Col. Roland Williams & Cap. Jno Frye to call together the Freeholders to meet this 13 June 1684, viz.:—

Lt Col. Moyle Johnson.	Owen Brambell.
Cap. Jno Yeamans.	Alex^r Duglas.
Hen. Winthorp.	Mr Chr. Keynell.
Jno Ravenscroft.	L. Law. Turton.
Wm Browne.	Pet . . . .
Math. Barton.	An . . . . rteen.
Juren Campbell.	Jon . . . .
Wm Grace.	Jon. (or Jam.) . . . .
Rob. Nickholls.	Th . . . .
Jas. Williams.	Ro . . . .
Tho. Everard.	[Part of page destroyed.]

1684, Sep. 4. Meeting of the Gentn of the Vestry—

Mr Wm Leader, Minister.

Coll. Ro. Williams.	Cap. Cha. Goss.
Nichs Rainsford, Esq.	Lieut. Laurence Turton.
Cap. Jno Frye.	Mr Hen. Winthorpe.
Cap. Cæsar Rodney.	Mr Chris. Keynell.

At a previous Meeting on 19 June it had been agreed that a Church or Chapel should be erected at the Road on the Ground the Old Church stood.

1684, Oct. 2. Cap. Jno Yeamans & Mr Peter Watson also present.

1685.* April 30. Present—

Col. Rowland Williams.	Mr Laurence Turton.
Cap. John Frye.	Mr John Crossfield.
Lt Col. Moyle Johnson.	

[At a previous meeting it was decided that the inhabitants of Bermudian Valley should erect their church & those of Old Road theirs. The Minister & clerk are to be paid by both, & the stipend of the minister is to be increased by 4000 lbs. yearly. Cap. Cæsar Rodney, Mr John Sampson, & Morgan Toole were the old sidesmen.] Cap. Chas. Goss, Chr. Keynell, Mr Jno Sampson mentioned. The Minister is pd 20,000 lbs. of sugar yearly.

1686,* April 19—

Mr Wm Leader, Minister.	Mr Henry Winthorpe.
The Hon. Col. Edwd Powell, Govr.	Mr Jno Sampson.
Hon. Col. Rowld Williams.	Cap. Chas. Goss.
Cap. Jno Frye.	Mr Owen Brambell.

1686, Nov. 11. A levy to be made on lands. On back are several names: Lt Will. Tremills, Bm Tremills, Wm Tremills, Jno Tremills, Robt Tremills, Wm Barns, Mr Pollington, Mr Tho. Taylor.

1688. A list of all the Lands & Negroes at Bermudian Valley, according to the Levy of 1 lb. of sugar per acre & 20 lbs. per slave:—

	Negros.	Acres.	Lbs. Sugar.
Mr Wm Leader	31	1150	1770
Cap. Jno Frye	70	995	2395
Mr Jno Roe	46	310	1230
Mrs Cath. Lingham	73	850	2310
Mrs Cammell	7	100	240
Lt Wm Tremills	7	300	440
Jas. Jones	3	90	150
Ambrose York	6	20	320
Mr Tho. Smith	14	450	73
Tho. Everard	4	115	—
Hen. Osborne	3	30	—
Collo Codrington & Cap. Frye for Horsnells Land	3	240	30
Cap. Shackerley's Land	—	200	—
Pet. Welch, Senr	6	128	—
. . . .	—	16	—
. . . . Crossfield	6	38	158
. . . . Hen. Winthorpe	26	250	770
. . . . Laurence Turton	22	200	640
. . . . all Johnson	—	75	75
	332	5811	12,451

A List of all the freemen in the parish of St Mary, Bermudian Valley, as they are assessed according to a Levy raised at the House of Mr Jno Sampson, April 16th, 1688:—

	Lbs. Sugar.
. . . . Tower	150
. . . . ffrere	100
. . . . Jackson	150
. . . . rew Courteen	100
. . . . ces Courage	100
. . . . n Andrews	50
Robert Nicholls	50
. . . . Sheers	150
Zacchariah Sennox	50
Benj. Tuck	150
Jno Butler	150
Tho. Bladwell	150
Alexr Douglas	150
Thurlo' O'Donnell	50
Arthur Hill	100
Jno Mayo	100
Tho. Mayers	100
Jas. Beard	50
Rob. Carpenter	50
Will. Griffin	100
. . . . Walters	100
Tho. Page	50
Adam Bryers	50
Jno Wilson	50
Phil. Godfrey	50
Rob. Blyther	150
Pat. Collonel	50
Walter Lane	150
Rob. Tremills	100
Simon Pereer	50
Pet. Welch, Jun.	100
Ed. Miner	100
Mathew Barton	200
Mr Jno Moore	200
34	3450

* These extracts I took from a very dilapidated page.—V. L. O.

1692. Mr Robt Freeman, Mr Tho. Chapman, Mr Math. Barton, Members of Vestry.

1693, Jan. 15. Mr Field, minister of St John's, to have 24*s.* for every sermon preached at the Valley.

Levy.

	Acres.	Negros.	£	*s.*	*d.*
. . . . Frye, Esq.	995	70	17	13	9
. . . . Steward	1150	39	17	6	0
. . . .	600	78	13	7	0
. . . . Roe	340	77	10	0	6
. . . . Winthorp	250	31	5	9	0
. . . . ce Turton	200	19	3	18	6
Jno Johnson	75	—	0	18	9
Tho. Smith of Nevis	450	—	5	12	6
Wm Tremills	78	2	1	1	6
Rob. Tremills	40	2	0	13	0
Jno Tremills	136	5	2	1	6
Eliz. Tremills	48	1	0	13	6
Mathew Tremills	48	0	0	12	0
Wm Moll	200	4	2	16	0
Jno Crossfield	40	5	0	17	6
Arch. Johnson	—	31	2	6	6
Eleanor Cammell	40	2	0	13	0
Mr Ambrose Yorke	220	13	3	14	0
Hockley Hole	50	—	0	12	6
Alexr Douglas	30	5	0	15	0
Mr Jno Butler	20	6	0	14	0
Mr Wm. Dunning	243	16	4	4	0
Mr Tho. Everit	45	9	1	4	9
Mr Mathew Barton	70	5	1	5	0
Mr Hen. Osborn	30	10	1	2	6
Tho. Duncomb, Esq.	100	—	1	5	0
Mr Esaiah Burges	100	—	1	5	0
Danl McDaniel	30	—	0	7	6
Mr Wm. Barns	100	—	1	5	0
Shakelys	200	—	2	10	0

	Acres.	Negros.	£	s.	d.
Coll. Chris. Codrington	120	—	1	10	0
Tho. Bladwell son Horsenail . .	120	8	2	2	0
Lt Rob. Shiers . .	—	—	1	10	0
Mr Benj. Tuck . .	—	—	1	10	0

	s.	d.		s.	d.
Cuthbert James	10	0	Rob. Jackson .	12	0
Jas. Read . .	12	0	Martin Albret .	6	0
Jno Maijo . .	15	0	Hen. Jones .	7	6
Jas. Corage .	9	0	Wm Cheffun .	6	0
And. Curteene .	12	0	Terence Stanley	15	0
Jno Andrews .	9	0	Danl Tourner .	15	0
Arth. Hill . .	12	0	Wm. Johnson .	12	0
Jno Curteen .	7	6	Wm. Johnson .	12	0
Rob. Walker .	12	0	Mrs Agnes Jones	15	0
Jno Newman .	12	0			

1694, Oct. 22. Mr Jas. Field, Minister.

1695, Jan. 23. Mr Tho. Power, Minister.

Levy for 1696.

	Acres.	Negros.	£	s.	d.
Coll. Chris. Codrington	544	—	9	1	4
Cap. Jno Frye, Esq. .	1000	72	20	5	4
Maj. Saml Martin .	550	—	9	3	4
Cap. Hen. Pearne .	750	74	16	4	0
Cap. Jno Roe . .	340	77	9	10	0
Mr Tho. Gateward .	550	14	9	17	4
Mr Hen. Winthorpe .	250	32	5	15	4
Lt Law. Turton . .	200	20	4	6	8
Mad. Ann Barnes .	300	—	5	0	0
Mr Wm. Dunning .	242	13	4	13	8
Mr Wm. Mould . .	200	2	3	8	8
Mr Amb. Yorke . .	152	12	3	2	8
Mr Tho. Horsenails, Ld	120	—	2	0	0
			£102	8	4

1696, Oct. 18. Cap. Hen. Pearne, Member of Vestry. "Order'd That the Church Wardens of St Mary's in the Valley do send two hhds. of Sugar for London to purchase Church Books, a pulpit Cloth, and Cushion of Green Velvet with Gold and Silk Fringe & St M. imbroidd in the midle of the pulpit Cloth, & that the Ten Commandments be sent for & set up at the East End of the Church." Sexton is pd 9*s.* per grave.

1697, Jan. 9. Mr Tho. Franklyn & Mr Jno Terry, Members of Vestry.

1698, Jan. 13. Richard Brocas, minister.

It is agreed upon by the Gentlemen above Named that the aforesaid Richard Brocass be moved & expelled out of the said parish of St Mary's, There being most notorious and opprobrious crimes alledged to his Charge by several of the parishioners which are insufferable in a man of his Coat. Agreed upon Nemine Contradicente.

1698, June 27. Mr Jas. Field to be Minister for one year, to have £60 c. & all perquisites. Cap. Jno Frye & Mr Jno Frye both present.

1698, Aug. 24. To Mr Steed, minister, £1 4*s.* for a sermon. To Mr Tho. Powers £1 16*s.* for ditto.

1698, Jan. 3. Lt Jno Gamble, Member of Vestry.

1699, June 6. Mr Abraham Slade, minister, to have £120 c. yearly.

1699, Oct. 9. Mr Saml Laffertey, minister.

1700, July 30. Mr Jas. Whitfield, minister for 6 mos.

1701, Feb. 18. Cap. Jno Frye, Junr, present.

1703, April 1. Mr Saml Frye, Member of Vestry.

1704, Jan. 8. Cap. Val. Morris, Member of Vestry.

1706, May 17. Letter read from Lt Genl Jno Johnson, Commander in Chief, presenting Jas. Field, B.A., to be still rector of St John's. He was accepted by the parish on 23rd following.

1706, June 7. Levy—

	Slaves.	Acres.
Col. John Frye . . .	103	560
Col. Hen. Pearne's Est. .	150	665
Cap. Jno Roe's Est. . .	101	410
Mr Hen. Winthorpe . .	38	190
Mr Saml Frye . . .	69	300
Cap. Antho Montirah . .	64	230
Lt Jarvis Turton . . .	54	200
Mr Wm Dunning . . .	66	288
Mr Math. Barton . . .	9	30
Mr Jno Benson . . .	24	70
Coll. Chr. Codrington . .	—	544
Maj. Martin's Est. . .	114	531
Cap. Ambrose Yorke . .	56	138
Lt Jno Martin . . .	6	200
Mr Jno Bezune, Sen. . .	22	70
Mr Wm Tremills . . .	2	30
Mr Jno Bezune, Junr . .	12	33
Mr Jno Poor . . .	13	96
Mr Rob. Dunning . .	—	40
Mr Tho. Horsnale . .	15	52
Lt Geo. Leonard . . .	16	62
Mr Mich. Bennett's Est. .	16	70
Mr Pat. Browne . . .	77	290
Cap. Chas. Callahane . .	31	164
Mr Rob. Shears . . .	26	60
Mr Isaac Wharf . . .	21	100
Mr Rob. Christian . .	9	30
Mr Tho. Laughlan . .	11	80
Mr Jas. Reed . . .	9	14
Jno Mayo	6	10
Lt Jno Stevens . . .	6	—
Jno Andrews . . .	—	7½
Mr Cha. Jacob . . .	4	20
Mrs Rebecca Johnson . .	—	—
Mr Jas. Field . . .	—	125
Mr Rob. Tremills . . .	—	—

1708, ... 14. Col. Jno Frye present.

1709, Oct. 5. Mr Fred. Woodside to preach 4 mos.

1710, April 12. Mr Fred. Woodside to be pd his 2 years' salary & to deliver up at his presentation.

1711-12, Jan. 22. Rev. Jas. Grigg, Rector; his Deacon's Orders da. at Fulham 20 Mar. 1708 & Lic. signed by Bishop of London da. 12 Mar. 1710. Presented by Hon. Walter Douglas, Comr in Chf., by letter of 18 Aug. 1711. *Re* Hen. Osborne's land by his will bequeathed to pious uses & otherwise disposed of by late Govr D. Parke.

1713-14, Feb. 23. Saml Lafferte gives up all claims as rector by presentation from Govr Walter Douglas.

1714, May 27. The 2 churchwardens with Mr Jas. Field to write to Mr Parrot & Mr Byam of London to send them a minister & M.A. at £200 a year.

1715. Cap. Jno Huyghne, Member of Vestry.

1715, May 26. Jas. Field, Commissary Genl of the Leewd Islands, Inducted the Rev. Mr Jno Simpson on the presentation from the Hon. Col. Danl Smith, Govr of the Charibbee Islands.

1716, April 26. A Regulation of the pews in the parish church of St Mary's in the Valley:—

1. Collo Valentine Morris.
2. Mr Barbottain & Mr Franklyn.
3. Mr Pern.
4. Collo John Frye.
5. Mr Samuel Martin & Madm Margt. Martin.
6. Capt Roe.

7. Cap[t] York.
8. The Reverend M[r] James Field & Sam. Frye.
9. The Minister's Pew.
10. Capt. Perrie.
11. M[r] Bezune.
12. John Tremills.
13. M[r] Denbo & the Land of William Tremills.
14. M[r] Jacobs on sufferance.
15. M[r] Stevens & M[r] Poor.
16. M[r] Gattagar & Tweedy.
17. John Maye & John Martin.
18. [*Blank.*]
19. Doctor William Young.
20. M[r] Bennett & Lightfoot.
21. M[r] Leonard.
22. M[r] Monteyro & M[r] Wharfe.
23. Church Warden's Pew.
24. M[r] William Dunning & his.
25. M[r] Jacob & M[r] Barton.
26. M[r] Samuel Winthorpe.
27. M[r] James Red & B . . . .
28. [*Blank.*]

Portion of letter from parishioners to Gov[r] Hamilton. The Rev. M[r] Simpson appears to have just died delirious & stabbed himself in the throat. His answer to above of 7th was da. at Nevis 19 Aug. 1717.

1717, Sep. 10. A rectory is ordered to be built on the glebe 46' long & 8' high, a porch 9' wide & 10' long.

1717-18, March 2. An Indenture da. 11 July 1717 between Hon. Jn[o] Yeamans of Antigua, Esq., & Eliz[th] his wife, & the Rev. Jn[o] Simpson of Antigua, cl'k, being a gift of 60 acres for glebe, bounded N. with Jn[o] Yeamans the top of Dildo Hill, W. with Chas. Jacobs, & S. with the sea.

1718, Aug. 21. Gov[r] Walter Hamilton's letter read presenting Rev. Jas. Knox. Col. Jn[o] Frye present in 1721.

1726. Hen. Douglas, Esq., Member of Vestry for several years.

1727, Jan. 8. Col. Jn[o] Frye & M[r] Jn[o] Frye, Jun[r].

Re Will of Hen. Osborne da. 26 May 1697. He left a dau. Arabella Osborne. Referred to Court of Chancery 10 Jan. 1720. Now present, H.M. Council & Gov[r] Hamilton, Geo. Jennings, Esq., Master in Chancery, Jn[o] Frye, Esq., Tho. Williams, Esq., Sam[l] Martin, Esq., s. & h. of Sam[l] Martin, dec[d], Complainants, Cæsar Rodney, Merch[t], Lucy Chester Parke, inf[t], & Edw[d] Chester, Sen., Merch[t], her father & Guardian, Defendants. The Hon. Col. Frye not present & party in this cause. The land contained 28 acres & was left for a charitable purpose to S[t] Mary's P'sh.

1729, Nov. 10. Col. Jn[o] Frye, Jn[o] Frye, Jun[r], Esq., & Sam[l] Frye, Esq., present.

1730, 7-ber 21. Rev. Geo. Holme, minister, to be Rector at £200 a year.

1735, Jan. 12. D[r] Rowl[d] Williams, Member of Vestry, & M[r] Perrie Yorke.

1737, April 9. M[r] Rowl[d] Oliver shews the will of Theophilus Field.

1738, Jan. 3. Col. Jn[o] Sawcolt, D[r] Walter Tullideph, Abrah. Picart de Lafertye.

1740, March 14. Letter read from Walt. Tullideph. M[r] Isaack Thibou claims the plant[n] of Theophilus Field, & offers to give up personalty by the deed of settlem[t] of the father & mother of Theoph. Field, da. 23 June 1727. £1000 each to the daus. was charged on the estate, & in default of issue it was to go to his 3 sisters.

1740. Cap. Geo. Moncrief of this p'sh. W[m] Byam, Esq., Treas[r].

1741. Rev. Geo. Holme, still rector.

1743. Jas. Salmond, Esq., Member of Vestry, & Jn[o] Brooke, Esq.

1747. Jn[o] Watkins, Esq., Member of Vestry, also Rob. Christian, Esq., D[r] Alex[r] Rouse, p[d].

1748, Sep. 13. Ordered "That one hundred and fifty pounds be allowed M[r] Rowland Oliver for his trouble as he has charged in his Acco[t]." The Nett legacy from Field = £1758 c.

1749, Dec. 14. This Legacy to be for clothing & schooling poor boys & binding apprentices.

1750. Geo. Leonard, Esq., Jn[o] Bolan, Esq., Fra. Frye, Esq., & Jn[o] Stevens, Esq., Members of Vestry.

1751, April 4. Turret 16' square for Rev. G. Holme, & cellar underneath 5' high.

1752, March 26. Eliz[th], dau. of Monteyro, chargeable to the p'sh to have £14. Jn[o] Dearmon Nanton, Esq., Member of Vestry.

1753. Jas. Doig, Esq., Member of Vestry, & Nisbet Darby, Esq.

1756, April 21. Hon. W. Tullideph, Esq.

1757. Francis Farley, Esq., Member of Vestry, & Jas. Ailhaud, Esq.

1758, Jan. 18. Rev. Geo. Holme resigns & is going to England.

1759. Jas. Emra, Esq., Member of Vestry.

1760. Baptist Looby, Esq., & M[r] Sam[l] Picart. Hon. Fra. Frye.

1760, May 15. Rev. David Hopkins, minister, is presented by Gov[r] Thomas.

1760, Nov. 4. Rev. Secum *vice* Hopkins who resigns.

1760, Nov. 20. Rev. Jn[o] Frew presented by Gov[r] Thomas.

1761, Jan. 7. W[m] Livingston, Esq., Member of Vestry, & Jos. or Jas. Weston, Esq.

In Lib. E, fo. 93 $\frac{L}{M}$, is this conveyance of land :—Nich[s] Rainsford from Cap. Jn[o] Frye, Bermudian Valley, where the church is now standing S. & N. 140' & E. & W. 120', bounded on all sides by said Frye. Dated 9 Aug. 1686, 2 Jas. II.

List of persons paying Church rate 1767, being a tax of 12[d] on each slave & 6[d] per acre :—

	Slaves.	Acres.
W[m] Allen	71	232
Mary Ailhaud . . .	14	22
Benj. Ailhaud . . .	19	—
Frances Byshop . . .	26	26
Tho. Burton . . .	50	14
Tho. Byshop . . .	26	20
Zacch. Byshop . . .	3	—
Andrew Browne . . .	35	—
John Brooke . . .	260	821
John Bolan	141	333
. . . . Bartlet . . .	4	—
. . . . Buckley . . .	7	—
. . . . ristian . . .	over 260	—
Rich. Chapman . . .	8	—
Est. of Wm. Codrington .	—	42
Geo. Dalzell	52	100
Burton Daxon . . .	82	150
Est. Jas. Doig (Inf[t]) . .	122	320
Bertie Entwisle . . .	40	—
Jn[o] Elliot	6	—
Ann Edgecomb . . .	12	12
Francis Farley . . .	50	171
The Hon. Fra[s] Frye . .	149	342
Est. Rowl[d] Frye . . .	236	588
John Foster	58	115
James Furlong . . .	52	79
Rachell Farley . . .	11	—
Edward Gratrix . . .	6	—
John Gilchrist . . .	66	112
Geo. Halloran . . .	65	140

	Slaves.	Acres.
John Harvey	194	493
Cath. Jacobs	19	—
Nichs Kirwan	89	200
Wm Livingston	256	885
Abra. Picart D'Laffertee .	55	137
Est. John Lynch	56	143
John Lindsay	114	231
Stephen Lynch	253	693
Rachell Lovey	20	28
Geo. Leonard	47	128
Col. Saml Martin	291	605
Valentine Morris	284	1004
Thos. Martin	123	330
John Ince Marchant . .	10	8
Alexr McPherson	14	11
John D. Nanton	124	201
Jas. Parker	57	—
Wm Woodley Parsons . .	116	199
John Rutherford	15	—
Wm Reese	22	—
James Russell	153	300
Ann Smith	14	4
John Stevens	89	105
Wm Salmond	177	306
Mary Trant	123	177
Isaac Thibou	(?) 120	—
Tho. Taylor	14	—
Walter Tullideph	144	236
Tho. Urlin	65	94
Richd N. Wesston . . .	27	29
Jos. Wesston	158	403
Saml Wesston	8	—
John Wesston	32	139
Saml Winthorpe	11	—
The Hon. Wm Young . .	233	460
	5610	12,350

Gross Tax, £589 5s. 0d. Nett Tax, £392 16s. 8d.

The following Church rate was levied 1780:—

	Slaves.	Acres.
Wm Allen	85	182
Ann Margt Allaire . . .	18	—
Thos. Byshopp	—	20
Andrew Browne	70	—
Alexr Brodie	—	42
John Brooke, decd . . .	247	744
John Bolt	80	188
Mary Christian	—	800
Est. Edward Codrington .	267	630
Ruth Courage	6	—
Est. James Doig	122	320
Jno Elliott, Sen. . . .	14	—
Jno Elliott, Jun. . . .	18	—
Rowld Frye	208	588
Est. Jno Foster, decd . .	61	115
Est. Fras Frye, decd . .	194	342
Est. Fras Farley, decd . .	9	171
Saml Gardner	69	105
Jno Gilchrist	72	112
Thos. Hawes	—	90
Jno Horsford	74	177
Trust Est. Geo. Halloran .	74	140
Zacch. Harris	5	—
Jno Halliday	137	303
Robt Harvey	306	703
Tho. Huyghue	8	—
Cath. Jacobs	18	—
Rachel Lovey	24	28
Est. Wm Livingston . .	196	735
Geo. Leonard . . .	51	128
Val. Morris . . .	196	451
Est. Col. Saml Martin, decd .	306	605
Est. Wm Merredith . .	—	15
Cath. Martin	100	240
Gilbert McConnell . . .	12	—
Margt Nanton	38	—
Kean Osborne	—	—
Wm Parker	3	—
Saml Parker	4	—
Abra. Picart D. La Ferte .	69	—
Saml Picart	36	50
Wm Reese	35	—
Lockhart Russell	—	199
Wm Salmond	212	456
Mary Smith	59	160
Walter Thibou	—	120
Est. Waltr Tullideph, decd .	325	536
Jos. Wesston	100	250
Saml Wesston	32	—
Josiah Wesston	20	—
Jno Wesston	60	139
Est. of Richd Wesston . .	34	—
T. Est. of Sir Wm Young, Bt	325	655
Jno Yeates	—	—
Edward Williams . . .	250	1030
Messrs. Entwisle & Brown .	74	553
Calahan McCarthy . . .	9	—
Saml Sedgwick	24	35
Saml Watkins	70	231

Charities.

Osborne's Land, £111 19s. 8d. for the year.

Legacy of Theoph. Field, £874 2s. 10½d. for the year, cash recd.

Parish Registers.*

(B. T. Leeward Islands, vol. 24.)

Baptized.

1734 July 20 Mary D. of Mr James Ailhand.

Buried.

1734 June 5 Mrs. Jane Fisher.

1734 Oct. 22 Mrs Berkly buried at the Road.

Monumental Inscriptions.

ST. MARY'S CHURCHYARD.

On a headstone:—In Memory of the Much Lamented | *MRS ANN SCHOLLAR* | late Wife of | *MR THOMAS SCHOLLAR* | at English Harbour Who Departed | this Life the 20th of Janr 1780 | Aged 25 Years | Here Lieys the .... (Remainder not decipherable.)

On a broken fragment:—.... E MEM .... | LOUISA CURT .... | only daughter of .... | JAMES CURT .... | Rector .... | Died January 18 .... | AGED 15 Years.

Sacred | To the memory of | SARAH FARQUHAR | who departed this life April 23rd 1813 | *Aged 33 Years.* (Six lines follow.)

Sacred
Memory ....
Mary ....
The Rev. ....

* Baptisms are complete from 1841, Marriages from 1833, and Burials from 1837.

VALLEY CHAPEL BURIAL-GROUND.

M S . | of | Mr Peter Corss | Who departed this Life | October 19th 1790. (Ten lines follow.)

Sufanah Ann Corbett | Died 12 March | 1829 | Aged 9 Yrs 5 Mos.

SACRED | To | The MEM . . . . of | SUSANNA | late Wife of Wm Hubbard | who departed this life | 19th Sepbr 1782 . Aged 50. (Four lines follow.)

On a headstone:—SACRed TO The Memory | of | MISS DEBORAH C. LAKE | WHO DEPARTED THIS LIFE | THE 11 OF FEBRUARY 1812 | AGED 26 YEARS | ErecteD By her ever DEAR AND | SORROWING relation AND FRIEND | Byron M . Roy.

On a white marble ledger:—SACRED | to the memory of | ELIZABETH FRANCES | *wife of Henry John Glanville* | chief justice of Dominica | born at Righton in Antigua | 29th March 1821 | married in Dominica | 6th February 1840 | died in this island | 16th September 1842. (Six lines follow.)

Beneath this stone also rest in peace | the mortal remains of | SARAH MARIA | daughter of | *Darius Davey* | who at the early age of | Eleven years | was summoned | to another and a better world | December 3rd 1842. (Seven lines follow.)

ERECTED | BY | JOHN DOBSON | in memory of his two dear children | JAMES DOBSON | who died Sep. 25th 1859 Aged 3 days | ALSO | WILLIAM DOBSON | who died Feb. 15th 1860 Aged 3 Years and 5 ms.

MISCELLANEOUS NOTES.

FULHAM PALACE MSS. (COLONIAL).

These papers consist of the correspondence which was carried on by the Bishops of London with the various Governors of the North American and West Indian colonies and the clergy. They are at present unsorted and the different colonies much mixed up, but a proper arrangement is in contemplation. From a few of the bundles which I had an opportunity of looking through, I was able to collect some notes about Antigua, but the most valuable paper amongst them was a complete transcript of the parish register of St. George's, Nevis, from 5 April 1716 to 25 March 1724. Doubtless in the great mass of documents other transcripts may be found.

1711, April 19. The Bishop of London writes to Governor Douglas about the Escheat of Mr. Osborne's estate in ye parish of St Marie's in Antigua, asking him to settle it for a glebe to the minister.

1712-13, Jan. 17. The original subscription list for building a new church in St Philip's parish. (See Vol. I., p. 87, for information on this matter.)

1716, May 14. Letter from William Lavington, Esq., to the Bishop about the same, enclosing an original petition signed by Isaac Grace, rector.

1716, April 18. Governor Walter Hamilton to the Bishop of London: "Mr. Charles Porter (who is now at my house) I am giving a Presentation to for the Parish of Falmouth in Antigua."

1717, Sep. 20. Charles Porter writes to the Bishop that he arrived a year and a half ago, that living is very dear, & his salary unpunctually paid.

1717-18, March 14. Governor Walter Hamilton to the Bishop about Mr. Field's absence from St John's, & is sending this letter by "Your kinsman Mr. Willett." (This last named was probably one of the Willetts of St. Christopher's.)

1719, July 15. Governor Walter Hamilton to the Bishop. Rev. Mr. Leslie whom I have presented to St Paul's, Falmouth. Mr. Samuel Sanders officiates in the room of Mr. Jefford, absent in Great Britain. Mr. Grace, who had formerly a presentation to a parish here, which he left years ago, & then filled up by Mr. Orr. Parishioners of St John's are uneasy at the long absence of Mr. Field.

1726, July. The Bishop writes about the heavy accusations by the Archbishop of Dublin against Mr. Metcalfe, the curate officiating at St John's, who is to be at once deprived.

1728, Dec. 1. The following list of clergy is sent to the Bishop:—

St John's. Rev. James Field, absent.

St Peter's. Rev. Samuel Sanderson, A.M. Oxon; ordained by Edwd. Bishop of Gloucester, in 1696.

St Philip's. Rev. Samuel Orr, A.M. Glascow; ordained at Fulham in 1710.

St Mary. Rev. James Knox, A.M. Glascow; licensed by the Bishop of London 1715.

St George's. Rev. Henry Husband, A.M. Oxon.

1729, April 10. Henry Husband writes to the Bishop that St Philip's is vacant by the death of Rev. Samuel Orr.

PARISH REGISTER OF ST. GEORGE, NEVIS.

Married.

1718 Nov. 20 Mr. Thomas Steevens of the Island Antigua, Merchant, and Mrs. Elizabeth Choppin.

HAMPSTEAD, CO. MIDDLESEX, CHURCHYARD.*

On a headstone north of Church and east of pathway:—

Here Lyeth ye Body of
MR RICHARD JAMES of this
Parifh who Died August the
8th 1751, Aged 36 Years (? 86)
Alfo the Body of
Mr JOHN JAMES of *ANTIGUA*
Merchant, Nephew of the
above Mr RICHARD JAMES
who Died October the 31st
1764 Aged 24 Years.
Here alfo Lyeth the Body
of Mrs ELIZABETH LOVEDAY
who Died June the 18th 1765
Aged 61 Years.

EXTRACTS FROM THE 'HISTORICAL REGISTER.'

1715, Feb. 15. Edward Perry, Esq; made Clerk of the Naval Stores or Navy Office in the Leeward Islands (pp. 47 and 51).

1717, May 10. John Floyer, Esq; appointed Clerk of the Naval Stores in the Leeward Islands (p. 24).

1718, Jan. 18. Col. Purcell made Governor of the Leeward-Islands (p. 4).

* Copied from the original in 1896 by Mr. R. Garraway Rice, F.S.A.

1728, Oct. 5. Died at Antigua, Samuel Pitman, Esq; Commander of the Pearl Man of War (p. 54).

1729, Oct. 18. About this Time came Advice of the Death of Capt. John Smith, Commander of his Majesty's Ship the Saphire, who dy'd at Antigua the 19th of August last (p. 58).

1735, April. Earl of Crawford made Colonel of the late General Jones's Regiment in the Leeward Islands (p. 18).

EXTRACTS FROM THE 'GENTLEMAN'S MAGAZINE,'

RELATING TO VARIOUS PERSONS CONNECTED WITH ANTIGUA, WHOSE PEDIGREES HAVE NOT BEEN TABULATED.

1743, Jan. James Gregory of St. Kitts, — Collector of Antigua in room of Mr. Arbuthnot, dec. (Promotions, p. 51.)

1751, July. John Saunders Seabright, Esq; clerk of the navy-office in the Leeward Islands, during life, on the death or surrender of Jn Floyer, Esq. (p. 333).

1757, *circa* March. John Chalmers of Antigua, esq. (p. 189).

1761, April 14. T. Cottle, Esq; Sollicitor Gen. (p. 189).

1764, April 30. Francis Forbes of the island of Barbuda, — to Miss Lindsay (p. 250).

1764, Aug. 8. Capt. Diamond, late in the Leeward island trade.

1765, April. Fra. Moore & J. Pyne, late of Antigua, merchant. Bankrupt (p. 200).

1765, Aug. Lieutenant Goddard of the 68th Regiment at Antigua (p. 443).

1766, Jan. 24. Edw. Griffiths, Esq; at Antigua, sollicitor-general of the ceded islands (p. 47).

1766, April. Edw. Hall, Esq; attorney-general of the Grenades, at Antigua (p. 247).

1766, June 4. Peter Burrell, Esq; formerly of Antigua, in May-fair (p. 294).

1766, Sep. 6. The King has been pleased to grant unto Geo. Thomas of Yapton-place, Sussex, Esq; and Governor of the Leeward Islands, and to his heirs male, the dignity of a Baronet (p. 439).

1766, Oct. Wm Woodley, Esq; — governor of the Leeward Islands in room of George Thomas, Esq. (p. 496).

1766, Nov. John Stuart, Esq; — appointed Vendue Master in the islands of Nevis, St Christophers, Montserrat, Antegoa, and other the Leeward Caribbee-islands in America (p. 552).

1784, July 31. At Hertford, Capt. Thomas Spence, in the Antigua trade, to Miss Susanna Platt (p. 636).

1785, Nov. 22. At Bath, Capt. John Mowbray, late commissioner of the dock-yard at Antigua (p. 1008).

1786, Oct. In Antigua, Lieut. Fred. Mouat, of Marines, son of Capt. M. of the royal navy (p. 998).

1791. D[r] James Grainger, who d. at Antigua, Dec. 24, 1767. List of his works (p. 614).

1791, Sep. 22. Tho. Lodington, esq. of Lamb's Conduit-street, one of the secondaries of the Court of Common Pleas, to Miss Day, of New Norfolk-street, daughter of the late John D. esq. of the island of Antigua (p. 873).

1793, Dec. 17. At Antigua, Lieut. Neate, of the 21st regiment, son of Tho. N. esq. of Bath (1794, p. 180).

1794, Jan. 8. At Wymondham, Nathaniel Watts, esq. many years a surveyor of the Kings works in Antigua, and several other of the British West-India islands (p. 91).

1794, Aug. 8. At Berwick, in his 22d year, of a decline, Mr Thomas Yelloly, surgeon of the royal artillery on the island of Antigua, to which situation he had only been a few months appointed. He was the eldest son of Mr Thomas Yelloly, master-gunner of that garrison etc. (p. 958).

1794, Oct. Lately. In the island of Antigua, of the yellow fever, Colin Patrick Scott, second son of the Rev. John S. minister of Muthill (p. 963).

1794, Nov. 15. At Antigua, of the yellow fever, in his 26th year, Henry Fairbairn, M.D. (1795, p. 166).

1795, April. Lately. At Paisley, in Scotland, in her 70th year, Mrs. Margaret Hutchinson. In consequence of the death of a brother in the island of Antigua, she, within these few years, succeeded to an inheritance of nearly 300,000 l. which as she has no other relations, will become a fund of division among a great number of legatees. By her will she has devised 1500 l. for the erection of a charity-school in the town of Paisley, to be under the direction of the magistrates for the time being, and sundry other patrons. She has likewise bequeathed 100 l. for the benefit of the town's hospital; 50 l. to the Sunday schools; 50 l. to the dispensary; 100 l. to the general Kirk sessions; and 200 l. as a fund for the support of four old people of the names of Hutchinson and Park (p. 354).

1795, June. At St John's, Antigua, Mr Patrick Cummings (p. 703).

1795, Oct. 15. At Antigua, Mr Charles Gibbons, a midshipman in the royal navy, and third son of Sir William G. bart. (p. 1055).

1796, Aug. At English Harbour, Antigua, Lieut. James Clerk, of his Majesty's ship Invincible, son to John C. of Eldin, esq. (p. 966).

1797, Sep. Lately. At Antigua, Dr John Robertson.

1798, Aug. 24. At his apartments in the Kings Bench prison, William Wilkinson, esq. of Antigua. He was one of those whose debt exceeded the limitations of the late insolvency act (p. 730).

1798, Sep. 30. At Antigua, of a fever, Mr. Henry Jones, acting lieutenant of his Majesty's frigate Solebay (1799, p. 165).

1801, Dec. 31. At Antigua, the lady of Brigadier-general Peter of Crossbasket (1802, p. 272).

1803, Jan. At Antigua, Mr John Masters Empson, surgeon of the Castor frigate. Of a malignant fever, David Roberts, esq. merchant (p. 86).

1803, Nov. 25. In New North-street, Queen-square, Robert Roberts, esq. late of Antigua, and brother to Dr R. physician to the army (p. 1188).

1804, June. At Antigua, in his 37th year, Mr Richard Spuring, sen. (p. 784).

1804, June. At Antigua, after three days illness, of the yellow fever, Lieut. George Mellis, of the 70th foot (p. 978).

1804, July 31. At Antigua, in his 25th year, much lamented by his family and friends, Capt. Thomas Winstanley, of the 70th regiment of foot, and third son of Clement W. esq. of Braunston (p. 1168).

1804, Aug. At Antigua, in the West Indies, where he was brigade-major to his uncle Brigadier-gen. Dunlop, Capt. Vans, of the 1st Foot-guards, eldest son of R. Vans Agnew, esq. of Barnbarrow (p. 1071).

1804, Sep. 27. In Charlotte street, Fitzroy-squa. Capt. Wm. Starke, formerly in the Antigua trade (p. 983).

1805, Aug. 30. At Antigua, of the yellow fever, Mr. Worthington Seaton, of his Majesty's ship Galatea, son of Mr. S. of Trinity-street, Bristol (p. 1171).

1805, Oct. 31. At Antigua, of the yellow fever, Capt. Thomas Henry Cray, of the 1st battalion of the 96th Foot.

1806, Oct. 31. At Antigua, Brigadier-general Crofton Vandeleur, of Kilruth, co. Clare in Ireland (p. 1251).

1807, June 24. At St John's, Antigua, the wife of Lieut-col. Carter, nephew of Sir John C. of Portsmouth. She had recently arrived from Trinidad, where her husband had died a short time before, and she was to have come to England in the Canada (p. 888).

1807, Nov. 25. At St John's, Antigua, after a few days illness, Major-gen. C. Archer, commander of the troops there.

1808, June 24. At Antigua, Master Ralph Cuming, and on the 25th, his father, Ralph Cuming, esq. M.D. of his Majesty's Naval Hospital at English Harbour, and late of Romsey, Hants. His loss will be severely felt, as he was bringing into practice a new method of cure for the yellow fever, and was besides a very skilful and able surgeon. (p. 851).

1808, Sep. On the island of Marigalante, John Brown, esq. a native of Belfast, and some years a merchant in Dublin. On his passage from Antigua, to another island, on a mercantile speculation, the ship he sailed in was captured etc. (p. 1126).

1808, Nov. At Antigua, Mr. John Newall, jun. late of Bristol; a young man of most promising abilities (1809, p. 277).

1808, Nov. 8. At Antigua, Capt Asa Rossiter, lately trading from Bristol to New York; a man of the strictest honour and integrity, whose loss will be severely felt by his relations and friends, but more particularly by his widow and five small children (1809, p. 182).

1809, June 5. At Port Royal, Martinique, after four days illness of a violent fever, aged 18, Miss Ramsay, only daughter of General R. adjutant-general to the Forces in the Leeward and Windward Islands (p. 678).

1809, Oct. 28. At Antigua, after a few days illness, and in his 23d year, Major George Gordon, of the 8th West India Regiment, nephew of Col. Gordon, and military secretary to the Earl of Harrington etc. He has left a disconsolate mother and sister to deplore his loss (p. 1236).

1810, May. Lately. At Antigua, Charles, the youngest son of the late Samuel Goodwin, esq. of Spath, co. Stafford (p. 500).

1810, Oct. 13. In his command at Antigua, Brigadier-gen. Robert Nicholson, senior lieut-colonel of the Royal Foot etc. (p. 583).

1810, Oct. 19. At Falmouth, in his 33d year, William-Camden Neild, esq. of the island of Antigua, one of the Kings Counsel for that and all the Leeward Islands, the eldest son of James Nield, esq. of Chelsea, well known as the benevolent Treasurer of the Society for the Relief of Small Debts (p. 583).

1810, Dec. 20. At Vera Cruz, of the yellow fever, Lieut. Wm Elliott, of the Implacable, second son of Governor E. of the Leeward Islands (1811, p. 395).

1810, Dec. 21. At Antigua, Mr R. Noton, R.N. 5th son of Mr N. of Hadley, Middlesex (1811, p. 293).

1811, Oct. 8. At Barnstaple, Mrs Kittoe, widow of the late G. K. esq. of Antigua (p. 487).

1814, Jan. At Antigua, J. Dover, first lieutenant of H.M's ship Barbadoes (p. 189).

1814, Mar. 27. At Chelsea, the wife of J. Mason Lewis, esq. commissioner of the Navy at Antigua (p. 418).

1816, Sep. 21. At Antigua, Lieut. J. Adamson, of the Royal Marines. He was on his return home from Trinidad, where he had been to settle his Black Corps as American Refugees, when, driven by a storm into Antigua, he was attacked by the fever then raging there, which terminated his existence after an illness of three days (p. 465).

1816, Sep. 29. At Antigua, Robert Mackay, esq. of Bighouse, N.B. (p. 566).

1816, Oct. 15. At Antigua, Lieut. Shortland, of H.M. ship Tigris (p. 625).

1816, Nov. At Antigua, Mrs S. Pele, eldest daughter of the late John Heaver, esq. (p. 626).

1817, Jan. At Antigua, on board the Childers, of a fever, Mr. Bishop, purser; also five successive pursers, several officers, and upwards of 30 of the crew, in one month. Mr Bishop was the last of three brothers who also fell victims to that destructive climate (p. 90).

1817, Feb. 11. At Antigua, in her 22d year, Louisa-Jane, wife of Lieut. Morgan, 1st West India regiment, and eldest daughter of the late Mr F. Hobson, of Wordsley, Staffordshire (p. 374).

1817, April. At Antigua, of the yellow fever, in his 20th year, Ensign Robinson, 63d reg. second son of Rev. R. G. Robinson, Vicar of Harborne, co. Stafford (p. 379).

1822, April. Aged 81, B. Butter, esq. for many years a resident of the island of Antigua, but late of Queen-square, Bath (p. 381).

1823, Oct. 31. At Speen-hill, aged 74, Wm. Brinton, esq. formerly of Antigua (p. 572).

1825, Aug. 15. In Nottingham-ter. Regent's-park, aged 44, Sarah Poole, wife of Philip Lyne, esq. formerly of Antigua (p. 188).

1827, Feb. 6. At Alphington, Exeter, the wife of Thos. Hoggard, esq. late of Antigua (p. 188).

1827, Sep. 27. At Antigua, Capt. Robert Dudgeon, of the 1st Royals etc.

1829, Dec. 21. In Upper Stamford-st. John Jacob Walter, esq. of Antigua (p. 649).

1831, Nov. 20. At Kensington, aged 62, Dorothy-Anne, widow of Henry Papps, esq. of Antigua (p. 569).

1835, Feb. 28. At Sion Hill, in his native island of Antigua, the Hon. John Duncombe Taylor, for many years an inhabitant of Clifton, Gloucestershire (p. 558).

1835, June 7. At Antigua, Lieut. C. M. Burrows, 36th regt. (p. 446).

1835, July 23. At Antigua, Wm. West, esq. M.D. (*Ibid.*)

1835, Oct. 21. At Antigua, Ensign and Adjutant Clarke, 36th foot (p. 335).

1835, Oct. 21. At Antigua, Mary-Redfern, wife of H. Armstrong, esq. eldest dau. of the Rev. Dr Bunting, of London. (*Ibid.*)

1839, June 4. At Antigua, Captain John McCausland 89th foot; Ensign 1812; Lieut. 1813; Capt. 1839 (p. 667).

1840, Dec. 27. Bucks. At the Cottage, Westbury, in the 51st year of his age, Benjamin Smyth, esq. formerly Colonial Secretary of Cape Breton, and Naval Officer General of the Islands of Antigua and Bermuda (p. 330).

1841, May 3. At Green Castle, in the Island of Antigua, of which place he had been a resident nearly forty years, Robert Briggs, esq. aged 57, father of Mrs Neville, of Bristol (p. 334).

1844, March 23. Aged 69, in Gloucester-road, Regents Park, Albert Francis Favey, esq. formerly of Antigua, and of Thornton Heath, Surrey (p. 552).

1845, July. Lately. At Demerara, Edmund Hayter Bingham, esq. 1st West India Regt. youngest son of the late Col. C. C. Bingham, Royal Art. to Cecilia-Lewis-Pauline, third dau. of Wm. B. Wolseley, esq. and great niece of Sir Chas. Wolseley, Bart. (p. 73).

1845. At the Cape, John W. Langford, esq. H. C. Bombay Civil Service, and eldest son of the late Edw. Langford, esq. of Bath, to Cecilia-Elizabeth, eldest dau. of Major Longmore, resident magistrate, and niece of Sir Benj. D'Urban, late Governor of the colony (p. 73).

1845, Sep. 29. In Norris-st, Haymarket, aged 45, John Gooch D'Urban, esq. Commander R.N. son of Sir Benjamin D'Urban, the late Governor of the Cape of Good Hope, etc. (p. 657).

WILLS AND ADMINISTRATIONS.

WILLS.

Roger Glover of London, merchant, now at Meavis. Will dated 14 Nov. 1636; proved 5 Sep. 1637 by Richard Rowe; power reserved to the others. (126 Goare.) William Hawkins, citizen & waxchandler of London, to be my overseer & to dispose of all goods in the ship "Increase" of London for the benefit of Richard Rowe of London, merchant, my loving brother Richard Glover of London, merchant, & my loving sisters Elizabeth & Sarah Glover, whom I appoint Ex'ors. My servant Roger the Indian £10. My niece Elizabeth Glover, dau. of my brother Joss Glover, £50. William Rowe, son of Richard Rowe, £30. My niece Elizabeth Pemmerton £40. John Worcester £10. Capt. John Sparrowe, Governor of Meavis, 2000 lbs. of tobacco. Mr. George Upcote of Meavis 500 lbs., & to Nicholas Godsalve, Secretary. 300 lbs. to my overseer. If I recover debts due from Thomas Littleton,* late Governor of Meavis, I give his son James Littleton £100 sterling. Witnessed by Thomas Sparrow, John Worcester, Thomas Hinde, Nicholas Godsalve, Scrivener.

Ralph Webster of Antigua, Gent. Will dated 13 April 1649†; proved 8 Oct. 1649 by William Webster. (149 Fairfax.) About to proceed to Antigua. All my plantations, slaves, etc., there held in partnership with Cap. Benjn Langham I give to my loving cozin Mr Wm Webster of London, Merch^t. To my loving mother Mrs Marie Webster £10. To my sister Mary wife of Robt Carter £20, & to each of his children Robt, Anne, & Mary Carter £20 each. To my loving cozin Eliz. wife of Wm Webster £20, & to each of his children, my little cozins W^m, Henry, Mathew, Eliz., & Kath. Webster £20 each. To my cozin Wm Webster, now residing with the said Wm Webster, £5. To Capt. Benjn Laugham my now partner £10. To Capt Joseph Lee £5. To Mr Thos. Akehurst £5. To Kath. Webster, dau. of the said Wm Webster, & my goddau. my 4 cottages in Bempton in Yorkshire. All the merchandise in the ship "Peter Bonadventure" of London, in which I take passage, to my cozin Wm Webster, & I appoint him Ex'or. Capt. Joseph Lee & Mr Tho. Akehurst to take charge of all my plantations for him. To my servant John Hobbs his freedom & 500 lbs. of tobacco. Witnessed by George Blanshard, Henry Kinge, ser., and Everard Frauncis, ser. to ye said ....

James Hewett of Nevis, planter. Will dated 9 Aug. 1649. Now bound for my native country in the ship "St. Peter" of Middleboroughe, being possessed of a moiety of a plantation at Ginger Land containing 27 mens lands‡ & ½ in breadth, & in length extending from Tumble downe Dick Gutt to Stepp Gutt; also a moiety of a parcell of land at India Castle bought of William Charley, containing 60,000 plants grounde; also a moiety of a parcell next Capt. Digbie's plantation which was first purchased of Margaret Meriton by Charley, who sold it to me & my planter Henry Marriott; also a moiety of a parcell containing 4000 plants of ground, purchased of Robert Littleton, lying at Ginger Land; also a moiety of 3 servants & 4 nigroes. To my father if living, Henry Hewett of Hennington under Castle Dunington, co. Leicester, yeoman, or to next-of-kin. Sarah Westberry, dau. of Richard Westberry, 1000 lbs. of tobacco. All residue at Nevis to my said planter Henry Merriott & Ex'or. Witnessed by Richard Westberry, Jenkin Rice, Miles Jones, William Denton, Nicholas Goodsalve, Scrivener. Copie from the Office of Nevis 27 March 1659. William Leach, clerk, Secretary.

On 24 July 1656 adm'on to John Hewett the only brother and principal legatee now living, Henry Marriott the sole Ex'or dying before testator.

Col. Henry Tillyer of Antigua, Esq. Will dated 30 Jan. 1649. (130 May.) My nephew Henry Devaulx all lands, & to be my sole heir & Ex'or on condition he live upon my plantation in Antigua, & does not sell or let it for 3 years, otherwise to my nephew Wm Devaulx, son of Thomas Devaulx. All goods sent in the ship the "Willing Mind" belonging to Martin Hardrett, & consigned to me by his son who died abroad, to be placed in the hands of my friends Henry Devaulx, Benjamin Langham, & Jacob Withers to sell. Witnessed by Benjamin Langham, Secretary of Antigua, Jacob Withers. Sworn on 8 April 1650 by the two witnesses before the Rt. Worshipful Captain Henry Ashton, Esq., Governor, etc. On 23 July 1652 Jacob Withers swore to the copy. On 19 Aug. 1661 commission to Magdalen Devaulx, sister of Henry Devaulx and Theodore Devaulx, niece and nephews by a sister of testator.

John Newbroughe of Bristol, merchant. Will dated upon Antiga 25 June 1658; commission 20 June 1662 to Joseph Newbroughe. (188 Laud.) My brother Joseph Newbroughe of Sturbridge in Old Swinford all sums, my other brothers. Mrs Hester Sandford of Martley, co. Worcester, £50. My friends Capt. Joseph Lee & Mr. Edmund Ditty to take charge of all goods on the Islands of Antega, Mountserott, Nevis, & St Christopher's. Brother Richard to preach my funeral sermon. Witnessed by Samuel Welborne, Henry Stodder, Michael Stodder.

Philip Gosse of Nevis, planter. Will proved 1664. (110 Bruce.) Stepney. Wife Joane estate in the hands of Capt. Francis Kennell of Nevis.

There was a Captain Charles Gosse living 1686 in St. Mary's, Antigua.

1681. (86 North.) John Bruning of Antigua.

Antegua. Tristram Stevens. Will dated 20 June 1684. My brother Robert Stevens £100 out of this plantation in 3 years. My wife Sarah for life ½ of my plantation formerly called Taylors Ridge, & ½ the negros, & at her death to my dau. Eliz. Stevens, & the whole of my estate in England left me by my father Tristram Stevens in Dover & Peckham. My said dau. sole Ex'trix, but if she die to return to my 2 brothers & sister, Richard, Robert, & Jane Stevens. Capt. Steven Lawler, Mr. Richard Francis, & Lieut. Richard Haddon, Trustees. Witnessed by Edward Scott, Thomas Beck, David Beck. By the Hon. Edward Powell, Deputy-Governor, appeared Thomas Beck and Edward Scott 11 Dec. 1684. On 15 Dec. 1684 Richard Francis, Gent., declined.

Codicil. 26 Oct. 1684. My friend Edward Perry, Jun., Ex'or in Trust. Witnessed by Robert Elbon, Thomas Beck. By the Governor Edward Powell appeared Thomas Beck 11 Dec. 1684.

On 6 July 1685 a commission issued to Elizabeth Stevens, "avice" and guardian of Elizabeth Stevens, a minor. Testator was formerly of St. Mary Magdalen, Bermondsey, but at Antigua, deceased. Proved 6 Nov. 1700 by Elizabeth Stevens the daughter, being of age. (93 Cann.)

1687. (102 Foot.) Edmund Clymer of Bristol, merchant. (See Vol. II., pp. 332, 333.)

1689. (61 Ent.) John Combes of Bristol and Antigua, merchant.

1693. (5 Coker.) Francis Le Cornu of Antigua.

* Captain Anthony Hylton settled in Nevis in July 1628, and was commissioned its first Governor in 1629. He was shortly after succeeded by Thomas Littleton, a London merchant, then by Captain Luke Stoakes and Captain Thomas Sparrowe.

† This is the earliest Antiguan will I have seen.—V. L. O.

‡ It would be interesting to know how much was contained in "one man's land." In Antigua the poor settlers were called "10-acre men," but persons of the rank of a gentleman were usually assigned 100 acres.

Thomas Lasher of London, merchant, bound to Antigua. Will dated 24 Feb. 1695; proved 27 July 1700 by Caleb Lasher. (102 Noel.) My brother Joshua Lasher 40s., sister Eliz. Guyon £12, & her husband Chas. Guyon 40s., brother Henry Guyon £60. All residue to my brother Caleb Lasher, citizen & girdler of London, & Ex'or. Witnessed by Jonathan Daniel, John Russell, John Hunter.

John Hamlin of Antigua, Gent. Will dated 23 March 1697-8; proved 5 July 1698 by Bastian Bayer. (166 Lort.) To Henry Smidmore & James Howie a ring each. Mr Cornelius Vogan all goods & furniture. John Burt for physic & care £6 c. My friend John Martin of Mercer's Creek £20 c. with my seal ring. Nephew John Hamlin, now aged 10, son of my brother Edward Hamlin of Burfield, co. Berks, deceased, £600, which Hon. Col. Bastian Bayer had out on mortgage, also £50 in the hands of Mr. Tho. Gandy, goldbeater in the Old Bayley. All residue to Col. Bastian Bayer as Ex'or on Trust for Antigua & Capt. John Otto. Revoke ring to James Howie. Witnessed by John Bowen, Martin Abbutt (or ? Albrett), Planche Bowles, Henry Smidmore, John Burtt, Cornelius Voeghan. True copy. Walter Quarme, Deputy-Secretary. By John Yeamans, Esq., 11 April 1698, appeared John Burtt, Martin Albrett, Henry Smidmore. Recorded also at St. John's.

"A Schedule of the goods and chattells of Left John Hamlin, taken the 23 of March 1697-8."

	£	s.	d.
Cash in his trunck	68	5	0
James Howie by bill	23	8	0
more lent him att times by Mingoe .	3	12	0
Capt. Wickham by bond . . .	6	0	0
Henry Smidmore	5	19	6
William Harrox for lent money .	13	0	0
Mr. Thomas Archer, cash lent . .	30	0	0
Six Negroes of my owne Sarah .	30	0	0
Nanny 30ll, Hater, a boy, 18 is .	48	0	0
Sneia, a girle, 12ll, Nanny, a girle, 15ll	27	0	0
Scanderbra, a Small boy . . .	6	0	0
a bay mare	25	0	0
a bay mare colt	12	0	0
Doctr Mackanen for a horse . .	15	0	0
One bay mare named Crab . .	36	0	0
One bay gelding Jack a dandy . .	26	0	0
to ten Swine great and small . .	7	0	0
55 Sheepe	49	0	0
40 goates	25	0	0
two ffeather beds, bolsters, and pillowes	10	0	0
one hundred acres of land in the body	100	0	0
John Pope's land in pope's head .	6	0	0
Collo Carlile for rent of itt . .	37	10	0
Sallary due to my selfe . . .	112	10	0
due to me from Collo Bayer plantacon	4	4	6
due from William Sigsworth for Nicholas Rich	5	0	0
George Rock for 10 sheepe . .	9	0	0
in my chest six duckaduns and a halfe	1	19	0
	£703	17	6

Recorded 13 April 1698. Letters of administration granted 11 April 1698 to Captain John Otto. Estate in Antigua appraised at £396.

Antigua. David Lockwood, mariner. Will dated 13 Sep., proved 6 Jan. 1699 by Anna Lockwood the widow; power reserved to Sir Richard Haddock, Knt. (10 Noel.) To my dear wife Anna Lockwood all my estate for life, then to my 4 daus. Sarah, Mary, Anna, & Rachel Lockwood equally. My dear brother Saml Lockwood & my friends Mr Richd Oliver & Nathl Sampson Ex'ors in Trust in Antigua, & to manage the ship "Princess Ann" of London which I command, & to send her home to her owner Mr Tho. Sands. My wife Anna & Sir Richd Haddock Ex'ors for all things not intrusted to the others. Witnessed by Edward Acton, Samuel Lawrence, John Allin, John Okey.

Antigua. Thomas Musgrave, Gent. Will dated 16 Nov. 1699; proved 20 Dec. 1700; commission to Robert Hartley the guardian of Richard Musgrave, Esq., the son and Ex'or of Edward Musgrave, Esq.,* deceased. The testator died a bachelor. (182 Noel.) My good friends Isaac Horsford & Anne Bradford, both of Antigua, have £50 in their hands for my funeral, & they are to sell my horse & apparel. To my niece Mrs Hartley, wife of Mr Hartley, bookseller, of London, £5. To my loving sister Mrs Anne Winder £100. All my estate both real & personal to my dear brother Edwd Musgrave of Westmoreland, Esq., & appoint him sole Ex'or. Antigua, 22 Aug. 1700. Deposition of John Smith, aged 27 and more, taken before Peter Lee, Esq., J.P., and an assistant of the Court of Common Pleas. Witnessed by John Hilliard and Robert Thomson, and on 23 Aug. 1700 was sworn Isaac Horsford, Gent. On same date appeared Shadrack Morgan of St. Bartholomew Exchange, London, aged 25 and more, merchant, and Thomas Webb of St. Michael's, Cornhill, 25 and more, merchant, and swore that on 16 Nov. 1699 Mr. Thomas Musgrave was then lodging at the house of Mr. Lightfoot of Antigua, etc.

John Roe of Antigua, Gent. Will dated 4 July 1700; proved 20 Aug. 1701 by Andrew Roe the brother, the adm'on being revoked; proved 3 Sep. 1708 by John Roe the son; power reserved to James Roe the son. (117 Dyer.) To my wife Margarett the furniture of her chamber, plate, a horse, & a negro boy & girl. To my 1st son John Roe my plantation called Shortshope of 284 acres in St. Mary's Parish, with the mill, stills, coppers, etc., & ½ of all my negros & cattle at 21. To my younger son James Roe my plantation in New Division of 175 acres near Five Islands Harbour, with the mill, stills, & coppers, & ½ of all my negros & cattle at 21. To each of my daus. £1000, to be paid in England at marriage; if either die the survivor to have £1500. My 2 sons Ex'ors. My friends Henry Pearne, Esq., Robt Amory, & John ffry, Gent., & my loving brother Andrew Roe Guardians. Witnessed by Samuel Martin, Elias Jamain, Thomas Gateward. On 8 Nov. 1700 commission to John Darby, the uncle & guardian of John, James, and Elizabeth Roe, minors, the children of John Roe at Antegoa, deceased, Margaret Roe his relict being there resident.

Samuel Poskins, Commander of the "Increase" of Bristoll from Antigua, now in Cork Harbour. Will dated 24 Sep. 1700. On 4 Dec. 1700 commission to James Wilcox. (183 Noel.) To my 1st brother John Poskins £10 & £5 to his child by his 1st wife. To my brother Francis Poskins £25. To my brother Richd Poskins £25. To my sister Ann Poskins £50. To my sister Ann Wilcox, the relict of Tho. Wilcox, £10. To my aunt Ann Hodge £10. I have on board 4 hogsheads of sugar & 6 of molasses which I give to my brothers & sisters, & all residue. I gave to Mr Chas. Harper of Antigua £85 11*s.* 0*d.*, which sum in sugar I expect on board the "Vine" ketch of Londonderry, Wm Wilson, master, his note for the same da. 27 July last. Mr Saml Phillipps' note for £11 15*s.* 0*d.* & Benjn Wickham's for £7 8*s.* 0*d.*, both of Antigua. Jas. Wilcox of Barbados, sadler, to be overseer. Witnessed by James Ithell, Arthur Lawrence, Owen Codden. Richard Hasell of Barbados,

* His will is recorded (86 Noel). He was of Ashby, co. Westmoreland, Esq. Sir Christopher and Sir Richard Musgrave, Barts., were his sons' guardians.

Notary Public, sends the copy. On 11 Dec. 1700 appeared Raines Trigg.

1707. (168 Poley.) Thomas Barker. 172. Francis Farnando, mariner. 178 and 9. Nathaniel Grafton and John Haley of H.M.S. "Jersey."

Thomas Newell, Captain of a company of Grenadiers in the Hon. Colonel James Jones' regiment of foot. Will dated 23 Aug. 1711; proved 3 Feb. 1712 by Peter Buor; power reserved to the others. (43 Leeds.) To be buried in Antigua. £300 equally amongst the children of my late sister Eliz. Dyos. All residue to my brothers Humphrey Newell & Andrew Newell, & appoint them Ex'ors in Gt Britain. My loving friends Richd Oliver & Joseph French, Esqres, both of Antigua, Ex'ors in this island, & I give them £10 apiece for mourning. To my servant Sarah Farrell £100 c., a negro girl Phillis, all household goods, & £10. Witnessed by Richard Worthington, John Gallagher, Charles Bowes.

Codicil. 24 Aug. 1711. Peter Buor, major in my Regt, to be another Ex'or. To Sarah Farrell £100. Witnessed by Gousse Bonin, John Buxton, H. Guichene, Peter Brothersam.

1712. Nicholas Roe, clothworker. Voyage to the West Indies, son Richard, dau. Mary, wife Kinborrow. (Barnes, vol. iii.)

1713. (147 Leeds.) Henry Smedmore, planter.

1714. (125 Aston.) John Singleton of H.M.S. "Jolly."

William Bridges of the Tower of London, Esq. Will dated 4 Oct., proved 4 Nov. 1714 by Elizabeth Bridges the sister and sole Ex'trix. (215 Aston.) All my estate to my dear sister Mrs. Eliz. Bridges, spinster, & sole Ex'trix. Witnessed by T. Tooke, Dr. Mercator, Joseph Hammett, Jonathan Jones. Recorded at Antigua.

Testator was I believe Agent of Barbados, M.P. Liskeard, co. Cornwall, Surveyor-General of Ordnance at the Tower, fourth son of Colonel Robert Bridges, Governor of Droghedah, born 10 July 1650, died 30 Oct. 1714, M.I. in Tower Chapel. (See Betham's 'Baronetage,' vol. iii., p. 192.)

1720. (170 Shaller.) Thomas Breton of St. Christopher's and Antigua.

Robert Tuite of Warrington, co. Lancaster, merchant. Will dated 13 April 1724; proved 19 Oct. 1726 by Robert Tuite the son; power reserved to the others. (195 Plymouth.) My sons Robert, Walter, & James, & my daus. Mary, Margaret, Ann, Elizabeth, & Elienor £400 apiece at 21. All sums owing from the West Indies to my son Robert Tuite, also plate. My sister Jane Reyly £15. Nephew Owen Reyly £10. Brother-in-law Robert Reyly £20. Kinswoman Bathia Pearse, dau. of Mr. Wm Pearse of London, £10. Sir Joseph Tuite, Bart., James Pearse of London, Esq., Patrick Cahill, Gent., Henry Peppard of Liverpoole, merchant, & my eldest son Robert Tuite, Ex'ors. To Sir Joseph Tuite & Jas. Pearse £20 each, & to Patrick Cahill & Henry Peppard £10 each. Witnessed by John Ansdell, Mary Dalton, Robert Bromley.

1725. (231 Romney.) George Harrison, mariner.

1726. (150 Plymouth.) Samuel Proctor, late of Finchley, now of Antigua, merchant. Wife Elizabeth sole heiress. (See Vol. III., p. 339.) Also the will of his wife Elizabeth.

1727. (177 Farrant.) James Anderson of the "Union" frigate bound to Antegoa.

John Filbrigge of Antegoa, Esq. Will dated 25 Feb. 1727; proved 12 Nov. 1728 by Anna Filbrigge the widow. (322 Brooke.) All my messuages & negros, all real & personal estate to my dear wife Anna, & appoint her sole Ex'trix. If she die all to my only dau. Frances Filbrigge. Antigua. By the Hon. Edward Byam, Esq., Lieut.-Governor, appeared on 30 March 1728 Christopher Stoodly, Esq., Stephen Blizard, Esq., and Thomas Stevenson, Surgeon, all of Antigua, and swore that they were present at testator's lodgings at St. John's Town where he lay dangerously ill on 25 Feb. last. Recorded in Secretary's Office in libro 2, fos. 403 and 404, 1 April 1728. John Catanaet, Deputy-Secretary, 4 April 1728.

1729. (233 Abbott.) Richard Staple of London, mariner, now of Antigua.

James Knox, Rector of St. Mary's Parish in the Island of Antegoa. Will dated 19 April 1729; proved 30 May 1741 by Elizabeth Knox the relict; the adm'on granted Feb. 1739 to her pending the arrival of the original will being revoked. (128 Spurway.) All my estate to my wife Eliz. & sole Ex'trix. Witnessed by John Gunthorpe, sen. and jun. Antigua. By His Excellency William Mathew, Esq., appeared the Hon. John Gunthorpe, Esq., and John Gunthorpe, jun., 19 May 1740.

1730. (263 Auber.) Charles McNeily of London and Antigua.

1733. (255 Price.) Clement Courland, master of H.M.S. "Ludlow Castle" at Antigua. 15 May 1733. No family named. Witnessed by David Bruce, John Hutten, Gul. Wyne, Notary Public.

John Stewart of Antigua, Gent. Will dated 17 Oct. 1734; on 15 Sep. 1735 commission to Alexander Inglis the attorney of Patrick Wilson. (194 Ducie.) Ensign in H.M. regiment of foot, commanded by the Hon. Brigadier Genl Edward Jones. To my friend Patrick Wilson of St John's, goldsmith, my pay & negros, & to be sole Ex'or. Witnessed by Walter Sydserfe, Walter Tullideph, William Wyne.

1735. (10 Ducie.) John Leste of Antigua, taylor. Proved 2 Jan. 1734 by the widow. All estate & slaves to my wife Sarah & sole Ex'trix. 14 April 1734. Witnessed by Robert Arbuthnot, George Fox.

Antigua. George Jenings, Esq.* Will dated 30 Nov. 1736; proved 31 Aug. 1737; commission to William Dunbar the attorney of Richard Oliver, Walter Sydserfe, and Anne Jenings the widow, the surviving Ex'ors. (184 Wake.) To my daus. Ann Mary Jenings & Sarah Jenings £1000 c. each at 21. To my son Saml my plantation. My wife Anne, my good friends Richd Oliver, Esq., & Wm Wyne, Gent., both of Antigua, Walter Sydserfe of Antigua, chyrurgeon, Ex'ors & Guardians. Witnessed by J. Senegat, Elizabeth Laferté, Abraham Picart de La Ferté. Antigua, 11 Dec. 1736. Before His Excellency William Mathew, Esq., were sworn J. Senegat, barber chyrurgeon, Elizabeth Laferté, spinster, and Abraham Picart de la Ferté, planter. Delacourt Walsh, Deputy-Secretary. Examined at Secretary's Office of Antigua 29 June 1737 per Martin Long. On 31 Aug. 1737 were sworn John Sutcliff of St. John's, Wapping, and Thomas Oliver of St. Mary, Whitechapple, both mariners. Recorded also at St. John's 5 Jan. 1736.

John Green of Antigua, mariner. Will dated 22 Dec. 1736. (234 Henchman.) My dau. Lucy Green £500 st. at 21. My friend Wm Wyne, Gent., a ring. All messuages & negros to my wife Frances, she & Wm Wyne Ex'ors. Witnessed by Abraham Picart Delaferté, Hugh Holmes, Samuel Hoskins. On 23 Nov. 1739 commission to Slingsby Bethell the attorney of Frances Adams, formerly Green, the wife of Roger (*sic*) Green, Esq., the relict, now residing at Cape Fear, North Carolina, William Wyne being dead.

John Wyne of Bartlett's Buildings, Holbourn, Gent. Will dated 13 Jan., proved 3 Feb. 1736 by Anne Wyne the relict. (45 Wake.) My cousen Wm Wyne of Antigua, Esq., & his wife £10 each, & to their son Madeira Wyne £5. My wife Anne Wyne the rectory of Morebath, co.

* Plan of the plantation of George Jennings, Esq., deceased, 330 acres; surveyed 7 July 1743. He was Master and Examiner in Chancery 1711-12.

Devon, & all residue, & Ex'trix. Witnessed by John Lewlinge, John Jocelyn, Thomas Bowker.

Antigua. James Seaborn Seaman. Will dated 15 Dec. 1737; proved 19 June 1739 by George Steygold the attorney of Philip Darby. (140 Henchman.) £50 for funeral. To Rebecca Lee of London £200, or to her 2 children if she be dead. To Mrs Eliz. Glanvile of this Island, widow, £20. To my uncle Tho. Vears of Norwich, co. Norfolk, my India boy Pero. All my clothing to Philip Darby, Chas. Morton, Jas. Gamble, & his son Edwd Gamble, all of this island. All residue to Philip Darby, & I appoint him sole Ex'or. Witnessed by Lustrania Ridd, Richard Nevill, De la Court Walsh. Antigua. Before the Hon. Edward Byam, Esq., Lieut.-Governor and Ordinary in the absence of the Commander-in-Chief, were sworn Lustrania Riddle of St. John's, widow, and Richard Nevill of St. John's, a common sentinel in the regiment of foot commanded by Brigadier Robert Murray, and De La Court Walsh of Antigua, Gent., now Deputy-Secretary. Testator was an Ensign in the said regiment and died at the house of Lustrania Riddle. The latter said that for years past she has wrote her name Ridd only. 30 Dec. 1737.

Henry William Erskine, now going to Antigua. Will dated 13 Dec. 1739; proved 2 Jan. 1740. (8 Spurway.) To John Erskine, saylor, my brother, & to Anne Erskine my sister all estate equally. Col. John Erskine of Carnock, my grandfather, & Mr Roger Hog, merchant in London, Ex'ors. On 2 Jan. 1740 appeared Joseph Herring of St. Botolph's, without Aldgate, watchmaker, and William Innes of Allhallows, Staining, factor. Testator was late of Antigua, but at sea deceased.

Edmund Barry of Bristol, mariner. Will dated 31 Oct. 1738; proved 22 May 1740 by Mary Barry the relict, but this probate void by reason of a will of later date proved in Jan. 1741. (133 Browne.) To my mother Margaret Barry & my brother David Barry £10 apiece. All residue to my dear wife Mary & sole Ex'trix. Witnessed by Mary Jones, Margaret Neady, Edward Gyles.

Edmund Barry, Commander of the snow the "Barrow," now at anchor in St. John's Harbour, Antigua. Will dated 16 Jan. 1739-40; proved 17 Jan. 1741. (3 Spurway.) To my beloved wife Mary Barry of Bristol & my mother Margaret Barry in Ireland all my estate equally. All my watches & apparel to my brother David Barry. Capt Joseph Little & Capt. George Gibbs, both in Antigua, Ex'ors. Witnessed by John Green, Jab. Blackall.

1741. (8 Spurway.) Henry W. Erskine going to Antigua.

[MEMORANDUM.—Between the years 1660 and 1742 *all* the books of wills in P.C.C. have been looked through and extracts made of Antiguan ones.—V. L. O.]

Francis Rufane of Antigua, Gent. Will dated 19 Sep. 1746; proved 11 Feb. 1760 by William Rufane the brother. (71 Lynch.) To be buried "with the usual solemnities belonging to officers of standing Regiments" at the discretion of my friend Henry Osborn, Gent. I am entitled to certain legacies by the will of my late father Majr Francis Rufane of Southampton, Gent., who died about 28 July 1743 leaving my mother Margt Rufane his widow & relict, & appointing her & my brother Majr Wm Rufane, late of Southampton, Gent., Ex'ors. To my said mother £100. To my sister Ann Duval of Southampton, widow, £50. To my niece Margt Duval, Spr, £50. To Eliz. Dorner, late servant to my mother, 5 gs. if living, if not to her niece Ann Ward, dau. of John Ward of Southampton, baker. My silver watch to Geo. Osborn Morgan, son of Eliz. Morgan, & my silver-hilted sword to his brother Henry Morgan. All sums due to me as a Lieut. bearing H.M. Comn & all residue to my elder brother Majr Wm Rufane, & appoint him Ex'or for England & Lieut. Wm Horn, Gent., of Antigua, for America. To the said Wm Horne & Eliz. his wife each a ring of 2 gs. To my friend Henry Osborn & to Mrs Eliz. Morgan, wife of Geo. Morgan, late of Antigua, taylor, each a ring of 2 gs. Witnessed by Isaac Anderson, William Weedon.

John Wills of St. John's, Antigua, but now of Dover, merchant. Will dated 28 Nov. 1766; proved 1 July 1767 by Joseph Moyne and Edward Burtenshaw. (288 Legard.) Very weak & infirm. To be buried at the discretion of my Ex'ors. To my son Joseph Wills my house in St John's, late in the occupation of Mr Nathl Booth, now of Mr Atkinson, & 4 negros at 21 if my friends John Payne, mercht, & John Williams, carpenter, both of St John's, think right, also my gold watch & 2 gold-headed canes. To my dau. Eliz. Wills my other house in St John's adjoining the first named, late in my own occupation, now in that of Capt Alexr Roland, & 6 negros at 18. All bonds equally between my son & dau. My wife Sarah being now with child Ex'ors to retain £200 for it. To each Ex'or 5 gs. All residue to my wife & son & dau. Joseph Moyne, sailmaker, & Edwd Burtenshaw, schoolmaster, both of Dover, Ex'ors. Witnessed by Sarah Balderson, Joshua Tolputt, Sampson Farbrace, Notary Public, Dover.

Nicholas Tuite of London, Esq. Will dated 5 Feb. 1772; proved 27 Nov. 1772 by Robert Tuite, Esq. (425 Taverner.) My lands at St Croix held under the King of Denmark by the late King's patent dated 5 July 1765. £100 to my Ex'ors for the poor of Montserrat. 40 pieces of eight for the Danish church of St Croix, likewise for Catharine Church there. £25 to be sent to John Lincoln & Mary his wife. Having allowed a small annuity to my kinswoman Mary Cahill, widow of Thos. Cahill of Cork, viz., £30 a year, this shall be continued, & the like annuity to Mrs Ann McNamara, widow of John McNamara. To my wife Ann Tuite & my son-in-law Tho. Selby, Esq., £100. Annuities to Biddy & Reily living near Grannard, co. Longford, of £10 a year, paid them by Mr John Nugent of Johnstown near Mullingar & repaid by my correspondent Mr Francis French of Dublin. To my wife Ann £2000 a year & £2000 at once, all my furniture & plate. Have already pd to my dau. Ellinor wife of Tho. Selby £11,000, give her £300 a year. Have agreed with Mr Wm Chippendale of C . . . . Mercht, to take my grandson Chas. Stapleton into partnership 24 J . . . . 1765, & again £3000, lend it him. My dau. Ann wife of Tho. Stapleton, Esq., has been pd £10,000, & I give her £200 a year. My dau. Winifred who mar. Justin McCarthy, Esq., has had £10,000 by deed of 13 Sep. 1765. To my son-in-law Tho. Selbye, Esq., £100. My s.-in-l. Tho. Stapleton £100. My s.-in-l. Justin McCarthy £100. My dear son Robt Tuite all residue & sole Ex'or. (See the Carter Pedigree, Vol. I., p. 123.)

Peter Blair, Esq. Will dated 18 Aug. 1773; proved 15 June 1774. (216 Bargrave.) My dear Willy, I have sent John's will home with power of attorney to Gathorne. I have been superceded as Surgeon by the Admiral, & am going to settle at Courland Bay, Tobago, where my gang of negros is. Your affectionate brother Peter Blair at St John's, Antigua. To Mr Wm Blair at Mrs. Barwels, Park Street, Westminster.

ADMINISTRATIONS (P.C.C.).*

1674, Oct. 11. Fo. 142. Daniel Ely of Antigua: to Daniel Ely the father.

1682, March 26. William Bonnell of Antego: to Anne Bonnell the sister, Jeremiah and Eleanor Bonnell the parents renouncing.

1684, July 10. Mary Butler of Antego, spinster; to Jane Taylor *alias* Butler the sister.

* No regular search has ever been made.

1688, March 5. Fo. 36. Robert Elton of Antegoa; previous grant March 1686, further one April 1689.

1693, March 31. Sir Samuel Foxon, late of St. Martin in the Fields and of Ireland; to George Moore, principal creditor, Dame Foxon not appearing.

1702, July 16. Gabriel Cox of St. Mildred Poultry, but at Antigua, deceased; to Elizabeth Cox, relict.

1710, Nov. Henry Slade of Antigua.

1739, Nov. 27. Thomas Science of Antigua, bachelor; to Martha Science, widow, the mother.

1741, Sep. 4. William Brice of Antigua; to Thomas Brice the brother.

1743, June 24. Thomas Bullen of St. John's, Cockles Point, Antigua; to Jemima Bullen the relict.

1763, Oct. 20. William Storton of Antigua, bachelor; to Elizabeth Maney the sister.

ADDITIONS AND CORRECTIONS TO VOLUMES I., II., AND III.

Volume I.

Page xiii. The following account of the settlement of St. Christopher's has been taken from "The True Travels and Adventures of Captain John Smith into Europe, Asia, Africa, and America, from the year 1592 to 1692." (Churchill's 'Voyages,' vol. ii., chapter xxv.)

The Beginning and Proceedings of the new Plantation of St. Christopher, by Captain Warner.

Master Ralph Merifield and others, having furnished this worthy Industrious Gentleman, he arrived at St. Christopher's, as is said, with fifteen Men, the 28th of January 1623, viz., William Tested, John Rhodes, Robert Bims, Mr. Benifield, Sergeant Jones, Mr. Ware, William Ryle, Rowland Grascock, Mr. Bond, Mr. Langley, Mr. Weaver, Edward Warner, their Captain's Son, and now Deputy Governour, till his Father's return, Sergeant Aplon, one Sailor and a Cook: At their arrival, they found three French Men, who sought to oppose Captain Warner, and to set the Indians upon us; but at last we all became Friends, and lived with the Indians a Month, then we built a Fort, and a House, and planting Fruits, by September we made a crop of Tobacco; but upon the nineteenth of September came a Hericano and blew it away, all this while we lived upon Cassada Bread, Potatoes, Plantanes, Pines, Turtles, Guanes, and Fish plenty; for drink we had Nicnobby. The 18th of March 1624, arrived Captain Jefferson, with three Men Passengers in the Hopewell of London, with some Trade for the Indians, and then we had another crop of Tobacco, in the mean time the French had planted themselves in the other end of the Isle; with this crop Captain Warner returned for England in September 1625.

In his absence came in a French Pinnace, under the command of Monsieur de Nombe, they told us, the Indians had slain some French Men in other of the Charibbe Isles, and that there were six Peryagoes, which are huge great Trees, formed as your Canoos, but so laid out on the sides with Boards, they will seem like a little Gally: Six of those, with about four or five hundred strange Indians came unto us, we bad them be gone, but they would not; whereupon we and the French joyned together, and upon the fifth of November set upon them, and put them to flight: upon New years Even they came again, found three English going about the Isle, whom they slew.

Until the fourth of August, we stood upon our Guard, living upon the spoil and did nothing. But now Captain Warner arriving again with near an hundred People, then we fell to work and planting as before; but upon the fourth of September, came such a Hericano, as blew down all our Houses, Tobacco, and two Drums into the air we know not whither, drove two Ships on Shoar that were both split; all our Provision thus lost, we were very miserable, living only on what we could get in the wild Woods, we made a small party of French and English to go aboard for Provision, but in their returning home, eight French Men were slain in the Harbour.

Thus we continued till near June that the Tortles came in 1627, but the French being like to starve, sought to surprize us, and all the Cassado, Potatoes, and Tobacco we had planted, but we did prevent them. The 26th of October, came in Captain William Smith, in the Hope-well, with some Ordnance, Shot and Powder, from the Earl of Carlisle, with Captain Pelham and thirty Men; about that time also came the Plow, also a small Ship of Bristow, with Captain Warner's Wife, and six or seven Women more.

Upon the 25th of November, the Indians set upon the French, for some injury about their Women, and slew six and twenty French Men, five English, and three Indians. Their Weapons are Bows and Arrows, their Bows are never bent, but the string lies flat to the Bow; their Arrows a small Reed, four or five feet long, headed some with the poisoned Sting of the Tail of a Stingray, some with Iron, some with Wood, but all so poisoned, that if they draw but blood, the hurt is incurable. The next day came in Captain Charles Saltonstall, a young Gentleman, Son of Sir Samuel Saltonstall, who brought with him good store of all Commodities to relieve the Plantation; but by reason some Hollanders, and others had been there lately before him, who carried away with them all the Tobacco, he was forced to put away all his Commodities upon trust till the next crop; in the mean time he resolved there to stay, and imploy himself and his Company in planting Tobacco, hoping thereby to make a Voyage, but before he could be ready to return for England, a Hericano happening, his Ship was split, to his great loss, being sole Merchant and owner himself, notwithstanding forced to pay to his Governour the fifth part of his Tobacco, and for fraught to England, three pence a pound and nine pence a pound custom, which amounts to more than threescore pound in the hundred pound, to the great discouragement of him and many others, that intended well to those Plantations. Nevertheless he is gone again this present year 1629, with a Ship of about three hundred Tuns, and very near two hundred People, with Sir William Tuffton Governour for the Barbadoes, and divers Gentlemen, and all manner of Commodities fit for a Plantation. Captain Prinn, Captain Stone, and divers others came in about Christmas; so that this last year, there hath been about thirty Sail of English, French, and Dutch Ships, and all the Indians forced out of the Isle, for they had done much mischief amongst the French, in cutting their Throats, burning their Houses, and spoiling their Tobacco; amongst the rest Tegramund, a little Child, the King's Son, his Parents being slain, or fled, was by great chance saved, and carefully brought to England, by Master Merifield, who brought him from thence, and bringeth him up as his own Children. It lieth seventeen degrees Northward of the Line, about an hundred and twenty Leagues from the Cape de tres Puntas, the nearest main Land in America, it is about eight Leagues in length, and four in breadth; an Island amongst 100 Isles in the West Indies, called the Caribbes, where ordinarily all them that frequent the West Indies, refresh themselves; those, most of them are Rocky, little, and Mountainous, yet frequented by the Canibals; many of them inhabited, as Saint Domingo, Saint Mattalin, Saint Lucia, Saint Vincent, Grenada, and Margarita, to the Southward; Northward, none but Saint Christopher's, and it but lately, yet they will be ranging Marigalanta, Guardalupo, Deceado, Mountserat, Antegna, Mevis, Bernardo, Saint Martin, and Saint Bartholomew, but the worst of the four Isles possessed by the Spaniard, as Porto ico or Jamaica, is better than all of them; as for Hispaniola, and Cuba, they are worthy the Title of two rich Kingdoms, the rest not respected by the Spaniards, for want of Harbours, and their better choice of good Land, and profit in the main. But Captain Warner, having been very familiar Captain Painton, in the Amazons, hearing his information of this St. Christopher's; and having made a year's trial, as it is said, returned for England, joyning with Master Merifield and his Friends, got Letters Patent from King James to plant and possess it. Since then, the Right Honourable the Earl of Carlisle hath got Letters Patents also, not only of that, but all the Caribe Isles about it, who is now chief Lord of them, and the English his Tenants that do possess them; over whom he appointeth such Governours and Officers as their affairs require; and although there be a great Custom imposed upon them, considering their other charges, both to feed and maintain themselves; yet there is there, and now a going, near upon the number of three thousand People; where by reason of the rockiness and thickness of the Woods in the Isle, it is difficult to pass, and such a snuff of the Sea goeth on the Shoar, ten may better defend, than fifty assault. In this Isle are many Springs, but yet Water is scarce again in many places; the Valleys and sides of the Hills very fertile, but the Mountains harsh, and of a sulphurous composition; all overgrown with Palmetas, Cotten Trees; Lignum vitæ, and divers other sorts, but none like any in Christendom, except those carried thither; the air very pleasant and healthful, but exceeding hot, yet so tempered with cool breaths, it seems very temperate to them, that are little used to it; the Trees being always green, the days and nights always very near equal in length, always Summer; only they have in their Seasons great Gusts and Rains, and sometimes a Hericano, which is an over grown, and a most violent storm.

In some of those Isles, are Cattel, Goats, and Hogs, but here none but what they must carry; Guanes they have, which is a little harmless Beast, like a Crocodile, or Aligator, very fat and good Meat: she lays Eggs in the Sand, as doth the Land Crabs, which live here in abundance, like Conies in Boroughs, unless about May, when they come down to the Seaside, to lay in the Sand, as the others; and all their Eggs are hatched by the heat of the Sun.

From May to September, they have good store of Tortoises that come out of the Sea to lay their Eggs in the Sand, and are hatched as the other; they will lay half a peck at a time, and near a bushel ere they have done, and are round like Tenis-balls; This Fish is like Veal in taste, the Fat of a brownish colour, very good and wholsom. We seek them in the Nights, where we find them on shoar, we turn them upon their backs, till the next day we fetch them home, for they can never return themselves, being so hard, a Cart may go over them; and so big, one will suffice forty or fifty Men to dinner. Divers sorts of other Fish they have in abundance, and Prawnes most great and excellent, but none will keep sweet scarce twelve hours.

The best and greatest Bird is a Passer Flaminga, which walking at her length, is as tall as a Man, Pigeons and Turtle Doves in abundance; some Parrots, wild Hawks, but divers other sorts of good Sea-fowl, whose Names we know not.

Cassado is a Root planted in the Ground, of a wonderful Increase, and will make very good White-bread, but the Juce Rank Poyson, yet boyled, better than Wine; Potatoes, Cabbages, and Radish plenty. Maize, like the Virginia Wheat; we have Pine-Apple, near so big as an Hartichock, but the most daintiest taste of any Fruit; Plantains, an excellent and most increasing Fruit, Apples, Prickle Pears, and Pease, but differing all from ours. There is Pepper that groweth in a little red Husk, as big as a Walnut, about four Inches in length, but the long Cods are small, and much stronger and better for use, than that from the East Indies. There is two sorts of Cotten, the silk Cotten as in the East Indies, groweth upon a small stalk, as good for Beds as Down; the other upon a shrub, and beareth a Cod bigger than a Walnut, full of Cotten Wool: Anotto also groweth upon a shrub, with a Cod like the other, and nine or ten on a bunch, full of Anotto, very good for Dyers, tho' wild; Sugar Canes, not tame, four or five foot high; also Mastick, and Locus-trees; great and hard Timber, Gourds, Musk-Melons, Water-Melons, Lettice, Parsly; all places naturally bear Purslain of itself; Sope-berries like a Musquet Bullet, that washeth as white as Sope; in the middle of the Root is a thing like a Sedge, a very good Fruit, we call Pengromes; a Pappaw is as great as an Apple, coloured like an Orange, and good to eat: a small hard Nut, like a Hazell Nut, grows close to the Ground, and like this grows on the Palmetas, which we call a Mucca Nut; Mustard-seed will grow to a great Tree, but bears no seed, yet the Leaves will make good Mustard; the Mancinel Tree, the Fruit is Poison; good Figs in abundance; but the Palmeta serveth to build Forts and Houses, the Leaves to cover them, and many other Uses; the juice we draw from them, till we suck them to Death, (is held restorative) and the top for meat doth serve us as Cabbage; but oft we want Powder'd Beef and Bacon, and many other needful necessaries.

By Thomas Simons, Rowland Grascocke,
Nicholas Burgh, and others.

Page xix. That Captain Henry Ashton succeeded Major Henry Huncks in 1640 as Governor of Antigua is shewn by the following very early will:—

Nicholas Saranck of Antigua, planter. Will dated 24 Dec. 1639; proved 13 March 1639-40. (58 Evelyn.) All estate to John Davies, planter. Witnessed by John Hall, Henry Rawlins, John Sigismund Cluver, Minister. Before Serjeant-Major Henry Huncks, Esq., Governor of Barbados and Antigua. Before Captain Henry Ashton, Esq., Governor of Antigua, sworn 30 Nov. 1640 Henry Huncks, the late Governor.

Page xxi. The thirteenth article of the Treaty reads:—That such particular persons as are in this island, together with Sir Sydenham Pointz, who have estates in Antegoa, may peaceably return thither . . . .

Page xxiii. *For* 1665 *read* 1655.

Page xxx. 1664, Sep. 20. List of the Council (Colonial Calendar):—

Rob. Carden.	John de Lamory.
Chas. Ghest.	Gyles Blizard.
Dan. Fitch.	Obad. Bradshaw.
Sam. Winthrop.	John Campbell.
Phil. Warner.	Wabrick Richard.
Hen. Ashton.	Rich[d] Ayres.
Rob. Poynte.	Mark Brewster.
Rich[d] Boraston.	Joseph Lee, Sec.
Jere. Watkins.	

Page xxxiii. Clause xv., second line, *for* vent *read* vent.

Page lxxi. General Codrington was succeeded by his son and heir, not a nephew.

Page lxxix. *For* Thomas Maris *read* Morris.

1729.

Page xcvii. Extract of a Letter from Charles Town, dated 5 Oct. 1728 :—

The Campbell of Bristol, Capt. Goodwin, from Bristol and Cork, was taken on the 27th of August last, as she was going from Barbadoes for St. Christopher's, by a French Pirate of 8 Guns and about 40 Men, 15 of whom were French, 15 Irish and Scotch, and the rest Indians, Negroes, and Mulattoes : She had several Passengers on Board her, whom the Pirate stripp'd ; and after having kept the Ship for about two Days, in which Time they plunder'd her of all that was valuable in her, they let her go, and on the first of September she arriv'd at St. Christopher's. On the 10th of September there was a Tornado at St. Christopher's, when the Campbell put to lea, and was soon after lost on the Point near the Fort on the Island of Nevis. Captain Goodwin came Passenger from Nevis in the Hampshire. On the 14th of October, the Earl of Londonderry, Captain General and Commander in Chief of the British Leeward Islands, arriv'd at Nevis in the Pearl Man of War from Antigua. ('Historical Register,' pp. 11, 12.)

Antigoa, October 22.

I wrote to you by Capt. Woodbridge, that Capt. Pitman, Commander of his Majesty's Ship the Pearl, dy'd here the 6th Instant: He is succeeded in his Command by Mr. Knight, the first Lieutenant of the said Ship. On the 13th his Excellency the Earl of Londonderry sailed from hence in the Pearl Man of War to visit St. Christopher's, and the other Islands under his Government, for the first Time, accompany'd by Lieutenant-General Matthews and others. Most of the Ships and Vessels which have arrived here from the Northward have met with very bad Weather, and either lost their Masts, Bowsprits, etc., or damag'd their Cargoes. On or about the 14th Instant, Capt. Miles, Master of the Sloop Mary, belonging to New-London, bound to Nevis, was taken up at Sea, together with two Sailors and three Passengers, in the Latitude of 21, by another Sloop, after they had been 17 Days upon the Bottom of the Vessel; but about six others were drowned: The Forepart of the Sloop being laden with Lumber, floated above the Water: They lived upon Raw Indian Corn which was stowed. The Lenox Man of War, Capt. Dent, has been supply'd here with Masts and other Necessaries, but will hardly sail for England 'till April. The French at Martinico have fitted out two Sloops in quest of a Pirate, and are to continue cruising three Months, unless they find her sooner. The Sloop Spy, George Wills Master, belonging to Bermuda, bound for Jamaica, was taken by a Spanish Launch within Musket Shot of Jamaica, and carry'd away in July last, as was at the same Time a Sloop belonging to Carolina .... The Squirrel Galley, Capt. Blines, arrived at Barbadoes the 23d of October, from Whydah in Guiney, from whence she sailed the 28th of July with the Feversham Man of War, with whom she kept Company as far as the Island of St. Thomas on the African Coast, belonging to the Portuguese, where she left Capt. Goodall, the Commander, at the Point of Death, who had been Speechless for some Days before. The Man of War's Third Lieutenant dy'd, and was bury'd on the Coast of Africa.

Antigua, Sep. 29.

An Act is passed for settling on his Excellency the Earl of Londonderry, their General, during his Government there, 3*s.* 6*d.* per Ton, according to the Register of each Vessel, clearing with the Produce of that Island, to be paid by the Treasurer; and for making some other Provisions as therein is specified: And in regard little Benefit will accrue from thence to his Excellency 'till next Year, (the Crop being over for this) they have made him a Present of a Thousand Pounds. 'Tis added, that they have a Prospect of a fine Crop next Season (pp. 14, 15).

Page xcvii. Du Tertre's work consists of four, not five volumes.

Page cxxiii. 1776, Feb. About the beginning of the present month William Salmond, Esq.; agent for the colony of Antigua, waited on Sir Ralph Payne, K.B. and presented his Excellency with a most magnificent sword set with diamonds, unanimously voted him by the council and general assembly of that island in testimony of their gratitude and approbation of his conduct during his administration. ('Gent. Mag.,' p. 94.)

1777, May 29. New York. On Tuesday last a small sloop, Alexander Hill master arrived here in 16 days from St. Eustatia, by whom we are informed that an account was just received there, that a ship of war, belonging to Admiral Young's squadron, had taken a rebel frigate, with Silas Deane of Connecticut on board, and carried her into Antigua. ('Town and Country Mag.,' p. 390.)

1778, Sep. 15. Admiral Young who is arrived from the Leeward Islands in his letter to Mr. Stephens dated at Spithead the 11th inst. incloses a list of ships which have been made prizes or destroyed by his Majesty's ships on that station, amounting in the whole to 222, 17 of which are privateers or armed vessels. ('Gent. Mag.,' p. 436.)

March. Two regiments embarked at St. Kitts on the 3rd of March, on board the Andromeda, bound to Antigua, where troops were collecting to go on an expedition. ('Town and Country Mag.,' p. 221.)

Page cxxiv. 1780, April. The Hon. Craister Greatheed, president of his majesty's council, and comptroller of the customs, in Antigua. (*Ibid.*, p. 223.)

April 13. Sir Adolphus Oughton, K.B. at Bath, Lieutenant General of his Majesty's Forces, Commander in Chief in North Britain, Colonel of the 31st regiment of foot, and Lieutenant Governor of Antigua. (*Ibid.*, p. 224.)

Aug. 8. The Leeward Islands & Jamaica fleet was captured off Cadiz on the voyage out. (*Ibid.*, p. 446.)

Aug. 28. Arrival announced of the Leeward Islands fleet of 110 sail at Falmouth. (*Ibid.*, p. 499.)

Page cxxv. 1781, June 29. Admiral Sir G. B. Rodney wrote: "Between Montserrat and Antigua, Sir S. Hood, with the remainder of the fleet, joined me—their necessities obliged me to anchor in St John's Road, having first despatched several quick-sailing vessels to St Lucia with assurance of speedy relief, in case of an attack by the enemy. Not a moment was lost at Antigua. The whole fleet was put to sea with all possible despatch. ('Gent. Mag.,' p. 389.)

Page cxxvii. 1784. Naval peace establishment for the Leeward Islands:—2 ships of 50 guns, 8 frigates 24 to 32 guns, 12 sloops 14 to 18 guns, in all 22 men of war. ('Town and Country Mag.,' p. 167.)

Page cxxviii. 1785, Sep. 13. A hurricane has done great damage. Antigua suffered a little. (*Ibid.*, p. 559.)

Page cxxix. For criticisms on Luffman's Letters see Dr. Adair's 'Defence of the Proprietors of the British Sugar Colonies,' pp. 94—109.

Page cliii. George S. Martin, John Duncombe Taylor, William Lee were Members of the Council in 1833, Colonel Francis G. Brown in 1834, and Bertie E. Jarvis in 1836. In 1834 there were 1980 whites and 33,432 negros and coloured persons.

Lieut.-Governor Light. Jane Smart married in 1805 Colonel Alexander Whalley Light, 25th Regiment, son of William Stratton Dundas Light, Paymaster-General in India, by Henrietta, daughter and heir of Chevalier Lüders and brother to Sir Henry Light, K.C.B., Lieut.-Governor of Antigua and Dominica, afterwards Governor of British Guiana 1838—48, grandsons of William Light, Esq., of Baglake and Broadstock, co. Dorset. ('Genealogist,' vol. vii., p. 188.)

The amount awarded under the Emancipation Act, including the slaves in Anguilla, amounted to £425,866, being at the rate of £14 2s. 8d. per slave. See the Appendix for list of all slave owners.

Dr. Walter Tullideph's Letter-Book.

Historical Notes.

1734, Oct. 21. We have now extraordinary fine weather . . . . it has been very sickly and mortal . . . . Mr. John Morrice, Coll. Wm Painter's wife, and a great many of inferior note are dead. Mr Wyne has laid down his clerkship in the office and Mr Dunbar has made choice of John Fyffe to succeed him without any gratuity. Our Assembly are about a Law to encourage white tradesmen to settle with us, and to lay a tax on negroe tradesmen.

1735, April 5. There is not any vessel gone from this to South Carolina this year yet . . . . We have many Irish vessells here at present, beef is like to be very low.

1735, July 23. We have had at least 14 severe earthquakes within these ten days, nor does ye earth yet seem to be free from motion . . . . we have fine rains and the prospect of a large forward crope for next year, altho' ye blast does much damadge in ye poor land.

1736, Jan. 15. The present circumstances of the Island from the horrid negroe conspiracy and dry weather has reduced us to great inconveniences . . . . As for the above plott no doubt it has made much noise in England; to be brief Mr Kerby's head man Court att the head of the Coromantees, and Thos Hansons, Junr, Carpt Tomboy, att the head of the Creoles, had for these 12 months past by degrees corrupted most of the negroe tradesmen and drivers, and brought them over att their publick feasts and entertainments and bound them by an oath to destroy all the whites, man, woman, & child; ye usual form for ye Coromantees was by a mixture of Grave dirt in rum or beer, which they drank, holding their hand over a white dunghill cock; to the Creoles was added alsoe kissing ye new testament, and so true were they one to the other that no plain discovery was made by any of them, nor should we ever come to the knowledge of it had not some of them been taken up (even after ye day designed for ye execution of their plott) for their impudence of Sundays to the Constables and severely whip't, & some distant hints by overhearing ye two chiefs talking of powder & ye like, ye frequent feastings, & crowning Court King at a military Coromantee dance to ye dram called ye Akim dance, a certain declaration of war. There was a ball to be kept at Mr Dunbar's great house the 11th of Octr wh was ye King's Coronation day, & Tomboy was to erect ye seats & lay such a quantity of powder under them as to blow up all the Gentry of the Island while they were in the height of their mirth, then three bodys, each consisting of 300 or 400 men, were to fall in upon three diffl quarters of the Town & putt all to the sword. We were saved by the Providence of the Almighty thus, the Genl had accots of Mr Guernier's his father-in-law's death we putt him into mourning, and by his order the ball was putt off till the 30th, being the King's birth day; this occasioned a warm dispute between the two chiefs, Tomboy being young & fiery was for falling on directly, but King Court being of a more phlegmatic temper opposed him, & was willing the business should be done with as little loss of their side as possible. About ye 13th or 14th ye plott began to be discovered, Court, Tomboy, & one Hercules, a Carpt, were broke on the wheel, & 9 more burnt . . . .

1737, Oct. 3. We have enjoyed exceeding fine weather since the beginning of May, so that our Island has putt on a new face. We are in great hopes of a plentifull crope after Christmas, our negroes very quiet, about 90 of ye ringleaders were putt to death & 50 bannished.

1738, April 17. Mr John Fyffe is in a very good way being deputy treasurer. Jas. Fyffe is gone down to live with Mr Gerrish at Mountserratt at £60 pr. ann. & found everything.

1738, Aug. 11. Sugars are now brought down with much adoe to 18s. c., cotton 12d pr. pd., rum fetches 16d cash.

Nov. 3. The small pox has run through this Island like wildfire, but has been very favourable; we have practised inoculation pretty much with great success.

1739, Aug. 3. Capt. Boscowen in a 20 Gun ship arrived here ye 27th July with an express to our General, & ye 28th a declaration was published here granting liberty to make reprisals on the Spaniards, she sailed the same day for Jamaica.

1739, Sep. 1. War has been proclaimed with Spain.

1739, Oct. 16. I shall be obliged to you if you'l send me two or three of the most modern & best books fitt for a country justice, for the General & Council have been pleased to conferr that honour on me.

1740, Sep. 2. About the storm, Moncrief's being lost.

1741-2, Jan. 9. Yr fleet passed here ye 4th inst. Govr Byam's & Jacob Thibou's death.

1742, June 6. Rum fallen to 2/9.

1743-4, Jan. 14. Mr Knowles' arrival here, his laying out £10,000 st. at English harbour.

[End of Volume I.]

Volume II.

1743-4, March 3. Our General went on board the Commodore abot 4 weeks agone & went to Barbadoes, where he was received in a very handsome manner, & had a review of all the Militia there, he returned again two days agoe, while he was there a vessell arrived f'm London 27 days passage, by whom the accots are that a French Warr is inevitable, ye 4 large ships yt was expected here is gone to Admirall Mathews, who 'tis thought will strike ye blow.

1744, April 10. We have severe drie weather which hath already shortned our crops ⅓d. The Woolwich man of warr arrived lately at Barbadoes f'm the Coast of Guinea, & the day after she left that Island in her voyage hither, she fell in with a Spanish Register ship of 34 Guns & 300 men, they engaged & ye Spaniard stood eight broadsides before he struck, she is carried into Barbadoes and is said to be worth £100,000 st., there was an 80 gun ship with 1300 men & three other Register ships came out with her, and 'tis said they are now at Martinico; Commodore Warren with all his force went out two days agone to endeavour to meet with them.

May 28. Warr was declared here the 24th inst. against France. Sugar hath been up at 28s. & 30s. Some French prizes are brought in here with bread & flower from Old France, & our Legislature intend to purchase them for ye use of the Public to humble our Merchants who want to raise flower to 20s., they have this 29th laid an Embargoe to prevent the exportation of provisions of all sorts to Leeward.

Sep. 15. We have only two Privateers belonging to this Island, who have destroyed two French Privateers, & therefore have done signal service to trade. Daniel Hill, Govr Thomas' overseer at Winthorpes, died about 3 weeks agone.

Nov. 18. Mrs McKinnen's death. Winthorps being settled by Gov. Thomas of Phil., & mill building this year.

1744-5, Jan. 9. Commodore Warren who hath not been here above 20 days hath already taken two of ye best French privateers, & run another ashore, a Danish sloop loaded with provisions off ye harbours of Martinique, & retaken an English Brigt belonging to North America, he hath been out these ten days again, & we expect he will not return without bringing something in with him. 70 pr. c^{t} Exchange.

1744-5, Feb. 28. The Lynn hath lately sent in two Outward bound Frenchmen & Capt. Douglass in the Mermaid, a Bourdeaux man, & a Brig^{t} f'm Cape Britton. Admiral Daverse sailed from hence ab^{t} ten days agone; while he stayed here the Weymouth, a fine 70 gun ship that came out for Mr Warren, was unfortunately lost by the carelessness of the pilot upon the reefs of Sandy Island, a great loss to these Islands. Mr Knowls was on board, and Admiral Daverse at an anchor in our Road.

1745, May 15. The French are now so much superiour to us by sea that our men of warr have ever since been laid up in English Harbour. We have been working at English Harbour ½ pr. cent. of our negroes these 12 months past, and there was an unlucky accident hapned there sometime agone; a quantity of damadged powder was careleslie put into a hutt without any watch upon it, by some means it was blown up and killed above 20 white people and several negroes.

May 19. A fleet of Jamaica ships past this Island in 30 days from Plymouth, by whom we are advised that one 70, one 60, and one 50-gun ship were ordered directly for this station, and they are expected hourlie under Commodore Lee.

Aug. 13. Mr James Stevenson keeps his health & is gone into partnership with one Dr Saml Young, a good natured countryman.

Oct. 5. Admirall Townsend arrived here this day 14 days with 8 saile of the line; there came with him 3 storeships for English Harbour; he went under sail yesterday and stood to the Southward with all his squadron, but whither bound is a secret.

Admiral Townsend with all his squadron sailed from hence ye 4th of Octr and blockaded Martinico ever since; the 31st of said month as he was cruizing a few leagues to leeward of Port Royall 43 sail of vessells came in sight, & as he had been informed by a Dutch sloop the day before that there was 8 men of warr with them, he prudently ordered his vessells to form into ye line, by which he lost two hours, but when they came nearer & found there was only two large ships, he then gave the Signall to his best sailing vessells to give chace, which they did and took 15 sail, sunk 5, burnt 8, & 8 run ashore; they had a 36 gun frigate was blown up, their 80 gun ship named the Magnanima was on a rock 40 hours, but got off, & she with the Ruby, a 60 gun ship, & about 5 sail of ye Merchantmen gott into Port Royall harbour . . . . The Admiral sent home the Otto sloop with an account of this victory, & we had a rejoicing for it here yesterday; he sent 3000 prisoners ashore to encrease their distress.

1745-6, Feb. 19. Admiral Townsend sailed hence with his squadron about 16 days agone for Cape Breton to the best of our judgement, and the 17th instant the Commodore sailed from hence with his squadron assisted with six privateers, and stood to the Southward to look out for a fleet of homeward bound Martinico merchantmen that were to sail the 16th under convoy of one 80, a 60, & 20 gun vessells.

1745-6, March 9. Out of the prizes brought in here by Mr Townsend one large ship is taken into the service of ye Crown & made a 20 gun ship, the rest loaded chiefly for Europe. Several privateers fitted out by merchants at Philadelphia & New York were cruising about. Admiral Townsend was within 5 days sail of Cape Bretton where he mett with a violent storm, whereby his ships suffered so much that he was obliged to bear up for this Island, & came in here 8 days agone.

1746, May 22. Our North America trade is intirely cutt off by ye great numbers of privateers, & ye King's ships being very inactive, which hath raised all kind of lumber & provisions very high.

Nov. 25. The danger to windward is not now so great, owing to the Leostaff privateer, fitted out by the merchants in London to cruize to windward of Barbadoes & these Islands. She was formerlie a man of war, mounts 24 guns, & 200 men; she with Capt. Denn's & Coll^{o} King's two privateers have lately taken 10 or 12 privateers & 3 row galleys. A smart engagement hapned in sight of Monk's Hill three days agone between a ship & snow. We think they were the Leostaff & a stout French privateer snow well manned, & sent out on purpose to take Capt. Tyrrell in ye Lime, because he is a vigilant officer; however it be the snow was taken & went to windward, & ye Leostaff carries all prizes to Barbadoes, where the Island advances the head money & waits till ye government can repay them.

1746-7, March 18. We don't expect our fleet till some time next month, under the command of Commodore Legg, who relieves the present. I wish he may protect trade better. Capt. Broderick in the Dreadnought hath taken one & demolished another, very stout privateers.

1747, May 31. Commodore Lee's tryall will hardly begin these four weeks, & on Aug. 22 Commodore Lee comes home in the Suffolk still under suspension. Mr Legg had appointed six Captains to trie him.

1748, June 25. An express arrived here with the King's Proclamation for a Cessation of Arms.

1748, Nov. 23. Last night the Admiral Osborne gave a handsome ball for the entertainment of the gentlemen & ladies of this Island, & there was a fine appearance, indeed this is leaveing us with a better grace than some other Admiralls have done before, & a suitable return to an elegant entertainment & ball we gave him soon after his arrival.

1749-50, March 20. Sugars from 27*s.* to 32*s.* Rum 2*s.* 6*d.*

1750, May 14. Our great Man goes in company with this vessell. His son Daniel was married last Tuesday to Mrs Lyons, the daughter of George Byam and widow of Henry Lyons's son, and come in this ship.

1751, Sep. 6. Our Island is likely to be ruined & deserted by the imprudence of people running in debt, & the severity of the merchants. Dr Husband is gone off to St Croix much in debt, many have gone in like manner, but what is worse a great number of the industrious midling people are gone there in an open manner this day, no less than 24 with their family & effects are gone off.

1751, Sep. 17. On the 8th inst. from 7 o'clock till 3 in the morning hap'ned here the most violent storm that was ever known in the memory of the oldest man liveing, many dwelling houses, windmills, & other works destroyed or much damaged, few escaped . . . . our canes being twisted or torn in pieces, many of our vessels are lost, those loading with sugar were all on shore, but were happily got off again; ye losses in buildings £100,000, & in our canes double that.

1752, May 11. We are obliged to send to Montserratt for water to drink & send our horses to drink at the creek; we have had little or no rains since Christmas; this severe drought succeeding the hurricane hath occasioned a very short crop this year.

1752, Aug. 19. I wrote the 10th inst. that Genl Mathew was dying, & the 16th that he departed this life the 14th at 10 o'clock. The Generall's son goes home in Burton.

1752, Dec. 25. To Richard Oliver, who has offered him a share in the "Langford."

1755, Jan. 20. It hath been very sickly . . . . we have lost many of the midling & lower class of people, of the soldiers about 30. Upon the death of Coll^{o} Gunthorpe the General was pleased to press me again to take my seat in Council, which I accordingly did last month, & Thos. Jarvis hath been since appointed another, Halliday hath filled mine, & think Wm Dunbar will that of Mr Jarvis's place in the Assembly. I dined with his Excellency New Year's day, I think, who received me very kindly. Coll° Martin was there the same day; Mrs Thomas was blooded that day therefore did not see her, but saw the rest of ye ladies, but not George. The General goes to Leeward the 31st inst.

1755, Feb. 24. Mr Otto was swore into the Councill last meeting & stands next to Coll° Lesley our President; at same time was Coll° Byam who is the next above me, Mr Oliver & Mr Jarvis below me. There is a mighty cock fight to be here the 21st March between St Kitts & this Island, which brings many of the Leeward people up & prevents his Excellency going down till that is over.

April 29. I have lost 100 hhds. at least by ye hurricane, ratts, & heavy rains. Our foolish affair of cocking & gameing hath drained us of our money; 'tis said the St Kitts gentry carried away above £4000 cash. I am afraid it is too true.

1755, Dec. 8. Commodore Frankland sent in here two French Guineamen, one from Angola with 500 slaves, the other from Papaw with 300. Nathl Booth was agent & sold them very well last week.

1756, March 2. Our Warwick, Capt. Shuldum, of 60 guns, was cruising about 15 leagues to windward of Martinico; she was unluckily taken & carried in there; we have now only one 50 gunship & a sloop, but expect a fleet dayly.

1757, March 4. Capt. Watkins of the Blandford, having lost his rudder, went into English Harbour; the Admiral was backward in supplying him with what he wanted; the Captain, poor man, wrote perhaps too freely to that great man, he confined him, held a Court Marshall, Capt. Cornish President, was removed from the command of that ship & may be some time before he gets another; this is now going on the 3^d that all our capital ships have been lying in St John's Road; the Edenburgh was sent to Jamaica to refitt some weeks agone for want of masts & other stores here, the Augusta went down with the last fleet to Jamaica, the Surprize to Windward of Barbadoes, the Saltash, Capt. Cumming, to Windward of us, the Tryal to Leeward attending the General who went down about 3 weeks agone & may be back in 10 days, the Sterling Castle, Anson, Bristol, Woolwich, Winchester, & the Blandford. We have no certainty yet when a Convoy will happen.

1757, April 30. Our Cork fleet is arrived some time past, & we now impatiently look out for our English fleet.

[End of VOLUME II.]

VOLUME III.

1764, June 8. Lieut. Ballingall of the 38th Reg^t sailed yesterday in the Tarne ship of warr with the whole regiment here for Ireland. I had the pleasure to pass the King's birthday* & the next in company of Lord Adam Gordon; he opened our ball with the General's daughter, was most elegantly entertained at noon with good turtles, the best beef, mutton, veal, poultry, the best of liquors; the General treated the Councill & Assembly with the King's officers. Lord Adam arrived here 3 or 4 days before & embark't the next day for St. Kitts, the next evening to meet the man of warr that had his regiment on board in order to proceed to Jamaica.

* George III. was born on the 4th June.

ABBOT. Page 1.

George Abbott of St. Christopher's, merchant. Will dated 1660; proved 6 Dec. 1660. (260 Nabbs.) My brothers & sisters' children in Lancashire. My plantation here to my wife's brother Capt. Geo. Hill. Church of St Ann, Sandy Point.

James Bevon of Nevis, Esq. 1720. My dau. Henrietta Bevon £1000 c. My grandchildren, the daus. of Richd Abbott, jun., & of Eliz. his late wife, viz., Eliz., Frances, & Anne, 12,000 lbs. each. John Dasent, a minor, the son of John Dasent, esq., lands at Saddle Hill. My son James Bevon.

In 1727 Thomas, Edward, and Richard Abbot were of Nevis.

Page 3. Robert Abbot, born 1852, was at Marlborough School 1867-71. Henry M. Abbott was resident at St. Kitts 1893, and William J. Abbott at Antigua 1894.

ALLEN. Page 6.

1710-11, March 27. Captain John Duer's land bounded S. with Mr. Leonard Allen. (Minutes of Assembly.)

1711, April 9. Petition of Robert Allen, son of William Allen, carpenter, for a grant of 4½ acres near the Body Ponds. (*Ibid.*)

1718, March 31. Allen petitioned for land for his son aged 6 or 7.

1768, May 10. William Allen a young man, son of Mr Allen, Keeper of the Horse-shoe-inn, in Blackman-street, Southwark, and who as appeared afterward was meerly a quiet spectator, being pursued, along with others, was unfortunately singled out, followed by three soldiers into a cowhouse, and shot dead!

A fine large marble tombstone, elegantly finished, was erected over the grave of Mr. Allen, junior, in Newington Churchyard, Surrey. On the four sides are the following inscriptions. North side:—

Sacred to the memory of
WILLIAM ALLEN,
An Englifhman of unfpotted life and amiable difpofition,
Who was inhumanly murdered, near St George's
fields, the 10th day of May, 1768, by Scottifh
detachments from the army.
His difconsolate parents, inhabitants of this parifh,
caufed this tomb to be erected to an only fon, loft
to them and to the world in his twentieth year,
as a monument of his virtues and their affection.

(South side, nine lines; east side, one line; west side, two lines.)

On the same monument is the following inscription:—

Here alfo lies interred,
The remains of SARAH NEWSHAM,
The *only* remaining child of
WILLIAM ALLEN.
Who survived a few months the cruel death of her
beloved brother.
She died December the 7th, 1768, aged 23 years.

(Noorthouck's 'History of London,' p. 445.)

(See William Allen's petition to the King in 'Gent. Mag.' for 1769, p. 484.)

ANDERSON. Page 7.

1713-14, Feb. 12. Sarah Anderson petitions for land E. and W. 36 feet, N. and S. 80', bounded E. with the Cross street leading from the Church, W. with her land, N. with Brown street, S. with George Forrest.

Joshua Gillyat of Antigua and Jamaica, d. at the latter island in 1791. ⅓ of his real estate of 900 acres descended to his granddau. Eliz. Anderson, dau. of Peter Anderson of

Antigua, who marr[d] a Miss Gillyat who d. v.p. (Jarvis Papers.)

1868. March. Lately. At Trinidad, aged 75, Thomas Anderson, esq, M.D. & J.P. etc. ('Gent. Mag.' p. 408.)

ARCHBOULD. Page 8.

Sarah, dau. of William Yeamans appears to have married 1, William Thomas; 2, Dr. Joshua Archbould; 3, Ernest Udney.

Lady Laroche, bapt. 25 March 1746-7, was a dau. of John, not William Yeamans.

ATHILL. Page 10.

Dorothy Athill, married 27 May 1828 Pierse Hackett, M.D. of Southampton.

Robert Mangles died at Sunninghill 31 July 1861, aged 80. He was brother to Ross. D. Mangles, M.P. for Guildford, and they were sons of James Mangles, M.P. (See 'Notes and Queries' for Jan. 1897.)

BAIJER. Page 18.

John Otto Baijer, in the army 1816, was at Eton 1793; was given a commission in the Guards by Geo. III., and became a distinguished officer.

Page 21. 1771, May 16. Ann Otto Baijer of Hummerton in the parish of St. John, Hackney, spinster, deceased. Administration to Jane Gillett, widow, the administratrix of John Otto Baijer the father, he dying before he had taken out administration.

John Otto Baijer of S[t] Thomas the Apostle, co. Devon, Esq. Will dated 8 June 1790; proved 1 July 1791 by the son. (348 Bevor.) Wife Sarah £250 a year. My daus. Ann wife of D[r] Tho. Oke, Edith O. Baijer, Fanny Cazell, wife of M[r] W[m] Cazell, Mary Williams, widow, Eliz. O. Baijer, & Barbara wife of M[r] Rob[t] Patch, £1000 each. My plantation & negros at Antigua, & all residue to my only son Baijer Otto Baijer. Witnessed by John Stoodly, George Short, William Branscombe. Recorded at Antigua 17 May 1792.

Page 23. 1779, March. The Hon. Edward Otto Bayer, president of the assembly of the island of Antigua. ('Town and Country Mag.,' p. 336.)

1783, Dec. 26. Zachary Bayley Edwards, esq. of Greenwich-park, to Miss Catherina Otto Bayer, of Farleigh-house, Somerset. (*Ibid.*, p. 718.)

1812, June. Grand Court, Spanish Town, Jamaica.

Four actions for assaults and false imprisonment have been brought during the present Grand Court against Samuel Otto Bayer, Esq., the first by the carpenter on Nonsuch estate, in S[t] Mary's; the second by the overseer on Unity estate, in the same parish; and the third and fourth by Messrs. Leith and O'Halloran, book-keepers on the first mentioned estate, of which he was respectively found guilty, and damages awarded against him; on the first action to the amount of 289 l., on the second 170 l., on the third 275 l., and on the fourth 165 l. ('Jamaica Mag.,' p. 354.)

Nov. In the above court, on Monday the 12th, the following actions for damages were tried against Samuel Otto Bayer, Esq. For an assault on, and false imprisonment of, Mr. White, book-keeper on Nonsuch estate, in St Mary's, found guilty and 250 l. damages awarded against him. For an assault on, and false imprisonment of, Messrs. M[c]Dermot and Creightney, two book-keepers on Unity estate, in the same parish, found guilty, and 200 l. damages awarded on each action. (*Ibid.*, p. 237.)

1839, Feb. 25. In Bentinck-st, aged 78, Baijer Otto Baijer, esq. of Antigua. ('Gent. Mag.,' p. 442.)

1839, July 23. At Antigua, the Hon. Owen Pell, member of Privy Council in that Island, to Elizabeth-Mary, dau. of the late Saml. Otto Baijer. (*Ibid.*, p. 419.)

1840, March 18. London. Robert Bayer Patch, esq. M.A. late Fellow of Wadham College, Oxford, eldest son of the late Robert Patch, esq of Exeter. He took the degree of M.A. Dec. 2, 1813. ('Gent. Mag.,' p. 551.)

1841, March 19. At Twickenham, aged 69, Sophia Otto, only dau. of the late J. O. Bayes (*sic*) esq. of Antigua. (*Ibid.*, p. 556.)

Page 30. Nicholas Otto-Baijer was buried 21 Oct. 1716, not 1706.

For Cazall *read* Cazal.

BANISTER. Page 34.

1771, Jan. 17. The Rev. Dr. Brownlow North, Dean of Canterbury, son of the Earl of Guildford, and brother to Lord North, to Miss Bannister, of Hill-street, Berkley square. ('Town and Country Mag.,' p. 56.)

1771, April 7. Sir George Osborne, Bart. Member for Bossiney, in Cornwall, and one of the Grooms of the Bed Chamber to his Majesty, to Miss Bannister, of Hill-street, Berkley-square. (*Ibid.*, p. 223.)

1789, May 5. In Harley-street, Mrs. Bannister, relict of John B. esq. By this lady's death, her jointure of 1000 l. a year devolves to her surviving daughters, Mrs. North, wife of Bishop of Winchester, and Mrs. Porter, and to Master Osborne, the only child of her eldest daughter, Lady O. the first wife of General Sir Geo. O. (*Ibid.*, p. 469.)

1796, Nov. 20. Mrs. North, lady of the Bp. of Winchester. (*Ibid.*, p. 972.)

CAMPTON, CO. BEDFORD.

('Collect. Top. et Gen.,' vol. iii., pp. 128—131.)

In the Osborn Columbarium below the chancel:—

ELIZABETH LADY OSBORN,
daughter of John Banister, Esq.
and wife to Sir George Osborn, Bt.
married April 6, 1771,
died, aged 26, March 8, 1773,
leaving one son John, born
Dec. y[e] 3[d], 1772.

Sir GEORGE OSBORN, Bart.
son of Sir Danvers and Lady Mary Osborn.
Born May 19th, 1742,
married first, Elizabeth daughter of
John Banister, Esq[r].
Secondly, the Lady Heneage, daughter of
Daniel Earl of Winchilsea and Nottingham.
A General in the Army,
and Colonel of the 40th Reg[t] of foot.
Died June 29th, 1818, leaving
issue one son John, by his first marriage.

Mrs. ELIZABETH BANISTER,
widow of John Banister, Esq. mother of
Elizabeth, married to Sir George Osborn, Bart.
Henrietta, married to the R[t] Rev. & Hon.
Brownlow North, Bishop of Winchester.
Anne, married to the Rev. Edmond Poulter,
Rector of Calborne & Crawley, Hants.
(Three lines.)
She departed this life on the fifth day of May 1789,
aged 61.

BARTER. Page 36.

See 'Unanswerable Arguments against the Abolition of the Slave Trade, with a Defence of the Proprietors of the British Sugar Colonies,' by James M. Adair, formerly M.D., Member of the Royal Medical Society, and F.R.C.P. Edinburgh. One of the Judges of the Courts of King's Bench and Common Pleas in the Island of Antigua, and Physician to the Commander-in-Chief and the Colonial Troops. London, 8vo., pp. 375.

Dedicated to Governor Sir Thomas Shirley, Bart., no date (1788—1791).

The author states that he was born at Inverness, that in the 1745 rising his father was senior captain, and himself, though not 17, second lieutenant in the Glasgow regiment, and they were both taken prisoners at the battle of Falkirk.

1802, April 24. At Harrowgate, in Yorkshire, James McKittrick Adair, M.D. ('Gent. Mag.,' p. 475.)

A later note on p. 582 says that he is recorded in vol. i. of 'Philip Thicknesse's Memoirs, 1788.'

BENDALL. Page 40.

Hopefor Bendall of Stepney, merchant. Will dated 14, proved 24 May 1710 by Joana Bendall the relict. (103 Smith.) My 1st son Hopefor Bendall, now in the West Indies, £5. My dau. Anne 1/16 of the ship "William & Mary," Joseph Kell master, also 1/16 of the ship "Invitation," Henry Simpson master. My son John Bendall £5, son Henry Bendall £5. All residue to my wife Joanna & sole Ex'trix, & at her death my mansion house at Mile End to my dau. Anne. Friend Arthur Bayly of Mile End overseer. Witnessed by Sarah Pack, Deabro Smith, W. Martyn.

The above named probably took out a grant of arms in 1692-3, and he was presumably the father of Hopefor Bendall of Antigua.

1691, Dec. 4. Joseph Haden (or Hayden) of St Mary Whitechapel, Bachr, about 25, & Alice Bendall, of Stepney, Midd., Spr, about 24, at own disposal; at St Dunstan's in the West, London. (Marriage Allegations: Vicar-General of the Archbishop of Canterbury.)

See also the licence for marriage of Patience Jackson of Stepney 1682, Aug. 12, alleged by Hopefor Bendall of Stepney, mariner.

BETHELL. Page 42.

Mary Slingsby, who married Sir Walter Bethell, was baptized 14 April 1582 at Knaresborough, and her marriage licence dated 1602. Their other son Henry Bethell was of Falthorpe, J.P., æt. 59 in 1665, and buried 27 Feb. 1667 at Alne. (See Hunter's 'Familiæ Minorum Gentium,' Harleian Society's Publications, pp. 916-918.) Slingsby Bethell the Sheriff of London married Mary, daughter of .... Burrel of co. Hunts. Priscilla died 1768, not 1758.

BLACKMAN. Page 44.

Rowland Blackman of the Middle Temple Esq

In the will of Hon. J. L. Blackman, the sixth line from end should read: "All residue to my son Rowld Blackman."

Page 46. *For* Longnet *read* Longuet.

Rowland St. John of London, merchant. Will dated 1694. (223 Box.) Bequeaths to Mrs Eliz. & Mrs Susan Blackman, daus. of Lucey Blackman, esq., £20 each, & sums to him & his wife for mourning.

1787, April. Samuel Blackman, esq. of Barbados. ('Town and Country Mag.,' p. 191.)

1792, July 20. The Lady of George Blackman, esq. of Chatham-place, a son. ('Gent. Mag.,' p. 671.)

1797, Jan. 9. In Craven-street, John Lucie Blackman, esq. West-India merchant. (*Ibid.*, p. 82.)

Page 50. 1814, Jan. 6. Aged 76, Mary, relict of Sir George Harnage, Bart. She was his cousin, the eldest surviving dau. of Lt.-Col. Henry Harnage, of Belliswardine, co. Salop; was married in 1791 to George Blackman, esq. who assumed the name of Harnage, and was created a Baronet in 1821: and was left his widow in 1836, having had issue the present Sir George Harnage, Capt. R.N. and three other sons. ('Gent. Mag.,' p. 216.)

BLAKE. Page 54.

Annabella Bunbury, wife of Sir Patrick Blake, 1st Bart., was born 1745; her marriage was dissolved by Act of Parliament in 1778, and she then married George Boscawen of St. Peter's, Thanet. Her portrait by Sir J. Reynolds was engraved in 1771 by Dixon.

Henry Blake of Mountserrat, merchant. Will dated 16 May 1723; proved 1 Sep. 1724 by James Kirwan and Nicholas French. (202 Bolton.) My brother Chr. Blake & my sisters Bridget Blake & Mary Blake of Ireland ⅔ of my real & personal estate. The children of Julian Blake, wife of Jefry Blake, £20. Megg Lynch *al's* Fallon & her children £20. Megg Kirwan *al's* Lynch, wife of John Kirwan of Blindwell, £10. Romish clergy of the Town of Gallway £10. Poor there £10. Rings of £2 to Ex'ors. All residue to my nearest kin. My friends Mr James Kirwan & Nicholas French, both of London, merchants, & Messrs. John Blake, senr, & Thirton Skerratt of Mountserrat, Ex'ors. Witnessed by Joseph Lynch, Thomas Martin. By Hon. Paul George, Esq., Governor of Montserrat, appeared Joseph Lynch 15 June 1724. Recorded 16 June 1724. George French, Deputy-Secretary. Lib. A., fo. 383.

Patrick Hynes of St. Christopher's. Will dated 1732. (109 Bedford.) Names as his Ex'ors Patrick Blake, Esq., of that island, and Martin Blake, Esq., of Moyne, co. Mayo.

1769, March 9. (6 Jenner.) Before Daniel van den Brink, Notary Public of Amsterdam, appeared Edward Blake of Bury St. Edmunds, co. Suffolk, Esq., lodging in this City, and made his brother Christopher Blake of London, Esq., his heir. Witnessed by Henry Pye Rich and Thomas Wilkieson, jun., merchants; proved 1 Jan. 1770 by Christopher Blake.

1772, March 29. The right hon. lord Montford, to Miss Blake, sister to Patrick Blake, Esq; member for Sudbury. ('Town and Country Mag.,' p. 166.)

1777. John Blake of Essex Street, Strand, witness to a Webb deed.

1785, Aug. 30. Capt. Robert Jones Adeane, esq. of Baberham, Cambridgeshire, to Miss Blake, only daughter of the late sir Patrick Blake. (*Ibid.*, p. 503.)

1787, Sep. Rob. Blake, esq. of Essex-street, Strand, to miss Goble, of Hempnetts, Sussex. (*Ibid.*, p. 431.)

1815. Robert Blake, then of Essex Street, Strand.

1825. John Goble Blake of Essex Street, Strand.

Messrs. Blake, White, Ainge, and Blake of 14 Essex Street, Strand.

PARISH REGISTER OF ST. ANTHONY, MONTSERRAT.

Baptized.

1729 .... S. of John Blake & Elizabeth his wife.

Married.

1725 Oct. 8 Gregory Skuret & Elen Blake; by L.

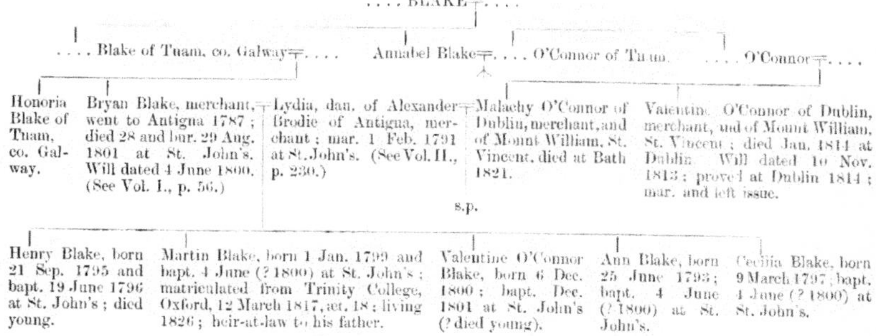
. . . . BLAKE ⊤ . . . .
. . . . Blake of Tuam, co. Galway ⊤ . . . .
Annabel Blake ⊤ . . . . O'Connor of Tuam.
. . . . O'Connor ⊤ . . . .
Honoria Blake of Tuam, co. Galway.
Bryan Blake, merchant, went to Antigua 1787; died 28 and bur. 29 Aug. 1801 at St. John's. Will dated 4 June 1800. (See Vol. I., p. 56.)
Lydia, dau. of Alexander Brodie of Antigua, merchant; mar. 1 Feb. 1791 at St. John's. (See Vol. II., p. 230.)
Malachy O'Connor of Dublin, merchant, and of Mount William, St. Vincent, died at Bath 1821.
Valentine O'Connor of Dublin, merchant, and of Mount William, St. Vincent; died Jan. 1814 at Dublin. Will dated 10 Nov. 1813; proved at Dublin 1814; mar. and left issue.
s.p.
Henry Blake, born 21 Sep. 1795 and bapt. 19 June 1796 at St. John's; died young.
Martin Blake, born 1 Jan. 1799 and bapt. 4 June (? 1800) at St. John's; matriculated from Trinity College, Oxford, 12 March 1817, æt. 18; living 1826; heir-at-law to his father.
Valentine O'Connor Blake, born 6 Dec. 1800; bapt. Dec. 1801 at St. John's (? died young).
Ann Blake, born 25 June 1793; bapt. 4 June (? 1800) at St. John's.
Cecilia Blake, born 9 March 1797; bapt. 4 June (? 1800) at St. John's.

PARISH REGISTER OF ST. PETER, MONTSERRAT.

Baptized.

1727 Sep. 7 Anne d. of John Blake & Elizabeth his wife.

1727-8 Feb. 25 Elizabeth d. of Edw[d] Blake & Elizabeth his wife.

1729 Oct. 5 [*blank*] of John Blake & Elizabeth his wife.

Married.

1727 May 21 Edward Blake & Elizabeth Butler; by B.

See later the will of Francis Browne of Montserrat.

Valentine O'Connor* of Dublin, merchant. Will dated 10 Nov. 1813; proved 1814 at Dublin. My son Hugh & son-in-law Maurice Blake of Tower hill, co. Mayo, Ex'ors. All real estates to my son Hugh & his heirs, remainder to Valentine O'Connor Blake, son of my son-in-law Maurice Blake, & to my granddaus. Mary & Honoria Blake, daus. of the said Maurice Blake, remainder as to ½ to my nephew & partner Hugh O'Connor, ¼ to my nephew Valentine O'Connor, & ¼ to my nephew Malachy O'Connor, the 3 sons of my late sister M[rs] Monica O'Connor. Niece Honoria O'Connor, dau. of my brother Malachy O'Connor, Esq., of Bath, £3000. Cousin Honoria Blake of Tuam, co. Galway, niece of my late aunt M[rs] Annabelle O'Connor of Tuam, £30 a year while unmarried. Granddaus. Mary & Honoria Blake £2000 each. Grandson Valentine O'Connor Blake £3500. Nieces Monica O'Connor & Christiana O'Connor £500 each. My late dear cousin Bryan Blake, Esq., of Antigua, who did not leave sufficient to pay even his debts, to his son Martin & dau. Cecilia Blake £500 each. My ⅔ of the estate & negros of Mount William in St Vincent to be sold.

On a map of co. Galway made in 1651 are the arms of Blake with the words, "Marilandiæ, Carolinæ, Verginiæ, Jamaica, Bermude, Barbude, Montserrat, et Sancti Christophore," shewing a very extensive colonial connection. (L. Archer's "M.I. in the West Indies," p. 31.)

BLIZARD. Page 57.

George Blizard of Spanish Town, Jamaica, bachelor, deceased. Adm'on 1785, Oct. 1, to John Buckmaster, attorney of William Blizard, now of St. Ann's, Jamaica. Later grant Aug. 1820.

In the will of William Blizard *for* Lesby *read* Lesly.

* Mr. Martin J. Blake of 9 Old Square, Lincoln's Inn, who has been preparing a genealogy of the various families of Blake in Ireland, kindly sent me the above will, together with O'Connor, Blake, and Lynch notes.

Page 58. John Blizard, sen., married Margaret dau. of Christopher Knight.

Jeremiah Blizard baptized 1734, married Mary dau. of Col. John Gunthorpe by Anne his wife.

Page 59. Frances wife of R. Donaldson was buried 17 July 1787 at St. George's.

Jonas L. Blizard, M.D., married Elizabeth dau. of Daniel Warner.

Page 62. 1693, Aug. 3. Giles Blizard ordered to appear. (Minutes of Assembly.)

1777, Nov. 24. Stephen Blizard, Esq: of Antigua. ('Town and Country Mag.' p. 716.)

BONNIN.

In French's 'History of Governor Parke's Administration' Captain Henry Beaulieu is called Boileau.

Baptized at Burnham, co. Bucks. ('Collect. Top. et Gen.,' vol. iv.)

1767, Aug. 19. Charles Henry son of Goussé Bonnin, Esq., and Dorothy his wife, daughter of Sir Charles Palmer of Dorney.

In Betham's 'Baronetage' he is described as of Antigua.

Leghorn, Italy. Sacred | to the memory of | Louisa Caroline | the infant daughter and second child | of | Henry Gousse Bonnin and | Charlotte his wife | born 24th July 1819 | died 20th Aug. 1821. ('Mis. Gen. et Her.' for 1896, vol. ii., Third Series, p. 116.)

BORASTON. Page 71.

1723, Oct. Petition of Richard Buraston of St. John's Town for land, W. with petitioner, S. with the Street, E. with Thomas Wise, N. with Edward Wise.

Mrs. Grace Duer in her will dated 14 Sep. 1700 names her grandsons Stephen & Richard Boraston, sons of her dau. Boraston, deceased.

BOTT. Page 72.

Mrs. Jane Bott was dau. of David Kennedy, Surgeon, whose will was dated 1 June 1809.

BROWN. Page 74.

Anthony Brown, baptized 1769, was of the firm of Brown, Cobbe, and Co., Bankers, of 67 Lombard Street. Mary Brown, baptized 1745, married . . . . Burke. See her will on p. 84. Refer also to M[rs] Sarah Garrett's will.

Jeremias Browne, son of James Browne of Nevis, gent., matriculated from Pembroke College, Oxford, 7 March, 1704-5, aged 18. See the Johnson Pedigree.

A Jeremiah Brown was Chief Justice of St. Christopher's in 1729.

Francis Browne of Mountserat, merchant. Will dated 4 Aug. 1701; proved 2 April 1702 by Andrew Browne the brother for Francis Browne the nephew. (57 Herne.) My niece Christian Blake, dau. of my sister Mary Blake *al's* Browne, £10. My father Mr. Francis Browne £5 a year. Poor here £6 c. Poor of Gallway in Ireland £6 st. My brother Mr. Patrick Browne* £50, which he received from Joseph & Daniel Alford, merchants in London. My 1/8 of the briganteen "Dragon" & cargoe effects in Mountserat & Antegua. All residue to my nephew Mr Francis Blake, son of my brother Andrew Browne of Gallway, the latter Ex'or in trust in England & Ireland. My brother Mr Patrick Browne & Mr Bartholomew Lynch, merchants in Mountserat, Ex'ors there & America. On 2 April 1702 Daniel & Tho. Alford of St Cath. Creechurch, London, merchants, swore that testator was late of Mountserat, but at St Cath. Creechurch, deceased; he came to England in Oct. last & died 19 days after in deponents' house.

Philip Browne of Nevis, Esq. Will dated 8 Dec. 1705; proved 25 Sep. 1708 by Christian Browne the relict. (196 Barrett.) My wife Christian Browne, formerly Chapman, on whom I have settled £3000, £200 c., furniture, plate with Mrs Mary Helme of London, & 6 negros. My father Mr Philip Browne £500 st. My mother Mrs Martha Browne of Ile Abbotts, co. Som. Nephew Chas. Browne, 1st son of my brother Francis Browne, 3 negros. Mr Robt Knight, son of Sir John Knight of Bristol, £100. My friend Col. Joseph Jory of London £50. Mr Joseph Martyn of Love Lane, London, merchant, £50. Phineas Andrues of Nevis £100. Poor of Ile Abbots £50, of St Thomas £50. All residue to the sons & daus. of my brothers Francis Browne & John Browne, decd, & of my sister Susanna wife of John Smith of Turke street, Bristol. My kinsman Charles B . . . ., Col. Joseph Jory, Joseph Martin, Phineas Andrues, & my wife Ex'ors. Witnessed by Elizabeth Pym, James Emra, James Pope, William Smith, John Huffame. Before Hon. William Burt, President, sworn 4 Jan., recorded 5 Jan. 1705-6. No. L., folios 195-7.

On 24 Oct. 1733 commission to Bluett Jones, son and Ex'or of Susanna Jones, widow, the dau. of Susanna Smith, wife of John Smith, and a residuary legatee of testator, all the residuary legatees being dead.

BUCKLEY. Page 81.

Buried at St. George's 1810, Nov. 6, Joseph Gravenor Buckley, in the Family Burying Ground on Gravenor's Estate.

His sister Mrs. Elizabeth Warner Frye was also buried there 9 Jan. 1802.

BURKE. Page 84.

Sarah Ward in her will of 19 April 1761 names her friend Ann Burke, daughter, and John Burke, son, of Walter Burke of Limerick, but now of Antigua, and Mary Burke.

Elizabeth Looby in her will dated 2 Sep. 1789 names Miss Mary daughter of Mr. Walter Burke, deceased. Mrs. Walrond £50 a year, and her son John Burke, Esq.

1814, Oct. 22. At Montserrat, Francis Burke, esq. to Rosina, fourth dau. of the late Dr. West of Antigua. ('Gent. Mag.,' p. 196.)

BURT. Page 88.

1788, June 12. At St. George's, Hanover-square, John Morgan, esq. M.P. for Monmouthshire to Miss Burt, da. of Cha. B. esq. of Albemarle-str. ('Gent. Mag.,' p. 657.)

1796. John Heyliger Burt, esq. of Cotton, Staffordshire, to Mrs. O'Keover, of Sheepy Magna, co. Leicester, widow of the late Rowland F. O'K. esq. of Oldbury. (*Ibid.*, p. 789.)

* This is evidently the Patrick Brown of Antigua whose will was dated 1705, and has been given in Vol. I., p. 74.

Louise daughter of Charles Pym Burt of St. Croix married George T. Smith of co. Carnarvon, and died March 1815.

1868, April. A. P. Burt, esq. to be Attorney General of Grenada. ('Gent. Mag.,' p. 532.)

DUTCH CHURCH, AUSTIN FRIARS, LONDON.

In south aisle, west end:—

Arms: . . . . *on a chevron three cross-crosslets fitchée between three bugles strung and garnished* (BURT); impaling, Quarterly: 1, ... *three hearts*; 2, ... *a cross-crosslet*; 3, ... *three nails*; 4. . . . . *transfixed by a sword erect, point downwards*.

Here lieth the body of
Mrs. PETRONELLA BURT, late Wife of
CHARLES PYM BURT, Esquire,
and Daughter of the late
Governor JOHN HEYLIGER,
of the Island of St. Eustatius, in America,
who died at Hampton in Middlesex,
the 8th day of June, 1770,
in the 29th Year of her age.
Haud ullam ingeniam parem.
Also Mrs. ANNA THOMPSON,
Widow of the late Mr. SAM. THOMPSON,
and Daughter of the said
IAN HEYLIGER,
died Sept. 13th, 1796, Aged 45 Years.

BURTON. Page 91.

William Painter in his will of 1721-2 names my grandson John Burton and his mother Elizabeth my daughter.

Dr. Adair wrote (*temp.* Governor Shirley) Miss Burton, the Mrs. Burtons, mothers of Rowland Burton, Esq., Chief Judge, and of John Burton, Esq., Counsellor-at-Law. There is now a lady in London who assisted her mother Mrs. Burton in the education of many ladies.

BUTLER. Page 93.

John Butler, son of William Butler of Nevis, Gent., matriculated from Magdalen College, Oxford, 13 May 1700, aged 15.

PARISH REGISTER OF ST. GEORGE, NEVIS.
(Fulham Palace MSS.)

Married.

1717 May 21 Mr. Roger Pemberton and Mrs. Frances Butler.

1718 July 10 Mr. James Symonds and Mrs. Mary Butler.

BYAM. Page 95.

Motto: *For* Daris *read* claris.

Page 97. Phyllis, another daughter of William Byam and Dorothy Knollys, married in 1645 Benjamin Cadman (born 1610), son of Benjamin Cadman of Yorkshire.

Edward Byam, President 1707, was never Governor of the Leeward Islands.

Henry Byam, D.D., entered Merchant Taylors' School in 1729, as did his elder brother Edward in 1725.

Page 101. Richard Scott Byam, M.D., *omit* Rev. He was buried 27 Dec. 1832 at St. James', Bath.

Page 105. William Byam, Esq., now residing in Featherstone Buildings, Holborn, but intending shortly on a voyage to Antigua. Will dated 18 March 1773. (114 Bevor.) Whereas my estates in Antigua were mortgaged by my late father to Messrs. Banister & Hammond, & I have further mortgaged them to the said John Banister, Esq.; subject to this I give all my estate in Antigua, real & personal, to my 1st son Edward Byam, charged with the following legacies :—£4000 to my son Samuel Byam at 16. £3000 to my dau. Lydia Byam at 16. To my wife Martha my house & lands in Pembrokeshire, & after her death to my dau. Lydia Byam. By agreement with John Banister all sugars are to be shipt to him, but the rum reserved to me after payment of the expenses of the estate; all surplus profits by the sale of rum to my wife. My mother-in-law M[rs] Ann Rogers of Goodwick, co. Pembroke, £30 a year. All residue to my son Edward Byam. Sam[l] Byam & Edw[d] Logan of Antigua, Esq[rs], Ex'ors. Witnessed by Joseph Pickering, Tobias Pickering, Samuel Mander.

On 18 March 1791 adm'on to Edward Byam the son, David Logan being dead, and Samuel Byam survived testator, but died before execution.

On 7 March 1800 adm'on of estate left unadministered by Edward Byam, Esq., deceased, granted to Rev. Samuel Byam his brother and Ex'or.

The following extract I made from the original paper sent me Jan. 1897 by the Hon. C. A. Shand of Byams, otherwise Fitche's Creek :—

[CEDAR HILL.]

"Appraisement made this 20th day of January 1795 of the Lands, Slaves, and dead stock, dwellings, mills, and works in the Island of Antigua belonging to Edward Byam, Jun[r], Esq."

	£	s.	d.
76 negro men. 88 women, 27 boys, 16 girls. 21 infants, 22 superannuated	23,270	15	0
32 oxen, 1 bull, 27 cows, 8 heifers, 12 calves, 8 horses, 1 mule	1,301	2	0

The Upper Estate of 211 acres.

A.	R.	P.			£	s.	d.	£	s.	d.
41	3	14	1st quality, @ £140	.	6,277	5	0			
54	2	5	2[d] " " 80	.	4,632	10	0			
36	3	35	3[d] " " 50	.	1,848	8	9			
74	2	26	pasture " 10	.	746	12	6			
								13,234	16	3

The Lower Estate, 277 acres.

A.	R.	P.			£	s.	d.	£	s.	d.
43	2	23	1st quality, @ £140	.	6,110	2	6			
77	3	2	2[d] " " 80	.	6,221	0	0			
20	3	19	3[d] " " 50	.	1,043	8	9			
135	1	34	pasture " 10	.	1,354	12	6			
								14,729	3	9

	£	s.	d.
Carts and plantation utensils	574	10	0
Carpenters' return, dwelling, pigeon, boiling, and curing houses	2,728	1	9
Masons' return	9,726	5	6
Coppersmiths' & plumbers' returns	1,714	7	3
2 mills	3,000	0	0
Total	£70,279	1	6

Signed by SAMUEL ATHILL.
THOMAS NORBURY KERBY.
THO[s] DUBERY HARMAN.
JOHN RONAN.
HENRY B. LIGHTFOOT.

Page 108. The Second Edition of 'Byam Memoirs' was 8vo.

1811, June. Lately. At Willesley near Tetbury, W. Byam, esq. ('Gent. Mag.,' p. 598.)

1864, Sep. 9. At Byam-house, Brighton, aged 69, Lieut.-Gen. Edward Byam, Col. of the 18th Hussars, etc. (*Ibid.*, p. 533.)

PARISH REGISTER OF ST. JAMES', BATH.

('Genealogist,' vol. ix., p. 112.)

Buried.

1832 Dec. 27 Richard Scott Byam, M.D., Aged 79.

CADE. Page 111.

Colonel John Buncle. *For* 1767 *read* 1667.

Captain John Cade was Member of the Council in 1671 and of Nevis 1672.

1683, June 26. John Bunkley of Autigua, deceased. Adm'on to Mounteney Bunkley, cousin-german and next-of-kin.

Elizabeth Boncle of London, widow. Will dated 13 June 1686; proved 26 Jan. 1687 by the son. (2 Exton.) To my son Seth Mountney Boncle £30, & £115 for my dau. Hannah Boncle. My dau. Margaret Carrington £35, dau. Eliz. Boncle £35, dau. Kath. Clowse, her 2 sons, £3 apiece. All residue to my son Seth Mountney Boncle & Ex'or. Witnessed by Isaac Burbidge, Thomas Hastings, Edmond Wynch, ser.

CARPENTER. Page 117.

William Carpenter, bound to sea. Will dated 9 Aug. 1675; proved 24 Dec. 1680 by Nathaniel Bridges. (161 Bath.) My estate, real & personal, to be sold & returned home to M[r] Nath[l] Bridges of London, merchant, from the Islands of Barbados, Montsirat, Antegua, & ⅓ to my mother M[rs] Jane Carpenter, ⅓ to M[r] John Blake of Barbados, merchant, ⅓ to M[r] Nath[l] Bridges & Ex'or. Witnessed by Bas. Hampshire, George Goode.

On 1 March 1686 adm'on to John Bridges, brother and administrator of Nathaniel Bridges, deceased, the Ex'or of testator, who was of Barbados.

Page 119. *Omit* the Russell portion of the tabular pedigree, which is incorrect. Colonel Randal Russell died 1678, leaving a wealthy widow Margaret, who married in or before 1682 Governor Thomas Hill. Her parentage is uncertain.

Page 122. PARISH REGISTER OF ST. PAUL, ANTIGUA.

Baptized.

1734 July 7 Joseph s. of Joseph Carpenter and Anne his wife.

Married.

1753 Feb. 10 Robert Carpenter and Arabella Browne; by L.

Buried.

1742 Jan. 7 George s. of Joseph Carpenter and Anne his wife.

CARTER. Page 123.

1772, Nov. 16. Nicholas Tuite, Esq; in Queen Anne-street. ('Town and Country Mag.,' p. 616.) See his will, *ante*, p. 404.

CARY. Page 125.

1684, June 30. Mr. Cary is Married to one M[rs] Right, a Turkey Merchant's daughter, and hath a good fortune wth her some say neere 2000[l]. (Jeaffreson MSS.)

Dorothy Cary, wife of Tobias Frere, was not related to Richard Cary of St. Dunstan's. Her father was Patrick Cary of St. Andrew, Holborn, Esq., whose will was dated and proved in 1669 (82 Coke).

ST. DUNSTAN'S IN THE EAST, LONDON.

Over against the pulpit, on one of the pillars in the middle aisle, is erected a white marble table, with the following inscription :—

Here lieth the Body of *Richard Cary*, Efq; who departed this Life the 25th of *January*, | 1726, aged 78 Years. He was the 2d Son of *Sherfhaw Cary*, of the City of *Briftol*, | Efq; by *Mary*, his Wife, eldeft Daughter of *John Scrope*, of *Caftle* Combe, in the | County of *Wilts*, Efq; by *Mary*, Daughter of *John Hungerford*, of *Cadnam*, Efq; | Here alfo lie the Bodies of *Jane* his Wife, *Richard* their Son, and *Jane* their | Daughter; *Martha*, his only furviving Child, married *Robert Elwes*, junr. of the | County of *Hertford*, Efq; who erected this Monument in Honour to his Memory. (Seymour's 'Survey of London,' vol. i., p. 298.)

The Carys were a very ancient family long resident in Bristol. Mr. H. F. Waters has printed several of their wills and pedigrees in the 'New England Hist. and Gen. Register,' which he very kindly shewed me. From these, from Wadley's Bristol Wills, and from information supplied by Mr. D. G. Cary-Elwes of Conway, Florida, the following short Pedigree has been drawn up:—

GERVASE CARY=Julian . . . . Masses for them ordered by William in 1395. (? his parents.)

William Cary of Bristol, Citizen, bur. at St. Werburgh. Will dated 4 May 1395; proved 8 May 1396, 20 Richard II. (See Wadley's Bristol Wills.)=Agnes . . . .

John Cary=. . . .

William Cary of Bristol, merchant; Mayor 1546; bur. at St. Nicholas. Will dated 2 April 1571; proved 10 June 1572. (P.C.C., 19 Daper.)=. . . .

Richard Cary of Bristol, merchant, 1st son, died, when Sheriff, of the plague; bur. at St. Nicholas. Will dated 11 June 1570; proved 3 Nov. 1570, v.p. (P.C.C., 31 Lyon.)=Anne . . . . 1st wife.

William Cary of Bristol, draper, bapt. 3 Oct. 1550; Mayor 1611; remar. when aged 80; bur. 1 March 1632. A will of this name was recorded 1633 at Bristol.=Elizabeth . . . . 1st wife.

Richard Cary of Bristol, 2nd son, bapt. 14 Aug. 1579; died about 1644; bur. at St. Nicholas.=Mary, dau. of Nicholas Shershaw of Abergavenny, co. Monmouth; died 1663.

Shershaw Cary of Bristol, merchant, 3rd son, died 24 Jan. 1681; bur. at Lisbon. Adm'on March 1681.=Mary, 1st dau. of John Scrope, Esq., of Castlecombe, co. Wilts; died 1650. 1st wife.

John Cary of Bristol, Gent., 1st son, born March 1647 (?); living 1700 in Ireland.=Mehitable, dau. of Mathew Warren; bapt. 20 Dec. 1652; living 1700.

Richard Cary* of Antigua, 2nd son, born April 1649. Took out a grant of arms.=Jane, dau. of Joseph Wright of London, Turkey Merchant, by Martha his wife.

Rev. Thomas Cary, 3rd son, Prebendary of Bristol, born 20 June 1650; B.A. Jesus College, Oxford, 1670; Vicar of St. Philip's, Bristol, etc.; died 1711.=Anna, dau. of James Harris of Bristol, merchant, by Mary his wife; born 9 Oct. 1662; living 1700.

* Of the children of Richard Cary and Jane Wright: Jane married 11 Nov. 1712 Henry Long, and after her death he married Margaret Webb, who, surviving him, married Edward Chester of Bygrave, co. Herts, Esq. Her will was proved P.C.C. 1735. Richard Cary, jun., was born 21 Feb. 1685, and was Captain in Alexander's Regiment of Foot and a bachelor in 1715. Joseph Cary, the other son, was born 31 Oct. 1688, and died a bachelor at St. John's July 1705. Martha Elwes became her father's heiress, the Egton Estate (? in Yorkshire) having been purchased about 1732 by her husband (as her father's Ex'or) of the Earl of Sussex for £38,000, and this was sold by their descendant in 1869 for £180,000.

CHESTER. Page 126.

Dame Magdalen Chester of St. Dunstan's in the East, London, late wife of Sir Robert Chester, Knt. Will dated 9 July, proved 8 Nov. 1585. (44 Brudenell.) To be buried near my 1st husband Sir James Granada, Knt, decd. Alex. Dyer, husband of my dau. Cath. Dyer, & their 2 children Robt & Mary. (Brown's 'Somersetshire Wills,' vol. vi., p. 62.)

1690. (116 Vere.) Robert Hawkins, fishmonger. Sons-in-law Hasledine Chester and Granado Chester.

1726, Dec. 18. (6 Farrant.) Ann Chester of Stratford Langhorne, co. Essex, spinster. Brothers Robert Chester, Esq., Edward Chester, Henry Chester. Sisters Jane, Mary, and Theodosia.

Page 130. The will of John Chevall of Creed Church was proved 1733. (111 Price.)

CLARKE. Page 137.

Samuel Clarke. Will dated 12 April 1669; proved 1671. (3 Duke.) Debts from Wm Mildon 9000 lbs. of sugar, Clement Harmond £8, Henry Aland at Nevis £390. My 2 brothers Tho. & Joseph Clarke overseers. My daus. Eliz. & Sarah £400 apiece, Mary £400, Joyce £400, Joseph £400. My wife & son Samuel Ex'ors. Col. Haggatt & cozen Deane.

Nathaniel Clarke appears to have made two wills, the one at Antigua as printed in Vol. I., p. 137, and the following one in London.

Nathaniel Clarke of Antigua, Esq., now in London, and bound for Ireland and soe to Antigua again. Will dated 8 Dec., proved 8 March 1674 by John Clarke the brother. Sentence 11 March 1674-5; testator died in London. (141 Dycer.) My nephew Nichs Clarke, now at Antigua, ½ of all my real & personal estate in Antigua in Old North Sound Division. My wife Mrs Anne Clarke ⅔ for life, & all goods in England or Ireland. My 1st brother Mr Samuel Clarke, now residing in London, £30 a year. To my 2nd brother Mr John Clarke, rector of Ashton, co. Northants, £20. After my wife's death ⅔ of my personal estate to be disposed of for my brother Samuel Clarke's children & my sister Luddington's children. My brother John sole Ex'or in trust. Witnessed by William and Robert Thory.

Captain Nathaniel Clarke was at the capture of Surinam in 1667.

CLOGSTOUN. Page 139.

The following additional information was sent me 23 Feb. 1895 by Mr. W. D. W. Lyons of the Board of Trade, Whitehall:—

Caroline Jane Walcott married 10 Aug. 1813 her second cousin Samuel Clogstoun, only son of Robert Clogstoun (who died 1799) by Letty Harman, daughter of Samuel Harman of Antigua (married 1785 and died 1810), niece of Jane Harman, who married 1753 John Lyons of Antigua and Bath: she was also niece of Dolly Harman, who married 31 Oct. 1791 Anthony Brown of Browne, Cobbe, and Co., Bankers, of 67 Lombard Street. He was Collector of Customs at Trinidad from 1814 to 1832, when he was transferred to be Collector at Tobago. She died 20 Jan. 1843.

Issue five sons and three daughters:—

1. Anthony B. James Clogstoun, born 1815; married 1840 Georgina Woodford Warner, daughter of Ashton Warner, Chief Justice of Trinidad, born 1819. He was Provost-Marshall of Trinidad 1845, and held this office till his death in 1850 or 1851. His widow died 29 Oct. 1882, aged 63. They left issue.
2. Edmund Clogstoun, born 1818.
3. Herbert M. Clogstoun, born 1820, Major R.E., V.C. (Indian Mutiny 1859); married died in India 1862. Left issue one son:—

   Herbert Frederick Clogstoun, C.S.I. (3 June 1893); entered the Madras Civil Service 1864. In 1894 was First Member of the Board of Revenue, Commissioner of Revenue Settlement, Director of the Department of Land Records and Agriculture, and Additional Member of the Council of Madras for making Laws and Regulations.

   [He died in London 22 Sep. 1895, aged 50.—V. L. O.]
4. Edward John Clogstoun, died 2 Jan. 1882.
5. Samuel Clogstoun, born dead .

1. Dora Browne Clogstoun, born 1814; married April 1845 Major Richard James Martin of the Guards and of Clairville Lodge, Oughterarde, co. Galway, second son of Nicholas Martin of Ross, co. Galway, who died 20 April 1811, by Elizabeth O'Hara, whom he married 1777, and who died 23 July 1838. Major Martin died and left two daughters. His widow Dora married secondly 4 Feb. 1856 James Valentine Browne, M.D., Professor of Surgery, Queen's College, Galway; she died 1859, and Dr. Browne died 1887.
2. Caroline Macnamara Clogstoun, born Feb. 1822; married 22 Oct. 1850 Rowland E. W. Pery Standish of Scaleby Castle, Cumberland, son of Rowland Stephenson of Farley Hill, Berks (who took the name of Standish 1834, and died 26 April 1843) by Lady Lucy Pery (whom he married 16 March 1816, and who died 23 Dec. 1845), third daughter of Edward Henry, 1st Earl of Limerick. Mr. Standish died s.p. 1893.
3. Augusta Mary Johnstone Clogstoun, married Captain George Wilder, R.H.A., her first cousin, second son of George Lodowick Wilder by Augusta Ivers Walcott, youngest daughter of Edmund Walcott Sympson of Winkton. They had issue George, who, on the death of his grandmother Mrs. Dixon (Augusta Ivers Walcott) in 1871, succeeded to Stanstead Park, and a daughter Augusta Margaret, married to Edward Alfred Collier. Captain Wilder died, and his widow married secondly, 1859, Arthur Richard Kenyon, born 1818 (nephew of 2nd Lord Kenyon), ninth son of Thomas Kenyon of Pradoe, co. Salop, born 1780; died 1851. Mr. Kenyon died 3 June 1888. Issue two sons and five daughters.

COCHRAN. Page 139.

Mountserat. John Cochran. Will dated 18 March 1698-9; proved 23 Aug. 1699 by William Cochran. (130 Pett.) My estate in the parish of Evendall in shire of Clydsdale & £100 to my brother Wm Cochran. My partner Alex^r Hamilton £30. Poor 2000 lbs. Major John Scott & Mr Joseph Alford £20 each. My brother Mungo Cochran ⅔ of the residue, sisters Barbara, Agnes, Janett, & Margaret Cochran ½ each. Brothers & sisters Ex'ors. Witnessed by Peter Hussey, John Wattson, Richard Jollings.

CODRINGTON. Page 145.

Colonel William Bate of Barbados, Member of Council 1666; Treasurer 1669—74 = ...

Richard Bate, purchased Foston, co. Derby, in = ... 1679; son-in-law 1683 of Samuel Newton (6 Lloyd) of Barbados, Esq.; Ex'or 1702 of Governor Christopher Codrington; dead 1720.

A dau., married Col. John Codrington of Barbados, Member of Council 1680.

Thomas Chambers of Derby, born 1660; bur. at All Saints. Will proved 1726. = Margaret Bagnold, born 1679; died 1735. Will dated 15 June 1734. (201 Ducie.)

William Bate of Foston, died 1726—35. = Arrabella Chambers, dau. and coheir.

Hannah Sophia Chambers, dau. and coheir, married 1725 Brownlow, Earl of Exeter.

Rev. Chambers Bate of Foston 1748.

Margaret Sophia Bate. — Sarah Bate.

Arrabella Bate, 2nd dau., born 1720; married 1746; died 1 Sep. 1804. = George René Aufrère of London, merchant, M.P. Stamford; born 7 March 1715; died 7 Jan. 1801, æt. 85, at his Villa at Chelsea.

Sophia Aufrère, only child, born at Neasdon Nov. 1752; married 1770; died 25 Jan. 1786. = Charles Anderson Pelham, 1st Lord Yarborough.

A quo Mr. D. G. Cary-Elwes, now of Florida.

Page 146. The following quarterings are from Stow MS. 707, printed in the 'Genealogist,' vol. xiv., p. 35:—

Richard Codrington of Codrington, co. Gloucester, descended from Thomas Codrington, temp. K. H. iii., conf.

I. *Arg., a fess emb. at the top Sa. betw. 3 lions pass. Gu.*

II. *Vt., on a bend Arg. 3 roses Gu., in chf. a dexter hand apaumée of the* 2nd.

III. *Az., 3 men's heads couped at the neck ppr. in helmets Arg.*

IV. *Chequée Or & Az., on a bend . . . . 3 lions pass. . . . .*

V. *Or, a cher. betw. 3 anchors Sa.*

VI. As I.

Crest: *From a crest coronet Or, a dragon's head Gu., its 2 wings displ. chequée Or & Az.*

Page 169. (*Circa* 1666.) "Council of Barbados under Francis Lord Willoughby of Parham. 1. Christopher Codrington, a young Man borne in the place, of an ambitious nature, hath no Estate in England, and was when he Entred upon the Governmt much in Debt there, hath been Taxed with horrid Crimes since his being in the Government."

Page 173. 1864, June 24. At Dodington, Gloucestershire, aged 59, Sir Christopher Wm. Codrington, bart. M.P. He was the son of the late Sir Bethel-Codrington, by Catherine Proby, sister of the second Lord Proby, and nephew of Sir Edward Codrington, was born in 1805, and was educated at Christ Church, Oxford. He married in December, 1836, Lady Georgiana Charlotte Annie, second dau. of the late Duke of Beaufort by his first wife. The baronetcy has been in dispute, and, according to the rules of the Heralds' College, has been sustained in the elder branch of the family, Sir Raimond Codrington being acknowledged as the baronet. The deceased was first elected for East Gloucestershire in 1834, on the death of Sir Wm. Guise, and has sat for it ever since. ('Gent. Mag.,' p. 257.)

1776, July 22. William Codrington, Esq; son of Sir William Codrington, Bart. to Miss Ward, daughter of the late Hon. William Ward. ('Town and Country Mag.,' p. 448.)

Chapter 18 in 'Worthies of All Souls,' by M. Burrows, 1874, relates to Codrington.

Page 174. The arms above the tomb in Bristol Cathedral are:—

Quarterly, 1 and 4, Argent, a fess embattled, counter-embattled sable fretty gules, between three lions passant of the last (CODRINGTON); 2, *Argent, a cherron between three escallops sable* (TREGARTHIAN); 3, *Sable, two groving irons in saltire between four pears or* (KELLOWAY).

John Kelloway of Collumpton (died 1530) married Joan Tregarthian and left coheiresses who married Greville of Penheale, Codrington of Codrington, Harwood, and Cooke. The arms are usually: *Argent, two groving irons in saltire sable between four pears or.* ('Notes and Queries,' First Series, vol. vii., p. 529, in the 'Herald and Genealogist,' vol. iv., p. 295.)

COLLINS. Page 175.

Captain John King, sen., in his will of 1736 names his daughter Sarah, wife of Nicholas Collins. She was probably identical with Sarah, wife of Nicholas Collins, Esq., who was buried 13 May 1740. He then married, 9 April 1741, Frances Yeamans; and Mary Crump, widow of Lynch, was apparently his third wife.

George Barret Collins was born 18 Dec. 1734, and entered Merchant Taylors' School 1743.

COLQUHOUN. Page 177.

1702. (18 Herne.) Adam Colhoun of London, merchant. Nephew Walter. Alexander Colhoun. St. Peter's, Cornhill.

Robert Colhoun was Treasurer of St. Christopher's in 1754. John Mills, Esq., of that island in his will of 1758 names his nephew William Colhoun of ditto, Esq.

See Vol. II., p. 231, for the will of Mrs. Elizabeth Catherine Colquhoun, dated 1820, naming her godson Arthur Colquhoun and his sister Margaret.

COULL. Page 178.

Mrs. Rachel Lovely was a Sanderson, not Coull.

The Westwood Estate of 250 acres in St. Vincent belonged to "Parson Cole of Antigua," and from a small note-book of mine relating to St. Vincent in 1801 had 139 slaves, and made 87 hogsheads of sugar and 49 puncheons of rum.

CRAWFORD. Page 182.

Alexander Crafford of Antigua, Gent. Will dated 24 Sep. 1706; proved 20 Dec. 1707 by William Crafford and John Chambers. (257 Poley.) Bound to England. My wife Dorothy £1000 c. of Ireland. My sons John & Wm £1500 c. at 21. My dau. Mary Crawford £500 c. at 21. My only brother Wm Crawford of Bellfast, merchant, £500 c. among my relations, he & John Chambers of Bellfast, merchant, Ex'ors. James Reade & Edwd Perrie of Antegua, merchants, Ex'ors. Witnessed by Daniell Mackinen, Samuel Proctor, Thomas Long, William Pearne, Peter Adams, Collin Maxwell.

(246 Barrett.) Arthur, Earl of Donegall, refers in his will proved 1708 to Thomas Crafford of Belfast, Gent., a trustee to testator's marriage settlement of 1692.

From a letter of 3 April 1749 written by Dr. Tullideph it appears that the Provost-Marshall had recently married a sister of Francis Farley. As Alexander Crawford was Marshall about 1750, and his eldest child was baptized 1 Feb. 1749, it is probable that he was the person referred to.

See 'Gent. Mag.' for 1773, p. 517, for an account of young Charles Crawford, then at Cambridge, caning Michael Lovell in Cheapside.

Dr. McKittrick Adair, 1788—91, refers to Mrs. Crawford, mother of the Colonel, and Mrs. Willock her sister.

1840. On the 10th inst. Miss Jane Crawford. ('Weekly Register' of Antigua for 17 March 1840.)

DANIEL. Page 188.

1763, Feb. 28. Earle Daniel, Esq., pays £600 st. to the heirs of Thomson for their 16 acres in St. Anthony's, Montserrat.

1766, Jan. 19. Dr. Walter Tullideph writes to Mr. William Daniel at Montserrat, on March 22 to Earl Daniel, Esq., and April 17: "Mr Daniel is my Attorney at Montserratt, a most worthy man; he comes home this year to borrow £7000 stg to pay off all his debts; not many years agone his father dyed & left him burthened with £26,000 stg which he hath now discharged, excepting the above sum; his Estates make above 300 hhds. Sept. 12. Mr Earl Daniel at London . . . . who owes me £1380; his brother Wm who is on Symes' estate."

1862, Dec. Geo. Webbe Daniell Esq. to be a M. of the Cl at Nevis. ('Gent. Mag.,' p. 766.)

DASENT. Page 190.

See the will of Mrs. Grace Parson (Vol. III., p. 258) dated 1735 wherein she mentions: my son-in-law John Dasent & Henrietta Dasent his wife my dau., granddau. Grace Dasent not 21.

Dr. McKittrick Adair 1788-91 refers to Mrs. Patterson, her sister Mrs. Peterson, and her mother Mrs. Dasent, Mrs. E. Horne, and her sister Mrs. Dasent.

John R. Dasent, Esq., J.P., Attorney-General, Member of H.M. Council, A.D.C. to Governor Sir Charles Brisbane. (St. Vincent Almanac, 1811 and 1815.)

1829. St. Vincent, Charlotte Parish. Union estate. John Roche Dasent, Esq., 818 acres, 563 negros, 780,800 lbs. of sugar, 39,960 gals. of rum.

The returns in 1801 had been 529 negros, 655 acres, 801 hogsheads sugar, 356 puncheons rum, 83 ditto molasses.

1863, Jan. 26. Very suddenly, at Rugby, aged 72, Charlotte Martha, widow of John Roche Dasent, esq. H.M's Attorney-General in the Island of St Vincent, West Indies. ('Gent. Mag.,' p. 394.)

1894, Feb. 24. At Ludford Rectory, Charles Underwood Dasent, priest, aged 68.

1896, June 11. At Tower Hill, near Ascot, Berks, in his eightieth year, after a long illness, Sir George Webbe Dasent, Knight, D.C.L., late one of Her Majesty's Civil Service Commissioners. His will was proved P.C.C. 15 Aug. 1896 by John R. Dasent, C.B., one of the sons.

Page 192. 1829. St. Vincent, Charlotte Parish. Three Rivers estate. Harry Hackshaw, Esq., 700 acres, 219 negros, 310,700 lbs. sugar, 10,230 gals. rum, 2000 gals. molasses.

In 1801 the returns had been: North part, 133 negros, 433 acres, 37 hhds. sugar, 90 puns. rum, 25 puns. molasses. South part, 86 negros, 200 acres, 62 hhds. sugar, 32 puns. rum.

1814, Jan. 18. In Alfred-place, Bedford-square, Wm. Alexander, esq. late of the Island of St Vincent. ('Gent. Mag.,' p. 299.)

PARISH REGISTER OF ST. GEORGE, NEVIS.

(Fulham Palace MSS.)

Baptized.

1718 May 29 Joseph the Son of John Dasent, Esqr, by Anne his wife.

1719 July 28 Hill the Son of John Dasent, Esqr, by Anne his wife.

Buried.

1716 June 20 Joseph the Son of John Dasent, Esqr, by Anne his wife.

DELAP. Page 196.

1751, July 12. James Delap is dead, Mr Halliday is one of his Executors. (Dr. Tullideph's Letter-Book.)

1767, Dec. 29. Hon. Rob. Delap, Esq; of the House of Assembly Jamaica. ('Gent. Mag.,' 1768, p. 47.)

DEWAR. Page 199.

John Panton of St. Christopher's, Esq. (196 Fox.) My son John. My wife Christian. On 31 Jan. 1746 adm'on of estate left unadministered by Christina Panton, widow, granted to Christina Dewar, wife of George Dewar, Esq., administratrix of the estate of John Panton, Esq., deceased, the son of testator, Christina Panton having died intestate.

1751, April 13. "Dr Dewar was married 14 days agone to a daugr of Dr Bennets of St Christopher's, an agreeable Lady."

1752, May 30. "A kinsman of mine Mr Willm Dewar, who proposes coming out here in a Mercantile way, his brother Dr Dewar here." (Dr. Tullideph's Letter-Book.)

1786, July 12. — Dewer, esq. of Andover, in the county of Southampton. ('Town and Country Mag.,' p. 447.)

1787, March 1. David Dewar, esq. of Enham, Hants, to miss Penelope Matthew, daughter of major-general Matthew. (*Ibid.*, p. 143.)

1788, Oct. 15. At Edinburgh, Jas. Dewar, esq. of Vogrie. ('Gent. Mag.,' p. 938.)

1862, June 5. Suddenly at the house of his friend (John Burrell, esq.) Camberwell, aged 38, Albemarle Bertie Dewar, esq. of Doles-hall, Hants, late Captain of the 87th R.I. Fusiliers, and eldest son of the late D. A. B. Dewar, esq. (*Ibid.*, p. 116.)

Page 201. The Dewar shield is from an old salver.

PARISH REGISTER OF ST. GEORGE, HANOVER SQUARE.

Married.

1821 May 12 David Albemarle Bertie Dewar, Esqr, of Hurstborne Tarrant, co. Southampton, B., & Anne Louisa Magenis, S. Lic.

DOIG. Page 204.

1750. James Doig styled a near relation by Dr. Walter Tullideph.

1752, May 6. Dr. W. Tullideph wrote to his brother Rev. Thomas Tullideph: "Young Doig goes home next month with his 2 eldest sisters & will see you on his way to Montrose."

July 7. John Lyndsey who was married last week to Mr. Doeg's eldest daughter.

1758. Provost Doig of Montrose was brother of James Doig of Antigua. The latter arrived in England on 2 Feb. 1758. On 21 Feb. Mr. Doig went up to town with his father . . . . his wife was yesterday delivered of a fine boy.

Sir James Carnegie of Pitarrow, 3rd Bart., M.P. Kincardineshire, married Christian, eldest daughter of David Doig, Esq., of Cookstown by Magdalen Swymmer, heiress of Balyordie.

DOUGLAS. Page 212.

John St. Leger Douglas of Pall Mall, co. Middlesex, Esq. Will dated 7 Dec. 1779. (559 Cornwallis.) All my plantations real & personal estate to my brother Lt Col. James Douglas & Alexr Douglas of Devonshire Sq., on trust. My dau. Mary Willett £6000. My dau. Charlotte £6000 at 21. Alexr Douglas £100. My said brother James £1000. Geo. Gavillear £100 & £20 a year for his services. Trustees to hold all my plantations in the Island of St Christopher's for my son Wm Douglas, remainder to my daus.; in the latter event £4000 to my brother James. Trustees to be Ex'ors. Witnessed by Edward Wilmot, Richard Wiles, Mark Clay.

1st Codicil. 15 Nov. 1781. To Charlotte Peacock *alias* Prescott of 6 Lower Brook str., Grosvenor sq., £200 a year. Witnessed by Edward Wilmot, Thomas White, J. Jones.

2nd Codicil. 6 Dec. 1782. Now of Albemarle str. My dau. Charlotte, now wife of John Leigh Douglas, Esq., Commander of H.M.S. Vigilant, her marriage articles dated 4th of this month, made between us & Alexr Douglas of Devonshire sq., & Ed. Wilmot of the Middle Temple, gent., of the 3d part, so revoke legacy. Witnessed by Thomas White, Richard Wiles, Claudy Martinet, servants to Mr. Douglas.

On 21 Nov. 1783 adm'on of testator, late of St. James, Westminster, granted to Richard Neave, Esq., the attorney of James Douglas, Esq., the brother, now at Naples, Alexander Douglas, Esq., the brother, not appearing.

On 24 Nov. 1829 adm'on of testator, a widower, granted to James Dalrymple, Esq., creditor. Alexander Douglas survived his co-ex'or James Dalrymple Douglas and died without proving the will. No residuary legatee was named. William Douglas and Charlotte Douglas, wife of John Leigh Douglas, the only children, being cited and not appearing.

On 31 Dec. 1832 adm'on of estate left unadministered by James Dalrymple, Esq., deceased, granted to Sir Thomas Neave, Bart., a creditor, the letters granted Nov. 1783 to Richard Neave, Esq., attorney of James Dalrymple, Esq. (in the will named James Douglas), being void by his death, and Alexander Douglas not appearing. William Douglas and Charlotte Douglas, widow, the children, not appearing.

On 11 Jan. 1851 adm'on of estate left unadministered by James Dalrymple, Esq., deceased, a creditor, and Sir Thomas Neave, Bart., deceased, a creditor, granted to Rev. Henry Lyttelton Neave, the son, the letters granted to Sir Richard Neave, Bart., attorney of James Dalrymple Douglas, expiring.

Walter Douglas left the University of Utrecht to go over with King William. The Duke of Queensbury was his patron. (French's 'Answer to a Libel, etc.')

Sir John St. Leger, Agent for Antigua, was so nearly related to Governor Walter Douglas that the Assembly would not re-elect him.

1774, July 29. Mrs. Douglas, aunt to John S[t] Leger Douglas, Esq; member for Hindon, in Wilts, at North-end, near Barnet. ('Town and Country Mag.,' p. 504.)

1782, May 18. Sir H. Hay Macdougall, bart., to Miss Isabella Douglas, 2[d] dau. of Adm. Sir Jas. D. ('Gent. Mag.' p. 261.)

1782, Dec. 4. J. Leigh Douglas, esq; of the navy, to Miss Charlotte Douglas, young. dau. of John S[t] Leger D., esq. (*Ibid.*, p. 598.)

1783, May 23. In Albemarle-street, John St. Leger Douglas, esq; M.P. for Weobly, co. Hereford. (*Ibid.*, p. 454.)

1804, Oct. Lately. Sir James Cockburn, of Langtown, bart. He married 1st, a natural daughter of Henry Douglas of London, West India merchant, with whom he was partner; 2[dly], a daughter of the Rev. Dr. Ayscough, dean of Bristol. (*Ibid.*, p. 983.)

PARISH REGISTER OF ST. GEORGE, HANOVER SQUARE.

Married.

1782 Dec. 4 John Leigh Douglas, Esq., & Charlotte Douglas. Lic. Witnesses, W[m] Douglas, Edw. Wilmot, "Temple."

DOW. Page 216.

1866, July 14. At Elwell, Weymouth, aged 71, William Dow, esq., Comm. R.N. The deceased was the fourth son of the late Archibald Dow, esq. and was born at Antigua, May 23, 1794. He entered the navy as second-class volunteer on board the Royal William in July 1806, and having afterwards served on board the Christian VII. and the Caledonia, was present at the storming and capture of a battery at Carri, near Marseilles, in 1813, and at the taking of a battery on Cape Croisette. Mr. Dow also contributed to the capture and destruction of two strong batteries and fourteen sail of vessels at Morjean, and assisted in escalading a tower at Port Nouvelle, in which action seven French vessels were destroyed. He subsequently served on the West Indian and South American stations until 1829. In 1836 he was appointed to the command of the Carron, in which vessel he proceeded to the West Indies, whence, in consequence of two severe attacks of yellow fever, he was invalided home in October of the same year. He became a Commander on the retired list in April 1857. Mr. Dow married in 1830, Caroline third dau. of Samuel Enderby, esq. of Croom's-hill, Blackheath, by whom he has had issue four daus. ('Gent. Mag.,' p. 413).

PEDIGREE OF DUER. Page 217.

JOHN DUER of Antigua, and of Fulham, co. Middlesex, Esq., died 1 Dec. 1764, æt. 67. (See Vol. I., p. 217.) = Frances, dau. of Colonel John Frye of Antigua; mar. 26 April 1739; died 3 July 1787, æt. 74. 2nd wife.

William Alexander, Major-General in the American Service, 2nd son of James Alexander by Maria his wife, dau. of John Spratt; died at Albany 15 Jan. 1783, æt. 56. = Sarah, dau. of Philip Livingston, Esq., by Katherine van Brugh his wife, and granddau. of Robert Livingston by Alida his wife, dau. of Philip Pieterse Schuyler, and widow of Rev. Nicolas Van Rensselaer. (See Burke's 'Extinct Peerage,' p. 610.)

William Duer, youngest son, born 18 March 1747 in co. Devon; A.D.C. to Lord Clive in India; removed to New York 1768, and became a Colonel in the American Service; died 7 May 1799 at New York. = Catharine Alexander, born in New York 8 March 1753; mar. 17 April 1779 at Basking Ridge, New Jersey; died 25 July 1826.

Mary Alexander, born at the manor house of Livingston 17 April 1749; mar. Robert Watts (born 23 Aug. 1743); died 1831. Issue 2 sons and 2 daus.

William Alexander Duer, LL.D., born 8 Sep. 1780 at Rynbeck; at one time Midshipman in U.S. Navy; Judge of Supreme Court 1822; President Columbia College 1829; died 31 May 1858. = Hannah Maria, youngest dau. of William Denning (who was born May 1746 and died 1819) by Amy Hauxhurst his wife; mar. 11 Sep. 1806 at Beverley, co. of Duchess, New York; died 17 July 1862.

John Duer, Judge of the Supreme Court, New York, born 7 Oct. 1782 at Albany. = Ann Bedford, dau. of George Bunner by Jane Cuyler his wife; mar. 18 Oct. 1804.

Alexander Duer, born 28 Aug. 1793; died 15 Aug. 1819. = Maria Wescott, died 8 March 1887.

- Catherine Duer, born April 1816; mar. 21 Jan. 1846 John V. Beam.
- Henrietta Duer, born 1818; mar. June 1844 David Gedney.
- Caroline Duer, spinster.

William Denning Duer of Hauxhurst, Wiehawken, Hudson co., New Jersey, born 6 Dec. 1812 at Rhinebeck; died 24 July 1863 at Hauxhurst. = Caroline, 1st dau. of James Gore King; mar. 8 May 1837 at Highwood, New Jersey.

Edward Duer, born 21 March 1815 at Rhinebeck; died 13 Dec. 1831.

John King Duer, Lieut.-Commander U.S. Navy, born 26 Dec. 1818 at Albany; died 14 June 1859. = Georgeanna Huyler.

- William Duer, born 4 July 1846; mar. 3 June 1884 Josephine Clark; s.p.
- John King Duer, born July 1852; s.p.
- Mary Duer, born 1842; mar. 8 April 1869 Charles Breck.

Henrietta Duer, died 18 Aug. 1824.

Frances Maria Duer, born 21 Dec. 1809 at New York; mar. 7 April 1836 Henry S. Hoyt.

Catherine Theodora Duer, born 24 Dec. 1811 at Rhinebeck; died 3 June 1877.

Eleanor Jones Duer, born 6 Feb. 18— at New York; mar. 17 May 1838 George Wilson, and died 17 Nov. 1892.

Sarah Henderson Duer, born 28 Jan. 1817 at Albany; died 5 Aug. 1856.

Edward Alexander Duer, born 14 March 1840 at Highwood. = Anna van Buren, dau. of John and granddau. of Martin, President U.S.A.; mar. 26 April 1870.

James Gore King Duer, born 9 Sep. 1841 at Highwood. = Elizabeth, dau. of Olando Meads; mar. 2 June 1864.

Rufus King Duer, Lieut.-Commander U.S. Navy, born 26 July 1843; died at sea 28 June 1869, bachelor.

William Alexander Duer, born 23 Nov. 1848; of 115 Broadway, New York City, 1895. = Ellen, dau. of William Travers; mar. 24 May 1877.

- Edward A. Duer, born 28 June 1871.
- Elizabeth V. Duer, born 21 Aug. 1874.
- Sarah G. Duer, born 25 Dec. 1876.
- Angelica Duer, born 17 Sep. 1878.

- John V. B. Duer, born 9 April 1882.
- James G. K. Duer, born 5 May 1885.
- William Duer, born Aug. 1886.

- Caroline K. Duer, born 27 Feb. 1865.
- Eleanor Duer, born 5 Oct. 1870; mar. 25 Oct. 1893 Joseph Laroque.
- Alice Maud Duer, born 28 July 1874.

- Catherine Alexander Duer, born 9 May 1878.

Elizabeth Dupper of Edmonton, co. Middlesex, widow. Will dated 1 Oct. 1733; proved 7 April 1734 by Slingsby Bethel; power reserved to the Hon. John Balchen. (83 Ockham.) To be buried near my late husband Edward Dupper, Esq., in the parish church of Edmonton at the discretion of my Ex'ors & of my dear dau. Eliz. wife of John Duer of Antego, Esq. To my said son-in-law & Eliz[th] £10 each, & to their 2 children Edward & Frances £5 each. John Toller, Esq., Capt. of H.M.S. Pearl, £50. My 2 Ex'ors £10 each. To my said dau. all linen & goods, use of plate, then to her said 2 children. All residue to John Balchen of Chelsea, Esq., Slingsby Bethel of London, merchant, Ex'ors for my said dau. & grandchildren. Witnessed by Nathaniel Carpenter, Thomas Beynon, Charles Lechmere.

Edward Duer of Chichester, Esq. Will dated 28 April 1787; proved 11 Nov. 1788 by the Rev. Rowland Duer, the brother, and John Duer. (529 Calvert.) To my wife Ann Costellon Duer £1025, plate, furniture, & ½ of the £100 annuity from my brother Rowland Duer, Esq., for his life. All securities, etc., in trust for my dau. Martha wife of W[m] Yeo, Esq. My said brother Rowland Duer & my friend John Drew, Esq., of Chichester, Ex'ors. Witnessed by William Fowler, Richard Dally, jun.

Edward Duer was at one time of Clare Hall, Cambridge. Of his half-brothers, Samuel was of Dominica in 1778 and William was then styled an "American."

The following notes were sent to me in 1895—7 by Mrs. John K. van Rensselaer of 40 East 29th Street, New York (V. L. O.):—

WILLIAM DUER.

Colonel in the army of the American Revolution. Probably born in Devonshire, England, 18 March 1747. Died in New York 7 May 1799. Married 17 April 1779, at Basking Ridge, New Jersey, Catherine Alexander, younger daughter of Major-General William Alexander (who unsuccessfully claimed the Earldom of Stirling) by his wife Sarah Livingston. The bride, in the absence of her father who was in command of the rebels at Valley Forge, was given away by General Washington.

"He first emigrated from England the country of his ancestors 1768, & after paying a short & last visit there in 1773 he returned to New York, married, & thus became the founder of a family in the New World." He bought the Falls of Miller, about five miles above Saratoga in the town of Argyle on the east bank of the Hudson River, New York, and there built a large house which is still (1895) known as Duer's Folly. (Family Bible *penes* the heirs of Denning Duer of Hauxhurst, New Jersey.)

Judge Duer was one of the Commissioners appointed by Congress to treat with the Indians in these parts—a man of exceeding good learning and parts living near Albany. (Journal kept by Ebenezer Elener during the Expedition to Canada in 1776, published by the New Jersey Historical Society, p. 122.)

William Duer one of the Commissioners appointed 10 Aug. 1776. (Thompson's 'History of Long Island,' p. 203.)

Treaty with the "Six Nation Indians," General Schuyler, Commissioner-in-Chief, William Duer, a Commissioner. (Colonial Documents *penes* O'Callaghan.)

William Duer, Commissioner of Commerce, properly appointed and authorized by the Delegates of the U.S.A. in Congress assembled. ('Documents on American Revolution,' by John Durand, pp. 120, 123, and 127.)

William Duer as Congressman signed an order to prevent the Moravians from being disturbed, a threat having been made to seize provisions and horses, etc., as they were non-combatants. (Journal kept by B . . . . 'Pennsylvania Mag.,' vol. xi., p. 325.)

William Duer, Member of State Assembly for the City and County of New York, and appointed Assistant Secretary of State. (New York Directory, 1786.)

Henrietta Frances Duer, born 14 Sep. 1781 at Rhinebeck, New York; died 4 Aug. 1782, spinster.

Frances Duer, born 18 Oct. 1785 at New York; mar. 11 Sep. 1805 Beverley Robinson, and had 2 sons and 2 daus.

Sarah Henrietta Duer, born 4 Nov. 1786 at New York; mar. 8 March 1805 John Witherspoon Smith; she died æt. 102. Had 7 daus.

Catherine Duer, born 13 March 1788 at New York; died 25 Jan. 1882, spinster.

Maria Theodora Duer, born 9 July 1789; mar. 14 June 1810 Beverley Chew, 1st son of John Chew by his wife Ann Foy, and had issue.

Caroline Duer, born 14 April 1795; died 1795.

Henrietta Elizabeth Duer, born 22 June 1790; mar. 1 Dec. 1813 Moris Robinson (son of Beverley Robinson and brother of Beverley Robinson who married her sister Frances Duer); she died 9 Aug. 1839 in London. They had 2 sons and 4 daus.

Elizabeth Denning Duer,* born 25 July 1821 at Albany; mar. 8 May 1845, at Morristown, New Jersey, Archibald Gracie King, son of James Gore King, and has issue; 3 children living 1895.

C. L. Henrietta Duer, born 28 May 1828 at Albany; died 8 Jan. 1832.

William Duer, a Judge, born 25 May 1805; first-cousin to his wife; died Aug. 1879. = Lucy, dau. of Beverley Chew by Maria T. Duer; born 31 Aug. 1816; mar. June 1835.

Anna H. Duer, born 21 July 1807; mar. 1 Nov. 1826 Rev. Pierre P. Irving, nephew of Washington Irving; she died 24 Aug. 1874, leaving 3 sons and 4 daus.

Jane Duer, born 1809; died Jan. 1894, spinster.

Catherine Duer, born 26 June 1814.

John Duer, born 26 June 1821; died 24 May 1874.

Harriet Robinson Duer, born 26 Feb. 1823.

George Wickham Duer, born 10 May 1812; first-cousin to his wife; died 1888. = Catherine, dau. of Beverley Robinson by Frances Duer his wife; mar. 24 Oct. 1844.

Morris R. Duer, s.p.

John Beverley Duer, mar. 5 Feb. 1894 Mary Hamilton.

Denning Duer, born 15 Sep. 1850. = Louise, dau. of Henry Suydam; mar. 12 Feb. 1874.

Caroline Suydam Duer, born 17 Aug. 1877.

Sarah Gracie Duer, born 2 Oct. 1838 at Highwood.

Amy Duer, born 20 March 1845.

John Duer, mar. 14 June 1871 Sarah Dupont.

Beverley Duer, mar. 19 April 1892. = Sophia Laurence, dau. of William Pool.

Beverley Duer, born 1893.

Irving Duer.

Theodora Duer.

Anna Duer.

Katherine Duer, mar. 3 Aug. 1881 Charles Vincent Smith.

* Their first daughter May, born 25 May 1848 at New York, married 4 Oct. 1871 John King van Rensselaer, son of Brigadier-General Henry van Rensselaer and grandson of the last Patron of the Manor of Rensselaerswyck (patent granted 19 June 1629), also grandson of John Alsop King, Governor of the State of New York. It is to this lady that I am indebted for these Duer Papers. (See a pedigree of Van Cortlandt, Philipse, Robinson, etc., in Burke's 'Landed Gentry.')

The Misses Duer of Chichester, England, daughters of Roland Duer, declared that the name was originally spelt D'eure. John Duer, Gent., commoner of Christ Church, married at seventeen Elizabeth Eyre, a relation of Mr. Duffer, a lawyer, at Engfield, Essex.* Returned to retrieve his affairs in Antigua. Had by her a son and a daughter. The latter died at Bellair,† near Exeter, where Mr. Duer lived twelve or fourteen years. The son was of Clare Hall, Cambridge, and is now in the King's service in Scotland. Mr. Duer's second wife was a descendant of Mr. Roland Frye of Antigua, by whom he had eight children: Roland, Frances, Theodora, Henrietta, Elizabeth, William, and John.

Mr. Duer was educated at a school in Codrington,‡ Beds. His estate is 3 or 4000 per annum. He now lives at Fulham, having retrieved his affairs . . . . estates, and laid up fortunes for his younger children. (Written probably in 1750.)

William Denning or Dunning of Antigua, born April 1740, emigrated *circa* 1760 to New York. He had relations who moved to Nova Scotia, one of whom was a Mrs. Odell.

Letter from Sir George Rose, M.P., to William Duer.

Duke Street, Westminster,
April 12th, 1778.

Dear William,

During three years that the unhappy Differences have prevailed between the two Parts of this Empire, neither I nor any one of your Family have heard from you, nor indeed of you except by the publick Prints, & it is nearly as long since I have written to you. While the Contention was violent I did not attempt a Correspondence because I did not conceive it could be attended with any good, but upon a supposition that there will now be a free Intercourse I cannot neglect to tell you we are all well, & to express to you my hopes that as the Concessions made by this Country are ample, & what those on your side of the water seemed to wish, such an end may be put to the business as may restore you to a communication with your Family & friends. I will not now enter into Particulars of Family matters; you may however suppose that there is one here for whom you must have the most anxious Concern, who has been as great a sufferer both in mind & circumstances, owing to the late occurances, as any person whatsoever in America, & whose happiness can only be restored by the event so much wished for. I have already told you we are all well; I mean by that all those you left here, & a little boy named William who you never saw. George goes to Westminster immediately. Your Brother John is still at Antigua, & Sam is going on remarkably well at Dominica. This will be delivered to you by Mr. Eden, one of the Commissioners sent from hence, in whom you may repose entire Confidence. I can only add my hearty prayers that the Negotiations may terminate in securing lasting peace & happiness to both countries, which every good & honest man must wish whatever part he may have taken or opinions he may have held. Dora joins in love to you, your other Sisters are not at present with us, & my determination to write to you was sudden. Your Uncle Frye is dead; he left the Bansted & his other Estates in Surray to your Uncle William, with remainder to Rowland Frye; the two Devonshire Estates & his personal fortune to William to dispose of as he pleases, & £100 to each of his Nephews & Nieces.

I am, Dear William,
Your affectionate Brother & faithful Friend,
George Rose.

* ? Enfield, Middlesex.

† Bellair is a neat villa in the parish of Heavitree, about one mile east of Exeter. (Jenkins' 'History,' 1806.)

‡ ? Caddington.

1783, Jan. 12. At Albany, in America, in his 57th year, Wm. Alexander, earl of Stirling, visc. Canada, maj.-gen. in the service of the United States, and commander in chief of the American forces in the northern department. ('Gent. Mag.,' p. 541; see 1776, pp. 444 and 505.)

Married September 11, 1806, at Beverley in the county of Duchess, New York, Mr. William A. Duer, to Miss (Hannah Maria) Denning, youngest daughter of the Hon. William Denning. (New York Papers.)

DUNBAR. Page 224.

Charles McNeily of London, merchant. (263 Auber.) Will dated 25 July 1730; proved 1 Sep. 1730. Wm Dunbar of London, merchant, Alex^r^ Browne of London, surgeon, Robt Lidderdale of London, merchant, £1500 on trust to pay the interest to my mother Jannett Baillie of the parish of Stranraver, co. Galloway, & at her death to Wm Dunbar, 2^d^ son of the said Wm Dunbar, at 21. £400 to the kirk session of the parish of Ballantry, baillery of Carrick, Ayrshire, for a school. £500 to my said trustees for Hellen Browne, dau. of the said Alex^r^ Browne, at 18. Wm Linn of London, merchant, £300. Walter Sidsearf of the Island of Antigua, surgeon, formerly my partner in that Island, all sums due there. Robt Lidderdale 20 gs. All residue to trustees & Ex'ors to sell for Wm Dunbar. Witnessed by Thomas Heacock, Thomas Cheslyn.

1752, March 4. The ½ per cent. charged on paying Mr Davison £265. I remember Mr Halliday excepted against such a charge in settling his acc^ts^ with his uncle Wm Dunbar. (Dr. Tullideph's Letter-Book.)

DUNCOMBE. Page 227.

Charles Byam Duer Duncombe, son of the late Alexander Duncombe, Esq., of 47 Royal York Crescent, Clifton, entered Rugby School 23 Sep. 1860, aged 15.

DUNNING. Page 229.

John Donning of Bristol, merchant. Will dated 2 March 1700; proved 26 April 1701 by James Donning. (49 Dyer.) My sisters Margaret, Mary, & Eliz^th^ £350 each. My brother Geo. £150 & goods I left in my house at Barbados & the negros. My brother James Donning a messuage in Bristol & all residue.

William Donning, Alderman of Bristol. Will dated 24 June 1692; proved 19 Aug. 1692 by Dorothy Donning, the relict. (150 Fane.) To my wife Dorothy £400, & my 3 daus. £100 each & all residue.

William Dunning of Antego, planter. Will dated 11 March 1709. (126 Young.) My father John Dunning of Ireland £12 a year. My dau. Mary Dunning £1000 c. Poor of St Mary's £10. All residue to my son Wm Dunning, he & Col. John Frye & Mr Jarvis Turton Ex'ors. Witnessed by Edward Wood, Agnas Martin, Samuel Drape, Notary Public. On 7 June 1711 commission to William Parrott, the attorney of John Frye, and William Dunning, the surviving Ex'ors.

This will corrects the tabular pedigree, but it still leaves it in uncertainty. There is no proof that Mary Wharfe's first husband was Thomas Dunning; it is much more likely that she was mother of Anna the wife of Robert Dunning.

EDWARDS. Page 235.

Zacchary Baily, clothier. Will dated 11 Aug. 1702; proved 2 Oct. 1704. (195 Ash.) Northwood Park, near Glassenbury, co. Som., to my son Edmond Baily, then to his son Zacchary Baily. My dau. Mary Baily £2100. My manor & farm of Chalcotts, co. Wilts, to my grandson Zacchary Baily, and in default of issue to my dau. Eliz. Harrington & her son John Harrington. My lands at West Harnam, after the death of my wife Abigal, to my said grandson. My 3 daus. Abigal Elton, Eliz. Harrington,

& Mary Baily. My wife £600. My sons-in-law Benj. Harrington & Abraham Elton. My mother Eliz. Baily. My brother Edmond Baily & his wife, brother-in-law John Hippey & his wife, brother-in-law Robert Merchant & his wife, my sister Alice. My sister Susanna Baily, brother-in-law Sam[l] Black, sister-in-law Jane Tooke.

1727. John Bayly of Westbury, co. Wilts, clothier. (180 Farrant.)

1729. Edmond Bayly of Westbury, co. Wilts, Gent. (30 Abbott.)

1771, May 25. Nathaniel Bailey Edwards, Esq; in the 21st year of his age, at Jamaica. ('Town and Country Mag.,' p. 335.)

1794, March 9. At Winchester-college, in his 17th year, of a nervous malignant fever, the eldest son of Bryan Edwards, esq. of the island of Jamaica. ('Gent. Mag.,' p. 284.)

1794, Nov. 4. At Bruges, in Flanders, much regretted by all who knew her, after a painful and lingering illness, Mrs. Jane Edwards, of St. Anne's, Jamaica, wife of W. E. esq. She has left a disconsolate husband and a large family to deplore their irreparable loss. ('Gent. Mag.,' p. 1205.)

Daniel Clutterbuck of Bradford Leigh, co. Wilts, Esq., and of Bath, banker, baptized at Avening, co. Gloucester, 20 Jan. 1744; died 11 June 1821, aged 77; buried at Bradford-on-Avon; married 1 Oct. 1773 Elizabeth daughter of Bryan Edwards of Jamaica, M.P. She died 28 April 1826, æt. 78; buried at Bradford. ('Gloucester Notes and Queries,' vol. v., p. 391.) If she was born 1748 and Bryan Edwards in 1743 they were probably brother and sister.

Bryan Edwards, who died 1835, æt. 29, could not have been son of Zacchary Edwards who died 1800.

William S. C. Mackie was baptized 13 June 1810 at St. John's, Antigua.

ELLYATT. Page 239.

Parish Register of St. George.

Buried.

1757 July 16 Mr James Griggs, buried in his own Estate by a Licence from his Excellency George Thomas, Esq[r].

Page 240. Ann wife of Colonel John Eliot was eldest daughter of Chief Justice Samuel Watkins.

Lieut.-Colonel Henry Augustus Montagu Cosby was knighted 9 Jan. 1784.

ELMES. Page 243.

1755, Dec. 8. M[r] Thos. Elmes dyed suddenly one day last week. (Dr. Tullideph's Letter-Book.)

1867, March 9. At 33 Ampthill-square, aged 66, Henry Spencer Papps, esq., solicitor, late of Hamilton, Canada West. He was the eldest son of the late Henry Papps, esq., of the Island of Antigua, by Dorothy Ann, dau. of Thomas Elmes, esq. and was born in Antigua in the year 1800. He was educated at Putney, under the Rev. W. Carmalt, and was admitted a solicitor in 1823. He was twice married: first in 1825, to Frances Ann, dau. of Alexander Forbes, esq; and secondly, to Laura Louisa, dau. of Mr. Simpson, of Hamilton, Canada West, and has left issue by both marriages. The deceased was buried at Kensal Green.—*Law Times.* ('Gent. Mag.,' p. 549.)

ENTWISLE. Page 245.

The Entwisle Pedigree has been taken from the one on record at the College of Arms.

FARLEY. Page 247.

1749, April 3. The Marshall hath been so busy courting . . . . he is married to a sister of Fran. Farley's. (Dr. Tullideph's Letter-Book.)

For an account of the connection between Farley and Parke, Watkins and Bird, see Vol. III., p. 207. Elizabeth Thomas, who married Hon. Francis Farley, was the only surviving child of William Thomas by Sarah his wife, consequently niece, *not* sister of Sir George Thomas, first Bart. Dr. McKittrick Adair (*circa* 1788—90) alludes to Mrs. Frances Farley, first wife of Mr. Simon Farley. Charles Manning, Esq., in his will of 1 March 1790, bequeathed £2000 for Mrs. Elizabeth Jesse, wife of Aaron Jesse, and her children Mary Elizabeth wife of Richard Jesse, merchant, Henrietta Farley, James Farley, Aaron Jesse, and Mary Jesse.

FIELD. Page 251.

James Field of New Windsor, co. Berks, Clerk. Will dated 26 Sep. 1728; proved 14 Feb. 1728 by Theophilus Field the son. (40 Abbott.) By Indenture dated 3 June 1717 between me & Rachel my late wife & the Hon. John Frye, Ashton Warner, Sam[l] Martin, & Isaac Herford, Esq[res], I settled my real & part of my personal estate. Furniture to my 3 daus., Mary, Kath., & Sophia. All residue to my son Theophilus. Tho. Stevens of S[t] John's Town & M[r] John Manwaring Ex'ors till my said son is 21 or arrives at Antigua. Witnessed by William Symonds, Kempe Parker, Nathaniel Richardson.

On 28 Aug. 1758 adm'on of estate left unadministered by Theophilus Field, deceased, the son, so far as relating to England, was granted to Catherine Thibou (wife of Isaac Thibou, Esq.), the daughter and only surviving legatee, Richard Oliver and Rowland Oliver, the surviving Ex'ors named in the will of the said Theophilus Field, having been cited but not appearing.

Buried at St. John's 1739, April 9, Mary Field of this Island. Her will was also recorded in P.C.C. (211 Henchman.)

FLEMING. Page 252.

John Fleming of Jamaica, merchant. Will proved 1692. (27 Fane.) My cousin Sam[l] Fleming, son of my uncle W[m] Fleming of Bishopsgate Street.

John Packer, M.D., of Chilton Foliat, co. Wilts. Will dated 1708. (99 Barrett.) £1700 on a mortgage on the lands of M[r] John Flemming of Clunne on the farmes of Shadwell & Broneth, co. Salop. £100 on bond of M[r] John Flemming, father & son.

Gabriel Wayne of Conham in the parish of St. Philip and St. Jacob, co. Gloucester, Gent. Will dated 9 Aug. 1721; proved 14 Feb. 1722. (P.C.C., Richmond.) My youngest son Mathew Wayne. Grandson Gabriel Wayne, 1st son of my 1st son John Wayne, £1000 at 23. My other grandson John Wayne, his brother. My dau. Eliz., wife of W[m] Clarke of Dublin. All residue to my son John Wayne & Ex'or. Witnessed by Benjamin Bathe, Jarrit Smith, John Jones.

James Hardwicke of Bristol, Esq. Will dated 11 Nov. 1733. (P.C.C., Wake.) My kinsman, the Hon. Gilbert Fleming, Esq., trustee to my marriage articles. Lands in co. Hereford. ('Gloucester Notes and Queries,' vol. v., p. 99.)

Gabriel Winstone Wayne of Lanverchon Lower, co. Monmouth, Gent. Will dated 28 April 1787; proved 24 Oct. 1788 by Alice Wayne the relict. (516 Calver.) My 1st son Gabriel Winstone Wayne £300 from the estate I sold to Chas. Coke, Esq., in Tortola. My son W[m], dau. Eliz. Wayne, son Philip, dau. Ann, dau. Cath., £300 each, all payable in 8 years. To my wife Alice all residue & Ex'trix. M[r] Nathan Windey, Attorney of Bristol, & M[r] Jenkins of Trostra, co. Monmouth, trustees, to sell my estate in Tortola.

1787, Nov. Lieut. Gab. Winstone Wayne. ('Town and Country Mag.,' p. 528.)

MARYLEBONE PARISH CHURCH.

On the south wall, under the gallery:—

Sacred to the Memory of
GILBERT FANE FLEMING Esqr
who was interr'd in this Church Dec^br XXVIII
MDCCLXXVI
This monument is here placed by his ever
affectionate and most truly grateful wife
Lady CAMILLA FLEMING.

('Mis. Gen. et Her.,' vol. i., Third Series, p. 131.)

FOOTE. Page 256.

Mr. Thomas Dickson Foote, C.M.G., was appointed a Member of the Executive Council 6 June 1891. His elder daughter married the late Mr. Robert Poole Griffith, M.R.C.S.; the younger is wife of Mr. Thomas Baines, who has been Solicitor- and Attorney-General, and is now a Puisne Judge of the Leeward Islands.

FRANKLIN. Page 258.

The will of Ann Franklin, widow, was also recorded P.C.C., 319 Browne.

FRASER. Page 259.

1750, April 20. Mr Frazer, the Collector at Parham, was this morning given over by the Doctors .... ill of a fever of which he died the next day. (Dr. Tullideph's Letter-Book.)

FREEMAN. Page 260.

Susanna Feilder of Oxford, spinster. Will proved 1730. (157 Auber.) My brother Tho. Hamond & Eliz. his wife £10 each. My nephew Arthur Freeman, Esq., & Dorothy his wife. My sister Marg^t Freeman.

Inigo Thomas matriculated from Magdalen College, Oxford, 26 Feb. 1783, aged 16; B.A. 1786; M.P. Weobly 1796—1800. Mr. F. Freeman Thomas, the present owner of Ratton, married in 1892 the Hon. Marie Adelaide, daughter of the first Lord Brassey.

Page 261. George Pelham Thomas, son of the Rev. Charles Edward Thomas, matriculated from Merton College, Oxford, 17 Jan. 1883, aged 18; B.A. 1887. Francis Inigo Thomas his brother matriculated from Pembroke College, Oxford, 30 Jan. 1844 (*sic* ? 1884), aged 18.

Page 262. John Cope Freeman was of a family long settled in Jamaica, whose pedigree limited space prevents me from here entering.

Page 266. 1794, Dec. 15. Suddenly dropped down dead, at the corner of Lilliput-alley, leading to the Parade, Bath, — Freeman, esq. a gentleman from the West Indies; who has left an amiable widow and five children. ('Gent. Mag.,' p. 1158.) This evidently refers to Thomas Freeman, Speaker of Antigua.

Buried at St. John's 1723, July 3, Alice the wife of Richard Willis.

Buried at St. George's 1774, Nov. 14, Benedick Freeman Willis, Esqr.

The will of Mrs. Elizabeth Freeman, widow of Captain William Freeman of St. Kitts, was proved 1719. (161 Browning.)

John Freeman of Ffawley Court, co. Bucks, Esq. Will dated 16 Feb. 1743; proved 1 Sep. 1752 by Sambrooke Freeman the son. (229 Bettesworth.) To my wife Susanna £2000, plate, jewells, horses, coaches, & use of furniture. My son John Freeman £4000. My son Jeremy Freeman £4000. My brother Tho. Cooke £50 a year by the first ship going to India. My nephew Tho. Cooke £100. All residue to my 1st son Sambrooke Freeman & sole Ex'or. My brother-in-law Sir Jeremy Sambrooke, Bart.

1st Codicil. 23 Feb. 1743. £500 already paid to my son Jeremy.

2nd Codicil. 31 March 1751. £1000 more paid to him.

3rd Codicil. Jan. 1752. £4000 already paid to my son John.

Sealed 28 Feb. 1752.

The arms of Smith are: *Ermine, three bezants.*

For V. J. C. Smith *read* V. T. C. Smith.

FRENCH. Page 273.

1809, April. At Lambeth, aged 63, Mr. James Andrew Bogle, heir to the dormant earldom of Monteith in Scotland. ('Gent. Mag.,' p. 478.)

See 'Notes and Queries,' vol. viii., Eighth Series, p. 48, for an unanswered inquiry as to the descendants of Nathaniel and Augustine Bogle French, merchants of Old South Sea House, Broad Street, about 1815.

1777, Jan. 17. The Rev. William Rugge, rector of Buckland, in Surrey, to Miss French, daughter of John French, Esq; of Percy Street. ('Town and Country Mag.,' p. 55.)

FRYE. Page 278.

The following deed has been supplied by Messrs. E. A. and George Fry:—

Indenture of four parts made 11 May 1804 between Bliss Leigh Frye of Wallington, co. Surrey, widow and relict of Rowland Frye, late of Wallington, Esq., deceased (which said Bliss Leigh Frye is daughter of Ann Spencer of Thorpe, co. Surrey, widow, deceased, and a legatee in her will), of the 1st part, Frances Spencer of Sutton, co. Lancaster, widow and administratrix of the Rev. Oliph Leigh Spencer, late of Buckland, co. Surrey, Clerk, deceased, who was one of the two sons of the said Ann Spencer and a legatee in her will, of the 2nd part, Richard Leigh Spencer of Gray's Inn, co. Middlesex, Gentleman, Henry Leigh Spencer of H.M. 20th Regiment of Dragoons, and Woolley Leigh John Spencer of High Street, Oxford, Esq., the three only children and the first two the administrators of the Rev. Woolley Leigh Spencer, late of Shepperton, co. Middlesex, Clerk, deceased, who was the first of the two sons of the said Ann Spencer, of the 3rd part, and William Morris Frye of Wallington, co. Surrey, Esq., of the 4th part. Whereas by Indentures of Lease and Release, dated 27 and 28 Jan. 1768, the Release being made between Barlow Trecothick, Esq., since deceased, of the 1st part, Thomas Wildman, Gentleman, of the 2nd part, the said Ann Spencer, of the 3rd part, and James Coulthard of Lincoln's Inn, Esq., and George Apthorpe, late of London, merchant, of the 4th part, reciting that the said Barlow Trecothick had purchased of the said Ann Spencer the manor, advowson, etc., therein mentioned for £38,500, and that the same were conveyed to him by Indentures of Lease and Release of the 25th and 26th Jan. preceding, and reciting difficulties *re* £3000 and £2000 claims, and that £2500, part of the purchase-money, should remain upon the security of the estate, it was witnessed that in consideration of those three sums Barlow Trecothick granted to Thomas Wildman the manor of Addington for Ann Spencer, subject to redemption on payment of £2625, and to the use of James Coulthard and George Apthorpe, subject to redemption on payment of £5000, on trust as to £3000 for the younger children of the said Ann Spencer by Henry Spencer her then late husband, according as they should be entitled by an Indenture dated 5 March 1744; and whereas the said younger children had no claim; and whereas Ann Spencer made her will 13 March 1768, she gave the said £5000 to Thomas Leigh Bennett and Hugh Stevenson on trust, and to pay £3000 to Oliph Leigh Spencer her younger son at 21 and £2000 to her daughter Bliss Leigh Spencer at 21 or marriage, £600 of the remaining £2500 to Woolley Leigh Spencer her son, and the residue to her younger children, and she died that month; and Oliph Leigh Spencer attained 21 and Bliss Leigh Spencer in 1767 married Rowland Frye; and whereas by Indenture of 1 July 1783 between James

Coulthard, the surviving Trustee, of the 1st part, James Trecothick of Addington, Esq., nephew and devisee of Barlow Trecothick, deceased, of the 2nd part, Thomas Leigh Bennett and Hugh Stevenson, of the 3rd part, Oliph Leigh Spencer, of the 4th part, and Rowland Frye and Bliss Leigh Frye his wife, of the 5th part. £4100 still due on the mortgage, £3075 of which was due to Oliph Leigh Spencer and £1025 to Rowland Frye and his wife, the ¾ of the hereditaments were granted to Oliph Leigh Spencer; and whereas by an Indenture of Assignment of 20 Feb. 1796, between Oliph Leigh Spencer, of the 1st part, and Frances Spencer (then Frances Cater) of the 2nd part, and Thomas Beaumont, Esq., and Woolley Leigh Spencer, of the 3rd part, reciting a marriage shortly after solemnized between Oliph Leigh Spencer and Frances Cator, the mortgaged premises and £2000, part of the money due thereon, should be vested in the said Thomas Beaumont and Woolley Leigh Spencer on trust, and Thomas Beaumont died in March 1796 and Oliph Leigh Spencer died Dec. 1796 intestate and without issue, and adm'on was granted to Frances Spencer his relict, and she became entitled to ½ of the said £3500, and Woolley Leigh Spencer and Bliss Spencer Frye, as next-of-kin, to the other ½, subject to the life interest of Frances Leigh Spencer; and whereas Woolley Leigh Spencer died Nov. 1797 leaving Mary Spencer his widow, and his sons, the said Woolley Leigh John Spencer, Richard Leigh Spencer, and Henry Leigh Spencer, so Mary Spencer became entitled to ⅓ of the £3075 and the said three sons to ⅔, and Mary Spencer died Oct. 1801 intestate; her said three only children became entitled to her share; and whereas Rowland Frye died Feb. 1801; and whereas by Indenture dated 16 June 1803, between Frances Spencer, of the 1st part, Bliss Leigh Frye, of the 2nd part, Richard Leigh Spencer and Henry Leigh Spencer, of the 3rd part, Woolley Leigh John Spencer, of the 4th part, and William Morris Frye, of the 5th part, Frances Spencer granted to William Morris Frye the £2000 settled on her in trust, ½ for Woolley Leigh John Spencer, Richard Leigh Spencer, and Henry Leigh Spencer, ¼ to Richard Leigh Spencer during her life, then for Bliss Leigh Spencer, and ¼ for the said three brothers. James Trecothick has paid off the mortgage with interest. (Division of proceeds in various shares given in detail.) Now William Morris Frye stands possessed of £883 Consols in trust for Frances Spencer, and at her death to pay to Bliss Leigh Frye. All parties quit-claim. Signed by Bliss Leigh Frye, Richard Leigh Spencer, Henry Leigh Spencer, Frances Spencer, Woolley Leigh John Spencer, William Morris Frye.

The seal used bears the arms of Leigh of Adington, co. Surrey: *Or, on a chevron sable three lions rampant argent.*

Crest: *On a mount vert a lion couchant gardant argent.*

George Frye of Liverpool, merchant. Will dated 5 May and proved 10 July 1667. (92 Carr.) Mrs. Hannah Drax £50. Brother John Frye £100. Wm Drax, Esq., £50. 1st son of my brother Wm Frye. My wife Margaret. My ship the "True Love," with my effects, from the Barbados. Estate in England & Ireland. Wife Margt, Wm Drax, Esq., & Tho. Sandiford Ex'ors.

William Frye of Wallington, co. Surrey, Esq. Will dated 4 May 1794; proved 10 March 1795 by the three Ex'ors. (165 Newcastle.) To be buried in Banstead Church. My late brother Rowland. My sister Henrietta Byam. My nephew Archibald Cochran. My nieces Jane Hulbert, Mary Mathew, Theodora Rose, Frances Duer, Eliz. Gracie Duer, & Eliz. Brown. My grt nieces Selena Honey, wife of Revd Wm Honey, Henrietta Maria Byam, & Eliz. Caroline wife of Mark Batt. My godson Peter Frye Honey. My grt. nephew Wm Morris Newton. My sister Eliz. Fra. Newton. My niece Henrietta Duer & her brother Rowland Duer. My nephew Revd Tho. Plan. My niece Mrs Ann Blake. Mrs Bliss Leigh Frye, wife of my nephew Rowland Frye. My cousin John Lucie Blackman of Craven Str., Strand, merchant, Geo. Blackman of Chatham Sq., Blackfriars, & Chr. Hall of the Inner Temple, Gent., Ex'ors.

1739, April 14. Letter from Dr. Tullideph mentioning "Saml Frye's widow . . . . & her sister Mrs Gamble."

Dorothy Frye was born 3 Oct 1768, descended from John Ffrye, Lieut. in the army of Charles I., who settled at Antigua about 1645. (Warner Pedigree in Davy's Suffolk Collections, British Museum.)

Page 285. Augusta Frye, Countess de Lubersac, was dead Jan. 1895. On the seal she used the horses were placed in pale, with one fleur-de-lis above and two below them.

William Edward Frye was at Eton in 1802, and later a Captain 58th Regiment.

1736, May 17. William Frye, Esq; President of the Council in the island of Montserrat. ('London Mag.,' p. 400.)

1774, March 20. The Hon. Francis Frye, Esq; at Antigua. ('Town and Country Mag.,' p. 336.)

Mar. at St George's, Hanover Square, 1818, Aug. 17, the Rev. Percival Frye, Clk., of the parish of Dinsdale, co. Durham, B., & Laura Augusta Hastings Scott Waring, of this parish, S., a minor. Lic. With the consent of her father John Scott Waring.

[End of Additions to Volume I.]

VOLUME II.

GALLWEY. Page 2.

Arms: *Quarterly, 1 and 4, per fess or and gules, in chief an eagle displayed sable, in base a castle argent.*

GAMBLE. Page 4.

1739. Samuel Frye's widow a sister of Mrs Gamble of Antigua & Cork. (Dr. Tullideph's Letter-Book.)

GARRETT. Page 7.

Joseph Merry, son of Joseph Merry by Frances Garrett, was a minor and an orphan in 1752; was aged 21 in Ap. 1754; got into debt at Antigua & fled to Jamaica. (Dr. Tullideph's Letter-Book.)

GILCHRIST. Page 16.

Dr. Adair, *temp.* Governor Shirley, refers to "Mrs. Gilchrist, her most amiable and accomplished daughter, the late Mrs. McConnell and her sisters."

GLOSTER. Page 20.

Elizabeth daughter of Thomas Jarvis, Esq., and Rachel Thibou his wife, baptized 3 March 1768; married 18 July 1785 Archibald Gloster, Esq., Member of Council and Attorney-General of Trinidad in 1807, later Chief Justice of Dominica; he died in Trinidad. Their other issue included:—1. Henry Gloster, Attorney-General and Judge of Berbice, who died there in 1842, leaving a widow and children; 2. Chester Gloster; 3. Mary Gloster; 4. Russell Gloster; 5. Eliza Gloster, who married . . . . Williams. (Mr. Thomas Bell's 'Jarvis Papers.')

GORDON. Page 22.

Gordon of Terpersy was a Cadet, House of Gordon of Lesmoir. ('Genealogist,' vol. xiv., part i., p. 16.)

1776, Jan. 4. Sir John Abdy, of Hanover-Street, to Miss Gordon, of Brewer Street. ('Town and Country Mag.,' p. 55.)

1788, Dec. James Gordon, esq. of Tobago, to Miss Mackay, of Turnham Green. (*Ibid.*, p. 624.)

1865, Sep. 9. At Brighton, Jane Eliza, widow of Wright Knox, esq., 87th Royal Fusiliers, late resident of Ithaca, youngest dau. of the late Capt. Francis Grant Gordon, R.N., and sister of the late Sir Willoughby Gordon, bart. ('Gent. Mag.')

PEDIGREE OF THE FAMILY OF GRANT OF CARRON, NORTH BRITAIN, AND OF THE ISLANDS OF ANTIGUA AND ST. VINCENT IN THE WEST INDIES.*

Colonel JOHN GRANT of Carron, killed at Carthagena 1741 = Ann Ogilvie.

Alexander = ... Grant of Auchterblair.

Lieut. Joseph = ... Grant of Col. Montgomerie's Highlanders.

Lewis Grant of Auchterblair, Captain Black Watch, purchased Carron; died 1756, æt. 62. Brother of Dr. Patrick Grant of Antigua. = Elizabeth Grant, died 1727.

Anna Grant, mar. Colonel John Grant of Lurg; died 1777.

Peggy Grant, mar. in 1766 Sir Alexander Grant of Dalvey.

Elizabeth Grant, marriage settlement dated 1771. She mar. 2ndly Dr. James T. Murray, and lived and died at Bath. (See 'Dict. Nat. Biog.,' vol. xxii., p. 385.) 2nd wife. = Captain James Grant of Carron and Wester Elchies, born 1727; heir 1770 to his uncle Patrick Grant of Antigua; died 1790 in Holyrood. = ... dau. of . . . . Grant. 1st wife.

Elizabeth Grant, mar. 1753 John Innes of Edengight, and was mother of Sir John Innes, Bart., of Balvenie.

Rev. Joseph Grant, died 17 June 1801 at Edinburgh. — Captain John Grant.

Captain Peter Grant. — Captain William Grant. — Effingham Grant.

Mary Ann How Grant. — Louisa Grant.

Charles Grant of the "Adelphi" Estate, St. Vincent, and of Carron, died 1821 at Marseilles. = Ann, dau. of John Mayer of Antigua by Esther Wickham his wife; mar. 1778; died 1796 at Antigua.

Eliza Wickham Grant, died 1790. — James Mayer Grant, Barrister-at-Law, 1st son and heir, died s.p. 14 Sep. 1808 at Bath.

Charles Grant of St. Vincent, Major in the Army, died 18 April 1828 at Tunbridge Wells, æt. 41. = A French lady at St. Croix.

Sarah Grant, died 1852. — Ann Montgomery Grant, born 1789; mar. Captain Birch, Adjutant 90th Regiment; he died 1844; she died 1868. (See the Birch Pedigree, entered under Wickham.)

George Colquhoun Grant, Treasurer of St. Vincent, died 1853. = Anne More Molyneux of Losely, co. Surrey.

Edward Effingham Grant. — Eight other children died young.

Louisa Ann Grant, only dau., born 16 Sep. 1815; mar. 11 April 1844, at Kensington, John Lister, M.D., of Shibden Hall, Yorkshire; he died 1867; she died 1892. ('Genealogist,' vol. xi., p. 100.)

James Mayer Grant, Lieut.-Governor of St. Lucia, died s.p. — Hay Grant.

Emily Grant, mar. at St. Vincent Robert Aitken of that island, and had issue.

Caroline Grant, mar. at St. Vincent Rev. Alexander Dasent (son of John Roche Dasent, Esq., of that island), and had issue; he was born 30 April 1822.

Barbara M. Grant, mar. Major-General Dawson Warren, C.B., and had issue.

* Most of this from information supplied by the Rev. Wickham M. Birch, Vicar of Ashburton.

1783, Jan. 18. In Billiter-lane, in the 49th year of his age, Alex. Grant, esq; many years an eminent West India merchant. ('Gent. Mag.,' p. 94.)

1862, Jan. 16. At the Lodge, Bembridge, Isle of Wight, aged 84, Sarah, relict of Charles Grant, esq. of Wester Elchies, Morayshire. (*Ibid.*, p. 381.)

Bond for £500, dated 1771 at Edinburgh, by James Grant of Carron and Lieut. William Grant, late of the 1st or Scotch Royal Regiment of Foot, and Mrs. Catherine Grant his spouse.

See MS. of Lord Adam Gordon in 'Genealogist' for 1897, p. 15, where a reference is given to "Chiefs of Grant" by Fraser, which I have not had an opportunity of consulting.

1896, Aug. 25. A marriage has been arranged between James William Hamilton Grant, eldest son of the late Henry Alexander Grant, of Wester Elchies, Morayshire, and Carron, Banffshire, and Mary, eldest daughter of the Right Hon. Lord Justice A. L. Smith and Lady Smith, of Salt Hill, Chichester, Sussex.

GUNTHORPE. Page 38.

Coke, solicitor to the people of England, tried in 1660 with other Roundheads ('Pepys' Diary,' vol. i., p. 78), and on 21 Oct. 1660 Pepys saw "Cooke's head set up for a traytor." Frances Stoughton, whose will was dated 9 Sep. 1693 and sworn 8 Feb. 1693-4, was probably the widow and executrix of Acquila Stoughton, whose will dated 17 July 1690 was recorded 21 June 1693. Mrs. Elizabeth Gunthorpe was dau. of Thomas Watkins. Mrs. Elizabeth Hesse remarried Aug. 1792 Admiral Phillips Cosby of Stradbally.

HALLIDAY. Page 43.

Elizabeth Halliday married Captain William Redman or Redmond. His will was dated 5 March 1697 and sworn 7 April 1698. Another of her sisters, Mary, married 6 May 1708 Major John Roach, and his will was dated 20 Feb. 1728-9. In 1752 William Dunbar had a nephew Mr. Halliday. William Woolsley Halliday, Esq., was apparently managing Lavingtons for Sir W. Abdy, Bart., about 1858; Mrs. Woolsley Halliday was living 1862, Mrs. Jane A. Halliday in 1861, and John Halliday, Esq., 1864.

Parish Register of St. Mary Cayon, St. Christopher.

Baptized.

1723 Oct. 22 Franses D. of Richard & Eliz. Wilson.
1726 May 6 Renolt S. of Richard & Eliz. Wilson.
1728 April 20 Spooner S. of Richard & Eliz. Wilson.

1866, Jan. 5. At Richmond-hill, Bath, aged 64, John Delap Wilson, esq. eldest son of the late John William Delap Wilson, formerly of Liddon House, Milford, Hants. ('Gent. Mag.,' p. 439.)

1867, June 30. At Peshawar, East Indies, of heat apoplexy, aged 34, Capt. John Edmund Delap Wilson, B.C.S. (*Ibid.*, p. 539.)

HAMILTON. Page 50.

Mrs. Anne Vaughan died 30 Aug. 1741, aged 64. Hannah Halfhide was born 8 Nov. 1707 and married 17 Jan. 1735. (See 'Mis. Gen. et Her.,' vol. iii., Second Series, p. 369, and vol. iv., p. 86, also 'Notes and Queries,' vol. vi., Seventh Series, pp. 168 and 238.)

1698. William Hamilton, late of St. Christopher's in the West Indies, merchant. (215 Lort.) My sister Lucy, now wife of Wm Ingles of Douglas, co. Clidsdale.

1722, April 18. Died at the Island of St. Christopher in North America Brigadier-General Hamilton, formerly Governor of the Leeward Islands.

1722, July 8. Dyed Suddenly at her House in Broad Street, the Relict of the late Gen^ll^ Hamilton, Governour of the Leeward Islands. (Mawson's Obits. in 'Genealogist.') This last notice is incorrect, as she survived for several years.

Mr. T. Colyer-Fergusson of Wombwell Hall, Gravesend, wrote me March 1897:—"An ancestor of mine, Charles Hamilton, settled in Nevis as a Doctor, and after making his fortune left about 1738 and returned to his home in Scotland. He was no relation to Governor Walter Hamilton; he is said to have married in Nevis, but I cannot find particulars."

John Hamilton, who was at Eton in 1796, owned most of the Island of Tobago, and died at Dover.

1840. The Honourable Henry Hamilton, President Administering the Government of Montserrat. This melancholy event took place at his residence in the town of Plymouth, Montserrat, at half-past 6 o'clock on the morning of the 10th instant, after an illness of a few days. (Antigua, the 'Weekly Register' for 17 March 1840.)

HANSON. Page 56.

Samuel Hanson of St. George's Parish, Barbados, Gent. Will dated 28 March 1687; proved 21 Feb. 1689 by Samuel Hanson the son. (23 Dyke.) My wife Margaret £150 a year charged on my plantation. 1st dau. Eliz. Hanson at 21 £1000 st., & £1000 at the birth of her 1st child, & £1000 for the 2^d^. My yst. dau. Silence Hanson at 21 ditto. To my son Samuel all lands, cattle, & Ex'or. Poor of Blewberry, co. Berks, where I was born, £6 a year. Capt. Humphry Southb. merchant in London, & Mr Tho. Lear, merchant of Barbados, £10 each & overseers. Witnessed by Henry St. John, William Bicknell, William Harding, William Marshall, Francis Gibbon. On 4 Aug. 1693 commission to Elizabeth Folkes, wife of Simon Folkes, Esq., daughter of Samuel Hanson, sen., Samuel Hanson, jun., the son being dead.

PARISH REGISTER OF ST. PAUL, ANTIGUA.

Baptized.

1747 Aug. 9 Jane D. of Francis Hanson and Anne his wife.

Buried.

1747 Sep. 29 Jane D. of Mr. Francis Hanson and Anne his wife.

HARMAN. Page 60.

Admiral Harman's portrait is at Greenwich.

1766. William Harman of Totnes, co. Devon, Esq., late Captain of H.M.S. "St. Ann." (63 Tyndall.) Brothers Edward and James, sisters Elizabeth and Mary. M.I. in the Chancel.

1840. On Sunday the 15th inst. Mary M. Harman, eldest daughter of the Honorable Samuel Harman . . . . her surviving parent . . . . (Antigua, the 'Weekly Register' for 17 March 1840.)

Page 62. 1772, June 29. Samuel Harman, Esq; in Soho. ('Town and Country Mag.,' p. 391.)

1788, March. Ph. Wright esq. of Camberwell, to Miss Letitia Harman. (*Ibid.*, p. 195.)

Captain Thomas Harman. Will dated 19 June 1675; proved 1677. (99 Hale.) My brother Mr Wm Harman the shipp. My brother Henry Harman £200. My uncle Mr Henry Harman, dec^d^. My brother Edward Harman, scrivener, dec^d^, his dau. Susan £100. My cousins Philip & Mary Harman, son & dau. of my brother Philip Harman, £200 each. My sister Ellen Holliday, wife of Samuel Holliday, her dau. Sarah Harman by my late brother-in-law Edward Harman. My father Mr Tho. Harman.

This will corrects the pedigree on p. 63.

Mr. Samuel Bruce Harman has sent me the following:—

Samuel Harman. Will dated 23 May 1810. On the point of leaving this Island. My estate called Harmans to my 1st son Sam. Bickerton Harman, subject to payment of £1000 st. each to Fred. Barkeley Harman my 2^d^ son, Athill Harman my 3^d^ son, Annie Ross Harman my only surviving dau. All my personal property to my sisters Anne Harman & Mary Harman, & name them joint Guardians & Ex'trices.

HART. Page 67.

John Hart was Governor of Maryland 1714—1720. He had previously served as an officer in Spain. His father was Merrick Hart of Crobert, co. Cavan, and his mother Lettice, daughter of the Venerable Thomas Vesey and sister of the Right Rev. John Vesey, Archbishop of Tuam. ('Notes and Queries' for 1896, p. 436, Jan. 1897, p. 31, and later.)

John Hart of Warfield, co. Berks, Esq., commonly called Governor Hart. My dau. Marylanda Hart ½ of her mother's personal estate, also £5000. Adeliza Gore, spr., £45 owing to her from Agmondesham Vesey, Esq. All my lands in England, Ireland, or the Plantations abroad, & all residue to my son Tho. Hart & Ex'or. Witnessed by Richard Roberts, James Neill, William Legard. Proved 26 Jan. 1740 by Thomas Hart, Esq., the son (12 Spurway). The last named married Oct. 1741 Jane, daughter of Sir John Cotton, sixth Bart., and died 26 Aug. 1756, æt. 43. M.I. at Warfield.

HAWES. Page 69.

Joseph Hawes of Antigua, planter, now in London. Will dated 31 March 1738; proved 18 Aug. 1739 by R. Bodicote; power reserved to Edward Evanson the surviving Ex'or. (179 Henchman.) Mr Richard Bodicote, James Parke, Esq., & Mr Edward Eavenson of Antigua, planter, all my negros & estate for my son Joseph Hawes at 21 & Guardians, he to choose others at the age of 14; if he die then all to my wife Elizabeth his mother if living, but if dead to my own sister Catherine Nibbs & to my wife's 3 sisters Henrietta, wife of James Parke, Esq., Amy Symes, & Catherine Symes equally. My trustees to be Ex'ors. Witnessed by Edward Mountague, John Hothersall.

HERBERT. Page 70.

(88 Cann.) 1685. Mountserrat. Edward Herbert of Bristol, merchant. Wife Anne 50,000 lbs. Shares of ships. Edmond Ellis, apprentice in plantation business. My son Thos. Herbert. Codicil in London.

(192 Vere.) 1691. Nevis. Thomas Harvey of Bristol, Gent. My dau.-in-l. Martha Parsons £200. Friend Tho. Tovey of Nevis £100. All residue to my wife Mary & son Thomas, & Ex'ors.

(51 Browning.) 1718. James Lytton of Nevis and Camberwell, co. Surrey. Niece Sarah Herbert & nephews Tho. Herbert & Joseph Herbert, dau. & sons of my brother-in-law Tho. Herbert & my sister Dorothy his wife. Niece Sarah Browne. Nephew Wm Carpenter.

PARISH REGISTER OF ST. GEORGE, NEVIS.

Baptized.

1716 Sep. 9 William Litton S. of Mr Thomas Herbert by Dorothy his wife.

1719 Aug. 20 John the S. of Mr Thomas Herbert, Senr, by Dorothy his wife.

1722 June 12 James the S. of Mr Thomas Herbert by Dorothy his wife.

1724 Dec. 1 Henry the S. of Mr Thomas Herbert by Dorothy his wife.

Married.

1724 June .. William Woolward, Mariner, & Anne Smith, widow.

William Woolward's wife Mary Herbert was sister to President Herbert.

HILL. Page 72.

The arms—*Sable, on a fess argent between three garbs . . . . a lion passant-guardant of the first*—were quartered by Mathew. ('Notes and Queries,' vol. ii., Eighth Series, p. 188.)

Oswald Wood, Provost-Marshal-General, by consent of the Executrix of the will of Daniel J. W. Hill of this Island, Esq., deceased, to be sold by execution a parcel of land on the Parade. Nathaniel J. Hill and Company to trade in the future as Hill and Moore. (Antigua, 'Weekly Register' for 17 March 1810.)

1812, April. Lately. At Antigua, Thomas T. Tucker, Esq., commander of his majesty's ship Cherub, to Miss Hill. ('Jamaica Mag.,' p. 143.)

1800, May. Lately. At Bermuda, John Noble Harvey, esq. to Miss M. Tucker, eldest dau. of the Hon. J. T. esq. Speaker of the Colonial Assembly. ('Gent. Mag.,' p. 484.)

HODGE. Page 76.

The following additional information was sent me in 1895 by Mr. Howard Williams Lloyd, of 43 Tulpehocken Street, Germantown, Philadelphia:—

"The only way I can account for part of the Hodge family settling in Philadelphia is that when Henry Hodge died 1694-5 at Antigua he left a young family, and his son Henry being thrown with the people called Quakers, who were numerous at that time at Antigua, Tortola, and Barbados, became convinced and joined their Society, or perhaps his mother was a 'Friend'; he then removed to Philadelphia, to be where they were free from persecution. The first record I have of him in Philadelphia is from the Philadelphia 'Society of Friends' Monthly Meeting Book' (Deaths and Burials), viz.: 'ffrance Hodge wife of Henry 11 mo. [old style Jan.] 11th, 1715.' He was a prominent merchant, and often acted as attorney for parties in Antigua, especially for Jonas Langford. The brief of title to one piece of real estate he possessed on what is now Clinton Street is as follows: '1728, 1st May, Deed to Henry Hodge for lot on North side of Pine St East of 11th St' [this property extended through to and across the present Clinton Street]. Henry Hodge died intestate leaving five children by his first wife, Knight Hodge, Henry Hodge, Margaret Rawle (wife of William Rawle), Frances Paschall (wife of John Paschall), and Mary Fisher, widow, and one child by his second wife, Thomas Hodge. 1734, Oct. 26 and July 27, deeds, Knight Hodge and Susanna his wife and Henry Hodge to their [step] mother Hannah Hodge. 1736, April 19, will of Hannah Hodge mentions her son Thomas Hodge. Henry Hodge on Oct. 3, 1727, was elected one of the Common Council [Alderman] of the City of Philadelphia. Among other family MSS. is the following: 'Release John and Frances Paschall to Thomas Hodge of Kingsessing [in Philadelphia Co.], yeoman,' unto a certain legacy left to said Frances Paschall by Christopher Knight her grandfather, deceased, of Antigua, and also to the estate of her father Henry Hodge, deceased . . . . Aug. 2, 1741—Signed John Paschall, Frances Paschall, and witnessed by George Wood and Joseph Fordham. Henry Hodge married for his second wife Hannah Scott, widow of Abraham Scott, also widow of John Scott; her maiden name was Lambert; she was of New Jersey. The entry in Philadelphia Monthly Meeting Book [this is an extract of the full entry]: 'Henry Hodge of Philada, merchant, and Hannah Scott, of the same place, widow, at Philads Meeting 7th mo. [Sep.] 12th, 1717.' I have no knowledge of any heraldic seal in the family.

"Children of Henry Hodge.

1. Knight Hodge, married at Philadelphia Friends' Meeting on 5th mo. [July] 25th 1728 Susannah Bickley, dau. of Abraham Bickley of Burlington, New Jersey. I believe he died in 1747 (Register of Wills, Philadelphia). Letters of adm'on granted 1747 (Book F, p. 83). I do not know whether he left issue or not.
2. Henry Hodge married Elizabeth . . . . Letters of adm'on granted on the estate of a Henry Hodge of Philadelphia 1754 (Book F, p. 530). The following entries are from Christ Episcopal Church Records, Philadelphia:—

Baptized.

1738 Oct. 4 Hodge, John Knight, s. Henry and Elizabeth, 2 wks.

Buried.

1738 Oct. 7 Hodge, John Knight, son of Henry.
1742 Dec. 25 Hodge, Henry, son of Henry.
1752 July 23 Hodge, John.
1759 Nov. 20 Hodge, Knight, son of Abraham.

[There are a couple of marriages, but I doubt if they belong to the same family.]

1743 May 29 Hodge, Susannah, and John Williams.
1754 Feb. 25 Hodge, Elizabeth, and Joseph Bond.

3. Margaret Hodge, married at Philadelphia Friends' Meeting on 6th mo. [Aug.] 29th 1728 to William Rawle, son of Francis and Martha Turner Rawle. They left numerous descendants, several of whom attained to positions of prominence.
4. Mary Hodge, born 1st mo. [March] 8th 1709 [this date is fixed by a piece of sample work with it on, now in the possession of the family], married at Philadelphia Friends' Meeting on 3rd mo. [May] 30th 1728 to John Fisher, son of John Fisher and Sarah, the latter deceased at the time of the wedding. Her husband died in 1740, and she married Jonathan Paschall. According to the will of John Fisher, proved at Philadelphia April 16, 1740, they had two sons and two daughters.
5. Frances Hodge, born 4 mo. [June] 15th 1710; died in Philadelphia 1st mo. [Jan.] 8th 1781; married at Philadelphia Friends' Meeting 2nd mo. [April] 25th 1728 Dr. John Paschall, son of Thomas Paschall and Margaret Jenkins Paschall his wife. Left numerous descendants. The Paschalls emigrated from near Bristol, England, to Pennsilvania in the fall of 1682.
6. Elizabeth Hodge, died 1719, I believe unmarried. The entry in Philadelphia Meeting Book of Deaths and Burials: 'Hodge, Elizabeth, 6 mo. [Aug.] 28th 1719. Parents, Henry and Frances, dec'd.' This looks as if you were wrong about Elizabeth marrying Henry Elliott.

"Notes on the second marriage of Henry Hodge:—Records of the Society of Friends, marriages at Chesterfield, New Jersey.—Certificates recorded (one for) John Scott and Hannah Lambert 2nd mo. [April] 4th 1695. Philadelphia marriages.—Certificates recorded (one for) Abraham Scott and Hannah Scott, widow, 5 mo. [July] 10, 1705. Same meeting.—Certificates recorded (one for) as given in my letter of March 8th. In an old family Bible printed in 1715 by John Basket, Oxford, etc., the above marriage is recorded, and the following: 'Thomas Hodge was born ye

8th day of 8 mo. 1718.' Wills registered at Philadelphia.—No. 3 of 1736, Hannah Hodge (Book F, p. 4). Philadelphia adm'ons.—Henry Hodge, 1731 (Book C, p. 192). Thomas Hodge, 1744 (Book E, p. 39). This is evidently the son by second marriage, I think s.p. Joseph Hodge, 1733 (Book C, p. 246). I do not identify him. The newspaper 'The Pennsilvania Gazette' for March 7th 1731-2 has a short obituary on Henry Hodge, 'a merchant and a man of good reputation.' Some of the family seem to have owned property in Pennsilvania as late as 1843, and they were resident of Antigua for the reason that there are recorded at West Chester, Chester Co., Pennsilvania, the following wills, certified to by the consul for the U.S.A. at St. John, Antigua, April 4, 1843, viz.: Isabella Hodge of Island of Antigua, widow and relict of Christopher Hodge, signed 21 Aug. 1795; proved Nov. 8, 1795 (Liber H, fo. F). Henry Hodge of the Island of Antigua, planter, signed 25 June 1811; mandamus signed 22 Jan. 1821 (Liber C, vol iii., fo. 47). Michael Hodge, Antigua, Dec. 21, 1807, sworn March 6, 1809 (Liber K, vol. vii., fo. 143, also P.C.C.). Langford Lovell Hodge, Island of Antigua, planter, signed Oct. 31, 1811, at Old Warren Cottage, Hampshire, in Great Britain; proved April 14, 1817 (Liber B, vol. ii., fo. 49), at Antigua.

HORNE. Page 82.

(23 Bath.) 1679, Jan. 29. John Horne of Exeter, merchant. 1st s. John £400, s. Tho. £200. Wife Ellenor.

(75 Hare.) 1683, Nov. 23. John Herault of Bristol, Gent. My kinsmen in France. Wife Rebecca. Wife's father Mr Thos. Horne.

(121 Cann.) 1685. Edward Horne, Citizen and Goldsmith of London. Brothers John Horne, Chas. Horne, Richd Horne. Sisters Ann Ferris & Mary Horne. Father Robert Horne.

(110 Coker.) 1693. John Horne of co. Essex, Gent. Plantation in Barbados. Bro. Tho. Horne. Father Sir Samuel Husbands & my mother Elizabeth.

(185 Pyne.) 1697, June 16. John Horne of Bristol, mercer. Father-in-law Wm Williams Turner & his wife Mary. My mother the manor of West Harnham, co. Wilts. Brother-in-law John Lloyd of Bristol, Esq. 1st s. Wm Horne, 2d & yst. s. Chas. Horne. Wife Dorothy, dau. Dorothy.

Thomas Horne, Citizen and Goldsmith of London, Ex'or of Samuel Horne, late of Antigua, Esq. Will dated 23 Dec. 1699; proved 13 June by Sir Thomas Cook, Alderman, and Thomas Rowe, and 17 Aug. 1700 by John Horne. (130 Noel.) My sister Hannah Horne £600. Sisters Susan Horne, Martha Horne, and Mary Towe, £200 each. Niece Anne Lee, dau. of my brother John Lee of Ken, co. Devon, £150. Niece Kath. Cooke, dau. of my brother Sir Tho. Cook, £300. Niece Hannah Cook his dau. £200. Cozen Tho. Rowe £100. Cozen John Horne of London, mercer, $\frac{1}{3}$ of effects in Antigua. All residue to my brother Sir Tho. Cook, he & my cozens Tho. Rowe & John Horne Ex'ors. Witnessed by Richard Woodward, John Tullidge, Henry Bedell, scr.

Dr. Adair, *temp.* Governor Shirley, names Mrs. E. Horne and her sister Mrs. Dasent.

1827, May 22. At Bath, the Rev. Chas. Paul, of White Lackington, Somerset, to Frances Kegan, third dau. of the late John Horne, esq. of St. Vincents. ('Gent. Mag.,' p. 557.)

HORSFORD. Page 86.

PARISH REGISTER OF ST. JOHN.

Baptized.

1740 Mar. 10 John the s. of George Horsford and Henrietta his wife.

1775 May 15 Alicia Mary the d. of John Horsford & Christian his wife.

1776 Jan. 4 Eliza Maria the d. of Yeamans Horsford & Eliza his wife.

1802 Feb. 24 Edward Byam. B. 30th Decer. 1800. Richard. B. 28 Decer. 1801. } of Valentine Horsford and Jane his wife.

1804 Feb. 3 James Payne s. of Valentine Horsford and Jane his wife; b. 20 May 1803.

Married.

1756 May 25 Burton Daxon and Henrietta Horsford (Widow). L.

1763 April 18 John Horseford to Christian Jenkins. L.

1826 Nov. 13 Robert Marsh Horsford of the Parish of St John's, Solicitor General, and Mary Furlonge of the same parish. S. L.

Buried.

1782 April 27 George Horseford.

1785 Mar. 1 Harriot Horseford.

1804 Dec. 26 Valentine Horseford.

Robert Marsh Horsford

PARISH REGISTER OF ST. PAUL.

Married.

1738 Dec. 14 Mr John Nanton & Mrs Martha Horsford.

1772 Aug. 12 Mr Isaac Horsford to Miss Marianne Stapleton Horn; pr Licence.

Buried.

1734 June 1 Mrs Mary Horsford.

1737 Aug. 7 Captn Paul Lee Horsford.

1754 Mar. 21 George Horsford, Esqr.

1754 Oct. 9 Mrs Catharine Horsford.

1767 Nov. 23 Isaac Horsford son of John Horsford.

1774 Jan. 9 Willm Entwisle son of John and Christian Horsford.

1774 Feb. .. Septimus Christian son of John and Christian Horsford.

PARISH REGISTER OF ST. PHILIP.

Buried.

1703 Oct. 28 Henry Housford.

HUMPHREYS. Page 91.

Sarah, only daughter of Rev. William Knight Humphreys, married George Scotland, C.B. She died 29 Jan. 1863.

Francis Freeland Humphreys, first son of Octavius Humphreys, Esq., of St. John's, entered the Government Service about 1887 as clerk in the General Post Office, and died on Tuesday 29 June 1897, aged 26.

HYNDMAN. Page 94.

1785, Aug. 29. John Hyndman, esq., of Hampstead. ('Town and Country Mag.,' p. 504.)

1803. A Mr. Hyndman was A.D.C. to Governor Prevost at Dominica, and left St. Kitts that year. (Matson Letters.)

John Beckler Hyndman was at Eton in 1829, became a West India merchant, and lived in Hyde Park Square. In 1840 Warwick Pearson Hyndman and Co. and Thomas W. Hyndman were trading at St. John's.

ILES. Page 95.

1786, April. Ellis Iles esq. of Montserrat, formerly speaker of the house of assembly of that island. ('Town and Country Mag.,' p. 223.)

PARISH REGISTER OF ST. GEORGE, NEVIS.

(Fulham Palace MSS.)

Baptized.

1717 Jan. 1 John the S. of Mr. Edward Iles by Sarah his wife.

1724 April 22 Joseph the S. of Mr. Thomas Iles, Planter, by Sarah his wife.

Buried.

1719 July 23 Mr. William Iles.

[There are other entries which were not taken.]

1862. Dec. John Alex[r] Iles to be a Member of the Executive Council of Nevis.

JARVIS. Page 96.

John Jarvis of Mountserrat, now of Bristol, merchant. Will dated 24 Jan. 1663; proved 18 March 1663. (31 Bruce.) My friends Gabriell Deane of Bristol, merchant, & English Smith of Bristol, gent., & John Abbot of Nevies, merchant, Ex'ors in Trust for my children John, Zachary, Marie, Martha, & Jane Jarvis at 21. Witnessed by Alice Grindham, John Hellier, Elizabeth Statham, Mary Smith, Anne Ellis.

1786, Jan. The hon. Thomas Jarvis, president and chief judge of the island of Antigua. ('Town and Country Mag.,' p. 112.)

1789, March 11. James Morley, esq. late of Bombay, to Miss Jarvis, of Welbeck-street, Cavendish-squ. dau. of the late Chief Judge of Antigua. ('Gent. Mag.,' p. 276.)

1801, Feb. 28. Hon. Thomas Jarvis, of Antigua, to Miss Blackwell. (*Ibid.*, p. 275.)

1808, Nov. 9. At Bath, Major-general Richardson, to Mrs. Scott, widow of the late David S. esq. of the island of Antigua. (*Ibid.*, p. 1039.)

1808, Dec. 10. At the house of Major-general Richardson, at Winchester, aged 25, T. Scott, esq. late of the island of Tobago. (*Ibid.*, p. 1190.)

1809, March 11. Rev. Charles Augustus North, third son of the Bishop of Winchester, to Rachel, third daughter of the late Thomas Jarvis, esq. of Laverstoke-house, Hants. (*Ibid.*, p. 277.)

1845, Dec. 22. At Bath, aged 42, Thomas Eden Blackwell, esq. late Capt. 91st Reg. eldest son of the late Maj.-Gen. Blackwell, C.B. He was appointed Ensign in 1822, Lieut. 1825, Captain 1830. (*Ibid.*, p. 220.)

1862, June 8. Jane, widow of Major General Blackwell, aged 78, etc. (*Ibid.*, p. 116.)

1862, Oct. 15. At sea, on board the R.M.S. "Seine," on his voyage to Antigua, aged 69, Bertie Entwisle Jarvis, esq. Senior Member of H.M.'s Council of that Island. (*Ibid.*, p. 789.)

1863, Dec. 15. At the Cathedral, St. John's, Antigua, Thomas Jarvis, esq. of Mount Joshua, to Annie, second dau. of his Excellency Col. Stephen J. Hill, C.B. Governor of the Leeward Islands. (*Ibid.*, p. 244.)

1866, Nov. 4. At 16 Earl's-terrace, Kensington, aged 59, the Rev. William Whitehead Blackwell, M.A. He was the youngest son of the late Maj.-gen. Blackwell, C.B. and was educated at Trinity Coll. Cambridge, where he graduated B.A. in 1829, and proceeded M.A. in 1845. He was for some time curate of Mells, co. York. ('Gent. Mag.,' p. 845.)

1867, Jan. 17. At Bath, Mrs. Frances Jarvis, widow of Col. Jarvis of Doddington Hall, Lincolnshire. (*Ibid.*, p. 393.)

1895, Nov. 4. On All Saints'-day, at the Cleave, Torquay, Frances Jane Jarvis, widow of the Rev. Charles Macquarie George Jarvis,* formerly rector of Doddington, Lincolnshire.

The following additional information has been supplied me by the Rev. Robert Eden Cole, Rector of Doddington, co. Lincoln, and Thomas Bell, Esq., of Dundee:—

Page 98. Thomas Jarvis married Jane Moll. My grandfather G. R. P. Jarvis left Antigua when so young (in 1786, aged 12), and spent so much of his early life in campaigning, that he knew little of his family, and the pedigrees here are very meagre. In one of these this Thomas Jarvis is represented as having married . . . . Delap. G. R. P. Jarvis always said that he was the twenty-first and youngest child of his parents, but I have only a list of eighteen names, one only (another Elizabeth) to be added to your 17; no doubt the rest died as infants.—R. E. Cole.

William B. Jarvis was born 4 Dec. 1759, married 24 July 1793, and died 23 March 1811. Abigail Nanton Weston his wife was daughter of John Weston, who died 3 Feb. 1797, æt. 61. She was born 18 May 1774 and died 9 March 1820. Their dau. Mary married 25 Jan. 1812 John Swinton Jarvis, and died 1841 at Antigua. Their other dau. Sophia was born 11 Dec. 1798.

The wife of James N. Jarvis was Georgina Lorne Campbell, who died at Bath 18 July 1879, æt. 75.

Page 99. Blackwell pedigree. A full account of Ebenezer Blackwell (a great friend of John Wesley) is given by Mr. J. B. Martin in a book called 'The Grasshopper in Lombard Street,' being a History of Martin's Bank, in which Ebenezer Blackwell was a partner.

The following entries in Mrs. Blackwell's (*i.e.* Mary Eden Blackwell) Bible give the dates of birth of her children by Ebenezer Blackwell, and of several grandchildren:—

"Eben[r] Blackwell married to Mary Eden at Blackheath Chappel by the Rev[d] M[r] Lowth Dec. 22nd, 1774.

"Mary Elizabeth Shepperd Freeman, d. of Eben[r] & Mary Blackwell, born Oct. 23rd, 1775, & bap[d] at Blackheath Chappel 20th Nov[r] following.

"Charlotte Martha, 2nd d. of Eben[r] & Mary Blackwell, born 31st March 1777, baptized at Blackheath Chapel in April.

"Nathaniel Shepherd Joseph James, son of Eben[r] & Mary Blackwell, born June 5th, 1778, bapt[d] July 15th at home.

"John Robert, 2nd son of Eben[r] & Mary Blackwell, born Aug[st] 22nd, 1779, bapt[d] Sept. 22nd at home.

"Philadelphia, 3rd d. of Eben[r] & Mary Blackwell, born Sept. 21, 1780, bapt. Oct. 8.

"Margaret, 4th d. of Eben[r] & Mary Blackwell, born March 5th, 1782, bapt[d] at home April 2nd.

"William, Earl of Banbury, was married to Charlotte Martha Blackwell by the Rev[d] D[r] Sturges at S[t] Thomas Church, Winchester, June 23rd, 1795.

"Nathaniel S. J. J. Blackwell was married to Jane Jarvis Feb. 4th, 1801, by the Rev[d] D[r] Sturges.

"Mary Elizabeth S. F. Blackwell was married to Thomas Jarvis, Esq[re], Feb. 28th, 1801, by the Rev[d] D[r] Sturges.

"Mary Wilhelmina, d. of Thomas & Mary Elizabeth Jarvis, was born 15th Dec[r] 1801, bapt[d] at home April 8th, 1802.

* Son of George Jarvis, born 16 Nov. 1804; entered Merchant Tailors' School 1816; B.A. Pembroke College, Cambridge, 1827; Rector of Doddington 1838 till his death 1861.

"George Ralph Payne Jarvis was married at St Thomas Church, Winchester, to Philadelphia Blackwell Dec. 2nd, 1802, by the Revd Robert Lowth.

"Thomas Eden, son of Nathaniel S. J. J. & Jane Blackwell, born Jan. 14, 1803, in Canada.

"Eden, son of Thomas & Mary Elizabeth S. F. Jarvis, was born on Feb. 13th, 1803, and died on the 14th, next day.

"Robert Edward, 2nd son of Nathaniel & Jane Blackwell, b. at Quebec Dec. 21st, 1804.

"Grace, 2nd d. of Thomas & Mary Elizabeth Jarvis, born Feb. 13th, 1804.

"Robert Eden, son of the late Thomas Jarvis & Mary Elizabeth Jarvis, born at Bath 29th March 1805; died at Winchester June 8th same year.

"Jane Mary, 1st d. of Nathaniel & Jane Blackwell, b. at Winchester 21st June 1811."

[There are other entries of the children of the Earl of Banbury and of G. R. P. and Philadelphia Jarvis, but I think you will not care for them.—R. E. Cole.]

Mrs. Blackwell (Mary Eden) died at Winchester 19th Sep. 1811, æt. 65. M.I. to her in the Cathedral there, as well as to her father Dr. Robert Eden, Archdeacon of Winchester and Prebendary of Winchester and Worcester, who died 1759, æt. 58.

General Nathaniel Blackwell. I have a note that he died of apoplexy at Cheltenham 27 Aug. 1833. [See his obituary in 'Gent. Mag.,' p. 271.—V. L. O.]

Charlotte Martha (Countess of Banbury) died in Paris 1818, æt. 38; as her husband, who lost his title in 1813, did in 1834, æt. 70. M.I. to them and some children in Winchester Cathedral.

Margaret Blackwell, the youngest daughter, died at Dover unmarried; was living 1816.

Nathaniel S. J. J. Blackwell and Jane Jarvis had three sons and two daughters:—

1. Thomas Eden Blackwell who died at Bath 22 Dec. 1845, æt. 42, leaving three daughters still living by his wife Elizabeth, who remarried at Bath, 2 Aug. 1853, the Rev. Arthur Maister, and died s.p. by him 189–.
2. Robert Edward Blackwell, Rector of Amberley, co. Gloucester, married Caroline Barbara Frith; died 1872.
3. William Whitehead Blackwell of Mells, co. Somerset, married Jane Lindsey Oct. 1834.

1. Jane Mary Blackwell, born 1811.
2. Theodosia Blackwell, died 1822.

Jane, wife of Nathaniel S. J. J. Blackwell, died 8 June 1862.

Page 99. Mrs. Sarah Hussey Gunman of Doddington Hall by her will, dated 27 Aug. 1824, bequeathed all her estate to her friend Lieut.-Colonel George R. P. Jarvis. He died 14 June 1851, æt. 77. Philadelphia his first wife had predeceased him 7 March 1816 at Dover. He married his second wife in 1830, and she died at Bath 17 Jan. 1867, æt. 91. For further information consult 'The History of Doddington,' by R. E. G. Cole, M.A., 1897.

Jacob Jarvis married firstly Grace Nibbs; his daughter Ann died single at Dover 1863.

John Swinton Jarvis was born 8 Oct. 1761 and died about 1844. His son William H. Jarvis died a bachelor in the West Indies. His son John A. Jarvis was buried 11 July 1828 at St. Andrew's, co. Fife. His daughter Mary M. Jarvis married Major George R. White. His youngest daughter Abigail Hardman Jarvis, born 1820, married Thomas Bell of Belmont, Dundee.

Mrs. Rachel North died at Quedgley Rectory, co. Gloucester, March 1856, æt. 70.

Mary Wilhelmina Jarvis married July 1835 and died at Winchester 16 July 1884, æt. 82, leaving two daughters Mary and Ella.

Grace Jarvis died single at Minchinhampton, co. Gloucester, 14 May 1869.

Page 100. John and Rachel Wilkins had issue: 1, Thomas; 2, Oswald; 3, Jackman; 4, Martin; 5, Louisa or Rachel who married first Lieut. Macquarie, by whom she had a daughter Louisa; and secondly . . . .

Elizabeth Jarvis married Archibald Gloster, Attorney-General of Trinidad.

David Scott of St. Andrew's and Antigua. 1st husband. ═ Christiana Jarvis, died at Southampton 31 Aug. 1842. ═ Major-General William Maddox Richardson, mar. at Bath 9 Nov. 1808. 2nd husband.

(by 2nd husband) s.p.

Children of David Scott and Christiana Jarvis:
- Thomas Scott of Tobago, died at Winchester 10 Dec. 1808, æt. 25.
- Eliza Scott, dead.
- Alexander Scott, died at Bath 1859. ═ Maria Elcock.

Children of Alexander Scott and Maria Elcock:
- Alexander Scott, mar. . . . . Wiltshire.
- Oswald Scott, died June 1828.
- George Sidney Scott, died in London May 1892. ═ . . . . (issue)
- Temple Scott, dead.
- Jackman Scott, mar. . . . . Gordon.
- Maria Harriet Scott.

Thomas Bell, J.P. of Belmont, Dundee, and Rossie, Fergandenry, Perthshire, born 1812; died 1887. Of the firm of Thomas Bell and Sons of Dundee. ═ Abigail Hardman, youngest child of John Swinton Jarvis of Antigua; born 1820; mar. 12 Feb. 1845 at St. Andrew's, co. Fife; died 4 May 1883; bur. at Dundee.

Children:
- Thomas Bell of Hazelwood, Broughton Ferry, North Britain, born 1848. ═ Jane Marshall, elder dau. of the late John Sharp, J.P., D.L., of Balmuir, co. Forfar; mar. 9 Sep. 1874.
- James Harriott Bell. — John William Bell. — Charles Hope Bell.
- George Jarvis Bell. — Edwin Weston Bell, died a bachelor 1894.
- Abigail Frances Jarvis Bell, only dau., mar. 1876. ═ David Robertson Soutar Kirkland.

Children of Thomas Bell and Jane Marshall:
- Thomas Norman Jarvis Bell, born 1879. — John Ronald Jarvis Bell, born 1894.
- Christian Rosa Bell, born 1875. — Evelyn Frances Jarvis Bell, born 1876.

Children of David Robertson Soutar Kirkland and Abigail Frances Jarvis Bell:
- John Luke Chaplin Kirkland. — Thomas Bell Kirkland.
- Abigail Hardman Kirkland. — Daisy Margaret Soutar Kirkland.
- Dorothea Mary Jarvis Kirkland. — Ethel Alice Jarvis Kirkland.

Dorothy Jarvis married, 11 March 1789, James Morley of the Bombay Civil Service; she died at Winchester 1 Nov. 1850, æt. 83; and he at Bath 22 Jan. 1798, æt. 55. M.I. to them and family in Winchester Cathedral. They had issue:—

1. Maria Morley, fourth daughter, who married 1815 Hon. Colonel Donald Ogilvie, son of the seventh Earl of Airlie, and died 1843.
2. Charles Morley.
3. Harriet Morley, who married Brownlow Poulter and had issue Brownlow and Dorothea Poulter.
(? 4.) Sarah, who married 1802 Sir William Ogilvy, eighth Bart., and died 26 May 1854.

Jane Jarvis married General Macquarie, Governor of New South Wales.

Notes contributed in 1895 by Thomas Bell, Esq., of Broughty Ferry:—

Old John Weston Died the 3rd February 1797, aged 61 Years.

Wm Blizard Jarvis Born 4th December 1759.

Abigail Nanton Weston, born 18th May 1774, & was married to Wm B. Jarvis the 24th July 1793.

Mary Jarvis, Daughter to W. B. Jarvis & A. N. Jarvis, was born Friday 27th Febry. 1795 at half past nine o'clock in the morning, & was Christened the 26th April following. Alexr Coates, Wm Mathew, Henry Jarvis, Ab. Picart, Walter Thibon, Edwd Barnes, God Fathers. Mrs Weston, Miss M. Nibbs, Mrs W. Weston, Mrs Mathew, God Mothers. She was Called Mary after Mr Jarvis' Mother.

11th xr 1798 Sophia Otto Jarvis was born at 11 o'clock P.M., was Christened 29 May 1799.

My Dear Mother Catherine Hanson Weston Died the 17th September at ½ past 9 A.M. 1803 & was buried last of the large . . . . directly opposite the North door of the Battery Church, Sunday.

Prayer Book. Abigail Nanton Jarvis. Antigua, 1794.

My dear Husband William Blizard Jarvis died the 23rd of March 1811.

My dear daughter Mary was married the 25th of January 1812, & on the 1st of December a fine Girl.

My dear Mother was married to Mr Hardman Aug. 22, 1818.

My dear Mother died March 9th, 1820, much regretted by her dear, fond children, who ever will lament the loss of so good a parent.

Died on Wednesday Morning the 8th inst. Mrs Abigail Nanton Hardman after a very sudden & short illness of only 24 hours. This lady was not only esteemed & respected by all who knew her, but she was most sincerely beloved by her Family & those Friends with whom she was most intimate. The goodness of her heart & the benignity of her conduct rendered her truly amiable, & her loss will ever be felt with the deepest sorrow among her family, for as a parent she was truly affectionate, & as a wife her Death will be remembered with the most heartfelt regret.

On Saturday last departed this life, after a long and painful illness, William B. Jarvis, Esq., for many Years Captain & Master Gunner of Fort James; the many amiable qualities which he possessed endeared him not only to his numerous relatives & friends, but to those strangers who, from the situation he held, so frequently experienced his generous heart & hospitable roof. He was a kind and affectionate husband & father, & a humane Master. His remains were interred on the North side of the Fort, followed by a most numerous & respectable assemblage of the inhabitants of the Island, who seemed to feel with the greatest regret the loss of so worthy & honourable a Member of Society.

In a testament (published 1822): "The Gift of John Swinton Jarvis to his son John Arthur Jarvis. Antigua, April 10th, 1828."

John Swinton Jarvis, born 8th October 1761.

July 19th, 1830, M. Jarvis.

My dear girl Abigail sailed in the Strathmore 3rd August 1831.

James Jarvis married Laura Campbell 3rd Febry 1831.

My dear Girl Mary arrived here on the 6th August, & my dear Sister Married on the 4th Do to James Norman 1832.

Miss Mary Martin Jarvis.

Mount Joshua was purchased by the President from one Joshua Burket, & the first letter he wrote Burket after from Joshua's (Mount Joshua) Burket got in a terrible passion.

In a small testament: "Jane Ogilvy of Clova, 1828."

St. Andrew's Parish, co. Fife.

8th February 1845. Were Contracted Thomas Bell, Merchant, of the Parish of Dundee, & Abigail Hardman* of this Parish. [They were married 12 Feb. 1845.] (General Registry Office, Edinburgh.)

John son of Colonel Jarvis, late from the West Indies, died on the 9th & was buried 11th of July 1828. (*Ibid.*)

George Ralph Payne Jarvis.

Jarvis: impaling, 1, Blackwell; 2, Sturges.

Mr. Thomas Bell sent me impressions of the three following seals:—

1. Crest and arms of Jarvis singly, with cinquefoils, not mullets.

2. Crest of Jarvis only in an oval.

3. Crest: *A stag lodged.* Arms: *Argent, six ostrich feathers, three, two, and one;* impaling, *Argent, on a chevron sable three crescents.*

JEAFFRESON. Page 106.

Christopher Jeaffreson, who died 1748. M.I. at Dullingham, also to Elizabeth his wife, who died 12 July 1778, æt. 78.

Christopher Jeaffreson died 1789, æt. 55. M.I. at Dullingham. Sarah his wife died 10 June 1792, æt. 62. M.I. at Dullingham.

Sarah Elizabeth Jeaffreson died 11 May 1804, æt. 40. M.I. at Dullingham.

Christopher Jeaffreson died Oct. 1824, æt. 63. M.I. to him and his wife Henrietta at Dullingham.

For further notes see Davy's Suffolk Collections, Add. MS. 19,137, fos. 141—9.

* The name Jarvis was here inserted after the entry was made.

JOHNSON. Page 111.

PARISH REGISTER OF LEE, CO. KENT.

Married.

1739-40 Jan. 1 John Johnson of St. Lawrence, near Guildhall, London, and Elizabeth Ann Warner of East Greenwich.

1746 Sep. 22 Edward Warner of St. Mary-le-Bow, London, and Katherine Johnson of Eltham; by Mr. Brian of Greenwich.

[Mem.—18 May 1767. The name of the Clergyman who married the above-named parties was Francis Byham, as Mrs. Warner informs me.—J. L., Rector.]

1788, Nov. The lady of Godschall Johnson, esq. of Bloomsbury square. ('Town and Country Mag.,' p. 580.)

1863, March 11. At Teneriffe, Canary Islands (at the house of her brother, Robt. Godschall Johnson, esq., H.M.'s Consul for that port), aged 27, Mary Godschall, dau. of the late Godschall Johnson, esq. many years H.M.'s Consul at Antwerp. ('Gent. Mag.,' p. 667.)

1865, June 28. At Montreal, Frank Travers, esq. Capt. 60th Royal Rifles, third son of the late Adm. Sir Eaton Travers, of Great Yarmouth, Norfolk, to Laura Wellwood, eldest dau. of Francis Godschall Johnson, esq. Judge of the Superior Court, L.C. (*Ibid.*, p. 235.)

John Godschall of London, merchant, and of East Sheen, co. Surrey, died 1691, leaving by Jane his wife an eldest son John, also of London, Turkey Merchant, and of East Sheen, who married at Westminster Abbey, 27 Sep. 1681, Bathia Charleton, and died 10 Oct. 1725 (Will P.C.C., 210 Romney), leaving, with other issue, a daughter Sarah, then widow of William Johnson of London.

KER. Page 118.

Colonel John Ker, who died 1731, was aged 59 in 1713.

John Ker, Colonel of the 38th Regiment, married Elizabeth second daughter of Chief Justice Samuel Watkins, and had five children.

Samuel W. Ker married Mary daughter of . . . . Furlong.

John Yeamans sold his share of Kerrs in 1752 to Dr. Patrick Grant, and Simon Farley his share (39 acres, at £80 per acre) to Mr. Jeaffreson.

Dr. S. A. Apreece, born 17 Dec. 1773, died v.p. 5 Dec. 1807 at Malvern.

Lady Davy died 8 May 1855.

(See Cole's 'History of Doddington, co. Lincoln.')

KERBY. Page 120.

For Francis *read* Mrs. Frances Stoughton.

Mrs. Hamilton Kerby died 26 April 1804 in Castle Street, Southwark.

Sarah Kerby married R. Pott in 1781.

PARISH REGISTER OF ST. JOHN, ANTIGUA.

Buried.

1758 May 11 Benjamin Kerby.

1759 May 16 Elizabeth Kirby.

KING. Page 125.

Nathaniel King of Nevis. Will dated 25 Jan. 1686-7. (139 Foot.) To be buried in St John's churchyard. £200 c. for a school, & to my trustees Mr Tho. Salt, minister, Lt-Col. John Netheway, Capt. Philip Lee, Esq., & Mr Joseph Loyd, mercht, £200 for the maintenance of 2 poor children. My brother Richd King & my sister Mary Chauncye's children moneys in the hands of Mr Henry Loyd of Bristol. My cozen Nathl King, son of my uncle Fulke King, my refining house.

Testator's sister Mary married Ichabod Chauncy, M.D., of Bristol, who died 1691, æt. 56. There is a very complete pedigree of his family in Dr. Howard's 'Mis. Gen. et Her.,' vol. i., Second Series, pp. 21—30, with arms and brasses.

KIRWAN. Page 128.

John F. Kirwan was appointed a Member of the Council Oct. 1867.

KNIGHT. Page 132.

Christopher Knight is supposed to have been a Quaker from co. Somerset. His second wife Margaret was widow of Henry Hodge. Christian, widow of his son Christopher Knight, married 23 Oct. 1718 John Price, whose will was dated 28 Nov. 1733, sworn 8 March 1733-4, by whom she had a daughter Christian Price, then under 17.

LAFERTY. Page 135.

Mr. Henry Wagner, F.S.A., kindly gave me the reference to the will of Francis De Monsallier of St. Leonard's, Shoreditch, merchant, dated 5 May 1725; proved 13 March 1729 by Lucy Pages and Elizabeth Fludyer the daughters. (61 Auber.) To my dau. Lucy Pages, wife of Solomon Pages, clerk, £600. My dau. Anna Maria Picart de Laferty, widow, £400. My dau. Eliz. Fludyer, widow, £500. My dau. Judith Romilly, wife of Stephen Romilly, mercht. All residue to my said 4 daus. My 2 daus. Lucy Pages & Eliz. Fludyer, Ex'trices. Witnessed by James de Val Frambert, Philippe Pittart, Anne Deval Frambert.

2nd Codicil dated 13 Oct. 1726.

The will of J. Barbottain was also proved P.C.C. (226 Romney).

LAFOREY. Page 136.

(159 Coke.) John de la fforest, chirurgeon, of the Prince of Orange. The Hague.

LANGFORD. Page 140.

The crest, as depicted on a wooden shield of arms at Mere Hall, is: *A demi-shoveller with wings displayed argent.* I have also an old eighteenth century seal of Oliver, impaling Langford, which must have been my great-great-grandfather's or else his father's. The same arms are also impaled in a lozenge on a silver salver in my possession bearing the date letter of 1802.

Page 142. John Collins matriculated from Queen's College, Oxford, 7 July 1739, æt. 17.

Page 156. William Langford of Ludlow "de bonis non" grant 1564. Margery his wife. Sentence 1556, 10 Ketchyn.

Thomas Rowland, merchant. Will dated 20 April 1584; proved P.C.C. 21 April 1586. 7th dau. Elizth. Godson & son-in-law Richard Langford.

PARISH REGISTER OF ST. STEPHEN, BRISTOL.

Married.

1581 Nov. 30 Thomas Rowland and Elizabeth Langford.

She was probably the widow of Richard Langford, who died 1580.

Will of John Rowland proved 18 May 1576 P.C.C. Bro. Nichs Langford & sister Joan his wife.

Jane Langforde, sick in the house of Thomas Slade of West Pennarde, co. Somerset. Nuncupative will dated 3 Dec. 1578; proved 6 May 1581 by Christopher Robinson, Notary Public, Attorney of Henry Hooper, Ex'or. (17 Darcy.) Church of West Pennarde 3*s.* 4*d.*; to each carrying her corpse 12d; ringers 12d. James Hooper her godson, son of Henry Hooper her brother-in-law, £20, & to his son Silvester Hooper £10. Henrie Langford her brother & Isodd Langford her sister equally between them £3. Wieffe of the said Tho. Slade 26*s.* 8*d.* above all charges, & to each of her children 2*s.* Sir John Gosse, Vicar or Curate of the parish church of Woodyates, co. Dorset, where she was borne, 6*s.* 8*d.* Her goddau. Jane Knighte, dau. of one Knighte dwelling about Crookethorne, co. Som., 6*s.* 8*d.*; every other of her godchildren 12d. Widow Slade of Botleye, co. Som., 5*s.* Joane Hooper *als* Laungforde, her sister, wieffe of the said Henrie Hooper, all apparel. To Laurence Walter, surgeon, £4. All residue of goods, cattall, etc., to Henry Hooper & Ex'or. Witnessed by William Guppye of Botlye, said widow Slade. Sentence annexed.

1578, Jan. 27. John Draper the elder, merchant. Richard Langford an overseer.

Robert Thorner of Baddesley, co. Southampton, Gent. Will dated 31 May, proved 8 Dec. 1690. (211 Dyke.) My lands at Pitton, co. Wilts, after my wife's death to Ellis Langford, son of Harry Langford, now in Jamaica, but if he be then dead to Edward Langford of London, goldsmith.

1652. John Langford of Pentridge, co. Dorset, deceased. Adm'on 4 May to Ellis Langford, cousin german and next-of-kin.

Chancery Inquisition p.m., 2 Edw. VI., Part 2, No. 83.

Henry Langford.

Dorset. Inquisition taken at Shurborn in the said county 8 Nov. 2 Edward VI. [1548] before Nicholas Halswell, Esq., escheator after the death of Henry Langford, by the oath of William Gerard, Esq., John Chandill, Esq., etc., jurors, who say that Henry Langeford was seised of the lordships and manors of Woddyattes and Gussage St. Andro within the parishes of Woddyattes and Iwerne in the said county, of the rectory of Woddyattes together with the advowson of the vicarage of Woddyattes, and three messuages, 200 acres of land, 30 acres of meadow, 100 acres of pasture, and 40 acres of wood in Pentryge and Wooddyattes, which the said Henry lately purchased of Richard Snell in his demesne as of fee.

The said manors of Woddyattes and Gussage St. Andro, the said rectory, and all the premises to the said manors belonging, are held of the King in chief by the service of the fortieth part of a knight's fee, and are worth per annum clear £13 9s. 10½d.

The said premises in Pentryge and Woddyattes are held of the King as of his manor of Cranborne in free socage, and not in chief, to wit, by fealty suit at court and the yearly rent of 2s., and are worth per annum clear £4 3s. 4d.

Henry Langeford died 27th day of August last past; William Langford is his son and next heir, and was aged 17 years on the last day of Nov. 1 Edward VI. [1547].

The following Pedigree corrects the one on page 157, but it is still very incomplete:—

HENRY LANGFORD, had a patent for lands 36 Henry VIII. (1545); died 27 Aug. last. Chancery Inq. p.m., 8 Nov., 2 Edward VI. (1548), seised of Manors of Woodyate and Gussage St. Andrew in Woodyate and Iwern, worth £13 9s. 10d. yearly; Rectory and advowson of the Vicarage of Woodyate; three messuages, 200 acres land, 30 acres meadow, 100 acres pasture, 40 acres wood, in Pentridge and Woodyate, worth £4 3s. 4d. yearly; all lands lately purchased of Richard Snell. ⚭ ....

Henry Langford, levies fine 30 Elizabeth (1588) on his Manor of Woodyate, with Rectory and advowson, and on one messuage, 1000 acres land, 50 acres meadow, 300 acres pasture, 150 acres wood, 100 acres heath, in Pentridge and Handley. ⚭ Susanna ...., party to fine 1588.

John Langford, trustee before 1585 for Ellis; died 1613. (67 Capell.) ⚭ Margaret ....

William Langford, son and heir, æt. 17 on 30 Nov. 1547; had livery of above lands 6 Edward VI., 1553. (Hutchins.)

Ellis Langford, Gent., died 3 April last, Chancery Inq. p.m. 7 June, 27 Elizabeth (1585), seised of the Manor of Gussage St. Andrew and one messuage, 200 acres land, 10 acres meadow, 300 acres pasture, 20 acres wood, in Iwern, worth £5 14s. 10d. yearly; bur. at Handley. Will dated 24 Dec., 23 Elizabeth; codicil 3 April 1585; proved P.C.C. (20 Brudenell.) ⚭ Joan Fry, sole Ex'trix 1585.

Bernard Langford of Pentridge, died 1605, v.p. (32 Hayes.) See Chancery suit, Knapton v. Fry, 1621. ⚭ Mary, dau. of John Pyne.

William Langford, 1st son and heir, æt. 18 on 23 Dec. 1584; held his father's manor and lands in 1588, which he alienated before 35 Elizabeth (1593); gave a 99 years' lease of his 284 acres 17 Jac. I. (1619); of New Sarum, late of Gussage, Gent., and æt. 55 in 1621; he was a Minister in 1622; died at Gussage 31 Aug. 1630. Inq. p.m. 4 April, 7 Car. I. (1631). In Hutchins he is called son and heir of Elizabeth, an error apparently for *Elizeus* or Ellis. ⚭ Elizabeth, dau. of John Pyne; living 1669; had dower of lands in Gussage.

Gideon Langford.

Henry Langford, æt. 40 in 1621.

Thomas Langford.

Ellis Langford.

Others.

John Langford, Gent., heir to his grandfather John 1613; died at Pentridge 26 Sep. last, Chancery Inq. p.m. 16 July, 11 Car. I. (1635), seised of the identical lands in Pentridge and Woodyate of £4 3s. 4d. yearly, which the first Henry had in 1548. ⚭ ....

Ellis Langford of Pitton in Alderbury, Wilts, Gent., son and heir, æt. over 27 in 1630; he and his cousin Arthur sold Gussage in 1664; died 1669. (143 Coke.) ⚭ Helena ....

Arthur Langford, son and heir, æt. 3 years 5 months 3 days at his father's death 1635; joined with his "cousin" Ellis 1664 in sale of Manor of Gussage for £1200.

Ellis Langford, son and heir, dead 1688. Had an only child Mary. See Chancery suit of Gostlett v. Langford 26 Nov., 1 William and Mary (1688). ⚭ Jane .... s.p.m.

Edward Langford of London, goldsmith, 1690.

Harry Langford of Jamaica 1690. ⚭ .... (? remar. Jonas Langford of Antigua).

Benjamin Langford.

Ellis Langford, heir 1690 to Robert Thorner of Pitton; godson of F. Rose of Jamaica 1693, then under 10 (? died at Antigua 1710-11).

THE BURIAL GROUND OF THE LANGFORD FAMILY
AT CASSADA GARDEN.

Chancery Inquisition p.m., 27 Eliz., Part 1, No. 119.

Elizeus Langford, Gentleman.

Dorset. Inquisition taken at Shireborne in the said county 7 June 27 Elizabeth [1585] before Edmund Wyndham, Esq., escheator after the death of Elizeus Langford, Gentleman, by the oath of Francis Whitington, Gentleman, Jasper Furlock, etc., jurors, who say that Elizeus Langford was seised in his demesne as of fee-tail of the manor of Gussage St. Andrew within the parish of Iwerne *alias* Iwerne Minster, and one messuage, one garden, one orchard, 200 acres of land, 10 acres of meadow, 300 acres of pasture, and 20 acres of wood in Iwerne Minster in county Dorset.

All the said premises are held of the Queen in chief, but by what part of a knight's fee the jurors know not, and are worth per annum clear £5 14s. 10½*d*.

Elizeus Langford died 3 April last past; William Langford is his son and next heir, and was aged 18 years on the 23rd day of Dec. last past.

Joan, late the wife of the said Elizeus, still survives.

Feet of Fines, P.R.O., Easter, 30 Eliz. [1588], Dorset.

Between James Howper, Gent., querent, and Henry Langford, Gent., and Susanna his wife, and Thomas Michell, Gent., deforcients.

Of the manor of Westwoodyatte *alias* Woodeate, and of the Rectory of ditto, and of one messuage, two dovecotes, one garden, one orchard, 1000 acres of land, 50 acres meadow, 300 acres pasture, 150 acres wood, and 100 acres heath and furze in ditto, Pentridge, and Handley, besides the advowson of the church of West Woodyatte *alias* Woodeate.

Plea of covenant summoned Henry Langford and Susanna his wife and Thomas Michell, recognise the manor and rectory and advowson to be the right of James Howper, as those which said James had of gift of Henry and Susanna Langford and Thomas Michell, and they remit and quitclaim from said Henry and Susanna Langford and Thomas Michell and heirs, and said Henry for ever, and warrant said James Howper against Henry and Susanna Langford and heirs of Henry, against said Thomas Michell and his heirs, and v. Francis Browne, arm., and his heirs, and v. Richard Wyvell, Gent., and Iseta his wife and heirs of Iseta, and v. Henry Howper, Gent., and Joan his wife and heirs of Joan for ever, and for this warrant and fine James gave Henry and Susanna Langford and Thomas Michell £160. (Sent me by Mr. E. A. Fry.)

There is a pedigree of Hooper of Boveridge in the 1623 'Visitation of Dorset.'

Chancery Inquisition p.m., 7 Chas. I., Part 1, No. 83.

William Langford.

Dorset. Inquisition taken at Sherborne in the said county 4 April 7 Charles I. [1631] before William Cox, Gentleman, escheator after the death of William Langford, by the oath of Robert Whetcombe, Gentleman, Richard Coothe, Gentleman, etc., jurors, who say that William Langford was seised in his demesne as of fee of the manor, capital messuage, and farm of Gussage St. Andree in county Dorset. So seised the said William Langford and John Penny by indentures dated 30 Dec. 17 James I. [1619] made between themselves by the names of William Langford of Gussage St. Andree in county Dorset, Gentleman, and John Penny of Stoke Verdon in county Wilts, Gentleman, of the one part, and Nicholas Morcombe of Blandford Forum in county Dorset, of the other part, in consideration of £250, to them in hand paid, granted to the said Nicholas the said manor for 99 years, he paying yearly for the same 4*d*.

To corroborate the said estate and term the said William Langford and Elizabeth his wife afterwards, to wit, in the Octaves of St. Hilary 17 James I., levied a fine at Westminster between the said Nicholas Morcombe, plaintiffs, and the said William and Elizabeth, deforcients, of the said premises by the name of one messuage, two barns, one garden, one orchard, 80 acres of land, 4 acres of meadow, and 200 acres of pasture in Gussage St. Andree and Handley, whereby they acknowleged the said premises to be the right of the said Nicholas, and the same remised to him and his heirs for ever.

The said manor and premises are held of the King in chief by the 100th part of a knight's fee, and are worth per annum clear during the said term 4*d*., but afterwards £3.

William Langford died at Gussage St. Andree the last day of Aug. 1630; Elizeus Langford, Gentleman, is his son and next heir, and was then aged 27 years and more.

Chancery Inquisition p.m., V. O., 11 Chas. I., Part 21, No. 91.

John Langford, Gentleman.

Dorset. Inquisition taken at Blandford Forum in the said county 16 July 11 Charles I. [1635] before Robert Hooper, Gentleman, escheator by virtue of his office after the death of John Langford, Gentleman, by the oath of William Clarke, Gentleman, Robert Chapman, etc., jurors, who say that John Langford was seised in his demesne as of fee of three messuages, 200 acres of land, 30 acres of meadow, 100 acres of pasture, and 40 acres of wood in Pentridge and Woodyates in the said county, which said premises are held of William, Earl of Salisbury, as of his honor of Gloucester, by knight's service, but by what part of a knight's fee the jurors know not; they are worth per annum clear £4 3s. 4*d*.

John Langford died at Pentridge 26 Sep. last past; Arthur Langford is his son and next heir, and was then aged 3 years 5 months and 3 days.

Gulielmus et Maria Rex & Regina, etc. Jane Langford, Maria Langford datm. cumquisdam ordo. coram nob. in cur. canc. nup. fact. riddit extitit in hec verba Lime vicesimo sexto die Nov. Anno quatro regni Jacobi Regis secundi.* Inter Elizam. Gostlet vid relict Benj. Gostlet Johem Harrington art. et Hellena ux ejus George Adams et Mariam ux ejus Elizam Gostlet spin Johem Gostlet & John Chetwin Quer, Janam Langford & Marian Langford, defendants. This cause coming this present day to be heard and debated in the presence of council, learned on both sides, the scope of the plaintiffs' bill appeared to be that on the fifth of Feb. 1661 Benjamin Gostlet made his will, and thereby (after some small leavings) gave the residue of his personal estate to the plaintiffs, Elizabeth his relict and Hellen, Mary, and Elizabeth his children, to the end that his executors in . . . . all convenient speed after his decease, purchase some lands in fee and settle the same to the uses following, viz., one moyety to the use of the plaintiff Elizabeth his relict for her life, and after her decease to the plaintiffs his children and their heirs share and share alike, and the other moyety he willed should be by his executors divided into so many parts as he should leave children, and to come immediately to them and their heirs share and share alike, but under several provisoes, and of his will appointed the said plaintiffs, John Gostlet, Chetwyn, together with Richard Thorne and Thomas Stearne, who are both since deceased, his executors in trust, and shortly after died, leaving only issue the said plaintiffs Hellen, Mary, and Elizabeth, and all the said executors undertook the trust, and pursuant thereto by Indentures of lease and release bearing date 30 April and 2 May 16 Charles II., and made between Ellis Langford and Arthur Langford, cousin of the

* Monday, 26 Nov. 4 James II. [1688].

said Ellis, of the first part, the said trustees, of the second part, and the said plaintiff Elizabeth Gostlet, of the third part, they, the said Ellis and Arthur Langford, in consideration of £1200 paid by the said trustees, being the said residue, did by the said Indenture and a fine thereupon levyed unto the said trustees and their heirs in trust for the said plaintiff the widow and the said other plaintiffs the children, all that the manor, capital messuage, demeanse, lands, and farm of Gussage with the appurt'ances in county Dorset, except some small cottages and lands, parcel of the said manor, and a counterpart of the said conveyance was sealed by the said trustees to the said Langfords, and the original deeds deposited in the hands of the said Ellis Langford, and the plaintiffs have ever since quietly enjoyed the said premises, but the said conveyances to the said trustees being left in the hands of the said plaintiff Adams, he, the said Adams, in the time of troubles in the West, to secure the said conveyances put them under ground, where they suffered so great damage by water that the letters thereof were quite wore out and the said deeds not legible. And the said Ellis Langford the vendor being dead, leaving Ellis his son and heir, who is also since dead, leaving only issue the defendant Mary and the other defendant Jane his relict, who have possessed themselves of the said original deeds and also of the said counterpart. And the said plaintiffs the children, being all come to one and twenty years, have consented to sell the premises and applyed themselves to the defendants for a copy of the counterparts, and also the said original deeds for the . . . . of a purchase. But the defendants, notwithstanding they claim no interest in any part of the said premises thereby mentioned to be conveyed as aforesaid, refused to produce the same. Therefore that the defendants may bring into court the said counterpart, also the said original deeds, that the plaintiffs may have authentic copies to be made use of in law or as occasion shall require, and to be relieved in the premises is the end of the Bill. Whereupon it was . . . . the defendants' counsel that the said defendants do by answer confess there was such agreement between the executors of Benjamine Gostlet and Ellis Langford for purchasing the manor of Gussage, with the appurtenances, and such conveyance thereon executed as in the Bill, and confess they have the original deeds relating to the premises in their custody, and also the counterparts of the plaintiffs' deed of purchase which they insist on the keeping of for maintenance of their [title] to the excepted premises in the Bill mentioned. Whereupon and upon hearing all what could be alledged on either side, it is hereby [ordered that?] said defendants do produce upon oath before Baron William Child, one of the masters of this court, all the deeds and writings which they have or ever had in their custody touching the estate in question or any part thereof, to the end the plaintiffs may have authentic copies of such of them as they shall think fit at their own charge, and that the counterpart of the plaintiffs' said deed of purchase from the Langfords bee, at the plaintiffs' charge, enrolled for safe custody, and the plaintiffs are to have such of the original deeds as the said master shall find belong solely to them. And the said master is also to tax the defendants their costs.

Vobis igit. p'fat Jane Langford and Marie Langford, etc. (order to enforce Jane and Mary to obey under pains and penalties, etc.). (Sent me by Mr. E. A. Fry.)

LAVINGTON. Page 166.

Jonah Lavington of Plymouth, co. Devon, apothecary. Will dated 31 May 1707; proved 29 March 1709 by John Lavington the son. (62 Lane.) Wife Kath. £100 & messuages, etc., in Ermington. My son John Lavington. Son-in-l. John Hunkyn & dau. Abigail his wife. Dau. Susanna Lavington £500. Brother Jonathan Lavington of Exon, sergemaker, £5, & to his children 1 g^{a} each. Andrew, John, & Jane Lavington, sons & dau. of my late brother John Tucker, deceased, 1 g. each. All residue to my son John, & Ex'or.

LEE. Page 172.

Obadiah Adney of London, Gent. Will dated 10 June 1689; proved 26 Feb. 1691 by Nathaniel Gale. (21 Fane.) My friend Mr Nathl Gale of London, brazier, after my father's death, all my estate in Wenlock, Kinton, & Alderton, co. Salop, now mortgaged for £300 to John Cook of Chishull, co. Essex, & all residue, & Ex'or. My friend Mr Ebenezer Tull, ser^{r}, in King Street, Guildhall, 10s. Witnessed by Richard Wootton, Thomas Bendish, jun., Thomas Simpson, King Street.

Richard Adney of London, Esq. Will dated 1726. (115 Plymouth.) Cozen Benj. Adney, s. of John Adney of co. Salop.

LEONARD. Page 175.

John Lennard (or Leonard) of St. Andrew, Holborne, jun., mariner. Will dated 24 Feb. 1715; proved 20 March 1721. (48 Marlboro'.) My father John Lennard 20s., & my mother Eliz. Lennard £200. All residue to my brothers Thos. & Henry & sister Jane Lennard equally. My bro. Tho. & sister Jane Ex'ors. Witnessed by Mary Rogers, Jane Griffiths.

Codicil. 7 June 1718. Now resident at Antigua. Wm Hill, esq., & Bartholomew Sanderson, merchants, Ex'ors here. Witnessed by Jn. Barke, Robert Smith, Samuel Nixon, William Hinde. By Governor Hamilton sworn 21 Sep. 1721 by William Hinde. Affidavit of George Jennings of Antigua, Gent., notary public. On 16 March 1721 appeared Thomas Leonard of Lyons' Inn, Gent., and Jane Leonard, spinster.

1752, Feb. 3. Dr. Walter Tullideph writes from Antigua to Mr. George Leonard at Tortola, where he was settling a new plantation, and living separated from his family: "Your boy George's education in England, your wife indisposed, Miss Ruth, your mother ailing, your works much injured by the hurricane, Dr. Turnbull makes a demand of your sister Turnbull's fortune in favour of his two sons." George was later sent to Cambridge.

1717. Anthony Fahie 200 acres and 90 negros in the French quarter of St. Kitts, but no land in the English quarter.

1777, Dec. George Fahie, Esq; in New Marybone street. ('Town and Country Mag.,' p. 715.)

Anthony Fahie, son of Antony Fahie of Isle of St. Christopher, Esq., Queen's College, matriculated 21 April 1738, aged 16.

1794, Jan. 18. In her 23d year, in the bloom of youth, beauty, and acknowledged worth, Mrs. Eleonara Leonard, daughter of the Hon. Henry Martin, late president of his Majesty's Virgin islands, and the wife of the Hon. George Leonard, the present president of the same government. She was buried, on the 19th, near the remains of her father, with all the honours and due solemnity which could be paid by a community conscious of the virtues which most cordially had endeared her to all ranks of inhabitants. ('Gent. Mag.,' p. 384.)

1833, Jan. 11. At Bermuda, in his 70th year, Sir William Charles Fahie, K.C.B. and K.F.M., Vice-Admiral of the Blue. Long notice follows. His wife d. Ap. 1817. (*Ibid.*, p. 561.)

1895, Nov. 16. At her residence on Balham-hill, Caroline Constance Carey, widow of Surgeon-Major Langer Carey, M.D., late R.A. and Royal Munster Fusiliers, daughter of the late Captain John Wilson, R.N., and granddaughter of Admiral Sir Wm. Chas. Fahie, K.C.B., late Commander-in-Chief in North America and the West Indies.

LESSLY. Page 178.

1768. (34 Secker.) Thomas Somers refers to Colonel Andrew Leslie, late of Antegoa, who has since come to England, and is residing in Little Chelsey, owes me a considerable sum.

LIGHTFOOT. Page 181.

Samuel Lightfoot married firstly Elizabeth, secondly Susannah Tremill.

1788, March. Geo. Cornelius Swann, esq. of York. ('Town and Country Mag.,' p. 196.)

LIVINGSTON. Page 190.

1774, March 21. William Levingstone, Esq; at Antigua. ('Town and Country Mag.,' p. 336.)

1803, July 25. At Spanish-town, Jamaica, the Hon. Francis Rigby Brodbelt, esq. to Miss Milward, daugh. of John Gardner M. esq. of the same place. ('Gent. Mag.,' 1804, p. 277.)

LOVELL. Page 196.

Michael Lovell was chairman 6 Oct. 1773 when Richard Oliver was polling for office of Lord Mayor. See 'Gent. Mag.,' p. 516, for his speech, also as to Charles Crauford of Antigua having publicly caned him.

LUCAS. Page 200.

Thomas Lucas of Hammersmith. Will dated 1718. (110 Browning.) To be buried in the vault with my father & mother in the church-yard of S[t] Peter's, Ipswich. My uncle Charles Lucas of Norwich, if living, £100. My aunt Mason of Norwich £100. Children of my late uncle Tho. Lucas £100.

Samuel Lucas of Bury St. Edmunds, co. Suffolk, clothier. Will dated 1728. (295 Brook.) Lands at Colchester, Ipswich. Bro. Joseph. Sister Sarah Darby.

John Lucas of Norwich, worsted weaver. Will dated 1738. (285 Brodrepp.) Brother Gibson Lucas. Brother Rich[d] Gay Lucas, clerk of G[t] Yarmouth.

Elizabeth Lucas of Bromley Street, St. Andrew, Holborn, spinster. Will dated 15 Feb. 1739; proved 22 Aug. 1740 by Elizabeth Bartholomew. (230 Brown.) To be buried in the parish church of Colekirk, co. Norfolk, in the grave of my mother Eliz. Lucas. Mrs. Eliz. Bartleme the £40 due by legacy from my cozen Lucas of Antegue, & my father's & mother's picture. M[rs] Merry 1 g[a]. M[rs] Anna Maria Scott of Islington, spinster, 3 g[as]. M[rs] Fuller of Yarmouth my own picture. M[rs] Tichburn's youngest dau. M[rs] Tichburn's picture. To M[r] Trescar Sir Anthony Dean's picture. To M[r] Jennings the Dutch Rat Catcher picture. M[rs] Eliz. Bartleme & M[rs] Unwin & M[rs] Ann Holliday Ex'trices. Witnessed by Thomas Collins, Ann Zouch, Elizabeth Scott. (Dr. Muskett gave me the reference to the above will.)

LYNCH. Page 205.

AMBROSE LYNCH of Galway, merchant, living in 1683 = ...

Bartholomew Lynch of Galway, merchant. = Mary, dau. of Thomas Blake (fitz John) of Mullaghmore, co. Galway, eldest brother of John Blake (fitz John) of Montserrat; Marriage Article dated 5 Feb. 1683.

Ambrose Lynch (fitz Bartholomew) of Antigua, merchant, born 4 Dec. 1685; signs petition 1712-13; witness 1719 and 1723 to will of Elizabeth Franklyn; joins the Troop 1719; Ex'or 1736 of Leonard Allen, and in 1737 of Richard French; died 1 and bur. 2 Sep. 1740. M.I. at St. John's. = Mary .... born 3 July 1703; died 3 Feb. 1741. M.I. at St. John's.	Thomas Lynch (fitz Bartholomew) of Galway, merchant. Will proved at Cork 28 June 1736.	Anne Lynch, died unmar. Will proved at Tuam 7 Nov. 1746.	Cecily Lynch, mar. .... Fahy; living in 1746.

Mary Lynch, bapt. 5 Nov. 1719. | Thomas Stephens Lynch, bapt. 12 July 1722.

1683, Feb. 5. Articles of agreement between Ambrose Lynch of Galway, merchant, and his son Bartholomew Lynch, of the one part, and Thomas Blake of Mullaghmore in the county Galway, Gent., and his daughter Mary Blake, of the other part, for and concerning a marriage between the said Bartholomew Lynch and the said Mary Blake. Witnesses, Patrick Browne, James Blake, Patrick Blake, Henry Blake. [Original now (1895) in possession of Martin J. Blake of Gold Square, Lincoln's Inn.]

Thomas Lynch (fitz Bartholomew) of Galway, merchant. Last will dated at Cork 3 and proved 28 June 1736 by Walter D'Arcy of Galway, merchant, one of the Ex'ors. I give my sister Anne Lynch, spinster, the yearly interest of £400 for the term of 16 years. To my sister Cecily Lynch, spinster, £30. To Doctor Ambrose Lynch of the Town of Galway £30. To my kinsman James Lynch £10. All the residue of my worldly substance to my brother Ambrose Lynch of Antigua, merchant. Ex'ors appointed were said Ambrose Lynch of Galway, Messrs. James D'Arcy and Walter D'Arcy of Galway, merch[ts], Joshua Beale of City of Cork, merch[t]. and said James Lynch of Galway. Witnesses, Nicholas Kirby, Dennis McCarthy, and John Long, Notary Public.

Ambrose Lynch (Bartholomew) of Antigua, merchant. A power of attorney dated Antigua, 17 August 1738, given by said Ambrose Lynch (Bartholomew) to his sisters Anne Lynch and Cecily Lynch, both of Galway, spinsters, and Martin Lynch and Andrew Lynch of Galway, to receive for the use and benefit of said Anne and Cecily Lynch all the moneys, goods, and effects of which his brother Thomas Lynch, late of Galway, merchant, deceased, was possessed or entitled to at the time of his death, and unto which said Ambrose Lynch (Bartholomew) hath or may have any right or title under the will of said Thomas Lynch, deceased. Witnesses, George Thompson and Edmond Terry. [Original now (1895) in possession of Martin J. Blake of Lincoln's Inn.]

Anne Lynch of Windfield, co. Galway, spinster. Last will dated 4 and proved at Tuam 7 Nov. 1746 by the Ex'ors Thomas Blake and Nicholas Blake. To my godchild

Demna Blake of Graige £10. To my sister Sisly Lynch *al's* Fahy £1 10*s*. To Mary Blake, second daughter of my kinsman Thomas Blake of Windfield, the bond passed by Walter D'Arcy of Dublin, merch', for my use for £120 sterl. To my kinsman Nicholas Blake fitz John £26 17*s*. 2*d*. My kinsmen s^d Thomas Blake and Nicholas Blake, both of Windfield, to be my Ex'ors. Witnesses, Mark Blake, Martin Blake, Thomas Hoth.

Petition of John Willett, late of London, merchant, now of Montserrat, that John Lynch of Montserrat, Esq., residuary legatee and Ex'or of John Roche, late of Montserrat, Esq., on 16 Feb. 1791 filed a Bill in the Court of Chancery against Richard Neave of London, Esq., and petitioner as his late partner *re* Richard Neave, and petitioner and their former co-partners Thomas Truman and James George Douglas, both deceased, and the said John Roche, and between them and Patrick Roche, father of John Roche, deceased.

Lewis Piers, Esq., formerly of Dublin, now of St. James, Clerkenwell, London. Will proved 1 Dec. 1738 by Elizabeth Piers the relict. (293 Brodrepp.) Whereas on 14 & 15 Feb. 1716 I, then of Dublin, made a settlement on my late wife Cecilia Piers *al's* Lynch of all the right I had in the plantations of Capt. Nich^s Lynch, fz. Nich^s, & of Mr Anguish Brown, both of Mountserrat, & conveyed the said estates to her in fee simple in order that she might convey them by will after our deaths, which she did shortly do, & settled them by will (recorded at Prerogative Court, Dublin) on Nich^s Lynch, fz. Marcus Lynch, fz. Andrew, & on his brother Wm Lynch, her nephews, charged with £200 to me, which sum I now give to my present wife Eliz. Piers *al's* Tadpole *al's* Parker, & all residue to her & her daus. Mrs Anne & Eliz. Tadpole. My late father Sir Henry Piers of Fristernaugh, co. Westmeath, Bart. My coming to London in 1717. My wife Eliz. Ex'trix 12 Feb. 1732. Witnessed by James Francis de Witte, John Vane, Mary Parker.

LUCIE. Page 202.

William Regemorter of North Creake, co. Norfolk, Gent., one of the sons of Ahasuerus Regemorter, late of London, M.D., deceased. Will dated 10 July 1684; proved 12 Feb. 1686 by Lucy Blackman. To Richd Teasdale of Stiffkey, farmer, 20*s*. Mr Wm Framingham of Stiffkey, Gent., 20*s*. My brother Mr Lucy Blackman of Stiffkey all estate & Ex'or.

LYONS. Page 214.

Christiana, wife of Charles Lyons, born 1690, was granddaughter maternally of John de Witt, who was killed in Holland in 1672. Mary Watson was of the Rockingham family.

Page 216. Sarah Wickham was a daughter and coheir of Colonel John Wickham. She was buried at St. Philip's 11 Aug. 1747.

Page 217. Algernon Wilson Lyons of Thames Ditton, M.B. London, 1890, is probably a member of this family.

1863, March 5. At Kentish-town, aged 67, Anthony Munton Lyons, esq. late Stipendiary Magistrate of Demerara. ('Gent. Mag.,' p. 534.)

1865, Aug. 31. At Hove, Brighton, Vice-Adm. John Lyons of Worthing, to Anna Maria, widow of Col. John L. Mowatt, of the Bengal Horse Artillery. (*Ibid.*, p. 507.)

Parish Register of St. George the Martyr, Queen Square.

Married.

1784 Nov. 6 Edmund Walcott, batch., of this parish, & Catherine Ann Lyons, sp., of St. Andrew's. (Extracted by Mr. G. S. Fry.)

McCARTHY. Page 224.

(135 Cottle.) 1682. Captain Florence Macartie.

MACKINEN. Page 226.

Binfield, co. Berks.

SACRED
to the Memory of Louisa Mackinnon
Relict of William Mackinnon Esquire,
whose Remains with her own
are interred in a Vault near this Stone
She was the Daughter of James Vernon Esquire
of Hilton in the County of Stafford
& born on the 21st Day of June 1738.
In her Character the exalted Christian Graces
of Piety Beneficence & Humility
were truly conspicuous
& She resigned her Spirit replete
with all the most angelic & ardent affections
that ever adorned
the Breast of Mother Wife or Child
with scarce a Struggle
into the hands of her Creator
on the 22nd Day of November 1816
with the confident Hope & Assurance
of a blessed *IMMORTALITY.*

St. Mary, Reading, co. Berks.

In south aisle, on a brass on south wall:—

In Memory of Major W. A. D. Mackinnon | 2nd Battalion Royal Berkshire Regiment | son of Lauchlan Bellingham Mackinnon | died 22nd January, 1889. | Major Mackinnon took part in the March on Candahar in 1880 | under General Roberts and was present at the battle of Candahar. | This Tablet is Erected by the Officers and N. C. Officers of the Battalion. ('Mis. Gen. et Her., vol. i., Third Series, p. 223.)

Parish Register of St. George, Hanover Square.

Married.

1823 July 17 Daniel Mackinnon, Esq., B., & Ann Jane Dent, S. Lic.

McNISH. Page 230.

1802, May 31. Rev. A. Brodie, M.A. to Miss Walter, daugh. of John W. esq. of Teddington. ('Gent. Mag.,' p. 583.)

1803, Nov. 22. At Twickenham, Middlesex, the wife of Rev. A. Brodie, a daughter. (*Ibid.*, p. 1084.)

Alexander, son of Alexander Brodie of London, Gent., matriculated from Trinity College, Oxford, 10 Feb. 1794, æt. 20, B.A. 1797, M.A. 1801, B. and D.D. 1811. One of this name was Vicar of Eastbourne 1809.

MANNING. Page 232.

1778, April 8. Henry Merttins Bird, Esq; of St. Mary Axe, to Miss Elizabeth Manning, daughter of William Manning, Esq; of the same place. ('Town and Country Mag.,' p. 223.)

1786, Oct. William Manning, jun. esq; of St. Mary Axe, to miss Smith, daughter of Abel Smith, esq. member of parliament for St. Germains, in Cornwall. (*Ibid.*, p. 614.)

1789, March 29. Mrs. Manning, lady of Wm. M. jun. esq. of Billiter-square, and daughter of the late Abel Smith, esq. ('Gent. Mag.,' p. 374.)

1791, Nov. 25. At his house at Totteridge, Herts, of a paralytic stroke, Wm. Manning, esq. a West India merchant, and one of the directors of the Royal Exchange Assurance office. (*Ibid.*, p. 1070.)

St. Thomas, Middle Island, St. Christopher.

Arms (but not copied by Mr. N. Darnell Davis).

Here lies in certain hope of a blessed resurrection, William Coventry, late of the parish of St. Thomas, Middle Island, Merchant, who departed this life August the 16th 1734, Aged 53 years. He was a tender and indulgent parent, an upright and a good Christian. His life was regularly sober and truly pious, and God Almighty, who visibly blessed his honest industry upon earth gave him here but . . . . etc. To his memory therefore, John Manning, Merchant, who married his only daughter, dutifully subscribes this monument.

In this tomb also is deposited the body of his grandson John Battry (?) Manning, who departed this life, September the 27th 1734, aged one year seven months, and ten days.

Totteridge, co. Herts.

(Cussans' 'Herts,' vol. ii., pp. 304-5.)

On the south side of a large altar-tomb of white marble, inclosed by an iron railing :—

Near this Place, lie the Remains of
WILLIAM MANNING, *ESQ*
who departed this Life on the 24th of November 1791, in
the Sixty Second Year of his Age.
This Monument is erected as a just Tribute to his Memory
by a grateful and affectionate Son.

At the west end of the tomb are these arms :—

Quarterly (azure and gules), a cross patonce between four trefoils slipped (or) for Manning.

On an inescutcheon: *Quarterly of four, 1 and 4, a chevron between three horses' heads erased: 2 and 3, six leaves erect, three and three.*

Another tomb adjoining to the grandson of the foregoing :—

WILLIAM HENRY MANNING, ESQ.
ELDEST SON OF
WILLIAM MANNING, ESQ.
OF THIS PARISH
DIED THE 13TH OF JULY, 1812
IN THE 20TH YEAR OF
HIS AGE.

A portrait of William Manning, Esq., M.P., Governor of the Bank of England, painted by I. Lonsdale and engraved by C. Turner, was published 18 Sep. 1813. On a shield are the following arms :—

Crest : *An eagle's head between two ostrichs' feathers, all issuing out of a ducal coronet.*

Arms: *Quarterly*, 1 *and* 4, *Azure and gules, a cross flory between four trefoils* (Manning); 2, *Gules, a chevron between three griffins' heads erased*; 3, *Argent, six leaves*; impaling, 1 *and* 4, *Or, a lion rampant between eight crosses patée fitchée* (Hunter); 2 *and* 3, *Argent, a* (?) *bear rampant.*

'Life of Cardinal Manning, Archbishop of Westminster,' by Edmund Sheridan Purcell, 2 vols. (Macmillan, 1895).

"Henry Edward Manning was born at Copped Hall, Hertfordshire, on the 15th of July 1807. He was the youngest son of William Manning, M.P., and of Mary his wife. His father, who was born 1st December 1763, was twice married. His first wife was Elizabeth, daughter of Abel Smith, banker of Nottingham, and sister of Robert, created Lord Carrington. Of this marriage there were two daughters: Elizabeth, who died unmarried; and Mary, who was married to Major-General Thomas Carey, of the Guernsey family of that name. About three years after the death of his first wife, Elizabeth, William Manning married secondly, in 1792, Mary the daughter of Henry Leroy Hunter of Beech Hill, Reading. William Manning died in 1835, and was buried at Sundridge, Kent, where Mary, his wife, who was born 4th July 1771, and died 12th May 1847, was likewise buried. Four sons and four daughters were the issue of the second marriage. Henry, the youngest, enjoyed the benefit of having many brothers and sisters. The Cardinal's eldest brother William, born July 1793, died in 1812. His sister Harriet also died in 1826, aged 20. Another sister Caroline, who married Colonel Austen, died in 1893, aged 92."

William Manning occupied Copped Hall, Totteridge, soon after 1792, subsequently purchasing it, but sold it about 1815.

In Totteridge Church are the tombs of the Cardinal's grandfather, who died in 1791, and of his eldest brother William.

"In the parish church of St. Giles, Speen, near Newbury, is to be found the marriage register of the Cardinal's grandfather, William Manning, and Elizabeth, daughter of William and Mary Ryan of St. Kitts, West Indies :— 'Elizabeth Ryan, baptized on 6th November, 1732, at the parish church of St. George, Basseterre, St. Kitts, married at Speen, Berks, 1st October, 1751, to William Manning.' Elizabeth Ryan was the owner of two estates in St. Kitts, and soon after the marriage, her husband, Mr. William Manning, founded the great West Indian house, afterwards known as Manning and Anderdon. It is said that he first started in business at Bristol, where he became acquainted with Isaac Disraeli, the father of Lord Beaconsfield. Subsequently he was established as a West Indian merchant at St. Mary Axe, London, and lived at Billiter Square, City.

"On his father's death in 1791, William Manning, the Cardinal's father, succeeded to the business, which was carried on in [3] New Bank Buildings, City, at a later period, in partnership with Mr. John Anderdon, and made a handsome fortune in the palmy days of West Indian prosperity. In those days the West Indian interest was a factor in the political world: accordingly William Manning entered Parliament as member for Plympton Earle in 1790. In 1807 he was elected member for Evesham; he represented afterwards Penryn, and supported West Indian and commercial interests in the House of Commons for about thirty-nine years. He was highly respected in the City; was for forty years a director of the Bank of England, and was governor in the years 1812-13. Mr. Manning sold his estate at Totteridge in 1815 and purchased Combe Bank in the parish of Sundridge, 3 miles from Sevenoaks. The depreciating value of West Indian property subsequently led to his financial ruin and bankruptcy in 1831. He died on the 17th of April 1835, at his house in Lower Gower Street, and was buried on the 24th inst. in the same vault with his daughter Harriet in Sundridge Church. The Cardinal married on 7th Nov. 1833 at Lavington, Caroline, 3rd dau. of the Revd. John Sargent and granddaughter of Mrs. Sargent of Lavington Manor; she died in July 1837 s.p."

Sundridge, co. Kent.

In a vault are deposited the Remains of
WILLIAM MANNING, Esq.
Formerly of Combe Bank, in this Parish,
Born December 1st, 1763,
And in a firm reliance on the merits of his Redeemer,
Departed this life on Good Friday, April 17th, 1835.
(Eight lines follow.)

ALSO OF
MARY MANNING
Beloved Wife of William Manning, Esq.,
Born July 4, 1771,
Died May 13, 1847.
(One line follows.)

In a church in the City of London :—

Sacred to the memory of
ELIZABETH MANNING,
Wife of William Manning, Esq., Merchant of London.
Died the 3rd of January 1780,
And was buried
Within the Walls of this Church.
This Tablet is erected by her Son,
William Manning, Esq.
(Two lines follow.)

St. Martin in the Fields, London.

Baptized.

1809 May 25 Henry Edward Manning, son of William Manning, Esq., and Mary his wife; born 15th July.

ANDERDON. Page 236.

1811, Dec. 14. At Bridgewater, Charles Anderdon, esq. father of C. P. A. esq. of Henlade-house, near Taunton, and brother of William and Edmund Anderdon, esqrs of Bristol. ('Gent. Mag.,' p. 659.)

MARTIN. Page 240.

George Martin, a noted Royalist, was in 1649 elected Sovereign of Belfast; his property was subsequently confiscated by the Roundheads, and he is supposed to have removed to the West Indies. (Betham's 'Baronetage,' vol. iv., p. 210.)

1770, Dec. Wm. Tyron, Esq; now Gov. of North Carolina, to be Gov. of New York. And Henry (*sic*) Martin, Esq; to be Gov. of North Carolina. ('Gent. Mag.,' p. 591.)

1778, Dec. The Hon. Josiah Martin, at Rockaway, in Long Island. ('Town and Country Mag.,' p. 716.)

1783, Dec. 24. The lady of Byam Martin, esq. of Upper Harley-Street, Cavendish-square, of a son. (*Ibid.*, p. 671.)

1786, March. Josiah Martin,* esq. of New Norfolk-street, Grosvenor-square, late his majesty's governor of North Carolina. (*Ibid.*, p. 224.)

1803, July 25. College of Fort William. The students now leaving College, on whom his Excellency was pleased to confer a degree of honour on this occasion, were: .... Mr. William Byam Martin, of the Establishment of Fort St. George. ('Gent. Mag.,' 1804, p. 582.)

1813, Dec. 12. Fell gallantly in an action near Bayonne, Lieut.-col. Samuel Coote Martin, 1st foot-guards, eldest son of the late Wm. Byam M. esq. of Whiteknights, Berks. The following is an extract from the letter of a brother officer: "Colonel Martin commanded the piquets which were attacked at day-light, on the 12th of December, by the Enemy in vast force. He repulsed them with great skill and gallantry; but at the conclusion of the contest he received a ball through the heart, which closed his honourable and virtuous life without a groan, deeply lamented by officers and men. He had greatly distinguished himself in the battle of the 9th." To his surviving parent, widow, and four infant children, his loss is indeed severe. (*Ibid.*, p. 701.)

Parish Chapel of St. Marylebone.

On the south-east wall below, on a white marble tablet on black marble :—

To the Memory | of | JOSIAH MARTIN | Esqre | Third Son of the first | Sir HENRY MARTIN B^art | Born the 14th of February 1772, | died the 5th of December 1849. | He was | an affectionate Relative, | and a liberal Friend | to the poor. ('Mis. Gen. et Her.,' vol. i., Third Series, p. 129.)

* He is stated to have been buried at St. George's, Hanover Square.

1863, Dec. 4. At Tunbridge Wells, Sir Henry Martin, bart. He was the son of the second baronet, by the dau. of Thomas Powell, esq. of the Chesnuts, near Tottenham, Middlesex. He was born in Weymouth-street in 1801, married, in 1825, his cousin Catherine, dau. of the late Admiral of the Fleet, Sir Thomas Byam Martin, G.C.B., and succeeded his father in 1842. Sir Henry was a man of antiquarian tastes, and was an occasional contributor to the 'Gentleman's Magazine.' ('Gent. Mag.,' p. 132.)

1865, Feb. 9. At Genoa, aged 61, Adm. Sir Henry Byam Martin, K.C.B. He was the second son of the late Adm. Sir Thomas Byam Martin, G.C.B., by the dau. of Capt. Thos. Fanshawe, R.N., and was born in 1803, etc. (*Ibid.*, p. 397.)

The following notes have been contributed by Mr. Edward Payson Payson, Counsellor-at-Law, of 150 Devonshire Street, Boston, Mass. :—

Samuel Martin of Green Castle, Antigua, who married Lydia Thomas, had three sons :—

I. Samuel, the progenitor of the present English branch.

II. Josiah, who married Mary Yeamans, as to whose early life I am uninformed. At Long Island he built a house, "Rock Hall"; was Aide-de-camp to the Royal Governor of the colony of New York in 1757; Member of the Governor's Council 1759—62; one of the Lords of Trade to the King for the trial of pirates; and died 21 Nov. 1778 at Rock Hall, aged 79; his wife died 30 Aug. 1805. Their children were :—

1. Elizabeth, married her cousin Josiah, afterwards Royal Governor of North Carolina.
2. Samuel, Physician, at Rock Hall, who gave his parole in £500 with sureties not to oppose the Whigs in 1776, and died 21 April 1804.
3. Alice, buried at Hempstead 10 Aug. 1815.
4. Rachel, married Thomas Bannister of Long Island.
5. Frances.
6. William (from Heralds' College pedigree: "a captain in 60th Reg. of foot, unmarried 1791"). (Information is particularly desired as to his descendants.)
7. Charles Yeamans. (See pedigree.)

III. William Thomas, who married Penelope Clark July 1728, was educated at Trinity College, Cambridge; M.D. 1728; died early; administration to his widow P.C.C. July 1735, leaving a daughter, who died young, and one son William, mentioned in will of his grandmother Lydia, and his stepfather Governor Edward Byam, born in All Hallows' Parish, Tower Hill, near London, 10 June 1733; intended for the University and his father's profession, but his death prevented, and he was educated at St. Paul's Classical School; afterwards in business in London; married Elizabeth, daughter of Captain Galpine, 1762; emigrated to Boston 1783; Citizen of Mass. by Special Act of 1787; Member of the General Court (Legislature) of Mass. 1792—98; Charter Trustee of Bowdoin College 1794—1813; died 15 June 1814; his wife died 1829. Children:—

1. William Clark, died s.p.
2. Samuel, married Hannah, daughter of Colonel John Morrill, and their

children all died unmarried except Penelope, who married Edward, eldest son of Rev. Dr. Edward Payson of Portland, Maine; and Hannah, who married James W. Tobey. Each left descendants.

3. Nathaniel, married Rhoda, daughter of Erastus Foote; and of their children Edward Byam married Sarah, daughter of Captain Norris; Erastus married Sarah Dallum; Emily married Henry Bennett, first President American Bible Society; and all these left descendants.

The line from Dr. William Thomas Martin will be found partially recorded in Heralds' College, London. The above facts as to Josiah come from parish records and historical manuscripts of the State of New York. Much of the same information is contained in a MS. left by Penelope, daughter of William the emigrant. Of Governor Josiah, son of Samuel and cousin of William the emigrant, there is a good deal of memoranda in American histories.

MEMORANDUM OF JOSIAH MARTIN.

From Martin pedigree, Heralds' College, 1791: "II. Josiah Martin of Long Island, near New York, and also of Antigua, died many years ago; married Mary, daughter of . . . . Yeamans of Antigua, living 1791." By Yeamans' pedigree (Sumner's 'History East Boston,' p. 231) Mary was daughter of William, a son of John Yeamans, Lieut.-Governor of Antigua.

Josiah is styled "Major" in the will of Governor Edward Byam dated 1734, and in the records of St. George Church both "Major" and "Colonel." He was President of the Council of Antigua for some years (1 Oliver). He emigrated to Long Island, America, about 1730 (?), where, in the midst of his retainers, he lived many years. He built "Rock Hall," near Far Rockaway, one of the still surviving manorial houses of that time, now the seat of the Hewlet family, containing his supposed portrait. In 1760 a house is advertised "near Rock Hall" (Hewlet Mem.) A Lieut. Josiah Martin was in Hale's 5th Conn. Regiment in Louisburg Expedition of 1745 (N.E.H.G.R. 24, p. 373). Josiah's name is frequent in the records of church of St. George's Parish, Hempstead, Long Island, from 1732, viz.:—

Baptized.

1732 Mar. 25 Mary daughter of Josiah and Elizabeth Martin.

(Mem.—Probably these names should be reversed, since Mary was wife of Josiah. See Martin pedigree later.)

1740 Oct. 14 Samuel son of Major Josiah and Mary Martin.

Before entries of 1745: "Samuel Martin and Alice Martin confirmed October 31."

1750 Mar. 12 Rachel daughter of Col. Josiah and Mrs. Mary Martin of Hempstead.

1754 Jan. 4 Frances daughter of Josiah and Mary Martin.

1757 Sep. 8 William son of Josiah and Mary Martin.

Clowes Mem. says a daughter married William McNiel. The Martin pedigree gives a son Charles Yeamans.

In 1751 Josiah subscribes £20 for an additional gallery.

In 1757 he was commissioned Aide-de-camp to the Royal Governor of New York (Calendar of New York Historical Manuscripts, English, 1644—1776, p. 672; a copy of an instrument endorsed "Draft of Commission for Aide-de-camp," *ibid.*, vol. 84, p. 63).

From 1759 till 1761 or 62 he was Member of the Legislature or Governor's Council of the colony of New York, first sitting 25 June 1759 under Governor James De Lancey (Journal Legislative Council of New York, p. 1371; New York Civil List of 1878, p. 19). He was one of the "Lords of Trade to the King" for the trial of pirates as a Member of His Majesty's Council for the province of New York (New Jersey Archives, vol. 9, p. 282).

The record of his death is "Died November 21, 1778, at his seat at Rockaway, the Hon. Josiah Martin, aged 79." (Hewlett Mem.) In Rev. Mr. Moore's 'History of St. George's Church' he is confused with his nephew Governor Josiah, who married his daughter Elizabeth, passed some time at, and sent his family from North Carolina to, Rockaway, and died in London in 1786.

His wife Mary died 1805 according to St. George's burial records: "Mrs. Mary Martin of Far Rockaway, August 30, 1805."

Of their children:—

1. Elizabeth, married Lieut.-Colonel Josiah Martin (her cousin), afterwards Governor of North Carolina. From St. George's Parish Records appear the baptisms:—

Baptized.

1762 April 19 Mary Elizabeth daughter to Samuel (Josiah ?) and Elizabeth Martin.

1768 Mar. 16 Alice daughter of Col. Josiah Martin and Mrs. Elizabeth Martin. Sponsors, Dr. Samuel Martin, Madam Mary Read, and Rachael Martin.

1771 June 21 Samuel George Thomas son of Josiah Martin, Esq., Governor of North Carolina, and Elizabeth Martin.

1775 Sep. 6 Augusta daughter of his Excellency Josiah Martin, Esq., Governor of North Carolina, and Elizabeth Martin.

From Martin pedigree: "Elizabeth, daughter of Josiah Martin, ob. at Long Island October 1778; m. Josiah Martin, late Governor of North Carolina, and sometime Colonel in the army; ob. 13 April 1786; bur. at St. George, Hanover Square."

2. Samuel, mentioned in Sabine's 'Loyalists' as having given his parole in 1776 in the sum of £500 with sureties not to oppose the Whigs; was a Physician; lived at Rock Hall; and is recorded as Vestryman of St. George's Parish 1770—1797, and frequently a Delegate to represent the church in convention, and as one of a Committee to protest against use of church as a granary by the troops; and under Burials: "Doctor Samuel Martin of Far Rockaway, April 21, 1806."
3. Alice. From St. George's Burials: "Miss Alice Martin of Rockaway, buried in ch. yd. Hempstead August 10, 1815." From Martin pedigree: "Samuel and Alice both living at Long Island and unmarried 1791."
4. Rachael, married Thomas Bannister, as appears in St. George's Records, thus: "1780, July 26, Baptised at Hempstead, Josiah Martin, son of Thomas and Rachael Bannister of Hempstead. Sponsors, Dr. Samuel Martin, Edward Winslow, Esq. (Muster Master-General), Mrs. Mary Martin." From Martin pedigree: "Rachael, mar. Bannister of Long Island, both living and have issue 1791."
5. Frances. No further information. Not given, as are the others, in Burke.
6. William. From Martin pedigree: "A captain in 60 Regt. of foot, unmar. 1791," *i.e.* at age of 34.
7. From Martin pedigree: "Charles Yeamans Martin of Antigua, mar. but s.p. 1791." From Burke: "Died issueless."

Clowes Mem., Hewlett Mem., speak of a Martin who married a Major McNiel of the British Army, and whose descendants are still in Queen's County.

I have lately learned that University of Pennsylvania Matriculate Catalogue shews "Gov. N. C." being error:—

"Josiah Martin, A.B., gratiæ causa 1757. A.M. gratiæ causa 1760, b. ; d. : s. Col. Josiah Martin, Gov. N. C., and entered May 25, 1754; studied at the Temple, London, Lawyer." I assume he was the Josiah whom your Vol. II. gives as son of Josiah the elder, and died 1762. Also from same, "Gov. N. C." being error:—

"Wm. Thomas Martin, b. : d. Philadelphia Aug. 28, 1754; s. Col. Josiah Martin, Gov. N. C. and Entered May 25, 1754. He died during his studentship, and Provost Wm. Smith, D.D., preached a sermon in Christ Church, Philadelphia, commemorative of his death." I find the sermon (vol. i., p. 5, 'Works of Wm. Smith, D.D.') prefaced with note of dedication to Samuel Martin, M.P. for Camelford, Secretary to Treasury, etc., as his cousin.

Neither name is among L. I. baptisms. Wm. Thos. Martin, M.D., was of Cambridge as stated by his granddaughter Penelope, as learned from his daughter-in-law in a genealogy left by her, also by his great-grandson John in minutes for publication and in other family papers. I notice that in his son William's certificate to Freedom of London the Wm. is omitted from the Doctor's name, but William records himself as "son of Dr. Wm. Thos. Martin;" and from Vicar-General's office, 22 July 1728, a licence issued for marriage of Wm. Thos. Martin of St. Edmund the King, London, Dr. of Physic, aged above 29 years, with Penelope Clark, etc.

I am just in receipt of a letter from J. W. Clark of the Registry of the University at Cambridge, saying: "William Thomas Martin matriculated as a pensioner from Trinity College 8 July 1721."

Page 242. The will of Adam Martin 1704 was also recorded P.C.C. (16 Barrett.)

MATHEW. Page 253.

H. Botham, Esq., was married to Lydia Payne Matthew in 1788, not 1780.

Lieut. Bertie Mathew as at Eton 1826.

MAYER. Page 262.

John Mayer and Esther Wickham also had a daughter who married . . . . Dalzell, and a daughter Ann who married, 1778, Charles Grant of St. Vincent; she died 1796; he died 1821.

MORRIS. Page 272.

1692, Oct. 10. Thomas Morris, of Antego, in the West Indies, Gent., Bach[r], ab[t] 20, & Mrs. Mary Sadler, of St. Martin's in the Fields, Midd., ab[t] 16, with consent of her guardian, John Fox, of Mortlake, Esq.; at S[t] Mary Hill, London. (Marriage Licences: Vicar-General of the Archbishop of Canterbury.)

1769, May 1. Miss Morris, the young lady who appeared with so much applause at Covent Garden theatre. ('Town and Country Mag.,' p. 279.)

MORSON. Page 279.

See pedigree of Akers in Burke's 'Landed Gentry.'

CHRIST CHURCH, NICHOLA TOWN, ST. KITTS.

(B. T. Leeward Islands, vol. 21.)

Buried.

1727 Jonas Acres 8ber 31[d].

MURRAY. Page 280.

1734, Aug. 27. To Mrs. Martha Murray at Dorchester, South Carolina. Your suit is determined thus: that the negros shall continue on the estate till the old man's debt of £300 is paid. Your share will be 4 negros.

1735, Nov. 8. To the same at Colonel Blake's: your little girl . . . . *re* the negros . . . . when Dr. Murray was here. "Your sister Bettey is married to a Scotch Taylor who has good business here in Town named George Swan."

1739, July 1. "Major Murray was married 14 days agone to Mrs. Otto & go to New England to-day, but will return again before Christmas." (Tullideph Letters.)

NANTON. Page 288.

1649. George Thompson of Antigua by his will gave 1000 lbs. of tobacco to his godchild George, son of Robert Nanton. (40 Fairfax.)

NIBBS. Page 292.

James Hawes in his will of 1738 names his own sister Catherine Nibbs.

1789, March 25. At Tortola, the Hon. Octavius Nibbs, for many years one of his Majesty's council for that island, and one of the assistant judges of the Court of Common Pleas. ('Gent. Mag.,' p. 573.)

1864, April 13. At Fiddington, Somerset, Capt. C. E. Evered, eldest son of the Rev. C. W. H. E. Rector of Otterhampton, Somerset, to Emily Mary, only surviving child of the late George Langford Nibbs, esq. of Keentharne-House, Fiddington. (*Ibid.*, p. 654.)

1897. On Sunday last the 7th inst., at his residence in Church Lane, Walter Selly Nibbs, merchant, of this island, at the age of 43 years and 9 months. A widowed sister and brother survive, etc. ('Antigua Standard' for 13 March 1897.)

NIHELL. Page 302.

John Trafford of Croston Hall, Lancashire, born 18 Feb. 1689; died 5 Dec. 1760; by his second wife Alice, daughter of James Shorrock, whom he married 18 Aug. 1756, had an only surviving child Catherine Eloisa, baptized 23 June 1757, who married Dr. Nihell. (Baines' 'Lancashire,' vol. iii., p. 239.)

1788, Aug. Dr. Nihell, of Bedford-street, Bedford-square, to Miss Trafford, of Croston-hall, Lancash. ('Town and Country Mag.,' p. 435.)

NISBET. Page 305.

Joseph Morton Landgrave of Carolina. Will dated 14 April 1685; proved 1688. (Exton.) S. Joseph £500. Dau. Deborah Blake £400. S. John £1000. Sister Rebecca Bowell. Wife Elinor.

John Morton of London, merchant. Will dated 27 Aug. 1694; proved 1699. (61 Pett.) Plantation in Carolina. Brother Joseph. Wife Ann £20. Dau. Ann £100. Sister Deborah Blake.

1773, July 17. James Lockhart, Esq; of Castlehill, to Miss Mary Nisbet, daughter of Walter Nisbet, Esq; late of the island of Nevis. ('Town and Country Mag.,' p. 391.)

1781, Oct. 5. At Salisbury, Dr. Nisbet, late of Nevis in the West Indies. ('Gent. Mag.,' p. 491.)

1804, Oct. 8. Jn. Nesbit Jordan, Emanuel Coll. Cam. M.A. Lambeth Degrees. (*Ibid.*, p. 770.)

1823, June 17. At Edinburgh, Josiah Nisbet, esq. of Madras Civil Service, to Rachel, dau. of Sir J. Marjoribanks, bart. M.P. (*Ibid.*, p. 177.)

1843, Dec. 4. At Bath, Clara-Amelia, only dau. of the late Major Harriott, of West Hall, Surrey, and wife of Robert Parry Nisbet, esq. of Southbroom House, Wilts. (*Ibid.*, 1844, p. 108.)

1864, Jan. 15. At Cheltenham, Mary Frances, relict of Capt. Josiah Nisbet, R.N. (*Ibid.*, p. 269.)

PEDIGREE OF NISBET.

ARMS.—*Three boars' heads couped within a bordure gules.*
CREST.—*A boar's head couped.*
MOTTO.—*Vis fortibus arma.*

ARCHIBALD NISBET of Carfin, co. Lanark. ╤ Emelia, dau. of Archibald, son of James, 3rd Earl of Moray, a descendant of James, King of Scotland.

A son, stated to have been father of Walter Nisbet ╤ . . . . of Nevis, but no proof.

Euphemia Nisbet, mar. Rev. David Blair, a Minister at Edinburgh and Chaplain to the King. Had issue Robert Blair the Poet.

Walter Nisbet of Mount Pleasant, Nevis, Member of Council 1759 till his death 1765. ╤ Mary, dau. of Walter Maynard,* Esq., of Nevis.

William Woolward† of Nevis, Esq., died 18 Feb. 1779. M.I. at St. John's, Nevis. ╤ Mary, dau. of Thomas Herbert, Esq.

Richard Nisbet of Nevis 1790 (a near relation).

Walter Nisbet, jun., of Mount Pleasant, Nevis, and Grafton Street, born 3 Jan. 1745; bapt. 28 April 1745 at St. James, Nevis; erected a chapel on his plantation 1793. ╤ Anne, dau. of Robert Parry of Plas Newydd, Llanrhaiadr, co. Denbigh; mar. 1784; died 2 Dec. 1819, æt. 67. M.I. at Walcot, Bath.

Josiah Nisbet, M.D., born 7 Aug. 1747; mar. 28 June 1779 at St. John's, Nevis; died 5 Oct. 1781 at Salisbury; bur. and M.I. at Stratford, near Old Sarum. 1st husband. ╤ Frances Herbert, only dau., bapt. May 1761 at St. George's, Nevis; died in London 6 May 1831, æt. 73; bur. and M.I. at Littleham, co. Devon. ╤ Horatio, Lord Nelson, mar. 11 March 1787 at St. John's, Nevis. 2nd husband. s.p.

Anne Nisbet, born 14 Feb. 1746; died spinster.

James Webb Nisbet, born 23 Aug. 1749; died a bachelor.

Mary Emelia Nisbet, born 4 Feb. 1752; mar. 17 July 1773 James Sinclair Lockhart of Cambusnethan House, co. Lanark.

Captain Josiah Nisbet, R.N., only son, died 1830. ═ Mary Frances Herbert, died 15 Jan. 1864 at Cheltenham.

Walter Nisbet, E.I.C.S., died a bachelor.

Josiah Nisbet, Madras Civil Service, died 1834. ╤ Rachel, dau. of Sir John Marjoribanks, Bart., M.P.; mar. 17 June 1823 at Edinburgh; died 1 Dec. 1874.

Caroline Nisbet, died 30 March 1867, æt. 77. M.I. at Walcot, Bath.

Robert Parry Nisbet, Bengal Civil Service, of Southbroom House, co. Wilts, died 1882. ╤ Clara Amelia, only dau. of Major Thomas Harriott of West Hall, co. Surrey; mar. 17 Nov. 1817; died 4 Dec. 1843 at Bath. M.I. at Southbroom.

Harry Nisbet, E.I.C.S., died 1890. ╤ Anne, sister of John Curtis Hayward of Quedgeley, co. Gloucester.

Rev. John Marjoribanks Nisbet, only son, matric. from Balliol College, Oxford, 17 Dec. 1842, æt. 18; B.A. 1846; M.A. 1851; Rector of Deal 1856—61; Vicar of Ramsgate 1861—67; Rector of St. Giles-in-the-Fields and Canon of Norwich 1867.

A dau., mar. Thomas Powney Marten, Esq., E.I.C.S., and had a son George Nisbet Marten, now of Marshalswick, St. Albans.

Colonel Robert Parry Nisbet, C.I.E., British Resident at Cashmere, born 1839; of 138 Cromwell Road 1896. ═ Anne Claxton, youngest dau. of John Delap Wilson‡ of Milford, co. Hants.

Harry Curtis Nisbet, a Solicitor for over 40 years; of 35 Lincoln's Inn Fields 1896, and the Old House, Wimbledon. ╤ . . . .

Walter Nisbet, 2nd son, matric. from Magdalen Hall, Oxford, 23 April 1858, æt. 22.

A dau., mar. Rev. Nicholas McGrath, Vicar of Bempton, Yorkshire.

Harry Bruce Nisbet, 1st son ═ Annabel, dau. of Thomas Godfrey Carey, Esq., H.M. Procureur at Guernsey.

* The present representative of the Maynards of Nevis is Mr. John S. Maynard, M.B.

† His nephew John Woolward of Ramsgate, Commander R.N., left a second son Rev. Alfred Gott Woolward, matriculated from Magdalen College, Oxford, 18 March 1837, æt. 16, B.A. 1841, M.A. 1846, Rector of Belton, co. Lincoln, 1844, till his death 25 Jan. 1873. Alfred Gott Woolward's first son Rev. Alfred Spencer Woolward matriculated from Keble College, Oxford, 14 Oct. 1878, æt. 19, B.A. 1882, M.A. 1885, Vicar of Totternhoe, co. Beds, since 1886. Crest: *An owl.*

‡ See Pedigree of Wilson of St. Kitts, Vol. II., p. 43.

LITTLEHAM, CO. DEVON.

On a small urn-shaped slab of white marble, surmounted by the arms of Nisbet :—

Crest : *A boar's head couped.*
Arms : *Three boars' heads couped within a bordure.*
Motto : *Vis fortibus arma.*

To the right on a lozenge, surmounted by a Viscount's coronet, the letter N :—

Sacred to the Memory of
Frances Herbert
Viscountess Nelson Duchess of Bronti
Widow of the late Admiral Lord Viscount Nelson
and to her son Josiah Nisbet Esq[r]
Captain in the Royal Navy
whom she survived eleven months
and died in London May 6th 1831
Aged 73 years.
This humble offering of affection
is erected by Frances Herbert Nisbet
in grateful remembrance of those virtues
which adorned a kind mother in law
and a good husband.

('Notes and Queries' for Nov. 1896, p. 439.)

STRATFORD SUB CASTRA, NEAR SALISBURY.

On a marble tablet on south wall of chancel within the altar-rails :—

Josiah Nisbet, M.D.,
of the Island of Nevis
Born 7th Augst. 1747 died 5th Octr. 1781.
This monument was erected to his memory
by his affectionate wife Frances Nisbet.

('Notes and Queries' for 1897, p. 408.)

NUGENT. Page 310.

Captain Thomas Nugent of Montnugent, co. Bucks. Will dated 15 June, proved 15 Nov. 1710 by the Hon. Christopher Nugent, commonly called Lord Delvin. (251 Smith.) £50 for funeral. To be buried at Paneridge. To my wife my messuage in Devonshire Street, S[t] Andrew's, Holborn, & £30 a year. M[r] Luke Nugent £20 for the poor. Garret Dardis my nephew's bond. All lands & manors at Montnugent, etc., to Dennis Daly of Gray's Inn, Esq., & Walter Nugent of Carpenter's Town, co. Westmeath, gent., on Trust to sell & pay to my residuary legatee. My plantation & negros in Monserat to my kinsman Chr. Nugent, called Lord Delvin, & all residue. Witnessed by John Eurs, Edmond Cullen, Michaell Berford.

Sir Ignatius Nugent, Knt. Will dated 1721. (207 Buckingham.) Wife Joyce. Son John. Brother Col. Chr. Nugent. (Testator was son of John Nugent of Killasonna, co. Longford, of the Earl of Westmeath's family.) He had been knighted by the Emperor Charles VI.

Hugh de Nugent is stated to have served in Ireland with Hugh de Lacy and his cousins Gilbert and Richard de Nugent, 1st and 2nd Barons of Delvin.

Page 311. *For* 2nd Baron *read* 10th. From Christopher, 11th, *not* 3rd Baron, descends the present Earl of Westmeath.

OLIVER. Page 318.

Captain Robert Porter and Grace his wife were of Antigua *temp.* death of Governor Parke 1710 (French). Thomas Oliver, who died 1803, was apparently residing on his plantation Bendals in 1787, when a pew in St. John's Church was allotted to him. Elizabeth Oliver, who died 1752, was aged 24 according to family list of interments.

Page 319. An old sampler has on it "Mary Oliver 1739."

Page 320. On Mr. George Gordon succeeding to Wincombe Park last year (1897) he very kindly allowed me to have Richard Oliver's books, from which the following bookplate has been taken :—

Richard Oliver A.M.

"1780, Feb. 15. M[r] Richard Oliver, born at Layton in Essex, admitted Fellow-Commoner and Pupil to M[r] Stevenson." (Clare College Records.)

Richard Oliver matriculated as a Fellow Commoner at Clare College on the 18th Dec. 1780. He proceeded to the degrees of B.A. in 1784, and M.A. in 1788. (Registry of Cambridge University.)

The later generations of pedigree have been also printed in Howard's 'Visitations of England,' vol. ii., p. 145.

Pew No. 68 in St. John's Church, Antigua, was allotted in 1806 to Richard Oliver and family, and pew No. 65 in 1822 to Mrs. Oliver.

EXTRACTS FROM DR. WALTER TULLIDEPH'S LETTER-BOOK.

1734, July 10. Per Capt. Oliver.

1736, April 28. Per Capt. Sam[l] Oliver.

1736, May 23. Yours of y[e] 31st Jan[y], p. y[e] "Fanny," Thos. Oliver.

1736, July 16. Per the "Resolution," Thos. Oliver.

1737, May 25. Sam[l] Oliver arrived here from Calis about 10 days agone, & in 6 days sailed directly for London. Johnny Martin sails in Tho[s] Oliver.

1739, July 1. Major Murray was married 14 days agone to Mrs. Otto & go to New England to-day, but will return again before Christmas.

1743, Oct. 12. Y[e] Antigua packet, Sam[l] Oliver.

1744, Oct. 28. Per Capt. Sam[l] Oliver. M[r] Rowl[d] Oliver *re* Williams' affairs.

1749-50. Rich[d] Oliver of London, Merch[t], his correspondent.

1752, April 11. Rich[d] Oliver, Ex'or to Tho. Martin.

1758, Oct. 16. To Rich[d] & Rich[d] Oliver.

1760, Feb. 22. I have some reason not to be so well pleased with the Olivers ; they are shy in advancing money equal to my wants on acc[t] of a late purchase of mine.

1762, April 6. I hope M[r] Oliver, Sen[r], is got well again.

1763, Aug. 27. To Thos. Oliver, Esq. "My very worthy friend your deceased father, for whose Death I am heartily concerned ;" if R. Oliver comes home this year.

1764, Aug. 11. Messrs. Rich[d] & Thos. Oliver alone.

1747. Capt. Samuel Oliver was seen after the Gale, with only a mainmast. ('Gent. Mag.,' p. 481.)

Page 321. Sir George Martin-Holloway was born in London 6 July 1833, as George Frederick Augustus Charles Martin, first son of George Frederick Martin by Hannah

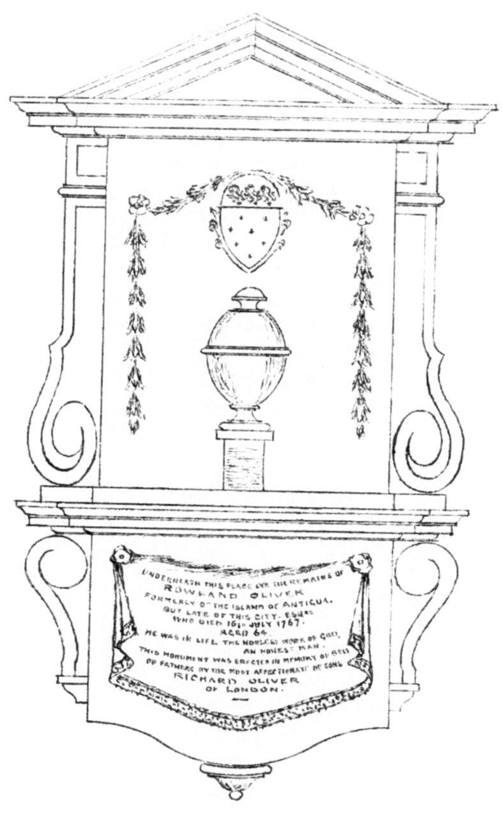

ST. MICHAEL'S CHURCH, BATH.

MARBLE TABLET OF VARIOUS COLOURS ON THE WALL OF THE TOWER.

Marriot his wife, and grandson of George Frederick Martin by Amelia Clemons his wife. For many years he carried ont the charitable schemes of his brother-in-law the late Thomas Holloway, patent medicine manufacturer, which resulted in the foundation of Holloway College at a cost of £800,000, and the Holloway Sanatorium for the Insane at a cost of £250,000. He took the name of Holloway by deed poll 20 Feb. 1884; was knighted in 1887; died at Cologne 14 Aug. 1895, and was interred at Sunninghill 22 Aug.; will dated 3 Aug. 1893; proved P.C.C. 31 Dec. 1895 by Walpole L. Greenwell, Vere L. Oliver, and Edward E. Greenwell the Ex'ors.

Mrs. F. V. Nash now resides at 4 Victoria Terrace, Weymouth, and has issue:—

1. Edith Vere, born July 1852 at Brighton; married 1892 at Tolpuddle Colonel Charles King, late of the Hampshire Regiment; s.p.
2. George, born 25 Jan. 1854, a planter in India, bachelor.
3. Rev. Cecil William, Vicar of Kincardine, N.B., M.A. Oxford, from Keble, born 24 June 1857; married Oct. 1885 Meriel, daughter of Rev. Fortescue Anderson, Vicar of North Berwick, and has issue:—
   Meriel Eileen Ella Vere, born 5 Aug. 1886 at Kincardine; Thomas; and a son born Jan. 1898.
4. Constance, born 15 March 1859.
5. Ada Maud, born 10 Feb. 1861; married at Tolpuddle 1884 Charles W. Sneyd-Kynnersley, Esq., Resident Councillor of Penang, son of the late Thomas Clement Sneyd-Kynnersley, J.P., D.L., cos. Stafford and Worcester (see Burke's 'Landed Gentry'), and has issue an only child Thomas.
6. Ella, born 19 Sep. 1862; married at St. John's, Weymouth, 20 April 1898, Percy Radcliffe, Esq., second son of the late James Radcliffe of Swinnow Hall, Wetherby, Yorkshire.
7. Mary Estella, born 29 March 1864; married at Tolpuddle James Edward Crane, Esq., of Southover House, Lord of the Manor of Tolpuddle, and has issue:—
   Malcolm, and a daughter Stella.
8. Mabel Helen, born at Weymouth 26 Feb. 1869.

Page 322. See a pedigree of the Hansons in Watson's 'History of Halifax' and Burke's 'Landed Gentry,' 1849 edition. Mary I. Oliver was married 4 March at the parish church of St. Michael, Crooked Lane. Susanna Dorothy Apreece, only sister of Sir Thomas Hussey Apreece, 1st Bart., was born 7 Jan. 1751; married . . . . Coles by whom she had a son Thomas Henry Coles, D.D. The latter's cousin Sir T. G. Apreece, Bart., shot himself in 1842 at Margate, and left all his property to St. George's Hospital. Dr. Coles had an only son Rev. Henry Apreece Coles, born 15 July and baptized 29 Sep. 1806, who was Vicar of Marnham, co. Notts, 1844—72, when he resigned and went to live at Leamington.—(R. E. Cole.)

Henry Oliver removed with his family to New Zealand in 1896.

Page 341. In 1771 Mr T. Oliver voted for the motion for dissolving the Society for supporting the Bill of Rights. ('Town and Country Mag.,' p. 221.)

Page 342. 1771, March 30. A copy of the Warrant of Commitment, by which Mr. Alderman Oliver is now detained in the Tower:—

Whereas the House of Commons have this day adjudged, that Richard Oliver, Esq; a Member of this House, having signed a warrant for the commitment of the Messenger of the House, for having executed the warrant of the Speaker, issued under an order of the House, and having held the said Messenger to bail, is guilty of a breach of the privilege of the House: and whereas the said House hath this day ordered the said Richard Oliver, Esq; one of the Aldermen of the City of London, and a Member of this House, to be for his said offence committed to the Tower of London.

These are therefore to require you to receive into your custody the body of the said Richard Oliver, Esq: and him safely to keep, during the pleasure of the said House, for which this shall be your sufficient warrant. Given under my hand the twenty-fifth day of March, one thousand seven hundred and seventy-one.

FLETCHER NORTON, Speaker.

To the Lieutenant of Tower of London,
or his Deputy.

('Town and Country Mag.,' p. 220.)

See a letter of Rd O. to the regt of Guards. (*Ibid.*, p. 276.)

1772, June 24. Yesterday came on the election for sheriffs for the year ensuing, when Mr. Alderman Oliver, and Watkin Lewes, Esq., were by the present sheriffs declared duly elected; but a poll being demanded in favour of Mr. Alderman Plumbe, notice was immediately given, that the books for that purpose would be opened in the afternoon at four o'clock, and closed at six in the evening; and afterwards to open at nine in the morning, and close at three in the afternoon, each day, during its continuance. (*Ibid.*, p. 334.)

July 2. Yesterday the poll finally ended at Guildhall for sheriffs; when the numbers were for alderman Oliver 1586, Mr. Lewes 1327, for alderman Plumbe 762. (*Ibid.*, p. 388.)

1772, Sep. 11. — Oliver, Esq. in Welbeck-street, a near relation to alderman Oliver. (*Ibid.*, p. 504.)

1772, Oct. 8. See Richard Oliver's Speech to the Livery. ('Gent. Mag.,' p. 490.)

On 23 Sep. the silver cup was presented (p. 436); his speech on 16 Dec. (p. 594).

1773, Jan. 31. His threatened duel with his co-sheriff Watkin Lewes averted (p. 99); as to short parliaments (pp. 101-109); 29 Sep., poll demanded (p. 466); Oct. 6. Poll for Lord Mayor Wilkes 1683, Bull 1649, Sawbridge 1177, Oliver 1093.

1774. Refuses to sign paper (p. 491).

1775. Speaks against long parliaments (p. 62).

Dec. Presents petition from W. I. merchants & planters (1776, p. 291).

1778, Nov. 24. A court of aldermen was held at Guildhall, at which were present the lord mayor, aldermen Alsop, Harley, Wilks, Bull, Kennet, Oliver, Lewes, Plomer, Thomas, Hayley, Newnham, Clark, Woolridge, Hart, Wright and Pugh.

Mr. Alderman Oliver arose in his place, and in a short speech, in which he thanked the aldermen for the polite and respectable behaviour always shewn him, desired, for reasons he had already given, and which have been since further strengthened by recent acts, to resign his gown as alderman of the Ward of Billingsgate, which resignation was accepted. Mr. Oliver, before he retired, wished that the court of aldermen might ever meet with that respect which their rank in the corporation merited; adding, that he left that court with an ardent desire, that whatever gentleman should succeed him, and indeed every present and future alderman, would prove themselves by their conduct the honest and faithful guardians of the liberties and franchises of this city.

The court then resolved unanimously, that the thanks of the court be given as follows:—

"Plumbe, Mayor, The first court held on Tuesday, the 24th day of November, 1778, and in the 19th year of the reign of King George the Third, of Great Britain, etc.

"Resolved unanimously, that the thanks of this court be given to Richard Oliver, Esq; late alderman of the Ward of Billingsgate, for his regular attendance, and salutary councils in this court; his wise, vigilant, and impartial administration of justice; his constant zeal for the honour, safety and prosperity of his fellow-citizen; and his inviolable attachment to the laws and liberties of his country.

"Ordered, that the said resolution be fairly transcribed, and signed by the Town Clerk, and published in the public papers. Rix." ('Town and Country Mag.,' pp. 666-7.)

1779, Dec. 22. Rowland Oliver, esq: of Bloomsbury. ('Gent. Mag.,' p. 616.)

1786, Feb. 25. John Pardoe, jun. esq. member for Plymouth, to miss Oliver, daughter of Thomas Oliver, esq. of Layton, in the county of Essex. ('Town and Country Mag.,' p. 167.)

Page 345. HOLY TRINITY CHURCH, TORONTO, CANADA.

Baptized.

1860 Feb. 10 Ethel Amy Harriett, dau. of Charles Langford and Amy Oliver. Gentleman. Ellah's Hotel. Born Jan. 12, 1860; privately bap. by W. Stewart Darling.

Page 346. Lieut.-Governor Thomas Oliver was residing in 1787 on his second wife's plantation at Antigua called Freemans or Friar's Hill, and had a pew in St. John's Church allotted to him.

Page 347. 1863, May 4. At North Stoke, Oxon, aged 71, James Elton, esq., late Recorder of Tiverton, Devon, in which neighbourhood he was some years since well known as an active master of fox-hounds, and a daring rider across country. ('Gent. Mag.,' p. 109.)

Page 354. EXTRACTS FROM THE WILLS IN THE GREAT ORPHAN BOOK, BRISTOL.

(Bristol and Gloucestershire Archaeological Society's Publications. By Rev. T. P. Wadley.)

1386. Walter Derby, burgess. Witnessed by John Oliver.

1387. Walter Frampton, burgess; legacy to Simon Olyver.

1389. Hugh le Hunt, burgess; legacy to Simon Olyver an Ex'or.

1389, Sep. 14. John Riper. Simon Olyver, overseer.

1391, Sep. 24. Henry London; legacies to Simon Olyver & the Mayor to see will fulfilled; proved 17 Ric. ii.

1392. Alan Wryngton. Arrangement with Simon Olyver as to sale of lands.

1392, Dec. 6. Wm. Somerwell, burgess. Sir John Olyver a witness.

1395. Tho. Spert, chancellor & canon of Wells. Ex'ors are to sell a tenement, once the property of Nich. Portbury, in the street of the blessed Mary in Foro, lately held by Simon Olyver.

1409, Feb. 26. Walter Seymour, burgess. A corner tenement in St Peter's street as one goes through the lane towards Wynche street, opposite the house where Simon Olyver dwells. (P.C.C., 20 March.)

1419, May 2. Simon Olyver, burgess. Testator describes himself as of the parish of St. Peter, & desires to be buried in the church there under the stone prepared by him for his monument, & under which his former wife Agnes lies. To his brother John Olyver his dwelling house & 4 shops built by him in St Peter's street, heretofore "ante edificac'oem p'me fact'," called "le plase sc'i Petri"; also his tenements in Lewynsmede. To Joan Boxwell, who was relict of Robert Boxwell, & guardian of testator's person after his wife Agnes departed, the sum of 12 marks 6*s.* 8*d.* for her good guardianship, the money to be levied by the persons appointed or his assigns, "temp'ibz obligac'onum a Joh'e Sherp," formerly Mayor of the town of Bristol, as it is more plainly contained in the letters of the bonds. Sir Thomas Lye, rector of St. Peter's, James Cokkes, and John Boxwell Ex'ors. Witnessed by Thomas Perys, Thomas Wylmott of Bristol, and others.

Proved before the commissary of the Prior of Worcester, "sede vacante," May 10, 1419; before the Mayor on Wednesday next before the feast of the Nativity of St. John Baptist, 7 Henry V.

1434, Sep. 16. Nich. Excestre, burgess. A hall & 14 shops opposite St Peter's place, situate between the shops of our Lady the Queen, which Simon Olyver lately caused to be built anew, & the lane called Stretedefence.

1474, Nov. 12. Wm. Canynges. A tenement with 14 shops opposite St Peter's Cross, between the shops of our Lady the Queen, which Simon Olyver lately caused to be built anew, & a lane called Strete of defence.

1557, June 19. Thomas Oliver, baker. Testator was of "the p'ishe of St Thomas th'appostell within the Cittie of Bristoll," and desired to be buried in the churchyard there. To the poor alms-people within that parish vj^s viij^d in bread. To dau. Elizabeth Oliver & her heirs a messuage in Reckcliffe streate, inhabited by Richd Rose, shoemaker, at 18. To wife Marg^t a messuage upon the Backe, inhabited by John Thomas. To son John at 21 all the rest of lands, tenements, rents, etc. Wife Marg^t to have the keeping of said son & dau. during their nonage, remainder to her, brother-in-law Richard Alkin, sister-in-law Eliz. Craddocke. To son John a goblet of silver, parcel gilt, & "haulf a dozen of Silver spones with Maydens' heddes." To dau. Eliz. "a standinge Cuppe of Silver, p'cell guilt, etc." Wife Marg^t residue & sole Ex'trix. Friends Richd Alkin & Tho. Craddocke, "my brother-lawes," overseers & X^s apiece. Wm Edmondes, Surgion, vi^s viij^d. Witnessed by Richard Woodcocke, saddler, William Dawemer, tailor, Randall Hassall, shearman, Richard Alkyn, and others. Proved 12 July 1557.

1567, Sep. 11. Richd Alkyne, soapmaker, of St Thomas' parish; sons John, Robt, Michael, Richard, & W^m, & daus. Joan, Frances, Eliz., Susan, Marg^t, & Sara £20 each. Wife Joan, sister Eliz. Wheitley, etc. Proved at London 20 Oct. 1567.

1574, Jan. 10. Wm Carr, merchant. To my servant Wm Oliver the lease in reversion of 21 years in one close of pasture called "Carrell's hamme" of 8 acres within the sea wall & 3 acres without, in Porteshedd.

1588, Sep. 13. John Caroe, vintner, of St Stephen's parish. A tenement upon Michael Hill, now or late in the tenure of Roger Oliver.

John Rowland of Bristol. Will proved P.C.C. 18 May 1576. My son Thomas, wife Eliz., father Rich[d] Rowland, brother Nich. Langford, & sister Joan his wife.

Joseph Hobbs of Bristol, sailmaker. Will dated 1688. (137 Exton.) John Oliver, ironmonger, overseer.

Jane Tayer of Bristol, widow. Will dated 25 Aug. 1698; proved 12 Sep. 1699. (150 Pett.) My niece Eliz. Timbrell £10. Aunt Eliz. Oliver 2 g[as]. My 2 daus. Frances Tayer & Mary Shute, wife of Chr. Shute, grocer.

William Adye of Malmesbury, co. Wilts, Gent. Will dated June 1703. (55 Ash.) Ruined fortune. Wife.

Frances Hodges of Bristol, widow. Will dated 1712. (70 Barnes.) Sister Ann Olver.

John Chapman of Bristol, skinner. Will dated 1718. (157 Tenison.) Arthur Oliver a witness.

Elizabeth Mounsey of Bristol, widow. Will dated 1719. (111 Browning.) Tho. Olliver of Bristol, weaver, £5.

Joseph Vigor, sen., of Bristol, merchant. Will dated 1726. (165 Brook.) My trusty & well beloved friend Edward Olver, ironmonger, of Bristol, a trustee, & 5 g[as] for his trouble.

Lydia Gregory of Bristol, widow. Will dated 16 Dec. 1728; proved 23 April 1731 by Susanna Oliver. (92 Isham.) My nephew Tho. Hersent £200, niece Susanna Oliver £300. Whereas my sister Sarah Hersent, deceased, desired that I would at my death give to the said Thos. Hersent, Susanna Oliver, & Benj. Biss (since deceased) £120 due from the estate of W[m] Penn, Esq., I do confirm the same. My niece Mary Galler of Darley, co. Hants, £5. Kinsman Tho. Carter of Southampton, pewterer, £5. Nephew Rich[d] Oliver a bed, etc. Kinsman John Gregory of Pill, co. Som., £50, & to his son John £10, & his 2 daus. £5 each. Sarah Whiting,* sister of the said John Gregory, £35, her 1st son £10, & her 2 daus. £5 each. Kinswoman Eliz. Paskin £35, her son £5, her dau. £10. My granddau. Eliz. Hiscox 25*s*. piece of gold. Friends Rachel Harford & Sarah Bush, both of Bristol, £20 for Quaker poor. Servant Ann Harris £10, a porringer marked I^G L, two spoons marked S. H., & my sister Hersent's linen. Frances Biss, mother of said Benj[n] Biss, £5. Mary Silcox & Hannah Godwin 1 ga. each. The debts of my late kinsman Benj. Biss to be paid. Alex[r] Arscott, gent., & James Boult, mercer, Trustees & 2 broad pieces of 23*s*. All residue to my said niece Susanna Oliver & sole Ex'trix. Witnessed by Samuel Reynell, jun., Rachell Harris.

Codicil. 29 Aug. 1730. Have purchased of Mary Horwood, widow, 2 messuages in parish of S[t] Philip & S[t] Jacob which are to be sold. Witnessed by Jo. Hipsly, John Godwin, Elinor Gifford.

Thomas Oliver of Worcester, Notary Public. Will dated 1735. (78 Ducie.) Brother Chr. Oliver. Aunt Dingley. Wife Eliz. The portions of my 3 eldest daus. Ann, Cath., & Mary have been paid. My 4 younger children by my said wife.

John Oliver, late of Bristol, now of H.M. sloop "Jamaica." Will dated 26 Sep. 1747; proved 12 July 1758 by Margaret Oliver, widow, the mother. (224 Hutton.) My father & mother Geo. & Marg[t] Oliver of Temple Parish all estate & Ex'ors. Witnessed by Henry Combe, Sarah Hickman, William Cory, William Bevan.

Helena Hart of Westbury-upon-Trim, co. Gloucester, widow. Will dated 30 Jan., proved 11 May 1752. (127 Bettesworth.) To be buried at Kelson churchyard near my brother & sister Gibbs. Niece Eliz. Warren, spinster, a tenement. Niece Eliz. Gibbs. Niece Dioness Gibbs. My late aunt Long. Sister Hannah Gibbs of Bath, spr., £10 a year. Niece Dioness,† wife of Joseph Oliver of Bristol, gent., £5 a year.

* 1706. (109 Eedes.) Nicholas Whiting of Bristol, soapmaker.
1706. (139 Eedes.) Jane Whiting of Bristol, widow.
1716. (128 Fox.) Samuel Whiteing of Bristol, Gent.

† She was daughter of Thomas Warren by Jane Gibbes, daughter of Alderman Henry Gibbes. (See 'Mis. Gen. et Her.,' vol. i., p. 6.)

A[o] 1276. Chancery Inquisition p.m. 4 Edw. I., No. 30.

Roger Oliver held his court in the town of Swaleclyve, co. Wilts, of John de Maunderyle in chief, and holds three messuages and 75 acres worth 51*s*. 7*d*. yearly. John Oliver, son of the said Roger, is his next heir and was aged 6 on the feast of St. Michael 3 Edw. I.

A[o] 1395. Chancery Inquisition p.m. 18 Ric. II., No. 112.

Inquisition taken at Bristol before William Frome, Mayor of the City and escheator, on Saturday next before the feast of the Conversion of St. Paul 18 Ric. II. [1395] by the oath of John Gibbys, Walter Herugge, etc., jurors, who say that it will not be to the damage of the King if he grants to Simon Olyver a messuage and waste place, which said messuage is worth per annum . . . . and the said waste place 3*s*. 4*d*. The said messuage is held . . . . in free burgage. The said waste place contains in length on the east part thereof 2 perches and 11 feet of land . . . . and in breadth from the south part to the corner thereof 3 perches . . . . [The heir's name is not given, and the Inquisition is torn away in places.]

A[o] 1592. Chancery Inquisition p.m. 12 Oct. 34 Eliz., Part 2, No. 48, and 36 Eliz., Part 1, No. 60.

John Ollyver was seised as of fee of a messuage called Ivyes and 84 acres in Sherston Magna, co. Wilts, also of a messuage called Hyde House and 102 acres in Sharston Pinckney *alias* Parva worth clear 63*s*. per annum, also lands held of the Queen by the service of the 10th part of a knight's fee. John Ollyver died 6 May 26 Eliz. [1584]. Henry Ollyver is his son and heir, and was then aged 6 and more. Henry Quintyn of Bupton is guardian in socage.

Wilts. Ancient Deeds at P.R.O.

B. 1868. No date. Grant by Nicholas de Nethemore to William Olyver and Agnes his wife of land in La Cleytelonde in the field of Langele Burel.

C. 2633. Release by Avelyne de Wychamtone to John Olyver of Bristol and Joan his wife of all her right in lands in East T . . . . Rammesbury, and Chiltone. Witnesses, Thomas Knap,* Mayor of Bristol, John Bannebury, Sheriff, and others, after Michaelmas 16 Ric. II. [1393].

A[o] 1327. Wilts. Feet of Fines 1 Edw. III.

(Hoare's 'Wilts,' vols. iv. and v., p. 223.)

John Oliver, sen., and Agnes his wife as to a messuage, mill, and 36 acres in Chilmark.

LEYTON, CO. ESSEX.

In the churchyard on the west side of the Pardoe tomb:—

Arms: *Argent, on a chevron embattled, counter embattled, between three towers sable, as many bombs of the field fired proper* (PARDOE); impaling, *Ermine, on a chief . . . . three lions rampant* . . . . (OLIVER).

Under this Tomb
are depofited the remains of
JANE the wife of JOHN PARDOE, Jun. Efq[r]:
Second daughter of THO[s] OLIVER Efq[r]
She departed this life the 20th day of April 1796,
in the 27th year of her age.
alfo of the faid JOHN PARDOE, who died the 26th day
of the fame month and year, aged 39.

(There are also inscriptions to Mr. Pardoe's parents and his children, etc.)

* Thomas Knappe was Mayor for the first time in 1386, and for the fifth and last time in 1403. John Bannebury died in 1404.

OSBORNE. Page 368.

1774, March 10. John Husband Osborn, Esq; at Montserrat, in the West Indies, a member of the assembly, and one of the judges of the courts of Kings-bench, and Common-pleas in that island. ('Town and Country Mag.,' p. 168.)

1864, April 23. In Paris, aged 79, the Hon. Theodosia, widow of Capt. Kean Osborn, 5th Dragoon Guards. ('Gent. Mag.,' p. 808.)

OTTLEY. Page 373.

Gilbert Franklyn was of Mereworth Castle, Kent, and a Member of the Council of Tobago.

1776, Oct. 11. Wm. Franklyn, eldest son of Gilbert Franklyn, Esq; of Bruton-street. ('Gent. Mag.,' p. 483.)

1806, March 1. At Mary-la-Bonne church, John Gilbert Francklin, esq. to Mrs. Stevenson, widow of the late Major-general S. of the Bengal Cavalry. (*Ibid.*, p. 280.)

1811, Dec. 30. At Blackmore, Essex, J. Gilbert Francklyn, esq. See 'Notes and Queries,' vol. vii., Eighth Series, p. 107. (*Ibid.*, p. 661.)

1812, Oct. 17. At Blackmore, Essex, Mrs. Franklyn, of Upper Norton-street. (*Ibid.*, p. 496.)

Page 374. Sir Richard Ottley was at Eton in 1791.

Page 375. 1772, April 21. Sir John Blois, Bart. to Miss Lucretia Ottley. ('Town and Country Mag.,' p. 223.)

1835, Oct. 8. The Rev. Lawrence Ottley, eld. son of Sir R. Ottley, to Eliz. eldest dau. of the Rev. J. Bickersteth, Vicar of Acton, Suff. ('Gent. Mag.,' p. 545.)

1861, Oct. 26. Louisa Elizabeth, wife of Captain William Vine, 6th Madras Light Cavalry, and dau. of the late William Young Ottley, esq. F.S.A. (*Ibid.*, p. 693.)

Rev. Francis John Ottley, at Eton 1841, Mathematical Master, was first son of Rev. John Bridges Ottley of Eling, co. Hants, M.A. Oriel. Rev. John Bridges Hooker assumed the name of Ottley in 1820.

1897, Dec. 4. On the 1st instant, at Templestowe, Torquay, the Rev. Warner Beckingham Ottley, late Indian Chaplain, Madras, last surviving son of the late William Young Ottley, Esq., and Sarah his wife, of 31 Devonshire Street, Portland Place, London, aged 78.

PARISH REGISTER OF ST. GEORGE, HANOVER SQUARE.

Married.

1761 May 26 Frederick Wollaston, of this parish, Clerk, W., & Priscilla Ottley, of St James, Westm^r, S., a minor, with consent of John Banister, Esq., & Wm Ottley, Esq., her Guardians appointed by the Lord High Chancellor. L.A.C.

ST. JAMES'S, BATH.

('Genealogist,' vol. ix., p. 110.)

Buried.

1775 Mar. 4 William Oattley (*sic*), Esq.

[END OF ADDITIONS TO VOLUME II.]

VOLUME III.

PARKE. Page 2.

Captain Byrd, from Cheshire, the first settler, married Mary daughter of Warham Horsemanden, a Kentish Cavalier, and lived on the site of Richmond; became Receiver-General of the King's Revenue, Colonel of Militia, and died in 1704, being succeeded by his son William, born 28 March 1674, died 26 Aug. 1744; admitted to the Bar of Middle Temple, F.R.S., President of Council, Receiver-General, Agent, etc.; 37 years Member of Council.

"Two years after coming into his inheritance—his father died in 1704—Colonel Byrd married Lucy Parke, daughter of the aide-de-camp of the Duke of Marlborough, who carried the news of the victory of Blenheim to Queen Anne. Another daughter was the progenitress of Martha Washington's first husband and of the wife of General Robert Edmund Lee.

"One of Kneller's portraits of Colonel Daniel Parke hangs in the dining-room at Brandon, another in the house of General Custis Lee at Lexington, Virginia. In both he is gorgeously attired in crimson velvet, with embroidery, and with a steenkirk and ruffles of costly lace, wears around his neck the queen's miniature set in pearls, presented to him by her placid majesty in reward for his good tidings, and looks prodigiously well pleased with himself, while the battle of Blenheim is raging in the background."

Mrs. Lucy Parke Byrd died at London in 1716 of small-pox. She left an only girl, Evelyn Byrd; she died at Westover, single, 13 Nov. 1737, æt. 28. Colonel Byrd remarried 1724 Miss Maria Taylor of Kensington.—('Century Magazine' for 1891, vol. xlii., pp. 163—178. Article on Colonel William Byrd of Westover, Virginia.)

PAYNE. Page 8.

1788, May. John Payne, esq; of Temford-hall, Bedfordshire, to Miss Campbell. ('Town and Country Mag.,' p. 291.)

1808, Sep. 22. At Tortola, Pickering Lettsom, esq. (son of Dr. L.) to Mrs. Georges, widow of William Payne G. esq. of Manchester-square, sister to Lord Lavington, and mother of Mrs. Charles Combe. ('Gent. Mag.,' p. 1038.)

1808, Sep. 29. At Tortola, Charles Combe, esq. youngest son of Dr. C. of Hart-street, Bloomsbury; a young gentleman whose untimely loss will long be regretted by many who well knew and justly estimated his merit. (*Ibid.*)

1808, Oct. 28. At Tortola, in his 28th year, Pickering Lettsom, esq. youngest son of Dr. L. (*Ibid.*, p. 1127.)

1809, Jan. 24. At Tortola, Mrs. Lettsom, relict of Pickering L. esq. (*Ibid.*, p. 278.)

PERRY. Page 20.

In 1789 the portrait of Micajah Perry was at Haberdasher's Hall. ('Gent. Mag.,' p. 888.)

PIGOTT. Page 26.

Rev. Richard Pigott, D.D., who married Hon. Dorothy Crosbie, was the second son of Emanuel Pigott and his third wife Judith Warburton. This Rev. Dr. Pigott inherited the Dysart estate from his third-cousin Thomas Pigott of Kilcromin and Grange, Queen's County, who married Mary Wheeler.

What is not generally known is that this Emanuel Pigott was really married three times, his second wife being Ann Phair, married in Diocese of Cork 1722; and in "The Index to the Marriage Licence Bonds of the Diocese of Cork and Ross" I find the following, viz.:—

"Aquila Stoughton and Hanna Scott mar. 1670."

Was this the "Aquila" who married Frances Proctor, widow, mother of the Frances Proctor who married Captain John Pigott, killed in Antigua 1710 (his first wife)?

(WM. JACKSON PIGOTT.)

POLLINGTON. Page 30.

1666-7, Jan. 18. Samuel Pollington of Antego. Adm'on to John Stoner, next-of-kin.

POWELL. Page 33.

1746, Aug. 27. Dr. Tullideph to Governor Thomas: The estate you sold to Powell, with an addition of 20 or 30 acres of Billie Richardson's, is now rented out of Powell's Executors for £550 st.

POYNTZ Page 36.

John Aston of London, merchant. Will dated 1715. (63 Fagg.) £600 given as a portion with my dau. Mary to her husband Wm Poyntz.

REDWOOD. Page 43.

John Redwood of St. Dunstan's, Gent. Will dated 1660. (15 Nabbs.) Wife Mary.

Nicholas Redwood of Exon, ironmonger. Will dated 1669. (22 Coke.) Son Nich. £80, son John £300, dau. Mary £500. Wife Charity.

John Avery of Bristol, plumber. Will dated 1713. (18 Aston.) Sarah Redwood £250, dau. of my sister Kath. Plumer, wife of Tho. Plumer.

Edward Morley of Bristol, tyler and plaisterer. Will dated 1722. (241 Marlborough.) Son-in-law Richard Redwood £100 at 21, dau.-in-law Eliz. Redwood, his sister, £100. My wife Eliz.

Christopher Redwood, late of Bristol, merchant. Will dated 1741. (136 Spurway.) Sister Frances Redwood £50. Wife Rebecca.

The following notes were sent to me by Mr. Boverton Redwood in 1896:—

COPY OF LETTER ADDRESSED TO "CHARLES REDWOOD, ESQ., COWBRIDGE, GLAMORGAN."

London,
15 Octo. 1829.

SIR,

On my arrival in town last Evg I found your letter, and in reply have to state I never knew a Robert Redwood. About the year 1660 Abraham Redwood, son of a Redwood who died in England, went to N. America, where he married. By his first wife he had a son Abraham, my Grandfather, who was born in 1700, & by his second wife another son William, who settled in Philadelphia & had several daughters, all well married there, & only one son by his 2d wife, born after he was 70, which son is now alive, unmarried, & is named William. My G. Father had three sons, Jonas Langford (my Father), William, & Abraham. My Father had two sons, myself & Jonas Langford, my younger brother, who died 1803 [or 1808—V. L. O.], unmarried. William had no children. Abraham had one son, Langford, who is now alive and at present in the United States, so, you see, for near 200 years there has been no Robert. I believe the head of our branch came from the West of England, all the three first generations having been brought up Quakers, & the whole of the before named were born in Rhode Island, N. America. I was sent to England for Education early in the American War, & have been occasionally in the W. Indies & America since the last time among the Islands in 1794; having many acquaintance W. Indians I am certain I should have heard of any Redwood in any superior situation in the Leeward Islands, certainly no governor of that name, Monserrat having never been a separate government, but always a part of the Leeward Islands Gov., till their division about 30 years ago, when Monserat was added to the govt of Antigua.

Between 20 & 30 years since there was a Phillip Redwood* Attorney-Gen. of Jamaica. I did not know him, but understand he died without children. A friend of mine in the Heralds' Office [Mr. Pulman—V. L. O.] told me he had occasion to examine some very old registers in the Church of St. Mary Ottery, Devon, & he observed the births & deaths of several of the name from 16 to 1700. I once knew a Capt. Redwood,* 5 Dragoon guards, whose Father was named Jeriniah,† & from the scripture name it is very probable he may have been descended from the same ancestor. The last of the name I saw was this summer at Taunton, in passing through, but seeing it was an old cloths & rag shop I did not stop to make any enquiries. I shall be happy if the foregoing proves of any service to you; at any rate you will not find a competitor in,

Sir,
Your most obt. Servant,
ABRM REDWOOD.

* 1810. Lately. Aged 60, Philip Redwood, esq. of York-place, Portman-square, late chief justice of the island of Jamaica, and Speaker of the Hon. House of Assembly. ('Gent. Mag.,' p. 287.) His father Stephen Richard Redwood, Esq., was born at Spanish Town 1 Dec. 1726 and died 8 Dec. 1781. (L. Archer's 'M.I.,' p. 66, and 'Gloucester Notes and Queries,' vol. iii., pp. 234, 358.)

1647, Aug. 19. Adm'on of Hugh Redwood, late of Bristol, but in parts, bachelor, deceased, granted to Robert Redwood the brother.

The following on a folio sheet, probably torn out of a Bible:—

Mary Williams
Jany the 5th, 1785.

Mary Ann Redwood was born the 5th Day of October 1786, at 3 o' th' Clock in the Morning, being one of twins.

Thomas Lewis Redwood was born thursday the 6th Day of December 1787, between 11 and 12 o' th' Clock at night, and about ten minutes after was born,

John Redwood, being two of twins, both of whome died about one o' th' Clock the Sunday Morning following.

Margaret Redwood was born Wednesday the 6th Day of May 1789, about 7 o' th' Clock in the Morning, and about one hour after was born,

Thos Redwood, the seventh child from Mary Ann, aged at this Day two years and seven months.

Jennet Redwood was born the 18th of October 1790, about 11 o' th' Clock at Night, being the first single child.

Isaac Redwood was born the 12th of August 1792, on Sunday night, between 9 & 10 o' th' Clock.

Arms: *Paly of six, or and ermine, a lion rampant sable, on a chief azure an embattled gateway proper, between two mullets of six points of the first* (REDWOOD).

Crest: *A rock, therefrom an eagle rising proper, charged on each wing with a mullet of six points, in the beak a staff raguly argent.*

Motto: *Lumen serimus antique.*

[No name of parish.]

Baptized.

1691	June	18	Charles S. of Charles Redwood & of Martha.
1692	Aug.	28	William S. of Charles Redwood & of Martha.
1697	July	30	Abraham S. of Richard Redwood.
1697	Oct.	31	Charles S. of Charles Redwood.
1702	June	7	John S. of John Redwood.
1707	June	17	Elizabeth D. of Christopher Redwood.
1709	May	5	Frances Redwood of Christopher and Elizabeth.
1711	Aug.	2	Thomas S. of Christopher and Elizabeth Redwood.
1713	Mar.	26	Chris. S. of Chris. Redwood and Elizabeth.
1715	July	20	Frances of Christopher & Elizabeth Redwood.
1718	Mar.	9	Hannah of Samuel & Ann Redwood.
1719	June	18	Mary of Christr & Eliz. Redwood.
1720	July	10	Stephen of Sam. & Ann Redwood.
1721	Aug.	25	Daniel of Christopher & Eliz. Redwood.
1722	Feb.	10	Grace of Sam. & Ann Redwood.

* 1804, Nov. 5. Capt. E. Redwood, of the 5th regiment of Dragoon-guards. ('Gent. Mag.,' p. 1169.)

† 1776, Aug. 28. Jerem. Redwood, sen. Esq; at Bromley, in Kent. (*Ibid.*, p. 436.)

1729 Feb. 1 Ann of James & Mary Redwood.
1734 Oct. 13 James of James & Mary Redwood.
1737 Aug. 7 Richard of James & Mary Redwood.

Buried.

1697 Sep. 10 Charles Redwood. In the Old Yard.
1698 Dec. 19 Charles Redwood. In the Old Yard.
1704 Oct. 10 George Redwood, from St Nicholas; in the Old Yard.
1705 Nov. 15 A Child of Christopher Redwood; in the Church.
1712 April 1 A Child of Mr Christopher Redwood; in the Church.
1712 Feb. 12 Mary Redwood. Old Yard.
1713 Jan. 10 A Child of Christopher Redwood. Church.
1719 Oct. 7 Mary of X'phor & Eliz. Redwood. Church.
1733 June 17 Christopher Redwood. Church.

PEDIGREE OF REDWOOD.

A short Pedigree of Redwood of Boverton appears in Burke's 'Landed Gentry,' 1858 Edition.

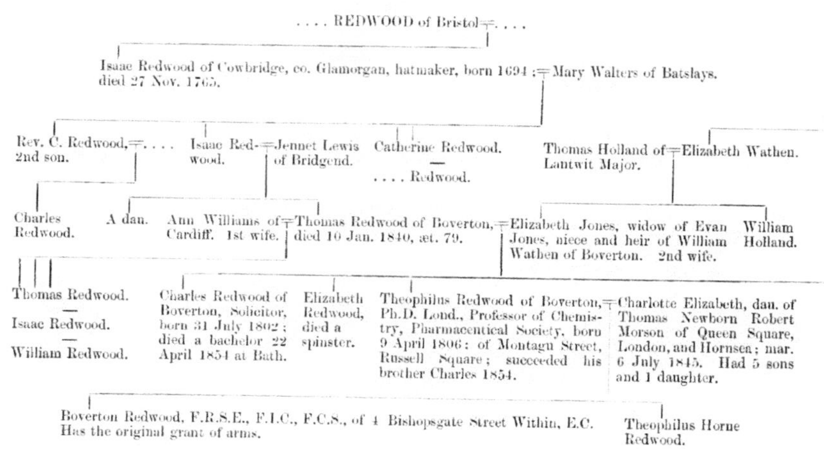
.... REDWOOD of Bristol=....
Isaac Redwood of Cowbridge, co. Glamorgan, hatmaker, born 1694; died 27 Nov. 1765.=Mary Walters of Batslays.
Rev. C. Redwood, 2nd son.=....
Isaac Redwood.=Jennet Lewis of Bridgend.
Catherine Redwood.
.... Redwood.
Thomas Holland of Lantwit Major.=Elizabeth Wathen.
Charles Redwood.
A dan.
Ann Williams of Cardiff. 1st wife.=Thomas Redwood of Boverton, died 10 Jan. 1840, æt. 79.=Elizabeth Jones, widow of Evan Jones, niece and heir of William Wathen of Boverton. 2nd wife.
William Holland.
Thomas Redwood.
Isaac Redwood.
William Redwood.
Charles Redwood of Boverton, Solicitor, born 31 July 1802; died a bachelor 22 April 1854 at Bath.
Elizabeth Redwood, died a spinster.
Theophilus Redwood of Boverton, Ph.D. Lond., Professor of Chemistry, Pharmaceutical Society, born 9 April 1806; of Montagu Street, Russell Square; succeeded his brother Charles 1854.=Charlotte Elizabeth, dau. of Thomas Newborn Robert Morson of Queen Square, London, and Hornsea; mar. 6 July 1845. Had 5 sons and 1 daughter.
Boverton Redwood, F.R.S.E., F.I.C., F.C.S., of 4 Bishopsgate Street Within, E.C. Has the original grant of arms.
Theophilus Horne Redwood.

[No name of parish.]
Underneath
Lieth the Bodies of the
Children of Isaac Redwood and
Mary his Wife. Rob. died Novr 10th 1723
Morgan died Feb. 28th 1732
Mary the Wife of Isaac Redwood
Died Octr 3rd 1750 in the 59th
Year of her Age.
As also Mary the Daur. of Tho. Lewis
Gent. and Anne his Wife who died
April 16th 1750.
Also 3 more of their Daurs. died
Decr 1st 1750.

Under lie three sisters in a Grave
They were a prize that God would have
Their Mother's Sorrow turn'd to Mirth
For they were all born at one birth.

Also underneath lies the
Body of the said Isaac Redwood
who departed this Life the 27th
day of November 1765 in the
72nd Year of his Age.

Here lieth the Body of Anne the
Wife of Thos Lewis Gent. who
departed this Life
March the [stone here broken]
9th 1791 aged 69 Years.
Also the body of the above
Thos Lewis Gent. who
departed this Life March the
28th 1807, aged 81 Years.

RICHARDSON. Page 46.

George Richardson of Nevis, vintner. Will dated 30 Dec. 13 H.M. reign. (153 Richmond.) Wife Eliz. ½ estate. Dau. Hester Richardson £100 c. at 21. All residue to my 2 sons John & Tho. Richardson. Friends Mr Tho. Minor, Mr. Soloman Israel, Mr. Hugh Gurnay Ex'ors. On 5 Feb. 1701-2 appeared the witnesses. True copy 1723. By Richard Abbott, Esq., President, 13 April 1723.

Zachariah Richardson. Will dated 1736. (41 Derby.) Suit obtained against Andrew Hamilton of Philadelphia. My wife's estate there. Wife Rebecca. My 5 sisters.

1746, Aug. 27. Dr. Tullideph wrote: "Dr. Richardson hath abt 90 Acres land and taken off his Crop with his new Windmill; he talks of going home if he can rent his Estate for £500 stg."

1789, Oct. 6. At Kirkton-hill, Wm. Richardson, esq. late of the island of St. Vincent, to Miss Eliz. Gardiner, da. of David G. esq. of Kirkton-hill. ('Gent. Mag.,' p. 954.)

ROACH. Page 48.

1710, July 3. Deposition of John Roach of Antegoa, merchant, that the last war and this, before the arrival of Governor Parke, he has been owner of a privateer. (French, p. 381.)

RODNEY. Page 49.

Dr. Tullideph wrote 1737 Aug. 15 that Cæsar Rodenay had quitted Antigua for debt, but that Dr. Sydserfe had got all his negros but 3 or 4 which he carried off with him. He announced his death in a letter dated 12 Nov. 1741.

RUSSELL. Page 60.

Colonel Randal Russell by his second wife Margaret (who remarried Governor Thomas Hill in 1682) had a son Edmund Russell and a daughter Mrs. Elizabeth Vernon; the pedigree on p. 61 requires correction on those points. See M.I. to Mr. Justice Cowper (Cussans' 'Herts,' vol. ii., p. 110), and a notice of his death in Mawson's Obits ('Genealogist,' vol. viii., p. 131).

1788, Dec. James Russel Maden, esq. of Green-street, Grosvenor-square. ('Town and Country Mag.,' p. 624.)

1792. Lately. Martin Madan, esq. of Epsom, Surrey, to Miss Anna Maria Ibbetson, daughter of the late Rev. J. I., D.D. archdeacon of St. Albans. ('Gent. Mag.,' p. 383.)

Lady Maitland died 22 Dec. 1805, æt. 75; he died 15 Feb. 1820, æt. 97. M.I. at Totteridge. (Cussans' 'Herts,' vol. ii., p. 301.)

Charles Wathan = Hannah . . . . Will dated 9 Nov. 1753; proved in Consistory Court of Llandaff 5 June 1775.

Mary Deere of Lantwit Major, widow. Will dated 13 Dec. 1742; proved at Llandaff 14 Feb. 1742. (37 Boycott.) Sister of Hannah.

Children of Charles and Hannah:
- Thomas Wathen. = ... (issue)
- William Wathen of Boverton in Lantwit Major, co. Glamorgan, and formerly of co. Gloucester, Gent. Will dated 23 May 1794; proved at Llandaff 13 Dec. 1796.
- Diana Wathen.
- Anne Wathen.
- Sarah Wathen.
- Mary Wathen.
- Elizabeth Wathen.
- Charles Wathen = ...
  - William Wathen.
  - Charles Wathen.

Lewis Redwood, Surgeon, of "The Lawn," Rhymney, co. Monmouth, and Boverton, born 15 April 1808; took out a grant of arms; succeeded his brother Charles 1854; dead. = Anna Maria, dau. of Joseph Hall and niece of James Williams Morgan, Sheriff of Radnor 1836.
- Two sons.
- Six daus.

A dau., died a spinster.

PARISH REGISTER OF ST. GEORGE, HANOVER SQUARE.

Married.

1819 Aug. 10 The Hon. James Henry Keith Stewart, B., & Henrietta Anne Madan of Ibstock, co. Leicester, S. Witnessed by Spencer Madan, S. Marlborough, Caroline Spencer Churchill, Charlotte Madan, Frances Madan, Penelope Frances Madan.

SAUNDERS. Page 70.

1719, July 15. Governor Hamilton writes: Mr Samuel Saunders officiates in the room of Mr. Jeffard, absent in Great Britain. 1728, Dec. 1, St Peter's Parish, Rev. Samuel Sanderson, A.M., Oxon. Ordained by Edwd, Bishop of Gloucester, in 1696 (Fulham Palace MSS.). He matriculated as son of Nath. of Wootton-under-Edge, co. Glouc., pleb. St Edmund Hall, 5 Feb. 1689-90, aged 16; B.A. 1693; M.A. 1696; Rector of Saxelby, co. Leic. 1707.

1777, Feb. 14. Gregory Saunders, Esq; at Tower-hill, late of the island of Antigua. ('Town and Country Mag.,' p. 168.)

SCOTLAND. Page 74.

1863, Jan. 29. At Kensington, Sarah, wife of George Scotland, esq. C.B. and only dau. of the late Rev. W. Humphrys, of the Island of Antigua. ('Gent. Mag.,' p. 395.)

SHAND. Page 78.

1787, June 21. At St. Kitts, Capt. Anth. Young, to Miss Rawling, dau. of Stidman R. esq. ('Gent. Mag.,' p. 738.)

1799. Stedman Rawlins Hartman then at Eton.

Stedman Rawlins, son of Stedman Rawlins of St. Christopher's in the West Indies, Esq., matriculated from Christ Church 22 Oct. 1801, aged 17.

1803, Aug. 22. At Eltham, Kent, Capt. Rawlins, of the 30th foot, to Miss Anne Taylor Rawlins, daughter of the late Stedman R. esq. of St. Kitt's, in the West Indies. ('Gent. Mag.,' p. 788.)

1862, July 10. At Neston, Liverpool, aged 74, Mary, relict of Francis Shand, esq. of Liverpool, and eldest dau. of the late Sir John Reid, bart. of Barra. (*Ibid.*, p. 237.)

SHEPHARD. Page 80.

Mary Stoodly of Yeovil, co. Somerset, spinster. Will dated 8 Sep. 1737; proved 26 July 1738. (185 Brodrepp.) My friend Mr Nathl Knott £500 given me by the will of my late uncle Chr. Stoodly of Antigua, merchant, all estate & Ex'or. Witnessed by William Knott, Thomas Templeman.

SMITH. Page 89.

Thomas Smith of Nevis, Gent. Will dated 1 May 1722; proved 10 Dec. 1735 by Martha Smith the relict. (257 Ducie.) Wife Martha all estate & Ex'trix. Witnessed by John Ruggles, J. Bernhofe, J. Nobbs, Henry Gray.

PARISH REGISTER OF ST. GEORGE, NEVIS.

(Fulham Palace MSS.)

Married.

1724 June — William Woolward, mariner, & Anne Smith, widow.

Buried.

1719 Nov. 30 Mrs. Elizabeth Smith, late wife of Mr. John Smith of Stony-hill.

Page 98. 1715, June 28. Captain Henry Smith try'd at the King's Bench Bar for the Murder of Colonel Park, Governor of Antegoa, and acquitted. ('Historical Register,' p. 63.)

Page 99. Captain Edward Smith of H.M.S. "Burford." See his pedigree in 'Gent. Mag.' for 1830, p. 488, wherein he is stated to have died at Antigua in 1742 of wounds received at Laquira, and to have been buried at Antigua 9 June 1742, aged 51. He was grandfather of Admiral Sir Sidney Smith.

STAPLETON. Page 103.

1809, March 5. At Hinckley, co. Leicester, William Francis Stapleton, second son of Major-gen. S. and nephew of Lord Le Despencer. ('Gent. Mag.,' p. 284.)

SWETE. Page 104.

There is a pedigree of Sweet of Cork from Devon in 'Gent. Mag.' for 1863, p. 580.

SYMES. Page 110.

Elizabeth Symes married firstly Joseph Hawes, whose will of 1738 refer to. Her sister Henrietta's first husband was James Parke, Esq., whose estate she administered May 1741. Two other sisters, Amy and Catherine, were living in 1738.

TANKARD. Page 118.

Rear-Admiral Richard Tyrrell, died 27 June 1766 at sea. Will dated 20 Feb. 1765; proved P.C.C. 5 Aug. 1766. (323 Tyndall.) = Russel, widow of . . . . Chester of Antigua and dau. of . . . . Tankard, etc.

Ann Tyrrell = ... Barnes.

Catherine Tyrrell. = ... Reily.

Richard Tyrrell Barnes, succeeded to "Tyrrells"; bankrupt 1797; died intestate 28 Nov. 1817; a widower. = ... s.p.

Ann Barnes, died 1826. Will dated 11 Jan. 1823; proved P.C.C. 26 Feb. 1827. = Roger Pattoun, died before 1826.

Mary Barnes, died 24 June 1796, intestate. Adm'on dated 16 Sep. 1799 to Anne Riley the dau. (P.C.C.) = Marcus Feely, died before 1796.

George Pattoun, Captain Royal Marines 1840, later Brevet-Major; died 25 Oct. 1859 at Gravesend, æt. 75. = ... born 19 Sep. 1802; died 21 May 1842 at Wortheim-on-the-Main, Baden.

Richard Tyrrell Robert Pattoun, Captain 54th Foot 1840, later Lieut.-Colonel 32nd Regiment; killed at Moultan 18—. = Essie Mercer, died s.p.

Anna Pattoun of Cape Town, died there about 1869. = James Mitchell Sparks, Captain 30th Regiment Royal African Corps, died at Grahamstown, South Africa, about 1824.

Eliza Pattoun, died intestate at Chatham 22 Oct. 1834. = ... Feely, died before wife. s.p.

Anne Pattoun, born 1823; of "Sunnylands," Dalwood, Honiton, Devon, 1897. = John Tombs, H.E.I.C. Engineers, died 1892.

William Henry Wilson Pattoun, Lieut. 61st Regiment, born 9 May 1832; wounded at Moultan, and died at Simla from effects 11 Nov. 1857, bachelor.

James Pattoun Sparks, C.B., General, 38th Regiment, born 1800; died at Reynoldstone, Swansea, South Wales, 1881. = Eliza Lucas, died at Reynoldstone, South Wales, 1879. s.p.

Mitchell George Sparks, Colonel 10th Regiment, born about 1802; died in India. = ... Barnes of Westbury, Wiltshire, died in India.

Henry Tombs, Ceylon Rifles (retired), living at Dalwood, South Devon, unmarried.

John Barnes Sparks, Colonel Bengal Staff Corps, born 1842; died in London 1893. = Eliza J. Clark or Buist of New Scone, Perth; died in India 1883.

Mary (?) Sparks, died in India. = ... Newmarch, who went to Canada.

James Noel Sparks, born in India 1869; of Jesus College, Cambridge, B.A. 1891.

Louisa Sarah Sparks, born in Scotland 1871; mar. 1891; died in India 1895. = S. P. Rice, Indian Civil Service. s.p.

John Barnes Sparks, Lieut. Royal Navy, born in India 1873.

B. Hilda Sparks, born in India 1875; now of Calcutta. = J. Longmuir of Calcutta, India.

Paper copy of a deed sent to me 6 Oct. 1896 by Lieut.-Colonel H. S. Knight of Winchester. Indorsed 27 Sep. 1840. Mrs. Anne Riley and others to James Foster Groom, Esq. Release, etc., on Mr. Groom's dividing £1115 as manager of Tyrrells in the Island of Antigua, and confirmation of his appointment as manager. Pering, Minet, and Smith, 5 Lawrence Pountney Place.

Notes by Mrs. Ann Tombs, daughter of Captain George Pattoun. (These are written in the margin in the original.)

Indenture made 27 Sep. 1840 between Anne Riley of Dobson's Terrace, Kennington, co. Surrey, widow, George Pattoun of Wortheim* in Germany, Esq., Captain Royal Marines, Richard Tyrrell Robert Pattoun, Esq., of Golden Square, Middlesex, Captain 54th Foot, Anna Sparks of Cape Town, widow, James Farrell of Dublin, Gent., and Marianne Louisa his wife, and Bridget Delia Farrell of Dublin, spinster, of the 1st part, James Foster Groom of Abchurch Lane, London, Gent., of the 2nd part. Whereas by the will of Richard Tyrrell, Rear-Admiral R.N., dated 20 Feb. 1765, his nephew Richard Tyrrell Barnes, son of testator's sister Ann Barnes, became seised of a plantation and slaves in Antigua charged with £10,000 currency for the children of testator's two sisters Catherine Reily and Ann Barnes: and whereas the only persons who became entitled to said £10,000 were Mary Reily who married Charles Reily, Ann Barnes who married Roger Pattoun,† Mary Barnes who married Marcus Feely, Catherine Barnes who married Martin Ford, and Charlotte Barnes who married Thomas Farrell, and which said Mary Reily was the only child of said Catherine Reily, and said Ann Pattoun, Mary Feely, Catherine Ford, and Charlotte Farrell were the only children of said Ann Barnes (except Richard Tyrrell Barnes); and whereas said Richard Tyrrell Barnes in Oct. 1797 obtained his discharge as an insolvent debtor, and David Sands and Richard England were appointed his assignees; and whereas by indentures of lease and release dated 19 and 20 Jan. 1802, enrolled at Antigua, between said Richard Tyrrell Barnes and David Sands and Richard England, Tyrrells or Orleans was conveyed to them in fee simple on trust to pay certain debts. Richard England died in 1812, and David Sands made his will 29 Aug. 1810 and appointed Edmund Baker of Broad Street, Golden Square, Gent., and testator's nephew James Henderson, his heir-at-law, Ex'ors, and died 1814; and whereas on 15 Feb. 1823 James Foster Groom was appointed assignee, and by indenture of 17 and 18 June 1831 between James Henderson and Edmund Baker, of one part, and James Foster Groom, of the other, all estate was conveyed to them on trust; and whereas Richard Tyrrell Barnes died 28 Nov. 1817 intestate and a widower s.p., leaving his sisters Ann Pattoun and Catherine Ford and Thomas Dennis Brown Feely, first son of said Mary Feely, deceased, and John Farrell, first son of said Charlotte Farrell, deceased, his coheirs: and whereas Catherine Ford (sister of Richard Tyrrell Barnes), widow, made her will 26 May 1821, and gave her share in said estate of her uncle Admiral Richard Tyrrell to her nephew George Pattoun,* and appointed Thomas

* My father went to London on this business leaving my mother, William, and self at our lodgings in Wertheim.

† Grandfather.

* Admiral Richard Tyrrell was my father's great-uncle; his mother was the Admiral's niece; and her children were my father George Pattoun, Richard Tyrrell Robert Pattoun, Mrs. Feely, and Mrs. Sparks.

[Continued on next page.

Catherine Barnes, died 1827. Will dated 26 May 1821; proved P.C.C. 3 Dec. 1835. = Martin Ford, died before 1827. (s.p.)

Charlotte Barnes, died intestate 1803. Adm'on 11 July 1821 to her son John. (P.C.C.) = Thomas Farrell.

Mary Reily, only child, died intestate 15 July 1795. Adm'on 26 June 1821 to Catherine Ford. = Charles Reily, died before his wife. (s.p.)

Thomas Dennis Brown Feely, 1st son, died s.p. 1828. Will dated 16 June 1828; set aside by agreement, Ann Riley becoming heir.

Ann Feely of Dobson's Terrace, Kennington, 1840, widow. = ... Riley.

John Farrell, only son, died bachelor, intestate, 1836—1840. Adm'on to James Farrell. (P.C.C.)

Marianne Louisa Farrell of Dublin 1840. = James Farrell of Dublin 1840.

Bridget Delia Farrell of Dublin 1840.

Anna Sparks, born about 1805; died 1843 at Cape Town, South Africa. = Thomas Solters Knight, Cape Mounted Rifles, died 1833.

Richard Sparks, died in infancy.

Mary Jane Sparks, born 1806; living at Cape Town, South Africa, 1897, unmarried.

Eliza Sparks, died in India about 18—, unmarried.

Robert Manners Sparks, born about 1815 in South Africa; died there about 1886; married, but left no issue.

Fanny Sparks, died at Cape Town, South Africa, unmarried.

Emily Sparks, died in South Africa about 1849. = Albert Kennedy of Deep River, George, South Africa.

Henry Solters Gunning Sparks Knight, Colonel 19th Regiment, now of "The Observatory," Harestock, Winchester, born 1828; served in Antigua, 67th Regiment, 1854.

Isabella Maria Knight, born 1830; died 1873, unmarried.

Benjamin Kennedy, born 1842; living in South Africa 1897. = Jessie, dau. of Dr. Reitz of Somerset West, South Africa.

George Tyrrell Sparks, born in India 1878; died at Simla, India, 1879.

Olive Margaret Sparks, born in India 1881; of Redhill, Surrey, 1897.

Jessie Emily Kennedy. = R. W. Wingfield of Cape Town 1897.

One dau. and two sons, infants.

May Kennedy = H. W. Fanner of Cape Town 1897.

Cyril Sparks Fanner, born at Cape Town about 1891.

Hilda Kennedy, now of Somerset West, South Africa, unmar.

Lane Ex'or, and by her codicil of 22 Dec. 1827 revoked same and gave one-half of her share to her nephews first son Geo. Pattoun and Richard Tyrrell Robert Pattoun as tenants in common, and the other half to her niece Ann Riley, and all residue to latter and Ex'trix *vice* Thomas Lane, and Catherine Ford died in 1827 and will was proved P.C.C. 3 Dec. 1835; and whereas Ann Pattoun (first sister of Richard Tyrrell Barnes), widow, made her will 11 Jan. 1823 and gave one-quarter share to her son George Pattoun, one-quarter to her son Richard Tyrrell Robert Pattoun, one-quarter to her daughter Anna Sparks, one-quarter to her daughter Eliza Feely, and appointed George Pattoun, Eliza Feely, and Mitchell James Sparks Ex'ors, and Ann Pattoun, the said testatrix, died 1826* (proved P.C.C. 26 Feb. 1827), and Eliza Feely† died 18 . . intestate s.p., leaving George Pattoun her first brother and heir-at-law; and whereas Thomas Dennis Brown Feely, another of the coheirs of Richard Tyrrell Barnes, deceased, by his will dated 16 June 1828 bequeathed to Catherine Buckley, formerly of the town of Clonmell, co. Tipperary (daughter of Mr. Patrick Buckley and Catherine his wife of ditto), all his estate, and testator died 1828 s.p., leaving Anne Riley his sister his heir-at-law, and will was registered P.C. Ireland; and whereas by indenture of 3 Jan. 1838 between Catherine Buckley (called Catherine Feely, widow), of the 1st part, and Anne Riley, of the 2nd, whereby it appears that Anne Riley denied that Thomas Dennis Brown Feely executed his will and claimed share as heir-at-law, and Catherine Buckley *alias* Feely claimed as Ex'trix and her dower as widow of Thomas Dennis Brown Feely under an alleged marriage, and Catherine Buckley *alias* Feely quitted claim to estate for £30 a year for her life, and Catherine Feely *alias* Buckley died shortly after; and whereas John Farrell the only other coheir of Richard Tyrrell Barnes died . . . . 18 . . intestate and unmarried, leaving Marianne Louisa, wife of said James Farrell, and Bridget Delia Farrell his only sisters and coheirs-at-law; and whereas Mary Reily was entitled to one-fifth of the £10,000 currency, survived her said husband, and died 15 July 1795 intestate, and adm'on was granted 26 June 1821 P.C.C. to Catherine Ford; and whereas Mary Feely, who was entitled to one-fifth of said legacy, survived her husband, and died 24 June 1796 intestate, and adm'on was granted 16 Sep. 1799 P.C.C. to Ann Riley her daughter; and whereas Charlotte Farrell, who was entitled to one-fifth of said legacy, died 1803 intestate, and adm'on was granted 11 July 1821 P.C.C. to John Farrell her only son: and whereas said Catherine Ford died, and adm'on of estate of Mary Rily left unadministered by said Catherine Ford was granted P.C.C. to Anne Riley; and whereas Ann Pattoun died and bequeathed her share of said legacy, but George Pattoun has not assented to it, and John Farrell died, and adm'on of estate of Charlotte Farrell left unadministered by him was in 1840 P.C.C. granted to said James Farrell; and whereas the only persons entitled to said estate now are George Pattoun three-sixteenths, viz., one-sixteenth as devisee of his mother Ann Pattoun, one-sixteenth as heir-at-law of his sister Eliza Feely,* and one-sixteenth as devisee of Catherine Ford; Richard Tyrrell Robert Pattoun two-sixteenths, one-sixteenth as devisee of his mother Ann Pattoun and one-sixteenth as devisee of Catherine Ford; Anna Sparks one-sixteenth as devisee of her mother Ann Pattoun; Anne Riley six-sixteenths, viz., two-sixteenths as devisee of Catherine Ford and four-sixteenths as heir of her brother Thomas Dennis Brown Feely; Marianne Louisa, wife of James Farrell, two-sixteenths as coheir to her brother said John Farrell; Bridget Delia Farrell two-sixteenths as the other coheir of her brother John Farrell. Whereas the only persons entitled to the balance of the £10,000 currency are Anne Riley as administratrix of Mary Riley, deceased, and as administratrix of Catherine Ford, deceased, and as administratrix of her mother Mary Feely, deceased: said George Pattoun as Ex'or of his mother Ann Pattoun, deceased: James Farrell as administrator of Charlotte Farrell, deceased; and whereas on 31 Dec. 1830 James Foster Groom took on the management for the beneficiaries; and whereas by an agreement dated 3 Aug. 1836 they agreed about his accounts and mode, and have done so up to June last, and there is a balance of £1445 6*s.* 8*d.*, and there is due to Anne Riley as balance of share £542 19*s.* 8*d.* sterling and interest £86 17*s.* 8*d.*, total £629 17*s.* 4*d.*, as administratrix of Mary Riley, deceased; £542 19*s.* 8*d.* and interest £86 17*s.* 8*d.*, total £629 17*s.* 4*d.*, as Ex'trix of Catherine Ford; and as administratrix of her mother Mary Feely £542 19*s.* 8*d.* and interest £86 17*s.* 8*d.*, total £629 17*s.* 4*d.*; and to George Pattoun as Ex'or of his mother £542 19*s.* 8*d.* and interest £86 17*s.* 8*d.*, total £629 17*s.* 4*d.*; and to James Farrell as administrator of Charlotte Farrell £512 19*s.* 8*d.* and interest £86 17*s.* 8*d.*, total £629 17*s.* 4*d.* James Foster Groom now distributes three sums of £289 1*s.* 4*d.* to Anne Riley, £289 1*s.* 4*d.* to George Pattoun, £289 1*s.* 1*d.* to James Farrell; and James Foster Groom is hereby released of all claims and indemnified. Whereas William Eales Ledeatt of Antigua, now in London, planter, has proposed to take a lease of said estate for fourteen years at £600 sterling a year from 1 Aug. 1840, and to purchase all the cattle and stores, and they appoint James Foster Groom to receive the rents and execute said lease, he to be paid two and a half per cent. commission.

* Three years after I was born. † Died at . . . . Street, Chatham.

* The aunt who lived with us till her death at Chatham.

Francis Tyssen, sen., of London, Esq., æt. 65 in 1687; owned plantations in Antigua; bur. at Dutch Church, Austin Fryers, 23 March 1699. Will dated 5 May 1690; proved 30 July 1700. = Dorothy Collent.

Francis Tyssen of Hackney, Esq., æt. 34 in 1687; owned the "Bridge" plantation in Antigua. Will dated 19 Aug., and proved 20 Dec. 1710. (278 Smith.) = Mary Western, died 9 April 1731.

Samuel Tyssen of Hackney, Esq.; inherited the "Bridge" plantation in Antigua. Will dated 12 Aug. 1743; proved 17 Jan. 1748. (28 Lisle.) = Sarah . . . . died May 1779, æt. 72.

William Tyssen of Cheshunt, co. Herts; owned a plantation of 250 acres in St. Paul's Parish, Antigua; died 1 Jan. 1778, æt. 55. = Mary Wootton, born 1746; mar. 12 Jan. 1762.

Sarah Tyssen, only dau., born 15 Feb. 1763; mar. at St. George, Hanover Square, 29 Nov. 1791; party to sale of 1815. = Sir John Tyrell of Boreham House, co. Essex, Bart., bapt. 20 July 1762; created Bart. 28 Sep. 1809; party to sale in 1815 of "Buckshornes" plantation, St. Paul's Parish, Antigua; died 3 Aug. 1832.

Page 119. 1747, May 29. To confer the order of Knighthood of the Bath on Rear Admiral Warren. The ceremony being perform'd in his majesty's closet. ('Gent. Mag.,' p. 248.)

Page 120. Francis Tyssen, sen., of London, Esq. Will dated 5 May 1690; proved P.C.C. 30 July 1700. My son & Ex'or Francis Tyssen of Shacklewell, co. Midd., Esq., lands in cos. Midd. & Hunt. to pay to my wife Dorothy £500 a year, also all my plantations in the Island of Antigua & Province of Zealand. Bason with coat of arms & crest. Dutch Church of Austin Fryers £100. Poor of Flushing £20. John Tyssen of Flushing.

Francis Tyssen of Hackney, Esq. Will dated 19 Aug., and proved 20 Dec. 1710. (278 Smith.) To my son Samuel the Bridge plantation in Antigua.

Francis Tyssen of Hackney, Esq. Will dated 1717. (222 Whitfield.) My wife Rachel. Dau. Mary £10,000. Brothers John Tyssen, Esq., Wm Tyssen, & Saml Tyssen.

The will of my late father Francis Tyssen of 1710. My mother Mary Tyssen. My wife's mother Mary Beauvoir.

John Tyssen, Esq. Will dated 1730. (266 Auber.) My son John Tyssen. My brother Saml Tyssen, Esq.

For a very complete pedigree of the Tyssens see Robinson's 'History of Hackney' and Berry's 'Essex Genealogies.'

DUTCH CHURCH, AUSTIN FRYERS.

Buried.

1699 Mar. 23 Mr. Francois Tijssen, Senr.

THIBOU. Page 125.

Lucy Thibou of French parentage, born in London (her mother Charlotte was buried 24 Nov. 1724 at St. John's), was under 50 in 1736. She married firstly Leonard Burroughs, an Englishman; secondly, 30 Oct. 1715, Peter Mercier, merchant, who was buried 13 Sep. 1733 at St. John's. By her first husband she had a son Benjamin who apparently removed to Bermuda, and a daughter Mary who married firstly John Tremills, and secondly Dr. Walter Tullideph.

THOMAS. Page 133.

Sarah, wife of William Thomas, was daughter of William Yeamans. She married secondly Dr. Joshua Archbold, who died 1758, and thirdly, 1759, Ernest Udney. Dr. Sydserfe was cousin to Dr. Walter Tullideph, a frequent correspondent of his.

TOBIN. Page 136.

Joseph Webbe Tobin, General R.A., son of James Tobin by Elizabeth Webbe his wife; born 1776; died 1863. = Harriet Boynes, mar. 1799.

Children:

- James Tobin, 2nd Lieut. R.A., born 1801; died
- Charles Tobin, Lieut. 58th Regiment, born 1802; died 1826.
- Mary Theodosia, dau. of Major Baynes, R.A., mar. 1847. = John Tobin, born 1804; died 1873. = Mary, widow of Major Good. s.p.
- Henry Tobin, born 1808. = ...
- George Edward Alexander Tobin, Captain 2nd Queen's, born 1815; died 1892. = Louisa, dau. of Captain Williams of Sowden, co. Devon; mar. 1847.
- Elizabeth Anne Tobin, born 1807; died 1879, spinster.
- Edward Tobin, born 1818; died 1819.

Children of John Tobin and Mary Theodosia:

- O'Hara John Tobin, Lieut. Royal Marines, born 1848. = Lillia, dau. of . . . . May, M.D.; mar. 1890.
- James Tobin, born 1849; died 1855.
- Margaret Anne Tobin, mar. Surgeon-Major Thorp; she died s.p. 1888.

Children of Henry Tobin:

- Helen Tobin.
- Jessie Tobin.

Children of George Edward Alexander Tobin and Louisa:

- Thomas George Webbe Tobin, Lieut. 6th Foot, born 1847. = Alice Maud, dau. of Captain Atwood, 27th Foot.
- Charles Villiers Tobin, born 1849; died 186–.
- Edward O'Hara Tobin, R.N., born 1852.
- Francis Tobin, born 1863; died 1864.
- William Henry John Tobin, born 1850. = Laura Browne, mar. 1878.
- Frederick John Tobin, born 1856; Major Royal Irish Rifles 1898; compiler of this pedigree. = Clara Edith Georgina, dau. of J. Waters of Parsonstown.
- Rev. Cecil Alexander Tobin, born 1856. = Geraldine Elizabeth, dau. of J. Brown, Colonel 1st Foot; mar. 1890.

Children of William Henry John Tobin and Laura Browne: Charles Tobin, born 1879. Laura Tobin. Frederica Tobin. George Henry Webbe Tobin. Constance Tobin. William Tobin. Eleanor Tobin.

Child of Rev. Cecil Alexander Tobin and Geraldine Elizabeth: Kathleen Tobin, born 1892.

ST. PAUL'S SCHOOL REGISTER.

1821 June 1 Walter Tobin, aged 9, son of James Webb Tobin, 17 Radcliffe Terrace.

1822 Feb. 5 Henry Hope Tobin, aged 8, son of James Webbe Tobin, 1 Little Carter Lane.

1863, Feb. 21. At Exmouth, aged 86, Gen. J. W. Tobin, Commanding 3rd Brigade R.A. etc. ('Gent. Mag.,' p. 528.)

PARISH REGISTER OF ST. GEORGE, NEVIS.

(Fulham Palace MSS.)

Married.

1718 July 10 Mr. James Symonds and Mrs. Mary Butler.

The following additional information has been sent to me by Major Tobin:—

James Tobin of Kilaghy, Knocknegonah, and Knockalny, co. Tipperary, was M.P. for Fethard 1688-9. One of this name was knighted in 1722 as appears by the record at Brussels: "Jacques Tobin, natif d'Irlande et domicilié en Flandres fût creé Chevalier et obtint des supports et une couronne au lieu de bournelits par lettres du 24 Fevrier 1722. Il portait pour armes de sinople à trois feuilles d'or tigées du meme."

John Tobin of Figtree Parish in the Island of Nevis died Oct. 1757.

His son James Tobin owned the Stoney Grove plantation in the said parish, and died 31 March 1770, æt. 72, leaving issue:—

1. James, who died at Bristol at an advanced age in 1817. Elizabeth his wife (*née* Webbe) died in York Place, Clifton, 8 July 1824 (see 'Gent. Mag.,' p. 94).
2. Walter, whose widow Sarah was party to a deed of 1798.
3. Henry Hope, died 1798—1803.
4. Lydia Thomas.
5. Anne.

Henry Hope Tobin, drowned 1831, had two brothers, Frederick, killed in California, and Walter. One of these wrote 'Travels with Sir Humphry Davy.'

Admiral Tobin's Christian names were George Webbe. Dorothy his widow died 10 April 1858, æt. 69. On the death of his mother in 1824 he inherited the Nevis estate, which was ultimately sold by his son. James Tobin, by Elizabeth Webbe his wife, had another daughter Frances, who married G. Bush of Bristol, and a son Joseph Webbe Tobin.

The crest of the Tobins is a bird; motto, "Avidus honoris."

TRANT. Page 140.

Sarah Vaudrey of Barbados, widow. Will dated 1698. (242 Lort.) Dau. Margaret Trant.

Thomas Duboys of Barbados, Esq. Will dated 1699. (171 Pett.) Brother-in-law Tho. Trant, Esq., & my sister Anne his wife, & their children.

Dame Hellen Trant, relict of Sir Patrick Trant, Bart., deceased, of St. Anne, Soho. Will dated 1729. (58 Abbott.) My grddau. the Hon. Mrs Hellen Fleming, dau. of the Rt Hon. Visct. Longford, late Lord Slane. £7000 due to me by Act of Parliament. Dau. Frances Trant. Son Sir Lawrence Trant, Bart.

Mrs. Mary Trant died 11 Feb. 1798, æt. 73. The English Ladies of Pontoise. 'Herald and Genealogist,' vol. iii., p. 521.

PARISH REGISTER OF ST. GEORGE, HANOVER SQUARE.

Married.

1815 June 12 Edward Trant Bontein, W., of this parish, & Mary Ann Stanley, S., of St Marylebone.

Baker's map of St. Kitts 1753 gives an estate in St. Paul's Parish as Dominick Trant's.

1789. Dominick Trant, esq. appointed King's advocate of the High Court of Admiralty in the kingdom of Ireland. ('Gent. Mag.,' p. 1216.)

1790, July. Lately at Cahir, co. Tipperary, in Ireland, Dominick Trant, esq. brother-in-law to the Lord Chancellor of that kingdom, King's advocate of the Court of Admiralty of Ireland, and late Chairman of the quarter sessions of the county of Tipperary. This gentleman had the misfortune (for such it must be deemed) to kill Sir John Colthurst in a duel. (*Ibid.*, p. 669.)

In Dublin the Hon. Miss Fitzgibbon, eldest daughter of the Lord Chancellor of Ireland. (*Ibid.*, p. 670.) See pedigree of Trant of Dovea in Burke's 'Landed Gentry.'

1801, March. Lately. In Hans-place, Sloane-street, the wife of James Trant, esq. a son and heir. (*Ibid.*, p. 274.)

TRAVERS. Page 144.

Indenture dated 14 Oct. 1634 by which Richard Traves, Citizen and Mercer of London, releases to his brother James Traves, Citizen and Mercer of London, all claim to certain messuages in the parish of St. Giles, Cripplegate, occupied by thirteen tenants. Indorsed "White Cross Street."

TUDWAY. Page 147.

In 1666 there was living at Reading, co. Berks, Elizabeth Tudway, a Quakeress. (Bisse, vol. i., p. 25.)

Rachell Tudway of Edmonton, co. Middlesex, spinster. Will dated 30 Nov. 1733; proved 5 Sep. 1735 by Clement Tudway. (194 Ducie.) My brother Mr John Creswill £20 a year, £200, & linen. Cousen Susannah Clowdsley £50. Cousen Eliz. Arnold £20. Cousen Eliz. Childe £20. Mrs Susannah Staresmore £5. Eliz. Bridgman £5. All residue to my loving brother Mr Clement Tudway & Ex'or. Witnessed by Joseph Kilpin, Robert Killingly, Sarah Killingly.

1861, June 19. At Wells, Somerset, aged 78, Frances Gould Tudway, relict of J. P. Tudway, esq. M.P. for Wells. ('Gent. Mag.,' p. 98.)

TULLIDEPH. Page 155.

David Ogilvie of St. Stephen, Coleman Street, London, clerk. Will dated 6 Nov., proved 20 Jan. 1723. On 8 May 1739 adm'on of estate left unadministered by Jane Ogilvie, widow, now deceased, granted to Thomas Ogilvie, Esq., the nephew. (14 Bolton.) My wife Jane. £200 to my nephew Tho. Ogilvie, s. of my eldest brother John Ogilvie. £200 to my brother Wm Ogilvie. £30 to the children of my niece Margt., dau. of my said brother John Ogilvie. £70 to my niece Isabell, the other dau. of my said bro. John. £100 to my said nephew Tho. Ogilvie & to the lairds of Innercarity & Balfour for the poor.

Nicholas Burroughs of Nevis. Will dated 9 Dec. 1723; proved 3 Oct. 1725 by John Burroughs the brother. (206 Romney.) My son John sole h. & Ex'or. Brother John Burroughs & Chr. Nichols, both of Bristol, & Roger Pemberton, Timothy Tyrrell, Pocock Walker, Esqres, & Jno Stephens, all of Nevis, guardians. Witnessed by Henry Hatsell, Thomas Lady, Thomas Herbro, James Stephens.

WARNER. Page 186.

In Canterbury Cathedral is a monument to Sir Charles Shipley, Governor of Grenada, who died there 30 Nov. 1815, æt. 58, and to Mary his widow, who died 6 Aug. 1820, æt. 58. (Cowper's 'M.I. Canterbury Cathedral.')

Robert S. A. Warner matriculated from Oriel College, Oxford, 15 Oct. 1877, æt. 18; B.A. 1882; Barrister-at-Law Inner Temple 1882.

Raymond J. R. Warner matriculated from Pembroke College, Oxford, 30 Oct. 1880, æt. 19.

Page 187. Phillis Maria Kirk of Eltham, co. Kent, widow. Will dated 1, proved 17 Aug. 1738. (199 Brodrepp.) My nephew & niece Sam. Byam & Grace his wife £20 each for mourning. Nieces Eliz. Anne Warner & Jane Warner £100 each, & £20 each for mourning. To Sam. Byam the picture of him & his said wife. Rev. Mr Peter £30. Mrs Mary Stonard £10, & her husband, & £20 for mourning. Nephew Joseph Warner £20 for mourning. Mr. Wm Tryon, Mr. Tho. Tryon, Mr Merry, Mr Smith, & Mr Percivall, who supported my late husband's pall, each a ga ring. Mr Tho. Smith of Gray's Inn £120, & all residue to him & the said Sam. Byam & Grace his wife in Trust for my goddau. Phillis Byam, dau. of said Saml & Grace Byam, at 21. Mr Tho. Smith sole Ex'or. Witnessed by John Marlow, David Jones.

Page 188. Elizabeth J. Ross was born 1789 at St. Vincent, was married 18 May 1809, and died 2 Sep. 1869.

Page 189. Frederick Warner, C.M.G., educated at Harrow, was of Woodford House, Trinidad, and at the time of his death, 18 Oct. 1889, senior unofficial Member of the Legislative Council. He was not Solicitor-General. His wife J. M. Gunthorpe was born 31 Oct. 1822.

Frederick Warner, born 19 Sep. 1859 at Woodford House, Trinidad, was educated at St. George's Hospital, F.R.C.S. Edinburgh, M.R.C.S. England, and now resides at 10 Brechin Place, South Kensington. He married, 19 Jan. 1887, Sydney Anne, younger daughter of Christopher Grove, Esq., of Amersham, co. Bucks, and has issue Brodrick Ashton, born 23 Dec. 1888, Jeannette Sydney, born 13 June 1890, and Christopher Frederick Ashton, born 18 Jan. 1895.

Broderick S. Warner was born 11 Nov. 1848, was of the Inner Temple, and died 13 Aug.

For Alice L. Warner *read* Alicia L. Warner.

Georgiana F. Warner was born 7 March. Mr. N. Cox is Inspector-General of Police, British Guiana.

Jeanetta Warner died 1867.

Page 196. The note about the English ladies of Pontoise was from the 'Herald and Genealogist,' vol. iii., p. 65.

WEBB. Page 214.

STRATFORD SUB CASTRA, NEAR SALISBURY.

In the chancel:—

Joseph Webb, Esq., of the Island of Nevis, died 1779, æt. 27.

Mr. John S. Maynard, M.B. Edinburgh, wrote me in 1896 that William Maynard of Nevis married Frances Webbe in 1737, and Webbe's New River Estate is still held by his family.

PARISH REGISTER OF ST. GEORGE, NEVIS.

(Fulham Palace MSS.)

Baptized.

1716 May 3 Frances the D. of Mr. George Webbe, Senr, by Elizabeth his wife.
1717 April 11 George the S. of Mr. George Webbe, Senr, by Elizabeth his wife.
1718 July 5 Mr. George Webbe, Senr.
1720 Sep. 16 Josiah the S. of Mr. George Webbe, Senr, by Elizabeth his wife.
1721 Jan. 2 John the S. of Mr. George Webbe, Senr, by Elizabeth his wife.

Buried.

1717 Oct. 27 George the S. of Mr. Josiah Webbe, Senr, by Anne his wife.
1718 May 27 Josiah the S. of Mr. Josiah Webbe, Senr, by Anne his wife.
1718 June 6 James the S. of Mr. George Webbe, Senr, by Elizabeth his wife.
1720 Feb. 10 Sarah the D. of Mr. George Webbe, Senr, by Elizabeth his wife.
1724 Aug. 21 Mrs. Anne Webbe, late Wife of Mr. Josiah Webbe, Senr.

WHITE. Page 224.

1802, Jan. 26. At Brighthelmstone, the wife of Michael White esq. of the island of St Vincent. ('Gent. Mag.,' p. 185.)

WILLIAMS. Page 231.

David Purviance of Antigua, Gent. Will dated 25 Aug. 1744; proved 22 Jan. 1746 by George Knox; power reserved to the others. (20 Potter.) My brother Robert Purviance £100; brother Joseph Purviance £50; sister Jennett Crawford, wife of Hugh Crawford, £50, & to each of her children £50; to each of the children of my sister Margaret Colhoun, deceased, late wife of . . . . Colhoun, deceased, £50. To my good friends His Excellency Wm Mathew, Daniel Mathew, Esq., his son & heir apparent, Hon. Geo. Lucas, Esq., Chas. Dunbar, Esq., Col. Andrew Lesley & Wm Lesley, & Richard Oliver, Esq., a mourning ring each of 21s. Revd Sam. Delap near Letterkenny in Ireland 5 gns.; my uncle Alex^{r} Purviance 10 gns. Hon. Ben. King, Esq., my gold toothpick case. Geo. Knox of Antigua my Barbuda horse & gold-headed cane. My dans.-in-law Martha, Mary, & Eliz. Williams, children of my late wife by a former husband, their mother's apparel & ornaments. All residue of my personal estate to my brother John Purviance of Letterleaque near Letterkenny, co. Donegal. All my real estate to my Ex'ors in trust to sell to buy a negro boy of £22 c. for George, youngest son of Wm Mackinen of Antigua, Esq. Hon. Ben. King, Esq., Walter Sydserfe, Esq., George Knox of Antigua, Gent., & my said brother John Purviance Ex'ors & 21s. rings. Witnessed by Nathaniel Messum, John Duer Duncombe, James Hornby.

WILLOUGHBY. Page 245.

Manton, co. Linc. "Here lyeth the body of Charles Pelham Esquire, sonne of Sir William Pelham, of Brocklesby, knight, and Anne his wife, Daughter of Charles Lord Willoughby of Parham etc. he died 1671. ('Gent. Mag.' for 1864, p. 367.)

Hugh, 15th Baron Willoughby, died at his house in Craven Street, Strand. He was a bigoted Presbyterian, and when the title came to him was in a very humble capacity in the army. (Cole's 'MSS. British Museum,' vol. xviii., p. 155.)

WISE. Page 254.

1686, Nov. 13. Elias Boudinot, of Stepney, Midd., Merch^{t}, Wid^{r}, about 44, & Susanna Papin, of the same, Wid., about 34; alleged by Daniel Brulon, of Stepney, Merch^{t}, at the French Chapel of the Savoy, or the Greek's Church, Midd. (Marriage Allegations; Vicar-General of the Archbishop of Canterbury.)

WOODLEY. Page 256.

Baptized at Richmond, co. Surrey, 13 March 1737-8, Joseph, a Black of riper years, Servt of Tobias Wall, Esqr. (J. Challenor C. Smith.)

1798, July 21. At Tavistock, Devon, William Maynard Mills, jun. esq. of Millikan-hall, eldest son of Wm. esq. of Bishop's Hull, co. Somerset, to Miss Eliz. Willesford, only daughter of the late Richard Vyvyan W.* esq. ('Gent. Mag.,' p. 808.)

1858, Sep. 17. Henry Maynard Mills, aged 11, son of Henry Mills, Barrister, 1 New Court, Temple (St. Paul's School Register, p. 338); as second son of Henry of London, Esq., he matriculated from Lincoln College, Oxon, 13 Oct. 1866, æt. 19; B.A. 1872; M.A. 1873; Barrister-at-Law Inner Temple 1875. (Foster.)

WYKE. Page 265.

William Irish, by Sarah Wyke his wife, had an only son and heir William, of the Hermitage and River Head Estates, Montserrat, whose daughter and heir Sarah married Rev. Harry Paxton, M.A., of Baythorne and Great Yeldham, co. Essex, Rector of Syderstone, co. Norfolk, and Vicar of Battisford, co. Suffolk, Chaplain to Horace, Earl of Orford, by whom she had five daughters, of whom Sarah Elizabeth the eldest married in 1818 John Norman, Esq. (Burke's 'Landed Gentry,' Supp., p. 248.)

* See his pedigree in Vivian's 'Visitations of Devon,' p. 787, where there is no mention of this match. His said daughter was baptized 30 May 1775 at Tavistock.

YEAMANS. Page 270.

1749, Nov. 22. William Yeamons lost his wife a few weeks agone, and the old man is now fond of his son John, but whether he will pay his debts I know not . . . . Jack Yeamans's mother died a few weeks agone.

1750, June. Levy on Ker's estate in right of Jack Yeamons' wife. (Tullideph Papers.)

Page 375. The following inscriptions, taken from 'Antigua and the Antiguans,' probably relate to memorials not now in existence:—

1. A mural monument in the churchyard to the memory of JAMES CULLEN, erected by his brother Robert Cullen, the architect of the church.
2. Memory of . . . . TROUHTON . . . . 1704.
3. FREDERICK COPE . . . . he was born in London of honest parents, on the 21st day of May, 1710, and died in Antigua, on the 8th . . . . 1739.
4. Major-General GEORGE W. RAMSAY, Governor in chief of Antigua, Montserrat, and Barbados, who departed this life, November 1st 1819, in the 58th year of his age.

WADLEY'S BRISTOL WILLS.

James Dowle, grocer. Will dated 1564. William Yeman a witness.

Michael Colstonne, draper. Will dated 1565. William Yemanns overseer.

William Yeman, glover, of Bristol. Will dated 21 Dec. 1573; proved 5 April 1574 at Bristol. To son Wm 2 houses in St Peter's, one in St James, £20, & best goblett. Wm Yeman, jr, grocer, to have the custody of said son. Dans. Alice, Margery, Kath., & Joan £20 apiece. Base dau. Kath. £5. All at age of 20. My father John Yeman a silver spoon. Wife Joan residue & Ex'trix. Wm Yeman the Yr, grocer, overseer.

John Boydell, vintner. Will dated 1575. Tenement in High Str. in the occupation of Wm Yeman the Elder.

William Yeman. Will dated 14 Nov., proved 7 Jan. 1580. Bur. at All Saints. S. Wm Yeman certain silver. Susan Yeman & her sister Mary Yeman £3 6s 8d. each at marriage. My dau. Joan Hunt £6 13s. 4d. Joan, Florence, & Alice Evenet, daus. of Edw. Evenet, £3 6s. 8d. each at marriage. Joan, dau. of John Yeman, shoemaker, 20s., also to her sister Annis Yeman, & her sister Grace Yeman in Cardiff. Cousin Joan, dau. of Stephen Tanner, 20s. Agnes, Mary, & Joan Yeman, daus. of Arthur Yeman in Cardiff. My s. Wm all residue & Ex'or. Well beloved in Christ Mr Tho. Colston & Tho. Fawkett overseers.

Thomas Pollington, merchant. Will dated 1587. William Yemans, grocer, an overseer.

Philip Seapulis, stationer. Will dated 1589. Alice & Eliz. Yeomans my maydes.

EXTRACTS FROM THE 'TOWN AND COUNTRY MAGAZINE.'

1771, May 16. Alexander Thompson, Esq; in Fenchurch-street, who came lately here from Antigua, for the benefit of his health (p. 280).

1772, Sep. 11. Henry Rice, Esq. of Antigua, at Cambridge (p. 504).

1777. Short description of Antigua, 32 lines (p. 412).

1779, July. Lieutenant O'Hara at Antigua (p. 448).

1785, Nov. 21. John Monttay, esq. of Bath, commissioner of the island of Antigua (p. 672).

1786, Nov. Lieutenant Mouat of the marines, at Antigua, in the West Indies, and son of captain Patrick Mouat of the royal navy (p. 615).

1787, March 13. Thomas Rodie, esq. of Liverpool, to miss Eliza Tannor, late of Antigua (p. 143).

1787, March. Alexander Scott, esq. of Antigua (p. 144).

1788, Feb. 4. Rich. Flint, esq. of Antigua, to miss Hannah Blundell, of the isle of Wight (p. 100).

[END OF ADDITIONS TO VOLUME III.]

MISCELLANEOUS NOTES AND WILLS.

JARRITT.

The following has been copied from an illustrated "Book of Common Prayer," 1768; on the flyleaf: "M. Bettey, The gift of her affectionate Mother December 17th - 64;" inside the cover, printed in capitals, on a small leather label: "M. Dafforne, May 8th 1772." I shall be pleased to return the original to any representative of the family wishing it.

ARTHUR SCHOMBERG.

George Jarritt was Born September 24, 1779, and Baptized at Maryleborn Church.

John Elliott Jarritt was Born April 19, 1782, and Baptized at Maryleborn Church.

Robert Jarritt was Born December 17, 1784, and Baptized at St. George's Church, Hanover Square.

Robert Jarritt was born at Spring Grove House, Old Sodbury, Gloucestershire, 29th November 1827, and Christened at Old Sodbury Church. Sponsors, Mr Thomas Iles, Mr Robert Collins, Miss Elizh Iles.

Maria Jarritt born at Betty's Hope, Antigua, 25th July 1830 and Baptized at Parham Church.

Mary Ann Jarritt born as above, 20th September 1832, Christened at Parham.

Margaret Eliza Jarritt born on Whitsunday 18th May 1834, Christened at Parham.

Henry Jarritt born 15th October 1835, Christened at Parham.

Robert Jarritt Senr Departed this Life 30th December 1835 at Betty's Hope Estr.

(Dr. Howard's 'Mis. Gen. et Her.,' Second Series, vol. vi.)

MEADE.

PARISH REGISTER OF ST. JOHN.

Married.

1712-3 26		James Meade and Mary Buckerill. L.
1727	June 20	James Spelling and Mary Meade; by L.

Buried.

1695	Aug. 20	Ellinor the wife of Thomas Mead.
1711	Sep. 9	Thomas Meade.
1720	Sep. 16	Katherine Meade.
1737	July 29	Catherine Meade of this Island.
1756	Mar. 12	Mary Meade.

(224 Collier.) Peter Lebeup of Albemarle Street, Esq., in his will dated 24 Nov. 1774 refers to £4000, the residue of a mortgage of £8000 charged on the estate of the late Thomas Mead, Esq., at Montserrat.

Henry Gillingham of the town and county of Southampton, now resident at Nevis. Will dated 15 Nov. 1662. (15 Bruce.) To be buried in the churchyard in the Leward side of this Island. Mrs Anne Woodward, sometime wife of Capt. Lawrence Broadbelt, Gent., deceased, £12 c. a year, & to her 4 children Richd, Eliz., Wm, & Geo. Broadbelt 15,000 lbs. of sugar to be laid out till they are 18 years of age. My friend Philip Gosse 2000 lbs. My servant Otto Curtess 10,000 lbs. Kinsman & servant Edmond Painter 3000 lbs. Francis Carlile & Wm Tilsed 1000 lbs. apiece & 1 year off their time of servitude as pr their indentures. Tho. Paynter my servant & kinsman 2000 lbs. & freedom. All other servants a year off their service. Friends Capt. Walter Symonds, Esq., Capt. Fra. Kaynell, & Mr John Hughes overseers & each a bever hat of £5. All produce to be consigned to Mr Fra. Sampson of London, merchant, or to Mr John Taylor of Southampton, merchant. Out of my estate in England to Mrs Ellinor Dormer £40. Children of my cousen James Paynter £50. Poor of Great Canfield, Dorset, £10. Cousin Mr Geo. Gillingham of Wimborne £5. Uncle John Gillingham £20. My 3 brothers Geo., John, & Richd Gillingham, & my sister Barbara Symonds ⅔ of estate, & brother Thos. Gillingham ⅓ & sole Ex'or. My uncle Col. Tho. Phillipps, Mr John Gillingham, Mr John Jaye, & Mr Rob. Gillingham overseers & £5 each. Witnessed by Wm Childes, Lancelott Lake, Rich. Sharpe. True copy, Wm Leach, ser., jun., Thomas Fenton, Nevis, 19 Nov. 1662. Before the Hon. Major James Russell, Governor, and his Council appeared Richard Sharpe. On 5 Feb. 1662 appeared Lieut. William Childes and Mr. Lancelot Lake.

Codicil. 16 Nov. 1662. Mrs Eliz. Lake my negro boy Charles. James Russell, son to Capt. Russell, my dun mare I bought of Mr Gardiner. Mrs Williams a negro boy. Mrs Margaret Kaynell 1000 lbs. Capt. Kaynell my rapier. Valentine Russell my ginny silver hat-band. Mrs Frances Russell my picture. Ed. Windover his freedom. Mathew, Saml, Arthur, & Richd 10s. each. Caroline & Catando 5s. each. On 1 Feb. 1663 commission to Ann Gillingham the widow and relict of Thomas Gillingham, Gent., the brother and Ex'or of the said Henry Gillingham, merchant, because the said Thomas Gillingham had died before he had carried the will into execution.

Nathaniel Gale, Citizen and Brewer of London. Will dated 27 March 1707. On 15 March 1745 adm'on of the estate of testator, late of St. Botolph's, Aldgate, but at Antigua, deceased, was granted to Esther Hollier, formerly Gale, wife of William Hollier, the only surviving child and residuary legatee. John Gale the son died in the lifetime of testator. The adm'on granted in Feb. 1734 as intestate to said Esther Hollier, then Gale (wife of John Gale), being declared void. (85 Edmunds.) Funeral not to exceed £50. £10 to Tho. Chamberlain for the poor of the Baptist Congregation. Wife Mary ⅓ of estate; s. Joseph, whom I have already paid several hundreds as well as his portion, & on account of his idle life, £10. My dau. Mary Gale £20, dau. Ann Gale £20, son Nathl Gale £20. My wife's dau. Hannah Lilly £10. My wife's son Tho. Lilly £5 at 21. ⅓ of my estate to my son John Gale, dau. Ester Gale, son Andrew Gale, & son Desiderius Gale; ⅓ to my 7 children John Gale, Esther Gale, Andrew Gale, Desiderius Gale, Mary Gale, Ann Gale, & Nathl Gale. A great part of my estate is in a plantation beyond the seas in the Island of Antegoa, & 2 small freeholds in Middlesex & Barkshire. My son John sole Ex'or. Witnessed by John Miller, William Jackson, Joseph Emes.

Thomas Butler of Camberwell, co. Surrey, Gent. Will dated 27 July 1739; proved 4 June 1744 by John Butler and James Butler; power reserved to Duke Butler the son. (138 Anstis.) To my wife Mary, over & above the £20 a year I settled on her at our marriage, £40 a year charged on my estate at Nevis, furniture, & pictures. Wm Fenton, sr, & James Symonds, Esqrs, now in the West Indies, & James Earl of Nevis, Esq., Tho. Hooke & John Hooke, my brothers-in-law, of Camberwell, Gentlemen, as many thousand pounds as I shall have daus. living & unmarried in Trust. My brothers-in-law Tho. & John Hooke £50 each. To the charity school here £20. To my trustees guinea rings. My 1st son Thos. Butler £50 a year & no more as he is a partner with me & has received his portion. My granddau. Sukey Butler his dau. £100 at 17. All my plantations & slaves to my 3 sons John, James, & Duke Butler. To my wife £40 a year more if Nevis be not plundered. £500 to the children of my dau. Sarah, wife of the Revd Wm Holford, clerk, at 17. £500 to the children of my dau. Bethia, wife of the Rev. Wm Vaughan, clerk, at 17. All residue to my said 3 sons. Trustees to be Ex'ors in trust & Guardians. £10 apiece to my son-in-law Tho. Pym & my dau. Elizabeth his wife. £10 apiece to my son-in-law Wm Clark & my dau. Henrietta his wife. All plate to my wife. Witnessed by John Sharpe, Hugh Hamersley, Thomas Waynes, clerks to Mr. Sharpe.

Thomas Hungerford of Bristol, merchant. Will dated 5 Dec. 1739; proved 14 June 1742. (188 Trenley.) To be buried in the new aisle of Clifton Church. My sons-in-law Richard Bayly, Esq., Amberson Tyte, Edward Oliver, & my grandson Geo. Tyte all my estate in trust. My dau. Rebecca Tyte £1000. My dau. Jane Oliver £900. Grandchild Ann Hungerford. My son Tho. Hungerford sole Ex'or. My leasehold estate at Yatton called Porter's Bargain. My late son-in-law Tho. Richton.

Elenor Garnier of St James in the Liberty of Westminster, widow. Will dated 2 Dec. 1740; proved 8 July 1742. (217 Trenley.) To be buried in the Chelsea College ground. All residue of my estate to my 4 daus. Isabella Chudleigh, Elenor Shelley, Margt Mathew, & Eliz. Laroche. My s.-in-law John Laroche Ex'or. My granddau. Diana Chudleigh, grandson John Garnier. Witnessed by William Lowther, Caleb Pott.

Ann Rigby, widow and relict of Richard Rigby, late of Mistley, co. Essex, Esq. Will dated 2 Feb. 1741. On 26 July 1744 adm'on granted to Richard Rigby, George Barker renouncing. (178 Anstis.) To my son Richard Rigby my ½ of a plantation in Antegoa with the negros, horses, cattle, coppers, mills, & stills which descended to me by the death of my late sister Elizabeth Perrie. By the will of my late husband I give to my daus. Ann Rigby & Martha Rigby £1000 each. All residue to my son. My brother-in-law George Barker, citizen & goldsmith of London, Ex'or. Witnessed by Edward Vernon, Rector of St. George's, Bloomsbury, Jonathan Perrie, Ja. Grewes.

Antigua. John Harrington of Southwall, co. Suffolk, mariner, H.M. Hulk "Ludlow Castle." Will dated 18 April 1744; proved 4 April 1745. (113 Seymer.)

Antigua. George Moyes of H.M.S. "Deal Castle." Will dated 4 July, proved 12 Nov. 1745. (304 Seymer.) All est. to Hans Injen. Witnessed by Gustavus Christian, William Higgin.

Edward Gregory of Antigua, cooper. Will dated 22 July 1745. (260 Edmunds.) My brothers Charles & Wm Gregory, & sister Susannah Gregory, £100 each. All residue to Wm Dickinson of this island, merchant, on trust for my wife Prudence, & at her death to raise £1000 c. for Capt. John Sutcliffe if then living, then to Mary Walker, wife of James Walker, blacksmith of Antigua, & to Robt Sutcliffe of London, merchant. My wife & Wm Dickinson Ex'ors. Witnessed by William Reed, George Roberts, James Hornby. By the Hon. George Lucas, Lieut.-Governor, appeared William Reed, merchant, and George Roberts, cooper, sworn 10 Jan. 1745. True copy, Edward

Gamble, Deputy-Secretary. Recorded 21 Jan. 1745. On 12 Sep. 1746 adm'on to Robert Sutcliffe the attorney of Prudence Gregory and William Dickinson.

Antigua. Samuel Secoryd *alias* Acroyde, mariner, of H.M.S. "Severn." Will dated 9 Dec. 1745; proved 19 Jan. 1747. (27 Strahan.) All pay to friend Tho. Smith of H.M.S. "Woolwich."

Peter Lynch of St. Christopher's. Will dated April 1746 at London; proved 5 Feb. 1747 by the two Ex'ors. (56 Strahan.) About to depart there from Great Britain this war time. My sister Ann Lynch, wife of Josias Brown of co. Galway, Gent., £300. M[r] Pierce Lynch, fz. Dom[r] of co. Galway, Gent., £100. Tho. Kenelly, late of Dublin, now at London, accomptant, £10. M[r] Nich[s] Lynch of London, merchant. Anthony Lynch, late of S[t] Christopher's, now of Hampton, co. Midx., Esq., £20. My dear brother Tho. Lynch of Clare Tuam, co. Galway, Gent., all residue, he to pay to M[r] W[m] Bourch of Billabanagher & M[r] Martin Brady £10. Nich. Lynch, merchant, & Anthony Lynch, Esq., Ex'ors. Witnessed by John Lewis Hansen, Nicholas Dawes, Richard Dawes.

William Mings, late belonging to H.M. Yard at English Harbour, Antigua. Will dated 28 Sep. 1747. (287 Potter.) All estate to friend John Stones of ditto. Witnessed by Thomas Walters, Richard Smith. On 17 Nov. 1747 adm'on to Hannah Mings, widow, the mother, John Stones renouncing. Testator died on board H.M.S. "Suffolk," a bachelor.

Index of Names.

Names in *Italics* have the arms given at those references.
" in SMALL CAPITALS are the headings of Pedigrees.
" with a prefix will be found under such prefix.

A

B

D

E

F

G

H

I

J

M

N

O

P

Q

R

S

T

Y

Z

London: Mitchell and Hughes, Printers, 140 Wardour Street, W.

Milton Keynes UK
Ingram Content Group UK Ltd.
UKHW042152050124
435443UK00003BB/36